Ninth Edition

Fundamentals oBusiness Law: Summarized Caes

Roger LeRoy Miller
Institute for University Studies
Arlington, Texas

(John Elk III/Lonely Planet Images/Getty Images)

SOUTH-WESTERN
CENGAGE Learning

Australia • Brazil • Japan • Korea • Mexico • Singapore • Spain • United Kingdom • United States

Fundamentals of Business Law: Summarized Cases

NINTH EDITION

Roger LeRoy Miller

Vice President and Editorial Director:
Jack Calhoun

Editor-in-Chief:
Rob Dewey

Senior Acquisitions Editor:
Vicky True-Baker

Senior Developmental Editor:
Jan Lamar

Executive Marketing Manager:
Lisa L. Lysne

Marketing Manager:
Laura-Aurora Stopa

Senior Marketing Communications Manager:
Sarah Greber

Production Manager:
Bill Stryker

Technology Project Manager:
Kristen Meere

Manufacturing Planner:
Kevin Kluck

Editorial Assistant:
Ben Genise

Compositor:
Parkwood Composition Service

Senior Art Director:
Michelle Kunkler

Internal Designer:
Bill Stryker

Cover Designer:
Rose Alcorn

Cover Images:
© Scott Cramer/iStockphoto

product information and technology assistance, contact us at
Cengage Learning Academic Resource Center
1-800-423-0563

permission to use material from this text or product, submit all requests online at **www.cengage.com/permissions**.

Further permissions questions can be emailed to
permissionrequest@cengage.com.

Library congress Control Number: 2011942269

ISBN-13 78-1-111-53062-4
ISBN-10: 111-53062-9

South-Wtern Cengage Learning
5191 Natp Blvd.
Mason, C 45040
USA

Cengage arning products are represented in Canada by Nelson Ecation, Ltd.

For your ourse and learning solutions, visit **www.cengage.com**.

Purchaseny of our products at your local college store or at our preferredonline store **www.cengagebrain.com**.

Printed in the United States
1 2 3 4 5 6 7 15 14 13 12 11

Contents in Brief

Unit One

The Legal Environment of Business 1

Chapter 1 **The Legal and Constitutional Environment of Business 2**

***Appendix to Chapter 1* 19**

Chapter 2 **Traditional and Online Dispute Resolution 28**

Chapter 3 **Ethics and Business Decision Making 50**

Unit Two

Torts and Crimes 67

Chapter 4 **Torts and Cyber Torts 68**

Chapter 5 **Intellectual Property and Internet Law 88**

Chapter 6 **Criminal Law and Cyber Crime 106**

Unit Three

Contracts 131

Chapter 7 **Nature and Classification 132**

Chapter 8 **Agreement in Traditional and E-Contracts 144**

Chapter 9 **Consideration, Capacity, and Legality 162**

Chapter 10 **Defenses to Contract Enforceability 178**

Chapter 11 **Third Party Rights and Discharge 193**

Chapter 12 **Breach and Remedies 211**

Unit Four

Sales and Lease Contracts 225

Chapter 13 **The Formation of Sales and Lease Contracts 226**

***Appendix to Chapter 13* 248**

Chapter 14 **Performance and Breach of Sales and Lease Contracts 252**

Chapter 15 **Warranties and Product Liability 269**

Unit Five

Negotiable Instruments 289

Chapter 16 **Negotiability, Transferability, and Liability 290**

Chapter 17 **Checks and Banking in the Digital Age 315**

Unit Six

Debtor-Creditor Relationships 335

Chapter 18 **Security Interests in Personal Property 336**

Chapter 19 **Creditors' Rights and Bankruptcy 354**

Chapter 20 **Mortgages and Foreclosures after the Recession 378**

Unit Seven

Employment Relations 395

Chapter 21 **Agency Relationships 396**

Chapter 22 **Employment, Immigration, and Labor Law 414**

Unit Eight

Business Organizations 443

Chapter 23 **Sole Proprietorships, Partnerships, and Limited Liability Companies 444**

Chapter 24 **Corporate Formation, Financing, and Termination 461**

Chapter 25 **Corporate Directors, Officers, and Shareholders 483**

Chapter 26 **Investor Protection, Insider Trading, and Corporate Governance 502**

Unit Nine

Property and Its Protection 525

Chapter 27 **Personal Property and Bailments 526**

Chapter 28 **Real Property and Landlord-Tenant Law 541**

Chapter 29 **Insurance, Wills, and Trusts 555**

Unit Ten

Special Topics 577

Chapter 30 **Liability of Accountants and Other Professionals 578**

Chapter 31 **International Law in a Global Economy 593**

Appendices

Appendix A **How to Brief Cases and Analyze Case Problems A–1**

Appendix B **The Constitution of the United States A–4**

Appendix C **The Uniform Commercial Code (Excerpts) A–11**

Appendix D **The Sarbanes-Oxley Act of 2002 (Excerpts and Explanatory Comments) A–120**

Appendix E **Sample Answers for Select *Questions with Sample Answer* A–126**

Appendix F **Sample Answers for *Case Problems with Sample Answer* A–128**

Appendix G **Answers to *Issue Spotters* A–135**

Glossary G–1

Table of Cases TC–1

Index I–1

Contents

Unit One

The Legal Environment of Business 1

Chapter 1 The Legal and Constitutional Environment of Business 2

Business Activities and the Legal Environment 2
Sources of American Law 3
The Common Law Tradition 5
Classifications of Law 6
The Constitution As It Affects Business 8
Family Winemakers of California v. Jenkins (2010) **9**
Bad Frog Brewery, Inc. v. New York State Liquor Authority (1998) **11**
Adapting the Law to the Online Environment The Supreme Court Upholds a Law that Prohibits Pandering Virtual Child Pornography 13
Trunk v. City of San Diego (2011) **14**
Reviewing . . . The Legal and Constitutional Environment of Business 15
Terms and Concepts • Chapter Summary • ExamPrep • For Review • Questions and Case Problems

Appendix to Chapter 1: Finding and Analyzing the Law 19

Finding Statutory and Administrative Law 19
Finding Case Law 19
Reading and Understanding Case Law 20

Chapter 2 Traditional and Online Dispute Resolution 28

The Judiciary's Role in American Government 28
Basic Judicial Requirements 29
Southern Prestige Industries, Inc. v. Independence Plating Corp. (2010) **30**
Gucci America, Inc. v. Wang Huoqing (2011) **32**
The State and Federal Court Systems 33
Following a State Court Case 36
Adapting the Law to the Online Environment The Duty to Preserve E-Evidence for Discovery 39
Downey v. Bob's Discount Furniture Holdings, Inc. (2011) **40**
The Courts Adapt to the Online World 41
Alternative Dispute Resolution 42
Reviewing . . . Traditional and Online Dispute Resolution 45
Terms and Concepts • Chapter Summary • ExamPrep • For Review • Questions and Case Problems

Chapter 3 Ethics and Business Decision Making 50

Business Ethics 50
Skilling v. United States (2010) **51**
Mathews v. B and K Foods, Inc. (2011) **52**
Krasner v. HSH Nordbank AG (2010) **53**
Ethical Transgressions by Financial Institutions 54
Approaches to Ethical Reasoning 55
Making Ethical Business Decisions 57
Practical Solutions to Corporate Ethics Questions 58
Business Ethics on a Global Level 58
Adapting the Law to the Online Environment Corporate Reputations under Attack 59
Reviewing . . . Ethics and Business Decision Making 60
Terms and Concepts • Chapter Summary • ExamPrep • For Review • Questions and Case Problems
Unit One Unit Case Study with Dissenting Opinion: *Paduano v. American Honda Motor Co.* 64

Unit Two

Torts and Crimes 67

Chapter 4 Torts and Cyber Torts 68

The Basis of Tort Law 68
Hamlin v. Hampton Lumber Mills, Inc. (2011) **69**
Intentional Torts against Persons 70
Orlando v. Cole (2010) **72**

Intentional Torts against Property 76
Unintentional Torts (Negligence) 78

Wolf v. Don Dingmann Construction, Inc. (2011) **81**

Strict Liability 83
Cyber Torts—Online Defamation 83

Reviewing . . . Torts and Cyber Torts 84

Terms and Concepts • Chapter Summary • ExamPrep • For Review • Questions and Case Problems

Chapter 5 Intellectual Property and Internet Law 88

Trademarks and Related Property 89

Coca-Cola Co. v. Koke Co. of America (1920) **89**

Cyber Marks 92
Patents 93

Adapting the Law to the Online Environment Should the Law Continue to Allow Business Process Patents? 95

Copyrights 96

UMG Recordings, Inc. v. Augusto (2011) **97**

Maverick Recording Co. v. Harper (2010) **99**

Trade Secrets 100
International Protection for Intellectual Property 101

Reviewing . . . Intellectual Property and Internet Law 102

Terms and Concepts • Chapter Summary • ExamPrep • For Review • Questions and Case Problems

Chapter 6 Criminal Law and Cyber Crime 106

Civil Law and Criminal Law 106
Criminal Liability 108
Types of Crimes 109

People v. Sisuphan (2010) **111**

Defenses to Criminal Liability 113

Management Perspective Can a Businessperson Use Deadly Force to Prevent a Crime on the Premises? 115

Constitutional Safeguards and Criminal Procedures 115

Herring v. United States (2009) **117**

Criminal Process 118
Cyber Crime 120

United States v. Oliver (2011) **121**

Adapting the Law to the Online Environment Student Plagiarism and the Computer Fraud and Abuse Act 124

Reviewing . . . Criminal Law and Cyber Crime 125

Terms and Concepts • Chapter Summary • ExamPrep • For Review • Questions and Case Problems

Unit Two Unit Case Study with Dissenting Opinion: *MedImmune, Inc. v. Genentech, Inc.* 129

Unit Three

Contracts 131

Chapter 7 Nature and Classification 132

An Overview of Contract Law 132
Elements of a Contract 133
Types of Contracts 134

Schwarzrock v. Remote Technologies, Inc. (2011) **135**

Quasi Contracts 136

Scheerer v. Fisher (2010) **137**

Interpretation of Contracts 138

U.S. Bank, N.A. v. Tennessee Farmers Mutual Insurance Co. (2009) **139**

Reviewing . . . Nature and Classification 140

Terms and Concepts • Chapter Summary • ExamPrep • For Review • Questions and Case Problems

Chapter 8 Agreement in Traditional and E-Contracts 144

Agreement 144

Lucy v. Zehmer (1954) **145**

Alexander v. Lafayette Crime Stoppers, Inc. (2010) **147**

Powerhouse Custom Homes, Inc. v. 84 Lumber Co. (2011) **151**

Agreement in E-Contracts 152
The Uniform Electronic Transactions Act 154

Management Perspective E-Mailed Credit-Card Receipts 155

Reviewing . . . Agreement in Traditional and E-Contracts 157

Terms and Concepts • Chapter Summary • ExamPrep • For Review • Questions and Case Problems

Chapter 9 Consideration, Capacity, and Legality 162

Consideration 162

Harvey v. Dow (2011) **165**

Contractual Capacity 166
Legality 168

Sturdza v. United Arab Emirates (2011) **169**
Lhotka v. Geographic Expeditions, Inc. (2010) **172**
Reviewing . . . Consideration, Capacity, and Legality 173
Terms and Concepts • Chapter Summary • ExamPrep • For Review • Questions and Case Problems

Chapter 10 Defenses to Contract Enforceability 178

Voluntary Consent 178
L&H Construction Co. v. Circle Redmont, Inc. (2011) **180**
The Statute of Frauds—Writing Requirement 182
The Sufficiency of the Writing 185
Beneficial Homeowner Service Corp. v. Steele (2011) **186**
The Parol Evidence Rule 187
Watkins v. Schexnider (2010) **188**
Reviewing . . . Defenses to Contract Enforceability 189
Terms and Concepts • Chapter Summary • ExamPrep • For Review • Questions and Case Problems

Chapter 11 Third Party Rights and Discharge 193

Assignments 193
Malone v. Flattery (2011) **195**
Delegations 196
Third Party Beneficiaries 198
Allan v. Nersesova (2010) **199**
Contract Discharge 200
Pack 2000, Inc. v. Cushman (2011) **201**
Reviewing . . . Third Party Rights and Discharge 206
Terms and Concepts • Chapter Summary • ExamPrep • For Review • Questions and Case Problems

Chapter 12 Breach and Remedies 211

Damages 211
Jamison Well Drilling, Inc. v. Pfeifer (2011) **212**
Hadley v. Baxendale (1854) **213**
B-Sharp Musical Productions, Inc. v. Haber (2010) **215**
Equitable Remedies 216
Recovery Based on Quasi Contract 218
Contract Provisions Limiting Remedies 218
Reviewing . . . Breach and Remedies 219
Terms and Concepts • Chapter Summary • ExamPrep • For Review • Questions and Case Problems

Unit Three Unit Case Study with Dissenting Opinion: *Braddock v. Braddock* 223

Unit Four Sales and Lease Contracts 225

Chapter 13 The Formation of Sales and Lease Contracts 226

The Scope of the UCC and Articles 2 (Sales) and 2A (Leases) 226
Adapting the Law to the Online Environment The Thorny Issue of Taxing Internet Sales 228
The Formation of Sales and Lease Contracts 230
Office Supply Store.com v. Kansas City School Board (2011) **233**
Jones v. Star Credit Corp. (1969) **236**
Title and Risk of Loss 236
United States v. 2007 Custom Motorcycle (2011) **237**
Contracts for the International Sale of Goods 241
Reviewing . . . The Formation of Sales and Lease Contracts 242
Terms and Concepts • Chapter Summary • ExamPrep • For Review • Questions and Case Problems

Appendix to Chapter 13: An Example of a Contract for the International Sale of Coffee 248

Chapter 14 Performance and Breach of Sales and Lease Contracts 252

Performance Obligations 252
Obligations of the Seller or Lessor 252
Maple Farms, Inc. v. City School District of Elmira (1974) **255**
Obligations of the Buyer or Lessee 256
Romero v. Scoggin-Dickey Chevrolet-Buick, Inc. (2010) **257**
Anticipatory Repudiation 258
Remedies of the Seller or Lessor 258
Remedies of the Buyer or Lessee 260
Les Entreprises Jacques Defour & Fils, Inc. v. Dinsick Equipment Corp. (2011) **261**
Limitation of Remedies 263
Reviewing . . . Performance and Breach of Sales and Lease Contracts 264
Terms and Concepts • Chapter Summary • ExamPrep • For Review • Questions and Case Problems

Chapter 15 Warranties and Product Liability 269

Warranties 269

Webster v. Blue Ship Tea Room, Inc. (1964) **271**

Lemon Laws 273

Product Liability 274

Strict Product Liability 274

Bruesewitz v. Wyeth, LLC (2011) **275**

Adapting the Law to the Online Environment Should Video Games Be Required to Have Warning Labels? 278

Defenses to Product Liability 278

Boles v. Sun Ergoline, Inc. (2010) **279**

Reviewing . . . Warranties and Product Liability 281

Terms and Concepts • Chapter Summary • ExamPrep • For Review • Questions and Case Problems

Unit Four Unit Case Study with Dissenting Opinion: *Casserlie v. Shell Oil Co.* 286

Unit Five

Negotiable Instruments 289

Chapter 16 Negotiability, Transferability, and Liability 290

Types of Instruments 290

Requirements for Negotiability 292

Reger Development, LLC v. National City Bank (2010) **295**

Las Vegas Sands, LLC v. Nehme (2011) **296**

Transfer of Instruments 297

Indorsements 298

Hammett v. Deutsche Bank National Co. (2010) **299**

Holder in Due Course (HDC) 301

Triffin v. Liccardi Ford, Inc. (2011) **303**

Signature and Warranty Liability 304

Defenses, Limitations, and Discharge 307

Reviewing . . . Negotiability, Transferability, and Liability 309

Terms and Concepts • Chapter Summary • ExamPrep • For Review • Questions and Case Problems

Chapter 17 Checks and Banking in the Digital Age 315

Checks 315

MidAmerica Bank, FSB v. Charter One Bank (2009) **316**

The Bank-Customer Relationship 318

Bank's Duty to Honor Checks 318

Auto-Owners Insurance Co. v. Bank One (2008) **320**

Bank's Duty to Accept Deposits 323

Cumis Mutual Insurance Society, Inc. v. Rosol (2011) **325**

Electronic Fund Transfers 326

E-Money and Online Banking 327

Reviewing . . . Checks and Banking in the Digital Age 328

Terms and Concepts • Chapter Summary • ExamPrep • For Review • Questions and Case Problems

Unit Five Unit Case Study with Dissenting Opinion: *Prestridge v. Bank of Jena* 333

Unit Six

Debtor-Creditor Relationships 335

Chapter 18 Security Interests in Personal Property 336

The Terminology of Secured Transactions 336

Creating a Security Interest 337

Perfecting a Security Interest 338

In re Camtech Precision Manufacturing, Inc. (2011) **340**

The Scope of a Security Interest 342

Priorities 343

Citizens National Bank of Jessamine County v. Washington Mutual Bank (2010) **344**

Rights and Duties of Debtors and Creditors 345

Default 347

Hicklin v. Onyx Acceptance Corp. (2009) **348**

Reviewing . . . Security Interests in Personal Property 349

Terms and Concepts • Chapter Summary • ExamPrep • For Review • Questions and Case Problems

Chapter 19 Creditors' Rights and Bankruptcy 354

Laws Assisting Creditors 354
BHP Land Services, Inc. v. Seymour (2011) **355**
Protection for Debtors 359
Bankruptcy Law 360
Chapter 7—Liquidation 360
Chapter 11—Reorganization 367
Adapting the Law to the Online Environment The Debt That Never Goes Away—It's Discharged in Bankruptcy but Still on the Debtor's Credit Report 368
Bankruptcy Relief under Chapter 12 and Chapter 13 369
Ransom v. FIA Card Services, N.A. (2011) **371**
United Student Aid Funds, Inc. v. Espinosa (2010) **372**
Reviewing . . . Creditors' Rights and Bankruptcy 372
Terms and Concepts • Chapter Summary • ExamPrep • For Review • Questions and Case Problems

Chapter 20 Mortgages and Foreclosures after the Recession 378

Mortgages 379
Real Estate Financing Law 381
In re Kitts (2011) **383**
Foreclosures 384
U.S. Bank National Association v. Ibanez (2011) **386**
Mitchell v. Valteau (2010) **387**
Reviewing . . . Mortgages and Foreclosures after the Recession 388
Terms and Concepts • Chapter Summary • ExamPrep • For Review • Questions and Case Problems
Unit Six Unit Case Study with Dissenting Opinion: *Central Virginia Community College v. Katz* 393

Unit Seven

Employment Relations 395

Chapter 21 Agency Relationships 396

Agency Relationships 396
Management Perspective Independent-Contractor Negligence 398
Lopez v. El Palmar Taxi, Inc. (2009) **399**
How Agency Relationships Are Formed 400
Laurel Creek Health Care Center v. Bishop (2010) **400**
Duties of Agents and Principals 401
Agent's Authority 403
Liability in Agency Relationships 405
Williams v. Pike (2011) **406**
How Agency Relationships Are Terminated 408
Reviewing . . . Agency Relationships 410
Terms and Concepts • Chapter Summary • ExamPrep • For Review • Questions and Case Problems

Chapter 22 Employment, Immigration, and Labor Law 414

Employment at Will 414
Management Perspective Can Parties Create and Modify Employment Contracts via E-Mail? 416
Wage and Hour Laws 416
Smith v. Johnson and Johnson (2010) **417**
Layoffs 418
Family and Medical Leave 419
Worker Health and Safety 419
Income Security 420
Employee Privacy Rights 422
National Aeronautics and Space Administration v. Nelson (2011) **423**
Employment Discrimination 423
Thompson v. North American Stainless, LP (2011) **428**
Immigration Law 431
Labor Unions 433
Reviewing . . . Employment, Immigration, and Labor Law 435
Terms and Concepts • Chapter Summary • ExamPrep • For Review • Questions and Case Problems
Unit Seven Unit Case Study with Dissenting Opinion: *Media General Operations, Inc. v. National Labor Relations Board* 441

Unit Eight

Business Organizations 443

Chapter 23 Sole Proprietorships, Partnerships, and Limited Liability Companies 444

Sole Proprietorships 444

Partnerships 445
Meinhard v. Salmon (1928) **448**
Limited Liability Partnerships 451
Limited Partnerships 451
Craton Capital, LP v. Natural Pork Production II, LLP (2011) **452**
Limited Liability Companies 453
Polk v. Polk (2011) **455**
Reviewing . . . Sole Proprietorships, Partnerships, and Limited Liability Companies 456
Terms and Concepts • Chapter Summary • ExamPrep • For Review • Questions and Case Problems

Chapter 24 **Corporate Formation, Financing, and Termination 461**

Corporate Nature and Classification 461
Adapting the Law to the Online Environment Economic Recession Fuels the "Amazon Tax" Debate 463
Rubin v. Murray (2011) **465**
Corporate Formation and Powers 466
Schultz v. General Electric Healthcare Financial Services (2010) **471**
Corporate Financing 471
Mergers and Acquisitions 473
American Standard, Inc. v. OakFabco, Inc (2010) **476**
Termination 477
Reviewing . . . Corporate Formation, Financing, and Termination 477
Terms and Concepts • Chapter Summary • ExamPrep • For Review • Questions and Case Problems

Chapter 25 **Corporate Directors, Officers, and Shareholders 483**

Roles of Directors and Officers 483
Duties and Liabilities of Directors and Officers 486
Henrichs v. Chugach Alaska Corp. (2011) **487**
Guth v. Loft, Inc. (1939) **488**
Roles of Shareholders 489
Adapting the Law to the Online Environment Moving Company Information to the Internet 491
Rights of Shareholders 492
Bezirdjian v. O'Reilly (2010) **494**
Duties and Liabilities of Shareholders 495
Major Business Forms Compared 496
Reviewing . . . Corporate Directors, Officers, and Shareholders 497
Terms and Concepts • Chapter Summary • ExamPrep • For Review • Questions and Case Problems

Chapter 26 **Investor Protection, Insider Trading, and Corporate Governance 502**

The Securities Act of 1933 502
Litwin v. Blackstone Group, LP (2011) **507**
The Securities Exchange Act of 1934 507
Adapting the Law to the Online Environment Corporate Blogs and Tweets Must Comply with the Securities Exchange Act 508
Securities and Exchange Commission v. Texas Gulf Sulphur Co. (1968) **509**
Gebhart v. Securities and Exchange Commission (2010) **512**
State Securities Laws 513
Corporate Governance 514
Online Securities Fraud and Ponzi Schemes 517
Reviewing . . . Investor Protection, Insider Trading, and Corporate Governance 518
Terms and Concepts • Chapter Summary • ExamPrep • For Review • Questions and Case Problems
Unit Eight Unit Case Study with Dissenting Opinion: *Notz v. Everett Smith Group, Ltd.* 523

Unit Nine

Property and Its Protection 525

Chapter 27 **Personal Property and Bailments 526**

Property Ownership 526
Acquiring Ownership of Personal Property 527
Goodman v. Atwood (2011) **528**
In re Estate of Piper (1984) **529**
Mislaid, Lost, and Abandoned Property 530
Bailments 531
LaPlace v. Briere (2009) **534**
Reviewing . . . Personal Property and Bailments 536
Terms and Concepts • Chapter Summary • ExamPrep • For Review • Questions and Case Problems

Chapter 28 **Real Property and Landlord-Tenant Law 541**

The Nature of Real Property 541
APL Limited v. State of Washington Department of Revenue (2010) **542**

Ownership Interests in Real Property 543
Transfer of Ownership 545
Scarborough v. Rollins (2010) **547**
Town of Midland v. Morris (2011) **548**
Leasehold Estates 549
Landlord-Tenant Relationships 550
Reviewing . . . Real Property and Landlord-Tenant Law 551
Terms and Concepts • Chapter Summary • ExamPrep • For Review • Questions and Case Problems

Chapter 29 Insurance, Wills, and Trusts 555

Insurance 555
Valero v. Florida Insurance Guaranty Association, Inc. (2011) **559**
Wills 560
In re Estate of Johnson (2011) **562**
Trusts 566
Garrigus v. Viarengo (2009) **568**
Reviewing . . . Insurance, Wills, and Trusts 569
Terms and Concepts • Chapter Summary • ExamPrep • For Review • Questions and Case Problems
Unit Nine Unit Case Study with Dissenting Opinion: *Kovarik v. Kovarik* 575

Unit Ten

Special Topics 577

Chapter 30 Liability of Accountants and Other Professionals 578

Potential Common Law Liability to Clients 578
Kelley v. Buckley (2011) **581**
Walsh v. State (2009) **582**
Potential Liability to Third Parties 583
Perez v. Stern (2010) **584**
The Sarbanes-Oxley Act 585
Potential Statutory Liability of Accountants under Securities Laws 586
Potential Criminal Liability 588
Confidentiality and Privilege 588
Reviewing . . . Liability of Accountants and Other Professionals 589
Terms and Concepts • Chapter Summary • ExamPrep • For Review • Questions and Case Problems

Chapter 31 International Law in a Global Economy 593

International Law—Sources and Principles 593
Spectrum Stores, Inc. v. Citgo Petroleum Corp. (2011) **595**
Doing Business Internationally 596
Regulation of Specific Business Activities 597
United States v. Inn Foods, Inc. (2009) **598**
Commercial Contracts in an International Setting 600
Payment Methods for International Transactions 601
U.S. Laws in a Global Context 602
Khulumani v. Barclay National Bank, Ltd. (2007) **603**
Reviewing . . . International Law in a Global Economy 603
Terms and Concepts • Chapter Summary • ExamPrep • For Review • Questions and Case Problems
Unit Ten Unit Case Study with Dissenting Opinion: *Dole Food Co. v. Patrickson* 608

Appendices

Appendix A How to Brief Cases and Analyze Case Problems A–1
Appendix B The Constitution of the United States A–4
Appendix C The Uniform Commercial Code (Excerpts) A–11
Appendix D The Sarbanes-Oxley Act of 2002 (Excerpts and Explanatory Comments) A–120
Appendix E Sample Answers for Select *Questions with Sample Answer* A–126
Appendix F Sample Answers for *Case Problems with Sample Answer* A–128
Appendix G Answers to *Issue Spotters* A–135

Glossary G–1
Table of Cases TC–1
Index I–1

Preface to the Instructor

A fundamental knowledge of the tenets of business law is crucial for anyone contemplating a career in business. Consequently, we have written *Fundamentals of Business Law: Summarized Cases,* Ninth Edition, with this goal in mind: to present a clear and comprehensive treatment of what every student should know about commercial law. While some of this may change, the fundamentals rarely do—and that's what students reading this text will acquire.

What's New in the Ninth Edition

Instructors have come to rely on the coverage, accuracy, and applicability of *Fundamentals of Business Law: Summarized Cases.* To make sure that our text engages your students' interest, solidifies their understanding of the legal concepts presented, and provides the best teaching tools available, we now offer the following items either in the text or in conjunction with the text.

New Chapter on *Mortgages and Foreclosures after the Recession*

For the Ninth Edition, we have included an entirely new chapter (Chapter 20) entitled ***Mortgages and Foreclosures after the Recession.*** This chapter examines some of the mortgage-lending practices that contributed to the Great Recession and discusses the legal reforms enacted in response to it.

New Numbered *Case Examples*

One of the more appreciated features of *Fundamentals of Business Law: Summarized Cases* has always been the numbered examples in each chapter that clarify legal principles for students. Because many instructors use cases to illustrate how the law applies to business, for this edition, rather than presenting more summarized cases in each chapter, we have expanded the in-text numbered examples to include ***Case Examples.***

These *Case Examples* are integrated appropriately throughout the text and present the facts, issues, and rulings from actual court cases. Students can quickly read through the *Case Examples* to see how courts apply the legal principles under discussion in the real world.

New Cases and Case Problems

The Ninth Edition of *Fundamentals of Business Law: Summarized Cases* is filled with new cases. New cases from 2010 and 2011 are included in every chapter. That means more than 75 percent of the cases are new to this edition. We have carefully selected the new cases using the criteria that (1) they illustrate important points of law, (2) they are of high interest to students and instructors, and (3) they are simple enough factually for business law students to understand. We have made it a point to find recent cases that enhance learning. We have also eliminated cases that are too difficult procedurally or factually.

Additionally, nearly every chapter features at least one new 2010 and 2011 case problem.

New Coverage of Hot Topics

To pique student interest from the outset, many chapters open with the latest news surrounding the legal topics under discussion. A section of text within that chapter further explores the topic.

For example, Chapter 5 discusses the patent infringement lawsuit filed by Apple, Inc., against Samsung for allegedly imitating the iPhone and iPad too closely. Chapter 20 discusses the $20 billion settlement paid by Bank of America in 2011 for fraud relating to mortgage securities. The employment and labor law chapter includes a discussion of the recently settled NFL lockout, as well as the United States Supreme Court's 2011 decision in a gender-discrimination case against Wal-Mart.

New *Video Questions*

In response to popular demand, we have created several new ***Video Questions*** for this edition. These questions refer students to the text's Web site to view a particular video clip before answering a series of questions in the book. Some of the new videos are clips from actual movies or television series, such as *Field of Dreams, Midnight Run,* and *Mary Tyler Moore.*

New *ExamPrep* Sections

In every chapter, we have added a new ***ExamPrep* section** that includes two ***Issue Spotters.*** These *Issue Spotters* facilitate student learning and review of the chapter materials. In addition, the section refers students to Appendix G for the answers to the *Issue Spotters.* The ***Before the Test*** portion of this section refers students to the text's Web site for additional study tools, such as *Flashcards* and *Interactive Quizzes* correlated to the chapter.

Practical and Effective Learning Tools

Today's business leaders must often think "outside the box" when making business decisions. For this reason, we have included numerous critical-thinking elements in the Ninth Edition that are designed to challenge students' understanding of the materials beyond simple retention. In addition, we have retained and improved the many practical features of this text to help students learn how the law applies to business.

Critical Thinking and Legal Reasoning

Every case presented in this text concludes with one critical thinking question. These questions include ***For Critical Analysis, What If the Facts Were Different?***, and ***Why Is This Case Important?***

This critical thinking emphasis is reiterated in the chapter-ending materials of selected chapters, which present special *Critical Thinking [Managerial or Legal] Questions*. **Suggested answers to these questions, as well as those following the cases, can be found in both the *Instructor's Manual* and the *Answers Manual* that accompany this text.**

Adapting the Law to the Online Environment

The Ninth Edition contains many new ***Adapting the Law to the Online Environment*** features, which examine cutting-edge cyberlaw issues coming before today's courts. Here are some examples:

- Should the Law Continue to Allow Business Process Patents? (Chapter 5)
- The Thorny Issue of Taxing Internet Sales (Chapter 13)
- Should Video Games Be Required to Have Warning Labels? (Chapter 14)
- Economic Recession Fuels the "Amazon Tax" Debate (Chapter 24)
- Corporate Blogs and Tweets Must Comply with the Securities Exchange Act (Chapter 26)

Each feature concludes with a *For Critical Analysis* section that asks the student to think critically about some facet of the issues discussed in the feature.

Management Perspective

Each ***Management Perspective*** feature begins with a section titled *Management Faces a Legal Issue* that describes a practical issue facing management—such as whether to include arbitration clauses in employment contracts. A section titled *What the Courts Say* comes next and discusses what the courts have concluded with respect to the specific issue. The feature concludes with *Implications for Managers*, a section indicating the importance of the courts' decisions for business management and offering some practical guidance.

Sample Answers

For those instructors who would like students to have sample answers available for some of the chapter-ending questions, we have included three new appendices of sample answers. Selected chapters include a ***Question with Sample Answer*** that is answered in Appendix E. Every chapter includes a ***Case Problem with Sample Answer*** that is based on an actual case and answered in Appendix F. In additiion, Appendix G provides answers to each of the ***Issue Spotters***, which are featured in every chapter of this Ninth Edition.

Students can compare their own answers to the answers provided to determine whether they have applied the law correctly and to learn what needs to be included when answering the end-of-chapter questions and case problems.

Reviewing . . . Features

Reviewing . . . features present a hypothetical scenario and ask a series of questions that require students to identify the issues and apply the legal concepts discussed in the chapter. Each chapter concludes with one of these features, which are intended to help students review the chapter materials in a simple and an interesting way.

Fundamentals of Business Law on the Web

For this edition of *Fundamentals of Business Law: Summarized Cases*, we have redesigned and streamlined the text's Web site so that users can easily locate the resources they seek. When you visit our Web site at **www.cengagebrain.com** and enter the ISBN 9781111530624, you will find a broad array of teaching/learning resources, including the following:

- ***Video Questions*** that appear in selected chapters.
- ***Interactive Quizzes*** for every chapter in this text that include a number of questions related to each chapter's contents.
- ***Terms and Concepts*** for every chapter in the text.
- ***Flashcards*** that provide students with an optional study tool to review the key terms in every chapter.
- ***Appendix A: How to Brief Cases and Analyze Case Problems***
- ***Legal reference materials*** including a "Statutes" page that offers links to the full text of selected statutes referenced in the text, a Spanish glossary, and links to other important legal resources available on the Web.

Business Law Digital Video Library

For this edition of *Fundamentals of Business Law: Summarized Cases,* we have included special *Video Questions* at the ends of selected chapters. Each of these questions directs students to the text's Web site at **www.cengagebrain.com**.

Once there, to view the specific video referenced in the *Video Question,* students click on the "Business Law Digital Video Library" link and type in their access code. After viewing the video online, students can return to the text's Web site and click on the relevant chapter's "Video Questions" link to view the series of questions based on the video they have just viewed. (An access code for the videos can be packaged with each new copy of this textbook for no additional charge. If *Business Law Digital Video Library* access did not come packaged with the textbook, it can be purchased online at **www.cengagebrain.com**.)

These videos can be used as homework assignments, discussion starters, or classroom demonstrations. By watching a video and answering the questions, students will gain an understanding of how the legal concepts they have studied in the chapter apply to the real-life situation portrayed in the video. **Suggested answers for all of the *Video Questions* are given in both the *Instructor's Manual* and the *Answers Manual* that accompany this text.**

Special Features and Pedagogy

In addition to the components of the *Fundamentals of Business Law: Summarized Cases* teaching/learning package described above, the Ninth Edition offers a number of special features and pedagogical devices, including those described here.

Case Presentation and Format

As discussed previously, we have carefully selected recent cases for each chapter that not only provide on-point illustrations of the legal principles discussed in the chapter but also are of high interest to students. The cases are numbered sequentially for easy referencing in class discussions, homework assignments, and examinations. The vast majority of cases in this text are new to the Ninth Edition.

Each case is presented in a special format, beginning with the case title and citation (including parallel citations). Whenever possible, we also include a URL just below the case citation that can be used to access the case online (a footnote to the URL explains how to find the specific case at that Web site).

After briefly outlining the ***Facts*** of the case, we present the legal ***Issue*** and the court's ***Decision.*** To enhance student understanding, we then paraphrase the ***Reason*** for the court's decision. Each case normally concludes with a ***For Critical Analysis*** question or a ***What If the Facts Were Different?*** question. For selected cases, we have included a section titled ***Why Is This Case Important?*** This section clearly sets forth the importance of the court's decision for businesspersons today.

We give special emphasis to *Classic Cases* by setting them off with a special heading and logo. These cases also include a section titled ***Impact of This Case on Today's Law*** that explains the significance of that particular decision for the evolution of the law in that area.

Other Pedagogical Devices within Each Chapter

- ***Learning Objectives*** (a series of brief questions at the beginning of each chapter designed to provide a framework for the student as he or she reads through the chapter).
- ***Numbered examples illustrating legal principles*** (we have added more for this edition to better clarify legal concepts).
- ***Exhibits.***

Chapter-Ending Pedagogy

- ***Reviewing . . .* features** (in every chapter).
- ***Terms and Concepts*** (with appropriate page references).
- ***Chapter Summary*** (in graphic format with page references).
- ***ExamPrep*** (in every chapter and features two *Issue Spotters* and a *Before the Test* section).
- ***For Review*** (the questions set forth in the chapter-opening *Learning Objectives* section are presented again to aid the student in reviewing the chapter).
- ***Questions and Case Problems*** (a compilation of hypothetical scenarios and case-based problems).
- ***Question with Sample Answer*** (in selected chapters).
- ***Case Problem with Sample Answer*** (in every chapter).
- ***A Question of Ethics*** (in every chapter).
- ***Critical Thinking Legal or Mangerial Question*** (in selected chapters).
- ***Video Question*** (in selected chapters).

Unit Case Study with Dissenting Opinion

At the end of each unit is a two-page feature entitled ***Unit Case Study with Dissenting Opinion.*** This feature focuses on a recent court case relating to a topic covered in the unit. Each feature opens with an introductory section, which discusses the background and significance of the case being presented.

Then, we present excerpts from the court's majority opinion and from a dissenting opinion in the case. The feature concludes with *Questions for Analysis*—a series of questions that prompt the student to think critically about the legal, ethical, economic, global, or general business implications of the case.

Suggested answers to all chapter-ending and unit-ending questions are included in both the *Instructor's Manual* and the *Answers Manual.*

Appendices

To help students learn how to find and analyze case law, we have included a special appendix at the end of Chapter 1. There, your students will find information, including an exhibit, on how to read case citations, how to locate cases in case reporters, and what the different components of URLs (Internet addresses) mean. The appendix to Chapter 1 also presents an annotated sample court case to help your students understand how to read and understand the cases presented within this text.

Additionally, we provide an appendix at the end of Chapter 13, which shows an actual international sales contract used by Starbucks Coffee Company. Annotations in the appendix explain the meaning and significance of specific clauses. At the end of the book, we have also included the following set of appendices:

A How to Brief Cases and Analyze Case Problems (also available on the Web site)

B The Constitution of the United States

C The Uniform Commercial Code (Excerpts)

D The Sarbanes-Oxley Act of 2002 (Excerpts and Explanatory Comments)

E Sample Answers for Select *Questions with Sample Answers*

F Sample Answers for *Case Problems with Sample Answer*

G Answers to the *Issue Spotters*

Supplemental Teaching Materials

Fundamentals of Business Law: Summarized Cases is accompanied by an expansive number of teaching and learning supplements. Individually and in conjunction with a number of our colleagues, we have developed supplementary teaching materials that we believe are the best available today. Each component of the supplements package is listed below.

Printed Supplements

- ***Instructor's Manual*** (Includes **additional cases on point** with at least one such case summary per chapter, answers to all *For Critical Analysis* questions in the cases, answers for the *Video Questions* at the ends of selected chapters, and answers to the *Unit Case Study with Dissenting Opinion* that concludes each unit. Also available on the *Instructor's Resource CD-ROM,* or IRCD, described below.)
- ***Study Guide.***
- A comprehensive ***Test Bank*** (also available on the IRCD).
- ***Answers to Questions and Case Problems and Alternate Problem Sets with Answers***—Provides answers to all the questions presented in the text, including those for each *Adapting the Law to the Online Environment* feature. It also provides alternate problem sets with answers (available on IRCD).

Software, Video, and Multimedia Supplements

- ***Instructor's Resource CD-ROM* (IRCD)**—The IRCD includes the following supplements: *Instructor's Manual, Answers Manual, Test Bank,* Case-Problem Cases, Case Printouts, ExamView, PowerPoint Slides, transparency masters, *Instructor's Manual* for the *Drama of the Law* video series, *Handbook of Landmark Cases and Statutes in Business Law and the Legal Environment, Handbook on Critical Thinking in Business Law and the Legal Environment,* and *A Guide to Personal Law.*
- **ExamView Testing Software** (available only on the IRCD).
- ***Business Law CourseMate***—Brings business law concepts to life with interactive learning, study, and exam preparation tools that support the printed textbook. Built-in engagement tracking tools allow you to assess your students' study activities. Additionally, *Business Law CourseMate* includes an interactive online textbook, which contains the entire contents of the printed textbook enhanced by the many advantages of a digital environment.
- ***Business Law Digital Video Library***—This dynamic video library features more than sixty videos that spark class discussion and clarify core legal principles. Access is available for free as an optional package item with each new text. If *Business Law Digital Video Library* access did not come packaged with the textbook, your students can purchase it online at **www.cengagebrain.com**.

For Users of the Eighth Edition

We thought that those of you who have been using the Eighth Edition of *Fundamentals of Business Law: Summarized Cases* would like to know some of the major changes that have been made for the Ninth Edition.

New Cases and Case Problems

You will find that most of the cases in this edition are new. Nearly every chapter has two new cases, and several chapters have three new cases, including many 2011 cases. In addition, each chapter also now includes one, two, or even three new case problems.

New Features and Special Pedagogy

We have added the following entirely new elements for the Ninth Edition:

- *Case Examples* that are numbered consecutively with the other in-text examples to illustrate legal principles, but are based on the facts and decisions of actual courts.
- ***ExamPrep* sections** in every chapter that include two *Issue Spotters*, as well as references to the *Interactive Quizzes* and *Flashcards* available on the text's Web site.
- Discussions of hot topics in selected chapter introductions and chapters.
- Appendix F, Sample Answers for *Case Problems with Sample Answers*.
- Appendix G, Answers to the *Issue Spotters*.

Significantly Revised Chapters

Every chapter of the Ninth Edition has been revised as necessary to incorporate new developments in the law or to streamline the presentations. Other major changes include the following:

- **Chapter 3** (Ethics and Business Decision Making)—This chapter has been substantially revised and refocused to be more pragmatic. The chapter now includes a step-by-step approach to making ethical business decisions, as well as a new feature discussing how companies and management can deal with attacks on a company's reputation.
- **Chapter 5** (Intellectual Property and Internet Law)—The materials on intellectual property rights in the online environment have been thoroughly revised and updated. A new subsection addresses the problem of counterfeit goods, and the discussion of domain names and cybersquatting has been updated. Several recent Supreme Court cases are discussed in the text, as well as the 2011 America Invents Act.
- **Chapter 6** (Criminal Law and Cyber Crime)—This chapter has been substantially revised to deal with the growing problem of cyber crime, including many types of Internet fraud, identity theft, phishing, and Ponzi schemes. It also covers some of the difficulties involved in prosecuting cyber crime.
- **Chapters 7 through 12** (the Contracts unit)—We have merged our discussion of online contracting and electronic signatures with our coverage of traditional contracts. We have added more examples, new *Case Examples*, and updates.
- **Chapters 13 through 15** (Sales and Lease Contracts)—We have streamlined and reorganized our materials so that we have an entire unit that deals with commercial transactions and aspects of the Uniform Commercial Code. We have focused on making these materials more comprehensible and readable, particularly in the area of secured transactions.
- **Chapter 20** (Mortgages and Foreclosures after the Recession)—This chapter is entirely new to this edition and provides a timely look at the mortgage crisis, predatory lending practices, and the laws enacted to address some of the problems that became evident during the recession.
- **Chapter 22** (Employment, Immigration, and Labor Law)—This chapter has been thoroughly revised and updated to include discussions of legal issues facing employers today. It includes an entirely new section on immigration law, a topic of increasing importance to employers. It also includes the 2009 changes to the Family and Medical Leave Act and the latest developments and United States Supreme Court decisions on constructive discharge, retaliation, religious discrimination, and age discrimination. It also discusses the 2009 equal pay legislation and the 2008 amendments to the Americans with Disabilities Act.
- **Chapter 26** (Investor Protection, Insider Trading, and Corporate Governance)—We have revamped this chapter to discuss the simplified registration process for "well-known seasoned issuers" and provide recent examples of insider trading and online securities fraud. A new feature discusses the disclosure of financial information on corporate blogs and tweets.
- **Chapter 30** (Liability of Accountants and Other Professionals)—This chapter has been updated to discuss how the Securities and Exchange Commission has recently adopted global accounting rules.

Acknowledgments

Numerous careful and conscientious users of *Fundamentals of Business Law: Summarized Cases* were kind enough to help us revise the book. In addition, the staff at Cengage/South-Western went out of its way to make sure that this edition came out early and in accurate form. In particular, we wish to thank Rob Dewey and Vicky True-Baker for their countless new ideas, many of which have been incorporated into the Ninth Edition. We also extend special thanks to Jan Lamar, our longtime developmental editor, for her many useful suggestions and for her efforts in coordinating reviews and ensuring the timely and accurate publication of all supplemental materials. We are particularly indebted to Laura-Aurora Stopa for her support and excellent marketing advice.

Our production manager and designer, Bill Stryker, made sure that we came out with an error-free, visually attractive edition. We will always be in his debt. We are also indebted to the staff at Parkwood Composition, our compositor. Their ability to generate the pages for this text quickly and accurately made it possible for us to meet our ambitious printing schedule.

We must especially thank Katherine Marie Silsbee and Vickie Reierson for their management of the project, as well as for the application of their superb research and editorial skills. We also wish to thank William Eric Hollowell, co-author of the *Instructor's Manual, Study Guide, Test Bank,* and *Online Legal Research Guide,* for his excellent research efforts. The copyediting services of Susan Bradley, and proofreading by Pat Lewis and Jeanne Yost, will not go unnoticed. We thank, too, Lavina Leed Miller, for her indexing expertise. We also thank Roxanna Lee for her proofreading and other assistance. Finally, our appreciation goes to Suzanne Jasin for her many special efforts on the projects.

Acknowledgments for the Ninth Edition

Kenneth Anderson
Mott Community College

John D. Grether
Northwood University

Curtis Hayes
Western New Mexico University

Christie Highlander
Southwestern Illinois College

Lori L. Pack
Suffolk Community College

We also wish to extend special thanks to the following individuals for their valuable input for the new Chapter 20 and for helping revise Chapter 28:

Robert C. Bird
University of Connecticut

Dean Bredeson
University of Texas at Austin

Corey Ciocchetti
University of Denver

Thomas D. Cavenagh
North Central College—Illinois

Joan Gabel
Florida State University

Eric D. Yordy
Northern Arizona University

Acknowledgments for Previous Editions

Jamie Baldwin
Embry Riddle Aeronautical University—Daytona Beach

Peter Dawson
Collin College

Douglas V. Jensen
Pierce College

Edward M. Kissling
Ocean County College

Nancy Lahmers
The Ohio State University

Robert M. Rowlands
Harrisburg Area Community College

John Spengler
University of Florida

Staci L. Thornsbury
York Technical College

Deborah Vinecour
SUNY Rockland Community College

We know that we are not perfect. If you or your students find something you don't like or want us to change, write to us or let us know via e-mail, using the "Contact Us" feature on this text's Web site. That is how we can make *Fundamentals of Business Law: Summarized Cases* an even better book in the future.

Roger LeRoy Miller

Dedication

To Amanda and Antoine,

You two prove that hard work equals fulfillment.

(But don't forget to play, too.)

R.L.M.

Unit One

The Legal Environment of Business

Unit Contents

1 The Legal and Constitutional Environment of Business

2 Traditional and Online Dispute Resolution

3 Ethics and Business Decision Making

(John Elk III/Lonely Planet Images/Getty Images)

Chapter 1

The Legal and Constitutional Environment of Business

Learning Objectives

After reading this chapter, you should be able to answer the following questions:

1. What is the common law tradition?
2. What is the difference between remedies at law and remedies in equity?
3. What constitutional clause gives the federal government the power to regulate commercial activities among the various states?
4. What is the Bill of Rights? What freedoms does the First Amendment guarantee?
5. Where in the U.S. Constitution can the due process clause be found?

The Learning Objectives above are designed to help improve your understanding of the chapter.

(John Elk III/Lonely Planet Images/Getty Images)

The law is of interest to all persons, not just to lawyers. Those entering the world of business will find themselves subject to numerous laws and government regulations. A basic knowledge of these laws and regulations is beneficial—if not essential—to anyone contemplating a successful career in today's business world.

Although the law has had and will continue to have different definitions, all the definitions are based on the general observation that, at a minimum, **law** consists of *enforceable rules governing relationships among individuals and between individuals and their society.* These "enforceable rules" may consist of unwritten principles of behavior established by a nomadic tribe. They may be set forth in an ancient or a contemporary law code. They may consist of written laws and court decisions created by modern legislative and judicial bodies, as in the United States. Regardless of how such rules are created, they all have one thing in common: they establish rights, duties, and privileges that are consistent with the values and beliefs of their society or its ruling group.

In this chapter, we first look at an important question for any student reading this text: How does the legal environment affect business decision making? We next describe the basic sources of American law, the common law tradition, and some general classifications of law. We conclude the chapter with a discussion of the U.S. Constitution as it affects business.

Business Activities and the Legal Environment

As those entering the business world will learn, laws and government regulations affect all business activities—hiring and firing decisions, workplace safety, the manufacturing and marketing of products, and business financing, to name just a few. To make good business decisions, a basic knowledge of the laws and regulations governing these activities is essential. Moreover, in today's setting, simply being aware of what conduct can lead to legal liability is not enough. Businesspersons are also under increasing pressure to make ethical decisions and to consider the consequences of their decisions for stockholders and employees (as will be discussed in Chapter 3).

As you will note, each chapter in this text covers a specific area of the law and shows how the legal rules in that area affect business activities. Although compartmentalizing the law in this fashion facilitates learning, it does not indicate the extent to which many different laws may apply to just one transaction.

Suppose that you are the president of NetSys, Inc., a company that creates and maintains computer network systems for other business firms. NetSys also markets software for internal computer networks. One day, Janet Hernandez, an operations officer for Southwest Distribution Corporation (SDC), contacts you by e-mail about a possible contract involving SDC's computer network.

In deciding whether to enter into a contract with SDC, you need to consider, among other things, the legal requirements for an enforceable contract. Are the requirements different for a contract for services and a contract for products? What are your options if SDC **breaches** (breaks, or fails to perform) the contract? The answers to these questions are part of contract law and sales law.

Other questions might concern payment under the contract. For example, if SDC pays with a check that is returned for insufficient funds, what are your options? Answers to these questions can be found in the laws that relate to negotiable instruments (such as checks) and creditors' rights. Also, a dispute may arise over the rights to NetSys's software, or there may be a question of liability if the software is defective. There may even be an issue as to whether you and Hernandez had the authority to make the deal in the first place. Resolutions of these questions may be found in the laws that relate to intellectual property, e-commerce, torts, product liability, agency, business organizations, or professional liability.

Finally, if any dispute cannot be resolved amicably, then the laws and the rules concerning courts and court procedures spell out the steps of a lawsuit. Exhibit 1–1 below illustrates the various areas of the law that may influence business decision making.

Sources of American Law

There are numerous sources of American law. **Primary sources of law**, or sources that establish the law, include the following:

- The U.S. Constitution and the constitutions of the various states.

• ***Exhibit*** **1–1 Areas of the Law That May Affect Business Decision Making**

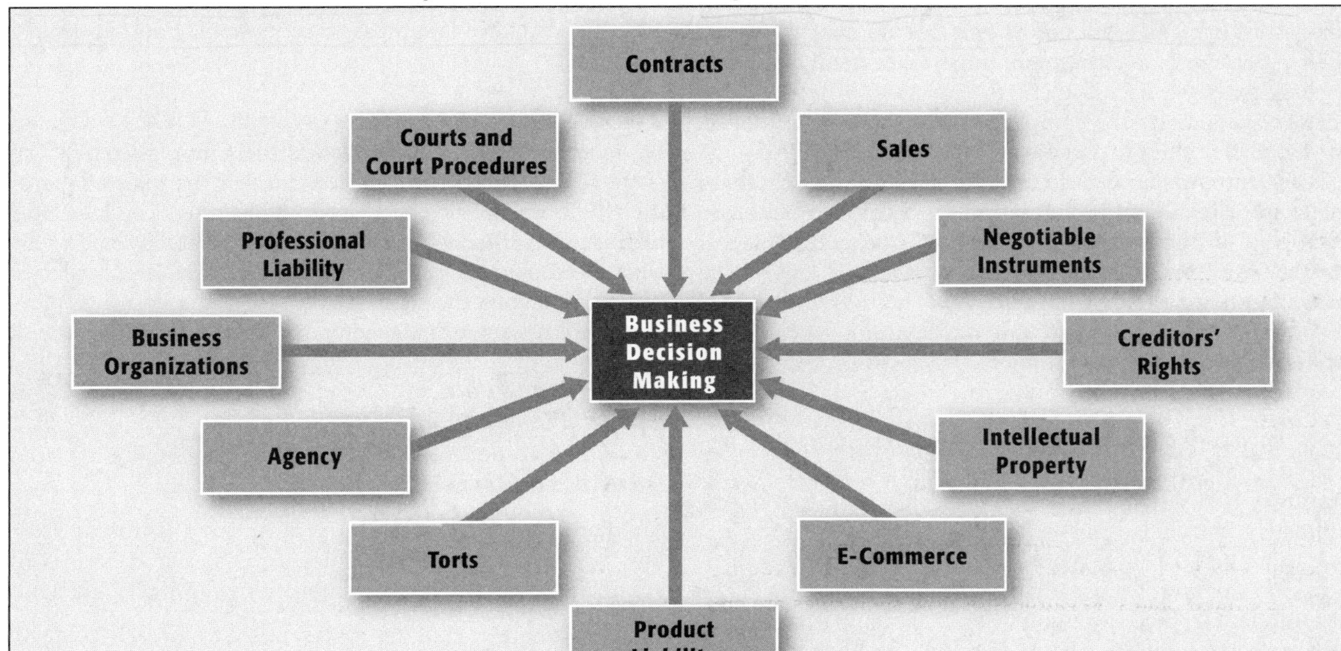

- Statutes, or laws, passed by Congress and by state legislatures.
- Regulations created by administrative agencies, such as the U.S. Food and Drug Administration.
- Case law (court decisions).

We describe each of these important primary sources of law in the following pages. (See the appendix at the end of this chapter for a discussion of how to find statutes, regulations, and case law.)

Secondary sources of law are books and articles that summarize and clarify the primary sources of law. Legal encyclopedias, compilations (such as *Restatements of the Law,* which summarize court decisions on a particular topic), official comments to statutes, treatises, articles in law reviews published by law schools, and articles in other legal journals are examples of secondary sources of law. Courts often refer to secondary sources of law for guidance in interpreting and applying the primary sources of law discussed here.

Constitutional Law

The federal government and the states have separate written constitutions that set forth the general organization, powers, and limits of their respective governments. **Constitutional law** is the law as expressed in these constitutions.

The U.S. Constitution is the supreme law of the land. As such, it is the basis of all law in the United States. A law in violation of the Constitution, if challenged, will be declared unconstitutional and will not be enforced no matter what its source. Because of its paramount importance in the American legal system, we discuss the U.S. Constitution later in this chapter and present the complete text of the Constitution in Appendix B.

The Tenth Amendment to the U.S. Constitution reserves to the states all powers not granted to the federal government. Each state in the union has its own constitution. Unless it conflicts with the U.S. Constitution or a federal law, a state constitution is supreme within the state's borders.

Statutory Law

Laws enacted by legislative bodies at any level of government, such as the statutes passed by Congress or by state legislatures, make up the body of law generally referred to as **statutory law.** When a legislature passes a statute, that statute ultimately is included in the federal code of laws or the relevant state code of laws. Whenever a particular statute is mentioned in this text, we usually provide a footnote showing its **citation** (a reference to a publication in which a legal authority—such as a statute or a court decision—or other source can be found). In the appendix following this chapter, we explain how you can use these citations to find statutory law.

Statutory law also includes local **ordinances**—statutes (laws, rules, or orders) passed by municipal or county governing units to govern matters not covered by federal or state law. Ordinances commonly have to do with city or county land use (zoning ordinances), building and safety codes, and other matters affecting only the local governing unit.

A federal statute, of course, applies to all states. A state statute, in contrast, applies only within the state's borders. State laws may vary from state to state. No federal statute may violate the U.S. Constitution, and no state statute or local ordinance may violate the U.S. Constitution or the relevant state constitution.

UNIFORM LAWS During the 1800s, the differences among state laws frequently created difficulties for businesspersons conducting trade and commerce among the states. To counter these problems, a group of legal scholars and lawyers formed the National Conference of Commissioners on Uniform State Laws (NCCUSL) in 1892 to draft **uniform laws** ("model statutes") for the states to consider adopting. The NCCUSL still exists today and continues to issue uniform laws: it has issued more than two hundred uniform acts since its inception.

Each state has the option of adopting or rejecting a uniform law. *Only if a state legislature adopts a uniform law does that law become part of the statutory law of that state.* Note that a state legislature may adopt all or part of a uniform law as it is written, or the legislature may rewrite the law however the legislature wishes. Hence, even though many states may have adopted a uniform law, those states' laws may not be entirely "uniform."

THE UNIFORM COMMERCIAL CODE (UCC) One of the more important uniform acts is the Uniform Commercial Code (UCC), which was created through the joint efforts of the NCCUSL and the American Law Institute.[1] The UCC was first issued in 1952 and has been adopted in all fifty states,[2] the District of Columbia, and the Virgin Islands. The UCC facilitates commerce among the states by providing a uniform, yet flexible, set of rules governing commercial transactions. Because of its importance in the area of commercial law, we cite the UCC frequently in this text. We also present excerpts of the UCC in Appendix C.

Administrative Law

Another important source of American law is **administrative law,** which consists of the rules, orders, and decisions of administrative agencies. An administrative agency is a federal,

1. This institute was formed in the 1920s and consists of practicing attorneys, legal scholars, and judges.
2. Louisiana has adopted only Articles 1, 3, 4, 5, 7, 8, and 9.

state, or local government agency established to perform a specific function. Rules issued by various administrative agencies now affect almost every aspect of a business's operations, including the firm's capital structure and financing, its hiring and firing procedures, its relations with employees and unions, and the way it manufactures and markets its products.

Case Law and Common Law Doctrines

The rules of law announced in court decisions constitute another basic source of American law. These rules of law include interpretations of constitutional provisions, of statutes enacted by legislatures, and of regulations created by administrative agencies. Today, this body of judge-made law is referred to as **case law.** Case law—the doctrines and principles announced in cases—governs all areas not covered by statutory law or administrative law and is part of our common law tradition. We look at the origins and characteristics of the common law tradition in some detail in the pages that follow.

The Common Law Tradition

Because of our colonial heritage, much of American law is based on the English legal system. A knowledge of this tradition is crucial to understanding our legal system today because judges in the United States still apply common law principles when deciding cases.

Early English Courts

After the Normans conquered England in 1066, William the Conqueror and his successors began the process of unifying the country under their rule. One of the means they used to do this was the establishment of the king's courts, or *curiae regis.* Before the Norman Conquest, disputes had been settled according to the local legal customs and traditions in various regions of the country. The king's courts sought to establish a uniform set of rules for the country as a whole. What evolved in these courts was the beginning of the **common law**—a body of general rules that applied throughout the entire English realm. Eventually, the common law tradition became part of the heritage of all nations that were once British colonies, including the United States.

Courts developed the common law rules from the principles underlying judges' decisions in actual legal controversies. Judges attempted to be consistent, and whenever possible, they based their decisions on the principles suggested by earlier cases. They sought to decide similar cases in a similar way and considered new cases with care, because they knew that their decisions would make new law. Each interpretation became part of the law on the subject and served as a legal **precedent**—that is, a court decision that furnished an example or authority for deciding subsequent cases involving identical or similar legal principles or facts.

In the early years of the common law, there was no single place or publication where court opinions, or written decisions, could be found. Beginning in the late thirteenth and early fourteenth centuries, however, portions of significant decisions from each year were gathered together and recorded in *Year Books.* The *Year Books* were useful references for lawyers and judges. In the sixteenth century, the *Year Books* were discontinued, and other reports of cases became available.

Stare Decisis

The practice of deciding new cases with reference to former decisions, or precedents, eventually became a cornerstone of the English and U.S. judicial systems. The practice forms a doctrine called ***stare decisis***[3] ("to stand on decided cases").

THE IMPORTANCE OF PRECEDENTS IN JUDICIAL DECISION MAKING Under the doctrine of *stare decisis,* once a court has set forth a principle of law as being applicable to a certain set of facts, that court and courts of lower rank must adhere to that principle and apply it in future cases involving similar fact patterns. *Stare decisis* has two aspects: first, decisions made by a higher court are binding on lower courts; and second, a court should not overturn its own precedents unless there is a strong reason to do so.

Controlling precedents in a *jurisdiction* (an area in which a court or courts have the power to apply the law—see Chapter 2) are referred to as binding authorities. A **binding authority** is any source of law that a court must follow when deciding a case. Binding authorities include constitutions, statutes, and regulations that govern the issue being decided, as well as court decisions that are controlling precedents within the jurisdiction. United States Supreme Court case decisions, no matter how old, remain controlling until they are overruled by a subsequent decision of the Supreme Court, by a constitutional amendment, or by congressional legislation.

***STARE DECISIS* AND LEGAL STABILITY** The doctrine of *stare decisis* helps the courts to be more efficient because if other courts have carefully reasoned through a similar case, their legal reasoning and opinions can serve as guides. *Stare decisis* also makes the law more stable and predictable. If the law on a given subject is well settled, someone bringing a case to court can usually rely on the court to make a decision based on what the law has been.

DEPARTURES FROM PRECEDENT Although courts are obligated to follow precedents, sometimes a court will depart

3. Pronounced *stahr*-ee dih-*si*-sis.

from the rule of precedent if it decides that a given precedent should no longer be followed. If a court decides that a precedent is simply incorrect or that technological or social changes have rendered the precedent inapplicable, the court might rule contrary to the precedent. Cases that overturn precedent often receive a great deal of publicity.

CASE EXAMPLE 1.1 In *Brown v. Board of Education of Topeka*,[4] the United States Supreme Court expressly overturned precedent when it concluded that separate educational facilities for whites and blacks, which had been upheld as constitutional in numerous previous cases,[5] were inherently unequal. The Court's departure from precedent in the *Brown* decision received a tremendous amount of publicity as people began to realize the ramifications of this change in the law. •

WHEN THERE IS NO PRECEDENT At times, cases arise for which there are no precedents within the jurisdiction. When hearing such cases, called "cases of first impression," courts often look at precedents established in other jurisdictions for guidance. Precedents from other jurisdictions, because they are not binding on the court, are referred to as **persuasive authorities.** A court may also consider various other factors, including legal principles and policies underlying previous court decisions or existing statutes, fairness, social values and customs, public policy, and data and concepts drawn from the social sciences.

Equitable Remedies and Courts of Equity

A **remedy** is the means given to a party to enforce a right or to compensate for the violation of a right. **EXAMPLE 1.2** Shem is injured because of Rowan's wrongdoing. If Shem files a lawsuit and is successful, a court can order Rowan to compensate Shem for the harm by paying Shem a certain amount. The compensation is Shem's remedy. •

The kinds of remedies available in the early king's courts of England were severely restricted. If one person wronged another, the king's courts could award as compensation either money or property, including land. These courts became known as *courts of law,* and the remedies were called *remedies at law.* Even though this system introduced uniformity in the settling of disputes, when plaintiffs wanted a remedy other than economic compensation, the courts of law could do nothing, so "no remedy, no right."

REMEDIES IN EQUITY *Equity* is a branch of law, founded on what might be described as notions of justice and fair dealing, that seeks to supply a remedy when no adequate remedy at law is available. When individuals could not obtain an adequate remedy in a court of law, they petitioned the king for relief. Most of these petitions were decided by an adviser to the king, called a *chancellor,* who had the power to grant new and unique remedies. Eventually, formal chancery courts, or *courts of equity,* were established. Thus, two distinct court systems were created, each having its own set of judges and its own set of remedies. The remedies granted by these courts were called *remedies in equity.*

Plaintiffs (those bringing lawsuits) had to specify whether they were bringing an "action at law" or an "action in equity," and they chose their courts accordingly. **EXAMPLE 1.3** A plaintiff might ask a court of equity to order the **defendant** (the person against whom a lawsuit is brought) to perform within the terms of a contract. A court of law could not issue such an order because its remedies were limited to payment of money or property as compensation for damages. A court of equity, however, could issue a decree for *specific performance*—an order to perform what was promised. A court of equity could also issue an *injunction,* directing a party to do or refrain from doing a particular act. In certain cases, a court of equity could allow for the *rescission* (cancellation) of the contract, thereby returning the parties to the positions that they held prior to the contract's formation. • Equitable remedies will be discussed in Chapter 12.

THE MERGING OF LAW AND EQUITY Today, in most states, the courts of law and equity have merged, and thus the distinction between the two courts has largely disappeared. A plaintiff may now request both legal and equitable remedies in the same action, and the trial court judge may grant either form—or both forms—of relief. The distinction between remedies at law and equity remains significant, however, because a court normally will grant an equitable remedy only when the remedy at law (monetary damages) is inadequate. To request the proper remedy, a businessperson (or her or his attorney) must know what remedies are available for the specific kinds of harms suffered. Exhibit 1–2 on the facing page summarizes the procedural differences (applicable in most states) between an action at law and an action in equity.

Classifications of Law

The law may be broken down according to several classification systems. For example, one classification system divides law into **substantive law** (all laws that define, describe, regulate, and create legal rights and obligations) and **procedural law** (all laws that establish the methods of enforcing the rights established by substantive law). **EXAMPLE 1.4** A state law that provides employees with the right to workers' compensation benefits for any on-the-job injuries they sustain is a substantive law because it creates legal rights (workers' compensation laws will be discussed in Chapter 22). Procedural laws,

4. 347 U.S. 483, 74 S.Ct. 686, 98 L.Ed. 873 (1954). See the appendix at the end of this chapter for an explanation of how to read legal citations.

5. See *Plessy v. Ferguson*, 163 U.S. 537, 16 S.Ct. 1138, 41 L.Ed. 256 (1896).

• ***Exhibit* 1–2 Procedural Differences between an Action at Law and an Action in Equity**

PROCEDURE	ACTION AT LAW	ACTION IN EQUITY
Initiation of lawsuit	By filing a complaint.	By filing a petition.
Decision	By jury or judge.	By judge (no jury).
Result	Judgment.	Decree.
Remedy	Monetary damages.	Injunction, specific performance, or rescission.

in contrast, establish the method by which an employee must notify the employer about an on-the-job injury, prove the injury, and periodically submit additional proof to continue receiving workers' compensation benefits. Note that a law regarding workers' compensation may contain both substantive and procedural provisions. •

Other classification systems divide law into federal law and state law or private law (dealing with relationships between persons) and public law (addressing the relationship between persons and their governments). Frequently, people use the term **cyberlaw** to refer to the emerging body of law that governs transactions conducted online. Cyberlaw is an informal term used to describe traditional legal principles that have been modified and adapted to fit situations that are unique to the online world. Of course, in some areas new statutes have been enacted, at both the federal and state levels, to cover specific types of problems stemming from online communications.

Civil Law and Criminal Law

Civil law spells out the rights and duties that exist between persons and between persons and their governments, and the relief available when a person's rights are violated. Typically, in a civil case, a private party sues another private party (although the government can also sue a party for a civil law violation) to make that other party comply with a duty or pay for the damage caused by the failure to comply with a duty. **EXAMPLE 1.5** If a seller fails to perform a contract with a buyer, the buyer may bring a lawsuit against the seller. The purpose of the lawsuit will be either to compel the seller to perform as promised or, more commonly, to obtain monetary damages for the seller's failure to perform. •

Much of the law that we discuss in this text is civil law. Contract law, for example, which we will discuss in Chapters 7 through 12, is civil law. The whole body of tort law (see Chapter 4) is civil law. Note that *civil law* is not the same as a *civil law system.* As you will read shortly, a **civil law system** is a legal system based on a written code of laws.

Criminal law has to do with wrongs committed against society for which society demands redress. Criminal acts are proscribed by local, state, or federal government statutes (see Chapter 6). Thus, criminal defendants are prosecuted by public officials, such as a district attorney, on behalf of the state, not by their victims or other private parties. Whereas in a civil case the object is to obtain a remedy (such as monetary damages) to compensate the injured party, in a criminal case the object is to punish the wrongdoer in an attempt to deter others from similar actions. Penalties for violations of criminal statutes consist of fines and/or imprisonment—and, in some cases, death. We will discuss the differences between civil and criminal law in greater detail in Chapter 6.

National and International Law

Although the focus of this book is U.S. business law, increasingly businesspersons in this country engage in transactions that extend beyond our national borders. In these situations, the laws of other nations or the laws governing relationships among nations may come into play. For this reason, those who pursue a career in business today should have an understanding of the global legal environment.

NATIONAL LAW The law of a particular nation, such as the United States or Sweden, is **national law.** National law, of course, varies from country to country because each country's law reflects the interests, customs, activities, and values that are unique to that nation's culture. Even though the laws and legal systems of various countries differ substantially, broad similarities do exist.

Two types of legal systems predominate around the globe today. One is the common law system of England and the United States, which we have already discussed. The other system is based on Roman civil law, or code law. The term *civil law,* as used here, refers not to civil as opposed to criminal law but to codified law—an ordered grouping of legal principles enacted into law by a legislature or governing body.

In a civil law system, the primary source of law is a statutory code, and case precedents are not judicially binding, as they normally are in a common law system. Although judges in a civil law system often refer to previous decisions as sources of legal guidance, they are not bound by precedent. In other words, the doctrine of *stare decisis* does not apply.

A third, less prevalent, legal system is common in Islamic countries, where the law is often influenced by *sharia,* the religious law of Islam. Although *sharia* affects the legal codes of many Muslim countries, the extent of its impact and its interpretation vary widely.

INTERNATIONAL LAW In contrast to national law, international law applies to more than one nation. **International law** can be defined as a body of written and unwritten laws observed by independent nations and governing the acts of individuals as well as governments. International law is an intermingling of rules and constraints derived from a variety of sources, including the laws of individual nations, the customs that have evolved among nations in their relations with one another, and treaties and international organizations. In essence, international law is the result of centuries-old attempts to reconcile the traditional need of each nation to be the final authority over its own affairs with the desire of nations to benefit economically from trade and harmonious relations with one another.

The key difference between national law and international law is that government authorities can enforce national law. If a nation violates an international law, however, the most that other countries or international organizations can do (if persuasive tactics fail) is to take coercive actions against the violating nation. Coercive actions range from the severance of diplomatic relations and boycotts to, as a last resort, war. We will examine international law in further detail in Chapter 31.

The Constitution As It Affects Business

Each of the sources of law discussed earlier helps to frame the legal environment of business. Because laws that govern business have their origin in the lawmaking authority granted by the U.S. Constitution, we examine that document more closely here. We focus on two areas of the Constitution of particular concern to business—the commerce clause and the Bill of Rights. As mentioned earlier, the Constitution provides the legal basis for both state and federal (national) powers. It is the supreme law in this country. If any law that conflicts with the Constitution is challenged in court, it will be declared invalid by the court.

The Commerce Clause

To prevent states from establishing laws and regulations that would interfere with trade and commerce among the states, the Constitution expressly delegated to the national government the power to regulate interstate commerce. Article I, Section 8, of the U.S. Constitution expressly permits Congress "to regulate Commerce with foreign Nations, and among the several States, and with the Indian Tribes." This clause, referred to as the **commerce clause,** has had a greater impact on business than any other provision in the Constitution.

Initially, the commerce clause was interpreted as being limited to *interstate* commerce (commerce among the states) and not applicable to *intrastate* commerce (commerce within a state). In 1824, however, in the landmark case *Gibbons v. Ogden*[6] the United States Supreme Court held that commerce within a state could also be regulated by the national government as long as the commerce *substantially affected* commerce involving more than one state.

THE COMMERCE CLAUSE AND THE EXPANSION OF NATIONAL POWERS In the *Gibbons* case, the commerce clause was expanded to regulate activities that "substantially affect interstate commerce." As the nation grew and faced new kinds of problems, the commerce clause became a vehicle for the additional expansion of the national government's regulatory powers. Even activities that seemed purely local came under the regulatory reach of the national government if those activities were deemed to substantially affect interstate commerce. **CASE EXAMPLE 1.6** In 1942, in *Wickard v. Filburn*[7] the Court held that wheat production by an individual farmer intended wholly for consumption on his own farm was subject to federal regulation. The Court reasoned that the home consumption of wheat reduced the market demand for wheat and thus could have a substantial effect on interstate commerce. •

THE COMMERCE CLAUSE TODAY Today, at least theoretically, the power over commerce authorizes the national government to regulate every commercial enterprise in the United States. Federal (national) legislation governs almost every major activity conducted by businesses—from hiring and firing decisions to workplace safety, competitive practices, and financing. Since 1995, however, the United States Supreme Court has imposed some curbs on the national government's regulatory authority under the commerce clause. In that year, the Court held—for the first time in sixty years—that Congress had exceeded its regulatory authority under the commerce clause. The Court struck down an act that banned the possession of guns within one thousand feet of any school because the act attempted to regulate an area that had "nothing to do with commerce."[8] Subsequently, the Court invalidated key portions of two other federal acts on the ground that they exceeded Congress's commerce clause authority.[9]

6. 22 U.S. (9 Wheat) 1, 6 L.Ed. 23 (1824).
7. 317 U.S. 111, 63 S.Ct. 82, 87 L.Ed. 122 (1942).
8. The United States Supreme Court held the Gun-Free School Zones Act of 1990 to be unconstitutional in *United States v. Lopez,* 514 U.S. 549, 115 S.Ct. 1624, 131 L.Ed.2d 626 (1995).
9. See *Printz v. United States,* 521 U.S. 898, 117 S.Ct. 2365, 138 L.Ed.2d 914 (1997), involving the Brady Handgun Violence Prevention Act of 1993; and *United States v. Morrison,* 529 U.S. 598, 120 S.Ct. 1740, 146 L.Ed.2d 658 (2000), concerning the federal Violence Against Women Act of 1994.

In one notable case, however, the Supreme Court did allow the federal government to regulate noncommercial activities taking place wholly within a state's borders. **CASE EXAMPLE 1.7** Several states have adopted laws that legalize marijuana for medical purposes. Marijuana possession, however, is illegal under the federal Controlled Substances Act (CSA).[10] After the federal government seized the marijuana that two seriously ill California women were using on the advice of their physicians, the women filed a lawsuit. They argued that it was unconstitutional for the federal statute to prohibit them from using marijuana for medical purposes that were legal within the state. The Court, however, held that Congress has the authority to prohibit the *intra*state possession and noncommercial cultivation of marijuana as part of a larger regulatory scheme (the CSA).[11] In other words, state medical marijuana laws do not insulate the users from federal prosecution. • Note that President Barack Obama has promised to end federal prosecution of persons legally using medical marijuana within their state.

THE REGULATORY POWERS OF THE STATES As part of their inherent sovereignty, state governments have the authority to regulate affairs within their borders. This authority stems, in part, from the Tenth Amendment to the Constitution, which reserves to the states all powers not delegated to the national government. State regulatory powers are often referred to as **police powers.** The term encompasses not only the enforcement of criminal law but also the right of state governments to regulate private activities in order to protect or promote the public order, health, safety, morals, and general welfare. Fire and building codes, antidiscrimination laws, parking regulations, zoning restrictions, licensing requirements, and thousands of other state statutes have been enacted pursuant to a state's police powers. Local governments, including cities, also exercise police powers.[12] Generally, state laws enacted pursuant to a state's police powers carry a strong presumption of validity.

10. 21 U.S.C. Sections 801 *et seq.*

11. *Gonzales v. Raich,* 545 U.S. 1, 125 S.Ct. 2195, 162 L.Ed.2d 1 (2005).

THE "DORMANT" COMMERCE CLAUSE The United States Supreme Court has interpreted the commerce clause to mean that the national government has the exclusive authority to regulate commerce that substantially affects trade and commerce among the states. This express grant of authority to the national government, which is often referred to as the "positive" aspect of the commerce clause, implies a negative aspect—that the states do not have the authority to regulate interstate commerce. This negative aspect of the commerce clause is often referred to as the "dormant" (implied) commerce clause.

The dormant commerce clause comes into play when state regulations affect interstate commerce. In this situation, the courts normally weigh the state's interest in regulating a certain matter against the burden that the state's regulation places on interstate commerce. Because courts balance the interests involved, predicting the outcome in a particular case can be extremely difficult.

The following case involved a Massachusetts law that provided exceptions to a regulatory system for "small" wineries. At issue was whether the law discriminated against out-of-state wineries in violation of the dormant commerce clause.

12. Local governments derive their authority to regulate their communities from the state because they are creatures of the state. In other words, they cannot come into existence unless authorized by the state to do so.

Case 1.1 Family Winemakers of California v. Jenkins[a]

United States Court of Appeals, First Circuit, 592 F.3d 1 (2010).
www.ca1.uscourts.gov/?content=opinions/main.php[b]

FACTS Before 2005, Massachusetts's winery licensing law allowed only in-state wineries to obtain licenses to combine distribution methods through wholesalers, retailers, and direct shipping to consumers. In 2006, after the United States Supreme Court held that similar laws discriminated against out-of-state wineries in violation of the commerce clause, Massachusetts enacted a new law regulating wineries. The new law did not distinguish between in-state and out-of-state wineries' eligibility for certain licenses but instead distinguished between "small" and "large" wineries through a gallonage cap. Wineries producing more than 30,000 gallons of wine a year—all of which were located outside Massachusetts—could apply for a "large winery shipment license." These wineries could choose to either remain completely within the three-tier system and distribute their wines solely through wholesalers or completely opt out of the three-tier system and sell their wines in Massachusetts exclusively through direct shipping to consumers. They could not do both. In contrast, "small" wineries—those producing 30,000 or fewer gallons per year (which included all of Massachusetts's wineries)—could simultaneously use the traditional wholesaler distribution method, direct distribution to retailers, and direct shipping to reach consumers. A group of California wineries and others sued the commonwealth in a federal court, claiming that Massachusetts's 2006

a. The case was brought against Eddie J. Jenkins, the chair of the Massachusetts Alcoholic Beverages Control Commission, in his official capacity.

b. When the page opens, type "Family Winemakers" in the "Short Title *contains*" box and then click on "Submit Search." Click on Opinion Number 09-01169P.01A to access the case. The U.S. Court of Appeals for the First Circuit maintains this Web site.

Case 1.1—Continues next page ➡

Case 1.1—Continued

law discriminated against out-of-state wineries in violation of the commerce clause. The district court agreed and prevented the law's enforcement. Massachusetts appealed.

ISSUE Did the Massachusetts law for licensing direct shipments of wine discriminate against out-of-state wineries and violate the dormant commerce clause?

DECISION Yes. The United States Court of Appeals for the First Circuit affirmed the lower court's decision. The reviewing court concluded that the Massachusetts state law regulating wineries purposefully discriminated against out-of-state commerce in violation of the dormant commerce clause.

REASON The federal appellate court noted that the evidence demonstrated the Massachusetts law gave preferential treatment to the "small" wineries. It stated, "State laws that alter conditions of competition to favor in-state interests over out-of-state competitors in a market have long been subject to invalidation." Because the state law conferred a "clear competitive advantage to 'small' wineries," which included all Massachusetts's wineries, it was discriminatory. Thus, the state law created a comparative disadvantage for "large" wineries, none of which were located in Massachusetts.

FOR CRITICAL ANALYSIS—Legal Consideration *Suppose most "small" wineries, as defined by the Massachusetts law, existed out of state. How could the law be discriminatory in that situation?*

Business and the Bill of Rights

The importance of having a written declaration of the rights of individuals eventually caused the first Congress of the United States to enact twelve amendments to the Constitution and submit them to the states for approval. The first ten of these amendments, commonly known as the **Bill of Rights**, were adopted in 1791 and embody a series of protections for the individual against various types of interference by the federal government.[13] Some constitutional protections apply to business entities as well. For example, corporations exist as separate legal entities, or legal persons, and enjoy many of the same rights and privileges as natural persons do. Summarized here are the protections guaranteed by these ten amendments (see the Constitution in Appendix B for the complete text of each amendment):

1. The First Amendment guarantees the freedoms of religion, speech, and the press and the rights to assemble peaceably and to petition the government.
2. The Second Amendment guarantees the right to keep and bear arms.
3. The Third Amendment prohibits, in peacetime, the lodging of soldiers in any house without the owner's consent.
4. The Fourth Amendment prohibits unreasonable searches and seizures of persons or property.
5. The Fifth Amendment guarantees the rights to *indictment* (formal accusation) by grand jury, to due process of law, and to fair payment when private property is taken for public use. The Fifth Amendment also prohibits compulsory self-incrimination and double jeopardy (trial for the same crime twice).
6. The Sixth Amendment guarantees the accused in a criminal case the right to a speedy and public trial by an impartial jury and with counsel. The accused has the right to cross-examine witnesses against him or her and to solicit testimony from witnesses in his or her favor.
7. The Seventh Amendment guarantees the right to a trial by jury in a civil (noncriminal) case involving at least twenty dollars.[14]
8. The Eighth Amendment prohibits excessive bail and fines, as well as cruel and unusual punishment.
9. The Ninth Amendment establishes that the people have rights in addition to those specified in the Constitution.
10. The Tenth Amendment establishes that those powers neither delegated to the federal government nor denied to the states are reserved for the states.

As originally intended, the Bill of Rights limited only the powers of the national government. Over time, however, the United States Supreme Court "incorporated" most of these rights into the protections against state actions afforded by the Fourteenth Amendment to the Constitution. That amendment, passed in 1868 after the Civil War, provides, in part, that "no State shall . . . deprive any person of life, liberty, or property, without due process of law."

Starting in 1925, the Supreme Court began to define various rights and liberties guaranteed in the national Constitution as constituting "due process of law," which was required of state governments under the Fourteenth Amendment. Today, most of the rights and liberties set forth in the Bill of Rights apply to state governments as well as to the national government.

We will look closely at several of the amendments in the previous list in Chapter 6, in the context of criminal law and procedures. Next, we examine some important constitutional guarantees, including the First Amendment's freedom of speech and freedom of religion, and the Fifth and Fourteenth Amendments' due process clause.

As you read through the following pages, keep in mind that none of these (or other) constitutional freedoms confers an absolute right. Ultimately, it is the United States Supreme Court, as the final interpreter of the Constitution, that gives meaning to these rights and determines their boundaries.

13. One of the proposed amendments was ratified more than two hundred years later (in 1992) and became the Twenty-seventh Amendment to the Constitution. See Appendix B.

14. Twenty dollars was forty days' pay for the average person when the Bill of Rights was written.

THE FIRST AMENDMENT—FREEDOM OF SPEECH A democratic form of government cannot survive unless people can freely voice their political opinions and criticize government actions or policies. Freedom of speech, particularly political speech, is thus a prized right, and traditionally the courts have protected this right to the fullest extent possible.

Symbolic speech—gestures, movements, articles of clothing, and other forms of expressive conduct—is also given substantial protection by the courts. The test is whether a reasonable person would interpret the conduct as conveying some sort of message. **CASE EXAMPLE 1.8** As a form of expression, Bryan has gang signs tattooed on his torso, arms, neck, and legs. If a reasonable person would interpret this conduct as conveying a message, then it might be a protected form of symbolic speech. •

Reasonable Restrictions. Expression—oral, written, or symbolized by conduct—is subject to reasonable restrictions. A balance must be struck between a government's obligation to protect its citizens and those citizens' exercise of their rights. Reasonableness is analyzed on a case-by-case basis. If a restriction imposed by the government is content neutral, then a court may allow it. To be content neutral, the restriction must be aimed at combating some secondary societal problem, such as crime, and not be aimed at suppressing the expressive conduct or its message. For instance, courts have often protected nude dancing as a form of symbolic expression. Nevertheless, the courts typically allow content-neutral laws that ban all public nudity. **CASE EXAMPLE 1.9** A man was charged with dancing nude at an annual anti-Christmas protest in Harvard Square under a statute banning public displays of open and gross lewdness. The man argued that the statute was overbroad and unconstitutional, and a trial court agreed. On appeal, however, a state appellate court upheld the statute as constitutional in situations in which there was an unsuspecting or unwilling audience.[15] •

Corporate Political Speech. Political speech by corporations also falls within the protection of the First Amendment. Many years ago, the United States Supreme Court reviewed a Massachusetts statute that prohibited corporations from making political contributions or expenditures that individuals were permitted to make. The Court ruled that the Massachusetts law was unconstitutional because it violated the right of corporations to freedom of speech.[16] The Court has also held that a law prohibiting a corporation from using bill inserts to express its views on controversial issues violated the First Amendment.[17]

Corporate political speech continues to be given significant protection under the First Amendment. In 2010, the Court overturned a twenty-year-old precedent when it ruled that corporations can spend freely to support or oppose candidates for president and Congress.[18]

Commercial Speech. The courts also give substantial protection to *commercial speech,* which consists of communications—primarily advertising and marketing—made by business firms that involve only their commercial interests. The protection given to commercial speech under the First Amendment is not as extensive as that afforded to noncommercial speech, however. A state may restrict certain kinds of advertising, for instance, in the interest of protecting consumers from being misled by the advertising practices. States also have a legitimate interest in the beautification of roadsides, and this interest allows states to place restraints on billboard advertising.

Generally, a restriction on commercial speech will be considered valid as long as it (1) seeks to implement a substantial government interest, (2) directly advances that interest, and (3) goes no further than necessary to accomplish its objective.

At issue in the following case was whether a government agency had unconstitutionally restricted commercial speech when it prohibited the inclusion of a certain illustration on beer labels.

15. *Commonwealth v. Ora,* 451 Mass. 125, 883 N.E.2d 1217 (2008).

16. *First National Bank of Boston v. Bellotti,* 435 U.S. 765, 98 S.Ct. 1407, 55 L.Ed.2d 707 (1978).

17. *Consolidated Edison Co. v. Public Service Commission,* 447 U.S. 530, 100 S.Ct. 2326, 65 L.Ed.2d 319 (1980).

18. *Citizens United v. Federal Election Commission,* ___ U.S. ___, 130 S.Ct. 876, 175 L.Ed.2d 753 (2010).

Case 1.2 Bad Frog Brewery, Inc. v. New York State Liquor Authority

United States Court of Appeals, Second Circuit, 134 F.3d 87 (1998).
www.findlaw.com/casecode/index.html[a]

FACTS Bad Frog Brewery, Inc., makes and sells alcoholic beverages. Some of the beverages feature labels with a drawing of a frog making the gesture generally known as "giving the finger." Bad Frog's authorized New York distributor, Renaissance Beer Company, applied to the New York State Liquor Authority (NYSLA) for brand label approval, as required by state law before the beer could be sold in New York. The NYSLA denied the application, in part, because "the label could appear in grocery and convenience stores, with obvious exposure on the shelf to children of tender age." Bad

a. Under the heading "US Courts of Appeals-Opinions and Resources," click on "2nd Circuit Court of Appeals." Enter "Bad Frog Brewery" in the "Party Name Search" box, and click on "search." On the resulting page, click on the case name to access the opinion.

Case 1.2—Continues next page ➥

Case 1.2—Continued

Frog filed a suit in a federal district court against the NYSLA, asking for, among other things, an injunction against the denial of the application. The court granted summary judgment in favor of the NYSLA. Bad Frog appealed to the U.S. Court of Appeals for the Second Circuit.

ISSUE Was the New York State Liquor Authority's ban of Bad Frog's beer labels a reasonable restriction on commercial speech?

DECISION No. The U.S. Court of Appeals for the Second Circuit reversed the judgment of the district court and remanded the case for judgment to be entered in favor of Bad Frog.

REASON The appellate court held that the NYSLA's denial of Bad Frog's application violated the First Amendment. The ban on the use of the labels lacked a "reasonable fit" with the state's interest in shielding minors from vulgarity, and the NYSLA did not adequately consider alternatives to the ban. The court acknowledged that the NYSLA's interest "in protecting children from vulgar and profane advertising" was "substantial." The question was whether banning Bad Frog's labels "directly advanced" that interest. "In view of the wide currency of vulgar displays throughout contemporary society, including comic books targeted directly at children, barring such displays from labels for alcoholic beverages cannot realistically be expected to reduce children's exposure to such displays to any significant degree." The court concluded that a "commercial speech limitation" must be "part of a substantial effort to advance a valid state interest, not merely the removal of a few grains of offensive sand from a beach of vulgarity." Finally, as to whether the ban on the labels was more extensive than necessary to serve this interest, the court pointed out that there were "numerous less intrusive alternatives." For example, the NYSLA's "concern could be less intrusively dealt with by placing restrictions on the permissible locations where the appellant's products may be displayed within * * * stores."

WHAT IF THE FACTS WERE DIFFERENT? *If Bad Frog had sought to use the offensive label to market toys instead of beer, would the court's ruling likely have been the same? Explain your answer.*

Unprotected Speech. The United States Supreme Court has made it clear that certain types of speech will not be given any protection under the First Amendment. Speech that harms the good reputation of another, or defamatory speech (see Chapter 4), will not be protected. Speech that violates criminal laws (such as threatening speech) is not constitutionally protected. Other unprotected speech includes *fighting words,* or words that are likely to incite others to respond violently.

The First Amendment, as interpreted by the Court, also does not protect obscene speech. Establishing an objective definition of obscene speech has proved difficult, however, and the Court has grappled with this problem from time to time. In *Miller v. California,*[19] the Court created a test for legal obscenity, which involved a set of requirements that must be met for material to be legally obscene. Under this test, material is obscene if (1) the average person finds that it violates contemporary community standards; (2) the work taken as a whole appeals to a prurient (arousing or obsessive) interest in sex; (3) the work shows patently offensive sexual conduct; and (4) the work lacks serious redeeming literary, artistic, political, or scientific merit.

Because community standards vary widely, the *Miller* test has had inconsistent application, and obscenity remains a constitutionally unsettled issue. Numerous state and federal statutes make it a crime to disseminate and possess obscene materials, including child pornography.

Online Obscenity. Congress's first two attempts at protecting minors from pornographic materials on the Internet—the Communications Decency Act (CDA) of 1996[20] and the Child Online Protection Act (COPA) of 1998[21]—failed. Ultimately, the United States Supreme Court struck down both the CDA and COPA as unconstitutional restraints on speech, largely because the wording of these acts was overbroad and would restrict nonpornographic materials.[22]

In 2000, Congress enacted the Children's Internet Protection Act (CIPA),[23] which requires public schools and libraries to block adult content from access by children by installing **filtering software** on computers. Such software is designed to prevent persons from viewing certain Web sites by responding to a site's Internet address or its meta tags, or key words. CIPA was also challenged on constitutional grounds, but the Supreme Court held that the act did not violate the First Amendment. The Court concluded that because libraries can disable the filters for any patrons who ask, the system is reasonably flexible and does not burden free speech to an unconstitutional extent.[24]

Because of the difficulties of policing the Internet, as well as the constitutional complexities of prohibiting online obscenity through legislation, it remains a continuing problem worldwide. The Federal Bureau of Investigation established an Anti-Porn Squad to target and prosecute companies that distribute child pornography in cyberspace. The Federal Communications Commission has also passed new obscenity regulations for television networks. For a discussion of how the law is evolving, see this chapter's *Adapting the Law to the Online Environment* feature on the facing page.

19. 413 U.S. 15, 93 S.Ct. 2607, 37 L.Ed.2d 419 (1973).

20. 47 U.S.C. Section 223(a)(1)(B)(ii).

21. 47 U.S.C. Section 231.

22. See *Reno v. American Civil Liberties Union,* 521 U.S. 844, 117 S.Ct. 2329, 138 L.Ed.2d 874 (1997); *Ashcroft v. American Civil Liberties Union,* 535 U.S. 564, 122 S.Ct. 1700, 152 L.Ed.2d 771 (2002); and *American Civil Liberties Union v. Ashcroft,* 322 F.3d 240 (3d Cir. 2003).

23. 17 U.S.C. Sections 1701–1741.

24. *United States v. American Library Association,* 539 U.S. 194, 123 S.Ct. 2297, 156 L.Ed.2d 221 (2003).

Adapting the Law to the Online Environment

The Supreme Court Upholds a Law That Prohibits Pandering Virtual Child Pornography

Millions of pornographic images of children are available on the Internet. Some are images of actual children engaged in sexual activity. Others are virtual (computer-generated) pornography—that is, images made to look like children engaged in sexual acts. Whereas child pornography is illegal, the United States Supreme Court has ruled that virtual pornography is legally protected under the First Amendment because it does not involve the exploitation of real children.[a] In its ruling, the Supreme Court struck down as overly broad, and therefore unconstitutional, provisions of the Child Pornography Prevention Act (CPPA) of 1996. Among other things, the act prohibited any visual depiction including a "computer-generated image" that "is, or appears to be, of a minor engaging in sexually explicit conduct."

This ruling and the difficulty in distinguishing between real and virtual pornography have created problems for prosecutors. Before they can convict someone of disseminating child pornography on the Internet, they must prove that the images depict real children. To help remedy this problem, Congress enacted the Protect Act of 2003 (here, *Protect* stands for "Prosecutorial Remedies and Other Tools to end the Exploitation of Children Today").[b]

The Protect Act's Pandering Provisions

One of the Protect Act's many provisions prohibits misrepresenting virtual child pornography as actual child pornography. The act makes it a crime to knowingly advertise, present, distribute, or solicit "any material or purported material in a manner that reflects the belief, or that is intended to cause another to believe, that the material or purported material" is illegal child pornography.[c] Thus, it may be a crime to intentionally distribute virtual child pornography.

The Protect Act's "pandering" provision was challenged in a subsequent case, *United States v. Williams.*[d] The defendant, Michael Williams, sent a message to an Internet chat room that read "Dad of Toddler has 'good' pics of her an [sic] me for swap of your toddler pics." A law enforcement agent responded by sending a private message to Williams that contained photos of a college-aged female, which were computer altered to look like photos of a ten-year-old girl. Williams requested explicit photos of the girl, but the agent did not respond. After that, Williams sent another public message that accused the agent of being a cop and included a hyperlink containing seven pictures of minors engaging in sexually explicit conduct.

Williams was arrested and charged with possession of child pornography and pandering material that appeared to be child pornography. He claimed that the Protect Act's pandering provision was—like its predecessor (the CPPA)—unconstitutionally overbroad and vague. (He later pleaded guilty to the charges but preserved the issue of constitutionality for appeal.)

Is the Protect Act Constitutional?

On appeal, the federal appellate court held that the pandering provision of the Protect Act was unconstitutional because it criminalized speech regarding child pornography. The court reasoned that, under the act, a person who distributes innocent pictures via the Internet (such as sending an e-mail labeled "good pictures of the kids in bed") could be penalized for offering child pornography.

The United States Supreme Court reversed that decision, ruling that the Protect Act was neither unconstitutionally overbroad nor impermissibly vague. The Court held that the statute was valid because it does not prohibit a substantial amount of protected speech. Rather, the act generally prohibits offers to provide, and requests to obtain, child pornography—both of which are unprotected speech. Thus, the act's pandering provisions remedied the constitutional defects of the CPPA, which had made it illegal to possess virtual child pornography.

FOR CRITICAL ANALYSIS

Why should it be illegal to "pander" virtual child pornography when it is not illegal to possess it?

a. *Ashcroft v. Free Speech Coalition,* 553 U.S. 234, 122 S.Ct. 1389, 152 L.Ed.2d 403 (2002).
b. 18 U.S.C. Section 2252A(a)(5)(B).
c. 18 U.S.C. Section 2252A(a)(3)(B).
d. 553 U.S. 285, 128 S.Ct. 1830, 170 L.Ed.2d 650 (2008).

THE FIRST AMENDMENT—FREEDOM OF RELIGION The First Amendment states that the government may neither establish any religion nor prohibit the free exercise of religious practices. The first part of this constitutional provision is referred to as the **establishment clause,** and the second part is known as the **free exercise clause.** Government action, both federal and state, must be consistent with this constitutional mandate.

The Establishment Clause. The establishment clause prohibits the government from establishing a state-sponsored religion, as well as from passing laws that promote (aid or endorse) religion or show a preference for one religion over another. The establishment clause does not require a complete separation of church and state, though. On the contrary, it requires the government to accommodate religions.

The establishment clause covers all conflicts about such matters as the legality of state and local government support for a particular religion, government aid to religious organizations and schools, the government's allowing or requiring school prayers, and the teaching of evolution versus fundamentalist theories of creation. For a government law or policy to be constitutional, it must not have the primary effect of advancing or inhibiting religion. Generally, federal or state regulation that does not promote religion or place a significant burden on religion is constitutional even if it has some impact on religion.

Religious displays on public property have often been challenged as violating the establishment clause, and the United States Supreme Court has ruled on several such cases. Generally, the Court has focused on the proximity of the religious display to nonreligious symbols, such as reindeer and candy canes, or to symbols from different religions, such as a menorah (a nine-branched candelabrum used in celebrating Hanukkah). **CASE EXAMPLE 1.10** The Court took a slightly different approach in 2005. The dispute involved a monument of the Ten Commandments on the Texas State Capitol grounds. The Court held that the monument did not violate the establishment clause because the Ten Commandments had historical, as well as religious, significance.[25] ●

The following case illustrates some of the factors that courts consider when deciding establishment clause cases.

25. *Van Orden v. Perry*, 545 U.S. 677, 125 S.Ct. 2854, 162 L.Ed.2d 607 (2005).

Case 1.3 Trunk v. City of San Diego

United States Court of Appeal, Ninth Circuit, 629 F.3d 1099 (2011).

FACTS Mount Soledad is a prominent hill in the La Jolla community of San Diego, California. There has been a cross on top of Mount Soledad since 1913. The cross is more than forty feet tall and is visible from miles away. Although the cross stood alone for most of its history, since the late 1990s it has been the centerpiece of a war memorial. This memorial features six walls around the base of the cross and more than two thousand stone plaques honoring individual veterans and groups of soldiers. The site was privately owned until 2006, when Congress authorized the property's transfer to the federal government "to preserve a historically significant war memorial." Shortly after the federal government took possession, Steve Trunk and the Jewish War Veterans filed lawsuits claiming that the cross display violated the establishment clause because it endorsed the Christian religion. The lawsuits were later consolidated (joined together). A federal district court determined that Congress had acted with a secular (nonreligious) purpose in acquiring the memorial and that the memorial did not have the effect of advancing religion. The court granted a summary judgment in favor of the government. The plaintiffs appealed.

ISSUE Did a forty-foot tall cross in the middle of a public war memorial violate the establishment clause?

DECISION Yes. The United States Court of Appeals for the Ninth Circuit ruled that the memorial as a whole violated the establishment clause.

REASON The court stated that the "heart of this controversy [was] the primary effect of the Memorial." Although the government's purpose in acquiring the memorial was nonreligious, the memorial could be seen as sending a message that endorses a particular religion–Christianity. The court noted that while not all cross displays at war memorials violate the U.S. Constitution, the cross in this case had to be evaluated in the context of its history and setting. The cross physically dominated the site, was originally dedicated to religious purposes, and had a long history of religious use (for example, Easter Sunday services). "From the perspective of drivers on Interstate 5, almost directly below, the Cross is the only visible aspect of the Memorial, and the secular elements cannot neutralize the appearance of [religious] sectarianism." The court reasoned that "the use of a distinctively Christian symbol to honor all veterans sends a strong message of endorsement and exclusion."

WHAT IF THE FACTS WERE DIFFERENT? *Suppose that the cross was only six feet tall and that the memorial had not had a long history of religious use. Would the outcome have been different? Why or why not?*

The Free Exercise Clause. The free exercise clause guarantees that a person can hold any religious belief that she or he wants, or a person can have no religious belief. The constitutional guarantee of personal religious freedom restricts only the actions of the government and not those of individuals or private businesses.

When religious *practices* work against public policy and the public welfare, however, the government can act. For instance, the government can require a child to receive certain types of vaccinations or medical treatment when that child's life is in danger—regardless of the child's or parent's religious beliefs. When public safety is an issue, an individual's religious beliefs often have to give way to the government's interests in protecting the public. **EXAMPLE 1.11** In the Muslim faith, it is wrong for a woman to appear in public without a scarf over her head. Due to public safety concerns, many courts today do not allow the wearing of any headgear in courtrooms. In 2008, a Muslim woman was prevented from entering a courthouse in Georgia because she refused to remove her headscarf. As she left, she uttered an expletive at a court official and was arrested and brought before the judge, who ordered her to serve ten days in jail. •

For business firms, an important issue involves the accommodation that businesses must make for the religious beliefs of their employees. Federal employment laws require business firms to accommodate employees' religious beliefs. If an employee's religion prohibits him or her from working on a certain day of the week or at a certain type of job, the employer must make a reasonable attempt to accommodate these religious requirements. Employers must reasonably accommodate an employee's religious beliefs even if the beliefs are not based on the tenets or dogma of a particular church, sect, or denomination. The only requirement is that the belief be religious in nature and sincerely held by the employee.

Fifth and Fourteenth Amendments—Due Process

Two other constitutional guarantees of great significance to Americans are mandated by the due process clauses of the Fifth and Fourteenth Amendments. Both the Fifth and the Fourteenth Amendments provide that no person shall be deprived "of life, liberty, or property, without due process of law." The **due process clause** of each of these constitutional amendments has two aspects—procedural and substantive. Note that the due process clause applies to "legal persons," such as corporations, as well as to individuals.

Procedural Due Process. Procedural due process requires that any government decision to take life, liberty, or property must be made fairly—that is, the government must give a person proper notice and an opportunity to be heard. Fair procedures must be used in determining whether a person will be subjected to punishment or have some burden imposed on him or her. Fair procedure has been interpreted as requiring that the person have at least an opportunity to object to a proposed action before a fair, neutral decision maker (who need not be a judge). **EXAMPLE 1.12** In most states, a driver's license is construed as a property interest. Therefore, the state must provide some sort of opportunity for the driver to object before suspending or terminating the person's license. •

Substantive Due Process. Substantive due process protects an individual's life, liberty, or property against certain government actions regardless of the fairness of the procedures used to implement them. Substantive due process limits what the government may do in its legislative and executive capacities. Legislation must be fair and reasonable in content and must further a legitimate governmental objective. Only when state conduct is arbitrary or shocks the conscience, however, will it rise to the level of violating substantive due process.

If a law or other governmental action limits a fundamental right, it will be held to violate substantive due process unless it promotes a compelling or overriding state interest. Fundamental rights include interstate travel, privacy, voting, marriage and family, and all First Amendment rights. Thus, a state must have a substantial reason for taking any action that infringes on a person's free speech rights. In situations not involving fundamental rights, a law or action does not violate substantive due process if it rationally relates to any legitimate governmental end. It is almost impossible for a law or action to fail the "rationality" test. Under this test, almost any government regulation of business will be upheld as reasonable.

Reviewing . . . The Legal and Constitutional Environment of Business

Suppose that the California legislature passes a law that severely restricts carbon dioxide emissions from automobiles in that state. A group of automobile manufacturers files a suit against the state of California to prevent the enforcement of the law. The automakers claim that a federal law already sets fuel economy standards nationwide and that these standards are essentially the same as carbon dioxide emission standards. According to the automobile manufacturers, it is unfair to allow California to impose more stringent regulations than those set by the federal law. Using the information presented in the chapter, answer the following questions.

1 Who are the parties (the plaintiffs and the defendant) in this lawsuit?
2 Are the plaintiffs seeking a legal remedy or an equitable remedy?
3 What is the primary source of the law that is at issue here?
4 Read through the appendix that follows this chapter, and then answer the following question: Where would you look to find the relevant California and federal laws?

Terms and Concepts

administrative law 4
Bill of Rights 10
binding authority 5
breach 3
case law 5
citation 4
civil law 7
civil law system 7
commerce clause 8
common law 5
constitutional law 4
criminal law 7
cyberlaw 7
defendant 6
due process clause 15
establishment clause 13
filtering software 12
free exercise clause 13
international law 8
law 2
national law 7
ordinance 4
persuasive authority 6
plaintiff 6
police powers 9
precedent 5
primary source of law 3
procedural law 6
remedy 6
secondary source of law 4
stare decisis 5
statutory law 4
substantive law 6
symbolic speech 11
uniform law 4

Chapter Summary: The Legal and Constitutional Environment of Business

Sources of American Law (See pages 3–5.)	1. *Constitutional law*—The law as expressed in the U.S. Constitution and the various state constitutions. The U.S. Constitution is the supreme law of the land. State constitutions are supreme within state borders to the extent that they do not violate the U.S. Constitution or a federal law. 2. *Statutory law*—Laws or ordinances created by federal, state, and local legislatures and governing bodies. None of these laws can violate the U.S. Constitution or the relevant state constitutions. Uniform laws, when adopted by a state legislature, become statutory law in that state. 3. *Administrative law*—The rules, orders, and decisions of federal or state government administrative agencies. 4. *Case law and common law doctrines*—Judge-made law, including interpretations of constitutional provisions, of statutes enacted by legislatures, and of regulations created by administrative agencies. The common law—the doctrines and principles embodied in case law—governs all areas not covered by statutory law (or agency regulations issued to implement various statutes).
The Common Law Tradition (See pages 5–6.)	1. *Common law*—Law that originated in medieval England with the creation of the king's courts, or *curiae regis,* and the development of a body of rules that were common to (or applied throughout) the land. 2. *Stare decisis*—A doctrine under which judges "stand on decided cases"—or follow the rule of precedent—in deciding cases. *Stare decisis* is the cornerstone of the common law tradition. 3. *Remedies*—A remedy is the means by which a court enforces a right or compensates for a violation of a right. Courts typically grant legal remedies (monetary damages) but may also grant equitable remedies (specific performance, injunction, or rescission) when the legal remedy is inadequate or unavailable.
Classifications of Law (See pages 6–8.)	The law may be broken down according to several classification systems, such as substantive or procedural law, federal or state law, and private or public law. Two broad classifications are civil and criminal law, and national and international law. Cyberlaw is not really a classification of law but a term that is used for the growing body of case law and statutory law that applies to Internet transactions.
The Constitution As It Affects Business (See pages 8–15.)	1. *Commerce clause*—Expressly permits Congress to regulate commerce. That power authorizes the national government, at least theoretically, to regulate every commercial enterprise in the United States. Under their police powers, state governments may regulate private activities to protect or promote the public order, health, safety, morals, and general welfare. 2. *Bill of Rights*—The first ten amendments to the U.S. Constitution. They embody a series of protections for individuals—and in some cases, business entities—against various types of interference by the federal government. One of the freedoms guaranteed by the Bill of Rights that affects businesses is the freedom of speech guaranteed by the First Amendment. Also important are the protections of the Fifth and the Fourteenth Amendments, which provide that no person shall be deprived of "life, liberty, or property, without due process of law."

ExamPrep

ISSUE SPOTTERS

—Check your answers to these questions against the answers provided in Appendix G.

1 The First Amendment to the U.S. Constitution provides protection for the free exercise of religion. A state legislature enacts a law that outlaws all religions that do not derive from the Judeo-Christian tradition. Is this law valid within that state? Why or why not?

2 Under what circumstance might a judge rely on case law to determine the intent and purpose of a statute?

BEFORE THE TEST

Go to **www.cengagebrain.com**, enter the ISBN 9781111530624, and click on "Find" to locate this textbook's Web site. Then, click on "Access Now" under "Study Tools," and select Chapter 1 at the top. There, you will find an Interactive Quiz that you can take to assess your mastery of the concepts in this chapter, as well as Flashcards and a Glossary of important terms.

For Review

1 What is the common law tradition?

2 What is the difference between remedies at law and remedies in equity?

3 What constitutional clause gives the federal government the power to regulate commercial activities among the various states?

4 What is the Bill of Rights? What freedoms does the First Amendment guarantee?

5 Where in the U.S. Constitution can the due process clause be found?

Questions and Case Problems

1–1 Remedies. Arthur Rabe is suing Xavier Sanchez for breaching a contract in which Sanchez promised to sell Rabe a Van Gogh painting for $150,000.

1 In this lawsuit, who is the plaintiff, and who is the defendant?

2 If Rabe wants Sanchez to perform the contract as promised, what remedy should Rabe seek?

3 Suppose that the court finds in Rabe's favor and grants a remedy. Sanchez then appeals the decision to a higher court. Read through the subsection entitled "Appellants and Appellees" in the appendix following this chapter. On appeal, which party in the Rabe-Sanchez case will be the appellant, and which party will be the appellee (or respondent)?

1–2 Question with Sample Answer This chapter discussed a number of sources of American law. Which source of law takes priority in each of the following situations, and why?

1 A federal statute conflicts with the U.S. Constitution.

2 A federal statute conflicts with a state constitution.

3 A state statute conflicts with the common law of that state.

4 A state constitutional amendment conflicts with the U.S. Constitution.

5 A federal administrative regulation conflicts with a state constitution.

—For a sample answer to Question 1–2, go to Appendix E at the end of this text.

1–3 Reading Citations. Assume that you want to read the court's entire opinion in the case of *Pack 2000, Inc. v. Cushman,* 126 Conn.App. 339, 11 A.3d 181 (2011). Read the section entitled "Finding Case Law" in the appendix that follows this chapter, and then explain specifically where you would find the court's opinion.

1–4 Case Problem with Sample Answer For decades, New York City has had to deal with the vandalism and defacement of public property caused by unauthorized graffiti. Among other attempts to stop the damage, in December 2005 the city banned the sale of aerosol spray-paint cans and broad-tipped indelible markers to persons under twenty-one years of age and prohibited them from possessing such items on property other than their own. By May 1, 2006, five people—all under age twenty-one—had been cited for violations of these regulations, while 871 individuals had been arrested for actually making graffiti. Artists who wished to create graffiti on legal surfaces, such as canvas, wood, and clothing, included college student Lindsey Vincenty, who was studying visual arts. Unable to buy her supplies in the city or to carry them in the city if she bought them elsewhere, Vincenty and others filed a suit in a federal district court on behalf of themselves and other young artists against Michael Bloomberg, the city's mayor, and others. The plaintiffs claimed that, among other things, the new rules violated their right to freedom of speech. They asked the court to enjoin the rules' enforcement. Should the court grant this request? Why or why not? [*Vincenty v. Bloomberg,* 476 F.3d 74 (2d Cir. 2007)]

—For a sample answer to Problem 1–4, go to Appendix F at the end of this text.

1–5 Due Process. In 2006, the Russ College of Engineering and Technology of Ohio University announced that an investigation had found "rampant and flagrant plagiarism" in the theses of mechanical engineering graduate students. Faculty singled out for "ignoring their ethical responsibilities and contributing to an atmosphere of negligence toward issues of academic misconduct" included Jay Gunasekera, professor of mechanical engineering and chair of the department. These findings were publicized in a press conference. The university then prohibited Gunasekera from advising graduate students. He filed a suit in a federal district court against Dennis Irwin, the dean of Russ College, and others, for violating his "due-process rights when they publicized accusations about his role in plagiarism by his graduate student advisees without providing him with a meaningful opportunity to clear his name" in public. Irwin asked the court to dismiss the suit. What does due process require in these circumstances? Why? [*Gunasekera v. Irwin,* 551 F.3d 461 (6th Cir. 2009)]

1–6 Commerce Clause. Under the federal Sex Offender Registration and Notification Act (SORNA), sex offenders must register as sex offenders and update their registration when they travel from one state to another. David Hall, a convicted sex offender in New York, moved from New York to Virginia, where he lived for part of a year. When he returned to New York, he was charged with the federal offense of failing to register as a sex offender while in Virginia, as required by SORNA. In his defense, he claimed that SORNA was unconstitutional because Congress had no authority to criminalize interstate travel since no commerce was involved. The district court dismissed the indictment. The government appealed, contending that the statute is valid under the commerce clause. Does that contention seem reasonable? Why or why not? [*United States v. Hall,* 591 F.3d 83 (2d Cir. 2010)]

1–7 Establishment Clause. James DeWeese, an Ohio judge, hung two posters in his courtroom, one showing the Bill of Rights and the other showing the Ten Commandments. The American Civil Liberties Union (ACLU) brought an action against DeWeese in a federal district court. The ACLU alleged that the Ten Commandments poster violated the establishment clause and requested an injunction to prevent DeWeese from continuing to display the poster in his courtroom. The district court ruled in the ACLU's favor. DeWeese appealed to the U.S. Court of Appeals for the Sixth Circuit, claiming that his purpose in displaying the Ten Commandments poster was not to promote religion. Rather, he claimed to be expressing his views about two warring legal philosophies that motivate behavior and consequences—moral relativism and moral absolutism (which was represented by the Ten Commandments). DeWeese also stated that he used the poster "occasionally in educational efforts" when speaking to community groups to "express his belief that God is the ultimate authority." Does displaying a poster of the Ten Commandments in a courtroom violate the establishment clause? Why or why not? How should the federal appellate court rule? [*American Civil Liberties Union of Ohio Foundation, Inc. v. DeWeese,* 633 F.3d 424 (6th Cir. 2011)]

1–8 A Question of Ethics *On July 5, 1884, Dudley, Stephens, and Brooks—"all able-bodied English seamen"—and a teenage English boy were cast adrift in a lifeboat following a storm at sea. They had no water with them in the boat, and all they had for sustenance were two one-pound tins of turnips. On July 24, Dudley proposed that one of the four in the lifeboat be sacrificed to save the others. Stephens agreed with Dudley, but Brooks refused to consent—and the boy was never asked for his opinion. On July 25, Dudley killed the boy, and the three men then fed on the boy's body and blood. Four days later, the men were rescued by a passing vessel. They were taken to England and tried for the murder of the boy. If the men had not fed on the boy's body, they would probably have died of starvation within the four-day period. The boy, who was in a much weaker condition, would likely have died before the rest. [*Regina v. Dudley and Stephens, *14 Q.B.D. (Queen's Bench Division, England) 273 (1884)]*

1. The basic question in this case is whether the survivors should be subject to penalties under English criminal law, given the men's unusual circumstances. You be the judge and decide the issue. Give the reasons for your decision.
2. Should judges ever have the power to look beyond the written "letter of the law" in making their decisions? Why or why not?

1–9 Critical Thinking Legal Question John's company is involved in a lawsuit with a customer, Beth. John argues that for fifty years higher courts in that state have decided cases involving circumstances similar to those of this case, in a way that indicates that this case should be decided in favor of John's company. Is this a valid argument? If so, must the judge in this case rule as those other judges did? What argument could Beth use to counter John's reasoning?

Appendix to Chapter 1: Finding and Analyzing the Law

The statutes, agency regulations, and case law referred to in this text establish the rights and duties of businesspersons engaged in various types of activities. The cases presented in the following chapters provide you with concise, real-life illustrations of how the courts interpret and apply these laws. Because of the importance of knowing how to find statutory, administrative, and case law, this appendix offers a brief introduction to how these laws are published and to the legal "shorthand" employed in referencing these legal sources.

Finding Statutory and Administrative Law

When Congress passes laws, they are collected in a publication titled *United States Statutes at Large*. When state legislatures pass laws, they are collected in similar state publications. Most frequently, however, laws are referred to in their codified form—that is, the form in which they appear in the federal and state codes. In these codes, laws are compiled by subject.

United States Code

The *United States Code* (U.S.C.) arranges all existing federal laws of a public and permanent nature by subject. Each of the fifty subjects into which the U.S.C. arranges the laws is given a title and a title number. For example, laws relating to commerce and trade are collected in "Title 15, Commerce and Trade." Titles are subdivided by sections. A citation to the U.S.C. includes title and section numbers. Thus, a reference to "15 U.S.C. Section 1" means that the statute can be found in Section 1 of Title 15. ("Section" may also be designated by the symbol §, and "Sections" by §§.) In addition to the print publication of the U.S.C., the federal government also provides a searchable online database of the *United States Code* at www.gpoaccess.gov/uscode/index.html.

Commercial publications of these laws and regulations are available and are widely used. For example, West Group publishes the *United States Code Annotated* (U.S.C.A.). The U.S.C.A. contains the complete text of laws included in the U.S.C., notes of court decisions that interpret and apply specific sections of the statutes, and the text of presidential proclamations and executive orders. The U.S.C.A. also includes research aids, such as cross-references to related statutes, historical notes, and library references. A citation to the U.S.C.A. is similar to a citation to the U.S.C.: "15 U.S.C.A. Section 1."

State Codes

State codes follow the U.S.C. pattern of arranging law by subject. The state codes may be called codes, revisions, compilations, consolidations, general statutes, or statutes, depending on the preferences of the state. In some codes, subjects are designated by number. In others, they are designated by name. For example, "13 Pennsylvania Consolidated Statutes Section 1101" means that the statute can be found in Title 13, Section 1101, of the Pennsylvania code. "California Commercial Code Section 1101" means the statute can be found in Section 1101 under the subject heading "Commercial Code" of the California code. Abbreviations may be used. For example, "13 Pennsylvania Consolidated Statutes Section 1101" may be abbreviated "13 Pa. C.S. § 1101," and "California Commercial Code Section 1101" may be abbreviated "Cal. Com. Code § 1101."

Administrative Rules

Rules and regulations adopted by federal administrative agencies are compiled in the *Code of Federal Regulations* (C.F.R.). Like the U.S.C., the C.F.R. is divided into fifty titles. Rules within each title are assigned section numbers. A full citation to the C.F.R. includes title and section numbers. For example, a reference to "17 C.F.R. Section 230.504" means that the rule can be found in Section 230.504 of Title 17.

Finding Case Law

Before discussing the case reporting system, we need to look briefly at the court system (which will be discussed in detail in Chapter 2). There are two types of courts in the United States: federal courts and state courts. Both the federal and state court systems consist of several levels, or tiers, of courts. *Trial courts,* in which evidence is presented and testimony is given, are on the bottom tier (which also includes lower courts handling specialized issues). Decisions from a trial court can be appealed to a higher court, which commonly would be an intermediate *court of appeals,* or an *appellate court.* Decisions from these intermediate courts of appeals may be appealed to an even higher court, such as a state supreme court or the United States Supreme Court.

State Court Decisions

Most state trial court decisions are not published. Except in New York and a few other states that publish selected opinions of their trial courts, decisions from state trial courts are merely filed in the office of the clerk of the court, where the decisions are available for public inspection. (Increasingly, they can be found online as well.) Written decisions of the appellate, or reviewing, courts, however, are published and distributed. As you will note, most of the state court cases presented in this book are from state appellate courts. The reported appellate decisions are published in volumes called *reports* or *reporters,* which are numbered consecutively. State appellate court decisions are found in the state reporters of that particular state.

REGIONAL REPORTERS Additionally, state court opinions appear in regional units of the *National Reporter System,* published by West Group. Most lawyers and libraries have the West reporters because they report cases more quickly and are distributed more widely than the state-published reports. In fact, many states have eliminated their own reporters in favor of West's National Reporter System. The National Reporter System divides the states into the following geographic areas: *Atlantic* (A., A.2d, or A.3d), *North Eastern* (N.E. or N.E.2d), *North Western* (N.W. or N.W.2d), *Pacific* (P., P.2d, or P.3d), *South Eastern* (S.E. or S.E.2d), *South Western* (S.W., S.W.2d, or S.W.3d), and *Southern* (So., So.2d, or So.3d). (The *2d* and *3d* in the abbreviations refer to *Second Series* and *Third Series,* respectively.) The states included in each of these regional divisions are indicated in Exhibit 1A–1 on the facing page, which illustrates West's National Reporter System.

CASE CITATIONS After appellate decisions have been published, they are normally referred to (cited) by the name of the case; the volume, name, and page number of the state's official reporter (if different from West's National Reporter System); the volume, name, and page number of the *National Reporter;* and the volume, name, and page number of any other selected reporter. This information is included in the *citation.* (Citing a reporter by volume number, name, and page number, in that order, is common to all citations.) When more than one reporter is cited for the same case, each reference is called a *parallel citation.*

Note that some states have adopted a "public domain citation system" that uses a somewhat different format for the citation. For example, in Wisconsin, a Wisconsin Supreme Court decision might be designated "2011 WI 40," meaning that the decision was the fortieth issued by the Wisconsin Supreme Court in the year 2011. Parallel citations to the *Wisconsin Reports* and West's *North Western Reporter* are still included after the public domain citation.

Consider the following case: *Orlando v. Cole,* 76 Mass. App.Ct. 1112, 921 N.E.2d 566 (2011). We see that the opinion in this case can be found in Volume 76 of the official *Massachusetts Appeals Court Reports,* on page 1112. The parallel citation is to Volume 921 of the *North Eastern Reporter, Second Series,* page 566.

When we present opinions in this text, we give the name of the court hearing the case and the year of the court's decision in addition to the reporter. A few states—including those with intermediate appellate courts, such as California, Illinois, and New York—have more than one reporter for opinions issued by their courts. Sample citations from these courts, as well as others, are listed and explained in Exhibit 1A–2 starting on page 22.

Federal Court Decisions

Federal district (trial) court decisions are published unofficially in West's *Federal Supplement* (F. Supp. or F.Supp.2d), and opinions from the circuit courts of appeals (federal reviewing courts) are reported unofficially in West's *Federal Reporter* (F., F.2d, or F.3d). Cases concerning federal bankruptcy law are published unofficially in West's *Bankruptcy Reporter* (Bankr.). The official edition of United States Supreme Court decisions is the *United States Reports* (U.S.), which is published by the federal government. Unofficial editions of Supreme Court cases include West's *Supreme Court Reporter* (S.Ct.) and the *Lawyers' Edition of the Supreme Court Reports* (L.Ed. or L.Ed.2d). Sample citations for federal court decisions are also listed and explained in Exhibit 1A–2 on pages 22 and 23.

Unpublished Opinions and Old Cases

Many court opinions that are not yet published or that are not intended for formal publication can be accessed through Westlaw® (abbreviated in citations as "WL"), an online legal database. When no citation to a published reporter is available for cases cited in this text, we give the WL citation (see Exhibit 1A–2 on page 24 for an example). Sometimes, both in this text and in other legal sources, you will see blanks left in a citation. This occurs when the decision will be published, but the particular volume number or page number is not yet available.

On a few occasions, this text cites opinions from old, classic cases dating to the nineteenth century or earlier. Some of these are from the English courts. The citations to these cases may not conform to the descriptions given above because the reporters in which they were published have since been replaced.

Reading and Understanding Case Law

The cases in this text have been condensed from the full text of the courts' opinions. For those wishing to review court cases for future research projects or to gain additional legal information, the following sections will provide useful insights into how to read and understand case law.

• *Exhibit* 1A–1 West's National Reporter System–Regional/Federal

Regional Reporters	Coverage Beginning	Coverage
Atlantic Reporter (A., A.2d, or A.3d)	1885	Connecticut, Delaware, District of Columbia, Maine, Maryland, New Hampshire, New Jersey, Pennsylvania, Rhode Island, and Vermont.
North Eastern Reporter (N.E. or N.E.2d)	1885	Illinois, Indiana, Massachusetts, New York, and Ohio.
North Western Reporter (N.W. or N.W.2d)	1879	Iowa, Michigan, Minnesota, Nebraska, North Dakota, South Dakota, and Wisconsin.
Pacific Reporter (P., P.2d, or P.3d)	1883	Alaska, Arizona, California, Colorado, Hawaii, Idaho, Kansas, Montana, Nevada, New Mexico, Oklahoma, Oregon, Utah, Washington, and Wyoming.
South Eastern Reporter (S.E. or S.E.2d)	1887	Georgia, North Carolina, South Carolina, Virginia, and West Virginia.
South Western Reporter (S.W., S.W.2d, or S.W.3d)	1886	Arkansas, Kentucky, Missouri, Tennessee, and Texas.
Southern Reporter (So., So.2d, or So.3d)	1887	Alabama, Florida, Louisiana, and Mississippi.
Federal Reporters		
Federal Reporter (F., F.2d, or F.3d)	1880	U.S. Circuit Courts from 1880 to 1912; U.S. Commerce Court from 1911 to 1913; U.S. District Courts from 1880 to 1932; U.S. Court of Claims (now called U.S. Court of Federal Claims) from 1929 to 1932 and since 1960; U.S. Courts of Appeals since 1891; U.S. Court of Customs and Patent Appeals since 1929; U.S. Emergency Court of Appeals since 1943.
Federal Supplement (F.Supp. or F.Supp.2d)	1932	U.S. Court of Claims from 1932 to 1960; U.S. District Courts since 1932; U.S. Customs Court since 1956.
Federal Rules Decisions (F.R.D.)	1939	U.S. District Courts involving the Federal Rules of Civil Procedure since 1939 and Federal Rules of Criminal Procedure since 1946.
Supreme Court Reporter (S.Ct.)	1882	United States Supreme Court since the October term of 1882.
Bankruptcy Reporter (Bankr.)	1980	Bankruptcy decisions of U.S. Bankruptcy Courts, U.S. District Courts, U.S. Courts of Appeals, and the United States Supreme Court.
Military Justice Reporter (M.J.)	1978	U.S. Court of Military Appeals and Courts of Military Review for the Army, Navy, Air Force, and Coast Guard.

NATIONAL REPORTER SYSTEM MAP

WASH. MONTANA N. DAK. MINN. OREGON IDAHO S. DAK. WIS. WYOMING MICH. NEVADA NEBR. IOWA UTAH CALIF. COLORADO KANSAS MO. ILL. IND. OHIO ARIZONA N. MEXICO OKLA. ARK. KY. TENN. TEXAS MISS. ALA. GA. LA. FLA. ALASKA HAWAII VT. ME. N.H. MASS. N.Y. R.I. CONN. PA. N.J. DEL. MD. W.VA. VA. N. CAR. S. CAR.

- Pacific
- North Western
- South Western
- North Eastern
- Atlantic
- South Eastern
- Southern

• ***Exhibit* 1A–2 How to Read Citations**

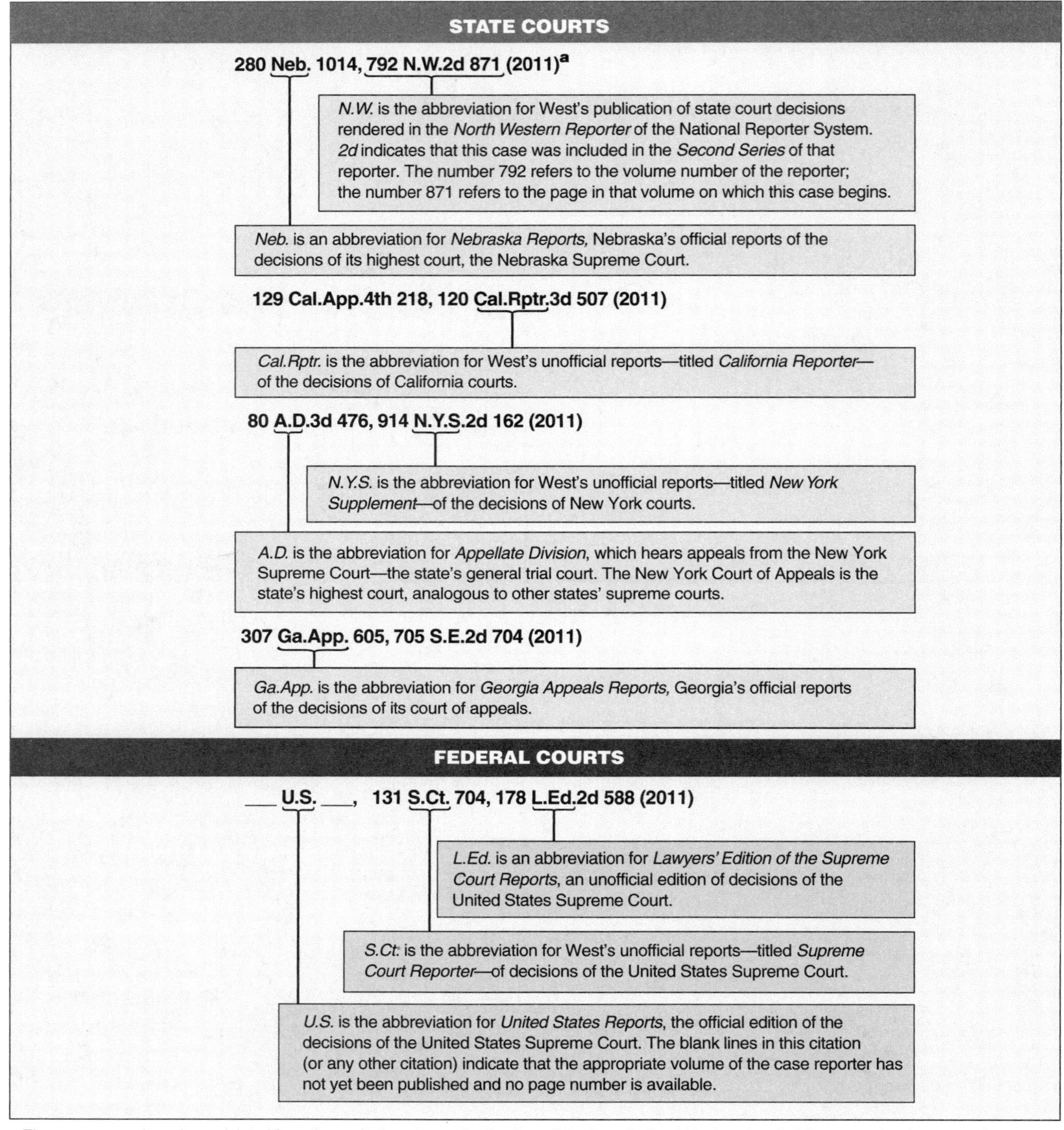
STATE COURTS
280 Neb. 1014, 792 N.W.2d 871 (2011)[a]
N.W. is the abbreviation for West's publication of state court decisions rendered in the North Western Reporter of the National Reporter System. 2d indicates that this case was included in the Second Series of that reporter. The number 792 refers to the volume number of the reporter; the number 871 refers to the page in that volume on which this case begins.
Neb. is an abbreviation for Nebraska Reports, Nebraska's official reports of the decisions of its highest court, the Nebraska Supreme Court.
129 Cal.App.4th 218, 120 Cal.Rptr.3d 507 (2011)
Cal.Rptr. is the abbreviation for West's unofficial reports—titled California Reporter—of the decisions of California courts.
80 A.D.3d 476, 914 N.Y.S.2d 162 (2011)
N.Y.S. is the abbreviation for West's unofficial reports—titled New York Supplement—of the decisions of New York courts.
A.D. is the abbreviation for Appellate Division, which hears appeals from the New York Supreme Court—the state's general trial court. The New York Court of Appeals is the state's highest court, analogous to other states' supreme courts.
307 Ga.App. 605, 705 S.E.2d 704 (2011)
Ga.App. is the abbreviation for Georgia Appeals Reports, Georgia's official reports of the decisions of its court of appeals.
FEDERAL COURTS
___ U.S. ___, 131 S.Ct. 704, 178 L.Ed.2d 588 (2011)
L.Ed. is an abbreviation for Lawyers' Edition of the Supreme Court Reports, an unofficial edition of decisions of the United States Supreme Court.
S.Ct. is the abbreviation for West's unofficial reports—titled Supreme Court Reporter—of decisions of the United States Supreme Court.
U.S. is the abbreviation for United States Reports, the official edition of the decisions of the United States Supreme Court. The blank lines in this citation (or any other citation) indicate that the appropriate volume of the case reporter has not yet been published and no page number is available.

a. The case names have been deleted from these citations to emphasize the publications. It should be kept in mind, however, that the name of a case is as important as the specific page numbers in the volumes in which it is found. If a citation is incorrect, the correct citation may be found in a publication's index of case names. In addition to providing a check on errors in citations, the date of a case is important because the value of a recent case as an authority is likely to be greater than that of older cases from the same court.

• ***Exhibit* 1A–2 How to Read Citations–Continued**

FEDERAL COURTS (Continued)

628 F.3d 1175 (9th Cir. 2011)

9th Cir. is an abbreviation denoting that this case was decided in the U.S. Court of Appeals for the Ninth Circuit.

761 F.Supp.2d 718 (S.D. Ohio 2011)

S.D. Ohio is an abbreviation indicating that the U.S. District Court for the Southern District of Ohio decided this case.

ENGLISH COURTS

9 Exch. 341, 156 Eng.Rep. 145 (1854)

Eng.Rep. is an abbreviation for *English Reports, Full Reprint,* a series of reports containing selected decisions made in English courts between 1378 and 1865.

Exch. is an abbreviation for *English Exchequer Reports*, which includes the original reports of cases decided in England's Court of Exchequer.

STATUTORY AND OTHER CITATIONS

18 U.S.C. Section 1961(1)(A)

U.S.C. denotes *United States Code*, the codification of *United States Statutes at Large.* The number 18 refers to the statute's U.S.C. title number and 1961 to its section number within that title. The number 1 in parentheses refers to a subsection within the section, and the letter A in parentheses to a subsection within the subsection.

UCC 2–206(1)(b)

UCC is an abbreviation for *Uniform Commercial Code*. The first number 2 is a reference to an article of the UCC, and 206 to a section within that article. The number 1 in parentheses refers to a subsection within the section, and the letter b in parentheses to a subsection within the subsection.

***Restatement (Third) of Torts,* Section 6**

Restatement (Third) of Torts refers to the third edition of the American Law Institute's *Restatement of the Law of Torts*. The number 6 refers to a specific section.

17 C.F.R. Section 230.505

C.F.R. is an abbreviation for *Code of Federal Regulations*, a compilation of federal administrative regulations. The number 17 designates the regulation's title number, and 230.505 designates a specific section within that title.

Continued

• ***Exhibit* 1A–2 How to Read Citations–Continued**

WESTLAW® CITATIONS[b]

2011 WL 213420

WL is an abbreviation for Westlaw. The number 2011 is the year of the document that can be found with this citation in the Westlaw database. The number 213420 is a number assigned to a specific document. A higher number indicates that a document was added to the Westlaw database later in the year.

UNIFORM RESOURCE LOCATORS (URLs)

http://www.westlaw.com[c]

The suffix *com* is the top level domain (TLD) for this Web site. The TLD *com* is an abbreviation for "commercial," which usually means that a for-profit entity hosts (maintains or supports) this Web site.

westlaw is the host name—the part of the domain name selected by the organization that registered the name. In this case, West registered the name. This Internet site is the Westlaw database on the Web.

www is an abbreviation for "World Wide Web." The Web is a system of Internet servers that support documents formatted in *HTML* (hypertext markup language) and other formats as well.

http://www.uscourts.gov

This is "The Federal Judiciary Home Page." The host is the Administrative Office of the U.S. Courts. The TLD *gov* is an abbreviation for "government." This Web site includes information and links from, and about, the federal courts.

http://www.law.cornell.edu/index.html

This part of a URL points to a Web page or file at a specific location within the host's domain. This page is a menu with links to documents within the domain and to other Internet resources.

This is the host name for a Web site that contains the Internet publications of the Legal Information Institute (LII), which is a part of Cornell Law School. The LII site includes a variety of legal materials and links to other legal resources on the Internet. The TLD *edu* is an abbreviation for "educational institution" (a school or a university).

http://www.ipl2.org/div/news

This part of the URL points to a static *news* page at this Web site, which provides links to online newspapers from around the world.

div is an abbreviation for "division," which is the way that the Internet Public Library tags the content on its Web site as relating to a specific topic.

ipl2 is an abbreviation for "Internet Public Library," which is an online service that provides reference resources and links to other information services on the Web. The IPL is supported chiefly by the School of Information at the University of Michigan. The TLD *org* is an abbreviation for "organization" (normally nonprofit).

b. Many court decisions that are not yet published or that are not intended for publication can be accessed through Westlaw, an online legal database.

c. The basic form for a URL is "service://hostname/path." The Internet service for all of the URLs in this text is *http* (hypertext transfer protocol). Because most Web browsers add this prefix automatically when a user enters a host name or a hostname/path, we have generally omitted the *http://* from the URLs listed in this text.

Case Titles and Terminology

The title of a case, such as *Adams v. Jones,* indicates the names of the parties to the lawsuit. The *v.* in the case title stands for *versus,* which means "against." Adams was the plaintiff, and Jones was the defendant. If the case is appealed, the appellate court will sometimes place the name of the party appealing the decision first, so the case may be called *Jones v. Adams.* Because some reviewing courts retain the trial court order of names, it is often impossible to distinguish the plaintiff from the defendant in the title of a reported appellate court decision.

The following terms and phrases are frequently encountered in court opinions and legal publications. Because it is important to understand what these terms and phrases mean, we define and discuss them here.

PLAINTIFFS AND DEFENDANTS The plaintiff in a lawsuit is the party that initiates the action. The defendant is the party against which a lawsuit is brought. Lawsuits frequently involve more than one plaintiff and/or defendant.

APPELLANTS AND APPELLEES The *appellant* is the party that appeals a case to another court or jurisdiction from the court or jurisdiction in which the case was originally brought. The *appellee* is the party against which the appeal is taken. Sometimes, the appellee is referred to as the *respondent.*

JUDGES AND JUSTICES The terms *judge* and *justice* are usually synonymous and represent two designations given to judges in various courts. All members of the United States Supreme Court, for example, are referred to as justices. And justice is the formal title usually given to judges of appellate courts, although this is not always the case. The term *justice* is commonly abbreviated to J., and *justices* to JJ. A Supreme Court case might refer to Justice Kagen as Kagen, J., or to Chief Justice Roberts as Roberts, C.J.

DECISIONS AND OPINIONS Most decisions reached by reviewing, or appellate, courts are explained in written *opinions.* The opinion contains the court's reasons for its decision, the rules of law that apply, and the judgment. When all judges or justices unanimously agree on an opinion, the opinion is written for the entire court and can be deemed a *unanimous opinion.* When there is not unanimous agreement, a *majority opinion* is written, outlining the views of the majority of the judges or justices deciding the case.

Often, a judge or justice who feels strongly about making a point that was not emphasized in the unanimous or majority opinion will write a *concurring opinion.* That means the judge or justice agrees (concurs) with the judgment given in the unanimous or majority opinion but for different reasons. When there is not a unanimous opinion, a *dissenting opinion* usually is written. (See the *Unit Case Study with Dissenting Opinion* on pages 64 and 65.) The dissenting opinion is important because it may form the basis of the arguments used years later in overruling the precedential majority opinion. Occasionally, a court issues a *per curiam* (by the court) opinion, which does not indicate which judge or justice authored the opinion.

A Sample Court Case

Knowing how to read and analyze a court opinion is an essential step in undertaking accurate legal research. A further step involves "briefing" the case. Legal researchers routinely brief cases by summarizing and reducing the texts of the opinions to their essential elements. The cases contained within the chapters of this text have already been analyzed and partially briefed by the authors, and the essential aspects of each case are presented in a convenient format consisting of four basic sections: *Facts, Issue, Decision,* and *Reason.*

Each case is followed by either a brief *For Critical Analysis* section, which presents a question regarding some issue raised by the case; a *Why Is This Case Important?* section, which explains the significance of the case; or a *What If the Facts Were Different?* question, which alters the facts slightly and asks you to consider how this would change the outcome. A section entitled *Impact of This Case on Today's Law* concludes the *Classic Cases* that appear throughout the text to indicate the significance of the case for today's legal landscape.

The sample court case we present and annotate in Exhibit 1A–3 on pages 26–27 is one that the Superior Court of New Jersey, Appellate Division—a state intermediate appellate court—decided in 2011. On behalf of Edward Fehr's boat, the *Gina Ariella,* Jack Aydelotte entered the Sterling Harbor Duke of Fluke Tournament in New Jersey. One of the issues before the court was the propriety of the *Gina Ariella's* disqualification from the tournament based on the judges' decision that Aydelotte had submitted "bad fish" in the competition for one of the prizes.

• ***Exhibit* 1A–3 A Sample Court Case**

This section contains the citation—the case name, the name of the court, the reporters in which the court's opinion can be found, and the year of the court's decision.

FEHR v. ALGARD

Superior Court of New Jersey, Appellate Division,

__ A.3d __ (2011).

This section identifies the parties and describes the events leading up to the trial and its appeal. The decision of the lower court is included, as well as the issue to be decided by the appellate court.

A *fluke* in this context is a flatfish, such as a flounder. *Fluke* has other meanings in the fishing industry—it can refer to part of an anchor, a harpoon, or a whale's tail.

A *contract* is an agreement between two or more parties that can be enforced in court. In a contract, each party agrees to perform, or to refrain from performing, some act now or in the future. A *breach of contract* is a failure to perform the obligations of a contract without a legal excuse.

A *summary judgment* is a judgment that a court enters without beginning or continuing a trial. This judgment can be entered only if no facts are in dispute and the only question is how the law applies to the facts.

In this case, *damages* consist of cash sought as a remedy for a breach of contract.

FACTS Cathy Algard owns Sterling Harbor Motel & Marina, Inc. (SHM). SHM sponsored the Sterling Harbor Duke of Fluke Tournament in Wildwood, New Jersey. Prizes included the "single heaviest **fluke** prize" for the contestant who caught the heaviest live flounder and the "five heaviest fluke prize" for the boat catching the five flounder with the greatest combined weight. On behalf of Edward Fehr's boat, the *Gina Ariella,* Jack Aydelotte presented the heaviest live flounder. He submitted five other fish for the five-fluke award. The judges ruled that two of the five had not been caught during the contest and disqualified the *Gina Ariella.* Fehr filed a suit in a New Jersey state court against Algard, alleging **breach of contract.** The court issued a **summary judgment** in Fehr's favor, crowned him the "Duke of Fluke," and awarded him **damages**. Algard appealed.

ISSUE Was the trial court correct in ruling that Fehr was entitled to the prize for the biggest flounder under the contract terms, even though the contest's judges had disqualified him for submitting day-old fish?

• ***Exhibit* 1A–3 A Sample Court Case–Continued**

This section contains the court's decision on the issue before it. An appellate court's decision is often phrased with reference to the decision of the lower court from which the case was appealed. For example, an appellate court may "affirm" or "reverse" a lower court's ruling.

DECISION No. A state appellate court **reversed** the judgment and **remanded** the case to give Algard an opportunity to prove that Aydelotte's deception warranted disqualification of the *Gina Ariella*.

This section contains the court's reasoning that led to its conclusion. The reasoning in this case covered the contract that existed between the contest's sponsors and contestants, and the terms of that contract, which consisted of the contest rules.

An appellate court's decision to *reverse* a judgment is to reject or overrule the judgment that was rendered in the lower court. To *remand* is to send back. Here, the appellate court sent this case back to the trial court to give the parties the opportunity to prove their claims.

REASON The court explained that the Tournament—like the offer of a prize in any contest—becomes a binding contract in favor of a contestant who complies with the rules. The question was whether Fehr complied and was therefore entitled to the receipt of an award. Fehr argued that he presented the heaviest live flounder and Algard's failure to award him the prize was a breach of contract. Algard pointed out that Aydelotte signed an entry form that proclaimed "anyone who is found to have provided false information is subject to immediate disqualification." The court stated, "The order of plaintiff's submissions for prizes should not allow the first fish to be considered for an award, if, in fact, he then tried to weigh-in day old fish." The court added, however, that "if the judges are found to have **acted in bad faith** and exceeded the rules in making a decision, plaintiff may prevail."

Every party to a contract is bound by a duty of good faith and fair dealing in its performance. Good faith conduct is honest, fair, and reasonable behavior in accord with the parties' agreed purpose and their justified expectations. To *act in bad faith* is to do something that undercuts the right of one of the parties to receive the benefits of the contract.

Chapter 2

Traditional and Online Dispute Resolution

Learning Objectives

After reading this chapter, you should be able to answer the following questions:

1. What is judicial review?
2. Before a court can hear a case, it must have jurisdiction. Over what must it have jurisdiction? How are the courts applying traditional jurisdictional concepts to cases involving Internet transactions?
3. What is the difference between a trial court and an appellate court?
4. What is discovery, and how does electronic discovery differ from traditional discovery?
5. What are three alternative methods of resolving disputes?

The Learning Objectives above are designed to help improve your understanding of the chapter.

(John Elk III/Lonely Planet Images/Getty Images)

Every society needs to have an established method for resolving disputes. This is particularly true in the business world—nearly every businessperson will face a lawsuit at some time in his or her career. For this reason, anyone involved in business needs to have an understanding of court systems in the United States, as well as the various methods of dispute resolution that can be pursued outside the courts.

After examining the judiciary's overall role in the American governmental scheme, this chapter discusses some basic requirements that must be met before a party may bring a lawsuit before a particular court. We then look at the court systems of the United States in some detail and, to clarify judicial procedures, follow a hypothetical case through a state court system. Throughout this chapter, we indicate how court doctrines and procedures are being adapted to the needs of a cyber age. The chapter concludes with an overview of some alternative methods of settling disputes, including online dispute resolution.

The Judiciary's Role in American Government

As you learned in Chapter 1, the body of American law includes the federal and state constitutions, statutes passed by legislative bodies, administrative law, and the case decisions and legal principles that form the common law. These laws would be meaningless, however, without the courts to interpret and apply them. This is the essential role of the judiciary—the courts—in the American governmental system: to interpret and to apply the law.

Judicial Review

As the branch of government entrusted with interpreting the laws, the judiciary can decide, among other things, whether the laws or actions of the other two branches are constitutional. The process for making such a determination is known as **judicial review.** The power of judicial review enables the judicial branch to act as a check on the other two branches of government, in line with the checks-and-balances system established by the U.S. Constitution. (Today, nearly all nations with constitutional democracies, including Canada, France, and Germany, have some form of judicial review.)

The Origins of Judicial Review

The power of judicial review was not mentioned in the Constitution, but the concept was not new at the time the nation was founded. Indeed, before 1789 state courts had already overturned state legislative acts that conflicted with state constitutions. Many of the founders expected the United States Supreme Court to assume a similar role with respect to the federal Constitution. Alexander Hamilton and James Madison both emphasized the importance of judicial review in their essays urging the adoption of the new Constitution.

Basic Judicial Requirements

Before a court can hear a lawsuit, certain requirements must be met. These requirements relate to *jurisdiction, venue,* and *standing to sue.* We examine these important concepts next.

Jurisdiction

In Latin, *juris* means "law," and *diction* means "to speak." Thus, "the power to speak the law" is the literal meaning of the term **jurisdiction.** Before any court can hear a case, it must have jurisdiction over the person (or company) against whom the suit is brought (the defendant) or over the property involved in the suit. The court must also have jurisdiction over the subject matter of the dispute.

JURISDICTION OVER PERSONS OR PROPERTY Generally, a court can exercise personal jurisdiction (*in personam* jurisdiction) over any person or business that resides in a certain geographic area. A state trial court, for example, normally has jurisdictional authority over residents (including businesses) in a particular area of the state, such as a county or district. A state's highest court (often called the state supreme court)[1] has jurisdiction over all residents of that state. A court can also exercise jurisdiction over property that is located within its boundaries. This jurisdiction is known as *im rem* jurisdiction.

Long Arm Statutes. Under the authority of a state **long arm statute,** a court can exercise personal jurisdiction over certain out-of-state defendants based on activities that took place within the state. Before exercising long arm jurisdiction over a nonresident, however, the court must be convinced that the defendant had sufficient contacts, or *minimum contacts,* with the state to justify the jurisdiction.[2] Generally, this means that the defendant must have enough of a connection to the state for the judge to conclude that it is fair for the state to exercise power over the defendant. If an out-of-state defendant caused an automobile accident or sold defective goods within the state, for instance, a court usually will find that minimum contacts exist to exercise jurisdiction over that defendant.

CASE EXAMPLE 2.1 After an Xbox game system caught fire in Bonnie Broquet's home in Texas and caused substantial personal injuries, Broquet filed a lawsuit in a Texas court against Ji-Haw Industrial Company, a nonresident company that made the Xbox components. Broquet alleged that Ji-Haw's components were defective and had caused the fire. Ji-Haw argued that the Texas court lacked jurisdiction over it, but in 2008, a state appellate court held that the Texas long arm statute authorized the exercise of jurisdiction over the out-of-state defendant.[3] ● Similarly, a state may exercise personal jurisdiction over a nonresident defendant who is sued for breaching a contract that was formed within the state, even when that contract was negotiated over the phone or through online and offline correspondence.

Corporate Contacts. Because corporations are considered legal persons, courts use the same principles to determine whether it is fair to exercise jurisdiction over a corporation.[4] A corporation normally is subject to personal jurisdiction in the state in which it is incorporated, has its principal office, and is doing business. Courts apply the minimum-contacts test to determine if they can exercise jurisdiction over out-of-state corporations.

The minimum-contacts requirement usually is met if the corporation advertises or sells its products within the state, or places its goods into the "stream of commerce" with the intent that the goods be sold in the state. **EXAMPLE 2.2** A business is incorporated under the laws of Maine but has a branch office and manufacturing plant in Georgia. The corporation also advertises and sells its products in Georgia. These activities would likely constitute sufficient contacts with the state of Georgia to allow a Georgia court to exercise jurisdiction over the corporation. ●

Some corporations, however, do not sell or advertise products or place any goods in the stream of commerce. Determining what constitutes minimum contacts in these situations can be more difficult. In the following case, the question before the court was whether a New Jersey firm had minimum contacts with a North Carolina firm.

1. As will be discussed shortly, a state's highest court is frequently referred to as the state supreme court, but there are exceptions. For example, in New York, the supreme court is a trial court.

2. The minimum-contacts standard was established in *International Shoe Co. v. State of Washington,* 326 U.S. 310, 66 S.Ct. 154, 90 L.Ed. 95 (1945).

3. *Ji-Haw Industrial Co. v. Broquet,* 2008 WL 441822 (Tex.App.—San Antonio 2008).

4. In the eyes of the law, corporations are "legal persons"—entities that can sue and be sued. See Chapter 24.

Case 2.1 Southern Prestige Industries, Inc. v. Independence Plating Corp.

Court of Appeals of North Carolina, 690 S.E.2d 768 (2010).
www.nccourts.org[a]

FACTS Independence Plating Corporation (the defendant) is a New Jersey corporation that provides metal-coating services. Its only office and all of its personnel are located in New Jersey. It does not advertise out of state, but it had a long-standing business relationship with Kidde Aerospace in North Carolina (filing under the name Southern Prestige Industries, Inc.). For almost a year, Independence and Kidde engaged in frequent transactions. On November 18, 2008, Kidde initiated an action for breach of contract in a North Carolina state court, alleging defects in the metal-plating process carried out by Independence. Independence filed a motion to dismiss for lack of personal jurisdiction, which the trial court denied. Independence appealed, arguing that it had insufficient contacts with North Carolina for the state to exercise jurisdiction.

ISSUE Did Independence Plating Corporation have sufficient minimum contacts with North Carolina for the state to exercise personal jurisdiction?

a. In the right-hand column of the page, click on "Court Opinions." When that page opens, select the year 2010 under the heading "Court of Appeals Opinions." Scroll down to February 2, 2010, and click on the case title under "Unpublished Opinions" to access the opinion. The North Carolina court system maintains this Web site.

DECISION Yes. The North Carolina appellate court affirmed the trial court's decision. Independence had sufficient minimum contacts with North Carolina to satisfy the due process of law requirements necessary for the state to exercise jurisdiction.

REASON The court looked at several factors in determining whether minimum contacts existed, including the quantity of the contacts and the nature and quality of the contacts, as well as the interests of the forum state. In this case, there were thirty-two separate purchase orders between the two parties in a period of less than twelve months. Independence sent invoices totaling more than $21,000, and these invoices were paid from Southern's corporate bank account. "North Carolina has a single 'manifest interest' in providing the plaintiff with 'a convenient forum for redressing injuries inflicted by' [the] defendant, an out-of-state merchant."

FOR CRITICAL ANALYSIS—Ethical Consideration *Was it fair for the North Carolina courts to require a New Jersey company to litigate in North Carolina? Explain.*

Jurisdiction over Subject Matter Jurisdiction over subject matter is a limitation on the types of cases a court can hear. In both the federal and state court systems, there are courts of *general* (unlimited) jurisdiction and courts of *limited jurisdiction*. An example of a court of general jurisdiction is a state trial court or a federal district court. An example of a state court of limited jurisdiction is a probate court. **Probate courts** are state courts that handle only matters relating to the transfer of a person's assets and obligations after that person's death, including matters relating to the custody and guardianship of children. An example of a federal court of limited subject-matter jurisdiction is a bankruptcy court. **Bankruptcy courts** handle only bankruptcy proceedings, which are governed by federal bankruptcy law (see Chapter 19).

A court's jurisdiction over subject matter usually is defined in the statute or constitution creating the court. In both the federal and state court systems, a court's subject-matter jurisdiction can be limited not only by the subject of the lawsuit but also by the amount in controversy, by whether a case is a felony (a more serious type of crime) or a misdemeanor (a less serious type of crime), or by whether the proceeding is a trial or an appeal.

Original and Appellate Jurisdiction The distinction between courts of original jurisdiction and courts of appellate jurisdiction normally lies in whether the case is being heard for the first time. Courts having original jurisdiction are courts of the first instance, or trial courts—that is, courts in which lawsuits begin, trials take place, and evidence is presented. In the federal court system, the *district courts* are trial courts. In the various state court systems, the trial courts are known by various names, as will be discussed shortly.

The key point is that any court having original jurisdiction normally is known as a trial court. Courts having appellate jurisdiction act as reviewing courts, or appellate courts. In general, cases can be brought before appellate courts only on appeal from an order or a judgment of a trial court or other lower court.

Jurisdiction of the Federal Courts Because the federal government is a government of limited powers, the jurisdiction of the federal courts is limited. Federal courts have subject-matter jurisdiction in two situations.

Federal Questions. Whenever a plaintiff's cause of action is based, at least in part, on the U.S. Constitution, a treaty, or a federal law, then a **federal question** arises, and the case comes under the judicial power of the federal courts. Any lawsuit involving a federal question, such as a person's rights under the U.S. Constitution, can originate in a federal court. Note that in a case based on a federal question, a federal court will apply federal law.

Diversity of Citizenship. U.S. district courts can exercise original jurisdiction over cases with **diversity of citizenship**.

The most common type of diversity jurisdiction has two requirements: (1) the plaintiff and defendant must be residents of different states and (2) the dollar amount in controversy must exceed $75,000. For purposes of diversity jurisdiction, a corporation is a citizen of both the state in which it is incorporated and the state in which its principal place of business is located. A case involving diversity of citizenship can be filed in the appropriate federal district court. If the case starts in a state court, it can sometimes be transferred, or "removed," to a federal court. A large percentage of the cases filed in federal courts each year are based on diversity of citizenship.

As noted, a federal court will apply federal law in cases involving federal questions. In a case based on diversity of citizenship, in contrast, a federal court will apply the relevant state law (which is often the law of the state in which the court sits).

EXCLUSIVE VERSUS CONCURRENT JURISDICTION When both federal and state courts have the power to hear a case, as is true in lawsuits involving diversity of citizenship, **concurrent jurisdiction** exists. When cases can be tried only in federal courts or only in state courts, **exclusive jurisdiction** exists. Federal courts have exclusive jurisdiction in cases involving federal crimes, bankruptcy, patents, and copyrights; in suits against the United States; and in some areas of admiralty law (law governing transportation on ocean waters). State courts also have exclusive jurisdiction over certain subject matter—for example, divorce and adoption.

When concurrent jurisdiction exists, a party may choose to bring a suit in either a federal court or a state court. A number of factors can affect a party's decision to litigate in a federal or a state court, such as the availability of different remedies, the distance to the respective courthouses, or the experience or reputation of a particular judge. For example, if the dispute involves a trade secret, a party might conclude that a federal court—which has exclusive jurisdiction over copyrights, patents, and trademarks—would have more expertise in the matter.

A party might also choose a federal court over a state court if he or she is concerned about bias in a state court. In contrast, a plaintiff might choose to litigate in a state court if it has a reputation for awarding substantial amounts of damages or if the judge is perceived as being pro-plaintiff. The concepts of exclusive jurisdiction and concurrent jurisdiction are illustrated in Exhibit 2–1 below.

Jurisdiction in Cyberspace

The Internet's capacity to bypass political and geographic boundaries undercuts the traditional basis on which courts assert personal jurisdiction. As already discussed, for a court to compel a defendant to come before it, there must be at least minimum contacts—the presence of a salesperson within the state, for example. Are there sufficient minimum contacts if the defendant's only connection to a jurisdiction is an ad on a Web site originating from a remote location?

THE "SLIDING-SCALE" STANDARD The courts have developed a standard—called a "sliding-scale" standard—for determining when the exercise of jurisdiction over an out-of-state defendant is proper. In developing this standard, the courts have identified three types of Internet business contacts: (1) substantial business conducted over the Internet (with contracts and sales, for example); (2) some interactivity through a Web site; and (3) passive advertising. Jurisdiction is proper for the first category, improper for the third, and may or may not be appropriate for the second. An Internet communication typically is considered passive if people have to voluntarily access it to read the message, and active if it is sent to specific individuals.

• ***Exhibit* 2–1 Exclusive and Concurrent Jurisdiction**

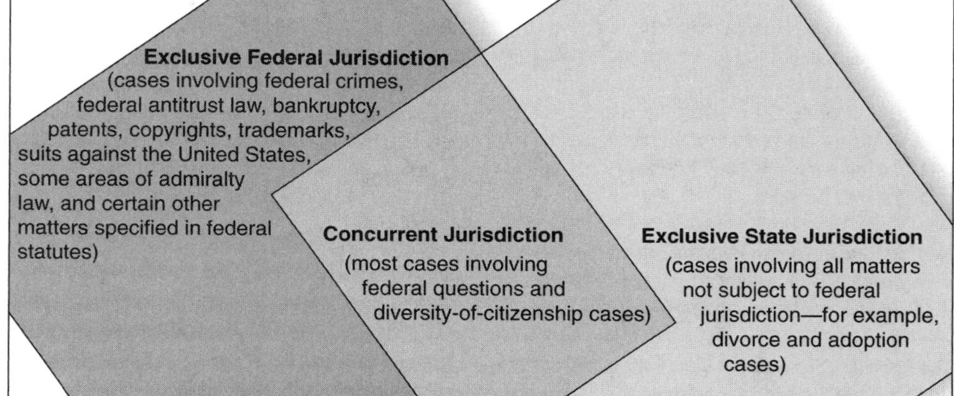

In certain situations, even a single contact can satisfy the minimum-contacts requirement. **CASE EXAMPLE 2.3** Daniel Crummey purchased a used recreational vehicle (RV) from sellers in Texas after viewing photos of it on eBay. The sellers' statements on eBay claimed that "Everything works great on this RV and it will provide comfort and dependability for years to come." Crummey picked up the RV in Texas, but on the drive home, the RV quit working. He filed a suit in Louisiana against the sellers alleging that the RV was defective, but the sellers claimed that the Louisiana court lacked jurisdiction. Because the sellers had used eBay to market and sell the RV to a Louisiana buyer—and had regularly sold to other remote parties—the court found that jurisdiction was proper.[5] •

5. *Crummey v. Morgan*, 965 So.2d 497 (La.App.1 Cir. 2007). Note that a single sale on eBay does not necessarily confer jurisdiction. Jurisdiction depends on whether the seller regularly uses eBay as a means for doing business with remote buyers. See *Boschetto v. Hansing*, 539 F.3d 1011 (9th Cir. 2008).

INTERNATIONAL JURISDICTIONAL ISSUES Because the Internet is global in scope, it obviously raises international jurisdictional issues. The world's courts seem to be developing a standard that echoes the minimum-contacts requirement applied by U.S. courts. Most courts are indicating that minimum contacts—doing business within the jurisdiction, for example—are enough to compel a defendant to appear and that a physical presence is not necessary. The effect of this standard is that a business firm has to comply with the laws in any jurisdiction in which it targets customers for its products. This situation is complicated by the fact that many countries' laws on particular issues—free speech, for example—are very different from U.S. laws.

The following case illustrates how federal courts apply a sliding-scale standard to determine if they can exercise jurisdiction over a foreign defendant whose only contact with the United States is through a Web site.

Case 2.2 Gucci America, Inc. v. Wang Huoqing

United States District Court, Northern District of California, ___ F.Supp.3d ___ (2011).

FACTS Gucci America, Inc., is a New York corporation headquartered in New York City. Gucci manufactures and distributes high-quality luxury goods, including footwear, belts, sunglasses, handbags, and wallets, which are sold worldwide. In connection with its products, Gucci uses twenty-one federally registered trademarks (trademark law will be discussed in Chapter 5). Gucci also operates a number of boutiques, some of which are located in California. Wang Huoqing, a resident of the People's Republic of China, operates numerous Web sites. When Gucci discovered that Huoqing's Web sites offered for sale counterfeit goods—products that bear Gucci's trademarks but are not genuine Gucci articles—it hired a private investigator in San Jose, California, to buy goods from the Web sites. The investigator purchased a wallet that was labeled Gucci but was counterfeit. Gucci filed a trademark infringement lawsuit against Huoqing in a federal district court in California seeking damages and an injunction to prevent further infringement. Huoqing was notified of the lawsuit via e-mail (see *service of process* on page 36) but did not appear in court. Gucci asked the court to enter a default judgment—that is, a judgment entered when the defendant fails to appear—but the court first had to determine whether it had personal jurisdiction over Huoqing based on the Internet sales.

ISSUE Can a U.S. federal court exercise personal jurisdiction over a resident of China whose only contact with the United States was through an interactive Web site that advertised and sold counterfeit goods?

DECISION Yes. The United States District Court for the Northern District of California held that it had personal jurisdiction over the foreign defendant, Huoqing. The court entered a default judgment against Huoqing and granted Gucci an injunction.

REASON The court reasoned that the due process clause allows a federal court to exercise jurisdiction over a defendant who has had sufficient minimum contacts with the court's forum—the place where the court exercises jurisdiction. Specific jurisdiction exists when (1) the nonresident defendant engages in some act or transaction with the forum "by which he purposefully avails himself of the privilege of conducting activities in the forum, thereby invoking the benefits and protections of its laws; (2) the claim must be one which arises out of or results from the defendant's forum-related activities; and (3) exercise of jurisdiction must be reasonable." To determine whether Huoqing had purposefully conducted business activities in Gucci's district through his Web sites, the court used a sliding-scale analysis. Under this analysis, passive Web sites do not create sufficient contacts for such a finding, but interactive sites may create sufficient contacts. Huoqing's Web sites were fully interactive. In addition, Gucci presented evidence that Huoqing had advertised and sold the counterfeited goods within the court's district, and that he had made one actual sale within the district—the sale to Gucci's private investigator.

WHAT IF THE FACTS WERE DIFFERENT? *Suppose that Gucci had* not *presented evidence that Huoqing had made one actual sale through his Web site to a resident (the private investigator) of the court's district. Would the court still have found that it had personal jurisdiction over Huoqing? Why or why not?*

Venue

Jurisdiction has to do with whether a court has authority to hear a case involving specific persons, property, or subject matter. **Venue**[6] is concerned with the most appropriate physical location for a trial. Two state courts (or two federal courts) may have the authority to exercise jurisdiction over a case, but it may be more appropriate or convenient to hear the case in one court than in the other.

Basically, the concept of venue reflects the policy that a court trying a suit should be in the geographic neighborhood (usually the county) where the incident leading to the lawsuit occurred or where the parties involved in the lawsuit reside. Venue in a civil case typically is where the defendant resides, whereas venue in a criminal case normally is where the crime occurred.

Pretrial publicity or other factors, though, may require a change of venue to another community, especially in criminal cases when the defendant's right to a fair and impartial jury has been impaired. **EXAMPLE 2.4** Police raided a compound of Mormon polygamists in Texas and removed many children from the ranch. Authorities suspected that some of the girls were being sexually and physically abused. The raid received a lot of media attention, and people living in the nearby towns would likely have been influenced by this publicity. In that situation, if the government filed criminal charges against a member of the religious sect, that individual might request—and would probably receive—a change of venue to another location. •

Standing to Sue

Before a person can bring a lawsuit before a court, the party must have **standing to sue**, or a sufficient stake in the matter to justify seeking relief through the court system. In other words, to have standing, a party must have a legally protected and tangible interest at stake in the litigation. The party bringing the lawsuit must have suffered a harm, or have been threatened by a harm, as a result of the action about which she or he has complained. Standing to sue also requires that the controversy at issue be a **justiciable**[7] **controversy**—a controversy that is real and substantial, as opposed to hypothetical or academic. As United States Supreme Court chief justice John Roberts recently noted, a lack of standing is like Bob Dylan's line in the song "Like a Rolling Stone": "When you got nothing, you got nothing to lose."[8]

CASE EXAMPLE 2.5 James Bush visited a Federal Bureau of Investigation (FBI) office in California in 2007. He filled out complaint forms indicating that he was seeking records under the Freedom of Information Act (FOIA) regarding the FBI's failure to investigate a police brutality claim. In 2008, Bush filed a suit against the U.S. Department of Justice in an attempt to compel the FBI to provide the requested records. The court dismissed the lawsuit on the ground that no justiciable controversy existed. Bush had failed to comply with the requirements of the FOIA when he filled out the forms, so the FBI was not obligated to provide any records. Thus, there was no actual controversy for the court to decide.[9] •

The State and Federal Court Systems

Each state has its own court system, and there is also a system of federal courts. Even though there are fifty-two court systems—one for each of the fifty states, one for the District of Columbia, plus a federal system—similarities abound. Exhibit 2–2 on the next page illustrates the basic organizational structure characteristic of the court systems in many states.

The State Court Systems

Typically, a state court system will include several levels of courts. As indicated in Exhibit 2–2, state courts may include (1) trial courts of limited jurisdiction, (2) trial courts of general jurisdiction, (3) appellate courts, and (4) the state's highest court (often called the state supreme court). Generally, any person who is a party to a lawsuit has the opportunity to plead the case before a trial court and then, if he or she loses, before at least one level of appellate court. Only if the case involves a federal statute or a federal constitutional issue may the decision of a state supreme court on that issue be further appealed to the United States Supreme Court.

The states use various methods to select judges for their courts. In most states, judges are elected, but in some states, they are appointed. Usually, states specify the number of years that a judge will serve. In contrast, judges in the federal court system are appointed by the president of the United States and, if they are confirmed by the Senate, hold office for life—unless they engage in blatantly illegal conduct.

TRIAL COURTS Trial courts are exactly what their name implies—courts in which trials are held and testimony taken. State trial courts have either general or limited jurisdiction. Trial courts that have general jurisdiction as to subject matter may be called county, district, superior, or circuit courts.[10] The jurisdiction of these courts is often determined by the size of the county in which the court sits. State trial courts of general jurisdiction have jurisdiction over a wide variety of subjects, including both civil disputes and criminal prosecutions. In some states, trial courts of general jurisdiction may hear appeals from courts of limited jurisdiction.

Some courts of limited jurisdiction are called special inferior trial courts or minor judiciary courts. **Small claims courts** are

6. Pronounced *ven*-yoo.
7. Pronounced jus-*tish*-uh-bul.
8. See *Sprint Communications Co. v. APCC Services, Inc.,* 554 U.S. 269, 128 S.Ct. 2531, 171 L.Ed.2d 424 (2008).
9. *Bush v. Department of Justice,* 2008 WL 5245046 (N.D.Cal. 2008).
10. The name in Ohio is court of common pleas, and the name in New York is supreme court.

• *Exhibit* **2–2 The State and Federal Court Systems**

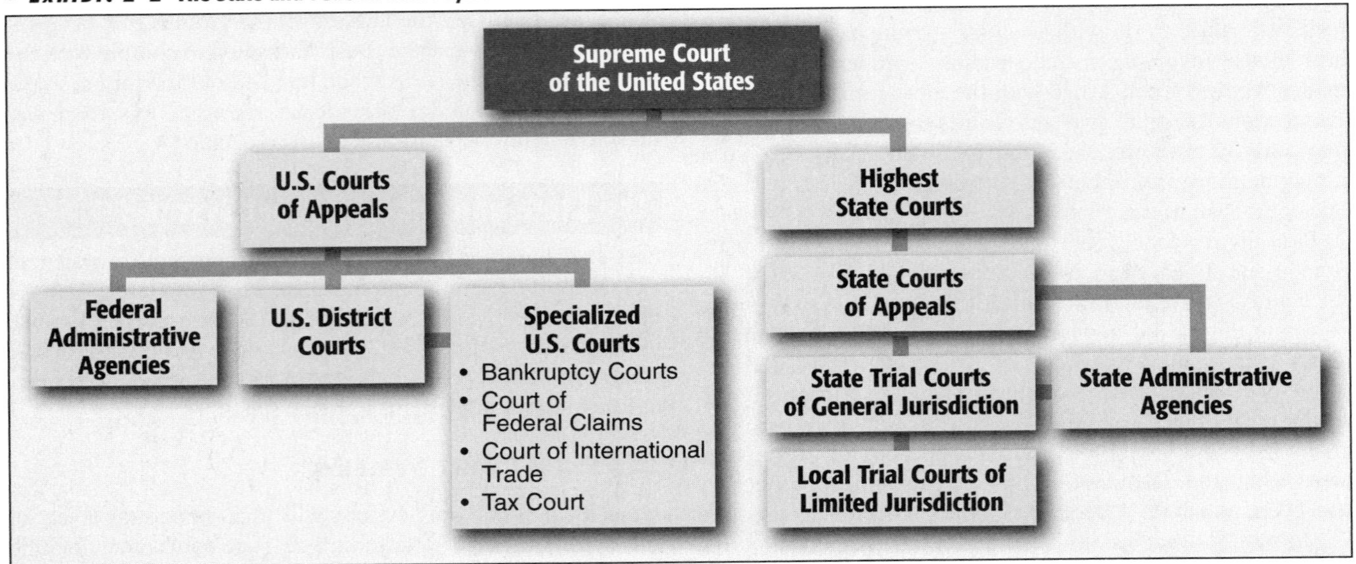

inferior trial courts that hear only civil cases involving claims of less than a certain amount, such as $5,000. Suits brought in small claims courts generally are conducted informally, and lawyers usually are not required. Another example of an inferior trial court is a local municipal court that hears mainly traffic cases. Decisions of small claims courts and municipal courts may sometimes be appealed to a state trial court of general jurisdiction. Other courts of limited jurisdiction as to subject matter include domestic relations or family courts, which handle primarily divorce actions and child-custody disputes, and probate courts. A few states have even established Islamic law courts, which are courts of limited jurisdiction that serve the American Muslim community.

APPELLATE, OR REVIEWING, COURTS Every state has at least one court of appeals (appellate court), which may be an intermediate appellate court or the state's highest court. About three-fourths of the states have intermediate appellate courts. Generally, courts of appeals do not conduct new trials in which evidence is submitted and witnesses are examined. Rather, an appellate court panel of three or more judges reviews the record of the case on appeal, which includes a transcript of the trial proceedings, and determines whether the trial court committed an error.

Usually, appellate courts focus on questions of law, not **questions of fact.** A question of fact deals with what really happened in regard to the dispute being tried—such as whether a party actually burned a flag. A **question of law** concerns the application or interpretation of the law—such as whether flag-burning is a form of speech protected by the First Amendment to the U.S. Constitution. Only a judge, not a jury, can rule on questions of law. Appellate courts normally defer (or give weight) to a trial court's findings on questions of fact because the trial court judge and jury were in a better position to evaluate testimony by directly observing witnesses' gestures, appearance, and nonverbal behavior during the trial. At the appellate level, the judges review the written transcript of the trial, which does not include these nonverbal elements.

An appellate court will challenge a trial court's finding of fact only when the finding is clearly erroneous—that is, when it is contrary to the evidence presented at trial—or when there is no evidence to support the finding. **EXAMPLE 2.6** A jury concludes that a manufacturer's product harmed the plaintiff, but no evidence was submitted to the court to support that conclusion. In this situation, the appellate court will hold that the trial court's decision was erroneous. •

HIGHEST STATE COURTS The highest appellate court in a state usually is called the supreme court but may be called by some other name. For example, in both New York and Maryland, the highest state court is called the court of appeals. The decisions of each state's highest court are final on all questions of state law. Only when issues of federal law are involved can a decision made by a state's highest court be overruled by the United States Supreme Court.

The Federal Court System

The federal court system is basically a three-tiered model consisting of (1) U.S. district courts (trial courts of general jurisdiction) and various courts of limited jurisdiction, (2) U.S. courts of appeals (intermediate courts of appeals), and (3) the United States Supreme Court. Unlike state court judges, who

• ***Exhibit* 2–3 Boundaries of the U.S. Courts of Appeals and U.S. District Courts**

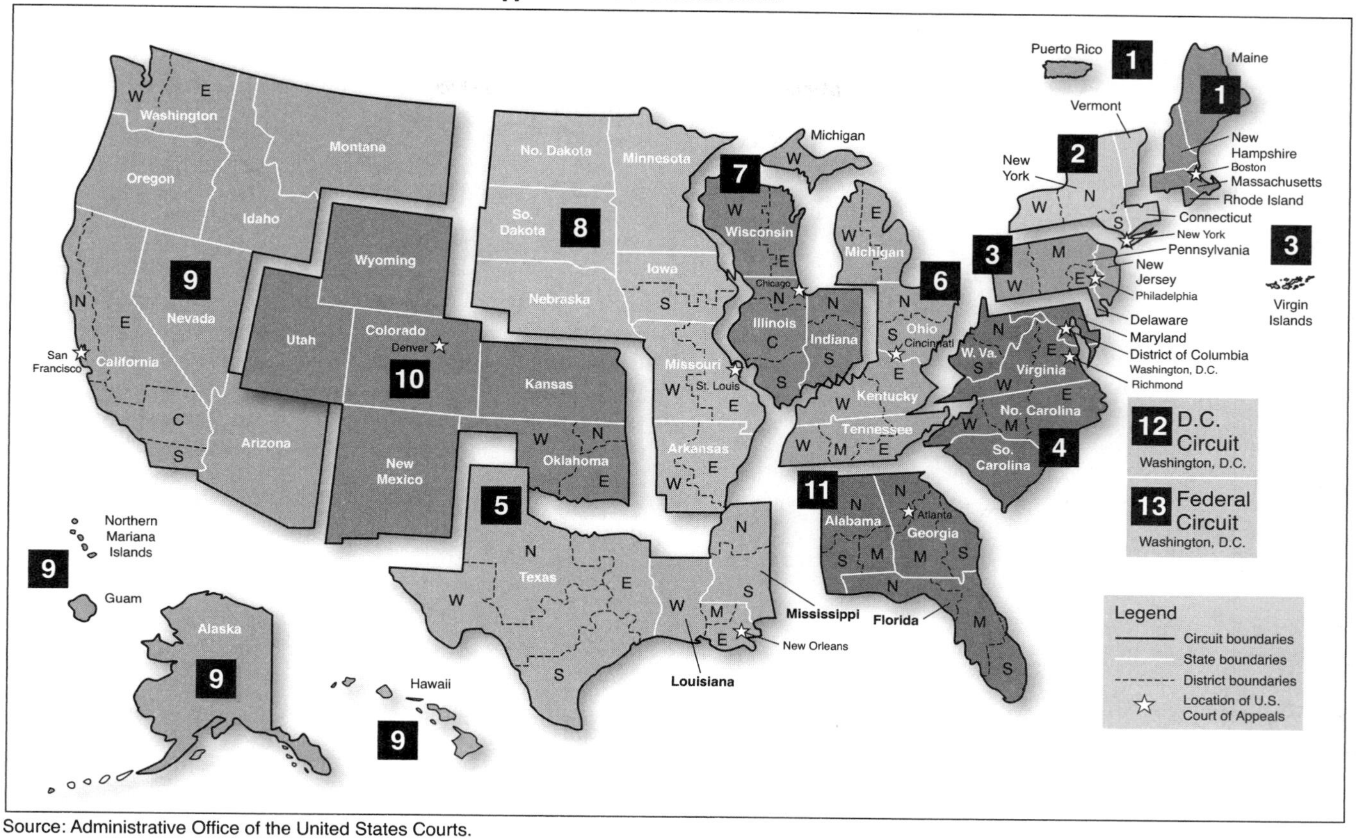

Source: Administrative Office of the United States Courts.

are usually elected, federal court judges—including the justices of the Supreme Court—are appointed by the president of the United States and confirmed by the U.S. Senate. All federal judges receive lifetime appointments because under Article III they "hold their offices during Good Behavior."

U.S. District Courts At the federal level, the equivalent of a state trial court of general jurisdiction is the district court. There is at least one federal district court in every state. The number of judicial districts can vary over time, primarily owing to population changes and corresponding caseloads. There are ninety-four federal judicial districts. U.S. district courts have original jurisdiction in federal matters. Federal cases typically originate in district courts. There are other courts with original, but special (or limited), jurisdiction, such as the federal bankruptcy courts and others shown in Exhibit 2–2 on the previous page.

U.S. Courts of Appeals In the federal court system, there are thirteen U.S. courts of appeals—also referred to as U.S. circuit courts of appeals. The federal courts of appeals for twelve of the circuits, including the U.S. Court of Appeals for the District of Columbia Circuit, hear appeals from the federal district courts located within their respective judicial circuits. The Court of Appeals for the Thirteenth Circuit, called the Federal Circuit, has national appellate jurisdiction over certain types of cases, such as cases involving patent law and cases in which the U.S. government is a defendant.

The decisions of the circuit courts of appeals are final in most cases, but appeal to the United States Supreme Court is possible. Exhibit 2–3 above shows the geographic boundaries of the U.S. circuit courts of appeals and the boundaries of the U.S. district courts within each circuit.

The United States Supreme Court The highest level of the three-tiered model of the federal court system is the United States Supreme Court. According to the language of Article III of the U.S. Constitution, there is only one national Supreme Court. All other courts in the federal system are considered "inferior." Congress is empowered to create other inferior courts as it deems necessary. The inferior courts that Congress has created include the second tier in our model—the U.S. courts of appeals—as well as the district courts and any other courts of limited, or specialized, jurisdiction.

The United States Supreme Court consists of nine justices. Although in rare instances the Supreme Court has original, or trial, jurisdiction (set forth in Article III, Section 2), most of its work is as an appeals court. The Court can review any case decided by any of the federal courts of appeals, and it also has appellate authority over some cases decided in the state courts.

Appeals to the Supreme Court. To bring a case before the Supreme Court, a party requests that the Court issue a writ of *certiorari.* A **writ of *certiorari***[11] is an order issued by the Supreme Court to a lower court requiring the latter to send it the record of the case for review. The Court will not issue a writ unless at least four of the nine justices approve of it. This is called the **rule of four.** Whether the Court will issue a writ of *certiorari* is entirely within its discretion. The Court is not required to issue one, and most petitions for writs are denied. (Thousands of cases are filed with the Court each year, but it hears, on average, fewer than one hundred of these cases.)[12] A denial is not a decision on the merits of a case, nor does it indicate agreement with the lower court's opinion. Furthermore, a denial of the writ has no value as a precedent.

Petitions Granted by the Court. Typically, the Court grants petitions when cases raise important constitutional questions or when the lower courts are issuing conflicting decisions on a significant issue. The justices, however, never explain their reasons for hearing certain cases and not others, so it is difficult to predict which type of case the Court might select.

Following a State Court Case

To illustrate the procedures that would be followed in a civil lawsuit brought in a state court, we present a hypothetical case and follow it through the state court system. The case involves an automobile accident in which Kevin Anderson, driving a Lexus, struck Lisa Marconi, driving a Ford Taurus. The accident occurred at the intersection of Wilshire Boulevard and Rodeo Drive in Beverly Hills, California. Marconi suffered personal injuries, incurring medical and hospital expenses as well as lost wages for four months. Anderson and Marconi are unable to agree on a settlement, and Marconi sues Anderson. Marconi is the plaintiff, and Anderson is the defendant. Both are represented by lawyers.

During each phase of the **litigation** (the process of working a lawsuit through the court system), Marconi and Anderson will have to observe strict procedural requirements. A large body of law—procedural law—establishes the rules and standards for determining disputes in courts. Procedural rules are very complex, and they vary from court to court and from state to state. There is a set of federal rules of procedure as well as various sets of rules for state courts. Additionally, the applicable procedures will depend on whether the case is a civil or criminal proceeding. Generally, the Marconi-Anderson civil lawsuit will involve the procedures discussed in the following subsections. Keep in mind that attempts to settle the case may be ongoing throughout the trial.

The Pleadings

The complaint and answer (and the counterclaim and reply)—all of which are discussed below—taken together are called the **pleadings.** The pleadings inform each party of the other's claims and specify the issues (disputed questions) involved in the case. The style and form of the pleadings may be quite different in different states.

The Plaintiff's Complaint Marconi's suit against Anderson commences when her lawyer files a **complaint** with the appropriate court. The complaint contains a statement alleging (1) the facts necessary for the court to take jurisdiction, (2) a brief summary of the facts necessary to show that the plaintiff is entitled to a remedy, and (3) a statement of the remedy the plaintiff is seeking. Complaints may be lengthy or brief, depending on the complexity of the case and the rules of the jurisdiction.

After the complaint has been filed, the sheriff, a deputy of the county, or another *process server* (one who delivers a complaint and summons) serves a **summons** and a copy of the complaint on defendant Anderson. The summons notifies Anderson that he must file an answer to the complaint with both the court and the plaintiff's attorney within a specified time period (usually twenty to thirty days). The summons also informs Anderson that failure to answer may result in a **default judgment** for the plaintiff, meaning the plaintiff could be awarded the damages alleged in her complaint. *Service of process* is essential in our legal system. No case can proceed to a trial unless the plaintiff can prove that he or she has properly served the defendant.

The Defendant's Answer The defendant's **answer** either admits the statements or allegations set forth in the complaint or denies them and outlines any defenses that the defendant may have. If Anderson admits to all of Marconi's allegations in his answer, the court will enter a judgment for Marconi. If Anderson denies any of Marconi's allegations, the litigation will go forward.

Anderson can deny Marconi's allegations and set forth his own claim that Marconi was in fact negligent and therefore owes him compensation for the damage to his Lexus. This is appropriately called a **counterclaim.** If Anderson files a counterclaim, Marconi will have to answer it with a pleading, normally called a **reply,** which has the same characteristics as an answer.

11. Pronounced sur-shee-uh-*rah*-ree.

12. In the Court's 1982–1983 term, for example, the Court issued opinions in 151 cases. In contrast, in its 2010–2011 term, the Court issued opinions in only 84 cases.

Anderson can also admit the truth of Marconi's complaint but raise new facts that may result in dismissal of the action. This is called raising an *affirmative defense*. For example, Anderson could assert the expiration of the time period under the relevant *statute of limitations* (a state or federal statute that sets the maximum time period during which a certain action can be brought or rights enforced) as an affirmative defense.

MOTION TO DISMISS A **motion to dismiss** requests the court to dismiss the case for stated reasons. Grounds for dismissal of a case include improper delivery of the complaint and summons, improper venue, and the plaintiff's failure to state a claim for which a court could grant relief (a remedy). For instance, if Marconi had suffered no injuries or losses as a result of Anderson's negligence, Anderson could move to have the case dismissed because Marconi would not have stated a claim for which relief could be granted.

If the judge grants the motion to dismiss, the plaintiff generally is given time to file an amended complaint. If the judge denies the motion, the suit will go forward, and the defendant must then file an answer. Note that if Marconi wishes to discontinue the suit because, for example, an out-of-court settlement has been reached, she can likewise move for dismissal. The court can also dismiss the case on its own motion.

Pretrial Motions

Either party may attempt to get the case dismissed before trial through the use of various pretrial motions. We have already mentioned the motion to dismiss. Two other important pretrial motions are the motion for judgment on the pleadings and the motion for summary judgment.

At the close of the pleadings, either party may make a **motion for judgment on the pleadings,** or on the merits of the case. The judge will grant the motion only when there is no dispute over the facts of the case and the sole issue to be resolved is a question of law. In deciding on the motion, the judge may consider only the evidence contained in the pleadings.

In contrast, in a **motion for summary judgment,** the court may consider evidence outside the pleadings, such as sworn statements (affidavits) by parties or witnesses, or other documents relating to the case. Either party can make a motion for summary judgment. As with the motion for judgment on the pleadings, a motion for summary judgment will be granted only if there are no genuine questions of fact and the sole question is a question of law.

Discovery

Before a trial begins, each party can use a number of procedural devices to obtain information and gather evidence about the case from the other party or from third parties. The process of obtaining such information is known as **discovery.** Discovery includes gaining access to witnesses, documents, records, and other types of evidence.

The Federal Rules of Civil Procedure and similar rules in the states set forth the guidelines for discovery activity. Generally, discovery is allowed regarding any matter that is not privileged and is relevant to the claim or defense of any party. Discovery rules also attempt to protect witnesses and parties from undue harassment and to safeguard privileged or confidential material from being disclosed. If a discovery request involves privileged or confidential business information, a court can deny the request and can limit the scope of discovery in a number of ways. For instance, a court can require the party to submit the materials to the judge in a sealed envelope so that the judge can decide if they should be disclosed to the opposing party.

Discovery prevents surprises at trial by giving parties access to evidence that might otherwise be hidden. This allows both parties to learn as much as they can about what to expect at a trial before they reach the courtroom. It also serves to narrow the issues so that trial time is spent on the main questions in the case.

DEPOSITIONS AND INTERROGATORIES Discovery can involve the use of depositions or interrogatories, or both. A **deposition** is sworn testimony by a party to the lawsuit or any witness. The person being deposed (the deponent) answers questions asked by the attorneys, and the questions and answers are recorded by an authorized court official and sworn to and signed by the deponent. (Occasionally, written depositions are taken when witnesses are unable to appear in person.) The answers given to depositions will, of course, help the attorneys prepare their cases. They can also be used in court to impeach (challenge the credibility of) a party or a witness who changes her or his testimony at the trial. In addition, the answers given in a deposition can be used as testimony if the witness is not available at trial.

Interrogatories are written questions for which written answers are prepared and then signed under oath. The main difference between interrogatories and written depositions is that interrogatories are directed to a party to the lawsuit (the plaintiff or the defendant), not to a witness, and the party can prepare answers with the aid of an attorney. The scope of interrogatories is broader because parties are obligated to answer the questions, even if that means disclosing information from their records and files.

REQUESTS FOR OTHER INFORMATION A party can serve a written request on the other party for an admission of the truth on matters relating to the trial. Any matter admitted under such a request is conclusively established for the trial. For example, Marconi can ask Anderson to admit that he was driving at a speed of forty-five miles an hour. A request for admission saves time at trial because the parties will not have to spend time proving facts on which they already agree.

A party can also gain access to documents and other items not in her or his possession in order to inspect and examine them. Likewise, a party can gain "entry upon land" to inspect the premises. Anderson's attorney, for example, normally can gain permission to inspect and photocopy Marconi's car repair bills.

When the physical or mental condition of one party is in question, the opposing party can ask the court to order a physical or mental examination. If the court issues the order, which it will do only if the need for the information outweighs the right to privacy of the person to be examined, the opposing party can obtain the results of the examination.

ELECTRONIC DISCOVERY Any relevant material, including information stored electronically, can be the object of a discovery request. The federal rules and most state rules now specifically allow all parties to obtain electronic "data compilations." Electronic evidence, or **e-evidence,** includes all types of computer-generated or electronically recorded information, such as e-mail, voice mail, spreadsheets, document preparation systems, and other data. E-evidence can reveal significant facts that are not discoverable by other means. For example, computers automatically record certain information about files—such as who created the file and when, and who accessed, modified, or transmitted it—on their hard drives. This information can be obtained only from the file in its electronic format—not from printed-out versions.

The Federal Rules of Civil Procedure deal with the preservation, retrieval, and production of electronic data. Although traditional means, such as interrogatories and depositions, are still used to find out about the e-evidence, a party must usually hire an expert to retrieve evidence in its electronic format. The expert uses software to reconstruct e-mail exchanges and establish who knew what and when they knew it. The expert can even recover files that the user thought had been deleted from a computer.

Electronic discovery, or e-discovery, has significant advantages over paper discovery. Back-up copies of documents and e-mail can provide useful—and often quite damaging—information about how a particular matter progressed over several weeks or months. E-discovery can uncover the proverbial smoking gun that leads to litigation success, but it is also time consuming and expensive, especially when lawsuits involve large firms with multiple offices. Also, many firms are finding it difficult to fulfill their duty to preserve e-evidence from a vast number of sources. For a discussion of some of the problems associated with preserving e-evidence for discovery, see this chapter's *Adapting the Law to the Online Environment* feature on the facing page.

Pretrial Conference

Either party or the court can request a pretrial conference, or hearing. Usually, the hearing consists of an informal discussion between the judge and the opposing attorneys after discovery has taken place. The purpose of the hearing is to explore the possibility of a settlement without trial and, if this is not possible, to identify the matters that are in dispute and to plan the course of the trial.

Jury Selection

A trial can be held with or without a jury. The Seventh Amendment to the U.S. Constitution guarantees the right to a jury trial for cases in *federal* courts when the amount in controversy exceeds $20, but this guarantee does not apply to state courts. Most states have similar guarantees in their own constitutions (although the threshold dollar amount is higher than $20). The right to a trial by jury does not have to be exercised, and many cases are tried without a jury. In most states and in federal courts, one of the parties must request a jury in a civil case, or the judge presumes the parties waive the right.

Before a jury trial commences, a jury must be selected. The jury selection process is known as ***voir dire.***[13] During *voir dire* in most jurisdictions, attorneys for the plaintiff and the defendant ask prospective jurors oral questions to determine whether a potential jury member is biased or has any connection with a party to the action or with a prospective witness. In some jurisdictions, the judge may do all or part of the questioning based on written questions submitted by counsel for the parties.

During *voir dire,* a party may challenge a prospective juror *peremptorily*—that is, ask that an individual not be sworn in as a juror without providing any reason. Alternatively, a party may challenge a prospective juror *for cause*—that is, provide a reason why an individual should not be sworn in as a juror. If the judge grants the challenge, the individual is asked to step down. A prospective juror may not be excluded from the jury by the use of discriminatory challenges, however, such as those based on racial criteria or gender.

The Trial

At the beginning of the trial, the attorneys present their opening arguments, setting forth the facts that they expect to prove during the trial. Then the plaintiff's case is presented. In our hypothetical case, Marconi's lawyer would introduce evidence (relevant documents, exhibits, and the testimony of witnesses) to support Marconi's position. The defendant has the opportunity to challenge any evidence introduced and to cross-examine any of the plaintiff's witnesses.

---

13. Pronounced vwahr *deehr.*

Adapting the Law to the Online Environment

The Duty to Preserve E-Evidence for Discovery

Today, less than 0.5 percent of new information is created on paper. Instead of sending letters and memos, people send e-mails and text messages, creating a massive amount of electronically stored information (ESI). The law requires parties to preserve ESI whenever there is a "reasonable anticipation of litigation."

Why Companies Fail to Preserve E-Evidence

Preserving e-evidence can be a challenge, though, particularly for large corporations that have electronic data scattered across multiple networks, servers, desktops, laptops, handheld devices, and even home computers. While many companies have policies regarding back-up of office e-mail and computer systems, these may cover only a fraction of the e-evidence requested in a lawsuit.

Technological advances further complicate the situation. Users of BlackBerrys, for example, can configure them so that messages are transmitted with limited or no archiving rather than going through a company's servers and being recorded. How can a company preserve e-evidence that is never on its servers? In one case, the court held that a company had a duty to preserve transitory "server log data," which exist only temporarily on a computer's memory.[a]

Potential Sanctions and Malpractice Claims

A court may impose sanctions (such as fines) on a party that fails to preserve electronic evidence or to comply with e-discovery requests. A firm may be sanctioned if it provides e-mails without the attachments, does not produce all of the e-evidence requested, or fails to suspend its automatic e-mail deletion procedures.[b] Nearly 25 percent of the reported opinions on e-discovery from 2008 involved sanctions for failure to preserve e-evidence.[c] Attorneys who fail to properly advise their clients concerning the duty to preserve e-evidence also often face sanctions and malpractice claims.[d]

Lessons from Intel

A party that fails to preserve e-evidence may even find itself at such a disadvantage that it will settle a dispute rather than continue litigation. For example, Advanced Micro Devices, Inc. (AMD), sued Intel Corporation, one of the world's largest microprocessor suppliers, for violating antitrust laws. Immediately after the lawsuit was filed, Intel began collecting and preserving the ESI on its servers. Although the company instructed its employees to retain documents and e-mails related to competition with AMD, many employees saved only copies of the e-mails that they had received and not e-mails that they had sent. In addition, Intel did not stop its automatic e-mail deletion system, causing other information to be lost. In the end, although Intel produced data that were equivalent to "somewhere in the neighborhood of a pile 137 miles high" in paper, its failure to preserve e-evidence led it to settle the dispute in 2008.[e]

FOR CRITICAL ANALYSIS

How might a large company protect itself from allegations that it intentionally failed to preserve electronic data?

a. See *Columbia Pictures v. Brunnell,* 2007 WL 2080419 (C.D.Cal. 2007).

b. See, for example, *John B. v. Goetz,* 531 F.3d 448 (6th Cir. 2008); and *Wingnut Films, Ltd. v. Katija Motion Pictures,* 2007 WL 2758571 (C.D.Cal. 2007).

c. Sheri Qualters. "25% of Reported E-Discovery Opinions in 2008 Involved Sanction Issues." *National Law Journal.* 12 Dec. 2008.

d. See, for example, *Qualcomm, Inc. v. Broadcom Corp.,* 539 F.Supp.2d 1214 (S.D.Cal. 2007).

e. See *In re Intel Corp. Microprocessor Antitrust Litigation,* 2008 WL 2310288 (D.Del. 2008). See also *Adams v. Gateway, Inc.,* 2006 WL 2563418 (D. Utah 2006).

At the end of the plaintiff's case, the defendant's attorney has the opportunity to ask the judge to direct a verdict for the defendant on the ground that the plaintiff has presented no evidence that would justify the granting of the plaintiff's remedy. This is called a **motion for a directed verdict** (known in federal courts as a *motion for judgment as a matter of law*). If the motion is not granted (it seldom is granted), the defendant's attorney then presents the evidence and witnesses for the defendant's case. At the conclusion of the defendant's case, the defendant's attorney has another opportunity to make a motion for a directed verdict. The plaintiff's attorney can challenge any evidence introduced and cross-examine the defendant's witnesses.

EXPERT WITNESSES Both plaintiffs and defendants may present testimony from expert witnesses—such as forensic scientists and physicians—as part of their cases. An expert witness is a person who, by virtue of education, training, skill, or experience, has scientific, technical, or other specialized knowledge in a particular area beyond that of an average person. In Marconi's case, her attorney might hire an accident reconstruction specialist to establish Anderson's negligence or a physician to confirm the extent of Marconi's injuries.

Normally, witnesses can testify only about the facts of a case—that is, what they personally observed. When witnesses are qualified as experts in a particular field, however, they can offer their opinions and conclusions about the evidence in that field. Because numerous experts are available for hire and their testimony is powerful and effective with juries, there is tremendous potential for abuse. Therefore, judges act as gatekeepers to ensure that the experts are qualified and that their opinions are based on scientific knowledge. If a party believes that the opponent's witness is not qualified as an expert, that party can make a motion asking the judge to exclude this evidence and prevent the expert witness from testifying.

In the following case, a federal district court had refused to allow an expert witness to testify at trial because the plaintiff had failed to file a discovery report outlining the expert witness's testimony and credentials. The appellate court had to decide whether to reverse the trial court's decision regarding the witness's testimony.

Case 2.3 Downey v. Bob's Discount Furniture Holdings, Inc.

United States Court of Appeals, First Circuit, 633 F.3d 1 (2011).

FACTS Yvette Downey bought a children's bedroom set from Bob's Discount Furniture Holdings, Inc., in 2004. Soon, Downey and her daughter, Ashley Celester, began to experience skin irritation. In July 2005, they discovered insects in their home, and some of the bugs were on Ashley's body. Downey immediately called Allegiance Pest Control and spoke to Edward Gordinier, a licensed and experienced exterminator. Gordinier inspected Downey's home that day. He found bedbugs throughout the house and identified Ashley's bedroom set as the main source of the infestation. Downey informed Bob's about the problem. Although Bob's retrieved the bedroom set and refunded the purchase price, it refused to pay for the costs of extermination or any other damages. Downey and her daughter filed a lawsuit in a federal district court seeking compensation for health problems, emotional distress, and economic loss. Before the trial, the plaintiffs named Gordinier as a witness but did not submit a written report describing his anticipated testimony or specifying his qualifications. Rule 26 of the Federal Rules of Civil Procedure requires that a written report be filed for an expert witness who is retained or specially employed to provide expert testimony. The plaintiffs asserted that Gordinier had not been specially employed as an expert and, therefore, no such disclosures were required. The defendants argued that Gordinier could not testify as to his expert opinion because the plaintiffs had not filed a written report. The district court agreed with the defendants and allowed Gordinier to testify only about the facts, such as his inspection of the premises, not about his opinion of the source of the bedbug infestation. The court granted a judgment for the defendants based, in part, on their claim that the plaintiffs had not proved that the furniture was infested with bedbugs when it was delivered. The plaintiffs appealed.

ISSUE Should the plaintiff's witness, Gordinier, have been allowed to give his professional opinion regarding the source of the bedbug infestation at trial, despite the plaintiff's failure to submit a written expert-witness report?

DECISION Yes. The United States Court of Appeals for the First Circuit decided that the trial court had abused its discretion by not allowing Gordinier's professional opinion as testimony. The court therefore reversed the district court's judgment and remanded the case for a new trial.

REASON The court reasoned that Rule 26 of the Federal Rules of Civil Procedure requires filing of a written report only for an expert witness who is "retained or specially employed to provide expert testimony in the case." The circumstances of this case indicated that Gordinier was not the type of expert witness that needed to file such a report. "For one thing, there is no evidence that Gordinier was a person who held himself out for hire as a purveyor [supplier] of expert testimony. For another thing, there is no evidence that he was charging a fee for his testimony."

FOR CRITICAL ANALYSIS—Legal Consideration *Why can only an expert testify about the source of a bedbug infestation?*

Closing Arguments After the defense concludes its presentation, the attorneys present their closing arguments, each urging a verdict in favor of her or his client. The judge instructs the jury in the law that applies to the case (these instructions are often called *charges*), and the jury retires to the jury room to deliberate on a verdict. In the Marconi-Anderson case, the jury will not only decide for the plaintiff or for the defendant but, if it finds for the plaintiff, will also decide on the amount of the **award**—that is, the compensation to be paid to her.

Posttrial Motions

After the jury has rendered its verdict, either party may make a posttrial motion. If Marconi wins and Anderson's attorney has previously moved for a directed verdict, Anderson's attorney may make a **motion for judgment *n.o.v.*** (from the Latin *non obstante veredicto,* which means "notwithstanding the verdict"—called *a motion for judgment as a matter of law* in the federal courts). Such a motion will be granted only if the jury's verdict was unreasonable and erroneous. If the judge grants the motion, the jury's verdict will be set aside, and a judgment will be entered in favor of the opposite party (Anderson).

Alternatively, Anderson could make a **motion for a new trial,** asking the judge to set aside the adverse verdict and to hold a new trial. The motion will be granted if, after looking at all the evidence, the judge is convinced that the jury was in error but does not feel that it is appropriate to grant judgment for the other side. A judge can also grant a new trial on the basis of newly discovered evidence, misconduct by the participants or the jury during the trial (such as when an attorney or jury member has made prejudicial and inflammatory remarks), or error by the judge.

The Appeal

Assume here that any posttrial motion is denied and that Anderson appeals the case. (If Marconi wins but receives a smaller monetary award than she sought, she can appeal also.) Keep in mind, though, that a party cannot appeal a trial court's decision simply because he or she is dissatisfied with the outcome of the trial. A party must have legitimate grounds to file an appeal—that is, he or she must be able to claim that the lower court committed an error. If Anderson has grounds to appeal the case, a notice of appeal must be filed with the clerk of the trial court within a prescribed time. Anderson now becomes the appellant, or petitioner, and Marconi becomes the appellee, or respondent.

FILING THE APPEAL Anderson's attorney files the record on appeal with the appellate court. The record includes the pleadings, the trial transcript, the judge's rulings on motions made by the parties, and other trial-related documents. Anderson's attorney will also provide the reviewing court with a condensation of the record, known as an *abstract,* and a brief. The **brief** is a formal legal document outlining the facts and issues of the case, the judge's rulings or jury's findings that should be reversed or modified, the applicable law, and arguments on Anderson's behalf (citing applicable statutes and relevant cases as precedents).

Marconi's attorney will file an answering brief. Anderson's attorney can file a reply to Marconi's brief, although it is not required. The reviewing court then considers the case.

APPELLATE REVIEW As mentioned earlier, a court of appeals does not hear evidence. Rather, it reviews the record for errors of law. Its decision concerning a case is based on the record on appeal, the abstracts, and the attorneys' briefs. The attorneys can present oral arguments, after which the case is taken under advisement. In general, appellate courts do not reverse findings of fact unless the findings are unsupported or contradicted by the evidence.

An appellate court has the following options after reviewing a case:

1. The court can *affirm* the trial court's decision.
2. The court can *reverse* the trial court's judgment if it concludes that the trial court erred or that the jury did not receive proper instructions.
3. The appellate court can *remand* (send back) the case to the trial court for further proceedings consistent with its opinion on the matter.
4. The court might also affirm or reverse a decision *in part.* For example, the court might affirm the jury's finding that Anderson was negligent but remand the case for further proceedings on another issue (such as the extent of Marconi's damages).
5. An appellate court can also *modify* a lower court's decision. If the appellate court decides that the jury awarded an excessive amount in damages, for example, the court might reduce the award to a more appropriate, or fairer, amount.

APPEAL TO A HIGHER APPELLATE COURT If the reviewing court is an intermediate appellate court, the losing party may decide to appeal to the state supreme court (the highest state court). Such a petition corresponds to a petition for a writ of *certiorari* from the United States Supreme Court. Although the losing party has a right to ask (petition) a higher court to review the case, the party does not have a right to have the case heard by the higher appellate court.

Appellate courts normally have discretionary power and can accept or reject an appeal. Like the United States Supreme Court, in general state supreme courts deny most appeals. If the appeal is granted, new briefs must be filed before the state supreme court, and the attorneys may be allowed or requested to present oral arguments. Like the intermediate appellate court, the supreme court may reverse or affirm the appellate court's decision or remand the case. At this point, the case typically has reached its end (unless a federal question is at issue and one of the parties has legitimate grounds to seek review by a federal appellate court).

Enforcing the Judgment

The uncertainties of the litigation process are compounded by the lack of guarantees that any judgment will be enforceable. Even if a plaintiff wins an award of damages in court, the defendant may not have sufficient assets or insurance to cover that amount. Usually, one of the factors considered before a lawsuit is initiated is whether the defendant has sufficient assets to cover the amount of damages sought, should the plaintiff win the case.

The Courts Adapt to the Online World

We have already mentioned that the courts have attempted to adapt traditional jurisdictional concepts to the online world. Not surprisingly, the Internet has also brought about changes in court procedures and practices, including new methods for filing pleadings and other documents and issuing decisions and opinions. Some jurisdictions are exploring the possibility of cyber courts, in which legal proceedings could be conducted totally online.

Electronic Filing

The federal court system has now implemented its electronic filing system, Case Management/Electronic Case Files (CM/ECF), in nearly all of the federal courts. The system is available in federal district, appellate, and bankruptcy courts, as well as the Court of International Trade and the Court of Federal Claims. More than 33 million cases are on the CM/ECF system. Users can create a document using conventional software, save it as a PDF file, and then log on to a court's Web site and submit the PDF to the court via the Internet. Access to the electronic documents filed on CM/ECF is available through a system called PACER (Public Access to Court Electronic Records), which is a service of the U.S. Judiciary.

More than 60 percent of the states have some form of electronic filing. Some states, including Arizona, California, Colorado, Delaware, Mississippi, New Jersey, New York, and Nevada, offer statewide e-filing systems. Generally, when electronic filing is made available, it is optional. Nonetheless, some state courts have now made e-filing mandatory in certain types of disputes, such as complex civil litigation.

Courts Online

Most courts today have Web sites, but the information provided varies. Some courts display only the names of court personnel and office phone numbers. Others add court rules and forms. Many appellate court sites include judicial decisions, although the decisions may remain online for only a limited time. In addition, in some states court clerks offer information about the court's **docket** (the court's schedule of cases to be heard) and other searchable databases online.

Appellate court decisions are often posted online immediately after they are rendered. Recent decisions of the U.S. courts of appeals, for example, are available online at their Web sites. The United States Supreme Court also has an official Web site and publishes its opinions there immediately after they are announced to the public.

Cyber Courts and Proceedings

Someday, litigants may be able to use cyber courts, in which judicial proceedings take place only on the Internet. The parties to a case could meet online to make their arguments and present their evidence. This might be done with e-mail submissions, through video cameras, in designated chat rooms, at closed sites, or through the use of other Internet facilities. These courtrooms could be efficient and economical. We might also see the use of virtual lawyers, judges, and juries—and possibly the replacement of court personnel with computer software.

Michigan has passed legislation creating cyber courts that will hear cases involving technology issues and high-tech businesses. Wisconsin recently enacted a rule authorizing the use of videoconferencing in both civil and criminal trials, at the discretion of the trial court.[14] In some situations, a Wisconsin judge can allow videoconferencing even over the objection of the parties, provided certain operational criteria are met.

The courts may also use the Internet in other ways. In a groundbreaking decision, for instance, a Florida county court granted "virtual" visitation rights in a couple's divorce proceeding. Each parent was ordered to set up a computerized videoconferencing system so that the child could visit with the parent who did not have custody via the Internet at any time.

Alternative Dispute Resolution

Litigation is expensive and time consuming. Because of the backlog of cases pending in many courts, several years may pass before a case is actually tried. For these and other reasons, more and more businesspersons are turning to **alternative dispute resolution (ADR)** as a means of settling their disputes.

The great advantage of ADR is its flexibility. Methods of ADR range from the parties sitting down together and attempting to work out their differences to multinational corporations agreeing to resolve a dispute through a formal hearing before a panel of experts. Normally, the parties themselves can control how they will attempt to settle their dispute, what procedures will be used, whether a neutral third party will be present or make a decision, and whether that decision will be legally binding or nonbinding.

Today, more than 90 percent of cases are settled before trial through some form of ADR. Indeed, most states either require or encourage parties to undertake ADR before trial. Many federal courts have instituted ADR programs as well. In the following pages, we examine the basic forms of ADR. Keep in mind, though, that new methods of ADR—and new combinations of existing methods—are constantly being devised and employed.

Negotiation

The simplest form of ADR is **negotiation,** a process in which the parties attempt to settle their dispute informally, with or without attorneys to represent them. Attorneys frequently advise their clients to negotiate a settlement voluntarily before they proceed to trial. Parties may even try to negotiate a settlement during a trial or after the trial but before an appeal. Negotiation traditionally involves just the parties themselves and (typically)

14. Wisconsin Statute Section 751.12.

their attorneys. The attorneys, though, are advocates—they are obligated to put their clients' interests first.

Mediation

In **mediation,** a neutral third party acts as a mediator and works with both sides in the dispute to facilitate a resolution. The mediator talks with the parties separately as well as jointly and emphasizes their points of agreement in an attempt to help the parties evaluate their options. Although the mediator may propose a solution (called a *mediator's proposal*), he or she does not make a decision resolving the matter. States that require parties to undergo ADR before trial often offer mediation as one of the ADR options or (as in Florida) the only option.

One of the main advantages of mediation is that it is not as adversarial as litigation. In trials, the parties "do battle" with each other in the courtroom, trying to prove one another wrong, while the judge is usually a passive observer. In mediation, the mediator takes an active role and attempts to bring the parties together so that they can come to a mutually satisfactory resolution. The mediation process tends to reduce the hostility between the disputants, allowing them to resume their former relationship without bad feelings. For this reason, mediation is often the preferred form of ADR for disputes involving business partners, employers and employees, or other parties involved in long-term relationships.

EXAMPLE 2.7 Two business partners, Mark Shalen and Charles Rowe, have a dispute over how the profits of their firm should be distributed. If the dispute is litigated, the parties will be adversaries, and their respective attorneys will emphasize how the parties' positions differ, not what they have in common. In contrast, when the dispute is mediated, the mediator emphasizes the common ground shared by Shalen and Rowe and helps them work toward agreement. The two men can work out the distribution of profits without damaging their continuing relationship as partners. •

Arbitration

A more formal method of ADR is **arbitration,** in which an arbitrator (a neutral third party or a panel of experts) hears a dispute and imposes a resolution on the parties. Arbitration is unlike other forms of ADR because the third party hearing the dispute makes a decision for the parties. Exhibit 2–4 below outlines the basic differences among the three traditional forms of ADR. Usually, the parties in arbitration agree that the third party's decision will be legally binding, although the parties can also agree to *nonbinding* arbitration. (Arbitration that is mandated by the courts often is nonbinding.) In nonbinding arbitration, the parties can go forward with a lawsuit if they do not agree with the arbitrator's decision.

In some respects, formal arbitration resembles a trial, although usually the procedural rules are much less restrictive than those governing litigation. In the typical arbitration, the parties present opening arguments and ask for specific remedies. Evidence is then presented, and witnesses may be called and examined by both sides. The arbitrator then renders a decision, which is called an award.

An arbitrator's award usually is the final word on the matter. Although the parties may appeal an arbitrator's decision, a court's review of the decision will be much more restricted in scope than an appellate court's review of a trial court's decision. The general view is that because the parties were free to frame the issues and set the powers of the arbitrator at the outset, they cannot complain about the results. The award will be set aside only if the arbitrator's conduct or "bad faith" substantially prejudiced the rights of one of the parties, if the award violates an established public policy, or if the arbitrator exceeded her or his powers (arbitrated issues that the parties did not agree to submit to arbitration).

ARBITRATION CLAUSES AND STATUTES Just about any commercial matter can be submitted to arbitration. Frequently, parties include an **arbitration clause** in a contract (a written

• ***Exhibit* 2–4 Basic Differences in the Traditional Forms of Alternative Dispute Resolution**

TYPE OF ADR	DESCRIPTION	NEUTRAL THIRD PARTY PRESENT	WHO DECIDES THE RESOLUTION
Negotiation	The parties meet informally with or without their attorneys and attempt to agree on a resolution.	No	The parties themselves reach a resolution.
Mediation	A neutral third party meets with the parties and emphasizes points of agreement to help them resolve their dispute.	Yes	The parties decide the resolution, but the mediator may suggest or propose a resolution.
Arbitration	The parties present their arguments and evidence before an arbitrator at a hearing, and the arbitrator renders a decision resolving the parties' dispute.	Yes	The arbitrator imposes a resolution on the parties that may be either binding or nonbinding.

agreement—see Chapter 7); the clause provides that any dispute that arises under the contract will be resolved through arbitration rather than through the court system. Parties can also agree to arbitrate a dispute after the dispute arises.

Most states have statutes under which arbitration clauses will be enforced. Some state statutes compel arbitration of certain types of disputes, such as those involving public employees. At the federal level, the Federal Arbitration Act (FAA), enacted in 1925, enforces arbitration clauses in contracts involving maritime activity and interstate commerce (though its applicability to employment contracts has been controversial, as discussed in a later subsection). Because of the breadth of the commerce clause (see Chapter 1), arbitration agreements involving transactions only slightly connected to the flow of interstate commerce may fall under the FAA.

CASE EXAMPLE 2.8 Vincent Concepcion and others sued AT&T Mobility, LLC, in a federal court in California. The customers claimed that AT&T had committed fraud when it offered a free cell phone to anyone who signed up for its service, but then charged each customer sales tax on the retail value of the free phone. Each contract included an arbitration clause and required plaintiffs to bring claims as individuals, not as part of a *class action* (a lawsuit in which an individual files a claim on behalf of many others). Nevertheless, the plaintiffs joined together, and AT&T filed a motion to compel arbitration. The district court denied the motion, finding that the arbitration clause was unfair under California case law, which held that class-action waivers in arbitration clauses were unfair in consumer contracts. On appeal, a federal appellate court also refused to compel arbitration. AT&T appealed to the United States Supreme Court. In 2011, the Court reversed and remanded the case for trial, holding that the Federal Arbitration Act preempted California's judicial rule against class arbitration waivers in consumer contracts.[15] The decision was a major victory for companies because the Court essentially held that arbitration clauses must be enforced, even if they may be considered unfair under state law. ●

THE ISSUE OF ARBITRABILITY Notice that in Case Example 2.8, the issue before the United States Supreme Court was *not* the basic controversy (whether charging tax on a free phone constituted fraud) but rather the issue of arbitrability—that is, whether the matter was one that had to be resolved by arbitration under the arbitration clause. Such actions, in which one party files a motion to compel arbitration, often occur when a dispute arises over an agreement that contains an arbitration clause. If the court finds that the subject matter in controversy is covered by the agreement to arbitrate—even when the claim involves the violation of a statute, such as an employment statute—then a party may be compelled to arbitrate the dispute. Usually, a court will allow the claim to be arbitrated if the court, in interpreting the statute, can find no legislative intent to the contrary.

No party, however, will be ordered to submit a particular dispute to arbitration unless the court is convinced that the party consented to do so. Additionally, the courts will not compel arbitration if it is clear that the prescribed arbitration rules and procedures are inherently unfair to one of the parties.

The terms of an arbitration agreement can limit the types of disputes that the parties agree to arbitrate. When the parties do not specify limits, however, disputes can arise as to whether a particular matter is covered by the arbitration agreement. Then it is up to the court to resolve the issue of arbitrability.

MANDATORY ARBITRATION IN THE EMPLOYMENT CONTEXT A significant question in the last several years has concerned mandatory arbitration clauses in employment contracts. Many claim that employees' rights are not sufficiently protected when workers are forced, as a condition of being hired, to agree to arbitrate all disputes and thus waive their rights under statutes specifically designed to protect employees. The United States Supreme Court, however, has generally held that mandatory arbitration clauses in employment contracts are enforceable.

CASE EXAMPLE 2.9 In a landmark decision, the Supreme Court held that a claim brought under a federal statute prohibiting age discrimination (see Chapter 22) could be subject to arbitration. The Court concluded that the employee had waived his right to sue when he agreed, as part of a required registration application to be a securities representative with the New York Stock Exchange, to arbitrate "any dispute, claim, or controversy" relating to his employment.[16] ●

Other Types of ADR

The three forms of ADR just discussed are the oldest and traditionally the most commonly used. In recent years, a variety of new types of ADR have emerged. Some parties today are using *assisted negotiation,* in which a third party participates in the negotiation process. The third party may be an expert in the subject matter of the dispute. In *early neutral case evaluation,* the parties explain the situation to the expert, and the expert assesses the strengths and weaknesses of each party's claims. Another form of assisted negotiation is the *mini-trial,* in which the parties present arguments before the third party (usually an expert), who renders an advisory opinion on how a court would likely decide the issue. This proceeding is designed to assist the parties in determining whether they should settle or take the dispute to court.

Other types of ADR combine characteristics of mediation with those of arbitration. In *binding mediation,* for example,

15. *AT&T Mobility, LLC v. Concepcion,* ___ U.S. ___, 131 S.Ct. 1740, 179 L.Ed.2d 472 (2011).

16. *Gilmer v. Interstate/Johnson Lane Corp.,* 500 U.S. 20, 111 S.Ct. 1647, 114 L.Ed.2d 26 (1991).

the parties agree that if they cannot resolve the dispute, the mediator may make a legally binding decision on the issue. In *mediation-arbitration,* or "med-arb," the parties agree to attempt to settle their dispute through mediation. If no settlement is reached, the dispute will be arbitrated.

Today's courts are also experimenting with a variety of ADR alternatives to speed up (and reduce the cost of) justice. Numerous federal courts now hold **summary jury trials,** in which the parties present their arguments and evidence and the jury renders a verdict. The jury's verdict is not binding, but it does act as a guide to both sides in reaching an agreement during the mandatory negotiations that immediately follow the trial. Other alternatives being employed by the courts include summary procedures for commercial litigation and the appointment of special masters to assist judges in deciding complex issues.

Providers of ADR Services

ADR services are provided by both government agencies and private organizations. A major provider of ADR services is the American Arbitration Association (AAA). Most of the largest U.S. law firms are members of this nonprofit association. Cases brought before the AAA are heard by an expert or a panel of experts in the area relating to the dispute and usually are settled quickly. The AAA has a special team devoted to resolving large, complex disputes across a wide range of industries.

Hundreds of for-profit firms around the country also provide various forms of dispute-resolution services. Typically, these firms hire retired judges to conduct arbitration hearings or otherwise assist parties in settling their disputes. The judges follow procedures similar to those of the federal courts and use similar rules. Generally, each party to the dispute pays a filing fee and a designated fee for a hearing session or conference.

Online Dispute Resolution

An increasing number of companies and organizations offer dispute-resolution services using the Internet. The settlement of disputes in these online forums is known as **online dispute resolution (ODR).** The disputes have most commonly involved disagreements over the rights to domain names or over the quality of goods sold via the Internet, including goods sold through Internet auction sites.

ODR may be best suited for resolving small- to medium-sized business liability claims, which may not be worth the expense of litigation or traditional ADR. Rules being developed in online forums, however, may ultimately become a code of conduct for everyone who does business in cyberspace. Most online forums do not automatically apply the law of any specific jurisdiction. Instead, results are often based on general, universal legal principles. As with most offline methods of dispute resolution, any party may appeal to a court at any time if the ADR is nonbinding arbitration.

Reviewing . . . Traditional and Online Dispute Resolution

Stan Garner resides in Illinois and promotes boxing matches for SuperSports, Inc., an Illinois corporation. Garner created the promotional concept of the "Ages" fights—a series of three boxing matches pitting an older fighter (George Foreman) against a younger fighter. The concept included titles for each of the three fights ("Challenge of the Ages," "Battle of the Ages," and "Fight of the Ages"), as well as promotional epithets to characterize the two fighters ("the Foreman Factor"). Garner contacted Foreman and his manager, who both reside in Texas, to sell the idea, and they arranged a meeting at Caesar's Palace in Las Vegas, Nevada. At some point in the negotiations, Foreman's manager signed a nondisclosure agreement prohibiting him from disclosing Garner's promotional concepts unless they signed a contract. Nevertheless, after negotiations fell through, Foreman used Garner's "Battle of the Ages" concept to promote a subsequent fight. Garner filed a lawsuit against Foreman and his manager in a federal district court in Illinois, alleging breach of contract. Using the information presented in the chapter, answer the following questions.

1. On what basis might the federal district court in Illinois exercise jurisdiction in this case?
2. Does the federal district court have original or appellate jurisdiction?
3. Suppose that Garner had filed his action in an Illinois state court. Could an Illinois state court exercise personal jurisdiction over Foreman or his manager? Why or why not?
4. Assume that Garner had filed his action in a Nevada state court. Would that court have personal jurisdiction over Foreman or his manager? Explain.

Terms and Concepts

alternative dispute resolution (ADR) 42
answer 36
arbitration 43
arbitration clause 43
award 40
bankruptcy court 30
brief 41
complaint 36
concurrent jurisdiction 31

counterclaim 36
default judgment 36
deposition 37
discovery 37
diversity of citizenship 30
docket 42
e-evidence 38
exclusive jurisdiction 31
federal question 30
interrogatories 37
judicial review 28
jurisdiction 29
justiciable controversy 33
litigation 36
long arm statute 29
mediation 43
motion for a directed verdict 39
motion for a new trial 41
motion for judgment *n.o.v.* 40
motion for judgment on the pleadings 37
motion for summary judgment 37
motion to dismiss 37
negotiation 42
online dispute resolution (ODR) 45
pleadings 36
probate court 30
question of fact 34
question of law 34
reply 36
rule of four 36
small claims court 33
standing to sue 33
summary jury trial 45
summons 36
venue 33
voir dire 38
writ of *certiorari* 36

Chapter Summary: Traditional and Online Dispute Resolution

The Judiciary's Role in American Government (See pages 28–29.)	The role of the judiciary—the courts—in the American governmental system is to interpret and apply the law. Through the process of judicial review—determining the constitutionality of laws—the judicial branch acts as a check on the executive and legislative branches of government.
Basic Judicial Requirements (See pages 29–33.)	1. *Jurisdiction*—Before a court can hear a case, it must have jurisdiction over the person against whom the suit is brought or the property involved in the suit, as well as jurisdiction over the subject matter. a. Limited versus general jurisdiction—Limited jurisdiction exists when a court is limited to a specific subject matter, such as probate or divorce. General jurisdiction exists when a court can hear any kind of case. b. Original versus appellate jurisdiction—Original jurisdiction exists when courts have authority to hear a case for the first time (trial courts). Appellate jurisdiction exists with courts of appeals, or reviewing courts; generally, appellate courts do not have original jurisdiction. c. Federal jurisdiction—Arises (1) when a federal question is involved (when the plaintiff's cause of action is based, at least in part, on the U.S. Constitution, a treaty, or a federal law) or (2) when a case involves diversity of citizenship and the amount in controversy exceeds $75,000. d. Concurrent versus exclusive jurisdiction—Concurrent jurisdiction exists when two different courts have authority to hear the same case. Exclusive jurisdiction exists when only state courts or only federal courts have authority to hear a case. 2. *Jurisdiction in cyberspace*—Because the Internet does not have physical boundaries, traditional jurisdictional concepts have been difficult to apply in cases involving online activities. Courts are developing standards for determining when jurisdiction over a Web site owner or operator located in another state is proper. 3. *Venue*—Venue has to do with the most appropriate location for a trial. 4. *Standing to sue*—A requirement that a party must have a legally protected and tangible interest at stake sufficient to justify seeking relief through the court system. The controversy at issue must also be a justiciable controversy—one that is real and substantial, as opposed to hypothetical or academic.
The State and Federal Court Systems (See pages 33–36.)	1. *Trial courts*—Courts of original jurisdiction, in which legal actions are initiated. a. State—Courts of general jurisdiction can hear any case; courts of limited jurisdiction include domestic relations courts, probate courts, traffic courts, and small claims courts. b. Federal—The federal district court is the equivalent of the state trial court. Federal courts of limited jurisdiction include the U.S. Tax Court, the U.S. Bankruptcy Court, and the U.S. Court of Federal Claims. 2. *Intermediate appellate courts*—Courts of appeals, or reviewing courts; generally without original jurisdiction. Many states have an intermediate appellate court; in the federal court system, the U.S. circuit courts of appeals are the intermediate appellate courts. 3. *Supreme (highest) courts*—Each state has a supreme court, although it may be called by some other name; appeal from the state supreme court to the United States Supreme Court is possible only if the case involves a federal question. The United States Supreme Court is the highest court in the federal court system.

Chapter Summary: Traditional and Online Dispute Resolution—Continued

Following a State Court Case (See pages 36–41.)	Rules of procedure prescribe the way in which disputes are handled in the courts. Rules differ from court to court, and separate sets of rules exist for federal and state courts, as well as for criminal and civil cases. A civil court case in a state court would involve the following procedures: 1. *The pleadings*— a. Complaint—Filed by the plaintiff with the court to initiate the lawsuit; served with a summons on the defendant. b. Answer—A response to the complaint in which the defendant admits or denies the allegations made by the plaintiff; may assert a counterclaim or an affirmative defense. c. Motion to dismiss—A request to the court to dismiss the case for stated reasons, such as the plaintiff's failure to state a claim for which relief can be granted. 2. *Pretrial motions (in addition to the motion to dismiss)*— a. Motion for judgment on the pleadings—May be made by either party; will be granted if the parties agree on the facts and the only question is how the law applies to the facts. The judge bases the decision solely on the pleadings. b. Motion for summary judgment—May be made by either party; will be granted if the parties agree on the facts. The judge applies the law in rendering a judgment. The judge can consider evidence outside the pleadings when evaluating the motion. 3. *Discovery*—The process of gathering evidence concerning the case. Discovery involves depositions, interrogatories, and various requests for information. Discovery may also involve electronically recorded information, such as e-mail, voice mail, document preparation systems, and other data compilations. 4. *Pretrial conference*—Either party or the court can request a pretrial conference to identify the matters in dispute after discovery has taken place and to plan the course of the trial. 5. *Trial*—Following jury selection (*voir dire*), the trial begins with opening statements from both parties' attorneys. The following events then occur: a. The plaintiff's introduction of evidence (including the testimony of witnesses) supporting the plaintiff's position. The defendant's attorney can challenge evidence and cross-examine witnesses. b. The defendant's introduction of evidence (including the testimony of witnesses) supporting the defendant's position. The plaintiff's attorney can challenge evidence and cross-examine witnesses. c. Closing arguments by the attorneys in favor of their respective clients, the judge's instructions to the jury, and the jury's verdict. 6. *Posttrial motions*— a. Motion for judgment *n.o.v.* ("notwithstanding the verdict")—Will be granted if the judge is convinced that the jury was in error. b. Motion for a new trial—Will be granted if the judge is convinced that the jury was in error; can also be granted on the grounds of newly discovered evidence, misconduct by the participants during the trial, or error by the judge. 7. *Appeal*—Either party can appeal the trial court's judgment to an appropriate court of appeals. After reviewing the record on appeal, the appellate court holds a hearing and renders its opinion.
The Courts Adapt to the Online World (See pages 41–42.)	Nearly all of the federal appellate courts and bankruptcy courts and a majority of the federal district courts have implemented electronic filing systems.
Alternative Dispute Resolution (See pages 42–45.)	1. *Negotiation*—The parties come together, with or without attorneys to represent them, and try to reach a settlement without the involvement of a third party. 2. *Mediation*—The parties themselves reach an agreement with the help of a neutral third party, called a mediator. The mediator may propose a solution but does not make a decision resolving the matter. 3. *Arbitration*—A more formal method of ADR in which the parties submit their dispute to a neutral third party, the arbitrator, who renders a decision. The decision may or may not be legally binding. 4. *Other types of ADR*—These include early neutral case evaluation, mini-trials, and summary jury trials. 5. *Providers of ADR services*—Hundreds of for-profit firms provide ADR services. 6. *Online dispute resolution*—A number of organizations now offer this service through online forums.

ExamPrep

ISSUE SPOTTERS

—Check your answers to these questions against the answers in Appendix G.

1 Sue contracts with Tom to deliver a quantity of computers to Sue's Computer Store. They disagree over the amount, the delivery date, the price, and the quality. Sue files a suit against Tom in a state court. Their state requires that their dispute be submitted to mediation or nonbinding arbitration. If the dispute is not resolved, or if either party disagrees with the decision of the mediator or arbitrator, will a court hear the case? Explain.

2 At the trial, after Sue calls her witnesses, offers her evidence, and otherwise presents her side of the case, Tom has at least two choices between courses of action. Tom can call his first witness. What else might he do?

BEFORE THE TEST

Go to **www.cengagebrain.com**, enter the ISBN 9781111530624, and click on "Find" to locate this textbook's Web site. Then, click on "Access Now" under "Study Tools," and select Chapter 2 at the top. There, you will find an Interactive Quiz that you can take to assess your mastery of the concepts in this chapter, as well as Flashcards and a Glossary of important terms.

For Review

1 What is judicial review?

2 Before a court can hear a case, it must have jurisdiction. Over what must it have jurisdiction? How are the courts applying traditional jurisdictional concepts to cases involving Internet transactions?

3 What is the difference between a trial court and an appellate court?

4 What is discovery, and how does electronic discovery differ from traditional discovery?

5 What are three alternative methods of resolving disputes?

Questions and Case Problems

2–1 Standing. Jack and Maggie Turton bought a house in Jefferson County, Idaho, located directly across the street from a gravel pit. A few years later, the county converted the pit to a landfill. The landfill accepted many kinds of trash that cause harm to the environment, including major appliances, animal carcasses, containers with hazardous content warnings, leaking car batteries, and waste oil. The Turtons complained to the county, but the county did nothing. The Turtons then filed a lawsuit against the county alleging violations of federal environmental laws pertaining to groundwater contamination and other pollution. Do the Turtons have standing to sue? Why or why not?

2–2 Question with Sample Answer Marya Callais, a citizen of Florida, was walking along a busy street in Tallahassee when a large crate flew off a passing truck and hit her, causing numerous injuries to Callais. She incurred a great deal of pain and suffering plus significant medical expenses, and she could not work for six months. She wishes to sue the trucking firm for $300,000 in damages. The firm's headquarters are in Georgia, although the company does business in Florida. In what court may Callais bring suit—a Florida state court, a Georgia state court, or a federal court? What factors might influence her decision?

—For a sample answer to Question 2–2, go to Appendix E at the end of this text.

2–3 Discovery. Advance Technology Consultants, Inc. (ATC), contracted with RoadTrac, LLC, to provide software and client software systems for the products of global positioning satellite (GPS) technology being developed by RoadTrac. RoadTrac agreed to provide ATC with hardware with which ATC's software would interface. Problems soon arose, however, and RoadTrac filed a lawsuit against ATC alleging breach of contract. During discovery, RoadTrac requested ATC's customer lists and marketing procedures. ATC objected to providing this information because RoadTrac and ATC had become competitors in the GPS industry. Should a party to a lawsuit have to hand over its confidential business secrets as part of a discovery request? Why or why not? What limitations might a court consider imposing before requiring ATC to produce this material?

2–4 Case Problem with Sample Answer Kathleen Lowden sued cellular phone company T-Mobile USA, Inc., contending that its service agreements were not enforceable under Washington state law. Lowden moved to create a class-action lawsuit, in which her claims would extend to similarly affected customers. She contended that T-Mobile had improperly charged her fees beyond the advertised price of service and charged her for roaming calls that should not have been classified as roaming. T-Mobile moved to force arbitration in accordance with provisions that were clearly set forth in the service agreement. The agreement also specified that no class-action lawsuit could be brought, so T-Mobile asked the court to dismiss the class-action request. Was T-Mobile correct that Lowden's only course of action would be to file arbitration personally? [*Lowden v. T-Mobile USA, Inc.*, 512 F.3d 1213 (9th Cir. 2008)]

—For a sample answer to Problem 2–4, go to Appendix F at the end of this text.

2–5 Discovery. Rita Peatie filed a suit in a Connecticut state court in October 2004 against Wal-Mart Stores, Inc., to recover for injuries to her head, neck, and shoulder. Peatie claimed that she had been struck two years earlier by a metal cylinder falling from a store ceiling. The parties agreed to nonbinding arbitration. Ten days before the hearing in January 2006, the plaintiff asked for, and was granted, four more months to conduct discovery. On the morning of the rescheduled hearing, she asked for more time, but the court denied this request. The hearing was held, and the arbitrator ruled in Wal-Mart's favor. Peatie filed a motion for a new trial, which was granted. Five months later, she sought through discovery to acquire any photos, records, and reports held by Wal-Mart regarding her alleged injury. The court issued a "protective order" against the request, stating that the time for discovery had long been over. On the day of the trial—four years after the alleged injury—the plaintiff asked the court to lift the order. Should the court do it? Why or why not? [*Peatie v. Wal-Mart Stores, Inc.*, 112 Conn. App. 8, 961 A.2d 1016 (2009)]

2–6 Arbitration. PRM Energy Systems, Inc. (PRM), owned technology patents and licensed Primenergy to use and to sublicense the technology in the United States. The agreement stated that all disputes would be settled by arbitration. Kobe Steel of Japan was interested in using the technology at its U.S. subsidiary; PRM directed Kobe to talk to Primenergy about that. Kobe talked to PRM directly about using the technology in Japan, but no agreement was reached. Primenergy then agreed to let Kobe use the technology in Japan without telling PRM. The dispute between PRM and Primenergy about Kobe went to arbitration as required by the license agreement. PRM sued Primenergy for fraud and theft of trade secrets. PRM also sued Kobe for using the technology in Japan without its permission. The district court ruled that PRM had to take all complaints about Primenergy to arbitration. PRM also had to take its complaint about Kobe to arbitration because the complaint involved a sublicense Kobe was granted by Primenergy. PRM appealed, contending that the fraud and theft of trade secrets went beyond the license agreement with Primenergy and that Kobe had no right to demand arbitration because it never had a right to use the technology under a license from PRM. Is PRM correct or must all matters go to arbitration? Explain. [*PRM Energy Systems v. Primenergy*, 592 F.3d 830 (8th Cir. 2010)]

2–7 Arbitration. From 1983 to 2002, Bruce Matthews played football in the National Football League (NFL) for the Houston Oilers and the Tennessee Titans. As part of his player contract, Matthews had agreed to submit any disputes with the NFL to final and binding arbitration. He had also signed a contract with the Titans stating that Tennessee law would determine all employment issues and matters related to workers' compensation benefits. Five years after he left the NFL, Matthews filed a workers' compensation claim (see Chapter 22) in California. The Titans and the NFL Management Council filed a grievance against Matthews, and the dispute was arbitrated. The arbitrator ruled that Matthews could pursue a workers' compensation claim in California but that the claim must proceed under Tennessee law. If California did not apply Tennessee law, then Matthews would be required to withdraw his claim. Unsatisfied with this ruling, the National Football League Players Association—on behalf of Matthews and all NFL players—filed a lawsuit asking the court to vacate the arbitration award. For what reasons will a court set aside an arbitrator's award? Should the court set aside the award in this case? Explain. [*National Football League Players Association v. National Football League Management Council*, ___ F.Supp.2d ___ (S.D.Cal. 2011)]

2–8 A Question of Ethics *Nellie Lumpkin, who suffered from various illnesses, including dementia, was admitted to the Picayune Convalescent Center, a nursing home. Because of Lumpkin's mental condition, her daughter, Beverly McDaniel, filled out the admissions paperwork and signed the admissions agreement. It included a clause requiring the parties to submit to arbitration any disputes that arose. After Lumpkin left the center two years later, she sued, through her husband, for negligent treatment and malpractice during her stay. The center moved to force the matter to arbitration. The trial court held that the arbitration agreement was not enforceable. The center appealed.* [Covenant Health & Rehabilitation of Picayune, LP v. Lumpkin, *23 So.3d 1092 (Miss.App. 2009)*]

1. Should a dispute involving medical malpractice be forced into arbitration? This is a claim of negligent care, not a breach of a commercial contract. Is it ethical for medical facilities to impose such a requirement? Is there really any bargaining over such terms?
2. Should a person with limited mental capacity be held to the arbitration clause agreed to by her next of kin who signed on her behalf?

2–9 Video Question To watch this chapter's video, *Jurisdiction in Cyberspace*, go to **www.cengagebrain.com**. Register the access code that came with your new book or log in to your existing account. Select the link for the "Business Law Digital Video Library Online Access" or "Business Law CourseMate." Click on "Complete Video List," view Video 1, and then answer the following questions:

1. What standard would a court apply to determine whether it has jurisdiction over the out-of-state computer firm in the video?
2. What factors is a court likely to consider in assessing whether sufficient contacts exist when the only connection to the jurisdiction is through a Web site?
3. How do you think a court would resolve the issue in this case?

Chapter 3

Ethics and Business Decision Making

Learning Objectives

After reading this chapter, you should be able to answer the following questions:

1. What is business ethics, and why is it important?
2. How can business leaders encourage their companies to act ethically?
3. How do duty-based ethical standards differ from outcome-based ethical standards?
4. What are six guidelines that an employee can use to evaluate whether his or her actions are ethical?
5. What types of ethical issues might arise in the context of international business transactions?

The Learning Objectives above are designed to help improve your understanding of the chapter.

(John Elk III/Lonely Planet Images/Getty Images)

In the early part of the first decade of the 2000s, ethics scandals erupted throughout corporate America. Heads of major corporations were tried for fraud, conspiracy, grand larceny, and obstruction of justice. Former multimillionaires (and even billionaires) who once ran multinational corporations received federal prison sentences. The giant energy company Enron in particular dominated headlines. Its investors lost around $60 billion when the company ceased to exist.

Fast-forward to 2009. One man, Bernard Madoff, was convicted of bilking investors out of more than $65 billion through a Ponzi scheme[1] that he had perpetrated for decades. He was sentenced to 150 years in prison—the maximum allowed. Madoff's victims included not just naïve retirees but also some of the world's largest and best-known financial institutions, such as the Royal Bank of Scotland and Japan's Nomura. And ethical lapses were not limited to Madoff. In 2010, the Securities and Exchange Commission imposed its largest-ever penalty against a Wall Street firm when it fined Goldman Sachs Group, Inc., $550 million for misleading investors in its marketing materials. Ethical problems in many financial institutions contributed to the onset of the deepest recession since the Great Depression of the 1930s. Not only did some $9 trillion in investment capital evaporate, but millions of workers lost their jobs.

The point is clear: the scope and scale of corporate unethical behavior, especially in the financial sector, skyrocketed in the first decade of the twenty-first century—with enormous repercussions for everyone, not just in the United States, but around the world. Indeed, the ethics scandals of the last fifteen years have taught businesspersons all over the world that business ethics cannot be taken lightly. Acting ethically in a business context can mean billions of dollars—made or lost—for corporations, shareholders, and employees, and can have far-reaching effects on society and the global economy.

Business Ethics

As you might imagine, business ethics is derived from the concept of ethics. **Ethics** can be defined as the study of what constitutes right or wrong behavior. It is the branch of

1. A Ponzi scheme is a type of illegal pyramid scheme named after Charles Ponzi, who duped thousands of New England residents into investing in a postage-stamp speculation scheme in the 1920s.

philosophy that focuses on morality and the way in which moral principles are derived and applied to one's conduct in daily life. Ethics has to do with questions relating to the fairness, justness, rightness, or wrongness of an action.

Business ethics focuses on what constitutes right or wrong behavior in the business world and on how businesspersons apply moral and ethical principles to situations that arise in the workplace. Because business decision makers often address more complex ethical dilemmas than they face in their personal lives, business ethics is more complicated than personal ethics.

Why Is Business Ethics Important?

To see why business ethics is so important, reread the first paragraph of this chapter. All of the corporate executives who are sitting behind bars could have avoided this outcome had they engaged in ethical decision making during their careers. As a result of their crimes, all of their companies suffered losses, and some were forced to enter bankruptcy, causing thousands of workers to lose their jobs.

If the executives had acted ethically, the corporations, shareholders, and employees of those companies would not have paid such a high price. Thus, an in-depth understanding of business ethics is important to the long-run viability of a corporation and to the well-being of its officers, directors, and employees. Finally, unethical corporate decision making can negatively affect suppliers, consumers, the community, and society as a whole.

The Moral Minimum

The minimum acceptable standard for ethical business behavior—known as the **moral minimum**—normally is considered to be compliance with the law. In many corporate scandals, had most of the businesspersons involved simply followed the law, they would not have gotten into trouble. Note, though, that in the interest of preserving personal freedom, as well as for practical reasons, the law does not—and cannot—codify all ethical requirements.

As they make business decisions, businesspersons must remember that just because an action is legal does not necessarily make it ethical. For instance, no law specifies the salaries that publicly held corporations can pay their officers. Nevertheless, if a corporation pays its officers an excessive amount relative to other employees, or to what officers at other corporations are paid, the executives' compensation might be challenged as unethical.

Short-Run Profit Maximization

Some people argue that a corporation's only goal should be profit maximization, which will be reflected in a higher market value. When all firms strictly adhere to the goal of profit maximization, resources tend to flow to where they are most highly valued by society. Thus, in theory, profit maximization ultimately leads to the most efficient allocation of scarce resources.

Corporate executives and employees have to distinguish, however, between *short-run* and *long-run* profit maximization. In the short run, a company may increase its profits by continuing to sell a product even though it knows that the product is defective. In the long run, though, because of lawsuits, large settlements, and bad publicity, such unethical conduct will cause profits to suffer. Thus, business ethics is consistent only with long-run profit maximization. An overemphasis on short-term profit maximization is the most common reason that ethical problems occur in business.

CASE EXAMPLE 3.1 When the powerful narcotic painkiller OxyContin was first marketed, its manufacturer, Purdue Pharma, claimed that it was unlikely to lead to drug addiction or abuse. Internal company documents later showed that the company's executives knew that OxyContin could be addictive, but they kept this risk a secret to boost sales and maximize short-term profits. Purdue Pharma and three former executives pleaded guilty to criminal charges that they misled regulators, patients, and physicians about OxyContin's risks of addiction. Purdue Pharma agreed to pay $600 million in fines and other payments. The three former executives agreed to pay $34.5 million in fines and were barred from federal health programs for a period of fifteen years. Thus, the company's focus on maximizing profits in the short run led to unethical conduct that hurt profits in the long run.[2] •

The following case provides an example of unethical—and illegal—conduct designed to enhance a company's short-term outlook that in the end destroyed the firm.

2. *United States v. Purdue Frederick Co.*, 495 F. Supp.2d 569 (W.D.Va. 2007).

Case 3.1 Skilling v. United States

Supreme Court of the United States, ___ U.S. ___, 130 S.Ct. 2896, 177 L.Ed.2d 619 (2010).

FACTS In August 2001, Jeffrey Skilling resigned his position as Enron Corporation's chief executive officer. Four months later, Enron filed for bankruptcy. An investigation uncovered a conspiracy to deceive investors about Enron's finances to ensure that its stock price remained high. Among other things, Skilling had concealed more than $2 billion in losses from Enron's

Case 3.1—Continues next page ➡

Case 3.1—Continued

struggling divisions. He had overstated Enron's profits in calls to investors and in press releases. To hide more losses, he had arranged deals between Enron's executives and third parties, which he falsely portrayed to Enron's accountants and to the Securities and Exchange Commission as producing income. Skilling was convicted in a federal district court of various crimes, including conspiring to commit fraud to deprive Enron and its shareholders of the "honest services" of its employees. He was sentenced to 292 months' imprisonment and three years' supervised release, and ordered to pay $45 million in restitution. Skilling appealed, and the U.S. Court of Appeals for the Fifth Circuit affirmed the trial court's ruling. Skilling appealed to the United States Supreme Court, arguing, among other things, that the honest-services statute is unconstitutionally vague or, in the alternative, that his conduct did not fall within the statute's compass.

ISSUE Is the honest-services fraud statute unconstitutionally vague?

DECISION Yes. The United States Supreme Court vacated the appellate court's ruling that Skilling's actions had violated the honest-services statute.

REASON The Supreme Court reasoned that the 1988 statute is so vague that it does not provide fair notice of the conduct that is prohibited, which makes it unconstitutional. Before 1988, most honest-services cases involved defendants who, in violation of a fiduciary duty, participated in bribery or kickback schemes. Although the honest-services doctrine originated from prosecutions involving bribery allegations, the statute prohibited "a wider range of offensive conduct." The Court acknowledged that upholding a conviction under this broad honest-services statute "would raise the due process concerns underlying the vagueness doctrine." There was no evidence that Skilling had solicited or accepted side payments from a third party in exchange for making misrepresentations about Enron's financial health, so there was no bribery involved. The Court remanded the case for further proceedings to determine how its decision would affect the other charges against Skilling.

FOR CRITICAL ANALYSIS—Ethical Consideration *During Skilling's tenure at Enron, the mood among the employees was upbeat because the company's future prospects appeared "rosy." Among other things, many employees invested all their pension funds in Enron stock. Is there anything unethical about this situation? Discuss.*

"Gray Areas" in the Law

In many situations, business firms can predict with a fair amount of certainty whether a given action would be legal. For instance, firing an employee solely because of that person's race or gender would clearly violate federal laws prohibiting employment discrimination. In some situations, though, the legality of a particular action may be less clear. In part, this is because there are so many laws regulating business that it is increasingly possible to violate one of them without realizing it. The law also contains numerous "gray areas," making it difficult to predict with certainty how a court will apply a given law to a particular action.

In addition, many rules of law require a court to determine what is "foreseeable" or "reasonable" in a particular situation. Because a business has no way of predicting how a specific court will decide these issues, decision makers need to proceed with caution and evaluate an action and its consequences from an ethical perspective. The same problem often occurs in cases involving the Internet because it is often unclear how a court will apply existing laws in the context of cyberspace. Generally, if a company can demonstrate that it acted in good faith and responsibly in the circumstances, it has a better chance of successfully defending its action in court or before an administrative law judge.

If a company discovers that a manager has behaved unethically or engaged in misconduct, the company should take prompt remedial action. The following case illustrates what can happen when a manager fails to follow the standards that apply to other employees.

Case 3.2 Mathews v. B and K Foods, Inc.

Missouri Court of Appeals, 332 S.W.3d 273 (2011).

FACTS Dianne Mathews was employed as a floral manager by B and K Foods, Inc. On July 15, 2010, her employment was terminated for submitting falsified time cards. On July 17, Mathews filed an application with the state for unemployment compensation (see Chapter 22). B and K objected, arguing that Mathews was not entitled to unemployment benefits because she had been discharged for misconduct in connection with work. At an administrative hearing held by the unemployment commission, the chief executive officer of B and K testified that it was company policy to deduct thirty minutes each day from the time sheets of employees, including managers, for a lunch break. When an individual was "not able to clock out for lunch" and worked straight through, that person could fill out a "no lunch" sheet for the day. Payroll would then add thirty minutes back to the person's work time. Mathews allegedly sometimes turned in "no lunch" sheets to cover time when she was running personal errands instead of working. Mathews admitted that she knew about the "no lunch" sheet policy and had used it on occasion but contended that her conduct was warranted. She claimed that a former employee who was a higher-level manager at B and K had told her that it was unnecessary to adjust her time card when she spent a few minutes on a personal errand. The unemployment commission concluded that Mathews was disqualified from seeking unemployment benefits due to misconduct. Mathews appealed.

Case 3.2–Continued

ISSUE Does it constitute work-related misconduct for an employee to turn in a "no lunch" sheet to get paid for times when she is running personal errands?

DECISION Yes. A state intermediate appellate court affirmed the decision of the state unemployment commission that Mathews was disqualified from receiving unemployment benefits.

REASON According to the court, "'work-related misconduct' must involve a willful violation of the rules or standards of the employer." The employer met its burden of proving such misconduct. B and K presented substantial evidence that Mathews had falsified time cards by turning in "no lunch" sheets for time she had spent running personal errands. Mathews admitted that she was familiar with the company's lunch policy. Furthermore, she was responsible for seeing that her subordinate employees followed the policy. The court accepted the B and K executive's statement that "they had no choice but to terminate [Mathews] because she was in a higher position and had a responsibility to enforce the lunch policy."

WHAT IF THE FACTS WERE DIFFERENT? *Suppose that Mathews had not admitted to knowing about the "no lunch sheet" policy. Would the result in this case have been different? Why or why not?*

The Importance of Ethical Leadership

Talking about ethical business decision making is meaningless if management does not set standards. Furthermore, managers must apply the same standards to themselves as they do to the employees of the company.

Attitude of Top Management One of the most important ways to create and maintain an ethical workplace is for top management to demonstrate its commitment to ethical decision making. A manager who is not totally committed to an ethical workplace rarely succeeds in creating one. Management's behavior, more than anything else, sets the ethical tone of a firm. Employees take their cues from management. **EXAMPLE 3.2** Devon, a SureTek employee, observes his manager cheating on her expense account. Devon quickly understands that such behavior is acceptable. Later, when Devon is promoted to a managerial position, he "pads" his expense account as well, knowing that he is unlikely to face sanctions for doing so. •

Managers who set unrealistic production or sales goals increase the probability that employees will act unethically. If a sales quota can be met only through high-pressure, unethical sales tactics, employees will try to act "in the best interest of the company" and will continue to behave unethically.

A manager who looks the other way when she or he knows about an employee's unethical behavior also sets an example—one indicating that ethical transgressions will be accepted. Managers have found that discharging even one employee for ethical reasons has a tremendous impact as a deterrent to unethical behavior in the workplace.

Behavior of Owners and Managers Business owners and managers sometimes take more active roles in fostering unethical and illegal conduct. This may indicate to their co-owners, co-managers, employees, and others that unethical business behavior will be tolerated.

The following case shows how a manager's sexist attitudes and actions affected the workplace environment. The case also underscores the limitations of the law with respect to this type of unethical business behavior.

Case 3.3 Krasner v. HSH Nordbank AG[a]

United States District Court, Southern District of New York, 680 F.Supp.2d 502 (2010).

FACTS David Krasner worked in the New York branch of HSH Nordbank AG (HSH), an international commercial bank headquartered in Germany. Krasner claimed that his supervisor, Roland Kiser, fostered an atmosphere "infected with overt sexism." According to Krasner, career advancement was based on "sexual favoritism," and women's advancement was governed by a "casting couch." Krasner alleged that Kiser and other male supervisors promoted a sexist and demeaning image of women in the workplace. Krasner also stated that Kiser pressured male subordinates, such as Krasner, to go to strip clubs with him when on business trips abroad. Krasner repeatedly objected to Kiser's and other supervisors' sexist attitudes, and particularly to Kiser's relationship with a female employee, Melissa Campfield. According to Krasner, Campfield was promoted at the expense of the "career advancement and reputations of other far more senior and qualified employees," including Krasner. Krasner complained both to Kiser and to the company's human resources department that Kiser's actions were violating the company's ethics policy. HSH investigated Krasner's complaints but found no violation of the law or of its own ethics policy. Shortly thereafter, Krasner was summarily terminated. Krasner sued HSH and Kiser in a federal district court, alleging that the defendants had discriminated against him on the basis of gender in

a. *AG* stands for *Actiengesellschaft,* a German term denoting a corporation.

Case 3.3–Continues next page ➡

Case 3.3–Continued

violation of Title VII of the Civil Rights Act of 1964.[b] The defendants moved to dismiss the case.

ISSUE If a man complains about the sexist attitudes of his supervisors at work and is subsequently fired, can he sue his employer for being discriminated against on the basis of his gender?

DECISION No. The federal district court granted the defendants' motions to dismiss. The court acknowledged that federal law prohibits employers from discriminating against an individual because of that individual's sex, but it did not find such discrimination in Krasner's case.

b. Title VII of the federal Civil Rights Act of 1964 prohibits employment discrimination on the basis of race, color, national origin, religion, or gender—see Chapter 22.

REASON Because Krasner did not contend that he had been disparaged, badly treated, or subjected to an unpleasant work atmosphere because he was a male, his complaint had to fail. Furthermore, the court noted that federal law prohibits a sexually hostile work environment where "the harassment is so pervasive that it changes the conditions of employment." But no law prohibits employers from maintaining "nasty, unpleasant workplaces, or even ones that are unpleasant for reasons that are sexual in nature." None of the alleged acts of harassment experienced by Krasner supported a claim that he was "being harassed because he is a male employee."

WHAT IF THE FACTS WERE DIFFERENT? *Assume that Krasner was a female employee who had experienced the same type of treatment that Krasner had. Would the female employee succeed in a Title VII claim of gender-based discrimination? Why or why not?*

Ethical Codes of Conduct

One of the most effective ways of setting a tone of ethical behavior within an organization is to create an ethical code of conduct. A well-written code of ethics explicitly states a company's ethical priorities and demonstrates the company's commitment to ethical behavior.

Ethics Training for Employees For an ethical code to be effective, its provisions must be clearly communicated to employees. Most large companies have implemented ethics training programs, in which managers discuss with employees on a face-to-face basis the firm's policies and the importance of ethical conduct. Some firms hold periodic ethics seminars during which employees can openly discuss any ethical problems that they may be experiencing and learn how the firm's ethical policies apply to those specific problems. Smaller firms should also offer some form of ethics training to employees because if a firm is accused of an ethics violation, the court will consider the presence or absence of such training in evaluating the firm's conduct.

The Sarbanes-Oxley Act and Web-Based Reporting Systems The Sarbanes-Oxley Act of 2002[3] requires companies to set up confidential systems so that employees and others can "raise red flags" about suspected illegal or unethical auditing and accounting practices. (Excerpts and explanatory comments on the Sarbanes-Oxley Act appear in Appendix D.)

Some companies have implemented online reporting systems to accomplish this goal. In one such system, employees can click on an icon on their computers that anonymously links them with EthicsPoint, an organization based in Portland, Oregon. Through EthicsPoint, employees can report suspicious accounting practices, sexual harassment, and other possibly unethical behavior. EthicsPoint, in turn, alerts management personnel or the audit committee at the designated company to the possible problem. Those who have used the system say that it is less inhibiting than calling a company's toll-free number.

3. 15 U.S.C. Sections 7201 *et seq.*

Ethical Transgressions by Financial Institutions

One of the best ways to learn the ethical responsibilities inherent in operating a business is to look at the mistakes made by other companies. In the following subsections, we describe some of the worst ethical failures of financial institutions during the latter part of the first decade of the 2000s. Many of these ethical wrongdoings received wide publicity and raised public awareness of the need for ethical leadership throughout all businesses.

Corporate Stock Buybacks

By now, you are probably aware that many well-known financial companies in the United States have either gone bankrupt, been taken over by the federal government, or been bailed out by U.S. taxpayers. What most people do not know is that those same corporations were using their own cash funds to prop up the value of their stock in the years just before the economic crisis that started in 2008.

The theory behind a **stock buyback** is simple—the management of a corporation believes that the market price of its shares is "below their fair value." Therefore, instead of issuing dividends to shareholders or reinvesting profits, management uses the company's funds to buy its shares in the open market, thereby boosting the price of the stock. From 2005 to 2007, stock buybacks for the top five hundred U.S. corporations added up to $1.4 *trillion*.

Who benefits from stock buybacks? The main individual beneficiaries are corporate executives who have been given **stock options,** which enable them to buy shares of the corporation's stock at a set price. When the market price rises above that level, the executives can profit by selling their shares. Although stock buybacks are legal and can serve legitimate purposes, they can easily be abused if managers use them just to increase the stock price in the short term so that they can profit from their options without considering the long-term needs of the company.

In the investment banking business, which almost disappeared entirely in the latter half of 2008, stock buybacks were particularly egregious. In the first half of 2008, Lehman Brothers Holdings was buying back its own stock—yet in September of that year, it filed for bankruptcy. According to financial writer Liam Denning, Lehman's buybacks were "akin to giving away the fire extinguisher even as your house begins to fill with smoke." Goldman Sachs, another investment bank, bought back $15 billion of its stock in 2007. By the end of 2008, U.S. taxpayers had provided $10 billion in bailout funds to that same company.

American International Group Example

For years, American International Group (AIG) was a respected, conservative worldwide insurance company based in New York. Then, during the first decade of the 2000s, it decided to enter an area in which it had little expertise—the issuance of insurance contracts guaranteeing certain types of complicated financial contracts. When many of those insured contracts failed, AIG experienced multibillion-dollar losses. Finally, the company sought a federal bailout that eventually amounted to almost $200 billion of U.S. taxpayers' funds.

While some company executives were testifying before Congress after receiving the funds, other AIG executives spent almost $400,000 on a retreat at a resort in California. In essence, U.S. taxpayers were footing the bill. To most observers, such arrogance was as incomprehensible as it was unethical.

Executive Bonuses

Until the economic crisis began in 2008, the bonuses paid in the financial industry did not make headlines. After all, times were good, and why shouldn't those responsible for record company earnings be rewarded? When investment banks and commercial banks began to fail, however, or had to be bailed out or taken over by the federal government, executive bonuses became an issue of paramount importance.

Certainly, the system of rewards in banking became perverse during the first decade of the 2000s. Executives and others in the industry were paid a percentage of their firm's profits, no matter how risky their investment actions had been. In other words, commissions and bonuses were based on sales of risky assets to investors. These included securities based on subprime mortgages, collateralized debt obligations, and other mortgages.

When the subprime mortgage crisis started, the worldwide house of cards came tumbling down, but those who had created and sold those risky assets suffered no liability—and even received bonuses. Of course, some of those firms that had enjoyed high short-run returns from their risky investments—and paid bonuses based on those profits—found themselves facing bankruptcy.

Consider Lehman Brothers before its bankruptcy. Its chief executive officer, Richard Fuld, Jr., earned almost $500 million between 2000 and the firm's demise in 2008. Even after Lehman Brothers entered bankruptcy, its new owners, Barclays and Nomura, legally owed $3.5 billion in bonuses to employees still on the payroll. In 2006, Goldman Sachs awarded its employees a total of $16.5 billion in bonuses, or an average of almost $750,000 for each employee.

By 2007, profits on Wall Street had already begun to drop—sometimes dramatically. Citigroup's profits, for example, were down 83 percent compared to the previous year. Bonuses, in contrast, declined by less than 5 percent. The bonus payout in 2007 for all Wall Street firms combined was $33.2 billion.

Approaches to Ethical Reasoning

Each individual, when faced with a particular ethical dilemma, engages in **ethical reasoning**—that is, a reasoning process in which the individual examines the situation at hand in light of his or her moral convictions or ethical standards. Businesspersons do likewise when making decisions with ethical implications.

How do business decision makers decide whether a given action is the "right" one for their firms? What ethical standards should be applied? Broadly speaking, ethical reasoning relating to business traditionally has been characterized by two fundamental approaches. One approach defines ethical behavior in terms of duty, which also implies certain rights. The other approach determines what is ethical in terms of the consequences, or outcome, of any given action. We examine each of these approaches here.

In addition to the two basic ethical approaches, several theories have been developed that specifically address the social responsibility of corporations. Because these theories also influence today's business decision makers, we conclude this section with a short discussion of the different views of corporate social responsibility.

Duty-Based Ethics

Duty-based ethical standards often are derived from revealed truths, such as religious precepts. They can also be derived through philosophical reasoning.

Religious Ethical Standards In the Judeo-Christian tradition, which is the dominant religious tradition in the United States, the Ten Commandments of the Old Testament establish fundamental rules for moral action. Other religions have their own sources of revealed truth. Religious rules generally are absolute with respect to the behavior of their adherents. **EXAMPLE 3.3** The commandment "Thou shalt not steal" is an absolute mandate for a person who believes that the Ten Commandments reflect revealed truth. Even a benevolent motive for stealing (such as Robin Hood's) cannot justify the act because the act itself is inherently immoral and thus wrong. ●

Kantian Ethics Duty-based ethical standards may also be derived solely from philosophical reasoning. The German philosopher Immanuel Kant (1724–1804), for example, identified some general guiding principles for moral behavior based on what he believed to be the fundamental nature of human beings. Kant believed that human beings are qualitatively different from other physical objects and are endowed with moral integrity and the capacity to reason and conduct their affairs rationally. Therefore, a person's thoughts and actions should be respected. When human beings are treated merely as a means to an end, they are being treated as the equivalent of objects and are being denied their basic humanity.

A central theme in Kantian ethics is that individuals should evaluate their actions in light of the consequences that would follow if *everyone* in society acted in the same way. This **categorical imperative** can be applied to any action. **EXAMPLE 3.4** Suppose that you are deciding whether to cheat on an examination. If you have adopted Kant's categorical imperative, you will decide *not* to cheat because if everyone cheated, the examination (and the entire education system) would be meaningless. ●

The Principle of Rights Because a duty cannot exist without a corresponding right, duty-based ethical standards imply that human beings have basic rights. The principle that human beings have certain fundamental rights (to life, liberty, and the pursuit of happiness, for example) is deeply embedded in Western culture. In particular, the natural law tradition embraces the concept that certain actions (such as killing another person) are morally wrong because they are contrary to nature (the natural desire to continue living). Those who adhere to this **principle of rights,** or "rights theory," believe that a key factor in determining whether a business decision is ethical is how that decision affects the rights of others. These others include the firm's owners, its employees, the consumers of its products or services, its suppliers, the community in which it does business, and society as a whole.

A potential dilemma for those who support rights theory, however, is that there are often conflicting rights and people may disagree on which rights are most important. When considering all those affected by a business decision, for example, how much weight should be given to employees relative to shareholders, customers relative to the community, or employees relative to society as a whole?

In general, rights theorists believe that whichever right is stronger in a particular circumstance takes precedence. **EXAMPLE 3.5** A firm can either keep a manufacturing plant open, saving the jobs of twelve workers, or shut the plant down and avoid contaminating a river with pollutants that would endanger the health of tens of thousands of people. In this situation, a rights theorist can easily choose which group to favor. Not all choices are so clear-cut, however. ●

Outcome-Based Ethics: Utilitarianism

"The greatest good for the greatest number" is a paraphrase of the major premise of the utilitarian approach to ethics. **Utilitarianism** is a philosophical theory developed by Jeremy Bentham (1748–1832) and modified by John Stuart Mill (1806–1873)—both British philosophers. In contrast to duty-based ethics, utilitarianism is outcome oriented. It focuses on the consequences of an action, not on the nature of the action itself or on any set of preestablished moral values or religious beliefs.

Under a utilitarian model of ethics, an action is morally correct, or "right," when, among the people it affects, it produces the greatest amount of good for the greatest number. When an action affects the majority adversely, it is morally wrong. Applying the utilitarian theory thus requires (1) a determination of which individuals will be affected by the action in question; (2) a **cost-benefit analysis,** which involves an assessment of the negative and positive effects of alternative actions on these individuals; and (3) a choice among alternative actions that will produce maximum societal utility (the greatest positive net benefits for the greatest number of individuals).

Corporate Social Responsibility

For many years, groups concerned with civil rights, employee safety and welfare, consumer protection, environmental preservation, and other causes have pressured corporate America to behave in a responsible manner with respect to these causes. Thus was born the concept of **corporate social responsibility**—the idea that those who run corporations can and should act ethically and be accountable to society for their actions. Just what constitutes corporate social responsibility has been debated for some time, and there are a number of different theories today.

Stakeholder Approach One view of corporate social responsibility stresses that corporations have a duty not just to shareholders, but also to other groups affected by corporate decisions (stakeholders). Under this approach, a corporation would consider the impact of its decision on the firm's employees, customers, creditors, suppliers, and the community in which the corporation operates. The reasoning behind this "stakeholder view" is that in some circumstances, one or more of these other groups may have a greater stake in company decisions than the shareholders do. Although this may be true, it is often difficult to decide which group's interests should receive greater weight if the interests conflict.

EXAMPLE 3.6 During 2008–2010, layoffs numbered in the millions. Nonetheless, some corporations succeeded in reducing labor costs without layoffs. To avoid slashing their workforces, these employers turned to alternatives such as four-day workweeks, voluntary furloughs, wage freezes, and pension cuts. Some companies asked for and received 1 percent wage cuts from their workers to prevent layoffs. •

CORPORATE CITIZENSHIP Another theory of social responsibility argues that corporations should behave as good citizens by promoting goals that society deems worthwhile and by taking positive steps toward solving social problems. The idea is that because business controls so much of the wealth and power of this country, business, in turn, has a responsibility to society to use that wealth and power in socially beneficial ways. Under a corporate citizenship view, companies are judged on how much they donate to social causes, as well as how they conduct their operations with respect to employment discrimination, human rights, environmental concerns, and similar issues.

Some corporations publish annual social responsibility reports, which may also be called corporate sustainability (*sustainability* refers to the capacity to endure) or citizenship reports. **EXAMPLE 3.7** The Hitachi Group releases an Annual Corporate Social Responsibility Report that outlines its environmental strategy, including its attempts to reduce carbon dioxide emissions (greenhouse gases). It typically discusses human rights policy and its commitment to human rights awareness. Symantec Corporation issued its first corporate responsibility report in 2008 to demonstrate its focus on critical environmental, social, and governance issues. Among other things, Symantec pointed out that it had adopted the Calvert Women's Principles, the first global code of corporate conduct designed to empower, advance, and invest in women worldwide. •

A Way of Doing Business. A survey of U.S. executives undertaken by the Boston College Center for Corporate Citizenship found that more than 70 percent of those polled agreed that corporate citizenship must be treated as a priority. More than 60 percent said that good corporate citizenship added to their companies' profits. Strategist Michelle Bernhart has argued that corporate social responsibility cannot attain its maximum effectiveness unless it is treated as a way of doing business rather than as a special program.

Not all socially responsible activities can benefit a corporation, however. Corporate responsibility is most successful when a company undertakes activities that are relevant and significant to its stakeholders and related to its business operations. **EXAMPLE 3.8** The Brazilian firm Companhia Vale do Rio Doce is one of the world's largest diversified metals and mining companies. In 2008, it invested more than $150 million in social projects, including health care, infrastructure, and education. At the same time, it invested more than $300 million in environmental protection. One of its projects involved the rehabilitation of native species in the Amazon Valley. To that end, it has planted almost 200 million trees in an attempt to restore 1,150 square miles of land where cattle breeding and farming have caused deforestation. •

The Employee Recruiting and Retention Advantage. One key corporate stakeholder is of course a company's workforce, which may include potential employees—job seekers. Surveys of college students about to enter the job market confirm that young people are looking for socially responsible employers. Younger workers generally are altruistic. They want to work for a company that allows them to participate in community projects. Corporations that engage in meaningful social activities find that they retain workers longer, particularly younger ones. **EXAMPLE 3.9** At the accounting firm PKF Texas, employees support a variety of business, educational, and philanthropic organizations. As a result, this company is able to recruit and retain a younger workforce. Its average turnover rate is half the industry average. •

Making Ethical Business Decisions

As Dean Krehmeyer, executive director of the Business Roundtable's Institute for Corporate Ethics, once said, "Evidence strongly suggests being ethical—doing the right thing—pays." Instilling ethical business decision making into the fabric of a business organization is no small task, even if ethics "pays." The job is to encourage people to understand that they have to think more broadly about how their decisions will affect employees, shareholders, customers, and even the community. Great companies, such as Enron and the worldwide accounting firm Arthur Andersen, were brought down by the unethical behavior of a few. A two-hundred-year-old British investment bank, Barings Bank, was destroyed by the actions of one employee and a few of his friends. Clearly, ensuring that all employees get on the ethical business decision-making "bandwagon" is crucial in today's fast-paced world.

The George S. May International Company has provided six basic guidelines to help corporate employees judge their actions. Each employee—no matter what her or his level in the organization—should evaluate her or his actions using the following six guidelines:

1. *The law.* Is the action you are considering legal? If you do not know the laws governing the action, then find out. Ignorance of the law is no excuse.
2. *Rules and procedures.* Are you following the internal rules and procedures that have already been laid out by your company? They have been developed to avoid problems. Is what you are planning to do consistent with your company's policies and procedures? If not, stop.
3. *Values.* Laws and internal company policies reinforce society's values. You might wish to ask yourself whether you are attempting to find a loophole in the law or in your company's policies. Next, you have to ask yourself whether you are following the "spirit" of the law as well as the letter of the law or the internal policy.
4. *Conscience.* If you feel any guilt, let your conscience be your guide. Alternatively, ask yourself whether you would be happy to be interviewed by the national news media about the actions you are going to take.
5. *Promises.* Every business organization is based on trust. Your customers believe that your company will do what it is supposed to do. The same is true for your suppliers and employees. Will your actions live up to the commitments you have made to others, both inside the business and outside?
6. *Heroes.* We all have heroes who are role models for us. Is what you are planning on doing an action that your "hero" would take? If not, how would your hero act? That is how you should be acting.

Practical Solutions to Corporate Ethics Questions

Corporate ethics officers and ethics committees require a practical method to investigate and solve specific ethics problems. Ethics consultant Leonard H. Bucklin of Corporate-Ethics.US has devised a procedure that he calls Business Process Pragmatism.[4] It involves the following five steps:

1. *Inquiry.* Of course, an understanding of the facts must be the initial action. The parties involved might include the mass media, the public, employees, or customers. At this stage of the process, the ethical problem or problems are specified. A list of relevant ethical principles is created.
2. *Discussion.* Here, a list of action options is developed. Each option carries with it certain ethical principles. Finally, resolution goals should also be listed.
3. *Decision.* Working together, those participating in the process create a consensus decision, or a consensus plan of action for the corporation.
4. *Justification.* Does the consensus solution withstand moral scrutiny? At this point in the process, reasons should be attached to each proposed action or series of actions. Will the stakeholders involved accept these reasons?
5. *Evaluation.* Do the solutions to the corporate ethics issue satisfy corporate values, community values, and individual values? Ultimately, can the consensus resolution withstand moral scrutiny of the decisions made and the process used to reach those decisions?

4. Corporate-Ethics.US and Business Process Pragmatism are registered trademarks.

Business Ethics on a Global Level

Given the various cultures and religions throughout the world, it is not surprising that conflicts in ethics frequently arise between foreign and U.S. businesspersons. **EXAMPLE 3.10** In certain countries, the consumption of alcohol and specific foods is forbidden for religious reasons. Under such circumstances, it would be thoughtless and imprudent for a U.S. businessperson to invite a local business contact out for a drink. •

The role played by women in other countries may also present some difficult ethical problems for firms doing business internationally. Equal employment opportunity is a fundamental public policy in the United States, and Title VII of the Civil Rights Act of 1964 prohibits discrimination against women in the employment context (see Chapter 22). Some other countries, however, offer little protection for women against gender discrimination in the workplace, including sexual harassment.

We look here at how laws governing workers in other countries, particularly developing countries, have created some especially difficult ethical problems for U.S. sellers of goods manufactured in foreign countries. We also examine some of the ethical ramifications of laws prohibiting U.S. businesspersons from bribing foreign officials to obtain favorable business contracts.

Employment Practices of Foreign Suppliers

Many U.S. businesses contract with companies in developing nations to produce goods, such as shoes and clothing, because the wage rates in those nations are significantly lower than wages in the United States. Yet what if a foreign company exploits its workers—by hiring women and children at below-minimum-wage rates, for example, or by requiring its employees to work long hours in a workplace full of health hazards? What if the company's supervisors routinely engage in workplace conduct that is offensive to women?

Given today's global communications network, few companies can assume that their actions in other nations will go unnoticed by "corporate watch" groups that discover and publicize unethical corporate behavior. (For a discussion of how the Internet has increased the ability of critics to publicize a corporation's misdeeds, see this chapter's *Adapting the Law to the Online Environment* feature below.) As a result, U.S. businesses today usually take steps to avoid such adverse publicity—either by refusing to deal with certain suppliers or by arranging to monitor their suppliers' workplaces to make sure that the employees are not being mistreated.

The Foreign Corrupt Practices Act

Another ethical problem in international business dealings has to do with the legitimacy of certain "side" payments to government officials. In the United States, the majority of contracts are formed within the private sector. In many foreign countries, however, government officials make the decisions on most major construction and manufacturing contracts because of extensive government regulation and control over trade and industry. Side payments to government officials in exchange for favorable business contracts are not unusual in such countries, where they are not considered to be unethical. In the past, U.S. corporations doing business in these countries largely followed the dictum "When in Rome, do as the Romans do."

In the 1970s, however, the U.S. press, and government officials as well, uncovered a number of business scandals involving large side payments by U.S. corporations to foreign representatives for the purpose of securing advantageous international trade contracts. In response to this unethical behavior, in 1977 Congress passed the Foreign Corrupt Practices Act[5] (FCPA), which prohibits U.S. businesspersons from bribing foreign officials to secure advantageous contracts.

Prohibition against the Bribery of Foreign Officials The first part of the FCPA applies to all U.S. companies and their directors, officers, shareholders, employees, and agents. This part prohibits the bribery of officials of foreign governments if the purpose of the payment is to get the officials to act in their official capacity to provide business opportunities.

The FCPA does not prohibit payment of substantial sums to minor officials whose duties are ministerial. These payments

5. 15 U.S.C. Sections 78dd-1 *et seq.*

Adapting the Law to the Online Environment

Corporate Reputations under Attack

In the pre-Internet days, disgruntled employees and customers wrote letters of complaint to corporate management or to the editors of local newspapers. Occasionally, an investigative reporter would write an exposé of alleged corporate misdeeds. Today, those unhappy employees and customers have gone online. To locate them, just type in the name of any major corporation. You will find electronic links to blogs, wikis, message boards, and online communities–many of which post unadorned criticisms of corporate giants. Some dissatisfied employees and consumers have even created rogue Web sites that mimic the look of the target corporation's official Web site, except that the rogue sites feature chat rooms and postings of "horror stories" about the corporation.

Damage to Corporate Reputations

Clearly, by providing a forum for complaints, the Internet has increased the potential for damage to the reputation of any major (or minor) corporation. Now a relatively small number of unhappy employees, for example, may make the entire world aware of a single incident that is not at all representative of how the corporation ordinarily operates.

Special Interest Groups Go on the Attack

Special interest groups are also using the Internet to attack corporations they do not like. Rather than writing letters or giving speeches to a limited audience, a special interest group can now go online and mercilessly "expose" what it considers to be a corporation's "bad practices." Wal-Mart and Nike in particular have been frequent targets for advocacy groups that believe those corporations exploit their workers.

Online Attacks: Often Inaccurate, but Probably Legal

Corporations often point out that many of the complaints and charges leveled against them are unfounded or exaggerated. Sometimes, management has tried to argue that the online attacks are libelous. The courts, however, disagree. To date, most courts have regarded online attacks simply as expressions of opinion and therefore a form of speech protected by the First Amendment.

In contrast, if employees breach company rules against the disclosure of internal financial information or trade secrets, the courts have been willing to side with the employers. Note, also, that a strong basis for successful lawsuits against inappropriate employee online disclosures always includes a clear set of written guidelines about what employees can do when they blog or generate other online content.

FOR CRITICAL ANALYSIS

How might online attacks actually help corporations in the long run? (Hint: Some online criticisms might be accurate.)

are often referred to as "grease," or facilitating payments. They are meant to accelerate the performance of administrative services that might otherwise be carried out at a slow pace. Thus, for example, if a firm makes a payment to a minor official to speed up an import licensing process, the firm has not violated the FCPA.

Generally, the act, as amended, permits payments to foreign officials if such payments are lawful within the foreign country. The act also does not prohibit payments to private foreign companies or other third parties unless the U.S. firm knows that the payments will be passed on to a foreign government in violation of the FCPA. Business firms that violate the FCPA may be fined up to $2 million. Individual officers or directors who violate the act may be fined up to $100,000 (the fine cannot be paid by the company) and may be imprisoned for up to five years.

ACCOUNTING REQUIREMENTS In the past, bribes were often concealed in corporate financial records. Thus, the second part of the FCPA is directed toward accountants. All companies must keep detailed records that "accurately and fairly" reflect the company's financial activities. In addition, all companies must have an accounting system that provides "reasonable assurance" that all transactions entered into by the company are accounted for and legal. These requirements assist in detecting illegal bribes. The FCPA further prohibits any person from making false statements to accountants or false entries in any record or account.

Reviewing . . . Ethics and Business Decision Making

Isabel Arnett was promoted to CEO of Tamik, Inc., a pharmaceutical company that manufactures a vaccine called Kafluk, which supposedly provides some defense against bird flu. The company began marketing Kafluk throughout Asia. After numerous media reports that bird flu might soon become a worldwide epidemic, the demand for Kafluk increased, sales soared, and Tamik earned record profits. Tamik's CEO, Arnett, then began receiving disturbing reports from Southeast Asia that in some patients, Kafluk had caused psychiatric disturbances, including severe hallucinations, and heart and lung problems. Arnett was informed that six children in Japan had committed suicide by jumping out of windows after receiving the vaccine. To cover up the story and prevent negative publicity, Arnett instructed Tamik's partners in Asia to offer cash to the Japanese families whose children had died in exchange for their silence. Arnett also refused to authorize additional research within the company to study the potential side effects of Kafluk. Using the information presented in the chapter, answer the following questions.

1 This scenario illustrates one of the main reasons why ethical problems occur in business. What is that reason?
2 Would a person who adheres to the principle of rights consider it ethical for Arnett not to disclose potential safety concerns and to refuse to perform additional research on Kafluk? Why or why not?
3 If Kafluk prevented fifty Asian people who were exposed to bird flu from dying, would Arnett's conduct in this situation be ethical under a utilitarian cost-benefit analysis? Why or why not?
4 Did Tamik or Arnett violate the Foreign Corrupt Practices Act in this scenario? Why or why not?

Terms and Concepts

business ethics 51
categorical imperative 56
corporate social responsibility 56
cost-benefit analysis 56
ethical reasoning 55
ethics 50
moral minimum 51
principle of rights 56
stock buyback 54
stock option 55
utilitarianism 56

Chapter Summary: Ethics and Business Decision Making

Business Ethics (See pages 50–54.)	1. *Ethics*—Business ethics focuses on how moral and ethical principles are applied in the business context. 2. *The moral minimum*—Lawful behavior is the moral minimum. The law has its limits, though, and some actions may be legal but not ethical.

Chapter Summary: Ethics and Business Decision Making—Continued

Business Ethics (Continued)	3. *Short-term profit maximization*—One of the more pervasive reasons why ethical breaches occur is the focus on short-term profit maximization. Executives should distinguish between short-run and long-run profit goals and focus on maximizing profits over the long run because only long-run profit maximization is consistent with business ethics. 4. *Legal uncertainties*—It may be difficult to predict with certainty whether particular actions are legal, given the numerous and frequent changes in the laws regulating business and the "gray areas" in the law. 5. *The importance of ethical leadership*—Management's commitment and behavior are essential in creating an ethical workplace. Management's behavior, more than anything else, sets the ethical tone of a firm and influences the behavior of employees. 6. *Ethical codes*—Most large firms have ethical codes or policies and training programs to help employees determine whether certain actions are ethical. In addition, the Sarbanes-Oxley Act requires firms to set up confidential systems so that employees and others can report suspected illegal or unethical auditing or accounting practices.
Ethical Transgressions by Financial Institutions (See pages 54–55.)	During the first decade of the 2000s, corporate wrongdoing in the U.S. financial markets escalated. A number of investment banking firms engaged in abusive use of stock buybacks and stock options. AIG, an insurance giant, was also on the brink of bankruptcy when the government stepped in with federal bailout funds. Exorbitant bonuses paid to Wall Street executives added to the financial industry's problems and fueled public outrage. U.S. taxpayers paid the price through the federal bailouts and a deepening nationwide recession.
Approaches to Ethical Reasoning (See pages 55–57.)	1. *Duty-based ethics*—Ethics based on religious beliefs; philosophical reasoning, such as that of Immanuel Kant; and the basic rights of human beings (the principle of rights). A potential problem for those who support this approach is deciding which rights are more important in a given situation. Management constantly faces ethical conflicts and trade-offs when considering all those affected by a business decision. 2. *Outcome-based ethics (utilitarianism)*—Ethics based on philosophical reasoning, such as that of John Stuart Mill. Applying this theory requires a cost-benefit analysis, weighing the negative effects against the positive and deciding which course of action produces the best outcome. 3. *Corporate social responsibility*—A number of theories based on the idea that corporations can and should act ethically and be accountable to society for their actions. These include the stakeholder approach and corporate citizenship.
Making Ethical Business Decisions (See pages 57–58.)	Making ethical business decisions is crucial in today's legal environment. Doing the right thing pays off in the long run, both in terms of increasing profits and avoiding negative publicity and the potential for bankruptcy. We provide six guidelines for making ethical business decisions on page 58.
Practical Solutions to Corporate Ethics Questions (See page 58.)	Corporate ethics officers and ethics committees require a practical method to investigate and solve specific ethics problems. For a five-step pragmatic procedure to solve ethical problems recommended by one expert, see page 58.
Business Ethics on a Global Level (See pages 58–60.)	Businesses must take account of the many cultural, religious, and legal differences among nations. Notable differences relate to the role of women in society, employment laws governing workplace conditions, and the practice of giving side payments to foreign officials to secure favorable contracts.

ExamPrep

ISSUE SPOTTERS

—Check your answers to these questions against the answers in Appendix G.

1 Delta Tools, Inc., markets a product that under some circumstances is capable of seriously injuring consumers. Does Delta owe an ethical duty to remove this product from the market, even if the injuries result only from misuse? Why or why not?

2 Acme Corporation decides to respond to what it sees as a moral obligation to correct for past discrimination by adjusting pay differences among its employees. Does this raise an ethical conflict among Acme's employees? Between Acme and its employees? Between Acme and its shareholders? Explain your answers.

BEFORE THE TEST

Go to **www.cengagebrain.com**, enter the ISBN 9781111530624, and click on "Find" to locate this textbook's Web site. Then, click on "Access Now" under "Study Tools," and select Chapter 3 at the top. There, you will find an Interactive Quiz that you can take to assess your mastery of the concepts in this chapter, as well as Flashcards and a Glossary of important terms.

For Review

1. What is business ethics, and why is it important?
2. How can business leaders encourage their companies to act ethically?
3. How do duty-based ethical standards differ from outcome-based ethical standards?
4. What are six guidelines that an employee can use to evaluate whether his or her actions are ethical?
5. What types of ethical issues might arise in the context of international business transactions?

Questions and Case Problems

3–1 Business Ethics. Jason Trevor owns a commercial bakery in Blakely, Georgia, that produces a variety of goods sold in grocery stores. Trevor is required by law to perform internal tests on food produced at his plant to check for contamination. Three times in 2008, the tests of food products that contained peanut butter were positive for salmonella contamination. Trevor was not required to report the results to U.S. Food and Drug Administration officials, however, so he did not. Instead, Trevor instructed his employees to simply repeat the tests until the outcome was negative. Therefore, the products that had originally tested positive for salmonella were eventually shipped out to retailers. Five people who ate Trevor's baked goods in 2008 became seriously ill, and one person died from salmonella. Even though Trevor's conduct was legal, was it unethical for him to sell goods that had once tested positive for salmonella? If Trevor had followed the six basic guidelines for making ethical business decisions, would he still have sold the contaminated goods? Why or why not?

3–2 Question with Sample Answer Shokun Steel Co. owns many steel plants. One of its plants is much older than the others. Equipment at that plant is outdated and inefficient, and the costs of production at that plant are now two times higher than at any of Shokun's other plants. The company cannot raise the price of steel because of competition, both domestic and international. The plant employs more than a thousand workers and is located in Twin Firs, Pennsylvania, which has a population of about 45,000. Shokun is contemplating whether to close the plant. What factors should the firm consider in making its decision? Will the firm violate any ethical duties if it closes the plant? Analyze these questions from the two basic perspectives on ethical reasoning discussed in this chapter.

—For a sample answer to Question 3–2, go to Appendix E at the end of this text.

3–3 Ethical Conduct. Unable to pay more than $1.2 billion in debt, Big Mountain Metals, Inc., filed a petition to declare bankruptcy in a federal bankruptcy court in July 2009. Big Mountain's creditors included Bank of New London and Suzuki Bank, among others. The court appointed Morgan Crawford to work as a "disinterested" (neutral) party with Big Mountain and the creditors to resolve their disputes; the court set an hourly fee as Crawford's compensation. Crawford told the banks that he wanted them to pay him an additional percentage fee based on the "success" he attained in finding "new value" to pay Big Mountain's debts. He said that without such a deal, he would not perform his mediation duties. Suzuki Bank agreed; the other banks disputed the deal, but no one told the court. In October 2010, Crawford asked the court for nearly $2.5 million in compensation, including the hourly fees, which totaled about $531,000, and the percentage fees. Big Mountain and others asked the court to deny Crawford any fees on the basis that he had improperly negotiated "secret side agreements." How did Crawford violate his duties as a "disinterested" party? Should he be denied compensation? Why or why not?

3–4 Corporate Social Responsibility. Methamphetamine (meth) is an addictive, synthetic drug made chiefly in small toxic labs (STLs) in homes, tents, barns, or hotel rooms. The manufacturing process is dangerous, often resulting in explosions, burns, and toxic fumes. The government has spent considerable resources to find and eradicate STLs, imprison meth dealers and users, treat addicts, and provide services for families affected by these activities. Meth cannot be made without ephedrine or pseudoephedrine, which are ingredients in cold and allergy medications. Arkansas has one of the highest numbers of STLs in the United States. In an effort to recoup the costs of dealing with the meth epidemic, twenty counties in Arkansas filed a suit in a federal district court against Pfizer, Inc., and other companies that make or distribute cold and allergy medications. What is the defendants' ethical responsibility in this case, and to whom do they owe it? Why? [*Ashley County, Arkansas v. Pfizer, Inc.*, 552 F.3d 659 (8th Cir. 2009)]

3–5  **Case Problem with Sample Answer** Havensure, LLC, an insurance broker, approached York International to determine whether it could provide insurance to York at a better rate than it currently was paying. York allowed Havensure to study its policies. Havensure realized that Prudential, an insurance provider for York, had a hidden broker fee in its premium that it used to pay the broker universal life resources (ULR) that provided the Prudential policy for York. Havensure told York that it could provide insurance at a lower price, so York had Havensure send requests for proposals to various insurance companies. To keep York's business, Prudential offered to match the lowest rate quoted, but Prudential told York that it would have to continue to buy the policy through the broker ULR, and not through Havensure. York agreed. Havensure then sued Prudential for wrongful interference with a business relationship (see Chapter 4). The trial court held for Prudential. Havensure appealed. The appeals court held that what Prudential did, by having a hidden fee for a broker, violated its ethical code and may have violated New York insurance law, but Havensure still had no case. Does it make sense that a firm violating its own rules, as well as possibly violating the law, has no obligation for the loss it may have imposed on another firm that is trying to compete for business? Explain your answer. [*Havensure, LLC v. Prudential Insurance,* 595 F.3d 312 (6th Cir. 2010)]

—To view a sample answer for Problem 3–5, go to Appendix F at the end of this text.

3–6 **Ethical Misconduct.** Frank A. Pasquale used the Social Security number of his father, Frank F. Pasquale, to obtain a credit card, which he used to charge a $7,500 item. Although he was employed by his father's firm, the son also collected unemployment benefits. Later, the son, claiming to act on behalf of Frank Pasquale Limited Partnership, misrepresented his status to obtain a $350,000 loan. His father—the only person authorized to borrow funds on behalf of the partnership—was unaware of his son's misdeeds. The loan went into default. When the father learned of the fraud, he confronted his son, who produced forged documents to show that the loan had been paid. Adams Associates, LLC, which had acquired the unpaid loan from the original lender, filed a suit in a New Jersey state court against the father and the son for damages. During the trial, another family member testified to the son's general "lack of ethics." Did the son deserve this characterization? Should the court issue a judgment against the father and the son? Explain. [*Adams Associates, LLC v. Frank Pasquale Limited Partnership,* __ A.3d __ (2011)]

3–7 **A Question of Ethics** *Steven Soderbergh is the Academy Award–winning director of* Erin Brockovich, Traffic, *and many other films. CleanFlicks, LLC, filed a suit in a federal district court against Soderbergh, fifteen other directors, and the Directors Guild of America. The plaintiff asked the court to rule that it had the right to sell DVDs of the defendants' films altered without the defendants' consent to delete scenes of "sex, nudity, profanity and gory violence." CleanFlicks sold or rented the edited DVDs under the slogan "It's About Choice" to consumers, sometimes indirectly through retailers. It would not sell to retailers that made unauthorized copies of the edited films. The defendants, with DreamWorks LLC and seven other movie studios that own the copyrights to the films, filed a counterclaim against CleanFlicks and others engaged in the same business, alleging copyright infringement. Those filing the counterclaim asked the court to enjoin (prevent) CleanFlicks and the others from making and marketing altered versions of the films.* [CleanFlicks of Colorado, LLC v. Soderbergh, *433 F.Supp.2d 1236 (D.Colo. 2006)]*

1. Movie studios often edit their films to conform to content and other standards and sell the edited versions to network television and other commercial buyers. In this case, however, the studios objected when CleanFlicks edited the films and sold the altered versions directly to consumers. Similarly, CleanFlicks made unauthorized copies of the studios' DVDs to edit the films, but objected to others' making unauthorized copies of the altered versions. Is there anything unethical about these apparently contradictory positions? Why or why not?
2. CleanFlicks and its competitors asserted, in part, that they were making "fair use" of the studios' copyrighted works. They argued that by their actions "they are criticizing the objectionable content commonly found in current movies and that they are providing more socially acceptable alternatives to enable families to view the films together, without exposing children to the presumed harmful effects emanating from the objectionable content." If you were the judge, how would you view this argument? Is a court the appropriate forum for making determinations of public or social policy? Explain.

3–8 **Critical Thinking Legal Question** Human rights groups, environmental activists, and other interest groups concerned with unethical business practices have often conducted publicity campaigns against various corporations that those groups feel have engaged in unethical practices. Can a small group of well-organized activists dictate how a major corporation conducts its affairs? Discuss fully.

3–9 **Video Question** To watch this chapter's videos, *Pharzime, Scene 1 and Scene 2,* go to **www.cengagebrain.com**. Register the access code that came with your new book or log in to your existing Cengage account. Select the link for the "Business Law Digital Video Library Online Access" or "Business Law CourseMate." Click on "Complete Video List," view Videos 79 and 80, and then answer the following questions:

1. In *Scene 1,* employees discuss whether to market their company's drug as a treatment for other conditions—even though it has only been approved for treating epilepsy. One employee argues that marketing the drug for more than the one treatment will increase the company's short-term profits and that obtaining approval for the other treatments will take too long. What theory describes this perspective?
2. In *Scene 2,* a new sales rep discusses the company's off-label marketing strategy with a veteran sales rep. Is it unethical or illegal for a sales rep to represent that he is a doctor when he has a doctorate in chemistry but is not actually a physician? Explain.

Unit One — Unit Case Study with Dissenting Opinion: *Paduano v. American Honda Motor Co.*

As mentioned on page 4 of Chapter 1, the U.S. Constitution is the supreme law of the land. Article VI of the Constitution provides that the Constitution, laws, and treaties of the United States are "the supreme Law of the Land." This article, commonly referred to as the supremacy clause, *is important in the ordering of state and federal relationships. When there is a direct conflict between a federal law and a state law, the state law is rendered invalid. Because some powers are concurrent (that is, shared by the federal government and the states), however, it is necessary to determine which law governs in a particular circumstance.*

Preemption *occurs when Congress chooses to act exclusively in a concurrent area. If Congress has chosen to act exclusively in an area, the federal statute will take precedence over a conflicting state law on the same subject under the doctrine of preemption.*

There is a strong presumption against preemption, however, because the states are independent "sovereigns" in our federal system. In areas in which the states have traditionally exercised their police power, on a subject such as consumer protection, for example, this presumption applies with particular force.

In this Unit Case Study with Dissenting Opinion, *we review* Paduano v. American Honda Motor Co.,[1] *a case in which a new-car buyer complained about the vehicle's inability to achieve the fuel economy advertised in the automaker's brochure. The defendant contended that federal law preempted the plaintiff's claims, which were founded on state law.*

1. 169 Cal.App.4th 1453, 88 Cal.Rptr.3d 90 (4 Dist. 2009).

CASE BACKGROUND

Gaetano Paduano bought a new Honda Civic Hybrid in California in June 2004. The Environmental Protection Agency's (EPA's) fuel economy estimate stated on the federally mandated new-car label was 47 miles per gallon (mpg) for city driving and 48 mpg for highway driving. Honda's sales brochure repeated the fuel economy estimate and added, "Just drive the Hybrid like you would a conventional car and save on fuel bills."

Paduano drove the vehicle for about a year but was frustrated with its fuel economy performance, which was less than half of the EPA estimate. A service employee at a Honda dealership told him that to achieve the estimate he would have to drive differently. The employee said, "It is very difficult to get MPG on [the] highway and to drive with traffic in a safe manner." The required "special" manner "would create a driving hazard." Paduano asked American Honda Motor Company to repurchase the vehicle. Honda refused.

Paduano filed a suit in a California state court against the automaker, alleging, among other things, deceptive advertising in violation of the state's Consumer Legal Remedies Act and Unfair Competition Law. Honda argued that the federal Energy Policy and Conservation Act (EPCA), which prescribed the EPA fuel economy estimate, preempted Paduano's claims. The court issued a summary judgment in Honda's favor. Paduano appealed to a state intermediate appellate court.

MAJORITY OPINION

AARON, J. [Judge]

* * * *

The basic rules of preemption are not in dispute: *Under the supremacy clause of the United States Constitution, Congress has the power to preempt state law concerning matters that lie within the authority of Congress.* In determining whether federal law preempts state law, a court's task is to discern congressional intent. Congress's express intent in this regard will be found when Congress explicitly states that it is preempting state authority. [Emphasis added.]

* * * *

Honda * * * argues that [the EPCA] prevents Paduano from pursuing his * * * claims. That provision states in pertinent part,

> When a requirement under [the EPCA] is in effect, a State or a political subdivision of a State may adopt or enforce a law or regulation on disclosure of fuel economy or fuel operating costs for an automobile covered by [the EPCA] only if the law or regulation is identical to that requirement.

* * * Honda goes on to assert that "Paduano's deceptive advertising and misrepresentation claims would impose *non* identical disclosure requirements."

Contrary to Honda's characterization * * *, Paduano's claims are based on statements Honda made in its advertising brochure to the effect that one may drive a Civic Hybrid in the same manner as one would a conventional car, and need not do anything "special," in order to achieve the beneficial fuel economy of the EPA estimates. * * * Paduano is challenging * * * Honda's * * * commentary in which it alludes to those estimates in a manner that may give consumers the misimpression that they will be able to achieve mileage close to the EPA estimates while driving a Honda hybrid in the same manner as they would a conventional vehicle. Paduano does not seek to require Honda to provide "additional alleged facts" regarding the Civic Hybrid's fuel economy, as Honda suggests, but rather, seeks to prevent Honda from making misleading claims about how easy it is to achieve better fuel economy. Contrary to Honda's assertions, if Paduano were to prevail on his claims, Honda would not have to do anything differently with regard to its disclosure of the EPA mileage estimates.

* * * *

* * * [The EPCA's] express preemption provisions do not purport to take away states' power to regulate the advertising of new vehicles, even when that advertising includes the EPA mileage estimates. *As long as a state's regulation does not require a manufacturer to provide a fuel estimate different from the EPA fuel economy estimate, or to make claims that go beyond, or are contrary to, what the federal scheme requires, the EPCA does not preempt such regulation.* * * * Allowing states to regulate false advertising and unfair business practices may further the goals of the EPCA, and we reject Honda's claim. [Emphasis added.]

* * * *

* * * We * * * conclude that federal law does not preempt Paduano's claims concerning Honda's advertising.

* * * *

The summary judgment is reversed. * * * The matter is remanded to the trial court for further proceedings.

DISSENTING OPINION

O'ROURKE, J. [Judge], * * * **dissenting** * * * .

* * * In my view, Paduano's false advertising claims under the Consumer Legal Remedies Act (CLRA) and Unfair Competition Law (UCL) are * * * preempted by the Energy Policy and Conservation Act of 1975 (EPCA) because those claims are necessarily predicated on Honda's representations about fuel economy and the Honda Civic Hybrid's asserted failure to meet the federal Environmental Protection Agency's (EPA) estimates as to fuel economy. * * * Paduano seeks to impose a legal duty on Honda to change its disclosures concerning fuel economy to something different from the EPA estimate. In such a case, the EPCA expressly preempts enforcement of his UCL and CLRA causes of action. * * * Accordingly, I respectfully dissent from * * * the majority opinion.

* * * *

Because Paduano's sought-after relief would require that Honda change its advertising to either eliminate or reduce the EPA mileage estimate, or include additional disclosures relating to the EPA mileage estimate and his car's fuel economy, his state law false advertising claims fail under express preemption principles as imposing a legal obligation related to fuel economy standards or they fail because they would impose disclosure requirements concerning fuel economy that are not identical to the EPCA.

This conclusion as to preemption is not impacted by the fact that Paduano's claims are made under consumer protection laws. A presumption against preemption is characteristically applied where the field is one that the states have traditionally occupied and regulated, but such a presumption is not triggered when the state regulates in an area where there has been a history of significant federal presence. In my view, the EPCA and its corresponding federal regulations reflect a significant federal presence with respect to the measurement and disclosure of automobile fuel economy estimates and standards, as well as the advertising concerning a new vehicle's fuel economy.

QUESTIONS FOR ANALYSIS

1. **Law.** What was the majority's decision on the principal issue before the court in this case? What were the reasons for this decision?
2. **Law.** How would the dissent apply the law to the facts differently than the majority did? What were the dissent's reasons?
3. **Ethics.** Suppose that the defendant automaker opposed this action solely to avoid paying for a car that had proved to be a "lemon." Would this have been unethical? Explain.
4. **Economic Dimensions.** Is either the majority's ruling or the dissent's position more favorable for the auto market? Why or why not?
5. **Implications for the Businessperson.** What does the interpretation of the law in this case suggest to businesspersons who sell products labeled with statements mandated by federal or state law?

Unit Two

Torts and Crimes

Unit Contents

4 Torts and Cyber Torts

5 Intellectual Property and Internet Law

6 Criminal Law and Cyber Crime

(Flickr/PetroleumJelliffe)

Chapter 4

Torts and Cyber Torts

Learning Objectives

After reading this chapter, you should be able to answer the following questions:

1. What is a tort?
2. What is the purpose of tort law? What are two basic categories of torts?
3. What are the four elements of negligence?
4. What is meant by strict liability? In what circumstances is strict liability applied?
5. What is a cyber tort, and how are tort theories being applied in cyberspace?

The Learning Objectives above are designed to help improve your understanding of the chapter.

(Flickr/PetroleumJelliffe)

Torts are wrongful actions.[1] Through tort law, society tries to ensure that those who have suffered injuries as a result of the wrongful conduct of others receive compensation from the wrongdoers. Although some torts, such as assault and trespass, originated in the English common law, the field of tort law continues to expand. As new ways to commit wrongs are discovered, such as the use of the Internet to commit wrongful acts, the courts are extending tort law to cover these wrongs. Many of the lawsuits brought by or against business firms are based on the tort theories discussed in this chapter. Some of the torts examined here can occur in any context, including the business environment. Others, traditionally referred to as **business torts,** involve wrongful interference with the business rights of others. Business torts include such vague concepts as *unfair competition* and *wrongfully interfering with the business relations of another.*

Torts committed via the Internet are sometimes referred to as **cyber torts.** We look at how the courts have applied traditional tort law to wrongful actions in the online environment in the concluding pages of this chapter.

1. The word *tort* is French for "wrong."

The Basis of Tort Law

Two notions serve as the basis of all torts: wrongs and compensation. Tort law is designed to compensate those who have suffered a loss or injury due to another person's wrongful act. In a tort action, one person or group brings a personal suit against another person or group to obtain compensation (monetary damages) or other relief for the harm suffered.

The Purpose of Tort Law

Generally, the purpose of tort law is to provide remedies for the invasion of various *protected interests.* Society recognizes an interest in personal physical safety, and tort law provides remedies for acts that cause physical injury or interfere with physical security and freedom of movement. Society recognizes an interest in protecting real and personal property, and tort law provides remedies for acts that cause destruction or damage to property. Society also recognizes an interest in protecting certain intangible interests, such as personal privacy, family relations, reputation, and dignity, and tort law provides remedies for invasion of these protected interests.

Damages Available in Tort Actions

Because the purpose of tort law is to compensate the injured party for the damage suffered, it is important to have a basic understanding of the types of damages that plaintiffs seek in tort actions.

COMPENSATORY DAMAGES **Compensatory damages** are intended to compensate or reimburse a plaintiff for actual losses—to make the plaintiff whole and put her or him in the same position that she or he would have been in had the tort not occurred. Compensatory damages awards are often broken down into *special damages* and *general damages.*

Special damages compensate the plaintiff for quantifiable monetary losses, such as medical expenses, lost wages and benefits (now and in the future), extra costs, the loss of irreplaceable items, and the costs of repairing or replacing damaged property. **CASE EXAMPLE 4.1** Seaway Marine Transport operates the *Enterprise,* a large cargo ship, which has twenty-two hatches for storing coal. When the *Enterprise* positioned itself to receive a load of coal on the shores of Lake Erie in Ohio, it struck a land-based coal-loading machine operated by Bessemer & Lake Erie Railroad Company. A federal court found Seaway liable for negligence and awarded $522,000 in special damages to compensate Bessemer for the cost of repairing the harm to the loading boom.[2] ●

General damages compensate individuals (not companies) for the nonmonetary aspects of the harm suffered, such as pain and suffering. A court might award general damages for physical or emotional pain and suffering, loss of companionship, loss of consortium (losing the emotional and physical benefits of a spousal relationship), disfigurement, loss of reputation, or loss or impairment of mental or physical capacity.

PUNITIVE DAMAGES Occasionally, **punitive damages** may also be awarded in tort cases to punish the wrongdoer and deter others from similar wrongdoing. Punitive damages are appropriate only when the defendant's conduct was particularly egregious (bad) or reprehensible (unacceptable). Usually, this means that punitive damages are available mainly in intentional tort actions and only rarely in negligence lawsuits (*intentional torts* and *negligence* will be explained later in this chapter). They may be awarded, however, in suits involving *gross negligence,* which can be defined as an intentional failure to perform a manifest duty in reckless disregard of the consequences of such a failure for the life or property of another.

Great judicial restraint is exercised in granting punitive damages to plaintiffs in tort actions, because punitive damages are subject to the limitations imposed by the due process clause of the U.S. Constitution (discussed in Chapter 1). The United States Supreme Court has held that a punitive damages award that is grossly excessive furthers no legitimate purpose and violates due process requirements.[3] Consequently, an appellate court will sometimes reduce the amount of punitive damages awarded to a plaintiff on the ground that it is excessive and thereby violates the due process clause.

Typically, appellate courts look at the ratio of the compensatory and punitive damages awarded to a plaintiff to determine whether the punitive damages award is grossly excessive. Nevertheless, as the following case illustrates, there is no strict formula for determining whether a punitive damages award is so excessive that it violates due process.

2. *Bessemer & Lake Erie Railroad Co. v. Seaway Marine Transport,* 596 F.3d 357 (6th Cir. 2010).

3. *State Farm Mutual Automobile Insurance Co. v. Campbell,* 538 U.S. 408, 123 S.Ct. 1513, 155 L.Ed.2d 585 (2003).

Case 4.1 Hamlin v. Hampton Lumber Mills, Inc.

Supreme Court of Oregon, 349 Or. 526, 246 P.3d 1121 (2011).

FACTS Hampton Lumber Mills, Inc., operates a lumber mill in Oregon. Ken Hamlin, a temporary employee, was injured while working at the mill. The company never instructed Hamlin on how to "lock out" the machinery to clear jams safely and avoid injury. Nor did it issue him the locks necessary to do so. Instead, Hamlin was told to watch the other employees and to do what they did. On the night he was injured, Hamlin was told to stand in a specified location, which later was determined to be unsafe. When a board became wedged between a conveyor belt and a bin, Hamlin was told to grab the board, and the machinery caught his glove and mangled his thumb. Hamlin was hospitalized and unable to work for four months. During that time, the mill twice told Hamlin that his job was secure. The agency through which he had been hired also informed Hamlin that under Oregon law he had the right to be reinstated when he recovered. During his recovery, Hamlin received workers' compensation benefits, and he filed a complaint with the Oregon Occupational Safety and Health Administration (OR-OSHA, see Chapter 22). When he was ready to work, the mill refused to reinstate him on the ground that he was a "safety risk." Hamlin filed an action against the mill for failing

Case 4.1—Continues next page ➡

Case 4.1–Continued

to reinstate him and claimed that the mill was retaliating against him for filing a complaint with OR-OSHA. A jury awarded him lost wages of $6,000 and punitive damages of $175,000. The mill appealed, claiming that the punitive damages award was so "grossly excessive" that it violated due process. The appellate court agreed, finding that the ratio between the punitive and compensatory damages (plus interest) awarded in the case was 22:1–well outside the 4:1 ratio that the defendant asserted was appropriate in such cases. Hamlin appealed to the state supreme court.

ISSUE Can the award of punitive damages be significantly greater than the compensatory damages and still not violate due process?

DECISION Yes. The Supreme Court of Oregon reversed the decision of the state appellate court.

REASON The state's highest court looked at decisions of the United States Supreme Court that offered three "guideposts" to determining whether punitive damages were grossly excessive: (1) the degree to which a defendant's misconduct is reprehensible, (2) the disparity or ratio between the punitive and compensatory damages awards, and (3) how the punitive damages award compares with civil penalties authorized by statute for comparable misconduct. Although the ratio of compensatory to punitive damages is an important consideration in most cases, the state supreme court reasoned that it is not the only consideration. "A state may be unable to achieve its goals of deterrence and retribution if awards of punitive damages must, in all instances, be closely proportional to compensatory damages." The court found that when the compensatory damages award is small, the ratio between punitive and compensatory damages is of limited assistance in determining whether the amount of punitive damages violates due process. In this case, $6,000 in lost wages is a relatively small amount, but the mill's conduct was reprehensible because it acted in reckless disregard of its employees' safety. Moreover, the Oregon legislature has protected similar interests in workplace safety by requiring employers to reinstate injured workers and by authorizing punitive damages against employers who breach their obligations to employees. The court concluded that the ratio between the punitive and compensatory damages "is higher than would be constitutionally permissible if the compensatory damages were more substantial, but is not so high that it makes the award 'grossly excessive.'"

FOR CRITICAL ANALYSIS—Legal Consideration *Why has the United States Supreme Court declined to articulate a hard-and-fast rule for when the ratio between compensatory and punitive damages is too great?*

Tort Reform

Critics contend that the current tort law system encourages trivial and unfounded lawsuits, which clog the courts and add unnecessary costs. In particular, they say, damages awards are often excessive and bear little relationship to the actual damage suffered. Such large awards encourage plaintiffs and their lawyers to bring frivolous suits. The result, in the critics' view, is a system that disproportionately rewards a few plaintiffs while imposing a "tort tax" on business and society as a whole. Furthermore, the tax manifests itself in other ways. Because physicians, hospitals, and pharmaceutical companies are worried about medical malpractice suits, they have changed their behavior. Physicians, for example, order more tests than necessary, adding to the nation's health-care costs.

TORT REFORM GOALS Critics wish to reduce both the number of tort cases brought each year and the amount of damages awarded. They advocate (1) limiting the amount of both punitive damages and general damages that can be awarded; (2) capping the amount that attorneys can collect in contingency fees (attorneys' fees that are based on a percentage of the damages awarded to the client); and (3) requiring the losing party to pay both the plaintiff's and the defendant's expenses to discourage the filing of meritless suits.

TORT REFORM LEGISLATION The federal government and a number of states have begun to take some steps toward tort reform. At the federal level, the Class Action Fairness Act of 2005[4] shifted jurisdiction over large interstate tort and product liability class-action lawsuits (lawsuits filed by a large number of plaintiffs) from the state courts to the federal courts. The intent was to prevent plaintiffs' attorneys from *forum shopping*—looking for a state court known to be sympathetic to their clients' cause and predisposed to award large damages in class-action suits.

At the state level, more than twenty states have placed caps ranging from $250,000 to $750,000 on general damages, especially in medical malpractice suits. More than thirty states have limited punitive damages, with some imposing outright bans.

Classifications of Torts

There are two broad classifications of torts: *intentional torts* and *unintentional torts* (torts involving negligence). The classification of a particular tort depends largely on how the tort occurs (intentionally or negligently) and the surrounding circumstances. In the following pages, you will read about these two classifications of torts.

Intentional Torts against Persons

An **intentional tort**, as the term implies, requires *intent*. The **tortfeasor** (the one committing the tort) must intend to commit an act, the consequences of which interfere with the personal or business interests of another in a way not permitted

4. 28 U.S.C. Sections 1453, 1711–1715.

by law. An evil or harmful motive is not required—in fact, the actor may even have a beneficial motive for committing what turns out to be a tortious act. In tort law, intent means only that the actor intended the consequences of his or her act or knew with substantial certainty that certain consequences would result from the act. The law generally assumes that individuals intend the *normal* consequences of their actions. Thus, forcefully pushing another—even if done in jest and without any evil motive—is an intentional tort if injury results, because the object of a strong push can ordinarily be expected to fall down.

This section discusses intentional torts against persons, which include assault and battery, false imprisonment, infliction of emotional distress, defamation, invasion of the right to privacy, appropriation, misrepresentation, abusive or frivolous litigation, and wrongful interference.

Assault and Battery

An **assault** is any intentional and unexcused threat of immediate harmful or offensive contact, including words or acts that create in another person a reasonable apprehension of harmful contact. An assault can be completed even if there is no actual contact with the plaintiff, provided the defendant's conduct creates a reasonable apprehension of imminent harm in the plaintiff. Tort law aims to protect individuals from having to expect harmful or offensive contact.

The *completion* of the act that caused the apprehension, if it results in harm to the plaintiff, is a **battery,** which is defined as an unexcused and harmful or offensive physical contact *intentionally* performed. **EXAMPLE 4.2** Ivan threatens Jean with a gun and then shoots her. The pointing of the gun at Jean is an assault; the firing of the gun (if the bullet hits Jean) is a battery. • The contact can be harmful, or it can be merely offensive (such as an unwelcome kiss). Physical injury need not occur. The contact can involve any part of the body or anything attached to it—for example, a hat, a purse, or a chair in which one is sitting. Whether the contact is offensive or not is determined by the *reasonable person standard.*[5] The contact can be made by the defendant or by some force the defendant sets in motion—for example, throwing a rock.

COMPENSATION If the plaintiff shows that there was contact, and the jury (or judge, if there is no jury) agrees that the contact was offensive, the plaintiff has a right to compensation. There is no need to show that the defendant acted out of malice. The person could have just been joking or playing around. The underlying motive does not matter, only the intent to bring about the harmful or offensive contact to the plaintiff. In fact, proving a motive is never necessary (but is sometimes relevant). A plaintiff may be compensated for the emotional harm or loss of reputation resulting from a battery, as well as for physical harm.

DEFENSES TO ASSAULT AND BATTERY A defendant who is sued for assault, battery, or both can raise any of the following legally recognized **defenses** (reasons why plaintiffs should not obtain what they are seeking):

1. *Consent.* When a person consents to the act that is allegedly tortious, this may be a complete or partial defense to liability (legal responsibility).
2. *Self-defense.* An individual who is defending her or his life or physical well-being can claim self-defense. In situations of both *real* and *apparent* danger, a person may use whatever force is *reasonably* necessary to prevent harmful contact.
3. *Defense of others.* An individual can act in a reasonable manner to protect others who are in real or apparent danger.
4. *Defense of property.* Reasonable force may be used in attempting to remove intruders from one's home, although force that is likely to cause death or great bodily injury can never be used just to protect property.

False Imprisonment

False imprisonment is the intentional confinement or restraint of another person's activities without justification. False imprisonment interferes with the freedom to move without restraint. The confinement can be accomplished through the use of physical barriers, physical restraint, or threats of physical force. Moral pressure or threats of future harm do not constitute false imprisonment. It is essential that the person under restraint does not wish to be restrained.

Businesspersons are often confronted with suits for false imprisonment after they have attempted to confine a suspected shoplifter for questioning. Under the "privilege to detain" granted to merchants in most states, a merchant can use *reasonable force* to detain or delay a person suspected of shoplifting the merchant's property. Although laws pertaining to the privilege to detain vary from state to state, generally they require that any detention be conducted in a *reasonable* manner and for only a *reasonable* length of time. Undue force or unreasonable detention can lead to liability for the business.

Intentional Infliction of Emotional Distress

The tort of *intentional infliction of emotional distress* can be defined as an intentional act that amounts to extreme and outrageous conduct resulting in severe emotional distress to another. **EXAMPLE 4.3** A prankster telephones a pregnant woman and says that her husband and son have been in a

5. The reasonable person standard is an objective test of how a reasonable person would have acted under the same circumstances. See "The Duty of Care and Its Breach" later in this chapter on pages 78 and 79.

horrible accident. As a result, the woman suffers intense mental anguish and a miscarriage. In this situation, the woman can sue for intentional infliction of emotional distress. •

Courts in most jurisdictions are wary of emotional distress claims and confine them to truly outrageous behavior. Generally, repeated annoyances (such as those experienced by a person who is being stalked), coupled with threats, are sufficient to support a claim. Acts that cause indignity or annoyance alone usually are not enough.

When the outrageous conduct consists of speech about a public figure, the First Amendment's guarantee of freedom of speech also limits emotional distress claims.

CASE EXAMPLE 4.4 *Hustler* magazine once printed a fake advertisement that showed a picture of the Reverend Jerry Falwell and described him as having lost his virginity to his mother in an outhouse while he was drunk. Falwell sued the magazine for intentional infliction of emotional distress and won, but the United States Supreme Court overturned the decision. The Court held that creators of parodies of public figures are protected under the First Amendment from intentional infliction of emotional distress claims. (The Court applied the same standards that apply to public figures in defamation lawsuits.)[6] •

6. *Hustler Magazine, Inc. v. Falwell*, 485 U.S. 46, 108 S.Ct. 876, 99 L.Ed.2d 41 (1988).

Defamation

As discussed in Chapter 1, the freedom of speech guaranteed by the First Amendment to the U.S. Constitution is not absolute. In interpreting the First Amendment, the courts must balance free speech rights against other strong social interests, including society's interest in preventing and redressing attacks on reputation.

Defamation of character involves wrongfully hurting a person's good reputation. The law has imposed a general duty on all persons to refrain from making *false,* defamatory *statements of fact* about others. Breaching this duty in writing or other permanent form (such as a digital recording) involves the tort of **libel.** Breaching this duty orally involves the tort of **slander.** The tort of defamation can also arise when a false statement of fact is made about a person's product, business, or legal ownership rights to property.

Often at issue in defamation lawsuits (including online defamation—see page 83) is whether the defendant made a statement of fact or a *statement of opinion.* Statements of opinion normally are not **actionable** (capable of serving as the basis of a lawsuit) because they are protected under the First Amendment. In other words, making a negative statement about another person is not defamation unless the statement is false and represents something as a fact ("Lane cheats on his taxes.") rather than a personal opinion ("Lane is a jerk.").

Whether an attorney's statement to a reporter about another attorney constituted fact or opinion was at issue in the following case.

Case 4.2 Orlando v. Cole

Appeals Court of Massachusetts, 76 Mass.App.Ct. 1112, 921 N.E. 2d 566 (2010).

FACTS In February 2005, Joseph Orlando, an attorney, was representing a high school student who had sued her basketball coach for sexual assault. The coach, Thomas Atwater, was apparently an acquaintance of Orlando's. After the alleged incident and before he had retained an attorney, Atwater approached Orlando and admitted that he had committed the act. Atwater signed an affidavit to that effect and then made a full confession to the police. A few days later, Orlando spoke to two newspaper reporters, gave them a copy of Atwater's affidavit, and explained the circumstances under which Atwater gave the affidavit. Before publishing the article, the reporters approached Garrick Cole, who was now representing Atwater, and asked for Cole's comments. Cole responded that the affidavit was "inaccurate" and called Orlando's actions "deceitful" and "fraudulent." The article further stated that "Cole would not say what he thought was inaccurate in the affidavit." Both Orlando's and Cole's comments were reported together in various publications. Orlando sued Cole for slander in a Massachusetts state court, alleging that Cole's comments were false, described conduct undertaken by Orlando in his profession and business, and imputed "an unfitness for or a misconduct in his office or employment." Orlando claimed that he had suffered harm to his reputation as an attorney as a result of Cole's comments. The trial court granted Cole's motion to dismiss the complaint, and Orlando appealed.

ISSUE Are Cole's statements that another attorney filed an "inaccurate" affidavit and engaged in "fraudulent" and "deceptive" conduct with regard to a case statements of fact that give rise to a defamation claim?

DECISION Yes. The Appeals Court of Massachusetts reversed the trial court's judgment and held that Cole's statements were "reasonably susceptible of a defamatory connotation [implication]." The appellate court remanded the case to allow for a jury trial.

REASON The reviewing court reasoned that the dismissal was premature by pointing out that "a statement is defamatory in the circumstances if it discredits a person in the minds of any considerable and respectable

Case 4.2–Continued

class of the community." The terms that Cole had used–"inaccurate," "fraudulent," and "deceitful"–implied professional misconduct. Further, those statements are capable of being proven false in a trial. They were not comments simply presented as opinions, nor did any cautionary language accompany them. They appeared to be based on undisclosed defamatory facts. A jury should be allowed to decide whether defamation had occurred.

FOR CRITICAL ANALYSIS—Legal Consideration *Orlando sued Cole for slander. Why didn't he sue Cole for libel, given that the comments were reported in various news publications?*

THE PUBLICATION REQUIREMENT The basis of the tort of defamation is the publication of a statement or statements that hold an individual up to contempt, ridicule, or hatred. In this instance, *publication* means that the defamatory statements are communicated to persons other than the defamed party. **EXAMPLE 4.5** If Thompson writes Andrews a private letter accusing him of embezzling funds, the action does not constitute libel. If Peters falsely states that Gordon is dishonest and incompetent when no one else is around, the action does not constitute slander. In neither situation was the message communicated to a third party. ●

The courts generally have held that even dictating a letter to a secretary constitutes publication, although the publication may be *privileged* (privileged communications will be discussed shortly). Moreover, if a third party merely overhears defamatory statements by chance, the courts usually hold that this also constitutes publication. Defamatory statements made via the Internet are also actionable. Note further that any individual who republishes or repeats defamatory statements is liable even if that person reveals the source of such statements.

DAMAGES FOR LIBEL Once a defendant's liability for libel is established, general damages are presumed as a matter of law. As mentioned earlier, general damages are designed to compensate the plaintiff for nonspecific harms such as disgrace or dishonor in the eyes of the community, humiliation, injured reputation, and emotional distress—harms that are difficult to measure. In other words, to recover damages in a libel case, the plaintiff need not prove that she or he was actually injured in any way as a result of the libelous statement.

DAMAGES FOR SLANDER In contrast to cases alleging libel, in a case alleging slander, the plaintiff must prove special damages to establish the defendant's liability. In other words, the plaintiff must show that the slanderous statement caused the plaintiff to suffer actual economic or monetary losses. Unless this initial hurdle of proving special damages is overcome, a plaintiff alleging slander normally cannot go forward with the suit and recover any damages. This requirement is imposed in cases involving slander because slanderous statements have a temporary quality. In contrast, a libelous (written) statement has the quality of permanence, can be circulated widely, and usually results from some degree of deliberation on the part of the author.

Exceptions to the burden of proving special damages in cases alleging slander are made for certain types of slanderous statements. If a false statement constitutes "slander *per se,*" no proof of special damages is required for it to be actionable. The following four types of utterances are considered to be slander *per se:*

1. A statement that another has a particular type of disease (historically, leprosy and sexually transmitted diseases, but now also including allegations of mental illness).
2. A statement that another has committed improprieties while engaging in a business, profession, or trade.
3. A statement that another has committed or has been imprisoned for a serious crime.
4. A statement that a person (usually only unmarried persons and sometimes only women) is unchaste or has engaged in serious sexual misconduct.

DEFENSES AGAINST DEFAMATION Truth is normally an absolute defense against a defamation charge. In other words, if the defendant in a defamation suit can prove that his or her allegedly defamatory statements were true, normally no tort has been committed. Other defenses to defamation may exist if the statement is privileged or concerns a public figure. Note that the majority of defamation actions in the United States are filed in state courts, and the states may differ both in how they define defamation and in the particular defenses they allow, such as privilege.

Privileged Communications. In some circumstances, a person will not be liable for defamatory statements because she or he enjoys a **privilege**, or immunity. Privileged communications are of two types: absolute and qualified.[7] Only in judicial proceedings and certain government proceedings is an *absolute* privilege granted. Thus, statements made in a courtroom by attorneys and judges during a trial are absolutely privileged,

7. Note that the term *privileged communication* in this context is not the same as privileged communication between a professional, such as an attorney, and his or her client.

as are statements made by government officials during legislative debate.

In other situations, a person will not be liable for defamatory statements because he or she has a *qualified,* or conditional, privilege. An employer's statements in written evaluations of employees are an example of a qualified privilege. Generally, if the statements are made in good faith and the publication is limited to those who have a legitimate interest in the communication, the statements fall within the area of qualified privilege.

EXAMPLE 4.6 Jorge applies for membership at the local country club. After the country club's board rejects his application, Jorge sues the club's office manager for making allegedly defamatory statements to the board concerning a conversation she had with Jorge. Assuming that the office manager had simply relayed what she thought was her duty to convey to the club's board, her statements would likely be protected by qualified privilege. •

The concept of conditional privilege rests on the assumption that in some situations, the right to know or speak is paramount to the right not to be defamed. Only if the privilege is abused or the statement is knowingly false or malicious will the person be liable for damages.

Public Figures. Public officials who exercise substantial governmental power and any persons in the public limelight are considered *public figures.* In general, public figures are considered fair game, and false and defamatory statements about them that appear in the media will not constitute defamation unless the statements are made with **actual malice.** To be made with actual malice, a statement must be made *with either knowledge of falsity or a reckless disregard of the truth.* Statements made about public figures, especially when the statements are made via a public medium, usually are related to matters of general interest. They are made about people who substantially affect all of us.

Furthermore, public figures generally have some access to a public medium for answering disparaging (belittling, discrediting) falsehoods about themselves; private individuals do not. For these reasons, public figures have a greater burden of proof in defamation cases (they must prove actual malice) than do private individuals.

CASE EXAMPLE 4.7 Lynne Spears, the mother of pop star Britney Spears, wrote a book in which she claimed that Sam Lutfi, Britney's former business manager, contributed to a mental breakdown that Britney experienced in 2008. Among other things, the book stated that Lutfi hid psychiatric drugs in Britney's food, disabled her cars and phones, and stole funds from her bank accounts. Lutfi filed a lawsuit for defamation and asserted that Lynne's statements were untrue, disparaging, and made with actual malice. A Los Angeles trial court found that Lutfi was a public figure and had presented enough evidence in his complaint for the case to go forward to trial. Lynne appealed, but the appellate court affirmed the ruling and refused to dismiss Lufti's complaint.[8] •

Invasion of the Right to Privacy

A person has a right to solitude and freedom from prying public eyes—in other words, to privacy. The United States Supreme Court has held that a fundamental right to privacy is implied by various amendments to the U.S. Constitution. Some state constitutions also explicitly provide for privacy rights. In addition, a number of federal and state statutes have been enacted to protect individual rights in specific areas. Tort law also safeguards these rights through the tort of *invasion of privacy.*

Generally, to sue successfully for invasion, a person must have a reasonable expectation of privacy, and the invasion must be highly offensive. Four acts can qualify as an invasion of privacy:

1. *Appropriation of identity.* Under the common law, using a person's name, picture, or other likeness for commercial purposes without permission is a tortious invasion of privacy. Most states today have also enacted statutes prohibiting appropriation (discussed further in the next subsection).
2. *Intrusion into an individual's affairs or seclusion.* For example, invading someone's home or illegally searching someone's briefcase is an invasion of privacy. The tort has been held to extend to eavesdropping by wiretap, the unauthorized scanning of a bank account, compulsory blood testing, and window peeping.
3. *False light.* Publication of information that places a person in a false light is another category of invasion of privacy. This could be a story attributing to the person ideas not held or actions not taken by the person. (Publishing such a story could involve the tort of defamation as well.)
4. *Public disclosure of private facts.* This type of invasion of privacy occurs when a person publicly discloses private facts about an individual that an ordinary person would find objectionable or embarrassing. A newspaper account of a private citizen's sex life or financial affairs could be an actionable invasion of privacy, even if the information revealed is true, because it is *not* a matter of legitimate public concern. Note, however, that news reports about public figures' personal lives are often not actionable because they *are* considered of legitimate public concern. For instance, when U.S. Congressman Anthony Weiner (a Democrat from New York) posted partially nude photos of himself on Twitter in 2011, it was of legitimate public concern. In contrast, the same inappropriate online communications by a neighbor might not be of legitimate public concern.

8. *Lutfi v. Spears,* 2010 WL 4723437 (2010).

Appropriation

The use by one person of another person's name, likeness, or other identifying characteristic, without permission and for the benefit of the user, constitutes the tort of **appropriation.** Under the law, an individual's right to privacy normally includes the right to the exclusive use of her or his identity.

CASE EXAMPLE 4.8 Vanna White, the hostess of the popular television game show *Wheel of Fortune,* brought a case against Samsung Electronics America, Inc. Without White's permission, Samsung had included in an advertisement a robotic image dressed in a wig, gown, and jewelry, posed in a scene that resembled the *Wheel of Fortune* set, in a stance for which White is famous. The court held in White's favor, holding that the tort of appropriation does not require the use of a celebrity's name or likeness. The court stated that Samsung's robot ad left "little doubt" as to the identity of the celebrity whom the ad was meant to depict.[9] •

The common law tort of appropriation in many states has become known as the right of publicity. Rather than being aimed at protecting a person's right to be left alone (privacy), this right aims to protect an individual's pecuniary (financial) interest in the commercial exploitation of his or her identity. Most states have also concluded that the right of publicity is inheritable and survives the death of the person who held the right. Normally, though, the person must provide for the passage of the right to another in her or his will.

CASE EXAMPLE 4.9 In a case involving Marilyn Monroe's right of publicity, a federal trial court held that Monroe's will did not specifically state a desire to pass the right to publicity to her heirs. Thus, the beneficiaries under her will did not have a right to prevent a company from marketing T-shirts and other merchandise using Monroe's name, picture, and likeness.[10] •

Fraudulent Misrepresentation

A misrepresentation leads another to believe in a condition that is different from the condition that actually exists. This is often accomplished through a false or incorrect statement. Although persons sometimes make misrepresentations accidentally because they are unaware of the existing facts, the tort of **fraudulent misrepresentation,** or fraud, involves *intentional* deceit for personal gain. The tort includes several elements:

1. The misrepresentation of facts or conditions with knowledge that they are false or with reckless disregard for the truth.
2. An intent to induce another to rely on the misrepresentation.
3. Justifiable reliance by the deceived party.
4. Damages suffered as a result of the reliance.
5. A causal connection between the misrepresentation and the injury suffered.

For fraud to occur, more than mere **puffery,** or *seller's talk,* must be involved. Fraud exists only when a person represents as a fact something she or he knows is untrue. For example, it is fraud to claim that a roof does not leak when one knows it does. Facts are objectively ascertainable, whereas seller's talk is not. "I am the best accountant in town" is seller's talk. The speaker is not trying to represent something as fact because the term *best* is a subjective, not an objective, term.

Normally, the tort of misrepresentation or fraud occurs only when there is reliance on a *statement of fact.* Sometimes, however, reliance on a *statement of opinion* may involve the tort of misrepresentation if the individual making the statement of opinion has a superior knowledge of the subject matter. For instance, when a lawyer makes a statement of opinion about the law in a state in which the lawyer is licensed to practice, a court would construe reliance on such a statement to be equivalent to reliance on a statement of fact.

Abusive or Frivolous Litigation

Persons or businesses generally have a right to sue when they have been injured. In recent years, however, an increasing number of meritless lawsuits are being filed—simply to harass the defendant. Defending oneself in legal proceedings can be costly, time consuming, and emotionally draining. Tort law recognizes that people have a right not to be sued without a legally just and proper reason, and therefore it protects individuals from the misuse of litigation. Torts related to abusive litigation include malicious prosecution and abuse of process.

If a party initiates a lawsuit out of malice and without probable cause (a legitimate legal reason), and ends up losing the suit, that party can be sued for *malicious prosecution.* In some states, the plaintiff (who was the defendant in the first proceeding) must also prove injury other than the normal costs of litigation, such as lost profits. *Abuse of process* can apply to any person using a legal process against another in an improper manner or to accomplish a purpose for which it was not designed. The key difference between the torts of abuse of process and malicious prosecution is the level of proof required to succeed.

Abuse of process does not require the plaintiff to prove malice or show that the defendant (who was previously the plaintiff) lost in a prior legal proceeding.[11] In addition, an abuse of

9. *White v. Samsung Electronics America, Inc.,* 971 F.2d 1395 (9th Cir. 1992).
10. *Shaw Family Archives, Ltd. v. CMG Worldwide, Inc.,* 486 F.Supp.2d 309 (S.D.N.Y. 2007).
11. See *Bernhard-Thomas Building Systems, LLC v. Dunican,* 918 A.2d 889 (Conn.App. 2007).

process claim is not limited to prior litigation. It can be based on the wrongful use of subpoenas, court orders to attach or seize real property, or other types of formal legal process.

Wrongful Interference

Business torts involving wrongful interference are generally divided into two categories: wrongful interference with a contractual relationship and wrongful interference with a business relationship.

WRONGFUL INTERFERENCE WITH A CONTRACTUAL RELATIONSHIP Three elements are necessary for *wrongful interference with a contractual relationship* to occur:

1. A valid, enforceable contract must exist between two parties.
2. A third party must know that this contract exists.
3. The third party must *intentionally* induce a party to breach the contract.

CASE EXAMPLE 4.10 A landmark case involved an opera singer, Joanna Wagner, who was under contract to sing for a man named Lumley for a specified period of years. A man named Gye, who knew of this contract, nonetheless "enticed" Wagner to refuse to carry out the agreement, and Wagner began to sing for Gye. Gye's action constituted a tort because it wrongfully interfered with the contractual relationship between Wagner and Lumley.[12] (Of course, Wagner's refusal to carry out the agreement also entitled Lumley to sue Wagner for breach of contract.) •

The body of tort law relating to intentional interference with a contractual relationship has expanded greatly in recent years. In principle, any lawful contract can be the basis for an action of this type. The contract could be between a firm and its employees or a firm and its customers. Sometimes, a competitor draws away one of a firm's key employees. To recover damages from the competitor, the original employer must show that the competitor knew of the contract's existence and intentionally induced the breach.

EXAMPLE 4.11 Sutter is under contract to do gardening work on Carlin's estate every week for fifty-two weeks at a specified price per week. Mellon, who needs gardening services and knows nothing about the Sutter-Carlin contract, contacts Sutter and offers to pay a wage substantially higher than that offered by Carlin. Sutter breaches his contract with Carlin so that he can work for Mellon. Carlin cannot sue Mellon because Mellon knew nothing of the Sutter-Carlin contract and was totally unaware that the higher wage he offered induced Sutter to breach that contract. •

12. *Lumley v. Gye*, 118 Eng.Rep. 749 (1853).

WRONGFUL INTERFERENCE WITH A BUSINESS RELATIONSHIP Businesspersons devise countless schemes to attract customers. They are prohibited, however, from unreasonably interfering with another's business in their attempts to gain a share of the market.

There is a difference between competitive methods and predatory behavior—actions undertaken with the intention of unlawfully driving competitors completely out of the market. Attempting to attract customers in general is a legitimate business practice, whereas specifically targeting the customers of a competitor is more likely to be predatory. **EXAMPLE 4.12** A shopping mall contains two athletic shoe stores: Joe's and SneakerSprint. Joe's cannot station an employee at the entrance of SneakerSprint to divert customers by telling them that Joe's will beat SneakerSprint's prices. This type of activity constitutes the tort of wrongful interference with a business relationship, which is commonly considered to be an unfair trade practice. If this type of activity were permitted, Joe's would reap the benefits of SneakerSprint's advertising. •

DEFENSES TO WRONGFUL INTERFERENCE A person can avoid liability for the tort of wrongful interference with a contractual or business relationship by showing that the interference was justified or permissible. Bona fide competitive behavior is a permissible interference even if it results in the breaking of a contract. **EXAMPLE 4.13** If Antonio's Meats advertises so effectively that it induces Sam's Restaurant to break its contract with Burke's Meat Company, Burke's Meat Company will be unable to recover against Antonio's Meats on a wrongful interference theory. After all, the public policy that favors free competition through advertising outweighs any possible instability that such competitive activity might cause in contractual relations. •

Although luring customers away from a competitor through aggressive marketing and advertising strategies obviously interferes with the competitor's relationship with its customers, courts typically allow such activities in the spirit of competition.

Intentional Torts against Property

Intentional torts against property include trespass to land, trespass to personal property, conversion, and disparagement of property. These torts are wrongful actions that interfere with individuals' legally recognized rights with regard to their land or personal property. The law distinguishes real property from personal property (see Chapters 27 and 28). *Real property* is land and things "permanently" attached to the land. *Personal property* consists of all other items, which are basically movable. Thus, a house and lot are real property, whereas the furniture inside a house is personal property. Cash and stocks and bonds are also personal property.

Trespass to Land

A **trespass to land** occurs anytime a person, without permission, enters onto, above, or below the surface of land that is owned by another; causes anything to enter onto the land; or remains on the land or permits anything to remain on it. Actual harm to the land is not an essential element of this tort because the tort is designed to protect the right of an owner to exclusive possession of her or his property.

Common types of trespass to land include walking or driving on someone else's land, shooting a gun over the land, throwing rocks at a building that belongs to someone else, building a dam across a river and thereby causing water to back up on someone else's land, and constructing a building so that part of it is on an adjoining landowner's property.

Trespass Criteria, Rights, and Duties Before a person can be a trespasser, the real property owner (or other person in actual and exclusive possession of the property) must establish that person as a trespasser. For example, "posted" trespass signs expressly establish as a trespasser a person who ignores these signs and enters onto the property. A guest in your home is not a trespasser—unless she or he has been asked to leave but refuses. Any person who enters onto your property to commit an illegal act (such as a thief entering a lumberyard at night to steal lumber) is established impliedly as a trespasser, without posted signs.

At common law, a trespasser is liable for damages caused to the property and generally cannot hold the owner liable for injuries sustained on the premises. This common law rule is being abandoned in many jurisdictions in favor of a *reasonable duty of care* rule that varies depending on the status of the parties. For instance, a landowner may have a duty to post a notice that guard dogs patrol the property. Also, under the *attractive nuisance* doctrine, children do not assume the risks of the premises if they are attracted to the property by some object, such as a swimming pool, an abandoned building, or a sand pile. Trespassers normally can be removed from the premises through the use of reasonable force without the owner's being liable for assault, battery, or false imprisonment.

Defenses against Trespass to Land One defense to a claim of trespass to land is to show that the trespass was warranted—for example, that the trespasser entered the property to assist someone in danger. Another defense is for the trespasser to show that he or she had a license to come onto the land. A *licensee* is one who is invited (or allowed to enter) onto the property of another for the licensee's benefit. A person who enters another's property to read an electric meter, for example, is a licensee. When you purchase a ticket to attend a movie or sporting event, you are licensed to go onto the property of another to view that movie or event. Note that licenses to enter are *revocable* by the property owner. If a property owner asks a meter reader to leave and the meter reader refuses to do so, the meter reader at that point becomes a trespasser.

Trespass to Personal Property

Whenever an individual wrongfully takes or harms the personal property of another or otherwise interferes with the lawful owner's possession of personal property, **trespass to personal property** occurs (also called *trespass to chattels* or *trespass to personalty*[13]). In this context, harm means not only destruction of the property, but also anything that diminishes its value, condition, or quality. Trespass to personal property involves intentional meddling with a possessory interest, including barring an owner's access to personal property.

EXAMPLE 4.14 Kelly takes Ryan's business law book as a practical joke and hides it so that Ryan is unable to find it for several days before the final examination. Here, Kelly has engaged in a trespass to personal property. (Kelly has also committed the tort of *conversion*—to be discussed next.) •

A complete defense to a claim of trespass to personal property is to show that the trespass was warranted. Most states, for example, allow automobile repair shops to hold a customer's car (under what is called an *artisan's lien*, which will be discussed in Chapter 19) when the customer refuses to pay for repairs already completed.

Conversion

Whenever a person wrongfully possesses or uses the personal property of another without permission, the tort of **conversion** occurs. Any act that deprives an owner of personal property or the use of that property without that owner's permission and without just cause can be conversion. Even the taking of electronic records and data can be a form of conversion.[14]

Often, when conversion occurs, a trespass to personal property also occurs because the original taking of the personal property from the owner was a trespass, and wrongfully retaining it is conversion. Conversion is the civil side of crimes related to theft, but it is not limited to theft. Even if the rightful owner consented to the initial taking of the property, so there was no theft or trespass, a failure to return the personal property may still be conversion. **EXAMPLE 4.15** Chen borrows Mark's iPod to use while traveling home from school for the holidays. When Chen returns to school, Mark asks for his iPod back. Chen tells Mark that she gave it to her little brother for Christmas. In this situation, Mark can sue Chen for conversion, and Chen will have to either return the iPod or pay damages equal to its value. •

---

13. Pronounced *per*-sun-ul-tee.

14. See, for example, *Thyroff v. Nationwide Mutual Insurance Co.*, 8 N.Y.3d 283, 864 N.E.2d 1272, 832 N.Y.S.2d 873 (2007).

Even if a person mistakenly believed that she or he was entitled to the goods, the tort of conversion may occur. In other words, good intentions are not a defense against conversion. In fact, conversion can be an entirely innocent act. Someone who buys stolen goods, for example, can be liable for conversion even if he or she did not know that the goods were stolen. If the true owner brings a tort action against the buyer, the buyer must either return the property to the owner or pay the owner the full value of the property, despite having already paid the purchase price to the thief. A successful defense against the charge of conversion is that the purported owner does not, in fact, own the property or does not have a right to possess it that is superior to the right of the holder.

Disparagement of Property

Disparagement of property occurs when economically injurious falsehoods are made about another's product or property, not about another's reputation. Disparagement of property is a general term for torts specifically referred to as *slander of quality* or *slander of title*. Publication of false information about another's product, alleging that it is not what its seller claims, constitutes the tort of **slander of quality,** or **trade libel.** To establish trade libel, the plaintiff must prove that the improper publication caused a third party to refrain from dealing with the plaintiff and that the plaintiff sustained economic damages (such as lost profits) as a result.

An improper publication may be both a slander of quality and defamation of character. For example, a statement that disparages the quality of a product may also, by implication, disparage the character of the person who would sell such a product.

When a publication denies or casts doubt on another's legal ownership of any property, and this results in financial loss to that property's owner, the tort of **slander of title** may exist. Usually, this is an intentional tort in which someone knowingly publishes an untrue statement about property with the intent of discouraging a third party from dealing with the person slandered. For instance, a car dealer would have difficulty attracting customers after competitors published a notice that the dealer's stock consisted of stolen automobiles.

Unintentional Torts (Negligence)

The tort of **negligence** occurs when someone suffers injury because of another's failure to live up to a required *duty of care.* In contrast to intentional torts, in torts involving negligence, the tortfeasor neither wishes to bring about the consequences of the act nor believes that they will occur. The actor's conduct merely creates a risk of such consequences. If no risk is created, there is no negligence. Moreover, the risk must be foreseeable—that is, it must be such that a reasonable person engaging in the same activity would anticipate the risk and guard against it. In determining what is reasonable conduct, courts consider the nature of the possible harm.

Many of the actions discussed earlier in the chapter in the section on intentional torts constitute negligence if the element of intent is missing. **EXAMPLE 4.16** Juan walks up to Maya and intentionally shoves her. Maya falls and breaks an arm as a result. In this situation, Juan has committed an intentional tort (assault and battery). If Juan carelessly bumps into Maya, however, and she falls and breaks an arm as a result, Juan's action will constitute negligence. In either situation, Juan has committed a tort. ●

To succeed in a negligence action, the plaintiff must prove each of the following:

1. *Duty*—That the defendant owed a duty of care to the plaintiff.
2. *Breach*—That the defendant breached that duty.
3. *Causation*—That the defendant's breach caused the plaintiff to suffer an injury.
4. *Damages*—That the injury suffered by the plaintiff is legally recognizable.

We discuss each of these four elements of negligence next.

The Duty of Care and Its Breach

Central to the tort of negligence is the concept of a **duty of care.** The basic principle underlying the duty of care is that people in society are free to act as they please so long as their actions do not infringe on the interests of others.

When someone fails to comply with the duty to exercise reasonable care, a potentially tortious act may have been committed. Failure to live up to a standard of care may be an act (accidentally setting fire to a building) or an omission (neglecting to put out a campfire). It may be a careless act or a carefully performed but nevertheless dangerous act that results in injury. Courts consider the nature of the act (whether it is outrageous or commonplace), the manner in which the act was performed (cautiously versus heedlessly), and the nature of the injury (whether it is serious or slight).

THE REASONABLE PERSON STANDARD Tort law measures duty by the **reasonable person standard.** In determining whether a duty of care has been breached, the courts ask how a reasonable person would have acted in the same circumstances. The reasonable person standard is said to be (though in an absolute sense it cannot be) objective. It is not necessarily how a particular person would act. It is society's judgment on how people *should* act. If the so-called reasonable person existed, he or she would be careful, conscientious, even tempered, and honest. The courts frequently use this hypothetical reasonable person in decisions relating to other areas of law as well. That individuals are required to exercise a reasonable standard of care in their activities is a pervasive concept in business law, and many of the issues discussed in subsequent chapters have to do with this duty.

In negligence cases, the degree of care to be exercised varies, depending on the defendant's occupation or profession, her or his relationship with the plaintiff, and other factors. Generally, whether an action constitutes a breach of the duty of care is determined on a case-by-case basis. The outcome depends on how the judge (or jury, if it is a jury trial) decides a reasonable person in the position of the defendant would act in the particular circumstances of the case.

THE DUTY OF LANDOWNERS Landowners are expected to exercise reasonable care to protect persons coming onto their property from harm. As mentioned earlier, in some jurisdictions, landowners are held to owe a duty to protect even trespassers against certain risks. Landowners who rent or lease premises to tenants (see Chapter 28) are expected to exercise reasonable care to ensure that the tenants and their guests are not harmed in common areas, such as stairways, entryways, and laundry rooms.

Duty to Warn Business Invitees of Risks. Retailers and other firms that explicitly or implicitly invite persons to come onto their premises are usually charged with a duty to exercise reasonable care to protect those persons, who are considered **business invitees.** **EXAMPLE 4.17** Liz enters a supermarket, slips on a wet floor, and sustains injuries as a result. The owner of the supermarket would be liable for damages if, when Liz slipped, there was no sign warning that the floor was wet. A court would hold that the business owner was negligent because the owner failed to exercise a reasonable degree of care in protecting the store's customers against foreseeable risks about which the owner knew or *should have known.* That a patron might slip on the wet floor and be injured was a foreseeable risk. The owner should have taken care to avoid this risk and warned the customer of it (by posting a sign or setting out orange cones, for example). •

The landowner also has a duty to discover and, within a reasonable amount of time, remove any hidden dangers that might injure a customer or other invitee. Store owners have a duty to protect customers from potentially slipping and injuring themselves on merchandise that has fallen off the shelves.

Obvious Risks Are an Exception. Some risks, of course, are so obvious that the owner need not warn of them. For instance, a business owner does not need to warn customers to open a door before attempting to walk through it. Other risks, however, may seem obvious to a business owner but may not be so in the eyes of another, such as a child. In addition, even if a risk is obvious, that does not necessarily excuse a business owner from the duty to protect its customers from foreseeable harm.

CASE EXAMPLE 4.18 Giorgio's Grill in Hollywood, Florida, is a restaurant that becomes a nightclub after hours. At those times, traditionally, as the manager of Giorgio's knew, the staff and customers threw paper napkins into the air as the music played. The napkins landed on the floor, but no one picked them up. One night, Jane Izquierdo went to Giorgio's. Although she had been to the club on other occasions and knew about the napkin-throwing tradition, she slipped and fell, breaking her leg. She sued Giorgio's for negligence but lost at trial because a jury found that the risk of slipping on the napkins was obvious. A state appellate court reversed, however, holding that the obviousness of a risk does not discharge a business owner's duty to its invitees to maintain the premises in a safe condition.[15] •

THE DUTY OF PROFESSIONALS If an individual has knowledge or skill superior to that of an ordinary person, the individual's conduct must be consistent with that status. Because professionals—including physicians, dentists, architects, engineers, accountants, lawyers, and others—are required to have a certain level of knowledge and training, a higher standard of care applies. In determining whether professionals have exercised reasonable care, the law takes their training and expertise into account. Thus, an accountant's conduct is judged not by the reasonable person standard, but by the reasonable accountant standard.

If a professional violates her or his duty of care toward a client, the professional may be sued for **malpractice,** which is essentially professional negligence. For example, a patient might sue a physician for *medical malpractice.* A client might sue an attorney for *legal malpractice.* We will discuss the liability of accountants and attorneys in more detail in Chapter 30.

Causation

Another element necessary to a negligence action is *causation.* If a person fails in a duty of care and someone suffers an injury, the wrongful activity must have caused the harm for the activity to be considered a tort. In deciding whether there is causation, the court must address two questions:

1. *Is there causation in fact?* Did the injury occur because of the defendant's act, or would it have occurred anyway? If an injury would not have occurred without the defendant's act, then there is causation in fact. **Causation in fact**

15. *Izquierdo v. Gyroscope, Inc.*, 946 So.2d 115 (Fla.App. 2007).

usually can be determined by the use of the *but for* test: "but for" the wrongful act, the injury would not have occurred. Theoretically, causation in fact is limitless. One could claim, for example, that "but for" the creation of the world, a particular injury would not have occurred. Thus, as a practical matter, the law has to establish limits, and it does so through the concept of proximate cause.

2. *Was the act the proximate cause of the injury?* **Proximate cause,** or legal cause, exists when the connection between an act and an injury is strong enough to justify imposing liability. Proximate cause is used by judges to limit the scope of the defendant's liability to a subset of the total number of potential plaintiffs that might have been harmed by the defendant's actions. **EXAMPLE 4.19** Ackerman carelessly leaves a campfire burning. The fire not only burns down the forest but also sets off an explosion in a nearby chemical plant that spills chemicals into a river, killing all the fish for a hundred miles downstream and ruining the economy of a tourist resort. Should Ackerman be liable to the resort owners? To the tourists whose vacations were ruined? These are questions of proximate cause that a court must decide. ●

Both of the questions listed above must be answered in the affirmative for liability in tort to arise. If a defendant's action constitutes causation in fact but a court decides that the action was not the proximate cause of the plaintiff's injury, the causation requirement has not been met—and the defendant normally will not be liable to the plaintiff.

Questions of proximate cause are linked to the concept of foreseeability because it would be unfair to impose liability on a defendant unless the defendant's actions created a foreseeable risk of injury.

The Injury Requirement and Damages

For a tort to have been committed, the plaintiff must have suffered a *legally recognizable* injury. To recover damages (receive compensation), the plaintiff must have suffered some loss, harm, wrong, or invasion of a protected interest. Essentially, the purpose of tort law is to compensate for legally recognized injuries resulting from wrongful acts. If no harm or injury results from a given negligent action, there is nothing to compensate—and no tort exists. **EXAMPLE 4.20** If you carelessly bump into a passerby, who stumbles and falls as a result, you may be liable in tort if the passerby is injured in the fall. If the person is unharmed, however, there normally cannot be a suit for damages because no injury was suffered. ●

Compensatory damages are the norm in negligence cases. As noted earlier, a court will award punitive damages only if the defendant's conduct was grossly negligent, reflecting an intentional failure to perform a duty with reckless disregard of the consequences to others.

Defenses to Negligence

Defendants often defend against negligence claims by asserting that the plaintiffs failed to prove the existence of one or more of the required elements for negligence. Additionally, there are three basic *affirmative* defenses in negligence cases (defenses that a defendant can use to avoid liability even if the facts are as the plaintiff state): *assumption of risk, superseding cause,* and *contributory and comparative negligence.*

ASSUMPTION OF RISK

A plaintiff who voluntarily enters into a risky situation, knowing the risk involved, will not be allowed to recover. This is the defense of **assumption of risk**. The requirements of this defense are (1) knowledge of the risk and (2) voluntary assumption of the risk. This defense frequently is asserted when the plaintiff is injured during recreational activities that involve known risk, such as skiing and skydiving. Note that assumption of risk can apply not only to participants in sporting events, but also to spectators and bystanders who are injured while attending those events.

Assumption of Risk Can Be Express or Implied.

The risk can be assumed by express agreement, or the assumption of risk can be implied by the plaintiff's knowledge of the risk and subsequent conduct. **EXAMPLE 4.21** Race car driver Bryan Stewart knows that there is a risk of being injured or killed in a crash whenever he enters a race. Therefore, a court will deem that Stewart has assumed the risk of racing. Of course, a person does not assume a risk different from or greater than the risk normally carried by the activity. Thus, Stewart would not assume the risk that the banking in the curves of the racetrack will give way during the race because of a construction defect. ●

Primary and Secondary Assumption of the Risk.

In some states, courts recognize two types of assumption of risk—primary and secondary. Primary assumption of risk completely bars a plaintiff's recovery because it relieves the defendant of the duty of care. Secondary assumption of risk constitutes a form of *contributory negligence* (see the facing page), which apportions fault between the parties but does not completely relieve the defendant of responsibility.

In the following case, the issue was whether a homeowner had primarily assumed the risk of injury at his house's construction site and was therefore barred from recovering for negligence on the part of the contractors.

Case 4.3 Wolf v. Don Dingmann Construction, Inc.

Court of Appeals of Minnesota, __ N.W.2d __ (2011).

FACTS Michael John Wolf contracted with Lumber One, Cold Spring, Inc., to remodel his home. Lumber One in turn awarded a subcontract to Don Dingmann Construction, Inc. Wolf lived in the house during the construction, and he was present at the job site on most days. Part of the project, which Wolf designed, included the construction of a loft. A ventilation pipe was to go from a fireplace in the den up through the loft. During construction, at Wolf's direction, the subcontractor left a large opening in the loft's floor to accommodate the pipe. One Friday, the subcontractor's owner, Don Dingmann, suggested removing the temporary stairs that led to the loft to prevent risk of injury over the weekend because guardrails had not yet been installed at the loft's edges. Wolf declined. The following Monday, while Dingmann was working in the loft, he saw Wolf climb the stairs from the den into the loft. A few minutes later, he found Wolf lying unconscious below the hole in the loft floor. Wolf filed a lawsuit in district court, alleging that Lumber One and Don Dingmann had negligently caused his fall. The defendants moved for summary judgment, arguing that they owed no duty to Wolf because the danger was open and obvious and because Wolf had assumed the risks associated with his presence on the job site. The district court agreed and granted summary judgment for the contractors. Wolf appealed.

ISSUE Did Wolf know about the risks associated with the construction site and voluntarily assume the risk of falling through a hole in the floor?

DECISION Yes. The state intermediate appellate court affirmed the lower court's judgment. Wolf undertook the risk at the construction site voluntarily, which relieved the contractors of their legal duty of care.

REASON The appellate court reasoned that "the undisputed facts establish that Wolf had personal knowledge and appreciation of the risk of falling. Wolf was familiar with the job site because he designed the loft, he lived in the home during construction, and he inspected the job site regularly." In addition, Dingmann and Wolf had discussed taking safety precautions because the loft lacked guardrails, but Wolf had declined them as unnecessary. Therefore, "even if the subcontractor was negligent by leaving the hole uncovered or failing to erect guardrails, Wolf's recovery is legally barred because primary assumption of risk is applicable when a defendant engages in negligence that is obvious."

FOR CRITICAL ANALYSIS—Ethical Consideration *Should courts apply the doctrine of assumption of risk to children? Discuss.*

When Courts Do Not Apply Assumption of Risk. Courts do not apply the assumption of risk doctrine in emergency situations. Nor does it apply when a statute protects a class of people from harm and a member of the class is injured by the harm. For instance, because federal and state statutes protect employees from harmful working conditions, employees do not assume the risks associated with the workplace. An employee who is injured generally will be compensated regardless of fault under state workers' compensation statutes (see Chapter 22).

SUPERSEDING CAUSE An unforeseeable intervening event may break the connection between a wrongful act and an injury to another. If so, the event acts as a *superseding cause*—that is, it relieves a defendant of liability for injuries caused by the intervening event. **EXAMPLE 4.22** Derrick, while riding his bicycle, negligently hits Julie, who is walking on the sidewalk. As a result of the impact, Julie falls and fractures her hip. While she is waiting for help to arrive, a small aircraft crashes nearby and explodes, and some of the fiery debris hits her, causing her to sustain severe burns. Derrick will be liable for Julie's fractured hip because the risk of hitting her with his bicycle was foreseeable. Normally, Derrick will not be liable for the burns caused by the plane crash—because the risk of a plane's crashing nearby and injuring Julie was not foreseeable. •

CONTRIBUTORY AND COMPARATIVE NEGLIGENCE All individuals are expected to exercise a reasonable degree of care in looking out for themselves. In the past, under the common law doctrine of **contributory negligence**, a plaintiff who was also negligent (failed to exercise a reasonable degree of care) could not recover anything from the defendant. Under this rule, no matter how insignificant the plaintiff's negligence was relative to the defendant's negligence, the plaintiff was precluded from recovering any damages. Today, only a few jurisdictions still hold to this doctrine.

In most states, the doctrine of contributory negligence has been replaced by a **comparative negligence** standard. Under this standard, both the plaintiff's and the defendant's negligence are computed, and the liability for damages is distributed accordingly. Some jurisdictions have adopted a "pure" form of comparative negligence that allows the plaintiff to recover, even if the extent of his or her fault is greater than that of the defendant.

For example, if the plaintiff was 80 percent at fault and the defendant 20 percent at fault, the plaintiff may recover 20 percent of his or her damages. Many states' comparative negligence statutes, however, contain a "50 percent" rule under which the plaintiff recovers nothing if she or he was more than 50 percent at fault. Following this rule, a plaintiff who is 35 percent at fault could recover 65 percent of his or her damages, but a plaintiff who is 65 percent (more than 50 percent) at fault could recover nothing.

Special Negligence Doctrines and Statutes

There are a number of special doctrines and statutes relating to negligence. We examine a few of them here.

RES IPSA LOQUITUR Generally, in lawsuits involving negligence, the plaintiff has the burden of proving that the defendant was negligent. In certain situations, however, under the doctrine of ***res ipsa loquitur***[16] (meaning "the facts speak for themselves"), the courts may infer that negligence has occurred. Then the burden of proof rests on the defendant—to prove she or he was *not* negligent. This doctrine is applied only when the event creating the damage or injury is one that ordinarily would occur only as a result of negligence.

CASE EXAMPLE 4.23 Mary Gubbins undergoes abdominal surgery and following the surgery has nerve damage in her spine near the area of the operation. She is unable to walk or stand for months, and even after regaining some use of her legs through physical therapy, her mobility is impaired and she experiences pain. In her subsequent negligence lawsuit, Gubbins can assert *res ipsa loquitur,* because the injury would never have occurred in the absence of the surgeon's negligence.[17] ●

NEGLIGENCE *PER SE* Certain conduct, whether it consists of an action or a failure to act, may be treated as **negligence *per se*** (*per se* means "in or of itself"). Negligence *per se* may occur if an individual violates a statute or ordinance and thereby causes the kind of harm that the statute was intended to prevent. The statute must clearly set out what standard of conduct is expected, when and where it is expected, and of whom it is expected. The standard of conduct required by the statute is the duty that the defendant owes to the plaintiff, and a violation of the statute is the breach of that duty.

CASE EXAMPLE 4.24 A Delaware statute states that anyone "who operates a motor vehicle and who fails to give full time and attention to the operation of the vehicle" is guilty of inattentive driving. Michael Moore was cited for inattentive driving after he collided with Debra Wright's car when he backed a truck out of a parking space. Moore paid the ticket, which meant that he pleaded guilty to violating the statute. The day after the accident, Wright began having back pain, which eventually required surgery. She sued Moore for damages, alleging negligence *per se.* The Delaware Supreme Court ruled that the inattentive driving statute set forth a sufficiently specific standard of conduct to warrant application of negligence *per se.*[18] ●

"DANGER INVITES RESCUE" DOCTRINE Sometimes, a person who is trying to avoid harm—such as an individual who swerves to avoid a head-on collision with a drunk driver—ends up causing harm to another (such as a cyclist riding in the bike lane) as a result. In those situations, the original wrongdoer (the drunk driver in this scenario) is liable to anyone who is injured, even if the injury actually resulted from another person's attempt to escape harm. The "danger invites rescue" doctrine extends the same protection to a person who is trying to rescue another from harm—the original wrongdoer is liable for injuries to an individual attempting a rescue. The idea is that the rescuer should not be held liable for *any* damages because he or she did not cause the danger and because danger invites rescue.

EXAMPLE 4.25 Ludley, while driving down a street, fails to see a stop sign because he is trying to break up a squabble between his two young children in the car's back seat. Salter, on the curb near the stop sign, realizes that Ludley is about to hit a pedestrian and runs into the street to push the pedestrian out of the way. If Ludley's vehicle hits Salter instead, Ludley will be liable for Salter's injury, as well as for *any* injuries the other pedestrian sustained. ● Rescuers may injure themselves, or the person rescued, or even a stranger, but the original wrongdoer will still be liable.

SPECIAL NEGLIGENCE STATUTES A number of states have enacted statutes prescribing duties and responsibilities in certain circumstances. For example, most states now have what are called **Good Samaritan statutes.** Under these statutes, someone who is aided voluntarily by another cannot turn around and sue the "Good Samaritan" for negligence. These laws were passed largely to protect physicians and medical personnel who voluntarily render medical services in emergency situations to those in need, such as individuals hurt in car accidents. Indeed, the California Supreme Court has interpreted the state's Good Samaritan statute to mean that a person who renders nonmedical aid is not immune from liability.[19] Thus, only medical personnel and persons rendering medical aid in emergencies are protected in California.

16. Pronounced *rehz ihp*-suh *low*-kwuh-tuhr.
17. *Gubbins v. Hurson,* 885 A.2d 269 (D.C. 2005).
18. *Wright v. Moore,* 931 A.2d 405 (Del.Supr. 2007).
19. *Van Horn v. Watson,* 45 Cal.4th 322, 197 P.3d 164, 86 Cal.Rptr.3d 350 (2008).

Many states have also passed **dram shop acts,**[20] under which a tavern owner or bartender may be held liable for injuries caused by a person who became intoxicated while drinking at the bar or who was already intoxicated when served by the bartender. Some states' statutes also impose liability on *social hosts* (persons hosting parties) for injuries caused by guests who became intoxicated at the hosts' homes. Under these statutes, it is unnecessary to prove that the tavern owner, bartender, or social host was negligent.

Strict Liability

Another category of torts is called **strict liability,** or *liability without fault.* Intentional torts and torts of negligence involve acts that depart from a reasonable standard of care and cause injuries. Under the doctrine of strict liability, liability for injury is imposed for reasons other than fault. Strict liability for damages proximately caused by an abnormally dangerous or exceptional activity is one application of this doctrine. Courts apply the doctrine of strict liability in such cases because of the extreme risk of the activity. Even if blasting with dynamite is performed with all reasonable care, there is still a risk of injury. Balancing that risk against the potential for harm, it seems reasonable to ask the person engaged in the activity to pay for injuries caused by that activity. Although there is no fault, there is still responsibility because of the dangerous nature of the undertaking.

There are other applications of the strict liability principle. Persons who keep dangerous animals, for example, are strictly liable for any harm inflicted by the animals. A significant application of strict liability is in the area of *product liability*—liability of manufacturers and sellers for harmful or defective products. Liability here is a matter of social policy and is based on two factors: (1) the manufacturer or seller can better bear the cost of injury because it can spread the cost throughout society by increasing prices of goods and services, and (2) the manufacturer or seller is making a profit from its activities and therefore should bear the cost of injury as an operating expense. We will discuss product liability in greater detail in Chapter 15.

Cyber Torts—Online Defamation

Torts can also be committed in the online environment. To date, most *cyber torts* have involved defamation, so this discussion will focus on how the traditional tort law concerning defamation is being adapted to apply to online defamation.

20. Historically, a *dram* was a small unit of liquid, and distilled spirits (strong alcoholic liquor) were sold in drams. Thus, a dram shop was a place where liquor was sold in drams.

Identifying the Author of Online Defamation

An initial issue raised by online defamation was simply discovering who was committing it. In the real world, identifying the author of a defamatory remark generally is an easy matter, but suppose that a business firm has discovered that defamatory statements about its policies and products are being posted in an online forum. Such forums allow anyone—customers, employees, or crackpots—to complain about a firm that they dislike while remaining anonymous.

Therefore, a threshold barrier to anyone who seeks to bring an action for online defamation is discovering the identity of the person who posted the defamatory message. An Internet service provider (ISP)—a company that provides connections to the Internet—can disclose personal information about its customers only when ordered to do so by a court.

Consequently, businesses and individuals are increasingly bringing lawsuits against "John Does" (John Doe, Jane Doe, and the like are fictitious names used in lawsuits when the identity of a party is not known or when a party wishes to conceal his or her name for privacy reasons). Then, using the authority of the courts, the plaintiffs can obtain from the ISPs the identity of the persons responsible for the defamatory messages.

Liability of Internet Service Providers

Recall from the discussion of defamation earlier in this chapter that those who repeat or otherwise disseminate defamatory statements made by others can be held liable for defamation. Thus, newspapers, magazines, and radio and television stations can be subject to liability for defamatory content that they publish or broadcast, even though the content was prepared or created by others. Applying this rule to cyberspace, however, raises an important issue: Should ISPs be regarded as publishers and therefore be held liable for defamatory messages that are posted by their users in online forums or other arenas?

Before 1996, the courts grappled with this question. Then Congress passed the Communications Decency Act (CDA), which states that "[n]o provider or user of an interactive computer service shall be treated as the publisher or speaker of any information provided by another information content provider."[21] Thus, under the CDA, ISPs generally are treated differently from publishers in other media and are not liable for publishing defamatory statements that come from a third party. Although the courts generally have construed the CDA as providing a broad shield to protect ISPs from liability for third party content, recently some courts have started establishing some limits to CDA immunity.

21. 47 U.S.C. Section 230.

Reviewing . . . Torts and Cyber Torts

Two sisters, Darla and Irene, are partners in an import business located in a small town in Rhode Island. Irene is also campaigning to be the mayor of their town. Both sisters travel to other countries to purchase the goods they sell at their retail store. Irene buys Indonesian goods, and Darla buys goods from Africa. After a tsunami destroys many of the cities in Indonesia to which Irene usually travels, she phones one of her contacts there and asks him to procure some items and ship them to her. He informs her that it will be impossible to buy these items now because the townspeople are being evacuated due to a water shortage. Irene is angry and tells her contact that if he cannot purchase the goods, he should take them without paying for them after the town has been evacuated. Darla overhears her sister's instructions and is outraged. They have a falling-out, and Darla decides that she no longer wishes to be in business with her sister. Using the information presented in the chapter, answer the following questions.

1. Suppose that Darla tells several of her friends about Irene's instructing her contact to take goods without paying for them after the tsunami. If Irene files a tort action against Darla alleging slander, will her suit be successful? Why or why not?
2. Now suppose that Irene wins the election and becomes the city's mayor. Darla then writes a letter to the editor of the local newspaper disclosing Irene's misconduct. If Irene accuses Darla of committing libel, what defenses could Darla assert?
3. If Irene accepts goods shipped from Indonesia that were wrongfully obtained, has she committed an intentional tort against property? Explain.
4. Suppose now that Darla was in the store one day with an elderly customer, Betty Green, who was looking for a graduation gift for her granddaughter. When Darla went to the counter to answer the phone, Green continued to wander around the store and eventually went through an open door into the stockroom area, where she fell over some boxes on the floor and fractured her hip. Green files a negligence action against the store. Did Darla breach her duty of care? Why or why not?

Terms and Concepts

actionable 72
actual malice 74
appropriation 75
assault 71
assumption of risk 80
battery 71
business invitee 79
business tort 68
causation in fact 79
comparative negligence 81
compensatory damages 69
contributory negligence 81
conversion 77
cyber tort 68
defamation 72
defense 71
disparagement of property 78
dram shop act 83
duty of care 78
fraudulent misrepresentation 75
Good Samaritan statute 82
intentional tort 70
libel 72
malpractice 79
negligence 78
negligence *per se* 82
privilege 73
proximate cause 80
puffery 75
punitive damages 69
reasonable person standard 78
res ipsa loquitur 82
slander 72
slander of quality (trade libel) 78
slander of title 78
strict liability 83
tort 68
tortfeasor 70
trespass to land 77
trespass to personal property 77

Chapter Summary: Torts and Cyber Torts

Intentional Torts against Persons (See pages 70–76.)	1. *Assault and battery*—An assault is an unexcused and intentional act that causes another person to be apprehensive of immediate harm. A battery is an assault that results in physical contact. 2. *False imprisonment*—The intentional confinement or restraint of another person's movement without justification. 3. *Intentional infliction of emotional distress*—An intentional act that amounts to extreme and outrageous conduct resulting in severe emotional distress to another.

Chapter Summary: Torts and Cyber Torts—Continued

Intentional Torts against Persons—(Continued)	4. *Defamation (libel or slander)*—A false statement of fact, not made under privilege, that is communicated to a third person and that causes damage to a person's reputation. For public figures, the plaintiff must also prove actual malice. 5. *Invasion of the right to privacy*—The use of a person's name or likeness for commercial purposes without permission, wrongful intrusion into a person's private activities, publication of information that places a person in a false light, or disclosure of private facts that an ordinary person would find objectionable. 6. *Appropriation*—The use of another person's name, likeness, or other identifying characteristic, without permission and for the benefit of the user. Courts disagree on the degree of likeness required. 7. *Fraudulent misrepresentation*—A false representation made by one party, through misstatement of facts or through conduct, with the intention of deceiving another and on which the other reasonably relies to his or her detriment. 8. *Abusive or frivolous litigation*—If a party initiates a lawsuit out of malice and without probable cause (a legitimate legal reason), and ends up losing the suit, that party can be sued for the tort of *malicious prosecution.* When a person uses a legal process against another in an improper manner or to accomplish a purpose for which it was not designed, that person can be sued for *abuse of process.* 9. *Wrongful interference*—The knowing, intentional interference by a third party with an enforceable contractual relationship or an established business relationship between other parties for the purpose of advancing the economic interests of the third party.
Intentional Torts against Property (See pages 76–78.)	1. *Trespass to land*—The invasion of another's real property without consent or privilege. 2. *Trespass to personal property*—Unlawfully damaging or interfering with the owner's right to use, possess, or enjoy her or his personal property. 3. *Conversion*—Wrongfully taking personal property from its rightful owner or possessor and placing it in the service of another. 4. *Disparagement of property*—Any economically injurious falsehood that is made about another's product or property; an inclusive term for the torts of slander of quality and slander of title.
Unintentional Torts (Negligence) (See pages 78–83.)	1. *Negligence*—The careless performance of a legally required duty or the failure to perform a legally required act. Elements that must be proved are that a legal duty of care exists, that the defendant breached that duty, and that the breach caused damage or injury to another. 2. *Defenses to negligence*—The basic affirmative defenses in negligence cases are assumption of risk, superseding cause, and contributory or comparative negligence. 3. *Special negligence doctrines and statutes*— a. *Res ipsa loquitur*—A doctrine under which a plaintiff need not prove negligence on the part of the defendant because "the facts speak for themselves." b. Negligence *per se*—A type of negligence that may occur if a person violates a statute or an ordinance and the violation causes another to suffer the kind of injury that the statute or ordinance was intended to prevent. c. Special negligence statutes—State statutes that prescribe duties and responsibilities in certain circumstances, the violation of which will impose civil liability. Dram shop acts and Good Samaritan statutes are examples of special negligence statutes.
Strict Liability (See page 83.)	Under the doctrine of strict liability, a person may be held liable, regardless of the degree of care exercised, for damages or injuries caused by her or his product or activity. Strict liability includes liability for harms caused by abnormally dangerous activities, by dangerous animals, and by defective products (product liability).
Cyber Torts—Online Defamation (See page 83.)	General tort principles are being extended to cover cyber torts, or torts that occur in cyberspace, such as online defamation. Federal and state statutes may also apply to certain forms of cyber torts. For example, under the federal Communications Decency Act of 1996, Internet service providers are not liable for defamatory messages posted by their subscribers.

ExamPrep

ISSUE SPOTTERS

—Check your answers to these questions against the answers provided in Appendix G.

1 Jana leaves her truck's motor running while she enters a Kwik-Pik Store. The truck's transmission engages and the vehicle crashes into a gas pump, starting a fire that spreads to a warehouse on the next block. The warehouse collapses, causing its billboard to fall and injure Lou, a bystander. Can Lou recover from Jana? Why or why not?

2 A water pipe bursts, flooding a Metal Fabrication Company utility room and tripping the circuit breakers on a panel in the room. Metal Fabrication contacts Nouri, a licensed electrician with five years' experience, to check the damage and turn the breakers back on. Without testing for short circuits, which Nouri knows that he should do, he tries to switch on a breaker. He is electrocuted, and his wife sues Metal Fabrication for damages, alleging negligence. What might the firm successfully claim in defense?

BEFORE THE TEST

Go to **www.cengagebrain.com**, enter the ISBN 9781111530624, and click on "Find" to locate this textbook's Web site. Then, click on "Access Now" under "Study Tools," and select Chapter 4 at the top. There, you will find an Interactive Quiz that you can take to assess your mastery of the concepts in this chapter, as well as Flashcards and a Glossary of important terms.

For Review

1 What is a tort?
2 What is the purpose of tort law? What are two basic categories of torts?
3 What are the four elements of negligence?
4 What is meant by strict liability? In what circumstances is strict liability applied?
5 What is a cyber tort, and how are tort theories being applied in cyberspace?

Questions and Case Problems

4–1 Liability to Business Invitees. Kim went to Ling's Market to pick up a few items for dinner. It was a stormy day, and the wind had blown water through the market's door each time it opened. As Kim entered through the door, she slipped and fell in the rainwater that had accumulated on the floor. The manager knew of the weather conditions but had not posted any sign to warn customers of the water hazard. Kim injured her back as a result of the fall and sued Ling's for damages. Can Ling's be held liable for negligence? Discuss.

4–2 Question with Sample Answer Lothar owns a bakery. He has been trying to obtain a long-term contract with the owner of Martha's Tea Salons for some time. Lothar starts an intensive advertising campaign on radio and television and in the local newspaper. The advertising is so persuasive that Martha decides to break her contract with Harley's Bakery so that she can patronize Lothar's bakery. Is Lothar liable to Harley's Bakery for the tort of wrongful interference with a contractual relationship? Is Martha liable for this tort? Explain.

—For a sample answer to Question 4–2, go to Appendix E at the end of this text.

4–3 Negligence. Shannon's physician gives her some pain medication and tells her not to drive after taking it because the medication induces drowsiness. In spite of the doctor's warning, Shannon decides to drive to the store while on the medication. Owing to her lack of alertness, she fails to stop at a traffic light and crashes into another vehicle, causing a passenger in that vehicle to be injured. Is Shannon liable for the tort of negligence?

4–4 Negligence and Multiparty Liability. Alice Banks was injured when a chair she was sitting on at an Elks club collapsed. As a result of her injury, Dr. Robert Boyce performed surgery on her back, fusing certain vertebrae. However, Boyce fused the wrong vertebrae and then had to perform a second surgery to correct the error. Then, during rehabilitation at a nursing home, Banks developed a serious infection that required additional surgeries and extensive care and treatment. She sued the Elks club and Boyce for negligence. The Elks club and Boyce filed motions against each other and also sued the nursing home. After complicated holdings by lower courts, the Tennessee high court reviewed the matter. Did the Elks club have primary liability for all injuries suffered by Banks after the initial accident, or did each of the defendants contribute separately to Banks's injuries? Explain your answer. [*Banks v. Elks Club Pride of Tennessee,* 301 S.W.3d 214 (Tenn. 2010)]

4–5 Case Problem with Sample Answer The *Northwest Herald,* a newspaper in Illinois, received e-mail reports regularly from area police departments about criminal arrests. That information was published in the paper, which is proper because it is public record. One day, an e-mail was received that stated that Carolene Eubanks had been charged with theft and obstruction of justice. This information was then placed in an issue of the newspaper, which was to be published four days later. Several hours later, the police issued another e-mail, which explained that Eubanks had not been charged with anything. Instead, the correct name was Barbara Bradshaw. Due to a long weekend, the second e-mail was not noticed until after the paper had been published. The following day, five days after the e-mails had been received, a correction was published. Eubanks sued the paper for libel and for invasion of privacy. Do you think Eubanks has a good case for either tort? Why or why not? [*Eubanks v. Northwest Herald Newspapers,* 397 Ill.App.3d 746, 922 N.E.2d 1196 (2010)]

—To view a sample answer for Problem 4–5, go to Appendix F at the end of this text.

4–6 Proximate Cause. Sixteen-year-old Galen Stoller was killed at a railroad crossing when an AMTRAK passenger train hit the vehicle he was driving on a county road in Rowe, New Mexico. His parents, Maida Henderson and Ken Stoller, filed a lawsuit against Burlington Northern & Santa Fe Railroad Corp. (BNSF), among others. The parents accused the railroad of negligence in the design and maintenance of the crossing. Specifically, they claimed that the railroad had failed to (1) clear excessive vegetation from the crossing area and (2) install active warning devices (such as flashing lights, bells, or gates to warn of approaching trains). The crossing was marked with a stop sign and a railroad-crossing symbol. Submitted photos revealed that the sign was unobstructed. Although it was clear that Galen's car was on the tracks when the train collided with the vehicle, the parties disputed whether Galen had stopped at the stop sign. New Mexico law requires "a traveler approaching an open, unguarded railroad crossing . . . to stop, look and listen for trains using the tracks." Under state law, a driver's failure to "stop, look and listen" will be deemed the sole proximate cause of the collision, unless sufficient evidence exists from which a jury could conclude that the railroad was also negligent. The district court granted a summary judgment in favor of the railroad, and the plaintiffs appealed. Was there sufficient evidence that the railroad was negligent? How should the appellate court rule concerning the proximate cause of the accident? Explain. [*Henderson v. National Railroad Passenger Corp.,* __ F.3d __ (10th Cir. 2011)]

4–7 Wrongful Interference. Medtronic, Inc., is a diversified medical technology company that develops therapies to treat a variety of medical conditions. The market is highly competitive, and Medtronic competes nationally and internationally with St. Jude Medical S.C., Inc. James Hughes worked for Medtronic as a district sales manager in Birmingham, Alabama. Hughes's employment contract prohibited him from working on competitors' products for one year after leaving Medtronic. After thirteen years with Medtronic, Hughes sought and accepted employment as a sales director for St. Jude in Orlando, Florida. In their negotiations, representatives of St. Jude told Hughes that they believed his employment contract with Medtronic was unenforceable. Medtronic filed a lawsuit in a Minnesota state court against Hughes and St. Jude, alleging wrongful interference. Which type of wrongful interference tort was most likely the basis for this lawsuit? What are its elements and defenses? Should the defendant be held liable? Why or why not? [*Medtronic, Inc. v. Hughes,* __ N.W.2d __ (Minn.App. 2011)]

4–8 A Question of Ethics *White Plains Coat & Apron Co. is a New York–based linen rental business. Cintas Corp. is a nationwide business that rents similar products. White Plains had five-year exclusive contracts with some of its customers. As a result of Cintas's soliciting of business, dozens of White Plains' customers breached their contracts and entered into rental agreements with Cintas. White Plains demanded that Cintas stop soliciting White Plains' customers. Cintas refused. White Plains filed a suit in a federal district court against Cintas, alleging wrongful interference with existing contracts. Cintas argued that it had no knowledge of any contracts with White Plains and had not induced any breach. The court dismissed the suit, ruling that Cintas had a legitimate interest as a competitor in soliciting business and making a profit. White Plains appealed to the U.S. Court of Appeals for the Second Circuit. [*White Plains Coat & Apron Co. v. Cintas Corp., *8 N.Y.3d 422, 867 N.E.2d 381 (2007)]*

1. What two important policy interests are at odds in wrongful interference cases? When there is an existing contract, which of these interests should be accorded priority?
2. The U.S Court of Appeals for the Second Circuit asked the New York Court of Appeals to answer a question: Is a general interest in soliciting business for profit a sufficient defense to a claim of wrongful interference with a contractual relationship? What do you think? Why?

4–9 Critical Thinking Legal Question What general principle underlies the common law doctrine that business owners have a duty of care toward their customers? Does the duty of care unfairly burden business owners? Why or why not?

4–10 Video Question To watch this chapter's video, *Jaws,* go to **www.cengagebrain.com**. Register the access code that came with your new book or log in to your existing Cengage account. Select the link for the "Business Law Digital Video Library Online Access" or "Business Law CourseMate." Click on "Complete Video List," view Video 56, and then answer the following questions:

1. In the video, the mayor (Murray Hamilton) and a few other men try to persuade Chief Brody (Roy Scheider) not to close the town's beaches. If Chief Brody keeps the beaches open and a swimmer is injured or killed because he failed to warn swimmers about the potential shark danger, has he committed a tort? If so, what kind of tort (intentional tort against persons, intentional tort against property, or negligence)? Explain your answer.
2. Can Chief Brody be held liable for any injuries or deaths to swimmers under the doctrine of strict liability? Why or why not?
3. Suppose that Chief Brody goes against the mayor's instructions and warns people to stay out of the water. Nevertheless, several swimmers do not heed his warning and are injured as a result. What defense or defenses could Chief Brody raise under these circumstances if he is sued for negligence?

Chapter 5

Intellectual Property and Internet Law

Learning Objectives

After reading this chapter, you should be able to answer the following questions:

1. What is intellectual property?
2. Why does the law protect trademarks and patents?
3. What laws protect authors' rights in the works they generate?
4. What are trade secrets, and what laws offer protection for this form of intellectual property?
5. What steps have been taken to protect intellectual property rights in today's digital age?

The Learning Objectives above are designed to help improve your understanding of the chapter.

(Flickr/PetroleumJelliffe)

Intellectual property is any property resulting from intellectual, creative processes—the products of an individual's mind. Although it is an abstract term for an abstract concept, intellectual property is nonetheless familiar to almost everyone. The information contained in books and computer files is intellectual property. The software you use, the movies you see, and the music you listen to are all forms of intellectual property.

A significant concern for many businesspersons is the need to protect their rights in intellectual property, which may be more valuable than their physical property, such as machines and buildings. Consider, for instance, the importance of intellectual property rights to technology companies, such as Apple, Inc., the maker of the iPhone and the iPad. Such companies derive most of their profits from their intellectual property rights, which is why Apple sued its rival Samsung Electronics Company in 2011. Apple claimed that Samsung's Galaxy line of mobile phones and tablets (which run Google's Android software) copied the look, design, and user interface of Apple's iPhone and iPad. Although Apple is one of Samsung's biggest customers and buys many of its components from Samsung, in this instance Apple was concerned about protecting its revenue from iPhone and iPad sales from competing Android products.

The need to protect creative works was first recognized in Article I, Section 8, of the U.S. Constitution (see Appendix B), and statutory protection of these rights began in the 1940s. Laws protecting patents, trademarks, and copyrights are explicitly designed to protect and reward inventive and artistic creativity. These laws continue to evolve to meet the challenges of modern society.

In today's global economy, however, protecting intellectual property in one country is no longer sufficient. Therefore, the United States is participating in international agreements to secure ownership rights in intellectual property in other countries. Protecting these rights in today's online environment has proved particularly challenging.

Trademarks and Related Property

A **trademark** is a distinctive mark, motto, device, or emblem that a manufacturer stamps, prints, or otherwise affixes to the goods it produces so that they may be identified on the market and their origins made known.

At common law, the person who used a symbol or mark to identify a business or product was protected in the use of that trademark. Clearly, by using another's trademark, a business could lead consumers to believe that its goods were made by the other business. The law seeks to avoid this kind of confusion.

In the following classic case concerning Coca-Cola, the defendants argued that the Coca-Cola trademark was entitled to no protection under the law because the term did not accurately represent the product.

Classic Case 5.1 Coca-Cola Co. v. Koke Co. of America

Supreme Court of the United States, 254 U.S. 143, 41 S.Ct. 113, 65 L.Ed. 189 (1920).

FACTS The Coca-Cola Company brought an action in a federal district court to enjoin other beverage companies from using the words *Koke* and *Dope* for their products. The defendants contended that the Coca-Cola trademark was a fraudulent representation and that Coca-Cola was therefore not entitled to any help from the courts. By use of the Coca-Cola name, the defendants alleged, the Coca-Cola Company represented that the beverage contained cocaine (from coca leaves). The district court granted the injunction, but the federal appellate court reversed. The Coca-Cola Company appealed to the United States Supreme Court.

ISSUE Did the marketing of products called Koke and Dope by the Koke Company of America and other firms constitute an unauthorized use of Coca-Cola's trademark?

DECISION Yes for Koke, but no for Dope. The Court enjoined (prevented) the competing beverage companies from calling their products Koke but did not prevent them from calling their products Dope.

REASON The Court noted that, to be sure, prior to 1900 the Coca-Cola beverage had contained a small amount of cocaine, but this ingredient had been deleted from the formula by 1906 at the latest, and the Coca-Cola Company had advertised to the public that no cocaine was present in its drink. Coca-Cola was a widely popular drink "to be had at almost any soda fountain." Because of the public's widespread familiarity with Coca-Cola, the retention of the name of the beverage (referring to coca leaves and kola nuts) was not misleading: "Coca-Cola probably means to most persons the plaintiff's familiar product to be had everywhere rather than a compound of particular substances." The name "Coke" was found to be so common a term for the trademarked product Coca-Cola that the defendants' use of the similar-sounding "Koke" as a name for their beverages was disallowed. The Court could find no reason to restrain the defendants from using the name "Dope," however.

WHAT IF THE FACTS WERE DIFFERENT? *Suppose that Coca-Cola had been trying to make the public believe that its product contained cocaine. Would the result in the case likely have been different? Explain your answer.*

IMPACT OF THIS CASE ON TODAY'S LAW *In this early case, the United States Supreme Court made it clear that trademarks and trade names (and nicknames for those marks and names, such as the nickname "Coke" for "Coca-Cola") that are in common use receive protection under the common law. This holding is significant historically because it is the predecessor to the federal statute later passed to protect trademark rights (the Lanham Act of 1946, to be discussed below).*

Statutory Protection of Trademarks

Statutory protection of trademarks and related property is provided at the federal level by the Lanham Act of 1946.[1] The Lanham Act was enacted, in part, to protect manufacturers from losing business to rival companies that used confusingly similar trademarks. The act incorporates the common law of trademarks and provides remedies for owners of trademarks who wish to enforce their claims in federal court. Many states also have trademark statutes.

Trademark Dilution Before 1995, federal trademark law prohibited only the unauthorized use of the same mark on competing—or on noncompeting but "related"—goods or services. Protection was given only when the unauthorized use would likely confuse consumers as to the origin of those goods and services. In 1995, Congress amended the Lanham Act by passing the Federal Trademark Dilution Act,[2] which allowed trademark owners to bring a suit in federal court for trademark *dilution*. Trademark dilution laws protect "distinctive" or "famous" trademarks (such as Jergens, McDonald's, Dell, and Apple) from certain unauthorized uses even when the use is on

1. 15 U.S.C. Sections 1051–1128.

2. 15 U.S.C. Section 1125.

noncompeting goods or is unlikely to confuse. More than half of the states have also enacted trademark dilution laws.

USE OF A SIMILAR MARK MAY CONSTITUTE TRADEMARK DILUTION A famous mark may be diluted not only by the use of an *identical* mark but also by the use of a *similar* mark, provided that it reduces the value of the famous mark.[3]

CASE EXAMPLE 5.1 Samantha Lundberg opened a coffee shop under the name "Sambuck's Coffeehouse" in Astoria, Oregon, even though she knew that "Starbucks" was one of the larger coffee chains in the nation. When Starbucks Corporation filed a dilution lawsuit, the federal court ruled that use of the "Sambuck's" mark constituted trademark dilution because it created confusion for consumers. Not only was there a "high degree" of similarity between the marks, but also both companies provided coffee-related services through "stand-alone" retail stores. Therefore, the use of the similar mark (Sambuck's) reduced the value of the famous mark (Starbucks).[4] •

Trademark Registration

Trademarks may be registered with the state or with the federal government. To register for protection under federal trademark law, a person must file an application with the U.S. Patent and Trademark Office in Washington, D.C. A mark can be registered (1) if it is currently in commerce or (2) if the applicant intends to put the mark into commerce within six months.

In special circumstances, the six-month period can be extended by thirty months, giving the applicant a total of three years from the date of notice of trademark approval to make use of the mark and file the required use statement. Registration is postponed until the mark is actually used. Nonetheless, during this waiting period, the applicant's trademark is protected against a third party who has neither used the mark previously nor filed an application for it. Registration is renewable between the fifth and sixth years after the initial registration and every ten years thereafter (every twenty years for trademarks registered before 1990).

Trademark Infringement

Registration of a trademark with the U.S. Patent and Trademark Office gives notice on a nationwide basis that the trademark belongs exclusively to the registrant. The registrant is also allowed to use the symbol ® to indicate that the mark has been registered. Whenever someone else uses that trademark in its entirety or copies it to a substantial degree, intentionally or unintentionally, the trademark has been *infringed* (used without authorization).

When a trademark has been infringed, the owner has a cause of action against the infringer. To succeed in a trademark infringement action, the owner must show that the defendant's use of the mark created a likelihood of confusion about the origin of the defendant's goods or services. The owner need not prove that the infringer acted intentionally or that the trademark was registered (although registration does provide proof of the date of inception of the trademark's use).

The most commonly granted remedy for trademark infringement is an *injunction* to prevent further infringement. Under the Lanham Act, a trademark owner that successfully proves infringement can recover actual damages, plus the profits that the infringer wrongfully received from the unauthorized use of the mark. A court can also order the destruction of any goods bearing the unauthorized trademark. In some situations, the trademark owner may also be able to recover attorneys' fees.

Distinctiveness of the Mark

A central objective of the Lanham Act is to reduce the likelihood that consumers will be confused by similar marks. For that reason, only those trademarks that are deemed sufficiently distinctive from all competing trademarks will be protected.

STRONG MARKS Fanciful, arbitrary, or suggestive trademarks are generally considered to be the most distinctive (strongest) trademarks because they are normally taken from outside the context of the particular product and thus provide the best means of distinguishing one product from another. Fanciful trademarks include invented words, such as "Xerox" for one manufacturer's copiers and "Kodak" for another company's photographic products. Arbitrary trademarks use common words that would not ordinarily be associated with the product, such as "Dutch Boy" as a name for paint.

A single letter used in a particular style can be an arbitrary trademark. **CASE EXAMPLE 5.2** Sports entertainment company ESPN sued Quiksilver, Inc., a maker of surfer clothing, alleging trademark infringement. ESPN claimed that Quiksilver had used on its clothing the stylized "X" mark that ESPN uses in connection with the "X Games," a competition focusing on extreme action sports such as skateboarding and snowboarding. Quiksilver filed counterclaims for trademark infringement and dilution, arguing that it has a long history of using the stylized X on its products. ESPN created the X Games in the mid-1990s, and Quiksilver has been using the X mark since 1994. ESPN, which has trademark applications pending for the stylized X, asked the court to dismiss Quiksilver's counterclaims. In 2008, a federal district court held that the X on Quiksilver's clothing is clearly an arbitrary mark. Noting that "the two Xs are similar enough that a consumer might well confuse them,"

---

3. See *Moseley v. V Secret Catalogue, Inc.*, 537 U.S. 418, 123 S.Ct. 1115, 155 L.Ed.2d 1 (2003).

4. *Starbucks Corp. v. Lundberg*, 2005 WL 3183858 (D.Or. 2005).

the court refused to dismiss Quiksilver's claims and allowed the dispute to go to trial.[5] ●

Suggestive trademarks bring to mind something about a product without describing the product directly. For instance, Blu-ray is a suggestive mark that is associated with the high-quality, high-definition video contained on a particular optical data storage disc. Although blue-violet lasers are used to read blu-ray discs, the term *blu-ray* does not directly describe the disc.

SECONDARY MEANING Descriptive terms, geographic terms, and personal names are not inherently distinctive and do not receive protection under the law *until* they acquire a secondary meaning. **CASE EXAMPLE 5.3** Frosty Treats, Inc., sells frozen desserts out of ice cream trucks. The video game series Twisted Metal depicts an ice cream truck with a clown character on it that is similar to the clowns on Frosty Treats' trucks. In the last game of the series, the truck bears the label "Frosty Treats." Frosty Treats sued for trademark infringement, but the court held that "Frosty Treats" is a descriptive term that is not protected by trademark law unless it has acquired a secondary meaning. To establish secondary meaning, Frosty Treats would have had to show that the public recognized its trademark and associated it with a single source. Because Frosty Treats failed to do so, the court entered a judgment in favor of the video game producer.[6] ●

A secondary meaning arises when customers begin to associate a specific term or phrase, such as *London Fog*, with specific trademarked items (coats with "London Fog" labels) made by a particular company. Whether a secondary meaning becomes attached to a term or name usually depends on how extensively the product is advertised, the market for the product, the number of sales, and other factors. Once a secondary meaning is attached to a term or name, a trademark is considered distinctive and is protected.

GENERIC TERMS Generic terms are terms that refer to an entire class of products, such as *bicycle* and *computer.* Generic terms receive no protection, even if they acquire secondary meanings. A particularly thorny problem for a business arises when its trademark acquires generic use. For instance, *aspirin* and *thermos* were originally trademarked products, but today the words are used generically. Other trademarks that have acquired generic use include *escalator, trampoline, raisin bran, dry ice, lanolin, linoleum, nylon,* and *cornflakes.*

5. *ESPN, Inc. v. Quiksilver, Inc.*, 586 F.Supp.2d 219 (S.D.N.Y. 2008).
6. *Frosty Treats, Inc. v. Sony Computer Entertainment America, Inc.*, 426 F.3d 1001 (8th Cir. 2005).

Service, Certification, and Collective Marks

A **service mark** is essentially a trademark that is used to distinguish the *services* (rather than the products) of one person or company from those of another. For instance, each airline has a particular mark or symbol associated with its name. Titles and character names used in radio and television are frequently registered as service marks.

Other marks protected by law include certification marks and collective marks. A **certification mark** is used by one or more persons, other than the owner, to certify the region, materials, mode of manufacture, quality, or other characteristic of specific goods or services. Certification marks include such marks as "Good Housekeeping Seal of Approval" and "UL Tested." When used by members of a cooperative, association, union, or other organization, a certification mark is referred to as a **collective mark.**

EXAMPLE 5.4 Collective marks appear at the ends of movie credits to indicate the various associations and organizations that participated in making the movie. The union marks found on the tags of certain products are also collective marks. ●

Trade Dress

The term **trade dress** refers to the image and overall appearance of a product. Trade dress is a broad concept and can include all or part of the total image or overall impression created by a product or its packaging. **EXAMPLE 5.5** The distinctive decor, menu, and style of service of a particular restaurant may be regarded as the restaurant's trade dress. Similarly, trade dress can include the layout and appearance of a mail-order catalogue, the use of a lighthouse as part of a golf hole's design, the fish shape of a cracker, or the G-shaped design of a Gucci watch. ●

Basically, trade dress is subject to the same protection as trademarks. In cases involving trade dress infringement, as in trademark infringement cases, a major consideration is whether consumers are likely to be confused by the allegedly infringing use.

Counterfeit Goods

Counterfeit goods copy or otherwise imitate trademarked goods, but they are not the genuine trademarked goods. The importation of goods bearing counterfeit (fake) trademarks poses a growing problem for U.S. businesses, consumers, and law enforcement. In addition to having negative financial effects on legitimate businesses, sales of certain counterfeit goods, such as pharmaceuticals and nutritional supplements, can present serious public health risks. It is estimated that nearly 7 percent of the goods imported into the United States are counterfeit.

THE STOP COUNTERFEITING IN MANUFACTURED GOODS ACT Congress enacted the Stop Counterfeiting in Manufactured Goods Act[7] (SCMGA) to combat counterfeit goods. The act made it a crime to intentionally traffic in, or attempt to traffic in, counterfeit goods or services, or to knowingly use a counterfeit mark on or in connection with goods or services. Before this act, the law did not prohibit the creation or shipment of counterfeit labels that were not attached to a product.[8] Therefore, counterfeiters would make labels and packaging bearing a fake trademark, ship the labels to another location, and then affix them to inferior products to deceive buyers. The SCMGA closed this loophole by making it a crime to traffic in counterfeit labels, stickers, packaging, and the like, whether or not they are attached to goods.

PENALTIES FOR COUNTERFEITING Persons found guilty of violating the SCMGA may be fined up to $2 million or imprisoned for up to ten years (or more if they are repeat offenders). If a court finds that the statute was violated, it must order the defendant to forfeit the counterfeit products (which are then destroyed), as well as any property used in the commission of the crime. The defendant must also pay restitution to the trademark holder or victim in an amount equal to the victim's actual loss. **CASE EXAMPLE 5.6** Wajdi Beydoun pleaded guilty to conspiring to import cigarette-rolling papers from Mexico that were falsely marked as "Zig-Zags" and sell them in the United States. The defendant was sentenced to prison and ordered to pay $566,267 in restitution. On appeal, the court affirmed the prison sentence but ordered the trial court to reduce the amount of restitution because it exceeded the actual loss suffered by the legitimate sellers of Zig-Zag rolling papers.[9] •

Trade Names

Trademarks apply to *products*. The term **trade name** is used to indicate part or all of a business's name, whether the business is a sole proprietorship, a partnership, or a corporation. Generally, a trade name is directly related to a business and its goodwill. A trade name may be protected as a trademark if it is the same as the company's trademarked product—for example, Coca-Cola. Unless it is also used as a trademark or service mark, a trade name cannot be registered with the federal government. A trade name is protected under the common law, however. As with trademarks, words must be unusual or fancifully used if they are to be protected as trade names. For instance, the courts held that the word *Safeway* was sufficiently fanciful to obtain protection as a trade name for a grocery chain.

7. Pub. L. No. 109-181 (2006), which amended 18 U.S.C. Sections 2318–2320.

8. See, for example, *Commonwealth v. Crespo,* 884 A.2d 960 (Pa. 2005).

9. *United States v. Beydoun,* 469 F.3d 102 (5th Cir. 2006).

Cyber Marks

In cyberspace, trademarks are sometimes referred to as **cyber marks.** We turn now to a discussion of how new laws and the courts are addressing trademark-related issues in cyberspace.

Domain Names

As e-commerce expanded worldwide, one issue that emerged involved the rights of a trademark owner to use the mark as part of a domain name. A **domain name** is part of an Internet address, such as "westlaw.com." Every domain name ends with a top level domain (TLD), which is the part to the right of the period that indicates the type of entity that operates the site (for example, *com* is an abbreviation for "commercial").

The second level domain (SLD)—the part of the name to the left of the period—is chosen by the business entity or individual registering the domain name. Competition for SLDs among firms with similar names and products has led to numerous disputes. By using the same, or a similar, domain name, parties have attempted to profit from a competitor's goodwill, sell pornography, offer for sale another party's domain name, or otherwise infringe on others' trademarks.

The Internet Corporation for Assigned Names and Numbers (ICANN), a nonprofit corporation, oversees the distribution of domain names and operates an online arbitration system. In 2011, ICANN's board of directors approved a significant change to the domain name system. The board voted to implement a plan that will dramatically increase the number of Internet domain name endings—by allowing generic TLDs, or gTLDs. In short, organizations can now apply for new domain names that can end with almost any word in any language. Despite the $185,000 application fee and $25,000 annual fee, ICANN anticipates that many companies and corporations will want gTLDs based on their brands. For example, Apple, Inc., might apply for a gTLD ending in *.ipad* or *.imac*, or Coca-Cola may want *.coke*. Many agree that gTLDs will inspire innovation and creativity, and provide firms with new ways to use the Internet.

Anticybersquatting Legislation

Cybersquatting occurs when a person registers a domain name that is the same as, or confusingly similar to, the trademark of another and then offers to sell the domain name back to the trademark owner. During the 1990s, cybersquatting led to so much litigation that Congress passed the Anticybersquatting Consumer Protection Act (ACPA) of 1999, which amended the Lanham Act—the federal law protecting trademarks discussed earlier. The ACPA makes it illegal to "register, traffic in, or use" a domain name (1) if the name is identical or confusingly similar to the trademark of another and (2) if the person registering, trafficking in, or using the domain name has a "bad faith intent" to profit from that trademark.

THE ONGOING PROBLEM OF CYBERSQUATTING Despite the ACPA, cybersquatting continues to present a problem for businesses, largely because more TLDs are now available and many more companies are registering domain names. Indeed, domain name registrars have proliferated. These companies charge a fee to businesses and individuals to register new names and to renew annual registrations (often through automated software). Many of these companies also buy and sell expired domain names. Although all registrars are supposed to relay information about these transactions to ICANN and the other companies that keep a master list of domain names, this does not always occur. The speed at which domain names change hands and the difficulty in tracking mass automated registrations have created an environment in which cyber-squatting can flourish.

Cybersquatters have also developed new tactics, such as *typosquatting* (registering a name that is a misspelling of a popular brand, for example, hotmial.com or myspac.com). Because many Internet users are not perfect typists, Web pages using these misspelled names can generate significant traffic. More traffic generally means increased profits (advertisers often pay Web sites based on the number of unique visits, or hits), which in turn provides incentive for more cybersquatters. Also, if the misspelling is significant, the trademark owner may have difficulty proving that the name is identical or confusingly similar to the owner's mark, as required by the ACPA.

Cybersquatting is costly for businesses, which must attempt to register all variations of a name to protect their domain name rights from would-be cybersquatters. Large corporations may have to register thousands of domain names across the globe just to protect their basic brands and trademarks.

APPLICABILITY OF THE ACPA AND SANCTIONS UNDER THE ACT The ACPA applies to all domain name registrations of trademarks. Successful plaintiffs in suits brought under the act can collect actual damages and profits or elect to receive statutory damages that range from $1,000 to $100,000.

Although some companies have successfully sued under the ACPA, there are roadblocks to pursuing such lawsuits. Some domain name registrars offer privacy services that hide the true owners of Web sites, making it difficult for trademark owners to identify cybersquatters. Thus, before a trademark owner can bring a suit, he or she has to ask the court for a subpoena to discover the identity of the owner of the infringing Web site. Because of the high costs of court proceedings, discovery, and even arbitration, many disputes over cybersquatting are settled out of court.

Meta Tags

Search engines compile their results by looking through a Web site's key-word field. *Meta tags,* or key words, may be inserted into this field to increase the likelihood that a site will be included in search engine results, even though the site may have nothing to do with the inserted words. Using this same technique, one site may appropriate the key words of other sites with more frequent hits so that the appropriating site appears in the same search engine results as the more popular sites. Using another's trademark in a meta tag without the owner's permission, however, normally constitutes trademark infringement.

Dilution in the Online World

As discussed earlier, trademark *dilution* occurs when a trademark is used, without authorization, in a way that diminishes the distinctive quality of the mark. Unlike trademark infringement, a claim of dilution does not require proof that consumers are likely to be confused by a connection between the unauthorized use and the mark. For this reason, the products involved do not have to be similar. **CASE EXAMPLE 5.7** In the first case alleging dilution on the Web, a court prohibited the use of "candyland.com" as the URL for an adult site. The suit was brought by the maker of the Candyland children's game and owner of the Candyland mark. Although consumers were not likely to connect candyland.com with the children's game, the court reasoned that the sexually explicit adult site would dilute the value of the Candyland mark.[10] •

Licensing

One way to make use of another's trademark or other form of intellectual property, while avoiding litigation, is to obtain a license to do so. A **license** in this context is an agreement permitting the use of a trademark, copyright, patent, or trade secret for certain limited purposes. The party that owns the intellectual property rights and issues the license is the *licensor,* and the party obtaining the license is the *licensee.*

A license grants only the rights expressly described in the license agreement. A licensor might, for example, allow the licensee to use the trademark as part of its company name, or as part of its domain name, but not otherwise use the mark on any products or services. Disputes frequently arise over licensing agreements, particularly when the license involves Internet uses. Typically, license agreements are very detailed and should be carefully drafted.

Patents

A **patent** is a grant from the government that gives an inventor the exclusive right to make, use, and sell an invention for a period of twenty years. Patents for designs, as opposed to inventions, are given for a fourteen-year period. For either a

10. *Hasbro, Inc. v. Internet Entertainment Group, Ltd.,* 1996 WL 84858 (W.D.Wash. 1996).

regular patent or a design patent, the applicant must demonstrate to the satisfaction of the U.S. Patent and Trademark Office that the invention, discovery, process, or design is *novel, useful,* and *not obvious* in light of current technology.

Until 2011, patent law in the United States differed from many other countries because the first person to invent a product or process obtained the patent rights rather than the first person to file for a patent. It was often difficult to prove who invented an item first, however, which prompted Congress to change the system in 2011 by passing the America Invents Act. Now, the first person to file an application for a patent on the product or process receives patent protection. In addition, under the new law there is a nine-month limit for challenging a patent on any ground.

The period of patent protection begins on the date when the patent application is filed, rather than when the patent is issued, which can sometimes be years later. After the patent period ends (either fourteen or twenty years later), the product or process enters the public domain, and anyone can make, sell, or use the invention without paying the patent holder.

Searchable Patent Databases

A significant development relating to patents is the availability online of the world's patent databases. The Web site of the U.S. Patent and Trademark Office provides searchable databases covering U.S. patents granted since 1976. The Web site of the European Patent Office provides online access to 50 million patent documents in more than seventy nations through a searchable network of databases. Businesses use these searchable databases in many ways. Because patents are valuable assets, businesses may need to perform patent searches to list or inventory their assets.

What Is Patentable?

Under federal law, "[w]hoever invents or discovers any new and useful process, machine, manufacture, or composition of matter, or any new and useful improvement thereof, may obtain a patent therefor, subject to the conditions and requirements of this title."[11] As mentioned, to be patentable, the item must be novel, useful, and not obvious.

Almost anything is patentable, except the laws of nature, natural phenomena, and abstract ideas (including algorithms). (See this chapter's *Adapting the Law to the Online Environment* feature on the facing page for a discussion of an emerging debate over whether business processes should be patentable.) Even artistic methods, certain works of art, and the structures of storylines are patentable, provided that they are novel and not obvious.

11. 35 U.S.C. Section 101.

Patent Infringement

If a firm makes, uses, or sells another's patented design, product, or process without the patent owner's permission, it commits the tort of patent infringement. Patent infringement may occur even though the patent owner has not put the patented product in commerce. Patent infringement may also occur even though not all features or parts of an invention are copied. (With respect to a patented process, however, all steps or their equivalent must be copied for infringement to exist.)

Patent Infringement Suits and High-Tech Companies

Obviously, companies that specialize in developing new technology stand to lose significant profits if someone makes, uses, or sells devices that incorporate their patented inventions. Because these firms hold numerous patents, they frequently are involved in patent infringement lawsuits. Many of the companies that make and sell electronics and computer software and hardware are based in foreign nations.

Foreign firms can apply for and obtain U.S. patent protection on items that they sell in the United States, just as U.S. firms can obtain protection in foreign nations where they sell goods. Nevertheless, as a general rule, no patent infringement occurs under U.S. law when a product patented in the United States is made and sold in another country by another firm. The United States Supreme Court has narrowly construed patent infringement as it applies to exported software.

CASE EXAMPLE 5.8 AT&T Corporation holds a patent on a device used to digitally encode, compress, and process recorded speech. AT&T brought an infringement case against Microsoft Corporation, which admitted that its Windows operating system incorporated software code that infringed on AT&T's patent. The case reached the United States Supreme Court on the question of whether Microsoft's liability extended to computers made in another country. The Court held that it did not. Microsoft was liable only for infringement in the United States and not for the Windows-based computers produced in foreign locations. The Court reasoned that Microsoft had not "supplied" the software for the computers but had only electronically transmitted a master copy, which the foreign manufacturers then copied and loaded onto the computers.[12] ●

Apple, Inc. v. Samsung Electronics Co. In 2011, Apple, Inc., filed a lawsuit against Samsung, alleging that Samsung's Galaxy mobile phones and tablets infringed on its patents. The complaint contained numerous claims, including infringement of trade dress (that Samsung copied the "look and feel" of Apple's iPhones and iPads) and trademarks (that Samsung's icons were nearly identical to Apple's). The

12. *Microsoft Corp. v. AT&T Corp.*, 550 U.S. 437, 127 S.Ct. 1746, 167 L.Ed.2d 737 (2007).

Adapting the Law to the Online Environment

Should the Law Continue to Allow Business Process Patents?

At one time, it was difficult for developers and manufacturers of software to obtain patent protection because many software products simply automate procedures that can be performed manually. In other words, it was thought that computer programs did not meet the "novel" and "not obvious" requirements for patents. This changed in 1981 when the United States Supreme Court held that a patent could be obtained for a *process* that incorporates a computer program.[a] Then, in a landmark 1998 case, *State Street Bank & Trust Co. v. Signature Financial Group, Inc.*,[b] a federal appellate court ruled that business processes are patentable.

Skyrocketing Demand

After the *State Street* case, numerous firms applied for and received patents on business processes or methods. Walker Digital obtained a business process patent for its "Dutch auction" system, which allows Priceline.com users to name their own price for airline tickets and hotels. Amazon.com patented its "one-click" online payment system.

The U.S. Patent and Trademark Office (USPTO) has issued thousands of business process patents, and many more applications are clogging its system. These applications frequently involve ideas about a business process, blurring the distinction between ideas (which are not patentable) and processes (which are). In addition, because business process patents often involve fields that provide services, such as accounting and finance, determining when a process originated or who first developed it can be difficult. Consequently, business process patents are more likely to lead to litigation than patents on tangible inventions, such as machines.

The *In re Bilski* Decision Significantly Limits Business Process Patents

In 2008, the same court that decided the *State Street* case made it more difficult to obtain patents for business processes when it reversed its earlier decision and invalidated "pure" business process patents.[c] In the *In re Bilski* case, two men had applied for a patent for a process that uses transactions to hedge the risk in commodity trading. The USPTO denied their application because it was not limited to a particular machine and did not describe any method for working out which transactions to perform. The men appealed.

After soliciting input from numerous interest groups, the appellate court established a new test for business process patents. A business process patent is valid only if the process (1) is carried out by a particular machine or apparatus or (2) transforms a particular article into a different state or object. Because the men's process did not meet the machine-or-transformation test, the court affirmed the USPTO's decision.

One of the dissenting judges in the *Bilski* case, Judge Haldane Robert Mayer, would have done away with business process patents altogether. He lamented that "the patent system is intended to protect and promote advances in science and technology, not ideas about how to structure commercial transactions." In Mayer's view, these patents "do not promote 'useful arts' because they are not directed to any technological or scientific innovation." Although they may use technology, such as computers, the creative part of business methods is in the thought process rather than the technology.

FOR CRITICAL ANALYSIS

Some patent experts think that the Bilski *decision, and sentiments such as those expressed by Judge Mayer, may signal an end to all business process patents in the near future. Should business process patents be severely limited or eliminated? Why or why not?*

a. *Diamond v. Diehr*, 450 U.S. 175, 101 S.Ct. 1048, 67 L.Ed.2d 155 (1981).
b. 149 F.3d 1368 (Fed.Cir. 1998).
c. *In re Bilski*, 545 F.3d 943 (Fed.Cir. 2008).

majority of the claims involved patent infringement, however. Apple claims that its design patents cover the graphical user interface, the device's shell, and the screen and button design. It also claims that it has patents covering the way information is displayed on iPhones and other devices, the way windows pop open, and the way information is scaled and rotated, as well as other aspects. Apple argues that Samsung's phones and tablets that use the Android system violate all of these patents. Although a court has ordered expedited discovery, this litigation will likely take years to resolve because of the number of claims and the complexity of the issues.[13]

13. *Apple, Inc. v. Samsung Electronics Co.*, 2011 WL 1938154 (2011). Note that Samsung has filed a countersuit against Apple.

Remedies for Patent Infringement

If a patent is infringed, the patent holder may sue for relief in federal court. The patent holder can seek an injunction against the infringer and can also request damages for royalties and lost profits. In some cases, the court may grant the winning party reimbursement for attorneys' fees and costs. If the court determines that the infringement was willful, the court can triple the amount of damages awarded (treble damages).

In the past, permanent injunctions were routinely granted to prevent future infringement. In 2006, however, the United States Supreme Court ruled that patent holders are not automatically entitled to a permanent injunction against future infringing activities. According to the Supreme Court, a patent holder must prove that it has suffered irreparable injury and that the public interest would not be disserved by a permanent injunction.[14] This decision gives courts discretion to decide what is equitable in the circumstances and allows them to consider what is in the public interest rather than just the interests of the parties. In one case, for example, a court determined that a patent holder was not entitled to an injunction against Microsoft because the public might suffer negative effects from changes in Microsoft's Office Suite.[15]

Copyrights

A **copyright** is an intangible property right granted by federal statute to the author or originator of certain literary or artistic productions. The Copyright Act of 1976,[16] as amended, governs copyrights. Works created after January 1, 1978, are automatically given statutory copyright protection for the life of the author plus 70 years. For copyrights owned by publishing houses, the copyright expires 95 years from the date of publication or 120 years from the date of creation, whichever is first. For works by more than one author, the copyright expires 70 years after the death of the last surviving author.

Copyrights can be registered with the U.S. Copyright Office in Washington, D.C. A copyright owner no longer needs to place a © or *Copr.* or *Copyright* on the work, however, to have the work protected against infringement. Chances are that if somebody created it, somebody owns it.

What Is Protected Expression?

Works that are copyrightable include books, records, films, artworks, architectural plans, menus, music videos, product packaging, and computer software. To be protected, a work must be "fixed in a durable medium" from which it can be perceived, reproduced, or communicated. Protection is automatic. Registration is not required.

To obtain protection under the Copyright Act, a work must be original and fall into one of the following categories:

1. Literary works (including newspaper and magazine articles, computer and training manuals, catalogues, brochures, and print advertisements).
2. Musical works and accompanying words (including advertising jingles).
3. Dramatic works and accompanying music.
4. Pantomimes and choreographic works (including ballets and other forms of dance).
5. Pictorial, graphic, and sculptural works (including cartoons, maps, posters, statues, and even stuffed animals).
6. Motion pictures and other audiovisual works (including multimedia works).
7. Sound recordings.
8. Architectural works.

SECTION 102 EXCLUSIONS It is not possible to copyright an *idea.* Section 102 of the Copyright Act specifically excludes copyright protection for any "idea, procedure, process, system, method of operation, concept, principle, or discovery, regardless of the form in which it is described, explained, illustrated, or embodied." Thus, others can freely use the underlying ideas or principles embodied in a work. What is copyrightable is the particular way in which an idea is *expressed.* Whenever an idea and an expression are inseparable, the expression cannot be copyrighted. Generally, anything that is not an original expression will not qualify for copyright protection. Facts widely known to the public are not copyrightable. Page numbers are not copyrightable because they follow a sequence known to everyone. Mathematical calculations are not copyrightable.

COMPILATIONS OF FACTS Unlike ideas, *compilations* of facts are copyrightable. Under Section 103 of the Copyright Act, a compilation is a work formed by the collection and assembling of preexisting materials or of data that are selected, coordinated, or arranged in such a way that the resulting work as a whole constitutes an original work of authorship. The key requirement for the copyrightability of a compilation is originality. **EXAMPLE 5.9** The White Pages of a telephone directory do not qualify for copyright protection because they simply list alphabetically names and telephone numbers. The Yellow Pages of a directory can be copyrightable, provided that the information is selected, coordinated, or arranged in an original way. Similarly, a compilation of information about yachts listed for sale may qualify for copyright protection.[17] •

Copyright Infringement

Whenever the form or expression of an idea is copied, an infringement of copyright occurs. The reproduction does not have to be exactly the same as the original, nor does it have to reproduce the original in its entirety. If a substantial part of the original is reproduced, copyright infringement has occurred.

REMEDIES FOR COPYRIGHT INFRINGEMENT Those who infringe copyrights may be liable for damages or criminal penalties. These range from actual damages or statutory damages, imposed at the court's discretion, to criminal proceedings for willful violations. Actual damages are based on the harm caused to the copyright holder by the infringement, while statutory damages, not to exceed $150,000, are provided for

14. *eBay, Inc. v. MercExchange, LLC,* 547 U.S. 388, 126 S.Ct. 1837, 164 L.Ed.2d 641 (2006).
15. See *Z4 Technologies, Inc. v. Microsoft Corp.,* 434 F.Supp.2d 437 (2006).
16. 17 U.S.C. Sections 101 *et seq.*
17. *BUC International Corp. v. International Yacht Council, Ltd.,* 489 F.3d 1129 (11th Cir. 2007).

under the Copyright Act. Criminal proceedings may result in fines and/or imprisonment. A court can also issue a permanent injunction against a defendant when the court deems it necessary to prevent future copyright infringement.

CASE EXAMPLE 5.10 Rusty Carroll operated an online term paper business, R2C2, Inc., that offered up to 300,000 research papers for sale at nine different Web sites. Individuals whose work was posted on these Web sites without their permission filed a lawsuit against Carroll for copyright infringement. A federal district court in Illinois ruled that an injunction was proper because the plaintiffs had shown that they had suffered irreparable harm and that monetary damages were inadequate to compensate them. Because Carroll had repeatedly failed to comply with court orders regarding discovery, the court found that the copyright infringement was likely to continue unless an injunction was issued. The court therefore issued a permanent injunction prohibiting Carroll and R2C2 from selling any term paper without sworn documentary evidence that the paper's author had given permission.[18] •

THE "FAIR USE" EXCEPTION An exception to liability for copyright infringement is made under the "fair use" doctrine. In certain circumstances, a person or organization can reproduce copyrighted material without paying royalties (fees paid to the copyright holder for the privilege of reproducing the copyrighted material). Section 107 of the Copyright Act provides as follows:

> [T]he fair use of a copyrighted work, including such use by reproduction in copies or phonorecords or by any other means specified by [Section 106 of the Copyright Act], for purposes such as criticism, comment, news reporting, teaching (including multiple copies for classroom use), scholarship, or research, is not an infringement of copyright. In determining whether the use made of a work in any particular case is a fair use the factors to be considered shall include–
>
> (1) the purpose and character of the use, including whether such use is of a commercial nature or is for nonprofit educational purposes;
> (2) the nature of the copyrighted work;
> (3) the amount and substantiality of the portion used in relation to the copyrighted work as a whole; and
> (4) the effect of the use upon the potential market for or value of the copyrighted work.

WHAT IS FAIR USE? Because these guidelines are very broad, the courts determine whether a particular use is fair on a case-by-case basis. Thus, even if a person who reproduces copyrighted material believes the fair use exception applies, that person may still be committing a violation. In determining whether a use is fair, courts have often considered the fourth factor to be the most important.

CASE EXAMPLE 5.11 The owner of copyrighted music, BMG Music Publishing, granted a license to Leadsinger, Inc., a manufacturer of karaoke devices. The license gave Leadsinger permission to reproduce the sound recordings, but not to reprint the song lyrics, which appeared at the bottom of a TV screen when the karaoke device was used. BMG demanded that Leadsinger pay a "lyric reprint" fee and a "synchronization" fee. Leadsinger refused to pay, claiming that its use of the lyrics was educational and thus did not constitute copyright infringement under the fair use exception. A federal appellate court disagreed. The court held that Leadsinger's display of the lyrics was not a fair use because it would have a negative effect on the value of the copyrighted work.[19] •

THE FIRST SALE DOCTRINE Section 109(a) of the Copyright Act—also known as the first sale doctrine—provides that "the owner of a particular copy or phonorecord lawfully made under [the Copyright Act], or any person authorized by such owner, is entitled, without the authority of the copyright owner, to sell or otherwise dispose of the possession of that copy or phonorecord." In other words, once a copyright owner sells or gives away a particular copy of a work, the copyright owner no longer has the right to control the distribution of that copy. Thus, for example, a person who buys a copyrighted book can sell it to another person.

In the following case, a music company sent promotional CDs to a group of people in the music industry. When those promotional CDs turned up for sale online, the music company filed a lawsuit for copyright infringement. The issue was whether the music company had given up its right to control further distribution of the promotional CDs under the first sale doctrine.

18. *Weidner v. Carroll,* No. 06-782-DRH, U.S. District Court for the Southern District of Illinois, January 21, 2010.

19. *Leadsinger, Inc. v. BMG Music Publishing,* 512 F.3d 522 (9th Cir. 2008).

Case 5.2 UMG Recordings, Inc. v. Augusto

United States Court of Appeals, Ninth Circuit, 628 F.3d 1175 (2011).

FACTS Universal Music Group (UMG) is the world's largest music company. It is made up of two core businesses–music recording and music publishing. UMG regularly ships specially produced promotional CDs to individuals such as music critics and radio programmers. The recipients have neither requested nor agreed to receive the CDs, and UMG does not receive

Case 5.2–Continues next page ➡

Case 5.2–Continued

payment for them. The CD labels state that the CDs are "the property of the record company," "licensed to the intended recipient," and for "Promotional Use Only–Not for Sale." Troy Augusto managed to obtain some of these promotional CDs from various sources and later sold them through online auction sites, such as eBay. After making several unsuccessful attempts to halt the auctions through eBay's dispute-resolution program, UMG filed a complaint in a federal district court alleging that Augusto had infringed UMG's copyrights. Augusto asserted that UMG's initial distribution of the CDs effectively transferred ownership of the CDs to the recipients. Thus, his resales were permitted under the first sale doctrine. UMG argued that the statements on the CD's labels and the circumstances of their distribution granted only a license to each recipient, not a transfer of ownership. The district court granted summary judgment in favor of Augusto, and UMG appealed.

ISSUE Did UMG, by sending promotional CDs to individuals in the music industry, lose its right to control further distribution of the CDs under the first sale doctrine?

DECISION Yes. The federal appellate court held that UMG had conveyed title of the copyrighted promotional CDs to the recipients rather than simply creating licenses.

REASON The court examined the nature and circumstances of UMG's distribution in determining that the recipients had acquired ownership of the CDs. "The promotional CDs are dispatched to the recipients without any prior arrangement as to those particular copies. The CDs are not numbered, and no attempt is made to keep track of where particular copies are or what use is made of them." Under the first sale doctrine, a copyright owner who transfers title in a particular copy to another cannot prevent resale of that copy. In addition, "although UMG places written restrictions in the labels of the CDs, it has not established that the restrictions on the CDs create a license agreement." Because there was no indication that the recipients had agreed to a license, no license was created. The court, therefore, affirmed the district court's order dismissing the copyright infringement action against Augusto.

FOR CRITICAL ANALYSIS—Social Consideration *What would be the implications for society if the first sale doctrine did not exist?*

Copyright Protection for Software

In 1980, Congress passed the Computer Software Copyright Act, which amended the Copyright Act of 1976 to include computer programs in the list of creative works protected by federal copyright law. Generally, the courts have extended copyright protection not only to those parts of a computer program that can be read by humans, such as the high-level language of a source code, but also to the binary-language object code of a computer program, which is readable only by the computer. Additionally, such elements as the overall structure, sequence, and organization of a program have been deemed copyrightable. Not all aspects of software are protected, however. For the most part, courts have not extended copyright protection to the "look and feel"—the general appearance, command structure, video images, menus, windows, and other screen displays—of computer programs.

Copyrights in Digital Information

Copyright law is probably the most important form of intellectual property protection on the Internet, largely because much of the material on the Web (software, for example) is copyrighted and in order to be transferred online, it must be "copied." Generally, anytime a party downloads software or music into a computer's random access memory, or RAM, without authorization, a copyright is infringed. Technology has vastly increased the potential for copyright infringement. **CASE EXAMPLE 5.12** In one case, a rap song that was included in the sound track of a movie had used only a few seconds from the guitar solo of another's copyrighted sound recording without permission. Nevertheless, a federal appellate court held that digitally sampling a copyrighted sound recording of any length constitutes copyright infringement.[20] •

In 1998, Congress implemented the provisions of the World Intellectual Property Organization (WIPO) treaty by updating U.S. copyright law. The law—the Digital Millennium Copyright Act of 1998—is a landmark step in the protection of copyright owners and, because of the leading position of the United States in the creative industries, serves as a model for other nations. Among other things, the act established civil and criminal penalties for anyone who circumvents (bypasses—or gets around—through clever maneuvering, for example) encryption software or other technological antipiracy protection. Also prohibited are the manufacture, import, sale, and distribution of devices or services for circumvention.

MP3 and File-Sharing Technology

Soon after the Internet became popular, a few enterprising programmers created software to compress large data files, particularly those associated with music, so that they could more easily be transmitted online. The best-known compression and decompression system is MP3, which enables music fans to download songs or entire CDs onto their computers or onto portable listening devices, such as iPods. The MP3 system also made it possible for music fans to access other fans' files by engaging in file-sharing via the Internet.

File-sharing is accomplished through **peer-to-peer (P2P) networking.** The concept is simple. Rather than going through a central Web server, P2P involves numerous personal comput-

20. *Bridgeport Music, Inc. v. Dimension Films,* 410 F.3d 792 (6th Cir. 2005).

ers (PCs) that are connected to the Internet. Individuals on the same network can access files stored on a single PC through a **distributed network,** which has parts dispersed in many locations. Persons scattered throughout the country or the world can work together on the same project by using file-sharing programs.

A newer method of sharing files via the Internet is **cloud computing,** which is essentially a subscription-based or pay-per-use service that extends a computer's software or storage capabilities. Cloud computing can deliver a single application through a browser to multiple users, or it may be a utility program to pool resources and provide data storage and virtual servers that can be accessed on demand. Amazon, Apple, Facebook, Google, IBM, and Sun Microsystems are using and developing cloud-computing services.

SHARING STORED MUSIC FILES When file-sharing is used to download others' stored music files, copyright issues arise. Recording artists and their labels stand to lose large amounts of royalties and revenues if relatively few CDs are purchased and then made available on distributed networks, from which everyone can get them for free. **CASE EXAMPLE 5.13** The issue of file-sharing infringement has been the subject of an ongoing debate since the highly publicized case of *A&M Records, Inc. v. Napster, Inc.*[21] Napster, Inc., operated a Web site with free software that enabled users to copy and transfer MP3 files via the Internet. When firms in the recording industry sued Napster, the court held that Napster was liable for contributory and vicarious[22] (indirect) copyright infringement because it had assisted others in obtaining unauthorized copies of copyrighted music. •

In the following case, a group of recording companies sued an Internet user who had downloaded a number of their copyrighted songs. The user then shared the audio files with others via a P2P network. One of the issues before the court was whether the user was an "innocent infringer"—that is, whether she was innocent of copyright infringement because she was unaware that the works were copyrighted.

21. 239 F.3d 1004 (9th Cir. 2001).

22. *Vicarious (indirect) liability* exists when one person is subject to liability for another's actions. A common example occurs in the employment context, when an employer is held vicariously liable by third parties for torts committed by employees in the course of their employment.

Case 5.3 Maverick Recording Co. v. Harper

United States Court of Appeals, Fifth Circuit, 598 F.3d 193 (2010).
www.ca5.uscourts.gov/Opinions/aspx[a]

FACTS Maverick Recording Company and several other music-recording firms (the plaintiffs) hired MediaSentry to investigate the infringement of their copyrights over the Internet. During its investigation, MediaSentry discovered that Whitney Harper was using a computer program to share digital audio files with other users of a peer-to-peer network. The shared files included a number of the plaintiffs' copyrighted works. The plaintiffs sued Harper for copyright infringement and sought $750 per infringed work (the minimum amount of damages set forth in the Copyright Act). Harper had downloaded thirty-seven copyrighted audio files. Harper asserted that she was an "innocent" infringer, citing Section 504(c)(2) of the Copyright Act, which provides that when an infringer was not aware that his or her acts constituted copyright infringement, "the court in its discretion may reduce the award of statutory damages to a sum of not less than $200." The trial court granted summary judgment for the plaintiffs on the issue of copyright infringement and prevented Harper from further downloading and sharing of the copyrighted works. The court, however, awarded the plaintiffs only $200 per infringed work. Both parties appealed. Harper claimed that there was insufficient evidence of copyright infringement. The plaintiffs argued that the district court had erred by failing to rule out the innocent infringer defense as a matter of law.

ISSUE Can a person who downloaded thirty-seven copyrighted audio files and then shared them with other users via a peer-to-peer network assert the innocent infringer defense?

DECISION No. The U.S. Court of Appeals for the Fifth Circuit affirmed the trial court's finding of copyright liability and reversed its finding that the innocent infringer defense presented an issue for trial. The court concluded that Harper was not an innocent infringer and that the district court had therefore erred in awarding damages of only $200 per infringement.

REASON The court looked at the language of the statute and determined that the innocent infringer defense is limited by Section 402(d) of the Copyright Act. "The plain language of the statute shows that the infringer's knowledge or intent does not affect its application." Harper contended that she was too young and naïve to understand that copyrights applied to downloaded music, but the court dismissed this argument. The court reasoned that the defendant's reliance on her own understanding of copyright law—or lack thereof—was irrelevant in the context of the Copyright Act. "Lack of legal sophistication cannot overcome a properly asserted limitation to the innocent infringer defense." The federal appellate court ruled that the plaintiffs must be awarded statutory damages of $750 per infringed work on remand.

a. In the box titled "and/or Title contains text," type in "Maverick." On the page that opens, click on the docket number beside the case title to access the opinion. The U.S. Court of Appeals for the Fifth Circuit maintains this Web site.

Case 5.3—Continues next page ➥

Case 5.3–Continued

FOR CRITICAL ANALYSIS—Ethical Consideration *In this and other cases involving similar rulings, the courts have held that when the published phonorecordings from which audio files were taken contained copyright notices, the innocent infringer defense does not apply. It is irrelevant that the notice is not provided in the online file. Is this fair? Explain.*

THE EVOLUTION OF FILE-SHARING TECHNOLOGIES After the *Napster* decision, the recording industry filed and won numerous lawsuits against companies that distribute online file-sharing software. Other companies then developed technologies that allow P2P network users to share stored music files, without paying a fee, more quickly and efficiently than ever. Software such as Morpheus, KaZaA, and LimeWire, for example, provides users with an interface that is similar to a Web browser.[23] When a user performs a search, the software locates a list of peers that have the file available for downloading. Because of the automated procedures, the companies do not maintain a central index and are unable to supervise whether users are exchanging copyrighted files.

In 2005, the United States Supreme Court clarified that companies that distribute file-sharing software intending that it be used to violate copyright laws can be liable for users' copyright infringement. **CASE EXAMPLE 5.14** In *Metro-Goldwyn-Mayer Studios, Inc. v. Grokster, Ltd.*,[24] music and film industry organizations sued Grokster, Ltd., and StreamCast Networks, Inc. for contributory and vicarious copyright infringement. The Supreme Court held that anyone who distributes file-sharing software "with the object of promoting its use to infringe copyright, as shown by clear expression or other affirmative steps taken to foster infringement, . . . is liable for the resulting acts of infringement by third parties." • Although the music and film industries won the *Grokster* case, they have not been able to prevent new technology from enabling copyright infringement.

Trade Secrets

The law of trade secrets protects some business processes and information that are not or cannot be patented, copyrighted, or trademarked against appropriation by a competitor. A **trade secret** is basically information of commercial value. This may include customer lists, plans, research and development, pricing information, marketing techniques, and production methods—anything that makes an individual company unique and that would have value to a competitor.

Unlike copyright and trademark protection, protection of trade secrets extends both to ideas and to their expression. (For this reason, and because there are no registration or filing requirements for trade secrets, trade secret protection may be well suited for software.) Of course, the secret formula, method, or other information must be disclosed to some persons, particularly to key employees. Businesses generally attempt to protect their trade secrets by having all employees who use the process or information agree in their contracts, or in confidentiality agreements, never to divulge it.[25]

State and Federal Law on Trade Secrets

Under Section 757 of the *Restatement of Torts,* those who disclose or use another's trade secret, without authorization, are liable to that other party if (1) they discovered the secret by improper means or (2) their disclosure or use constitutes a breach of a duty owed to the other party. The theft of confidential business data by industrial espionage, as when a business taps into a competitor's computer, is a theft of trade secrets without any contractual violation and is actionable in itself.

Although trade secrets have long been protected under the common law, today most states' laws are based on the Uniform Trade Secrets Act, which has been adopted in forty-seven states. Additionally, in 1996 Congress passed the Economic Espionage Act, which made the theft of trade secrets a federal crime. We will examine the provisions and significance of this act in Chapter 6, in the context of crimes related to business.

Trade Secrets in Cyberspace

Today's computer technology undercuts a business firm's ability to protect its confidential information, including trade secrets. For instance, a dishonest employee could e-mail trade secrets in a company's computer to a competitor or a future employer. If e-mail is not an option, the employee might walk out with the information on a flash pen drive.

For a comprehensive summary of trade secrets and other forms of intellectual property, see Exhibit 5–1 on the facing page.

23. Note that in 2005, KaZaA entered into a settlement agreement with four major music companies that had alleged copyright infringement. KaZaA agreed to offer only legitimate, fee-based music downloads in the future.

24. 545 U.S. 913, 125 S.Ct. 2764, 162 L.Ed.2d 781 (2005). Grokster, Ltd., later settled this dispute out of court and stopped distributing its software.

25. See, for example, *Verigy US, Inc. v. Mayder,* 2008 WL 564634 (N.D.Cal. 2008); and *Gleeson v. Preferred Sourcing, LLC,* 883 N.E.2d 164 (Ind.App. 2008).

• ***Exhibit* 5–1 Forms of Intellectual Property**

	DEFINITION	HOW ACQUIRED	DURATION	REMEDY FOR INFRINGEMENT
Patent	A grant from the government that gives an inventor exclusive rights to an invention.	By filing a patent application with the U.S. Patent and Trademark Office and receiving its approval.	Twenty years from the date of the application; for design patents, fourteen years.	Monetary damages, including royalties and lost profits, *plus* attorneys' fees. Damages may be tripled for intentional infringements.
Copyright	The right of an author or originator of a literary or artistic work, or other production that falls within a specified category, to have the exclusive use of that work for a given period of time.	Automatic (once the work or creation is put in tangible form). Only the *expression* of an idea (and not the idea itself) can be protected by copyright.	For authors: the life of the author, plus 70 years. For publishers: 95 years after the date of publication or 120 years after creation.	Actual damages plus profits received by the party who infringed *or* statutory damages under the Copyright Act, *plus* costs and attorneys' fees in either situation.
Trademark (service mark and trade dress)	Any distinctive word, name, symbol, or device (image or appearance), or combination thereof, that an entity uses to distinguish its goods or services from those of others. The owner has the exclusive right to use that mark or trade dress.	1. At common law, ownership created by use of the mark. 2. Registration with the appropriate federal or state office gives notice and is permitted if the mark is currently in use or will be within the next six months.	Unlimited, as long as it is in use. To continue notice by registration, the owner must renew by filing between the fifth and sixth years, and thereafter, every ten years.	1. Injunction prohibiting the future use of the mark. 2. Actual damages plus profits received by the party who infringed (can be increased under the Lanham Act). 3. Destruction of articles that infringed. 4. *Plus* costs and attorneys' fees.
Trade Secret	Any information that a business possesses and that gives the business an advantage over competitors (including formulas, lists, patterns, plans, processes, and programs).	Through the originality and development of the information and processes that constitute the business secret and are unknown to others.	Unlimited, so long as not revealed to others. Once revealed to others, it is no longer a trade secret.	Monetary damages for misappropriation (the Uniform Trade Secrets Act also permits punitive damages if willful), *plus* costs and attorneys' fees.

International Protection for Intellectual Property

For many years, the United States has been a party to various international agreements relating to intellectual property rights. For example, the Paris Convention of 1883, to which 172 countries are signatory, allows parties in one country to file for patent and trademark protection in any of the other member countries. Other international agreements include the Berne Convention, the Agreement on Trade-Related Aspects of Intellectual Property Rights (or more simply, the TRIPS agreement), and the Madrid Protocol.

The Berne Convention

Under the Berne Convention of 1886, an international copyright agreement, if a U.S. citizen writes a book, every country that has signed the convention must recognize the U.S. author's copyright in the book. Also, if a citizen of a country that has not signed the convention first publishes a book in one of the 164 countries that have signed, all other countries that have signed the convention must recognize that author's copyright. Copyright notice is not needed to gain protection under the Berne Convention for works published after March 1, 1989.

This convention and other international agreements have given some protection to intellectual property on a worldwide level. None of them, however, has been as significant and far reaching in scope as the agreement discussed next.

The TRIPS Agreement

Representatives from more than one hundred nations signed the TRIPS agreement in 1994. The agreement established, for the first time, standards for the international protection of intellectual property rights, including patents, trademarks, and copyrights for movies, computer programs, books, and music. The TRIPS agreement provides that each member country must include in its domestic laws broad intellectual property rights and effective remedies (including civil and criminal penalties) for violations of those rights.

Generally, the TRIPS agreement forbids member nations from discriminating against foreign owners of intellectual property rights (in the administration, regulation, or adjudication of such rights). In other words, a member nation cannot give its own nationals (citizens) favorable treatment without offering the same treatment to nationals of all member countries. **EXAMPLE 5.15** A U.S. software manufacturer brings a suit for the infringement of intellectual property rights under Germany's national laws. Because Germany is a member nation, the U.S. manufacturer is entitled to receive the same treatment as a German manufacturer. ● Each member nation must also ensure that legal procedures are available for parties who wish to bring actions for infringement of intellectual property rights. Additionally, a related document established a mechanism for settling disputes among member nations.

The Madrid Protocol

In the past, one of the difficulties in protecting U.S. trademarks internationally was that registering a trademark in foreign countries was a time-consuming and expensive process. The filing fees and procedures for trademark registration vary significantly among individual countries. The Madrid Protocol, which was signed into law in 2003, may help to resolve these problems. The Madrid Protocol is an international treaty that has been signed by eighty-four countries. Under its provisions, a U.S. company wishing to register its trademark abroad can submit a single application and designate other member countries in which it would like to register the mark. The treaty was designed to reduce the costs of obtaining international trademark protection by more than 60 percent.

Although the Madrid Protocol may simplify and reduce the cost of trademark registration in foreign nations, whether it will provide significant benefits remains unclear. Even with an easier registration process, trademark owners must still be concerned that some member countries may not enforce the law and protect the mark.

Reviewing . . . Intellectual Property and Internet Law

Two computer science majors, Trent and Xavier, have an idea for a new video game, which they propose to call "Hallowed." They form a business and begin developing their idea. Several months later, Trent and Xavier run into a problem with their design and consult with a friend, Brad, who is an expert in creating computer source codes. After the software is completed but before Hallowed is marketed, a video game called Halo 2 is released for both the Xbox and PlayStation 3 systems. Halo 2 uses source codes similar to those of Hallowed and imitates Hallowed's overall look and feel, although not all the features are alike. Using the information presented in the chapter, answer the following questions.

1 Would the name *Hallowed* receive protection as a trademark or as trade dress?
2 If Trent and Xavier had obtained a business process patent on Hallowed, would the release of Halo 2 infringe on their patent? Why or why not?
3 Based only on the facts described above, could Trent and Xavier sue the makers of Halo 2 for copyright infringement? Why or why not?
4 Suppose that Trent and Xavier discover that Brad took the idea of Hallowed and sold it to the company that produced Halo 2. Which type of intellectual property issue does this raise?

Terms and Concepts

certification mark 91
cloud computing 99
collective mark 91
copyright 96
cyber mark 92
cybersquatting 92
distributed network 99
domain name 92
intellectual property 88
license 93
patent 93
peer-to-peer (P2P) networking 98

service mark 91
trade dress 91
trade name 92
trade secret 100
trademark 89

Chapter Summary: Intellectual Property and Internet Law

Trademarks and Related Property (See pages 89–92.)	1. A *trademark* is a distinctive mark, motto, device, or emblem that a manufacturer stamps, prints, or otherwise affixes to the goods it produces so that they may be identified on the market and their origin vouched for. 2. The major federal statutes protecting trademarks and related property are the Lanham Act of 1946 and the Federal Trademark Dilution Act of 1995. Generally, to be protected, a trademark must be sufficiently distinctive from all competing trademarks. 3. *Trademark infringement* occurs when one uses a mark that is the same as, or confusingly similar to, the protected trademark, service mark, trade name, or trade dress of another without permission when marketing goods or services.
Cyber Marks (See pages 92–93.)	A *cyber mark* is a trademark in cyberspace. Trademark infringement in cyberspace occurs when one person uses, in a domain name or in meta tags, a name that is the same as, or confusingly similar to, the protected mark of another.
Patents (See pages 93–96.)	1. A *patent* is a grant from the government that gives an inventor the exclusive right to make, use, and sell an invention for a period of twenty years (fourteen years for a design patent) from the date when the application for a patent is filed. To be patentable, an invention (or a discovery, process, or design) must be genuine, novel, useful, and not obvious in light of current technology. Computer software may be patented. 2. Almost anything is patentable, except the laws of nature, natural phenomena, and abstract ideas (including algorithms). Even business processes or methods are patentable if they relate to a machine or transformation. 3. *Patent infringement* occurs when one uses or sells another's patented design, product, or process without the patent owner's permission. The patent holder can sue the infringer in federal court and request an injunction, but must prove irreparable injury to obtain a permanent injunction against the infringer. The patent holder can also request damages and attorneys' fees.
Copyrights (See pages 96–100.)	1. A *copyright* is an intangible property right granted by federal statute to the author or originator of certain literary or artistic productions. The Copyright Act of 1976, as amended, governs copyrights. 2. *Copyright infringement* occurs whenever the form or expression of an idea is copied without the permission of the copyright holder. An exception applies if the copying is deemed a "fair use." 3. To protect copyrights in digital information, Congress passed the Digital Millennium Copyright Act of 1998. 4. Technology that allows users to share files online often raises copyright infringement issues. 5. The United States Supreme Court has ruled that companies that provide file-sharing software to users can be held liable for contributory and vicarious copyright liability if they take affirmative steps to promote copyright infringement.
Trade Secrets (See page 100.)	*Trade secrets* include customer lists, plans, research and development, and pricing information, for example. Trade secrets are protected under the common law and, in some states, under statutory law against misappropriation by competitors.
International Protection for Intellectual Property (See pages 100–102.)	Various international agreements provide international protection for intellectual property. A landmark agreement is the 1994 Agreement on Trade-Related Aspects of Intellectual Property Rights (TRIPS), which provides for enforcement procedures in all countries signatory to the agreement.

ExamPrep

ISSUE SPOTTERS

—Check your answers to these questions against the answers provided in Appendix G.

1 Global Products develops, patents, and markets software. World Copies, Inc., sells Global's software without the maker's permission. Is this patent infringement? If so, how might Global save the cost of suing World for infringement and at the same time profit from World's sales?

2 Eagle Corporation began marketing software in 2000 under the mark "Eagle." In 2009, Eagle.com, Inc., a different company selling different products, begins to use "eagle" as part of its URL and registers it as a domain name. Can Eagle Corporation stop this use of "eagle"? If so, what must the company show?

BEFORE THE TEST

Go to **www.cengagebrain.com**, enter the ISBN 9781111530624, and click on "Find" to locate this textbook's Web site. Then, click on "Access Now" under "Study Tools," and select Chapter 5 at the top. There, you will find an Interactive Quiz that you can take to assess your mastery of the concepts in this chapter, as well as Flashcards and a Glossary of important terms.

For Review

1 What is intellectual property?
2 Why does the law protect trademarks and patents?
3 What laws protect authors' rights in the works they generate?
4 What are trade secrets, and what laws offer protection for this form of intellectual property?
5 What steps have been taken to protect intellectual property rights in today's digital age?

Questions and Case Problems

5–1 Patent Infringement. John and Andrew Doney invented a hard-bearing device for balancing rotors. Although they registered their invention with the U.S. Patent and Trademark Office, it was never used as an automobile wheel balancer. Some time later, Exetron Corp. produced an automobile wheel balancer that used a hard-bearing device with a support plate similar to that of the Doneys' device. Given that the Doneys had not used their device for automobile wheel balancing, does Exetron's use of a similar device infringe on the Doneys' patent? Explain.

5–2 Copyright Infringement. In which of the following situations would a court likely hold Maruta liable for copyright infringement?

1 At the library, Maruta photocopies ten pages from a scholarly journal relating to a topic on which she is writing a term paper.
2 Maruta makes leather handbags and sells them in her small shop. She advertises her handbags as "Vutton handbags," hoping that customers might mistakenly assume that they were made by Vuitton, the well-known maker of high-quality luggage and handbags.
3 Maruta owns a video store. She purchases one copy of several popular movie DVDs from various distributors. Then, using blank DVDs, she burns copies of the movies to rent or sell to her customers.
4 Maruta teaches Latin American history at a small university. She has a digital video recorder and frequently records television programs relating to Latin America and puts them on DVDs. She then takes the DVDs to her classroom so that her students can watch them.

5–3 Copyright Infringement. Professor Littrell is teaching a summer seminar in business torts at State University. Several times during the course, he makes copies of relevant sections from business law texts and distributes them to his students. Littrell does not realize that the daughter of one of the textbook authors is a member of his seminar. She tells her father about Littrell's copying activities, which have taken place without her father's or his publisher's permission. Her father sues Littrell for copyright infringement. Littrell claims protection under the fair use doctrine. Who will prevail? Explain.

5–4 Copyright Infringement. Redwin Wilchcombe is a musician and music producer. In 2002, Wilchcombe met Jonathan Smith, known as Lil Jon, a member of Lil Jon & The East Side Boyz (LJESB). Lil Jon and LJESB are under contract to give TeeVee Toons, Inc. (TVT), all rights to LJESB's recordings and Lil Jon's songs. At Lil Jon's request, based on his idea, and with his suggestions, Wilchcombe composed, performed, and recorded a song titled *Tha Weedman* for LJESB's album *Kings of Crunk*. They did not discuss payment and Wilchcombe was not paid, but he was given credit on the album as a producer. By 2005, the album had sold 2 million copies. Wilchcombe filed a suit against TVT and the others, alleging copyright infringement. The defendants asserted that they had a license to use the song. Wilchcombe argued that he had never granted a license to anyone. Do these facts indicate that the defendants had a license to use Wilchcombe's song? If so, what does that mean for Wilchcombe's cause? Explain. [*Wilchcombe v. TeeVee Toons, Inc.*, 555 F.3d 949 (11th Cir. 2009)]

5–5 Case Problem with Sample Answer Peggy Hamilton was a major shareholder in Carbon Processing and Reclamation, LLC (CPR). After a dispute, she sold her interest in the company and signed a confidentiality agreement not to divulge company business to anyone. A year later, when William Jones, the owner of CPR, left on a trip, he let an employee, Jesse Edwards, drive his company car. There were boxes containing some detailed company records in the car. Edwards and his wife, Channon, were in the middle of a divorce, and she suspected him of hiding financial information from her.

When Channon saw the boxes in the car her husband was driving, she got a car key from Hamilton, who still had one from when she was an owner. Channon used the key to get into the boxes of company information. Jones then sued Hamilton for breach of the confidentiality agreement, contending that allowing Channon to have access to the files was assisting in the theft of trade secrets. The trial court dismissed the claim, but Jones appealed. Could Hamilton's actions be the basis for a claim of trade secret violation? What factors should be taken into consideration? [*Jones v. Hamilton,* 53 So.3d 134 (Ala.Civ.App. 2010)]

—For a sample answer to Problem 5–5, go to Appendix F at the end of this text.

5–6 Copyright Infringement. United Fabrics International, Inc., purchased a fabric design from an Italian design house, Contromoda, and registered a copyright to the design with the U.S. Copyright Office. When Macy's, Inc., began selling garments with a similar design, United filed a copyright infringement lawsuit against Macy's and others. In its defense, Macy's claimed that United did not own a valid copyright to the design. Ownership of a copyright is a requirement to establish an infringement claim. The district court held that the evidence was insufficient to establish United's ownership of the design and, for that reason, dismissed the action. United appealed, arguing that its copyright in the design should be presumptively valid because the copyright had been registered with the U.S. Copyright Office. How should the federal appellate court rule? Should the owner of a registered copyright have to prove that the copyright is valid to establish infringement? Or, should the party contesting the validity of a copyright have to show that it is invalid? Explain your answer. [*United Fabrics International, Inc. v. C&J Wear, Inc.*, 630 F.3d 1255 (9th Cir. 2011)]

5–7 A Question of Ethics *Custom Copies, Inc., in Gainesville, Florida, is a copy shop, reproducing and distributing, for profit, on request, material published and owned by others. One of the copy shop's primary activities is the preparation and sale of coursepacks, which contain compilations of readings for college courses. For a particular coursepack, a teacher selects the readings and delivers a syllabus to the copy shop, which obtains the materials from a library, copies them, and then binds and sells the copies. Blackwell Publishing, Inc., in Malden, Massachusetts, publishes books and journals in medicine and other fields and owns the copyrights to these publications. Blackwell and others filed a suit in a federal district court against Custom Copies, alleging copyright infringement for its "routine and systematic reproduction of materials from plaintiffs' publications, without seeking permission," to compile coursepacks for classes at the University of Florida. The plaintiffs asked the court to issue an injunction and award them damages, as well as the profit from the infringement. The defendant filed a motion to dismiss the complaint.* [Blackwell Publishing, Inc. v. Custom Copies, Inc., __ *F.Supp.2d* __ *(N.D.Fla. 2007)]*

1. Custom Copies argued, in part, that it did not "distribute" the coursepacks. Does a copy shop violate copyright law if it only copies materials for coursepacks? Does the copying fall under the "fair use" exception? Should the court grant the defendants' motion? Why or why not?
2. What is the potential impact if copies of a book or journal are created and sold without the permission of, and the payment of royalties or a fee to, the copyright owner? Explain.

5–8 Critical Thinking Legal Question In the United States, patent protection is granted to the first person to invent a given product or process, even though another person may be the first to file for a patent on the same product or process. What are the advantages of this patenting procedure? Can you think of any disadvantages? Explain.

5–9 Video Question To watch this chapter's video, *The Jerk,* go to **www.cengagebrain.com**. Register the access code that came with your new book or log in to your existing Cengage account. Select the link for the "Business Law Digital Video Library Online Access" or "Business Law CourseMate." Click on "Complete Video List," view Video 66, and then answer the following questions:

1. In the video, Navin (Steve Martin) creates a special handle for Fox's (Bill Macy's) glasses. Can Navin obtain a patent or a copyright protecting his invention? Explain.
2. Suppose that after Navin legally protects his idea, Fox steals it and decides to develop it for himself, without Navin's permission. Has Fox committed infringement? If so, what kind: trademark, patent, or copyright?
3. Suppose that after Navin legally protects his idea, he realizes he doesn't have the funds to mass-produce the special handle. Navin therefore agrees to allow Fox to manufacture the product. Has Navin granted Fox a license? Explain.
4. Assume that Navin is able to manufacture his invention. What might Navin do to ensure that his product is identifiable and can be distinguished from other products?

Chapter 6

Criminal Law and Cyber Crime

Learning Objectives

After reading this chapter, you should be able to answer the following questions:

1. What two elements must exist before a person can be held liable for a crime? Can a corporation commit crimes?
2. What are five broad categories of crimes? What is white-collar crime?
3. What defenses might be raised by criminal defendants to avoid liability for criminal acts?
4. What constitutional safeguards exist to protect persons accused of crimes?
5. How has the Internet expanded opportunities for identity theft?

The Learning Objectives above are designed to help improve your understanding of the chapter.

(Flickr/Petroleumjelliffe)

Criminal law is an important part of the legal environment of business. Various sanctions are used to bring about a society in which individuals engaging in business can compete and flourish. These sanctions include damages for various types of tortious conduct (see Chapter 4), damages for breach of contract (see Chapter 12), and equitable remedies (see Chapter 1). Additional sanctions are imposed under criminal law. Many statutes regulating business provide for criminal as well as civil sanctions.

Crime is a serious problem in the United States. Some fear that the nation's economic difficulties will lead to even higher crime rates. Moreover, the government's ability to pay for prisons has declined due to the economic slowdown. Many prisons are at twice their capacity, and inmates are not receiving adequate medical care. Overcrowding became so severe in California prisons that in 2011 the United States Supreme Court ruled that conditions there violated the Eighth Amendment's prohibition against cruel and unusual punishment.[1] As a result, 46,000 inmates had to be released from California prisons.

In this chapter, following a brief summary of the major differences between criminal and civil law, we look at how crimes are classified and what elements must be present for criminal liability to exist. We then examine various categories of crimes, the defenses that can be raised to avoid liability for criminal actions, and the rules of criminal procedure. We conclude the chapter with a discussion of crimes that occur in cyberspace, often referred to as *cyber crime.*

Civil Law and Criminal Law

Remember from Chapter 1 that *civil law* spells out the duties that exist between persons or between persons and their governments, excluding the duty not to commit crimes. Contract

1. See *Brown v. Plata,* ___ U.S. ___, 131 S.Ct. 1910, 179 L.Ed.2d 969 (2011).

law, for example, is part of civil law. The whole body of tort law, which deals with the infringement by one person on the legally recognized rights of another, is also an area of civil law.

Criminal law, in contrast, has to do with crime. A **crime** can be defined as a wrong against society set forth in a statute and, if committed, punishable by society through fines and/or imprisonment—and, in some instances, death. As mentioned in Chapter 1, because crimes are *offenses against society as a whole,* criminals are prosecuted by a public official, such as a district attorney (D.A.), rather than by the crime victims. Victims often report the crime to the police, but ultimately it is the D.A.'s office that decides whether to file criminal charges and to what extent to pursue the prosecution or carry out additional investigation.

Key Differences between Civil Law and Criminal Law

Because the state has extensive resources at its disposal when prosecuting criminal cases, there are procedural safeguards to protect the rights of defendants. We look here at one of these safeguards—the higher burden of proof that applies in a criminal case—as well as the harsher sanctions for criminal acts than for civil wrongs. Exhibit 6–1 below summarizes these and other key differences between civil law and criminal law.

BURDEN OF PROOF In a civil case, the plaintiff usually must prove his or her case by a *preponderance of the evidence.* Under this standard, the plaintiff must convince the court that, based on the evidence presented by both parties, it is more likely than not that the plaintiff's allegation is true.

In a criminal case, in contrast, the state must prove its case **beyond a reasonable doubt.** If the jury views the evidence in the case as reasonably permitting either a guilty or a not guilty verdict, then the jury's verdict must be *not* guilty. In other words, the government (prosecutor) must prove beyond a reasonable doubt that the defendant committed every essential element of the offense with which she or he is charged. If the jurors are not convinced of the defendant's guilt beyond a reasonable doubt, they must find the defendant not guilty. Note also that in a criminal case, the jury's verdict normally must be unanimous—agreed to by all members of the jury—to convict the defendant.[2] (In a civil trial by jury, in contrast, typically only three-fourths of the jurors need to agree.)

CRIMINAL SANCTIONS The sanctions imposed on criminal wrongdoers are also harsher than those that are applied in civil cases. Remember from Chapter 4 that the purpose of tort law is to allow persons harmed by the wrongful acts of others to obtain compensation from the wrongdoer rather than to punish the wrongdoer. In contrast, criminal sanctions are designed to punish those who commit crimes and to deter others from committing similar acts in the future. Criminal sanctions include fines as well as the much harsher penalty of the loss of one's liberty by incarceration in a jail or prison. The harshest criminal sanction is, of course, the death penalty.

Civil Liability for Criminal Acts

Some torts, such as assault and battery, provide a basis for a criminal prosecution as well as a tort action. **EXAMPLE 6.1** Joe is walking down the street, minding his own business, when suddenly a passerby attacks him. In the ensuing struggle, the attacker stabs Joe several times, seriously injuring him. A police officer restrains and arrests the wrongdoer. In this situation, the attacker may be subject to both criminal prosecution by the state and a tort lawsuit brought by Joe. •

2. Note that there are exceptions—a few states allow jury verdicts that are not unanimous. Arizona, for example, allows six of eight jurors to reach a verdict in criminal cases. Louisiana and Oregon have also relaxed the requirement of unanimous jury verdicts.

• ***Exhibit* 6–1 Key Differences between Civil Law and Criminal Law**

ISSUE	CIVIL LAW	CRIMINAL LAW
Party who brings suit	The person who suffered harm.	The state.
Wrongful act	Causing harm to a person or to a person's property.	Violating a statute that prohibits some type of activity.
Burden of proof	Preponderance of the evidence.	Beyond a reasonable doubt.
Verdict	Three-fourths majority (typically).	Unanimous (almost always).
Remedy	Damages to compensate for the harm or a decree to achieve an equitable result.	Punishment (fine, imprisonment, or death).

• *Exhibit* **6–2 Tort Lawsuit and Criminal Prosecution for the Same Act**

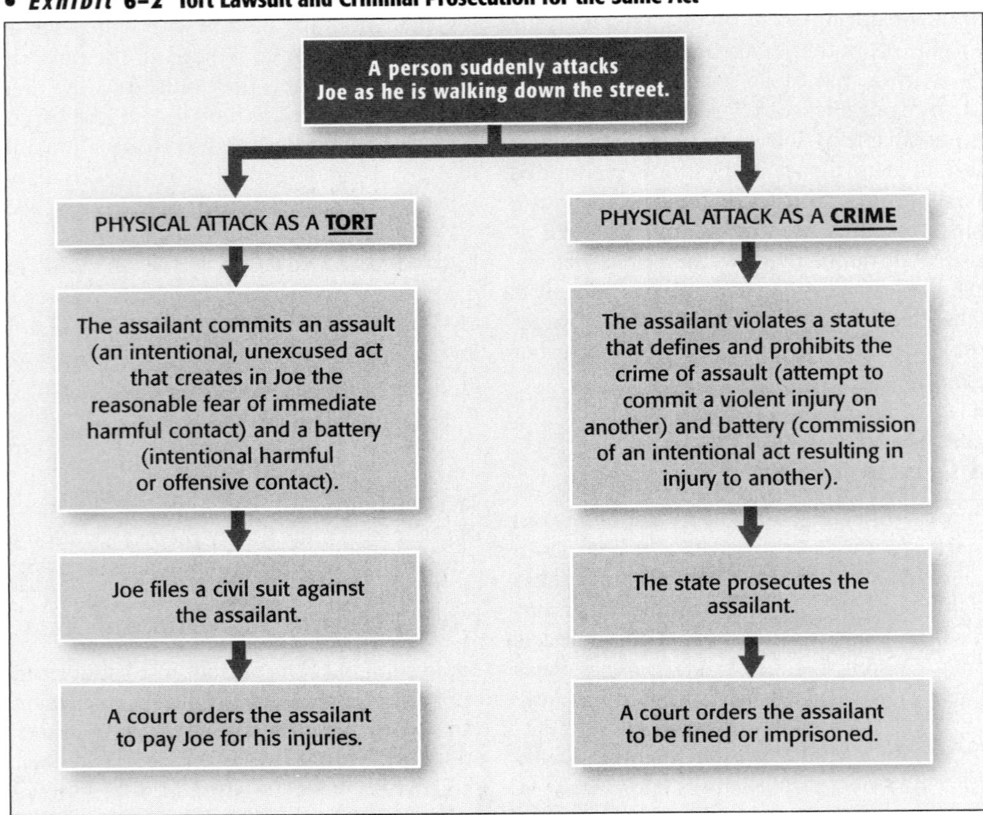

Exhibit 6–2 above illustrates how the same act can result in both a tort action and a criminal action against the wrongdoer.

Criminal Liability

Two elements must exist simultaneously for a person to be convicted of a crime: (1) the performance of a prohibited act and (2) a specified state of mind or intent on the part of the actor. Additionally, to establish criminal liability, there must be a *concurrence* between the act and the intent. In other words, these two elements must occur together.

The Criminal Act

Every criminal statute prohibits certain behavior. Most crimes require an act of *commission*—that is, a person must *do* something in order to be accused of a crime. In criminal law, a prohibited act is referred to as the ***actus reus,***[3] or guilty act. In some situations, an act of *omission* can be a crime, but only when a person has a legal duty to perform the omitted act, such as failing to file a tax return.

The *guilty act* requirement is based on one of the premises of criminal law—that a person is punished for harm done to society. For a crime to exist, the guilty act must cause some harm to a person or to property. Thinking about killing someone or about stealing a car may be wrong, but the thoughts do no harm until they are translated into action. Of course, a person can be punished for attempting murder or robbery, but normally only if he or she took substantial steps toward the criminal objective.

State of Mind

Mens rea[4] is a wrongful state of mind or intent and generally is required to establish criminal liability. What constitutes such a mental state varies according to the wrongful action. For murder, the act is the taking of a life, and the mental state is the intent to take life. For theft, the guilty act is the taking of another person's property, and the mental state involves both the knowledge that the property belongs to another and the intent to deprive the owner of it.

3. Pronounced *ak*-tuhs *ray*-uhs.

4. Pronounced *mehns ray*-uh.

A guilty mental state can be attributed to acts of negligence or recklessness as well. *Criminal negligence* involves the mental state in which the defendant takes an unjustified, substantial, and foreseeable risk that results in harm. Under the Model Penal Code, a defendant is negligent even if she or he was not actually aware of the risk but *should have been aware* of it.[5] A defendant is criminally reckless if he or she consciously disregards a substantial and unjustifiable risk.

Corporate Criminal Liability

As will be discussed in Chapter 24, a *corporation* is a legal entity created under the laws of a state. At one time, it was thought that a corporation could not incur criminal liability because, although a corporation is a legal person, it can act only through its agents (corporate directors, officers, and employees). Therefore, the corporate entity itself could not "intend" to commit a crime. Over time, this view has changed. Obviously, corporations cannot be imprisoned, but they can be fined.

LIABILITY OF THE CORPORATE ENTITY Today, corporations normally are liable for the crimes committed by their agents and employees within the course and scope of their employment.[6] For such criminal liability to be imposed, the prosecutor typically must show that the corporation could have prevented the act or that a supervisor within the corporation authorized or had knowledge of the act. In addition, corporations can be criminally liable for failing to perform specific duties imposed by law.

CASE EXAMPLE 6.2 A prostitution ring, the Gold Club, was operating out of Economy Inn and Scottish Inn motels in West Virginia. A motel manager gave discounted rates to the prostitutes, and they paid him in cash. The corporation that owned the motels received a portion of the funds generated by the Gold Club's illegal operations. At trial, a jury found that the corporation was criminally liable because a supervisor within the corporation—the motel manager—knew of the prostitution and the corporation allowed it to continue. The motel manager was sentenced to fifteen months in prison, and the corporation was ordered to forfeit the Scottish Inn property.[7] •

LIABILITY OF CORPORATE OFFICERS AND DIRECTORS Corporate directors and officers are personally liable for the crimes they commit, regardless of whether the crimes were committed for their personal benefit or on the corporation's behalf. Additionally, corporate directors and officers may be held liable for the actions of employees under their supervision. Under what has become known as the *responsible corporate officer doctrine,* a court may impose criminal liability on a corporate officer regardless of whether she or he participated in, directed, or even knew about a given criminal violation.

CASE EXAMPLE 6.3 The Roscoe family owned a corporation that operated an underground storage tank that leaked gasoline. After the leak occurred, an employee, John Johnson, notified the state environmental agency, and the Roscoes hired an environmental services firm to clean up the spill. The clean-up did not occur immediately, however, and the state sent many notices to John Roscoe, a corporate officer, warning him that the company was violating federal and state laws. Roscoe gave the letters to Johnson, who passed them on to the environmental services firm, but nothing was cleaned up. The state eventually filed criminal charges against the corporation and the Roscoes individually, and they were convicted under the responsible corporate officer doctrine. The Roscoes were in positions of responsibility, they had influence over the corporation's actions, and their failure to act caused a violation of environmental laws.[8] •

Types of Crimes

Federal, state, and local laws provide for the classification and punishment of hundreds of thousands of different criminal acts. Traditionally, though, crimes have been grouped into five broad categories, or types: violent crime (crimes against persons), property crime, public order crime, white-collar crime, and organized crime. Within each of these categories, crimes may also be separated into more than one classification. *Cyber crime*—crime committed in cyberspace—is less a category of crime than a new way to commit crime (see page 120).

Violent Crime

Crimes against persons, because they cause others to suffer harm or death, are referred to as *violent crimes.* Murder is a violent crime. So, too, is sexual assault, or rape. **Robbery**—defined as the taking of cash, personal property, or any other article of value from a person by means of force or fear—is another violent crime. Typically, states have more severe penalties for *aggravated robbery*—robbery with the use of a deadly weapon.

Assault and battery, which were discussed in Chapter 4 in the context of tort law, are also classified as violent crimes. Remember that assault can involve an object or force put into motion by a person. **EXAMPLE 6.4** In 2009, on the anniversary of an abortion rights ruling, a man drove his vehicle into an abortion clinic building in Saint Paul, Minnesota. The police arrested him for aggravated assault, even though no one was injured. •

5. Model Penal Code Section 2.02(2)(d).
6. See Model Penal Code Section 2.07.
7. *United States v. Singh,* 518 F.3d 236 (4th Cir. 2008).
8. *People v. Roscoe,* 169 Cal.App.4th 829, 87 Cal.Rptr.3d 187 (3 Dist. 2008).

Each of these violent crimes is further classified by degree, depending on the circumstances surrounding the criminal act. These circumstances include the intent of the person who committed the crime, whether a weapon was used, and (in cases other than murder) the level of pain and suffering experienced by the victim.

Property Crime

The most common type of criminal activity is property crime—crimes in which the goal of the offender is to obtain some form of economic gain or to damage property. Robbery is a form of property crime, as well as a violent crime, because the offender seeks to gain the property of another. We look here at a number of other crimes that fall within the general category of property crime.

BURGLARY Traditionally, **burglary** was defined under the common law as breaking and entering the dwelling of another at night with the intent to commit a felony. Originally, the definition was aimed at protecting an individual's home and its occupants. Most state statutes have eliminated some of the requirements found in the common law definition. The time of day at which the breaking and entering occurs, for example, is usually immaterial. State statutes frequently omit the element of breaking, and some states do not require that the building be a dwelling. When a deadly weapon is used in a burglary, the person can be charged with *aggravated burglary* and punished more severely.

LARCENY Under the common law, the crime of **larceny** involved the unlawful taking and carrying away of someone else's personal property with the intent to permanently deprive the owner of possession. Put simply, larceny is stealing or theft. Whereas robbery involves force or fear, larceny does not. Therefore, picking pockets is larceny, not robbery. Similarly, taking company products and supplies home for personal use, if one is not authorized to do so, is larceny. (Note that a person who commits larceny generally can also be sued under tort law because the act of taking possession of another's property involves a trespass to personal property.)

Most states have expanded the definition of property that is subject to larceny statutes. Stealing computer programs or computer time may constitute larceny even though the "property" consists of magnetic impulses. So, too, can the theft of natural gas or Internet and television cable service. The common law distinguished between grand and petit larceny depending on the value of the property taken. Many states have abolished this distinction, but in those that have not, grand larceny (or theft) is a felony, and petit larceny (or theft) is a misdemeanor.

OBTAINING GOODS BY FALSE PRETENSES It is a criminal act to obtain goods by means of false pretenses, such as buying groceries with a check knowing that you have insufficient funds to cover it or offering to sell someone the latest iPad knowing that you do not actually own the iPad. Statutes dealing with such illegal activities vary widely from state to state.

RECEIVING STOLEN GOODS It is a crime to receive stolen goods. The recipient of such goods need not know the true identity of the owner or the thief. All that is necessary is that the recipient knows or should have known that the goods are stolen, which implies an intent to deprive the owner of those goods.

ARSON The willful and malicious burning of a building (and, in some states, personal property) owned by another is the crime of **arson.** At common law, arson traditionally applied only to burning down another person's house. The law was designed to protect human life. Today, arson statutes have been extended to cover the destruction of any building, regardless of ownership, by fire or explosion.

Every state has a special statute that covers the act of burning a building for the purpose of collecting insurance. **EXAMPLE 6.5** Benton owns an insured apartment building that is falling apart. If he sets fire to it himself or pays someone else to do so, he is guilty not only of arson but also of defrauding the insurer, which is attempted larceny. • Of course, the insurer need not pay the claim when insurance fraud is proved.

FORGERY The fraudulent making or altering of any writing (including electronic records) in a way that changes the legal rights and liabilities of another is **forgery.** **EXAMPLE 6.6** Without authorization, Severson signs Bennett's name to the back of a check made out to Bennett and attempts to cash it. Severson has committed the crime of forgery. • Forgery also includes changing trademarks, falsifying public records, counterfeiting, and altering a legal document.

Public Order Crime

Historically, societies have always outlawed activities that are considered to be contrary to public values and morals. Today, the most common public order crimes include public drunkenness, prostitution, gambling, and illegal drug use. These crimes are sometimes referred to as victimless crimes because they normally harm only the offender. From a broader perspective, however, they are deemed detrimental to society as a whole because they may create an environment that gives rise to property and violent crimes. **EXAMPLE 6.7** A man traveling on a Continental Airlines flight became angry and yelled obscenities at a flight attendant after a beverage cart struck his knee. The pilot diverted the plane to another airport, and the man was removed and arrested. He later pleaded guilty to interfering with a flight crew and was sentenced to two years in prison. •

White-Collar Crime

Crimes that typically occur only in the business context are popularly referred to as **white-collar crimes.** Although there is no official definition of white-collar crime, the term is commonly used to mean an illegal act or series of acts committed by an individual or business entity using some nonviolent means. Usually, this kind of crime is committed in the course of a legitimate occupation. Corporate crimes fall into this category. In addition, certain property crimes, such as larceny and forgery, may also be white-collar crimes if they occur within the business context.

EMBEZZLEMENT When a person who is entrusted with another person's funds or property fraudulently appropriates it, **embezzlement** occurs. Typically, embezzlement is carried out by an employee who steals funds. Banks are particularly prone to this problem, but embezzlement can occur in any firm. In a number of businesses, corporate officers or accountants have fraudulently converted funds for their own benefit and then "fixed" the books to cover up their crime. Embezzlement is not larceny, because the wrongdoer does not physically take the property from the possession of another, and it is not robbery, because force or fear is not used.

Embezzlement occurs whether the embezzler takes the funds directly from the victim or from a third person. If the financial officer of a large corporation pockets checks from third parties that were given to her to deposit into the corporate account, she is embezzling. Frequently, an embezzler takes a relatively small amount at one time but does so repeatedly over a long period. This might be done by underreporting income or deposits and embezzling the remaining amount, for example, or by creating fictitious persons or accounts and writing checks to them from the corporate account. Even an employer's failure to remit state withholding taxes that were collected from employee wages can constitute embezzlement.

The intent to return the embezzled property—or its actual return—is not a defense to the crime of embezzlement, as the following case illustrates.

Case 6.1 People v. Sisuphan

Court of Appeal of California, First District, 181 Cal.App.4th 800, 104 Cal.Rptr.3d 654 (2010).

FACTS Lou Sisuphan was the director of finance at a Toyota dealership. His responsibilities included managing the financing contracts for vehicle sales and working with lenders to obtain payments. Sisuphan complained repeatedly to management about the attitude of Ian McClelland, another employee. The general manager, Michael Christian, would not terminate McClelland "because he brought a lot of money into the dealership." One day, McClelland accepted $22,600 in cash and two checks from a customer. McClelland placed the cash and the checks in a large envelope. As he tried to drop the envelope into the safe through a mechanism at its top, the envelope became stuck. While McClelland went for assistance, Sisuphan wiggled the envelope free and kept it. On McClelland's return, Sisuphan told him that the envelope had dropped into the safe. When the payment turned up missing, Christian told all the managers he would not bring criminal charges if the payment was returned. Sisuphan told Christian that he had taken the envelope, and he returned the cash and checks to Christian. Sisuphan claimed that he had no intention of stealing the payment but had taken it to get McClelland fired. Christian fired Sisuphan the next day, and the district attorney later charged Sisuphan with embezzlement. After a jury trial, Sisuphan was found guilty. Sisuphan appealed, arguing that the trial court had erred by excluding evidence that he had returned the funds.

ISSUE Did Sisuphan take the funds with the intent to defraud his employer?

DECISION Yes. The appellate court affirmed Sisuphan's conviction for embezzlement. Sisuphan had the required intent at the time of taking the funds, and the evidence that he repaid the dealership was properly excluded.

REASON The court reasoned that evidence of repayment is admissible only if it shows that a defendant's intent at the time of the taking was not fraudulent. In determining whether Sisuphan's intent was fraudulent at the time of the taking, the main issue was not whether he intended to spend the cash that he had taken. Rather, the deciding factor was whether Sisuphan intended to use the funds "for a purpose other than that for which the dealership entrusted it to him." Sisuphan's stated purpose was to get McClelland fired. Because this purpose was beyond the scope of his responsibility, it was "outside the trust afforded him by the dealership" and indicated that he had fraudulent intent.

FOR CRITICAL ANALYSIS—Legal Consideration *Why was Sisuphan convicted of embezzlement instead of larceny? What is the difference between these two crimes?*

MAIL AND WIRE FRAUD One of the more potent weapons against white-collar criminals is the Mail Fraud Act of 1990.[9] Under this act, it is a federal crime (mail fraud) to use the mails to defraud the public. Illegal use of the mails must involve (1) mailing or causing someone else to mail a writing—something written, printed, or photocopied—for the purpose of executing a scheme to defraud and (2) a contemplated or an organized scheme to defraud by false pretenses.

Federal law also makes it a crime to use wire (for example, the telephone), radio, or television transmissions to

9. 18 U.S.C. Sections 1341–1342.

defraud.[10] Violators may be fined up to $1,000, imprisoned for up to five years, or both. If the violation affects a financial institution, the violator may be fined up to $1 million, imprisoned for up to thirty years, or both.

CASE EXAMPLE 6.8 Gabriel Sanchez and Timothy Lyons set up six charities and formed North American Acquisitions (NAA) to solicit donations on the charities' behalf through telemarketing. NAA raised more than $6 million, of which less than $5,000 was actually spent on charitable causes. The telemarketers kept 80 percent of the donated funds as commissions, the NAA took 10 percent, and the rest went to Sanchez. Lyons and Sanchez were prosecuted for mail fraud and sentenced to fifteen years in prison. They appealed. A federal appellate court affirmed their convictions, ruling that the government can use these antifraud laws to prohibit professional fund-raisers from obtaining funds through false pretenses or by making false statements.[11] •

BRIBERY The crime of bribery involves offering to give something of value to someone in an attempt to influence that person, who usually, but not always, is a public official, to act in a way that serves a private interest. Three types of bribery are considered crimes: bribery of public officials, commercial bribery, and bribery of foreign officials. As an element of the crime of bribery, intent must be present and proved. The bribe itself can be anything the recipient considers to be valuable. Realize that the *crime of bribery occurs when the bribe is offered*—it is not required that the bribe be accepted. *Accepting a bribe* is a separate crime.

Commercial bribery involves corrupt dealings between private persons or businesses. Typically, people make commercial bribes to obtain proprietary information, cover up an inferior product, or secure new business. Industrial espionage sometimes involves commercial bribes. **EXAMPLE 6.9** Kent works at the firm of Jacoby & Meyers. He offers to pay Laurel, an employee in a competing firm, in exchange for that firm's trade secrets and pricing schedules. Kent has committed commercial bribery. • So-called kickbacks, or payoffs for special favors or services, are a form of commercial bribery in some situations. Bribing foreign officials to obtain favorable business contracts is a crime. The Foreign Corrupt Practices Act of 1977 was passed to curb the use of bribery by U.S. businesspersons in securing foreign contracts.

BANKRUPTCY FRAUD Federal bankruptcy law (see Chapter 19) allows individuals and businesses to be relieved of oppressive debt through bankruptcy proceedings. Numerous white-collar crimes may be committed during the many phases of a bankruptcy proceeding. A creditor, for example, may file a false claim against the debtor. Also, a debtor may attempt to protect assets from creditors by fraudulently transferring property to favored parties. For instance, a company-owned automobile may be "sold" at a bargain price to a trusted friend or relative. Closely related to the crime of fraudulent transfer of property is the crime of fraudulent concealment of property, such as hiding gold coins.

THE THEFT OF TRADE SECRETS Trade secrets constitute a form of intellectual property that can be extremely valuable for many businesses. The Economic Espionage Act of 1996[12] made the theft of trade secrets a federal crime. The act also made it a federal crime to buy or possess trade secrets of another person, knowing that the trade secrets were stolen or otherwise acquired without the owner's authorization.

Violations of the act can result in steep penalties. An individual who violates the act can be imprisoned for up to ten years and fined up to $500,000. If a corporation or other organization violates the act, it can be fined up to $5 million. Additionally, the law provides that any property acquired as a result of the violation, such as airplanes and automobiles, and any property used in the commission of the violation, such as computers and other electronic devices, are subject to criminal *forfeiture*—meaning that the government can take the property. A theft of trade secrets conducted via the Internet, for example, could result in the forfeiture of every computer or other device used to commit or facilitate the crime.

INSIDER TRADING An individual who obtains *inside information*—that is, information that has not been made available to the public—about the plans of a publicly listed corporation can often make stock-trading profits by purchasing or selling corporate securities based on the information. Insider trading is a violation of securities law and will be considered more fully in Chapter 26.

Organized Crime

As mentioned, white-collar crime takes place within the confines of the legitimate business world. *Organized crime,* in contrast, operates *illegitimately* by, among other things, providing illegal goods and services. For organized crime, the traditional preferred markets are gambling, prostitution, illegal narcotics, and loan sharking (lending at higher than legal interest rates), along with counterfeiting and credit-card scams.

MONEY LAUNDERING The profits from organized crime and illegal activities amount to billions of dollars a year, particularly the profits from illegal drug transactions and, to a lesser extent, from racketeering, prostitution, and gambling.

10. 18 U.S.C. Section 1343.

11. *United States v. Lyons,* 569 F.3d 995 (9th Cir. 2009).

12. 18 U.S.C. Sections 1831–1839.

Under federal law, banks, savings and loan associations, and other financial institutions are required to report currency transactions involving more than $10,000. Consequently, those who engage in illegal activities face difficulties in depositing their cash profits from illegal transactions.

As an alternative to simply storing cash from illegal transactions in a safe-deposit box, wrongdoers and racketeers have invented ways to launder "dirty" money to make it "clean" through legitimate business. **Money laundering** is engaging in financial transactions to conceal the identity, source, or destination of illegally gained funds.

EXAMPLE 6.10 Harris, a successful drug dealer, becomes a partner with a restaurateur. Little by little, the restaurant shows increasing profits. As a partner in the restaurant, Harris is able to report the "profits" of the restaurant as legitimate income on which he pays federal and state taxes. He can then spend those funds without worrying that his lifestyle may exceed the level possible with his reported income. •

THE RACKETEER INFLUENCED AND CORRUPT ORGANIZATIONS ACT In 1970, in an effort to curb the apparently increasing entry of organized crime into the legitimate business world, Congress passed the Racketeer Influenced and Corrupt Organizations Act (RICO).[13] The statute, which was enacted as part of the Organized Crime Control Act, makes it a federal crime to (1) use income obtained from racketeering activity to purchase any interest in an enterprise, (2) acquire or maintain an interest in an enterprise through racketeering activity, (3) conduct or participate in the affairs of an enterprise through racketeering activity, or (4) conspire to do any of the preceding activities.

RICO incorporates by reference twenty-six separate types of federal crimes and nine types of state felonies[14] and declares that if a person commits two of these offenses, he or she is guilty of "racketeering activity." Under the criminal provisions of RICO, any individual found guilty is subject to a fine of up to $25,000 per violation, imprisonment for up to twenty years, or both. Additionally, the statute provides that those who violate RICO may be required to forfeit (give up) any assets, in the form of property or cash, that were acquired as a result of the illegal activity or that were "involved in" or an "instrumentality of" the activity.

In the event of a RICO violation, the government can seek civil penalties, including the divestiture of a defendant's interest in a business (called forfeiture) or the dissolution of the business. Moreover, in some cases, the statute allows private individuals to sue violators and potentially recover three times their actual losses (treble damages), plus attorneys' fees, for business injuries caused by a violation of the statute. This is perhaps the most controversial aspect of RICO and one that continues to cause debate in the nation's federal courts.

13. 18 U.S.C. Sections 1961–1968.

14. See 18 U.S.C. Section 1961(1)(A).

Classification of Crimes

Depending on their degree of seriousness, crimes typically are classified as felonies or misdemeanors. **Felonies** are serious crimes punishable by death or by imprisonment for more than a year. Many states also define different degrees of felony offenses and vary the punishment according to the degree.

Misdemeanors are less serious crimes, punishable by a fine or by confinement for up to a year. In most jurisdictions, **petty offenses** are considered to be a subset of misdemeanors. Petty offenses are minor violations, such as jaywalking and violations of building codes. Even for petty offenses, however, a guilty party can be put in jail for a few days, fined, or both, depending on state or local law.

Defenses to Criminal Liability

Persons charged with crimes may be relieved of criminal liability if they can show that their criminal actions were justified under the circumstances. In certain circumstances, the law may also allow a person to be excused from criminal liability because she or he lacks the required mental state. We look at several of the defenses to criminal liability here.

Note that procedural violations, such as obtaining evidence without a valid search warrant, may also operate as defenses. As you will read later in this chapter, evidence obtained in violation of a defendant's constitutional rights normally may not be admitted in court. If the evidence is suppressed, then there may be no basis for prosecuting the defendant.

Justifiable Use of Force

One of the best-known defenses to criminal liability is that of **self-defense.** Other situations, however, also justify the use of force: the defense of one's dwelling, the defense of other property, and the prevention of a crime. In all of these situations, it is important to distinguish between deadly and nondeadly force. *Deadly force* is likely to result in death or serious bodily harm. *Nondeadly force* is force that reasonably appears necessary to prevent the imminent use of criminal force.

Generally speaking, people can use the amount of nondeadly force that seems necessary to protect themselves, their dwellings, or other property or to prevent the commission of a crime. Deadly force can be used in self-defense if the defender *reasonably believes* that imminent death or grievous bodily harm will otherwise result, if the attacker is using unlawful force (an example of lawful force is that exerted by a police officer), and if the defender has not initiated or provoked the attack. Deadly force normally can be used to defend a dwelling only if the unlawful entry is violent and the person believes deadly force is necessary to prevent imminent death or great bodily harm.

In some jurisdictions, however, deadly force can also be used if the person believes it is necessary to prevent the commission of a felony in the dwelling. Many states are expanding the situations in which the use of deadly force can be justified. (See this chapter's *Management Perspective* feature on the facing page for further discussion.)

Necessity

Sometimes, criminal defendants can be relieved of liability by showing that a criminal act was necessary to prevent an even greater harm. **EXAMPLE 6.11** Trevor is a convicted felon and, as such, is legally prohibited from possessing a firearm. While he and his wife are in a convenience store, a man draws a gun, points it at the cashier, and demands all the cash. Afraid that the man will start shooting, Trevor grabs the gun and holds on to it until police arrive. In this situation, if Trevor is charged with possession of a firearm, he can assert the defense of necessity. •

Insanity

A person who suffers from a mental illness may be incapable of the state of mind required to commit a crime. Thus, insanity can be a defense to a criminal charge. Note that an insanity defense does not allow a person to avoid prison. It simply means that if the defendant successfully proves insanity, she or he will be placed in a mental institution.

The courts have had difficulty deciding what the test for legal insanity should be, and psychiatrists as well as lawyers are critical of the tests used. Almost all federal courts and some states use the relatively liberal substantial-capacity test set forth in the Model Penal Code:

> A person is not responsible for criminal conduct if at the time of such conduct as a result of mental disease or defect he or she lacks substantial capacity either to appreciate the wrongfulness of his [or her] conduct or to conform his [or her] conduct to the requirements of the law.

Some states use the *M'Naghten* test,[15] under which a criminal defendant is not responsible if, at the time of the offense, he or she did not know the nature and quality of the act or did not know that the act was wrong. Other states use the irresistible-impulse test. A person operating under an irresistible impulse may know an act is wrong but cannot refrain from doing it. Under any of these tests, proving insanity is extremely difficult. For this reason, the insanity defense is rarely used and usually is not successful.

Mistake

Everyone has heard the saying "Ignorance of the law is no excuse." Ordinarily, ignorance of the law or a mistaken idea about what the law requires is not a valid defense. A *mistake of fact,* as opposed to a *mistake of law,* can excuse criminal responsibility if it negates the mental state necessary to commit a crime. **EXAMPLE 6.12** If Oliver Wheaton mistakenly walks off with Julie Tyson's briefcase because he thinks it is his, there is no crime. Theft requires knowledge that the property belongs to another. (If Wheaton's act causes Tyson to incur damages, however, she may sue him in a civil action for trespass to personal property or conversion—torts that were discussed in Chapter 4.) •

Duress

Duress exists when the *wrongful threat* of one person induces another person to perform an act that she or he would not otherwise have performed. In such a situation, duress is said to negate the mental state necessary to commit a crime because the defendant was forced or compelled to commit the act. Duress can be used as a defense to most crimes except murder. The states vary in how duress is defined and what types of crimes it can excuse, however. Generally, to successfully assert duress as a defense, the defendant must reasonably believe in the immediate danger, and the jury (or judge) must conclude that the defendant's belief was reasonable.

Entrapment

Entrapment is a defense designed to prevent police officers or other government agents from enticing persons to commit crimes in order to later prosecute them for those crimes. In the typical entrapment case, an undercover agent *suggests* that a crime be committed and somehow pressures or induces an individual to commit it. The agent then arrests the individual for the crime.

For entrapment to succeed as a defense, both the suggestion and the inducement must take place. The defense is intended not to prevent law enforcement agents from setting a trap for an unwary criminal but rather to prevent them from pushing the individual into it. The crucial issue is whether the person who committed a crime was predisposed to commit the illegal act or did so because the agent induced it.

Statute of Limitations

With some exceptions, such as for the crime of murder, statutes of limitations apply to crimes just as they do to civil wrongs. In other words, the state must initiate criminal prosecution within a certain number of years. If a criminal action is brought after the statutory time period has expired, the accused person can raise the statute of limitations as a defense.

---

15. A rule derived from *M'Naghten's* Case, 8 Eng.Rep. 718 (1843).

MANAGEMENT PERSPECTIVE • Can a Businessperson Use Deadly Force to Prevent a Crime on the Premises?

Management Faces a Legal Issue

Traditionally, the justifiable use of force, or self-defense, doctrine required prosecutors to distinguish between deadly and nondeadly force. In general, state laws have allowed individuals to use the amount of *nondeadly force* that is reasonably necessary to protect themselves, or their dwellings, businesses, or other property. Most states have allowed a person to use *deadly force* only when the person reasonably believed that imminent death or bodily harm would otherwise result. Additionally, the attacker had to be using unlawful force, and the defender had to have no other possible response or alternative way out of the life-threatening situation.

What the Courts Say

Today, many states still have "duty-to-retreat" laws. Under these laws, when a person's home is invaded or an assailant approaches, the person is required to retreat and cannot use deadly force unless her or his life is in danger.[a] Other states, however, are taking a very different approach and expanding the occasions when deadly force can be used in self-defense. Because such laws allow or even encourage the defender to stay and use force, they are known as "stand-your-ground" laws.

Florida, for example, enacted a statute that allows the use of deadly force to prevent the commission of a "forcible felony," including not only murder but also such crimes as robbery, carjacking, and sexual battery.[b] Under this law, a Florida resident has a right to shoot an intruder in his or her home or a would-be carjacker even if there is no physical threat to the owner's safety. At least thirteen other states have passed similar laws that eliminate the duty to retreat.

In a number of states, a person may use deadly force to prevent someone from breaking into his or her home, car, or place of business. For example, courts in Louisiana now allow a person to use deadly force to repel an attack while he or she is lawfully in a home, car, or place of business without imposing any duty to retreat.[c] Courts in Connecticut allow the use of deadly force not only to prevent a person from unlawful entry, but also when reasonably necessary to prevent arson or some other violent crime from being committed on the premises.[d]

Implications for Managers

The stand-your-ground laws that many states have enacted often include places of business as well as homes and vehicles. Consequently, businesspersons in those states can be less concerned about the duty-to-retreat doctrine. In addition, business liability insurance often costs less in states without a duty to retreat, because many statutes provide that the business owner is not liable in a civil action for injuries to the attacker. Even in states that impose a duty to retreat, there is no duty to retreat if doing so would increase rather than diminish the danger. Nevertheless, business owners should use deadly force only as a last resort to prevent the commission of crime at their business premises.

a. See, for example, *State v. Sandoval,* 342 Or. 506, 156 P.3d 60 (2007).
b. Florida Statutes Section 776.012.
c. See, for example, *State v. Johnson,* 948 So.2d 1229 (La.App. 3d Cir. 2007); and Louisiana Statutes Annotated Section 14:20.
d. See, for example, *State v. Terwilliger,* 105 Conn.App. 219, 937 A.2d 735 (2008); and Connecticut General Statutes Section 53a-20.

Immunity

At times, the government may wish to obtain information from a person accused of a crime. Accused persons are understandably reluctant to give information if it will be used to prosecute them, and they cannot be forced to do so. The privilege against **self-incrimination** is guaranteed by the Fifth Amendment to the U.S. Constitution, which reads, in part, "nor shall [any person] be compelled in any criminal case to be a witness against himself." When the state wishes to obtain information from a person accused of a crime, the state can grant *immunity* from prosecution or agree to prosecute for a less serious offense in exchange for the information. Once immunity is given, the person can no longer refuse to testify on Fifth Amendment grounds because he or she now has an absolute privilege against self-incrimination.

Often, a grant of immunity from prosecution for a serious crime is part of the **plea bargaining** between the defendant and the prosecuting attorney. The defendant may be convicted of a lesser offense, while the state uses the defendant's testimony to prosecute accomplices for serious crimes carrying heavy penalties.

Constitutional Safeguards and Criminal Procedures

Criminal law brings the power of the state, with all its resources, to bear against the individual. Criminal procedures are designed to protect the constitutional rights of individuals and to prevent the arbitrary use of power on the part of the government.

The U.S. Constitution provides specific safeguards for those accused of crimes, as mentioned in Chapter 1. Most of these safeguards protect individuals against state government actions, as well as federal government actions, by virtue of the due process clause of the Fourteenth Amendment. These protections are set forth in the Fourth, Fifth, Sixth, and Eighth Amendments.

Fourth Amendment Protections

The Fourth Amendment protects the "right of the people to be secure in their persons, houses, papers, and effects." Before searching or seizing private property, law enforcement officers must obtain a **search warrant**—an order from a judge or other public official authorizing the search or seizure.

To obtain a search warrant, law enforcement officers must convince a judge that they have reasonable grounds, or **probable cause**, to believe a search will reveal a specific illegality. Probable cause requires the officers to have trustworthy evidence that would convince a reasonable person that the proposed search or seizure is more likely justified than not. Furthermore, the Fourth Amendment prohibits general warrants. It requires a particular description of what is to be searched or seized. General searches through a person's belongings are impermissible. The search cannot extend beyond what is described in the warrant. Although search warrants require specificity, if a search warrant is issued for a person's residence, items that are in that residence may be searched even if they do not belong to that individual.

Because of the strong governmental interest in protecting the public, a warrant normally is not required for the seizure of spoiled or contaminated food. Nor are warrants required for searches of businesses in such highly regulated industries as liquor, guns, and strip mining. The standard used for highly regulated industries is sometimes applied in other contexts as well.

Fifth Amendment Protections

The Fifth Amendment offers significant protections for accused persons. One is the guarantee that no one can be deprived of "life, liberty, or property without due process of law." Remember from Chapter 1 that *due process of law* has both procedural and substantive aspects. Basically, the law must be carried out in a fair and orderly way. In criminal cases, due process means that defendants should have an opportunity to object to the charges against them before a fair, neutral decision maker, such as a judge. Two other important Fifth Amendment provisions protect persons against double jeopardy and self-incrimination.

DOUBLE JEOPARDY The Fifth Amendment also protects persons from **double jeopardy** (being tried twice for the same criminal offense). The prohibition against double jeopardy means that once a criminal defendant is acquitted (found "not guilty") of a particular crime, the government may not retry him or her for the same crime.

The prohibition against double jeopardy does not preclude the crime victim from bringing a civil suit against that same person to recover damages, however. In other words, a person found "not guilty" of assault and battery in a state criminal case can be sued for damages by the victim in a civil tort case. Additionally, a state's prosecution of a crime will not prevent a separate federal prosecution relating to the same activity (and vice versa), provided the activity can be classified as a different crime. Therefore, a person who is found not guilty of police brutality in a state court can still be prosecuted in a federal court for civil rights violations resulting from the same action.

SELF-INCRIMINATION The Fifth Amendment grants a privilege against self-incrimination. Thus, an accused person cannot be compelled to give testimony that might subject her or him to any criminal prosecution. The Fifth Amendment's guarantee against self-incrimination extends only to natural persons.

Because a corporation is a legal entity and not a natural person, the privilege against self-incrimination does not apply to it. Similarly, the business records of a partnership do not receive Fifth Amendment protection. When a partnership is required to produce these records, it must do so even if the information incriminates the persons who constitute the business entity. Sole proprietors who have not incorporated normally cannot be compelled to produce their business records. These individuals have full protection against self-incrimination because they function in only one capacity. There is no separate business entity (see Chapter 23).

Protections under the Sixth and Eighth Amendments

The Sixth Amendment guarantees several important rights for criminal defendants: the right to a speedy trial, the right to a jury trial, the right to a public trial, the right to confront witnesses, and the right to counsel. The Sixth Amendment right to counsel is one of the rights of which a suspect must be advised when he or she is arrested. In many cases, a statement that a criminal suspect makes in the absence of counsel is not admissible at trial unless the suspect has knowingly and voluntarily waived this right.

The Eighth Amendment prohibits excessive bail and fines, as well as cruel and unusual punishment. Under this amendment, prison officials are required to provide humane conditions of confinement, including adequate food, clothing, shelter, and medical care. If a prisoner has a serious medical problem, for instance, and a correctional officer is deliberately indifferent to it, a court could find that the prisoner's Eighth

Amendment rights were violated. Critics of the death penalty claim that it constitutes cruel and unusual punishment.[16]

The Exclusionary Rule and the *Miranda* Rule

Two other procedural protections for criminal defendants are the exclusionary rule and the *Miranda* rule.

THE EXCLUSIONARY RULE Under what is known as the **exclusionary rule,** all evidence obtained in violation of the constitutional rights spelled out in the Fourth, Fifth, and Sixth Amendments, as well as all evidence derived from illegally obtained evidence, normally must be excluded from the trial. Evidence derived from illegally obtained evidence is known as the "fruit of the poisonous tree." For example, if a confession is obtained after an illegal arrest, the arrest is "the poisonous tree," and the confession, if "tainted" by the arrest, is the "fruit."

The purpose of the exclusionary rule is to deter police from conducting warrantless searches and engaging in other misconduct. The rule is sometimes criticized because it can lead to injustice. Many a defendant has "gotten off on a technicality" because law enforcement personnel failed to observe procedural requirements. Even though a defendant may be obviously guilty, if the evidence of that guilt was obtained improperly (without a valid search warrant, for example), it normally cannot be used against the defendant in court.

If a suspect is arrested on the basis of a police officer's mistaken belief that there is an outstanding arrest warrant for that individual, should evidence found during a search incident to the arrest be excluded from the trial? This question arose in the following case.

16. See *Baze v. Rees,* 553 U.S. 35, 128 S.Ct. 1520, 170 L.Ed.2d 420 (2008).

Case 6.2 Herring v. United States

Supreme Court of the United States, 555 U.S. 135, 129 S.Ct. 695, 172 L.Ed.2d 496 (2009).
www.findlaw.com/casecode/supreme.html[a]

FACTS The Dale County, Alabama, sheriff's office maintains copies of arrest warrants in a computer database. When a warrant is recalled, Sharon Morgan, the warrant clerk, enters this information in the database and also throws out the physical copy. In July 2004, Sandy Pope, the warrant clerk in the sheriff's department in neighboring Coffee County, asked Morgan if there were any outstanding warrants for the arrest of Bennie Herring. Morgan checked her database and told Pope that there was a warrant. Coffee County officers arrested Herring. A search revealed methamphetamine in his pocket and an illegal gun in his truck. Meanwhile, Morgan learned that a mistake had been made: the warrant had been recalled. Herring was charged in a federal district court with illegal possession of a gun and drugs. He filed a motion to exclude the evidence on the ground that his arrest had been illegal. The court denied the motion, the U.S. Court of Appeals for the Eleventh Circuit affirmed the denial, and Herring appealed.

ISSUE Is evidence found during a search incident to an arrest that was based on a mistake admissible in the prosecution of the suspect?

DECISION Yes. The United States Supreme Court affirmed the lower court's judgment.

REASON The Court reasoned that the abuses that gave rise to the exclusionary rule involved intentional conduct that was clearly unconstitutional—for example, entering homes or businesses, sometimes forcibly, without search warrants or probable cause. The exclusionary rule applies in such cases because its deterrent effect on police misconduct outweighs the substantial social cost of "letting guilty and possibly dangerous defendants go free." But when a police mistake leading to an unlawful search is the result of an isolated instance of negligence—not "systemic error or reckless disregard of constitutional requirements"—the exclusionary rule does not apply. Thus, a police officer's reasonable reliance on mistaken information in a sheriff's computer database that an arrest warrant is outstanding does not require the exclusion of subsequently acquired evidence. Because there is "no basis for believing that application of the exclusionary rule in those circumstances would have any significant effect in deterring the errors," the evidence need not be excluded.

a. In the "Browse Supreme Court Opinions" section, click on "2009." On that page, scroll to the name of the case and click on it to access the opinion. FindLaw maintains this Web site.

WHY IS THIS CASE IMPORTANT? *This was the first time that the United States Supreme Court found that an exception existed to bar application of the exclusionary rule when a police officer honestly and reasonably relied in good faith on a warrant that later proved to be a mistake. The Court decided that the police clerk's negligence in mistakenly identifying an arrest warrant for the defendant did not justify application of the exclusionary rule. Because the officer's error was not "deliberate" and the officers involved were not "culpable" (at fault), the evidence discovered after the defendant's subsequent arrest was admissible at trial. Courts in the future will apply the "deliberate and culpable" test to determine whether to admit evidence obtained as a result of a police error or unconstitutional search.*

THE *MIRANDA* RULE In *Miranda v. Arizona,*[17] a case decided in 1966, the United States Supreme Court established the rule that individuals who are arrested must be informed of certain constitutional rights, including their Fifth Amendment right to remain silent and their Sixth Amendment right to counsel. If the arresting officers fail to inform a criminal suspect of these constitutional rights, any statements the suspect makes normally will not be admissible in court.

Over time, as part of a continuing attempt to balance the rights of accused persons against the rights of society, the United States Supreme Court has carved out numerous exceptions to the *Miranda* rule. For example, the Court has recognized a "public safety" exception, holding that certain statements—such as statements concerning the location of a weapon—are admissible even if the defendant was not given *Miranda* warnings. Additionally, a suspect must unequivocally and assertively request to exercise his or her right to counsel in order to stop police questioning. Saying "Maybe I should talk to a lawyer" during an interrogation after being taken into custody is not enough. Police officers are not required to decipher the suspect's intentions in such situations.

Criminal Process

As mentioned, a criminal prosecution differs significantly from a civil case in several respects. These differences reflect the desire to safeguard the rights of the individual against the state. Exhibit 6–3 on the facing page summarizes the major procedural steps in processing a criminal case. Here, we discuss three phases of the criminal process—arrest, indictment or information, and trial—in more detail.

Arrest

Before a warrant for arrest can be issued, there must be probable cause to believe that the individual in question has committed a crime. As discussed earlier, *probable cause* can be defined as a substantial likelihood that the person has committed or is about to commit a crime. Note that probable cause involves a likelihood, not just a possibility. Arrests can be made without a warrant if there is no time to get one, but the action of the arresting officer is still judged by the standard of probable cause.

Indictment or Information

Individuals must be formally charged with having committed specific crimes before they can be brought to trial. If issued by a grand jury, this charge is called an **indictment.**[18] A **grand jury** usually consists of more jurors than the ordinary trial jury. A grand jury does not determine the guilt or innocence of an accused party. Rather, its function is to hear the state's evidence and to determine whether a reasonable basis (probable cause) exists for believing that a crime has been committed and that a trial ought to be held.

Usually, grand juries are used in cases involving serious crimes, such as murder. For lesser crimes, an individual may be formally charged with a crime by what is called an **information,** or criminal complaint. An information will be issued by a government prosecutor if the prosecutor determines that there is sufficient evidence to justify bringing the individual to trial.

Trial

At a criminal trial, the accused person does not have to prove anything. The entire burden of proof is on the prosecutor (the state). The prosecution must show that, based on all the evidence presented, the defendant's guilt is established *beyond a reasonable doubt.* If there is a reasonable doubt as to whether a criminal defendant committed the crime with which she or he has been charged, then the verdict must be "not guilty." Note that giving a verdict of "not guilty" is not the same as stating that the defendant is innocent. It merely means that not enough evidence was properly presented to the court to prove guilt beyond a reasonable doubt.

Courts have complex rules about what types of evidence may be presented and how the evidence may be brought out in criminal cases. These rules are designed to ensure that evidence in trials is relevant, reliable, and not prejudicial toward the defendant.

Sentencing Guidelines

In 1984, Congress passed the Sentencing Reform Act. This act created the U.S. Sentencing Commission, which was charged with the task of standardizing sentences for federal crimes. The commission's guidelines, which became effective in 1987, established a range of possible penalties for each federal crime and required the judge to select a sentence from within that range. In other words, the guidelines originally established a mandatory system because judges were not allowed to deviate from the specified sentencing range. Some federal judges felt uneasy about imposing long prison sentences on certain criminal defendants, particularly first-time offenders, and in illegal substances cases involving small quantities of drugs.[19]

In 2005, the United States Supreme Court held that certain provisions of the federal sentencing guidelines were unconstitutional.[20] Essentially, the Court's ruling changed the federal

17. 384 U.S. 436, 86 S.Ct. 1602, 16 L.Ed.2d 694 (1964).
18. Pronounced in-*dyte*-ment.
19. See, for example, *United States v. Angelos,* 345 F.Supp.2d 1227 (D. Utah 2004).
20. *United States v. Booker,* 543 U.S. 220, 125 S.Ct. 738, 160 L.Ed.2d 621 (2005).

• ***Exhibit* 6–3 Major Procedural Steps in a Criminal Case**

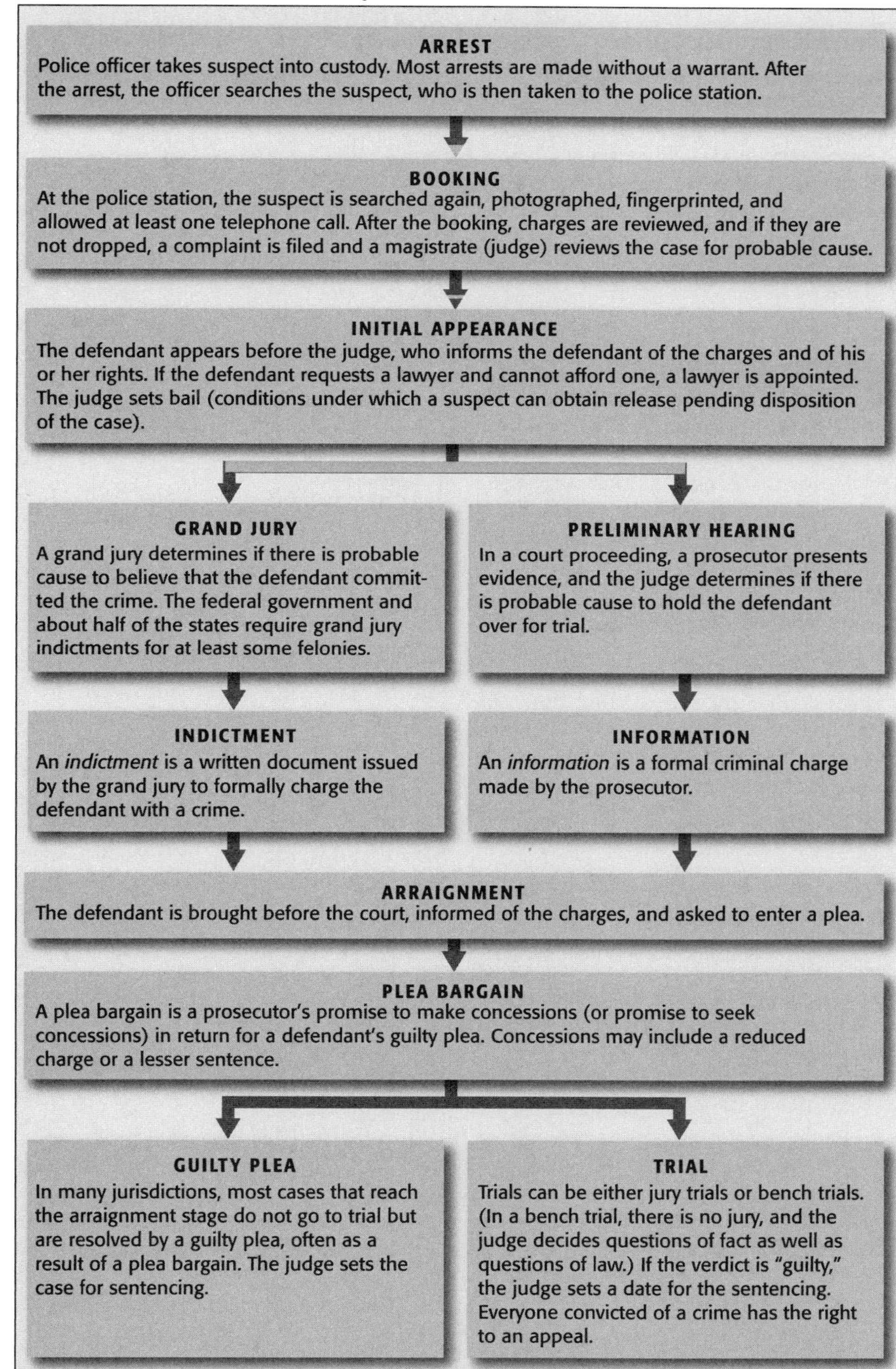
ARREST
Police officer takes suspect into custody. Most arrests are made without a warrant. After the arrest, the officer searches the suspect, who is then taken to the police station.
BOOKING
At the police station, the suspect is searched again, photographed, fingerprinted, and allowed at least one telephone call. After the booking, charges are reviewed, and if they are not dropped, a complaint is filed and a magistrate (judge) reviews the case for probable cause.
INITIAL APPEARANCE
The defendant appears before the judge, who informs the defendant of the charges and of his or her rights. If the defendant requests a lawyer and cannot afford one, a lawyer is appointed. The judge sets bail (conditions under which a suspect can obtain release pending disposition of the case).
GRAND JURY
A grand jury determines if there is probable cause to believe that the defendant committed the crime. The federal government and about half of the states require grand jury indictments for at least some felonies.
PRELIMINARY HEARING
In a court proceeding, a prosecutor presents evidence, and the judge determines if there is probable cause to hold the defendant over for trial.
INDICTMENT
An *indictment* is a written document issued by the grand jury to formally charge the defendant with a crime.
INFORMATION
An *information* is a formal criminal charge made by the prosecutor.
ARRAIGNMENT
The defendant is brought before the court, informed of the charges, and asked to enter a plea.
PLEA BARGAIN
A plea bargain is a prosecutor's promise to make concessions (or promise to seek concessions) in return for a defendant's guilty plea. Concessions may include a reduced charge or a lesser sentence.
GUILTY PLEA
In many jurisdictions, most cases that reach the arraignment stage do not go to trial but are resolved by a guilty plea, often as a result of a plea bargain. The judge sets the case for sentencing.
TRIAL
Trials can be either jury trials or bench trials. (In a bench trial, there is no jury, and the judge decides questions of fact as well as questions of law.) If the verdict is "guilty," the judge sets a date for the sentencing. Everyone convicted of a crime has the right to an appeal.

sentencing guidelines from mandatory to advisory. Depending on the circumstances of the case, a federal trial judge may now depart from the guidelines if he or she believes that it is reasonable to do so. Sentencing guidelines still exist and provide for enhanced punishment for certain types of crimes and violations of securities laws (see Chapter 26). In 2009, the Court considered the sentencing guidelines again and held that a sentencing judge cannot presume that a sentence within the applicable guidelines is reasonable.[21] The judge must take into account the various sentencing factors that apply to an individual defendant before concluding that a particular sentence is reasonable.

Cyber Crime

The U.S. Department of Justice broadly defines **computer crime** as any violation of criminal law that involves knowledge of computer technology for its perpetration, investigation, or prosecution. A number of white-collar crimes, such as fraud, embezzlement, and theft of intellectual property, are now committed with the aid of computers and are thus considered computer crimes.

Many computer crimes fall under the broad label of **cyber crime,** which describes any criminal activity occurring via a computer in the virtual community of the Internet. Most cyber crimes are not new crimes. Rather, they are existing crimes in which the Internet is the instrument of wrongdoing. Here, we look at several types of activity that constitute cyber crimes against persons or property.

Cyber Fraud

Fraud is any misrepresentation knowingly made with the intention of deceiving another and on which a reasonable person would and does rely to her or his detriment. **Cyber fraud** is fraud committed over the Internet. Frauds that were once conducted solely by mail or phone can now be found online, and new technology has led to increasingly creative ways to commit fraud.

ONLINE AUCTION FRAUD Online auction fraud, in its most basic form, is a simple process. A person puts up an expensive item for auction, on either a legitimate or a fake auction site, and then refuses to send the product after receiving payment. Or, as a variation, the wrongdoer may provide the purchaser with an item that is worth less than the one offered in the auction. The larger online auction sites, such as eBay, try to protect consumers against such schemes by providing warnings about deceptive sellers or offering various forms of insurance.

The nature of the Internet, however, makes it nearly impossible to completely block fraudulent auction activity. Because users can assume multiple identities, it is very difficult to pinpoint fraudulent sellers—they will simply change their screen names with each auction.

ONLINE RETAIL FRAUD Somewhat similar to online auction fraud is online retail fraud, in which consumers pay directly (without bidding) for items that are never delivered. Because most consumers will purchase items only from reputable, well-known sites such as Amazon.com, criminals have had to take advantage of some of the complexities of cyberspace to lure unknowing customers. As with other forms of online fraud, it is difficult to determine the actual extent of online sales fraud, but anecdotal evidence suggests that it is a substantial problem.

CASE EXAMPLE 6.13 Jeremy Jaynes grossed more than $750,000 per week selling nonexistent or worthless products such as "penny stock pickers" and "Internet history erasers." By the time he was arrested, he had amassed an estimated $24 million from his various fraudulent schemes.[22] •

Cyber Theft

In cyberspace, thieves are not subject to the physical limitations of the "real" world. A thief can steal data stored in a networked computer with Internet access from anywhere on the globe. Only the speed of the connection and the thief's computer equipment limit the quantity of data that can be stolen.

IDENTITY THEFT Not surprisingly, there has been a marked increase in identity theft in recent years. **Identity theft** occurs when the wrongdoer steals a form of identification—such as a name, date of birth, or Social Security number—and uses the information to access the victim's financial resources. This crime existed to a certain extent before the widespread use of the Internet. Thieves would rifle through garbage to find credit-card or bank account numbers and then use those numbers to purchase goods or to withdraw funds from the victims' accounts.

The Internet has provided even easier access to private data. Frequent Web surfers surrender a wealth of information about themselves without knowing it. Many Web sites use "cookies" to collect data on those who visit their sites. The data may include the areas of the site the user visits and the links on which the user clicks. Furthermore, Web browsers often store information such as the consumer's name and

21. *Nelson v. United States,* 555 U.S. 350, 129 S.Ct. 890, 172 L.Ed.2d 719 (2009).

22. *Jaynes v. Commonwealth of Virginia,* 276 Va.App. 443, 666 S.E.2d 303 (2008).

e-mail address. Finally, every time a purchase is made online, the item is linked to the purchaser's name, allowing Web retailers to amass a database of who is buying what.

In the following case, the defendant was charged with identity theft and mail fraud stemming from his role in a scheme to file fraudulent claims for unemployment benefits. The court had to decide whether to suppress evidence of the crime that officers found at the defendant's girlfriend's house.

Case 6.3 United States v. Oliver

United States Court of Appeals, Fifth Circuit, 630 F.3d 397 (2011).
www.ca5.uscourts.gov/Opinions.aspx[a]

FACTS Lonnie Oliver, Jr., was arrested by officers investigating a scheme to file fraudulent claims for unemployment benefits. Oliver and others were suspected of gaining access to people's names and Social Security numbers and using this information to receive unemployment benefits. After he was read his *Miranda* rights, Oliver confessed to his role in the scheme. Oliver also consented to a search of his car, but he refused to consent to a search of his home. Oliver's co-defendant then told the police that Oliver had stored a laptop computer and a cardboard box containing items related to the scheme at the apartment of Erica Armstrong, Oliver's girlfriend. Acting on this information, agents went to Armstrong's apartment, and she gave them the box and the laptop computer. Inside the box, officers found hundreds of personal identifiers of victims, along with credit and debit cards. They also found a notebook labeled "business ideas" with Oliver's notes for the scheme. After the laptop was seized, officers obtained a warrant to search its contents and found evidence that Oliver had used it to submit fraudulent unemployment claims. Oliver filed a motion to suppress the evidence in the cardboard box on the ground that it had been obtained unconstitutionally because he had not consented to the search. Further, he claimed that the evidence found on the laptop should also be excluded as "fruit of the poisonous tree" (see page 117) because the warrant to search the laptop was issued on the basis of an affidavit that relied, in part, on the evidence in the box. The district court denied the motion. Oliver appealed.

ISSUE Were the searches of Oliver's laptop and box lawful under the Fourth Amendment?

DECISION Yes. A federal appellate court affirmed the lower court's decision that the search was legal and that the evidence in the box and on the laptop computer was admissible.

REASON The court explained that the private search doctrine legitimized the search of the box and that the independent source doctrine applied to the computer. Under the private search doctrine, when a private individual examines the contents of a closed container, a subsequent search of the container by government officials does not constitute an unlawful search for purposes of the Fourth Amendment. In this case, Armstrong testified that she had looked through the contents of the box before the police showed up at her apartment. Even though the officers were unaware of her actions at that time, the private search doctrine applied and legitimized the officers' search. As for the laptop, under the independent source doctrine, evidence obtained through a legal, independent source need not be suppressed. Both Oliver and his co-defendant had admitted to using a laptop computer to submit fraudulent unemployment claims. Therefore, police had an independent source for obtaining a warrant to search the laptop, despite whether its original seizure was legal.

WHAT IF THE FACTS WERE DIFFERENT? *Suppose that Armstrong had not looked through the cardboard box before the police searched it. Would the box's contents have been admissible? Why or why not?*

a. Under the heading "Search for opinions where," type "09-10133" in the "and/or Docket number is:" box and click on "Search." In the result, click on the docket number to access the opinion. The U.S. Court of Appeals for the Fifth Circuit maintains this Web site.

PHISHING A distinct form of identity theft known as **phishing** has added a different wrinkle to the practice. In a phishing attack, the perpetrators "fish" for financial data and passwords from consumers by posing as a legitimate business such as a bank or credit-card company. The "phisher" sends an e-mail asking the recipient to "update" or "confirm" vital information, often with the threat that an account or some other service will be discontinued if the information is not provided. Once the unsuspecting individual enters the information, the phisher can use it to masquerade as that person or to drain his or her bank or credit account.

EXAMPLE 6.14 Customers of Wachovia Bank received official-looking e-mails telling them to type in personal information on a Web form to complete a mandatory installation of a new Internet security certificate. But the Web site was bogus. When people filled out the forms, their computers were infected and funneled their data to a computer server. The cyber criminals then sold the data. •

VISHING When phishing involves some form of voice communication, the scam is known as **vishing.** In one variation, the consumer receives an e-mail saying there is a problem with an account and that she or he should call a certain telephone number to resolve the problem. Sometimes, the e-mail even says that a telephone call is being requested so that the recipient will know that this is not a phishing attempt. Of course, the goal is to get the consumer to divulge passwords and account information during the call. Vishing scams use Voice over Internet Protocol (VoIP) service, which enables telephone calls to be made over the Internet. Such calls are inexpensive and make it easy for scammers to hide their identity.

EMPLOYMENT FRAUD Cyber criminals also look for victims at online job-posting sites. Claiming to be an employment officer in a well-known company, the criminal sends bogus e-mail messages to job seekers. The message asks the unsuspecting job seeker to reveal enough information to allow for identity theft. **CASE EXAMPLE 6.15** The job site Monster.com had to ask all of its users to change their passwords because cyber thieves had broken into its databases and stolen user identities and passwords. The theft of 4.5 million users' personal information from Monster.com was one of Britain's largest cyber theft cases.[23] ●

CREDIT-CARD THEFT Credit-card theft was mentioned previously in connection with identity theft. An important point to note, however, is that stolen credit cards are much more likely to hurt merchants and credit-card issuers (such as banks) than consumers. In most situations, the legitimate holders of credit cards are not held responsible for the costs of purchases made with a stolen number. That means the financial burden must be borne either by the merchant or by the credit-card company. Most credit-card issuers require merchants to cover the costs—especially if the address to which the goods are sent does not match the billing address of the credit card.

Additionally, companies take risks by storing their online customers' credit-card numbers. By doing so, companies can provide quicker service because a consumer can make a purchase by providing a code or clicking on a particular icon without entering a lengthy card number. These electronic warehouses are quite tempting to cyber thieves, however.

Hacking

A **hacker** is someone who uses one computer to break into another. The danger posed by hackers has increased significantly because of **botnets,** or networks of computers that have been appropriated by hackers without the knowledge of their owners. A hacker will secretly install a program on thousands, if not millions, of personal computer "robots," or "bots," that allows him or her to forward transmissions to an even larger number of systems.

EXAMPLE 6.16 In 2011, someone hacked into Sony Corporation's PlayStation 3 video gaming and entertainment networks. The incident forced the company to temporarily shut down its online gaming services and affected more than 100 million online accounts that provide gaming, chat, and music-streaming services. ●

MALWARE Botnets are one of the latest forms of **malware,** a term that refers to any program that is harmful to a computer or, by extension, a computer user. A **worm,** for example, is a software program that is capable of reproducing itself as it spreads from one computer to the next. **EXAMPLE 6.17** In 2009, within three weeks, the computer worm called "Conflicker" spread to more than 1 million personal computers around the world. It was transmitted to some computers through the use of Facebook and Twitter. This worm also infected servers and devices plugged into infected computers via USB ports, such as iPods and USB flash drives. ●

A **virus,** another form of malware, is also able to reproduce itself, but must be attached to an "infested" host file to travel from one computer network to another. For example, hackers are now capable of corrupting banner ads that use Adobe's Flash Player. When an Internet user clicks on the banner ad, a virus is installed. Worms and viruses can be programmed to perform a number of functions, such as prompting host computers to continually "crash" and reboot, or otherwise infect the system.

SERVICE-BASED HACKING A recent trend in business computer applications is the use of "software as a service." Instead of buying software to install on a computer, the user connects to Web-based software. The user can write e-mails, edit spreadsheets, and the like using his or her Web browser. Cyber criminals have adapted this method and now offer "crimeware as a service."

A would-be thief no longer has to be a computer hacker to create a botnet or steal banking information and credit-card numbers. He or she can rent the online services of cyber criminals to do the work on such sites as NeoSploit. The thief can even target individual groups, such as U.S. physicians or British attorneys. The cost of renting a Web site to do the work is only a few cents per target computer.

CYBERTERRORISM Hackers who break into computers without authorization often commit cyber theft, but sometimes their principal aim is to prove how smart they are by gaining access to others' password-protected computers. **Cyberterrorists** are hackers who, rather than trying to gain attention, strive to remain undetected so that they can exploit computers for a serious impact. Just as terrorists destroyed the World Trade Center towers and a portion of the Pentagon on September 11, 2001, cyberterrorists might explode "logic

23. John Bingham, "Monster.com Hacking Follows Tradition of Cyber Theft," *Telegraph.co.uk.*, January 28, 2009.

bombs" to shut down central computers. Such activities obviously can pose a danger to national security.

Cyberterrorists, as well as hackers, may target businesses. The goals of a hacking operation might include a wholesale theft of data, such as a merchant's customer files, or the monitoring of a computer to discover a business firm's plans and transactions. A cyberterrorist might also want to insert false codes or data. For example, the processing control system of a food manufacturer could be changed to alter the levels of ingredients so that consumers of the food would become ill.

A cyberterrorist attack on a major financial institution, such as the New York Stock Exchange or a large bank, could leave securities or money markets in flux and seriously affect the daily lives of millions of citizens. Similarly, any prolonged disruption of computer, cable, satellite, or telecommunications systems due to the actions of expert hackers would have serious repercussions on business operations—and national security—on a global level.

Spam

Businesses and individuals alike are targets of **spam,** or unsolicited "junk e-mails" that flood virtual mailboxes with advertisements, solicitations, and other messages. Considered relatively harmless in the early days of the Internet's popularity, by 2012 spam accounted for roughly 75 percent of all e-mails. Far from being harmless, the unwanted files can wreak havoc on business operations.

STATE REGULATION In an attempt to combat spam, thirty-six states have enacted laws that prohibit or regulate its use. Many state laws that regulate spam require the senders of e-mail ads to instruct the recipients on how they can "opt out" of further e-mail ads from the same sources. For instance, in some states an unsolicited e-mail ad must include a toll-free phone number or return e-mail address through which the recipient can contact the sender to request that no more ads be e-mailed.

THE CAN-SPAM ACT In 2003, Congress enacted the Controlling the Assault of Non-Solicited Pornography and Marketing (CAN-SPAM) Act. The legislation applies to any "commercial electronic mail messages" that are sent to promote a commercial product or service. Significantly, the statute preempts state antispam laws except for those provisions in state laws that prohibit false and deceptive e-mailing practices.

Generally, the act permits the use of unsolicited commercial e-mail but prohibits certain types of spamming activities, including the use of a false return address and the use of false, misleading, or deceptive information when sending e-mail. The statute also prohibits the use of "dictionary attacks"—sending messages to randomly generated e-mail addresses—and the "harvesting" of e-mail addresses from Web sites with specialized software.

CASE EXAMPLE 6.18 In 2007, federal officials arrested Robert Alan Soloway, considered one of the world's most prolific spammers. Because Soloway had been using botnets to send out hundreds of millions of unwanted e-mails, he was charged under anti–identity theft laws for the appropriation of other people's domain names, among other crimes. In 2008, Soloway, known as the "Spam King," pleaded guilty to mail fraud and failure to pay taxes.[24] ● Arresting prolific spammers, however, has done little to curb spam, which continues to flow at a rate of billions of messages per day.

THE U.S. SAFE WEB ACT After the CAN-SPAM Act prohibited false and deceptive e-mails originating in the United States, spamming from servers located in other nations increased. These cross-border spammers generally were able to escape detection and legal sanctions because the Federal Trade Commission (FTC) lacked the authority to investigate foreign spamming.

Congress sought to rectify the situation by enacting the U.S. Safe Web Act of 2006. This act allows the FTC to cooperate and share information with foreign agencies in investigating and prosecuting those involved in Internet fraud and deception, including spamming, spyware, and various Internet frauds. It also provides Internet service providers (ISPs) with a "safe harbor" (immunity from liability) for supplying information to the FTC concerning possible unfair or deceptive conduct in foreign jurisdictions.

Prosecution of Cyber Crime

Cyber crime has raised new issues in the investigation of crimes and the prosecution of offenders. Determining the "location" of a cyber crime and identifying a criminal in cyberspace are two significant challenges for law enforcement.

JURISDICTION AND IDENTIFICATION CHALLENGES A threshold issue is, of course, jurisdiction. A person who commits an act against a business in California, where the act is a cyber crime, might never have set foot in California but might instead reside in New York, or even in Canada, where the act may not be a crime. If the crime was committed via e-mail, the question arises as to whether the e-mail would constitute sufficient minimum contacts (see Chapter 2 on page 29) for the victim's state to exercise jurisdiction over the perpetrator.

Identifying the wrongdoer can also be difficult. Cyber criminals do not leave physical traces, such as fingerprints or DNA samples, as evidence of their crimes. Even electronic "footprints" can be hard to find and follow. For example, e-mail may be sent through a remailer, an online service that guarantees that a message cannot be traced to its source.

---

24. " 'Spam King of Seattle' Soloway Pleads Guilty," *SC Magazine,* March 17, 2008: n.p. Web.

THE COMPUTER FRAUD AND ABUSE ACT For these reasons, laws written to protect physical property are often difficult to apply in cyberspace. Nonetheless, governments at both the state and the federal level have taken significant steps toward controlling cyber crime, both by applying existing criminal statutes and by enacting new laws that specifically address wrongs committed in cyberspace.

Perhaps the most significant federal statute specifically addressing cyber crime is the Counterfeit Access Device and Computer Fraud and Abuse Act of 1984.[25] This act is commonly known as the Computer Fraud and Abuse Act, or CFAA. Among other things, the CFAA provides that a person who accesses a computer online, without authority, to obtain classified, restricted, or protected data (or attempts to do so) is subject to criminal prosecution. Such data could include financial and credit records, medical records, legal files, military and national security files, and other confidential information in government or private computers. The crime has two elements: accessing a computer without authority and taking the data.

This theft is a felony if it is committed for a commercial purpose or for private financial gain, or if the value of the stolen data (or computer time) exceeds $5,000. Penalties include fines and imprisonment for up to twenty years. For a discussion of a case involving students who were accused of violating the CFAA, see this chapter's *Adapting the Law to the Online Environment* feature below.

25. 18 U.S.C. Section 1030.

Adapting the Law to the Online Environment

Student Plagiarism and the Computer Fraud and Abuse Act

The Computer Fraud and Abuse Act (CFAA) is primarily a criminal statute in that its main purpose is to deter computer hackers. Nevertheless, in certain circumstances, private parties may bring a civil suit alleging a violation of the act. One case arose when four high school students were required to submit written assignments to an online anti-plagiarism service, which then archived the students' work.

Fighting Student Plagiarism

Instructors in high schools, colleges, and universities worldwide face a plagiarism problem of epic proportions. Any student can access various online sources from which work can be plagiarized. As a result, several companies, including iParadigms, LLC, have created software and other services to help instructors detect plagiarism. One of iParadigms' products is Turnitin Plagiarism Detection Service. Instructors can require their students to submit written assignments to Turnitin, which then compares the students' work with more than 10 billion Web pages; 70 million student papers; 10,000 newspapers, magazines, and scholarly journals; plus thousands of books. Students who submit their work to Turnitin must agree to allow iParadigms to archive their papers in the Turnitin master file.

Does Gaining Unauthorized Access to an Online Service Violate the Computer Fraud and Abuse Act?

Four high school students who were required to submit their assignments to Turnitin filed a suit in a federal district court, claiming that the archiving of their papers infringed their copyright interests. The court found that the archiving of the papers qualified as a "fair use" and thus did not infringe the students' copyright interests (see Chapter 5 for a full discussion of copyright law). Hence, the court granted summary judgment for iParadigms, LLC, a decision that was upheld on appeal by the U.S. Court of Appeals for the Fourth Circuit.[a]

Meanwhile, iParadigms had counterclaimed, alleging that one of the high school students had gained unauthorized access to the company's online services in violation of the CFAA. Using a password and login ID obtained via the Internet, the student had registered and submitted papers to Turnitin, misrepresenting himself as a student of a university that he had never attended.

Was this a violation of the CFAA? The federal district court did not believe so. On appeal, though, the decision was reversed and remanded. The appellate court observed that iParadigms had to spend costly resources to determine whether there was a glitch in its online registration program. These expenses fell under the economic damages part of the act, which defines *loss* as:

> any reasonable cost to any victim, including the cost of responding to an offense, conducting a damage assessment, and restoring . . . the system . . . to its condition prior to the offense, and any revenue lost, cost incurred, or other consequential damages incurred because of interruption to service.[b]

The federal appeals court also ruled in iParadigms' favor on a separate counterclaim, finding that the defendant had violated the Virginia Computer Crimes Act.[c] The consequential damages presented by iParadigms fit within the "any damages" language of the Virginia law.

FOR CRITICAL ANALYSIS

What might have motivated the four high school students to bring their lawsuit?

a. *A.V. ex rel. Vanderhye v. iParadigms, LLC,* 562 F.3d 630 (4th Cir. 2009).

b. 18 U.S.C. Section 1030(a)(11).

c. Virginia Code Annotated Sections 18.2-152.3 and 18.2-152.6.

Reviewing . . . Criminal Law and Cyber Crime

Edward Hanousek worked for Pacific & Arctic Railway and Navigation Company (P&A) as a roadmaster of the White Pass & Yukon Railroad in Alaska. As an officer of the corporation, Hanousek was responsible "for every detail of the safe and efficient maintenance and construction of track, structures, and marine facilities of the entire railroad," including special projects. One project was a rock quarry, known as "6-mile," above the Skagway River. Next to the quarry, and just beneath the surface, ran a high-pressure oil pipeline owned by Pacific & Arctic Pipeline, Inc., P&A's sister company. When the quarry's backhoe operator punctured the pipeline, an estimated 1,000 to 5,000 gallons of oil were discharged into the river. Hanousek was charged with negligently discharging a harmful quantity of oil into a navigable water of the United States in violation of the criminal provisions of the Clean Water Act (CWA). Using the information presented in the chapter, answer the following questions.

1 Did Hanousek have the required mental state *(mens rea)* to be convicted of a crime? Why or why not?
2 Which theory discussed in the chapter would enable a court to hold Hanousek criminally liable for violating the statute regardless of whether he participated in, directed, or even knew about the specific violation?
3 Could the quarry's backhoe operator who punctured the pipeline also be charged with a crime in this situation? Explain.
4 Suppose that at trial, Hanousek argued that he could not be convicted because he was not aware of the requirements of the CWA. Would this defense be successful? Why or why not?

Terms and Concepts

actus reus 108
arson 110
beyond a reasonable doubt 107
botnet 122
burglary 110
computer crime 120
crime 107
cyber crime 120
cyber fraud 120
cyberterrorist 122
double jeopardy 116
duress 114
embezzlement 111
entrapment 114
exclusionary rule 117
felony 113
forgery 110
grand jury 118
hacker 122
identity theft 120
indictment 118
information 118
larceny 110
malware 122
mens rea 108
misdemeanor 113
money laundering 113
petty offense 113
phishing 121
plea bargaining 115
probable cause 116
robbery 109
search warrant 116
self-defense 113
self-incrimination 115
spam 123
virus 122
vishing 121
white-collar crime 111
worm 122

Chapter Summary: Criminal Law and Cyber Crime

Civil Law and Criminal Law (See pages 106–108.)	1. *Civil law*—Spells out the duties that exist between persons or between citizens and their governments, excluding the duty not to commit crimes. 2. *Criminal law*—Has to do with crimes, which are defined as wrongs against society set forth in statutes and, if committed, punishable by society through fines and/or imprisonment—and, in some cases, death. Because crimes are *offenses against society as a whole,* they are prosecuted by a public official, not by victims. 3. *Key differences*—An important difference between civil and criminal law is that the standard of proof is higher in criminal cases. 4. *Civil liability for criminal acts*—A criminal act may give rise to both criminal liability and tort liability.
Criminal Liability (See pages 108–109.)	1. *Guilty act*—In general, some form of harmful act must be committed for a crime to exist. 2. *Intent*—An intent to commit a crime, or a wrongful mental state, is generally required for a crime to exist. 3. *Liability of corporations*—Corporations normally are liable for the crimes committed by their agents and employees within the course and scope of their employment. Corporations cannot be imprisoned, but they can be fined.

Continued

Chapter Summary: Criminal Law and Cyber Crime—Continued

Criminal Liability—Continued	4. *Liability of corporate officers and directors*—Corporate directors and officers are personally liable for the crimes they commit and may be held liable for the actions of employees under their supervision.
Types of Crimes (See pages 109–113.)	Crimes fall into five general categories: violent crime, property crime, public order crime, white-collar crime, and organized crime. Each type of crime may also be classified according to its degree of seriousness. Felonies are serious crimes punishable by death or by imprisonment for more than one year. Misdemeanors are less serious crimes punishable by fines or by confinement for up to one year.
Defenses to Criminal Liability (See pages 113–115.)	Defenses to criminal liability include justifiable use of force, necessity, insanity, mistake, duress, entrapment, the statute of limitations, and, in some cases, immunity.
Constitutional Safeguards and Criminal Procedures (See pages 115–118.)	1. *Fourth Amendment*—Provides protection against unreasonable searches and seizures and requires that probable cause exist before a warrant for a search or an arrest can be issued. 2. *Fifth Amendment*—Requires due process of law, prohibits double jeopardy, and protects against self-incrimination. 3. *Sixth Amendment*—Provides guarantees of a speedy trial, a trial by jury, a public trial, the right to confront witnesses, and the right to counsel. 4. *Eighth Amendment*—Prohibits excessive bail and fines, and cruel and unusual punishment. 5. *Exclusionary rule*—A criminal procedural rule that prohibits the introduction at trial of all evidence obtained in violation of constitutional rights, as well as any evidence derived from the illegally obtained evidence. 6. *Miranda rule*—A rule holding that individuals who are arrested must be informed of certain constitutional rights.
Criminal Process (See pages 118–120.)	1. *Arrest, indictment, and trial*—Procedures governing arrest, indictment, and trial for a crime are designed to safeguard the rights of the individual against the state. See Exhibit 6–3 on page 119 for a summary of the procedural steps involved in prosecuting a criminal case. 2. *Sentencing guidelines*—The federal government has established sentencing laws or guidelines, which are no longer mandatory but provide a range of penalties for each federal crime.
Cyber Crime (See pages 120–124.)	1. *Cyber fraud*—Occurs when misrepresentations are knowingly made over the Internet to deceive another; for example, online auction fraud and online retail fraud. 2. *Cyber theft*—In cyberspace, thieves can steal data from computers worldwide. Phishing, vishing, employment fraud, and credit-card theft are variations of identity theft. 3. *Hacking*—A hacker is a person who uses one computer to break into another. Cyberterrorists may target businesses to find out a firm's plans or transactions, or insert false codes or data to damage a firm's product. A cyberterrorist attack could have serious repercussions, including jeopardizing national security. 4. *Spam*—Unsolicited junk e-mail accounts for about three-quarters of all e-mails. Laws to combat spam have been enacted by thirty-six states and the federal government, but the flow of spam continues. 5. *Prosecution of cyber crime*—Prosecuting cyber crime is difficult. Identifying the wrongdoer through electronic footprints is complicated, and jurisdictional issues may arise when the suspect lives in another jurisdiction or nation. A significant federal statute addressing cyber crime is the Computer Fraud and Abuse Act of 1984.

ExamPrep

ISSUE SPOTTERS

—Check your answers to these questions against the answers provided in Appendix G.

1 Ethan walks off with Floyd's bowling ball mistakenly believing that it is his. Is this theft? Why or why not?

2 Daisy takes her roommate's credit card, intending to charge expenses that she incurs on a vacation. Her first stop is a gas station, where she uses the card to pay for gas. With respect to the gas station, has she committed a crime? If so, what is it?

BEFORE THE TEST

Go to **www.cengagebrain.com**, enter the ISBN 9781111530624, and click on "Find" to locate this textbook's Web site. Then, click on "Access Now" under "Study Tools," and select Chapter 6 at the top. There, you will find an Interactive Quiz that you can take to assess your mastery of the concepts in this chapter, as well as Flashcards and a Glossary of important terms.

For Review

1 What two elements must exist before a person can be held liable for a crime? Can a corporation commit crimes?
2 What are five broad categories of crimes? What is white-collar crime?
3 What defenses might be raised by criminal defendants to avoid liability for criminal acts?
4 What constitutional safeguards exist to protect persons accused of crimes?
5 How has the Internet expanded opportunities for identity theft?

Questions and Case Problems

6–1 Double Jeopardy. Armington, while robbing a drugstore, shot and seriously injured Jennings, a drugstore clerk. Armington was subsequently convicted of armed robbery and assault and battery in a criminal trial. Jennings later brought a civil tort suit against Armington for damages. Armington contended that he could not be tried again for the same crime, as that would constitute double jeopardy, which is prohibited by the Fifth Amendment to the U.S. Constitution. Is Armington correct? Explain.

6–2 Property Crimes. Which, if any, of the following crimes necessarily involves illegal activity on the part of more than one person?

(a) Bribery
(b) Forgery
(c) Embezzlement
(d) Larceny
(e) Receiving stolen property

6–3 Cyber Scam. Kayla, a student at Learnwell University, owes $20,000 in unpaid tuition. If Kayla does not pay the tuition, Learnwell will not allow her to graduate. To obtain the funds to pay the debt, she sends e-mail letters to people that she does not personally know asking for financial help to send Milo, her disabled child, to a special school. In reality, Kayla has no children. Is this a crime? If so, which one?

6–4 Credit Cards. Oleksiy Sharapka ordered merchandise online using stolen credit cards. He had the items sent to outlets of Mail Boxes, Etc., and then arranged for someone to deliver the items to his house. He subsequently shipped the goods overseas, primarily to Russia. Sharapka was indicted in a federal district court. At the time of his arrest, government agents found in his possession, among other things, more than three hundred stolen credit-card numbers, including numbers issued by American Express. There was evidence that he had used more than ten of the American Express numbers to buy goods worth between $400,000 and $1 million from at least fourteen vendors. Did Sharapka commit any crimes? If so, who were his victims? Explain. [*United States v. Sharapka,* 526 F.3d 58 (1st Cir. 2008)]

6–5 Case Problem with Sample Answer Three police officers, including Maria Trevizo, were on patrol in Tucson, Arizona, near a neighborhood associated with the Crips gang, when they pulled over a car with a suspended registration. Each officer talked to one of the three occupants. Trevizo spoke with Lemon Johnson, who was wearing clothing consistent with Crips membership. Visible in his jacket pocket was a police scanner, and he said that he had served time in prison for burglary. Trevizo asked him to get out of the car and patted him down "for officer safety." She found a gun. Johnson was charged in an Arizona state court with illegal possession of a weapon. What standard should apply to an officer's patdown of a passenger during a traffic stop? Should a search warrant be required? Could a search proceed solely on the basis of probable cause? Would a reasonable suspicion short of probable cause be sufficient? Why? Discuss. [*Arizona v. Johnson,* 555 U.S. 323, 129 S.Ct. 781, 172 L.Ed.2d 694 (2009)]

—For a sample answer to Problem 6–5, go to Appendix F at the end of this text.

6–6 Sentencing Guidelines. Paul Wilkinson worked for a company that sold fuel to the military at various bases. He paid a competitor's employee to provide him with information about bids made for contracts in which the two companies were bidding. This information allowed Wilkinson to rig his company's bids to win contracts. When the scam was uncovered, he was indicted for conspiracy to defraud the government, commit wire fraud, and steal trade secrets. He pleaded guilty to the charges under a plea arrangement. Given the nature of the offenses, the Sentencing Guidelines provided for a prison term of fifty-one to sixty-three months and no possibility of probation. Due to his cooperation, the prosecution recommended fifty-one months. Wilkinson's attorney argued for a prison term of ten to sixteen months. The judge sentenced Wilkinson to no prison term, but three years' probation and eight hundred hours of community service. The government appealed, claiming that the sentence was too light and in violation of the Sentencing Guidelines. Can the trial judge give such a sentence under the Sentencing Guidelines? Why or why not? [*United States v. Wilkinson*, 590 F.3d 259 (4th Cir. 2010)]

6–7 **Fourth Amendment.** While awaiting trial, Charles E. Byrd was held in a minimum-security jail. Several fights had broken out at the jail, and the guards suspected that some of the inmates possessed contraband. One day, a team of officers wearing T-shirts and jeans showed up at the jail. They ordered the inmates to form a line and then took several inmates at a time into a room for a strip search. Byrd was ordered to remove all his clothing except his boxer shorts. A female officer searched Byrd while several male officers stood by watching. During the search, the officer felt around Byrd's inner and outer thighs, felt across his genitals on the outside of his boxer shorts, and squeezed his buttocks to check his anus for drugs. Byrd later filed a grievance with the jail and then a lawsuit against the sheriff's department, claiming that the search was unreasonable and violated his Fourth Amendment rights. Is a cross-gender strip search constitutionally unreasonable if no immediate emergency exists? Why or why not? When would such a search be permissible? [*Byrd v. Maricopa County Sheriff's Department*, 629 F.3d. 1135 (9th Cir. 2011)]

6–8 **A Question of Ethics** *Davis Omole had good grades in high school, played on the football and chess teams, and went on to college. Twenty-year-old Omole was also one of the chief architects of a scheme through which more than one hundred individuals were defrauded. Omole worked at a cell phone store, where he stole customers' personal information. He and others used the stolen identities to create one hundred different accounts on eBay, through which they held more than three hundred auctions listing for sale items that they did not own and did not intend to sell—cell phones, plasma televisions, stereos, and more. They collected $90,000 through these auctions. To avoid getting caught, they continuously closed and opened the eBay accounts, activated and deactivated cell phone and e-mail accounts, and changed mailing addresses and post office boxes. Omole, who had previously been convicted in a state court for Internet fraud, was convicted in a federal district court of identity theft and wire fraud. [*United States v. Omole*, 523 F.3d 691 (7th Cir. 2008)]*

1 Before Omole's trial, he sent e-mails to his victims, ridiculing them and calling them stupid for having been cheated. During his trial, he displayed contempt for the court. What do these factors show about Omole's ethics?

2 Under the federal sentencing guidelines, Omole could have been imprisoned for more than eight years, but he received a sentence of only three years, two of which were the mandatory sentence for identity theft. Was this sentence too lenient? Explain.

6–9 **Critical Thinking Legal Question** Ray steals a purse from an unattended car at a gas station. Because the purse contains money and a handgun, Ray is convicted of grand theft of property (cash) and grand theft of a firearm. On appeal, Ray claims that he is not guilty of grand theft of a firearm because he did not know that the purse contained a gun. Can Ray be convicted of grand theft of a firearm even though he did not know that the gun was in the purse?

6–10 **Video Question** To watch this chapter's video, *Twelve Angry Men*, go to **www.cengagebrain.com**. Register the access code that came with your new book or log in to your existing account. Select the link for the "Business Law Digital Video Library Online Access" or "Business Law CourseMate." Click on "Complete Video List," view Video 70, and then answer the following questions:

1 One juror says that at the beginning of the trial he felt that the defendant was guilty and that "nobody proved otherwise." Does a criminal defendant have to offer evidence of his or her innocence? What must the prosecution show to establish that a defendant is guilty? How does the burden of proof differ in criminal and civil cases?

2 It is clear that all of the jurors except one (Henry Fonda) believe that the defendant is guilty. How many jurors does it usually take to render a verdict in a criminal case?

3 When the holdout juror says that under the U.S. Constitution "the defendant does not even have to open his mouth," to which provision is he referring?

Unit Two

Unit Case Study with Dissenting Opinion: *MedImmune, Inc. v. Genentech, Inc.*

Under Article III of the U.S. Constitution, the jurisdiction of the federal courts is limited to actual "Cases" or "Controversies." The Declaratory Judgment Act also requires the existence of an "actual controversy" before a court can act.[1] *As you read in Chapter 5 on intellectual property, a* license agreement *permits the use of a trademark, copyright, patent, or trade secret for certain purposes.*

In this Unit Case Study with Dissenting Opinion, *we look at* MedImmune, Inc. v. Genentech, Inc.,[2] *a case involving a dispute between the holder of a patent license and the owner of the patent over the patent's validity. The petitioner in this case is seeking a* declaratory judgment, *which is a court ruling that establishes the rights and obligations of the parties but does not include any provisions to enforce those rights or obligations. Is this an "actual controversy" on which a court can issue a declaratory judgment? Or does the licensee first have to breach the license agreement and subject itself to a possible suit for patent infringement, with a potential assessment of treble (triple) damages and a loss of the license?*

1. 28 U.S.C. Section 2201(a).
2. 549 U.S. 118, 127 S.Ct. 764, 166 L.Ed.2d 604 (2007).

CASE BACKGROUND

MedImmune, Inc., makes and sells Synagis, a drug to prevent respiratory disease in children. In 1997, MedImmune entered into a license agreement with Genentech, Inc. The license covered a patent relating to the production of "chimeric antibodies" and a pending patent application relating to "the coexpression of immunoglobulin chains in recombinant host cells." MedImmune agreed to pay royalties on sales of "Licensed Products," which the agreement defined as a specified antibody, "the manufacture, use or sale of which * * * would, if not licensed * * * infringe [the covered patents]."

In December 2001, the "coexpression" application became the "Cabilly II" patent. Genentech contended that the Cabilly II patent covered Synagis and demanded the payment of royalties. MedImmune believed that the patent was invalid, but considered Genentech's demand a threat to terminate the license agreement and sue for patent infringement if MedImmune did not pay. In such a suit, MedImmune could be ordered to pay treble damages and be enjoined from selling Synagis, which accounted for more than 80 percent of its revenue. Unwilling to take this risk, MedImmune paid the royalties and filed a suit in a federal district court against Genentech, seeking a declaratory judgment. The court dismissed the suit, and MedImmune appealed to the U.S. Court of Appeals for the Federal Circuit, which affirmed the dismissal. MedImmune appealed to the United States Supreme Court.

MAJORITY OPINION

Justice *SCALIA* delivered the opinion of the Court.

* * * *

The Declaratory Judgment Act provides that, "in a case of actual controversy within its jurisdiction * * * any court of the United States * * * may declare the rights and other legal relations of any interested party seeking such declaration, whether or not further relief is or could be sought." * * * [T]he phrase "case of actual controversy" in the Act refers to the type of "Cases" and "Controversies" that are justiciable [real issues able to be resolved by a court] under Article III.

* * * *Basically, the question in each case is whether the facts alleged, under all the circumstances, show that there is a substantial controversy, between parties having adverse legal interests, of sufficient immediacy and reality to warrant the issuance of a declaratory judgment.* [Emphasis added.]

There is no dispute that these standards would have been satisfied if petitioner [MedImmune] had taken the final step of refusing to make royalty payments under the 1997 license agreement. * * * Petitioner's own acts, in other words, eliminate the imminent threat of harm. The question before us is whether this causes the dispute no longer to be a case or controversy within the meaning of Article III.

Our analysis must begin with the recognition that, where threatened action by government is concerned, we do not require a plaintiff to expose himself to liability before bringing suit to challenge the basis for the threat—for example, the constitutionality of a law threatened to be enforced. The plaintiff's own action (or inaction) in failing to violate the law eliminates the imminent threat of prosecution, but nonetheless does not eliminate Article III jurisdiction. * * * *Simply not doing what [a plaintiff] claim[s] the right to do * * * [does] not preclude subject-matter jurisdiction because the threat-eliminating behavior [is] effectively coerced.* The dilemma posed by that coercion—putting the challenger to the choice between abandoning his rights or risking prosecution—is a dilemma that it was the very purpose of the Declaratory Judgment Act to ameliorate. [Emphasis added.]

[United States] Supreme Court jurisprudence is more rare regarding application of the Declaratory Judgment Act to situations

Continued

in which the plaintiff's self-avoidance of imminent injury is coerced by threatened enforcement action of a private party rather than the government. Lower federal courts, however (and state courts interpreting [state] declaratory judgment Acts requiring "actual controversy"), have long accepted jurisdiction in such cases.

The only Supreme Court decision in point is, fortuitously, close on its facts to the case before us. * * * [In that case] royalties were being paid under protest and under the compulsion of an injunction decree, and unless the injunction decree [was] modified, the only other course of action was to defy it, and to risk not only actual but treble damages in infringement suits. We concluded that "the requirements of a case or controversy are met where payment of a claim is demanded as of right and where payment is made, but where the involuntary or coercive nature of the exaction preserves the right to recover the sums paid or to challenge the legality of the claim."

* * * *

We hold that petitioner was not required, insofar as Article III is concerned, to break or terminate its 1997 license agreement before seeking a declaratory judgment in federal court that the underlying patent is invalid, unenforceable, or not infringed. *The Court of Appeals erred in affirming the dismissal of this action for lack of subject-matter jurisdiction.* [Emphasis added.]

The judgment of the Court of Appeals is reversed, and the cause is remanded for proceedings consistent with this opinion.

It is so ordered.

DISSENTING OPINION

Justice *THOMAS*, dissenting.

We granted *certiorari* in this case to determine whether a patent licensee in good standing must breach its license prior to challenging the validity of the underlying patent * * * . The answer to that question is yes. We have consistently held that parties do not have standing to obtain rulings on matters that remain hypothetical or conjectural. We have also held that the declaratory judgment procedure cannot be used to obtain advance rulings on matters that would be addressed in a future case of actual controversy. MedImmune has sought a declaratory judgment for precisely that purpose, and I would therefore affirm the Court of Appeals' holding that there is no Article III jurisdiction over MedImmune's claim. The Court reaches the opposite result * * * . I respectfully dissent.

* * * *

Article III of the Constitution limits the judicial power to the adjudication of "Cases" or "Controversies." * * * In the constitutional sense, a "Controversy" is distinguished from a difference or dispute of a hypothetical or abstract character; from one that is academic or moot. The controversy must be definite and concrete, touching the legal relations of parties having adverse legal interests. * * * It must be a real and substantial controversy * * * , as distinguished from an opinion advising what the law would be upon a hypothetical state of facts.

* * * *

The facts before us present no case or controversy under Article III. * * * MedImmune's actions in entering into and continuing to comply with the license agreement deprived Genentech of any cause of action against MedImmune. Additionally, MedImmune had no cause of action against Genentech. * * *

* * * MedImmune wants to know whether, if it decides to breach its license agreement with Genentech, and if Genentech sues it for patent infringement, it will have a successful affirmative defense. Presumably, upon a favorable determination, MedImmune would then stop making royalty payments, knowing in advance that the federal courts stand behind its decision. * * * MedImmune has therefore asked the courts to render an opinion advising what the law would be upon a hypothetical state of facts. A federal court cannot, consistent with Article III, provide MedImmune with such an opinion.

* * * To hold a patent valid if it is not infringed is to decide a hypothetical case. Of course, MedImmune presents exactly that case. * * * [Thus] I would hold that this case presents no actual case or controversy.

QUESTIONS FOR ANALYSIS

1. **Law.** What was the majority's decision on the principal question before the Court in this case? What were the reasons for this decision?
2. **Law.** How did the dissent interpret the issue before the Court? What were the reasons for this interpretation?
3. **Ethics.** Suppose that either or both of the parties in this case had asserted their respective positions only to increase their profits. Would this have been unethical? Explain.
4. **Economic Dimensions.** This case resolved what seems to be a technical question in a dispute between a pharmaceutical maker and a biotechnology firm. What is the practical importance of the ruling?
5. **Implications for the Businessperson.** What does the outcome of this case suggest to the smaller start-up company that relies on a license to obtain patented technology?

Unit Three

Contracts

Unit Contents

7 Nature and Classification

8 Agreement in Traditional and E-Contracts

9 Consideration, Capacity, and Legality

10 Defenses to Contract Enforceability

11 Third Party Rights and Discharge

12 Breach and Remedies

(AP Photo/Carlos Osorio)

Chapter 7

Nature and Classification

Learning Objectives

After reading this chapter, you should be able to answer the following questions:

1. What is a contract? What is the objective theory of contracts?
2. What are the four basic elements necessary to the formation of a valid contract?
3. What is the difference between an implied contract and a quasi contract?
4. How does a void contract differ from a voidable contract? What is an unenforceable contract?
5. What rules guide the courts in interpreting contracts?

The Learning Objectives above are designed to help improve your understanding of the chapter.

(AP Photo/Carlos Osorio)

Contract law deals with, among other things, the formation and keeping of promises. A **promise** is an assertion that something either will or will not happen in the future.

Like other types of law, contract law reflects our social values, interests, and expectations at a given point in time. It shows, for example, what kinds of promises our society thinks should be legally binding. It distinguishes between promises that create only *moral* obligations (such as a promise to take a friend to lunch) and promises that are legally binding (such as a promise to pay for merchandise purchased).

Contract law also demonstrates what excuses our society accepts for breaking certain types of promises. In addition, it shows what promises are considered to be contrary to public policy—against the interests of society as a whole—and therefore legally invalid. When the person making a promise is a child or is mentally incompetent, for example, a question will arise as to whether the promise should be enforced. Resolving such questions is the essence of contract law.

An Overview of Contract Law

Before we look at the numerous rules that courts use to determine whether a particular promise will be enforced, it is necessary to understand some fundamental concepts of contract law. In this section, we describe the sources and general function of contract law and introduce the objective theory of contracts.

Sources of Contract Law

The common law governs all contracts except when it has been modified or replaced by statutory law, such as the Uniform Commercial Code (UCC),[1] or by administrative agency regulations. Contracts relating to services, real estate,

1. See Chapter 13 for further discussions of the significance and coverage of the Uniform Commercial Code (UCC). Excerpts from the UCC are presented in Appendix C at the end of this book.

employment, and insurance, for example, generally are governed by the common law of contracts.

Contracts for the sale and lease of goods, however, are governed by the UCC—to the extent that the UCC has modified general contract law. The relationship between general contract law and the law governing sales and leases of goods will be explored in detail in Chapter 13. In this unit covering the common law of contracts (Chapters 7 through 12), we indicate briefly in footnotes the areas in which the UCC has significantly altered common law contract principles.

The Function of a Contract

No aspect of modern life is entirely free of contractual relationships. You acquire rights and obligations, for example, when you borrow funds, buy or lease a house, obtain insurance, form a business, and purchase goods or services. Contract law is designed to provide stability and predictability for both buyers and sellers in the marketplace.

Contract law assures the parties to private agreements that the promises they make will be enforceable. Clearly, many promises are kept because the parties involved feel a moral obligation to do so or because keeping a promise is in their mutual self-interest. The **promisor** (the person making the promise) and the **promisee** (the person to whom the promise is made) may decide to honor their agreement for other reasons. Nevertheless, the rules of contract law are often followed in business agreements to avoid potential problems.

By supplying procedures for enforcing private agreements, contract law provides an essential condition for the existence of a market economy. Without a legal framework of reasonably ensured expectations within which to plan and venture, businesspersons would be able to rely only on the good faith of others. Duty and good faith are usually sufficient, but when dramatic price changes or adverse economic conditions make it costly to comply with a promise, these elements may not be enough. Contract law is necessary to ensure compliance with a promise or to entitle the innocent party to some form of relief.

The Definition of a Contract

A **contract** is an agreement that can be enforced in court. It is formed by two or more parties who agree to perform or to refrain from performing some act now or in the future. Generally, contract disputes arise when there is a promise of future performance. If the contractual promise is not fulfilled, the party who made it is subject to the sanctions of a court (see Chapter 12). That party may be required to pay monetary damages for failing to perform the contractual promise. In limited instances, the party may be required to perform the promised act.

The Objective Theory of Contracts

In determining whether a contract has been formed, the element of intent is of prime importance. In contract law, intent is determined by what is referred to as the **objective theory of contracts**, not by the personal or subjective intent, or belief, of a party. The theory is that a party's intention to enter into a contract is judged by outward, objective facts as interpreted by a *reasonable person*, rather than by the party's own secret, subjective intentions. Objective facts include (1) what the party said when entering into the contract, (2) how the party acted or appeared, and (3) the circumstances surrounding the transaction. Intent to form a contract may be manifested by conduct, as well as by words, oral or written.

Elements of a Contract

The many topics that will be discussed in the following chapters on contract law require an understanding of the basic elements of a valid contract and the way in which a contract is created. You will also need an understanding of the types of circumstances in which even legally valid contracts will not be enforced.

Requirements of a Valid Contract

The following list briefly describes the four requirements that must be met for a valid contract to exist. If any of these elements is lacking, no contract will have been formed. (Each item will be explained more fully in subsequent chapters.)

1. *Agreement.* An agreement to form a contract includes an *offer* and an *acceptance*. One party must offer to enter into a legal agreement, and another party must accept the terms of the offer (see Chapter 8).
2. *Consideration.* Any promises made by the parties must be supported by legally sufficient and bargained-for consideration (something of value received or promised to convince a person to make a deal) (see Chapter 9).
3. *Contractual capacity.* Both parties entering into the contract must have the contractual capacity to do so. The law must recognize them as possessing characteristics that qualify them as competent parties (see Chapter 9).
4. *Legality.* The contract's purpose must be to accomplish some goal that is legal and not against public policy (see Chapter 9).

Defenses to the Enforceability of a Contract

Even if all of the elements of a valid contract are present, a contract may be unenforceable if the following requirements are not met.

1. *Voluntary consent.* The apparent consent of both parties must be voluntary. For example, if a contract was formed as a result of fraud, a mistake, or duress, the contract may not be enforceable.
2. *Form.* The contract must be in whatever form the law requires. For example, some contracts must be in writing to be enforceable.

The failure to fulfill either requirement may be raised as a *defense* to the enforceability of an otherwise valid contract (see Chapter 10).

Types of Contracts

There are numerous types of contracts. They are categorized based on legal distinctions as to their formation, performance, and enforceability. Exhibit 7–1 below illustrates three classifications, or categories, of contracts based on their mode of formation.

Contract Formation

As you can see in Exhibit 7–1, three classifications of contracts are based on how and when a contract is formed. The best way to explain each type of contract is to compare one type with another, as we do in the following pages.

BILATERAL VERSUS UNILATERAL CONTRACTS Every contract involves at least two parties. The **offeror** is the party making the offer. The **offeree** is the party to whom the offer is made. The offeror always promises to do or not to do something and thus is also a promisor. Whether the contract is classified as *bilateral* or *unilateral* depends on what the offeree must do to accept the offer and bind the offeror to a contract.

Bilateral Contracts. If the offeree can accept simply by promising to perform, the contract is a **bilateral contract.** Hence, a bilateral contract is a "promise for a promise." An example of a bilateral contract is a contract in which one person agrees to buy another person's automobile for a specified price. No performance, such as the payment of funds or delivery of goods, need take place for a bilateral contract to be formed. The contract comes into existence at the moment the promises are exchanged.

EXAMPLE 7.1 Javier offers to buy Ann's digital camera for $200. Javier tells Ann that he will give her the cash for the camera on the following Friday, when he gets paid. Ann accepts Javier's offer and promises to give him the camera when he pays her on Friday. Javier and Ann have formed a bilateral contract. ●

Unilateral Contracts. If the offer is phrased so that the offeree can accept only by completing the contract performance, the contract is a **unilateral contract.** Hence, a unilateral contract is a "promise for an act." In other words, the contract is formed not at the moment when promises are exchanged but rather when the contract is *performed.* **EXAMPLE 7.2** Reese says to Celia, "If you drive my car from New York to Los Angeles, I'll give you $1,000." Only on Celia's completion of the act—bringing the car to Los Angeles—does she fully accept Reese's offer to pay $1,000. If she chooses not to accept the offer to drive the car to Los Angeles, there are no legal consequences. ●

In the following case, the court was asked to resolve a dispute that arose from an employer's refusal to pay a bonus to a former employee. The court's resolution depended, in part, on whether the parties' employment contract was bilateral or unilateral.

• ***Exhibit* 7–1 Classifications Based on Contract Formation**

Case 7.1 Schwarzrock v. Remote Technologies, Inc.

Court of Appeals of Minnesota, __ N.W.2d __ (2011).

FACTS Remote Technologies, Inc., is a Minnesota-based manufacturer of home-theater and home-automation controls. Remote employs product trainers to conduct training sessions for its dealers. Nick Schwarzrock contacted Peter Baker, Remote's vice president of sales and marketing, to apply for employment. Baker offered Schwarzrock a position as a trainer. In a letter, Baker wrote that the compensation was "$60,000 per year salary, plus bonus." The day after starting work, Schwarzrock signed an employment agreement (EA) that expressly "superseded all previous correspondence." The EA stated, in part, that the salary "constitutes the full and exclusive . . . compensation for . . . the performance of all Employee's promises." Less than three months later, Baker fired Schwarzrock for "lots of reasons." Schwarzrock filed a suit in a Minnesota state court against Remote. Among other things, he alleged breach of contract to recover what he believed he was owed as a bonus. On this claim, the court held that there was no breach of contract and that the bonus was discretionary. Schwarzrock appealed.

ISSUE Was Schwarzrock's employment agreement a bilateral contract?

DECISION No. The state intermediate appellate court affirmed the lower court's judgment that it was a unilateral contract.

REASON An employer's offer of a position on certain terms for an indefinite period becomes a unilateral contract on the employee's acceptance. Schwarzrock argued that "salary, plus bonus" was "an essential term of a bilateral negotiated contract," but he provided no proof that such a contract existed. Instead, the court reasoned that the EA was a unilateral offer of employment by Remote that specifically made any bonus subject to the employer's discretion. The EA explicitly stated that "any additional compensation to Employee (whether a bonus or other form of additional compensation) shall rest in the sole discretion of [the employer]." Schwarzrock accepted this offer when he signed the EA and continued working. Both Remote's EA and Baker's letter expressed the employer's intent to offer a salary and a potential bonus to Schwarzrock. Baker's letter may have implied that the bonus was not discretionary, but the EA clarified or modified the offer by clearly stating that it was.

WHAT IF THE FACTS WERE DIFFERENT? *Suppose that the court had ruled that Schwarzrock was employed under a bilateral contract, as he alleged. Would the result have been different? Explain.*

Revocation of Offers for Unilateral Contracts. A problem arises in unilateral contracts when the promisor attempts to *revoke* (cancel) the offer after the promisee has begun performance but before the act has been completed. **EXAMPLE 7.3** Roberta offers to buy Ed's sailboat, moored in San Francisco, on delivery of the boat to Roberta's dock in Newport Beach, three hundred miles south of San Francisco. Ed rigs the boat and sets sail. Shortly before his arrival at Newport Beach, Ed receives a radio message from Roberta withdrawing her offer. Roberta's offer is to form a unilateral contract, and only Ed's delivery of the sailboat at her dock is an acceptance. •

In contract law, offers are normally *revocable* (capable of being taken back, or canceled) until accepted. Under the traditional view of unilateral contracts, Roberta's revocation would terminate the offer. Because of the harsh effect on the offeree of the revocation of an offer to form a unilateral contract, the modern-day view is that once performance has been *substantially* undertaken, the offeror cannot revoke the offer. Thus, in our example, even though Ed has not yet accepted the offer by complete performance, Roberta is prohibited from revoking it. Ed can deliver the boat and bind Roberta to the contract.

Formal versus Informal Contracts

Another classification system divides contracts into formal contracts and informal contracts. **Formal contracts** are contracts that require a special form or method of creation (formation) to be enforceable.[2] For example, *negotiable instruments,* which include checks, drafts, promissory notes, and certificates of deposit (see Chapter 16), are formal contracts because, under the Uniform Commercial Code, a special form and language are required to create them. Letters of credit, which are frequently used in international sales contracts (see Chapter 31), are another type of formal contract.

Informal contracts (also called *simple contracts*) include all other contracts. No special form is required (except for certain types of contracts that must be in writing), as the contracts are usually based on their substance rather than their form. Typically, businesspersons put their contracts in writing to ensure that there is some proof of a contract's existence should problems arise.

Express versus Implied Contracts

Contracts may also be formed and categorized as *express* or *implied* by the

2. See *Restatement (Second) of Contracts,* Section 6, which explains that formal contracts include (1) contracts under seal, (2) recognizances, (3) negotiable instruments, and (4) letters of credit.

conduct of the parties. In an **express contract,** the terms of the agreement are fully and explicitly stated in words, oral or written. A signed lease for an apartment or a house is an express written contract. If a classmate accepts your offer to sell your textbooks from last semester for $300, an express oral contract has been made.

A contract that is implied from the conduct of the parties is called an **implied contract,** or an implied-in-fact contract. This type of contract differs from an express contract in that the *conduct* of the parties, rather than their words, creates and defines at least some of the terms of the contract. Normally, if the following conditions are met, a court will hold that an implied contract was formed:

1. The plaintiff furnished some service or property.
2. The plaintiff expected to be paid for that service or property, and the defendant knew or should have known that payment was expected (by using the objective-theory-of-contracts test discussed on page 133).
3. The defendant had a chance to reject the services or property and did not.

EXAMPLE 7.4 A business owner needs an accountant to complete his tax return this year. He notices an accountant's office in the neighborhood. He drops by the firm's office, explains his problem to an accountant, and learns what fees will be charged. The next day, he returns and gives the receptionist all of the necessary information and documents, such as W-2 forms. Then he walks out the door without saying anything expressly to the accountant. In this situation, the business owner has entered into an implied contract to pay the accountant the usual and reasonable fees for her services. The contract is implied by the owner's conduct and by hers. She expects to be paid for completing the tax return. By bringing in the records she will need to do the work, the owner has implied an intent to pay her. •

Contract Performance

Contracts are also classified according to their state of performance. A contract that has been fully performed on both sides is called an **executed contract.** A contract that has not been fully performed on either side is called an **executory contract.** If one party has fully performed but the other has not, the contract is said to be executed on the one side and executory on the other, but the contract is still classified as executory.

EXAMPLE 7.5 You agreed to buy ten tons of coal from Western Coal Company. Western has delivered the coal to your steel mill, where it is now being burned. At this point, the contract is an executory contract—it is executed on the part of Western and executory on your part. After you pay Western for the coal, the contract will be executed on both sides. •

Contract Enforceability

A **valid contract** has the four elements necessary for contract formation: (1) an agreement (offer and acceptance) (2) supported by legally sufficient consideration (3) for a legal purpose and (4) made by parties who have the legal capacity to enter into the contract. As you can see in Exhibit 7–2 on the facing page, valid contracts may be enforceable, voidable, or unenforceable. Additionally, a contract may be referred to as a *void contract.* We look next at the meaning of the terms *voidable, unenforceable,* and *void* in relation to contract enforceability.

VOIDABLE CONTRACTS A **voidable contract** is a *valid* contract but one that can be avoided at the option of one or both of the parties. The party having the option can elect either to avoid any duty to perform or to *ratify* (make valid) the contract. If the contract is avoided, both parties are released from it. If it is ratified, both parties must fully perform their respective legal obligations.

As a general rule, for example, contracts made by minors are voidable at the option of the minor (see Chapter 9). Additionally, contracts entered into under fraudulent conditions are voidable at the option of the defrauded party. Contracts entered into under legally defined duress or undue influence are also voidable (see Chapter 10).

UNENFORCEABLE CONTRACTS An **unenforceable contract** is one that cannot be enforced because of certain legal defenses against it. It is not unenforceable because a party failed to satisfy a legal requirement of the contract; rather, it is a valid contract rendered unenforceable by some statute or law. For example, some contracts must be in writing (see Chapter 10), and if they are not, they will not be enforceable except in certain exceptional circumstances.

VOID CONTRACTS A **void contract** is no contract at all. The terms *void* and *contract* are contradictory. None of the parties has any legal obligations if a contract is void. A contract can be void because, for example, one of the parties was previously determined by a court to be legally insane (and thus lacked the legal capacity to enter into a contract) or because the purpose of the contract was illegal.

Quasi Contracts

Quasi contracts, or contracts *implied in law,* are wholly different from actual contracts. Express contracts and implied contracts are actual or true contracts formed by the words or actions of the parties. The word *quasi* is Latin for "as if" or "analogous to." Quasi contracts are not true contracts because they do not arise from any agreement, express or implied, between the parties themselves. Rather, quasi contracts are

• *Exhibit* **7–2 Enforceable, Voidable, Unenforceable, and Void Contracts**

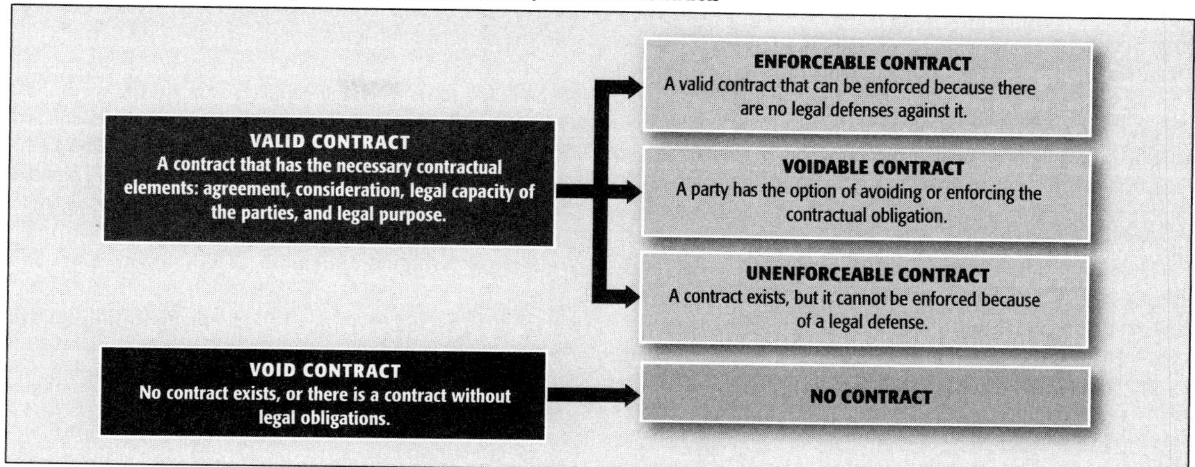

fictional contracts that courts can impose on the parties "as if" the parties had entered into an actual contract. They are equitable rather than legal contracts.

Usually, quasi contracts are imposed to avoid the *unjust enrichment* of one party at the expense of another. The doctrine of unjust enrichment is based on the theory that individuals should not be allowed to profit or enrich themselves inequitably at the expense of others.

When the court imposes a quasi contract, a plaintiff may recover in ***quantum meruit,***[3] a Latin phrase meaning "as much as he or she deserves." *Quantum meruit* essentially describes the extent of compensation owed under a contract implied in law. The following case illustrates an application of the principle of *quantum meruit.*

3. Pronounced *kwahn*-tuhm *mehr*-oo-wit.

Case 7.2 Scheerer v. Fisher

Court of Appeals of North Carolina, 688 S.E.2d 472 (2010).
www.nccourts.org[a]

FACTS In January 2007, David Scheerer, a licensed real estate agent, told Jack Fisher, the manager of Renaissance Ventures, LLC, that two parcels of property were for sale. Fisher asked Scheerer to investigate the costs of developing the properties, which he did. After Scheerer had negotiated the terms of the sale with the property owners, Fisher executed purchase contracts for a combined price of $20 million. The contracts stated that the sellers would pay Scheerer a 2 percent commission. Fisher, who had previously dealt with Scheerer, orally promised to pay Scheerer a 2 percent commission for his role as Fisher's buying agent. In April 2007, through no fault of Scheerer or the sellers, Fisher and Renaissance rescinded (canceled) the offers to buy the properties. Shortly thereafter, Fisher arranged for Anthony Antonio to purchase the same properties for substantially less than $20 million and then *assign* (transfer the rights under a contract to someone else—see Chapter 11) the new purchase contracts to Fisher. Scheerer and the property sellers had no knowledge of the relationship between Fisher and Antonio. Indeed, during this time, Fisher continued to discuss with Scheerer the amount he would subsequently offer the original sellers for the properties. After Antonio bought the properties, he assigned the contracts to Fisher, at which point Scheerer learned of the relationship. Scheerer, who had received a commission from the sellers only, sued Fisher for breach of implied contract and to recover in *quantum meruit* for his services. The trial court dismissed the complaint for failure to state a claim, and Scheerer appealed.

a. In the right-hand column, click on "Court Opinions." When that page opens, click on "2010" under "Court of Appeals Opinions." When the list of 2010 opinions appears, scroll down to "Jan 19, 2010" and click on the case title to access the opinion. The North Carolina Courts maintain this Web site.

ISSUE Could Scheerer recover in *quantum meruit* for the amount of the commission that he would have received under the original contract, which was cancelled by Fisher?

DECISION Yes. The North Carolina appellate court reversed the trial court's decision and reinstated the case. Scheerer had stated a valid claim for recovery in *quantum meruit.*

REASON The reviewing court accepted the plaintiffs' allegations that "(1) plaintiffs provided services to defendants; (2) defendants knowingly

Case 7.2—Continues next page ➡

Case 7.2–Continued

and voluntarily accepted the services; (3) plaintiffs did not perform these services gratuitously; (4) defendants were ready, willing, and able buyers and in fact closed on the properties after rescinding the first contract and arranging for Antonio to purchase and assign the properties." Moreover, defendant Fisher continued to mislead the plaintiffs by discussing with them the possibility of subsequent offers to purchase the properties. Fisher took action to deny Scheerer compensation that Scheerer had earned for services rendered. "Although the original contract he [Scheerer] negotiated failed to close, the law implies a promise to pay some reasonable compensation for services rendered."

WHAT IF THE FACTS WERE DIFFERENT? *Suppose that Fisher had not ultimately obtained the properties (through Antonio and the assignment) and had shown no further interest in the properties after he rescinded the first contract. Would Scheerer still have had a valid claim against Fisher for recovery in* quantum meruit*? Why or why not?*

Limitations on Quasi-Contractual Recovery

Although quasi contracts exist to prevent unjust enrichment, the party who obtains a benefit is not liable for the fair value in some situations. Basically, a party who has conferred a benefit on someone else unnecessarily or as a result of misconduct or negligence cannot invoke the doctrine of quasi contract. The enrichment in those situations will not be considered "unjust."

CASE EXAMPLE 7.6 Qwest Wireless, LLC, provides wireless phone services in Arizona and thirteen other states. Qwest marketed and sold handset insurance to its wireless customers, although it did not have a license to sell insurance in Arizona or in any other state. Patrick and Vicki Van Zanen sued Qwest in a federal court for unjust enrichment based on its receipt of sales commissions for the insurance. The court agreed that Qwest had violated the insurance-licensing statute, but found that the sales commissions did not constitute unjust enrichment because the customers had, in fact, received the insurance. Qwest had not retained a benefit (the commissions) without paying for it (providing insurance). Thus, the Van Zanens and other customers did not suffer unfair detriment.[4] •

When an Actual Contract Exists

The doctrine of quasi contract generally cannot be used when an actual contract covers the area in controversy. This is because a remedy already exists if a party is unjustly enriched as a result of a breach of contract: the nonbreaching party can sue the breaching party for breach of contract. **EXAMPLE 7.7** Fung contracts with Cameron to deliver a furnace to a building owned by Bateman. Fung delivers the furnace, but Cameron never pays Fung. Bateman has been unjustly enriched in this situation, to be sure. Nevertheless, Fung cannot recover from Bateman in quasi contract because Fung had an actual contract with Cameron. Fung already has a remedy—he can sue for breach of contract to recover the price of the furnace from Cameron. In this situation, the court does not need to impose a quasi contract to achieve justice. •

4. *Van Zanen v. Qwest Wireless, LLC*, 522 F.3d 1127 (10th Cir. 2008).

Interpretation of Contracts

Sometimes, parties agree that a contract has been formed but disagree on its meaning or legal effect. One reason that this may happen is that one of the parties is not familiar with the legal terminology used in the contract. To an extent, *plain language laws* have helped to avoid this difficulty. Sometimes, though, a dispute may still arise over the meaning of a contract simply because the rights or obligations under the contract are not expressed clearly—no matter how "plain" the language used.

In this section, we look at some common law rules of contract interpretation. These rules, including the *plain meaning rule* and various other rules that have evolved, provide the courts with guidelines for deciding disputes over how contract terms or provisions should be interpreted. Exhibit 7–3 on the facing page provides a brief graphic summary of how these rules are applied.

The Plain Meaning Rule

When a contract's writing is clear and unequivocal, a court will enforce it according to its obvious terms. The meaning of the terms must be determined from *the face of the instrument*—from the written document alone. This is sometimes referred to as the *plain meaning rule.*

Under this rule, if a contract's words appear to be clear and unambiguous, a court cannot consider *extrinsic evidence,* which is any evidence not contained in the document itself. Admissibility of extrinsic evidence can significantly affect how a court interprets ambiguous contractual provisions and thus can affect the outcome of litigation.

Other Rules of Interpretation

Generally, a court will interpret the language to give effect to the parties' intent *as expressed in their contract.* This is the primary purpose of the rules of interpretation—to determine the parties' intent from the language used in their agreement and to give effect to that intent. Normally, a court will not make or remake a contract, nor will it interpret the language according to what the parties *claim* their intent was when they made the

• *Exhibit* **7–3 Rules of Contract Interpretation**

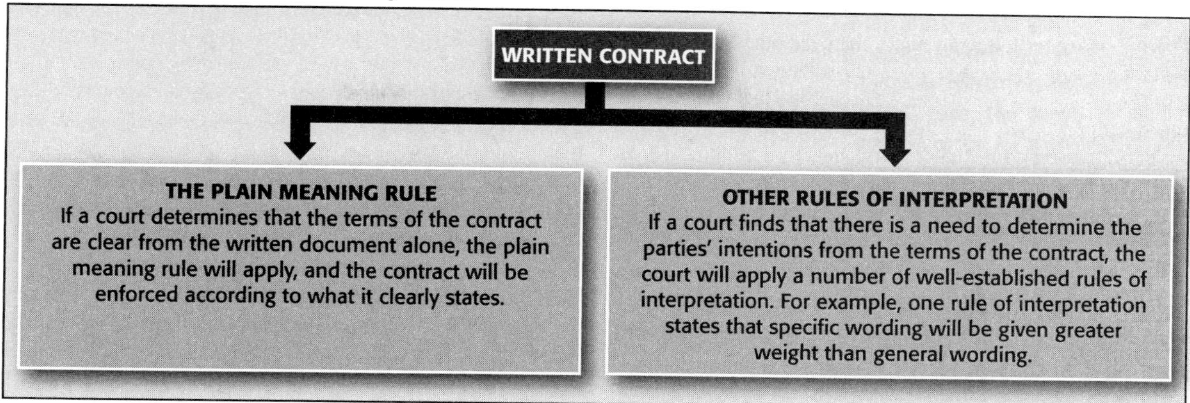

contract. Nevertheless, if a court finds that, even after applying the rules of interpretation, the terms are susceptible to more than one meaning, the court may permit extrinsic evidence to prove what the parties intended. The courts use the following rules in interpreting contractual terms:

1. Insofar as possible, a reasonable, lawful, and effective meaning will be given to all of a contract's terms.
2. A contract will be interpreted as a whole. Individual, specific clauses will be considered subordinate to the contract's general intent. All writings that are a part of the same transaction will be interpreted together.
3. Terms that were the subject of separate negotiation will be given greater consideration than standardized terms and terms that were not negotiated separately.
4. A word will be given its ordinary, commonly accepted meaning, and a technical word or term will be given its technical meaning, unless the parties clearly intended something else.
5. Specific and exact wording will be given greater consideration than general language.
6. Written or typewritten terms prevail over preprinted terms.
7. Because a contract should be drafted in clear and unambiguous language, a party that uses ambiguous expressions is held to be responsible for the ambiguities. Thus, when the language has more than one meaning, it will be interpreted *against* the party that drafted the contract.
8. Evidence of *trade usage, prior dealing,* and *course of performance* may be admitted to clarify the meaning of an ambiguously worded contract. (We will define and discuss these terms in Chapter 13.) What each of the parties does pursuant to the contract will be interpreted as consistent with what the other does and with any relevant usage of trade and course of dealing or performance.

Express terms (terms expressly stated in the contract) are given the greatest weight, followed by course of performance, course of dealing, and custom and usage of trade—in that order. When considering custom and usage, a court will look at the trade customs and usage common to the particular business or industry and to the locale in which the contract was made or is to be performed.

In the following case, the court was asked to interpret the phrase *increase of hazard* as it appeared in an insurance policy.

Case 7.3 U.S. Bank, N.A. v. Tennessee Farmers Mutual Insurance Co.

Tennessee Supreme Court, 277 S.W.3d 381 (2009).

FACTS Jessica Robbins bought a house in Humboldt, Tennessee. U.S. Bank, N.A.,[a] financed the purchase. Tennessee Farmers Mutual Insurance Company issued the homeowner's insurance policy. The policy included a "standard mortgage clause" that promised payment to the bank unless the house was lost due to an "increase in hazard" that the bank knew about but did not tell the insurer. When Robbins fell behind on her mortgage payments, the bank started foreclosure proceedings. No one told the insurer. Robbins filed for bankruptcy, which postponed foreclosure. Meanwhile, the house "blew up," in Robbins's words, and was destroyed in a fire caused by

a. The abbreviation *N.A.* stands for *National Association,* which means the bank was chartered by the federal government under the National Bank Act.

Case 7.3—Continues next page ➡

Case 7.3—Continued

chemicals used to make methamphetamine. The bank filed a claim under the policy, but the insurer refused to pay. The bank then filed a suit in a Tennessee state court against the insurer, claiming breach of contract. The insurer argued that it had not been told by the bank of an "increase in hazard"—that is, the foreclosure. The court ruled in favor of the bank, an appellate court reversed in favor of the insurer, and the bank appealed.

ISSUE Does the phrase *increase of hazard,* by its ordinary meaning, include the commencement of foreclosure proceedings?

DECISION No. The Tennessee Supreme Court reversed the judgment of the appellate court and remanded the case to the trial court. The failure to notify the insurer of the foreclosure did not breach the terms of the policy.

REASON An insurance policy is subject to the same rules of construction as any other contract and should be interpreted and enforced as written. Its terms should be given their plain, ordinary meaning because "the primary rule of contract interpretation is to ascertain and give effect to the intent of the parties." In cases involving standard mortgage clauses that require notice of an "increase of hazard," other courts have found that the plain meaning of the words refers to physical conditions on the property that pose a risk, not to events such as foreclosure. Thus, the bank was not required to notify the insurer under the terms of the policy, and the lack of notice did not invalidate the coverage. Besides, the house "burned not because of an impending foreclosure sale, but rather due to a mishap during an occupant's production of an illegal substance."

WHY IS THIS CASE IMPORTANT? *This case underscores the importance of insurance to businesses that lend money or otherwise extend credit secured by the property of a borrower who retains its possession. Those businesses should be certain that their interests are protected by the applicable policy. The court's interpretation of the policy at issue here—and the reasoning that determined the outcome—emphasize the significance of the words used in an insurance contract.*

Reviewing . . . Nature and Classification

Mitsui Bank hired Ross Duncan as a branch manager in one of its Southern California locations. At that time, Duncan received an employee handbook informing him that Mitsui would review his performance and salary level annually. In 2008, Mitsui decided to create a new lending program to help financially troubled businesses stay afloat. It hired Duncan as the credit development officer (CDO) and gave him a written compensation plan. Duncan's compensation was to be based on the new program's success and involved a bonus and commissions based on new loans and sales volume. The written plan also stated, "This compensation plan will be reviewed and potentially amended after one year and will be subject to such review and amendment annually thereafter." Duncan's efforts as CDO were successful, and the business-lending program he developed grew to represent 25 percent of Mitsui's business in 2009 and 40 percent by 2010. Nevertheless, Mitsui not only refused to give Duncan a raise in 2009 but also amended his compensation plan to significantly reduce his compensation and to change his performance evaluation schedule to every six months. When he had still not received a raise by 2010, Duncan retired as CDO and filed a lawsuit claiming breach of contract. Using the information presented in the chapter, answer the following questions.

1. What are the four requirements of a valid contract?
2. Did Duncan have a valid contract with Mitsui for employment as credit development officer? If so, was it a bilateral or a unilateral contract?
3. What are the requirements of an implied contract?
4. Can Duncan establish an implied contract based on the employment manual or the written compensation plan? Why or why not?

Terms and Concepts

bilateral contract 134
contract 133
executed contract 136
executory contract 136
express contract 136
formal contract 135
implied contract 136
informal contract 135
objective theory of contracts 133
offeree 134
offeror 134
promise 132
promisee 133
promisor 133
quantum meruit 137
quasi contract 136
unenforceable contract 136
unilateral contract 134
valid contract 136
void contract 136
voidable contract 136

Chapter Summary: Nature and Classification

An Overview of Contract Law **(See pages 132–133.)**	1. *Sources of contract law*—The common law governs all contracts except when it has been modified or replaced by statutory law, such as the Uniform Commercial Code (UCC), or by administrative agency regulations. The UCC governs contracts for the sale or lease of goods (see Chapter 13). 2. *The function of a contract*—Contract law establishes what kinds of promises will be legally binding and supplies procedures for enforcing legally binding promises, or agreements. 3. *The definition of a contract*—A contract is an agreement that can be enforced in court. It is formed by two or more competent parties who agree to perform or to refrain from performing some act now or in the future. 4. *Objective theory of contracts*—In contract law, intent is determined by objective facts, not by the personal or subjective intent, or belief, of a party.
Elements of a Contract **(See pages 133–134.)**	1. *Requirements of a valid contract*—The four requirements of a valid contract are agreement, consideration, contractual capacity, and legality. 2. *Defenses to the enforceability of a contract*—Even if the four requirements of a valid contract are met, a contract may be unenforceable if it lacks voluntary consent or is not in the required form.
Types of Contracts **(See pages 134–136.)**	1. *Bilateral*—A promise for a promise. 2. *Unilateral*—A promise for an act (acceptance is the completed—or substantial—performance of the contract by the offeree). 3. *Formal*—Requires a special form for contract formation. 4. *Informal*—Requires no special form for contract formation. 5. *Express*—Formed by words (oral, written, or a combination). 6. *Implied*—Formed at least in part by the conduct of the parties. 7. *Executed*—A fully performed contract. 8. *Executory*—A contract not yet fully performed. 9. *Valid*—A contract that has the necessary contractual elements of offer and acceptance, consideration, parties with legal capacity, and a legal purpose. 10. *Voidable*—A contract in which a party has the option of avoiding or enforcing the contractual obligation. 11. *Unenforceable*—A valid contract that cannot be enforced because of a legal defense. 12. *Void*—No contract exists, or there is a contract without legal obligations.
Quasi Contracts **(See pages 136–138.)**	A quasi contract, or a contract implied in law, is a contract that is imposed by law to prevent unjust enrichment.
Interpretation of Contracts **(See pages 138–140.)**	Increasingly, plain language laws require private contracts to be written in plain language so that the terms are clear and understandable to the parties. Under the plain meaning rule, a court will enforce the contract according to its plain terms, the meaning of which must be determined from the written document alone. Other rules applied by the courts when interpreting contracts are set out on pages 138 and 139.

ExamPrep

ISSUE SPOTTERS

—Check your answers to these questions against the answers provided in Appendix G.

1 Joli signs and returns a letter from Kerin, referring to a book for sale and its price. When Kerin delivers the book, Joli sends it back, claiming that they have no contract. Kerin claims they do. What standard determines whether these parties have a contract?

2 Dyna tells Ed that she will pay Ed $1,000 to set fire to Dyna's store, so that she can collect funds under a fire insurance policy. Ed sets fire to the store, but Dyna refuses to pay. Can Ed recover? Why or why not?

BEFORE THE TEST

Go to **www.cengagebrain.com**, enter the ISBN 9781111530624, and click on "Find" to locate this textbook's Web site. Then, click on "Access Now" under "Study Tools," and select Chapter 7 at the top. There, you will find an Interactive Quiz that you can take to assess your mastery of the concepts in this chapter, as well as Flashcards and a Glossary of important terms.

For Review

1 What is a contract? What is the objective theory of contracts?
2 What are the four basic elements necessary to the formation of a valid contract?
3 What is the difference between an implied contract and a quasi contract?
4 How does a void contract differ from a voidable contract? What is an unenforceable contract?
5 What rules guide the courts in interpreting contracts?

Questions and Case Problems

7–1 Contract Classification. Jay's Flying Advertising, LLC, contracted with Big Bob's Burger restaurant to fly an advertisement above the Connecticut beaches. The advertisement offered $5,000 to any person who could swim from the Connecticut beaches to Long Island across the Long Island Sound in less than a day. Frank Dimitri saw the streamer and accepted the challenge. He started his marathon swim that same day at 10 A.M. After he had been swimming for four hours and was about halfway across the sound, Dimitri saw another plane pulling a streamer that read, "Big Bob's Burger revokes." Is there a contract between Dimitri and Big Bob's? If there is a contract, what type (types) of contract is (are) formed?

7–2 Question with Sample Answer Janine was hospitalized with severe abdominal pain and placed in an intensive care unit. Her doctor told the hospital personnel to order around-the-clock nursing care for Janine. At the hospital's request, a nursing services firm, Nursing Services Unlimited, provided two weeks of in-hospital care and, after Janine was sent home, an additional two weeks of at-home care. During the at-home period of care, Janine was fully aware that she was receiving the benefit of the nursing services. Nursing Services later billed Janine $4,000 for the nursing care, but Janine refused to pay on the ground that she had never contracted for the services, either orally or in writing. In view of the fact that no express contract was ever formed, can Nursing Services recover the $4,000 from Janine? If so, under what legal theory? Discuss.

—For a sample answer to Question 7–2, go to Appendix E at the end of this text.

7–3 Contract Interpretation. Lisa and Darrell Miller married in 1983 and had two children, Landon and Spencer. The Millers divorced in 2003 and entered into a "Joint Custody Implementation Plan" (JCIP). Under the JCIP, Darrell agreed to "begin setting funds aside for the minor children to attend post-secondary education necessary to pay tuition, books, supplies, and room and board not to exceed four (4) years." After Landon's eighteenth birthday, Darrell filed a petition in a Louisiana state court to reduce the amount of the child support that he was paying to Lisa. In response, she asked the court to order Darrell to pay the boys' college expenses but offered no evidence to support the request. Darrell contended that the JCIP was not clear on this point. Do the rules of contract interpretation, applied to the phrasing of the Millers' JCIP, support Lisa's request or Darrell's contention? Explain. [*Miller v. Miller,* 1 So.3d 815 (La.App. 2009)]

7–4 Case Problem with Sample Answer Robert Gutkowski, a sports marketing expert, met numerous times with George Steinbrenner, the owner of the New York Yankees, and other Yankees executives over a ten-year period to discuss and help launch the Yankees Entertainment and Sports Network (YES Network). He was paid as a consultant for several years during that time. When the parties quit working together, Gutkowski sued, contending that he had been made promises to be given an ownership share in YES as part of the compensation for his work. While he was paid as a consultant, he was not given a share of YES or hired as a regular executive for YES. He contended that, by industry standards, a reasonable value for his services would be a 2 to 3 percent ownership share of YES. There was no written contract for such a share, but Gutkowski claimed that he was due this compensation to prevent unjust enrichment of the Yankees for exploiting his expertise. Does Gutkowski have a good claim for payment based on *quantum meruit?* Explain your answer. [*Gutkowski v. Steinbrenner,* 680 F.Supp.2d 602 (S.D.N.Y. 2010)]

—For a sample answer for Problem 7–4, go to Appendix F at the end of this text.

7–5 Types of Contracts. Kim Panenka asked to borrow $4,750 from her sister, Kris, so that Kim could make her mortgage payment. Kris deposited a check for that amount into Kim's bank account. Hours later, Kim asked to borrow another $1,100. Kris took a cash advance on her credit card and deposited this amount into Kim's account. About a week later, Kim asked Kris for $845.40 to pay a dental bill. Kris paid the bill by credit card. After Kris asked for repayment several times and did not receive payment, she filed a suit against her sister in a Wisconsin state court. At the trial, Kim admitted that she had asked for the funds and that it had not been a gift, but she testified that the sisters had a long history of paying for things for each other without expecting repayment. Kris countered that she had "loaned" Kim these amounts. Can the court impose a contract between the sisters? Explain. [*Panenka v. Panenka,* 331 Wis.2d 731, 795 N.W.2d 493 (2011)]

7–6  **A Question of Ethics** *International Business Machines Corp. (IBM) hired Niels Jensen in 2000 as a software sales representative. In 2001, IBM presented a new "Software*

*Sales Incentive Plan" (SIP) at a conference for its sales employees. A brochure given to the attendees stated, "[T]here are no caps to your earnings; the more you sell, * * * the more earnings for you." The brochure outlined how the plan worked and referred the employees to the "Sales Incentives" section of IBM's corporate intranet for more details. Jensen was given a "quota letter" that said he would be paid $75,000 as a base salary and, if he attained his quota, an additional $75,000 as incentive pay. In September, Jensen closed a deal with the U.S. Department of the Treasury's Internal Revenue Service worth more than $24 million to IBM. Relying on the SIP brochure, Jensen estimated his commission to be $2.6 million. IBM paid him less than $500,000, however. Jensen filed a suit in a federal district court against IBM, contending that the SIP brochure and quota letter constituted a unilateral offer that became a binding contract when Jensen closed the sale. In view of these facts, consider the following questions. [*Jensen v. International Business Machines Corp.*, 454 F.3d 382 (4th Cir. 2006)]*

1 Would it be fair to the employer in this case to hold that the SIP brochure and the quota letter created a unilateral contract if IBM did not *intend* to create such a contract? Would it be fair to the employee to hold that no contract was created? Explain.

2 The "Sales Incentives" section of IBM's intranet included a clause providing that "[m]anagement will decide if an adjustment to the payment is appropriate" when an employee closes a large transaction. Jensen's quota letter stated, "[The SIP] program does not constitute a promise by IBM to make any distributions under it. IBM reserves the right to adjust the program terms or to cancel or otherwise modify the program at any time." How do these statements affect your answers to the above questions? From an ethical perspective, would it be fair to hold that a contract exists despite these statements?

7–7 **Critical Thinking Legal Question** Review the basic requirements for a valid contract listed at the beginning of this chapter. In view of those requirements, analyze the relationship entered into when a student enrolls in a college or university. Has a contract been formed? If so, is it a bilateral contract or a unilateral contract? Discuss.

Chapter 8

Agreement in Traditional and E-Contracts

Learning Objectives

After reading this chapter, you should be able to answer the following questions:

1. What elements are necessary for an effective offer? What are some examples of nonoffers?
2. In what circumstances will an offer be irrevocable?
3. What are the elements that are necessary for an effective acceptance?
4. How do shrink-wrap and click-on agreements differ from other contracts? How have traditional laws been applied to these agreements?
5. What is the Uniform Electronic Transactions Act? What are some of the major provisions of this act?

The Learning Objectives above are designed to help improve your understanding of the chapter.

(AP Photo/Carlos Osorio)

In Chapter 7, we pointed out that promises and agreements, and the knowledge that some of those promises and agreements will be legally enforced, are essential to civilized society. The homes we live in, the food we eat, the clothes we wear, the cars we drive, the books we read, the concerts and professional sporting events we attend—all of these have been purchased through contractual agreements. Contract law developed over time, through the common law tradition, to meet society's need to know with certainty what kinds of promises, or contracts, will be enforced and the point at which a valid and binding contract is formed.

For a contract to be valid and enforceable, the requirements listed in Chapter 7 must be met. In this chapter, we look closely at the first of these requirements, *agreement.* Agreement is required to form a contract, regardless of whether it is formed in the traditional way by exchanging paper documents or online by exchanging electronic messages or documents. In today's world, many contracts are formed via the Internet. We discuss online offers and acceptances and examine some laws that have been created to apply to electronic contracts, or *e-contracts,* in the latter part of this chapter.

Agreement

An essential element for contract formation is **agreement**—the parties must agree on the terms of the contract. Ordinarily, agreement is evidenced by two events: an *offer* and an *acceptance.* One party offers a certain bargain to another party, who then accepts that bargain.

Requirements of the Offer

An **offer** is a promise or commitment to perform or refrain from performing some specified act in the future. The party making an offer is called the *offeror,* and the party to whom the offer is made is called the *offeree.* Three elements are necessary for an offer to be effective:

1. There must be a serious, objective intention by the offeror.

2. The terms of the offer must be reasonably certain, or definite, so that the parties and the court can ascertain the terms of the contract.
3. The offer must be communicated to the offeree.

Once an effective offer has been made, the offeree's acceptance of that offer creates a legally binding contract (providing the other essential elements for a valid and enforceable contract are present).

INTENTION The first requirement for an effective offer is a serious, objective intention on the part of the offeror. Intent is not determined by the *subjective* intentions, beliefs, or assumptions of the offeror. Rather, it is determined by what a reasonable person in the offeree's position would conclude the offeror's words and actions meant. Offers made in obvious anger, jest, or undue excitement do not meet the serious-and-objective-intent test. Because these offers are not effective, an offeree's acceptance does not create an agreement.

EXAMPLE 8.1 Linda and Dena ride to school each day in Dena's new automobile, which has a market value of $20,000. One cold morning, they get into the car, but Dena cannot get the car started. She yells in anger, "I'll sell this car to anyone for $500!" Linda drops $500 on Dena's lap. A reasonable person—taking into consideration Dena's frustration and the obvious difference in value between the market price of the car and the proposed purchase price—would realize that Dena's offer was not made with serious and objective intent. No agreement was formed. ●

In the classic case presented next, the court considered whether an offer made "after a few drinks" met the serious-intent requirement.

Classic Case 8.1 Lucy v. Zehmer

Supreme Court of Appeals of Virginia, 196 Va. 493, 84 S.E.2d 516 (1954).

FACTS W. O. Lucy and A. H. Zehmer had known each other for fifteen to twenty years. For some time, Lucy had been wanting to buy Zehmer's farm. Zehmer had always told Lucy that he was not interested in selling. One night, Lucy stopped in to visit with the Zehmers at a restaurant they operated. Lucy said to Zehmer, "I bet you wouldn't take $50,000 for that place." Zehmer replied, "Yes, I would, too; you wouldn't give fifty." Throughout the evening, the conversation returned to the sale of the farm. At the same time, the parties were drinking whiskey. Eventually, Zehmer wrote up an agreement, on the back of a restaurant check, for the sale of the farm, and he asked his wife, Ida, to sign it–which she did. When Lucy brought an action in a Virginia state court to enforce the agreement, Zehmer argued that he had been "high as a Georgia pine" at the time and that the offer had been made in jest: "two doggoned drunks bluffing to see who could talk the biggest and say the most." Lucy claimed that he had not been intoxicated and did not think Zehmer had been, either, given the way Zehmer handled the transaction. The trial court ruled in favor of the Zehmers, and Lucy appealed.

ISSUE Can the agreement be avoided on the basis of intoxication?

DECISION No. The agreement to sell the farm was binding.

REASON The court held that the evidence given about the nature of the conversation, the appearance and completeness of the agreement, and the signing all tended to show that a serious business transaction, not a casual jest, was intended. The court had to look into the objective meaning of the words and acts of the Zehmers: "An agreement or mutual assent is of course essential to a valid contract, but the law imputes to a person an intention corresponding to the reasonable meaning of his words and acts. If his words and acts, judged by a reasonable standard, manifest an intention to agree, it is immaterial what may be the real but unexpressed state of mind."

WHAT IF THE FACTS WERE DIFFERENT? *Suppose that the day after Lucy signed the agreement, he decided that he did not want the farm after all, and Zehmer sued Lucy to perform the contract. Would this change in the facts alter the court's decision that Lucy and Zehmer had created an enforceable contract? Why or why not?*

IMPACT OF THIS CASE ON TODAY'S LAW *This is a classic case in contract law because it so clearly illustrates the objective theory of contracts with respect to determining whether an offer was intended. Today, the objective theory of contracts continues to be applied by the courts, and the* Lucy v. Zehmer *decision is routinely cited as a significant precedent in this area.*

Expressions of Opinion. An expression of opinion is not an offer. It does not demonstrate an intention to enter into a binding agreement. **CASE EXAMPLE 8.2** Hawkins took his son to McGee, a physician, and asked McGee to operate on the son's hand. McGee said that the boy would be in the hospital three or four days and that the hand would *probably* heal a few days later. The son's hand did not heal for a month, but nonetheless the father did not win a suit for breach of contract. The court held that McGee did not make an offer to heal the son's hand in three or four days.

He merely expressed an opinion as to when the hand would heal.[1] •

Statements of Future Intent. A statement of an *intention* to do something in the future is not an offer. **EXAMPLE 8.3** If Samir says, "I *plan* to sell my stock in Novation, Inc., for $150 per share," no contract is created if John "accepts" and tenders $150 per share for the stock. Samir has merely expressed his intention to enter into a future contract for the sale of the stock. If John accepts and tenders the $150 per share, no contract is formed, because a reasonable person would conclude that Samir was only *thinking about* selling his stock, not promising to sell it. •

Preliminary Negotiations. A request or invitation to negotiate is not an offer; it only expresses a willingness to discuss the possibility of entering into a contract. Examples are statements such as "Will you sell Forest Acres?" and "I wouldn't sell my car for less than $8,000." A reasonable person in the offeree's position would not conclude that such statements indicated an intention to enter into binding obligations.

Likewise, when the government and private firms need to have construction work done, they invite contractors to submit bids. The *invitation* to submit bids is not an offer, and a contractor does not bind the government or private firm by submitting a bid. (The bids that the contractors submit are offers, however, and the government or private firm can bind the contractor by accepting the bid.)

Advertisements, Catalogues, and Circulars. In general, advertisements, mail-order catalogues, price lists, and circular letters (meant for the general public) are treated as invitations to negotiate, not as offers to form a contract.[2] **CASE EXAMPLE 8.4** An advertisement on the *Science*NOW Web site asked readers to submit "news tips," which the organization would then investigate for possible inclusion in its magazine or on the Web site. Erik Trell, a professor and physician, submitted a manuscript in which he claimed to have solved a famous mathematical problem. When *Science*NOW did not publish the information, Trell filed a lawsuit for breach of contract. He claimed that the *Science*NOW ad was an offer, which he had accepted by submitting his manuscript. The court dismissed Trell's suit, holding that the ad was not an offer, but merely an invitation.[3] •

Price lists are another form of invitation to negotiate or trade. A seller's price list is not an offer to sell at that price; it merely invites the buyer to offer to buy at that price. In fact, the seller usually puts "prices subject to change" on the price list. Only in rare circumstances will a price quotation be construed as an offer.

Although most advertisements and the like are treated as invitations to negotiate, this does not mean that an advertisement can never be an offer. On some occasions, courts have construed advertisements to be offers because the ads contained definite terms that invited acceptance (such as an ad offering a reward for the return of a lost dog).

Auctions. In an auction, a seller "offers" goods for sale through an auctioneer, but this is not an offer to form a contract. Rather, it is an invitation asking bidders to submit offers. In the context of an auction, a bidder is the offeror, and the auctioneer is the offeree. The offer is accepted when the auctioneer strikes the hammer. Before the fall of the hammer, a bidder may revoke (take back) her or his bid, or the auctioneer may reject that bid or all bids. Typically, an auctioneer will reject a bid that is below the price the seller is willing to accept.

When the auctioneer accepts a higher bid, he or she rejects all previous bids. Because rejection terminates an offer (as will be discussed later), those bids represent offers that have been terminated. Thus, if the highest bidder withdraws his or her bid before the hammer falls, none of the previous bids is reinstated. If the bid is not withdrawn or rejected, the contract is formed when the auctioneer announces, "Going once, going twice, sold!" (or something similar) and lets the hammer fall.

Auctions with and without Reserve. Traditionally, auctions have been either *with reserve* or *without reserve.* In an auction with reserve, the seller (through the auctioneer) may withdraw the goods at any time before the auctioneer closes the sale by announcement or by the fall of the hammer. All auctions are assumed to be auctions with reserve unless the terms of the auction are explicitly stated to be without reserve. In an auction without reserve, the goods cannot be withdrawn by the seller and must be sold to the highest bidder. In auctions with reserve, the seller may reserve the right to confirm or reject the sale even after "the hammer has fallen." In this situation, the seller is obligated to notify those attending the auction that sales of goods made during the auction are not final until confirmed by the seller.[4]

Agreements to Agree. Traditionally, agreements to agree—that is, agreements to agree to the material terms of a contract at some future date—were not considered to be binding contracts. The modern view, however, is that agreements to agree may be enforceable agreements (contracts) if it is clear that the parties intend to be bound by the agreements. In other words, under the modern view the emphasis is on the parties' intent rather than on form.

---

1. *Hawkins v. McGee,* 84 N.H. 114, 146 A. 641 (1929).
2. *Restatement (Second) of Contracts,* Section 26, Comment b.
3. *Trell v. American Association for the Advancement of Science,* __ F.Supp.2d __ (W.D.N.Y. 2007).
4. These rules apply under both the common law of contracts and the Uniform Commercial Code, or UCC. See UCC 2–328.

CASE EXAMPLE 8.5 After a customer was injured and nearly drowned on a water ride at one of its amusement parks, Six Flags, Inc., filed a lawsuit against the manufacturer that had designed the ride. The defendant manufacturer claimed that there was no binding contract between the parties, only preliminary negotiations that were never formalized into a contract to construct the ride. The court, however, held that a faxed document specifying the details of the water ride, along with the parties' subsequent actions (beginning construction and handwriting notes on the fax), was sufficient to show an intent to be bound. Because of the court's finding, the manufacturer was required to provide insurance for the water ride at Six Flags, and its insurer was required to defend Six Flags in the personal-injury lawsuit that arose out of the incident.[5] •

Increasingly, the courts are holding that a preliminary agreement constitutes a binding contract if the parties have agreed on all essential terms and no disputed issues remain to be resolved. In contrast, if the parties agree on certain major terms but leave other terms open for further negotiation, a preliminary agreement is binding only in the sense that the parties have committed themselves to negotiate the undecided terms in good faith in an effort to reach a final agreement.

DEFINITENESS The second requirement for an effective offer involves the definiteness of its terms. An offer must have reasonably definite terms so that a court can determine if a breach has occurred and give an appropriate remedy.[6] Generally, a contract must include the following terms, either expressed in the contract or capable of being reasonably inferred from it:

1. The identification of the parties.
2. The identification of the object or subject matter of the contract (also the quantity, when appropriate), including the work to be performed, with specific identification of such items as goods, services, and land.
3. The consideration to be paid.
4. The time of payment, delivery, or performance.

An offer may invite an acceptance to be worded in such specific terms that the contract is made definite. **EXAMPLE 8.6** Marcus Business Machines contacts your corporation and offers to sell "from one to ten MacCool copying machines for $1,600 each; state number desired in acceptance." Your corporation agrees to buy two copiers. Because the quantity is specified in the acceptance, the terms are definite, and the contract is enforceable. •

COMMUNICATION The third requirement for an effective offer is communication—the offer must be communicated to the offeree. **EXAMPLE 8.7** Tolson advertises a reward for the return of her lost cat. Dirk, not knowing of the reward, finds the cat and returns it to Tolson. Ordinarily, Dirk cannot recover the reward because an essential element of a reward contract is that the one who claims the reward must have known it was offered. A few states would allow recovery of the reward, but not on contract principles—Dirk would be allowed to recover on the basis that it would be unfair to deny him the reward just because he did not know about it. •

The following case illustrates the importance of the communication requirement in contract formation.

5. *Six Flags, Inc. v. Steadfast Insurance Co.*, 474 F.Supp.2d 201 (D.Mass. 2007).
6. *Restatement (Second) of Contracts*, Section 33.

Case 8.2 Alexander v. Lafayette Crime Stoppers, Inc.

Court of Appeal of Louisiana, Third District, 28 So.3d 1253 (2010).
www.la3circuit.org/opinions.htm[a]

FACTS In 2002, several Louisiana women were murdered, and the Multi Agency Homicide Task Force was established to investigate the murders. Investigators believed one individual had committed these murders and referred to this person as the "South Louisiana Serial Killer." In April 2003, the Baton Rouge Crime Stoppers (BRCS) began publicizing a reward offer in newspapers, television stations, and billboards regarding the South Louisiana Serial Killer. A short time later, Lafayette Crime Stoppers (LCS) also publicized a reward offer. Both offers promised to give rewards for information leading to the arrest of the killer, included a telephone number to call with information, and stated that the offers expired on August 1, 2003. Dianne Alexander was attacked in her home, but her son chased the attacker from the property. Thanks to the Alexanders' assistance, the suspect—who was also being investigated as the possible serial killer—was subsequently arrested and indicted. On August 14, 2003, when Alexander sought to collect the advertised reward, LCS told her that she was not eligible to receive it. Alexander and her son sued LCS and BRCS in a Louisiana state court to recover the amount of the awards—$100,000 and $50,000, respectively. BRCS and LCS (the defendants) asserted that Alexander and her son (the plaintiffs) had not complied with the "form, terms, or conditions" required by the reward offers because they did not provide information to Crime Stoppers via the tipster hotline before August 1, 2003. The trial court granted the defendants' motion for summary judgment, and the plaintiffs appealed.

a. Under "2010," click on "February." When that page opens, select "February 3, 2010." When you reach the page for February 3, 2010, scroll down the list to the case title and docket number (CA 09-11927) to access the opinion. The judicial branch of Louisiana maintains this Web site.

Case 8.2—Continues next page ➡

Case 8.2–Continued

ISSUE Did the Alexanders communicate their acceptance of the reward to the offerors before the expiration date?

DECISION No. The Louisiana appellate court affirmed the trial court's judgment granting the defendants' motions for summary judgment.

REASON The court reviewed the offers presented in press releases by both crime-stopper organizations and found that the offers were irrevocable because they specified a period of time for acceptance. Such an offer is accepted when acceptance is received by the offeror or someone authorized to receive acceptance on the offeror's behalf. Although Alexander and her son admitted that they had not contacted either crime-stopper organization before August 1, 2003, they argued that they had accepted the organizations' offers by performance when they provided information to law enforcement officials. The court disagreed, however, finding that while the plaintiffs provided information concerning the serial killer to local law enforcement and to the task force, neither of those parties were authorized to receive acceptance. Because the plaintiffs did not notify the offerors of their acceptance of the reward before August 1, the offers had expired.

WHAT IF THE FACTS WERE DIFFERENT? *Suppose that the plaintiffs had learned about the reward offer after the killer had already been arrested and indicted due to their assistance but before the August 1, 2003, deadline. If they had then called in their information on the tip line, would they have been legally entitled to claim the reward in this circumstance? Explain.*

Termination of the Offer

The communication of an effective offer to an offeree gives the offeree the power to transform the offer into a binding, legal obligation (a contract) by an acceptance. This power of acceptance does not continue forever, though. It can be terminated by either the *action of the parties* or by *operation of law*.

Termination by Action of the Parties

An offer can be terminated by the action of the parties in any of three ways: by revocation, by rejection, or by counteroffer.

Revocation of the Offer. The offeror's act of withdrawing an offer is referred to as **revocation.** Unless an offer is irrevocable, the offeror usually can revoke the offer (even if he or she has promised to keep the offer open), as long as the revocation is communicated to the offeree before the offeree accepts. Revocation may be accomplished by an express repudiation of the offer (for example, with a statement such as "I withdraw my previous offer of October 17") or by the performance of acts that are inconsistent with the existence of the offer and that are made known to the offeree.

EXAMPLE 8.8 Michelle offers to sell some land to Gary. A month passes, and Gary, who has not accepted the offer, learns that Michelle has sold the property to Liam. Because Michelle's sale of the land to Liam is inconsistent with the continued existence of the offer to Gary, the offer to Gary is effectively revoked. •

The general rule followed by most states is that a revocation becomes effective when the offeree or the offeree's agent (a person who acts on behalf of another) actually receives it. Therefore, a letter of revocation mailed on April 1 and delivered at the offeree's residence or place of business on April 3 becomes effective on April 3.

An offer made to the general public can be revoked in the same manner in which the offer was originally communicated. **EXAMPLE 8.9** An electronic goods retailer offers a $10,000 reward to anyone providing information leading to the apprehension of the persons who burglarized its downtown store. The offer is published in three local papers and in four papers in neighboring communities. To revoke the offer, the retailer must publish the revocation in all seven papers for the same number of days it published the offer. The revocation is then accessible to the general public, and the offer is revoked even if some particular offeree does not know about the revocation. •

Irrevocable Offers. Although most offers are revocable, some can be made irrevocable. Increasingly, courts refuse to allow an offeror to revoke an offer when the offeree has changed position because of justifiable reliance on the offer (under the doctrine of *detrimental reliance,* or *promissory estoppel,* which will be discussed in Chapter 9). In some circumstances, "firm offers" made by merchants may also be considered irrevocable. We will discuss these offers in Chapter 13.

Another form of irrevocable offer is an option contract. An **option contract** is created when an offeror promises to hold an offer open for a specified period of time in return for a payment (consideration) given by the offeree. An option contract takes away the offeror's power to revoke an offer for the period of time specified in the option. If no time is specified, then a reasonable period of time is implied.

Option contracts are frequently used in conjunction with the sale of real estate. **EXAMPLE 8.10** Tyrell agrees to lease a house from Jackson, the property owner. The lease contract includes a clause stating that Tyrell is paying an additional $15,000 for an option to purchase the property within a specified period of time. If Tyrell decides not to purchase the house after the specified period has lapsed, he loses the $15,000, and Jackson is free to sell the property to another buyer. •

Rejection of the Offer by the Offeree. If the offeree rejects the offer—by words or by conduct—the offer is terminated.

Any subsequent attempt by the offeree to accept will be construed as a new offer, giving the original offeror (now the offeree) the power of acceptance.

Like a revocation, a rejection of an offer is effective only when it is actually received by the offeror or the offeror's agent. **EXAMPLE 8.11** Goldfinch Farms offers to sell specialty Maitake mushrooms to a Japanese buyer, Kinoko Foods. If Kinoko rejects the offer by sending a letter via U.S. mail, the rejection will not be effective (and the offer will not be terminated) until Goldfinch receives the letter. •

Merely inquiring about an offer does not constitute rejection. **EXAMPLE 8.12** A friend offers to buy your Wii gaming system with additional accessories for $300. You respond, "Is this your best offer?" or "Will you pay me $375 for it?" A reasonable person would conclude that you did not reject the offer but merely made an inquiry for further consideration of the offer. You can still accept and bind your friend to the $300 purchase price. When the offeree merely inquires as to the firmness of the offer, there is no reason to presume that she or he intends to reject it. •

Counteroffer by the Offeree. A **counteroffer** is a rejection of the original offer and the simultaneous making of a new offer. **EXAMPLE 8.13** Burke offers to sell his home to Lang for $270,000. Lang responds, "Your price is too high. I'll offer to purchase your house for $250,000." Lang's response is called a counteroffer because it rejects Burke's offer to sell at $270,000 and creates a new offer by Lang to purchase the home at a price of $250,000. •

At common law, the **mirror image rule** requires that the offeree's acceptance match the offeror's offer exactly. In other words, the terms of the acceptance must "mirror" those of the offer. If the acceptance materially changes or adds to the terms of the original offer, it will be considered not an acceptance but a counteroffer—which, of course, need not be accepted. The original offeror can, however, accept the terms of the counteroffer and create a valid contract.

TERMINATION BY OPERATION OF LAW The power of the offeree to transform the offer into a binding, legal obligation can be terminated by operation of law through the occurrence of any of the following events:

1. Lapse of time.
2. Destruction of the specific subject matter of the offer.
3. Death or incompetence of the offeror or the offeree.
4. Supervening illegality of the proposed contract.

Lapse of Time. An offer terminates automatically by law when the period of time *specified in the offer* has passed. If the offer states that it will be left open until a particular date, then the offer will terminate at midnight on that day. If the offer states that it will be left open for a number of days, such as ten days, this time period normally begins to run when the offer is actually received by the offeree, not when it is formed or sent. When the offer is delayed (through the misdelivery of mail, for example), the period begins to run from the date the offeree would have received the offer, but only if the offeree knows or should know that the offer is delayed.[7]

EXAMPLE 8.14 Beth offers to sell her boat to Jonah, stating that the offer will remain open until May 20. Unless Jonah accepts the offer by midnight on May 20, the offer will lapse (terminate). Now suppose that Beth writes a letter to Jonah, offering to sell him her boat if Jonah accepts the offer within twenty days of the letter's date, which is May 1. Jonah must accept within twenty days after May 1, or the offer will terminate. Suppose that instead of including the date May 1 in her letter, Beth simply writes to Jonah offering to sell him her boat if Jonah accepts within twenty days. In this instance, Jonah must accept within twenty days of receiving the letter. The same rule would apply if Beth used insufficient postage and Jonah received the letter ten days late without knowing that it had been delayed. If, however, Jonah knew that the letter was delayed, the offer would lapse twenty days after the day he ordinarily would have received the offer had Beth used sufficient postage. •

If the offer does not specify a time for acceptance, the offer terminates at the end of a *reasonable* period of time. A reasonable period of time is determined by the subject matter of the contract, business and market conditions, and other relevant circumstances. An offer to sell farm produce, for example, will terminate sooner than an offer to sell farm equipment because farm produce is perishable and subject to greater fluctuations in market value.

Destruction of the Subject Matter. An offer is automatically terminated if the specific subject matter of the offer is destroyed before the offer is accepted. **EXAMPLE 8.15** Bekins offers to sell his prize cow to Yates. If the cow becomes ill and dies before Yates accepts, the offer is automatically terminated. (Note that if Yates had accepted the offer before the cow died, a contract would have been formed. Nonetheless, because the cow was dead, a court would likely excuse Bekins's obligation to perform the contract on the basis of impossibility of performance—see Chapter 11.) •

Death or Incompetence of the Offeror or Offeree. An offeree's power of acceptance is terminated when the offeror or offeree dies or is deprived of legal capacity to enter into the proposed contract, *unless the offer is irrevocable.* A revocable offer is personal to both parties and normally cannot pass to a decedent's heirs or estate or to the guardian of a mentally incompetent

7. *Restatement (Second) of Contracts,* Section 49.

person. This rule applies whether or not one party had notice of the death or incompetence of the other party.

EXAMPLE 8.16 Kapola, who is quite ill, writes to her friend Amanda, offering to sell Amanda her grand piano for only $400. That night, Kapola dies. The next day, Amanda, not knowing of Kapola's death, writes a letter to Kapola, accepting the offer and enclosing a check for $400. Is there a contract? No. There is no contract because the offer automatically terminated on Kapola's death. •

Supervening Illegality of the Proposed Contract. A statute or court decision that makes an offer illegal automatically terminates the offer. **EXAMPLE 8.17** Acme Finance Corporation offers to lend Carlos $20,000 at 15 percent interest annually, but before Carlos can accept, the state legislature enacts a statute prohibiting loans at interest rates greater than 12 percent. In this situation, the offer is automatically terminated. (If the statute is enacted after Carlos accepts the offer, a valid contract is formed, but the contract may still be unenforceable—see Chapter 9.) •

Acceptance

An **acceptance** is a voluntary act by the offeree that shows assent, or agreement, to the terms of an offer. The offeree's act may consist of words or conduct. The acceptance must be unequivocal and must be communicated to the offeror.

WHO CAN ACCEPT? Generally, a third person cannot substitute for the offeree and effectively accept the offer. After all, the identity of the offeree is as much a condition of a bargaining offer as any other term contained therein. Thus, except in special circumstances, only the person to whom the offer is made or that person's agent can accept the offer and create a binding contract. For instance, Lottie makes an offer to Paul. Paul is not interested, but his friend José accepts the offer. No contract is formed.

UNEQUIVOCAL ACCEPTANCE To exercise the power of acceptance effectively, the offeree must accept unequivocally. This is the mirror image rule. If the acceptance is subject to new conditions or if the terms of the acceptance materially change the original offer, the acceptance may be deemed a counteroffer that implicitly rejects the original offer.

Certain terms, when included in an acceptance, will not change the offer sufficiently to constitute rejection. **EXAMPLE 8.18** In response to an art dealer's offer to sell a painting, the offeree, Ashton Gibbs, replies, "I accept. Please send a written contract." Gibbs is requesting a written contract but is not making it a condition for acceptance. Therefore, the acceptance is effective without the written contract. In contrast, if Gibbs replies, "I accept *if* you send a written contract," the acceptance is expressly conditioned on the request for a writing, and the statement is not an acceptance but a counteroffer. (Notice how important each word is!) •

SILENCE AS ACCEPTANCE Ordinarily, silence cannot constitute acceptance, even if the offeror states, "By your silence and inaction, you will be deemed to have accepted this offer." This general rule applies because an offeree should not be put under a burden of liability to act affirmatively in order to reject an offer. No consideration—that is, nothing of value—has passed to the offeree to impose such a liability.

In some instances, however, the offeree does have a duty to speak. If so, his or her silence or inaction will operate as an acceptance. Silence may be an acceptance when an offeree takes the benefit of offered services even though he or she had an opportunity to reject them and knew that they were offered with the expectation of compensation.

EXAMPLE 8.19 John is a student who earns extra income by washing store windows. John taps on the window of a store, catches the attention of the store's manager, and points to the window and raises his cleaner, signaling that he will be washing the window. The manager does nothing to stop him. Here, the store manager's silence constitutes an acceptance, and an implied contract is created. The store is bound to pay a reasonable value for John's work. •

Silence can also operate as an acceptance when the offeree has had prior dealings with the offeror. If a merchant, for example, routinely receives shipments from a supplier and in the past has always notified the supplier when defective goods are rejected, then silence constitutes acceptance. Also, if a buyer solicits an offer specifying that certain terms and conditions are acceptable, and the seller makes the offer in response to the solicitation, the buyer has a duty to reject—that is, a duty to tell the seller that the offer is not acceptable. Failure to reject (silence) will operate as an acceptance.

COMMUNICATION OF ACCEPTANCE In a bilateral contract, communication of acceptance is necessary because acceptance is in the form of a promise (not performance), and the contract is formed when the promise is made (rather than when the act is performed). Communication of acceptance is not necessary if the offer dispenses with the requirement, however, or if the offer can be accepted by silence.[8]

Because a unilateral contract calls for the full performance of some act, acceptance is usually evident, and notification is unnecessary. Nevertheless, exceptions do exist, such as when the offeror requests notice of acceptance or has no way of determining whether the requested act has been performed.

8. Under UCC 2–206(1)(b), an order or other offer to buy goods that are to be promptly shipped may be treated as either a bilateral or a unilateral offer and can be accepted by a promise to ship or by actual shipment.

In the following case, one of the parties argued that communication of acceptance was not necessary, because the parties had dispensed with the requirement by establishing a deadline for objections. According to this argument, if no objection was offered, acceptance could be assumed. The court had to decide whether this line of reasoning was acceptable or not.

Case 8.3 Powerhouse Custom Homes, Inc. v. 84 Lumber Co.

Court of Appeals of Georgia, 307 Ga.App. 605, 705 S.E.2d 704 (2011).

FACTS Powerhouse Custom Homes, Inc., entered into a credit agreement to obtain building materials from 84 Lumber Company. Eventually, Powerhouse owed 84 Lumber a balance of $95,260.42 under the agreement. When Powerhouse failed to pay, 84 Lumber filed a suit in a Georgia state court to collect. Before the trial, 84 Lumber filed a discovery request for admissions with respect to the debt. (A request for admissions is a written request that a party admit certain facts–in this case, facts concerning the existence and amount of the debt.) Powerhouse did not respond to the request, which meant that the facts included in the request were deemed admitted. Later, while taking part in court-ordered mediation, the parties agreed to a deadline for objections to any agreements they might reach during mediation. Powerhouse then proposed to pay a sum less than the amount owed, but 84 Lumber did not respond to this proposal before the deadline. Afterward, 84 Lumber filed a motion for summary judgment with the trial court. The court granted summary judgment in 84 Lumber's favor for the entire debt. Powerhouse appealed, arguing that 84 Lumber had accepted its proposal to pay a lesser amount by not objecting to it before the agreed-on deadline had elapsed.

ISSUE Did 84 Lumber, by its failure to object to Powerhouse's proposal to settle the debt for less than what was owed, unequivocally accept the offer?

DECISION No. A state intermediate appellate court affirmed the lower court's judgment. For a contract to be formed, an offer must be accepted unequivocally. Without such an acceptance, there is no enforceable contract.

REASON Powerhouse made an offer of a proposed settlement, but 84 Lumber did not communicate its acceptance. Thus, the court reasoned that the parties did not reach an agreement. Because 84 Lumber had not agreed to Powerhouse's proposal, the ten-day deadline did not apply. Meanwhile, Powerhouse had not responded to 84 Lumber's request for admission, so its facts were deemed admitted. Powerhouse was liable for the entire debt, plus interest, attorneys' fees, and costs.

FOR CRITICAL ANALYSIS—Economic Consideration *Why do judgments often include awards of interest, attorneys' fees, and costs?*

MODE AND TIMELINESS OF ACCEPTANCE Acceptance in bilateral contracts must be timely. The general rule is that acceptance in a bilateral contract is timely if it is made before the offer is terminated. Problems may arise, though, when the parties involved are not dealing face to face. In such situations, the offeree should use an authorized mode of communication.

The Mailbox Rule. Acceptance takes effect, thus completing formation of the contract, at the time the offeree sends or delivers the communication via the mode expressly or impliedly authorized by the offeror. This is the so-called **mailbox rule,** also called the *deposited acceptance rule,* which the majority of courts follow. Under this rule, if the authorized mode of communication is the mail, then an acceptance becomes valid when it is dispatched (placed in the control of the U.S. Postal Service)—*not* when it is received by the offeror.

The mailbox rule does not apply to instantaneous forms of communication, such as when the parties are dealing face to face, by telephone, or by fax. There is still some uncertainty in the courts as to whether e-mail should be considered an instantaneous form of communication to which the mailbox rule does not apply. If the parties have agreed to conduct transactions electronically and if the Uniform Electronic Transactions Act (UETA—see page 154) applies, then e-mail is considered sent when it either leaves the sender's control or is received by the recipient. This rule, which takes the place of the mailbox rule when the UETA applies, essentially allows an e-mail acceptance to become effective when sent (as it would if sent by U.S. mail).

Authorized Means of Communication. A means of communicating acceptance can be expressly authorized by the offeror or impliedly authorized by the facts and circumstances surrounding the situation. An acceptance sent by means not expressly or impliedly authorized normally is not effective until it is received by the offeror.

When an offeror specifies how acceptance should be made (for example, by overnight delivery), express authorization is said to exist, and the contract is not formed unless the offeree uses that specified mode of acceptance. Moreover, both offeror and offeree are bound in contract the moment this means of acceptance is employed. **EXAMPLE 8.20** Shaylee & Perkins, a Massachusetts firm, offers to sell a container of antique furniture to Leaham's Antiques in Colorado. The offer states that Leaham's must accept the offer via FedEx overnight delivery. The acceptance is effective (and a binding contract is formed) the moment that Leaham's gives the overnight envelope containing the acceptance to the FedEx driver. •

If the offeror does not expressly authorize a certain mode of acceptance, then acceptance can be made by any reasonable means.[9] Courts look at the prevailing business usages and the surrounding circumstances to determine whether the mode of acceptance used was reasonable. Usually, the offeror's choice of a particular means in making the offer implies that the offeree can use the *same or a faster means* for acceptance. Thus, if the offer is made via priority mail, it would be reasonable to accept the offer via priority mail or by a faster method, such as by fax or overnight delivery.

Substitute Method of Acceptance. If the offeror authorizes a particular method of acceptance, but the offeree accepts by a different means, the acceptance may still be effective if the substituted method serves the same purpose as the authorized means. The use of a substitute method of acceptance is not effective on dispatch, though, and no contract will be formed until the acceptance is received by the offeror. Thus, if an offer specifies FedEx overnight delivery but the offeree accepts by overnight delivery from another carrier, such as UPS, the acceptance will still be effective, but not until the offeror receives it.

Agreement in E-Contracts

Numerous contracts are formed online. Electronic contracts, or **e-contracts,** must meet the same basic requirements (agreement, consideration, contractual capacity, and legality) as paper contracts. Disputes concerning e-contracts, however, tend to center on contract terms and whether the parties voluntarily agreed to those terms.

Online contracts may be formed not only for the sale of goods and services but also for *licensing*. The "sale" of software generally involves a license, or a right to use the software, rather than the passage of title (ownership rights) from the seller to the buyer.

EXAMPLE 8.21 Galynn wants to obtain software that will allow her to work on spreadsheets on her BlackBerry. She goes online and purchases GridMagic. During the transaction, she has to click on several on-screen "I agree" boxes to indicate that she understands that she is purchasing only the right to use the software and will not obtain any ownership rights. After she agrees to these terms (the licensing agreement), she can download the software. •

9. Note that UCC 2–206(1)(a) states specifically that an acceptance of an offer for the sale of goods can be made by any medium that is *reasonable* under the circumstances.

As you read through the following subsections, keep in mind that although we typically refer to the offeror and the offeree as a *seller* and a *buyer,* in many online transactions these parties would be more accurately described as a *licensor* and a *licensee.*

Online Offers

Sellers doing business via the Internet can protect themselves against contract disputes and legal liability by creating offers that clearly spell out the terms that will govern their transactions if the offers are accepted. All important terms should be conspicuous and easy to view.

Displaying the Offer The seller's Web site should include a hypertext link to a page containing the full contract so that potential buyers are made aware of the terms to which they are assenting. The contract generally must be displayed online in a readable format such as a twelve-point typeface. All provisions should be reasonably clear. **EXAMPLE 8.22** Netquip sells heavy equipment, such as trucks and trailers, online at its Web site. Because Netquip's pricing schedule is very complex, the schedule must be fully provided and explained on the Web site. In addition, the terms of the sale (such as any warranties and the refund policy) must be fully disclosed. •

Provisions to Include An important rule to keep in mind is that the offeror controls the offer and thus the resulting contract. The seller should therefore determine the terms she or he wants to include in a contract and provide for them in the offer. In some instances, a standardized contract form may suffice. At a minimum, an online offer should include the following provisions:

1. *Acceptance of terms.* A clause that clearly indicates what constitutes the buyer's agreement to the terms of the offer, such as a box containing the words "I accept" that the buyer can click on to indicate acceptance.
2. *Payment.* A provision specifying how payment for the goods (including any applicable taxes) must be made.
3. *Return policy.* A statement of the seller's refund and return policies.
4. *Disclaimer.* Disclaimers of liability for certain uses of the goods. For example, an online seller of business forms may add a disclaimer that the seller does not accept responsibility for the buyer's reliance on the forms rather than on an attorney's advice.
5. *Limitation on remedies.* A provision specifying the remedies available to the buyer if the goods are found to be defective or if the contract is otherwise breached. Any limitation of remedies should be clearly spelled out.
6. *Privacy policy.* A statement indicating how the seller will use the information gathered about the buyer.

7. *Dispute resolution.* Provisions relating to dispute settlement, such as an arbitration clause or a *forum-selection clause* (discussed next).

Dispute-Settlement Provisions Online offers frequently include provisions relating to dispute settlement. For example, the offer might include an arbitration clause specifying that any dispute arising under the contract will be arbitrated in a designated forum.

Many online contracts also contain a **forum-selection clause** indicating the forum, or location (such as a court or jurisdiction), for the resolution of any dispute arising under the contract. As discussed in Chapter 2, significant jurisdictional issues may occur when parties are at a great distance, as they often are when they form contracts via the Internet. A forum-selection clause will help to avert future jurisdictional problems and also help to ensure that the seller will not be required to appear in court in a distant state.

Online Acceptances

The *Restatement (Second) of Contracts*—a compilation of common law contract principles—states that parties may agree to a contract "by written or spoken words or by other action or by failure to act."[10] The Uniform Commercial Code (UCC), which governs sales contracts, has a similar provision. Section 2–204 of the UCC states that any contract for the sale of goods "may be made in any manner sufficient to show agreement, including conduct by both parties which recognizes the existence of such a contract."

Click-on Agreements The courts have used these provisions to conclude that a binding contract can be created by conduct, including the act of clicking on a box indicating "I accept" or "I agree" to accept an online offer. The agreement resulting from such an acceptance is often called a **click-on agreement** (*click-on license* or *click-wrap agreement*).

Generally, the law does not require that the parties have read all of the terms in a contract for it to be effective. Therefore, clicking on a box that states "I agree" to certain terms can be enough. The terms may be contained on a Web site through which the buyer is obtaining goods or services, or they may appear on a computer screen when software is loaded from a CD-ROM or DVD or downloaded from the Internet.

Shrink-Wrap Agreements A **shrink-wrap agreement** (or *shrink-wrap license*) is an agreement whose terms are expressed inside a box in which the goods are packaged. (The term *shrink-wrap* refers to the plastic that covers the box.) Usually, the party who opens the box is told that she or he agrees to the terms by keeping whatever is in the box. Similarly, when the purchaser opens a software package, he or she agrees to abide by the terms of the limited license agreement.

EXAMPLE 8.23 John orders a new computer from a national company, which ships the computer to him. Along with the computer, the box contains an agreement setting forth the terms of the sale, including what remedies are available. The document also states that John's retention of the computer for longer than thirty days will be construed as an acceptance of the terms. •

In most instances, a shrink-wrap agreement is not between a retailer and a buyer, but between the manufacturer of the hardware or software and the ultimate buyer-user of the product. The terms generally concern warranties, remedies, and other issues associated with the use of the product.

Shrink-Wrap Agreements and Enforceable Contract Terms. In some cases, the courts have enforced the terms of shrink-wrap agreements in the same way as the terms of other contracts. These courts have reasoned that by including the terms with the product, the seller proposed a contract that the buyer could accept by using the product after having an opportunity to read the terms.

Shrink-Wrap Terms That May Not Be Enforced. Sometimes, however, courts have refused to enforce certain terms in shrink-wrap agreements because the buyer did not expressly consent to them. An important factor is when the parties form their contract. Suppose that a buyer orders a product over the telephone. If the contract is formed at that time and the seller does not mention terms, such as an arbitration clause or a forum-selection clause, clearly the buyer has not expressly consented to these terms. If the clauses are included in the shrink-wrap agreement, a court may conclude that they are proposals for additional terms, and not part of the original contract, because the buyer did not discover them until *after* the contract was formed.

Browse-Wrap Terms Like the terms of a click-on agreement, **browse-wrap terms** can occur in a transaction conducted over the Internet. Unlike a click-on agreement, however, browse-wrap terms do not require an Internet user to assent to the terms before, say, downloading or using certain software. In other words, a person can install the software without clicking "I agree" to the terms of a license. Browse-wrap terms are often unenforceable because they do not satisfy the agreement requirement of contract formation.[11]

E-Signature Technologies

Today, numerous technologies allow electronic documents to be signed. An **e-signature** has been defined as "an electronic sound, symbol, or process attached to or logically associated

10. *Restatement (Second) of Contracts,* Section 19.

11. See, for example, *Jesmer v. Retail Magic, Inc.*, 863 N.Y.S.2d 737 (2008).

with a record and executed or adopted by a person with the intent to sign the record."[12] Thus, e-signatures include encrypted digital signatures, names (intended as signatures) at the ends of e-mail messages, and "clicks" on a Web page if the click includes the identification of the person.

The technologies for creating e-signatures generally fall into one of two categories, *digitized handwritten signatures* and *digital signatures based on a public-key infrastructure*. A digitized signature is a graphical image of a handwritten signature that is often created using a digital pen and pad, such as an ePad, and special software. For security reasons, the strokes of a person's signature can be measured by software to authenticate the person signing (this is referred to as signature dynamics).

In a public-key infrastructure (such as an asymmetric cryptosystem), two mathematically linked but different keys are generated—a private signing key and a public validation key. A digital signature is created when the signer uses the private key to create a unique mark on an electronic document. The appropriate software enables the recipient of the document to use the public key to verify the identity of the signer. A **cybernotary,** or legally recognized certification authority, issues the key pair, identifies the owner of the keys, and certifies the validity of the public key. The cybernotary also serves as a repository for public keys.

Federal Law on E-Signatures and E-Documents

In 2000, Congress enacted the Electronic Signatures in Global and National Commerce Act (E-SIGN Act),[13] which provides that no contract, record, or signature may be "denied legal effect" solely because it is in electronic form. In other words, under this law, an electronic signature is as valid as a signature on paper, and an e-document can be as enforceable as a paper one.

For an e-signature to be enforceable, the contracting parties must have agreed to use electronic signatures. For an electronic document to be valid, it must be in a form that can be retained and accurately reproduced.

The E-SIGN Act does not apply to all types of documents, however. Contracts and documents that are exempt include court papers, divorce decrees, evictions, foreclosures, health-insurance terminations, prenuptial agreements, and wills. Also, the only agreements governed by the UCC that fall under this law are those covered by Articles 2 and 2A and UCC 1–107 and 1–206. Despite these limitations, the E-SIGN Act significantly expanded the possibilities for contracting online.

The Fair and Accurate Credit Transactions (FACT) Act of 2003[14] was passed to combat identity theft (see page 120). One provision of the FACT Act involves how credit-card receipts should be handled to avoid fraud. See this chapter's *Management Perspective* feature on the facing page for more details on how this provision may affect online transactions.

Partnering Agreements

One way that online sellers and buyers can prevent disputes over signatures in their e-contracts, as well as disputes over the terms and conditions of those contracts, is to form partnering agreements. In a **partnering agreement,** a seller and a buyer who frequently do business with each other agree in advance on the terms and conditions that will apply to all transactions subsequently conducted electronically. The partnering agreement can also establish special access and identification codes to be used by the parties when transacting business electronically.

A partnering agreement reduces the likelihood that disputes will arise under the contract because the buyer and the seller have agreed in advance to the terms and conditions that will accompany each sale. Furthermore, if a dispute does arise, a court or arbitration forum will be able to refer to the partnering agreement when determining the parties' intent.

The Uniform Electronic Transactions Act

Although most states have laws governing e-signatures and other aspects of electronic transactions, these laws are far from uniform. In an attempt to create more uniformity among the states, in 1999 the National Conference of Commissioners on Uniform State Laws and the American Law Institute promulgated the Uniform Electronic Transactions Act (UETA). To date, the UETA has been adopted, at least in part, by forty-eight states.

The primary purpose of the UETA is to remove barriers to e-commerce by giving the same legal effect to electronic records and signatures as is given to paper documents and signatures. As mentioned earlier, the UETA broadly defines an *e-signature* as "an electronic sound, symbol, or process attached to or logically associated with a record and executed or adopted by a person with the intent to sign the record."[15] A **record** is "information that is inscribed on a tangible medium or that is stored in an electronic or other medium and is retrievable in perceivable [visual] form."[16]

The UETA does not create new rules for electronic contracts but rather establishes that records, signatures, and contracts may not be denied enforceability solely due to their electronic form. The UETA does not apply to all writings and signatures. It covers only electronic records and electronic signatures *relating to a transaction.* A *transaction* is defined as an interaction between two or more people relating to business, commercial, or governmental activities.[17]

12. This definition is from the Uniform Electronic Transactions Act.
13. 15 U.S.C. Sections 7001 *et seq.*
14. 15 U.S.C. Sections 1681 *et seq.*

15. UETA 102(8).
16. UETA 102(15).
17. UETA 2(12) and 3.

MANAGEMENT PERSPECTIVE • E-Mailed Credit-Card Receipts

Management Faces a Legal Issue

As consumers engage in more transactions on the Internet, retailers are printing out fewer credit-card receipts than they did previously. Merchants who do print out paper receipts must follow strict guidelines. The Fair and Accurate Credit Transactions (FACT) Act of 2003 prohibits merchants from printing more than the last five digits of the card number or the expiration date on any receipt provided to the cardholder at the point of sale of the transaction. This prohibition applies only to receipts that are "electronically printed." Congress did not specifically indicate what is meant by the words *electronically printed.* Thus, online retailers have faced the legal issue of whether e-mailed receipts are subject to the FACT Act's so-called truncation (shortening) requirement.

What the Courts Say

The question is whether a Web page screen shot counts as a receipt under the FACT Act. At least two court cases have examined this issue. The first one involved reservations for rental motorcycles. The motorcycle rental store sent out an online reservation confirmation that included credit cards' expiration dates on the renters' computer screens. The plaintiffs contended that the confirmations they received were "electronically printed" receipts subject to the FACT Act's truncation requirement. The defendant moved for summary judgment on the ground that the receipts did not violate the act. The court granted the motion, observing that "[w]hen one refers to a printed receipt, what springs to mind is a tangible document."[a]

A similar case concerned the online sale of contact lenses by a popular telemarketing and online retailer. Again, the plaintiff received an e-mail confirmation that included his credit card's expiration date, and again, the court sided with the defendant. The court pointed out that the legislative history of the FACT Act clearly shows that Congress intended this law to apply to physically printed paper receipts. The FACT Act "makes no use of terms like 'Internet' or 'e-mail' that would signal an intent to reach paperless receipts transmitted to the consumer via e-mail."[b]

Implications for Managers

At this time, credit-card receipts sent via e-mail by online retailers appear not to be subject to the FACT Act's truncation requirement. Nonetheless, the prudent online retailer might wish to conform to the FACT Act provisions simply as a good business practice. After all, hackers can sometimes illegally access e-mail correspondence. Moreover, Congress may amend the FACT Act to include e-mail receipts because online retailing is growing dramatically in the United States and elsewhere.

a. *Kelleher v. Eaglerider, Inc.,* 2010 WL 4386837 (N.D.Ill. 2010).
b. *Shlahtichman v. 1-800 Contacts, Inc.,* 615 F.3d 794 (7th Cir. 2010).

The act specifically does not apply to wills or testamentary trusts or to transactions governed by the UCC (other than those covered by Articles 2 and 2A).[18] In addition, the provisions of the UETA allow the states to exclude its application to other areas of law.

The Federal E-SIGN Act and the UETA

Congress passed the E-SIGN Act in 2000, a year after the UETA was presented to the states for adoption. Thus, a significant issue was to what extent the federal E-SIGN Act preempted the UETA as adopted by the states. The E-SIGN Act[19] refers explicitly to the UETA and provides that if a state has enacted the uniform version of the UETA, it is not preempted by the E-SIGN Act. In other words, if the state has enacted the UETA without modification, state law will govern. The problem is that many states have enacted nonuniform (modified) versions of the UETA, largely for the purpose of excluding other areas of state law from the UETA's terms. The E-SIGN Act specifies that those exclusions will be preempted to the extent that they are inconsistent with the E-SIGN Act's provisions.

The E-SIGN Act, however, explicitly allows the states to enact alternative requirements for the use of electronic records or electronic signatures. Generally, however, the requirements must be consistent with the provisions of the E-SIGN Act, and the state must not give greater legal status or effect to one specific type of technology. Additionally, if a state enacts alternative requirements *after* the E-SIGN Act was adopted, the state law must specifically refer to the E-SIGN Act. The relationship between the UETA and the E-SIGN Act is illustrated in Exhibit 8–1 on the next page.

Highlights of the UETA

We look next at selected provisions of the UETA. Our discussion is, of course, based on the act's uniform provisions. Keep in mind that the states that have enacted the UETA may have adopted slightly different versions.

AGREEMENT The UETA will not apply to a transaction unless each of the parties has previously agreed to conduct

18. UETA 3(b).
19. 15 U.S.C. Section 7002(2)(A)(i).

transactions by electronic means. The agreement need not be explicit, however, and it may be implied by the conduct of the parties and the surrounding circumstances.[20] In the comments that accompany the UETA, the drafters stated that it may be reasonable to infer that a person who gives out a business card with an e-mail address on it has consented to transact business electronically.[21] The party's agreement may also be inferred from a letter or other writing, as well as from some verbal communication. Nothing in the UETA requires that the agreement to conduct transactions electronically be made electronically.

Note, however, that some courts have required that the parties' agreement to conduct transactions electronically be clear and unequivocal. For example, in one Louisiana case, the fact that the parties had *negotiated* the terms of previous contracts via e-mail was not sufficient evidence by itself to show that the parties had *agreed* to transact business electronically.[22]

A person who has previously agreed to an electronic transaction can also withdraw his or her consent and refuse to conduct further business electronically. Additionally, the act expressly gives parties the power to vary the UETA's provisions by contract. In other words, *parties can opt out of all or some of the terms of the UETA*. If the parties do not opt out of the terms of the UETA, however, the UETA will govern their electronic transactions.

20. UETA 5(b).
21. UETA 5, Comment 4B.
22. *EPCO Carbondioxide Products, Inc. v. St. Paul Travelers Insurance Co.*, 2007 WL 1347785 (W.D.La. 2007).

ATTRIBUTION In the context of electronic transactions, the term *attribution* refers to the procedures that may be used to ensure that the person sending an electronic record is the same person whose e-signature accompanies the record. Under the UETA, if an electronic record or signature is the act of a particular person, the record or signature may be attributed to that person. If a person types her or his name at the bottom of an e-mail purchase order, that name will qualify as a "signature" and be attributed to the person whose name appears. Just as in paper contracts, one may use any relevant evidence to prove that the record or signature is or is not the act of the person.[23]

Note that even if an individual's name does not appear on a record, the UETA states that the effect of the record is to be determined from the context and surrounding circumstances. In other words, a record may have legal effect even if no one has signed it. **EXAMPLE 8.24** Darby sends a fax to Corina. The fax contains a letterhead identifying Darby as the sender, but Darby's signature does not appear on the faxed document. Depending on the circumstances, the fax may be attributed to Darby. •

The UETA does not contain any express provisions about what constitutes fraud or whether an *agent* (a person who acts on behalf of another—see Chapter 21) is authorized to enter a contract. Under the UETA, other state laws control if any issues relating to agency, authority, forgery, or contract formation arise. If existing state law requires a document to be notarized, the UETA provides that this requirement is satisfied by the electronic signature of a notary public or other person authorized to verify signatures.

23. UETA 9.

• ***Exhibit* 8–1 The E-SIGN Act and the UETA**

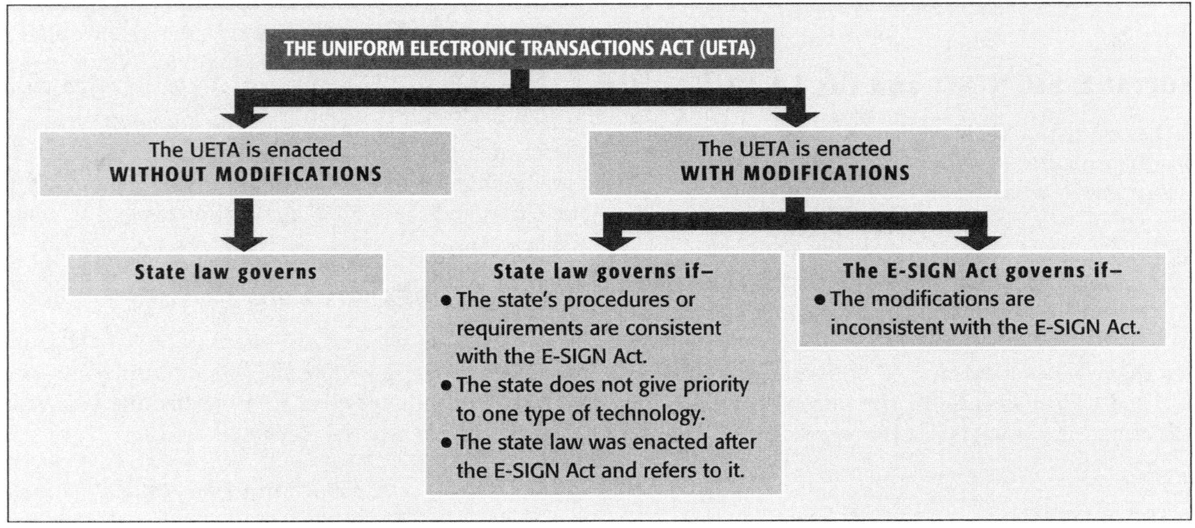

THE EFFECT OF ERRORS The UETA encourages, but does not require, the use of security procedures (such as encryption) to verify changes to electronic documents and to correct errors. Section 10 of the UETA provides that if the parties have agreed to a security procedure and one party does not detect an error because he or she did not follow the procedure, the conforming party can legally avoid the effect of the change or error. If the parties have not agreed to use a security procedure, then other state laws (including contract law governing mistakes—see Chapter 10) will determine the effect of the error on the parties' agreement. To avoid the effect of errors, a party must promptly notify the other party of the error and of her or his intent not to be bound by the error. In addition, the party must take reasonable steps to return any benefit received: parties cannot avoid a transaction if they have benefited.

TIMING Section 15 of the UETA sets forth provisions relating to the sending and receiving of electronic records. These provisions apply unless the parties agree to different terms. Under Section 15, an electronic record is considered *sent* when it is properly directed to the intended recipient in a form readable by the recipient's computer system. Once the electronic record leaves the control of the sender or comes under the control of the recipient, the UETA deems it to have been sent. An electronic record is considered *received* when it enters the recipient's processing system in a readable form—*even if no individual is aware of its receipt.*

Additionally, the UETA provides that, unless otherwise agreed, an electronic record is to be sent from or received at the party's principal place of business. If a party has no place of business, the provision then authorizes the place of sending or receipt to be the party's residence. If a party has multiple places of business, the record should be sent from or received at the location that has the closest relationship to the underlying transaction.

Reviewing . . . Agreement in Traditional and E-Contracts

Ted and Betty Hyatt live in California, a state that has extensive statutory protection for consumers. The Hyatts decided to buy a computer so that they could use e-mail to stay in touch with their grandchildren, who live in another state. Over the phone, they ordered a computer from CompuEdge, Inc. When the box arrived, it was sealed with a brightly colored sticker warning that the terms enclosed within the box would govern the sale unless the customer returned the computer within thirty days. Among those terms was a clause that required any disputes to be resolved in Tennessee state courts. The Hyatts then signed up for Internet service through CyberTool, an Internet service provider. They downloaded CyberTool's software and clicked on the "quick install" box that allowed them to bypass CyberTool's "Terms of Service" page. It was possible to read this page by scrolling to the next screen, but the Hyatts did not realize this. The terms included a clause that stated all disputes were to be submitted to a Virginia state court. As soon as the Hyatts attempted to e-mail their grandchildren, they experienced problems using CyberTool's e-mail service, which continually stated that the network was busy. They also were unable to receive the photos sent by their grandchildren. Using the information presented in the chapter, answer the following questions.

1. Did the Hyatts accept the list of contract terms included in the computer box? Why or why not? What is the name used for this type of e-contract?
2. What type of agreement did the Hyatts form with CyberTool?
3. Suppose that the Hyatts experienced trouble with the computer's components after they had used the computer for two months. What factors will a court consider in deciding whether to enforce the forum-selection clause? Would a court be likely to enforce the clause in this contract? Why or why not?
4. Are the Hyatts bound by the contract terms specified on CyberTool's "Terms of Service" page that they did not read? Which of the required elements for contract formation might the Hyatts claim were lacking? How might a court rule on this issue?

Terms and Concepts

acceptance 150
agreement 144
browse-wrap term 153
click-on agreement 153
counteroffer 149
cybernotary 154
e-contract 152
e-signature 153
forum-selection clause 153
mailbox rule 151
mirror image rule 149
offer 144
option contract 148
partnering agreement 154
record 154
revocation 148
shrink-wrap agreement 153

Chapter Summary: Agreement in Traditional and E-Contracts

Requirements of the Offer (See pages 144–148.)	1. *Intent*—There must be a serious, objective intention by the offeror to become bound by the offer. Nonoffer situations include (a) expressions of opinion; (b) statements of intention; (c) preliminary negotiations; (d) generally, advertisements, catalogues, price lists, and circulars; (e) solicitations for bids made by an auctioneer; and (f) traditionally, agreements to agree in the future. 2. *Definiteness*—The terms of the offer must be sufficiently definite to be ascertainable by the parties or by a court. 3. *Communication*—The offer must be communicated to the offeree.
Termination of the Offer (See pages 148–150.)	1. *By action of the parties*— a. Revocation—Unless the offer is irrevocable, it can be revoked at any time before acceptance without liability. Revocation is not effective until received by the offeree or the offeree's agent. Some offers, such as a merchant's firm offer and option contracts, are irrevocable. b. Rejection—Accomplished by words or actions that demonstrate a clear intent not to accept the offer; not effective until received by the offeror or the offeror's agent. c. Counteroffer—A rejection of the original offer and the making of a new offer. 2. *By operation of law*— a. Lapse of time—The offer terminates (1) at the end of the time period specified in the offer or (2) if no time period is stated in the offer, at the end of a reasonable time period. b. Destruction of the specific subject matter of the offer—Automatically terminates the offer. c. Death or incompetence of the offeror or offeree—Terminates the offer unless the offer is irrevocable. d. Illegality—Supervening illegality terminates the offer.
Acceptance (See pages 150–152.)	1. Can be made only by the offeree or the offeree's agent. 2. Must be unequivocal. Under the common law (mirror image rule), if new terms or conditions are added to the acceptance, it will be considered a counteroffer. 3. Acceptance of a unilateral offer is effective on full performance of the requested act. Generally, no communication is necessary. 4. Acceptance of a bilateral offer can be communicated by the offeree by any authorized mode of communication and is effective on dispatch. If the offeror does not specify the mode of communication, acceptance can be made by any reasonable means. Usually, the same means used by the offeror or a faster means can be used.
Online Offers (See pages 152–153.)	The terms of contract offers presented via the Internet should be as inclusive as the terms in an offer made in a written (paper) document. The offer should be displayed in an easily readable format and should include some mechanism, such as an "I agree" or "I accept" box, by which the customer may accept the offer. Because jurisdictional issues frequently arise with online transactions, the offer should include dispute-settlement provisions, as well as a forum-selection clause.
Online Acceptances (See page 153.)	1. *Click-on agreement*— a. Definition—An agreement created when a buyer, completing a transaction on a computer, is required to indicate her or his assent to be bound by the terms of an offer by clicking on a box that says, for example, "I agree." The terms of the agreement may appear on the Web site through which the buyer is obtaining goods or services, or they may appear on a computer screen when software is downloaded. b. Enforceability—The courts have enforced click-on agreements, holding that by clicking on "I agree," the offeree has indicated acceptance by conduct. Browse-wrap terms (terms in a license that an Internet user does not have to read prior to downloading the product, such as software), however, may not be enforced on the ground that the user is not made aware that he or she is entering into a contract. 2. *Shrink-wrap agreement*— a. Definition—An agreement whose terms are expressed inside a box in which the goods are packaged. The party who opens the box is informed that, by keeping the goods that are in the box, he or she agrees to the terms of the shrink-wrap agreement. b. Enforceability—The courts have often enforced shrink-wrap agreements, even if the purchaser-user of the goods did not read the terms of the agreement. A court may deem a shrink-wrap agreement unenforceable, however, if the buyer learns of the shrink-wrap terms after the parties entered into the agreement.

Chapter Summary: Agreement in Traditional and E-Contracts—Continued

E-Signatures (See pages 153–154.)	The Uniform Electronic Transactions Act (UETA) defines an e-signature as "an electronic sound, symbol, or process attached to or logically associated with a record and executed or adopted by a person with the intent to sign the record." 1. *E-signature technologies*—The two main categories are digitized handwritten signatures and digital signatures based on a public-key infrastructure. 2. *Federal law on e-signatures and e-documents*—The Electronic Signatures in Global and National Commerce Act (E-SIGN Act) of 2000 gave validity to e-signatures by providing that no contract, record, or signature may be "denied legal effect" solely because it is in an electronic form. 3. *Partnering agreements*—To reduce the likelihood that disputes will arise under their e-contracts, parties who frequently do business with each other online may form a partnering agreement, setting out the terms and conditions that will apply to all their subsequent electronic transactions.
The Uniform Electronic Transactions Act (UETA) (See pages 154–157.)	This uniform act has been adopted, at least in part, by most states, to create rules to support the enforcement of e-contracts. Under the UETA, contracts entered into online, as well as other documents, are presumed to be valid. The UETA does not apply to certain transactions governed by the UCC or to wills or testamentary trusts.

ExamPrep

ISSUE SPOTTERS

—**Check your answers to these questions against the answers in Appendix G.**

1 Joe advertises in the *New York Times* that he will pay $5,000 to anyone giving him information as to the whereabouts of Elaine. Max sees a copy of the ad in a Tokyo newspaper, in Japanese, and sends Joe the requested information. Does Max get the reward? Why or why not?

2 Applied Products, Inc., does business with Beltway Distributors, Inc., online. Under the Uniform Electronic Transactions Act, what determines the effect of the electronic documents evidencing the parties' deal? Is a party's "signature" necessary? Explain.

BEFORE THE TEST

Go to **www.cengagebrain.com**, enter the ISBN 9781111530624, and click on "Find" to locate this textbook's Web site. Then, click on "Access Now" under "Study Tools," and select Chapter 8 at the top. There, you will find an Interactive Quiz that you can take to assess your mastery of the concepts in this chapter, as well as Flashcards and a Glossary of important terms.

For Review

1 What elements are necessary for an effective offer? What are some examples of nonoffers?

2 In what circumstances will an offer be irrevocable?

3 What are the elements that are necessary for an effective acceptance?

4 How do shrink-wrap and click-on agreements differ from other contracts? How have traditional laws been applied to these agreements?

5 What is the Uniform Electronic Transactions Act? What are some of the major provisions of this act?

Questions and Case Problems

8–1 Agreement. Ball writes to Sullivan and inquires how much Sullivan is asking for a specific forty-acre tract of land Sullivan owns. In a letter received by Ball, Sullivan states, "I will not take less than $60,000 for the forty-acre tract as specified." Ball immediately sends Sullivan a fax stating, "I accept your offer for $60,000 for the forty-acre tract as specified." Discuss whether Ball can hold Sullivan to a contract for sale of the land.

8–2 **Acceptances.** Chernek, the sole owner of a small business, has a large piece of used farm equipment for sale. He offers to sell the equipment to Bollow for $10,000. Discuss the legal effects of the following events on the offer:

1. Chernek dies prior to Bollow's acceptance, and at the time she accepts, Bollow is unaware of Chernek's death.
2. The night before Bollow accepts, a fire destroys the equipment.
3. Bollow pays $100 for a thirty-day option to purchase the equipment. During this period, Chernek dies, and Bollow accepts the offer, knowing of Chernek's death.
4. Bollow pays $100 for a thirty-day option to purchase the equipment. During this period, Bollow dies, and Bollow's estate accepts Chernek's offer within the stipulated time period.

8–3 **Online Acceptance.** Anne is a reporter for the *Daily Business Journal,* a print publication consulted by investors and other businesspersons. She often uses the Internet to perform research for the articles that she writes for the publication. While visiting the Web site of Cyberspace Investments Corp., Anne reads a pop-up window that states, "Our business newsletter, *E-Commerce Weekly,* is available at a one-year subscription rate of $5 per issue. To subscribe, enter your e-mail address below and click 'SUBSCRIBE.' By subscribing, you agree to the terms of the subscriber's agreement. To read this agreement, click 'AGREEMENT.'" Anne enters her e-mail address, but does not click on "AGREEMENT" to read the terms. Has Anne entered into an enforceable contract to pay for *E-Commerce Weekly?* Explain.

8–4 **Revocation.** On Thursday, Dennis mailed a letter to Tanya's office offering to sell his car to her for $3,000. On Saturday, having changed his mind, Dennis sent a fax to Tanya's office revoking his offer. Tanya did not go to her office over the weekend and thus did not learn about the revocation until Monday morning, just a few minutes after she had mailed a letter of acceptance to Dennis. When Tanya demanded that Dennis sell his car to her as promised, Dennis claimed that no contract existed because he had revoked his offer prior to Tanya's acceptance. Is Dennis correct? Explain.

8–5 **Online Acceptance.** Internet Archive (IA) is devoted to preserving a record of resources on the Internet for future generations. IA uses the "Wayback Machine" to automatically browse Web sites and reproduce their contents in an archive. IA does not ask the owners' permission before copying their material but will remove it on request. Suzanne Shell, a resident of Colorado, owns www.profane-justice.org, which is dedicated to providing information to individuals accused of child abuse or neglect. The site warns, "IF YOU COPY OR DISTRIBUTE ANYTHING ON THIS SITE YOU ARE ENTERING INTO A CONTRACT." The terms, which can be accessed only by clicking on a link, include, among other charges, a fee of $5,000 for each page copied "in advance of printing." Neither the warning nor the terms require a user to indicate assent. When Shell discovered that the Wayback Machine had copied the contents of her site—approximately eighty-seven times between May 1999 and October 2004—she asked IA to remove the copies from its archive and pay her $100,000. IA removed the copies and filed a suit in a federal district court against Shell, who responded, in part, with a counterclaim for breach of contract. IA filed a motion to dismiss this claim. Did IA contract with Shell? Explain. [*Internet Archive v. Shell,* 505 F.Supp.2d 755 (D.Colo. 2007)]

8–6  **Case Problem with Sample Answer** Evelyn Kowalchuk, an eighty-eight-year-old widow, and her son, Peter, put their savings into accounts managed by Matthew Stroup. Later, they initiated an arbitration proceeding before the National Association of Securities Dealers (NASD), asserting that Stroup fraudulently or negligently handled their accounts. They asked for an award of $832,000. After the hearing, but before a decision was rendered, Stroup offered to pay the Kowalchuks $285,000, and they e-mailed their acceptance. Stroup signed a settlement agreement and faxed it to the Kowalchuks for their signatures. Meanwhile, the NASD issued an award in the Kowalchuks' favor for $88,788. Stroup immediately told them that he was withdrawing his settlement "offer." When Stroup did not pay according to its terms, the Kowalchuks filed a suit in a New York state court against him for breach of contract. Did these parties have a contract? Why or why not? [*Kowalchuk v. Stroup,* 873 N.Y.S.2d 43 (N.Y.A.D. 1 Dept. 2009)]

—To view a sample answer for Problem 8–6, go to Appendix F at the end of this text.

8–7 **Offer and Acceptance.** In 1996, Troy Blackford was gambling at Prairie Meadows Casino when he destroyed a slot machine. After pleading guilty to criminal mischief, Blackford was banned from the casino. In 1998, Blackford was found in the casino, escorted out, and charged with trespass. In 2006, he gambled at the casino again and won $9,387. When Blackford went to collect his winnings, casino employees learned who he was and refused to pay. He sued for breach of contract, contending that he and the casino had an enforceable contract because he had accepted its offer to gamble. The casino argued that it had not made an offer and in fact had banned Blackford from the premises. The trial court held in favor of the casino. The appellate court reversed and ordered a new trial. The casino appealed to the Iowa high court for review. Did the casino make a valid offer to Blackford to gamble and thus create an enforceable contract between them? Explain your answer. [*Blackford v. Prairie Meadows Racetrack and Casino,* 778 N.W.2d 184 (Iowa 2010)]

8–8 **Acceptance.** In August, Kathy Wright entered into a written agreement with a real estate agent, Jennifer Crilow, to sell certain real estate in Ohio. The agreement ran until February 28. A "protection period" provision in the agreement stated that if the property sold within six months after the agreement expired to a party who had been shown the property during the term of the agreement, Crilow would be paid a commission. In January, Crilow switched agencies and asked Wright to sign a new contract. They orally agreed on the terms, which included an expiration date of April 30. Crilow sent Wright a written copy of the agreement. Wright crossed out the protection period provision and signed and returned the copy. Crilow filed it without reviewing it. Before April 30, Crilow showed Wright's property to Michael Ballway. Less than six months later—after the agreement had expired but within the protection period—Ballway bought the property. Crilow filed a suit against Wright in an Ohio state court seeking a commission on the sale. Did the parties' contract include the protection period provision? Does Wright owe Crilow a commission? Explain. [*Crilow v. Wright*, __ N.E.2d __ (Ohio App. 5 Dist. 2011)]

8–9  **A Question of Ethics** *In 2000 and 2001, Dewayne Hubbert, Elden Craft, Chris Grout, and Rhonda Byington bought computers from Dell Corp. through its Web site. Before buying, Hubbert and the others configured their own computers. To make a purchase, each buyer completed forms on five Web pages. On each page, Dell's "Terms and Conditions of Sale" were accessible by clicking on a blue hyperlink. A statement on three of the pages reads, "All sales are subject to Dell's Term[s] and Conditions of Sale," but a buyer was not required to click an assent to the terms to complete a purchase. The terms were also printed on the backs of the invoices and on separate documents contained in the shipping boxes with the computers. Among those terms was a "Binding Arbitration" clause. The computers contained Pentium 4 microprocessors, which Dell advertised as the fastest, most powerful Intel Pentium processors available. In 2002, Hubbert and the others filed a suit in an Illinois state court against Dell, alleging that this marketing was false, misleading, and deceptive. The plaintiffs claimed that the Pentium 4 microprocessor was slower and less powerful, and provided less performance, than either a Pentium III or an AMD Athlon, and at a greater cost. Dell asked the court to compel arbitration. [*Hubbert v. Dell Corp.*, *359 Ill.App.3d 976, 835 N.E.2d 113, 296 Ill.Dec. 258 (5 Dist. 2005)]*

1 Should the court enforce the arbitration clause in this case? If you were the judge, how would you rule on this issue?

2 In your opinion, do shrink-wrap, click-on, and browse-wrap terms impose too great a burden on purchasers? Why or why not?

3 An ongoing complaint about shrink-wrap, click-on, and browse-wrap terms is that sellers (often large corporations) draft them and buyers (typically individual consumers) do not read them. Should purchasers be bound in contract by terms that they have not even read? Why or why not?

8–10  **Video Question** To watch this chapter's video, *Jack's Restaurant, Scene 2,* go to **www.cengagebrain.com**. Register the access code that came with your new book or log in to your account. Select the link for the "Business Law Digital Video Library Online Access" or "Business Law CourseMate." Click on "Complete Video List," view Video 77, and then answer the following questions:

1 In regard to the sale of Jack's Restaurant, Jack (the seller) says that he is going to retain the rights to the restaurant's frozen food line. The buyers, however, thought that their sales agreement included the rights to all of the restaurant's signature dishes—whether fresh or frozen. Did the parties have an "agreement to agree" on the terms of the sale of the restaurant? Why or why not?

2 Suppose that Jack previously offered to sell the restaurant to these particular buyers and they had all agreed on the price and date for delivery. Would such an offer meet the definiteness requirement, even if no terms pertained to the frozen food line? Explain.

Chapter 9

Consideration, Capacity, and Legality

Learning Objectives

After reading this chapter, you should be able to answer the following questions:

1. What is consideration? What is required for consideration to be legally sufficient?
2. In what circumstances might a promise be enforced despite a lack of consideration?
3. Does a minor have the capacity to enter into an enforceable contract? What does it mean to disaffirm a contract?
4. Under what circumstances will a covenant not to compete be enforceable? When will such covenants not be enforced?
5. What is an exculpatory clause? In what circumstances might exculpatory clauses be enforced? When will they not be enforced?

The Learning Objectives above are designed to help improve your understanding of the chapter.

(AP Photo/Carlos Osorio)

Courts generally want contracts to be enforceable, and much of the law is devoted to aiding the enforceability of contracts. Before a court will enforce a contractual promise, however, it must be convinced that there was some exchange of consideration underlying the bargain. Furthermore, not all people can make legally binding contracts at all times. Contracts entered into by persons lacking the capacity to do so may be voidable. Similarly, contracts calling for the performance of an illegal act are illegal and thus void—they are not contracts at all. In this chapter, we first examine the requirement of consideration and then look at contractual capacity and legality.

Consideration

In every legal system, some promises will be enforced, and other promises will not be enforced. The simple fact that a party has made a promise, then, does not mean that the promise is enforceable. Under the common law, a primary basis for the enforcement of promises is consideration. **Consideration** usually is defined as the value given in return for a promise.

Elements of Consideration

Often, consideration is broken down into two parts: (1) something of *legally sufficient value* must be given in exchange for the promise, and (2) there must be a *bargained-for exchange.*

LEGALLY SUFFICIENT VALUE The "something of legally sufficient value" may consist of (1) a promise to do something that one has no prior legal duty to do (to pay on receipt of certain goods, for example), (2) the performance of an action that one is otherwise not obligated to undertake (such as providing accounting services), or (3) the refraining from an action that one has a legal right to undertake (called a forbearance).

Consideration in bilateral contracts normally consists of a promise in return for a promise, as explained in Chapter 7. In contrast, unilateral contracts involve a promise in return for a performance. **EXAMPLE 9.1** Anita says to her neighbor, "If you paint my garage, I will pay you $800." Anita's neighbor paints the garage. The act of painting the garage is the consideration that creates Anita's contractual obligation to pay her neighbor $800. ●

BARGAINED-FOR EXCHANGE The second element of consideration is that it must provide the basis for the bargain struck between the contracting parties. The promise given by the promisor must induce the promisee to incur a legal detriment either now or in the future, and the detriment incurred must induce the promisor to make the promise. This element of bargained-for exchange distinguishes contracts from gifts.

EXAMPLE 9.2 Roberto says to his son, "In consideration of the fact that you are not as wealthy as your brothers, I will pay you $5,000." The fact that the word *consideration* is used does not, by itself, mean that consideration has been given. Indeed, Roberto's promise is not enforceable, because the son need not do anything to receive the $5,000 promised. Because the son does not need to give Roberto something of legal value in return for his promise, there is no bargained-for exchange. Rather, Roberto has simply stated his motive for giving his son a gift. ●

Adequacy of Consideration

Adequacy of consideration involves how much consideration is given. Essentially, it concerns the fairness of the bargain. On the surface, when the items exchanged are of unequal value, fairness would appear to be an issue. A court generally will not question the adequacy of consideration, however, based solely on a comparison of values of the things exchanged. Something need not be of direct economic or financial value to be regarded as legally sufficient consideration. Under the doctrine of freedom of contract, courts leave it up to the parties to decide what something is worth, and parties are usually free to bargain as they wish. If people could sue merely because they had entered into an unwise contract, the courts would be overloaded with frivolous suits.

Nevertheless, a large disparity in the amount or value of the consideration exchanged may raise a red flag, causing a court to look more closely at the bargain. This is because shockingly inadequate consideration can indicate that fraud, duress, or undue influence was involved or that the element of bargained-for exchange was lacking. Judges are uneasy about enforcing unequal bargains and generally try to make sure that a contract was, in fact, formed with mutual assent.

Agreements That Lack Consideration

Sometimes, one or both of the parties to a contract may think that they have exchanged consideration when in fact they have not. Here, we look at some situations in which the parties' promises or actions do not qualify as contractual consideration.

PREEXISTING DUTY Under most circumstances, a promise to do what one already has a legal duty to do does not constitute legally sufficient consideration. A sheriff, for example, cannot collect a reward for information leading to the capture of a criminal if the sheriff already has a legal duty to capture the criminal.

Likewise, if a party is already bound by contract to perform a certain duty, that duty cannot serve as consideration for a second contract. **EXAMPLE 9.3** Bauman-Bache, Inc., begins construction on a seven-story office building and after three months demands an extra $75,000 on its contract. If the extra $75,000 is not paid, the firm will stop working. The owner of the land, finding no one else to complete construction, agrees to pay the extra $75,000. The agreement is not enforceable because it is not supported by legally sufficient consideration; Bauman-Bache had a preexisting contractual duty to complete the building. ●

Unforeseen Difficulties. The preexisting duty rule is intended to prevent extortion and the "holdup game." If, during performance of a contract, extraordinary difficulties arise that were totally unforeseen at the time the contract was formed, a court may allow an exception to the rule.

Suppose that in Example 9.3 above, Bauman-Bache had asked for the extra $75,000 because it encountered a rock formation that no one knew existed, and the landowner had agreed to pay the extra amount to excavate the rock. In this situation, the court may refrain from applying the preexisting duty rule and enforce the agreement to pay the extra $75,000. Note, however, that for the rule to be waived, the difficulties must be truly unforeseen and not be the types of risks ordinarily assumed in business. In Example 9.3, if the construction was taking place in an area where rock formations were common, a court would likely enforce the preexisting duty rule on the basis that Bauman-Bache had assumed the risk that it would encounter rock.

Rescission and New Contract. The law recognizes that two parties can mutually agree to rescind, or cancel, their contract, at least to the extent that it is executory (still to be carried out). **Rescission**[1] is the unmaking of a contract so as to return the parties to the positions they occupied before the contract was made. Sometimes, parties rescind a contract and make a new contract at the same time. When this occurs, it is often difficult to determine whether there was consideration for the new

1. Pronounced reh-*sih*-zhen.

contract or whether the parties had a preexisting duty under the previous contract. If a court finds there was a preexisting duty, then the new contract will be invalid because there was no consideration.

PAST CONSIDERATION Promises made in return for actions or events that have already taken place are unenforceable. These promises lack consideration in that the element of bargained-for exchange is missing. In short, you can bargain for something to take place now or in the future but not for something that has already taken place. Therefore, **past consideration** is no consideration.

EXAMPLE 9.4 Blackmon became friends with Iverson when Iverson was a high school student who showed tremendous promise as an athlete. One evening, Blackmon suggested that Iverson use "The Answer" as a nickname in the summer league basketball tournaments. Blackmon said that Iverson would be "The Answer" to all of the National Basketball Association's woes. Later that night, Iverson said that he would give Blackmon 25 percent of any proceeds from the merchandising of products that used "The Answer" as a logo or a slogan. Because Iverson's promise was made in return for past consideration (Blackmon's earlier suggestion), it was unenforceable. In effect, Iverson stated his intention to give Blackmon a gift.[2] •

ILLUSORY PROMISES If the terms of the contract express such uncertainty of performance that the promisor has not definitely promised to do anything, the promise is said to be *illusory*—without consideration and unenforceable. **EXAMPLE 9.5** The president of Tuscan Corporation says to his employees, "All of you have worked hard, and if profits remain high, a 10 percent bonus at the end of the year will be given—if management thinks it is warranted." This is an *illusory promise,* or no promise at all, because performance depends solely on the discretion of the president (the management). There is no bargained-for consideration. The statement declares merely that management may or may not do something in the future. •

Sometimes, option-to-cancel clauses in term contracts present problems in regard to consideration. When the promisor has the option to cancel the contract before performance has begun, then the promise is illusory. Suppose that Abe contracts to hire Chris for one year at $5,000 per month, reserving the right to cancel the contract at any time. On close examination of these words, you can see that Abe has not actually agreed to hire Chris, as Abe could cancel without liability before Chris started performance. This contract is therefore illusory.

But if Abe instead reserves the right to cancel the contract at any time *after* Chris has begun performance by giving Chris *thirty days' notice,* the promise is not illusory. Abe, by saying that he will give Chris thirty days' notice, is relinquishing the opportunity (legal right) to hire someone else instead of Chris for a thirty-day period. If Chris works for one month, at the end of which Abe gives him thirty days' notice, Chris has an enforceable claim for $10,000 in salary.[3]

Settlement of Claims

Businesspersons and others often enter into contracts to settle legal claims. It is important to understand the nature of the consideration given in these settlement agreements, or contracts. Claims are commonly settled through an *accord and satisfaction,* in which a debtor offers to pay a lesser amount than the creditor says is owed. Claims may also be settled by the signing of a *release* or a *covenant not to sue.*

ACCORD AND SATISFACTION In an **accord and satisfaction,** a debtor offers to pay, and a creditor accepts, a lesser amount than the creditor originally claimed was owed. The *accord* is the agreement under which one of the parties promises to give or perform, and the other to accept, in satisfaction of a claim, something other than that on which the parties originally agreed. *Satisfaction* is the performance (usually payment), which takes place after the accord is executed. A basic rule is that there can be no satisfaction unless there is first an accord. For accord and satisfaction to occur, the amount of the debt *must be in dispute.*

Liquidated Debts. If a debt is *liquidated,* accord and satisfaction cannot take place. A **liquidated debt** is one whose amount has been ascertained, fixed, agreed on, settled, or exactly determined. **EXAMPLE 9.6** Barbara Kwan signs an installment loan contract with her banker. In the contract, Kwan agrees to pay a specified rate of interest on a specified amount of borrowed funds at monthly intervals for two years. Because both parties know the precise amount of the total obligation, it is a liquidated debt. •

In the majority of states, acceptance of (an accord for) a lesser sum than the entire amount of a liquidated debt is not satisfaction, and the balance of the debt is still legally owed. The reason for this rule is that the debtor has given no consideration to satisfy the obligation of paying the balance to the creditor—because the debtor has a preexisting legal obligation to pay the entire debt.

Unliquidated Debts. An *unliquidated debt* is the opposite of a liquidated debt. The amount of the debt is *not* settled, fixed, agreed on, ascertained, or determined, and reasonable persons may differ over the amount owed. In these circumstances, acceptance of payment of the lesser sum operates as a satisfaction, or discharge, of the debt because there is valid consideration—the parties give up a legal right to contest the amount in dispute.

2. *Blackmon v. Iverson,* 324 F.Supp.2d 602 (E.D.Pa. 2003).

3. For another example, see *Vanegas v. American Energy Services,* 302 S.W.3d 299 (Tex. 2009).

RELEASE A **release** is a contract in which one party forfeits the right to pursue a legal claim against the other party. It bars any further recovery beyond the terms stated in the release. Releases will generally be binding if they are (1) given in good faith, (2) stated in a signed writing (required by many states), and (3) accompanied by consideration. Clearly, parties are better off if they know the extent of their injuries or damages before signing releases.

EXAMPLE 9.7 Lucy's car is damaged in an accident caused by Donovan's negligence. Donovan offers to give Lucy $3,000 if she will release him from further liability resulting from the accident. Lucy believes that this amount will cover her repairs, so she agrees and signs the release. Later, Lucy discovers that the repairs to her car will cost $4,200. Can Lucy collect the balance from Donovan? Normally, the answer is no. She is limited to the $3,000 in the release. Why? The reason is that a valid contract existed. Lucy and Donovan both voluntarily consented to the terms (hence, agreement existed), and sufficient consideration was present. The consideration was the legal detriment Lucy suffered (she forfeited her right to sue to recover damages, should they be more than $3,000) in exchange for Donovan's promise to give her $3,000. •

COVENANT NOT TO SUE Unlike a release, a **covenant not to sue** does not always bar further recovery. The parties simply substitute a contractual obligation for some other type of legal action based on a valid claim. Suppose (in Example 9.7) that Lucy agrees with Donovan not to sue for damages in a tort action if he will pay for the damage to her car. If Donovan fails to pay, Lucy can bring an action for breach of contract.

Promissory Estoppel

Under the doctrine of **promissory estoppel** (also called *detrimental reliance*), a person who has reasonably and substantially relied on the promise of another can obtain some measure of recovery. Promissory estoppel is applied in a variety of contexts and allows a party to recover on a promise even though it was made *without consideration.* Under this doctrine, a court may enforce an otherwise unenforceable promise to avoid the injustice that would otherwise result.

REQUIREMENTS TO STATE A CLAIM For the doctrine to be applied, the following elements are required:

1. There must be a clear and definite promise.
2. The promisor should have expected that the promisee would rely on the promise.
3. The promisee reasonably relied on the promise by acting or refraining from some act.
4. The promisee's reliance was definite and resulted in substantial detriment.
5. Enforcement of the promise is necessary to avoid injustice.

If these requirements are met, a promise may be enforced even though it is not supported by consideration. In essence, the promisor (the offeror) will be estopped (prevented) from asserting lack of consideration as a defense.

Promissory estoppel is similar in some ways to the doctrine of quasi contract that was discussed in Chapter 7. In both situations, a court is acting in the interests of equity and imposes contract obligations on the parties to prevent unfairness even though no actual contract exists. In quasi contracts, however, no promise at all was made, whereas with promissory estoppel, a promise was made and relied on, but it was unenforceable.

APPLICATION OF THE DOCTRINE Promissory estoppel was originally applied to situations involving gifts (I promise to pay you $1,000 a week so that you will not have to work) and donations to charities (I promise to contribute $50,000 a year to the All Saints Orphanage). Later, courts began to apply the doctrine to avoid inequity or hardship in other situations, including business transactions. **EXAMPLE 9.8** An employer, Jay Bailey, orally promises to pay each of his five employees $2,000 a month for the remainder of their lives after they retire. When Sal Hernandez retires, he receives the monthly amount for two years, but then Bailey stops paying. Under the doctrine of promissory estoppel, Hernandez can sue Bailey in an attempt to enforce his promise. •

In the following case, a daughter built a house on her parents' land with their help and permission. When the parents refused to deed the land on which the house was built to her, she filed a lawsuit against them on a claim of promissory estoppel.

Case 9.1 Harvey v. Dow

Supreme Judicial Court of Maine, 11 A.3d 303, 2011 ME 4 (2011).

FACTS Jeffrey and Kathryn Dow own 125 acres of land in Corinth, Maine. The Dows saw the land as their children's heritage, and the subject of the children's living on the land was often discussed within the family. With the Dows' permission, their daughter Teresa installed a mobile home and built a garage on the land. After Teresa married Jarrod Harvey, the Dows agreed to finance the construction of a house on the land for the couple. When Jarrod died in a motorcycle accident, however, Teresa financed the house with life insurance proceeds. The construction cost about $200,000. Jeffrey performed a substantial amount of work on the house, including general carpentry, much of the foundation work, and helping to install the underground electrical lines. Teresa then asked her

Case 9.1—Continues next page ➡

Case 9.1–Continued

parents for a deed to the property so that she could obtain a mortgage. They refused. Teresa filed a suit in a Maine state court against her parents. The court rejected the claim that she was entitled to a judgment on a theory of promissory estoppel. Teresa appealed.

ISSUE Did Teresa detrimentally rely on her parents' promise to convey the land to her when she and her husband built a house on it?

DECISION Yes. The Supreme Judicial Court of Maine vacated the lower court's judgment and remanded the case for the entry of a judgment in Teresa's favor. The state's highest court held that the Dows showed a present commitment to transfer land to their daughter or to forgo a challenge to her ownership of it.

REASON The court reasoned that the Dows' support and encouragement of their daughter's construction of a house on the land "conclusively demonstrated" their intent. For years, they had made general promises to convey the land to their children, including Teresa. In addition, Jeffrey had approved the site for the house, obtained the building permit, and built much of the house himself. The court explained, "Statements or conduct representing a present commitment to do or refrain from doing something in the future reasonably can be expected to induce reliance and the promisee's reliance on such statements is reasonable."

FOR CRITICAL ANALYSIS—Legal Consideration *On remand, the lower court was ordered to determine the appropriate remedy. Should Teresa be awarded specific performance to compel a transfer of the land? Or should she obtain damages? Discuss.*

Contractual Capacity

Contractual capacity is the legal ability to enter into a contractual relationship. Courts generally presume the existence of contractual capacity, but in some situations, capacity is lacking or may be questionable. A person who has been determined by a court to be mentally incompetent, for example, cannot form a legally binding contract with another party. In other situations, a party may have the capacity to enter into a valid contract but may also have the right to avoid liability under it. For example, minors—or *infants,* as they are commonly referred to in the law—usually are not legally bound by contracts. In this section, we look at the effect of youth, intoxication, and mental incompetence on contractual capacity.

Minors

Today, in almost all states, the *age of majority* (when a person is no longer a minor) for contractual purposes is eighteen years—the so-called coming of age. (Note that the age of majority may still be twenty-one for other purposes, such as the purchase and consumption of alcohol.) In addition, some states provide for the termination of minority on marriage. Minority status may also be terminated by a minor's **emancipation,** which occurs when a child's parent or legal guardian relinquishes the legal right to exercise control over the child. Normally, minors who leave home to support themselves are considered emancipated. Several jurisdictions permit minors to petition a court for emancipation. For business purposes, a minor may petition a court to be treated as an adult.

The general rule is that a minor can enter into any contract an adult can, provided that the contract is not one prohibited by law for minors (for example, the sale of alcoholic beverages or tobacco). A contract entered into by a minor, however, is voidable at the option of that minor, subject to certain exceptions (to be discussed shortly). To exercise the option to avoid a contract, a minor need only manifest an intention not to be bound by it. The minor "avoids" the contract by disaffirming it.

DISAFFIRMANCE The legal avoidance, or setting aside, of a contractual obligation is referred to as **disaffirmance.** To disaffirm, a minor must express through words or conduct, his or her intent not to be bound to the contract. The minor must disaffirm the entire contract, not merely a portion of it. For instance, a minor cannot decide to keep part of the goods purchased under a contract and return the remaining goods. When a minor disaffirms a contract, the minor can recover any property that she or he transferred to the adult as consideration for the contract, even if it is then in the possession of a third party.

A contract can ordinarily be disaffirmed at any time during minority or for a reasonable time after the minor comes of age. What constitutes a "reasonable" time may vary. Two months would probably be considered reasonable, but except in unusual circumstances, a court may not find it reasonable to wait a year or more after coming of age to disaffirm. If an individual fails to disaffirm an executed contract within a reasonable time after reaching the age of majority, a court will likely hold that the contract has been ratified (*ratification* will be discussed shortly).

Note that an adult who enters into a contract with a minor cannot avoid his or her contractual duties on the ground that the minor can do so. Unless the minor exercises the option to disaffirm the contract, the adult party normally is bound by it.

A Minor's Obligations on Disaffirmance. Although all states' laws permit minors to disaffirm contracts (with certain exceptions), including executed contracts, state laws differ on the extent of a minor's obligations on disaffirmance. Courts in most states hold that the minor need only return the goods (or other consideration) subject to the contract, provided the goods are in the minor's possession or control. Even if the minor returns damaged goods, the minor often is entitled to disaffirm the contract and obtain a refund of the purchase price.

A growing number of states place an additional duty on the minor to restore the adult party to the position she or he held before the contract was made. These courts may hold a minor responsible for damage, ordinary wear and tear, and depreciation of goods that the minor used prior to disaffirmance.

EXAMPLE 9.9 Sixteen-year-old Joseph Dodson bought a truck for $4,900 from a used-car dealer. Although the truck developed mechanical problems nine months later, Dodson continued to drive it until the engine blew up and it stopped running. Dodson then disaffirmed the contract and attempted to return the truck to the dealer for a refund of the full purchase price. The dealer refused to accept the truck or to provide a refund. Dodson filed a suit. Ultimately, the Tennessee Supreme Court allowed Dodson to disaffirm the contract but required him to compensate the seller for the depreciated value—not the purchase price—of the truck.[4] •

Exceptions to a Minor's Right to Disaffirm. State courts and legislatures have carved out several exceptions to the minor's right to disaffirm. Some contracts, such as marriage contracts and contracts to enlist in the armed services, cannot be avoided on the ground of public policy. Other contracts may not be disaffirmed for different reasons.

Although ordinarily minors can disaffirm contracts even when they have misrepresented their age, a growing number of states have enacted laws to prohibit disaffirmance in such situations. Some state laws also prohibit minors from disaffirming contracts entered into by a minor who is engaged in business as an adult.

In addition, a minor who enters into a contract for necessaries may disaffirm the contract but remains liable for the reasonable value of the goods used. **Necessaries** include whatever is reasonably needed to maintain the minor's standard of living. In general, food, clothing, shelter, and medical services are necessaries. What is a necessary for one minor, however, may be a luxury for another, depending on the minors' customary living standard. In addition, what a court considers to be a necessary may depend on what the minor's parents provide. **EXAMPLE 9.10** If Shannon is a minor whose parents provide her with a residence, then a contract that Shannon enters to lease an apartment normally will not be classified as a contract for necessaries. •

4. *Dodson v. Shrader*, 824 S.W.2d 545 (Tenn. 1992).

RATIFICATION In contract law, **ratification** is the act of accepting and giving legal force to an obligation that previously was not enforceable. A minor who has reached the age of majority can ratify a contract expressly or impliedly. *Express* ratification occurs when the individual, on reaching the age of majority, states orally or in writing that she or he intends to be bound by the contract. *Implied* ratification takes place when the minor, on reaching the age of majority, indicates an intent to abide by the contract.

EXAMPLE 9.11 Lin enters into a contract to sell her laptop to Andrew, a minor. Andrew does not disaffirm the contract. If, on reaching the age of majority, he writes a letter to Lin stating that he still agrees to buy the laptop, he has expressly ratified the contract. If, instead, Andrew takes possession of the laptop as a minor and continues to use it well after reaching the age of majority, he has impliedly ratified the contract. •

If a minor fails to disaffirm a contract within a reasonable time after reaching the age of majority, then a court must determine whether the conduct constitutes implied ratification or disaffirmance. Generally, courts presume that a contract that is *executed* (fully performed by both sides) was ratified. A contract that is still *executory* (not yet performed by both parties) is normally considered to be disaffirmed.

PARENTS' LIABILITY As a general rule, parents are not liable for the contracts made by minor children acting on their own, except contracts for necessaries, which the parents are legally required to provide. This is why businesses ordinarily require parents to cosign any contract made with a minor. The parents then become personally obligated to perform the conditions of the contract, even if their child avoids liability. (Parents can sometimes be held liable for a minor's torts, however, depending on state law.)

Intoxication

Intoxication is a condition in which a person's normal capacity to act or think is inhibited by alcohol or some other drug. A contract entered into by an intoxicated person can be either voidable or valid (and thus enforceable). If the person was sufficiently intoxicated to lack mental capacity, then the transaction may be voidable at the option of the intoxicated person even if the intoxication was purely voluntary. If, despite intoxication, the person understood the legal consequences of the agreement, the contract is enforceable. Courts look at objective indications of the situation to determine if the intoxicated person possessed or lacked the required capacity.

For the contract to be voidable, the person must prove that the intoxication impaired her or his reason and judgment so severely that she or he did not comprehend the legal consequences of entering into the contract. In addition, the person claiming intoxication must be able to return all consideration received. As a practical matter, courts rarely permit contracts to be avoided on the ground of intoxication, because it is difficult to determine whether a party was sufficiently intoxicated to avoid legal duties.

Mental Incompetence

Contracts made by mentally incompetent persons can be void, voidable, or valid. We look here at the circumstances that determine when these classifications apply.

WHEN THE CONTRACT WILL BE VOID If a court has previously determined that a person is mentally incompetent and has appointed a guardian to represent the person, any contract made by that mentally incompetent person is *void*—no contract exists. Only the guardian can enter into a binding contract on behalf of the mentally incompetent person.

WHEN THE CONTRACT WILL BE VOIDABLE If a court has not previously judged a person to be mentally incompetent but in fact the person was incompetent at the time, the contract may be *voidable*. A contract is voidable if the person did not know he or she was entering into the contract or lacked the mental capacity to comprehend its nature, purpose, and consequences. In such situations, the contract is voidable at the option of the mentally incompetent person but not the other party. The contract may then be disaffirmed or ratified (if the person regains mental competence). Like intoxicated persons, mentally incompetent persons must return any consideration and pay for the reasonable value of any necessaries they receive.

EXAMPLE 9.12 Milo, a mentally incompetent man who had not been previously declared incompetent by a judge, agrees to sell twenty lots in a prime residential neighborhood to Pierce. At the time of entering into the contract, Milo is confused over which lots he is selling and how much they are worth. As a result, he contracts to sell the properties for substantially less than their market value. If the court finds that Milo was unable to understand the nature and consequences of the contract, the contract is voidable. Milo can avoid the sale, provided that he returns any consideration that he received. •

WHEN THE CONTRACT WILL BE VALID A contract entered into by a mentally incompetent person (whom a court has not previously declared incompetent) may also be valid if the person had capacity *at the time the contract was formed.* An otherwise incompetent person who understands the nature, purpose, and consequences at the time of entering into a contract is bound by it. Some people who are incompetent due to age or illness have *lucid intervals*—temporary periods of sufficient intelligence, judgment, and will—during which they will be considered to have legal capacity to enter into contracts.

Legality

For a contract to be valid and enforceable, it must be formed for a legal purpose. Legality is the fourth requirement for a valid contract to exist. A contract to do something that is prohibited by federal or state statutory law is illegal and, as such, is void from the outset and thus unenforceable. Additionally, a contract to commit a tortious act (see Chapter 4) or to commit an action that is contrary to public policy is illegal and unenforceable.

Contracts Contrary to Statute

Statutes often set forth rules specifying which terms and clauses may be included in contracts and which are prohibited. We examine here several ways in which contracts may be contrary to a statute and thus illegal.

CONTRACTS TO COMMIT A CRIME Any contract to commit a crime is a contract in violation of a statute. Thus, a contract to sell illegal drugs in violation of criminal laws is unenforceable, as is a contract to cover up a corporation's violation of the Sarbanes-Oxley Act (see Chapter 26). Similarly, a contract to smuggle undocumented workers from another country into the United States for an employer is illegal (see Chapter 22). If the object or performance of a contract is rendered illegal by statute *after* the contract has been formed, the contract is considered to be discharged by law.

USURY Almost every state has a statute that sets the maximum rate of interest that can be charged for different types of transactions, including ordinary loans. A lender who makes a loan at an interest rate above the lawful maximum commits **usury.** Although usurious contracts are illegal, most states simply limit the interest that the lender may collect on the contract to the lawful maximum interest rate in that state. In a few states, the lender can recover the principal amount of the loan but no interest.

Although usury statutes place a ceiling on allowable rates of interest, exceptions are made to facilitate business transactions. For example, many states exempt corporate loans from the usury laws. In addition, almost all states have special statutes allowing much higher interest rates on small loans to help those borrowers who need funds and could not otherwise obtain loans.

GAMBLING Gambling is the creation of risk for the purpose of assuming it. Any scheme that involves the distribution of property by chance among persons who have paid valuable consideration for the opportunity (chance) to receive the property is gambling. Traditionally, the states have deemed gambling contracts illegal and thus void. All states have statutes that regulate gambling, and many states allow certain forms of gambling, such as horse racing, poker machines, and charity-sponsored bingo. In addition, nearly all states allow state-operated lotteries and gambling on Indian reservations. Regardless, even in states that permit certain types of gambling, courts often find that gambling contracts are illegal.

EXAMPLE 9.13 Casino gambling and video poker machines are legal in Louisiana. Nevertheless, Louisiana courts refused to enforce a contract between a gaming company and a restaurant relating to the installation of video poker machines. Gaming Venture, Inc. (GVI), had entered into two contracts with Tastee Restaurant Corporation. One was a licensing agreement, and the other was a gaming device placement agreement that authorized GVI to install poker machines in various Tastee locations. When several Tastee restaurants refused to install the machines, GVI sued for breach of contract. The state appellate court held that the two agreements were illegal and void. For them to have been enforceable, GVI would have needed prior approval of the two contracts from the state video gaming commission. Without that, the contracts were illegal gambling contracts.[5] ●

5. *Gaming Venture, Inc. v. Tastee Restaurant Corp.*, 996 So.2d 515 (La.App. 5 Cir. 2008).

LICENSING STATUTES All states require members of certain professions—including physicians, lawyers, real estate brokers, accountants, architects, electricians, and stockbrokers—to have licenses. Some licenses are obtained only after extensive schooling and examinations, which indicate to the public that a special skill has been acquired. Others require only that the particular person be of good moral character and pay a fee.

Whether a contract with an unlicensed person is legal and enforceable depends on the purpose of the licensing statute. If the statute's purpose is to protect the public from unauthorized practitioners, then a contract involving an unlicensed practitioner generally is illegal and unenforceable. If the purpose is merely to raise government revenues, however, a contract with an unlicensed person may be enforced (and the unlicensed practitioner fined).

Can a member of a profession licensed in one jurisdiction recover on a contract to perform professional services in another jurisdiction? What if the contract was the result of a winning entry in an international competition? The court in the following case was asked these questions.

Case 9.2 Sturdza v. United Arab Emirates

District of Columbia Court of Appeals, 11 A.3d 251 (2011).

FACTS The United Arab Emirates (UAE) held a competition for the design of a new embassy in Washington, D.C. At the conclusion of the competition, the UAE informed Elena Sturdza–an architect licensed in Maryland and Texas but not in the District of Columbia–that she had won. Sturdza and the UAE began to negotiate a contract. For two years, they exchanged proposals. Then, without explanation, the UAE stopped communicating with Sturdza. No contract between the UAE and Sturdza was ever signed. About two years later, Sturdza learned that the UAE had contracted with a District of Columbia architect, Angelos Demetriou, to use his design for its embassy. Believing that Demetriou's design "copied and appropriated many of the design features that had been the hallmark of [her] design," Sturdza filed a suit in a federal district court against the UAE, alleging breach of contract. The court issued a summary judgment in the UAE's favor. Sturdza appealed to the U.S. Court of Appeals for the District of Columbia Circuit. This court asked the District of Columbia Court of Appeals "precisely how D.C. law applies" in this situation.

ISSUE Can an architect who is licensed in Maryland sue to enforce a contract under which she was to perform architectural services in the District of Columbia?

DECISION No. The District of Columbia appellate court answered the question it was asked by the federal court to resolve. According to the licensing statute, an architect cannot recover on a contract to perform architectural services in the District of Columbia if he or she lacks a District of Columbia license.

REASON Sturdza argued that the licensing statute should not apply to architects who submit plans in international architectural design competitions. The court held, however, that licensing requirements are necessary to ensure the safety of those who work in and visit buildings in the District of Columbia, as well as the safety of neighboring buildings. Besides, the statute contains no exception for international design competitions or any other type of client or service. "We must apply the statute as it is written and not create *ad hoc* [impromptu] exceptions by judicial decree based on nebulous [unclear] policy considerations."

FOR CRITICAL ANALYSIS—Global Consideration *The architectural services at the center of this case were to be performed for a foreign embassy. Should the court have made an exception for such a circumstance? Why or why not?*

Contracts Contrary to Public Policy

Although contracts involve private parties, some are not enforceable because of the negative impact they would have on society. These contracts are said to be *contrary to public policy*. Examples include a contract to commit an immoral act, such as selling a child, and a contract that prohibits marriage.

EXAMPLE 9.14 Everett offers a young man $10,000 if he refrains from marrying Everett's daughter. If the young man accepts, no contract is formed (the contract is void) because it is contrary to public policy. Thus, if the man marries Everett's daughter, Everett cannot sue him for breach of contract. • Business contracts that may be contrary to public policy include contracts in *restraint of trade* and *unconscionable contracts or clauses*.

CONTRACTS IN RESTRAINT OF TRADE The United States has a strong public policy favoring competition in the economy. Thus, contracts that restrain trade, or anticompetitive agreements, generally are unenforceable because they are contrary to public policy. An exception is recognized when the restraint is reasonable and is an ancillary (secondary) part of the contract. Such restraints often are included in contracts for the sale of an ongoing business and employment contracts.

Covenants Not to Compete and the Sale of an Ongoing Business. Many contracts involve a type of restraint called a **covenant not to compete,** or a restrictive covenant (promise). A covenant not to compete may be created when a seller agrees not to open a new store in a certain geographic area surrounding the old store. Such an agreement enables the seller to sell, and the purchaser to buy, the goodwill and reputation of an ongoing business without having to worry that the seller will open a competing business a block away. Provided the restrictive covenant is reasonable and is an ancillary part of the sale of an ongoing business, it is enforceable.

Covenants Not to Compete in Employment Contracts. Agreements not to compete can also be included in **employment contracts** (contracts stating the terms and conditions of employment). People in middle- and upper-level management positions commonly agree not to work for competitors or not to start a competing business for a specified period of time after terminating employment. Such agreements generally are legal in most states so long as the specified period of time (of restraint) is not excessive in duration and the geographic restriction is reasonable. What constitutes a reasonable time period may be shorter in the online environment than in conventional employment contracts because the restrictions would apply worldwide.

To be reasonable, a restriction on competition must protect a legitimate business interest and must not be any greater than necessary to protect that interest.[6] **EXAMPLE 9.15** Safety and Compliance Management, Inc. (S&C), provides drug-testing services. S&C hired Angela Burgess to retrieve specimens from clients and transport them to the lab. She signed a covenant not to compete "in any area of business" conducted by S&C for a period of two years from the date of termination. When Burgess quit her job and went to work at a nearby hospital, S&C filed a lawsuit claiming that she was breaching the noncompete agreement. The hospital also offered drug-testing services, and Burgess sometimes collected specimens from patients. The court, however, found that because S&C's noncompete agreement failed to specify the activities that Burgess was prohibited from performing, it was too broad and indefinite to be enforceable. The noncompete agreement imposed a greater limitation on Burgess than was necessary for the protection of S&C and was thus unreasonable.[7] •

Enforcement Problems. The laws governing the enforceability of covenants not to compete vary significantly from state to state. In some states, such as Texas, such a covenant will not be enforced unless the employee has received some benefit in return for signing the noncompete agreement. This is true even if the covenant is reasonable as to time and area. If the employee receives no benefit, the covenant will be deemed void. California prohibits the enforcement of covenants not to compete altogether.

Occasionally, depending on the jurisdiction, courts will *reform* covenants not to compete. If a covenant is found to be unreasonable in time or geographic area, the court may convert the terms into reasonable ones and then enforce the reformed covenant. This presents a problem, however, in that the judge has implicitly become a party to the contract. Consequently, courts usually resort to contract **reformation** only when necessary to prevent undue burdens or hardships.

UNCONSCIONABLE CONTRACTS OR CLAUSES Ordinarily, a court does not look at the fairness or equity of a contract, or, as discussed earlier, inquire into the adequacy of consideration. Persons are assumed to be reasonably intelligent, and the courts will not come to their aid just because they have made unwise or foolish bargains. In certain circumstances, however, bargains are so oppressive that the courts relieve innocent parties of part or all of their duties. Such bargains are

6. See, for example, *Gould & Lamb, LLC v. D'Alusio*, 949 So.2d 1212 (Fla.App. 2007); and *Freeman v. Brown Hiller, Inc.*, 102 Ark.App. 76, 281 S.W.3d 749 (2008).

7. *Stultz v. Safety and Compliance Management, Inc.*, 285 Ga.App. 799, 648 S.E.2d 129 (2007).

• ***Exhibit* 9–1 Unconscionability**

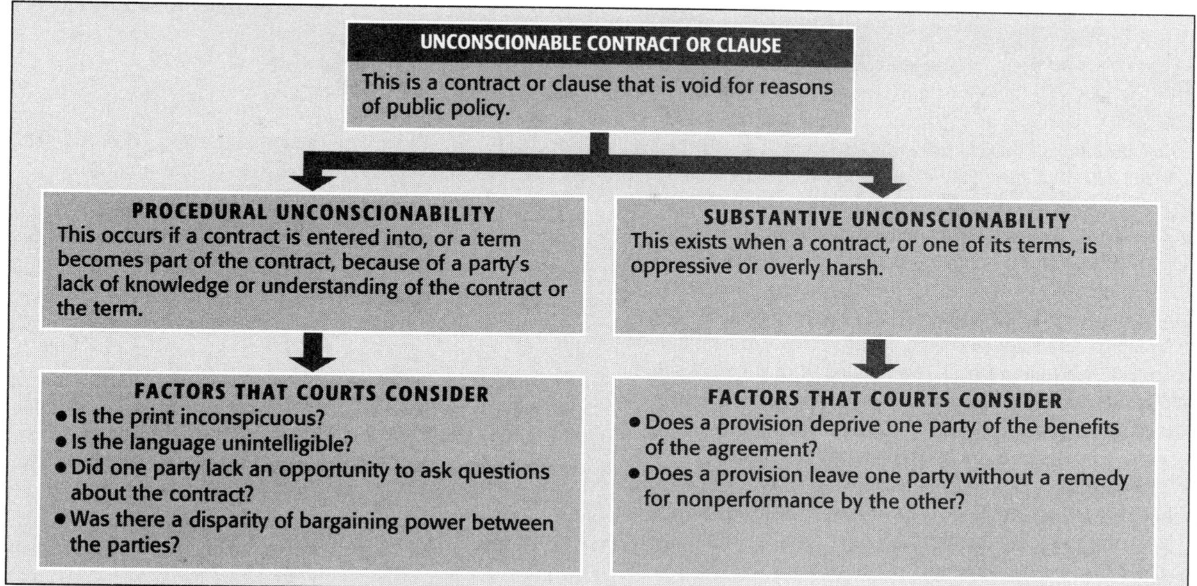

deemed **unconscionable**[8] because they are so unscrupulous or grossly unfair as to be "void of conscience."

The Uniform Commercial Code (UCC) incorporates the concept of unconscionability in its provisions with regard to the sale and lease of goods.[9] A contract can be unconscionable on either procedural or substantive grounds, as discussed in the following subsections and illustrated graphically in Exhibit 9–1 above.

Procedural Unconscionability. Procedural unconscionability often involves inconspicuous print, unintelligible language (legalese), or the lack of an opportunity to read the contract or ask questions about its meaning. This type of unconscionability typically arises when a party's lack of knowledge or understanding of the contract terms deprived him or her of any meaningful choice.

Procedural unconscionability can also occur when there is such a disparity in bargaining power between the two parties that the weaker party's consent is not voluntary. This type of situation often involves an *adhesion contract,* which is a standard-form contract written exclusively by one party (the dominant party, usually the seller or creditor) and presented to the other (the adhering party, usually the buyer or borrower) on a take-it-or-leave-it basis. In other words, the adhering party has no opportunity to negotiate the terms of the contract. Not all adhesion contracts are unconscionable, only those that unreasonably favor the drafter.

8. Pronounced un-*kon*-shun-uh-bul.

9. See UCC 2–302 and 2–719.

Substantive Unconscionability. Substantive unconscionability occurs when contracts, or portions of contracts, are oppressive or overly harsh. Courts generally focus on provisions that deprive one party of the benefits of the agreement or leave that party without remedy for nonperformance by the other. **EXAMPLE 9.16** A person with little income and only an eighth-grade education agrees to purchase a computer for $4,500 and signs a two-year installment contract. The same type of computer usually sells for $1,000 on the market. Despite the general rule that the courts will not inquire into the adequacy of the consideration, some courts have held that this type of contract is unconscionable because the contract terms are so oppressive as to "shock the conscience" of the court. •

Substantive unconscionability can arise in a wide variety of business contexts. For example, a contract clause that gives the business entity unrestricted access to the courts but requires the other party to arbitrate any dispute with the firm may be unconscionable. Similarly, an arbitration clause in a credit-card agreement that prevents credit cardholders from obtaining relief for abusive debt-collection practices under consumer law may be unconscionable. Contracts drafted by insurance companies and cell phone providers have been struck down as substantively unconscionable when they included provisions that were overly harsh or one sided.

In the following case, the question was whether an arbitration clause was both procedurally and substantively unconscionable.

Case 9.3 Lhotka v. Geographic Expeditions, Inc.

California Court of Appeal, First District, 181 Cal.App.4th 816, 104 Cal.Rptr.3d 844 (2010).

FACTS Sandra Menefee and her son Jason Lhotka went on an expedition up Mount Kilimanjaro that had been arranged by Geographic Expeditions, Inc. (GeoEx). GeoEx's limitation-of-liability and release form, which both Lhotka and Menefee signed as a requirement for participating in the expedition, provided that each of them released GeoEx from all liability in connection with the trek and waived any claims for liability "to the maximum extent permitted by law." The release also provided that in the event of a dispute, the dispute would be mediated and then, if not yet resolved, arbitrated in San Francisco. The maximum recovery was limited to the amount paid for the trip with GeoEx. The release also stated, "I agree to fully indemnify [compensate] GeoEx for all its costs (including attorneys' fees) if I commence an action or claim against GeoEx based upon claims I have previously released or waived by signing this release." GeoEx led Menefee and Lhotka to believe that other travel companies required similar releases. Menefee paid $16,831 for herself and Lhotka to go on the trip. While on the trip, Lhotka died of an altitude-related illness. Lhotka's wife and others (the plaintiffs) sued GeoEx for wrongful death under various theories of liability. The trial court found that the release was unconscionable and refused to grant GeoEx's motion to compel arbitration. GeoEx appealed.

ISSUE Was GeoEx's arbitration clause procedurally and substantively unconscionable because it required all expedition participants to sign a release (without modification) limiting their potential recovery to the amount that they had paid for the trip?

DECISION Yes. The California appellate court affirmed the trial court's order denying GeoEx's motion to compel arbitration.

REASON Because GeoEx explicitly advised potential participants in its expeditions that they had to sign an unmodified release form to participate, and that other travel companies were no different, GeoEx led the plaintiffs to understand that no negotiations were possible. The court noted that "This [was] a sufficient basis for us to conclude that the plaintiffs lacked bargaining power." To be sure, the plaintiffs could have chosen not to sign. But this "take it or leave it" option created oppression that arose from an inequality of bargaining power and justified a finding of procedural unconscionability. As to the substantive unconscionability issue, the reviewing court pointed out that the arbitration provision in the GeoEx release limited any recovery that the plaintiffs could obtain to the amount they paid GeoEx. This provision guaranteed that the plaintiffs could not possibly obtain anything approaching full compensation for their harm. Further, GeoEx's arbitration scheme "provided a potent disincentive for an aggrieved client to pursue any claim, in any form–and may well guarantee that GeoEx wins even if it loses." Therefore, the arbitration clause was so one sided as to be substantively unconscionable.

FOR CRITICAL ANALYSIS—Economic Consideration *What did the court mean when it said that GeoEx's one-sided arbitration scheme "may well guarantee that GeoEx wins even if it loses"?*

EXCULPATORY CLAUSES Often closely related to the concept of unconscionability are **exculpatory clauses,** which release a party from liability in the event of monetary or physical injury, *no matter who is at fault.* Indeed, courts sometimes refuse to enforce such clauses because they deem them to be unconscionable. Exculpatory clauses found in rental agreements for commercial property are frequently held to be contrary to public policy, and such clauses are almost always unenforceable in residential property leases. Exculpatory clauses in the employment context may be deemed unconscionable when they attempt to remove the employer's potential liability for injuries to employees.

Although courts view exculpatory clauses with disfavor, they do enforce such clauses when they do not contravene public policy, are not ambiguous, and do not claim to protect parties from liability for intentional misconduct. Businesses such as health clubs, racetracks, skiing facilities, horse-rental operations, and skydiving organizations frequently use exculpatory clauses to limit their liability for patrons' injuries. Because these services are not essential, the firms offering them are sometimes considered to have no relative advantage in bargaining strength, and anyone contracting for their services is considered to do so voluntarily.

The Effect of Illegality

In general, an illegal contract is void: the contract is deemed never to have existed, and the courts will not aid either party. In most illegal contracts, both parties are considered to be equally at fault—*in pari delicto.* If the contract is executory (not yet fulfilled), neither party can enforce it. If it has been executed, neither party can recover damages.

The courts usually are not concerned if one wrongdoer in an illegal contract is unjustly enriched at the expense of the other—except under certain circumstances (to be discussed shortly). The main reason for this hands-off attitude is a belief that a plaintiff who has broken the law by entering into an illegal bargain should not be allowed to obtain help from the courts. Another justification is the hoped-for deterrent effect: a plaintiff who suffers a loss because of an illegal bargain will presumably be deterred from entering into similar illegal bargains in the future.

There are exceptions to the general rule that neither party to an illegal bargain can sue for breach and neither party can recover for performance rendered. We look at these exceptions here.

JUSTIFIABLE IGNORANCE OF THE FACTS When one of the parties to a contract is relatively innocent (has no reason to know that the contract is illegal), that party can often recover any benefits conferred in a partially executed contract. In this situation, the courts will not enforce the contract but will allow the parties to return to their original positions.

A court may sometimes permit an innocent party who has fully performed under a contract to enforce the contract against the guilty party. **EXAMPLE 9.17** A trucking company contracts with Gillespie to carry crated goods to a specific destination for a normal fee of $5,000. The trucker delivers the crates and later finds out that they contained illegal goods. Although the shipment, use, and sale of the goods are illegal under the law, the trucker, being an innocent party, can normally still legally collect the $5,000 from Gillespie. •

MEMBERS OF PROTECTED CLASSES When a statute protects a certain class of people, a member of that class can enforce an illegal contract even though the other party cannot. **EXAMPLE 9.18** Statutes prohibit certain employees (such as flight attendants) from working more than a specified number of hours per month. These employees thus constitute a class protected by statute. An employee who is required to work more than the maximum can recover for those extra hours of service. •

Other examples of statutes designed to protect a particular class of people are **blue sky laws**—state laws that regulate the offering and sale of securities for the protection of the public (see Chapter 26)—and state statutes regulating the sale of insurance. If an insurance company violates a statute when selling insurance, the purchaser can nevertheless enforce the policy and recover from the insurer.

WITHDRAWAL FROM AN ILLEGAL AGREEMENT If the illegal part of a bargain has not yet been performed, the party rendering performance can withdraw from the contract and recover the performance or its value. **EXAMPLE 9.19** Marta and Ande decide to wager (illegally) on the outcome of a boxing match. Each deposits money with a stakeholder, who agrees to pay the winner of the bet. At this point, each party has performed part of the agreement, but the illegal part of the agreement will not occur until the money is paid to the winner. Before such payment occurs, either party is entitled to withdraw from the agreement by giving notice to the stakeholder of his or her withdrawal. •

SEVERABLE, OR DIVISIBLE, CONTRACTS A contract that is *severable,* or divisible, consists of distinct parts that can be performed separately, with separate consideration provided for each part. With an *indivisible* contract, in contrast, the parties intended that complete performance by each party would be essential, even if the contract contains a number of seemingly separate provisions.

If a contract is divisible into legal and illegal portions, a court may enforce the legal portion but not the illegal one, so long as the illegal portion does not affect the essence of the bargain. This approach is consistent with the basic policy of enforcing the legal intentions of the contracting parties whenever possible.

EXAMPLE 9.20 Cole signs an employment contract that includes an overly broad and thus illegal covenant not to compete. In that situation, a court might allow the employment contract to be enforceable but reform the unreasonably broad covenant by converting its terms into reasonable ones. Alternatively, the court could declare the covenant illegal (and thus void) and enforce the remaining employment terms. •

FRAUD, DURESS, OR UNDUE INFLUENCE Often, one party to an illegal contract is more at fault than the other. When a party has been induced to enter into an illegal bargain through fraud, duress, or undue influence on the part of the other party to the agreement, the first party will be allowed to recover for the performance or its value.

Reviewing . . . Consideration, Capacity, and Legality

Renee Beaver started racing go-karts competitively in 2008, when she was fourteen. Many of the races required her to sign an exculpatory clause to participate, which she or her parents regularly signed. In 2011, right before her birthday, she participated in the annual Elkhart Grand Prix, a series of races in Elkhart, Indiana. During the event in which she drove, a piece of foam padding used as a course barrier was torn from its base and ended up on the track. A portion of the padding struck Beaver in the head, and another portion was thrown into oncoming traffic, causing a multikart collision during which she sustained severe injuries. Beaver filed an action against the race organizers for negligence. The organizers could not locate the exculpatory clause that Beaver was supposed to have signed. Race organizers argued that she must have signed one to enter the race, but even if she had not signed one, her actions showed her intent to be bound by its terms. Using the information presented in the chapter, answer the following questions.

1. Did Beaver have the contractual capacity to enter a contract with an exculpatory clause? Why or why not?
2. Assuming that Beaver did, in fact, sign the exculpatory clause, did she later disaffirm or ratify the contract? Explain.
3. Now assume that Beaver had stated that she was eighteen years old at the time that she signed the exculpatory clause. How might this affect Beaver's ability to disaffirm or ratify the contract?
4. If Beaver did not actually sign the exculpatory clause, could a court conclude that she impliedly accepted its terms by participating in the race? Why or why not?

Terms and Concepts

accord and satisfaction 164
blue sky laws 173
consideration 162
contractual capacity 166
covenant not to compete 170
covenant not to sue 165
disaffirmance 166
emancipation 166
employment contract 170
exculpatory clause 172
liquidated debt 164
necessaries 167
past consideration 164
promissory estoppel 165
ratification 167
reformation 170
release 165
rescission 163
unconscionable 171
usury 168

Chapter Summary: Consideration, Capacity, and Legality

CONSIDERATION	
Elements of Consideration (See pages 162–163.)	Consideration has two parts: 1. Something of *legally sufficient value* must be given in exchange for a promise. 2. There must be a *bargained-for exchange.*
Adequacy of Consideration (See page 163.)	Legal sufficiency means that something of legal value must be given in exchange for a promise. Adequacy relates to "how much" consideration is given and whether a fair bargain was reached. Courts will inquire into the adequacy of consideration only when fraud, undue influence, duress, or unconscionability may be involved.
Agreements That Lack Consideration (See pages 163–164.)	Consideration is lacking in the following situations: 1. *Preexisting duty*—A promise to do what one already has a legal duty to do is not legally sufficient consideration for a new contract. 2. *Past consideration*—Actions or events that have already taken place do not constitute legally sufficient consideration. 3. *Illusory promises*—When the nature or extent of performance is too uncertain, the promise is rendered illusory (without consideration and unenforceable).
Settlement of Claims (See pages 164–165.)	Disputes may be settled by the following, which are enforceable provided there is consideration: 1. *Accord and satisfaction*—An *accord* is an agreement in which a debtor offers to pay a lesser amount than the creditor claims is owed. *Satisfaction* takes place when the accord is executed. 2. *Release*—An agreement in which, for consideration, a party forfeits the right to seek further recovery beyond the terms specified in the release. 3. *Covenant not to sue*—An agreement not to sue on a present, valid claim.
Promissory Estoppel (See pages 165–166.)	The equitable doctrine of promissory estoppel applies when a promisor should have expected a promise to induce definite and substantial action or forbearance by the promisee, and the promisee does act in reliance on the promise. Such a promise is binding, even though there is no consideration, if injustice can be avoided only by enforcement of the promise. Also known as the doctrine of *detrimental reliance.*
CONTRACTUAL CAPACITY	
Minors (See pages 166–167.)	1. *General rule*—Contracts with minors are voidable at the option of the minor. 2. *Disaffirmance*—The legal avoidance of a contractual obligation. a. Disaffirmance can take place (in most states) at any time during minority and within a reasonable time after the minor has reached the age of majority. b. The minor must disaffirm the entire contract, not just part of it. c. When disaffirming executed contracts, the minor has a duty to return the received goods if they are still in the minor's control or (in some states) to pay their reasonable value. d. A minor who has committed an act of fraud (such as misrepresenting her or his age) will be denied the right to disaffirm by some courts.

Chapter Summary: Consideration, Capacity, and Legality—Continued

Minors—Continued	e. A minor may disaffirm a contract for necessaries but remains liable for the reasonable value of the goods. 3. *Ratification*—The acceptance, or affirmation, of a legal obligation; may be express or implied. a. *Express ratification*—Occurs when the minor, in writing or orally, explicitly assumes the obligations imposed by the contract. b. *Implied ratification*—Occurs when the conduct of the minor is inconsistent with disaffirmance or when the minor fails to disaffirm an executed contract within a reasonable time after reaching the age of majority. 4. *Parents' liability*—Generally, except for contracts for necessaries, parents are not liable for the contracts made by minor children acting on their own. Parents may be liable for minors' torts in certain circumstances, however.
Intoxication (See pages 167–168.)	1. A contract entered into by an intoxicated person is voidable at the option of the intoxicated person if the person was sufficiently intoxicated to lack mental capacity, even if the intoxication was voluntary. 2. A contract with an intoxicated person is enforceable if, despite being intoxicated, the person understood the legal consequences of entering into the contract.
Mental Incompetence (See page 168.)	1. A contract made by a person previously judged by a court to be mentally incompetent is void. 2. A contract made by a person who is mentally incompetent, but has not been previously declared incompetent by a court, is voidable at the option of that person.
	LEGALITY
Contracts Contrary to Statute (See pages 168–169.)	1. *Contracts to commit a crime*—Any contract to commit a crime, such as selling illegal drugs, is a contract in violation of a statute. 2. *Usury*—Usury occurs when a lender makes a loan at an interest rate above the lawful maximum. The maximum rate of interest varies from state to state. 3. *Gambling*—Gambling contracts that contravene (go against) state statutes are deemed illegal and thus void. 4. *Licensing statutes*—Contracts entered into by persons who do not have a license, when one is required by statute, will not be enforceable *unless* the underlying purpose of the statute is to raise government revenues (and not to protect the public from unauthorized practitioners).
Contracts Contrary to Public Policy (See pages 170–172.)	1. *Contracts in restraint of trade*—Contracts to reduce or restrain free competition are illegal and prohibited by statutes. An exception is a *covenant not to compete.* Such covenants usually are enforced by the courts if the terms are secondary to a contract (such as a contract for the sale of a business or an employment contract) and are reasonable as to time and area of restraint. Courts tend to scrutinize covenants not to compete closely and, at times, may reform them if they are overbroad rather than declaring the entire covenant unenforceable. 2. *Unconscionable contracts and clauses*—When a contract or contract clause is so unfair that it is oppressive to one party, it may be deemed unconscionable; as such, it is illegal and cannot be enforced. 3. *Exculpatory clauses*—An exculpatory clause is a clause that releases a party from liability in the event of monetary or physical injury, no matter who is at fault. In certain situations, exculpatory clauses may be contrary to public policy and thus unenforceable.
The Effect of Illegality (See pages 172–173.)	1. *General rule*—In general, an illegal contract is void, and the courts will not aid either party when both parties are considered to be equally at fault *(in pari delicto).* If the contract is executory, neither party can enforce it. If the contract is executed, neither party can recover damages. 2. *Exceptions*—The general rule that neither party to an illegal bargain will be able to recover has several exceptions, including justifiable ignorance of the facts; members of protected classes; withdrawal from an illegal agreement; severable, or divisible, contracts; and fraud, duress, or undue influence.

ExamPrep

ISSUE SPOTTERS

—Check your answers to these questions against the answers provided in Appendix G.

1 In September, Sharyn agrees to work for Totem Productions, Inc., at $500 a week for a year beginning January 1. In October, Sharyn is offered the same work at $600 a week by Umber Shows, Ltd. When Sharyn tells Totem about

the other offer, they tear up their contract and agree that Sharyn will be paid $575. Is the new contract binding? Explain.

2 Sun Airlines, Inc., prints on its tickets that it is not liable for any injury to a passenger caused by the airline's negligence. If the cause of an accident is found to be the airline's negligence, can Sun use the clause as a defense to liability? Why or why not?

BEFORE THE TEST

Go to **www.cengagebrain.com**, enter the ISBN 9781111530624, and click on "Find" to locate this textbook's Web site. Then, click on "Access Now" under "Study Tools," and select Chapter 9 at the top. There, you will find an Interactive Quiz that you can take to assess your mastery of the concepts in this chapter, as well as Flashcards and a Glossary of important terms.

For Review

1 What is consideration? What is required for consideration to be legally sufficient?
2 In what circumstances might a promise be enforced despite a lack of consideration?
3 Does a minor have the capacity to enter into an enforceable contract? What does it mean to disaffirm a contract?
4 Under what circumstances will a covenant not to compete be enforceable? When will such covenants not be enforced?
5 What is an exculpatory clause? In what circumstances might exculpatory clauses be enforced? When will they not be enforced?

Questions and Case Problems

9–1 Contract Modification. Tabor is a buyer of file cabinets manufactured by Martin. Martin's contract with Tabor calls for delivery of fifty file cabinets at $40 per cabinet in five equal installments. After delivery of two installments (twenty cabinets), Martin informs Tabor that because of inflation, Martin is losing money and will promise to deliver the remaining thirty cabinets only if Tabor will pay $50 per cabinet. Tabor agrees in writing to do so. Discuss whether Martin can legally collect the additional $100 on delivery to Tabor of the next installment of ten cabinets.

9–2 Intoxication. After Kira had had several drinks one night, she sold Charlotte a diamond necklace worth thousands of dollars for just $100. The next day, Kira offered the $100 to Charlotte and requested the return of her necklace. Charlotte refused to accept the $100 or return the necklace, claiming that there was a valid contract of sale. Kira explained that she had been intoxicated at the time the bargain was made and thus the contract was voidable at her option. Was Kira correct? Explain.

9–3 Consideration. Ben hired Lewis to drive his racing car in a race. Tuan, a friend of Lewis, promised to pay Lewis $3,000 if he won the race. Lewis won the race, but Tuan refused to pay the $3,000. Tuan contended that no legally binding contract had been formed because he had received no consideration from Lewis for his promise to pay the $3,000. Lewis sued Tuan for breach of contract, arguing that winning the race was the consideration given in exchange for Tuan's promise to pay the $3,000. What rule of law discussed in this chapter supports Tuan's claim? Explain.

9–4 Substantive Unconscionability. Erica Bishop lived in public housing with her children. Her lease stated that only she and her children, who were listed on the lease, could live in the apartment, and that she was responsible for the actions of all household members. Any violations of the lease by any household member, including criminal activity, would be grounds for eviction. Bishop's son Derek committed an armed robbery at a store next to the apartment building. Bishop was given thirty days to vacate the apartment due to breach of the lease. She sued, arguing that Derek had moved out of the apartment months before the robbery, but she admitted he had been in the apartment right before the robbery. The trial court held that since Derek had visited the apartment right before the robbery, he was a household member and Bishop had to vacate. She appealed, contending that the lease was invalid because it was substantively unconscionable. Does Erica have grounds for a reversal in her favor? Discuss. [*Bishop v. Housing Authority of South Bend,* 920 N.E.2d 772 (Ind.App. 2010)]

9–5 Case Problem with Sample Answer In 2002, Farrokh and Scheherezade Sharabianlou were looking for a location for a printing business. They signed a purchase agreement to buy a building owned by Berenstein Associates for $2 million and deposited $115,000 in escrow until the time of the final purchase. The agreement contained a clause requiring an environmental assessment of the property. This study indicated the presence of tricholoroethene and other chemicals used in dry cleaning, and it recommended further study of the contamination. Because of this issue, the bank would not provide financing for the purchase. When the deal fell apart, the Berensteins sued for breach of contract. The Sharabianlous sought the return of their $115,000 deposit and rescission of the contract. The trial court awarded the Berensteins $428,660 in damages due to the reduced value of their property when it was later sold to another party at a lower price. The Sharabianlous appealed. Do they have a good argument for rescission? Explain your answer. [*Sharabianlou v. Karp*, 181 Cal.App.4th 1133, 105 Cal.Rptr.3d 300 (1st Dist. 2010)]

—For a sample answer to Problem 9–5, go to Appendix F at the end of this text.

9–6 Licensing Statutes. PEMS Co. International, Inc., agreed to find a buyer for Rupp Industries, Inc. A commission of 2 percent of the purchase price was to be paid by the buyer. PEMS analyzed Rupp's operational and financial conditions, paid legal fees, carefully managed Rupp's confidential data, and screened more than a dozen potential buyers. Using PEMS's services, an investment group that became Rupp Industries Acquisition, Inc. (RIA), acquired key information about Rupp and bought the company for $20 million. RIA changed Rupp's name to Temp-Air, Inc. No one paid PEMS's commission. PEMS filed a suit in a Minnesota state court against Temp-Air, alleging breach of contract. Temp-Air responded that PEMS had been acting as a broker in the transaction without having obtained a broker's license. Thus, because state law required a broker to have a license, PEMS was barred from maintaining this suit. PEMS argued that it had acted not as a broker but as a "finder." The applicable statute defines a broker as any person who deals with the sale of a business. What determines whether a contract with an unlicensed person is enforceable? Assuming that the statute in this case was intended to protect the public, can PEMS collect its commission? Explain. [*PEMS Co. International, Inc. v. Temp-Air, Inc.*, __ N.W.2d __ (Minn. App. 2011)]

9–7 Consideration. In March 1997, Leonard Kranzler loaned Lewis Saltzman $100,000. Saltzman signed a written memo that stated, "Loaned to Lewis Saltzman $100,000 to be paid back with interest." Saltzman made fifteen payments on the loan, but these payments did not cover the entire amount. The last payment was made in July 2005. In June 2007—more than ten years after the date of the loan but less than two years after the date of the last payment—Kranzler filed a suit in an Illinois state court against Saltzman, seeking to recover the outstanding principal and interest. Saltzman admitted that he had borrowed the funds and had made payments on the loan, but he claimed that Kranzler's complaint was barred by a ten-year statute of limitations. Does Kranzler need to prove a new promise with new consideration to collect the unpaid debt? Explain. [*Kranzler v. Saltzman*, 347 Ill.Dec. 519, 942 N.E.2d 722 (1 Dist. 2011)]

9–8  **A Question of Ethics** *Claudia Aceves obtained a loan of $845,000 to buy a home in Los Angeles, California. Less than two years into the loan, Aceves could no longer afford the monthly payments. U.S. Bank, which held her mortgage, declared her in default and notified her that it planned to foreclose on her home. (Foreclosure is a process that allows a lender to repossess and sell the property that secures a loan.) Aceves filed for bankruptcy. Filing a petition in bankruptcy automatically stays, or suspends, any action by a mortgagee (lender) against the debtor. Aceves hoped to set up a new, affordable schedule of payments. On learning of the filing, U.S. Bank offered to modify Aceves's mortgage if she would forgo bankruptcy. In reliance on that promise, she allowed the bankruptcy court to lift the automatic stay. Once the stay was lifted, the bank did not work with Aceves to modify her loan. Instead, it foreclosed on her home and initiated eviction proceedings. She filed a lawsuit in a California state court against the bank, alleging a cause of action for promissory estoppel.* [Aceves v. U.S. Bank, N.A., *129 Cal.App.4th 218, 120 Cal.Rptr.3d 507 (2 Dist. 2011)]*

1 Is Aceves likely to succeed in her claim of promissory estoppel? Why or why not? How does this theory relate to the ethical principles discussed in Chapter 3?
2 Did either the borrower or the lender—or both—behave unethically in the circumstances of this case? Explain.

9–9  **Critical Thinking Legal Question** Under what circumstances should courts examine the adequacy of consideration?

Chapter 10

Defenses to Contract Enforceability

Learning Objectives

After reading this chapter, you should be able to answer the following questions:

1. In what types of situations might voluntary consent to a contract's terms be lacking?
2. What is the difference between a mistake of value or quality and a mistake of fact?
3. What are the elements of fraudulent misrepresentation?
4. What contracts must be in writing to be enforceable?
5. What is parol evidence? When is it admissible to clarify the terms of a written contract?

The Learning Objectives above are designed to help improve your understanding of the chapter.

(AP Photo/Carlos Osorio)

An otherwise valid contract may still be unenforceable if the parties have not genuinely agreed to its terms. Lack of **voluntary consent** (assent) is a *defense* to the enforcement of a contract. If one party does not voluntarily consent to the terms of a contract, then there is no genuine "meeting of the minds," and the courts will not enforce the contract, as we will discuss in the first part of this chapter.

A contract that is otherwise valid may also be unenforceable if it is not in the proper form. For example, if a contract is required by law to be in writing and there is no written evidence of the contract, it may not be enforceable. In the second part of this chapter, we examine the kinds of contracts that require a writing under what is called the *Statute of Frauds*. The chapter concludes with a discussion of the parol evidence rule, under which courts determine the admissibility at trial of evidence extraneous (external) to written contracts.

Voluntary Consent

Voluntary consent may be lacking because of mistake, fraudulent misrepresentation, undue influence, or duress. Generally, a party who demonstrates that he or she did not voluntarily consent to the terms of a contract can choose either to carry out the contract or to rescind (cancel) it and thus avoid the entire transaction.

Mistakes

We all make mistakes, so it is not surprising that mistakes are made when contracts are created. In certain circumstances, contract law allows a contract to be avoided on the basis of mistake. It is important to distinguish between *mistakes of fact* and *mistakes of value or quality*. Only a mistake of fact makes a contract voidable.

EXAMPLE 10.1 Paco buys a violin from Beverly for $250. Although the violin is very old, neither party believes that it is valuable. Later, however, an antiques dealer informs the parties that the violin is rare and worth thousands of dollars. Here, both parties were mistaken, but the mistake is a mistake of *value* rather than a mistake of *fact* that warrants contract rescission. Therefore, Beverly cannot rescind the contract. •

Mistakes of fact occur in two forms—*unilateral* and *bilateral (mutual)*. A **unilateral mistake** is made by only one of the contracting parties, whereas, a **bilateral mistake** is made by both. We look next at these two types of mistakes and illustrate them graphically in Exhibit 10–1 below.

Unilateral Mistakes

A unilateral mistake occurs when only one party is mistaken as to a **material fact**—that is, a fact important to the subject matter of the contract. Generally, a unilateral mistake does not give the mistaken party any right to relief from the contract. In other words, the contract normally is enforceable against the mistaken party.

EXAMPLE 10.2 Elena intends to sell her motor home for $17,500. When she learns that Chin is interested in buying a used motor home, she faxes a letter offering to sell the vehicle to him. When typing the fax, however, she mistakenly keys in the price of $15,700. Chin immediately sends Elena a fax accepting her offer. Even though Elena intended to sell her motor home for $17,500, she has made a unilateral mistake and is bound by the contract to sell the vehicle to Chin for $15,700. •

There are at least two exceptions to this rule.[1] First, if the *other* party to the contract knows or should have known that a mistake of fact was made, the contract may not be enforceable. **EXAMPLE 10.3** In Example 10.2, if Chin knew that Elena intended to sell her motor home for $17,500, then Elena's unilateral mistake (stating $15,700 in her offer) may render the resulting contract unenforceable. •

The second exception arises when a unilateral mistake of fact was due to a mathematical mistake in addition, subtraction, division, or multiplication and was made inadvertently and without gross (extreme) negligence. If a contractor's bid was significantly low because he or she made a mistake in addition when totaling the estimated costs, any contract resulting from the bid normally may be rescinded. Of course, in both situations, the mistake must still involve some material fact.

Bilateral (Mutual) Mistakes

A bilateral mistake is a "mutual misunderstanding concerning a basic assumption on which the contract was made."[2] When both parties are mistaken about the same material fact, the contract can be rescinded by either party. Note that, as with unilateral mistakes, the mistake must be about a material fact. When a bilateral mistake occurs, normally the contract is voidable by the adversely affected party and can be rescinded, or canceled.

CASE EXAMPLE 10.4 Steven Simkin married Laura Blank in 1973. When they divorced in 2006, they agreed to split their assets equally. At the time of the agreement, both parties believed that they owned an account with Bernard L. Madoff Investment Securities worth $5.4 million. Simkin kept the account and paid his wife more than $6.5 million—including $2.7 million to offset the funds in the Madoff account—to settle the divorce. Later, they discovered that the Madoff account had no funds because of a Ponzi scheme (see page 50). Simkin filed a lawsuit seeking rescission of the divorce agreement due to mutual mistake. Blank filed a motion to dismiss, which the lower court granted. Simkin appealed. A New York appellate court reversed, concluding that he had stated a claim for bilateral

1. The *Restatement (Second) of Contracts,* Section 153, liberalizes the general rule to take into account the modern trend of allowing avoidance in some circumstances even though only one party has been mistaken.

2. *Restatement (Second) of Contracts,* Section 152.

• ***Exhibit* 10–1 Mistakes of Fact**

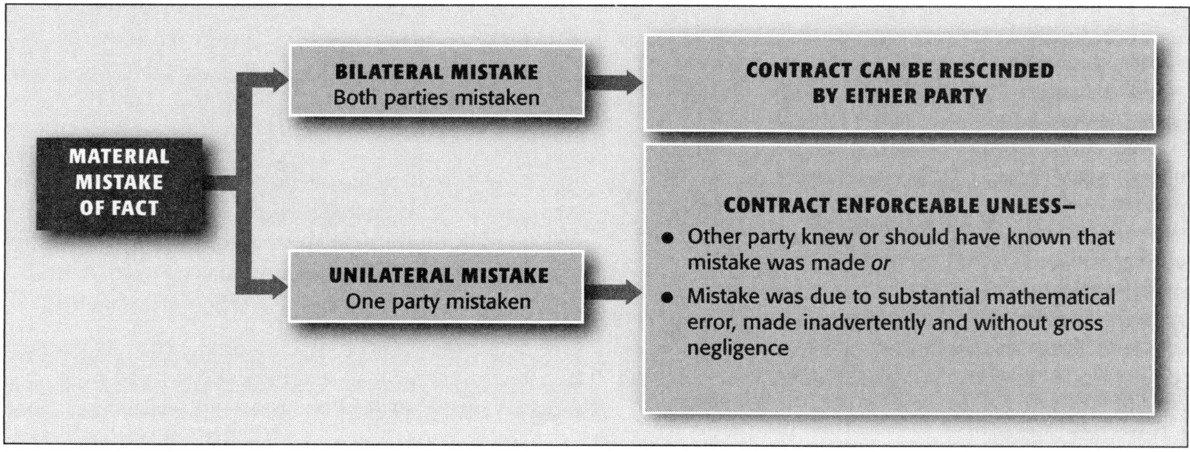

mistake. Because both parties had been mistaken concerning a material fact—that the Madoff account was their largest asset—the divorce settlement could possibly be rescinded (depending on the outcome after a full trial on the issues).[3] •

A word or term in a contract may be subject to more than one reasonable interpretation. If the parties to the contract attach materially different meanings to the term, their mutual misunderstanding may allow the contract to be rescinded.

CASE EXAMPLE 10.5 In a classic case, *Raffles v. Wichelhaus,*[4] Wichelhaus purchased a shipment of cotton from Raffles to arrive on a ship called the *Peerless* from Bombay, India. Wichelhaus meant a ship called *Peerless* sailing from Bombay in October, but Raffles meant a different ship called *Peerless* sailing from Bombay in December. When the goods arrived on the December *Peerless* and Raffles tried to deliver them, Wichelhaus refused to accept them. The British court held for Wichelhaus, concluding that a mutual mistake had been made because the parties had attached materially different meanings to an essential term of the contract (which ship *Peerless* was to transport the goods). •

In the following case, the court had to grapple with the question of whether a mutual mistake of fact had occurred.

3. *Simkin v. Blank*, 80 A.D.3d 401, 915 N.Y.S.2d 47 (N.Y.A.D. 1 Dept. 2011).

4. 159 Eng.Rep. 375 (1864).

Case 10.1 L&H Construction Co. v. Circle Redmont, Inc.

District Court of Appeal of Florida, Fifth District, 55 So.3d 630 (2011).
www.5dca.org/opinions.shtml[a]

FACTS L&H Construction Company was a general contractor involved in the renovation of the Thomas Edison historic site in West Orange, New Jersey, for the National Park Service. L&H contracted with Circle Redmont, Inc., which is based in Melbourne, Florida, to make a cast-iron staircase and a glass flooring system. Circle's original proposal was to "engineer, fabricate, and install" the staircase and flooring system. During negotiations, however, installation and its costs were cut from the deal. In the final agreement, payment was due on "Supervision of Installation" instead of "Completion of Installation." Nevertheless, the final agreement stated that Circle would "engineer, fabricate, and install." Later, Circle claimed that this was a mistake. L&H insisted that installation was included. L&H filed a suit in a Florida state court against Circle. The court found that the word *install* in the phrase "engineer, fabricate, and install" was the result of a mutual mistake. L&H appealed.

ISSUE Was the use of the word *install* in the phrase, "engineer, fabricate, and install" a mutual mistake of fact?

a. In the "Search Opinions" section, in the "Search for this:" box, type "Redmont" and click on "Submit." In the result, click on the appropriate link to view the opinion. The Florida Fifth District Court of Appeal maintains this Web site.

DECISION Yes. A state intermediate appellate court upheld the lower court's decision on the question of whether the use of the word *install* in the parties' agreement was a mutual mistake.

REASON The appellate court explained that the contract between these parties was ambiguous. The proposal indicated that Circle would "engineer, fabricate, and install" the staircase and flooring system, but the agreement stated that L&H's final payment was due on "Supervision" of the installation. According to the testimony of Circle's witnesses, the final agreement stated the parties' understanding–Circle would only supervise the installation, not perform it. Installation was cut from the contract as a cost-saving measure at the request of L&H's president. The trial court determined that these witnesses were credible.

WHAT IF THE FACTS WERE DIFFERENT? *Suppose that Circle Redmont had intentionally misled L&H to believe that installation was included in the price. Would the court's decision on the mutual mistake issue have been different? Discuss.*

Fraudulent Misrepresentation

Although fraud is a tort (see Chapter 4), the presence of fraud also affects the authenticity of the innocent party's consent to a contract. When an innocent party is fraudulently induced to enter into a contract, the contract usually can be avoided because she or he has not *voluntarily* consented to the terms.[5] Normally, the innocent party can either cancel the contract and be restored to her or his original position or enforce the contract and seek damages for harms resulting from the fraud.

Generally, fraudulent misrepresentation refers only to misrepresentation that is consciously false and is intended to mislead another. Typically, fraud involves three elements:

1. A misrepresentation of a material fact must occur.
2. There must be an intent to deceive.
3. The innocent party must justifiably rely on the misrepresentation.

5. *Restatement (Second) of Contracts*, Sections 163 and 164.

MISREPRESENTATION HAS OCCURRED The first element of proving fraud is to show that misrepresentation of a material fact has occurred. This misrepresentation can occur by words or actions. For instance, an art gallery owner's statement "This painting is a Picasso" is a misrepresentation of fact if the painting was done by another artist.

Statements of opinion and representations of future facts (predictions) generally are not subject to claims of fraud. Every person is expected to exercise care and judgment when entering into contracts, and the law will not come to the aid of one who simply makes an unwise bargain. Statements such as "This land will be worth twice as much next year" and "This car will last for years and years" are statements of opinion, not fact. Contracting parties should recognize them as opinions and not rely on them. A fact is objective and verifiable; an opinion is usually subject to debate. Therefore, a seller is allowed to use *puffery* to sell her or his goods without being liable for fraud.

Nevertheless, in certain situations, such as when a naïve purchaser relies on an opinion from an expert, the innocent party may be entitled to rescission or reformation. (*Reformation* is an equitable remedy by which a court alters the terms of a contract to reflect the true intentions of the parties.)

Misrepresentation by Conduct. Misrepresentation also occurs when a party takes specific action to conceal a fact that is material to the contract.[6] For example, if a seller, by her or his actions, prevents a buyer from learning of some fact that is material to the contract, such behavior constitutes misrepresentation by conduct.

CASE EXAMPLE 10.6 Actor Tom Selleck contracted to purchase a horse named Zorro for his daughter from Dolores Cuenca. Cuenca acted as though Zorro was fit to ride in competitions, when in reality the horse suffered from a medical condition. Selleck filed a lawsuit against Cuenca for wrongfully concealing the horse's condition and won. In 2009, a jury awarded Selleck more than $187,000 for Cuenca's misrepresentation by conduct.[7] •

Another example of misrepresentation by conduct is the untruthful denial of knowledge or information concerning facts that are material to the contract when such knowledge or information is requested.

Misrepresentation of Law. Misrepresentation of law *ordinarily* does not entitle a party to be relieved of a contract. **EXAMPLE 10.7** Debbie has a parcel of property that she is trying to sell to Barry. Debbie knows that a local ordinance prohibits building anything higher than three stories on the property. Nonetheless, she tells Barry, "You can build a condominium fifty stories high if you want to." Barry buys the land and later discovers that Debbie's statement is false. Normally, Barry cannot avoid the contract because under the common law, people are assumed to know state and local laws. • Exceptions to this rule occur, however, when the misrepresenting party is in a profession known to require greater knowledge of the law than the average citizen possesses, such as real estate brokers or lawyers.

Misrepresentation by Silence. Ordinarily, neither party to a contract has a duty to come forward and disclose facts, and a contract normally will not be set aside because certain pertinent information has not been volunteered. **EXAMPLE 10.8** Jake is selling a car that has been in an accident and has been repaired. He does not need to volunteer this information to a potential buyer. If, however, the purchaser asks him if the car has had extensive bodywork and he lies, he has committed a fraudulent misrepresentation. •

Generally, if the seller knows of a serious defect or a serious potential problem that the buyer cannot reasonably be expected to discover, the seller may have a duty to speak. Normally, the seller must disclose only "latent" defects—that is, defects that could not readily be ascertained. Thus, termites in a house may not be a latent defect because a buyer could normally discover their presence through a termite inspection. Also, when the parties are in a *fiduciary relationship*—one of trust, such as with business partners or a physician and patient—there is a duty to disclose material facts. Failure to do so may constitute fraud.

INTENT TO DECEIVE The second element of fraud is knowledge on the part of the misrepresenting party that facts have been misrepresented. This element, usually called ***scienter,***[8] or "guilty knowledge," generally signifies that there was an intent to deceive. *Scienter* clearly exists if a party knows that a fact is not as stated. *Scienter* also exists if a party makes a statement that he or she believes not to be true or makes a statement recklessly, without regard to whether it is true or false. Finally, this element is met if a party says or implies that a statement is made on some basis, such as personal knowledge or personal investigation, when it is not.

RELIANCE ON THE MISREPRESENTATION The third element of fraud is *justifiable reliance* on the misrepresentation of fact. The deceived party must have a justifiable reason for relying on the misrepresentation, and the misrepresentation must be an important factor (but not necessarily the sole factor) in inducing the party to enter into the contract.

Reliance is not justified if the innocent party knows the true facts or relies on obviously extravagant statements. **EXAMPLE 10.9** If a used-car dealer tells you, "This old Cadillac will get over sixty miles to the gallon," you normally would not be justified in relying on this statement. Suppose, however, that Merkel, a

6. *Restatement (Second) of Contracts,* Section 160.

7. *Selleck v. Cuenca,* Case No. GIN056909, North County of San Diego, California, decided September 9, 2009.

8. Pronounced sy-*en*-ter.

bank director, induces O'Connell, a co-director, to sign a statement that the bank has sufficient assets to meet its liabilities by telling O'Connell, "We have plenty of assets to satisfy our creditors." This statement is false. If O'Connell knows the true facts or, as a bank director, should know the true facts, he is not justified in relying on Merkel's statement. If O'Connell does not know the true facts, however, *and has no way of finding them out,* he may be justified in relying on the statement. •

Injury to the Innocent Party Most courts do not require a showing of injury when the action is to rescind the contract. These courts hold that because rescission returns the parties to the positions they held before the contract was made, a showing of injury to the innocent party is unnecessary.

To recover damages caused by fraud, however, proof of harm is universally required. The measure of damages is ordinarily equal to the property's value had it been delivered as represented, less the actual price paid for the property. In actions based on fraud, courts often award *punitive,* or *exemplary, damages,* which are granted to a plaintiff over and above the compensation for the actual loss. As pointed out in Chapter 4, punitive damages are based on the public-policy consideration of punishing the defendant or setting an example to deter similar wrongdoing by others.

Undue Influence

Undue influence arises from relationships in which one party can greatly influence another party, thus overcoming that party's free will. A contract entered into under excessive or undue influence lacks voluntary consent and is therefore voidable.[9]

There are various types of relationships in which one party may dominate another party, thus unfairly influencing him or her. Minors and elderly people, for example, are often under the influence of guardians (persons legally responsible for others). If a guardian induces a young or elderly ward (a person whom the guardian looks after) to enter into a contract that benefits the guardian, the guardian may have exerted undue influence. Undue influence can arise from a number of confidential or fiduciary relationships, including attorney-client, physician-patient, parent-child, husband-wife, and trustee-beneficiary.

The essential feature of undue influence is that the party being taken advantage of does not, in reality, exercise free will in entering into a contract. It is not enough that a person is elderly or suffers from some mental or physical impairment. There must be clear and convincing evidence that the person did not act out of her or his free will.

9. *Restatement (Second) of Contracts,* Section 177.

Duress

Consent to the terms of a contract is not voluntary if one of the parties is forced into the agreement. Forcing a party to enter into a contract because of the fear created by threats is referred to as **duress.**[10] In addition, blackmail or extortion to induce consent to a contract constitutes duress. Generally, for duress to occur, the threatened act must be wrongful or illegal. Threatening to exercise a legal right, such as the right to sue someone, ordinarily is not illegal and usually does not constitute duress.

Duress is both a defense to the enforcement of a contract and a ground for rescission of a contract. Therefore, a party who signs a contract under duress can choose to carry out the contract or to avoid the entire transaction. (The wronged party usually has this choice in cases in which consent is not voluntary.) Economic need generally is not sufficient to constitute duress, even when one party exacts a very high price for an item the other party needs. If the party exacting the price also creates the need, however, economic duress may be found.

The Statute of Frauds—Writing Requirement

Every state has a statute that stipulates what types of contracts must be in writing or be evidenced by a record. In this text, we refer to such a statute as the **Statute of Frauds.** The primary purpose of the statute is to ensure that, for certain types of contracts, there is reliable evidence of the contracts and their terms. These types of contracts are those historically deemed to be important or complex. Although the statutes vary slightly from state to state, the following types of contracts are normally required to be in writing or evidenced by a written (or electronic) memorandum:

1. Contracts involving interests in land.
2. Contracts that cannot by their terms be performed within one year from the date of formation.
3. Collateral contracts, such as promises to answer for the debt or duty of another.
4. Promises made in consideration of marriage.
5. Under the Uniform Commercial Code (UCC—see Chapter 13), contracts for the sale of goods priced at $500 or more.

Agreements or promises that fit into one or more of these categories are said to "fall under" or "fall within" the Statute of Frauds. (Certain exceptions are made to the Statute of Frauds, however, as you will read later in this section.)

The actual name of the Statute of Frauds is misleading because it does not apply to fraud. Rather, the statute denies

10. *Restatement (Second) of Contracts,* Sections 174 and 175.

enforceability to certain contracts that do not comply with its requirements.

Contracts Involving Interests in Land

Land is a form of *real property,* or real estate, which includes not only land but all physical objects that are permanently attached to the soil, such as buildings, plants, trees, and the soil itself. Under the Statute of Frauds, a contract involving an interest in land must be evidenced by a writing to be enforceable.[11] **EXAMPLE 10.10** If Carol contracts orally to sell Seaside Shelter to Axel but later decides not to sell, Axel cannot enforce the contract. Similarly, if Axel refuses to close the deal, Carol cannot force Axel to pay for the land by bringing a lawsuit. The Statute of Frauds is a *defense* to the enforcement of this type of oral contract. •

A contract for the sale of land ordinarily involves the entire interest in the real property, including buildings, growing crops, vegetation, minerals, timber, and anything else affixed to the land. Therefore, a *fixture* (personal property so affixed or so used as to become a part of the realty) is treated as real property.

The Statute of Frauds requires written contracts not just for the sale of land but also for the transfer of other interests in land, such as mortgages, easements, and leases. We will describe these other interests in Chapters 20 and 28.

The One-Year Rule

Contracts that cannot, *by their own terms,* be performed within one year *from the day after* the contract is formed must be in writing to be enforceable. Because disputes over such contracts are unlikely to occur until some time after the contracts are made, resolution of these disputes is difficult unless the contract terms have been put in writing. The one-year period begins to run *the day after the contract is made.*

EXAMPLE 10.11 Superior University forms a contract with Kimi San stating that San will teach three courses in history during the coming academic year (September 15 through June 15). If the contract is formed in March, it must be in writing to be enforceable—because it cannot be performed within one year. If the contract is not formed until July, however, it will not have to be in writing to be enforceable—because it can be performed within one year. • Exhibit 10–2 below illustrates the one-year rule.

Normally, the test for determining whether an oral contract is enforceable under the one-year rule of the Statute of Frauds is whether performance is *possible* within one year from the day after the date of contract formation—not whether the agreement is *likely* to be performed within one year. When performance of a contract is objectively impossible during the one-year period, the oral contract will be unenforceable.

EXAMPLE 10.12 Bankers Life orally contracts to lend $40,000 to Janet Lawrence "as long as Lawrence and Associates operates its financial consulting firm in Omaha, Nebraska." The contract does not fall within the Statute of Frauds—no writing is required—because Lawrence and Associates could go out of business in one year or less. In this event, the contract would be fully performed within one year. Similarly, an oral contract for lifetime employment does not fall within the Statute of Frauds. Because an employee who is hired "for life" can die within a year, the courts reason that the contract can be performed within one year.[12] •

11. In some states, the contract will be enforced if each party admits to the existence of the oral contract in court or admits to its existence during discovery before trial (see Chapter 2).

12. See, for example, *Gavengno v. TLT Construction Corp.,* 67 Mass.App.Ct. 1102, 851 N.E.2d 1133 (2006).

• ***Exhibit* 10–2 The One-Year Rule**

Under the Statute of Frauds, contracts that by their terms are impossible to perform within one year from the day after the date of contract formation must be in writing to be enforceable. Put another way, if it is at all possible to perform an oral contract within one year from the day after the contract is made, the contract will fall outside the Statute of Frauds and be enforceable.

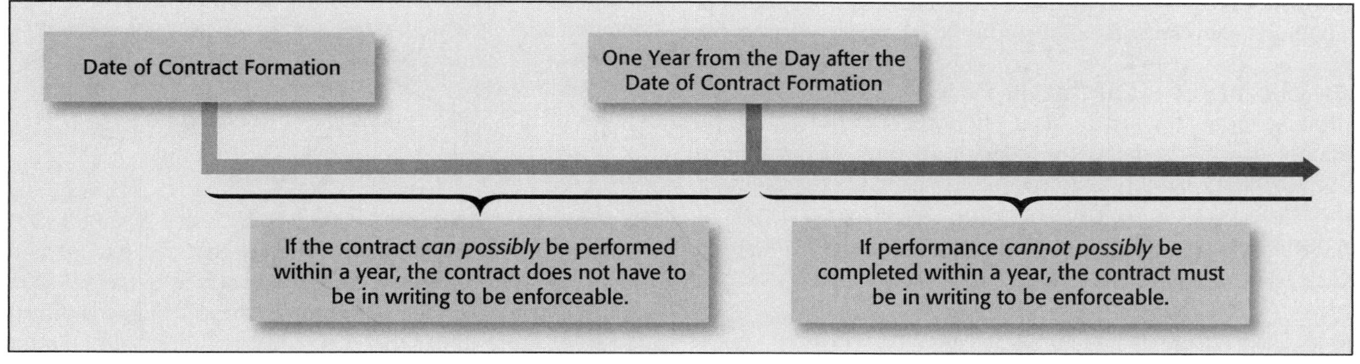
Date of Contract Formation
One Year from the Day after the Date of Contract Formation
If the contract *can possibly* be performed within a year, the contract does not have to be in writing to be enforceable.
If performance *cannot possibly* be completed within a year, the contract must be in writing to be enforceable.

Collateral Promises

A **collateral promise,** or secondary promise, is one that is ancillary (subsidiary) to a principal transaction or primary contractual relationship. In other words, a collateral promise is one made by a third party to assume the debts or obligations of a primary party to a contract if that party does not perform. Any collateral promise of this nature falls under the Statute of Frauds and therefore must be in writing to be enforceable. To understand this concept, it is important to distinguish between primary and secondary promises and obligations.

PRIMARY VERSUS SECONDARY OBLIGATIONS A contract in which a party assumes a primary obligation normally does not need to be in writing to be enforceable. **EXAMPLE 10.13** Kenneth orally contracts with Joanne's Floral Boutique to send his mother a dozen roses for Mother's Day. Kenneth promises to pay the boutique when he receives the bill for the flowers. Kenneth is a direct party to this contract and has incurred a *primary* obligation under the contract. Because he is a party to the contract and has a primary obligation to Joanne's Floral Boutique, this contract does not fall under the Statute of Frauds and does not have to be in writing to be enforceable. If Kenneth fails to pay and the florist sues him for payment, Kenneth cannot raise the Statute of Frauds as a defense. He cannot claim that the contract is unenforceable because it was not in writing. •

In contrast, a contract in which a party assumes a secondary obligation does have to be in writing to be enforceable. **EXAMPLE 10.14** Kenneth's mother borrows $10,000 from the Medford Trust Company on a promissory note payable in six months. Kenneth promises the bank officer handling the loan that he will pay the $10,000 *if his mother does not pay the loan on time.* Kenneth, in this situation, becomes what is known as a *guarantor* on the loan. He is guaranteeing to the bank (the creditor) that he will pay the loan if his mother fails to do so. This kind of collateral promise, in which the guarantor states that he or she will become responsible only if the primary party does not perform, must be in writing to be enforceable. • We will return to the concept of guaranty and the distinction between primary and secondary obligations in Chapter 19, in the context of creditors' rights.

AN EXCEPTION—THE "MAIN PURPOSE" RULE An oral promise to answer for the debt of another is covered by the Statute of Frauds *unless* the guarantor's purpose in accepting secondary liability is to secure a personal benefit. Under the "main purpose" rule, this type of contract need not be in writing.[13] The assumption is that a court can infer from the circumstances of a case whether a "leading objective" of the promisor was to secure a personal benefit.

EXAMPLE 10.15 Carrie Braswell contracts with Custom Manufacturing Company to have some machines custom made for her factory. She promises Newform Supply, Custom's supplier, that if Newform continues to deliver the materials to Custom for the production of the custom-made machines, she will guarantee payment. This promise need not be in writing, even though the effect may be to pay the debt of another, because Braswell's main purpose is to secure a benefit for herself. •

Another typical application of the main purpose doctrine occurs when one creditor guarantees the debtor's debt to another creditor to forestall litigation. This allows the debtor to remain in business long enough to generate profits sufficient to pay *both* creditors. In this situation, the guaranty does not need to be in writing to be enforceable.

Promises Made in Consideration of Marriage

A unilateral promise to make a monetary payment or to give property in consideration of marriage must be in writing. **EXAMPLE 10.16** Baumann promises to pay Joe Villard $10,000 if Villard marries Baumann's daughter. Because the promise is in consideration of marriage, it must be in writing to be enforceable. • The same rule applies to **prenuptial agreements**—agreements made before marriage (also called *antenuptial agreements*) that define each partner's ownership rights in the other partner's property. A prospective wife or husband may wish to limit the amount the prospective spouse can obtain if the marriage ends in divorce. Prenuptial agreements made in consideration of marriage must be in writing to be enforceable.

Generally, courts tend to give more credence to prenuptial agreements that are accompanied by consideration. **EXAMPLE 10.17** Maureen, who is not wealthy, marries Kaiser, who has a net worth of $300 million. Kaiser has several children, and he wants them to receive most of his wealth on his death. Prior to their marriage, Maureen and Kaiser draft and sign a prenuptial agreement in which Kaiser promises to give Maureen $100,000 per year for the rest of her life if they divorce. As consideration for consenting to this amount, Kaiser offers Maureen $1 million. If Maureen consents to the agreement and accepts the $1 million, very likely a court would hold that this prenuptial agreement is valid, should it ever be contested. •

Contracts for the Sale of Goods

The Uniform Commercial Code (UCC—see Chapter 13) includes Statute of Frauds provisions that require written evidence or an electronic record of a contract. Section 2–201 requires a writing or memorandum for the sale of goods priced at $500 or more under the UCC (this low threshold amount

13. *Restatement (Second) of Contracts,* Section 116.

may be increased in the future). A writing that will satisfy the UCC requirement need only state the quantity term; other terms agreed on need not be stated "accurately" in the writing, as long as they adequately reflect both parties' intentions.

The contract will not be enforceable, however, for any quantity greater than that set forth in the writing. In addition, the writing must have been signed by the person to be charged—that is, by the person who refuses to perform or the one being sued. Beyond these two requirements, the writing need not designate the buyer or the seller, the terms of payment, or the price.

Exceptions to the Statute of Frauds

Exceptions to the applicability of the Statute of Frauds are made in certain situations. We describe those situations here.

PARTIAL PERFORMANCE In cases involving oral contracts for the transfer of interests in land, if the purchaser has paid part of the price, taken possession, and made valuable improvements to the property, and if the parties cannot be returned to their positions prior to the contract, a court may grant *specific performance* (performance of the contract according to its precise terms). Whether a court will enforce an oral contract for an interest in land when partial performance has taken place is usually determined by the degree of injury that would be suffered if the court chose *not* to enforce the oral contract. In some states, mere reliance on certain types of oral contracts is enough to remove them from the Statute of Frauds. Under the UCC, an oral contract for goods priced at $500 or more is enforceable to the extent that a seller accepts payment or a buyer accepts delivery of the goods.[14]

ADMISSIONS In some states, if a party against whom enforcement of an oral contract is sought admits in pleadings, testimony, or otherwise in court proceedings that a contract for sale was made, the contract will be enforceable.[15] A contract subject to the UCC will be enforceable, but only to the extent of the quantity admitted.[16] **EXAMPLE 10.18** The president of Ashley Corporation admits under oath that an oral agreement was made with Com Best to pay $10,000 for certain business equipment. In this situation, a court will enforce the agreement only to the extent admitted (the $10,000), even if Com Best claims that the agreement involved $20,000 of equipment. •

PROMISSORY ESTOPPEL In some states, an oral contract that would otherwise be unenforceable under the Statute of Frauds may be enforced under the doctrine of promissory estoppel, or detrimental reliance, discussed in Chapter 9. Section 139 of the *Restatement (Second) of Contracts* provides that an oral promise can be enforceable, notwithstanding the Statute of Frauds, if the promisee has justifiably relied on it to her or his detriment. For the contract to be enforceable, the reliance must have been foreseeable to the person making the promise, and enforcing the promise must be the only way to avoid injustice.

SPECIAL EXCEPTIONS UNDER THE UCC Special exceptions to the applicability of the Statute of Frauds exist for sales contracts. Oral contracts for customized goods may be enforced in certain circumstances. Another exception has to do with oral contracts *between merchants* that have been confirmed in writing. We will examine these exceptions in more detail in Chapter 13. Exhibit 10–3 on the following page graphically summarizes the types of contracts that fall under the Statute of Frauds and the various exceptions that apply.

The Sufficiency of the Writing

A written contract will satisfy the writing requirement of the Statute of Frauds. A *written memorandum* (written or electronic evidence of the oral contract) signed by the party against whom enforcement is sought will also satisfy the writing requirement. The signature need not be placed at the end of the document but can be anywhere in the writing. It can even be initials rather than the full name. As discussed in Chapter 8, in today's business world there are many ways to create signatures electronically, and electronic signatures generally satisfy the Statute of Frauds.

What Constitutes a Writing?

A writing can consist of any confirmation, invoice, sales slip, check, fax, or e-mail—or such items in combination. The written contract need not consist of a single document to constitute an enforceable contract. One document may incorporate another document by expressly referring to it. Several documents may form a single contract if they are physically attached—such as by staple, paper clip, or glue—or even if they are only placed in the same envelope.

EXAMPLE 10.19 Simpson orally agrees to sell some land next to a shopping mall to Terro Properties. Simpson gives Terro an unsigned memo that contains a legal description of the property, and Terro gives Simpson an unsigned first draft of their contract. Simpson sends Terro a signed letter that refers to the memo and to the first and final drafts of the contract. Terro sends Simpson an unsigned copy of the final draft of the contract with a signed check stapled to it. Together, the documents can constitute a writing sufficient to satisfy the Statute of Frauds and bind both parties to the terms of the contract as evidenced by the writings. •

14. UCC 2–201(3)(c).
15. *Restatement (Second) of Contracts*, Section 133.
16. UCC 2–201(3)(b).

• *Exhibit* 10–3 Contracts Subject to the Statute of Frauds

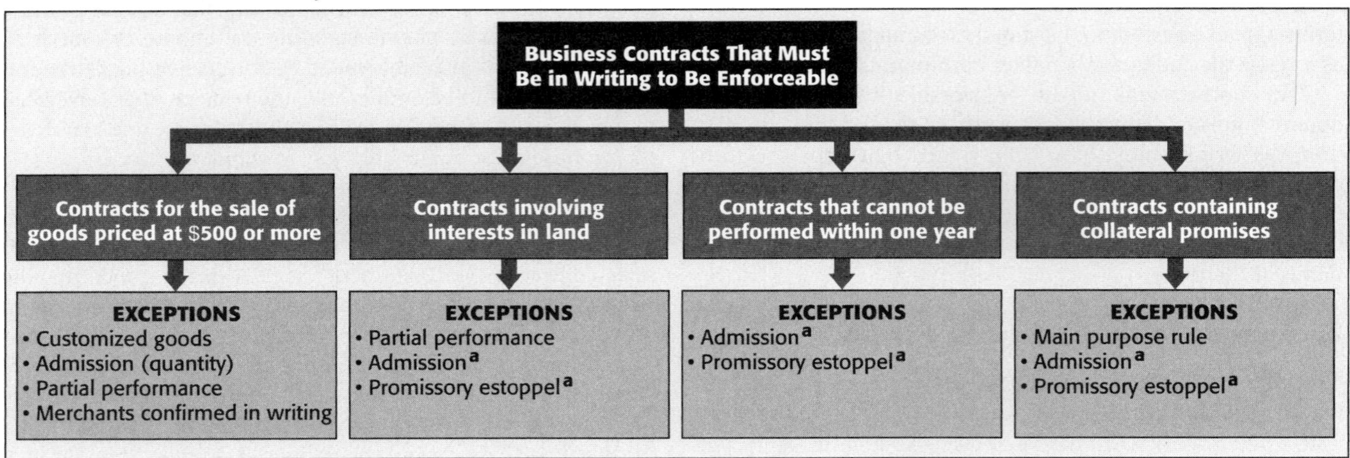

a. Some states follow Section 133 (on admissions) and Section 139 (on promissory estoppel) of the *Restatement (Second) of Contracts*.

What Must Be Contained in the Writing?

A memorandum or note evidencing the oral contract need only contain the essential terms of the contract, not every term. There must, of course, also be some indication that the parties voluntarily agreed to the terms. A faxed memo of the terms of an agreement could be sufficient if it showed that there was a meeting of the minds and that the faxed terms were not just part of the preliminary negotiations.[17] Under the UCC, in regard to the sale of goods, the writing need only state the quantity and be signed by the party against whom enforcement is sought.

Because only the party against whom enforcement is sought must have signed the writing, a contract may be enforceable by one of its parties but not by the other. **EXAMPLE 10.20** Rock orally agrees to buy Betty Devlin's lake house and lot for $350,000. Devlin writes Rock a letter confirming the sale by identifying the parties and the essential terms of the sales contract—price, method of payment, and legal address—and signs the letter. Devlin has made a written memorandum of the oral land contract. Because she has signed the letter, she normally can be held to the oral contract by Rock. Devlin cannot enforce the agreement against Rock, however. Because he has not signed or entered into a written contract or memorandum, Rock can plead the Statute of Frauds as a defense. •

In the following case, the court was presented with a written document that the plaintiff sought to enforce. The writing, however, was missing at least one essential element to satisfy the Statute of Frauds—the signatures of the parties against whom the enforcement was being sought.

17. See, for example, *Coca-Cola Co. v. Babyback's International, Inc.*, 841 N.E.2d 557 (Ind.App. 2006).

Case 10.2 Beneficial Homeowner Service Corp. v. Steele

Supreme Court of New York, Suffolk County, 30 Misc.3d 1208(A) (2011).

FACTS Beneficial Homeowner Service Corporation filed a suit in a New York state court against Stephen and Susan Steele to foreclose on a mortgage. (Foreclosure is a process that allows a lender to repossess and sell the property that secures a loan.) A mortgage is a written instrument that gives a creditor an interest in the property that the debtor provides as security for the payment of the loan (see Chapter 20). In this case, Beneficial (the lender) claimed that the loan was secured by real property in East Hampton, New York. Beneficial sought $91,614.34 in unpaid principal, plus interest. The lender, based on its assertion that both Stephen and Susan Steele had signed the loan agreement, filed a motion for summary judgment. Among the documents that Beneficial filed with the court was a copy of the loan agreement. There were two problems–the agreement identified Stephen Steele as the sole obligor (the party owing the obligation), and it had not been signed.

ISSUE Does the Statute of Frauds require the borrowers' signatures on a contract that gives the lender an interest in real property, such as in a mortgage loan?

Case 10.2–Continued

DECISION Yes. The court denied Beneficial's motion for summary judgment. Because a mortgage involves the transfer of an interest in real property, the loan agreement to which it relates must be in writing to satisfy the Statute of Frauds. To be enforceable, the writing must be signed by the parties to be charged.

REASON Beneficial was seeking to foreclose on a mortgage that purportedly constituted security for a certain loan agreement. Beneficial sought to enforce the agreement against two parties–Stephen and Susan Steele–who had not signed it. In fact, Susan was not even mentioned in the agreement as a party to it. The lender's assertions about the document were "painfully obvious misstatements of facts" and meant that the agreement was most likely unenforceable. The court ordered a hearing to determine whether Beneficial had acted in good faith.

WHAT IF THE FACTS WERE DIFFERENT? *Suppose that at the hearing, the Steeles admitted they had an obligation to pay the outstanding loan amount. Would the result have been different? Explain.*

The Parol Evidence Rule

Sometimes, a written contract does not include—or contradicts—an oral understanding reached by the parties before or at the time of contracting. For instance, a landlord might tell a person who agrees to rent an apartment that she or he can have a cat, whereas the lease contract clearly states that no pets are allowed. In determining the outcome of such disputes, the courts look to a common law rule governing the admissibility in court of oral evidence, or *parol evidence.*

Under the **parol evidence rule,** if a court finds that a written contract represents the complete and final statement of the parties' agreement, then it will not allow either party to present parol evidence (testimony or other evidence of communications between the parties that are not contained in the contract itself). In other words, a party cannot introduce in court evidence of the parties' prior negotiations, prior agreements, or contemporaneous oral agreements if that evidence contradicts or varies the terms of the parties' written contract.[18]

Exceptions to the Parol Evidence Rule

Because of the rigidity of the parol evidence rule, courts make several exceptions. These exceptions are discussed next.

CONTRACTS SUBSEQUENTLY MODIFIED Evidence of a *subsequent modification* of a written contract can be introduced in court. Oral modifications may not be enforceable, however, if they come under the Statute of Frauds—for example, if they increase the price of the goods for sale to $500 or more or increase the term for performance to more than one year. Also, oral modifications will not be enforceable if the original contract provides that any modification must be in writing.[19]

VOIDABLE OR VOID CONTRACTS Oral evidence can be introduced in all cases to show that the contract was voidable or void (for example, induced by mistake, fraud, or misrepresentation). In this situation, if deception led one of the parties to agree to the terms of a written contract, oral evidence indicating fraud should not be excluded. Courts frown on bad faith and are quick to allow the introduction at trial of parol evidence when it establishes fraud.

CONTRACTS CONTAINING AMBIGUOUS TERMS When the terms of a written contract are ambiguous, evidence is admissible to show the meaning of the terms.

INCOMPLETE CONTRACTS Evidence is admissible when the written contract is incomplete in that it lacks one or more of the essential terms. The courts allow evidence to "fill in the gaps" in the contract.

PRIOR DEALING, COURSE OF PERFORMANCE, OR USAGE OF TRADE Under the UCC, evidence can be introduced to explain or supplement a written contract by showing a prior dealing, course of performance, or usage of trade.[20] This is because when buyers and sellers deal with each other over extended periods of time, certain customary practices develop. These practices are often overlooked in the writing of the contract, so courts allow the introduction of evidence to show how the parties have acted in the past.

Usage of trade—practices and customs generally followed in a particular industry—can also shed light on the meaning of certain contract provisions, and thus evidence of trade usage may be admissible. We will discuss these terms in further detail in Chapter 13, in the context of sales contracts.

CONTRACTS SUBJECT TO AN ORALLY AGREED-ON CONDITION PRECEDENT As you will read in Chapter 11, sometimes the parties agree that a condition must be fulfilled before a party is required to perform the contract. This is called a *condition precedent.* If the parties have orally agreed on a condition precedent and the condition does not conflict with the terms of a written agreement, then a court may allow parol evidence to prove the oral condition. The parol

18. *Restatement (Second) of Contracts,* Section 213.

19. UCC 2–209(2), (3).

20. UCC 1–205, 2–202.

evidence rule does not apply here because the existence of the entire written contract is subject to an orally agreed-on condition. Proof of the condition does not alter or modify the written terms but affects the *enforceability* of the written contract.

EXAMPLE 10.21 A city leases property for an airport from a well-established helicopter business. The lease is renewable every five years. During the second five-year lease, a dispute arises, and the parties go to mediation. They enter into a settlement memorandum under which they agree to amend the lease agreement subject to the approval of the city council. The city amends the lease, but the helicopter business refuses to sign it, contending that the council has not given its approval. In this situation, the council's approval is a condition precedent to the formation of the settlement memorandum contract. Therefore, the parol evidence rule does not apply, and oral evidence is admissible to show that no agreement exists as to the terms of the settlement. •

CONTRACTS WITH AN OBVIOUS CLERICAL ERROR When an obvious or gross clerical (or typographic) error exists that clearly would not represent the agreement of the parties, parol evidence is admissible to correct the error. **EXAMPLE 10.22** Davis agrees to lease 1,000 square feet of office space from Stone Enterprises at the current monthly rate of $3 per square foot. The signed written lease provides for a monthly lease payment of $300 rather than the $3,000 agreed to by the parties. Because the error is obvious, Stone Enterprises would be allowed to admit parol evidence to correct the mistake. •

In the following case, the court addressed the issue of whether parol evidence could be admitted to clarify the parties' intent in a purchase and sale of property.

Case 10.3 Watkins v. Schexnider

Court of Appeal of Louisiana, Third Circuit, 31 So.3d 609 (2010).

FACTS In 2000, Pamela Watkins purchased a home from Sandra Schexnider. The home purchase agreement stated that Watkins would pay off the balance of the mortgage in monthly payments until the note was paid in full. "Then the house will be hers." The agreement also stipulated that Watkins would pay for insurance on the property. Watkins regularly paid the note and insurance. The home was destroyed following Hurricane Rita in 2005, and the mortgage was satisfied by the insurance proceeds. Watkins claimed that she owned the land, but Schexnider refused to transfer title to her. Schexnider asserted that she had sold only the house to Watkins, not the land. Watkins filed a petition in a Louisiana state court for specific performance of the agreement.[a] The trial court denied her claim for specific performance, concluding that the "clear wording of the contract" indicated that Watkins was purchasing only the house, not the property. Because the contract was clear on its face, the court refused to admit parol evidence to the contrary. Watkins appealed.

ISSUE Were the terms of the contract unclear as to whether Watkins would receive title to the house only or to the house and the land on which it sits?

a. *Specific performance* is an equitable remedy that requires a party who has breached (broken) a contract to perform the specific terms promised in the contract—see Chapter 12.

DECISION Yes. The Court of Appeal of Louisiana held that parol evidence should have been admitted to clarify the meaning of the contract. In light of the parol evidence, the court concluded that (1) the parties intended to transfer ownership of both the house and the land, and (2) it ordered that title to the property be transferred to Watkins.

REASON The court reasoned that parol evidence is allowed "in many instances in order to discern the intention of the parties in contracts to sell real estate." Here, an ambiguity arose because Schexnider claimed that the contract conveyed only the house and yet failed to put any such provision in writing. Rarely does a party intend to sell a house and not the land on which it sits. Therefore, a person who intends to sell only the house normally will indicate this intention in the contract. Further, Schexnider, when showing the house, had taken Watkins around the property and had pointed out the property lines. A witness, Marla Raffield (Watkins's daughter-in-law), testified that she had been present when the property boundaries were shown. The court concluded that "the land was included as part of the sale."

FOR CRITICAL ANALYSIS—Ethical Consideration *The parol evidence rule is centuries old and is an important rule of contract law. Why should the courts allow exceptions to this rule?*

Integrated Contracts

The determination of whether parol evidence will be allowed basically depends on whether the written contract is intended to be a complete and final statement of the terms of the agreement. If it is so intended, it is referred to as an **integrated contract**, and extraneous evidence (evidence from outside the contract) is excluded.

An integrated contract can be either completely or partially integrated. If it contains all of the terms of the parties' agreement, then it is completely integrated. If it contains

• ***Exhibit* 10–4 The Parol Evidence Rule**

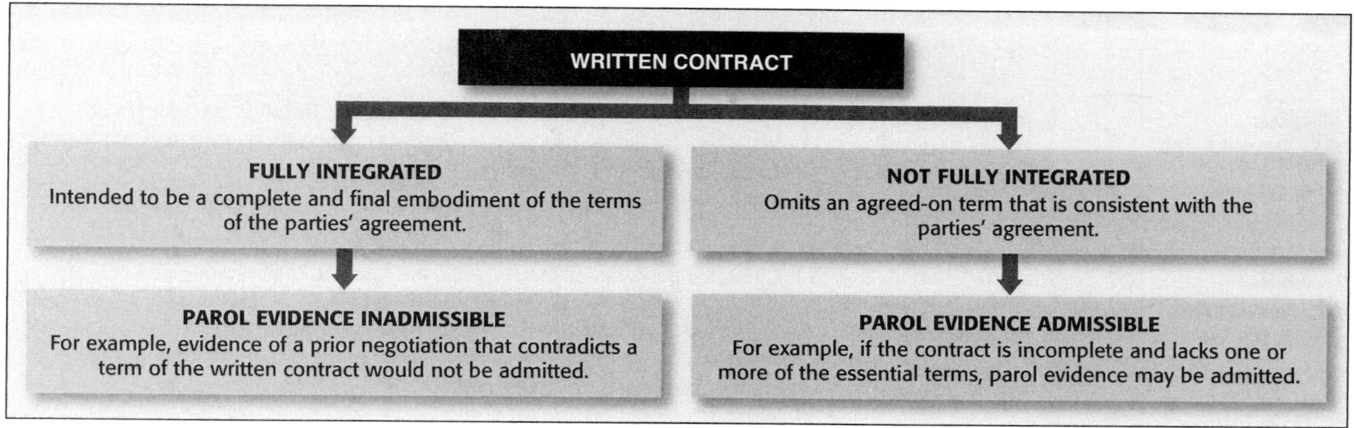

only some of the terms that the parties agreed on and not others, it is partially integrated. If the contract is only partially integrated, evidence of consistent additional terms is admissible to supplement the written agreement.[21] Note that for both completely and partially integrated contracts, courts exclude any evidence that *contradicts* the writing and allow parol evidence only to add to the terms of a partially integrated contract. Exhibit 10–4 above illustrates the relationship between integrated contracts and the parol evidence rule.

WRITTEN CONTRACT
FULLY INTEGRATED
Intended to be a complete and final embodiment of the terms of the parties' agreement.
NOT FULLY INTEGRATED
Omits an agreed-on term that is consistent with the parties' agreement.
PAROL EVIDENCE INADMISSIBLE
For example, evidence of a prior negotiation that contradicts a term of the written contract would not be admitted.
PAROL EVIDENCE ADMISSIBLE
For example, if the contract is incomplete and lacks one or more of the essential terms, parol evidence may be admitted.

21. *Restatement (Second) of Contracts,* Section 216.

Reviewing . . . Defenses to Contract Enforceability

Charter Golf, Inc., manufactures and sells golf apparel and supplies. Ken Odin had worked as a Charter sales representative for six months when he was offered a position with a competing firm. Charter's president, Jerry Montieth, offered Odin a 10 percent commission "for the rest of his life" if Ken would turn down the offer and stay on with Charter. He also promised that Odin would not be fired unless he was dishonest. Odin turned down the competitor's offer and stayed with Charter. Three years later, Charter fired Odin for no reason. Odin sued, alleging breach of contract. Using the information presented in the chapter, answer the following questions.

1 Would a court likely decide that Montieth's employment contract with Odin falls within the Statute of Frauds? Why or why not?
2 Assume that the court does find that the contract falls within the Statute of Frauds and that the state in which the court sits recognizes every exception to the Statute of Frauds discussed in the chapter. What exception provides Odin with the best chance of enforcing the oral contract in this situation?
3 Now suppose that Montieth had taken out a pencil, written "10 percent for life" on the back of a register receipt, and handed it to Odin. Would this satisfy the Statute of Frauds? Why or why not?
4 Assume that Odin had signed a written employment contract at the time he was hired by Charter, but it was not completely integrated. Would a court allow Odin to present parol evidence of Montieth's subsequent promises? Explain.

Terms and Concepts

bilateral mistake 179
collateral promise 184
duress 182
integrated contract 188
material fact 179
parol evidence rule 187
prenuptial agreement 184
***scienter* 181**
Statute of Frauds 182
unilateral mistake 179
voluntary consent 178

Chapter Summary: Defenses to Contract Enforceability

VOLUNTARY CONSENT	
Mistakes (See pages 178–180.)	1. *Unilateral*—Generally, the mistaken party is bound by the contract *unless* (a) the other party knows or should have known of the mistake or (b) the mistake is an inadvertent mathematical error—such as an error in addition or subtraction—committed without gross negligence. 2. *Bilateral (mutual)*—When both parties are mistaken about the same material fact, such as identity, either party can avoid the contract.
Fraudulent Misrepresentation (See pages 180–182.)	When fraud occurs, usually the innocent party can enforce or avoid the contract. The following elements are necessary to establish fraud: 1. A misrepresentation of a material fact must occur. 2. There must be an intent to deceive. 3. The innocent party must justifiably rely on the misrepresentation.
Undue Influence (See page 182.)	Undue influence arises from special relationships, such as fiduciary or confidential relationships, in which one party's free will has been overcome by the undue influence exerted by the other party. Usually, the contract is voidable.
Duress (See page 182.)	Duress is the tactic of forcing a party to enter a contract under the fear of a threat—for example, the threat of violence or serious economic loss. The party forced to enter the contract can rescind the contract.
FORM	
The Statute of Frauds—Writing Requirement (See pages 182–185.)	1. *Applicability*—The following types of contracts fall under the Statute of Frauds and must be in writing to be enforceable: a. Contracts involving interests in land—The statute applies to any contract for an interest in realty, such as a sale, a lease, or a mortgage. b. Contracts that cannot by their terms be performed within one year—The statute applies only to contracts that are objectively impossible to perform fully within one year from (the day after) the contract's formation. c. Collateral promises—The statute applies only to express contracts made between the guarantor and the creditor whose terms make the guarantor secondarily liable. *Exception:* the "main purpose" rule. d. Promises made in consideration of marriage—The statute applies to promises to make a monetary payment or give property in consideration of a promise to marry and to prenuptial agreements made in consideration of marriage. e. Contracts for the sale of goods priced at $500 or more—Under the Statute of Frauds provision in Section 2–201 of the Uniform Commercial Code. 2. *Exceptions*—Partial performance, admissions, and promissory estoppel.
The Sufficiency of the Writing (See pages 185–187.)	To constitute an enforceable contract under the Statute of Frauds, a writing must be signed by the party against whom enforcement is sought, name the parties, identify the subject matter, and state with reasonable certainty the essential terms of the contract. Under the UCC, a contract for a sale of goods is not enforceable beyond the quantity of goods shown in the contract.
The Parol Evidence Rule (See pages 187–189.)	The parol evidence rule prohibits the introduction at trial of evidence of the parties' prior negotiations, prior agreements, or contemporaneous oral agreements that contradicts or varies the terms of the parties' written contract. The written contract is assumed to be the complete embodiment of the parties' agreement. Exceptions are made in certain circumstances.

ExamPrep

ISSUE SPOTTERS

—Check your answers to these questions against the answers provided in Appendix G.

1 Elle, an accountant, certifies several audit reports to Flite Corporation, Elle's client, knowing that Flite intends to use the reports to obtain loans from Good Credit Company (GCC). Elle believes that the reports are true and does not

intend to deceive GCC, but does not check the reports before certifying them. Can Elle be held liable to GCC? Why or why not?

2 My-T Quality Goods, Inc., and Nu! Sales Corporation orally agree to a deal. My-T writes up the essential terms on company letterhead stationery and files the memo in My-T's office. If Nu! Sales later refuses to complete the transaction, is this memo a sufficient writing to enforce the contract against it? Explain your answer.

BEFORE THE TEST

Go to **www.cengagebrain.com**, enter the ISBN 9781111530624, and click on "Find" to locate this textbook's Web site. Then, click on "Access Now" under "Study Tools," and select Chapter 10 at the top. There, you will find an Interactive Quiz that you can take to assess your mastery of the concepts in this chapter, as well as Flashcards and a Glossary of important terms.

For Review

1. In what types of situations might voluntary consent to a contract's terms be lacking?
2. What is the difference between a mistake of value or quality and a mistake of fact?
3. What are the elements of fraudulent misrepresentation?
4. What contracts must be in writing to be enforceable?
5. What is parol evidence? When is it admissible to clarify the terms of a written contract?

Questions and Case Problems

10–1 Voluntary Consent. Jerome is an elderly man who lives with his nephew, Philip. Jerome is totally dependent on Philip's support. Philip tells Jerome that unless Jerome transfers a tract of land he owns to Philip for a price 30 percent below market value, Philip will no longer support and take care of him. Jerome enters into the contract. Discuss fully whether Jerome can set aside this contract.

10–2 The One-Year Rule. On May 1, by telephone, Yu offers to hire Benson to perform personal services. On May 5, Benson returns Yu's call and accepts the offer. Discuss fully whether this contract falls under the Statute of Frauds in the following circumstances:

1. The contract calls for Benson to be employed for one year, with the right to begin performance immediately.
2. The contract calls for Benson to be employed for nine months, with performance of services to begin on September 1.
3. The contract calls for Benson to submit a written research report, with a deadline of two years for submission.

10–3 Collateral Promises. Jeremy took his mother on a special holiday to Mountain Air Resort. Jeremy was a frequent patron of the resort and was well known by its manager. The resort required each of its patrons to make a large deposit to ensure payment of the room rental. Jeremy asked the manager to waive the requirement for his mother and told the manager that if his mother for any reason failed to pay the resort for her stay there, he would cover the bill. Relying on Jeremy's promise, the manager waived the deposit requirement for Jeremy's mother. After she returned home from her holiday, Jeremy's mother refused to pay the resort bill. The resort manager tried to collect the sum from Jeremy, but Jeremy also refused to pay, stating that his promise was not enforceable under the Statute of Frauds. Is Jeremy correct? Explain.

10–4 Fraudulent Misrepresentation. Ricky and Sherry Wilcox hired Esprit Log and Timber Frame Homes to build a log house, which the Wilcoxes intended to sell. They paid Esprit \$125,260 for materials and services. They eventually sold the home for \$1,620,000 but sued Esprit due to construction delays. The logs were supposed to arrive at the construction site precut and predrilled, but that did not happen. So it took five extra months to build the house while the logs were cut and drilled one by one. The Wilcoxes claimed that the interest they paid on a loan for the extra construction time cost them about \$200,000. The jury agreed and awarded them that much in damages, plus \$250,000 in punitive damages and \$20,000 in attorneys' fees. Esprit appealed, claiming that the evidence did not support the verdict because the Wilcoxes had sold the house for a good price. Is Esprit's argument credible? Explain your answer. [*Esprit Log and Timber Frame Homes, Inc. v. Wilcox,* 302 Ga.App. 550, 691 S.E.2d 344 (2010)]

10–5 Case Problem with Sample Answer When Hurricane Katrina hit the Gulf Coast in 2005, Evangel Temple Assembly of God in Wichita Falls, Texas, contacted Wood Care Centers, Inc., about leasing a facility it owned to house evacuees from the hurricane. Evangel and Wood Care reached an agreement and signed a twenty-year lease at \$10,997 per month. One clause said that Evangel could terminate the lease at any time by giving Wood Care notice and paying 10 percent of the balance remaining on the lease. Another clause stated that if the facility was not given a property tax exemption, Evangel had the option to terminate the lease. Nine months later, the last of the evacuees left the facility, and Evangel notified Wood Care that it would end the lease. Wood Care demanded the 10 percent payment. Evangel claimed that it did not need to make the payment because if the facility converted back to a "non-church" use, it would lose its tax-exempt status and Evangel could simply terminate the lease. Evangel's pastor testified that the parties understood that this would be the scenario at the time the lease was signed. The trial court held that Evangel owed nothing. Wood Care appealed, contending that the trial court improperly allowed parol evidence to interpret the contract. Was the trial court's acceptance of parol evidence correct? Why or why not? [*Wood Care Centers, Inc. v. Evangel Temple Assembly of God of Wichita Falls,* 307 S.W.3d 816 (Tex.App.—Fort Worth 2010)]

—For a sample answer to Problem 10–5, go to Appendix F at the end of this text.

10–6 Sufficiency of the Writing. Newmark & Co. Real Estate, Inc., contacted 2615 East 17 Street Realty, LLC (the landlord), in New York City to negotiate a lease of real property on behalf of an unnamed client. When the parties appeared close to agreeing to the terms of the lease, Newmark e-mailed the landlord a separate agreement that set out the terms for the payment of Newmark's commission for brokering the deal. The agreement set forth the amount of commission that the parties had discussed. The landlord e-mailed the agreement back, but requested to pay the commission in installments. Newmark consented, revised the agreement, and e-mailed a final copy to the landlord. The landlord did not object further, but neither did it pay the commission. Newmark filed a suit in a New York state court against the landlord to collect. Can an e-mail constitute a writing for purposes of the Statute of Frauds? Does the e-mail in this case qualify? Explain. [*Newmark & Co. Real Estate, Inc. v. 2615 East 17 Street Realty, LLC,* 80 A.D.3d 476, 914 N.Y.S.2d 162 (1 Dept. 2011)]

10–7 Fraudulent Misrepresentation. Charter One Bank acquired a fifteen-story commercial building in Cleveland, Ohio, through a foreclosure proceeding. Kaczmar Architects, Inc., inspected the building and recommended changes to the sprinklers, fire standpipe, fire hose cabinet, and fire pump system. No action was taken. Charter One hired Ehle Morrison Group, Ltd. (EMG), to sell the building. Tenants complained to EMG about the taste and odor of the water. A fire inspector told EMG that the fire standpipe was cut and capped, that there was no fire pump, that the drinking-water and fire-suppression systems were linked, and that the water gauge on the top floor showed the pressure was not sufficient to run the sprinklers on that floor. EMG sold the building to Northpoint Properties, Inc., without disclosing Kaczmar's recommendations or the fire inspector's report. Northpoint spent $280,000 to repair the water and fire-suppression systems and then filed a suit in an Ohio state court against Charter One, alleging fraud. Is the seller liable for not disclosing the building's defects? Discuss. [*Northpoint Properties, Inc. v. Charter One Bank,* __ Ohio App.3d __, __ N.E.2d __ (8 Dist. 2011)]

10–8 A Question of Ethics *On behalf of BRJM, LLC, Nicolas Kepple offered Howard Engelsen $210,000 for a parcel of land known as lot five on the north side of Barnes Road in Stonington, Connecticut. Engelsen's company, Output Systems, Inc., owned the land. Engelsen had the lot surveyed and obtained an appraisal. The appraiser valued the property at $277,000, after determining that it was three acres and thus could not be subdivided because it did not meet the town's minimum legal requirement of 3.7 acres for subdivision. Engelsen responded to Kepple's offer with a counteroffer of $230,000, which Kepple accepted. On May 3, 2002, the parties signed a contract. When Engelsen refused to go through with the deal, BRJM filed a suit in a Connecticut state court against Output, seeking specific performance and other relief. The defendant asserted the defense of mutual mistake on at least two grounds. [*BRJM, LLC v. Output Systems, Inc., *100 Conn.App. 143, 917 A.2d 605 (2007)]*

1. In the counteroffer, Engelsen asked Kepple to remove from their contract a clause requiring written confirmation of the availability of a "free split," which meant that the property could be subdivided without the town's prior approval. Kepple agreed. After signing the contract, Kepple learned that the property was *not* entitled to a free split. Would this circumstance qualify as a mistake on which the *defendant* could avoid the contract? Why or why not?
2. After signing the contract, Engelsen obtained a second appraisal that established the size of lot five as 3.71 acres, which meant that it could be subdivided, and valued the property at $490,000. Can the defendant avoid the contract on the basis of a mistake in the first appraisal? Explain.

10–9 Critical Thinking Legal Question Describe the types of individuals who might be capable of exerting undue influence on others.

10–10 Video Question To watch this chapter's video, *Mistake,* go to **www.cengagebrain.com**. Register the access code that came with your new book or log in to your existing account. Select the link for the "Business Law Digital Video Library Online Access" or "Business Law CourseMate." Click on "Complete Video List," view Video 18, and then answer the following questions:

1. What kind of mistake is involved in the dispute shown in the video (bilateral or unilateral, mistake of fact or mistake of value)?
2. According to the chapter, in what two situations would the supermarket be able to rescind a contract to sell peppers to Melnick at the incorrectly advertised price?
3. Does it matter if the price that was advertised was a reasonable price for the peppers? Why or why not?

Chapter 11

Third Party Rights and Discharge

Learning Objectives

After reading this chapter, you should be able to answer the following questions:

1. What is the difference between an assignment and a delegation?
2. What rights can be assigned despite a contract clause expressly prohibiting assignment?
3. What factors indicate that a third party beneficiary is an intended beneficiary?
4. How are most contracts discharged?
5. What is a contractual condition, and how might a condition affect contractual obligations?

The Learning Objectives above are designed to help improve your understanding of the chapter.

(AP Photo/Carlos Osorio)

Because a contract is a private agreement between the parties who have entered into that contract, it is fitting that these parties alone should have rights and liabilities under the contract. This concept is referred to as **privity of contract,** and it establishes the basic principle that third parties have no rights in contracts to which they are not parties.

You may be convinced by now that for every rule of contract law, there is an exception. As times change, so must the laws. When justice cannot be served by adherence to a rule of law, exceptions to the rule must be made. In this chapter, we look at some exceptions to the rule of privity of contract. These exceptions include *assignments* and *delegations,* as well as *third party beneficiary contracts.*

We also examine how contractual obligations can be *discharged.* Normally, contract discharge is accomplished by both parties performing the acts promised in the contract. In the latter part of this chapter, we look at the degree of performance required to discharge a contractual obligation, as well as at some other ways in which contract discharge can occur.

Assignments

In a bilateral contract, the two parties have corresponding rights and duties. One party has a *right* to require the other to perform some task, and the other has a *duty* to perform it. Sometimes, though, a party will transfer her or his rights under the contract to someone else. The transfer of contract *rights* to a third person is known as an **assignment.** (The transfer of contract duties is a *delegation,* as will be discussed later in this chapter.)

Assignments are important because they are often used in business financing. Lending institutions, such as banks, frequently assign the rights to receive payments under their loan contracts to other firms, which pay for those rights. If you obtain a loan from your local bank to purchase a car, you may later receive a notice stating that your bank has transferred (assigned) its rights to receive payments on the loan to another firm and that you should make your payments to that other firm.

Lenders that make *mortgage loans* (see Chapter 20) often assign their rights to collect the mortgage payments to a third party, such as Chase Home Mortgage Company. Following an assignment, the home buyer is notified that future payments must be made to the third party, rather than to the original lender. Billions of dollars change hands daily in the business world in the form of assignments of rights in contracts.

Effect of an Assignment

In an assignment, the party assigning the rights to a third party is known as the **assignor,**[1] and the party receiving the rights is the **assignee.**[2] Other terms traditionally used to describe the parties in assignment relationships are the **obligee** (the person to whom a duty, or obligation, is owed) and the **obligor** (the person who is obligated to perform the duty).

When rights under a contract are assigned unconditionally, the rights of the *assignor* (the party making the assignment) are extinguished. The third party (the *assignee,* or the party receiving the assignment) has a right to demand performance from the other original party to the contract (the obligor, the person who is obligated to perform). **EXAMPLE 11.1** Brent (the *obligor*) owes Alex $1,000, and Alex, the obligee, assigns to Carmen the right to receive the $1,000 (thus, Alex is now the assignor). Here, a valid assignment of a debt exists. Carmen, the assignee, can enforce the contract against Brent, the obligor, if Brent fails to perform (pay the $1,000). • Exhibit 11–1 below illustrates assignment relationships.

The assignee obtains only those rights that the assignor originally had. Also, the assignee's rights are subject to the defenses that the obligor has against the assignor. **EXAMPLE 11.2** Brent owes Alex $1,000 under a contract in which Brent agreed to buy Alex's MacBook Pro laptop. Alex assigns his right to receive the $1,000 to Carmen. Brent, in deciding to purchase the laptop, relied on Alex's fraudulent misrepresentation that the computer had eight megabytes of memory. When Brent discovers that the computer has only four megabytes of memory, he tells Alex that he is going to return the laptop and cancel the contract. Even though Alex has assigned his "right" to receive the $1,000 to Carmen, Brent need not pay Carmen the $1,000—Brent can raise the defense of Alex's fraudulent misrepresentation to avoid payment. •

1. Pronounced uh-*sye*-nore.
2. Pronounced uh-*sye*-nee.

Rights That Cannot Be Assigned

As a general rule, all rights can be assigned. Exceptions are made, however, in the following special circumstances.

WHEN A STATUTE EXPRESSLY PROHIBITS ASSIGNMENT If a statute expressly prohibits assignment, the particular right in question cannot be assigned. **EXAMPLE 11.3** Marn is a new employee of CompuFuture, Inc. CompuFuture is an employer governed by workers' compensation statutes (see Chapter 22) in this state, so Marn is a covered employee. Marn has a relatively high-risk job. In need of a loan, she borrows from Stark, assigning to Stark all workers' compensation benefits due her should she be injured on the job. A state statute prohibits the assignment of *future* workers' compensation benefits, and thus such rights cannot be assigned. •

WHEN A CONTRACT IS PERSONAL IN NATURE When a contract is for personal services, the rights under the con-

• ***Exhibit* 11–1 Assignment Relationships**
In the assignment relationship illustrated here, Alex assigns his *rights* under a contract that he made with Brent to a third party, Carmen. Alex thus becomes the *assignor* and Carmen the *assignee* of the contractual rights. Brent, the *obligor,* now owes performance to Carmen instead of to Alex. Alex's original contract rights are extinguished after the assignment.

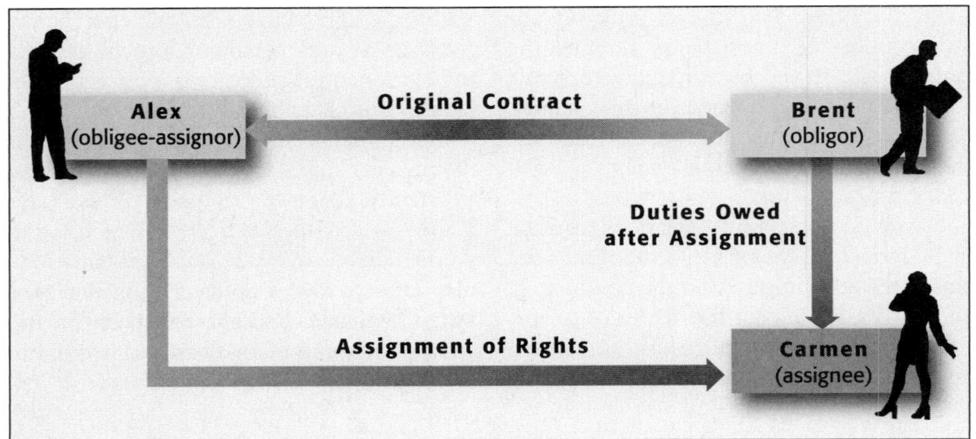

tract normally cannot be assigned unless all that remains is a monetary payment.[3] **EXAMPLE 11.4** Brent signs a contract to be a tutor for Alex's children. Alex then attempts to assign to Carmen his right to Brent's services. Carmen cannot enforce the contract against Brent. Brent may not like Carmen's children or for some other reason may not want to tutor them. Because personal services are unique to the person rendering them, rights to receive personal services cannot be assigned. ●

At the center of the following case was a right of first refusal in a real estate contract—that is, the right to buy the property before it is offered for sale to others. The court had to determine whether the right was assignable or personal to the party who contracted for it.

Case 11.1 Malone v. Flattery

Court of Appeals of Iowa, 797 N.W.2d 624 (2011).
www.iowacourts.gov/Court_of_Appeals/Opinions[a]

FACTS Leo and Grace Flattery sold their farm to Stanek Cattle Company. The Flatterys, however, kept the acre of land on which their home was located. The contract gave Stanek an easement–which is a right to cross a piece of land–that was "binding on the Sellers' and Buyer's personal representatives, distributees, heirs, successors, transferees and assigns." Stanek also "shall have a right of first refusal to acquire the one-acre tract. In the event that the Sellers intend to sell the one-acre tract, the Sellers will notify the Buyer," who could then exercise the right to buy it. A year later, Stanek sold the farm to William and Sharon Malone. Seven years later, without notice to the Malones, the Flatterys transferred their interest in the acre to Timothy and Deann Crall. The Malones filed a suit in an Iowa state court against the Flatterys to rescind (cancel) the transfer to the Cralls and enforce the right of first refusal. The court issued a judgment in the Flatterys' favor. The Malones appealed.

ISSUE Was the right of first refusal granted by the Flatterys to Stanek assignable to a third party?

a. Click on "Opinions Archive." On that page, under "2011," in the "February 9, 2011" row, click on "Opinions." In the result, scroll to "No. 0-912/10-0904," the number of the case, and click on the appropriate link to view the opinion. The Iowa Judicial Branch maintains this Web site.

DECISION No. A state intermediate appellate court affirmed the lower court's judgment in favor of the Flatterys. Stanek's right of first refusal was personal and not assignable. Stanek did not exercise the right before selling the property to the Malones, and the right terminated with that sale.

REASON There is a presumption that a right of first refusal is personal and not assignable. This can be overcome by language in a contract that makes the right assignable or refers to the "successors" or "assigns" of the party to whom the right is transferred (as stated in the easement clause). The reason for this presumption is that a right of first refusal is a restraint on the transfer of land ownership that "can impede the marketability of real estate." Construing the right narrowly limits its duration. In this case, the contract between the Flatterys and Stanek did not state that the right was assignable, and the clause that granted it did not mention the buyer's "successors" or "assigns." Thus, Stanek's right of first refusal was personal and not assignable (to the Malones).

FOR CRITICAL ANALYSIS—Economic Consideration *What underlies the policy against assignments of rights of first refusal and other restraints on the transfer of land ownership?*

WHEN AN ASSIGNMENT WILL SIGNIFICANTLY CHANGE THE RISK OR DUTIES OF THE OBLIGOR A right cannot be assigned if assignment will significantly increase or alter the risks or the duties of the obligor (the party owing performance under the contract).[4] **EXAMPLE 11.5** Alex has a hotel, and to insure it, he takes out a policy with Northwest Insurance Company. The policy insures against fire, theft, floods, and vandalism. Alex attempts to assign the insurance policy to Carmen, who also owns a hotel. The assignment is ineffective because it may substantially alter the insurance company's duty of performance and the risk that the company undertakes. An insurance company evaluates the particular risk of a certain party and tailors its policy to fit that risk. If the policy is assigned to a third party, the insurance risk is materially altered. ●

3. *Restatement (Second) of Contracts*, Sections 317 and 318.
4. See Section 2–210(2) of the Uniform Commercial Code (UCC).

WHEN THE CONTRACT PROHIBITS ASSIGNMENT If a contract stipulates that the right cannot be assigned, then *ordinarily* it cannot be assigned. **EXAMPLE 11.6** Brent agrees to build a house for Alex. The contract between Brent and Alex states, "This contract cannot be assigned by Alex without Brent's consent. Any assignment without such consent renders this contract void, and all rights hereunder will thereupon terminate." Alex then assigns his rights to Carmen, without first obtaining Brent's consent. Carmen cannot enforce the contract against Brent. ● This rule has several exceptions:

1. A contract cannot prevent an assignment of the right to receive funds. This exception exists to encourage the free flow of funds and credit in modern business settings.
2. The assignment of ownership rights in real estate often cannot be prohibited because such a prohibition is contrary to public policy in most states. Prohibitions of this kind are

called restraints against **alienation** (the voluntary transfer of land ownership).

3. The assignment of negotiable instruments (see Chapter 16) cannot be prohibited.
4. In a contract for the sale of goods, the right to receive damages for breach of contract or for payment of an account owed may be assigned even though the sales contract prohibits such an assignment.[5]

Notice of Assignment

Once a valid assignment of rights has been made to a third party, the third party should notify the obligor of the assignment (for example, in Exhibit 11–1 on page 194, Carmen should notify Brent). Giving notice is not legally necessary to establish the validity of the assignment because an assignment is effective immediately, whether or not notice is given. Two major problems arise, however, when notice of the assignment is *not* given to the obligor:

1. If the assignor assigns the same right to two different persons, the question arises as to which one has priority—that is, which one has the right to the performance by the obligor. Although the rule most often observed in the United States is that the first assignment in time is the first in right, some states follow the English rule, which basically gives priority to the first assignee who gives notice.

   EXAMPLE 11.7 Brent owes Alex $5,000 on a contractual obligation. On May 1, Alex assigns this monetary claim to Carmen, but she does not give notice of the assignment to Brent. On June 1, for services Dorman has rendered to Alex, Alex assigns the same monetary claim (to collect $5,000 from Brent) to Dorman. Dorman immediately notifies Brent of the assignment. In the majority of states, Carmen would have priority because the assignment to her was first in time. In some states, however, Dorman would have priority because he gave first notice. •
2. Until the obligor has notice of an assignment, the obligor can discharge his or her obligation by performance to the assignor, and this performance constitutes a discharge to the assignee. Once the obligor receives proper notice, only performance to the assignee can discharge the obligor's obligations.

   EXAMPLE 11.8 Suppose that Alex, in the above example, assigns to Carmen his right to collect $5,000 from Brent, and Carmen does not give notice to Brent. Brent subsequently pays Alex the $5,000. Although the assignment was valid, Brent's payment to Alex is a discharge of the debt, and Carmen's failure to notify Brent of the assignment causes her to lose the right to collect the $5,000 from Brent. (Note that Carmen still has a claim against Alex for the $5,000.) If Carmen had given Brent notice of the assignment, however, Brent's payment to Alex would not have discharged the debt. •

5. UCC 2–210(2).

Delegations

Just as a party can transfer rights to a third party through an assignment, a party can also transfer duties. Duties are not assigned, however; they are *delegated*. Normally, a **delegation of duties** does not relieve the party making the delegation (the **delegator**) of the obligation to perform in the event that the party to whom the duty has been delegated (the **delegatee**) fails to perform. No special form is required to create a valid delegation of duties. As long as the delegator expresses an intention to make the delegation, it is effective; the delegator need not even use the word *delegate*. Exhibit 11–2 on the facing page graphically illustrates delegation relationships.

Duties That Cannot Be Delegated

As a general rule, any duty can be delegated. This rule has some exceptions, however. Delegation is prohibited in the following circumstances:

1. When the duties are personal in nature.
2. When performance by a third party will vary materially from that expected by the obligee.
3. When the contract expressly prohibits delegation.

WHEN THE DUTIES ARE PERSONAL IN NATURE When special trust has been placed in the obligor or when performance depends on the personal skill or talents of the obligor, contractual duties cannot be delegated. **EXAMPLE 11.9** Horton, who is impressed with Brower's ability to perform veterinary surgery, contracts with Brower to have her perform surgery on Horton's prize-winning stallion in July. Brower later decides that she would rather spend the summer at the beach, so she delegates her duties under the contract to Kuhn, who is also a competent veterinary surgeon. The delegation is not effective without Horton's consent, no matter how competent Kuhn is, because the contract is for *personal* performance. •

In contrast, nonpersonal duties may be delegated. Assume that Brower contracts with Horton to pick up and deliver heavy construction machinery to Horton's property. Brower delegates this duty to Kuhn, who is in the business of delivering heavy machinery. This delegation is effective because the performance required is of a *routine* and *nonpersonal* nature.

WHEN PERFORMANCE BY A THIRD PARTY WILL VARY MATERIALLY FROM THAT EXPECTED BY THE OBLIGEE When performance by a third party will vary materially from

• ***Exhibit* 11–2 Delegation Relationships**
In the delegation relationship illustrated here, Brent delegates his *duties* under a contract that he made with Alex to a third party, Carmen. Brent thus becomes the *delegator* and Carmen the *delegatee* of the contractual duties. Carmen now owes performance of the contractual duties to Alex. Note that a delegation of duties normally does not relieve the delegator (Brent) of liability if the delegatee (Carmen) fails to perform the contractual duties.

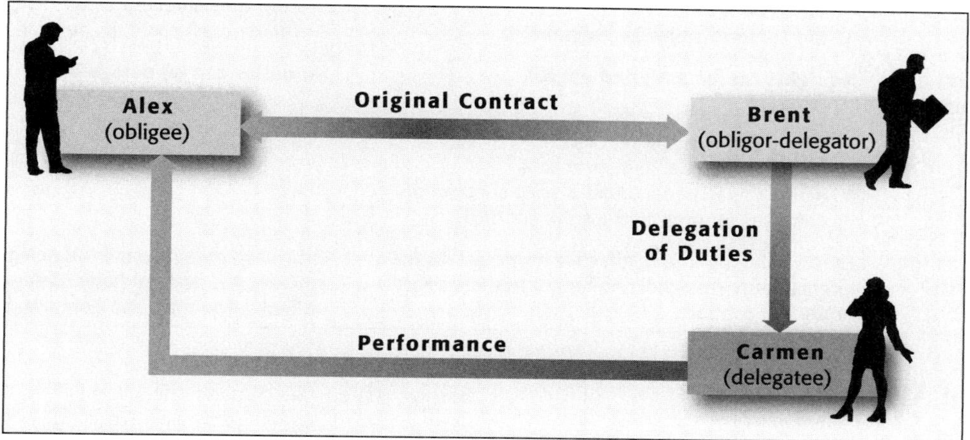

that expected by the obligee under the contract, contractual duties cannot be delegated.

EXAMPLE 11.10 Alex Payton is a wealthy philanthropist who recently established a charitable foundation. Payton has known Brenda Murdoch for twenty years and knows that Murdoch shares his beliefs on many humanitarian issues. He contracts with Murdoch to be in charge of allocating funds among various charitable causes. Six months later, Murdoch is experiencing health problems and delegates her duties to Drew Cole. Payton does not approve of Cole as a replacement. In this situation, Payton can claim the delegation was not effective because it *materially altered his expectations* under the contract. Payton had reasonable expectations about the types of charities to which Murdoch would give the foundation's funds, and the substitution of Cole's performance materially changes those expectations. •

WHEN THE CONTRACT PROHIBITS DELEGATION When the contract expressly prohibits delegation by including an *antidelegation clause,* the duties cannot be delegated.

EXAMPLE 11.11 R.W. Stern Company contracts with Jan Pearson, a certified public accountant, to perform its annual audits for the next five years. If the contract prohibits delegation, then Pearson cannot delegate her duty to perform the audit to another accountant at the same firm. In some situations, however, when the duties are completely impersonal in nature, courts have held that the duties can be delegated notwithstanding an antidelegation clause. •

Effect of a Delegation

If a delegation of duties is enforceable, the obligee must accept performance from the delegatee. **EXAMPLE 11.12** Brent delegates his duty (to pick up and deliver heavy construction machinery to Alex's property) to Carmen. In that situation, Alex (the obligee) must accept performance from Carmen (the delegatee) because the delegation was effective. The obligee can legally refuse performance from the delegatee only if the duty is one that cannot be delegated. •

A valid delegation of duties does not relieve the delegator of obligations under the contract. **EXAMPLE 11.13** If Carmen (the delegatee) fails to perform, Brent (the delegator) is still liable to Alex (the obligee). The obligee can also hold the delegatee liable if the delegatee made a promise of performance that will directly benefit the obligee. In this situation, there is an "assumption of duty" on the part of the delegatee, and breach of this duty makes the delegatee liable to the obligee. For example, if Carmen (the delegatee) promises Brent (the delegator), in a contract, to pick up and deliver the construction equipment to Alex's property but fails to do so, Alex (the obligee) can sue Brent, Carmen, or both. • Although there are many exceptions, the general rule today is that the obligee can sue both the delegatee and the delegator.

Exhibit 11–3 on the following page summarizes the basic principles of the laws governing assignments and delegations.

• *Exhibit* 11–3 **Assignments and Delegations**

Which rights can be assigned, and which duties can be delegated?	**All rights can be assigned *unless:*** 1. A statute expressly prohibits assignment. 2. The contract is for personal services. 3. The assignment will materially alter the obligor's risk or duties. 4. The contract prohibits assignment.	**All duties can be delegated *unless:*** 1. Performance depends on the obligor's personal skills or talents. 2. Performance by a third party will vary materially from that expected by the obligee. 3. The contract prohibits delegation.
What if the contract prohibits assignment or delegation?	**No rights can be assigned *except:*** 1. Rights to receive funds. 2. Ownership rights in real estate. 3. Rights to negotiable instruments. 4. Rights to payments under a sales contract or damages for breach of a sales contract.	**No duties can be delegated.**
What is the effect on the original party's rights?	On a valid assignment, effective immediately, the original party (assignor) no longer has any rights under the contract.	On a valid delegation, if the delegatee fails to perform, the original party (delegator) is liable to the obligee (who may also hold the delegatee liable).

"Assignment of All Rights"

Sometimes, a contract provides for an "assignment of all rights." The traditional view was that under this type of assignment, the assignee did not assume any duties. This view was based on the theory that the assignee's agreement to accept the benefits of the contract was not sufficient to imply a promise to assume the duties of the contract.

Modern authorities, however, take the view that the probable intent in using such general words is to create both an assignment of rights and an assumption of duties.[6] Therefore, when general words are used (for example, "I assign the contract" or "all my rights under the contract"), the contract is construed as implying both an assignment of rights and an assumption of duties.

Third Party Beneficiaries

As mentioned earlier in this chapter, to have contractual rights, a person normally must be a party to the contract. In other words, privity of contract must exist. An exception to the doctrine of privity exists when the original parties to the contract intend, *at the time of contracting,* that the contract performance directly benefit a third person. In this situation, the third person becomes a **third party beneficiary** of the contract. As an **intended beneficiary** of the contract, the third party has legal rights and can sue the promisor directly for breach of the contract.

Who, though, is the promisor? In bilateral contracts, both parties to the contract are promisors because they both make promises that can be enforced. In third party beneficiary contracts, courts determine the identity of the promisor by asking which party made the promise that benefits the third party—that person is the promisor. Allowing the third party to sue the promisor directly in effect circumvents the "middle person" (the promisee) and thus reduces the burden on the courts. Otherwise, the third party would sue the promisee, who would then sue the promisor.

Types of Intended Beneficiaries

The law distinguishes between *intended* beneficiaries and *incidental* beneficiaries. Only intended beneficiaries acquire legal rights in a contract. One type of intended beneficiary is a *creditor beneficiary.* A creditor beneficiary benefits from a contract in which one party (the promisor) promises another party (the promisee) to pay a debt that the promisee owes to a third party (the creditor beneficiary). As an intended beneficiary, the creditor beneficiary can sue the promisor directly to enforce the contract.

Another type of intended beneficiary is a *donee* beneficiary. When a contract is made for the express purpose of giving a *gift* to a third party, the third party (the donee beneficiary) can sue the promisor directly to enforce the promise. The most common donee beneficiary contract is a life insurance contract.

EXAMPLE 11.14 Akins (the promisee) pays premiums to Standard Life, a life insurance company, and Standard Life (the promisor) promises to pay a certain amount on Akins's death to anyone Akins designates as a beneficiary. The designated beneficiary is a donee beneficiary under the life insurance policy and can enforce the promise made by the insurance company to pay her or him on Akins's death. •

As the law concerning third party beneficiaries evolved, numerous cases arose in which the third party beneficiary did not fit readily into either the creditor beneficiary or the donee beneficiary category. Thus, the modern view, and the one adopted

6. See UCC 2–210(1), (4); and *Restatement (Second) of Contracts,* Section 328.

by the *Restatement (Second) of Contracts,* does not draw such clear lines and distinguishes only between intended beneficiaries (who can sue to enforce contracts made for their benefit) and incidental beneficiaries (who cannot sue, as will be discussed shortly).

In the following case, however, the court uses the traditional terminology when deciding whether an aggrieved owner of a condominium unit was an intended third party beneficiary of another owner's contract with the condominium association.

Case 11.2 Allan v. Nersesova[a]

Court of Appeals of Texas, Dallas, 307 S.W.3d 564 (2010).
www.5thcoa.courts.state.tx.us[b]

FACTS Autumn Allan and Aslan Koraev both owned units in the Boardwalk on the Parkway Condominiums. Allan's unit was directly beneath Koraev's. Between March 2005 and July 2007, Allan's unit suffered eight incidents of water and sewage incursion as a result of plumbing problems and misuse of appliances in Koraev's unit. Allan sued Koraev and others for breach of contract. The trial jury found for Allan on her claims for breach of contract against Koraev. Koraev moved for judgment notwithstanding the verdict, asserting that Allan had failed to prove as a matter of law the existence of a contract between her and Koraev. The trial court granted the motion, and Allan appealed.

ISSUE Was Allan an intended third party beneficiary of the contract between Koraev and the condominium association?

a. Ekaterina Nersesova was sued in her official capacity as property manager of Aslan Koraev's condominium unit.

b. In the left-hand column, select "Search Opinions." When that page opens, key in the title of this case and click on the "Search" box. From the search results, select the file number that precedes the case title to access the opinion. The Fifth District Court of Appeals in Dallas, Texas, maintains this Web site.

DECISION Yes. The Court of Appeals of Texas concluded that the governing documents made Allan an intended creditor beneficiary of the contract between Koraev and the association.

REASON Allan was a creditor beneficiary because she benefited from Koraev's contractual promises to comply with the condominium association's terms and to pay for damages that he caused to other units. Consequently, the trial court "erred by granting Koraev's motion for judgment notwithstanding the verdict on Allan's claim for breach of contract." The court reasoned that "A third party, such as Allan, may sue to enforce a contract as a third-party beneficiary . . . if the contracting parties entered into the contract directly and primarily for the third-party's benefit." Because the governing documents stated that each owner had to comply strictly with their provisions, failure to comply created grounds for an action by the condominium association or an aggrieved (wronged) owner. Clearly, Allan was an aggrieved owner. "Koraev's failure to perform the contract between himself and the Association was a breach of his duty not to cause damage to Allan's unit. As an intended creditor beneficiary, Allan had standing to bring suit against Koraev for his breach of the governing documents."

FOR CRITICAL ANALYSIS—Legal Consideration *Why did the court use the term* creditor beneficiary *to describe Allan?*

When the Rights of an Intended Beneficiary Vest

An intended third party beneficiary cannot enforce a contract against the original parties until the rights of the third party have *vested,* meaning that the rights have taken effect and cannot be taken away. Until these rights have vested, the original parties to the contract—the promisor and the promisee—can modify or rescind the contract without the consent of the third party. When do the rights of third parties vest? Generally, the rights vest when one of the following occurs:

1. When the third party demonstrates express consent to the agreement, such as by sending a letter or note acknowledging awareness of, and consent to, a contract formed for her or his benefit.
2. When the third party materially alters his or her position in detrimental reliance on the contract, such as when a donee beneficiary contracts to have a home built in reliance on the receipt of funds promised to him or her in a donee beneficiary contract.
3. When the conditions for vesting are satisfied. For example, the rights of a beneficiary under a life insurance policy vest when the insured person dies.

If the contract expressly reserves to the contracting parties the right to cancel, rescind, or modify the contract, the rights of the third party beneficiary are subject to any changes that result. In such a situation, the vesting of the third party's rights does not terminate the power of the original contracting parties to alter their legal relationships.

Intended versus Incidental Beneficiaries

The benefit that an **incidental beneficiary** receives from a contract between two parties is *unintentional.* Because the benefit is unintentional, an incidental beneficiary cannot sue to enforce the contract.

In determining whether a party is an intended or an incidental beneficiary, the courts focus on the parties' intent, as expressed in the contract language and implied by the surrounding circumstances. Any beneficiary who is not deemed an intended beneficiary is considered incidental. Although no single test can embrace all possible situations, courts often apply the *reasonable person* test: Would a reasonable person in the position of the beneficiary believe that the promisee intended to confer on the beneficiary the right to enforce the contract? In addition, the presence of one or more of the following factors strongly indicates that the third party is an intended beneficiary to the contract:

1. Performance is rendered directly to the third party.
2. The third party has the right to control the details of performance.
3. The third party is expressly designated as a beneficiary in the contract.

Exhibit 11–4 below illustrates the distinction between intended and incidental beneficiaries.

Contract Discharge

The most common way to **discharge**, or terminate, one's contractual duties is by the **performance** of those duties. The duty to perform under a contract may be *conditioned* on the occurrence or nonoccurrence of a certain event, or the duty may be *absolute*. In addition to performance, a contract can be discharged in numerous other ways, including discharge by agreement of the parties and discharge by operation of law. We discuss these methods of contract discharge in this section.

Conditions of Performance

In most contracts, promises of performance are not expressly conditioned or qualified. Instead, they are *absolute promises*. They must be performed, or the party promising the act will be in breach of contract. **EXAMPLE 11.15** JoAnne contracts to sell Alfonso a painting for $10,000. The parties' promises are unconditional: JoAnne's transfer of the painting to Alfonso and Alfonso's payment of $10,000 to JoAnne. The payment does not have to be made if the painting is not transferred. •

In some situations, however, contractual promises are conditioned. A **condition** is a possible future event, the occurrence or nonoccurrence of which will trigger the performance of a legal obligation or terminate an existing obligation under a contract. If the condition is not satisfied, the obligations of the parties are discharged. **EXAMPLE 11.16** Alfonso, in the above example, offers to purchase JoAnne's painting only if an independent appraisal indicates that it is worth at least $10,000. JoAnne accepts Alfonso's offer. Their obligations (promises) are conditioned on the outcome of the appraisal. Should this condition not be satisfied (for example, if the appraiser deems the market value of the painting to be only $5,000), their obligations to each other are discharged and cannot be enforced. •

We look next at three types of conditions that can be present in any given contract: *conditions precedent, conditions subsequent,* and *concurrent conditions.*

CONDITIONS PRECEDENT A condition that must be fulfilled before a party's promise becomes absolute is called a **condition precedent.** The condition precedes the absolute duty to perform. For instance, insurance contracts frequently specify that certain conditions, such as passing a physical

• ***Exhibit* 11–4 Third Party Beneficiaries**

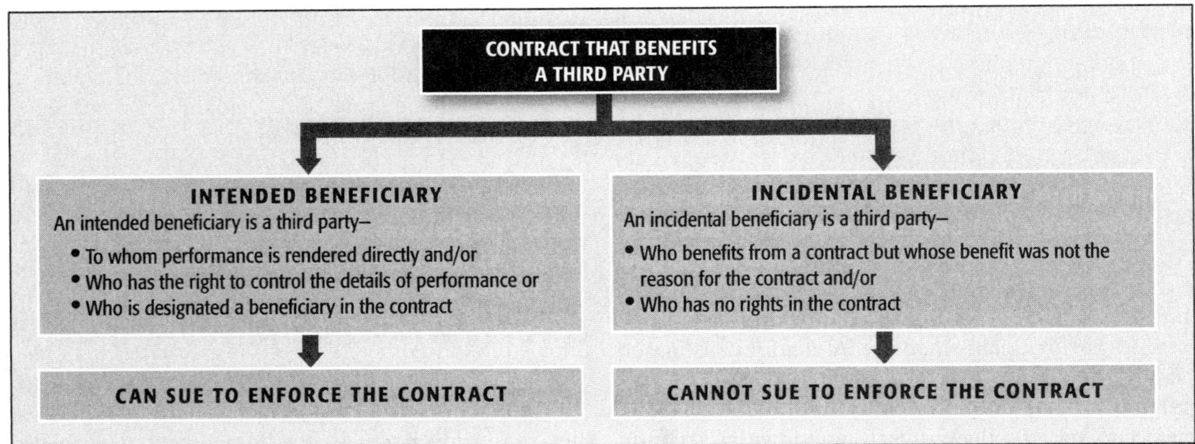

examination, must be met before the insurance company will be obligated to perform under the contract.

Sometimes, a lease of real property (see Chapter 28) includes an option to buy that property. The lease in the following case required timely rent payments as a condition of exercising such an option, but the lessee often failed to make the payments on time. The court had to decide whether the lessee could still exercise the option even though it had not strictly complied with the condition precedent.

Case 11.3 Pack 2000, Inc. v. Cushman

Appellate Court of Connecticut, 126 Conn.App. 339, 11 A.3d 181 (2011).
www.jud.state.ct.us[a]

FACTS Eugene Cushman agreed to transfer two Midas muffler shops to Pack 2000, Inc. The deal included leases for the real estate on which the shops were located. Each lease provided Pack with an option to buy the leased real estate subject to certain conditions. Pack was to pay rent by the first day of each month, make payments on the notes by the eighth day of each month, and pay utilities and other accounts on time. Pack, however, was often late in making these payments. The utility and phone companies threatened to cut off services, an insurance company canceled Pack's liability coverage, and other delinquencies prompted collection calls and letters. When Pack sought to exercise the options to buy the real estate, Cushman responded that Pack had not complied with the conditions. Pack filed a suit in a Connecticut state court against Cushman, seeking specific performance of the options. The court rendered a judgment in Pack's favor. Cushman appealed.

a. In the left column, in the "Opinions" pull-out menu, click on "Appellate Court." On that page, in the "Search the Archives:" section, click on "Appellate Court Archive." In the result, click on "2011." Scroll to the "Published in Connecticut Law Journal–2/1/11" section, and click on the docket number next to the title of the case to view the opinion. The Connecticut judicial branch maintains this Web site.

ISSUE Can Pack exercise its option to buy the leased real estate even though it did not strictly comply with the condition precedent that required it to make payments on time?

DECISION No. A state intermediate appellate court reversed the lower court's judgment and remanded the case for the entry of a judgment for Cushman. A party retains its right to exercise an option to buy real estate only by complying strictly with any conditions precedent to its exercise of the option.

REASON The leases provided Pack with the option to buy the leased real estate. But to take advantage of the options, Pack had to comply with the condition precedent of making periodic payments to Cushman and to certain third parties by specific dates. Pack was often late in making these payments and thus did not strictly comply with the condition. The court reasoned that because of this failure of strict compliance, Pack lost the right to exercise the options to buy the real estate.

WHAT IF THE FACTS WERE DIFFERENT? *Suppose that Pack had not made any late payments. Would the result have been different? Explain.*

CONDITIONS SUBSEQUENT When a condition operates to terminate a party's absolute promise to perform, it is called a **condition subsequent.** The condition follows, or is subsequent to, the absolute duty to perform. If the condition occurs, the party need not perform any further. **EXAMPLE 11.17** A law firm hires Julia Darby, a recent law school graduate and a newly licensed attorney. Their contract provides that the firm's obligation to continue employing Darby is discharged if she fails to maintain her license to practice law. This is a condition subsequent because a failure to maintain the license will discharge a duty that has already arisen. •

Generally, conditions precedent are common, and conditions subsequent are rare. The *Restatement (Second) of Contracts* deletes the terms *condition subsequent* and *condition precedent* and refers to both simply as "conditions."[7]

CONCURRENT CONDITIONS When each party's absolute duty to perform is conditioned on the other party's absolute duty to perform, **concurrent conditions** are present. These conditions exist only when the parties expressly or impliedly are to perform their respective duties *simultaneously.*

EXAMPLE 11.18 If a buyer promises to pay for goods when they are delivered by the seller, each party's absolute duty to perform is conditioned on the other party's absolute duty to perform.

7. *Restatement (Second) of Contracts,* Section 224.

The buyer's duty to pay for the goods does not become absolute until the seller either delivers or attempts to deliver the goods. Likewise, the seller's duty to deliver the goods does not become absolute until the buyer pays or attempts to pay for the goods. Therefore, neither can recover from the other for breach without first tendering performance. •

Discharge by Performance

The contract comes to an end when both parties fulfill their respective duties by performing the acts they have promised. Performance can also be accomplished by tender. **Tender** is an unconditional offer to perform by a person who is ready, willing, and able to do so. Therefore, a seller who places goods at the disposal of a buyer has tendered delivery and can demand payment according to the terms of the agreement. A buyer who offers to pay for goods has tendered payment and can demand delivery of the goods.

Once performance has been tendered, the party making the tender has done everything possible to carry out the terms of the contract. If the other party then refuses to perform, the party making the tender can consider the duty discharged and sue for breach of contract.

COMPLETE PERFORMANCE When a party performs exactly as agreed, there is no question as to whether the contract has been performed. When a party's performance is perfect, it is said to be complete.

Normally, conditions expressly stated in the contract must fully occur in all aspects for complete performance (strict performance) of the contract to take place. Any deviation breaches the contract and discharges the other party's obligations to perform. For example, most construction contracts require the builder to meet certain specifications. If the specifications are conditions, complete performance is required to avoid material breach. (*Material breach* will be discussed shortly.) If the conditions are met, the other party to the contract must then fulfill her or his obligation to pay the builder. If the specifications are not conditions and if the builder, without the other party's permission, fails to meet the specifications, performance is not complete. What effect does such a failure have on the other party's obligation to pay? The answer is part of the doctrine of *substantial performance.*

SUBSTANTIAL PERFORMANCE A party who in good faith performs substantially all of the terms of a contract can enforce the contract against the other party under the doctrine of substantial performance. Note that good faith is required. Intentionally failing to comply with the terms is a breach of the contract.

To qualify as substantial performance, the performance must not vary greatly from the performance promised in the contract, and it must create substantially the same benefits as those promised in the contract. If the omission, variance, or defect in performance is unimportant and can easily be compensated for by awarding damages, a court is likely to hold that the contract has been substantially performed.

Courts decide whether the performance was substantial on a case-by-case basis, examining all of the facts of the particular situation. If performance is substantial, the other party's duty to perform remains absolute (except that the party can sue for damages due to the minor deviations).

CASE EXAMPLE 11.19 Wisconsin Electric Power Company (WEPCO) contracted with Union Pacific Railroad to transport coal to WEPCO from mines in Colorado. The contract required WEPCO to notify Union Pacific monthly of how many tons of coal (below a certain maximum) it wanted to have shipped the next month. Union Pacific was to make "good faith reasonable efforts" to meet the schedule. The contract also required WEPCO to supply the railcars. When WEPCO did not supply the railcars, Union Pacific used its own railcars and delivered 84 percent of the requested coal. A federal appellate court held that in this situation, the delivery of 84 percent of the contracted amount constituted substantial performance.[8] •

PERFORMANCE TO THE SATISFACTION OF ANOTHER Contracts often state that completed work must personally satisfy one of the parties or a third person. The question is whether this satisfaction becomes a condition precedent, requiring actual personal satisfaction or approval for discharge, or whether the performance need only satisfy a *reasonable person* (substantial performance).

When the subject matter of the contract is *personal,* a contract to be performed to the satisfaction of one of the parties is conditioned, and performance must actually satisfy that party. For example, contracts for portraits, works of art, and tailoring are considered personal. Therefore, only the personal satisfaction of the party fulfills the condition—unless a court finds that the party is expressing dissatisfaction simply to avoid payment or otherwise is not acting in good faith.

Most other contracts need to be performed only to the satisfaction of a reasonable person unless they *expressly state otherwise.* When such contracts require performance to the satisfaction of a third party (for example, "to the satisfaction of Robert Ames, the supervising engineer"), the courts are divided. A majority of courts require the work to be satisfactory to a reasonable person, but some courts hold that the personal satisfaction of the third party designated in the contract (Robert Ames, in this example) must be met. Again, the personal judgment must be made honestly, or the condition will be excused.

8. *Wisconsin Electric Power Co. v. Union Pacific Railroad Co.,* 557 F.3d 504 (7th Cir. 2009).

MATERIAL BREACH OF CONTRACT A **breach of contract** is the nonperformance of a contractual duty. A breach is *material* when performance is not at least substantial.[9] If there is a material breach, the nonbreaching party is excused from the performance of contractual duties and can sue for damages caused by the breach. If the breach is minor (not material), the nonbreaching party's duty to perform may sometimes be suspended until the breach is remedied, but the duty is not entirely excused. Once the minor breach is cured, the nonbreaching party must resume performance of the contractual obligations.

Any breach entitles the nonbreaching party to sue for damages, but only a material breach discharges the nonbreaching party from the contract. The policy underlying these rules is that contracts should go forward when only minor problems occur, but contracts should be terminated if major problems arise.[10]

CASE EXAMPLE 11.20 Su Yong Kim sold an apartment building in Portland, Oregon. At the time of the sale, the building's plumbing violated the city's housing code. The contract provided that Kim would correct the violations within eight months after the contract was signed. A year later, Kim had not made the necessary repairs, and the new owners were being fined for continuing code violations. The buyers stopped making payments, and the dispute ended up in court. The court found that the seller's failure to make the required repairs was a material breach of the contract. The buyers had purchased the building to lease to tenants. Instead, they were losing tenants and paying fines due to the substandard plumbing. The buyers were not obligated to continue to perform their obligation to make payments under the contract.[11] ●

ANTICIPATORY REPUDIATION OF A CONTRACT Before either party to a contract has a duty to perform, one of the parties may refuse to perform her or his contractual obligations. This is called **anticipatory repudiation.**[12] When anticipatory repudiation occurs, it is treated as a material breach of contract, and the nonbreaching party is permitted to bring an action for damages immediately, even though the scheduled time for performance under the contract may still be in the future.[13] Until the nonbreaching party treats this early repudiation as a breach, however, the breaching party can retract the anticipatory repudiation by proper notice and restore the parties to their original obligations.[14]

An anticipatory repudiation is treated as a present, material breach for two reasons. First, the nonbreaching party should not be required to remain ready and willing to perform when the other party has already repudiated the contract. Second, the nonbreaching party should have the opportunity to seek a similar contract elsewhere and may have the duty to do so to minimize his or her loss.

Quite often, an anticipatory repudiation occurs when market prices change significantly, making performance of the contract extremely unfavorable to one of the parties.

EXAMPLE 11.21 Shasta Corporation contracts to manufacture and sell 100,000 personal computers to New Age, Inc., a retailer of computer equipment. Delivery is to be made two months from the date of the contract. One month later, three suppliers of computer parts raise their prices to Shasta. Because of these higher prices, Shasta stands to lose $500,000 if it sells the computers to New Age at the contract price. Shasta writes to New Age, stating that it cannot deliver the 100,000 computers at the contract price. Even though you may sympathize with Shasta, its letter is an anticipatory repudiation of the contract. New Age can treat the repudiation as a material breach and immediately pursue remedies, even though the contract delivery date is still a month away. ●

Discharge by Agreement

Any contract can be discharged by agreement of the parties. The agreement can be contained in the original contract, or the parties can form a new contract for the express purpose of discharging the original contract.

DISCHARGE BY MUTUAL RESCISSION *Rescission* is the process in which the parties cancel the contract and are returned to the positions they occupied before the contract's formation. For **mutual rescission** to take place, the parties must make another agreement that also satisfies the legal requirements for a contract—there must be an offer, an acceptance, and consideration. Ordinarily, if the parties agree to rescind the original contract, their promises not to perform those acts promised in the original contract will be legal consideration for the second contract. Agreements to rescind executory contracts (in which neither party has performed) are enforceable even if they are made orally and the original agreement was in writing.

Under the Uniform Commercial Code, however, an agreement rescinding a contract for the sale of goods, regardless of price, must be in writing (or contained in an electronic record) when the contract requires a written rescission. Also, agreements to rescind contracts involving transfers of realty must be evidenced by a writing or other record.

When one party has fully performed, an agreement to rescind the original contract usually is not enforceable unless additional consideration or restitution is made. Because the performing

---

9. *Restatement (Second) of Contracts,* Section 241.
10. See UCC 2–612, which deals with installment contracts for the sale of goods.
11. *Kim v. Park,* 192 Or.App. 365, 86 P.3d 63 (2004).
12. *Restatement (Second) of Contracts,* Section 253; and UCC 2–610.
13. The doctrine of anticipatory repudiation first arose in the landmark case of *Hochster v. De La Tour,* 2 Ellis and Blackburn Reports 678 (1853), when an English court recognized the delay and expense inherent in a rule requiring a nonbreaching party to wait until the time of performance before suing for an anticipatory repudiation.
14. See UCC 2–611.

party has received no consideration for the promise to call off the original bargain, additional consideration is necessary.

Discharge by Novation The process of **novation** substitutes a third party for one of the original parties. Essentially, the parties to the original contract and one or more new parties all get together and agree to the substitution. The requirements of a novation are as follows:

1. The existence of a previous, valid obligation.
2. Agreement by all of the parties to a new contract.
3. The extinguishing of the old obligation (discharge of the prior party).
4. A new, valid contract.

EXAMPLE 11.22 Union Corporation contracts to sell its pharmaceutical division to British Pharmaceuticals, Ltd. Before the transfer is completed, Union, British Pharmaceuticals, and a third company, Otis Chemicals, execute a new agreement to transfer all of British Pharmaceuticals' rights and duties in the transaction to Otis Chemicals. As long as the new contract is supported by consideration, the novation will discharge the original contract (between Union and British Pharmaceuticals) and replace it with the new contract (between Union and Otis Chemicals). •

A novation expressly or impliedly revokes and discharges a prior contract. The parties involved may expressly state in the new contract that the old contract is now discharged. If the parties do not expressly discharge the old contract, it will be impliedly discharged if the new contract's terms are inconsistent with the old contract's terms.

Discharge by Accord and Satisfaction As Chapter 9 explained, in an accord and satisfaction, the parties agree to accept performance different from the performance originally promised. An *accord* is an executory contract (one that has not yet been performed) to perform some act to satisfy an existing contractual duty that is not yet discharged.[15] A *satisfaction* is the performance of the accord agreement. An accord and its satisfaction discharge the original contractual obligation.

Once the accord has been made, the original obligation is merely suspended until the accord agreement is fully performed. If it is not performed, the party to whom performance is owed can bring an action on the original obligation or for breach of the accord.

EXAMPLE 11.23 Shep obtains a judgment against Marla for $8,000. Later, both parties agree that the judgment can be satisfied by Marla's transfer of her automobile to Shep. This agreement to accept the auto in lieu of $8,000 is the accord. If Marla transfers her automobile to Shep, the accord agreement is fully performed, and the $8,000 debt is discharged. If Marla refuses to transfer her car, the accord is breached. Because the original obligation is merely suspended, Shep can sue to enforce the judgment for $8,000 or bring an action for breach of the accord. •

Discharge by Operation of Law

Under some circumstances, contractual duties may be discharged by operation of law. These circumstances include material alteration of the contract, the running of the relevant statute of limitations, bankruptcy, and impossibility of performance.

Material Alteration To discourage parties from altering written contracts, the law allows an innocent party to be discharged when one party has materially altered a written contract without the knowledge or consent of the other party. For example, if a party alters a material term of the contract—such as the quantity term or the price term—without the knowledge or consent of the other party, the party who was unaware of the alteration can treat the contract as discharged or terminated.

Statutes of Limitations Statutes of limitations limit the period during which a party can sue on a particular cause of action. After the applicable limitations period has passed, a suit can no longer be brought. For example, the limitations period for bringing lawsuits for breach of oral contracts is usually two to three years; for written contracts, four to five years; and for recovery of amounts awarded in judgment, ten to twenty years, depending on state law. Lawsuits for breach of a contract for the sale of goods must be brought within four years after the cause of action has accrued. By original agreement, the parties can agree to reduce this four-year period to not less than a one-year period. They cannot, however, agree to extend it beyond the four-year limitations period.

Bankruptcy A proceeding in bankruptcy attempts to allocate the debtor's assets to the creditors in a fair and equitable fashion. Once the assets have been allocated, the debtor receives a *discharge in bankruptcy* (see Chapter 19). A discharge in bankruptcy ordinarily bars the creditors from enforcing most of the debtor's contracts.

When Performance Is Impossible After a contract has been made, performance may become impossible in an objective sense. This is known as **impossibility of performance** and may discharge the contract.[16] Performance may also become so difficult or costly due to some unforeseen

15. *Restatement (Second) of Contracts,* Section 281.

16. *Restatement (Second) of Contracts,* Section 261.

event that a court will consider it commercially unfeasible, or impracticable, as will be discussed later in the chapter.

Objective Impossibility. *Objective impossibility* ("It can't be done") must be distinguished from subjective impossibility ("I'm sorry, I simply can't do it"). An example of subjective impossibility occurs when a party cannot deliver goods on time because of freight car shortages or cannot make payment on time because the bank is closed. In effect, the nonperforming party is saying, "It is impossible for *me* to perform," rather than "It is impossible for *anyone* to perform." Accordingly, such excuses do not discharge a contract, and the nonperforming party is normally held in breach of contract. Three basic types of situations will generally qualify as grounds for the discharge of contractual obligations based on impossibility of performance:[17]

1. *When a party whose personal performance is essential to the completion of the contract dies or becomes incapacitated prior to performance.* **EXAMPLE 11.24** Fred, a famous dancer, contracts with Ethereal Dancing Guild to play a leading role in its new ballet. Before the ballet can be performed, Fred becomes ill and dies. His personal performance was essential to the completion of the contract. Thus, his death discharges the contract and his estate's liability for his nonperformance. •
2. *When the specific subject matter of the contract is destroyed.* **EXAMPLE 11.25** A-1 Farm Equipment agrees to sell Gudgel the green tractor on its lot and promises to have the tractor ready for Gudgel to pick up on Saturday. On Friday night, however, a truck veers off the nearby highway and smashes into the tractor, destroying it beyond repair. Because the contract was for this specific tractor, A-1's performance is rendered impossible owing to the accident. •
3. *When a change in the law renders performance illegal.* **EXAMPLE 11.26** A contract to build an apartment building becomes impossible to perform when the zoning laws are changed to prohibit the construction of residential rental property at the planned location. •

Temporary Impossibility. An occurrence or event that makes performance temporarily impossible operates to suspend performance until the impossibility ceases. Then, ordinarily, the parties must perform the contract as originally planned. If, however, the lapse of time and the change in circumstances surrounding the contract make it substantially more burdensome for the parties to perform the promised acts, the contract is discharged.

For instance, actor Gene Autry was drafted into the U.S. Army in 1942. Being drafted rendered his contract with a Hollywood movie company temporarily impossible to perform, and it was suspended until the end of World War II. When Autry got out of the army, the purchasing power of the dollar had declined so much that performance of the contract would have been substantially burdensome to him. Therefore, the contract was discharged.[18]

CASE EXAMPLE 11.27 On August 22, 2005, Keefe Hurwitz contracted to sell his home in Madisonville, Louisiana, to Wesley and Gwendolyn Payne for a price of $241,500. On August 26—just four days after the parties signed the contract—Hurricane Katrina made landfall and caused extensive property damage to the house. The cost of repairs was estimated at $60,000 and Hurwitz would have to make the repairs before the *closing date* (see Chapter 20). Hurwitz did not have the funds and refused to pay $60,000 for the repairs only to sell the property to the Paynes for the previously agreed-on price of $241,500. The Paynes filed a lawsuit to enforce the contract. Hurwitz claimed that Hurricane Katrina had made it impossible for him to perform and had discharged his duties under the contract. The court, however, ruled that Hurricane Katrina had caused only a temporary impossibility. Hurwitz was required to pay for the necessary repairs and to perform the contract as written. In other words, he could not obtain a higher purchase price to offset the cost of the repairs.[19] •

Commercial Impracticability

Courts may excuse parties from their performance obligations when the performance becomes much more difficult or expensive than the parties originally contemplated at the time the contract was formed. For someone to invoke the doctrine of **commercial impracticability** successfully, however, the anticipated performance must become extremely difficult or costly.[20]

The added burden of performing not only *must be extreme but also must not have been known by the parties when the contract was made.* For instance, in one classic case, a court held that a contract could be discharged because a party would otherwise have to pay ten times more than the original estimate to excavate a certain amount of gravel.[21] In another case, the court allowed a party to rescind a contract for the sale of land because of a potential problem with contaminated groundwater under the land. The court found that "the potential for substantial and unbargained-for" liability made contract performance economically impracticable. Interestingly, the court in that case also noted that the possibility of "environmental degradation with consequences extending well beyond the

17. *Restatement (Second) of Contracts,* Sections 262–266; and UCC 2–615.

18. See *Autry v. Republic Productions,* 30 Cal.2d 144, 180 P.2d 888 (1947).
19. *Payne v. Hurwitz,* 978 So.2d 1000 (La.App. 1st Cir. 2008).
20. *Restatement (Second) of Contracts,* Section 264.
21. *Mineral Park Land Co. v. Howard,* 172 Cal. 289, 156 P. 458 (1916).

• *Exhibit* **11–5 Contract Discharge**

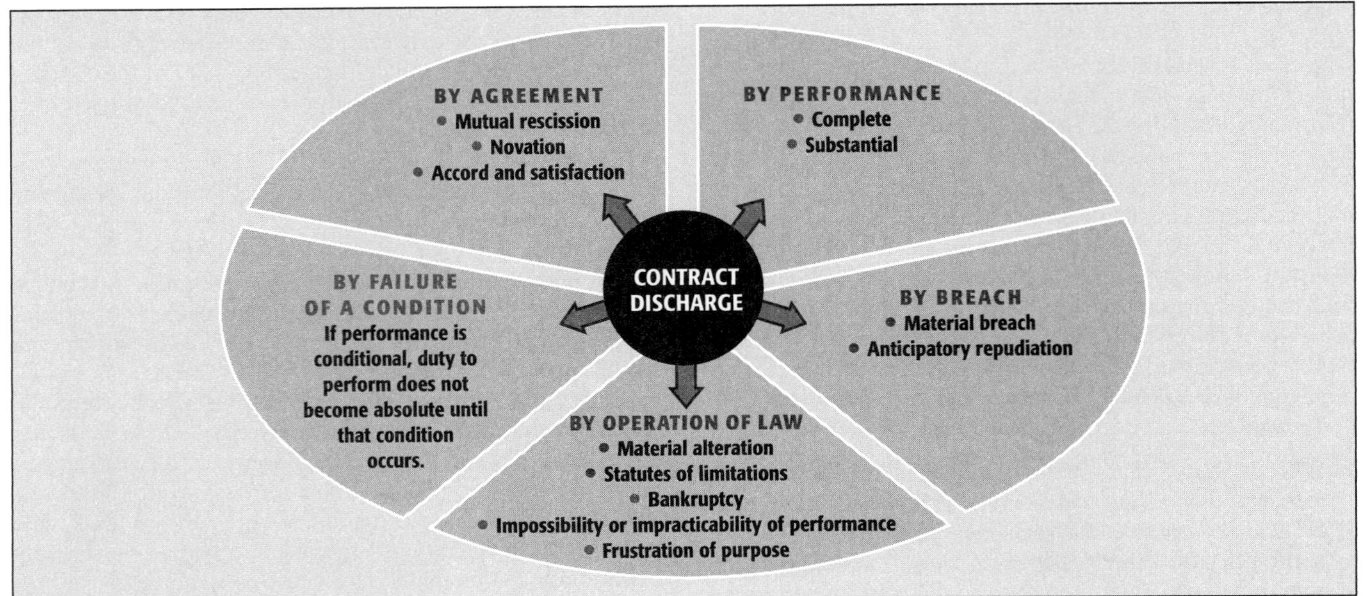

parties' land sale" was just as important to its decision as the economic considerations.[22]

FRUSTRATION OF PURPOSE Closely allied with the doctrine of commercial impracticability is the doctrine of **frustration of purpose.** In principle, a contract will be discharged if supervening circumstances make it impossible to attain the purpose both parties had in mind when making the contract. As with commercial impracticability, the supervening event must not have been foreseeable at the time of the contracting.

See Exhibit 11–5 above for a visual summary of the ways in which a contract can be discharged.

22. *Cape-France Enterprises v. Estate of Peed,* 305 Mont. 513, 29 P.3d 1011 (2001).

Reviewing . . . Third Party Rights and Discharge

Myrtle Jackson owns several commercial buildings that she leases to businesses, one of which is a restaurant. The lease states that tenants are responsible for securing all necessary insurance policies but the landlord is obligated to keep the buildings in good repair. The owner of the restaurant, Joe McCall, tells his restaurant manager to purchase insurance, but the manager never does so. Jackson tells her son-in-law, Rob Dunn, to perform any necessary maintenance for the buildings. Dunn knows that the ceiling in the restaurant needs repair but fails to do anything about it. One day a customer, Ian Faught, is dining in the restaurant when a chunk of the ceiling falls on his head and fractures his skull. Faught files suit against the restaurant and discovers that there is no insurance policy in effect. Faught then files a suit against Jackson, arguing that he is an intended third party beneficiary of the lease provision requiring insurance and thus can sue Jackson for failing to enforce the lease (which requires the restaurant to carry insurance). Using the information presented in the chapter, answer the following questions.

1. Can Jackson delegate her duty to maintain the buildings to Dunn? Why or why not?
2. Who can be held liable for Dunn's failure to fix the ceiling, Jackson or Dunn?
3. Was Faught an intended third party beneficiary of the lease between Jackson and McCall? Why or why not?
4. Suppose that Jackson tells Dan Stryker, a local builder to whom she owes $50,000, that he can collect the rents from the buildings' tenants until the debt is satisfied. Is this a valid assignment? Why or why not?

Terms and Concepts

alienation 196	**condition precedent 200**	**intended beneficiary 198**
anticipatory repudiation 203	**condition subsequent 201**	**mutual rescission 203**
assignee 194	**delegatee 196**	**novation 204**
assignment 193	**delegation of duties 196**	**obligee 194**
assignor 194	**delegator 196**	**obligor 194**
breach of contract 203	**discharge 200**	**performance 200**
commercial impracticability 205	**frustration of purpose 206**	**privity of contract 193**
concurrent conditions 201	**impossibility of performance 204**	**tender 202**
condition 200	**incidental beneficiary 199**	**third party beneficiary 198**

Chapter Summary: Third Party Rights and Discharge

THIRD PARTY RIGHTS	
Assignments (See pages 193–196.)	1. An assignment is the transfer of rights under a contract to a third party. The person assigning the rights is the *assignor,* and the party to whom the rights are assigned is the *assignee.* The assignee has a right to demand performance from the other original party to the contract. 2. Generally, all rights can be assigned, except in certain circumstances. 3. The assignee should notify the obligor of the assignment. Although not legally required, notification avoids two potential problems: a. If the assignor assigns the same right to two different persons, generally the first assignment in time is the first in right, but in some states the first assignee to give notice takes priority. b. Until the obligor is notified of the assignment, the obligor can tender performance to the assignor. If the assignor accepts the performance, the obligor's duties under the contract are discharged without benefit to the assignee.
Delegations (See pages 196–198.)	1. A delegation is the transfer of duties under a contract to a third party (the *delegatee*), who then assumes the obligation of performing the contractual duties previously held by the one making the delegation (the *delegator*). 2. As a general rule, any duty can be delegated, except in certain circumstances. 3. A valid delegation of duties does not relieve the delegator of obligations under the contract. If the delegatee fails to perform, the delegator is still liable to the obligee. 4. An "assignment of all rights" or an "assignment of the contract" is often construed to mean that both the rights and the duties arising under the contract are transferred to a third party.
Third Party Beneficiaries (See pages 198–200.)	A third party beneficiary contract is one made for the purpose of benefiting a third party. 1. *Intended beneficiary*—One for whose benefit a contract is created. When the promisor (the one making the contractual promise that benefits a third party) fails to perform as promised, the third party can sue the promisor directly. Examples of third party beneficiaries are creditor and donee beneficiaries. 2. *Incidental beneficiary*—A third party who indirectly (incidentally) benefits from a contract but for whose benefit the contract was not specifically intended. Incidental beneficiaries have no rights to the benefits received and cannot sue to have the contract enforced.
CONTRACT DISCHARGE	
Conditions of Performance (See pages 200–202.)	Contract obligations may be subject to the following types of conditions: 1. *Condition precedent*—A condition that must be fulfilled before a party's promise becomes absolute. 2. *Condition subsequent*—A condition that operates to terminate a party's absolute promise to perform. 3. *Concurrent conditions*—Conditions that must be performed simultaneously. Each party's absolute duty to perform is conditioned on the other party's absolute duty to perform.

Continued

Chapter Summary: Third Party Rights and Discharge—Continued

Discharge by Performance (See pages 202–203.)	A contract may be discharged by complete (strict) performance or by substantial performance. In some instances, performance must be to the satisfaction of another. Totally inadequate performance constitutes a material breach of the contract. An anticipatory repudiation of a contract allows the other party to sue immediately for breach of contract.
Discharge by Agreement (See pages 203–204.)	Parties may agree to discharge their contractual obligations in several ways: 1. *By mutual rescission*—The parties mutually agree to rescind (cancel) the contract. 2. *By novation*—A new party is substituted for one of the primary parties to a contract. 3. *By accord and satisfaction*—The parties agree to render and accept performance different from that on which they originally agreed.
Discharge by Operation of Law (See pages 204–206.)	Parties' obligations under contracts may be discharged by operation of law owing to one of the following: 1. Material alteration. 2. Statutes of limitations. 3. Bankruptcy. 4. Impossibility of performance. 5. Commercial impracticability. 6. Frustration of purpose.

ExamPrep

ISSUE SPOTTERS

—Check your answers to these questions against the answers provided in Appendix G.

1 Eagle Company contracts to build a house for Frank. The contract states that "any assignment of this contract renders the contract void." After Eagle builds the house, but before Frank pays, Eagle assigns its right to payment to Good Credit Company. Can Good Credit enforce the contract against Frank? Why or why not?

2 Ready Foods contracts to buy from Speedy Distributors two hundred carloads of frozen pizzas. Before Ready or Speedy starts performing, can they call off the deal? What if Speedy has already shipped the pizzas? Explain your answers.

BEFORE THE TEST

Go to **www.cengagebrain.com**, enter the ISBN 9781111530624, and click on "Find" to locate this textbook's Web site. Then, click on "Access Now" under "Study Tools," and select Chapter 11 at the top. There, you will find an Interactive Quiz that you can take to assess your mastery of the concepts in this chapter, as well as Flashcards and a Glossary of important terms.

For Review

1 What is the difference between an assignment and a delegation?
2 What rights can be assigned despite a contract clause expressly prohibiting assignment?
3 What factors indicate that a third party beneficiary is an intended beneficiary?
4 How are most contracts discharged?
5 What is a contractual condition, and how might a condition affect contractual obligations?

Questions and Case Problems

11–1 Third Party Beneficiaries. Wilken owes Rivera $2,000. Howie promises Wilken that he will pay Rivera the $2,000 in return for Wilken's promise to give Howie's children guitar lessons. Is Rivera an intended beneficiary of the Howie-Wilken contract? Explain.

11–2 Conditions of Performance. The Caplans own a real estate lot, and they contract with Faithful Construction, Inc., to build a house on it for $360,000. The specifications list "all plumbing bowls and fixtures . . . to be Crane brand." The Caplans leave on vacation, and during their absence Faithful is unable to buy and install Crane plumbing fixtures. Instead, Faithful installs Kohler brand fixtures, an equivalent in the industry. On completion of the building contract, the Caplans inspect the work, discover the substitution, and refuse to accept the house, claiming Faithful has breached the conditions set forth in the specifications. Discuss fully the Caplans' claim.

11–3 Assignments. Hensley purchased a house but was unable to pay the full purchase price. She borrowed funds from Thrift Savings and Loan, which in turn took a mortgage at 6.5 percent interest on the house. The mortgage contract did not prohibit the assignment of the mortgage. Hensley secured a job in another city and sold the house to Sylvia. The purchase price included payment to Hensley of the value of her equity and the assumption of the mortgage debt still owed to Thrift. At the time the contract between Hensley and Sylvia was made, Thrift did not know about or consent to the sale. Based on these facts, if Sylvia defaults in making the house payments to Thrift, what are Thrift's rights? Discuss.

11–4 Assignment and Delegation. Bruce Albea Contracting, Inc., was the general contractor on a state highway project. Albea and its *sureties* (the companies that consented to guarantee the financial liabilities involved) agreed to be liable for all work on the project. Albea subcontracted with APAC-Southeast, Inc., an asphalt company. The contract stated that it could not be assigned without Albea's consent. Later, Albea and APAC got into a dispute because APAC wanted to be paid more for its asphalt. APAC then sold and assigned its assets, including the contract, to Matthews Contracting Co. Albea was informed of the assignment and did not approve it but allowed Matthews to work. Matthews demanded higher payments for asphalt, and Albea agreed because no other contractor would step in at the original price. Albea suffered a loss on the job and could not pay its bills, so Albea's sureties paid Matthews $2.7 million for work performed. APAC sued Albea and its sureties for $1.2 million for work it had performed before the contract was delegated to Matthews. The trial court granted APAC $1.2 million. On appeal, the defendants argued that APAC had breached the contract by assignment without consent. Did APAC breach the contract with Albea? Did Albea owe APAC anything? Explain your answers. [*Western Surety Co. v. APAC-Southeast, Inc.,* 302 Ga.App. 654, 691 S.E.2d 234 (2010)]

11–5 Case Problem with Sample Answer Just Homes, LLC (JH), hired Mike Building & Contracting, Inc., to do $1.35 million worth of renovation work on three homes. Community Preservation Corp. (CPC) supervised Mike's work on behalf of JH. The contract stated that in the event of a dispute, JH would have to obtain the project architect's certification to justify terminating Mike. As construction progressed, relations between Mike and CPC worsened. At a certain point in the project, Mike requested partial payment, and CPC recommended that JH not make it. Mike refused to continue work without further payment. JH evicted Mike from the project. Mike sued for breach of contract. JH contended that it had the right to terminate the contract due to CPC's negative reports and Mike's failure to agree with the project's engineer. Mike moved for summary judgment for the amounts owed for work performed, claiming that JH had not fulfilled the condition precedent—that is, JH never obtained the project architect's certification for Mike's termination. Which of the two parties involved breached the contract? Explain your answer. [*Mike Building & Contracting, Inc. v. Just Homes, LLC,* 27 Misc.3d 833, 901 N.Y.S.2d 458 (2010)]

—For a sample answer to Problem 11–5, go to Appendix F at the end of this text.

11–6 Conditions of Performance. James Maciel leased an apartment in Regent Village, a university-owned housing facility for Regent University (RU) students in Virginia Beach, Virginia. The lease ran until the end of the fall semester. Maciel had an option to renew the lease semester by semester as long as he maintained his status as an RU student. When Maciel completed his coursework for the spring semester, he told RU that he intended to withdraw. The university told him that he could stay in the apartment until May 31, the final day of the spring semester. Maciel asked for two additional weeks, but the university denied the request. On June 1, RU changed the locks on the apartment. Maciel entered through a window and e-mailed the university that he planned to stay "for another one or two weeks." Charged in a Virginia state court with trespassing, Maciel argued that he had "legal authority" to occupy the apartment. Was Maciel correct? Explain. [*Maciel v. Commonwealth,* __ S.E.2d __ (Va.App. 2011)]

11–7 Assignment. Mary Kazery entered into a lease with Courtesy Inns, Inc. The initial term was one year, with a renewal option of twenty years and four subsequent options of ten years each. During the first renewal term, Courtesy assigned its interest in the lease to George Wilkinson. A year later, Kazery transferred her interest in the property to her son, Arnold. Less than a year later, Arnold transferred his interest to his son, Sam, who became the sole owner of the property. No one notified Wilkinson. For the next twenty years, Wilkinson paid the rent to Arnold and renewed the lease by notice to Arnold. At the end of the third term, Wilkinson wrote to Arnold that he was exercising the fourth option. More than ten months later, Sam filed a suit in a Mississippi state court against Wilkinson, claiming that the lease was void because Wilkinson had not given proper notice to renew. Who should have notified Wilkinson that Sam had been assigned Arnold's interest in the property? What effect does the lack of notice have on Wilkinson's discharge of his duties under the lease? Did he give proper notice to renew? Discuss. [*Kazery v. Wilkinson,* 52 So.3d 1270 (Miss. App. 2011)]

11–8 A Question of Ethics *King County, Washington, hired Frank Coluccio Construction Co. (FCCC) to act as general contractor for a public works project involving the construction of a small utility tunnel under the Duwamish Waterway. FCCC hired Donald B. Murphy Contractors, Inc. (DBM), as a subcontractor. DBM was responsible for constructing an access shaft at the eastern end of the tunnel. Problems arose during construction, including a "blow-in" of the access shaft that caused it to fill with water, soil, and debris. FCCC and DBM incurred substantial expenses from the repairs and delays. Under the project contract, King County was supposed to buy an insurance policy to "insure* *against physical loss or damage by perils included under an 'All-Risk' Builder's Risk policy." Any claim under this policy was to be filed through the insured. King County, which had general property damage insurance, did not obtain an all-risk builder's risk policy. For the losses attributable to the blow-in, FCCC and DBM submitted builder's risk claims, which the county denied. FCCC filed a suit in a Washington state court against King County, alleging, among other claims, breach of contract.* [Frank Coluccio Construction Co., Inc. v. King County, *136 Wash.App. 751, 150 P.3d 1147 (Div. 1 2007)*]

1 King County's property damage policy specifically excluded, at the county's request, coverage of tunnels. The county drafted its contract with FCCC to require the all-risk builder's risk policy and authorize itself to "sponsor" claims. When FCCC and DBM filed their claims, the county secretly colluded with its property damage insurer to deny payment. What do these facts indicate about the county's ethics and legal liability in this situation?

2 Could DBM, as a third party to the contract between King County and FCCC, maintain an action on the contract against King County? Discuss.

3 All-risk insurance is a promise to pay on the "fortuitous" happening of a loss or damage from any cause except those that are specifically excluded. Payment usually is not made on a loss that, at the time the insurance was obtained, the claimant subjectively knew would occur. If a loss results from faulty workmanship on the part of a contractor, should the obligation to pay under an all-risk policy be discharged? Explain.

11–9 **Critical Thinking Legal Question** If intended third party beneficiaries could not sue the promisor directly to enforce a contract, what would their legal remedy be?

11–10 **Video Question** To watch this chapter's video, *Third Party Beneficiaries,* go to **www.cengagebrain.com**. Register the access code that came with your new book or log in to your existing account. Select the link for the "Business Law Digital Video Library Online Access" or "Business Law CourseMate." Click on "Complete Video List," view Video 20, and then answer the following questions:

1 Discuss whether a valid contract was formed when Oscar and Vinny bet on the outcome of a football game. Would Vinny be able to enforce the contract in court? Discuss fully.

2 Is the Fresh Air Fund an incidental or an intended beneficiary? Explain your answer.

3 Can Maria sue to enforce Vinny's promise to donate Oscar's winnings to the Fresh Air Fund? Why or why not?

Chapter 12

Breach and Remedies

Learning Objectives

After reading this chapter, you should be able to answer the following questions:

1. What is the difference between compensatory damages and consequential damages? What are nominal damages, and when do courts award nominal damages?
2. What is the standard measure of compensatory damages when a contract is breached? How are damages computed differently in construction contracts?
3. Under what circumstances is the remedy of rescission and restitution available?
4. When do courts grant specific performance as a remedy?
5. What is a limitation-of-liability clause, and when will courts enforce it?

The Learning Objectives above are designed to help improve your understanding of the chapter.

(AP Photo/Carlos Osorio)

Normally, people enter into contracts to secure some advantage. When it is no longer advantageous for a party to fulfill her or his contractual obligations, that party may *breach*, or fail to perform, the contract. Once one party breaches the contract, the other party—the nonbreaching party—can choose one or more of several remedies. A *remedy* is the relief provided to an innocent party when the other party has breached the contract. It is the means employed to enforce a right or to redress an injury. While there may not be a remedy for every situation, there is a remedy available for nearly every contract breach.

The most common remedies available to a nonbreaching party under contract law include damages, rescission and restitution, specific performance, and reformation. Courts distinguish between *remedies at law* and *remedies in equity*. Today, the remedy at law normally is monetary damages. We discuss this remedy in the first part of this chapter. Equitable remedies include rescission and restitution, specific performance, and reformation, all of which we examine later in this chapter. Usually, a court will not award an equitable remedy unless the remedy at law is inadequate. We also look at some special legal doctrines and concepts relating to remedies.

Damages

A breach of contract entitles the nonbreaching party to sue for monetary damages. Tort law damages are designed to compensate a party for harm suffered as a result of another's wrongful act. In the context of contract law, damages are designed to compensate the nonbreaching party for the loss of the bargain, including lost profits. Often, courts say that innocent parties are to be placed in the position they would have occupied had the contract been fully performed.[1]

Types of Damages

There are basically four broad categories of damages:

1. Compensatory—to cover direct losses and costs.
2. Consequential—to cover indirect and foreseeable losses.

1. *Restatement (Second) of Contracts,* Section 347.

3. Punitive—to punish and deter wrongdoing.
4. Nominal—to recognize wrongdoing when no monetary loss is shown.

Compensatory and punitive damages were discussed in Chapter 4 in the context of tort law. Here, we look at these types of damages, as well as consequential and nominal damages, in the context of contract law.

COMPENSATORY DAMAGES Damages that compensate the nonbreaching party for the *loss of the bargain* are known as *compensatory damages*. These damages compensate the injured party only for damages actually sustained and proved to have arisen directly from the loss of the bargain caused by the breach of contract. They simply replace what was lost because of the wrong or damage.

The standard measure of compensatory damages is the difference between the value of the breaching party's promised performance under the contract and the value of her or his actual performance. This amount is reduced by any loss that the injured party has avoided.

EXAMPLE 12.1 Matt contracts with Marinot Industries to perform certain personal services exclusively for Marinot during August for a payment of $4,000. Marinot cancels the contract and is in breach. Matt is able to find another job during August but can earn only $3,000. He normally can sue Marinot for breach and recover $1,000 as compensatory damages. He may also recover from Marinot the amount that he spent to find the other job. • Expenses that are directly incurred because of a breach of contract—such as those incurred to obtain performance from another source—are called **incidental damages.**

The measurement of compensatory damages varies by type of contract. Certain types of contracts deserve special mention—contracts for the sale of goods, contracts for the sale of land, and construction contracts.

Sale of Goods. In a contract for the sale of goods, the usual measure of compensatory damages is the difference between the contract price and the market price. **EXAMPLE 12.2** Medik Laboratories contracts to buy ten model UTS 400 network servers from Cal Industries for $4,000 each. Cal Industries, however, fails to deliver the ten servers to Medik. The market price of the servers at the time Medik learns of the breach is $4,500. Therefore, Medik's measure of damages is $5,000 (10 × $500), plus any incidental damages (expenses) caused by the breach. • When the buyer breaches and the seller has not yet produced the goods, compensatory damages normally equal the seller's lost profits on the sale, rather than the difference between the contract price and the market price.

Sale of Land. Ordinarily, because each parcel of land is unique, the remedy for a seller's breach of a contract for a sale of real estate is specific performance—that is, the buyer is awarded the parcel of property for which he or she bargained (*specific performance* will be discussed more fully later in this chapter). When this remedy is unavailable (because the property has been sold, for example) or when the buyer is the party in breach, the measure of damages is typically the difference between the contract price and the market price of the land. The majority of states follow this rule.

Construction Contracts. The measure of damages in a building or construction contract varies depending on which party breaches and when the breach occurs. If the owner breaches *before performance has begun,* the contractor can recover only the profits that would have been made on the contract (that is, the total contract price less the cost of materials and labor). If the owner breaches *during performance,* the contractor can recover the profits plus the costs incurred in partially constructing the building. If the owner breaches *after the construction has been completed,* the contractor can recover the entire contract price, plus interest.

When the contractor breaches the construction contract—either by failing to begin construction or by stopping work partway through the project—the measure of damages is the cost of completion, which includes reasonable compensation for any delay in performance. If the contractor finishes late, the measure of damages is the loss of use. Exhibit 12–1 on page 214 summarizes the rules concerning the measurement of damages in breached construction contracts.

How should a court rule when the performance of both parties—the construction contractor and the owner—falls short of what their contract required? That was the issue in the following case.

Case 12.1 Jamison Well Drilling, Inc. v. Pfeifer

Court of Appeals of Ohio, Third District, 2011 Ohio 521 (2011).

FACTS Jamison Well Drilling, Inc., contracted to drill a water well for Ed Pfeifer in Crawford County, Ohio. Pfeifer agreed to pay Jamison $4,130 for the labor and supplies. Jamison drilled the well and installed a storage tank. The Ohio Department of Health requires that a well be lined with a minimum of twenty-five vertical feet of casing, but Jamison installed only eleven feet of casing in the drilled well. The county health department later tested the water in the well for bacteria and repeatedly found that the levels were too high. The state health department investigated and discovered that the well's casing did not comply with its requirements. The department ordered that the well be abandoned and sealed. Pfeifer used the storage tank but

Case 12.1–Continued

paid Jamison nothing. Jamison filed a suit in an Ohio state court against Pfeifer to recover the contract price and other costs. The court entered a judgment for Jamison for $970 for the storage tank. Jamison appealed.

ISSUE Does Pfeifer have to pay the full contract price to Jamison when the well cannot be used because it does not meet health department standards?

DECISION No. A state appellate court affirmed the lower court's decision. The judgment had struck a balance that realized the completed construction project had value and the storage tank was functional, but the well was not usable.

REASON The court reasoned that the parties entered into a contract for the drilling of a well for a certain price. The work also included the installation of a storage tank. The drilled well was not in compliance with state law and consequently had to be sealed and abandoned. Pfeifer may have assumed the risk that the well could not be used due to inadequate water production, but he did not assume the risk that it would have to be sealed for noncompliance with state law.

Thus, Jamison was not entitled to the full contract price of $4,130. Yet the storage tank was usable, and Pfeifer had kept it. Because it would not be fair to allow Pfeifer to keep the tank without paying for it, Jamison should recover the cost of the tank only.

WHAT IF THE FACTS WERE DIFFERENT? *Suppose that Pfeifer had paid Jamison for the work before the well was ordered sealed and had later filed a suit to recover for breach of contract. What would have been the measure of damages?*

CONSEQUENTIAL DAMAGES Foreseeable damages that result from a party's breach of contract are called **consequential damages**, or *special damages*. They differ from compensatory damages in that they are caused by special circumstances beyond the contract itself and flow from the consequences, or results, of a breach.

When a seller fails to deliver goods, knowing that the buyer is planning to use or resell those goods immediately, a court may award consequential damages (in addition to compensatory damages) for the loss of profits from the planned resale. **EXAMPLE 12.3** Gilmore contracts to have a specific item shipped to her—one that she desperately needs to repair her printing press. In her contract with the shipper, Gilmore states that she must receive the item by Monday, or she will not be able to print her paper and will lose $3,000. If the shipper is late, Gilmore normally can recover the consequential damages caused by the delay (that is, the $3,000 in losses). •

To recover consequential damages, the breaching party must know (or have reason to know) that special circumstances will cause the nonbreaching party to suffer an additional loss. This rule was enunciated in the following classic case. In reading this decision, it is helpful to understand that in the mid-nineteenth century, large flour mills customarily kept more than one main crankshaft on hand in the event that one broke and had to be repaired.

Classic Case 12.2 Hadley v. Baxendale

Court of Exchequer, 156 Eng.Rep. 145 (1854).

FACTS The Hadleys (the plaintiffs) ran a flour mill in Gloucester, England. The main crankshaft attached to the steam engine in the mill broke, causing the mill to shut down. The crankshaft had to be sent to a foundry located in Greenwich so that a new shaft could be made to fit the other parts of the engine. Baxendale, the defendant, was a common carrier that transported the shaft from Gloucester to Greenwich. The freight charges were collected in advance, and Baxendale promised to deliver the shaft the following day. It was not delivered for a number of days, however. As a consequence, the mill was closed for several days. The Hadleys sued to recover the profits lost during that time. Baxendale contended that the loss of profits was "too remote" to be recoverable. The court held for the plaintiffs, and the jury was allowed to take into consideration the lost profits. The defendant appealed.

ISSUE Did Baxendale have reason to know that a delay in delivering the crankshaft would cause the mill to shut down?

DECISION No. The Court of Exchequer reversed the decision of the lower court and ordered a new trial at which the lost profits could not be awarded.

REASON According to the court, to collect consequential damages, the plaintiffs would have to have given express notice of the special circumstances that cause the loss of profit. The only circumstances communicated by the Hadleys to Baxendale at the time the contract was made were that (1) the item to be transported was a broken crankshaft of a mill and (2) the Hadleys were the owners and operators of that mill. The court reasoned that these circumstances did not reasonably indicate that the mill would have to stop operations if the delivery of the crankshaft was delayed.

FOR CRITICAL ANALYSIS—E-Commerce Consideration *If a Web merchant loses business due to a computer system's failure that*

Case 12.2–Continues next page ➡

Classic Case 12.2–Continued

can be attributed to malfunctioning software, can the merchant recover the lost profits from the software maker? Explain.

IMPACT OF THIS CASE ON TODAY'S LAW *This case established the rule that when damages are awarded, compensation is given only for those injuries that the defendant could reasonably have foreseen as a probable result of the usual course of events following a breach. Today, the rule enunciated by the court in this case still applies. To recover consequential damages, the plaintiff must show that the defendant had reason to know or foresee that a particular loss or injury would occur.*

PUNITIVE DAMAGES Punitive, or exemplary, damages, generally are not awarded in an action for breach of contract. Such damages have no legitimate place in contract law because they are, in essence, penalties, and a breach of contract is not unlawful in a criminal sense. A contract is simply a civil relationship between the parties. The law may compensate one party for the loss of the bargain—no more and no less.

In a few situations, when a person's actions cause both a breach of contract and a tort, punitive damages may be available. Overall, though, punitive damages are almost never available in contract disputes.

NOMINAL DAMAGES When no actual damage or financial loss results from a breach of contract and only a technical injury is involved, the court may award **nominal damages** to the innocent party. Nominal damages awards are often small, such as one dollar, but they do establish that the defendant acted wrongfully. Most lawsuits for nominal damages are brought as a matter of principle under the theory that a breach has occurred and some damages must be imposed regardless of actual loss.

EXAMPLE 12.4 Hernandez contracts to buy potatoes at fifty cents a pound from Stanley. Stanley breaches the contract and does not deliver the potatoes. Meanwhile, the price of potatoes falls. Hernandez is able to buy them in the open market at half the price he agreed to pay Stanley. Hernandez is clearly better off because of Stanley's breach. Thus, because Hernandez sustained only a technical injury and suffered no monetary loss, if he sues for breach of contract and wins, the court will likely award only nominal damages. •

Mitigation of Damages

In most situations, when a breach of contract occurs, the injured party is held to a duty to mitigate, or reduce, the damages that he or she suffers. Under this doctrine of **mitigation of damages,** the required action depends on the nature of the situation.

In the majority of states, a person whose employment has been wrongfully terminated has a duty to mitigate damages incurred because of the employer's breach of the employment contract. In other words, wrongfully terminated employees have a duty to take similar jobs if they are available. If the employees fail to do this, the damages they receive will be equivalent to their salaries less the incomes they would have received in similar jobs obtained by reasonable means. Normally, the employee is under no duty to take a job that is not of the same type and rank.

CASE EXAMPLE 12.5 Harry De La Concha was employed by Fordham University. De La Concha claimed that he was injured in an altercation with Fordham's director of human resources and filed for workers' compensation benefits. (These benefits are available for on-the-job injuries regardless of fault, as you will read in Chapter 22.) Fordham then fired De La Concha, who sought to be reinstated by arguing that he had been terminated in retaliation for filing a workers' compensation claim. The New York state workers' compensation board held that De La Concha had failed to mitigate his damages because he had not even looked for another job, and a state court affirmed the decision. Because De La Concha had failed to mitigate his damages, any compensation he received would

• ***Exhibit* 12–1 Measurement of Damages–Breach of Construction Contracts**

PARTY IN BREACH	TIME OF BREACH	MEASUREMENT OF DAMAGES
Owner	Before construction has begun.	Profits (contract price less cost of materials and labor).
Owner	During construction.	Profits, plus costs incurred up to time of breach.
Owner	After construction is completed.	Full contract price, plus interest.
Contractor	Before construction has begun.	Cost in excess of contract price to complete work.
Contractor	Before construction is completed.	Generally, all costs incurred by owner to complete.

be reduced by the amount he could have obtained from other employment.[2] •

Some states require a landlord to use reasonable means to find a new tenant if a tenant abandons the premises and fails to pay rent. If an acceptable tenant becomes available, the landlord is required to lease the premises to this tenant to mitigate the damages recoverable from the former tenant. The former tenant is still liable for the difference between the amount of the rent under the original lease and the rent received from the new tenant. If the landlord has not taken reasonable steps to find a new tenant, a court will likely reduce any award by the amount of rent the landlord could have received had he or she done so.

Liquidated Damages versus Penalties

A **liquidated damages** provision in a contract specifies that a certain dollar amount is to be paid in the event of a future default or breach of contract. (*Liquidated* means determined, settled, or fixed.) Liquidated damages differ from penalties. A **penalty** specifies a certain amount to be paid in the event of a default or breach of contract and is designed to penalize the breaching party. Liquidated damages provisions normally are enforceable. In contrast, if a court finds that a provision calls for a penalty, the agreement as to the amount will not be enforced, and recovery will be limited to actual damages.[3]

To determine whether a particular provision is for liquidated damages or for a penalty, the court must answer two questions:

1. At the time the contract was formed, was it apparent that damages would be difficult to estimate in the event of a breach?
2. Was the amount set as damages a reasonable estimate and not excessive?[4]

If the answers to both questions are yes, the provision normally will be enforced. If either answer is no, the provision usually will not be enforced. Liquidated damages provisions are frequently used in construction contracts because it is difficult to estimate the amount of damages that would be caused by a delay in completing the work.

EXAMPLE 12.6 Ray Curl is a construction contractor. He enters into a contract with a developer to build a home in a new subdivision. The contract includes a clause that requires Curl to pay $300 for every day he is late in completing the project. This is a liquidated damages provision because it specifies a reasonable amount that Curl must pay to the developer if his performance is late. •

In the following case, the issue before the court was whether a clause in a contract was an enforceable liquidated damages provision or an unenforceable penalty.

2. *De La Concha v. Fordham University,* 814 N.Y.S.2d 320, 28 A.3d 963 (2006).
3. This is also the rule under the UCC. See UCC 2–718(1).
4. *Restatement (Second) of Contracts,* Section 356(1).

Case 12.3 B-Sharp Musical Productions, Inc. v. Haber

New York Supreme Court, 27 Misc.3d 41, 899 N.Y.S.2d 792 (2010).

FACTS B-Sharp Musical Productions, Inc., and James Haber entered into a contract under which B-Sharp was to provide a designated sixteen-piece band on a specified date to perform at Haber's son's bar mitzvah. Haber was to pay approximately $30,000 for the band's services. The contract contained a liquidated damages clause stating, "If [the contract] is terminated in writing by [Haber] for any reason within ninety (90) days prior to the engagement, the remaining balance of the contract will be immediately due and payable. If [the contract] is terminated in writing by [Haber] for any reason before the ninety (90) days period, 50% of the balance will be immediately due and payable."

Fewer than ninety days before the date of the bar mitzvah, Haber sent a letter to B-Sharp notifying it that he was canceling the contract. After Haber refused B-Sharp's demand that he pay the remaining amount due under the contract—approximately $25,000—B-Sharp sued Haber and his wife in a New York state court to recover the damages. The court granted B-Sharp's motion for summary judgment, enforcing the liquidated damages clause, and the defendants appealed.

ISSUE Was the liquidated damages clause, which specified the amount to be paid to the band in the event that the performance was cancelled, enforceable?

DECISION Yes. The New York Supreme Court upheld the civil court's judgment. The clause was a reasonable estimate of damages given that B-Sharp most likely would not be able to rebook another performance that close to the contracted performance for the Haber bar mitzvah.

Case 12.3—Continues next page ➡

Case 12.3–Continued

REASON The court determined that the clause in question was "not an unenforceable penalty." The clause used an estimate of B-Sharp's probable loss in the event of a cancellation as the measure of loss. This estimate reflected an understanding that "although the expense and possibility of rebooking a cancelled [performance] could not be ascertained with certainty, as a practical matter, the expense would become greater, and the possibility would be less, the closer to the [performance] the cancellation was made, until a point was reached, [ninety] days before the [performance], that any effort to rebook could not be reasonably expected."

FOR CRITICAL ANALYSIS—Ethical Consideration *Why did the court determine that the contract clause at issue provided for enforceable liquidated damages and not for an unenforceable penalty?*

Equitable Remedies

Sometimes, damages are an inadequate remedy for a breach of contract. In these situations, the nonbreaching party may ask the court for an equitable remedy. Equitable remedies include *rescission and restitution, specific performance,* and *reformation.*

Rescission and Restitution

As discussed in previous chapters, *rescission* is essentially an action to undo, or cancel, a contract—to return nonbreaching parties to the positions that they occupied before the transaction. The rescission discussed here refers to *unilateral* rescission, in which only one party wants to undo the contract. In *mutual* rescission (see page 203), both parties agree to undo the contract. Mutual rescission discharges the contract. Unilateral rescission generally is available as a remedy for breach of contract.

When fraud, mistake, duress, undue influence, lack of capacity, or failure of consideration is present, rescission is available. Rescission may also be available by statute. The failure of one party to perform under a contract entitles the other party to rescind the contract. The rescinding party must give prompt notice to the breaching party.

RESTITUTION To rescind a contract, both parties generally must make **restitution** to each other by returning goods, property, or funds previously conveyed.[5] If the property or goods can be returned, they must be. If the property or goods have been consumed, restitution must be made in an equivalent dollar amount.

Essentially, restitution involves the recapture of a benefit conferred on the defendant that has unjustly enriched her or him. **EXAMPLE 12.7** Andrea pays $32,000 to Miles in return for his promise to design a house for her. The next day, Miles calls Andrea and tells her that he has taken a position with a large architectural firm in another state and cannot design the house. Andrea decides to hire another architect that afternoon. Andrea can require restitution of $32,000 because Miles has received an unjust benefit of $32,000. •

5. *Restatement (Second) of Contracts,* Section 370.

RESTITUTION IS NOT LIMITED TO RESCISSION CASES Restitution may be required when a contract is rescinded, but the right to restitution is not limited to rescission cases. Because an award of restitution basically gives back or returns something to its rightful owner, a party can seek restitution in actions for breach of contract, tort actions, and other types of actions. For instance, restitution can be obtained when funds or property has been transferred by mistake or because of fraud or incapacity. Similarly, restitution might be available when there has been misconduct by a party with a special relationship with the other party. Even in criminal cases a court can order restitution of funds or property obtained through embezzlement, conversion, theft, or copyright infringement.

Specific Performance

The equitable remedy of **specific performance** calls for the performance of the act promised in the contract. This remedy is attractive to a nonbreaching party because it provides the exact bargain promised in the contract. It also avoids some of the problems inherent in a suit for monetary damages, such as collecting a judgment and arranging another contract. Moreover, the actual performance may be more valuable than the monetary damages.

Normally, however, specific performance will not be granted unless the party's legal remedy (monetary damages) is inadequate.[6] For this reason, contracts for the sale of goods rarely qualify for specific performance. Monetary damages ordinarily are adequate in sales contracts because substantially identical goods can be bought or sold in the market. Only if the goods are unique will a court grant specific performance. For instance, paintings, sculptures, and rare books and coins are often unique, and monetary damages will not enable a buyer to obtain substantially identical substitutes in the market.

SALE OF LAND A court will grant specific performance to a buyer in an action for a breach of contract involving the sale of land. In this situation, the legal remedy of monetary damages will not compensate the buyer adequately because every parcel

6. *Restatement (Second) of Contracts,* Section 359.

of land is unique. The same land in the same location obviously cannot be obtained elsewhere. Only when specific performance is unavailable (for example, when the seller has sold the property to someone else) will damages be awarded instead.

CASE EXAMPLE 12.8 Howard Stainbrook entered into a contract to sell Trent Low forty acres of land for $45,000. Low agreed to pay for a survey of the property and other costs in addition to the price. He gave Stainbrook a check for $1,000 to show his intent to fulfill the contract. One month later, Stainbrook died. His son David became the executor of the estate. After he discovered that the timber on the property was worth more than $100,000, David asked Low to withdraw his offer to buy the forty acres. Low refused and filed a suit against David seeking specific performance of the contract. The court found that because Low had substantially performed his obligations under the contract and offered to perform the rest, he was entitled to specific performance.[7] •

CONTRACTS FOR PERSONAL SERVICES Personal-service contracts require one party to work personally for another party. Courts normally refuse to grant specific performance of contracts for personal services. This is because ordering a party to perform personal services against his or her will amounts to a type of involuntary servitude, which is contrary to the public policy expressed in the Thirteenth Amendment to the U.S. Constitution. Moreover, the courts do not want to monitor contracts for personal services, which usually require the exercise of personal judgment or talent.

EXAMPLE 12.9 If Nicole contracts with a surgeon to remove a brain tumor and he refuses to perform, the court will not compel (nor would Nicole want) the surgeon to perform under these circumstances. There is no way the court can ensure meaningful performance in such a situation.[8] • If a contract is not deemed personal, the remedy at law of monetary damages may be adequate if substantially identical service (for example, lawn mowing) is available from other persons.

7. *Stainbrook v. Low,* 842 N.E.2d 386 (Ind.App. 2006).

Reformation

Reformation is an equitable remedy used when the parties have *imperfectly* expressed their agreement in writing. Reformation allows a court to rewrite the contract to reflect the parties' true intentions. Courts order reformation most often when fraud or mutual mistake is present. **EXAMPLE 12.10** If Carson contracts to buy a forklift from Shelley but the written contract refers to a crane, a mutual mistake has occurred. Accordingly, a court could reform the contract so that the writing conforms to the parties' original intention as to which piece of equipment is being sold. • Exhibit 12–2 below graphically presents the remedies, including reformation, that are available to the nonbreaching party.

Courts frequently reform contracts in two other situations. The first occurs when two parties who have made a binding oral contract agree to put the oral contract in writing but, in doing so, they make an error in stating the terms. Usually, the courts allow into evidence the correct terms of the oral contract, thereby reforming the written contract. The second situation occurs when the parties have executed a written covenant not to compete (see Chapter 9). If the covenant not to compete is for a valid and legitimate purpose (such as the sale of a business) but the area or time restraints are unreasonable, some courts will reform the restraints by making them reasonable and will enforce the entire contract as reformed. Other courts, however, will throw out the entire restrictive covenant as illegal.

8. Similarly, courts often refuse to order specific performance of construction contracts because courts are not set up to operate as construction supervisors or engineers.

• ***Exhibit*** **12–2 Remedies for Breach of Contract**

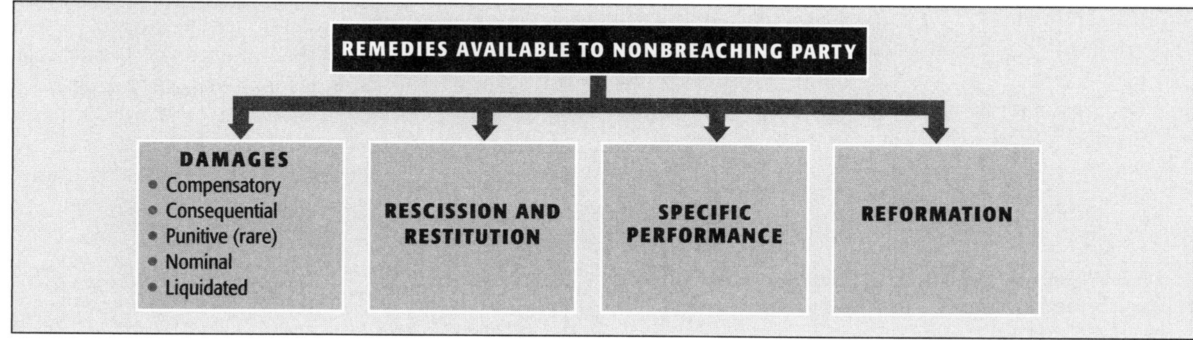

Recovery Based on Quasi Contract

In some situations, when no actual contract exists, a court may step in to prevent one party from being unjustly enriched at the expense of another party. As discussed in Chapter 7, *quasi contract* is a legal theory under which an obligation is imposed in the absence of an agreement. A quasi contract is not a true contract but rather a fictional contract that is imposed on the parties to prevent unjust enrichment.

When Quasi Contract Is Used

Quasi contract allows a court to act as if a contract exists when there is no actual contract or agreement between the parties. A court can also use this theory when the parties entered into a contract, but it is unenforceable for some reason.

Quasi-contractual recovery is often granted when one party has partially performed under a contract that is unenforceable. It provides an alternative to suing for damages and allows the party to recover the reasonable value of the partial performance. **EXAMPLE 12.11** Ericson contracts to build two oil derricks for Petro Industries. The derricks are to be built over a period of three years, but the parties do not create a written contract. Therefore, the Statute of Frauds will bar the enforcement of the contract.[9] After Ericson completes one derrick, Petro Industries informs him that it will not pay for the derrick. Ericson can sue Petro Industries under the theory of quasi contract. •

The Requirements of Quasi Contract

To recover on a quasi contract theory, the party seeking recovery must show the following:

1. The party conferred a benefit on the other party.
2. The party conferred the benefit with the reasonable expectation of being paid.
3. The party did not act as a volunteer in conferring the benefit.
4. The party receiving the benefit would be unjustly enriched if allowed to retain the benefit without paying for it.

Applying these requirements to Example 12.11, Ericson can sue in quasi contract because all of the conditions for quasi-contractual recovery have been fulfilled. Ericson conferred a benefit on Petro Industries by building the oil derrick. Ericson build the derrick with the reasonable expectation of being paid. He did not intend to act as a volunteer. Petro Industries would be unjustly enriched if it was allowed to keep the derrick without paying Ericson for the work. Therefore, Ericson should be able to recover the reasonable value of the oil derrick that was built (under the theory of *quantum meruit*[10]—see page 137). The reasonable value is ordinarily equal to the fair market value.

9. Contracts that by their terms cannot be performed within one year from the day after the date of contract formation must be in writing to be enforceable (see Chapter 10).
10. Pronounced *kwahn*-tuhm *mehr*-oo-wuht.

Contract Provisions Limiting Remedies

A contract may include provisions stating that no damages can be recovered for certain types of breaches or that damages will be limited to a maximum amount. The contract may also provide that the only remedy for breach is replacement, repair, or refund of the purchase price. Provisions stating that no damages can be recovered are called *exculpatory clauses* (see Chapter 9). Provisions that affect the availability of certain remedies are called *limitation-of-liability clauses.*

What the UCC Allows

The Uniform Commercial Code (UCC) provides that in a contract for the sale of goods, remedies can be limited. We will examine the UCC provisions on limitation-of-liability clauses in Chapter 14, in the context of the remedies available on the breach of a contract for the sale or lease of goods.[11]

Enforceability of Limitation-of-Liability Clauses

Whether a limitation-of-liability clause in a contract will be enforced depends on the type of breach that is excused by the provision. For instance, a provision excluding liability for fraudulent or intentional injury will not be enforced. Likewise, a clause excluding liability for illegal acts, acts that are contrary to public policy, or violations of law will not be enforced.

CASE EXAMPLE 12.12 Engineering Consulting Services, Ltd. (ECS), contracted with RSN Properties, Inc., a real estate developer, to perform soil studies for $2,200 and render an opinion on the use of septic systems in a particular subdivision being developed. A clause in the contract limited ECS's liability to RSN to the value of the engineering services or the sum of $50,000, whichever was greater. ECS concluded that most of the lots were suitable for septic systems. RSN proceeded with the development in reliance on ECS's conclusions, which turned out to be incorrect. RSN filed a breach of contract lawsuit against ECS and argued that the limitation of liability was against public policy and unenforceable. The court, however, held that the "contract represented a reasonable allocation of risks in an arm's-length business transaction, and did not violate public policy for professional engineering practice." The court therefore enforced the limitation-of-liability clause.[12] •

A clause that excludes liability for negligence may be enforced in some situations when the parties have roughly equal bargaining positions. If the limitation-of-liability clause is contained in a contract between persons with unequal bargaining power or is part of an adhesion contract, then it may not be enforced.

11. UCC 2–719.
12. *RSN Properties, Inc. v. Engineering Consulting Services, Ltd.*, 301 Ga.App. 52, 686 S.E.2d 853 (2009).

Reviewing . . . Breach and Remedies

Kyle Bruno enters into a contract with X Entertainment to be a stuntman in a movie being produced. Bruno is widely known as the best motorcycle stuntman in the business, and the movie to be produced, *Xtreme Riders,* has numerous scenes involving high-speed freestyle street-bike stunts. Filming is set to begin August 1 and end by December 1 so that the film can be released the following summer. Both parties to the contract have stipulated that the filming must end on time in order to capture the profits from the summer movie market. The contract states that Bruno will be paid 10 percent of the net proceeds from the movie for his stunts. The contract also includes a liquidated damages provision, which specifies that if Bruno breaches the contract, he will owe X Entertainment $1 million. In addition, the contract includes a limitation-of-liability clause stating that if Bruno is injured during filming, X Entertainment's liability is limited to nominal damages. Using the information presented in the chapter, answer the following questions.

1. One day, while Bruno is preparing for a difficult stunt, he gets into an argument with the director and refuses to perform any stunts. Can X Entertainment seek specific performance of the contract? Why or why not?
2. Suppose that while performing a high-speed wheelie on a motorcycle, Bruno is injured by an intentionally reckless act of an X Entertainment employee. Will a court be likely to enforce the limitation-of-liability clause? Why or why not?
3. What factors would a court consider to determine if the $1 million liquidated damages clause is valid or is a penalty?
4. Suppose that there was no liquidated damages clause (or the court refused to enforce it) and X Entertainment breached the contract. The breach caused the release of the film to be delayed until after summer. Could Bruno seek consequential (special) damages for lost profits from the summer movie market in that situation? Explain.

Terms and Concepts

consequential damages 213
incidental damages 212
liquidated damages 215
mitigation of damages 214
nominal damages 214
penalty 215
restitution 216
specific performance 216

Chapter Summary: Breach and Remedies

COMMON REMEDIES AVAILABLE TO NONBREACHING PARTY	
Damages (See pages 211–216.)	The legal remedy designed to compensate the nonbreaching party for the loss of the bargain. By awarding monetary damages, the court tries to place the parties in the positions that they would have occupied had the contract been fully performed. The nonbreaching party frequently has a duty to *mitigate* (lessen or reduce) the damages incurred as a result of the contract's breach. There are four broad categories of damages: 1. *Compensatory damages*—Damages that compensate the nonbreaching party for injuries actually sustained and proved to have arisen directly from the loss of the bargain resulting from the breach of contract. a. In breached contracts for the sale of goods, the usual measure of compensatory damages is the difference between the contract price and the market price. b. In breached contracts for the sale of land, the measure of damages is ordinarily the same as in contracts for the sale of goods. c. In breached construction contracts, the measure of damages depends on which party breaches and at what stage of construction the breach occurs. 2. *Consequential damages*—Damages resulting from special circumstances beyond the contract itself; the damages flow only from the consequences of a breach. For a party to recover consequential damages, the damages must be the foreseeable result of a breach of contract, and the breaching party must have known at the time the contract was formed that special circumstances existed that would cause the nonbreaching party to incur additional loss on breach of the contract. Also called *special damages.* 3. *Punitive damages*—Damages awarded to punish the breaching party. Usually not awarded in an action for breach of contract unless a tort is involved.

Continued

Chapter Summary: Breach and Remedies—Continued

Damages—Continued	4. *Nominal damages*—Damages small in amount (such as one dollar) that are awarded when a breach has occurred but no actual injury has been suffered. Liquidated damages may be specified in a contract as the amount to be paid to the nonbreaching party in the event the contract is breached in the future. Clauses providing for liquidated damages are enforced if the damages were difficult to estimate at the time the contract was formed and if the amount stipulated is reasonable.
Rescission and Restitution (See page 216.)	1. *Rescission*—A remedy whereby a contract is canceled and the parties are restored to the original positions that they occupied before the transaction. The rescinding party must give prompt notice of the rescission to the breaching party. 2. *Restitution*—When a contract is rescinded, both parties must make restitution to each other by returning the goods, property, or funds previously conveyed. Restitution prevents the unjust enrichment of the parties.
Specific Performance (See pages 216–217.)	An equitable remedy calling for the performance of the act promised in the contract. This remedy is available only in special situations—such as those involving contracts for the sale of unique goods or land—and when monetary damages would be an inadequate remedy. Specific performance is not available as a remedy for breached contracts for personal services.
Reformation (See page 217.)	An equitable remedy allowing a contract to be "reformed," or rewritten, to reflect the parties' true intentions. Available when an agreement is imperfectly expressed in writing.
Recovery Based on Quasi Contract (See page 218.)	An equitable theory imposed by the courts to obtain justice and prevent unjust enrichment in a situation in which no enforceable contract exists. The party seeking recovery must show the following: 1. A benefit was conferred on the other party. 2. The party conferring the benefit did so with the expectation of being paid. 3. The benefit was not volunteered. 4. The party receiving the benefit would be unjustly enriched if allowed to retain the benefit without paying for it.
CONTRACT DOCTRINES RELATING TO REMEDIES	
Contract Provisions Limiting Remedies (See page 218.)	A contract may provide that no damages (or only a limited amount of damages) can be recovered in the event the contract is breached. Under the Uniform Commercial Code, remedies may be limited in contracts for the sale of goods. Clauses excluding liability for fraudulent or intentional injury or for illegal acts cannot be enforced. Clauses excluding liability for negligence may be enforced if both parties hold roughly equal bargaining power.

ExamPrep

ISSUE SPOTTERS

—Check your answers to these questions against the answers provided in Appendix G.

1 Greg contracts to build a storage shed for Haney, who pays Greg in advance, but Greg completes only half the work. Haney pays Ipswich $500 to finish the shed. If Haney sues Greg, what would be the measure of recovery?

2 Lyle contracts to sell his ranch to Marley, who is to take possession on June 1. Lyle delays the transfer until August 1. Marley incurs expenses in providing for livestock that he bought for the ranch. When they made the contract, Lyle had no reason to know of the livestock. Is Lyle liable for Marley's expenses in providing for the cattle? Why or why not?

BEFORE THE TEST

Go to **www.cengagebrain.com**, enter the ISBN 9781111530624, and click on "Find" to locate this textbook's Web site. Then, click on "Access Now" under "Study Tools," and select Chapter 12 at the top. There, you will find an Interactive Quiz that you can take to assess your mastery of the concepts in this chapter, as well as Flashcards and a Glossary of important terms.

For Review

1 What is the difference between compensatory damages and consequential damages? What are nominal damages, and when do courts award nominal damages?
2 What is the standard measure of compensatory damages when a contract is breached? How are damages computed differently in construction contracts?
3 Under what circumstances is the remedy of rescission and restitution available?
4 When do courts grant specific performance as a remedy?
5 What is a limitation-of-liability clause, and when will courts enforce it?

Questions and Case Problems

12–1 Liquidated Damages. Carnack contracts to sell his house and lot to Willard for $100,000. The terms of the contract call for Willard to make a deposit of 10 percent of the purchase price as a down payment. The terms further stipulate that should the buyer breach the contract, Carnack will retain the deposit as liquidated damages. Willard makes the deposit, but because her expected financing of the $90,000 balance falls through, she breaches the contract. Two weeks later, Carnack sells the house and lot to Balkova for $105,000. Willard demands her $10,000 back, but Carnack refuses, claiming that Willard's breach and the contract terms entitle him to keep the deposit. Discuss who is correct.

12–2 Mitigation of Damages. Lauren Barton, a single mother with three children, lived in Portland, Oregon. Cynthia VanHorn also lived in Oregon until she moved to New York City to open and operate an art gallery. VanHorn asked Barton to manage the gallery under a one-year contract for an annual salary of $72,000. To begin work, Barton relocated to New York. As part of the move, Barton transferred custody of her children to her husband, who lived in London, England. In accepting the job, Barton also forfeited her husband's alimony and child-support payments, including unpaid amounts of nearly $30,000. Before Barton started work, VanHorn repudiated the contract. Unable to find employment for more than an annual salary of $25,000, Barton moved to London to be near her children. Barton filed a suit in an Oregon state court against VanHorn, seeking damages for breach of contract. Should the court hold, as VanHorn argued, that Barton did not take reasonable steps to mitigate her damages? Why or why not?

12–3 Damages. Tyna Ek met Russell Peterson in Seattle, Washington. Peterson persuaded Ek to buy a boat that he had once owned, the *O'Hana Kai,* which was in Juneau, Alaska. Ek paid the boat's current owner $43,000 for the boat, and in January 2000, she and Peterson entered into a contract, under which Peterson agreed to make the vessel seaworthy so that within one month it could be transported to Seattle, where he would pay its moorage costs. He would renovate the boat at his own expense in return for a portion of the profit on its resale in 2001. On the sale, Ek would recover her costs, and then Peterson would be reimbursed for his. Ek loaned Peterson her cell phone so that they could communicate while he prepared the vessel for the trip to Seattle. In March, Peterson, who was still in Alaska, borrowed $4,000 from Ek. Two months later, Ek began to receive unanticipated, unauthorized bills for vessel parts and moorage, the use of her phone, and charges on her credit card. She went to Juneau to take possession of the boat. Peterson moved it to Petersburg, Alaska, where he registered it under a false name, and then to Taku Harbor, where the police seized it. Ek filed a suit in an Alaska state court against Peterson, alleging breach of contract and seeking damages. If the court finds in Ek's favor, what should her damages include? Discuss. [*Peterson v. Ek,* 93 P.3d 458 (Alaska 2004)]

12–4 Remedies. On July 7, 2000, Frances Morelli agreed to sell to Judith Bucklin a house at 126 Lakedell Drive in Warwick, Rhode Island, for $77,000. Bucklin made a deposit on the house. The closing at which the parties would exchange the deed for the price was scheduled for September 1. The agreement did not state that "time is of the essence," but it did provide, in "Paragraph 10" that "[i]f Seller is unable to [convey good, clear, insurable, and marketable title], Buyer shall have the option to: (a) accept such title as Seller is able to convey without abatement or reduction of the Purchase Price, or (b) cancel this Agreement and receive a return of all Deposits." An examination of the public records revealed that the house did not have marketable title. Wishing to be flexible, Bucklin offered Morelli time to resolve the problem, and the closing did not occur as scheduled. Morelli decided "the deal is over" and offered to return the deposit. Bucklin refused and, in mid-October, decided to exercise her option under Paragraph 10(a). She notified Morelli, who did not respond. Bucklin filed a suit in a Rhode Island state court against Morelli. In whose favor should the court rule? Should damages be awarded? If not, what is the appropriate remedy? Why? [*Bucklin v. Morelli,* 912 A.2d 931 (R.I. 2007)]

12–5 Case Problem with Sample Answer Middleton Motors, Inc., a struggling Ford dealership in Madison, Wisconsin, sought managerial and financial assistance from Lindquist Ford, Inc., a successful Ford dealership in Bettendorf, Iowa. While the two dealerships negotiated the terms for the services and a cash infusion, Lindquist sent Craig Miller, its general manager, to assume control of Middleton. After about a year, the parties had not agreed on the terms, Lindquist had not invested any funds, Middleton had not made a profit, and Miller was fired without being paid. Lindquist and Miller filed a suit in a federal district court against Middleton based on quasi contract, seeking to recover Miller's pay for his time. What are the requirements to recover on a quasi-contract theory? Which of these requirements is most likely to be disputed in this case? Why? [*Lindquist Ford, Inc. v. Middleton Motors, Inc.*, 557 F.3d 469 (7th Cir. 2009)]

—For a sample answer to Problem 12–5, go to Appendix F at the end of this text.

12–6 Liquidated Damages versus Penalties. Planned Pethood Plus, Inc., is a veterinarian-owned clinic. It borrowed $389,000 from KeyBank at an interest rate of 9.3 percent per year for ten years. The loan had a "prepayment penalty" clause that clearly stated that if the loan was repaid early, a specific formula would be used to assess a lump-sum payment to extinguish the obligation. The sooner the loan was paid off, the higher the prepayment penalty. After a year, the veterinarians decided to pay off the loan. KeyBank invoked a prepayment penalty of $40,525.92, which was equal to 10.7 percent of the balance due. The veterinarians sued, contending that the prepayment penalty was unenforceable as a penalty. The bank countered that the amount was not a penalty but liquidated damages and that the sum was reasonable. The trial court agreed with the bank, and the veterinarians appealed. Was the loan's prepayment charge reasonable, and should it have been enforced? Why or why not? [*Planned Pethood Plus, Inc. v. KeyCorp, Inc.*, 228 P.3d 262 (Colo.App. 2010)]

12–7 Damages. Before buying a house in Rockaway, New Jersey, Dean and Donna Testa hired Ground Systems, Inc. (GSI), to inspect the sewage and water disposal system. Steve Austin, the GSI inspector, told Dean that the system included a tank, a distribution box, pipes, and a leach field (where contaminants are removed from the sewage). Austin's written report described a split system with a watertight septic tank and a separate kitchen and laundry wastewater tank. The Testas bought the house. Ten years later, when they tried to sell the house, a prospective buyer withdrew from the sale after receiving an inspection report that evaluated the septic system as "unsatisfactory." The Testas arranged for the installation of a new system. During the work, Dean saw that the old system was not as Austin had described—there was no distribution box or leach field, and there was only one tank, which was not watertight. The Testas filed a suit in a New Jersey state court against GSI, alleging breach of contract. If GSI was liable, what would be the measure of the damages? [*Testa v. Ground Systems, Inc.*, 206 N.J. 330, 20 A.3d 435 (2011)]

12–8 A Question of Ethics *In 2004, Tamara Cohen, a real estate broker, began showing property in Manhattan to Steven Galistinos, who represented comedian Jerry Seinfeld and his wife, Jessica. According to Cohen, she told Galistinos that her commission would be 5 or 6 percent, and he agreed. According to Galistinos, there was no such agreement. Cohen spoke with Maximillan Sanchez, another broker, about a townhouse owned by Ray and Harriet Mayeri. According to Cohen, Sanchez said that the commission would be 6 percent, which they agreed to split equally. Sanchez later acknowledged that they agreed to split the fee, but claimed that they did not discuss a specific amount. On a Friday in February 2005, Cohen showed the townhouse to Jessica. According to Cohen, she told Jessica that the commission would be 6 percent, with the Seinfelds paying half, and Jessica agreed. According to Jessica, there was no such conversation. Later that day, Galistinos asked Cohen to arrange for the Seinfelds to see the premises again. Cohen told Galistinos that her religious beliefs prevented her from showing property on Friday evenings or Saturdays before sundown. She suggested the following Monday or Tuesday, but Galistinos said that Jerry would not be available and asked her to contact Carolyn Liebling, Jerry's business manager. Cohen left Liebling a message. Over the weekend, the Seinfelds toured the building on their own and agreed to buy the property for $3.95 million. Despite repeated attempts, they were unable to contact Cohen. [*Cohen v. Seinfeld*, *15 Misc.3d 1118(A), 839 N.Y.S.2d 432 (Sup. 2007)]*

1. The contract between the Seinfelds and the Mayeris stated that the sellers would pay Sanchez's fee and the "buyers will pay buyer's real estate broker's fees." The Mayeris paid Sanchez $118,500, which is 3 percent of $3.95 million. The Seinfelds refused to pay Cohen. She filed a suit in a New York state court against them, asserting, among other things, breach of contract. Should the court order the Seinfelds to pay Cohen? If so, is she entitled to a full commission even though she was not available to show the townhouse when the Seinfelds wanted to see it? Explain.
2. What obligation do parties involved in business deals owe to each other with respect to their religious beliefs? How might the situation in this case have been avoided?

12–9 Critical Thinking Legal Question Review the discussion of the doctrine of mitigation of damages in this chapter. What are some of the advantages and disadvantages of this doctrine?

12–10 Video Question To watch this chapter's video, *Midnight Run*, go to **www.cengagebrain.com**. Register the access code that came with your new book or log in to your existing account. Select the link for the "Business Law Digital Video Library Online Access" or "Business Law CourseMate." Click on "Complete Video List," view Video 57, and then answer the following questions:

1. Eddie (Joe Pantoliano) and Jack (Robert De Niro) negotiate a contract for Jack to find "the Duke," a mob accountant who embezzled funds, and bring him back for trial. Assume that the contract is valid. If Jack breaches the contract by failing to bring in the Duke, what kinds of remedies, if any, can Eddie seek? Explain your answer.
2. Would the equitable remedy of specific performance be available to either Jack or Eddie in the event of a breach? Why or why not?
3. Now assume that the contract between Eddie and Jack is unenforceable. Nevertheless, Jack performs his side of the bargain by bringing in the Duke. Does Jack have any legal recourse in this situation? Explain.

Unit Three Unit Case Study with Dissenting Opinion: *Braddock v. Braddock*

Fraudulent misrepresentation, as discussed in Chapter 10, is one of the events that may cause a contract to lack voluntary consent. To be fraudulent, there must be a misrepresentation of a present, material fact. A representation, or prediction, of a future fact does not qualify. The misrepresentation must be consciously false and intended to mislead an innocent party, who must justifiably rely on it. When an innocent party is fraudulently induced to enter into a contract, the party can rescind the contract and be restored to her or his original position or enforce the contract and seek damages for injuries resulting from the fraud.

In this Unit Case Study with Dissenting Opinion, *we set out* Braddock v. Braddock,[1] *a case in which an individual sacrificed his career and relocated his home and family based on his cousin's representations about a newly formed entrepreneurial venture. What was presented to the individual about his place in the new enterprise did not occur. Were the cousin's statements fraudulent? Or were they simply expressions of expectation—predictions of future possibilities—subject to contingencies that neither party could control?*

1. 60 A.D.3d 84, 871 N.Y.S.2d 68 (1 Dept. 2009).

CASE BACKGROUND

David Braddock wanted to form Broad Oak Energy, Inc. (BOE), to tap oil and gas reserves in Louisiana and Texas. He asked his cousin John, an investment banker in New York, to find an investor to provide BOE with $75 to $150 million. David assured John that he would be BOE's chief financial officer (CFO) and land manager and that he would receive half as much stock in the company as would be issued to David, who would serve as the company's chief executive officer. John quit his job, agreed to accept a significantly reduced fee to find an investor for BOE, and moved his family to Texas. As a result of John's efforts, Warburg Pincus, LLC, agreed to provide $150 million in start-up capital.

A couple of weeks later, David told John that Warburg Pincus insisted John not be made CFO or land manager. David offered him the position of landman, a substantially reduced position with lesser salary, benefits, and terms. Surprised, John nevertheless cooperated. He signed "engagement agreements" to accept the lesser position as an "employee at will," subject to discharge for any reason at any time. Stress soon began to take a toll on his health, and he was granted a conditional medical leave of absence. The next month, BOE terminated his employment.

John filed a suit in a New York state court against David, asserting that these circumstances constituted fraud. The court dismissed the complaint. John appealed to a state intermediate appellate court.

MAJORITY OPINION

SAXE, J. [Judge]

* * * *

To plead a claim for [fraud], a plaintiff must assert the misrepresentation of a material fact, which was known by the defendant to be false and intended to be relied on when made, and that there was justifiable reliance and resulting injury. The complaint here sufficiently sets forth these elements. [Emphasis added.]

* * * *

[John's] allegations satisfy the particularity requirement for a fraud claim.

* * * *

* * * Since David and John are cousins, John's reliance on David's good faith may be found to be reasonable even where it might not be reasonable in the context of an arm's length transaction with a stranger. Family members stand in a fiduciary relationship [one of trust] toward one another in a co-owned business venture. * * * Under the circumstances alleged here, John had reason to believe that David would treat him, in their interaction, with good faith and integrity.

* * * *

The situation presented here should be distinguished from cases in which a plaintiff who was involved in a business deal claims that, in the original discussions of the deal, misrepresentations were made as to its terms but the falsity of those representations was revealed by the time the deal was executed. In such cases, the ultimate terms of the deal, if agreed upon, are all that the plaintiff is entitled to, and he will not be permitted to seek damages based upon the original misrepresentations, because he did not rely on them in electing to go through with the deal. Here, in contrast, John's subsequent execution of documents that fundamentally altered the originally promised terms of his position with the company was not merely an election to enter into the deal anyway. First of all, even before he executed * * * the agreements * * *, the deal was essentially under way, at least on his part, in that

Continued

he had already sacrificed his former life and undertaken tasks to forward the venture, and he was no longer in a position to reject the offered terms or even to negotiate effectively. Indeed, when the allegations are understood in the context of an ongoing attempt by John to salvage something from his dashed expectations, the fact that he subsequently acceded to new and lesser terms should not justify holding * * * that he did not reasonably rely on his cousin's alleged misrepresentations and false assurances, to his own severe detriment.

If all these interactions had been between strangers conducting an arm's length business transaction, strict reliance on the signed written documents, to the exclusion of the parties' words and conduct, would be appropriate. But the expectation of the good faith of a family member in circumstances such as these may justify some reliance on assurances that are not incorporated into written documents drafted and executed later.

* * * *

Here, * * * the issues of material misrepresentation and reasonable reliance are not subject to summary disposition [settlement], and the fiduciary relationship between the parties, with its concomitant [associated] mutual obligation to act in good faith, makes John's reliance on David's assurances all the more reasonable.

* * * *

* * * Defendants' motion to dismiss the complaint for failure to state a cause of action * * * [is] denied * * * so as to reinstate the [plaintiff's fraud] cause of action.

DISSENTING OPINION

***LIPPMAN*, P.J. [Presiding Justice], (dissenting).**

* * * *

* * * It is, in essence, alleged that John's entire course of conduct in providing investment banking services for a discounted fee, giving up his lucrative New York employment as an investment banker and advisor, moving to Texas and agreeing to take the non-executive position with BOE from which he was eventually dismissed * * * was induced by David's * * * assurances.

* * * *

* * * At the time of David's nominal assurances, BOE was but an unfunded shell requiring for its viability an enormous infusion of capital. And, while John was confident of procuring financing for the venture, there had been, at the time, neither a commitment of funds nor even the emergence of a leading candidate to provide such a commitment. Moreover, John, in addition to being an experienced investment banker and financial consultant, was, by reason of his own prior professional involvement in oil and gas ventures and his extensive familial connections to the industry, particularly well aware of the risks such ventures entailed. * * * In these circumstances, * * * no promise of high executive-level employment in the company * * * could reasonably have been viewed as an "assurance" or a "guarantee." * * * What he now terms "assurances" and "guarantees" could have been reasonably understood as only expressions of expectation or intent, the realization of which would depend upon contingencies not within the power of the parties to foreseeably accommodate to their stated objectives.

* * * While he may have had a moral claim to rely upon his cousin even when objective circumstances counseled otherwise, there is no legal right to recovery in fraud that may be vindicated upon such a predicate.

Accordingly, I would affirm the dismissal of plaintiffs' fraud cause of action.

QUESTIONS FOR ANALYSIS

1. **Law.** What did the majority conclude on the issue before the court in this case? What reasoning supported this conclusion?
2. **Law.** On what important point did the dissent disagree with the majority, and why?
3. **Ethics.** How do you view David's statements and John's actions? Did David take unethical advantage of his cousin, luring him in bad faith? Was John too willing to rely on assurances that he should have known from experience would not occur? Discuss.
4. **Economic Dimensions.** What does this case indicate about employment and employment contracts?
5. **Implications for the Investor.** Why would an investor like Warburg Pincus not want someone like John in an executive role in an enterprise for which the investor was providing significant capital?

Unit Four

Sales and Lease Contracts

Unit Contents

13 The Formation of Sales and Lease Contracts

14 Performance and Breach of Sales and Lease Contracts

15 Warranties and Product Liability

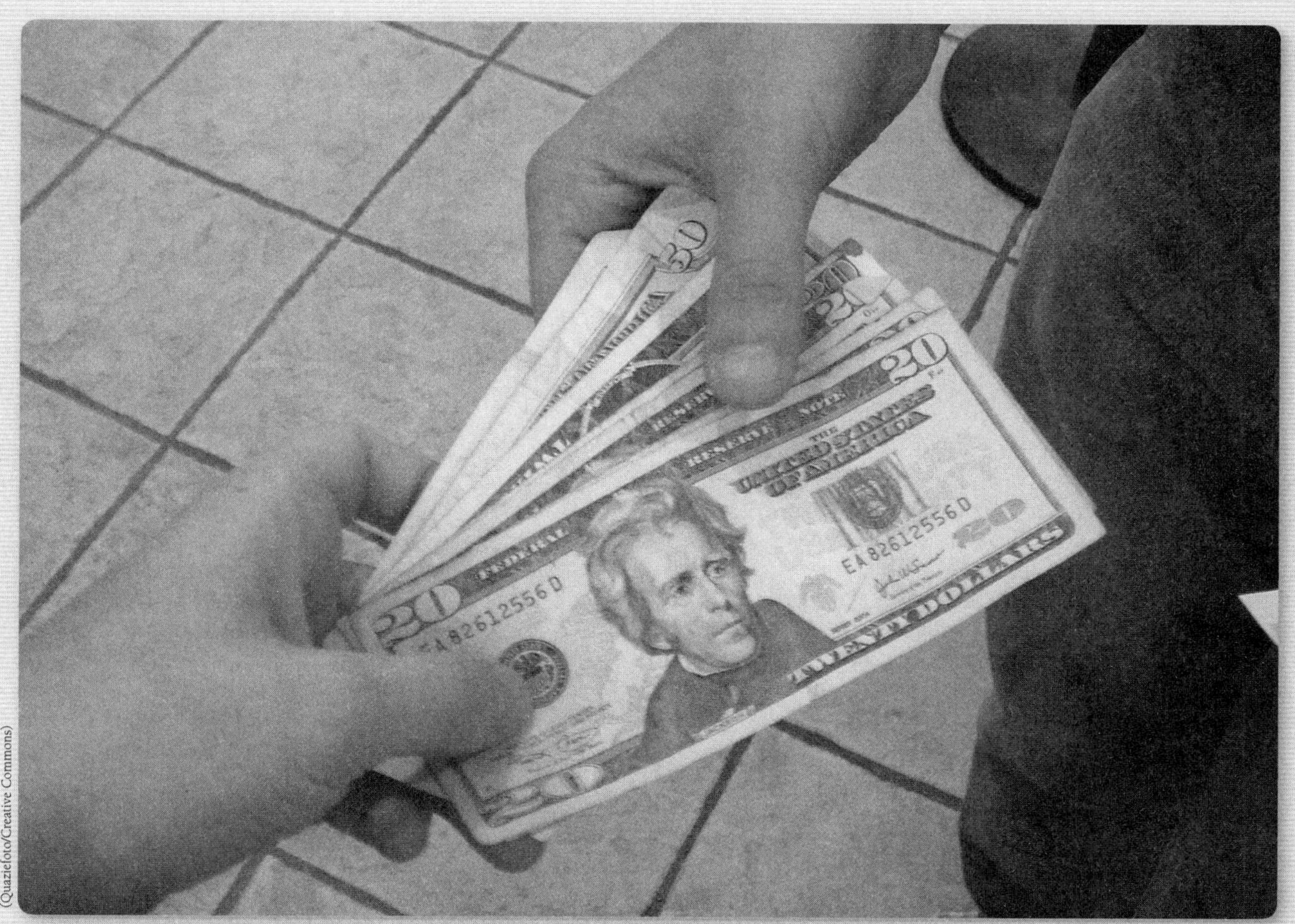

(Quaziefoto/Creative Commons)

Chapter 13

The Formation of Sales and Lease Contracts

Learning Objectives

After reading this chapter, you should be able to answer the following questions:

1. How do Article 2 and Article 2A of the UCC differ? What types of transactions does each article cover?
2. What is a merchant's firm offer?
3. In a sales contract, if an offeree includes additional or different terms in an acceptance, will a contract result? If so, what happens to these terms?
4. Risk of loss does not necessarily pass with title. If the parties to a contract do not expressly agree when risk passes and the goods are to be delivered without movement by the seller, when does risk pass?
5. What law governs contracts for the international sale of goods?

The Learning Objectives above are designed to help improve your understanding of the chapter.

(Quaziefoto/Creative Commons)

The law generally encourages commerce, because most Americans believe that free commerce will benefit our nation. This is particularly true with respect to the Uniform Commercial Code (UCC). The UCC facilitates commercial transactions by making the laws governing sales and lease contracts uniform, clearer, simpler, and more readily applicable to the numerous difficulties that can arise during such transactions. Recall from Chapter 1 that the UCC is one of many uniform (model) acts drafted by the National Conference of Commissioners on Uniform State Laws and submitted to the states for adoption. Once a state legislature has adopted a uniform act, the act becomes statutory law in that state. Thus, when we turn to sales and lease contracts, we move away from common law principles and into the area of statutory law.

We open this chapter with a discussion of the general coverage of the UCC and its significance. We look at the scope of the UCC's Article 2 (on sales) and Article 2A (on leases) as a background to the formation of contracts for the sale and lease of goods. Because international sales transactions are increasingly commonplace in the business world, we conclude this chapter with an examination of the United Nations Convention on Contracts for the International Sale of Goods, which governs international sales contracts.

The Scope of the UCC and Articles 2 (Sales) and 2A (Leases)

The UCC attempts to provide a consistent and integrated framework of rules to deal with all phases ordinarily arising in a commercial sales or lease transaction from start to finish. For example, consider the following events, all of which may occur during a single transaction:

1. *A contract for the sale or lease of goods is formed and executed.* Article 2 and Article 2A of the UCC provide rules governing all aspects of this transaction.
2. *The transaction may involve a payment—by check, electronic fund transfer, or other means.* Article 3 (on negotiable instru-

ments), Article 4 (on bank deposits and collections), Article 4A (on fund transfers), and Article 5 (on letters of credit) cover this part of the transaction.

3. *The transaction may involve a bill of lading or a warehouse receipt that covers goods when they are shipped or stored.* Article 7 (on documents of title) deals with this subject.
4. *The transaction may involve a demand by the seller or lender for some form of security for the remaining balance owed.* Article 9 (on secured transactions) covers this part of the transaction.

The UCC has been adopted in whole or in part by all of the states.[1] Because of its importance in the area of commercial transactions, we present excerpts from the UCC in Appendix C at the end of this text.

Article 2—Sales

Article 2 of the UCC governs **sales contracts,** or contracts for the sale of goods. To facilitate commercial transactions, Article 2 modifies some of the common law contract requirements that were discussed in Chapters 7 through 12. To the extent that it has not been modified by the UCC, however, the common law of contracts also applies to sales contracts.

In general, the rule is that when a UCC provision addresses a certain issue, the UCC governs; when the UCC is silent, the common law governs. The relationship between general contract law and the law governing sales of goods is illustrated in Exhibit 13–1 below. (For a discussion of some problems surrounding state taxation of sales that take place over the Internet, see this chapter's *Adapting the Law to the Online Environment* feature on the following page.)

Keep in mind that Article 2 deals with the sale of *goods.* It does not deal with real property (real estate), services, or intangible property such as stocks and bonds. Thus, if a dispute involves real estate or services, the common law applies. Also note that in some situations, the rules under the UCC can vary quite a bit, depending on whether the buyer or the seller is a merchant. We look now at how the UCC defines three important terms: *sale, goods,* and *merchant status.*

WHAT IS A SALE? The UCC defines a **sale** as "the passing of title [evidence of ownership] from the seller to the buyer for a price" [UCC 2–106(1)]. The price may be payable in cash (or its equivalent) or in other goods or services.

WHAT ARE GOODS? To be characterized as a *good,* the item of property must be *tangible,* and it must be *movable.*

1. Louisiana has not adopted Articles 2 and 2A, however.

• ***Exhibit* 13–1 The Law Governing Contracts**
This exhibit graphically illustrates the relationship between general contract law and statutory law (UCC Articles 2 and 2A) governing contracts for the sale and lease of goods. Sales contracts are not governed exclusively by Article 2 of the UCC but are also governed by general contract law whenever it is relevant and has not been modified by the UCC.

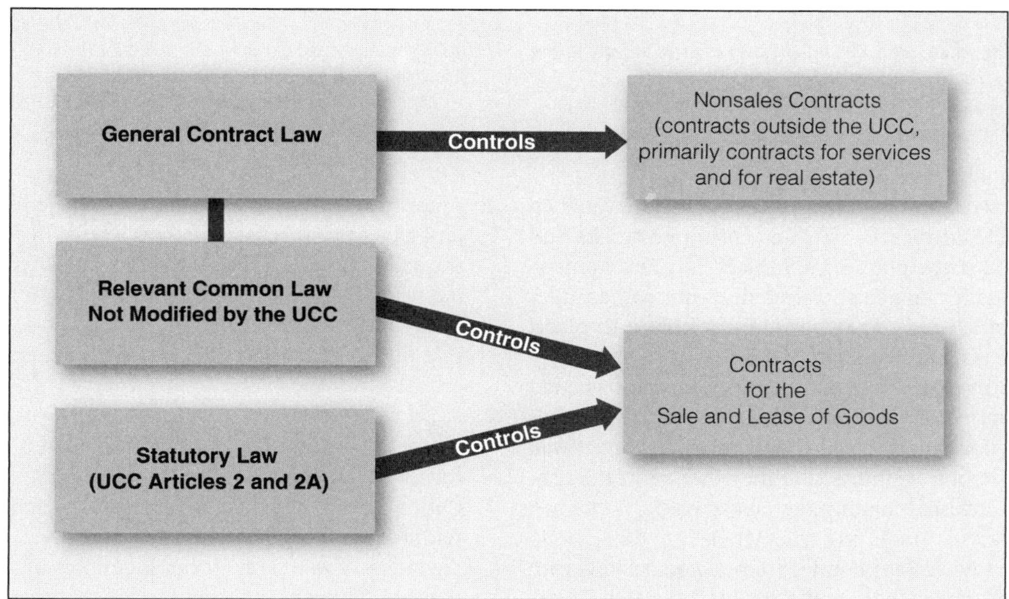

Adapting the Law to the Online Environment

The Thorny Issue of Taxing Internet Sales

From the very beginning of e-commerce, cities and states have complained that they are losing millions, if not billions, of dollars of potential tax revenues because nearly all e-commerce companies do not collect state and local sales taxes. Although most states have laws requiring their residents to report purchases from other states and to pay taxes on those purchases (so-called use taxes), few (if any) U.S. consumers ever comply with these laws. Certainly, the possibility of avoiding sales taxes has likely contributed to the growth of e-commerce. Not surprisingly, retailers with investment in physical sales outlets have complained to local, state, and federal governments about this "sales tax inequity."

Local Governments Are Suing Online Travel Companies

One recent trend in the effort to collect taxes from e-commerce has focused on online travel companies, including Travelocity, Priceline.com, Hotels.com, and Orbitz.com. By 2011, at least a dozen cities, including Atlanta, Charleston, Philadelphia, and San Antonio, had filed suits claiming that the online travel companies owed taxes on hotel reservations that they had booked. All of the cities involved in the suits impose hotel occupancy taxes. In Atlanta, for example, the local statute authorizes the city to devise "a rate of taxation, the manner of imposition, payment, and collection of the tax, and all other procedures related to the tax."[a]

At issue in the lawsuits is not whether the online travel companies owe hotel occupancy tax, but rather the amount of tax that they owe and the procedure that should be used to collect it. Online travel companies, such as Hotels.com, typically purchase blocks of hotel rooms at a wholesale rate and subsequently resell the rooms to customers at a marked-up retail rate, keeping the difference as profit. The company forwards to the hotel an amount intended to cover the hotel occupancy tax on the wholesale price of the rooms sold. The hotel then remits to the city taxing authority the tax on the rooms sold by the online travel agency. Thus, the online travel companies do not remit taxes directly to any city authorities.

In calculating the amount of tax owed, the online travel companies assess the occupancy tax rates on the wholesale prices of the rooms, rather than the retail prices that they charge. The cities claim that the online travel companies should be assessing the hotel occupancy tax on the retail prices of the rooms. The cities also want the online companies to register with the local jurisdictions and to collect and remit the required taxes directly.

What the Courts Have Been Deciding

More than a dozen cases have been brought against online travel agencies, but so far the courts have been divided. Many of these cases have been brought in federal district courts, and those courts have often ruled in favor of the cities.[b]

Some state courts have also upheld the cities' claims. In one case, for example, the Supreme Court of Georgia reversed the lower court's dismissal and remanded the case for trial on Atlanta's claim concerning the city's hotel tax ordinance.[c] Given that most cities and counties have found themselves in dire financial straits since the latest recession, we can expect to see more such suits around the country.

FOR CRITICAL ANALYSIS

Why do you think that cities and states have not brought similar lawsuits against e-commerce retailers such as Amazon.com?

a. OCGA Section 48-13-53, which is the Enabling Statutes for the city of Atlanta.

b. See, for example, *City of Goodlettsville v. Priceline.com, Inc.*, 605 F.Supp.2d 982 (M.D.Tenn. 2009); and *City of Findlay v. Hotels.com*, 561 F.Supp.2d 917 (N.D. Ohio 2008).

c. *City of Atlanta v. Hotels.com, L.P.*, 285 Ga. 231, 674 S.E.2d 898 (2009).

Tangible property has physical existence—it can be touched or seen. **Intangible property**—such as corporate stocks and bonds, patents and copyrights, and ordinary contract rights—has only conceptual existence and thus does not come under Article 2. A movable item can be carried from place to place. Hence, real estate is excluded from Article 2.

Two issues often give rise to disputes in determining whether the object of a contract is goods and thus whether Article 2 is applicable. One problem has to do with *goods associated with real estate*, such as crops or timber, and the other concerns contracts involving a combination of *goods and services.*

Goods Associated with Real Estate. Goods associated with real estate often fall within the scope of Article 2. Section 2–107 provides the following rules:

1. A contract for the sale of minerals or the like (including oil and gas) or a structure (such as a building) is a contract for the sale of goods if *severance, or separation, is to be made by the seller.* If the *buyer* is to sever (separate) the minerals or structure from the land, the contract is considered to be a sale of real estate governed by the principles of real property law, not the UCC.
2. A sale of growing crops (such as potatoes, carrots, and wheat) or timber to be cut is considered to be a contract for the sale of goods *regardless of who severs them.*
3. Other "things attached" to realty but capable of severance without material harm to the land are considered goods *regardless of who severs them.* Examples of "things attached" that are severable without harm to realty include a window air conditioner in a house and stools in a restaurant.

Thus, the removal and sale of these items would be considered a sale of goods. The test is whether removal will cause substantial harm to the real property to which the item is attached.

Goods and Services Combined. In cases involving contracts in which goods and services are combined, the courts generally use the **predominant-factor test** to determine whether a contract is primarily for the sale of goods or for the sale of services.[2] This determination is important because the UCC will apply to services provided under a mixed contract that is predominantly for goods, even though the majority of courts treat services as being excluded by the UCC.

In other words, if a court decides that a mixed contract is primarily a goods contract, *any* dispute, even a dispute over the services portion, will be decided under the UCC. Likewise, any disagreement over a predominantly services contract will not be decided using the UCC, even if the dispute involves the goods portion of the contract. If the transaction is not covered by the UCC, then UCC provisions, including those relating to implied warranties, will not apply.

CASE EXAMPLE 13.1 Gene and Martha Jannusch agreed to sell Festival Foods, a concessions business, to Lindsey and Louann Naffziger for a price of $150,000. The deal included a truck, a trailer, freezers, roasters, chairs, tables, a fountain service, signs, and lighting. The Naffzigers paid $10,000 down with the balance to come from a bank loan. They took possession of the equipment and began to use it immediately in Festival Foods operations at various events. After six events, the Naffzigers returned the truck and all the equipment and wanted out of the deal. They said that the business did not generate as much income as they expected. The Jannusches sued the Naffzigers for the balance due on the purchase price, claiming that the Naffzigers could no longer reject the goods under the UCC. The Naffzigers claimed that the UCC did not apply because the deal primarily involved the sale of a business rather than the sale of goods. The court found that the UCC governed under the predominant purpose test. The primary value of the contract was in the goods, not the value of the business. The parties had agreed on the essential terms of the contract (such as the price), thus a contract had been formed, and the Naffzigers had breached it. The Naffzigers took possession of the business. They had no right to return it.[3] •

WHO IS A MERCHANT? Article 2 governs the sale of goods in general. It applies to sales transactions between all buyers and sellers. In a limited number of instances, however, the UCC presumes that certain special business standards ought to be imposed on merchants because they possess a relatively high degree of commercial expertise.[4] Such standards do not apply to the casual or inexperienced seller or buyer (a "consumer"). Section 2–104 sets out three ways in which merchant status can arise:

1. A merchant is a person who *deals in goods of the kind* involved in the sales contract. Thus, a retailer, a wholesaler, or a manufacturer is a merchant of those goods sold in the business. A merchant for one type of goods is not necessarily a merchant for another type. For instance, a sporting equipment retailer is a merchant when selling tennis rackets but not when selling a used computer.
2. A merchant is a person who, by occupation, *holds himself or herself out as having special knowledge and skill* related to the practices or goods involved in the transaction. Note that this broad definition may include banks or universities as merchants.
3. A person who *employs a merchant as a broker, agent, or other intermediary* has the status of merchant in that transaction. Hence, if an art collector hires a broker to purchase or sell art for her, the collector is considered a merchant in the transaction.

In summary, a person is a **merchant** when she or he, acting in a mercantile capacity, possesses or uses an expertise specifically related to the goods being sold. This basic distinction is not always clear-cut. For instance, state courts appear to be split on whether farmers should be considered merchants. In some states, farmers are considered merchants because they sell products or livestock on a regular basis. In other states, courts have held that the drafters of the UCC did not intend to include farmers as merchants.

Article 2A—Leases

Leases of personal property (goods) have become increasingly common. In this context, a **lease** is a transfer of the right to possess and use goods for a period of time in exchange for payment. Article 2A of the UCC was created to fill the need for uniform guidelines in this area. Article 2A covers any transaction that creates a lease of goods, as well as subleases of goods [UCC 2A–102, 2A–103(1)(k)]. Except that it applies to leases, rather than sales, of goods, Article 2A is essentially a repetition of Article 2 and varies only to reflect differences between sales and lease transactions. (Note that Article 2A is

2. UCC 2–314(1) does stipulate that serving food or drinks is a "sale of goods" for purposes of the implied warranty of merchantability, as will be discussed in Chapter 15. The UCC also specifies that selling unborn animals and rare coins qualifies as a "sale of goods."

3. *Jannusch v. Naffziger*, 379 Ill.App.3d 381, 883 N.E.2d 711 (2008).

4. The provisions that apply only to merchants deal principally with the Statute of Frauds, firm offers, confirmatory memorandums, warranties, and contract modifications. These special rules reflect expedient business practices commonly known to merchants in the commercial setting. They will be discussed later in this chapter.

not concerned with leases of real property, such as land or buildings. The laws governing leases of real property will be discussed in Chapter 28.)

DEFINITION OF A LEASE AGREEMENT Article 2A defines a **lease agreement** as a lessor and lessee's bargain with respect to the lease of goods, as found in their language and as implied by other circumstances, including course of dealing and usage of trade or course of performance [UCC 2A–103(1)(k)]. A **lessor** is one who transfers the right to the possession and use of goods under a lease [UCC 2A–103(1)(p)]. A **lessee** is one who acquires the right to the temporary possession and use of goods under a lease [UCC 2A–103(1)(o)]. In other words, the lessee is the party who is leasing the goods from the lessor. Article 2A applies to all types of leases of goods, including commercial leases and consumer leases. Special rules apply to certain types of leases, however, including consumer leases.

CONSUMER LEASES A *consumer lease* involves three elements: (1) a lessor who regularly engages in the business of leasing or selling; (2) a lessee (except an organization) who leases the goods "primarily for a personal, family, or household purpose"; and (3) total lease payments that are less than a dollar amount set by state statute [UCC 2A–103(1)(e)]. To ensure special protection for consumers, certain provisions of Article 2A apply only to consumer leases. For instance, one provision states that a consumer may recover attorneys' fees if a court finds that a term in a consumer lease contract is unconscionable [UCC 2A–108(4)(a)].

The Formation of Sales and Lease Contracts

In regard to the formation of sales and lease contracts, Article 2 and Article 2A of the UCC modify common law contract rules in several ways. Remember, though, that parties to sales contracts are free to basically establish whatever terms they wish. The UCC comes into play only when the parties have failed to provide in their contract for a contingency that later gives rise to a dispute. The UCC makes this clear time and again by using such phrases as "unless the parties otherwise agree" or "absent a contrary agreement by the parties."

Offer

In general contract law, the moment a definite offer is met by an unqualified acceptance, a binding contract is formed. In commercial sales transactions, the verbal exchanges, correspondence, and actions of the parties may not reveal exactly when a binding contractual obligation arises. The UCC states that an agreement sufficient to constitute a contract can exist even if the moment of its making is undetermined [UCC 2–204(2), 2A–204(2)].

OPEN TERMS Remember from Chapter 8 that under the common law of contracts, an offer must be definite enough for the parties (and the courts) to ascertain its essential terms when it is accepted. In contrast, the UCC states that a sales or lease contract will not fail for indefiniteness even if one or more terms are left open as long as (1) the parties intended to make a contract and (2) there is a reasonably certain basis for the court to grant an appropriate remedy [UCC 2–204(3), 2A–204(3)].

EXAMPLE 13.2 Mike agrees to lease a highly specialized computer work station from Office Mart. Mike and one of Office Mart's sales representatives sign a lease agreement that leaves some of the details blank, to be "worked out" the following week, when the leasing manager will be back from her vacation. In the meantime, Office Mart obtains the necessary equipment from one of its suppliers and spends several days modifying the equipment to suit Mike's needs. When the leasing manager returns, she calls Mike and tells him that his work station is ready. Mike says he is no longer interested in the work station, as he has arranged to lease the same type of equipment for a lower price from another firm. Office Mart sues Mike to recover its costs in obtaining and modifying the equipment, and one of the issues before the court is whether the parties had an enforceable contract. The court will likely hold that they did, based on their intent and conduct, despite the "blanks" in their written agreement. •

Open Price Term. If the parties have not agreed on a price, the court will determine a "reasonable price at the time for delivery" [UCC 2–305(1)]. If either the buyer or the seller is to determine the price, the price is to be fixed (set) in good faith [UCC 2–305(2)]. Under the UCC, *good faith* means honesty in fact and the observance of reasonable commercial standards of fair dealing in the trade [UCC 2–103(1)(b)]. The concepts of *good faith* and *commercial reasonableness* permeate the UCC.

Sometimes, the price fails to be fixed (specified) through the fault of one of the parties. In that situation, the other party can treat the contract as canceled or specify a reasonable price. **EXAMPLE 13.3** Perez and Merrick enter into a contract for the sale of unfinished doors and agree that Perez will determine the price. Perez refuses to specify the price. Merrick can either treat the contract as canceled or set a reasonable price [UCC 2–305(3)]. •

Open Payment Term. When parties do not specify payment terms, payment is due at the time and place at which the buyer is to receive the goods [UCC 2–310(a)]. The buyer can tender payment using any commercially normal or acceptable means, such as a check or credit card. If the seller demands payment in cash, however, the buyer must be given a reasonable time to obtain it [UCC 2–511(2)].

CASE EXAMPLE 13.4 Max Alexander agreed to purchase hay from Wagner's farm. Alexander left his truck and trailer at the farm for the seller to load the hay. Nothing was said about when payment was due, and the parties were unaware of the UCC's rules. When Alexander came back to get the hay, a dispute broke out. Alexander claimed that he had been given less hay than he had ordered and argued that he did not have to pay at that time. Wagner refused to release the hay (or the vehicles on which the hay was loaded) until Alexander paid for it. Eventually, Alexander jumped into his truck and drove off without paying for the hay—for which he was later prosecuted for the crime of theft (see Chapter 6). Because the parties had failed to specify when payment was due, UCC 2–310(a) controlled, and payment was due at the time Alexander picked up the hay.[5] •

Open Delivery Term. When no delivery terms are specified, the buyer normally takes delivery at the seller's place of business [UCC 2–308(a)]. If the seller has no place of business, the seller's residence is used. When goods are located in some other place and both parties know it, delivery is made there. If the time for shipment or delivery is not clearly specified in the sales contract, the court will infer a "reasonable" time for performance [UCC 2–309(1)].

Duration of an Ongoing Contract. A single contract might specify successive performances but not indicate how long the parties are required to deal with each other. In this situation, either party may terminate the ongoing contractual relationship. Principles of good faith and sound commercial practice call for reasonable notification before termination, however, to give the other party time to make substitute arrangements [UCC 2–309(2), (3)].

Options and Cooperation Regarding Performance. When the contract contemplates shipment of the goods but does not specify the shipping arrangements, the *seller* has the right to make these arrangements in good faith, using commercial reasonableness in the situation [UCC 2–311].

When a sales contract omits terms relating to the assortment of goods, the *buyer* can specify the assortment. **EXAMPLE 13.5** Petry Drugs, Inc., agrees to purchase one thousand toothbrushes from Marconi's Dental Supply. The toothbrushes come in a variety of colors, but the contract does not specify color. Petry, the buyer, has the right to take six hundred blue toothbrushes and four hundred green ones if it wishes. Petry, however, must exercise good faith and commercial reasonableness in making its selection [UCC 2–311]. •

Open Quantity Term. Normally, if the parties do not specify a quantity, a court will have no basis for determining a remedy. This is because there is almost no way to determine objectively what is a reasonable quantity of goods for someone to buy (whereas a court can objectively determine a reasonable price for particular goods by looking at the market). Nevertheless, the UCC recognizes two exceptions involving requirements and output contracts [UCC 2–306(1)].

In a **requirements contract,** the buyer agrees to purchase and the seller agrees to sell all or up to a stated amount of what the buyer *needs* or *requires*. **EXAMPLE 13.6** Umpqua Cannery forms a contract with Al Garcia. The cannery agrees to purchase from Garcia, and Garcia agrees to sell to the cannery, all of the green beans that the cannery needs or requires during the following summer. • There is implicit consideration in a requirements contract because the buyer (the cannery, in this situation) gives up the right to buy green beans from any other seller, and this forfeited right creates a legal detriment (that is, consideration). Requirements contracts are common in the business world and normally are enforceable. In contrast, if the buyer promises to purchase only if the buyer *wishes* to do so, or if the buyer reserves the right to buy the goods from someone other than the seller, the promise is illusory (without consideration) and unenforceable by either party.

In an **output contract,** the seller agrees to sell and the buyer agrees to buy all or up to a stated amount of what the seller *produces*. **EXAMPLE 13.7** Al Garcia forms a contract with Umpqua Cannery. Garcia agrees to sell to the cannery, and the cannery agrees to purchase from Garcia, all of the beans that Garcia produces on his farm during the following summer. • Again, because the seller essentially forfeits the right to sell goods to another buyer, there is implicit consideration in an output contract.

The UCC imposes a *good faith limitation* on requirements and output contracts. The quantity under such contracts is the amount of requirements or the amount of output that occurs during a *normal* production year. The actual quantity purchased or sold cannot be unreasonably disproportionate to normal or comparable prior requirements or output [UCC 2–306(1)].

MERCHANT'S FIRM OFFER

Under regular contract principles, an offer can be revoked at any time before acceptance. The major common law exception is an *option contract* (discussed in Chapter 8), in which the offeree pays consideration for the offeror's irrevocable promise to keep the offer open for a stated period. The UCC creates a second exception for firm offers made by a merchant to sell, buy, or lease goods.

A **firm offer** arises when a merchant-offeror gives *assurances* in a *signed writing* that the offer will remain open. The merchant's firm offer is irrevocable without the necessity of consideration[6] for the stated period or, if no definite period is stated, a reasonable period (neither period to exceed three months) [UCC 2–205, 2A–205]. **EXAMPLE 13.8** Osaka, a used-car dealer, writes a letter to Saucedo on January 1 stating,

5. *State v. Alexander,* 186 Or.App. 600, 64 P.3d 1148 (2003).

6. If the offeree pays consideration, then an option contract (not a merchant's firm offer) is formed.

"I have a 2011 Suzuki SX4 on the lot that I'll sell you for $22,500 any time between now and January 31." This writing creates a firm offer, and Osaka will be liable for breach if he sells that Suzuki SX4 to someone other than Saucedo before January 31. ●

It is necessary that the offer be both *written* and *signed* by the offeror.[7] When a firm offer is contained in a form contract prepared by the offeree, the offeror must also sign a separate assurance of the firm offer. This requirement ensures that the offeror is aware of the offer. For instance, an offeree might respond to an initial offer by sending its own form contract containing a clause stating that the offer will remain open for three months. If the firm offer is buried amid copious language in one of the pages of the offeree's form contract, the offeror may inadvertently sign the contract without realizing that it contains a firm offer, thus defeating the purpose of the rule—which is to give effect to a merchant's deliberate intent to be bound to a firm offer.

Acceptance

Acceptance of an offer to buy, sell, or lease goods generally may be made in any reasonable manner and by any reasonable means. The UCC permits acceptance of an offer to buy goods "either by a prompt *promise* to ship or by the prompt or current shipment of conforming or nonconforming goods" [UCC 2–206(1)(b)]. *Conforming goods* accord with the contract's terms; *nonconforming goods* do not.

The prompt shipment of nonconforming goods constitutes both an acceptance, which creates a contract, and a breach of that contract. This rule does not apply if the seller **seasonably** (within a reasonable amount of time) notifies the buyer that the nonconforming shipment is offered only as an *accommodation,* or as a favor. The notice of accommodation must clearly indicate to the buyer that the shipment does not constitute an acceptance and that, therefore, no contract has been formed.

EXAMPLE 13.9 McFarrell Pharmacy orders five cases of Johnson & Johnson 3-by-5-inch gauze pads from H.T. Medical Supply, Inc. If H.T. ships five cases of Xeroform 3-by-5-inch gauze pads instead, the shipment acts as both an acceptance of McFarrell's offer and a *breach* of the resulting contract. McFarrell may sue H.T. for any appropriate damages. If, however, H.T. notifies McFarrell that the Xeroform gauze pads are being shipped *as an accommodation*—because H.T. has only Xeroform pads in stock—the shipment will constitute a counteroffer, not an acceptance. A contract will be formed only if McFarrell accepts the Xeroform gauze pads. ●

Communication of Acceptance Under the common law, because a unilateral offer invites acceptance by a performance, the offeree need not notify the offeror of performance unless the offeror would not otherwise know about it. In other words, a unilateral offer can be accepted by beginning performance. The UCC is more stringent than the common law in this regard because it requires notification. Under the UCC, if the offeror is not notified within a reasonable time that the offeree has accepted the contract by beginning performance, then the offeror can treat the offer as having lapsed before acceptance [UCC 2–206(2), 2A–206(2)].

Additional Terms Recall from Chapter 8 that under the common law, the *mirror image rule* requires that the terms of the acceptance exactly match those of the offer. Thus, if Alderman makes an offer to Beale, and Beale in turn accepts but in the acceptance makes some slight modification to the terms of the offer, there is no contract. The UCC dispenses with the mirror image rule. Generally, the UCC takes the position that if the offeree's response indicates a *definite* acceptance of the offer, a contract is formed even if the acceptance includes additional or different terms from those contained in the offer [UCC 2–207(1)]. Whether the additional terms become part of the contract depends, in part, on whether the parties are nonmerchants or merchants.

Rules When One Party or Both Parties Are Nonmerchants. If one (or both) of the parties is a *nonmerchant,* the contract is formed according to the terms of the original offer submitted by the original offeror and not according to the additional terms of the acceptance [UCC 2–207(2)].

EXAMPLE 13.10 Tolsen offers in writing to sell his iPad and thirteen additional apps to Valdez for $1,500. Valdez faxes a reply to Tolsen stating, "I accept your offer to purchase your iPad and thirteen additional apps for $1,500. I *would like* a box of laser printer paper and two extra toner cartridges to be included in the purchase price." Valdez has given Tolsen a definite expression of acceptance (creating a contract), even though the acceptance also *suggests* an added term for the offer. Because Tolsen is not a merchant, the additional term is merely a proposal (suggestion), and Tolsen is not legally obligated to comply with that term. ●

In the following case, the court had to decide whether an additional term that appeared in the invoice sent with the goods was part of the parties' contract. This additional term was a forum-selection clause (see page 153).

7. *Signed* includes any symbol executed or adopted by a party with a present intention to authenticate a writing [UCC 1–201(39)]. A complete signature is not required. Therefore, initials, a thumbprint, a trade name, or any mark used in lieu of a written signature will suffice, regardless of its location on the document.

Case 13.1 Office Supply Store.com v. Kansas City School Board

Missouri Court of Appeals, 334 S.W.3d 574 (2011).
www.courts.mo.gov[a]

FACTS Office Supply Store.com is a domain name registered to Office Supply Store, Inc., a corporation based in Bellevue, Washington. Employees of the Kansas City School District in Missouri allegedly ordered $17,642.54 worth of office supplies–without the authority or approval of their employer–from Office Supply Store.com. The Office Supply invoice that was sent with the goods (after the order had been placed) identified Los Angeles, California, as the "legal venue" for deciding disputes. When the goods were not paid for, Office Supply filed a suit against the Kansas City School Board and others, including some of the district's employees, in a California state court. The defendants did not respond. The court entered a default judgment in Office Supply's favor for more than $30,000 in damages, interest, attorneys' fees, and court costs. Office Supply asked a Missouri state court to formally register the judgment so that it could be enforced. The defendants appealed this registration.

a. In the "Quick Links" column, click on "Opinions & Minutes." On the next page, in the "Missouri Court of Appeals, Western District" row, click on "opinions." On that page, type "Office Supply" in the "Step 2. Search Opinion" box, and click on "Search." In the result, click on the case title to access the opinion. The Missouri courts maintain this Web site.

ISSUE Is a forum-selection clause enforceable when it was included as an additional term in a seller's invoice that was received at the time the goods were delivered?

DECISION No. A state appellate court reversed the lower court's decision.

REASON Under UCC 2–207, additional terms included in an invoice delivered by a seller to a nonmerchant buyer with the purchased goods do not become part of the parties' contract, unless that buyer expressly agreed to them. This law has been adopted in both California and Missouri. In this case, the school board and the district's employees did not fit the definition of a *merchant* under the UCC. Thus, the court reasoned that the forum-selection clause could only be construed as a proposal for an addition to the contract. There was no evidence that the defendants had agreed to the clause.

FOR CRITICAL ANALYSIS—Ethical Consideration *Should the court have allowed the default judgment to be registered so that it could have been enforced? Why or why not?*

Rules When Both Parties Are Merchants. The drafters of the UCC created a special rule for merchants to avoid the "battle of the forms," which occurs when two merchants exchange separate standard forms containing different contract terms. Under UCC 2–207(2), in contracts *between merchants,* the additional terms *automatically* become part of the contract unless one of the following conditions exists:

1. The original offer expressly limited acceptance to its terms.
2. The new or changed terms materially alter the contract.
3. The offeror objects to the new or changed terms within a reasonable period of time.

Generally, if the modification does not involve an unreasonable element of surprise or hardship for the offeror, the court will hold that the modification did not materially alter the contract. Courts also consider the parties' prior dealings and course of performance when determining whether the alteration is material.

Conditioned on Offeror's Assent. Regardless of merchant status, the UCC provides that the offeree's expression cannot be construed as an acceptance if it contains additional or different terms that are explicitly conditioned on the offeror's assent to those terms [UCC 2–207(1)]. **EXAMPLE 13.11** Philips offers to sell Hundert 650 pounds of turkey thighs at a specified price and with specified delivery terms. Hundert responds, "I accept your offer for 650 pounds of turkey thighs *on the condition that you give me ninety days to pay for them.*" Hundert's response will be construed not as an acceptance but as a counteroffer, which Philips may or may not accept. •

Consideration

The common law rule that a contract requires consideration also applies to sales and lease contracts. Unlike the common law, however, the UCC does not require a contract modification to be supported by new consideration. An agreement modifying a contract for the sale or lease of goods "needs no consideration to be binding" [UCC 2–209(1), 2A–208(1)]. Of course, a contract modification must be sought in good faith [UCC 1–304].

In some situations, an agreement to modify a sales or lease contract without consideration must be in writing to be enforceable. If the contract itself prohibits any changes to the contract unless they are in a signed writing, for instance, then only those changes agreed to in a signed writing are enforceable. If a consumer (nonmerchant buyer) is dealing with a merchant and the merchant supplies the form that contains a prohibition against oral modification, the consumer must sign a separate acknowledgment of such a clause [UCC 2–209(2), 2A–208(2)]. Also, any modification that brings a sales contract under Article 2's Statute of Frauds provision (discussed next) usually must be in writing to be enforceable.

The Statute of Frauds

The UCC contains Statute of Frauds provisions covering sales and lease contracts. Under these provisions, sales contracts for goods priced at $500 or more and lease contracts requiring payments of $1,000 or more must be in writing to be enforceable [UCC 2–201(1), 2A–201(1)]. (These low threshold amounts may eventually be raised.)

SUFFICIENCY OF THE WRITING The UCC has greatly relaxed the requirements for the sufficiency of a writing to satisfy the Statute of Frauds. A writing or a memorandum will be sufficient as long as it indicates that the parties intended to form a contract and as long as it is signed by the party (or agent of the party—see Chapter 21) against whom enforcement is sought. The contract normally will not be enforceable beyond the quantity of goods shown in the writing, however. All other terms can be proved in court by oral testimony. For leases, the writing must reasonably identify and describe the goods leased and the lease term.

SPECIAL RULES FOR CONTRACTS BETWEEN MERCHANTS Once again, the UCC provides a special rule for merchants in sales transactions (there is no corresponding rule that applies to leases under Article 2A). Merchants can satisfy the Statute of Frauds if, after the parties have agreed orally, one of the merchants sends a signed written confirmation to the other merchant within a reasonable time. The communication must indicate the terms of the agreement, and the merchant receiving the confirmation must have reason to know of its contents. Unless the merchant who receives the confirmation gives written notice of objection to its contents within ten days after receipt, the writing is sufficient against the receiving merchant, even though she or he has not signed anything [UCC 2–201(2)]. Generally, courts even hold that it is sufficient if a merchant sends an e-mail confirmation of the agreement.

EXAMPLE 13.12 Alfonso is a merchant-buyer in Cleveland. He contracts over the telephone to purchase $4,000 worth of spare aircraft parts from Goldstein, a merchant-seller in New York City. Two days later, Goldstein sends a written and signed confirmation detailing the terms of the oral contract, and Alfonso subsequently receives it. If Alfonso does not notify Goldstein in writing of his objection to the contents of the confirmation within ten days of receipt, Alfonso cannot raise the Statute of Frauds as a defense against the enforcement of the oral contract. •

EXCEPTIONS In addition to the special rules for merchants, the UCC defines three exceptions to the writing requirements of the Statute of Frauds. An oral contract for the sale of goods priced at $500 or more or the lease of goods involving total payments of $1,000 or more will be enforceable despite the absence of a writing in the circumstances discussed in the following subsections [UCC 2–201(3), 2A–201(4)].

Specially Manufactured Goods. An oral contract is enforceable if (1) it is for goods that are specially manufactured for a particular buyer or specially manufactured or obtained for a particular lessee, (2) these goods are not suitable for resale or lease to others in the ordinary course of the seller's or lessor's business, and (3) the seller or lessor has substantially started to manufacture the goods or has made commitments for their manufacture or procurement. In this situation, once the seller or lessor has taken action, the buyer or lessee cannot repudiate the agreement claiming the Statute of Frauds as a defense.

EXAMPLE 13.13 Womach orders custom-made draperies for her new boutique. The price is $6,000, and the contract is oral. When the merchant-seller manufactures the draperies and tenders delivery to Womach, she refuses to pay for them even though the job has been completed on time. Womach claims that she is not liable because the contract was oral. Clearly, if the unique style and color of the draperies make it improbable that the seller can find another buyer, Womach is liable to the seller. Note that the seller must have made a substantial beginning in manufacturing the specialized item prior to the buyer's repudiation. (Here, the manufacture was completed.) Of course, the court must still be convinced by evidence of the terms of the oral contract. •

Admissions. An oral contract for the sale or lease of goods is enforceable if the party against whom enforcement of the contract is sought admits in pleadings, testimony, or other court proceedings that a contract for sale was made. In this situation, the contract will be enforceable even though it was oral, but enforceability will be limited to the quantity of goods admitted.

CASE EXAMPLE 13.14 Gerald Lindgren, a farmer, agreed by phone to sell his crops to Glacial Plains Cooperative. The parties reached four oral agreements: two for the delivery of soybeans and two for the delivery of corn. Lindgren made the soybean deliveries and part of the first corn delivery, but he sold the rest of his corn to another dealer. Glacial Plains bought corn elsewhere, paying a higher price, and then sued Lindgren for breach of contract. In papers filed with the court, Lindgren acknowledged his oral agreements with Glacial Plains and admitted that he did not fully perform. The court applied the admissions exception and held that the four agreements were enforceable.[8] •

8. *Glacial Plains Cooperative v. Lindgren,* 759 N.W.2d 661 (Minn.App. 2009).

Partial Performance. An oral contract for the sale or lease of goods is enforceable if payment has been made and accepted or goods have been received and accepted. This is the "partial performance" exception. The oral contract will be enforced at least to the extent that performance *actually* took place.

EXAMPLE 13.15 Allan orally contracts to lease to Opus Enterprises a thousand chairs at $2 each to be used during a one-day concert. Before delivery, Opus sends Allan a check for $1,000, which Allan cashes. Later, when Allan attempts to deliver the chairs, Opus refuses delivery, claiming the Statute of Frauds as a defense, and demands the return of its $1,000. Under the UCC's partial performance rule, Allan can enforce the oral contract by tender of delivery of five hundred chairs for the $1,000 accepted. Similarly, if Opus had made no payment but had accepted the delivery of five hundred chairs from Allan, the oral contract would have been enforceable against Opus for $1,000, the lease payment due for the five hundred chairs delivered. •

Parol Evidence

Recall from Chapter 10 that *parol evidence* is testimony or other evidence of the parties' prior negotiations, prior agreements, or contemporaneous oral agreements. When the parties to a sales contract set forth its terms in a confirmatory memorandum or in other writing that is intended as a complete and final statement of their agreement, it is considered *fully integrated* and the *parol evidence rule* applies. The terms of a fully integrated contract cannot be contradicted by evidence of any prior agreements or contemporaneous oral agreements. If, however, the writing contains some of the terms the parties agreed on but not others, then the contract is not fully integrated.

When a court finds that the terms of the sales contract are *not fully integrated,* then the court may allow evidence of *consistent additional terms* to explain or supplement the terms stated in the contract. The court may also allow the parties to submit evidence of *course of dealing, usage of trade,* or *course of performance* when the contract was only partially integrated [UCC 2–202, 2A–202]. A court will not under any circumstances allow the parties to submit evidence that contradicts the stated terms (this is also the rule under the common law of contracts).

Course of Dealing and Usage of Trade

Under the UCC, the meaning of any agreement, evidenced by the language of the parties and by their actions, must be interpreted in light of commercial practices and other surrounding circumstances. In interpreting a commercial agreement, the court will assume that the course of prior dealing between the parties and the usage of trade were taken into account when the agreement was phrased.

A **course of dealing** is a sequence of previous actions and communications between the parties to a particular transaction that establishes a common basis for their understanding [UCC 1–303(b)]. A course of dealing is restricted to the sequence of actions and communications between the parties that occurred prior to the agreement in question. Under the UCC, a course of performance (discussed next) or course of dealing between the parties—or one that the parties are (or should be) aware of because it is widely used in the particular trade or industry—is relevant in ascertaining the meaning of the parties' agreement, may give particular meaning to specific terms of the agreement, and may supplement or qualify the terms of the agreement [UCC 1–303(d)].

Usage of trade is any practice or method of dealing having such regularity of observance in a place, vocation, or trade as to justify an expectation that it will be observed with respect to the transaction in question [UCC 1–303(c)]. Further, the express terms of an agreement and an applicable course of dealing or usage of trade will be construed to be consistent with each other whenever reasonable. When such a construction is *unreasonable,* however, the express terms in the agreement will prevail [UCC 1–303(e)].

Course of Performance

A **course of performance** is the conduct that occurs under the terms of a particular agreement. Presumably, the parties themselves know best what they meant by their words, and the course of performance actually undertaken under their agreement is the best indication of what they meant [UCC 1–303(a), 2–208(1), 2A–207(1)].

EXAMPLE 13.16 Janson's Lumber Company contracts with Barrymore to sell Barrymore a specified number of "two-by-fours." The lumber in fact does not measure 2 inches by 4 inches but rather 1⅞ inches by 3¾ inches. Janson's agrees to deliver the lumber in five deliveries, and Barrymore, without objection, accepts the lumber in the first three deliveries. On the fourth delivery, however, Barrymore objects that the two-by-fours do not measure 2 inches by 4 inches. The course of performance in this transaction—that is, the fact that Barrymore accepted three deliveries without objection under the agreement—is relevant in determining that here the term *two-by-four* actually means "1⅞ by 3¾." Janson's can also prove that two-by-fours need not be exactly 2 inches by 4 inches by applying usage of trade, course of prior dealing, or both. Janson's can, for example, show that in previous transactions, Barrymore took 1⅞-by-3¾-inch lumber without objection. In addition, Janson's can show that in the lumber trade, two-by-fours are commonly 1⅞ inches by 3¾ inches. •

Rules of Construction

The UCC provides *rules of construction* for interpreting contracts. Express terms, course of performance, course of dealing, and usage of trade are to be construed together when they do not contradict one another. When such a construction is unreasonable, however, the following order of priority controls: (1) express terms, (2) course of performance, (3) course of dealing, and (4) usage of trade [UCC 1–303(e), 2–208(2), 2A–207(2)].

Unconscionability

As discussed in Chapter 9, an unconscionable contract is one that is so unfair and one sided that it would be unreasonable to enforce it. The UCC allows the court to evaluate a contract or any clause in a contract, and if the court deems it to have been unconscionable at the time it was made, the court can (1) refuse to enforce the contract, (2) enforce the remainder of the contract without the unconscionable clause, or (3) limit the application of any unconscionable clauses to avoid an unconscionable result [UCC 2–302, 2A–108]. The following classic case illustrates an early application of the UCC's unconscionability provisions.

Classic Case 13.2 Jones v. Star Credit Corp.

Supreme Court of New York, Nassau County, 59 Misc.2d 189, 298 N.Y.S.2d 264 (1969).

FACTS The Joneses, the plaintiffs, agreed to purchase a freezer for $900 as the result of a salesperson's visit to their home. Tax and financing charges raised the total price to $1,234.80. At trial, the freezer was found to have a maximum retail value of approximately $300. The plaintiffs, who had made payments totaling $619.88, brought a suit in a New York state court to have the purchase contract declared unconscionable under the UCC.

ISSUE Should the law deny enforcement of this contract on the ground of unconscionability?

DECISION Yes. The court held that the contract was unenforceable as it stood, and the contract was reformed so that no further payments were required.

REASON The court relied on UCC 2–302(1), which states that if "the court as a matter of law finds the contract or any clause of the contract to have been unconscionable at the time it was made, the court may . . . so limit the application of any unconscionable clause as to avoid any unconscionable result." The court then examined the disparity between the $900 purchase price and the $300 retail value, as well as the fact that the credit charges alone exceeded the retail value. These excessive charges were exacted despite the seller's knowledge of the plaintiffs' limited resources. The court reformed the contract so that the plaintiffs' payments, amounting to more than $600, were regarded as payment in full.

FOR CRITICAL ANALYSIS—Social Consideration *Why didn't the court rule that the Joneses, as adults, had made a decision of their own free will and therefore were bound by the terms of the contract, regardless of the difference between the freezer's contract price and its retail value?*

IMPACT OF THIS CASE ON TODAY'S LAW *This early case illustrates the approach that many courts today take when deciding whether a sales contract is unconscionable–an approach that focuses on "excessive" price and unequal bargaining power.*

Title and Risk of Loss

Before the creation of the UCC, *title*—the right of ownership—was the central concept in sales law, controlling all issues of rights and remedies of the parties to a sales contract. In some situations, title is still relevant under the UCC, and the UCC has special rules for determining who has title. (These rules do not apply to leased goods, obviously, because title remains with the lessor, or owner, of the goods.) In most situations, however, the UCC has replaced the concept of title with three other concepts: (1) identification, (2) risk of loss, and (3) insurable interest.

Identification

Before any interest in specific goods can pass from the seller or lessor to the buyer or lessee, the goods must exist and be identified as the specific goods designated in the contract. **Identification** takes place when specific goods are designated as the subject matter of a sales or lease contract. Title and risk of loss cannot pass from seller to buyer unless the goods are identified to the contract. (As mentioned, title to leased goods does not pass to the lessee.) Identification is significant because it gives the buyer or lessee the right to insure the goods and the right to recover from third parties who damage the goods.

The parties can agree in their contract on when identification will take place (although it will not effectively pass title and risk of loss to the buyer on future goods, such as unborn cattle). If the parties do not so specify, however, the UCC provisions discussed here determine when identification takes place [UCC 2–501(1), 2A–217].

EXISTING GOODS If the contract calls for the sale or lease of specific goods that are already in existence, identification takes place at the time the contract is made. **EXAMPLE 13.17** You contract to purchase or lease a fleet of five cars designated by their vehicle identification numbers (VINs). Because the cars are identified by their VINs, identification has taken place, and you acquire an insurable interest in them at the time of contracting. ●

FUTURE GOODS If a sale involves unborn animals to be born within twelve months after contracting, identification takes place when the animals are conceived. If a lease involves any unborn animals, identification occurs when the animals are conceived. If a sale involves crops that are to be harvested within twelve months (or the next harvest season occurring after contracting, whichever is longer), identification takes place when the crops are planted. Otherwise, identification takes place when they begin to grow. In a sale or lease of any other future goods, identification occurs when the goods are shipped, marked, or otherwise designated by the seller or lessor as the goods to which the contract refers.

GOODS THAT ARE PART OF A LARGER MASS As a general rule, goods that are part of a larger mass are identified when the goods are marked, shipped, or somehow designated by the seller or lessor as the particular goods that are the subject of the contract. **EXAMPLE 13.18** A buyer orders 1,000 cases of beans from a 10,000-case lot. Until the seller separates the 1,000 cases of beans from the 10,000-case lot, title and risk of loss remain with the seller. ●

A common exception to this rule involves fungible goods. **Fungible goods** are goods that are alike by physical nature, by agreement, or by trade usage, such as specific grades or types of wheat, oil, and wine, that are usually stored in large containers. If more than one person owns an interest in the fungible goods as *tenants in common* (a type of joint ownership in which each party owns an undivided interest that passes to her or his heirs after death), a seller-owner can pass title and risk of loss to the buyer without an actual separation. The buyer replaces the seller as an owner in common [UCC 2–105(4)].

Passage of Title

Once goods exist and are identified, the provisions of UCC 2–401 apply to the passage of title. In nearly all subsections of UCC 2–401, the words "unless otherwise explicitly agreed" appear, meaning that any explicit understanding between the buyer and the seller determines when title passes. Without an explicit agreement to the contrary, *title passes to the buyer at the time and the place the seller performs by delivering the goods* [UCC 2–401(2)]. For instance, if a person buys cattle at a livestock auction, title will pass to the buyer when the cattle are physically delivered to him or her (unless, of course, the parties agree otherwise).

If a seller gives up possession or control of goods, but keeps a "certificate of origin" supposedly showing ownership, has there been a delivery sufficient to pass title? That was the question in the following case.

Case 13.3 United States v. 2007 Custom Motorcycle

United States District Court, District of Arizona, __ F.Supp.2d __ (2011).

FACTS Timothy Allen commissioned a custom motorcycle from Indy Route 66 Cycles, Inc., a company based in Indianapolis, Indiana. Indy built the motorcycle and issued a "Certificate of Origin" in April 2007. Two years later, federal law enforcement officers arrested Allen on drug charges and seized his home and other property in Phoenix, Arizona. The officers also seized the Indy-made motorcycle from the garage of the home of Allen's sister, Tena. The government alleged that the motorcycle was subject to forfeiture as the proceeds of drug trafficking. Indy filed a claim in a federal district court against the government. Indy argued that it owned the motorcycle, as evidenced by the "Certificate of Origin," which the company still possessed. Indy claimed that it had been keeping the motorcycle in storage. The government asserted that the motorcycle had been delivered to Allen in April 2007 and that Indy thus did not have standing to make its claim. The government filed a motion to strike the claim.

ISSUE Did ownership to the motorcycle pass at the time that Indy gave Allen possession and control over it?

DECISION Yes. The district court issued a ruling in the government's favor and granted the motion to strike Indy's claim.

REASON Under UCC 2–401(2), "unless otherwise explicitly agreed, title passes to the buyer at the time and place at which the seller completes his performance with reference to the physical delivery of the goods." In the sales transaction in this case, the parties did not "otherwise explicitly agree" to different terms. Thus, the critical factor was whether Indy had delivered the motorcycle to Allen. Testimony by Indy's former vice president, Vince Ballard, was "inconclusive." Although Ballard implied that Indy had delivered the motorcycle to Allen, he also asserted that Indy had kept it in storage. Yet the motorcycle was found in Tena's garage. This "strongly indicates that claimant delivered it to [Timothy] Allen." Thus, Indy had given up possession of the motorcycle to Allen. This was sufficient to pass title even though Indy had kept a "Certificate of Origin." As a consequence, the motorcycle was subject to forfeiture as the proceeds of drug trafficking.

WHAT IF THE FACTS WERE DIFFERENT? *Suppose that Indy had given the "Certificate of Origin" to Allen and had kept the motorcycle. Would the result have been different? Explain.*

SHIPMENT AND DESTINATION CONTRACTS Unless otherwise agreed, delivery arrangements can determine when title passes from the seller to the buyer. In a **shipment contract,** the seller is required or authorized to ship goods by carrier, such as a trucking company. Under a shipment contract, the seller is required only to deliver conforming goods into the hands of a carrier, and title passes to the buyer at the time and place of shipment [UCC 2–401(2)(a)]. Generally, *all contracts are assumed to be shipment contracts if nothing to the contrary is stated in the contract.*

In a **destination contract,** the seller is required to deliver the goods to a particular destination, usually directly to the buyer, but sometimes to another party designated by the buyer. Title passes to the buyer when the goods are *tendered* at that destination [UCC 2–401(2)(b)]. As you will read in Chapter 14, *tender of delivery* occurs when the seller places or holds conforming goods at the buyer's disposal (with any necessary notice), enabling the buyer to take possession [UCC 2–503(1)].

DELIVERY WITHOUT MOVEMENT OF THE GOODS When the sales contract does not call for the seller to ship or deliver the goods (when the buyer is to pick up the goods), the passage of title depends on whether the seller must deliver a **document of title,** such as a bill of lading or a warehouse receipt, to the buyer. A *bill of lading* is a receipt for goods that is signed by a carrier and serves as a contract for the transport of the goods. A *warehouse receipt* is a receipt issued by a warehouser for goods stored in a warehouse.

When a document of title is required, title passes to the buyer *when and where the document is delivered.* Thus, if the goods are stored in a warehouse, title passes to the buyer when the appropriate documents are delivered to the buyer. The goods never move. In fact, the buyer can choose to leave the goods at the same warehouse for a period of time, and the buyer's title to those goods will be unaffected.

When no documents of title are required and delivery is made without moving the goods, title passes at the time and place the sales contract is made, if the goods have already been identified. If the goods have not been identified, title does not pass until identification occurs [UCC 2–401(3)].

EXAMPLE 13.19 Juarez sells lumber to Bodan. They agree that Bodan will pick up the lumber at the lumberyard. If the lumber has been identified (segregated, marked, or in any other way distinguished from all other lumber), title passes to Bodan when the contract is signed. If the lumber is still in large storage bins at the lumberyard, title does not pass to Bodan until the particular pieces of lumber to be sold under this contract are identified. •

SALES OR LEASES BY NONOWNERS Problems occur when persons who acquire goods with *imperfect* titles attempt to sell or lease them. Sections 2–402 and 2–403 of the UCC deal with the rights of two parties who lay claim to the same goods, sold with imperfect titles. Generally, a buyer acquires at least whatever title the seller has to the goods sold.

Void Title. A buyer may unknowingly purchase goods from a seller who is not the owner of the goods. If the seller is a thief, the seller's title is *void*—legally, no title exists. Thus, the buyer acquires no title, and the real owner can reclaim the goods from the buyer. If the goods were only leased, the same result would occur because the lessor has no leasehold interest to transfer.

EXAMPLE 13.20 If Saki steals diamonds owned by Maren, Saki has a *void title* to those diamonds. If Saki sells the diamonds to Shannon, Maren can reclaim them from Shannon even though Shannon acted in good faith and honestly was not aware that the goods were stolen. • (Article 2A contains similar provisions for leases.)

Voidable Title. A seller has *voidable title* if the goods that she or he is selling were obtained by fraud, paid for with a check that is later dishonored, purchased from a minor, or purchased on credit when the seller was insolvent. (Under the UCC, a person is **insolvent** when that person ceases to pay his or her debts in the ordinary course of business, cannot pay his or her debts as they become due, or is insolvent within the meaning of federal bankruptcy law [UCC 1–201(23)].)

In contrast to a seller with *void title,* a seller with *voidable title* has the power to transfer good title to a good faith purchaser for value. A **good faith purchaser** is one who buys without knowledge of circumstances that would make a person of ordinary prudence inquire about the validity of the seller's title to the goods. One who purchases *for value* gives legally sufficient consideration (value) for the goods purchased. The original owner cannot recover goods from a good faith purchaser for value [UCC 2–403(1)].[9] If the buyer of the goods is not a good faith purchaser for value, then the actual owner of the goods can reclaim them from the buyer (or from the seller, if the goods are still in the seller's possession). Exhibit 13–2 on the facing page illustrates these concepts.

The Entrustment Rule. According to Section 2–403(2), entrusting goods to a merchant *who deals in goods of that kind* gives the merchant the power to transfer all rights to a *buyer in the ordinary course of business.* This is known as the **entrustment rule.** Entrusting includes both turning over the goods to the merchant and leaving purchased goods with the merchant for later delivery or pickup [UCC 2–403(3)]. Article 2A provides a similar rule for leased goods [UCC 2A–305(2)].

9. The real owner could, of course, sue the person who initially obtained voidable title to the goods.

• ***Exhibit* 13–2 Void and Voidable Titles**

If goods are transferred from their owner to another by theft, the thief acquires no ownership rights. Because the thief's title is *void,* a later buyer can acquire no title, and the owner can recover the goods. If the transfer occurs by fraud, the transferee acquires a *voidable* title. A later good faith purchaser for value can acquire good title, and the original owner cannot recover the goods.

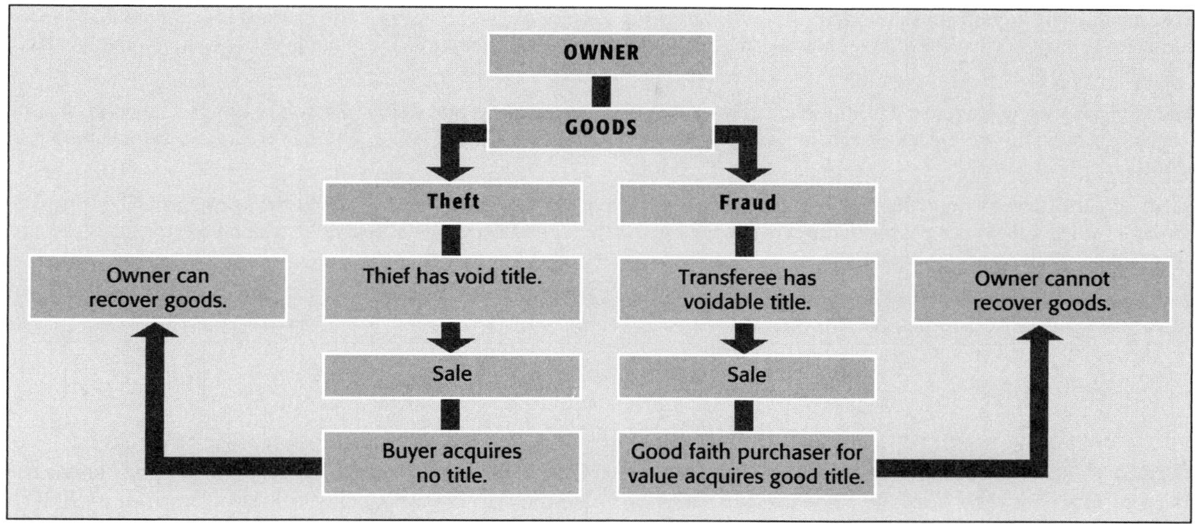

A buyer in the ordinary course of business is a person who, in good faith and without knowledge that the sale violates the ownership rights or security interest of a third party, buys in ordinary course from a person (other than a pawnbroker) in the business of selling goods of that kind [UCC 1–201(9)]. (A *security interest* is any interest in personal property that secures the payment of or the performance of an obligation—see Chapter 18.)

The entrustment rule basically allows innocent buyers to obtain legitimate title to goods purchased from merchants, even if the merchants do not have good title. **EXAMPLE 13.21** Jan leaves her watch with a jeweler to be repaired. The jeweler sells new and used watches. The jeweler sells Jan's watch to Kim, a customer, who does not know that the jeweler has no right to sell it. Kim, as a good faith buyer, gets good title against Jan's claim of ownership.[10] Kim, however, obtains only those rights held by the person entrusting the goods (here, Jan). Suppose that in fact Jan had stolen the watch from Greg and then left it with the jeweler to be repaired. The jeweler then sells it to Kim. In this situation, Kim gets good title against Jan, who entrusted the watch to the jeweler, but not against Greg (the real owner), who neither entrusted the watch to Jan nor authorized Jan to entrust it. •

10. Jan, of course, can sue the jeweler for the tort of trespass to personalty or conversion (see Chapter 4) for the equivalent cash value of the watch.

Risk of Loss

Under the UCC, risk of loss does not necessarily pass with title. When risk of loss passes from a seller or lessor to a buyer or lessee is generally determined by the contract between the parties. Sometimes, the contract states expressly when the risk of loss passes. At other times, it does not, and a court must interpret the performance and delivery terms of the contract to determine whether the risk has passed.

DELIVERY WITH MOVEMENT OF THE GOODS—CARRIER CASES When the contract involves movement of the goods through a common carrier but does not specify when risk of loss passes, the courts first look for specific delivery terms in the contract. The terms that have traditionally been used in contracts within the United States are listed and defined in Exhibit 13–3 on the following page. These terms determine which party will pay the costs of delivering the goods and who bears the risk of loss. If the contract does not include these terms, then the courts must decide whether the contract is a shipment or a destination contract.

Shipment Contracts. In a shipment contract, the seller or lessor is required or authorized to ship goods by carrier, but is not required to deliver them to a particular final destination. The risk of loss in a shipment contract passes to the buyer or lessee when the goods are delivered to the carrier [UCC 2–319(1)(a), 2–509(1)(a), 2A–219(2)(a)].

• *Exhibit* 13–3 Contract Terms–Definitions

The contract terms listed and defined in this exhibit help to determine which party will bear the costs of delivery and when risk of loss will pass from the seller to the buyer.

F.O.B. (free on board)—Indicates that the selling price of goods includes transportation costs to the specific F.O.B. place named in the contract. The seller pays the expenses and carries the risk of loss to the F.O.B. place named [UCC 2–319(1)]. If the named place is the place from which the goods are shipped (for example, the seller's city or place of business), the contract is a shipment contract. If the named place is the place to which the goods are to be shipped (for example, the buyer's city or place of business), the contract is a destination contract.
F.A.S. (free alongside ship)—Requires that the seller, at his or her own expense and risk, deliver the goods alongside the vessel in the manner usual in that port or on a dock designated and provided by the buyer [UCC 2–319(2)]. An F.A.S. contract is essentially an F.O.B. contract for ships.
C.I.F. or **C.&F.** (cost, insurance, and freight or just cost and freight)—Requires, among other things, that the seller "put the goods in the possession of a carrier" before risk passes to the buyer [UCC 2–320(2)]. (These are basically pricing terms, and the contracts remain shipment contracts, not destination contracts.)
Delivery ex-ship (delivery from the carrying vessel)—Means that risk of loss does not pass to the buyer until the goods are properly unloaded from the ship or other carrier [UCC 2–322].

EXAMPLE 13.22 A seller in Texas sells five hundred cases of grapefruit to a buyer in New York, F.O.B. Houston (free on board in Houston—that is, the buyer pays the transportation charges from Houston). The contract authorizes shipment by carrier. It does not require that the seller tender the grapefruit in New York. Risk passes to the buyer when conforming goods are properly placed in the possession of the carrier. If the goods are damaged in transit, the loss is the buyer's. (Actually, buyers have recourse against carriers, subject to certain limitations, and buyers usually insure the goods from the time the goods leave the seller.) •

Destination Contracts. In a destination contract, the risk of loss passes to the buyer or lessee when the goods are tendered to the buyer or lessee at the specified destination [UCC 2–319(1)(b), 2–509(1)(b), 2A–219(2)(b)]. In Example 13.22, if the contract had been F.O.B. New York, the risk of loss during transit to New York would have been the seller's.

Delivery without Movement of the Goods

The UCC also addresses situations in which the contract does not require the goods to be shipped or moved. Frequently, the buyer or lessee is to pick up the goods from the seller or lessor, or the goods are held by a bailee. Under the UCC, a **bailee** is a party who, by a bill of lading, warehouse receipt, or other document of title, acknowledges possession of goods and/or contracts to deliver them. A warehousing company, for example, or a trucking company that normally issues documents of title for the goods it receives is a bailee.[11]

Goods Held by the Seller. When the seller keeps the goods for pick up, a document of title usually is not used. If the seller is a merchant, risk of loss to goods held by the seller passes to the buyer when the buyer *actually takes physical possession of the goods* [UCC 2–509(3)]. In other words, the merchant bears the risk of loss between the time the contract is formed and the time the buyer picks up the goods.

If the seller is not a merchant, the risk of loss to goods held by the seller passes to the buyer on *tender of delivery* [UCC 2–509(3)]. This means that the seller bears the risk of loss until he or she makes the goods available to the buyer and notifies the buyer that the goods are ready to be picked up. With respect to leases, the risk of loss passes to the lessee on the lessee's receipt of the goods if the lessor is a merchant. Otherwise, the risk passes to the lessee on tender of delivery [UCC 2A–219(2)(c)].

Goods Held by the Bailee. When a bailee is holding goods for a person who has contracted to sell them and the goods are to be delivered without being moved, the goods are usually represented by a document of title, such as a bill of lading or a warehouse receipt. Risk of loss passes to the buyer when (1) the buyer receives a negotiable document of title for the goods, (2) the bailee acknowledges the buyer's right to possess the goods, or (3) the buyer receives a nonnegotiable document of title or a writing (record) directing the bailee to deliver the goods *and* has had a *reasonable* time to present the document to the bailee and demand the goods. Obviously, if the bailee refuses to honor the document, the risk of loss remains with the seller [UCC 2–503(4)(b), 2–509(2)].

With respect to leases, if goods held by a bailee are to be delivered without being moved, the risk of loss passes to the

11. Bailments will be discussed in Chapter 27.

lessee on acknowledgment by the bailee of the lessee's right to possession of the goods [UCC 2A–219(2)(b)].

RISK OF LOSS WHEN THE CONTRACT IS BREACHED When a sales or lease contract is breached, the transfer of risk operates differently depending on which party breaches. Generally, the party in breach bears the risk of loss.

When the Seller or Lessor Breaches. If the goods are so nonconforming that the buyer has the right to reject them, the risk of loss does not pass to the buyer until (1) the defects are **cured** (that is, until the goods are repaired, replaced, or discounted in price by the seller); or (2) the buyer accepts the goods in spite of their defects (thus waiving the right to reject). **EXAMPLE 13.23** A buyer orders ten white refrigerators from a seller, F.O.B. the seller's plant. The seller ships amber refrigerators instead. The amber refrigerators (nonconforming goods) are damaged in transit. The risk of loss falls on the seller. Had the seller shipped white refrigerators (conforming goods) instead, the risk would have fallen on the buyer [UCC 2–510(1)]. •

If a buyer accepts a shipment of goods and later discovers a defect, acceptance can be revoked. Revocation allows the buyer to pass the risk of loss back to the seller, at least to the extent that the buyer's insurance does not cover the loss [UCC 2–510(2)].

When the Buyer or Lessee Breaches. The general rule is that when a buyer or lessee breaches a contract, the risk of loss immediately shifts to the buyer or lessee. This rule has three important limitations:

1. The seller or lessor must already have identified the contract goods.
2. The buyer or lessee bears the risk for only a commercially reasonable time after the seller or lessor has learned of the breach.
3. The buyer or lessee is liable only to the extent of any deficiency in the seller's insurance coverage [UCC 2–510(3), 2A–220(2)].

Insurable Interest

Parties to sales and lease contracts often obtain insurance coverage to protect against damage, loss, or destruction of goods. Any party purchasing insurance, however, must have a sufficient interest in the insured item to obtain a valid policy. Insurance laws—not the UCC—determine sufficiency (see Chapter 29). The UCC is helpful, however, because it contains certain rules regarding insurable interests in goods.

INSURABLE INTEREST OF THE BUYER OR LESSEE A buyer or lessee has an **insurable interest** in identified goods. The moment the contract goods are identified by the seller or lessor, the buyer or lessee has a special property interest that allows the buyer or lessee to obtain necessary insurance coverage for those goods even before the risk of loss has passed [UCC 2–501(1), 2A–218(1)]. Buyers obtain an insurable interest in crops at the time of identification. **EXAMPLE 13.24** In March, a farmer sells a cotton crop that he hopes to harvest in October. When the crop is planted, the buyer acquires an insurable interest in it because those goods (the cotton crop) are identified to the sales contract between the seller and the buyer. •

INSURABLE INTEREST OF THE SELLER OR LESSOR A seller has an insurable interest in goods if she or he retains title to the goods. Even after title passes to the buyer, a seller who has a security interest in the goods (a right to secure payment—see Chapter 18) still has an insurable interest and can insure the goods [UCC 2–501(2)]. Hence, both a buyer and a seller can have an insurable interest in identical goods at the same time. Of course, the buyer or seller must sustain an actual loss to have the right to recover from an insurance com-pany. In regard to leases, the lessor retains an insurable interest in leased goods until the lessee exercises an option to buy and the risk of loss has passed to the lessee [UCC 2A–218(3)].

Contracts for the International Sale of Goods

International sales contracts between firms or individuals located in different countries are governed by the 1980 United Nations Convention on Contracts for the International Sale of Goods (CISG). The CISG governs international contracts only if the countries of the parties to the contract have ratified the CISG and if the parties have not agreed that some other law will govern their contract. As of 2011, the CISG had been adopted by seventy-seven countries, including the United States, Canada, Mexico, some Central and South American countries, and most European nations.

Applicability of the CISG

Essentially, the CISG is to international sales contracts what Article 2 of the UCC is to domestic sales contracts. As discussed in this chapter, in domestic transactions the UCC applies when the parties to a contract for a sale of goods have failed to specify in writing some important term concerning price, delivery, or the like. Similarly, whenever the parties subject to the CISG have failed to specify in writing the precise terms of a contract for the international sale of goods, the CISG will be applied. Unlike the UCC, *the CISG does not apply to consumer sales,* and neither the UCC nor the CISG applies to contracts for services.

Businesspersons must take special care when drafting international sales contracts to avoid problems caused by distance, including language differences and varying national laws. The appendix at the end of this chapter, which shows an actual international sales contract used by Starbucks Coffee Company, illustrates many of the special terms and clauses that are typically contained in international contracts for the sale of goods. Annotations in the exhibit explain the meaning and significance of specific clauses in the contract. (See Chapter 31 for a discussion of other laws that frame global business transactions.)

A Comparison of CISG and UCC Provisions

The provisions of the CISG, although similar for the most part to those of the UCC, differ from them in certain respects. For example, the CISG does not include any Statute of Frauds provisions. Under Article 11 of the CISG, an international sales contract does not need to be evidenced by a writing or to be in any particular form.

We look here at some differences between the UCC and the CISG with respect to contract formation. In the following chapters, we will continue to point out differences between the CISG and the UCC as they relate to the topics covered. These topics include performance, remedies, and warranties.

OFFERS Some differences between the UCC and the CISG have to do with offers. For instance, the UCC provides that a merchant's firm offer is irrevocable, even without consideration, if the merchant gives assurances in a signed writing. In contrast, under the CISG, an offer can become irrevocable without a signed writing. Article 16(2) of the CISG provides that an offer will be irrevocable if the merchant-offeror simply states orally that the offer is irrevocable or if the offeree reasonably relies on the offer as being irrevocable. In both of these situations, the offer will be irrevocable even without a writing and without consideration.

Another difference is that, under the UCC, if the price term is left open, the court will determine "a reasonable price at the time for delivery" [UCC 2–305(1)]. Under the CISG, however, the price term must be specified, or at least provisions for its specification must be included in the agreement. Otherwise, normally no contract will exist.

ACCEPTANCES Like UCC 2–207, the CISG provides that a contract can be formed even though the acceptance contains additional terms, unless the additional terms materially alter the contract. Under the CISG, however, the definition of a "material alteration" includes almost any change in the terms. If an additional term relates to payment, quality, quantity, price, time and place of delivery, extent of one party's liability to the other, or the settlement of disputes, the CISG considers the added term a "material alteration." In effect, then, the CISG requires that the terms of the acceptance mirror those of the offer.

Additionally, under the UCC, an acceptance is effective on dispatch. Under the CISG, however, a contract is not created until the offeror receives the acceptance. (The offer becomes irrevocable, however, when the acceptance is sent.) Also, in contrast to the UCC, the CISG provides that acceptance by performance does not require that the offeror be notified of the performance.

Reviewing . . . The Formation of Sales and Lease Contracts

Guy Holcomb owns and operates Oasis Goodtime Emporium, an adult entertainment establishment. Holcomb wanted to create an adult Internet system for Oasis that would offer customers adult theme videos and "live" chat room programs using performers at the club. On May 10, Holcomb signed a work order authorizing Crossroads Consulting Group (CCG) "to deliver a working prototype of a customer chat system, demonstrating the integration of live video and chatting in a Web browser." In exchange for creating the prototype, Holcomb agreed to pay CCG $64,697. On May 20, Holcomb signed an additional work order in the amount of $12,943 for CCG to install a customized firewall system. The work orders stated that Holcomb would make monthly installment payments to CCG, and both parties expected the work would be finished by September. Due to unforeseen problems largely attributable to system configuration and software incompatibility, the project required more time than anticipated. By the end of the summer, the Web site was still not ready, and Holcomb had fallen behind in the payments to CCG. CCG was threatening to cease work and file suit for breach of contract unless the bill was paid. Rather than make further payments, Holcomb wanted to abandon the Web site project. Using the information presented in the chapter, answer the following questions.

1. Would a court be likely to decide that the transaction between Holcomb and CCG was covered by the Uniform Commercial Code (UCC)? Why or why not?
2. Would a court be likely to consider Holcomb a merchant under the UCC? Why or why not?
3. Did the parties have a valid contract under the UCC? Explain.
4. Suppose that Holcomb and CCG meet in October in an attempt to resolve their problems. At that time, the parties reach an oral agreement that CCG will continue to work without demanding full payment of the past-due amounts and Holcomb will pay CCG $5,000 per week. Assuming that the contract falls under the UCC, is the oral agreement enforceable? Why or why not?

Terms and Concepts

bailee 240
course of dealing 235
course of performance 235
cured 241
destination contract 238
document of title 238
entrustment rule 238
firm offer 231
fungible goods 237
good faith purchaser 238
identification 236
insolvent 238
insurable interest 241
intangible property 228
lease 229
lease agreement 230
lessee 230
lessor 230
merchant 229
output contract 231
predominant-factor test 229
requirements contract 231
sale 227
sales contract 227
seasonably 232
shipment contract 238
tangible property 238
usage of trade 235

Chapter Summary: The Formation of Sales and Lease Contracts

The Scope of the UCC and Articles 2 (Sales) and 2A (Leases) (See pages 226–230.)	1. *The UCC*—The UCC attempts to provide a consistent, uniform, and integrated framework of rules to deal with all phases *ordinarily arising* in a commercial sales or lease transaction, including contract formation, passage of title and risk of loss, performance, remedies, payment for goods, warehoused goods, and secured transactions. 2. *Article 2 (sales)*—Article 2 governs contracts for the sale of goods (tangible, movable personal property). The common law of contracts also applies to sales contracts to the extent that the common law has not been modified by the UCC. If there is a conflict between a common law rule and the UCC, the UCC controls. 3. *Article 2A (leases)*—Article 2A governs contracts for the lease of goods. Except that it applies to leases, instead of sales, of goods, Article 2A is essentially a repetition of Article 2 and varies only to reflect differences between sales and lease transactions.
The Formation of Sales and Lease Contracts (See pages 230–236.)	1. *Offer*— a. Not all terms have to be included for a contract to be formed (only the subject matter and quantity term must be specified). b. The price does not have to be included for a contract to be formed. c. Particulars of performance can be left open. d. A written and signed offer by a *merchant,* covering a period of three months or less, is irrevocable without payment of consideration. 2. *Acceptance*— a. Acceptance may be made by any reasonable means of communication; it is effective when dispatched. b. An offer can be accepted by a promise to ship or by prompt shipment of conforming goods, or by prompt shipment of nonconforming goods if not accompanied by a notice of accommodation. c. Acceptance by performance requires notice within a reasonable time; otherwise, the offer can be treated as lapsed. d. A definite expression of acceptance creates a contract even if the terms of the acceptance vary from those of the offer, unless the varied terms in the acceptance are expressly conditioned on the offeror's assent to those terms. 3. *Consideration*—A modification of a contract for the sale of goods does not require consideration. 4. *The Statute of Frauds*— a. All contracts for the sale of goods priced at $500 or more must be in writing. A writing is sufficient as long as it indicates a contract between the parties and is signed by the party against whom enforcement is sought. A contract is not enforceable beyond the quantity shown in the writing. d. A written and signed offer by a *merchant,* covering a period of three months or less, is irrevocable without payment of consideration. 2. *Acceptance*— a. Acceptance may be made by any reasonable means of communication; it is effective when dispatched. b. An offer can be accepted by a promise to ship or by prompt shipment of conforming goods, or by prompt shipment of nonconforming goods if not accompanied by a notice of accommodation.

Continued

Chapter Summary: The Formation of Sales and Lease Contracts—Continued

The Formation of Sales and Lease Contracts—Continued	c. Acceptance by performance requires notice within a reasonable time; otherwise, the offer can be treated as lapsed. d. A definite expression of acceptance creates a contract even if the terms of the acceptance vary from those of the offer, unless the varied terms in the acceptance are expressly conditioned on the offeror's assent to those terms. 3. *Consideration*—A modification of a contract for the sale of goods does not require consideration. 4. *The Statute of Frauds*— a. All contracts for the sale of goods priced at $500 or more must be in writing. A writing is sufficient as long as it indicates a contract between the parties and is signed by the party against whom enforcement is sought. A contract is not enforceable beyond the quantity shown in the writing. b. When written confirmation of an oral contract *between merchants* is not objected to in writing by the receiver within ten days, the contract is enforceable. c. Exceptions to the Statute of Frauds include specially manufactured goods, admissions, and partial performance. 5. *Parol evidence rule*— a. The terms of a clearly and completely worded written contract cannot be contradicted by evidence of prior agreements or contemporaneous oral agreements. b. Evidence is admissible to clarify the terms of a writing if the contract terms are ambiguous or if evidence of course of dealing, usage of trade, or course of performance is necessary to learn or to clarify the parties' intentions. 6. *Unconscionability*—An unconscionable contract is one that is so unfair and one sided that it would be unreasonable to enforce it. If the court deems a sales contract to have been unconscionable at the time it was made, the court can (a) refuse to enforce the contract, (b) refuse to enforce the unconscionable clause, or (c) limit the application of any unconscionable clauses to avoid an unconscionable result.
Title and Risk of Loss (See pages 236–241.)	1. *Shipment contract*—In the absence of an agreement, title and risk (in a lease, only risk) pass on the seller's or lessor's delivery of conforming goods to the carrier [UCC 2–319(1)(a), 2–401(2)(a), 2–509(1)(a), 2A–219(2)(a)]. 2. *Destination contract*—In the absence of an agreement, title and risk pass on the seller's or lessor's *tender* of delivery of conforming goods to the buyer or lessee at the point of destination [UCC 2–319(1)(b), 2–401(2)(b), 2–509(1)(b), 2A–219(2)(b)]. 3. *Delivery without movement of the goods*—In the absence of an agreement, if the goods are not represented by a document of title, title passes on the formation of the contract, and risk passes on the buyer's or lessee's receipt of the goods if the seller or lessor is a merchant or on the tender of delivery if the seller or lessor is a nonmerchant. 4. *Sales and leases by nonowners*—Between the owner and a good faith purchaser or between the lessee and a sublessee: a. Void title—Owner prevails. b. Voidable title—Buyer prevails [UCC 2–403(1)]. c. Entrusting to a merchant—Buyer or sublessee prevails [UCC 2–403(2), (3); 2A–305(2)]. 5. *Risk of loss when the contract is breached*— a. If the seller or lessor breaches by tendering nonconforming goods that are rejected by the buyer or lessee, the risk of loss does not pass to the buyer or lessee until the defects are cured (unless the buyer or lessee accepts the goods in spite of their defects, thus waiving the right to reject) [UCC 2–510(1)]. b. If the buyer or lessee breaches the contract, the risk of loss immediately shifts to the buyer or lessee for goods that are identified to the contract. The buyer or lessee bears the risk for only a commercially reasonable time after the seller or lessor has learned of the breach [UCC 2–510(3), 2A–220(2)].
Contracts for the International Sale of Goods (See pages 241–242.)	International sales contracts are governed by the United Nations Convention on Contracts for the International Sale of Goods (CISG)—if the countries of the parties to the contract have ratified the CISG (and if the parties have not agreed that some other law will govern their contract). Essentially, the CISG is to international sales contracts what Article 2 of the UCC is to domestic sales contracts. Whenever parties who are subject to the CISG have failed to specify in writing the precise terms of a contract for the international sale of goods, the CISG will be applied.

ExamPrep

ISSUE SPOTTERS

—Check your answers to these questions against the answers provided in Appendix G.

1 E-Design, Inc., orders 150 computer desks. Fav-O-Rite Supplies, Inc., ships 150 printer stands. Is this an acceptance of the offer or a counteroffer? If it is an acceptance, is it a breach of the contract? What if Fav-O-Rite told E-Design it was sending the printer stands as "an accommodation"?

2 Truck Parts, Inc. (TPI), often sells supplies to United Fix-It Company (UFC), which services trucks. Over the phone, they negotiate for the sale of eighty-four sets of tires. TPI sends a letter to UFC detailing the terms and two weeks later ships the tires. Do TPI and UFC have an enforceable contract? Why or why not?

BEFORE THE TEST

Go to **www.cengagebrain.com**, enter the ISBN 9781111530624, and click on "Find" to locate this textbook's Web site. Then, click on "Access Now" under "Study Tools," and select Chapter 13 at the top. There, you will find an Interactive Quiz that you can take to assess your mastery of the concepts in this chapter, as well as Flashcards and a Glossary of important terms.

For Review

1 How do Article 2 and Article 2A of the UCC differ? What types of transactions does each article cover?

2 What is a merchant's firm offer?

3 In a sales contract, if an offeree includes additional or different terms in an acceptance, will a contract result? If so, what happens to these terms?

4 Risk of loss does not necessarily pass with title. If the parties to a contract do not expressly agree when risk passes and the goods are to be delivered without movement by the seller, when does risk pass?

5 What law governs contracts for the international sale of goods?

Questions and Case Problems

13–1 Statute of Frauds. Fresher Foods, Inc., orally agreed to purchase one thousand bushels of corn for $1.25 per bushel from Dale Vernon, a farmer. Fresher Foods paid $125 down and agreed to pay the remainder of the purchase price on delivery, which was scheduled for one week later. When Fresher Foods tendered the balance of $1,125 on the scheduled day of delivery and requested the corn, Vernon refused to deliver it. Fresher Foods sued Vernon for damages, claiming that Vernon had breached their oral contract. Can Fresher Foods recover? If so, to what extent?

13–2 Merchant's Firm Offer. On September 1, Jennings, a used-car dealer, wrote a letter to Wheeler, stating, "I have a 1955 Thunderbird convertible in mint condition that I will sell you for $13,500 at any time before October 9. [signed] Peter Jennings." By September 15, having heard nothing from Wheeler, Jennings sold the Thunderbird to another party. On September 29, Wheeler accepted Jennings's offer and tendered the $13,500. When Jennings told Wheeler he had sold the car to another party, Wheeler claimed Jennings had breached their contract. Is Jennings in breach? Explain.

13–3 **Question with Sample Answer** M.M. Salinger, Inc., a retailer of flat-screen television sets, orders one hundred model HD-X sets from manufacturer Fulsom. The order specifies the price and that the television sets are to be shipped via InterAmerican Freightways on or before October 30. Fulsom receives the order on October 5. On October 8, Fulsom writes Salinger a letter indicating that it has received the order and that it will ship the sets as directed, at the specified price. Salinger receives this letter on October 10. On October 28, Fulsom, in preparing the shipment, discovers it has only ninety HD-X sets in stock. Fulsom ships the ninety HD-X sets and ten television sets of a different model, stating clearly on the invoice that the ten sets are being shipped only as an accommodation. Salinger claims that Fulsom is in breach of contract. Fulsom claims that there was not an acceptance and, therefore, no contract was formed. Explain who is correct, and why.

—For a sample answer to Question 13–3, go to Appendix E at the end of this text.

13–4 Offer. In 1998, Johnson Controls, Inc. (JCI), began buying auto parts from Q. C. Onics Ventures, LP. For each part, JCI would inform Onics of its need and ask the price. Onics would analyze the specifications, contact its suppliers, and respond with a formal quotation. A quote listed a part's number and description, the price per unit, and an estimate of units available for a given year. A quote did not state payment terms, an acceptance date, the time of performance, warranties, or quantities. JCI would select a supplier and issue a purchase order for a part. The purchase order required the seller to supply all of JCI's requirements for the part but gave the buyer the right to end the deal at any time. Using this procedure, JCI issued hundreds of purchase orders. In July 2001, JCI terminated its relationship with Onics and began buying parts through another supplier. Onics filed a suit in a federal district court against JCI, alleging breach of contract. Which documents—the price quotations or the purchase orders—constituted offers? Which were acceptances? What effect would the answers to these questions have on the result in this case? Explain. [*Q. C. Onics Ventures, LP v. Johnson Controls, Inc.*, __ F.Supp.2d __ (N.D.Ind. 2006)]

13–5 **Case Problem with Sample Answer** Clear Lakes Trout Co. operates a fish hatchery in Idaho. Rodney and Carla Griffith are trout growers. Clear Lakes agreed to sell "small trout" to the Griffiths, who agreed to sell the trout back when they had grown to "market size." At the time, in the trade "market size" referred to fish approximating one-pound live weight. The parties did business without a written agreement until September 1998, when they executed a contract with a six-year duration. The contract did not define "market size." All went well until September 2001, after which there was a demand for larger fish. Clear Lakes began taking deliveries later and in smaller loads, leaving the Griffiths with overcrowded ponds and other problems. In 2003, the Griffiths refused to accept more fish and filed a suit in an Idaho state court against Clear Lakes, alleging breach of contract. Clear Lakes argued that there was no contract because the parties had different interpretations of "market size." Clear Lakes claimed that "market size" varied according to whatever its customers demanded. The Griffiths asserted that the term referred to fish of about one-pound live weight. Is outside evidence admissible to explain the terms of a contract? Are there any exceptions that could apply in this case? If so, what is the likely result? Explain. [*Griffith v. Clear Lakes Trout Co.*, 143 Idaho 733, 152 P.3d 604 (2007)]

—For a sample answer to Problem 13–5, go to Appendix F at the end of this text.

13–6 **Additional Terms.** Continental Insurance Co. issued a policy to cover shipments by Oakley Fertilizer, Inc. Oakley agreed to ship three thousand tons of fertilizer by barge from New Orleans, Louisiana, to Ameropa North America in Caruthersville, Missouri. Oakley sent Ameropa a contract form that set out these terms and stated that title and risk would pass to the buyer after the seller was paid for the goods. Ameropa e-mailed a different form that set out the same essential terms but stated that title and risk of loss would pass to the buyer when the goods were loaded onto the barges in New Orleans. The cargo was loaded onto barges but had not yet been delivered when it was damaged in Hurricane Katrina. Oakley filed a claim for the loss with Continental but was denied coverage. Oakley filed a suit in a Missouri state court against the insurer. Continental argued that title and risk passed to Ameropa before the damage as specified in the buyer's form under Section 2–207(3) of the Uniform Commercial Code because the parties did not have a valid contract under UCC 2–207(1). Apply UCC 2–207 on additional terms in an acceptance to these facts. Is Continental correct? Explain. [*Oakley Fertilizer, Inc. v. Continental Insurance Co.*, 276 S.W.3d 342 (Mo.App.E.D. 2009)]

13–7 **Acceptance.** JMAM, LLC, is a wholesaler of costume jewelry, doing business as "Joan Rivers Worldwide Enterprises." B.S. International, Ltd. (BSI), makes costume jewelry. JMAM and BSI did business under an agreement written by JMAM that set forth certain terms. One of the terms specified that JMAM would receive credit from BSI for any items rejected by JMAM's customers. JMAM had presented the terms to BSI with a cover letter stating, "By signing below, you the vendor agree to [these] terms." Steven Baracsi, BSI's owner, had signed the letter and returned it. For the next six years, BSI made jewelry for JMAM, which sold the jewelry to QVC, Inc. Items rejected by QVC were sent back to JMAM, which applied the cost as a credit against BSI invoices. The items, however, were never returned to BSI. When a dispute arose over the orders, BSI filed a suit in a Rhode Island state court against JMAM, claiming that it was owed $41,294.21 for items delivered but not returned. BSI showed the court a copy of JMAM's terms. Across the bottom had been typed a "P.S. [Post Script]" requiring the return of rejected merchandise. Baracsi testified that he had mailed this page to JMAM. James Halliday, JMAM's chief financial officer, testified that he had never seen it. When do additional terms become part of a contract between merchants? Was BSI's "P.S." part of this contract? Discuss. [*B.S. International, Ltd. v. JMAM, LLC*, 13 A.3d 1057 (R.I. 2011)]

13–8 **Delivery without Movement of the Goods.** Aleris International, Inc., rented a John Deere 644J loader from Holt Equipment Co. Four months later, the parties signed a sales contract for the loader, which was still in Aleris's possession. This agreement provided that "despite physical delivery of the equipment, title shall remain in the seller" until Aleris paid the full price or the parties signed an installment contract, a loan agreement, or a lease for it. The next month, Aleris filed for bankruptcy in a federal court. Holt filed a claim with the court to repossess the loader. Holt asserted that under UCC 2–401, it was the owner. Holt cited the sales contract provision that referred to the seller's retention of title and to the fact that Aleris had not fully paid for the loader. Which provision of UCC 2–401 applies in this case? What are its rules? Under these rules, who is entitled to the loader, and why? [*In re Aleris International, Ltd.*, __ Bankr. __ (D.Del. 2011)]

13–9 **A Question of Ethics** *Daniel Fox owned Fox & Lamberth Enterprises, Inc., a kitchen and bath remodeling business, in Dayton, Ohio. Fox leased a building from Carl and Bellulah Hussong. Craftsmen Home Improvement, Inc., also remodeled baths and kitchens. When Fox planned to close his business, Craftsmen expressed an interest in buying his showroom assets. Fox set a price of $50,000. Craftsmen's owners agreed and gave Fox a list of the desired items and "A Bill of Sale" that set the terms for payment. The parties did not discuss Fox's arrangement with the Hussongs, but Craftsmen expected to negotiate a new lease and* *extensively modified the premises, including removing some of the displays to its own showroom. When the Hussongs and Craftsmen could not agree on new terms, Craftsmen told Fox that the deal was off.* [Fox & Lamberth Enterprises, Inc. v. Craftsmen Home Improvement, Inc., __ *N.E.2d* __ *(2 Dist. 2006)*]

1. In Fox's suit in an Ohio state court for breach of contract, Craftsmen raised the Statute of Frauds as a defense. What are the requirements of the Statute of Frauds? Did the deal between Fox and Craftsmen meet these requirements? Did it fall under one of the exceptions? Explain.
2. Craftsmen also claimed that the "predominant factor" of its agreement with Fox was a lease for the Hussongs' building. What is the predominant-factor test? Does it apply here? In any event, is it fair to hold a party to a contract to buy a business's assets when the buyer is unable to negotiate a favorable lease of the premises on which the assets are located? Discuss.

13–10  **Video Question** To watch this chapter's video, *Sales and Lease Contracts,* go to **www.cengagebrain.com**. Register the access code that came with your new book or log in to your existing account. Select the link for the "Business Law Digital Video Library Online Access" or "Business Law CourseMate." Click on "Complete Video List," view Video 26, and then answer the following questions:

1. Is Anna correct in assuming that a contract can exist even though the sales price for the computer equipment was not specified? Explain.
2. According to the Uniform Commercial Code (UCC), what conditions must be satisfied in order for a contract to be formed when certain terms are left open? What terms (in addition to price) can be left open?
3. Are the e-mail messages that Anna refers to sufficient proof of the contract? Why or why not?
4. Would parol evidence be admissible? Explain.

Appendix to Chapter 13:

An Example of a Contract for the International Sale of Coffee

1 OVERLAND COFFEE IMPORT CONTRACT
OF THE
GREEN COFFEE ASSOCIATION
OF
NEW YORK CITY, INC.*

Contract Seller's No.: 504617
Buyer's No.: P9264
Date: 10/11/12

2 SOLD BY: XYZ Co.
TO: Starbucks

3 QUANTITY: Five Hundred (Bags) Tons of Mexican coffee
weighing about 152.117 lbs. per bag.

4 PACKAGING: Coffee must be packed in clean sound bags of uniform size made of sisal, henequen, jute, burlap, or similar woven material, without inner lining or outer covering of any material properly sewn by hand and/or machine.
Bulk shipments are allowed if agreed by mutual consent of Buyer and Seller.

5 DESCRIPTION: High grown Mexican Altura

6 PRICE: At Ten/$10.00 dollars U. S. Currency, per lb. net, (U.S. Funds)
Upon delivery in Bonded Public Warehouse at Laredo, TX
(City and State)

PAYMENT: Cash against warehouse receipts

Bill and tender to DATE when all import requirements and governmental regulations have been satisfied, and coffee delivered or discharged (as per contract terms). Seller is obliged to give the Buyer two (2) calendar days free time in Bonded Public Warehouse following but not including date of tender.

7 ARRIVAL: During December via truck
(Period) (Method of Transportation)
from Mexico for arrival at Laredo, TX, USA
(Country of Exportation) (Country of Importation)
Partial shipments permitted.

8 ADVICE OF ARRIVAL: Advice of arrival with warehouse name and location, together with the quantity, description, marks and place of entry, must be transmitted directly, or through Seller's Agent/Broker, to the Buyer or his Agent/Broker. Advice will be given as soon as known but not later than the fifth business day following arrival at the named warehouse. Such advice may be given verbally with written confirmation to be sent the same day.

9 WEIGHTS: (1) DELIVERED WEIGHTS: Coffee covered by this contract is to be weighed at location named in tender. Actual tare to be allowed.
(2) SHIPPING WEIGHTS: Coffee covered by this contract is sold on shipping weights. Any loss in weight exceeding 1/2 percent at location named in tender is for account of Seller at contract price.
(3) Coffee is to be weighed within fifteen (15) calendar days after tender. Weighing expenses, if any, for account of Seller (Seller or Buyer)

10 MARKINGS: Bags to be branded in English with the name of Country of Origin and otherwise to comply with laws and regulations of the Country of Importation, in effect at the time of entry, governing marking of import merchandise. Any expense incurred by failure to comply with these regulations to be borne by Exporter/Seller.

11 RULINGS: The "Rulings on Coffee Contracts" of the Green Coffee Association of New York City, Inc., in effect on the date this contract is made, is incorporated for all purposes as a part of this agreement, and together herewith, constitute the entire contract. No variation or addition hereto shall be valid unless signed by the parties to the contract.
Seller guarantees that the terms printed on the reverse hereof, which by reference are made a part hereof, are identical with the terms as printed in By-Laws and Rules of the Green Coffee Association of New York City, Inc., heretofore adopted.
Exceptions to this guarantee are:

12 ACCEPTED: XYZ Co. Seller
BY ______ Agent
Starbucks Buyer
BY ______ Agent

COMMISSION TO BE PAID BY: Seller
ABC Brokerage Broker(s)

13 When this contract is executed by a person acting for another, such person hereby represents that he is fully authorized to commit his principal.

* Reprinted with permission of The Green Coffee Association of New York City, Inc.

An Example of a Contract for the International Sale of Coffee, Continued

❶ This is a contract for a sale of coffee to be *imported* internationally. If the parties have their principal places of business located in different countries, the contract may be subject to the United Nations Convention on Contracts for the International Sale of Goods (CISG). If the parties' principal places of business are located in the United States, the contract may be subject to the Uniform Commercial Code (UCC).

❷ Quantity is one of the most important terms to include in a contract. Without it, a court may not be able to enforce the contract.

❸ Weight per unit (bag) can be exactly stated or approximately stated. If it is not so stated, usage of trade in international contracts determines standards of weight.

❹ Packaging requirements can be conditions for acceptance and payment. Bulk shipments are not permitted without the consent of the buyer.

❺ A description of the coffee and the "markings" constitute express warranties. Warranties in contracts for domestic sales of goods are discussed generally in Chapter 15. International contracts rely more heavily on descriptions and models or samples.

❻ Under the UCC, parties may enter into a valid contract even though the price is not set. Under the CISG, a contract must provide for an exact determination of the price.

❼ The terms of payment may take one of two forms: credit or cash. Credit terms can be complicated. A cash term can be simple, and payment may be by any means acceptable in the ordinary course of business (for example, a personal check or a letter of credit). If the seller insists on actual cash, the buyer must be given a reasonable time to get it. See Chapter 14.

❽ *Tender* means the seller has placed goods that conform to the contract at the buyer's disposition. What constitutes a valid tender is explained in Chapter 14. This contract requires that the coffee meet all import regulations and that it be ready for pickup by the buyer at a "Bonded Public Warehouse." (A *bonded warehouse* is a place in which goods can be stored without paying taxes until the goods are removed.)

❾ The delivery date is significant because, if it is not met, the buyer may hold the seller in breach of the contract. Under this contract, the seller can be given a "period" within which to deliver the goods, instead of a specific day, which could otherwise present problems. The seller is also given some time to rectify goods that do not pass inspection (see the "Guarantee" clause on page two of the contract on the next page). For a discussion of the remedies of the buyer and seller, see Chapter 14.

❿ As part of a proper tender, the seller (or its agent) must inform the buyer (or its agent) when the goods have arrived at their destination. The responsibilities of agents are set out in Chapter 21.

⓫ In some contracts, delivered and shipped weights can be important. During shipping, some loss can be attributed to the type of goods (spoilage of fresh produce, for example) or to the transportation itself. A seller and buyer can agree on the extent to which either of them will bear such losses.

⓬ Documents are often incorporated in a contract by reference, because including them word for word can make a contract difficult to read. If the document is later revised, the whole contract might have to be reworked. Documents that are typically incorporated by reference include detailed payment and delivery terms, special provisions, and sets of rules, codes, and standards.

⓭ In international sales transactions, and for domestic deals involving certain products, brokers are used to form the contracts. When so used, the brokers are entitled to a commission. See Chapter 21.

Continued

An Example of a Contract for the International Sale of Coffee, Continued

TERMS AND CONDITIONS

14 **ARBITRATION:** All controversies relating to, in connection with, or arising out of this contract, its modification, making or the authority or obligations of the signatories hereto, and whether involving the principals, agents, brokers, or others who actually subscribe hereto, shall be settled by arbitration in accordance with the "Rules of Arbitration" of the Green Coffee Association of New York City, Inc., as they exist at the time of the arbitration (including provisions as to payment of fees and expenses). Arbitration is the sole remedy hereunder, and it shall be held in accordance with the law of New York State, and judgment of any award may be entered in the courts of that State, or in any other court of competent jurisdiction. All notices or judicial service in reference to arbitration or enforcement shall be deemed given if transmitted as required by the aforesaid rules.

15 **GUARANTEE:** (a) If all or any of the coffee is refused admission into the country of importation by reason of any violation of governmental laws or acts, which violation existed at the time the coffee arrived at Bonded-Public Warehouse, seller is required, as to the amount not admitted and as soon as possible, to deliver replacement coffee in conformity to all terms and conditions of this contract, excepting only the Arrival terms, but not later than thirty (30) days after the date of the violation notice. Any payment made and expenses incurred for any coffee denied entry shall be refunded within ten (10) calendar days of denial of entry, and payment shall be made for the replacement delivery in accordance with the terms of this contract. Consequently, if Buyer removes the coffee from the Bonded Public Warehouse, Seller's responsibility as to such portion hereunder ceases.

16 (b) Contracts containing the overstamp "No Pass-No Sale" on the face of the contract shall be interpreted to mean: If any or all of the coffee is not admitted into the country of Importation in its original condition by reason of failure to meet requirements of the government's laws or Acts, the contract shall be deemed null and void as to that portion of the coffee which is not admitted in its original condition. Any payment made and expenses incurred for any coffee denied entry shall be refunded within ten (10) calendar days of denial of entry.

CONTINGENCY: This contract is not contingent upon any other contract.

CLAIMS: Coffee shall be considered accepted as to quality unless within *fifteen* (15) calendar days after delivery at Bonded Public Warehouse or within *fifteen* (15) calendar days after all Government clearances have been received, whichever is later, either:

(a) Claims are settled by the parties hereto, or,

17 (b) Arbitration proceedings have been filed by one of the parties in accordance with the provisions hereof.

(c) If neither (a) nor (b) has been done in the stated period or if any portion of the coffee has been removed from the Bonded Public Warehouse before representative sealed samples have been drawn by the Green Coffee Association of New York City, Inc., in accordance with its rules, Seller's responsibility for quality claims ceases for that portion so removed.

(d) Any question of quality submitted to arbitration shall be a matter of allowance only, unless otherwise provided in the contract.

18 **DELIVERY:** (a) No more than three (3) chops may be tendered for each lot of 250 bags.

(b) Each chop of coffee tendered is to be uniform in grade and appearance. All expense necessary to make coffee uniform shall be for account of seller.

(c) Notice of arrival and/or sampling order constitutes a tender, and must be given not later than the fifth business day following arrival at Bonded Public Warehouse stated on the contract.

INSURANCE: Seller is responsible for any loss or damage, or both, until Delivery and Discharge of coffee at the Bonded Public Warehouse in the Country of Importation.

19 All Insurance Risks, costs and responsibility are for Seller's Account until Delivery and Discharge of coffee at the Bonded Public Warehouse in the Country of Importation.

Buyer's insurance responsibility begins from the day of importation or from the day of tender, whichever is later.

20 **FREIGHT:** Seller to provide and pay for all transportation and related expenses to the Bonded Public Warehouse in the Country of Importation.

EXPORT DUTIES/TAXES: Exporter is to pay all Export taxes, duties or other fees or charges, if any, levied because of exportation.

21 **IMPORT DUTIES/TAXES:** Any Duty or Tax whatsoever, imposed by the government or any authority of the Country of Importation, shall be borne by the Importer/Buyer.

INSOLVENCY OR FINANCIAL FAILURE OF BUYER OR SELLER: If, at any time before the contract is fully executed, either party hereto shall meet with creditors because of inability generally to make payment of obligations when due, or shall suspend such payments, fail to meet his general trade obligations in the regular course of business, shall file a petition in bankruptcy or, for an arrangement, shall become insolvent, or commit an act of bankruptcy, then the other party may at his option, expressed in writing, declare the aforesaid to constitute a breach and default of this contract, and may, in addition to other remedies, decline to deliver further or make payment or may sell or purchase for the defaulter's account, and may collect damage for any injury or loss, or shall account for the profit, if any, occasioned by such sale or purchase.

22 This clause is subject to the provisions of (11 USC 365 (e) 1) if invoked.

23 **BREACH OR DEFAULT OF CONTRACT:** In the event either party hereto fails to perform, or breaches or repudiates this agreement, the other party shall subject to the specific provisions of this contract be entitled to the remedies and relief provided for by the Uniform Commercial Code of the State of New York. The computation and ascertainment of damages, or the determination of any other dispute as to relief, shall be made by the arbitrators in accordance with the Arbitration Clause herein.

Consequential damages shall not, however, be allowed.

An Example of a Contract for the International Sale of Coffee, Continued

14 Arbitration is the settling of a dispute by submitting it to a disinterested party (other than a court) that renders a decision. The procedures and costs can be provided for in an arbitration clause or incorporated through other documents. To enforce an award rendered in an arbitration, the winning party can "enter" (submit) the award in a court "of competent jurisdiction." For a general discussion of arbitration and other forms of dispute resolution (other than courts), see Chapter 2.

15 When goods are imported internationally, they must meet certain import requirements before being released to the buyer. Because of this, buyers frequently want a guaranty clause that covers the goods not admitted into the country and that either requires the seller to replace the goods within a stated time or allows the contract for those goods not admitted to be void.

16 In the "Claims" clause, the parties agree that the buyer has a certain time within which to reject the goods. The right to reject is a right by law and does not need to be stated in a contract. If the buyer does not exercise the right within the time specified in the contract, the goods will be considered accepted. See Chapter 14.

17 Many international contracts include definitions of terms so that the parties understand what they mean. Some terms are used in a particular industry in a specific way. Here, the word *chop* refers to a unit of like-grade coffee bean. The buyer has a right to inspect ("sample") the coffee. If the coffee does not conform to the contract, the seller must correct the nonconformity.

18 The "Delivery," "Insurance," and "Freight" clauses, with the "Arrival" clause on page one of the contract, indicate that this is a destination contract. The seller has the obligation to deliver the goods to the destination, not simply deliver them into the hands of a carrier. Under this contract, the destination is a "Bonded Public Warehouse" in a specific location. The seller bears the risk of loss until the goods are delivered at their destination. Typically, the seller will have bought insurance to cover the risk.

19 Delivery terms are commonly placed in all sales contracts. Such terms determine who pays freight and other costs, and, in the absence of an agreement specifying otherwise, who bears the risk of loss. International contracts may use these delivery terms or they may use INCOTERMS, which are published by the International Chamber of Commerce. For example, the INCOTERM "DDP" ("delivered duty paid") requires the seller to arrange shipment, obtain and pay for import or export permits, and get the goods through customs to a named destination.

20 Exported and imported goods are subject to duties, taxes, and other charges imposed by the governments of the countries involved. International contracts spell out who is responsible for these charges. See Chapter 31.

21 This clause protects a party if the other party should become financially unable to fulfill the obligations under the contract. Thus, if the seller cannot afford to deliver, or the buyer cannot afford to pay, for the stated reasons, the other party can consider the contract breached. This right is subject to "11 USC 365(e)(1)," which refers to a specific provision of the U.S. Bankruptcy Code dealing with executory contracts. Bankruptcy provisions are covered in Chapter 19.

22 In the "Breach or Default of Contract" clause, the parties agreed that the remedies under this contract are the remedies (except for consequential damages) provided by the UCC, as in effect in the state of New York. The amount and "ascertainment" of damages, as well as other disputes about relief, are to be determined by arbitration. Breach of contract and contractual remedies in general are explained in Chapter 14. Arbitration is discussed in Chapter 2.

23 Three clauses frequently included in international contracts are omitted here. There is no "choice-of-language" clause designating the official language to be used in interpreting the contract terms. There is no "choice-of-forum" clause designating the place in which disputes will be litigated, except for arbitration (law of New York State). Finally, there is no "*force majeure*" clause relieving the sellers or buyers from nonperformance due to events beyond their control.

Chapter 14

Performance and Breach of Sales and Lease Contracts

Learning Objectives

After reading this chapter, you should be able to answer the following questions:

1. What are the respective obligations of the parties under a contract for the sale or lease of goods?
2. What is the perfect tender rule?
3. What options are available to the nonbreaching party when the other party to a sales or lease contract repudiates the contract prior to the time for performance?
4. What remedies are available to a seller or lessor when the buyer or lessee breaches the contract?
5. In contracts subject to the UCC, are parties free to limit the remedies available to the nonbreaching party on a breach of contract? If so, in what ways?

The Learning Objectives above are designed to help improve your understanding of the chapter.

(Quaziefoto/Creative Commons)

The performance required of the parties under a sales or lease contract consists of the duties and obligations each party has under the terms of the contract. Keep in mind that a party's "duties and obligations" include those specified by the agreement, by custom, and by the Uniform Commercial Code (UCC). In addition to those requirements, the UCC also imposes a duty of good faith on the parties involved in sales or lease contracts. This duty basically requires honesty and fair dealing. In this chapter, we examine the performance obligations of the parties under a sales or lease contract.

Sometimes, circumstances make it difficult for a person to carry out the promised performance, and the contract is breached. When breach occurs, the aggrieved party looks for remedies—which we discuss in the second half of this chapter.

Performance Obligations

As discussed in previous chapters and noted in this chapter's introduction, the standards of good faith and commercial reasonableness are read into every contract. These standards provide a framework for the entire agreement. If a sales contract leaves open some particulars of performance, for instance, the parties must exercise good faith and commercial reasonableness when later specifying the details.

In the performance of a sales or lease contract, the basic obligation of the seller or lessor is to *transfer and deliver conforming goods.* The basic obligation of the buyer or lessee is to *accept and pay for conforming goods* in accordance with the contract [UCC 2–301, 2A–516(1)]. Overall performance of a sales or lease contract is controlled by the agreement between the parties. When the contract is unclear and disputes arise, the courts look to the UCC and impose standards of good faith and commercial reasonableness.

Obligations of the Seller or Lessor

The major obligation of the seller or lessor under a sales or lease contract is to tender conforming goods to the buyer or lessee. Goods that conform to the contract description in every way are called **conforming goods.** To fulfill the contract, the seller or lessor must either deliver or tender delivery of conforming goods to the buyer or lessee. **Tender of delivery** occurs when the seller or lessor makes conforming goods available to the buyer or lessee and gives the buyer or lessee whatever notification is reasonably necessary to enable the buyer or lessee to take delivery [UCC 2–503(1), 2A–508(1)].

Tender must occur at a *reasonable hour* and in a *reasonable manner.* In other words, a seller cannot call the buyer at 2:00 A.M. and say, "The goods are ready. I'll give you twenty minutes to get them." Unless the parties have agreed otherwise, the goods must be tendered for delivery at a reasonable hour and kept available for a reasonable period of time to enable the buyer to take possession of them [UCC 2–503(1)(a)].

Normally, all goods called for by a contract must be tendered in a single delivery—unless the parties have agreed that the goods may be delivered in several lots or *installments* [UCC 2–307, 2–612, 2A–510]. Hence, an order for 1,000 shirts cannot be delivered 2 shirts at a time. If, however, the parties agree that the shirts will be delivered in four lots of 250 each as they are produced (for summer, fall, winter, and spring stock), then delivery may occur in this manner.

Place of Delivery

The UCC provides for the place of delivery pursuant to a contract only if the contract does not. The buyer and seller (or lessor and lessee) may agree that the goods will be delivered to a particular destination where the buyer or lessee will take possession. If the contract does not designate the place of delivery, then the goods must be made available to the buyer at the *seller's place of business* or, if the seller has none, at the seller's residence [UCC 2–308(a)]. If, at the time of contracting, the parties know that the goods identified to the contract are located somewhere other than the seller's business, then *the location of the goods* is the place for their delivery [UCC 2–308(b)].

EXAMPLE 14.1 Li Wan and Jo Boyd both live in San Francisco. In San Francisco, Wan contracts to sell Boyd five used trucks, which both parties know are located in a Chicago warehouse. If nothing more is specified in the contract, the place of delivery for the trucks is Chicago. Wan may tender delivery either by giving Boyd a negotiable or nonnegotiable document of title or by obtaining the bailee's (warehouser's) acknowledgment that the buyer is entitled to possession.[1] ●

Delivery via Carrier

In many instances, it is clear from surrounding circumstances or delivery terms in the contract (such as F.O.B. or F.A.S. terms, shown in Exhibit 13–3 on page 240) that the parties intended the goods to be moved by a carrier. In carrier contracts, the seller fulfills the obligation to deliver the goods through either a shipment contract or a destination contract.

SHIPMENT CONTRACTS Recall from Chapter 13 that a *shipment contract* requires or authorizes the seller to ship goods by a carrier, rather than to deliver them at a particular destination [UCC 2–319, 2–509(1)(a)]. Under a shipment contract, unless otherwise agreed, the seller must do the following:

1. Put the goods into the hands of the carrier.
2. Make a contract for their transportation that is reasonable according to the nature of the goods and their value. (For example, certain types of goods need refrigeration in transit.)
3. Obtain and promptly deliver or tender to the buyer any documents necessary to enable the buyer to obtain possession of the goods from the carrier.
4. Promptly notify the buyer that shipment has been made [UCC 2–504].

If the seller fails to notify the buyer that shipment has been made or fails to make a proper contract for transportation, the buyer can treat the contract as breached and reject the goods, but only if a *material loss* of the goods or a significant *delay* results. Of course, the parties can agree that a lesser amount of loss or that any delay will be grounds for rejection.

DESTINATION CONTRACTS In a *destination contract,* the seller agrees to deliver conforming goods to the buyer at a particular destination. The seller must provide the buyer with any documents of title necessary to enable the buyer to obtain delivery from the carrier [UCC 2–503].

The Perfect Tender Rule

As previously noted, the seller or lessor has an obligation to ship or tender *conforming goods,* and the buyer or lessee is required to accept and pay for the goods according to the terms of the contract. Under the common law, the seller was obligated to deliver goods that conformed to the terms of the contract in every detail. This was called the *perfect tender* doctrine. The UCC preserves the perfect tender doctrine by stating that if goods or tender of delivery fails *in any respect* to conform to the contract, the buyer or lessee has the right to accept the goods, reject the entire shipment, or accept part and reject part [UCC 2–601, 2A–509].

EXAMPLE 14.2 A lessor contracts to lease fifty NEC monitors to be delivered at the lessee's place of business on or before October 1. On September 28, the lessor discovers that it

1. If the seller delivers a nonnegotiable document of title or merely instructs the bailee in a writing (or electronic record) to release the goods to the buyer without the bailee's *acknowledgment* of the buyer's rights, this is also a sufficient tender, unless the buyer objects [UCC 2–503(4)]. Risk of loss, however, does not pass until the buyer has a reasonable amount of time in which to present the document or to give the bailee instructions for delivery, as discussed in Chapter 13.

has only thirty NEC monitors in inventory, but that it will have another forty NEC monitors within the next two weeks. The lessor tenders delivery of the thirty NEC monitors on October 1, with the promise that the other monitors will be delivered within two weeks. Because the lessor failed to make a perfect tender of fifty NEC monitors, the lessee has the right to reject the entire shipment and hold the lessor in breach. •

Exceptions to the Perfect Tender Rule

Because of the rigidity of the perfect tender rule, several exceptions to the rule have been created, some of which are discussed here.

AGREEMENT OF THE PARTIES Exceptions to the perfect tender rule may be established by agreement. If the parties have agreed, for example, that defective goods or parts will not be rejected if the seller or lessor is able to repair or replace them within a reasonable period of time, the perfect tender rule does not apply.

CURE The UCC does not specifically define the term *cure,* but it refers to the right of the seller or lessor to repair, adjust, or replace defective or nonconforming goods [UCC 2–508, 2A–513]. When any tender of delivery is rejected because of nonconforming goods and the time for performance has not yet expired, the seller or lessor can notify the buyer or lessee promptly of the intention to cure and can then do so *within the contract time for performance* [UCC 2–508(1), 2A–513(1)].

Once the time for performance has expired, the seller or lessor still has a reasonable time in which to cure if, at the time of delivery, he or she had *reasonable grounds to believe that the nonconforming goods would be acceptable to the buyer or lessee* [UCC 2–508(2), 2A–513(2)]. A seller or lessor may sometimes tender nonconforming goods with a price allowance (discount), which can also serve as "reasonable grounds" to believe the buyer or lessee will accept the nonconforming tender.

The right to cure means that, to reject goods, the buyer or lessee must inform the seller or lessor of a particular defect. For instance, if a lessee refuses a tender of goods as nonconforming but does not disclose the nature of the defect to the lessor, the lessee cannot later assert the defect as a defense if the defect is one that the lessor could have cured. Generally, buyers and lessees must act in good faith and state specific reasons for refusing to accept goods [UCC 2–605, 2A–514].

SUBSTITUTION OF CARRIERS When an agreed-on manner of delivery (such as the carrier to be used to transport the goods) becomes impracticable or unavailable through no fault of either party, but a commercially reasonable substitute is available, the seller must use this substitute performance, which is sufficient tender to the buyer [UCC 2–614(1)].

EXAMPLE 14.3 A sales contract calls for a large generator to be delivered via Roadway Trucking Corporation on or before June 1. The contract terms clearly state the importance of the delivery date. The employees of Roadway Trucking go on strike. The seller is required to make a reasonable substitute tender, perhaps by another trucking firm or by air freight, if that is available. Note that the seller normally will be responsible for any additional shipping costs, unless other arrangements have been made in the sales contract. •

INSTALLMENT CONTRACTS An **installment contract** is a single contract that requires or authorizes delivery in two or more separate lots to be accepted and paid for separately. With an installment contract, a buyer or lessee can reject an installment *only if the nonconformity substantially impairs the value* of the installment and cannot be cured [UCC 2–307, 2–612(2), 2A–510(1)]. If the buyer or lessee subsequently accepts a nonconforming installment and fails to notify the seller or lessor of cancellation, however, the contract is reinstated [UCC 2–612(3), 2A–510(2)].

Unless the contract provides otherwise, the entire installment contract is breached only when one or more nonconforming installments *substantially* impair the value of the *whole contract.* **EXAMPLE 14.4** A contract calls for the parts of a machine to be delivered in installments. The first part is necessary for the operation of the machine, but when it is delivered, it is irreparably defective. The failure of this first installment will be a breach of the whole contract because the machine will not operate without the first part. The situation would likely be different, however, if the contract had called for twenty carloads of plywood and only 6 percent of one carload had deviated from the thickness specifications in the contract. It is unlikely that a court would find that a defect in 6 percent of one installment substantially impaired the value of the whole contract. •

The point to remember is that the UCC significantly alters the right of the buyer or lessee to reject the entire contract if the contract requires delivery to be made in several installments. The UCC strictly limits rejection to cases of *substantial* nonconformity.

COMMERCIAL IMPRACTICABILITY Occurrences unforeseen by either party when a contract was made may make performance commercially impracticable. When this occurs, the rule of perfect tender no longer holds. According to UCC 2–615(a) and 2A–405(a), a delay in delivery or nondelivery in whole or in part is not a breach when performance has been made impracticable "by the occurrence of a contingency the nonoccurrence of which was a basic assumption on which the contract was made." The seller or lessor must, however, notify the buyer or lessee as soon as practicable that there will be a delay or nondelivery.

Foreseeable versus Unforeseeable Contingencies. The doctrine of commercial impracticability extends only to problems that could not have been foreseen. **EXAMPLE 14.5** A major oil company that receives its supplies from the Middle East has a contract to supply a buyer with 100,000 gallons of oil. Because of an oil embargo by the Organization of Petroleum Exporting Countries, the seller is unable to secure oil supplies to meet the terms of the contract. Because of the same embargo, the seller cannot secure oil from any other source. This situation comes fully under the commercial impracticability exception to the perfect tender doctrine. •

Can unanticipated increases in a seller's costs, which make performance "impracticable," constitute a valid defense to performance on the basis of commercial impracticability? The court dealt with this question in the following classic case.

Classic Case 14.1 Maple Farms, Inc. v. City School District of Elmira

Supreme Court of New York, 76 Misc.2d 1080, 352 N.Y.S.2d 784 (1974).

FACTS On June 15, 1973, Maple Farms, Inc., formed an agreement with the city school district of Elmira, New York, to supply the school district with milk for the 1973–1974 school year. The agreement was in the form of a requirements contract, under which Maple Farms would sell to the school district all the milk the district required at a fixed price—which was the June market price of milk. By December 1973, the price of raw milk had increased by 23 percent over the price specified in the contract. This meant that if the terms of the contract were fulfilled, Maple Farms would lose $7,350. Because it had similar contracts with other school districts, Maple Farms stood to lose a great deal if it was held to the price stated in the contracts. When the school district would not agree to release Maple Farms from its contract, Maple Farms brought an action in a New York state court for a declaratory judgment (a determination of the parties' rights under a contract). Maple Farms contended that the substantial increase in the price of raw milk was an event not contemplated by the parties when the contract was formed and that, given the increased price, performance of the contract was commercially impracticable.

ISSUE Can Maple Farms be released from the contract on the ground of commercial impracticability?

DECISION No. The court ruled that performance in this case was not impracticable.

REASON The court reasoned that commercial impracticability arises when an event occurs that is totally unexpected and unforeseeable by the parties. The increased price of raw milk was not totally unexpected, given that in the previous year, the price of milk had risen 10 percent and that the price of milk had traditionally varied. Additionally, the general inflation of prices in the United States should have been anticipated. Maple Farms had reason to know these facts and could have included a clause in its contract with the school district to protect itself from its present situation. The court also noted that, for the school district, the primary purpose of the contract was to protect itself (for budgeting purposes) against price fluctuations.

WHAT IF THE FACTS WERE DIFFERENT? *Suppose that the court had ruled in the plaintiff's favor. How might that ruling have affected the plaintiff's contracts with other parties?*

IMPACT OF THIS CASE ON TODAY'S LAW *This case is a classic illustration of the UCC's commercial impracticability doctrine. Under this doctrine, parties who freely enter into contracts normally will not be excused from their contractual obligations simply because changed circumstances make performance difficult or unprofitable. Rather, to be excused from performance, a party must show that the changed circumstances were unforeseeable at the time the contract was formed. This principle continues to be applied today.*

Partial Performance. Sometimes, an unforeseen event only *partially* affects the capacity of the seller or lessor to perform, and the seller or lessor is thus able to fulfill the contract *partially* but cannot tender total performance. In this event, the seller or lessor is required to allocate in a fair and reasonable manner any remaining production and deliveries among those to whom it is contractually obligated to deliver the goods, and this allocation may take into account its regular customers [UCC 2–615(b), 2A–405(b)]. The buyer or lessee must receive notice of the allocation and has the right to accept or reject it [UCC 2–615(c), 2A–405(c)].

EXAMPLE 14.6 A Florida orange grower, Best Citrus, Inc., contracts to sell this season's crop to a number of customers, including Martin's grocery chain. Martin's contracts to purchase two thousand crates of oranges. Best Citrus has sprayed some of its orange groves with a chemical called Karmoxin. The Department of Agriculture discovers that persons who eat products sprayed with Karmoxin may develop cancer. The department issues an order prohibiting the sale of these products. Best Citrus picks only those oranges not sprayed with Karmoxin, but there are not enough to meet all the contracted-for deliveries. In this situation, Best Citrus is required to allocate its production. It notifies Martin's that it cannot deliver the full quantity specified in the contract and indicates the amount it will be able to deliver. Martin's can either accept or reject the allocation, but Best Citrus has no further contractual liability. ●

DESTRUCTION OF IDENTIFIED GOODS Sometimes, an unexpected event, such as a fire, totally destroys goods through no fault of either party and before risk passes to the buyer or lessee. In such a situation, *if the goods were identified at the time the contract was formed,* the parties are excused from performance [UCC 2–613, 2A–221]. If the goods are only partially destroyed, however, the buyer or lessee can inspect them and either treat the contract as void or accept the goods with a reduction of the contract price.

EXAMPLE 14.7 Atlas Sporting Equipment agrees to lease to River Bicycles sixty bicycles of a particular model that has been discontinued. No other bicycles of that model are available. River specifies that it needs the bicycles to rent to tourists. Before Atlas can deliver the bicycles, they are destroyed by a fire. In this situation, Atlas is not liable to River for failing to deliver the bicycles. The goods were destroyed through no fault of either party, before the risk of loss passed to the lessee. The loss was total, so the contract is avoided. Clearly, Atlas has no obligation to tender the bicycles, and River has no obligation to pay for them. ●

ASSURANCE AND COOPERATION Two other exceptions to the perfect tender doctrine apply equally to parties to sales and lease contracts: the right of assurance and the duty of cooperation.

The Right of Assurance. The UCC provides that if one party to a contract has "reasonable grounds" to believe that the other party will not perform as contracted, he or she may *in writing* "demand adequate assurance of due performance" from the other party. Until such assurance is received, he or she may "suspend" further performance (such as payments due under the contract) without liability. What constitutes "reasonable grounds" is determined by commercial standards. If such assurances are not forthcoming within a reasonable time (not to exceed thirty days), the failure to respond may be treated as a *repudiation* of the contract [UCC 2–609, 2A–401].

CASE EXAMPLE 14.8 Two companies that make road-surfacing materials, Koch Materials Company and Shore Slurry Seal, Inc., enter into a contract. Koch obtains a license to use Novachip, a special material made by Shore, and Shore agrees to buy all of its asphalt from Koch for the next seven years. A few years into the contract term, Shore notifies Koch that it is planning to sell its assets to Asphalt Paving Systems, Inc. Koch demands assurances that Asphalt Paving will continue the deal, but Shore refuses to provide assurances. In this situation, Koch can treat Shore's failure to give assurances as a repudiation and file a suit against Shore for breach of contract.[2] ●

The Duty of Cooperation. Sometimes, the performance of one party depends on the cooperation of the other. The UCC provides that when such cooperation is not forthcoming, the other party can suspend her or his own performance without liability and hold the uncooperative party in breach or proceed to perform the contract in any reasonable manner [UCC 2–311(3)].

EXAMPLE 14.9 Aman is required by contract to deliver 1,200 model HE washing machines to various locations in California. Deliveries are to be made on or before October 1, and the locations are to be specified later by Farrell. Aman has repeatedly requested the delivery locations, but Farrell has not responded. On October 1, the washing machines are ready to be shipped, but Farrell still refuses to give Aman the delivery locations. Aman does not ship on October 1. Can Aman be held liable? The answer is no. Aman is excused for any resulting delay of performance because of Farrell's failure to cooperate. ●

Obligations of the Buyer or Lessee

The main obligation of the buyer or lessee under a sales or lease contract is to pay for the goods tendered in accordance with the contract. Once the seller or lessor has adequately tendered delivery, the buyer or lessee is obligated to accept the goods and pay for them according to the terms of the contract.

Payment

In the absence of any specific agreements, the buyer or lessee must make payment at the time and place the goods are *received* [UCC 2–310(a), 2A–516(1)]. When a sale is made on credit, the buyer is obligated to pay according to the specified credit terms (for example, 60, 90, or 120 days), not when the goods are received. The credit period usually begins on the *date of shipment* [UCC 2–310(d)]. Under a lease contract, a lessee must pay the lease payment that was specified in the contract [UCC 2A–516(1)].

Payment can be made by any means agreed on by the parties—cash or any other method generally acceptable in the commercial world. If the seller demands cash when the buyer offers a check, credit card, or the like, the seller must permit the buyer reasonable time to obtain legal tender [UCC 2–511].

2. *Koch Materials Co. v. Shore Slurry Seal, Inc.*, 205 F.Supp.2d 324 (D.N.J. 2002).

The Right of Inspection

Unless the parties otherwise agree, or for C.O.D. (collect on delivery) transactions, the buyer or lessee has an absolute right to inspect the goods before making payment. This right allows the buyer or lessee to verify, before making payment, that the goods tendered or delivered are what were contracted for or ordered. If the goods are not what were ordered, the buyer or lessee has no duty to pay. *An opportunity for inspection is therefore a condition precedent to the right of the seller or lessor to enforce payment* [UCC 2–513(1), 2A–515(1)].

Inspection can take place at any reasonable place and time and in any reasonable manner. Generally, what is reasonable is determined by custom of the trade, past practices of the parties, and the like. The buyer bears the costs of inspecting the goods (unless otherwise agreed), but if the goods are rejected because they are not conforming, the buyer can recover the costs of inspection from the seller [UCC 2–513(2)].

The following case focuses on the buyer's right to inspect the goods before acceptance, as well as the buyer's right to reject nonconforming goods.

Case 14.2 Romero v. Scoggin-Dickey Chevrolet-Buick, Inc.

Court of Appeals of Texas, Amarillo, ___ S.W.3d ___ (2010).

FACTS Jessie Romero wanted to buy a 2006 Silverado pickup from the Scoggin-Dickey Chevrolet-Buick, Inc., dealership in Lubbock, Texas. In his discussion with a sales representative, Fred Morales, Romero proposed to purchase the pickup by assigning the dealership the factory rebates, supplying two trade-in vehicles, and paying the cash difference. After negotiating a value for the trade-in vehicles—which Romero did not have on the lot at that time—Romero and Morales signed a contract order in which Scoggin-Dickey agreed to sell Romero the 2006 Silverado pickup for $21,888. In return, Romero agreed to trade in the two vehicles (having a negotiated combined net value of $15,000), assign factory rebates totaling $3,000, and pay $4,333.52 in cash. Romero paid the cash, assigned the rebates, and took possession of the 2006 Silverado pickup. At that time, Romero did not deliver the trade-in vehicles to Scoggin-Dickey, nor did Scoggin-Dickey transfer title to the 2006 Silverado pickup to Romero. Subsequently, after inspecting the trade-in vehicles, Scoggin-Dickey determined that the vehicles had very little commercial value. So it took back the pickup and offered to partially refund Romero's down payment. Romero rejected the offer and filed a suit. The trial court held that Scoggin-Dickey had a right to inspect the trade-in vehicles under UCC Section 2–513 and, upon inspection, had validly exercised its right to reject the vehicles tendered by Romero. Romero appealed, arguing that Scoggin-Dickey had no legal right to inspect and/or reject the trade-in vehicles after the contract order had been executed.

ISSUE Did the dealership have a right to inspect Romero's trade-in vehicles even after the sales contract on the truck had been signed?

DECISION Yes. The Texas appellate court affirmed the trial court's judgment. Scoggin-Dickey had a right to inspect Romero's trade-in vehicles and to reject the goods if they did not conform to their description in the contract.

REASON The court indicated that "Unless the parties agree otherwise, a buyer has a right to inspect goods identified to a contract for sale at any reasonable place and time and in any reasonable manner prior to payment or acceptance of the goods. This is an implied condition in all contracts for sale." Further, if the goods are nonconforming, the buyer has an absolute right to reject. In addition, execution of the contract order did not constitute a "sale," because ownership of the 2006 Silverado pickup was not transferred to Romero, nor was ownership of the two trade-in vehicles transferred to the dealership as part of the payment for the Silverado.

FOR CRITICAL ANALYSIS—Legal Consideration *Why didn't the "contract order" signed by the parties constitute a binding contract for the sale of goods?*

Acceptance

A buyer or lessee demonstrates acceptance of the delivered goods by doing any of the following:

1. If, after having had a reasonable opportunity to inspect the goods, the buyer or lessee signifies to the seller or lessor that the goods either are conforming or are acceptable in spite of their nonconformity [UCC 2–606(1)(a), 2A–515(1)(a)].
2. If the buyer or lessee has had a reasonable opportunity to inspect the goods and has *failed to reject* them within a reasonable period of time, then acceptance is presumed [UCC 2–602(1), 2–606(1)(b), 2A–515(1)(b)].
3. In sales contracts, if the buyer *performs any act inconsistent with the seller's ownership,* then the buyer will be deemed to have accepted the goods. For example, any use or resale of the goods—except for the limited purpose of testing or

inspecting the goods—generally constitutes an acceptance [UCC 2–606(1)(c)].

If some of the goods delivered do not conform to the contract and the seller or lessor has failed to cure, the buyer or lessee can make a *partial* acceptance [UCC 2–601(c), 2A–509(1)]. The same is true if the nonconformity was not reasonably discoverable before acceptance. (In the latter situation, the buyer or lessee may be able to revoke the acceptance, as will be discussed later in this chapter.)

A buyer or lessee cannot accept less than a single commercial unit, however. The UCC defines a *commercial unit* as a unit of goods that, by commercial usage, is viewed as a "single whole" for purposes of sale, and its division would materially impair the character of the unit, its market value, or its use [UCC 2–105(6), 2A–103(1)(c)]. A commercial unit can be a single article (such as a machine), a set of articles (such as a suite of furniture or an assortment of sizes), a quantity (such as a bale, a gross, or a carload), or any other unit treated in the trade as a single whole.

Anticipatory Repudiation

What if, before the time for contract performance, one party clearly communicates to the other the intention not to perform? As discussed in Chapter 11, such an action is a breach of the contract by anticipatory repudiation.

When anticipatory repudiation occurs, the nonbreaching party has a choice of two responses: (1) treat the repudiation as a final breach by pursuing a remedy or (2) wait to see if the repudiating party will decide to honor the contract despite the avowed intention to renege [UCC 2–610, 2A–402]. In either situation, the nonbreaching party may suspend performance.

The UCC permits the breaching party to "retract" his or her repudiation (subject to some limitations). This can be done by any method that clearly indicates the party's intent to perform. Once retraction is made, the rights of the repudiating party under the contract are reinstated. There can be no retraction, however, if since the time of the repudiation the other party has canceled or materially changed position or otherwise indicated that the repudiation is final [UCC 2–611, 2A–403].

EXAMPLE 14.10 On April 1, Cora, who owns a small inn, purchases a suite of furniture from Tom Horton, proprietor of Horton's Furniture Warehouse. The contract states, "Delivery must be made on or before May 1." On April 10, Tom informs Cora that he cannot make delivery until May 10 and asks her to consent to the modified delivery date. In this situation, Cora has the option of either treating Tom's notice of late delivery as a final breach of contract and pursuing a remedy or agreeing to the changed delivery date. Suppose that Cora does neither for two weeks. On April 24, Tom informs Cora that he will be able to deliver the furniture by May 1 after all. In effect, he has retracted his repudiation, reinstating the rights and obligations of the parties under the original contract. Note that if Cora had indicated after Tom's repudiation that she was canceling the contract, he would not have been able to retract his repudiation. •

Remedies of the Seller or Lessor

When the buyer or lessee is in breach, the seller or lessor has numerous remedies available under the UCC. Generally, the remedies available to the seller or lessor depend on the circumstances at the time of the breach, such as which party has possession of the goods, whether the goods are in transit, and whether the buyer or lessee has rejected or accepted the goods.

When the Goods Are in the Possession of the Seller or Lessor

Under the UCC, if the buyer or lessee breaches the contract before the goods have been delivered to her or him, the seller or lessor has the right to pursue the following remedies:

1. Cancel (rescind) the contract.
2. Resell the goods and sue to recover damages.
3. Sue to recover the purchase price or lease payments due.
4. Sue to recover damages for the buyer's nonacceptance.

The Right to Cancel the Contract If the buyer or lessee breaches the contract, the seller or lessor can choose to cancel (rescind) the contract [UCC 2–703(f), 2A–523(1)(a)]. The seller must notify the buyer or lessee of the cancellation, and at that point all remaining obligations of the seller or lessor are discharged. The buyer or lessee is not discharged from all remaining obligations, however. He or she is in breach, and the seller or lessor can pursue remedies available under the UCC for breach.

The Right to Withhold Delivery In general, sellers and lessors can withhold or discontinue performance of their obligations under sales or lease contracts when the buyers or lessees are in breach. This is true whether a buyer or lessee has wrongfully rejected or revoked acceptance of contract goods (rejection and revocation of acceptance will be discussed later), failed to make a payment, or repudiated the contract [UCC 2–703(a), 2A–523(1)(c)]. The seller or lessor can also refuse to deliver the goods to a buyer or lessee who is insolvent (unable to pay debts as they become due), unless the buyer or lessee pays in cash [UCC 2–702(1), 2A–525(1)].

The Right to Resell or Dispose of the Goods When a buyer or lessee breaches or repudiates a sales contract while the seller or lessor is still in possession of the goods, the seller or lessor can resell or dispose of the goods. The seller can retain any profits made as a result of the sale and can hold the buyer or lessee liable for any loss [UCC 2–703(d), 2–706(1), 2A–523(1)(e), 2A–527(1)]. The seller must give the original buyer reasonable notice of the resale, unless the goods are perishable or will rapidly decline in value [UCC 2–706(2), (3)].

When the goods contracted for are unfinished at the time of breach, the seller or lessor can either (1) cease manufacturing the goods and resell them for scrap or salvage value or (2) complete the manufacture and resell or dispose of them, holding the buyer or lessee liable for any deficiency. In choosing between these two alternatives, the seller or lessor must exercise reasonable commercial judgment to mitigate the loss and obtain maximum value from the unfinished goods [UCC 2–704(2), 2A–524(2)]. Any resale of the goods must be made in good faith and in a commercially reasonable manner.

In sales transactions, the seller can recover any deficiency between the resale price and the contract price, along with **incidental damages,** defined as the costs resulting from the breach [UCC 2–706(1), 2–710]. In lease transactions, the lessor may lease the goods to another party and recover from the original lessee, as damages, any unpaid lease payments up to the beginning date of the lease term under the new lease. The lessor can also recover any deficiency between the lease payments due under the original lease contract and those due under the new lease contract, along with incidental damages [UCC 2A–527(2)].

The Right to Recover the Purchase Price or the Lease Payments Due Under the UCC, an unpaid seller or lessor can bring an action to recover the purchase price or payments due under the lease contract, plus incidental damages [UCC 2–709(1), 2A–529(1)]. If a seller or lessor is unable to resell or dispose of goods and sues for the contract price or lease payments due, the goods must be held for the buyer or lessee. The seller or lessor can resell or dispose of the goods at any time prior to collection (of the judgment) from the buyer or lessee, but must credit the net proceeds from the sale to the buyer or lessee.

EXAMPLE 14.11 Southern Realty contracts to purchase one thousand pens with its name inscribed on them from Gem Point. When Gem Point tenders delivery of the pens, Southern Realty wrongfully refuses to accept them. In this situation, Gem Point can bring an action for the purchase price because it delivered conforming goods, and Southern Realty refused to accept or pay for the goods. Gem Point obviously cannot resell the pens inscribed with the buyer's business name, so this situation falls under UCC 2–709. Gem Point is required to make the pens available for Southern Realty, but can resell them (in the event that it can find a buyer) at any time before collecting the judgment from Southern Realty. •

The Right to Recover Damages If a buyer or lessee repudiates a contract or wrongfully refuses to accept the goods, a seller or lessor can maintain an action to recover the damages that were sustained. Ordinarily, the amount of damages equals the difference between the contract price or lease payments and the market price or lease payments at the time and place of tender of the goods, plus incidental damages [UCC 2–708(1), 2A–528(1)]. When the ordinary measure of damages is inadequate to put the seller or lessor in as good a position as the buyer's or lessee's performance would have, the UCC provides an alternative. In that situation, the proper measure of damages is the lost profits of the seller or lessor, including a reasonable allowance for overhead and other expenses [UCC 2–708(2), 2A–528(2)].

When the Goods Are in Transit

If the seller or lessor has delivered the goods to a carrier or a bailee but the buyer or lessee has not yet received them, the goods are said to be *in transit*. If, while the goods are in transit, the seller or lessor learns that the buyer or lessee is insolvent, the seller or lessor can stop the carrier or bailee from delivering the goods, regardless of the quantity of goods shipped. If the buyer or lessee is in breach but is not insolvent, the seller or lessor can stop the goods in transit only if the quantity shipped is at least a carload, a truckload, a planeload, or a larger shipment [UCC 2–705(1), 2A–526(1)].

EXAMPLE 14.12 Arturo Ortega orders a truckload of lumber from Timber Products, Inc., to be shipped to Ortega six weeks later. Ortega, who owes Timber Products for a past shipment, promises to pay the debt immediately and to pay for the current shipment as soon as it is received. After the lumber has been shipped, a bankruptcy court judge notifies Timber Products that Ortega has filed a petition in bankruptcy and listed Timber Products as one of his creditors (see Chapter 19). If the goods are still in transit, Timber Products can stop the carrier from delivering the lumber to Ortega. •

Requirements for Stopping Delivery To stop delivery, the seller or lessor must *timely notify* the carrier or other bailee that the goods are to be returned or held for the seller or lessor. If the carrier has sufficient time to stop delivery, it must hold and deliver the goods according to the instructions of the seller or lessor, who is liable to the carrier for any additional costs incurred [UCC 2–705(3), 2A–526(3)].

The sellor or lessor has the right to stop delivery of the goods under UCC 2–705(2) and 2A–526(2) until the time when:

1. The buyer or lessee obtains possession of the goods.
2. The carrier or the bailee acknowledges the rights of the buyer or lessee in the goods (by reshipping or holding the goods for the buyer or lessee, for example).
3. A negotiable document of title covering the goods has been properly transferred to the buyer (in sales transactions only), giving the buyer ownership rights in the goods [UCC 2–702].

REMEDIES ONCE THE GOODS ARE RECLAIMED Once the seller or lessor reclaims the goods in transit, she or he can pursue the remedies allowed to sellers and lessors when the goods are in their possession.

When the Goods Are in the Possession of the Buyer or Lessee

When the buyer or lessee breaches a sales or lease contract and the goods are in the buyer's or lessee's possession, the seller or lessor can sue to recover the purchase price of the goods or the lease payments due, plus incidental damages [UCC 2–709(1), 2A–529(1)].

In some situations, a seller may also have a right to reclaim the goods from the buyer. For instance, in a sales contract, if the buyer has received the goods on credit and the seller discovers that the buyer is insolvent, the seller can demand return of the goods [UCC 2–702(2)]. Ordinarily, the demand must be made within ten days of the buyer's receipt of the goods.[3] The seller's right to reclaim the goods is subject to the rights of a good faith purchaser or other subsequent buyer in the ordinary course of business who purchases the goods from the buyer before the seller reclaims them.

In regard to lease contracts, if the lessee is in default (fails to make payments that are due, for example), the lessor may reclaim the leased goods that are in the lessee's possession [UCC 2A–525(2)].

Remedies of the Buyer or Lessee

When the seller or lessor breaches the contract, the buyer or lessee has numerous remedies available under the UCC. Like the remedies available to sellers and lessors, the remedies of buyers and lessees depend on the circumstances existing at the time of the breach.

When the Seller or Lessor Refuses to Deliver the Goods

If the seller or lessor refuses to deliver the goods or the buyer or lessee has rejected the goods, the remedies available to the buyer or lessee include the right to:

1. Cancel (rescind) the contract.
2. Obtain goods that have been paid for if the seller or lessor is insolvent.
3. Sue to obtain specific performance if the goods are unique or if damages are an inadequate remedy.
4. Buy other goods (obtain *cover*—defined at bottom right) and obtain damages from the seller.
5. Sue to obtain identified goods held by a third party (*replevy* goods).
6. Sue to obtain damages.

THE RIGHT TO CANCEL THE CONTRACT When a seller or lessor fails to make proper delivery or repudiates the contract, the buyer or lessee can cancel, or rescind, the contract. On notice of cancellation, the buyer or lessee is relieved of any further obligations under the contract but retains all rights to other remedies against the seller [UCC 2–711(1), 2A–508(1)(a)]. (The right to cancel the contract is also available to a buyer or lessee who has rightfully rejected goods or revoked acceptance, as will be discussed shortly.)

THE RIGHT TO OBTAIN THE GOODS ON INSOLVENCY If a buyer or lessee has made a partial or full payment for goods that are in the possession of a seller or lessor who is or becomes insolvent, the buyer or lessee has a right to obtain the goods. To exercise this right, the goods must be identified to the contract and the buyer or lessee must pay any remaining balance of the price to the seller or lessor [UCC 2–502, 2A–522].

THE RIGHT TO OBTAIN SPECIFIC PERFORMANCE A buyer or lessee can obtain specific performance when the goods are unique and the remedy at law is inadequate [UCC 2–716(1), 2A–521(1)]. Ordinarily, a successful suit for monetary damages is sufficient to place a buyer or lessee in the position he or she would have occupied if the seller or lessor had fully performed. When the contract is for the purchase of a particular work of art or a similarly unique item, however, monetary damages may not be sufficient. Under these circumstances, equity will require that the seller or lessor perform exactly by delivering the particular goods identified to the contract (a remedy of specific performance).

CASE EXAMPLE 14.13 Doreen Houseman and Eric Dare bought a house together and a pedigreed dog. When the couple separated, they agreed that Dare would keep the house (and pay Houseman for her interest in it) and Houseman would keep the dog. Houseman allowed Dare to take the dog for visits, but after one visit, Dare kept the dog. Houseman filed a lawsuit seeking specific performance of their agreement. The court found that because pets have special subjective value to their owners, a dog can be unique goods. Thus, an award of specific performance was appropriate.[4] •

THE RIGHT OF COVER In certain situations, buyers and lessees can protect themselves by obtaining **cover**—that is, by purchasing or leasing other goods to substitute for those due

3. The seller can demand and reclaim the goods at any time, though, if the buyer misrepresented his or her solvency in writing within three months prior to the delivery of the goods.

4. *Houseman v. Dare*, 405 N.J.Super. 538, 966 A.2d 24 (2009).

under the contract. This option is available when the seller or lessor repudiates the contract or fails to deliver the goods, or when a buyer or lessee has rightfully rejected goods or revoked acceptance.

In obtaining cover, the buyer or lessee must act in good faith and without unreasonable delay [UCC 2–712, 2A–518]. After purchasing or leasing substitute goods, the buyer or lessee can recover damages from the seller or lessor. The measure of damages is the difference between the cost of cover and the contract price (or lease payments), plus incidental and consequential damages, less the expenses (such as delivery costs) that were saved as a result of the breach [UCC 2–712, 2–715, 2A–518]. Consequential damages are any losses suffered by the buyer or lessee that the seller or lessor could have foreseen (had reason to know about) at the time of contract formation and any injury to the buyer's or lessee's person or property proximately resulting from the contract's breach [UCC 2–715(2), 2A–520(2)].

Buyers and lessees are not required to cover, and failure to do so will not bar them from using any other remedies available under the UCC. A buyer or lessee who fails to cover, however, may *not* be able to collect consequential damages that could have been avoided by purchasing or leasing substitute goods.

THE RIGHT TO REPLEVY GOODS Buyers and lessees also have the right to replevy goods. **Replevin**[5] is an action to recover specific goods in the hands of a party who is wrongfully withholding them from the other party. Outside the UCC, the term *replevin* refers to a *prejudgment process* (a proceeding that takes place prior to a court's judgment) that permits the seizure of specific personal property in which a party claims a right or an interest. Under the UCC, the buyer or lessee can replevy goods subject to the contract if the seller or lessor has repudiated or breached the contract. To maintain an action to replevy goods, usually buyers and lessees must show that they are unable to cover for the goods after a reasonable effort [UCC 2–716(3), 2A–521(3)].

5. Pronounced ruh-*pleh*-vun.

THE RIGHT TO RECOVER DAMAGES If a seller or lessor repudiates the sales contract or fails to deliver the goods, the buyer or lessee can sue for damages. The measure of recovery is the difference between the contract price (or lease payments) and the market price of (or lease payments that could be obtained for) the goods at the time the buyer (or lessee) *learned* of the breach. The market price or market lease payments are determined at the place where the seller or lessor was supposed to deliver the goods. The buyer or lessee can also recover incidental and consequential damages, less the expenses that were saved as a result of the breach [UCC 2–713, 2A–519].

EXAMPLE 14.14 Schilling orders ten thousand bushels of wheat from Valdone for $7 a bushel, with delivery due on June 14 and payment due on June 20. Valdone does not deliver on June 14. On June 14, the market price of wheat is $7.50 per bushel. Schilling chooses to do without the wheat. He sues Valdone for damages for nondelivery. Schilling can recover $0.50 × 10,000, or $5,000, plus any expenses the breach may have caused him. The measure of damages is the market price less the contract price on the day Schilling was to have received delivery. Any expenses Schilling saved by the breach would be deducted from the damages. •

In the following case, a contract for the sale of goods was breached less than a month after the parties entered into it. The market price of the goods was equal to the contract price, but the buyer had also paid a commercial trucking company to pick up the goods. The question before the court was whether the shipping amount could be included in the damages.

Case 14.3 Les Entreprises Jacques Defour & Fils, Inc. v. Dinsick Equipment Corp.

United States District Court, Northern District of Illinois, __ F.Supp.2d __ (2011).

FACTS Les Entreprises Jacques Defour & Fils, Inc., is a Canadian corporation in the business of highway construction. Its principal place of business is in Baie-Saint-Paul, Quebec, Canada. Dinsick Equipment Corporation is a U.S. firm that sells new and used industrial equipment from its base of operations in Plainfield, Illinois. Les Entreprises contracted to buy a 30,000-gallon industrial tank from Dinsick and wired the price of $70,000 directly to the seller's bank account. Less than a week later, Dinsick told Les Entreprises that the tank could be picked up in Joplin, Missouri. The buyer paid Xaak Transport, Inc., to pick up the tank, but when Xaak went to Joplin, the tank was not there. Les Entreprises paid Xaak $7,459 for its services and then contacted Dinsick, which agreed to reimburse the $70,000. When Dinsick did not refund the price, however, Les Entreprises filed a suit in a federal district court against the seller.

ISSUE In addition to the contract price, can Les Entreprises (the buyer) recover damages for the amount it paid to a trucking company to pick up goods that Dinsick (the seller) had failed to deliver?

DECISION Yes. The federal district court issued a judgment in favor of Les Entreprises. The judgment included an award of compensatory

Case 14.3—Continues next page ➥

Case 14.3–Continued

damages in the amount of $70,000 for the tank and incidental damages of $7,459 for the transport.

REASON To establish a breach of contract, the plaintiff must show (1) an enforceable contract, (2) substantial performance by the nonbreaching party, (3) a breach by the other party, and (4) damages. In this case, Les Entreprises agreed–as evidenced by Dinsick's invoice–to buy an industrial tank. The buyer deposited the funds into the seller's account, which shows substantial performance. Dinsick failed to tender or deliver the tank and later failed to refund the price. These circumstances show that Dinsick breached the contract with Les Entreprises. As for the amount of the damages in addition to the price of the tank, Les Entreprises–on Dinsick's notice that the tank was ready for pickup–paid Xaak to transport it. Because shipping costs were key to the performance of the contract, this was a reasonable expense.

FOR CRITICAL ANALYSIS—Technological Consideration *What did the act of wiring the full payment directly to the seller's bank account demonstrate? Are there other methods of payment that could have accomplished the same purpose? Explain.*

When the Seller or Lessor Delivers Nonconforming Goods

When the seller or lessor delivers nonconforming goods, the buyer or lessee has several remedies available under the UCC.

THE RIGHT TO REJECT THE GOODS If either the goods or the tender of the goods by the seller or lessor fails to conform to the contract *in any respect,* the buyer or lessee can reject the goods in whole or in part [UCC 2–601, 2A–509]. If the buyer or lessee rejects the goods, she or he may then obtain cover, cancel the contract, or sue for damages for breach of contract, just as if the seller or lessor had refused to deliver the goods (see the earlier discussion of these remedies).

CASE EXAMPLE 14.15 Jorge Jauregui contracted to buy a Kawai RX5 piano from Bobb's Piano Sales. Bobb's represented that the piano was in new condition and qualified for the manufacturer's warranty. Jauregui paid the contract price, but the piano was delivered with "unacceptable damage," according to Jauregui, who videotaped its condition. Jauregui rejected the piano and filed a lawsuit for breach of contract. The court ruled that Bobb's had breached the contract by delivering nonconforming goods. Jauregui was entitled to damages equal to the contract price with interest, plus the sales tax, delivery charge, and attorneys' fees.[6] •

Timeliness and Reason for Rejection Are Required. The buyer or lessee must reject the goods within a reasonable amount of time after delivery and must *seasonably* (timely) notify the seller or lessor [UCC 2–602(1), 2A–509(2)]. If the buyer or lessee fails to reject the goods within a reasonable amount of time, acceptance will be presumed.

When rejecting goods, the buyer or lessee must also designate defects that would have been apparent to the seller or lessor on reasonable inspection. Failure to do so precludes the buyer or lessee from using such defects to justify rejection or to establish breach when the seller could have cured the defects if they had been disclosed in a timely fashion [UCC 2–605, 2A–514].

Duties of Merchant Buyers and Lessees When Goods Are Rejected. What happens if a *merchant buyer* or *lessee* rightfully rejects goods and the seller or lessor has no agent or business at the place of rejection? In that situation, the merchant buyer or lessee has a good faith obligation to follow any reasonable instructions received from the seller or lessor with respect to the goods [UCC 2–603, 2A–511]. The buyer or lessee is entitled to be reimbursed for the care and cost entailed in following the instructions. The same requirements hold if the buyer or lessee rightfully revokes his or her acceptance of the goods at some later time [UCC 2–608(3), 2A–517(5)]. (Revocation of acceptance will be discussed shortly.)

If no instructions are forthcoming and the goods are perishable or threaten to decline in value quickly, the buyer can resell the goods in good faith, taking the appropriate reimbursement from the proceeds and a selling commission (not to exceed 10 percent of the gross proceeds) [UCC 2–603(1), (2); 2A–511(1), (2)]. If the goods are not perishable, the buyer or lessee may store them for the seller or lessor or reship them to the seller or lessor [UCC 2–604, 2A–512].

REVOCATION OF ACCEPTANCE Acceptance of the goods precludes the buyer or lessee from exercising the right of rejection, but it does not necessarily prevent the buyer or lessee from pursuing other remedies. In certain circumstances, a buyer or lessee is permitted to *revoke* her or his acceptance of the goods. Acceptance of a lot or a commercial unit can be revoked if the nonconformity *substantially* impairs the value of the lot or unit and if one of the following factors is present:

1. Acceptance was predicated on the reasonable assumption that the nonconformity would be cured, and it has not been cured within a reasonable time [UCC 2–608(1)(a), 2A–517(1)(a)].
2. The buyer or lessee did not discover the nonconformity before acceptance, either because it was difficult to discover before acceptance or because assurances made by the seller or lessor that the goods were conforming kept the buyer or lessee from inspecting the goods [UCC 2–608(1)(b), 2A–517(1)(b)].

6. *Jauregui v. Bobb's Piano Sales & Service, Inc.*, 922 So.2d 303 (Fla.App. 2006).

Revocation of acceptance is not effective until the seller or lessor is notified, which must occur within a reasonable time after the buyer or lessee either discovers or *should have discovered* the grounds for revocation. Additionally, revocation must occur before the goods have undergone any substantial change (such as spoilage) not caused by their own defects [UCC 2–608(2), 2A–517(4)]. Once acceptance is revoked, the buyer or lessee can pursue remedies, just as if the goods had been rejected.

THE RIGHT TO RECOVER DAMAGES FOR ACCEPTED GOODS A buyer or lessee who has accepted nonconforming goods may also keep the goods and recover damages caused by the breach. To do so, the buyer or lessee must notify the seller or lessor of the breach within a reasonable time after the defect was or should have been discovered. Failure to give notice of the defects (breach) to the seller or lessor bars the buyer or lessee from pursuing any remedy [UCC 2–607(3), 2A–516(3)]. In addition, the parties to a sales or lease contract can insert a provision requiring the buyer or lessee to give notice of any defects in the goods within a set period.

When the goods delivered are not as promised, the measure of damages equals the difference between the value of the goods as accepted and their value if they had been delivered as warranted [UCC 2–714(2), 2A–519(4)]. The buyer or lessee is also entitled to incidental and consequential damages when appropriate [UCC 2–714(3), 2A–519(3)]. The UCC also permits the buyer or lessee, with proper notice to the seller or lessor, to deduct all or any part of the damages from the price or lease payments still due under the contract [UCC 2–717, 2A–516(1)].

CASE EXAMPLE 14.16 James Fitl attended a sports-card show in San Francisco, California, where he met Mark Strek, an exhibitor at the show. Fitl bought a 1952 Mickey Mantle Topps baseball card for $17,750 from Strek, who had represented that the card was in near-mint condition. Strek delivered it to Fitl in Nebraska, and Fitl placed it in a safe-deposit box. Two years later, Fitl sent the card to Professional Sports Authenticators (PSA), a sports-card grading service. PSA told Fitl that the card was ungradable because it had been discolored and doctored. Fitl complained to Strek, who refused to refund the purchase price because of the amount of time that had gone by. Fitl then filed a lawsuit, and the court awarded him $17,750, plus his court costs. Strek appealed. The Nebraska Supreme Court affirmed Fitl's right to recover damages. The court held that Fitl had reasonably relied on Strek's representation that the card was "authentic," which it was not, and that Fitl had given Strek timely notice of the card's defects when they were discovered.[7] ●

Limitation of Remedies

The parties to a sales or lease contract can vary their respective rights and obligations by contractual agreement. For example, a seller and buyer can expressly provide for remedies in addition to those provided in the UCC. They can also provide remedies in lieu of those provided in the UCC, or they can change the measure of damages. The seller can provide that the buyer's only remedy on breach of warranty will be repair or replacement of the item, or the seller can limit the buyer's remedy to return of the goods and refund of the purchase price. In sales and lease contracts, an agreed-on remedy is in addition to those provided in the UCC unless the parties expressly agree that the remedy is exclusive of all others [UCC 2–719(1), 2A–503(1), (2)].

Exclusive Remedies

If the parties state that a remedy is exclusive, then it is the sole remedy. **EXAMPLE 14.17** Standard Tool Company agrees to sell a pipe-cutting machine to United Pipe & Tubing Corporation. The contract limits United's remedy exclusively to repair or replacement of any defective parts. Thus, repair or replacement of defective parts is the buyer's exclusive remedy under this contract. ●

When circumstances cause an exclusive remedy to fail in its essential purpose, however, it is no longer exclusive, and the buyer or lessee may pursue other remedies available under the UCC [UCC 2–719(2), 2A–503(2)]. **EXAMPLE 14.18** In the example just given, suppose that Standard Tool Company is unable to repair a defective part, and no replacement parts are available. In this situation, because the exclusive remedy failed in its essential purpose, the buyer normally will be entitled to seek other remedies provided to a buyer by the UCC. ●

Limitations on Consequential Damages

As discussed in Chapter 12, *consequential damages* are special damages that compensate for indirect losses (such as lost profits) resulting from a breach of contract that were reasonably foreseeable. Under the UCC, parties to a contract can limit or exclude consequential damages, provided the limitation is not unconscionable. When the buyer or lessee is a consumer, any limitation of consequential damages for personal injuries resulting from consumer goods is *prima facie*[8] unconscionable. The limitation of consequential damages is not necessarily unconscionable when the loss is commercial in nature—for example, lost profits and property damage [UCC 2–719(3), 2A–503(3)].

7. *Fitl v. Strek,* 269 Neb. 51, 690 N.W.2d 605 (2005).

8. *Prima facie* is Latin for "at first sight." Legally, it refers to a fact that is presumed to be true unless contradicted by evidence.

Statute of Limitations

An action for breach of contract under the UCC must be commenced *within four years after the cause of action accrues*—that is, within four years after the breach occurs [UCC 2–725(1)]. In addition to filing suit within the four-year period, a buyer or lessee who has accepted nonconforming goods usually must notify the breaching party of the breach within a reasonable time, or the aggrieved party is barred from pursuing any remedy [UCC 2–607(3)(a), 2A–516(3)]. The parties can agree in their contract to reduce this period to not less than one year, but cannot extend it beyond four years [UCC 2–725(1), 2A–506(1)]. A cause of action accrues for breach of warranty when the seller or lessor tenders delivery. This is the rule even if the aggrieved party is unaware that the cause of action has accrued [UCC 2–725(2), 2A–506(2)].

Reviewing . . . Performance and Breach of Sales and Lease Contracts

GFI, Inc., a Hong Kong company, makes audio decoder chips, one of the essential components used in the manufacture of MP3 players. Egan Electronics contracts with GFI to buy 10,000 chips on an installment contract, with 2,500 chips to be shipped every three months, F.O.B. Hong Kong via Air Express. At the time for the first delivery, GFI delivers only 2,400 chips but explains to Egan that while the shipment is less than 5 percent short, the chips are of a higher quality than those specified in the contract and are worth 5 percent more than the contract price. Egan accepts the shipment and pays GFI the contract price. At the time for the second shipment, GFI makes a shipment identical to the first. Egan again accepts and pays for the chips. At the time for the third shipment, GFI ships 2,400 of the same chips, but this time GFI sends them via Hong Kong Air instead of Air Express. While in transit, the chips are destroyed. When it is time for the fourth shipment, GFI again sends 2,400 chips, but this time Egan rejects the chips without explanation. Using the information presented in the chapter, answer the following questions.

1 Did GFI have a legitimate reason to expect that Egan would accept the fourth shipment? Why or why not?
2 Does the substitution of carriers in the third shipment constitute a breach of the contract by GFI? Explain.
3 Suppose that the silicon used for the chips becomes unavailable for a period of time and that GFI cannot manufacture enough chips to fulfill the contract, but does ship as many as it can to Egan. Under what doctrine might a court release GFI from further performance of the contract?
4 Under the UCC, does Egan have a right to reject the fourth shipment? Why or why not?

Terms and Concepts

conforming goods 252	**incidental damages 259**	**replevin 261**
cover 260	**installment contract 254**	**tender of delivery 253**

Chapter Summary: Performance and Breach of Sales and Lease Contracts

REQUIREMENTS OF PERFORMANCE	
Obligations of the Seller or Lessor (See pages 252–256.)	1. The seller or lessor must tender *conforming* goods to the buyer or lessee. Tender must take place at a *reasonable hour* and in a *reasonable manner.* Under the perfect tender doctrine, the seller or lessor must tender goods that conform exactly to the terms of the contract [UCC 2–503(1), 2A–508(1)]. 2. If the seller or lessor tenders nonconforming goods prior to the performance date and the buyer or lessee rejects them, the seller or lessor may *cure* (repair or replace the goods) within the contract time for performance [UCC 2–508(1), 2A–513(1)]. If the seller or lessor had reasonable grounds to believe that the buyer or lessee would accept the tendered goods, on the buyer's or lessee's rejection the seller or lessor has a reasonable time to substitute conforming goods without liability [UCC 2–508(2), 2A–513(2)]. 3. If the agreed-on means of delivery becomes impracticable or unavailable, the seller must substitute an alternative means (such as a different carrier) if one is available [UCC 2–614(1)].

Chapter Summary: Performance and Breach of Sales and Lease Contracts—Continued

Obligations of the Seller or Lessor—Continued	4. If a seller or lessor tenders nonconforming goods in any one installment under an installment contract, the buyer or lessee may reject the installment only if its value is substantially impaired and cannot be cured. The entire installment contract is breached only when one or more nonconforming installments *substantially* impair the value of the *whole* contract [UCC 2–612, 2A–510]. 5. When performance becomes commercially impracticable owing to circumstances that were not foreseeable when the contract was formed, the perfect tender rule no longer holds [UCC 2–615, 2A–405].
Obligations of the Buyer or Lessee (See pages 256–258.)	1. On tender of delivery by the seller or lessor, the buyer or lessee must pay for the goods at the time and place the goods are *received,* unless the sale is made on credit. Payment may be made by any method generally acceptable in the commercial world unless the seller demands cash [UCC 2–310, 2–511]. In lease contracts, the lessee must make lease payments in accordance with the contract [UCC 2A–516(1)]. 2. Unless otherwise agreed, the buyer or lessee has an absolute right to inspect the goods before acceptance [UCC 2–513(1), 2A–515(1)]. 3. The buyer or lessee can manifest acceptance of delivered goods expressly in words or by conduct or by failing to reject the goods after a reasonable period of time following inspection or after having had a reasonable opportunity to inspect them [UCC 2–606(1), 2A–515(1)]. A buyer will be deemed to have accepted goods if he or she performs any act inconsistent with the seller's ownership [UCC 2–606(1)(c)]. 4. The buyer or lessee can make a partial acceptance if some of the goods do not conform to the contract and the seller or lessor failed to cure [2–601(c), 2A–509(1)].
Anticipatory Repudiation (See page 258.)	If, before the time for performance, one party clearly indicates to the other an intention not to perform, under UCC 2–610 and 2A–402, the aggrieved party may do the following: 1. Await performance by the repudiating party for a commercially reasonable time. 2. Resort to any remedy for breach. 3. In either situation, suspend performance.
	REMEDIES FOR BREACH OF CONTRACT
Remedies of the Seller or Lessor (See pages 258–260.)	1. *When the goods are in the possession of the seller or lessor*—The seller or lessor may do the following: a. Cancel the contract [UCC 2–703(f), 2A–523(1)(a)]. b. Withhold delivery [UCC 2–703(a), 2A–523(1)(c)]. c. Resell or dispose of the goods [UCC 2–703(d), 2–706(1), 2A–523(1)(e), 2A–527(1)]. d. Sue to recover the purchase price or lease payments due [UCC 2–709(1), 2A–529(1)]. e. Sue to recover damages [UCC 2–708, 2A–528]. 2. *When the goods are in transit*—The seller or lessor may stop the carrier or bailee from delivering the goods [UCC 2–705, 2A–526]. 3. *When the goods are in the possession of the buyer or lessee*—The seller or lessor may do the following: a. Sue to recover the purchase price or lease payments due [UCC 2–709(1), 2A–529(1)]. b. Reclaim the goods. A seller may reclaim goods received by an insolvent buyer if the demand is made within ten days of receipt (reclaiming goods excludes all other remedies) [UCC 2–702(2)]; a lessor may repossess goods if the lessee is in default [UCC 2A–525(2)].
Remedies of the Buyer or Lessee (See pages 260–262.)	1. *When the seller or lessor refuses to deliver the goods*—The buyer or lessee may do the following: a. Cancel the contract [UCC 2–711(1), 2A–508(1)(a)]. b. Recover the goods if the seller or lessor becomes insolvent within ten days after receiving the first payment and the goods are identified to the contract [UCC 2–502, 2A–522]. c. Obtain specific performance (when the goods are unique and when the remedy at law is inadequate) [UCC 2–716(1), 2A–521(1)]. d. Obtain cover [UCC 2–712, 2A–518]. e. Replevy the goods (if cover is unavailable) [UCC 2–716(3), 2A–521(3)]. f. Sue to recover damages [UCC 2–713, 2A–519].

Continued

Chapter Summary: Performance and Breach of Sales and Lease Contracts—Continued

Remedies of the Buyer or Lessee—Continued	2. *When the seller or lessor delivers or tenders delivery of nonconforming goods*—The buyer or lessee may do the following: a. Reject the goods [UCC 2–601, 2A–509]. b. Revoke acceptance if the nonconformity *substantially* impairs the value of the unit or lot and if one of the following factors is present: (1) Acceptance was predicated on the reasonable assumption that the nonconformity would be cured and it was not cured within a reasonable time [UCC 2–608(1)(a), 2A–517(1)(a)]. (2) The buyer or lessee did not discover the nonconformity before acceptance, either because it was difficult to discover before acceptance or because the seller's or lessor's assurance that the goods were conforming kept the buyer or lessee from inspecting the goods [UCC 2–608(1)(b), 2A–517(1)(b)]. c. Accept the goods and recover damages [UCC 2–607, 2–714, 2–717, 2A–519].
Limitation of Remedies **(See pages 263–264.)**	1. Remedies may be limited in sales or lease contracts by agreement of the parties. If the contract states that a remedy is exclusive, then that is the sole remedy unless the remedy fails in its essential purpose. Sellers and lessors can also limit the rights of buyers and lessees to consequential damages unless the limitation is unconscionable [UCC 2–719, 2A–503]. 2. The UCC has a four-year statute of limitations for actions involving breach of contract. By agreement, the parties to a sales or lease contract can reduce this period to not less than one year, but they cannot extend it beyond four years [UCC 2–725(1), 2A–506(1)].

ExamPrep

ISSUE SPOTTERS

—Check your answers to these questions against the answers provided in Appendix G.

1 Country Fruit Stand orders eighty cases of peaches from Down Home Farms. Without stating a reason, Down Home untimely delivers thirty cases instead of eighty. Does Country have the right to reject the shipment? Explain.

2 Brite Images, Inc. (BI), agrees to sell Catalog Corporation (CC) five thousand posters of celebrities, to be delivered on May 1. On April 1, BI repudiates the contract. CC informs BI that it expects delivery. Can CC sue BI without waiting until May 1? Why or why not?

BEFORE THE TEST

Go to **www.cengagebrain.com**, enter the ISBN 9781111530624, and click on "Find" to locate this textbook's Web site. Then, click on "Access Now" under "Study Tools," and select Chapter 14 at the top. There, you will find an Interactive Quiz that you can take to assess your mastery of the concepts in this chapter, as well as Flashcards and a Glossary of important terms.

For Review

1 What are the respective obligations of the parties under a contract for the sale or lease of goods?

2 What is the perfect tender rule?

3 What options are available to the nonbreaching party when the other party to a sales or lease contract repudiates the contract prior to the time for performance?

4 What remedies are available to a seller or lessor when the buyer or lessee breaches the contract?

5 In contracts subject to the UCC, are parties free to limit the remedies available to the nonbreaching party on a breach of contract? If so, in what ways?

Questions and Case Problems

14–1 Remedies. Genix, Inc., has contracted to sell Larson five hundred washing machines of a certain model at list price. Genix is to ship the goods on or before December 1. Genix produces one thousand washing machines of this model but has not yet prepared Larson's shipment. On November 1, Larson repudiates the contract. Discuss the remedies available to Genix in this situation.

14–2 Breach. Cummings ordered two model X Super Fidelity speakers from Jamestown Wholesale Electronics, Inc. Jamestown shipped the speakers via United Parcel Service, C.O.D. (collect on delivery), although Cummings had not requested or agreed to a C.O.D. shipment of the goods. When the speakers were delivered, Cummings refused to accept them because he would not be able to inspect them before payment. Jamestown claimed that it had shipped conforming goods and that Cummings had breached their contract. Had Cummings breached the contract? Explain.

14–3 Anticipatory Repudiation. Moore contracted in writing to sell her 2002 Ford Taurus to Hammer for $8,500. Moore agreed to deliver the car on Wednesday, and Hammer promised to pay the $8,500 on the following Friday. On Tuesday, Hammer informed Moore that he would not be buying the car after all. By Friday, Hammer had changed his mind again and tendered $8,500 to Moore. Although Moore had not sold the car to another party, she had refused the tender and to deliver. Hammer claimed that Moore had breached their contract. Moore contended that Hammer's repudiation released her from her duty to perform under the contract. Who is correct, and why?

14–4 Acceptance. In April 2007, Stark, Ltd., applied for credit and opened an account with Quality Distributors, Inc., to obtain snack foods and other items for Stark's convenience stores. For three months, Quality delivered the goods and Stark paid the invoices. In July, Quality was dissolved, and its assets were distributed to J. F. Hughes Co. Hughes continued to deliver the goods to Stark, which continued to pay the invoices until November, when Stark began to experience financial difficulties. By January 2008, Stark owed Hughes $54,241.77. Hughes then dealt with Stark only on a collect-on-delivery basis until Stark's stores closed in 2009. Hughes filed a lawsuit in a state court against Stark and its owner to recover amounts due on unpaid invoices. To successfully plead its case, Hughes had to show that there was a contract between the parties. One question was whether Stark had manifested acceptance of the goods delivered by Hughes. How does a buyer manifest acceptance? Was there an acceptance in this case?

14–5  **Case Problem with Sample Answer** Flint Hills Resources, LP, a crude oil refiner, agreed to buy "approximately 1,000 barrels per day" of Mexican natural gas condensate from JAG Energy Inc., an oil broker. Four months into the contract, Pemex, the only authorized seller of freshly extracted Mexican condensate, warned Flint Hills that some companies might be selling stolen Mexican condensate. Fearing potential criminal liability, Flint Hills refused to accept more deliveries from JAG without proof of the title to its product. JAG promised to forward documents showing its chain of title. When, after several weeks, JAG did not produce the documents, Flint Hills canceled their agreement. JAG filed a suit in a federal district court against Flint Hills, alleging breach. Did Flint Hills have a right to demand assurance of JAG's title to its product? If so, did the buyer act reasonably in exercising that right? Explain. [*Flint Hills Resources, LP v. JAG Energy, Inc.*, 559 F.3d 373 (5th Cir. 2009)]

—For a sample answer to Problem 14–5, go to Appendix F at the end of this text.

14–6 Breach and Damages. Before Chad DeRosier could build a house on his undeveloped property, he needed to have some fill dirt dumped onto the land. Utility Systems of America, Inc., was doing roadwork nearby, and DeRosier asked Utility if it would like to dump extra fill dirt onto his property. Utility said it would, and DeRosier got the necessary permits. The permit was for 1,500 cubic yards of fill dirt, which was how much DeRosier needed. DeRosier gave Utility a copy of the permit. Later, DeRosier found a mountain of fill dirt on his land—6,500 cubic yards. So 5,000 cubic yards of fill dirt had to be removed. Utility denied responsibility but said that it would remove the fill dirt for $9,500. DeRosier sued and hired another company to remove the fill dirt and to do certain foundation work. He paid $46,629 to that contractor. The district court held that Utility had breached its contract and ordered it to pay DeRosier $22,829 in general damages, and $8,000 in consequential damages. Utility appealed. Because Utility charged nothing for the fill dirt, was there a breach of contract? If a breach occurred, would the damages be greater than $9,500? Could consequential damages be justified? Discuss. [*DeRosier v. Utility Systems of America, Inc.*, 780 N.W.2d 1 (Minn.App. 2010)]

14–7 Remedies of the Buyer. Woodridge USA Properties, LP, bought eighty-seven commercial truck trailers under a contract with Southeast Trailer Mart (STM), Inc. Southeastern Freight Lines, Inc., owned the lot in Atlanta, Georgia, where the trailers were stored. Gerald McCarty, an independent sales agent who arranged the deal, showed Woodridge the documents of title. They did not indicate that Woodridge was the buyer. Woodridge asked McCarty to hold the documents and sell the trailers for Woodridge. Within three months, all of the trailers had been sold, but McCarty had not given the proceeds to Woodridge. Woodridge—without mentioning the title documents—asked STM to refund the contract price. STM refused. Later, Woodridge filed a suit in a federal district court against STM, claiming that the title documents had been defective and seeking damages. Does Woodridge have a right to recover damages for accepted goods? What would be the measure of the damages? Explain. [*Woodridge USA Properties, L.P. v. Southeast Trailer Mart, Inc.*, __ F.3d __ (11th Cir. 2011)]

14–8  **A Question of Ethics** *Scotwood Industries, Inc., sells calcium chloride flake for use in ice melt products. Between July and September 2004, Scotwood delivered thirty-seven shipments of flake to Frank Miller & Sons, Inc. After each delivery,*

Scotwood billed Miller, which paid thirty-five of the invoices and processed 30 to 50 percent of the flake. In August, Miller began complaining about the product's quality. Scotwood assured Miller that it would remedy the situation. Finally, in October, Miller told Scotwood, "This is totally unacceptable. We are willing to discuss Scotwood picking up the material." Miller claimed that the flake was substantially defective because it was chunked. Calcium chloride maintains its purity for up to five years, but if it is exposed to and absorbs moisture, it chunks, making it unusable. In response to Scotwood's suit to collect payment on the unpaid invoices, Miller filed a counterclaim in a federal district court for breach of contract, seeking to recover based on revocation of acceptance, among other things. [Scotwood Industries, Inc. v. Frank Miller & Sons, Inc., *435 F.Supp.2d 1160 (D.Kan. 2006)]*

1 What is revocation of acceptance? How does a buyer effectively exercise this option? Do the facts in this case support this theory as a ground for Miller to recover damages? Why or why not?

2 Is there an ethical basis for allowing a buyer to revoke acceptance of goods and recover damages? If so, is there an ethical limit to this right? Discuss.

14–9 **Critical Thinking Legal Question** Under what circumstances should courts not allow fully informed contracting parties to agree to limit remedies?

Chapter 15

Warranties and Product Liability

Learning Objectives

After reading this chapter, you should be able to answer the following questions:

1. What factors determine whether a seller's or lessor's statement constitutes an express warranty or mere puffery?
2. What implied warranties arise under the UCC?
3. Can a manufacturer be held liable to any person who suffers an injury proximately caused by the manufacturer's negligently made product?
4. What are the elements of a cause of action in strict product liability?
5. What defenses to liability can be raised in a product liability lawsuit?

The Learning Objectives above are designed to help improve your understanding of the chapter.

(Quazie foto/Creative Commons)

Warranty is an age-old concept. In sales and lease law, a warranty is an assurance or guarantee by the seller or lessor of certain facts concerning the goods being sold or leased. Sellers and lessors warrant to those who purchase or lease their goods that the goods are as represented or will be as promised.

The Uniform Commercial Code (UCC) has numerous rules governing product warranties as they occur in sales and lease contracts. Those rules are the subject matter of the first part of this chapter. A natural addition to the discussion is *product liability:* Who is liable to consumers, users, and bystanders for physical harm and property damage caused by a particular good or its use? Product liability encompasses the contract theory of warranty, as well as the tort theories of negligence and strict liability (discussed in Chapter 4).

Warranties

Most goods are covered by some type of warranty designed to protect consumers. Article 2 (on sales) and Article 2A (on leases) of the UCC designate several types of warranties that can arise in a sales or lease contract, including warranties of title, express warranties, and implied warranties. We discuss these types of warranties in the following subsections, as well as a federal statute that is designed to prevent deception and make warranties more understandable.

Warranties of Title

Under the UCC, three types of title warranties—*good title, no liens,* and *no infringements*—can automatically arise in sales and lease contracts. In most sales, sellers warrant that they have good and valid title to the goods sold and that transfer of the title is rightful [UCC 2–312(1)(a)]. If the buyer subsequently learns that the seller did not have good title to goods that were purchased, the buyer can sue the seller for breach of this warranty. (There is no warranty of good title in lease contracts because title to the goods does not pass to the lessee, as discussed in Chapter 13.)

An additional warranty of title shields buyers and lessees who are *unaware* of any encumbrances, or **liens** (claims, charges, or liabilities—see Chapter 19), against goods at the time the contract is made [UCC 2–312(1)(b), 2A–211(1)]. This warranty protects buyers who, for example, unknowingly purchase goods that are subject to a creditor's security interest (an interest in the goods that secures payment or performance, to be discussed in Chapter 18). If a creditor legally repossesses the goods from a buyer *who had no actual knowledge of the security interest,* the buyer can recover from the seller for breach of warranty.

Finally, when the seller or lessor is a merchant, he or she automatically warrants that the buyer or lessee takes the goods *free of infringements.* In other words, a merchant promises that the goods delivered are free from any copyright, trademark, or patent claims of a third person [UCC 2–312(3), 2A–211(2)].

Express Warranties

A seller or lessor can create an **express warranty** by making representations concerning the quality, condition, description, or performance potential of the goods. Under UCC 2–313 and 2A–210, express warranties arise when a seller or lessor indicates any of the following:

1. That the goods conform to any *affirmation* (declaration that something is true) or *promise of fact* that the seller or lessor makes to the buyer or lessee about the goods. Such affirmations or promises are usually made during the bargaining process. Statements such as "these drill bits will penetrate stainless steel—and without dulling" are express warranties.
2. That the goods conform to any *description* of them. For example, a label that reads "Crate contains one 150-horsepower diesel engine" or a contract that calls for the delivery of a "camel's-hair coat" creates an express warranty.
3. That the goods conform to any *sample or model* of the goods shown to the buyer or lessee.

BASIS OF THE BARGAIN To create an express warranty, a seller or lessor does not have to use formal words such as *warrant* or *guarantee* [UCC 2–313(2), 2A–210(2)]. It is only necessary that a reasonable buyer or lessee would regard the representation of fact as part of the basis of the bargain [UCC 2–313(1), 2A–210(1)]. Just what constitutes the basis of the bargain is hard to say. The UCC does not define the concept, and it is a question of fact in each case whether a representation was made at such a time and in such a way that it induced the buyer or lessee to enter into the contract.

STATEMENTS OF OPINION AND VALUE Only statements of fact create express warranties. If the seller or lessor makes a statement that relates to the supposed value or worth of the goods, or makes a statement of opinion or recommendation about the goods, the seller or lessor is not creating an express warranty [UCC 2–313(2), 2A–210(2)].

EXAMPLE 15.1 A seller claims, "This is the best used car to come along in years. It has four new tires and a 250-horsepower engine just rebuilt this year." The seller has made several *affirmations of fact* that can create a warranty: the automobile has an engine, it has a 250-horsepower engine, it was rebuilt this year, there are four tires on the automobile, and the tires are new. The seller's *opinion* that the vehicle is "the best used car to come along in years," however, is known as "puffery" and creates no warranty. (*Puffery* is the expression of opinion by a seller or lessor that is not made as a representation of fact.) •

A statement relating to the value of the goods, such as "this is worth a fortune" or "anywhere else you'd pay $10,000 for it," usually does not create a warranty. If the seller or lessor is an expert and gives an opinion as an expert to a layperson, though, then a warranty may be created. It is not always easy to determine whether a statement constitutes an express warranty or puffing. The reasonableness of the buyer's or lessee's reliance appears to be the controlling criterion in many cases.

CASE EXAMPLE 15.2 A tobacco farmer read an advertisement for Chlor-O-Pic, a chemical fumigant, which stated that, if applied as directed, Chlor-O-Pic would give "season-long control with application in fall, winter, or spring" against black shank disease, a fungal disease that destroys tobacco crops. The farmer bought Chlor-O-Pic and applied it as directed to his tobacco crop. Nonetheless, the crop developed black shank disease. The farmer sued the manufacturer of Chlor-O-Pic, arguing that he had purchased the product in reliance on a "strong promise" of "season-long control." The court found that the manufacturer's strong promise had created an express warranty and that the farmer was entitled to the value of the damaged crop.[1] •

Implied Warranties

An **implied warranty** is one that *the law derives* by implication or inference because of the circumstances of a sale, rather than by the seller's express promise. In an action based on breach of implied warranty, it is necessary to show that an implied warranty existed and that the breach of the warranty proximately caused[2] the damage sustained. We look here at some of the implied warranties that arise under the UCC.

IMPLIED WARRANTY OF MERCHANTABILITY Every sale or lease of goods made *by a merchant who deals in goods of the kind sold or leased* automatically gives rise to an **implied warranty of merchantability** [UCC 2–314, 2A–212]. **EXAMPLE 15.3** A

1. *Triple E, Inc. v. Hendrix & Dail, Inc.*, 344 S.C. 186, 543 S.E.2d 245 (2001). See also *Nomo Agroindustrial Sa De CV v. Enza Zaden North America, Inc.*, 492 F.Supp.2d 1175 (D.Ariz. 2007).
2. Proximate, or legal, cause exists when the connection between an act and an injury is strong enough to justify imposing liability—see Chapter 4.

merchant who is in the business of selling ski equipment makes an implied warranty of merchantability every time she sells a pair of skis. A neighbor selling his skis at a garage sale does not (because he is not in the business of selling goods of this type). •

Merchantable Goods. Goods that are *merchantable* are "reasonably fit for the ordinary purposes for which such goods are used." They must be of at least average, fair, or medium-grade quality. The quality must be comparable to a level that will pass without objection in the trade or market for goods of the same description. To be merchantable, the goods must also be adequately packaged and labeled, and they must conform to the promises or affirmations of fact made on the container or label, if any.

The warranty of merchantability may be breached even though the merchant did not know or could not have discovered that a product was defective (not merchantable). Of course, merchants are not absolute insurers against all accidents occurring in connection with their goods. For instance, a bar of soap is not unmerchantable merely because a user could slip and fall by stepping on it.

CASE EXAMPLE 15.4 Darrell Shoop bought a Dodge Dakota truck that had been manufactured by DaimlerChrysler Corporation. Almost immediately, he had problems with the truck. During the first eighteen months, the engine, suspension, steering, transmission, and other components required repairs twelve times, including at least five times for the same defect, which remained uncorrected. Shoop eventually traded in the truck and filed a lawsuit against DaimlerChrysler for breach of the implied warranty of merchantability. The court held that Shoop could maintain an action against DaimlerChrysler and use the fact that the truck had required a significant number of repairs as evidence that it was unmerchantable.[3] •

Merchantable Food. The UCC recognizes the serving of food or drink to be consumed on or off the premises as a sale of goods subject to the implied warranty of merchantability [UCC 2–314(1)]. "Merchantable" food means food that is fit to eat. Courts generally determine whether food is fit to eat on the basis of consumer expectations. The courts assume that consumers should reasonably expect on occasion to find cherry pits in cherry pie or a nutshell in a package of shelled nuts, for example—because such substances are natural incidents of the food. In contrast, consumers would not reasonably expect to find an inchworm in a can of peas or a piece of glass in a soft drink—because these substances are not natural to the food product.

In the following classic case, the court had to determine whether a fish bone was a substance that one should reasonably expect to find in fish chowder.

3. *Shoop v. DaimlerChrysler Corp.*, 371 Ill.App.3d 1058, 864 N.E.2d 785, 309 Ill.Dec. 544 (2007).

Classic Case 15.1 Webster v. Blue Ship Tea Room, Inc.

Supreme Judicial Court of Massachusetts, 347 Mass. 421, 198 N.E.2d 309 (1964).

FACTS Blue Ship Tea Room, Inc., was located in Boston in an old building overlooking the ocean. Priscilla Webster, who had been born and raised in New England, went to the restaurant and ordered fish chowder. The chowder was milky in color. After three or four spoonfuls, she felt something lodged in her throat. As a result, she underwent two esophagoscopies. In the second esophagoscopy, a fish bone was found and removed. Webster filed a lawsuit against the restaurant in a Massachusetts state court for breach of the implied warranty of merchantability. The jury rendered a verdict for Webster, and the restaurant appealed to the state's highest court.

ISSUE Does serving fish chowder that contains a bone constitute a breach of an implied warranty of merchantability by the restaurant?

DECISION No. The Supreme Judicial Court of Massachusetts held that Webster could not recover against Blue Ship Tea Room because no breach of warranty had occurred.

REASON The court, citing UCC Section 2–314, stated that "a warranty that goods shall be merchantable is implied in a contract for their sale if the seller is a merchant with respect to goods of that kind. Under this section the serving for value of food or drink to be consumed either on the premises or elsewhere is a sale. . . . Goods to be merchantable must at least be . . . fit for the ordinary purposes for which such goods are used." The question here was whether a fish bone made the chowder unfit for eating. In the judge's opinion, "the joys of life in New England include the ready availability of fresh fish chowder. We should be prepared to cope with the hazards of fish bones, the occasional presence of which in chowders is, it seems to us, to be anticipated, and which, in the light of a hallowed tradition, do not impair their fitness or merchantability."

FOR CRITICAL ANALYSIS—E-Commerce Consideration *If Webster had made the chowder herself from a recipe that she had found on the Internet, could she have successfully brought an action against its author for a breach of the implied warranty of merchantability? Explain.*

IMPACT OF THIS CASE ON TODAY'S LAW *This classic case, phrased in memorable language, was an early application of the UCC's implied warranty of merchantability to food products. The case established the rule that consumers should expect to find, on occasion, elements of food products that are natural to the product (such as fish bones in fish chowder). Courts today still apply this rule.*

Implied Warranty of Fitness for a Particular Purpose The **implied warranty of fitness for a particular purpose** arises when any seller or lessor (merchant or nonmerchant) knows the particular purpose for which a buyer or lessee will use the goods *and* knows that the buyer or lessee is relying on the skill and judgment of the seller or lessor to select suitable goods [UCC 2–315, 2A–213].

A "particular purpose" of the buyer or lessee differs from the "ordinary purpose for which goods are used" (merchantability). Goods can be merchantable but unfit for a particular purpose. **EXAMPLE 15.5** You need a gallon of paint to match the color of your living room walls—a light shade somewhere between coral and peach. You take a sample to your local hardware store and request a gallon of paint of that color. Instead, you are given a gallon of bright blue paint. Here, the salesperson has not breached any warranty of implied merchantability—the bright blue paint is of high quality and suitable for interior walls—but he or she has breached an implied warranty of fitness for a particular purpose. •

A seller or lessor is not required to have actual knowledge of the buyer's or lessee's particular purpose, so long as the seller or lessor "has reason to know" the purpose. For an implied warranty to be created, however, the buyer or lessee must have *relied* on the skill or judgment of the seller or lessor in selecting or furnishing suitable goods.

Warranties Implied from Prior Dealings or Trade Custom Implied warranties can also arise (or be excluded or modified) as a result of course of dealing or usage of trade [UCC 2–314(3), 2A–212(3)]. In the absence of evidence to the contrary, when both parties to a sales or lease contract have knowledge of a well-recognized trade custom, the courts will infer that both parties intended for that trade custom to apply to their contract. **EXAMPLE 15.6** Suppose that it is an industry-wide custom to lubricate new cars before they are delivered to buyers. Vera buys a new car from Bender Chevrolet. After the purchase, Vera discovers that Bender failed to lubricate the car before delivering it to her. In this situation, Vera can hold the dealer liable for damages resulting from the breach of an implied warranty. (This, of course, would also be negligence on the part of the dealer.) •

Overlapping Warranties

Sometimes, two or more warranties are made in a single transaction. An implied warranty of merchantability, an implied warranty of fitness for a particular purpose, or both can exist in addition to an express warranty. For instance, when a sales contract for a new car states that "this car engine is warranted to be free from defects for 36,000 miles or thirty-six months, whichever occurs first," there is an express warranty against all defects and an implied warranty that the car will be fit for normal use.

The rule under the UCC is that express and implied warranties are construed as *cumulative* if they are consistent with one another [UCC 2–317, 2A–215]. In other words, courts interpret two or more warranties as being in agreement with each other unless this construction is unreasonable. If it is unreasonable, then a court will hold that the warranties are inconsistent and apply the following rules to interpret which warranty is most important:

1. *Express* warranties displace inconsistent *implied* warranties, except for implied warranties of fitness for a particular purpose.
2. Samples take precedence over inconsistent general descriptions.
3. Exact or technical specifications displace inconsistent samples or general descriptions.

Warranty Disclaimers

The UCC generally permits warranties to be disclaimed or limited by specific and unambiguous language, provided that the buyer or lessee is protected from surprise. The manner in which a seller or lessor can disclaim warranties varies depending on the type of warranty.

Express Warranties A seller or lessor can disclaim all oral express warranties by including in the contract a written (or an electronically recorded) disclaimer in language that is clear and conspicuous, and called to a buyer's or lessee's attention [UCC 2–316(1), 2A–214(1)]. This allows the seller or lessor to avoid false allegations that oral warranties were made, and it ensures that only representations made by properly authorized individuals are included in the bargain.

Note, however, that a buyer or lessee must be made aware of any warranty disclaimers or modifications *at the time the contract is formed.* In other words, any oral or written warranties—or disclaimers—made during the bargaining process as part of a contract's formation cannot be modified at a later time by the seller or lessor.

Implied Warranties Generally, unless circumstances indicate otherwise, the implied warranties of merchantability and fitness are disclaimed by expressions such as "as is" or "with all faults." The phrase must be one that in common understanding for *both* parties calls the buyer's or lessee's attention to the fact that there are no implied warranties [UCC 2–316(3)(a), 2A–214(3)(a)]. (Note, however, that some states have laws that forbid "as is" sales. Other states do not allow disclaimers of warranties of merchantability for consumer goods.)

CASE EXAMPLE 15.7 Mandy Morningstar advertised a "lovely, eleven-year-old mare" with extensive jumping ability for sale. After examining the horse twice, Sue Hallett contracted to buy the horse. She signed a contract that described the horse as an eleven-year-old mare and as being sold "as is." Shortly after the purchase, a veterinarian determined that the horse was actually sixteen years old and in no condition for jumping. Hallett stopped payment, and Morningstar filed a lawsuit for breach of contract. The court held that the statement in the contract describing the horse as eleven years old constituted an express warranty, which Morningstar had breached. Although the "as is" clause effectively disclaimed any implied warranties (of merchantability and fitness for a particular purpose, such as jumping), the court ruled that it did not disclaim the express warranty concerning the horse's age.[4] •

Disclaimer of the Implied Warranty of Merchantability. To specifically disclaim an implied warranty of merchantability, a seller or lessor must mention the word *merchantability* [UCC 2–316(2), 2A–214(2)]. The disclaimer need not be written, but if it is, the writing (or record) must be conspicuous [UCC 2–316(2), 2A–214(4)]. Under the UCC, a term or clause is conspicuous when it is written or displayed in such a way that a reasonable person would notice it. Conspicuous terms include words set in capital letters, in a larger font size, or in a different color so as to be set off from the surrounding text.

Disclaimer of the Implied Warranty of Fitness. To specifically disclaim an implied warranty of fitness for a particular purpose, the disclaimer *must* be in a writing (or record) and must be conspicuous. The word *fitness* does not have to be mentioned; it is sufficient if, for example, the disclaimer states, "There are no warranties that extend beyond the description on the face hereof."

Buyer's or Lessee's Examination or Refusal to Inspect. If a buyer or lessee actually examines the goods (or a sample or model) as fully as desired before entering into a contract, or if the buyer or lessee refuses to examine the goods on the seller's or lessor's request that he or she do so, *there is no implied warranty with respect to defects that a reasonable examination would reveal or defects that are actually found* [UCC 2–316(3)(b), 2A–214(2)(b)].

EXAMPLE 15.8 Azumi buys a lamp at Gershwin's Store. No express warranties are made. Gershwin asks Azumi to inspect the lamp before buying it, but she refuses. Had Azumi inspected the lamp, she would have noticed that the base was obviously cracked and the electrical cord was pulled loose. If the lamp later cracks or starts a fire in Azumi's home and she is injured, she normally will not be able to hold Gershwin's liable for breach of the warranty of merchantability. Because Azumi refused to examine the lamp when asked by Gershwin, Azumi will be deemed to have assumed the risk that it was defective. •

WARRANTY DISCLAIMERS AND UNCONSCIONABILITY The UCC sections dealing with warranty disclaimers do not refer specifically to unconscionability as a factor. Ultimately, however, the courts will test warranty disclaimers with reference to the UCC's unconscionability standards [UCC 2–302, 2A–108]. Such factors as lack of bargaining position, take-it-or-leave-it choices, and a buyer's or lessee's failure to understand or know of a warranty disclaimer will become relevant to the issue of unconscionability.

Magnuson-Moss Warranty Act

The Magnuson-Moss Warranty Act of 1975[5] was designed to prevent deception in warranties by making them easier to understand. The act modifies UCC warranty rules to some extent when *consumer* transactions are involved. The UCC, however, remains the primary codification of warranty rules for commercial transactions.

Under the Magnuson-Moss Act, no seller or lessor is required to give an express written warranty for consumer goods sold. If a seller or lessor chooses to make an express written warranty, however, and the goods are priced at more than $25, the warranty must be labeled as "full" or "limited." A *full warranty* requires free repair or replacement of any defective part. If the product cannot be repaired within a reasonable time, the consumer has the choice of a refund or a replacement without charge. A full warranty can be for an unlimited or limited time period, such as a "full twelve-month warranty." A *limited warranty* is one in which the buyer's recourse is limited in some fashion, such as to replacement of an item. The fact that only a limited warranty is being given must be conspicuously stated.

The Magnuson-Moss Act further requires the warrantor to make certain disclosures fully and conspicuously in a single document in "readily understood language." It must state the names and addresses of the warrantor(s), specifically what is warranted, and the procedures for enforcing the warranty. It must also clarify that the buyer has legal rights and explain any limitations on warranty relief.

Lemon Laws

Some purchasers of defective automobiles—called "lemons"—found that the remedies provided by the UCC were inadequate due to limitations imposed by the seller. In response to the frustrations of these buyers, all of the states have enacted *lemon laws*. Basically, state lemon laws provide remedies to consumers who buy automobiles that repeatedly fail to meet standards of quality and performance because they are "lemons." Although lemon laws vary by state, typically they apply to automobiles under warranty that are defective in a way that significantly affects the vehicle's value or use. Lemon laws do not necessarily cover used-car purchases (unless the

4. *Morningstar v. Hallett*, 858 A.2d 125 (Pa.Super.Ct. 2004).

5. 15 U.S.C. Sections 2301–2312.

car is covered by a manufacturer's extended warranty) or vehicles that are leased.[6]

Generally, the seller or manufacturer is given a number of opportunities to remedy the defect (usually four). If the seller fails to cure the problem despite a reasonable number of attempts (as specified by state law), the buyer is entitled to a new car, replacement of defective parts, or return of all consideration paid. Buyers who prevail in a lemon law dispute may also be entitled to reimbursement for their attorneys' fees.

In most states, lemon laws require an aggrieved new-car owner to give the dealer or manufacturer an opportunity to solve the problem. If the problem persists, the owner must then submit complaints to the arbitration program specified in the manufacturer's warranty before taking the case to court. Most major automobile companies operate their own arbitration panels, but some use independent arbitration services, such as those provided by the Better Business Bureau. Decisions by arbitration panels are binding on the manufacturer—that is, cannot be appealed by the manufacturer to the courts—but usually are not binding on the purchaser.

Product Liability

Those who make, sell, or lease goods can be held liable for physical harm or property damage caused by those goods to a consumer, user, or bystander. This is called **product liability.** Product liability claims may be based on the warranty theories just discussed, as well as on the theories of negligence, misrepresentation, and strict liability. We look here at product liability based on negligence and misrepresentation.

Negligence

Chapter 4 defined *negligence* as the failure to exercise the degree of care that a reasonable, prudent person would have exercised under the circumstances. If a manufacturer fails to exercise "due care" to make a product safe, a person who is injured by the product may sue the manufacturer for negligence.

DUE CARE MUST BE EXERCISED The manufacturer must exercise due care in designing the product, selecting the materials, using the appropriate production process, assembling the product, and placing adequate warnings on the label informing the user of dangers of which an ordinary person might not be aware. The duty of care also extends to the inspection and testing of any purchased products that are used in the final product sold by the manufacturer.

PRIVITY OF CONTRACT NOT REQUIRED A product liability action based on negligence does not require *privity of contract* between the injured plaintiff and the defendant manufacturer. As discussed in Chapter 11, *privity of contract* refers to the relationship that exists between the promisor and the promisee of a contract. Privity is the reason that only the parties to a contract normally can enforce that contract.

In the context of product liability law, privity is not required. This means that a person who was injured by a product need not be the one who actually purchased the product—that is, need not be in privity—to maintain a negligence suit against the manufacturer or seller of a defective product. A manufacturer is liable for its failure to exercise due care to *any person* who sustains an injury proximately caused by a negligently made (defective) product. Relative to the long history of the common law, this exception to the privity requirement is a fairly recent development, dating to the early part of the twentieth century.

Misrepresentation

When a user or consumer is injured as a result of a manufacturer's or seller's fraudulent misrepresentation, the basis of liability may be the tort of fraud. The intentional mislabeling of packaged cosmetics, for instance, or the intentional concealment of a product's defects would constitute fraudulent misrepresentation. The misrepresentation must be of a material fact, and the seller must have intended to induce the buyer's reliance on the misrepresentation. Misrepresentation on a label or advertisement is enough to show an intent to induce the reliance of anyone who may use the product. In addition, the buyer must have relied on the misrepresentation.

Strict Product Liability

Under the doctrine of strict liability (discussed in Chapter 4), people may be liable for the results of their acts regardless of their intentions or their exercise of reasonable care. In addition, liability does not depend on privity of contract. The injured party does not have to be the buyer or a third party beneficiary (see Chapter 11), as required under contract warranty theory. In the 1960s, courts applied the doctrine of strict liability in several landmark cases involving manufactured goods, and it has since become a common method of holding manufacturers liable.

Strict Product Liability and Public Policy

The law imposes strict product liability as a matter of public policy. This public policy rests on the threefold assumption that (1) consumers should be protected against unsafe products; (2) manufacturers and distributors should not escape liability for faulty products simply because they are not in privity of contract with the ultimate user of those products; and (3) manufacturers, sellers, and lessors of products generally are in a better position than consumers to bear the costs associated

6. Note that in some states, such as California, these laws may extend beyond automobile purchases and apply to other consumer goods.

with injuries caused by their products—costs that they can ultimately pass on to all consumers in the form of higher prices.

California was the first state to impose strict product liability in tort on manufacturers. In a landmark decision, *Greenman v. Yuba Power Products, Inc.*,[7] the California Supreme Court set out the reason for applying tort law rather than contract law in cases involving consumers injured by defective products. According to the court, the "purpose of such liability is to ensure that the costs of injuries resulting from defective products are borne by the manufacturers . . . rather than by the injured persons who are powerless to protect themselves."

Public policy may be expressed in a statute or in the common law. Sometimes, public policy may be revealed in a court's interpretation of a statute, as in the following case.

7. 59 Cal.2d 57, 377 P.2d 897, 27 Cal.Rptr. 697 (1963).

Case 15.2 Bruesewitz v. Wyeth, LLC

Supreme Court of the United States, __ U.S. __, 131 S.Ct. 1068, 179 L.Ed.2d 1 (2011).
www.supremecourt.gov[a]

FACTS When Hannah Bruesewitz was six months old, her pediatrician administered a dose of the DTP vaccine according to the Centers for Disease Control's recommended childhood immunization schedule. Within twenty-four hours, Hannah began to experience seizures. She suffered over one hundred seizures during the next month. Her doctors diagnosed her with "residual seizure disorder" and "developmental delay." Hannah's parents, Russell and Robalee Bruesewitz, filed a claim for relief in a federal claims court under the National Childhood Vaccine Injury Act (NCVIA) of 1986, which set up a no-fault compensation program for persons injured by vaccines. The claim was denied. The Bruesewitzes then filed a suit in a Pennsylvania state court against Wyeth, LLC, the maker of the vaccine, alleging strict product liability. The suit was moved to a federal district court. The court held that the claim was preempted by the NCVIA, which includes provisions protecting manufacturers from liability for "a vaccine's unavoidable, adverse side effects." The U.S. Court of Appeals for the Third Circuit affirmed the district court's judgment. The Bruesewitzes appealed to the United States Supreme Court.

ISSUE Was the Bruesewitzes' strict product liability claim against Wyeth for the injuries suffered by their child from vaccination preempted by the NCVIA?

a. In the "Supreme Court Documents" column, in the "Opinions" pull-down menu, select "Bound Volumes." On the next page, in the "For Search Term:" box, type "Bruesewitz" and click on "Search." In the result, click on the name of the case to access the opinion. The United States Supreme Court maintains this Web site.

DECISION Yes. The United States Supreme Court affirmed the lower court's judgment. The NCVIA preempted the Bruesewitzes' claim against Wyeth for injury to their daughter caused by the DTP vaccine's side effects.

REASON The court reasoned that Congress enacted the NCVIA as a matter of public policy to stabilize the vaccine market and facilitate compensation. In the no-fault compensation program set up by the NCVIA, a person with a vaccine-related claim files a petition with the U.S. Court of Federal Claims. The court may award compensation for legal, medical, rehabilitation, counseling, special education, and vocational training expenses, as well as for diminished earning capacity, pain and suffering, and death. The awards are funded by a tax on the vaccine. In exchange for the "informal, efficient" compensation program, vaccine manufacturers who comply with the regulatory requirements are "immunized" from liability. The statute thus strikes a balance between paying victims harmed by vaccines and protecting the vaccine industry from collapsing under the costs of tort liability.

FOR CRITICAL ANALYSIS—Political Consideration *If the public wants to change the policy outlined in this case, which branch of the government–and at what level–should be lobbied to make the change? Explain.*

Requirements for Strict Liability

After the *Restatement (Second) of Torts* was issued in 1964, Section 402A became a widely accepted statement of how the doctrine of strict liability should be applied to sellers of goods (including manufacturers, processors, assemblers, packagers, bottlers, wholesalers, distributors, retailers, and lessors). The bases for an action in strict liability that are set forth in Section 402A of the *Restatement* can be summarized as the following series of six requirements. Depending on the jurisdiction, if these requirements are met, a manufacturer's liability to an injured party can be almost unlimited.

1. The product must be in a *defective condition* when the defendant sells it.
2. The defendant must normally be engaged in the *business of selling* (or otherwise distributing) that product.
3. The product must be *unreasonably dangerous* to the user or consumer because of its defective condition (in most states).

4. The plaintiff must incur *physical harm* to self or property by use or consumption of the product.
5. The defective condition must be the *proximate cause* of the injury or damage.
6. The *goods must not have been substantially changed* from the time the product was sold to the time the injury was sustained.

PROVING A DEFECTIVE CONDITION Under these requirements, in any action against a manufacturer, seller, or lessor, the plaintiff does not have to show why or in what manner the product became defective. The plaintiff does, however, have to prove that the product was defective at the time it left the hands of the seller or lessor and that this defective condition made it "unreasonably dangerous" to the user or consumer. Unless evidence can be presented that will support the conclusion that the product was defective when it was sold or leased, the plaintiff normally will not succeed. If the product was delivered in a safe condition and subsequent mishandling made it harmful to the user, the seller or lessor usually is not strictly liable.

UNREASONABLY DANGEROUS PRODUCTS The *Restatement* recognizes that many products cannot possibly be made entirely safe for all consumption, and thus holds sellers or lessors liable only for products that are *unreasonably* dangerous. A court may consider a product so defective as to be an **unreasonably dangerous product** in either of the following situations.

1. The product is dangerous beyond the expectation of the ordinary consumer.
2. A less dangerous alternative was economically feasible for the manufacturer, but the manufacturer failed to produce it.

As will be discussed next, a product may be unreasonably dangerous due to a flaw in the manufacturing process, a design defect, or an inadequate warning.

Product Defects—*Restatement (Third) of Torts*

Because Section 402A of the *Restatement (Second) of Torts* did not clearly define such terms as "defective" and "unreasonably dangerous," they were interpreted differently by different courts. In 1997, to address these concerns, the American Law Institute issued the *Restatement (Third) of Torts: Products Liability*. This *Restatement* defines the three types of product defects that have traditionally been recognized in product liability law—manufacturing defects, design defects, and inadequate warnings.

MANUFACTURING DEFECTS According to Section 2(a) of the *Restatement (Third) of Torts: Products Liability,* a product "contains a manufacturing defect when the product departs from its intended design even though all possible care was exercised in the preparation and marketing of the product." Basically, a manufacturing defect is a departure from a product's design specifications, which results in products that are physically flawed, damaged, or incorrectly assembled. A glass bottle that is made too thin and explodes in a consumer's face is an example of a manufacturing defect.

Usually, such defects occur when a manufacturer fails to assemble, test, or adequately check the quality of a product. Liability is imposed on the manufacturer (and on the wholesaler and retailer) regardless of whether the manufacturer's quality control efforts were "reasonable." The idea behind holding defendants strictly liable for manufacturing defects is to encourage greater investment in product safety and stringent quality control standards.

CASE EXAMPLE 15.9 Kevin Schmude purchased an eight-foot ladder and used it to install radio-frequency shielding in a hospital room. While Schmude was standing on the ladder, it collapsed, and he was seriously injured. He filed a lawsuit against the ladder's maker, Tricam Industries, Inc., based on a manufacturing defect. Experts testified that when the ladder was assembled, the preexisting holes in the top cap did not properly line up with the holes in the rear right rail and backing plate. As a result of the misalignment, the rivet at the rear legs of the ladder was more likely to fail. A jury concluded that this manufacturing defect made the ladder unreasonably dangerous and awarded Schmude more than $677,000 in damages.[8] •

DESIGN DEFECTS Unlike a product with a manufacturing defect, a product with a design defect is made in conformity with the manufacturer's design specifications, but nevertheless results in injury to the user because the design itself is faulty. The product's design creates an unreasonable risk to the user. A product "is defective in design when the foreseeable risks of harm posed by the product could have been reduced or avoided by the adoption of a reasonable alternative design by the seller or other distributor, or a predecessor in the commercial chain of distribution, and the omission of the alternative design renders the product not reasonably safe."[9]

Test for Design Defects. To successfully assert a design defect, a plaintiff has to show that a reasonable alternative design was available and that the defendant's failure to adopt the alternative design rendered the product unreasonably dangerous. In other words, a manufacturer or other defendant is liable only when the harm was reasonably preventable.

CASE EXAMPLE 15.10 Gillespie, who cut off several of his fingers while operating a table saw, filed a lawsuit against the maker of the table saw. Gillespie alleged that the blade guards on the saw were defectively designed. At trial, however, an

8. *Schmude v. Tricam Industries, Inc.*, 550 F.Supp.2d 846 (E.D.Wis. 2008).
9. *Restatement (Third) of Torts: Products Liability,* Section 2(b).

expert testified that the alternative design for blade guards used for table saws could not have been used for the particular cut that Gillespie was performing at the time he was injured. The court found that Gillespie's claim about defective blade guards failed because there was no proof that the "better" design of guard would have prevented his injury.[10] ●

Factors to Be Considered. According to the *Restatement (Third) of Torts,* a court can consider a broad range of factors in deciding claims of design defects. These factors include the magnitude and probability of the foreseeable risks, as well as the relative advantages and disadvantages of the product as designed and as it alternatively could have been designed. Basically, most courts engage in a risk-utility analysis, determining whether the risk of harm from the product as designed outweighs its utility to the user and to the public.

CASE EXAMPLE 15.11 Jodie Bullock smoked cigarettes manufactured by Philip Morris for forty-five years. When she was diagnosed with lung cancer, Bullock brought a product liability suit against Philip Morris. She presented evidence that by the late 1950s, scientists had proved that smoking caused lung cancer. Nonetheless, Philip Morris had issued full-page announcements stating that there was no proof that smoking caused cancer and that "numerous scientists" questioned "the validity of the statistics." At trial, the judge instructed the jury to consider the gravity of the danger posed by the design, as well as the likelihood that the danger would cause injury. The jury found that there was a defect in the design of the cigarettes and that they had been negligently designed. It awarded Bullock $850,000 in compensatory damages and $28 million in punitive damages. Philip Morris appealed, claiming that no evidence had been offered to show that there was a safer design for cigarettes, but the reviewing court found that the jury had been properly instructed. The court affirmed the award but remanded the case for a reconsideration of the proper amount of punitive damages.[11] ●

INADEQUATE WARNINGS A product may also be deemed defective because of inadequate instructions or warnings. A product will be considered defective "when the foreseeable risks of harm posed by the product could have been reduced or avoided by the provision of reasonable instructions or warnings by the seller or other distributor, or a predecessor in the commercial chain of distribution, and the omission of the instructions or warnings renders the product not reasonably safe."[12] Generally, a seller must also warn consumers of the harm that can result from the *foreseeable misuse* of its product.

Important factors for a court to consider include the risks of a product, the "content and comprehensibility" and "intensity of expression" of warnings and instructions, and the "characteristics of expected user groups."[13] Courts apply a "reasonableness" test to determine if the warnings adequately alert consumers to the product's risks. For example, children will likely respond more readily to bright, bold, simple warning labels, while educated adults might need more detailed information.

There is no duty to warn about risks that are obvious or commonly known. Warnings about such risks do not add to the safety of a product and could even detract from it by making other warnings seem less significant. The obviousness of a risk and a user's decision to proceed in the face of that risk may be a defense in a product liability suit based on a warning defect. (This defense and other defenses in product liability suits will be discussed later in this chapter.)

An action alleging that a product is defective due to an inadequate label can be based on state law. For a discussion of a case involving a state law that required warning labels on violent video games, see this chapter's *Adapting the Law to the Online Environment* feature on the following page.

Market-Share Liability

Generally, in all cases involving product liability, a plaintiff must prove that the defective product that caused her or his injury was the product of a specific defendant. In a few situations, however, courts have dropped this requirement when a plaintiff cannot prove which of many distributors of a harmful product supplied the particular product that caused the injuries. Under a theory of **market-share liability,** all firms that manufactured and distributed the product during the period in question are held liable for the plaintiff's injuries in proportion to the firms' respective shares of the market for that product during that period.

CASE EXAMPLE 15.12 A man with hemophilia (a blood-clotting disorder) received injections of a blood protein known as antihemophiliac factor (AHF) concentrate. When he later tested positive for the AIDS (acquired immune deficiency syndrome) virus, he sued. Because it was not known which manufacturer was responsible for the particular AHF received by the plaintiff, the court held that all of the manufacturers of AHF could be held liable under a market-share theory of liability.[14] ●

Courts in many jurisdictions do not recognize this theory of liability, believing that it deviates too significantly from

10. *Gillespie v. Sears, Roebuck & Co.,* 386 F.3d 21 (1st Cir. 2004).
11. *Bullock v. Philip Morris USA, Inc.,* 159 Cal.App.4th 655, 71 Cal.Rptr.3d 775 (2008).
12. *Restatement (Third) of Torts: Products Liability,* Section 2(c).
13. *Restatement (Third) of Torts: Products Liability,* Section 2, Comment h.
14. *Smith v. Cutter Biological, Inc.,* 72 Haw. 416, 823 P.2d 717 (1991). See also *Sutowski v. Eli Lilly & Co.,* 92 Ohio St.3d 347, 696 N.E.2d 187 (1998); and *In re Methyl Tertiary Butyl Ether (MTBE) Products Liability Litigation,* 447 F.Supp.2d 289 (S.D.N.Y. 2006).

Adapting the Law to the Online Environment

Should Video Games Be Required to Have Warning Labels?

Just about any product that you purchase in the physical world has one or more warning labels. Indeed, some critics argue that these labels have become so long and so ubiquitous that consumers now ignore them. In other words, putting warnings on just about everything defeats their original purpose. In the online environment, warning labels are not so extensive—at least not yet.

So far, video games have largely escaped mandated warning labels, although the video game industry has instituted a voluntary rating system to provide consumers and retailers with information about a video game's content. The Entertainment Software Rating Board assigns each video game one of six age-specific ratings, ranging from "Early Childhood" to "Adults Only."

Should video games, whether they are downloaded from the manufacturer's site or bought on a CD-ROM or DVD, have additional warnings that would advise potential users (or their parents) that the games might be overly violent? When the California legislature enacted a new law imposing restrictions and a labeling requirement on the sale or rental of "violent video games" to minors, this issue became paramount.[a]

Video Software Dealers Sue the State

Immediately after the labeling requirement was enacted, the Video Software Dealers Association, along with the Entertainment Software Association, brought a suit in federal district court seeking to invalidate the law. The court granted summary judgment in favor of the plaintiffs and also denied California's cross motion for summary judgment in its favor.

The act defined a violent video game as one in which "the range of options available to a player includes killing, maiming, dismembering, or sexually assaulting an image of a human being." While agreeing that some video games are unquestionably violent by everyday standards, the trial court pointed out, as did the federal court that heard the appeal, that many video games are based on popular novels or motion pictures and have extensive plot lines.

Accordingly, the court found that the definition of a violent video game was unconstitutionally vague and thus violated the First Amendment's guarantee of freedom of speech. The court also noted the existence of the voluntary rating system. The state appealed, but the U.S. Court of Appeals for the Ninth Circuit also found that the statute's definition of a violent video game was unconstitutionally broad.[b] The state appealed again.

The United States Supreme Court's Decision

In 2011, the United States Supreme Court affirmed the decision in favor of video game and software industries. The Court noted that video games are entitled to First Amendment protection. Because California had failed to show that the statute was justified by a compelling government interest and that the law was narrowly tailored to serve that interest, the Court ruled that the statute was unconstitutional.[c]

FOR CRITICAL ANALYSIS

Why would some legislators believe that the six-part voluntary labeling system for video games is not sufficient to protect minors?

a. California Civil Code Sections 1746–1746.5.

b. *Video Software Dealers Association v. Schwarzenegger*, 556 F.3d 950 (9th Cir. 2009).

c. *Brown v. Entertainment Merchants Association*, ___ U.S. ___, 131 S.Ct. 2729, 180 L.Ed.2d 708 (2011).

traditional legal principles.[15] In jurisdictions that do recognize market-share liability, it is usually applied in cases involving drugs or chemicals, when it is difficult or impossible to determine which company made a particular product.

Other Applications of Strict Liability

Almost all courts extend the strict liability of manufacturers and other sellers to injured bystanders. **EXAMPLE 15.13** A forklift that Trent is operating will not go into reverse, and as a result, it runs into a bystander. In this situation, the bystander can sue the manufacturer of the defective forklift under strict liability (and possibly bring a negligence action against the forklift operator as well). •

Strict liability also applies to suppliers of component parts. **EXAMPLE 15.14** Toyota buys brake pads from a subcontractor and puts them in Corollas without changing their composition. If those pads are defective, both the supplier of the brake pads and Toyota will be held strictly liable for the injuries caused by the defects. •

Defenses to Product Liability

Defendants in product liability suits can raise a number of defenses. One defense, of course, is to show that there is no basis for the plaintiff's claim. For example, in a product

15. For the Illinois Supreme Court's position on market-share liability, see *Smith v. Eli Lilly & Co.*, 137 Ill.2d 252, 560 N.E.2d 324, 148 Ill.Dec. 22 (1990). Pennsylvania law also does not recognize market-share liability. See *Bortell v. Eli Lilly & Co.*, 406 F.Supp.2d 1 (D.D.C. 2005).

liability case based on negligence, if a defendant can show that the plaintiff has *not* met the requirements (such as causation) for an action in negligence, generally the defendant will not be liable. Similarly, in a case involving strict product liability, a defendant can claim that the plaintiff failed to meet one of the requirements. If the defendant, for instance, establishes that the goods were altered after they were sold, the defendant normally will not be held liable.[16] A defendant may also assert that the statute of limitations for a product liability claim has lapsed.[17] Several other defenses may also be available to defendants, as discussed next. Today, some defendants are raising the defense of preemption—that government regulations preempt claims for product liability.

16. See, for example, *Edmondson v. Macclesfield L-P Gas Co.*, 642 S.E.2d 265 (N.C.App. 2007); and *Pichardo v. C. S. Brown Co.*, 35 A.D.3d 303, 827 N.Y.S.2d 131 (N.Y.App. 2006).

17. Similar state statutes, called *statutes of repose,* place outer time limits on product liability actions.

Assumption of Risk

Assumption of risk can sometimes be used as a defense in a product liability action. To establish such a defense, the defendant must show that (1) the plaintiff knew and appreciated the risk created by the product defect and (2) the plaintiff voluntarily assumed the risk, even though it was unreasonable to do so. (See Chapter 4 for a more detailed discussion of assumption of risk.)

In the following case, an injured user of a tanning booth had signed an *exculpatory clause* (see page 172 in Chapter 9) stating that she was using the booth at her own risk and that she released the manufacturer, among others, from any liability for injuries. The issue before the court was whether a manufacturer, by means of an exculpatory clause, could be relieved from strict product liability for faulty products.

Case 15.3 Boles v. Sun Ergoline, Inc.

Supreme Court of Colorado, 222 P.3d 724 (2010).

FACTS Executive Tans operated an upright tanning booth, which was manufactured by Sun Ergoline, Inc. Before using the booth, Savannah Boles signed a release form provided by Executive Tans that contained the following exculpatory agreement: "I have read the instructions for proper use of the tanning facilities and do so at my own risk and hereby release the owners, operators, franchisor, or manufacturers, from any damage or harm that I might incur due to use of the facilities." After Boles entered the booth, several of her fingers came in contact with an exhaust fan located at the top of the booth, partially amputating them. Boles sued Sun Ergoline in a Colorado state court, asserting a strict product liability claim for personal injury. Sun Ergoline moved for summary judgment on the ground that Boles's claim was barred by the release that she had signed before using its product. The trial court agreed and granted Sun Ergoline's motion. The court of appeals affirmed the trial court's judgment, finding that the language of the release was broad enough to include any damage or harm that might occur due to Boles's use of the facilities. The court of appeals also found no violation of public policy. Boles appealed to the Colorado Supreme Court.

ISSUE Was Boles's strict product liability claim against the manufacturer of a tanning booth that partially amputated her fingers barred by assumption of risk because she had signed an exculpatory clause?

DECISION No. The Supreme Court of Colorado reversed the judgment of the appellate court and directed it to remand the case for further proceedings consistent with its opinion. The court concluded that, as a matter of public policy, assumption of risk (via the exculpatory clause) was not appropriate in a strict liability context.

REASON The reviewing court reasoned that strict product liability "is premised on the concept of enterprise liability for casting a defective product into the stream of commerce." In a strict product liability situation, the focus is on the nature of the product rather than on the conduct of the manufacturer or the person injured. The court also stated that strict product liability is driven by public policy considerations. One such consideration is the deliberate creation of economic incentives for manufacturers to improve product safety and take advantage of their unique "position to spread the risk of loss among all who use the product." The *Restatement (Third) of Torts* prohibits exculpatory agreements that bar or reduce otherwise valid product liability claims for personal injuries made by ordinary consumers against sellers or distributors of new products. "An agreement releasing the manufacturer from strict product liability for personal injury, in exchange for nothing more than an individual consumer's right to have or use the product, necessarily violates the public policy of this jurisdiction and is void."

FOR CRITICAL ANALYSIS—Ethical Consideration *Why would the enforcement of the exculpatory clause in this case conflict with the rationale underlying strict product liability?*

Product Misuse

Similar to the defense of voluntary assumption of risk is that of product misuse, which occurs when a product is used for a purpose for which it was not intended. The courts have severely limited this defense, however, and it is now recognized as a defense only when the particular use was not reasonably foreseeable. If the misuse is foreseeable, the seller must take measures to guard against it.

Comparative Negligence (Fault)

Developments in the area of comparative negligence, or fault (discussed in Chapter 4), have also affected the doctrine of strict liability. In the past, the plaintiff's conduct was not a defense to liability for a defective product. Today, courts in many jurisdictions consider the negligent or intentional actions of both the plaintiff and the defendant when apportioning liability and awarding damages.[18] This means that a defendant may be able to limit at least some of its liability for injuries caused by its defective product if it can show that the plaintiff's misuse of the product contributed to the injuries. When proved, comparative negligence differs from other defenses in that it does not completely absolve the defendant of liability, but it can reduce the amount of damages that will be awarded to the plaintiff.

CASE EXAMPLE 15.15 Dan Smith, a mechanic in Alaska, was not wearing a hard hat at work when he was asked to start a diesel engine of an air compressor. Because the compressor was an older model, he had to prop open a door to start it. When Smith got the engine started, the door fell from its position and hit his head. The injury caused him to suffer from seizures and epilepsy. Smith sued the manufacturer, claiming that the engine was defectively designed. The manufacturer argued that Smith had been negligent by failing to wear his hard hat and by propping the door open in an unsafe manner. Smith's attorney claimed that the plaintiff's ordinary negligence could not be used as a defense in product liability cases, but the Alaska Supreme Court disagreed. Alaska, like many other states, allows comparative negligence to be raised as a defense in product liability lawsuits.[19] •

Commonly Known Dangers

The dangers associated with certain products (such as sharp knives and guns) are so commonly known that manufacturers need not warn users of those dangers. If a defendant succeeds in convincing the court that a plaintiff's injury resulted from a commonly known danger, the defendant normally will not be liable.

CASE EXAMPLE 15.16 A classic case on this issue involved a plaintiff who was injured when an elastic exercise rope that she had purchased slipped off her foot and struck her in the eye, causing a detachment of the retina. The plaintiff claimed that the manufacturer should be liable because it had failed to warn users that the exercise rope might slip off a foot in such a manner. The court stated that to hold the manufacturer liable in these circumstances "would go beyond the reasonable dictates of justice in fixing the liabilities of manufacturers." After all, stated the court, "[a]lmost every physical object can be inherently dangerous or potentially dangerous in a sense. . . . A manufacturer cannot manufacture a knife that will not cut or a hammer that will not mash a thumb or a stove that will not burn a finger. The law does not require [manufacturers] to warn of such common dangers."[20] •

Knowledgeable User

A related defense is the *knowledgeable user* defense. If a particular danger (such as electrical shock) is or should be commonly known by particular users of the product (such as electricians), the manufacturer of electrical equipment need not warn these users of the danger.

CASE EXAMPLE 15.17 The parents of a group of teenagers who had become overweight and developed health problems filed a product liability lawsuit against McDonald's. The teenagers claimed that the well-known fast-food chain should be held liable for failing to warn customers of the adverse health effects of eating its food products. The court rejected this claim, however, based on the knowledgeable user defense. The court found that it is well known that the food at McDonald's contains high levels of cholesterol, fat, salt, and sugar and is therefore unhealthful. The court's opinion, which thwarted numerous future lawsuits against fast-food restaurants, stated: "If consumers know (or reasonably should know) the potential ill health effects of eating at McDonald's, they cannot blame McDonald's if they, nonetheless, choose to satiate [satisfy] their appetite with a surfeit [excess] of super-sized McDonald's products."[21] •

---

18. See, for example, *Industrial Risk Insurers v. American Engineering Testing, Inc.*, 318 Wis.2d 148, 769 N.W.2d 82 (Wis.App. 2009).

19. *Smith v. Ingersoll-Rand Co.*, 14 P.3d 990 (Alaska 2000). See also *Winschel v. Brown*, 171 P.3d 142 (Alaska 2007).

20. *Jamieson v. Woodward & Lothrop*, 247 F.2d 23, 101 D.C.App. 32 (1957).

21. *Pelman v. McDonald's Corp.*, 237 F.Supp.2d 512 (S.D.N.Y. 2003).

Reviewing . . . Warranties and Product Liability

Shalene Kolchek bought a Great Lakes Spa from Val Porter, a dealer who was selling spas at the state fair. Porter told Kolchek that Great Lakes spas are "top of the line" and "the Cadillac of spas" and indicated that the spa she was buying was "fully warranted for three years." Kolchek signed an installment sale contract; then Porter handed her the manufacturer's paperwork and arranged for the spa to be delivered and installed for her. Three months later, Kolchek noticed that one corner of the spa was leaking onto her new deck and causing damage. She complained to Porter, but he did nothing about the problem. Kolchek's family continued to use the spa. Using the information presented in the chapter, answer the following questions.

1. Did Porter's statement that the spa was "top of the line" and "the Cadillac of spas" create any type of warranty? Why or why not?
2. Did Porter breach the implied warranty of merchantability? Why or why not?
3. One night, Kolchek's six-year-old daughter, Litisha, was in the spa with her mother. Litisha's hair became entangled in the spa's drain, and she was sucked down and held under water for a prolonged period, causing her to suffer brain damage. Under which theory or theories of product liability can Kolchek sue Porter to recover for Litisha's injuries?
4. If Kolchek had negligently left Litisha alone in the spa before the incident described in the previous question, what defense to liability might Porter assert?

Terms and Concepts

express warranty 270
implied warranty 270
implied warranty of fitness for a particular purpose 272
implied warranty of merchantability 270
lien 269
market-share liability 277
product liability 274
unreasonably dangerous product 276

Chapter Summary: Warranties and Product Liability

WARRANTIES	
Warranties of Title (See pages 269–270.)	In most sales, sellers warrant that they have good and valid title to the goods sold and that transfer of the title is rightful [UCC 2–312(1)(a)]. A second warranty of title shields buyers and lessees who are *unaware* of any encumbrances, or liens, against goods at the time the contract is made [UCC 2–312(1)(b), 2A–211(1)]. Third, when the seller or lessor is a merchant, he or she automatically warrants that the buyer or lessee takes the goods *free of infringements* [UCC 2–312(3), 2A–211(2)].
Express Warranties (See page 270.)	Under the UCC, an express warranty arises under the UCC when a seller or lessor indicates, as part of the basis of the bargain, any of the following [UCC 2–313, 2A–210]: 1. An affirmation or promise of fact. 2. A description of the goods. 3. A sample shown as conforming to the contract goods.
Implied Warranty of Merchantability (See pages 270–271.)	When a seller or lessor is a merchant who deals in goods of the kind sold or leased, the seller or lessor warrants that the goods sold or leased are properly packaged and labeled, are of proper quality, and are reasonably fit for the ordinary purposes for which such goods are used [UCC 2–314, 2A–212].
Implied Warranty of Fitness for a Particular Purpose (See page 272.)	Arises when the buyer's or lessee's purpose or use is expressly or impliedly known by the seller or lessor, and the buyer or lessee purchases or leases the goods in reliance on the seller's or lessor's selection [UCC 2–315, 2A–213]. Other implied warranties can arise as a result of course of dealing or usage of trade [UCC 2–314(3), 2A–212(3)].
Overlapping Warranties (See page 272.)	The UCC construes warranties as cumulative if they are consistent with each other. If warranties are inconsistent, then express warranties take precedence over implied warranties, except for the implied warranty of fitness for a particular purpose. Also, samples take precedence over general descriptions, and exact or technical specifications displace inconsistent samples or general descriptions.

Continued

Chapter Summary: Warranties and Product Liability—Continued

Warranty Disclaimers (See pages 272–273.)	Express warranties can be disclaimed in language that is clear and conspicuous and called to the buyer's or lessee's attention at the time the contract is formed. A disclaimer of the implied warranty of merchantability must specifically mention the word *merchantability.* The disclaimer need not be in writing, but if it is written, it must be conspicuous. A disclaimer of the implied warranty of fitness *must* be in writing and be conspicuous, though it need not mention the word *fitness*.
Magnuson-Moss Warranty Act (See page 273.)	Under the Magnuson-Moss Warranty Act, express written warranties covering consumer goods priced at more than $25, *if made,* must be labeled as one of the following: 1. Full warranty—Free repair or replacement of defective parts; refund or replacement for goods if they cannot be repaired in a reasonable time. 2. Limited warranty—When less than a full warranty is being offered.
PRODUCT LIABILITY	
Liability Based on Negligence or Misrepresentation (See pages 274–275.)	1. The manufacturer must use due care in designing the product, selecting materials, using the appropriate production process, assembling and testing the product, and placing adequate warnings on the label or product. 2. Privity of contract is not required. A manufacturer is liable for failure to exercise due care to any person who sustains an injury proximately caused by a negligently made (defective) product. 3. Fraudulent misrepresentation of a product may result in product liability based on the tort of fraud.
Requirements for Strict Liability (See pages 275–276.)	1. The defendant must sell the product in a defective condition. 2. The defendant must normally be engaged in the business of selling that product. 3. The product must be unreasonably dangerous to the user or consumer because of its defective condition (in most states). 4. The plaintiff must incur physical harm to self or property by use or consumption of the product. 5. The defective condition must be the proximate cause of the injury or damage. 6. The goods must not have been substantially changed from the time the product was sold to the time the injury was sustained.
Product Defects—*Restatement (Third) of Torts* (See pages 276–277.)	A product may be defective in three basic ways: 1. In its manufacture. 2. In its design. 3. In the instructions or warnings that come with it.
Market-Share Liability (See pages 277–278.)	When plaintiffs cannot prove which of many distributors of a defective product supplied the particular product that caused the plaintiffs' injuries, some courts apply market-share liability. All firms that manufactured and distributed the harmful product during the period in question are then held liable for the plaintiffs' injuries in proportion to the firms' respective shares of the market, as directed by the court.
Other Applications of Strict Liability (See page 278.)	1. Manufacturers and other sellers are liable for harms suffered by bystanders as a result of defective products. 2. Suppliers of component parts are strictly liable for defective parts that, when incorporated into a product, cause injuries to users.
Defenses to Product Liability (See pages 278–280.)	1. *Assumption of risk*—The user or consumer knew of the risk of harm and voluntarily assumed it. 2. *Product misuse*—The user or consumer misused the product in a way unforeseeable by the manufacturer. 3. *Comparative negligence*—Liability may be distributed between the plaintiff and the defendant under the doctrine of comparative negligence if the plaintiff's misuse of the product contributed to the risk of injury. 4. *Commonly known dangers*—If a defendant succeeds in convincing the court that a plaintiff's injury resulted from a commonly known danger, such as the danger associated with using a sharp knife, the defendant will not be liable. 5. *Knowledgeable user*—If a particular danger is or should be commonly known by particular users of the product, the manufacturer of the product need not warn these users of the danger.

ExamPrep

ISSUE SPOTTERS

—Check your answers to these questions against the answers provided in Appendix G.

1 Rim Corporation makes tire rims, which it sells to Superior Vehicles, Inc., who installs them onto cars. One set of rims is defective, which an inspection would reveal. Superior does not inspect the rims. The car with the defective rims is sold to Town Auto Sales, which sells the car to Uri. Soon, the car is in an accident caused by the defective rims, and Uri is injured. Is Superior Vehicles liable? Explain your answer.

2 Real Chocolate Company makes a box of candy, which it sells to Sweet Things, Inc., a distributor. Sweet sells the box to a Tasty Candy store, where Jill buys it. Jill gives it to Ken, who breaks a tooth on a stone the same size and color as a piece of the candy. If Real, Sweet, and Tasty were not negligent, can they be liable for the injury? Why or why not?

BEFORE THE TEST

Go to **www.cengagebrain.com**, enter the ISBN 9781111530624, and click on "Find" to locate this textbook's Web site. Then, click on "Access Now" under "Study Tools," and select Chapter 15 at the top. There, you will find an Interactive Quiz that you can take to assess your mastery of the concepts in this chapter, as well as Flashcards and a Glossary of important terms.

For Review

1 What factors determine whether a seller's or lessor's statement constitutes an express warranty or mere puffery?
2 What implied warranties arise under the UCC?
3 Can a manufacturer be held liable to any person who suffers an injury proximately caused by the manufacturer's negligently made product?
4 What are the elements of a cause of action in strict product liability?
5 What defenses to liability can be raised in a product liability lawsuit?

Questions and Case Problems

15–1 Product Liability. Carmen buys a television set manufactured by AKI Electronics. She is going on vacation, so she takes the set to her mother's house for her mother to use. Because the set is defective, it explodes, causing considerable damage to her mother's house. Carmen's mother sues AKI for the damage to her house. Discuss the theories under which Carmen's mother can recover from AKI.

15–2 Warranty Disclaimers. Tandy purchased a washing machine from Marshall Appliances. The sales contract included a provision explicitly disclaiming all express or implied warranties, including the implied warranty of merchantability. The disclaimer was printed in the same size and color as the rest of the contract. The machine turned out to be a "lemon" and never functioned properly. Tandy sought a refund of the purchase price, claiming that Marshall had breached the implied warranty of merchantability. Can Tandy recover her money, notwithstanding the warranty disclaimer in the contract? Explain.

15–3 Product Liability. Jason Clark, an experienced hunter, bought a paintball gun. Clark practiced with the gun and knew how to screw in the carbon dioxide cartridge, pump the gun, and use its safety and trigger. Although Clark was aware that he could purchase protective eyewear, he chose not to buy it. Clark had taken gun safety courses and understood that it was "common sense" not to shoot anyone in the face. Clark's friend, Chris Wright, also owned a paintball gun and was similarly familiar with the gun's use and its risks. Clark, Wright, and their friends played a game that involved shooting paintballs at cars whose occupants also had the guns. One night, while Clark and Wright were cruising with their guns, Wright shot at Clark's car, but hit Clark in the eye. Clark filed a product liability lawsuit against the manufacturer of Wright's paintball gun to recover for the injury. Clark claimed that the gun was defectively designed. During the trial, Wright testified that his gun "never malfunctioned." In whose favor should the court rule? Why?

15–4 Express Warranties. Videotape is recorded magnetically. The magnetic particles that constitute the recorded image are bound to the tape's polyester base. The binder that holds the particles to the base breaks down over time. This breakdown, which is called sticky shed syndrome, causes the image to deteriorate. The Walt Disney Co. made many of its movies available on tape. Buena Vista Home Entertainment, Inc., sold the tapes, which it described as part of a "Gold Collection" or "Masterpiece Collection." The advertising included such statements as "Give Your Children The Memories Of A Lifetime—Collect Each Timeless Masterpiece!" and "Available

For A Limited Time Only!" Charmaine Schreib and others who bought the tapes filed a suit in an Illinois state court against Disney and Buena Vista, alleging, among other things, breach of warranty. The plaintiffs claimed that the defendants' marketing promised the tapes would last for generations. In reality, the tapes were as subject to sticky shed syndrome as other tapes. Did the ads create an express warranty? In whose favor should the court rule on this issue? Explain. [*Schreib v. The Walt Disney Co.*, __ N.E.2d __ (Ill.App. 1 Dist. 2006)]

15–5 **Case Problem with Sample Answer** Peter and Tanya Rothing operate Diamond R Stables near Belgrade, Montana, where they bred, trained, and sold horses. Arnold Kallestad owns a ranch in Gallatin County, Montana, where he grows hay and grain, and raises Red Angus cattle. For more than twenty years, Kallestad has sold between 300 and 1,000 tons of hay annually, sometimes advertising it for sale in the *Bozeman Daily Chronicle*. In 2001, the Rothings bought hay from Kallestad for $90 a ton. They received delivery on April 23. In less than two weeks, at least nine of the Rothings' horses exhibited symptoms of poisoning that was diagnosed as botulism. Before the outbreak was over, nineteen animals died. Robert Whitlock, associate professor of medicine and the director of the Botulism Laboratory at the University of Pennsylvania, concluded that Kallestad's hay was the source. The Rothings filed a suit in a Montana state court against Kallestad, claiming, in part, breach of the implied warranty of merchantability. Kallestad asked the court to dismiss this claim on the ground that, if botulism had been present, it had been in no way foreseeable. Should the court grant this request? Why or why not? [*Rothing v. Kallestad*, 337 Mont. 193, 159 P.3d 222 (2007)]

—For a sample answer to Problem 15–5, go to Appendix F at the end of this text.

15–6 **Defenses to Product Liability.** Terry Kunkle and VanBuren High School hosted a Christmas party in Berkeley County, South Carolina. Guests had drinks and hors d'oeuvres at a residence and adjourned to dinner in a barn across a public road. Brandon Stroud ferried the guests to the barn in a golf car made by Textron, Inc. The golf car was not equipped with lights, and Textron did not warn against its use on public roads at night. South Carolina does not require golf cars to be equipped with lights, but does ban their operation on public roads at night. As Stroud attempted to cross the road at 8:30 P.M., his golf car was struck by a vehicle driven by Joseph Thornley. Stroud was killed. His estate filed a suit in a South Carolina state court against Textron, alleging strict product liability and product liability based on negligence. The estate claimed that the golf car was defective and unreasonably dangerous. What might Textron assert in its defense? Explain. [*Moore v. Barony House Restaurant, LLC*, 382 S.C. 35, 674 S.E.2d 500 (S.C.App. 2009)]

15–7 **Product Liability.** Yun Tung Chow tried to unclog a floor drain in the kitchen of the restaurant where he worked. He used a drain cleaner called Lewis Red Devil Lye that contained crystalline sodium hydroxide. The product label said to wear eye protection, to put one tablespoon of lye directly into the drain, and to keep your face away from the drain because there could be dangerous backsplash. Not wearing eye protection, Chow mixed three spoonfuls of lye in a can and poured that mixture down the drain while bending over it. Liquid splashed back into his face, causing injury. He sued for product liability based on inadequate warnings and a design defect. The trial court granted summary judgment to the manufacturer; Chow appealed. An expert for Chow stated that the product was defective because it had a tendency to backsplash. Is that a convincing argument? Why or why not? [*Yun Tung Chow v. Reckitt & Coleman, Inc.*, 69 A.D.3d 413, 891 N.Y.S.2d 402 (N.Y.A.D. 1 Dept. 2010)]

15–8 **Theory of Recovery.** David Dobrovolny bought a Ford F-350 pickup truck from Ainsworth Motors in Ainsworth, Nebraska. Fourteen months later, the truck spontaneously caught fire in his driveway. No one was injured, and no property other than the truck was damaged, but the truck was completely destroyed. Dobrovolny filed a suit in a Nebraska state court against Ford Motor Co. on a theory of strict product liability, alleging that the truck's electrical system and other potential ignition sources had not been properly insulated from the combustible materials in the engine. Dobrovolny sought to recover the cost of the truck. Nebraska recognizes strict product liability, but the state's courts limit its application to situations involving personal injuries rather than property damage. How is the court likely to rule on Dobrovolny's claim? Why? Is there another basis for liability discussed in this chapter on which Dobrovolny might recover? [*Dobrovolny v. Ford Motor Co.*, 281 Neb. 86, 793 N.W.2d 445 (2011)]

15–9 **A Question of Ethics** *Susan Calles lived with her four daughters, Amanda, age 11, Victoria, age 5, and Jenna and Jillian, age 3. In March 1998, Calles bought an Aim N Flame utility lighter, which she stored on the top shelf of her kitchen cabinet. A trigger can ignite the Aim N Flame after an "ON/OFF" switch is slid to the "on" position. On the night of March 31, Calles and Victoria left to get videos. Jenna and Jillian were in bed, and Amanda was watching television. Calles returned to find fire trucks and emergency vehicles around her home. Robert Finn, a fire investigator, determined that Jenna had started a fire using the lighter. Jillian suffered smoke inhalation, was hospitalized, and died on April 21. Calles filed a suit in an Illinois state court against Scripto-Tokai Corp., which distributed the Aim N Flame, and others. In her suit, which was grounded in part in strict liability claims, Calles alleged that the lighter was an "unreasonably dangerous product." Scripto filed a motion for summary judgment. [*Calles v. Scripto-Tokai Corp.*, *224 Ill.2d 247, 864 N.E.2d 249, 309 Ill.Dec. 383 (2007)]*

1 A product is "unreasonably dangerous" when it is dangerous beyond the expectation of the ordinary consumer. Whose expectation—Calles's or Jenna's—applies here? Why? Does the lighter pass this test? Explain.

2 A product is also "unreasonably dangerous" when a less dangerous alternative was economically feasible for its maker, who failed to produce it. Scripto contended that because its product was "simple" and the danger was "obvious," it should not be liable under this test. Do you agree? Why or why not?

3 Calles presented evidence as to the likelihood and seriousness of injury from lighters that do not have child-safety devices. Scripto argued that the Aim N Flame is a useful, inexpensive, alternative source of fire and is safer than a match. Calles admitted that she was aware of the dangers presented by lighters in the hands of children. Scripto admitted that it had been a defendant in at least twenty-five suits for injuries that occurred under similar circumstances. With these factors in mind, how should the court rule? Why?

15–10 VIDEO **Video Question** To watch this chapter's video, *Matilda,* go to **www.cengagebrain.com**. Register the access code that came with your new book or log in to your existing account. Select the link for the "Business Law Digital Video Library Online Access" or "Business Law CourseMate." Click on "Complete Video List," view Video 71, and then answer the following questions:

1 What warranties of title arise in the sales of used cars by dealers?

2 In the video, a father (Danny DeVito) uses a tool to turn back the numbers on a vehicle's odometer. When he sells this car, if he tells the buyer the mileage is only 60,000 knowing that it is really 120,000, has he breached an express warranty? What if the seller did not make any oral statements about the car's mileage, could the buyer claim an express warranty existed? Explain.

3 What would a person who buys the car in the video have to show to prove that the seller breached the implied warranty of merchantability?

Unit Four Unit Case Study with Dissenting Opinion: *Casserlie v. Shell Oil Co.*

As discussed in Chapter 13, in contrast to the rule under the common law of contracts, a contract for a sale of goods will not fail for indefiniteness even if one or more of its terms are left open. For example, under Section 2–305(1) of the Uniform Commercial Code (UCC), if the parties have not agreed on a price, a court will determine a "reasonable price at the time for delivery." If either the buyer or the seller is to determine the price, the price is to be set in good faith [UCC 2–305(2)]. In this context, good faith *means "honesty in fact and the observance of reasonable commercial standards of fair dealing in the trade" [UCC 2–103(1)(b)].*

In this Unit Case Study with Dissenting Opinion, *we review the case of* Casserlie v. Shell Oil Co.,[1] *in which a group of service station dealers brought an action against a gasoline distributor, claiming that the distributor engaged in bad faith in setting the price of gas under the open term provision of their contracts. Is a subjective inquiry into the distributor's motive required to make this determination?*

1. 121 Ohio St.3d 55, 902 N.E.2d 1 (2009).

CASE BACKGROUND

Donald Casserlie is one of a group of independent Shell Oil Company service station lessee-dealers in Cleveland, Ohio. The dealers lease gas stations, including equipment and land, from Shell.

In the 1990s, they contracted to buy gas only from Shell at a price set by Shell at the time of delivery. Shell charged the dealers a price that was based on such factors as the price of its competitor British Petroleum and the street price of gas in Cleveland. The price was referred to as the dealer-tank-wagon (DTW) price because it included the cost of delivery of the gas to the stations. Shell also sells gas to jobbers, which are independent companies operating non-Shell-owned gas stations. Jobbers buy gas at the oil company's terminal and thus pay the "rack price," which does not include delivery costs.

Casserlie and other dealers filed a suit in an Ohio state court against Shell, alleging that the DTW prices were being set in bad faith. The dealers contended that the pricing was commercially unreasonable and part of a plan to drive them out of business. They charged that Shell's goal was to take over the gas stations to profit from all of the sales, including nonfuel sales, not just from wholesale gas sales and rental income. The court issued a summary judgment in Shell's favor. A state intermediate appellate court affirmed the judgment. The dealers appealed to the Ohio Supreme Court.

MAJORITY OPINION

MOYER, C.J. [Chief Justice]

* * * *

It is not disputed that the latter half of the definition of good faith, "the observance of reasonable commercial standards of fair dealing in the trade," requires only an objective analysis. The issue before us is whether there is room for a subjective inquiry within the honesty-in-fact analysis in these circumstances.

The UCC does not define the term "honesty in fact."

Comment 3 to UCC 2–305 * * * provides, * * * "In the normal case a 'posted price' or a future seller's or buyer's 'given price,' 'price in effect,' 'market price,' or the like satisfies the good faith requirement."

Comment 3 * * * provides a safe harbor where a "posted price" satisfies good faith in its entirety.

* * * *

* * * By its language, the safe harbor does not apply when it is not the "normal case" or when the price setter is not imposing a "posted price," "given price," "price in effect," "market price," or the like. *As long as a price is commercially reasonable, it qualifies as the "normal case."* The touchstone of prices set through open-price-term contracts under UCC 2–305(2) is reasonableness. *A price that is nondiscriminatory among similarly situated buyers correspondingly qualifies as a "posted price" or the like.* A discriminatory price could not be considered a "posted" or "market" price, because, in effect, the seller is not being "honest in fact" about the price that it is charging as a posted price, since it is charging a different price to other buyers. [Emphasis added.]

Therefore, a price that is both commercially reasonable and nondiscriminatory fits within the limits of the safe harbor and complies with the statute's good-faith requirement.

* * * *

The facts of this case demonstrate that the prices set by Shell were both commercially reasonable and nondiscriminatory. * * * The only evidence of bad faith was that the prices set were too high for dealers to remain profitable and compete with jobbers in the Cleveland area. However, Shell is not required to sell gasoline at a price that is profitable for buyers. A good-faith price under UCC 2–305 is not synonymous with a fair market price or the lowest price available. * * * The DTW prices set by the company were within the range set by its competitors.

* * * *

* * * The only other argument of discrimination put forth by the dealers is that jobbers were charged significantly less, specifically, the rack price rather than the DTW price. Jobbers and dealers are not, however, similarly situated buyers. The price difference is partially explained by the fact that the DTW price includes a delivery charge, while the rack price does not. * * * Jobbers perform additional functions compared to dealers, such as maintaining the properties they own and bearing the risk of environmental liability. Because jobbers relieve Shell of these obligations, they are charged a lower price.

* * * *

When a price that has been left open in a contract is fixed at a price posted by a seller or buyer, and the posted price is both commercially reasonable and nondiscriminatory, the price setter has acted in good faith as required by [UCC 2–305(2)] and a subjective inquiry into the motives of the price setter is not permitted. In this case, the dealers have not provided any evidence that the prices set by Shell were commercially unreasonable or discriminatory. The posted-price safe harbor therefore applies, and we affirm the judgment of the court of appeals.

DISSENTING OPINION

***PFEIFER*, J. [Justice], dissenting.**

* * * *

"Good faith" is generally treated as incorporating both subjective and objective standards. Although [UCC 2–305] deals exclusively with open-price terms, it does not define "good faith" differently from its customary meaning. Many different jurisdictions in many different contexts, including in the context of an open-price term, define "good faith" as requiring both subjective and objective analysis.

* * * The courts agree that it is not possible to determine whether a party acted in "good faith" without a subjective inquiry.

* * * *

"Good faith" in the context of open-price terms should be subject to both objective and subjective inquiry. Even courts and commentators who have written in favor of the safe-harbor presumption have concluded that an intent to drive a contractual partner out of business might overcome the presumption. I can conceive of situations in which nondiscriminatory pricing could violate "good faith." For instance, in this case, it is alleged that Shell charged all of its similarly situated [dealers] the same price, and it is alleged that that price was set too high for them to profitably operate a gas station. In that situation, even though the pricing was nondiscriminatory, it was designed to drive a contractual partner out of business.

* * * A court's analysis of a merchant's good faith, then, should be both subjective and objective. Furthermore, the safe-harbor presumption * * * only applies in the normal case; at a minimum, the appellants should be allowed to attempt to establish that this is not a normal case. I would reverse the judgment of the court of appeals and remand the case for further consideration.

QUESTIONS FOR ANALYSIS

1. **Law.** What was the majority's reasoning in this case? How did this affect the outcome?
2. **Law.** Why did the dissent disagree with the majority? If the court had adopted the dissent's position, how would this have affected the result?
3. **Technology.** By what method could the distributor ensure the most immediate payment for its products from the dealers?
4. **Economic Dimensions.** If the distributor granted credit to the dealers, how might it guarantee or secure payment for its products on default?
5. **Implications for the Businessperson.** How might tariffs levied on imported oil affect the price of gas in Cleveland? What does this indicate about the ramifications of global developments for domestic businesses?

Unit Five

Negotiable Instruments

Unit Contents

16 Negotiability, Transferability, and Liability

17 Checks and Banking in the Digital Age

Chapter 16

Negotiability, Transferability, and Liability

Learning Objectives

After reading this chapter, you should be able to answer the following questions:

1. What requirements must an instrument meet to be negotiable?
2. What are the requirements for attaining the status of a holder in due course (HDC)?
3. What is the difference between signature liability and warranty liability?
4. Certain defenses are valid against all holders, including HDCs. What are these defenses called? Name four defenses that fall within this category.
5. Certain defenses can be used against an ordinary holder but are not effective against an HDC. What are these defenses called? Name four defenses that fall within this category.

The Learning Objectives above are designed to help improve your understanding of the chapter.

Most commercial transactions would be inconceivable without negotiable instruments. A **negotiable instrument** is a signed writing (record) that contains an unconditional promise or order to pay an exact sum on demand or at a specified future time to a specific person or order, or to bearer. Most negotiable instruments are paper documents, which is why they are sometimes referred to as *commercial paper.* The checks you write are negotiable instruments.

A negotiable instrument can function as a substitute for cash or as an extension of credit. For a negotiable instrument to operate *practically* as either a substitute for cash or a credit device, or both, it is essential that the instrument be *easily transferable without danger of being uncollectible.* Each rule described in the following pages can be examined in light of this essential function of negotiable instruments.

Negotiable instruments must meet special requirements relating to form and content that are imposed by Article 3 of the Uniform Commercial Code (UCC) and discussed throughout this chapter. Article 3 also governs the process of *negotiation* (transferring an instrument from one party to another), as will be discussed. Article 4 of the UCC, which governs bank deposits and collections, will be discussed in Chapter 17.

Types of Instruments

UCC 3–104(b) defines *instrument* as a "negotiable instrument."[1] For that reason, whenever the term *instrument* is used in this book, it refers to a negotiable instrument. The UCC specifies four types of negotiable instruments: *drafts, checks, promissory notes,* and *certificates of deposit* (CDs). These instruments are frequently divided into the two classifications that we will discuss in the following subsections: *orders to pay* (drafts and checks) and *promises to pay* (promissory notes and CDs).

Negotiable instruments may also be classified as either demand instruments or time instruments. A *demand instrument*

1. Note that all of the references to Article 3 of the UCC in this chapter are to the 1990 version of Article 3, which has been adopted by nearly every state.

is payable on demand—that is, it is payable immediately after it is issued and thereafter for a reasonable period of time. A *time instrument* is payable at a future date.

Drafts and Checks (Orders to Pay)

A **draft** is an unconditional written order to pay rather than a promise to pay. Drafts involve three parties. The party creating the draft (the **drawer**) orders another party (the **drawee**) to pay funds, usually to a third party (the **payee**). The most common type of draft is a check, but drafts other than checks may be used in commercial transactions.

TIME DRAFTS AND SIGHT DRAFTS A *time draft* is payable at a definite future time. A *sight draft* (or demand draft) is payable on sight—that is, when it is presented to the drawee (usually a bank or financial institution) for payment. A sight draft may be payable on acceptance. **Acceptance** is the drawee's written promise to pay the draft when it comes due. Usually, an instrument is accepted by writing the word *accepted* across its face, followed by the date of acceptance and the signature of the drawee. A draft can be both a time and a sight draft; such a draft is payable at a stated time after sight (a draft that states it is payable ninety days after sight, for instance).

Exhibit 16–1 below shows a typical time draft. For the drawee to be obligated to honor the order, the drawee must be obligated to the drawer either by agreement or through a debtor-creditor relationship. **EXAMPLE 16.1** On January 16, OurTown Real Estate orders $1,000 worth of office supplies from Eastman Supply Company, with payment due in ninety days. Also on January 16, OurTown sends Eastman a draft drawn on its account with the First National Bank of Whiteacre as payment. In this scenario, the drawer is OurTown, the drawee is OurTown's bank (First National Bank of Whiteacre), and the payee is Eastman Supply Company. •

TRADE ACCEPTANCES A *trade acceptance* is a type of draft that is commonly used in the sale of goods. In this draft, the seller is both the drawer and the payee. The buyer to whom credit is extended is the drawee.

EXAMPLE 16.2 Jackson Street Bistro buys its restaurant supplies from Osaka Industries. When Jackson requests supplies, Osaka creates a draft ordering Jackson to pay Osaka for the supplies within ninety days. Jackson accepts the draft by signing its face and is then obligated to make the payment. This is a trade acceptance and can be sold to a third party if Osaka is in need of cash before the payment is due. • (If the draft orders the buyer's bank to pay, it is called a *banker's acceptance.*)

CHECKS As mentioned, the most commonly used type of draft is a **check.** The writer of the check is the drawer, the bank on which the check is drawn is the drawee, and the person to whom the check is payable is the payee. Checks are demand instruments because they are payable on demand.

Checks will be discussed more fully in Chapter 17, but it should be noted here that with certain types of checks, such as *cashier's checks,* the bank is both the drawer and the drawee. The bank customer purchases a cashier's check from the bank—that is, pays the bank the amount of the check—and indicates to whom the check should be made payable. The bank, not the

• ***Exhibit* 16–1 A Typical Time Draft**

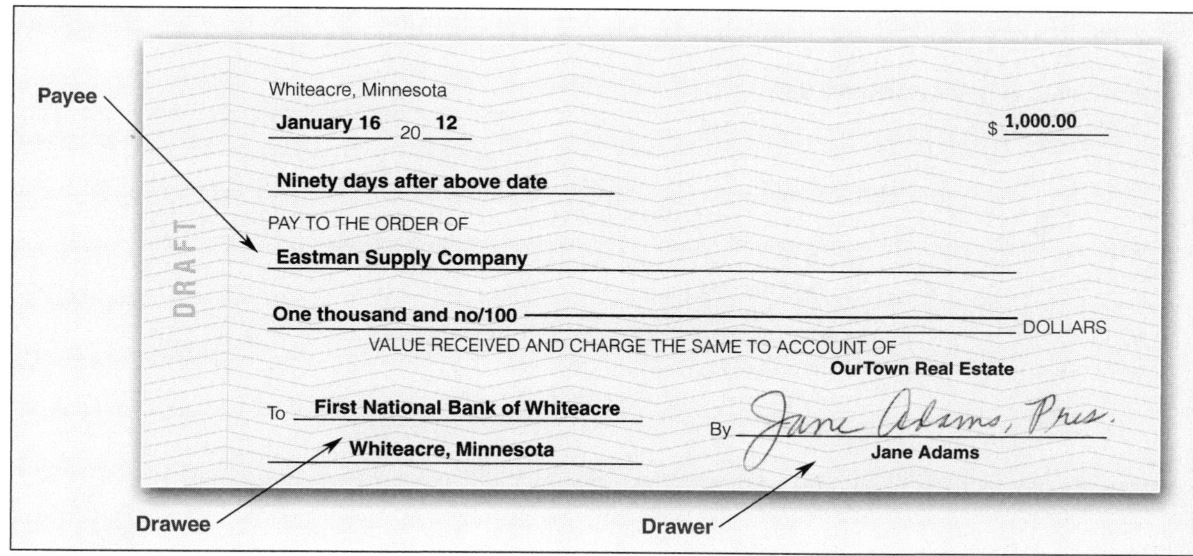

customer, is the drawer of the check, as well as the drawee. A cashier's check functions the same as cash because the bank has committed itself to paying the stated amount on demand.

Promissory Notes and Certificates of Deposit (Promises to Pay)

A **promissory note** is a written promise made by one person (the **maker** of the promise to pay) to another (usually a payee). A promissory note, which is often referred to simply as a *note,* can be made payable at a definite time or on demand. It can name a specific payee or merely be payable to bearer (bearer instruments will be discussed later in this chapter). **EXAMPLE 16.3** On April 30, Laurence and Margaret Roberts, who are called co-makers, sign a writing unconditionally promising to pay "to the order of" the First National Bank of Whiteacre $3,000 (with 8 percent interest) on or before June 29. This writing is a promissory note. ● A typical promissory note is shown in Exhibit 16–2 below.

CASE EXAMPLE 16.4 Joseph Cotton borrowed funds from a bank for his education and signed a promissory note for their repayment. The bank assigned the note to the U.S. Department of Education, and Cotton failed to pay the debt. The government then received a court order allowing it to garnish (take a percentage of) Cotton's wages and his federal income tax refund. Cotton filed a lawsuit seeking to avoid payment and claiming that the debt was invalid because he had not signed any document promising to pay the government. The court found that the signature on Cotton's employment records matched the one on the bank's note, which had been validly assigned to the government. Thus, the government was entitled to enforce the note.[2] ●

2. *Cotton v. U.S. Department of Education,* 2006 WL 3313753 (M.D.Fla. 2006).

A **certificate of deposit (CD)** is a type of note. A CD is issued when a party deposits funds with a bank that the bank promises to repay, with interest, on a certain date [UCC 3–104(j)]. The bank is the maker of the note, and the depositor is the payee. **EXAMPLE 16.5** On February 15, Sara Levin deposits $5,000 with the First National Bank of Whiteacre. The bank issues a CD, in which it promises to repay the $5,000, plus 3.25 percent annual interest, on August 15. ●

Certificates of deposit in small denominations (for amounts up to $100,000) are often sold by savings and loan associations, savings banks, commercial banks, and credit unions. Certificates of deposit for amounts over $100,000 are called large or jumbo CDs. Exhibit 16–3, on the top of the facing page, shows a typical small CD.

Because CDs are time deposits, the purchaser-payee typically is not allowed to withdraw the funds before the date of maturity (except in limited circumstances, such as disability or death). If a payee wants to access the funds prior to the maturity date, he or she can sell (negotiate) the CD to a third party.

Exhibit 16–4, on the bottom of the facing page, summarizes the types of negotiable instruments.

Requirements for Negotiability

For an instrument to be negotiable, it must meet the following requirements:

1. Be in writing.
2. Be signed by the maker or the drawer.
3. Be an unconditional promise or order to pay.
4. State a fixed amount of money.
5. Be payable on demand or at a definite time.
6. Be payable to order or to bearer, unless it is a check.

● ***Exhibit* 16–2 A Typical Promissory Note**

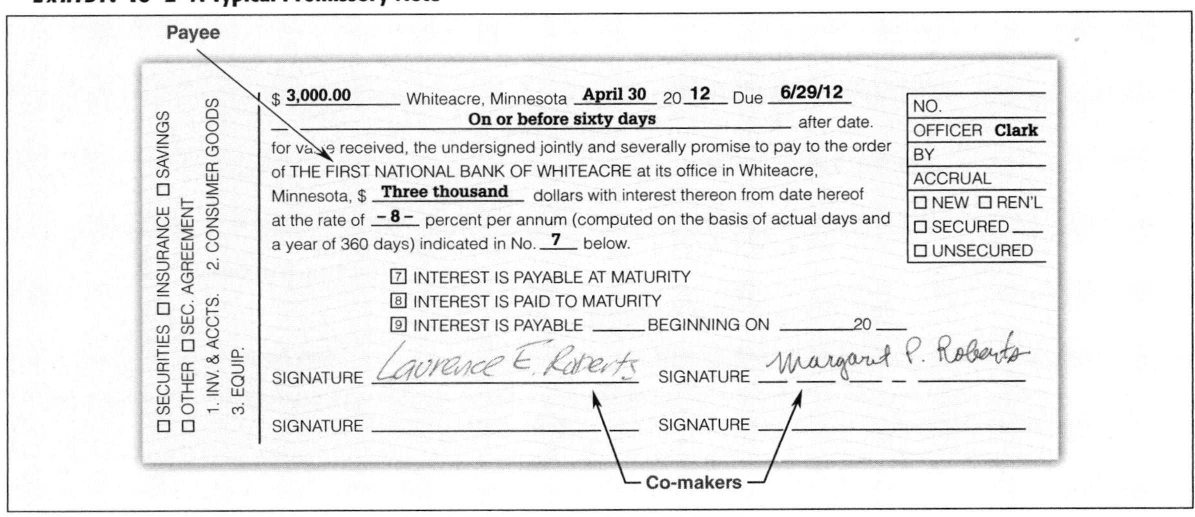

☐ SECURITIES ☐ INSURANCE ☐ SAVINGS
☐ OTHER ☐ SEC. AGREEMENT
1. INV. & ACCTS. 2. CONSUMER GOODS
3. EQUIP.

$ **3,000.00** Whiteacre, Minnesota **April 30** 20 **12** Due **6/29/12**

On or before sixty days after date.

for value received, the undersigned jointly and severally promise to pay to the order of THE FIRST NATIONAL BANK OF WHITEACRE at its office in Whiteacre, Minnesota, $ **Three thousand** dollars with interest thereon from date hereof at the rate of **-8-** percent per annum (computed on the basis of actual days and a year of 360 days) indicated in No. **7** below.

7 INTEREST IS PAYABLE AT MATURITY
8 INTEREST IS PAID TO MATURITY
9 INTEREST IS PAYABLE ____ BEGINNING ON ____ 20 __

SIGNATURE *Laurence E. Roberts* SIGNATURE *Margaret P. Roberts*

SIGNATURE ____ SIGNATURE ____

NO.
OFFICER **Clark**
BY
ACCRUAL
☐ NEW ☐ REN'L
☐ SECURED
☐ UNSECURED

• *Exhibit* **16–3 A Typical Small Certificate of Deposit**

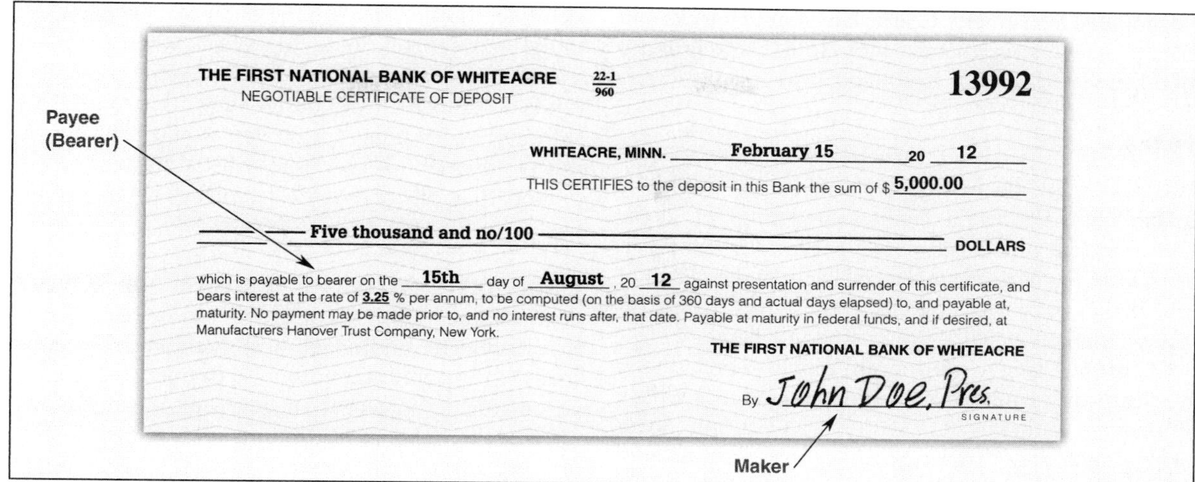
THE FIRST NATIONAL BANK OF WHITEACRE 22-1/960 13992
NEGOTIABLE CERTIFICATE OF DEPOSIT

WHITEACRE, MINN. February 15 20 12

THIS CERTIFIES to the deposit in this Bank the sum of $ 5,000.00

Five thousand and no/100 DOLLARS

which is payable to bearer on the 15th day of August, 20 12 against presentation and surrender of this certificate, and bears interest at the rate of 3.25 % per annum, to be computed (on the basis of 360 days and actual days elapsed) to, and payable at, maturity. No payment may be made prior to, and no interest runs after, that date. Payable at maturity in federal funds, and if desired, at Manufacturers Hanover Trust Company, New York.

THE FIRST NATIONAL BANK OF WHITEACRE

By John Doe, Pres.
SIGNATURE

Written Form

Negotiable instruments must be in written form [UCC 3–103(a)(6), (9)]. This is because negotiable instruments must possess the quality of certainty that only formal, written expression can give. The writing must have the following qualities:

1. The writing must be on material that lends itself to *permanence.* Instruments carved in blocks of ice or recorded on other impermanent surfaces would not qualify as negotiable instruments. **EXAMPLE 16.6** Suzanne writes in the sand, "I promise to pay $500 to the order of Jack." This cannot be a negotiable instrument because, although it is in writing, it lacks permanence. •
2. The writing must also have *portability.* Although the UCC does not explicitly state this requirement, if an instrument is not movable, it obviously cannot meet the requirement that it be freely transferable. **EXAMPLE 16.7** Charles writes on the side of a cow, "I promise to pay $500 to the order of Jason." Technically, this would meet the requirements of a negotiable instrument—except for portability. A cow cannot easily be transferred in the ordinary course of business. Thus, the "instrument" is nonnegotiable. •

• *Exhibit* **16–4 Basic Types of Negotiable Instruments**

INSTRUMENTS	CHARACTERISTICS	PARTIES
ORDERS TO PAY:		
Draft	An order by one person to another person or to bearer [UCC 3–104(e)].	Drawer—The person who signs or makes the order to pay [UCC 3–103(a)(3)].
Check	A draft drawn on a bank and payable on demand [UCC 3–104(f)].[a] (With certain types of checks, such as cashier's checks, the bank is both the drawer and the drawee—see Chapter 17 for details.)	Drawee—The person to whom the order to pay is made [UCC 3–103(a)(2)]. Payee—The person to whom payment is ordered.
PROMISES TO PAY:		
Promissory note	A promise by one party to pay funds to another party or to bearer [UCC 3–104(e)].	Maker—The person who promises to pay [UCC 3–103(a)(5)]. Payee—The person to whom the promise is made.
Certificate of deposit	A note issued by a bank acknowledging a deposit of funds made payable to the holder of the note [UCC 3–104(j)].	

a. Under UCC 4–105(1), banks include savings banks, savings and loan associations, credit unions, and trust companies. (Trust companies are organizations that perform the fiduciary functions of trusts and agencies.)

The UCC nevertheless gives considerable leeway as to what can be a negotiable instrument. Courts have found checks and notes written on napkins, menus, tablecloths, shirts, and a variety of other materials to be negotiable instruments.

Signatures

For an instrument to be negotiable, it must be signed by (1) the maker, if it is a note or a certificate of deposit, or (2) the drawer, if it is a draft or a check [UCC 3–103(a)(3)]. If a person signs an instrument as an authorized agent of the maker or drawer, the maker or drawer has effectively signed the instrument. (Agents' signatures will be discussed in Chapter 21.)

The UCC is quite lenient with regard to what constitutes a signature. Nearly any symbol executed or adopted by a person with the intent to authenticate a written or electronic document can be a signature. A signature can be made manually or by some device, such as a rubber stamp or thumbprint, and can consist of any name, including a trade or assumed name, or a word, mark, or symbol [UCC 3–401(b)]. If necessary, *parol evidence* (see Chapter 10) is admissible to identify the signer. When the signer is identified, the signature becomes effective.

The location of the signature on the document is unimportant, although the usual place is the lower right-hand corner. A *handwritten* statement on the body of the instrument, such as "I, Jerome Garcia, promise to pay Elena Greer," is sufficient to act as a signature.

Unconditional Promise or Order to Pay

The terms of the promise or order must be included in the writing on the face of a negotiable instrument. The terms must also be *unconditional*—that is, they cannot be conditioned on the occurrence or nonoccurrence of some other event or agreement [UCC 3–104(a)].

PROMISE OR ORDER For an instrument to be negotiable, it must contain an express order or promise to pay. If a buyer executes a promissory note using the words "I promise to pay Jonas $1,000 on demand for the purchase of these goods," then this requirement for a negotiable instrument is satisfied. A mere acknowledgment of the debt, such as an I.O.U. ("I owe you"), might logically *imply* a promise, but it is not sufficient under the UCC because the promise must be an affirmative (express) undertaking [UCC 3–103(a)(9)]. If such words as "to be paid on demand" or "due on demand" are added to an I.O.U., however, the need for an express promise to pay is satisfied.[3]

An *order* is associated with three-party instruments, such as checks, drafts, and trade acceptances. An order directs a third party to pay the instrument as drawn. In the typical check, for example, the word *pay* (to the order of a payee) is a command to the drawee bank to pay the check when presented—thus, it is an order. A command, such as "pay," is mandatory even if it is accompanied by courteous words as in "Please pay" or "Kindly pay." Stating "I wish you would pay" does not fulfill this requirement. An order may be addressed to one party or to more than one party, either jointly ("to A *and* B") or alternatively ("to A *or* B") [UCC 3–103(a)(6)].

UNCONDITIONALITY OF PROMISE OR ORDER Only unconditional promises or orders can be negotiable. A promise or order is conditional (and therefore *not* negotiable) if it states (1) an express condition to payment, (2) that the promise or order is subject to or governed by another writing, or (3) that the rights or obligations with respect to the promise or order are stated in another writing.

A mere reference to another writing, however, does not make the promise or order conditional [UCC 3–106(a)]. For example, the words "As per contract" or "This debt arises from the sale of goods X and Y" do not render an instrument nonnegotiable. Similarly, a statement in the instrument that payment can be made only out of a particular fund or source will not render the instrument nonnegotiable [UCC 3–106(b)(ii)]. **EXAMPLE 16.8** The terms of Biggs's note state that payment will be made out of the proceeds of next year's cotton crop. This does not make the note nonnegotiable—although the payee of such a note may find the note commercially unacceptable and refuse to take it. •

A Fixed Amount of Money

Negotiable instruments must state with certainty a fixed amount of money to be paid at any time the instrument is payable [UCC 3–104(a)]. The term *fixed amount* means an amount that is ascertainable from the face of the instrument. A demand note payable with 8 percent interest meets the requirement of a fixed amount because its amount can be determined at the time it is payable or at any time thereafter [UCC 3–104(a)].

The rate of interest may also be determined with reference to information that is not contained in the instrument if that information is readily ascertainable by reference to a formula or a source described in the instrument [UCC 3–112(b)]. For instance, an instrument that is payable at the *legal rate of interest* (a rate of interest fixed by statute) is negotiable. Mortgage notes tied to a variable rate of interest (a rate that fluctuates as a result of market conditions) are also negotiable.

UCC 3–104(a) provides that a fixed amount is to be *payable in money*. The UCC defines money as "a medium of exchange authorized or adopted by a domestic or foreign government as a part of its currency" [UCC 1–201(24)]. Thus, a note that promises "to pay on demand $1,000 in gold" is not negotiable because gold is not a medium of exchange adopted by the U.S. government. An instrument payable in the United States

3. A certificate of deposit (CD) is an exception in this respect. A CD does not have to contain an express promise because the bank's acknowledgment of the deposit and the other terms of the instrument clearly indicate a promise by the bank to repay the funds [UCC 3–104(j)].

with a face amount stated in a foreign currency is negotiable, however, and can be paid in the foreign currency or in the equivalent of U.S. dollars [UCC 3–107].

Payable on Demand or at a Definite Time

To determine the value of a negotiable instrument, it is necessary to know when the maker, drawee, or acceptor (an **acceptor** is a drawee that promises to pay an instrument when it is presented later for payment) is required to pay the instrument. A negotiable instrument must therefore "be payable on demand or at a definite time" [UCC 3–104(a)(2)].

PAYABLE ON DEMAND Instruments that are payable on demand include those that contain the words "Payable at sight" or "Payable upon presentment." **Presentment** means a demand made by or on behalf of a person entitled to enforce an instrument to either pay or accept the instrument [UCC 3–501]. Thus, presentment occurs when a person brings the instrument to the appropriate party for payment or acceptance.

The very nature of the instrument may indicate that it is payable on demand. For example, a check, by definition, is payable on demand [UCC 3–104(f)]. If no time for payment is specified and the person responsible for payment must pay on the instrument's presentment, the instrument is payable on demand [UCC 3–108(a)].

In the following case, the issue before the court was whether a promissory note was a demand note.

Case 16.1 Reger Development, LLC v. National City Bank

United States Court of Appeals, Seventh Circuit, 592 F.3d 759 (2010).
www.ca7.uscourts.gov[a]

FACTS Kevin Reger is the principal and sole member of Reger Development, LLC. National City Bank had loaned funds to Reger Development for several projects. In June 2007, National City offered the company a line of credit to finance potential development opportunities. Reger Development then executed a form contract, which was structured as a promissory note. One clause in the contract read, in part, "PAYMENT: Borrower will pay this loan in full immediately upon Lender's demand." Several other provisions of the note also referred to payment being made on the lender's demand. About a year later, the bank asked Reger Development to pay down some of the loan and stated that it would be reducing the amount of cash available through the line of credit. Kevin Reger "expressed surprise" about these developments and asked if the bank would call in the line of credit if Reger Development did not agree to the requests. The bank said that there was a possibility that it would demand payment of the line. Reger Development then sued National City in an Illinois state court, alleging that the bank had breached the terms of the note. National City removed the case to a federal district court based on diversity jurisdiction. The court granted the bank's motion to dismiss the complaint for failure to state a cause of action under which relief could be granted, and Reger Development appealed. The main question before the court was whether the note entitled National City to demand payment from Reger Development at will.

a. Select "Opinions" under the "Case Information" heading. When the page opens, enter "09" and "2821" in the "Case Number" boxes, respectively, and click on "List Case(s)." On the page that appears next, click on the link to the case number to access the opinion. The U.S. Court of Appeals for the Seventh Circuit maintains this Web site.

ISSUE Was a contract executed for a line of credit that stated it was a promissory note, but required the borrower (Reger Development) to pay the loan on the lender's demand, a demand instrument?

DECISION Yes. The U.S. Court of Appeals for the Seventh Circuit affirmed the district court's dismissal of Reger Development's complaint. The promissory note was a demand instrument, and thus National City had the right to collect payment from Reger Development at any time on demand.

REASON The appellate court reasoned that although a covenant of fair dealing and good faith is implied in every contract, "the duty to act in good faith does not apply to lenders seeking payment on demand notes." Reger Development alleged that National City had arbitrarily and capriciously demanded payment, even though Reger Development was not in default, and that National City had unilaterally changed the fundamental terms of the contract. The appellate court, however, pointed out that explicit contract language set forth the lender's right to demand payment at any time. National City had the "right to collect scheduled monthly interest payments and [did] not deviate from the structure of a demand note."

FOR CRITICAL ANALYSIS—Ethical Consideration *In its opinion, the court pointed out "the duty to act in good faith does not apply to lenders seeking payment on demand notes." Why is this so?*

PAYABLE AT A DEFINITE TIME If an instrument is not payable on demand, to be negotiable it must be payable at a definite time. An instrument is payable at a definite time if it states that it is payable (1) on a specified date, (2) within a definite period of time (such as thirty days) after being presented for payment, or (3) on a date or time readily ascertainable at the time the promise or order is issued [UCC 3–108(b)]. The maker or drawee in a time draft, for example, is under no obligation to pay until the specified time.

When an instrument is payable by the maker or drawer on or before a stated date, it is clearly payable at a definite time. The maker or drawer has the *option* of paying before the stated maturity date, but the holder can still rely on payment being made by the maturity date. The option to pay early does not violate the definite-time requirement. In contrast, an instrument that is undated and made payable "one month after date" is clearly nonnegotiable. There is no way to determine the maturity date from the face of the instrument.

ACCELERATION CLAUSE An **acceleration clause** allows a payee or other holder of a time instrument to demand payment of the entire amount due, with interest, if a certain event occurs, such as a default in the payment of an installment when due. (A **holder** is any person in possession of an instrument drawn, issued, or indorsed to him or her, to his or her order, to bearer, or in blank [UCC 1–201(20)].)

Under the UCC, instruments that include acceleration clauses are negotiable because (1) the exact value of the instrument can be ascertained and (2) the instrument will be payable on a specified date if the event allowing acceleration does not occur [UCC 3–108(b)(ii)]. Thus, the specified date is the outside limit used to determine the value and negotiability of the instrument.

EXTENSION CLAUSE The reverse of an acceleration clause is an **extension clause,** which allows the date of maturity to be extended into the future [UCC 3–108(b)(iii), (iv)]. To keep the instrument negotiable, the interval of the extension must be specified if the right to extend the time of payment is given to the maker or drawer of the instrument. If, however, the holder of the instrument can extend the time of payment, the extended maturity date does not have to be specified.

Payable to Order or to Bearer

Because one of the functions of a negotiable instrument is to serve as a substitute for cash, freedom to transfer is essential. To ensure a proper transfer, the instrument must be "payable to order or to bearer" at the time it is issued or first comes into the possession of the holder [UCC 3–104(a)(1)]. An instrument is not negotiable unless it meets this requirement.

ORDER INSTRUMENTS An **order instrument** is an instrument that is payable (1) "to the order of an identified person" or (2) "to an identified person or order" [UCC 3–109(b)]. An identified person is the person "to whom the instrument is initially payable" as determined by the intent of the maker or drawer [UCC 3–110(a)]. The identified person, in turn, may transfer the instrument to whomever he or she wishes. Thus, the maker or drawer is agreeing to pay either the person specified on the instrument or whomever that person might designate. In this way, the instrument retains its transferability.

Note that in order instruments, the person specified must be identified with *certainty* because the transfer of an order instrument requires the *indorsement,* or signature, of the payee (*indorsements* will be discussed at length later in this chapter). An order instrument made "Payable to the order of my nicest cousin," for instance, is not negotiable because it does not clearly specify the payee.

BEARER INSTRUMENTS A **bearer instrument** is an instrument that does not designate a specific payee [UCC 3–109(a)]. The term **bearer** refers to a person in possession of an instrument that is payable to bearer or indorsed in blank (with a signature only, as will be discussed shortly) [UCC 1–201(5), 3–109(a), 3–109(c)]. This means that the maker or drawer agrees to pay anyone who presents the instrument for payment.

Any instrument containing terms such as "Payable to Kathy Esposito or bearer" or "Pay to the order of cash" is a bearer instrument. In addition, an instrument that "indicates that it is not payable to an identified person" is a bearer instrument [UCC 3–109(a)(3)]. Thus, an instrument "payable to X" or "payable to Batman" can be negotiated as a bearer instrument, just as though it were payable to cash. An instrument made payable to a *nonexistent organization* or company is not a negotiable bearer instrument, however [UCC 3–109, Comment 2].

The bearer instrument at the center of the following case was a *gambling marker*—that is, a credit instrument that allows a gambler to receive tokens or chips from a casino based on a prior credit application. The question before the court was whether the gambling marker was negotiable.

Case 16.2 Las Vegas Sands, LLC v. Nehme

United States Court of Appeals, Ninth Circuit, 632 F.3d 526 (2011).
www.ca9.uscourts.gov[a]

FACTS Amine Nehme, a California resident, applied for credit at the Venetian Resort Hotel Casino in Las Vegas, Nevada. Nehme was granted $500,000 in credit. He soon accrued more than $1.2 million in gambling debts to the Venetian, which he paid. About a year later, Nehme deposited

a. In the left column, in the "Opinions" pull-out menu, click on "Published." On the next page, click on "Advanced Search." In the "by Case No.:" box, type "09-16740," and click on "Search." In the result, click on the name of the case to access the opinion. The U.S. Court of Appeals for the Ninth Circuit maintains this Web site.

Case 16.2–Continued

$1,000 with the Venetian and signed a gambling marker for $500,000. Generally, a gambling marker is an instrument that is dated, bears the gambler's name—as well as the name and account number of the gambler's bank—and states the instruction "Pay to the Order of" the casino. In this case, though, the line following "Pay to the Order of" was apparently left blank, which made the marker a bearer instrument. Nehme quickly lost $500,000 gambling, and he left the casino. The Venetian presented the marker for payment to Bank of America, Nehme's bank, which returned it for insufficient funds. The casino's owner, Las Vegas Sands, LLC, applied Nehme's deposit against the marker and filed a suit against him to recover the remainder—$499,000—plus interest, claiming that he had failed to pay a negotiable instrument. A federal district court issued a summary judgment in the Venetian's favor. Nehme appealed.

ISSUE Was a gambling marker under which Nehme borrowed funds from a casino a negotiable instrument?

DECISION Yes. The U.S. Court of Appeals for the Ninth Circuit agreed with the lower court that the marker was a negotiable instrument. To determine whether Nehme could establish a defense to liability, the appellate court reversed the lower court's judgment and remanded the case for a trial.

REASON In Nevada, a negotiable instrument is defined as an unconditional order to pay a fixed amount of money, payable on demand or at a definite time, and stating no "undertaking" in addition to the payment of money [Nevada Revised Statutes Section 104.3104, Nevada's version of UCC 3–104]. A check is defined as a draft "payable on demand and drawn on a bank." The court reasoned that the gambling marker fits these definitions. It specifies a fixed amount of money, $500,000. It does not state a time for payment and thus is payable on demand. It is unconditional and states no "undertaking" by Nehme in addition to the payment of a fixed sum. The Venetian can thus enforce the marker against Nehme unless he can establish a defense to liability.

WHAT IF THE FACTS WERE DIFFERENT? *Suppose that the marker had stated "Payable to the Order of the Venetian." Could the casino have transferred it for collection? If so, how?*

Factors That Do Not Affect Negotiability

Certain ambiguities or omissions will not affect the negotiability of an instrument. The UCC provides the following rules for clearing up ambiguous terms:

1. Unless the date of an instrument is necessary to determine a definite time for payment, the fact that an instrument is *undated* does not affect its negotiability. A typical example is an undated check, which is still negotiable. If a check is not dated, its date is the date of its issue, meaning the date the maker first delivers the check to another person to give that person rights in the check [UCC 3–113(b)].
2. Antedating or postdating an instrument does not affect the instrument's negotiability [UCC 3–113(a)]. *Antedating* occurs when a party puts a date on the instrument that is before the actual date; *postdating* occurs when a party puts a date on an instrument that is after the actual date.

   EXAMPLE 16.9 On May 1, Avery draws a check on her account with First State Bank made payable to Consumer Credit Corporation. Avery postdates the check "May 15." Consumer Credit can negotiate the check, and, unless Avery tells First State otherwise, the bank can charge the amount of the check to Avery's account before May 15 [UCC 4–401(c)]. ●
3. Handwritten terms outweigh typewritten and printed terms (preprinted terms on forms, for example), and typewritten terms outweigh printed terms [UCC 3–114]. **EXAMPLE 16.10** Like most checks, your check is printed "Pay to the order of" with a blank next to it. In handwriting, you insert in the blank, "Anita Delgado or bearer." The handwritten terms will outweigh the printed form (an order instrument), and the check will be a bearer instrument. ●
4. Words outweigh figures unless the words are ambiguous [UCC 3–114]. This rule is important when the numerical amount and the written amount on a check differ. **EXAMPLE 16.11** Rob issues a check payable to Standard Appliance Company. For the amount, he fills in the numbers "$100" and writes in the words "One thousand and 00/100" dollars. The check is payable in the amount of $1,000. ●
5. When an instrument does not specify a particular interest rate but simply states "with interest," the interest rate is the *judgment rate of interest* (a rate of interest fixed by statute that is applied to a monetary judgment awarded by a court until the judgment is paid or terminated) [UCC 3–112(b)].
6. A check is negotiable even if there is a notation on it stating that it is "nonnegotiable" or "not governed by Article 3." Any other instrument, in contrast, can be made nonnegotiable by the maker's or drawer's conspicuously noting on it that it is "nonnegotiable" or "not governed by Article 3" [UCC 3–104(d)].

Transfer of Instruments

Once issued, a negotiable instrument can be transferred by *assignment* or by *negotiation*. Only a transfer by negotiation can result in the party obtaining the instrument receiving the rights of a holder.

Transfer by Assignment

Recall from Chapter 11 that an assignment is a transfer of rights under a contract. Under general contract principles, a transfer by assignment to an assignee gives the assignee only those rights that the assignor possessed. Any defenses that can be raised against an assignor can normally be raised against the assignee. This same principle applies when a negotiable instrument, such as a promissory note, is transferred by assignment. The transferee is then an *assignee* rather than a *holder*. Sometimes, a transfer fails to qualify as a negotiation because it fails to meet one or more of the requirements of a negotiable instrument, discussed above. When this occurs, the transfer becomes an assignment.

Transfer by Negotiation

Negotiation is the transfer of an instrument in such form that the transferee (the person to whom the instrument is transferred) becomes a holder [UCC 3–201(a)]. Under UCC principles, a transfer by negotiation creates a holder who, at the very least, receives the rights of the previous possessor [UCC 3–203(b)]. Unlike an assignment, a transfer by negotiation can make it possible for a holder to receive more rights in the instrument than the prior possessor had [UCC 3–202(b), 3–305, 3–306]. A holder who receives greater rights is known as a *holder in due course,* a concept we will discuss later in this chapter.

There are two methods of negotiating an instrument so that the receiver becomes a holder. The method used depends on whether the instrument is order paper or bearer paper.

NEGOTIATING ORDER INSTRUMENTS An order instrument contains the name of a payee capable of indorsing it, as in "Pay to the order of Lloyd Sorenson." If the instrument is an order instrument, it is negotiated by delivery with any necessary indorsements. **EXAMPLE 16.12** National Express Corporation issues a payroll check "to the order of Lloyd Sorenson." Sorenson takes the check to the bank, signs his name on the back (an indorsement), gives it to the teller (a delivery), and receives cash. Sorenson has *negotiated* the check to the bank [UCC 3–201(b)]. •

Negotiating order instruments requires both delivery and indorsement (indorsements will be discussed shortly). If Sorenson had taken the check to the bank and delivered it to the teller without signing it, the transfer would not qualify as a negotiation. In that situation, the transfer would be treated as an assignment, and the bank would become an assignee rather than a holder.

NEGOTIATING BEARER INSTRUMENTS If an instrument is payable to bearer, it is negotiated by delivery—that is, by transfer into another person's possession. Indorsement is not necessary [UCC 3–201(b)]. The use of bearer instruments thus involves more risk through loss or theft than the use of order instruments.

EXAMPLE 16.13 Richard Kray writes a check "payable to cash" and hands it to Jessie Arnold (a delivery). Kray has issued the check (a bearer instrument) to Arnold. Arnold places the check in her wallet, which is subsequently stolen. The thief has possession of the check. At this point, the thief has no rights to the check. If the thief "delivers" the check to an innocent third person, however, negotiation will be complete. All rights to the check will be passed absolutely to that third person, and Arnold will lose all rights to recover the proceeds of the check from that person [UCC 3–306]. Of course, Arnold could attempt to recover the amount from the thief if the thief can be found. •

Indorsements

Indorsements are required whenever the instrument being negotiated is classified as an order instrument. An **indorsement** is a signature with or without additional words or statements. It is most often written on the back of the instrument itself. If there is no room on the instrument, the indorsement can be on a separate piece of paper that is firmly affixed to the instrument, such as with staples [UCC 3–204(a)]. A person who transfers an instrument by signing (indorsing) it and delivering it to another person is an *indorser*. The person to whom the check is indorsed and delivered is the *indorsee*.

We examine here the four categories of indorsements: blank, special, qualified, and restrictive. Note that a single indorsement may have characteristics of more than one category. In other words, these categories are not mutually exclusive.

Blank Indorsements

A **blank indorsement** does not specify a particular indorsee and can consist of a mere signature [UCC 3–205(b)]. Hence, a check payable "to the order of Alan Luberda" is indorsed in blank if Luberda simply writes his signature on the back of the check—as shown in Exhibit 16–5 below. An order instrument indorsed in blank becomes a bearer instrument and can be negotiated by delivery alone, as already discussed. In other words, a blank indorsement converts an order instrument to a bearer instrument, which anybody can cash.

• ***Exhibit* 16–5 A Blank Indorsement**

Alan Luberda

Special Indorsements

A **special indorsement** contains the signature of the indorser and identifies the person to whom the instrument is made payable; that is, it names the indorsee [UCC 3–205(a)]. For instance, words such as "Pay to the order of Clay" or "Pay to Clay," followed by the signature of the indorser, create a special indorsement. When an instrument is indorsed in this way, it is an order instrument.

To avoid the risk of loss from theft, a holder may convert a blank indorsement to a special indorsement by writing, above the signature of the indorser, words identifying the indorsee [UCC 3–205(c)]. This changes the bearer instrument back to an order instrument.

EXAMPLE 16.14 A check is made payable to Peter Rabe. He indorses the check in blank by simply signing his name on the back and delivers the check to Anthony Bartomo. Anthony is unable to cash the check immediately and wants to avoid any risk should he lose the check. He therefore prints "Pay to Anthony Bartomo" above Peter's blank indorsement (see Exhibit 16–6 below). In this manner, Anthony has converted Peter's blank indorsement into a special indorsement. Further negotiation now requires Anthony Bartomo's indorsement plus delivery. •

• ***Exhibit* 16–6 A Special Indorsement**

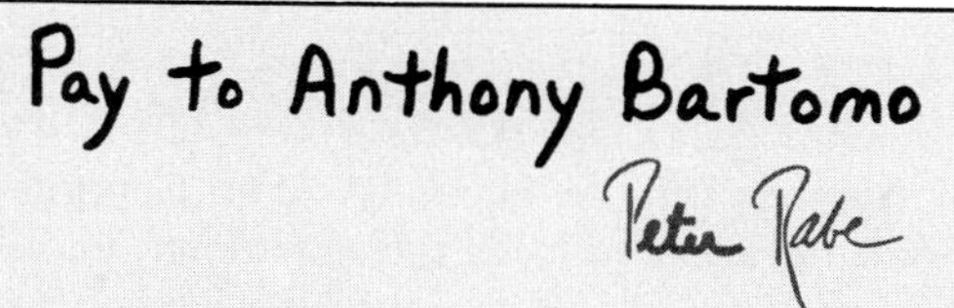

• ***Exhibit* 16–7 A Qualified Indorsement**

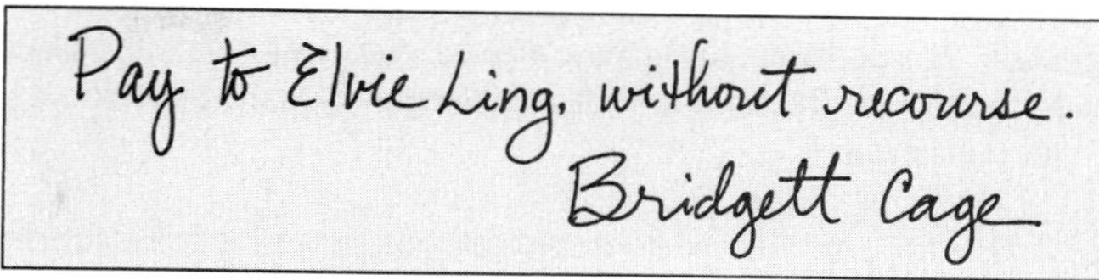

THE EFFECT OF QUALIFIED INDORSEMENTS Qualified indorsements are often used by persons (agents) acting in a representative capacity, such as insurance agents who receive checks payable to them that are really intended as payment to the insurance company.

The "without recourse" indorsement relieves the agent from any liability on a check. If the instrument is dishonored, the holder cannot obtain recovery from the agent who indorsed "without recourse" unless the indorser has breached one of the transfer warranties (relating to title, signature, and material alteration) that will be discussed later in this chapter.

Qualified Indorsements

Generally, an indorser, *merely by indorsing,* impliedly promises to pay the holder or any subsequent indorser the amount of the instrument in the event that the drawer or maker defaults on the payment [UCC 3–415(a)]. Usually, then, indorsements are *unqualified indorsements;* that is, the indorser is guaranteeing payment of the instrument in addition to transferring title to it. An indorser who does not wish to be liable on an instrument can use a **qualified indorsement** to disclaim this liability [UCC 3–415(b)]. The notation "without recourse" is commonly used to create a qualified indorsement, such as the one shown in Exhibit 16–7 on the upper right of this page.

SPECIAL VERSUS BLANK QUALIFIED INDORSEMENTS A qualified indorsement can be accompanied by either a special indorsement or a blank indorsement. A special qualified indorsement includes the name of the indorsee as well as the words *without recourse.* The special indorsement makes the instrument an order instrument, and it requires an indorsement, plus delivery, for negotiation. A blank qualified indorsement makes the instrument a bearer instrument, and only delivery is required for negotiation. In either situation, the instrument can be further negotiated.

The case that follows illustrates the effect of a blank qualified indorsement.

Case 16.3 Hammett v. Deutsche Bank National Co.

United States District Court, Eastern District of Virginia, ___ F.Supp.2d ___ (2010).

FACTS Vernon Hammett and others (the plaintiffs) purchased a residential property in Alexandria, Virginia. As part of that transaction, the plaintiffs executed a promissory note in favor of Encore Credit Corporation in the amount of $475,000. The note was secured by the property being purchased. Subsequently, the note was negotiated by delivery to Deutsche Bank National Company and related entities (the defendants). The note had an attached allonge,[a] which contained a blank indorsement reading as follows: "Pay to The Order of ____ without Recourse Encore Credit Corp. A California Corporation." At some point after executing the note, the plaintiffs refused to continue making the payments due under the note. As holder of the note, Deutsche Bank initiated foreclosure proceedings on the property and subsequently purchased the property at the foreclosure sale. (*Foreclosure* occurs when a homeowner fails to make payments on the home loan.) The plaintiffs brought an action against Deutsche Bank in a Virginia state court, alleging that the defendants had no rights in the note. The defendants removed the action to a federal district court and then filed a motion to dismiss the case.

a. An *allonge* (pronounced uh-*lonj*) is a piece of paper firmly attached to a negotiable instrument on which indorsements can be made if there is no room on the instrument.

Case 16.3—Continues next page ➡

Case 16.3—Continued

ISSUE If a borrower, to purchase a home, executes a note with a blank endorsement, can the current holder of the note enforce it by foreclosing on the homeowner?

DECISION Yes. The federal district court dismissed the case. Deutsche Bank, as holder of the note, was entitled to enforce the instrument.

REASON The court reasoned that the note had included a blank qualified indorsement and thus only delivery of the instrument was required for negotiation. "If an instrument has a blank endorsement, it is considered 'payable to bearer' and it may be negotiated by transfer of possession alone." Because the face of the note showed that it had a blank indorsement, it was indeed negotiable by a simple change in possession. Thus, it was enforceable by its current possessor, Deutsche Bank. The court further stated that "by their own allegations, Plaintiffs admit that they 'refused to pay' on the Note. To permit parties to the [instrument] to object to its payment, on any of the grounds stated, would greatly impair the negotiability of bills and notes, their most distinguishing, most useful, and most valued feature."

WHAT IF THE FACTS WERE DIFFERENT? *Suppose that the indorsement at issue in this case had been written on a separate document that was not firmly affixed to the note. Would this document have constituted an allonge? Would Deutsche Bank be entitled to enforce the note? Explain.*

Restrictive Indorsements

A **restrictive indorsement** requires the indorsee to comply with certain instructions regarding the funds involved, but it does not prohibit the further negotiation of an instrument [UCC 3–206(a)]. Although most indorsements are nonrestrictive because there are no instructions or conditions attached to the payment of funds, many forms of restrictive indorsements do exist, including those discussed here.

CONDITIONAL INDORSEMENTS When payment depends on the occurrence of some event specified in the indorsement, the instrument has a conditional indorsement. **EXAMPLE 16.15** Ken Barton indorses a check, "Pay to Lars Johansen if he completes the renovation of my kitchen by June 1, 2012. [Signed] Ken Barton." Barton has created a conditional indorsement. • A conditional indorsement (on the back of the instrument) does not prevent further negotiation of the instrument.

INDORSEMENTS FOR DEPOSIT OR COLLECTION A common type of restrictive indorsement is one that makes the indorsee (almost always a bank) a collecting agent of the indorser [UCC 3–206(c)]. **EXAMPLE 16.16** Stephanie Mallak has received a check and wants to deposit it into her checking account at the bank. She can indorse the check "For deposit [or collection] only. [Signed] Stephanie Mallak" (see Exhibit 16–8 below). She may also wish to write her bank account number on the check. A "For Deposit" or "For Collection" indorsement locks the instrument into the bank-collection process and thus prohibits further negotiation except by the bank. Following this indorsement, only the bank can acquire the rights of a holder. •

TRUST (AGENCY) INDORSEMENTS An indorsement to a person who is to hold or use the funds for the benefit of the indorser or a third party is called a **trust indorsement** (also known as an *agency indorsement*) [UCC 3–206(d), (e)]. **EXAMPLE 16.17** Robert Emerson asks his accountant, Ada Johnson, to pay some bills for his invalid wife, Sarah, while he is out of the country. He indorses a check as follows: "Pay to Ada Johnson as Agent for Sarah Emerson." This agency indorsement obligates Johnson to use the funds only for the benefit of Sarah Emerson. • Exhibit 16–9 on the top of the facing page shows sample trust (agency) indorsements.

Miscellaneous Indorsement Problems

Of course, a significant problem occurs when an indorsement is forged or unauthorized. The UCC's rules concerning unauthorized or forged signatures and indorsements will be discussed later in this chapter, in the context of signature liability, and again in Chapter 17, in the context of the bank's liability for payment of an instrument over an unauthorized signature. Two other problems that may arise with indorsements concern misspelled names and multiple payees.

• ***Exhibit* 16–8 "For Deposit" and "For Collection" Indorsements**

For deposit only Stephanie Mallak	or	For collection only Stephanie Mallak

• *Exhibit* **16–9 Trust (Agency) Indorsements**

Pay to Ada Johnson in trust for Sarah Emerson Robert Emerson	or	Pay to Ada Johnson as Agent for Sarah Emerson Robert Emerson

MISSPELLED NAMES An indorsement should be identical to the name that appears on the instrument. A payee or indorsee whose name is misspelled can indorse with the misspelled name, the correct name, or both [UCC 3–204(d)]. For example, if Sheryl Kruger receives a check payable to the order of Sherrill Krooger, she can indorse the check either "Sheryl Kruger" or "Sherrill Krooger," or both. The usual practice is to indorse with the name as it appears on the instrument, followed by the correct name.

ALTERNATIVE OR JOINT PAYEES An instrument payable to two or more persons *in the alternative* (for example, "Pay to the order of Tuan or Johnson") requires the indorsement of only one of the payees. In contrast, if an instrument is made payable to two or more persons *jointly* (for example, "Pay to the order of Sharrie and Bob Covington"), all of the payees' indorsements are necessary for negotiation.

If an instrument payable to two or more persons does not clearly indicate whether it is payable in the alternative or jointly (for example, "Pay to the order of John and/or Sara Fitzgerald"), then the instrument is payable to the persons alternatively [UCC 3–110(d)]. The same principles apply to special indorsements that indicate more than one identified person to whom the indorser intends to make the instrument payable [UCC 3–205(a)].

CASE EXAMPLE 16.18 Hyatt Corporation hired Skyscraper Building Maintenance, LLC, to perform maintenance services at some of its Florida hotels. Under an agreement with Skyscraper, J&D Financial Corporation asked Hyatt to make checks for the services payable to Skyscraper and J&D. Hyatt issued many checks to the two payees, but two of the checks that a bank negotiated were indorsed only by Skyscraper and were made payable to "J&D Financial Corp. Skyscraper Building Maint." Parties listed in this manner—without including an "and" or "or" between them—are referred to as *stacked payees.* J&D and Hyatt filed a lawsuit and claimed that the checks were payable *jointly,* requiring indorsement by both payees. The bank argued that the checks were payable to J&D and Skyscraper *alternatively*. A state court found that the bank was not liable because a check payable to stacked payees is ambiguous (unclear) and thus payable alternatively under UCC 3–110(d). Consequently, the bank could negotiate the check when it was indorsed by only one of the two payees.[4] •

Holder in Due Course (HDC)

Often, whether a holder is entitled to obtain payment will depend on whether the holder is a *holder in due course*. An ordinary holder obtains only those rights that the transferor had in the instrument, as mentioned previously. In this respect, a holder has the same status as an *assignee* (see Chapter 11). Like an assignee, a holder normally is subject to the same defenses that could be asserted against the transferor.

In contrast, a **holder in due course** is a holder who, by meeting certain acquisition requirements (to be discussed shortly), takes an instrument *free* of most of the defenses and claims that could be asserted against the transferor.

EXAMPLE 16.19 Marcia Cambry signs a $1,000 note payable to Alex Jerrod in payment for some ancient Roman coins. Jerrod negotiates the note to Alicia Larson, who promises to pay Jerrod for it in thirty days. During the next month, Larson learns that Jerrod has breached his contract with Cambry by delivering coins that were not from the Roman era, as promised, and that for this reason Cambry will not honor the $1,000 note. Whether Larson can hold Cambry liable on the note depends on whether Larson has met the requirements for HDC status. If Larson has met these requirements and thus has HDC status, Larson is entitled to payment on the note. If Larson has not met these requirements, she has the status of an ordinary holder, and Cambry's defense of breach of contract against payment to Jerrod will also be effective against Larson. •

Requirements for HDC Status

The basic requirements for attaining HDC status are set forth in UCC 3–302. A holder of a negotiable instrument is an HDC if she or he takes the instrument (1) for value; (2) in good faith; and (3) without notice that it is defective (such as when the instrument is overdue, dishonored, irregular, or incomplete). We now examine each of these requirements.

4. *Hyatt Corp. v. Palm Beach National Bank,* 840 So.2d 300 (Fla.App. 2003).

• ***Exhibit* 16–10 Taking for Value**
By exchanging defective goods for the note, Jerrod breached his contract with Cambry. Cambry could assert this defense if Jerrod presented the note to her for payment. Jerrod exchanged the note for Larson's promise to pay in thirty days, however. Because Larson did not take the note for value, she is not a holder in due course. Thus, Cambry can assert against Larson the defense of Jerrod's breach when Larson submits the note to Cambry for payment. In contrast, if Larson had taken the note for value, Cambry could not assert that defense and would be liable to pay the note.

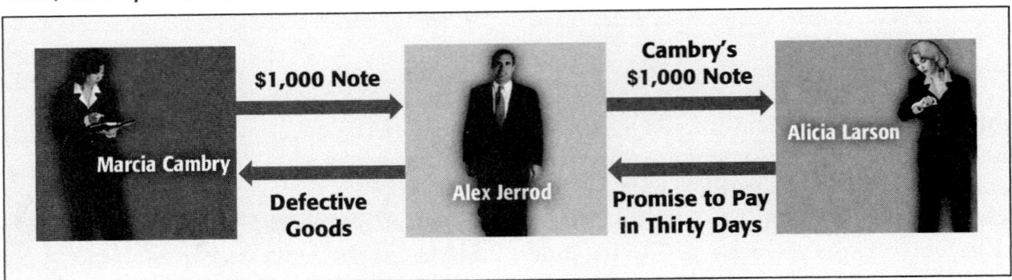

TAKING FOR VALUE An HDC must have given *value* for the instrument [UCC 3–302(a)(2)(i)]. A person who receives an instrument as a gift or inherits it has not met the requirement of value. In these situations, the person becomes an ordinary holder and does not possess the rights of an HDC.

Under UCC 3–303(a), a holder takes an instrument for value if the holder has done any of the following:

1. Performed the promise for which the instrument was issued or transferred.
2. Acquired a security interest or other lien in the instrument, excluding a lien obtained by a judicial proceeding (see Chapters 18 and 19).
3. Taken the instrument in payment of, or as security for, a preexisting claim. **EXAMPLE 16.20** Zon owes Dwyer $2,000 on a past-due account. If Zon negotiates a $2,000 note signed by Gordon to Dwyer and Dwyer accepts it to discharge the overdue account balance, Dwyer has given value for the instrument. •
4. Given a negotiable instrument as payment for the instrument. **EXAMPLE 16.21** Filip issued a $500 negotiable promissory note to Paulene. The note is due six months from the date issued. Paulene needs cash and does not want to wait for the maturity date to collect. She negotiates the note to her friend Kristen, who pays her $200 in cash and writes her a check—a negotiable instrument—for the balance of $300. Kristen has given full value for the note by paying $200 in cash and issuing Paulene the check for $300. •
5. Given an irrevocable commitment (such as a letter of credit) as payment for the instrument.

If a person promises to perform or give value in the future, that person is not an HDC. A holder takes an instrument for value *only to the extent that the promise has been performed* [UCC 3–303(a)(1)]. Therefore, in the Larson-Cambry scenario, which was presented earlier as Example 16.19, Larson is not an HDC because she did not take the instrument (Cambry's note) for value—she has not yet paid Jerrod for the note. Thus, Cambry's defense of breach of contract is valid against Larson as well as Jerrod. Exhibit 16–10 above illustrates these concepts.

TAKING IN GOOD FAITH To qualify as an HDC, a holder must take the instrument in *good faith* [UCC 3–302(a)(2)(ii)]. This means that the holder must have acted honestly in the process of acquiring the instrument. UCC 3–103(a)(4) defines *good faith* as "honesty in fact and the observance of reasonable commercial standards of fair dealing."

The good faith requirement applies only to the *holder*. It is immaterial whether the transferor acted in good faith. Thus, even a person who takes a negotiable instrument from a thief may become an HDC if the person acquired the instrument in good faith and had no reason to be suspicious of the transaction. The purchaser must have honestly believed that the instrument was not defective, however. If a person purchases a $10,000 note for $300 from a stranger on a street corner, the issue of good faith can be raised on the grounds of both the suspicious circumstances and the grossly inadequate consideration (value).

As mentioned earlier in this chapter, postdating a check does not affect its negotiability. Banks are permitted to make payment on postdated checks unless their customers have notified them otherwise. But suppose that a state statute prohibits a check-cashing service from paying a postdated check. Does a service that cashes such a check fail to comply with "reasonable commercial standards" and thereby fail to meet the good faith requirement for HDC status? That was the question in the following case.

Case 16.4 Triffin v. Liccardi Ford, Inc.

Superior Court of New Jersey, Appellate Division, 417 N.J.Super. 453, 10 A.3d 227 (2011).
lawlibrary.rutgers.edu/search.shtml[a]

FACTS Liccardi Ford, Inc., issued a postdated check that was made payable to one of Liccardi's employees, Charles Stallone, Jr. The company did not give the check to Stallone, however, because he was suspected of embezzlement. The check disappeared from the company offices. When the disappearance was discovered, Liccardi immediately asked its bank to stop payment on the check. Meanwhile, JCNB Check Cashing, Inc., cashed the check for Stallone before the issue date on the face of the check and then deposited the check in its bank account. Liccardi's bank refused to honor the check and returned it to JCNB. Eighteen months later, Robert Triffin bought the dishonored check from JCNB and filed a suit in a New Jersey state court against Liccardi to recover its amount, plus interest. The court granted Liccardi's motion to dismiss the complaint. Triffin appealed.

ISSUE Did the check-cashing service that cashed a post-dated check take the instrument in good faith and thus qualify as an HDC?

DECISION No. A state intermediate appellate court affirmed the decision of the lower court to dismiss Triffin's complaint. The check-cashing service (JCNB) was not a holder in due course when it obtained the check from Stallone. Triffin did not take the check as an HDC, because he bought it with notice that it had been dishonored.

REASON If JCNB had qualified as an HDC, it could have assigned its interest to Triffin, who could have enforced JCNB's rights as its assignee. The check, however, was postdated. Under New Jersey state law, a check-cashing service is prohibited from "cashing or advancing any money on a postdated check." This statute defines the "reasonable commercial standards" that JCNB was required to follow. By cashing the check, JCNB failed to follow those standards and violated state law. Therefore, JCNB did not take the check in good faith and did not become an HDC. Triffin could not then, by taking an assignment of the check, assert the rights of an HDC. Instead, Triffin took the check subject to the issuer's defense that the check was stolen.

WHAT IF THE FACTS WERE DIFFERENT? *Suppose that the postdated check at the heart of this case had instead been a money order. Further suppose that the serial number in the upper corner was not part of the sequence of numbers in the bottom corner. Would the outcome have been different? Explain.*

a. In the "Search the N.J. Courts Decisions" section, in the "Please enter your search term(s) below" box, type "Liccardi," and click on "Search!" In the result, click on the name of the case to access the opinion. Rutgers University School of Law in Camden, New Jersey, maintains this Web site.

TAKING WITHOUT NOTICE The final requirement for HDC status involves *notice* [UCC 3–302]. A person will not qualify for HDC protection if he or she is *on notice* (knows or has reason to know) that the instrument being acquired is defective in any one of the following ways [UCC 3–302(a)]:

1. It is overdue.
2. It has been dishonored.
3. It is part of a series of which at least one instrument has an uncured (uncorrected) default.
4. It contains an unauthorized signature or has been altered.
5. There is a defense against the instrument or a claim to the instrument.
6. The instrument is so irregular or incomplete as to call into question its authenticity.

A holder will be deemed to have notice if she or he (1) has actual knowledge of the defect; (2) has received written notice (such as a letter listing the serial numbers of stolen bearer instruments); or (3) has reason to know that a defect exists, given all the facts and circumstances known at the time in question [UCC 1–201(25)]. The holder must also have received the notice "at a time and in a manner that gives a reasonable opportunity to act on it" [UCC 3–302(f)]. A purchaser's knowledge of certain facts, such as insolvency proceedings against the instrument's maker or drawer, does not constitute notice that the instrument is defective [UCC 3–302(b)].

Overdue Instruments. What constitutes notice that an instrument is overdue depends on whether it is a demand instrument (payable on demand) or a time instrument (payable at a definite time). A purchaser has notice that a *demand instrument* is overdue if she or he either takes the instrument knowing that demand has been made or takes the instrument an unreasonable length of time after its issue. For a check, a "reasonable time" is ninety days after the date of the check. For all other demand instruments, what will be considered a reasonable time depends on the circumstances [UCC 3–304(a)].

Normally, a *time instrument* is overdue the day after its due date. Hence, anyone who takes a time instrument after the due date is on notice that it is overdue [UCC 3–304(b)(2)]. Thus, if a promissory note due on May 15 is purchased on May 16, the purchaser will be an ordinary holder, not an HDC. If an instrument states that it is "Payable in thirty days," counting begins the day after the instrument is dated. Thus, a note dated December 1 that is payable in thirty days is due by midnight on December 31. If the payment date falls on a Sunday or holiday, the instrument is payable on the next business day.

Dishonored Instruments. An instrument is **dishonored** when it is presented in a timely manner for payment or acceptance, whichever is required, and payment or acceptance is refused. The holder is on notice if he or she (1) has actual knowledge of the dishonor or (2) has knowledge of facts that would lead him or her to suspect that an instrument has been dishonored [UCC 3–302(a)(2)]. Conversely, if a person purchasing an instrument does not know and has no reason to know that it has been dishonored, the person is *not* put on notice and therefore can become an HDC.

Notice of Claims or Defenses. A holder cannot become an HDC if she or he has notice of any claim to the instrument or any defense against it [UCC 3–302(a)(2)]. Any obvious irregularity on the face of an instrument that calls into question its validity or terms of ownership, or that creates an ambiguity as to the party to pay, will bar HDC status. For instance, if an instrument is so incomplete on its face that an element of negotiability is lacking (for example, the amount is not filled in), the purchaser cannot become an HDC. A good forgery of a signature or the careful alteration of an instrument, however, can go undetected by reasonable examination. In that situation, the purchaser can qualify as an HDC.

Holder through an HDC

A person who does not qualify as an HDC but who derives his or her title through an HDC can acquire the rights and privileges of an HDC. This rule, which is sometimes called the **shelter principle,** is set out in UCC 3–203(b). The shelter principle extends the benefits of HDC status and is designed to aid the HDC in readily disposing of the instrument. Under this rule, anyone—no matter how far removed from an HDC—who can ultimately trace his or her title back to an HDC may acquire the rights of an HDC. By extending the benefits of HDC status, the shelter principle promotes the marketability and free transferability of negotiable instruments.

There are some limitations on the shelter principle, though. Certain persons who formerly held instruments cannot improve their positions by later reacquiring the instruments from HDCs [UCC 3–203(b)]. If a holder participated in fraud or illegality affecting the instrument, or had notice of a claim or defense against an instrument, that holder is not allowed to improve her or his status by repurchasing the instrument from a later HDC.

Signature and Warranty Liability

Liability on negotiable instruments can arise either from a person's signature or from the warranties that are implied when the person presents the instrument for negotiation. Signature liability requires the transferor's signature whereas no signature is required to impose warranty liability. We discuss signature liability (both primary and secondary) and warranty liability in the subsections that follow.

Signature Liability

The general rule is that every party, except a qualified indorser,[5] who signs a negotiable instrument is either primarily or secondarily liable for payment of that instrument when it comes due. Signature liability is contractual liability—no person will be held contractually liable for an instrument that he or she has not signed.

PRIMARY LIABILITY A person who is primarily liable on a negotiable instrument is absolutely required to pay the instrument—unless, of course, he or she has a valid defense to payment [UCC 3–305]. Only *makers* and *acceptors* of instruments are primarily liable.

The maker of a promissory note unconditionally promises to pay the note. It is the maker's promise to pay that makes the note a negotiable instrument. If the instrument was incomplete when the maker signed it, the maker is obligated to pay it according to its stated terms or according to terms that were agreed on and later filled in to complete the instrument [UCC 3–115, 3–407(a), 3–412]. **EXAMPLE 16.22** Tristan executes a preprinted promissory note to Sharon, without filling in the blank for a due date. If Sharon does not complete the form by adding the date, the note will be payable on demand. If Sharon subsequently fills in a due date that Tristan authorized, the note is payable on the stated due date. In either situation, Tristan (the maker) is obligated to pay the note. •

As mentioned earlier, an *acceptor* is a drawee that promises to pay an instrument, such as a *trade acceptance* or a *certified check* (to be discussed in Chapter 17), when it is presented for payment. Once a drawee indicates acceptance by signing the draft, the drawee becomes an acceptor and is obligated to pay the draft when it is presented for payment [UCC 3–409(a)]. Failure to pay an accepted draft when presented leads to primary signature liability.

SECONDARY LIABILITY *Drawers* and *indorsers* are secondarily liable. On a negotiable instrument, secondary liability is similar to the liability of a guarantor in a simple contract in

5. A qualified indorser—one who indorses "without recourse"—undertakes no contractual obligation to pay. A qualified indorser merely assumes warranty liability, which will be discussed later in this chapter.

the sense that it is *contingent liability.* In other words, a drawer or an indorser will be liable only if the party that is responsible for paying the instrument refuses to do so (dishonors the instrument). The drawer's secondary liability on drafts and checks does not arise until the drawee fails to pay or to accept the instrument, whichever is required [UCC 3–412, 3–415].

Dishonor of an instrument thus triggers the liability of parties who are secondarily liable on the instrument—that is, the drawer and *unqualified* indorsers. **EXAMPLE 16.23** Nina Lee writes a check on her account at Universal Bank payable to the order of Stephen Miller. Universal Bank refuses to pay the check when Miller presents it for payment, thus dishonoring the check. In this situation, Lee will be liable to Miller on the basis of her secondary liability. ● Drawers are secondarily liable on drafts unless they disclaim their liability by drawing the instruments "without recourse" (if the draft is a check, however, a drawer cannot disclaim liability) [UCC 3–414(e)].

Parties are secondarily liable on a negotiable instrument only if the following events occur:[6]

1. The instrument is properly and timely presented.
2. The instrument is dishonored.
3. Timely notice of dishonor is given to the secondarily liable party.

Proper Presentment. As previously explained, *presentment* occurs when a person presents an instrument either to the party liable on the instrument for payment or to a drawee for acceptance. The UCC requires that a holder present the instrument to the appropriate party, in a timely fashion, and give reasonable identification if requested [UCC 3–414(f), 3–415(e), 3–501]. The party to whom the instrument must be presented depends on the type of instrument involved. A note or CD must be presented to the maker for payment. A draft is presented to the drawee for acceptance, payment, or both. A check is presented to the drawee for payment [UCC 3–501(a), 3–502(b)].

Presentment can be made by any commercially reasonable means, including oral, written, or electronic communication [UCC 3–501(b)]. It is ordinarily effective when the demand for payment or acceptance is received (unless presentment takes place after an established cutoff hour, in which case it may be treated as occurring the next business day).

Timely Presentment. Timeliness is important for proper presentment [UCC 3–414(f), 3–415(e), 3–501(b)(4)]. Failure to present an instrument on time is the most common reason for improper presentment and leads to unqualified indorsers being discharged from secondary liability. The holder of a domestic check must present that check for payment or collection within thirty days of its *date* to hold the drawer secondarily liable, and within thirty days after its indorsement to hold the indorser secondarily liable. The time for proper presentment for different types of instruments is shown in Exhibit 16–11 below.

Dishonor. As mentioned previously, an instrument is dishonored when the required acceptance or payment is refused or cannot be obtained within the prescribed time. An instrument is also dishonored when the required presentment is excused (as it would be, for example, if the maker had died) and the instrument is not properly accepted or paid [UCC 3–502(e), 3–504].

In certain situations, a postponement of payment or a refusal to pay an instrument will *not* dishonor the instrument. When presentment is made after an established cutoff hour (not earlier than 2:00 P.M.), for instance, a bank can postpone payment until the following business day without dishonoring the instrument. In addition, when the holder refuses to exhibit the instrument, to give reasonable identification (sometimes even a thumbprint), or to sign a receipt for the

6. These requirements are necessary for a secondarily liable party to have signature liability on a negotiable instrument, but they are not necessary for a secondarily liable party to have warranty liability (as will be discussed later in the chapter).

• ***Exhibit* 16–11 Time for Proper Presentment**

TYPE OF INSTRUMENT	FOR ACCEPTANCE	FOR PAYMENT
Time	On or before due date.	On due date.
Demand	Within a reasonable time (after date of issue or after secondary party becomes liable on the instrument).	Within a reasonable time.
Check	Not applicable.	Within thirty days of its date, to hold drawer secondarily liable. Within thirty days of indorsement, to hold indorser secondarily liable.

payment on the instrument, a bank's refusal to pay does not dishonor the instrument.

Proper Notice. Once an instrument has been dishonored, proper notice must be given to secondary parties (drawers and indorsers) for them to be held contractually liable. Notice may be given in any reasonable manner, including an oral, written, or electronic communication, as well as notice written or stamped on the instrument itself. The bank must give any necessary notice before its midnight deadline (midnight of the next banking day after receipt). Notice by any party other than a bank must be given within thirty days following the day of dishonor or the day on which the person who is secondarily liable receives notice of dishonor [UCC 3–503].

UNAUTHORIZED SIGNATURES Unauthorized signatures arise in two situations—when a person forges another person's name on a negotiable instrument and when an *agent* (see Chapter 21) who lacks authority signs an instrument on behalf of a principal. The general rule is that an unauthorized signature is wholly inoperative and will not bind the person whose name is signed or forged.

EXAMPLE 16.24 Parker finds Dolby's checkbook lying in the street, writes out a check to himself, and forges Dolby's signature. Banks normally have a duty to determine whether a person's signature on a check is forged. If a bank fails to determine that Dolby's signature is not genuine and cashes the check for Parker, the bank will generally be liable to Dolby for the amount. • (The liability of banks for paying checks with forged signatures will be discussed further in Chapter 17.) Similarly, if an agent lacks the authority to sign the principal's name or has exceeded the authority given by the principal, the signature does not bind the principal but will bind the "unauthorized signer" [UCC 3–403(a)].

There are two exceptions to the general rule that an unauthorized signature will not bind the person whose name is signed:

1. When the person whose name is signed ratifies (affirms) the signature, he or she will be bound [UCC 3–403(a)].
2. When the negligence of the person whose name was forged substantially contributed to the forgery, a court may not allow the person to deny the effectiveness of an unauthorized signature [UCC 3–115, 3–406, 4–401(d)(2)].

SPECIAL RULES FOR UNAUTHORIZED INDORSEMENTS Generally, when an indorsement is forged or unauthorized, the burden of loss falls on the first party to take the instrument with the forged or unauthorized indorsement. The reason for this general rule is that the first party to take an instrument is in the best position to prevent the loss. **EXAMPLE 16.25** Jen Nilson steals a check that is payable to Inga Leed and drawn on Universal Bank. Nilson indorses the check "Inga Leed" and presents the check to Universal Bank for payment. The bank, without asking Nilson for identification, pays the check, and Nilson disappears. In this situation, Leed will not be liable on the check because her indorsement was forged. The bank will bear the loss, which it might have avoided if it had requested identification from Nilson. •

There are two important exceptions to this general rule, which cause the loss to fall on the maker or drawer. These exceptions arise when an indorsement is made by an imposter or by a fictitious payee.

Imposter Rule. An **imposter** is one who, by her or his personal appearance or use of the mails, Internet, telephone, or other communication, induces a maker or drawer to issue an instrument in the name of an impersonated payee. If the maker or drawer believes the imposter to be the named payee at the time of issue, the indorsement by the imposter is not treated as unauthorized when the instrument is transferred to an innocent party. This is because the maker or drawer *intended* the imposter to receive the instrument. In this situation, under the UCC's *imposter rule,* the imposter's indorsement will be effective—that is, not considered a forgery—insofar as the drawer or maker is concerned [UCC 3–404(a)].

EXAMPLE 16.26 Carol impersonates Donna and induces Edward to write a check payable to the order of Donna. Carol, continuing to impersonate Donna, negotiates the check to First National Bank as payment on her loan there. As the drawer of the check, Edward is liable for its amount to First National. •

Fictitious Payee Rule. When a person causes an instrument to be issued to a payee who will have *no interest* in the instrument, the payee is referred to as a **fictitious payee.** A fictitious payee can be a person or firm that does not truly exist, or it may be an identifiable party that will not acquire any interest in the instrument. Under the UCC's *fictitious payee rule,* the payee's indorsement is not treated as a forgery, and an innocent holder can hold the maker or drawer liable on the instrument [UCC 3–404(b), 3–405].

Situations involving fictitious payees most often arise when (1) a dishonest employee deceives the employer into signing an instrument payable to a party with no right to receive payment on the instrument or (2) a dishonest employee or agent has the authority to issue an instrument on behalf of the employer. Regardless of whether a dishonest employee actually signs the check or merely supplies his or her employer with names of fictitious creditors (or with true names of creditors having fictitious debts), the result is the same under the UCC.

Warranty Liability

In addition to the signature liability, transferors make certain implied warranties regarding the instruments that they are negotiating. Warranty liability arises even when a transferor does not indorse (sign) the instrument [UCC 3–416, 3–417]. Warranty liability is particularly important when a holder cannot hold a party liable on her or his signature, such as when a person delivers a bearer instrument. Unlike secondary signature liability, warranty liability is not subject to the conditions of proper presentment, dishonor, or notice of dishonor.

Warranties fall into two categories: those that arise on the *transfer* of a negotiable instrument and those that arise on *presentment*. Both transfer and presentment warranties attempt to shift liability back to a wrongdoer or to the person who dealt face to face with the wrongdoer and thus was in the best position to prevent the wrongdoing.

TRANSFER WARRANTIES The UCC describes five **transfer warranties** [UCC 3–416].[7] For transfer warranties to arise, an instrument *must be transferred for consideration*. One who transfers an instrument for consideration makes the following warranties to all subsequent transferees and holders who take the instrument in good faith (with some exceptions, as will be noted shortly):

1. The transferor is entitled to enforce the instrument.
2. All signatures are authentic and authorized.
3. The instrument has not been altered.
4. The instrument is not subject to a defense or claim of any party that can be asserted against the transferor.
5. The transferor has no knowledge of any insolvency (bankruptcy) proceedings against the maker, the acceptor, or the drawer of the instrument.

Parties to Whom Warranty Liability Extends. Transfer of order paper, for consideration, by indorsement and delivery extends warranty liability to any subsequent holder who takes the instrument in good faith. The warranties of a person who transfers *without indorsement* (by the delivery of a bearer instrument), however, will extend the transferor's warranties only to the immediate transferee [UCC 3–416(a)].

Recovery for Breach of Warranty. A transferee or holder who takes an instrument in good faith can sue on the basis of a breach of warranty as soon as he or she has reason to know of the breach [UCC 3–416(d)]. Notice of a claim for breach of warranty must be given to the warrantor within thirty days after the transferee or holder has reason to know of the breach and the identity of the warrantor, or the warrantor is not liable for any loss caused by a delay [UCC 3–416(c)]. The transferee or holder can recover damages for the breach in an amount equal to the loss suffered (but not more than the amount of the instrument), plus expenses and any loss of interest caused by the breach [UCC 3–416(b)]. These warranties can be disclaimed with respect to any instrument except a check [UCC 3–416(c)].

PRESENTMENT WARRANTIES Any person who presents an instrument for payment or acceptance makes the following **presentment warranties** to any other person who in good faith pays or accepts the instrument [UCC 3–417(a), 3–417(d)]:

1. The person obtaining payment or acceptance is entitled to enforce the instrument or is authorized to obtain payment or acceptance on behalf of a person who is entitled to enforce the instrument. (This is, in effect, a warranty that there are no missing or unauthorized indorsements.)
2. The instrument has not been altered.
3. The person obtaining payment or acceptance has no knowledge that the signature of the issuer of the instrument is unauthorized.[8]

These warranties are referred to as presentment warranties because they protect the person to whom the instrument is presented. They often have the effect of shifting liability back to the party that was in the best position to prevent the wrongdoing. The second and third warranties do not apply to makers, acceptors, and drawers. It is assumed that a drawer or a maker will recognize his or her own signature and that a maker or an acceptor will recognize whether an instrument has been materially altered.

Defenses, Limitations, and Discharge

Persons who would otherwise be liable on negotiable instruments may be able to avoid liability by raising certain defenses. There are two general categories of defenses—*universal defenses* and *personal defenses,* which are discussed below.

Universal Defenses

Universal defenses (also called *real defenses*) are valid against *all* holders, including HDCs and holders who take through an HDC. Universal defenses include those described below.

FORGERY Forgery of a maker's or drawer's signature cannot bind the person whose name is used unless that person ratifies (approves or validates) the signature or is barred from denying

7. An amendment to UCC 3–416(a) adds a sixth warranty: "with respect to a remotely created consumer item, that the person on whose account the item is drawn authorized the issuance of the item in the amount for which the item is drawn." A "remotely created consumer item" is an item, such as an electronic check, that is not created by the payor bank and does not contain the drawer's handwritten signature, but was authorized by the consumer. A bank that accepts and pays the instrument warrants to the next bank in the collection chain that the consumer authorized the item in that amount.

8. As discussed in Footnote 7, amendments to Article 3 of the UCC provide additional protection for "remotely created" consumer items in the context of presentment [see Amended UCC 3–417(a)(4)].

it (because the forgery was made possible by the maker's or drawer's negligence, for example) [UCC 3–403(a)]. Thus, when a person forges an instrument, the person whose name is forged normally has no liability to pay any holder or any HDC the value of the forged instrument.

FRAUD IN THE EXECUTION If a person is deceived into signing a negotiable instrument, believing that she or he is signing something other than a negotiable instrument (such as a receipt), *fraud in the execution,* or fraud in the inception, is committed against the signer [UCC 3–305(a)(1)]. Fraud in the execution is a universal defense.

The defense of fraud in the execution cannot be raised, however, if a reasonable inquiry would have revealed the nature and terms of the instrument. Thus, the signer's age, experience, and intelligence are relevant because they frequently determine whether the signer should have known the nature of the transaction before signing.

MATERIAL ALTERATION An alteration is material if it changes the obligations of the parties in the instrument *in any way.* Examples include any unauthorized addition of words or numbers or other changes to complete an incomplete instrument that affect the obligation of a party to the instrument [UCC 3–407(a)]. Making any change in the amount, the date, or the rate of interest—even if the change is only one penny, one day, or 1 percent—is material. It is not a material alteration, however, to correct the maker's address or to change the figures on a check so that they agree with the written amount. If the alteration is not material, any holder is entitled to enforce the instrument according to its terms.

Material alteration is a *complete defense* against an ordinary holder, but only a partial defense against an HDC. An ordinary holder can recover nothing on an instrument if it has been materially altered [UCC 3–407(b)]. In contrast, when the holder is an HDC and an original term, such as the monetary amount payable, has been *altered,* the HDC can enforce the instrument against the maker or drawer according to the *original* terms but not for the altered amount.

If the instrument was originally incomplete and was later completed in an unauthorized manner, however, alteration no longer can be claimed as a defense against an HDC, and the HDC can enforce the instrument as completed [UCC 3–407(b)].

DISCHARGE IN BANKRUPTCY Discharge in bankruptcy (see Chapter 19) is an absolute defense on any instrument, regardless of the status of the holder, because the purpose of bankruptcy is to settle finally all of the insolvent party's debts [UCC 3–305(a)(1)].

MINORITY Minority, or infancy, is a universal defense only to the extent that state law recognizes it as a defense to a simple contract (see Chapter 9). Because state laws on minority vary, so do determinations of whether minority is a universal defense against an HDC [UCC 3–305(a)(1)(i)].

ILLEGALITY Certain types of illegality constitute universal defenses. Other types constitute personal defenses—that is, defenses that are effective against ordinary holders but not against HDCs. If a statute provides that an illegal transaction is void, then the defense is universal—that is, absolute against both an ordinary holder and an HDC. If the law merely makes the instrument voidable, then the illegality is still a personal defense against an ordinary holder but not against an HDC [UCC 3–305(a)(1)(ii)].

MENTAL INCAPACITY If a person has been declared by a court to be mentally incompetent, then any instrument issued thereafter by that person is void. The instrument is void *ab initio* (from the beginning) and unenforceable by any holder or HDC [UCC 3–305(a)(1)(ii)]. Mental incapacity in these circumstances is thus a universal defense. If a court has not declared the person to be mentally incompetent, however, then mental incapacity operates as a defense against an ordinary holder but not against an HDC.

EXTREME DURESS When a person signs and issues a negotiable instrument under such extreme duress as an immediate threat of force or violence (for example, at gunpoint), the instrument is void and unenforceable by any holder or HDC [UCC 3–305(a)(1)(ii)]. (Ordinary duress is a defense against ordinary holders but not against HDCs.)

Personal Defenses

Personal defenses (sometimes called *limited defenses*), such as those described here, can be used to avoid payment to an ordinary holder of a negotiable instrument, but not to an HDC or a holder with the rights of an HDC.

BREACH OF CONTRACT OR BREACH OF WARRANTY When there is a breach of the underlying contract for which the negotiable instrument was issued, the maker of a note can refuse to pay it, or the drawer of a check can order his or her bank to stop payment on the check. Breach of warranty can also be claimed as a defense to liability on the instrument.

LACK OR FAILURE OF CONSIDERATION The absence of consideration (value) may be a successful personal defense in some instances [UCC 3–303(b), 3–305(a)(2)]. **EXAMPLE 16.27**

Tara gives Clem, as a gift, a note that states, "I promise to pay you $100,000." Clem accepts the note. Because there is no consideration for Tara's promise, a court will not enforce the promise. •

FRAUD IN THE INDUCEMENT (ORDINARY FRAUD) A person who issues a negotiable instrument based on false statements by the other party will be able to avoid payment on that instrument, unless the holder is an HDC.

ILLEGALITY As mentioned, if a statute provides that an illegal transaction is voidable, the defense is personal.

MENTAL INCAPACITY If a maker or drawer issues a negotiable instrument while mentally incompetent but has not been declared incompetent by a court, the instrument is voidable [UCC 3–305(a)(1)(ii)]. In this situation, mental incapacity can serve only as a personal defense.

Federal Limitations on the Rights of HDCs

Under the HDC doctrine, a consumer who purchased a defective product (such as a defective automobile) would continue to be liable to HDCs even if the consumer returned the defective product to the retailer. To protect consumers, in 1976 the Federal Trade Commission (FTC) issued a rule that effectively abolished the HDC doctrine in consumer transactions.

Discharge from Liability

Discharge from liability on an instrument can occur in several ways. The liability of all parties to an instrument is discharged when the party primarily liable on it pays to the holder the full amount due [UCC 3–602, 3–603]. Payment by any other party discharges only the liability of that party and subsequent parties.

Intentional cancellation of an instrument discharges the liability of all parties [UCC 3–604]. Intentionally writing "Paid" across the face of an instrument cancels it, as does intentionally tearing it up. If a holder intentionally crosses out a party's signature, that party's liability and the liability of subsequent indorsers who have already indorsed the instrument are discharged. Materially altering an instrument may discharge the liability of any party affected by the alteration, as previously discussed [UCC 3–407(b)]. (An HDC may be able to enforce a materially altered instrument against its maker or drawer according to the instrument's original terms, however.)

Discharge of liability can also occur when a holder impairs another party's right of recourse (right to seek reimbursement) on the instrument [UCC 3–605]. This occurs when, for example, the holder releases, or agrees not to sue, a party against whom the indorser has a right of recourse.

Reviewing . . . Negotiability, Transferability, and Liability

Robert Durbin, a student, borrowed funds from a bank for his education and signed a promissory note for their repayment. The bank lent the funds under a federal program designed to assist students at postsecondary institutions. Under this program, repayment ordinarily begins nine to twelve months after the student borrower fails to carry at least one-half of the normal full-time course load at his or her school. The federal government guarantees that the note will be fully paid. If the student defaults on the payments, the lender presents the current balance—principal, interest, and costs—to the government. When the government pays the balance, it becomes the lender, and the borrower owes the government directly. After Durbin defaulted on his note, the government paid the lender the balance due and took possession of the note. Durbin then refused to pay the government, claiming that the government was not the holder of the note. The government filed a suit in a federal district court against Durbin to collect the amount due. Using the information presented in the chapter, answer the following questions.

1 Using the categories discussed in the chapter, what type of negotiable instrument was the note that Durbin signed (an order to pay or a promise to pay)? Explain.
2 Suppose that the note did not state a specific interest rate but instead referred to a statute that established the maximum interest rate for government-guaranteed student loans. Would the note fail to meet the requirements for negotiability in that situation? Why or why not?
3 How does a party who is not named by a negotiable instrument (in this situation, the government) obtain a right to enforce the instrument?
4 Suppose that in court, Durbin argues that because the school closed down before he could finish his education, there was a failure of consideration: he did not get something of value in exchange for his promise to pay. Assuming that the government is a holder of the promissory note, would this argument likely be successful against it? Why or why not?

Terms and Concepts

acceleration clause 296
acceptance 291
acceptor 295
bearer 296
bearer instrument 296
blank indorsement 298
certificate of deposit (CD) 292
check 291
dishonor 304
draft 291
drawee 291
drawer 291
extension clause 296
fictitious payee 306
holder 296
holder in due course (HDC) 301
imposter 306
indorsement 298
maker 292
negotiable instrument 290
negotiation 298
order instrument 296
payee 291
personal defense 308
presentment 295
presentment warranties 307
promissory note 292
qualified indorsement 299
restrictive indorsement 300
shelter principle 304
special indorsement 298
transfer warranties 307
trust indorsement 300
universal defense 307

Chapter Summary: Negotiability, Transferability, and Liability

Types of Instruments (See pages 290–292.)	The UCC specifies four types of negotiable instruments: drafts, checks, promissory notes, and certificates of deposit (CDs). These instruments fall into two basic classifications: 1. *Demand instruments versus time instruments*—A demand instrument is payable on demand (when the holder presents it to the maker or drawer). A time instrument is payable at a future date. 2. *Orders to pay versus promises to pay*—Checks and drafts are *orders* to pay. Promissory notes and CDs are *promises* to pay.
Requirements for Negotiability (See pages 292–297.)	To be negotiable, an instrument must meet the requirements stated below. 1. *Be in writing*—A writing can be on anything that is readily transferable and has a degree of permanence [UCC 3–103(a)(6), (9)]. 2. *Be signed by the maker or drawer*—The signature can be anyplace on the face of the instrument, can be in any form (including a rubber stamp), and can be made in a representative capacity [UCC 3–103(a)(3), 3–401(b)]. 3. *Be an unconditional promise or order to pay*— a. A promise must be more than a mere acknowledgment of a debt [UCC 3–103(a)(6), (9)]. b. The words "I/We promise" or "Pay" meet this criterion. c. Payment cannot be expressly conditioned on the occurrence of an event and cannot be made subject to or governed by another contract [UCC 3–106]. 4. *State a fixed amount of money*— a. An amount is considered a fixed sum if it is ascertainable from the face of the instrument or (for the interest rate) readily determinable by a formula described in the instrument [UCC 3–104(a), 3–112(b)]. b. Any medium of exchange recognized as the currency of a government is money [UCC 1–201(24)]. 5. *Be payable on demand or at a definite time*— a. Any instrument that is payable on sight, presentation, or issue, or that does not state any time for payment, is a demand instrument [UCC 3–104(a)(2)]. b. An instrument is still payable at a definite time, even if it is payable on or before a stated date or within a fixed period after sight or if the drawer or maker has an option to extend the time for a definite period [UCC 3–108(a), (b), (c)]. c. Acceleration clauses do not affect the negotiability of the instrument. 6. *Be payable to order or bearer*— a. An order instrument must identify the payee with certainty. b. An instrument that indicates it is not payable to an identified person is payable to bearer [UCC 3–109(a)(3)].

Chapter Summary: Negotiability, Transferability, and Liability—Continued

Factors That Do Not Affect Negotiability (See page 297.)	Certain ambiguities or omissions will not affect an instrument's negotiability.
Transfer of Instruments (See pages 297–298.)	1. *Transfer by assignment*—A transfer by assignment to an assignee gives the assignee only those rights that the assignor possessed. Any defenses against payment that can be raised against an assignor normally can be raised against the assignee. 2. *Transfer by negotiation*—An order instrument is negotiated by indorsement and delivery. A bearer instrument is negotiated by delivery only.
Indorsements (See pages 298–301.)	The four categories of indorsements include the following: 1. *Blank indorsements*—Do not specify a particular indorsee and can consist of a mere signature (see Exhibit 16–5 on page 298). 2. *Special indorsements*—Contain the signature of the indorser and identify the indorsee (see Exhibit 16–6 on page 299). 3. *Qualified indorsements*—Contain language, such as the notation "without recourse," that indicates the indorser is not guaranteeing payment of the instrument (see Exhibit 16–7 on page 299). 4. *Restrictive indorsements*—Require the indorsee to comply with certain instructions regarding the funds involved, but do not prohibit further negotiation of an instrument.
Holder in Due Course (HDC) (See pages 301–304.)	1. *Holder*—A person in the possession of an instrument drawn, issued, or indorsed to him or her, to his or her order, to bearer, or in blank. A holder obtains only those rights that the transferor had in the instrument. 2. *Holder in due course (HDC)*—A holder who, by meeting certain acquisition requirements (summarized next), takes an instrument free of most defenses and claims to which the transferor was subject. 3. *Requirements for HDC status*—To be an HDC, a holder must take the instrument: a. For value—A holder must give value to become an HDC and can take an instrument for value in any of the five ways listed on page 302 [UCC 3–303]. b. In good faith—Good faith is defined as "honesty in fact and the observance of reasonable commercial standards of fair dealing" [UCC 3–103(a)(4)]. c. Without notice—To be an HDC, a holder must not be on notice that the instrument is defective because it is overdue, has been dishonored, is part of a series of which at least one instrument has an uncured defect, contains an unauthorized signature or has been altered, or is so irregular or incomplete as to call its authenticity into question. 4. *Shelter principle*—A holder who cannot qualify as an HDC has the *rights* of an HDC if he or she derives title through an HDC, unless the holder engaged in fraud or illegality affecting the instrument [UCC 3–203(b)].
Signature and Warranty Liability (See pages 304–307.)	Liability on negotiable instruments can arise either from a person's signature or from the (transfer and presentment) warranties that are implied when a person presents the instrument for negotiation. 1. *Signature liability*—Every party (except a qualified indorser) who signs a negotiable instrument is either primarily or secondarily liable for payment of the instrument when it comes due. a. Primary liability—Makers and acceptors are primarily liable (an *acceptor* is a drawee that promises in writing to pay an instrument when it is presented for payment at a later time) [UCC 3–115, 3–407, 3–409, 3–412]. b. Secondary liability—Drawers and indorsers are secondarily liable [UCC 3–412, 3–414, 3–415, 3–501, 3–502, 3–503]. Parties are secondarily liable on an instrument only if (1) presentment is proper and timely, (2) the instrument is dishonored, and (3) they received timely notice of dishonor. 2. *Transfer warranties*—Any person who transfers an instrument for consideration makes the following warranties to subsequent transferees and holders [UCC 3–416]: a. The transferor is entitled to enforce the instrument. b. All signatures are authentic and authorized. c. The instrument has not been altered. d. The instrument is not subject to a defense or claim of any party that can be asserted against the transferor.

Continued

Chapter Summary: Negotiability, Transferability, and Liability—Continued

Signature and Warranty Liability—Continued	e. The transferor has no knowledge of any insolvency proceedings against the maker, the acceptor, or the drawer of the instrument. 3. *Presentment warranties*—Any person who presents an instrument for payment or acceptance makes the following warranties to any other person who in good faith pays or accepts the instrument [UCC 3–417(a), 3–417(d)]: a. The person obtaining payment or acceptance is entitled to enforce the instrument or is authorized to obtain payment or acceptance on behalf of a person who is entitled to enforce the instrument. (This is, in effect, a warranty that there are no missing or unauthorized indorsements.) b. The instrument has not been altered. c. The person obtaining payment or acceptance has no knowledge that the signature of the drawer of the instrument is unauthorized.
Defenses, Limitations, and Discharge (See pages 307–309.)	1. *Universal (real) defenses*—The following defenses are valid against all holders, including HDCs and holders with the rights of HDCs [UCC 3–305, 3–403, 3–407]: a. Forgery. b. Fraud in the execution. c. Material alteration. d. Discharge in bankruptcy. e. Minority—if the contract is voidable under state law. f. Illegality, mental incapacity, or extreme duress—if the contract is void under state law. 2. *Personal (limited) defenses*—The following defenses are valid against ordinary holders but not against HDCs or holders with the rights of HDCs [UCC 3–303, 3–305]: a. Breach of contract or breach of warranty. b. Lack or failure of consideration (value). c. Fraud in the inducement. d. Illegality and mental incapacity—if the contract is voidable. e. Ordinary duress or undue influence that renders the contract voidable. 3. *Federal limitations on the rights of HDCs*—A rule issued by the Federal Trade Commission in 1976 essentially abolished the HDC doctrine in consumer credit transactions. 4. *Discharge from liability*—All parties to a negotiable instrument will be discharged when the party primarily liable on it pays to the holder the full amount due. Discharge can also occur in other circumstances (if the instrument has been canceled or materially altered, for example) [UCC 3–602 through 3–605].

ExamPrep

ISSUE SPOTTERS

—Check your answers to these questions against the answers provided in Appendix G.

1 Sabrina owes $600 to Yale, who asks Sabrina to sign an instrument for the debt. If included on that instrument, which of the following would prevent its negotiability—"I.O.U. $600," "I promise to pay $600," or an instruction to Sabrina's bank stating, "I wish you would pay $600 to Yale"?

2 Rye signs corporate checks for Suchin Corporation. Rye writes a check payable to U-All Company, to which Suchin owes no money. Rye signs the check, forges U-All's indorsement, and cashes the check at Viceroy Bank, the drawee. Does Suchin have any recourse against the bank for the payment? Why or why not?

BEFORE THE TEST

Go to **www.cengagebrain.com**, enter the ISBN 9781111530624, and click on "Find" to locate this textbook's Web site. Then, click on "Access Now" under "Study Tools," and select Chapter 16 at the top. There, you will find an Interactive Quiz that you can take to assess your mastery of the concepts in this chapter, as well as Flashcards and a Glossary of important terms.

For Review

1 What requirements must an instrument meet to be negotiable?
2 What are the requirements for attaining the status of a holder in due course (HDC)?
3 What is the difference between signature liability and warranty liability?
4 Certain defenses are valid against all holders, including HDCs. What are these defenses called? Name four defenses that fall within this category.
5 Certain defenses can be used against an ordinary holder but are not effective against an HDC. What are these defenses called? Name four defenses that fall within this category.

Questions and Case Problems

16–1 Indorsements. A check drawn by David for $500 is made payable to the order of Matthew and issued to Matthew. Matthew owes his landlord $500 in rent and transfers the check to his landlord with the following indorsement: "For rent paid. [Signed] Matthew." Matthew's landlord has contracted to have Lambert do some landscaping on the property. When Lambert insists on immediate payment, the landlord transfers the check to Lambert without indorsement. Later, to pay for some palm trees purchased from Green's Nursery, Lambert transfers the check with the following indorsement: "Pay to Green's Nursery, without recourse. [Signed] Lambert." Green's Nursery sends the check to its bank indorsed "For deposit only. [Signed] Green's Nursery."

1 Classify each of these indorsements.
2 Was the transfer from Matthew's landlord to Lambert, without indorsement, an assignment or a negotiation? Explain.

16–2 Question with Sample Answer Muriel Evans writes the following note on the back of an envelope: "I, Muriel Evans, promise to pay Karen Marvin or bearer $100 on demand." Is this a negotiable instrument? Discuss fully.

—For a sample answer to Question 16–2, go to Appendix E at the end of this text.

16–3 Signature Liability. Marion makes a promissory note payable to the order of Perry. Perry indorses the note by writing "without recourse, Perry" and transfers the note for value to Steven. Steven, in need of cash, negotiates the note to Harriet by indorsing it with the words "Pay to Harriet, [signed] Steven." On the due date, Harriet presents the note to Marion for payment, only to learn that Marion has filed for bankruptcy and will have all debts (including the note) discharged in bankruptcy. Discuss fully whether Harriet can hold Marion, Perry, or Steven liable on the note.

16–4 Holder in Due Course. American International Group, Inc. (AIG), an insurance company, issued a check to Jermielem Merriwether in connection with a personal-injury matter. Merriwether presented the check to A-1 Check Cashing Emporium (A-1) for payment. A-1's clerk forgot to have Merriwether sign the check. When he could not reach Merriwether and ask him to come back to A-1 to sign the check, the clerk printed Merriwether's name on the back and deposited it for collection. When the check was not paid, A-1 sold it to Robert Triffin, who is in the business of buying dishonored checks. When Triffin could not get the check honored, he sued AIG, contending that he, through A-1, had the right to collect on the check as a holder in due course (HDC). The trial court rejected that claim. Triffin appealed. On what basis could he claim HDC status? [*Triffin v. American International Group, Inc.,* __ A.2d __ (N.J.Super. 2008)]

16–5 Transfer and Holder in Due Course. Germanie Fequiere executed and delivered a promissory note in the principal amount of $240,000 to BNC Mortgage. As security for the note, Fequiere executed and delivered a mortgage on real property. BNC endorsed the promissory note in blank. Several years later, when Fequiere failed to make payments on the note, Chase Home Finance, LLC—the holder in due course of the note and holder of the mortgage—moved to foreclose on the property. Fequiere defended that Chase could not foreclose on the property because the mortgage on the property had not been properly transferred from BNC to Chase. Assuming that is true, does that mean Chase cannot, as holder of the negotiable note, act to foreclose on the collateral—that is, the property secured by the mortgage? Explain your answer. [*Chase Home Finance, LLC v. Fequiere,* 119 Conn.App. 570, 989 A.2d 606 (2010)]

16–6 Case Problem with Sample Answer Michael Scotto borrowed $2,970 from Cindy Vinueza. Both of their signatures appeared at the bottom of an instrument that stated in its entirety, "I, Michael Scotto, owe Cindy Vinueza $2,970 (two thousand and nine-hundred & seventy dollars) & agree to pay her back in full. Signed on this 26th day of September 2009." More than a year later, Vinueza filed a suit in a New York state court against Scotto to recover $3,600, offering as evidence only this instrument. Scotto admitted that he had borrowed the funds, but he contended—without proof—that he had paid Vinueza in full. Is this instrument negotiable? If it is a negotiable instrument, which type is it? In the suit, which party is likely to prevail? Why? [*Vinueza v. Scotto,* 30 Misc.3d 1229 (2011)]

—For a sample answer to Problem 16–6, go to Appendix F at the end of this text.

16–7 Negotiation. Sandra Ford signed a note and a mortgage on her home in Westwood, New Jersey, to borrow $403,750 from Argent Mortgage Co. Argent transferred the note and mortgage to Wells Fargo Bank, N.A., without indorsement. The following spring, Ford stopped making payments on the note. Wells Fargo filed a suit in a New Jersey state court against Ford to foreclose on the mortgage—that is, to repossess and auction off Ford's home to obtain the amount due on the note. Ford asserted that Argent had committed fraud in connection with the note by providing misleading information and charging excessive fees. Ford contended that Wells Fargo was subject to these defenses because the bank was not a holder in due course of the note. Was the transfer of the note from Argent to Wells Fargo a negotiation or an assignment? What difference does it make? If Argent indorsed the note to Wells Fargo now, would the bank's status change? Discuss. [*Wells Fargo Bank, N.A. v. Ford,* 418 N.J.Super. 592, 15 A.3d 327 (App.Div. 2011)]

16–8 Defenses. Thomas and Heidi Klutz, who did business as Hit Enterprises, LLC, obtained a franchise from Kahala Franchise Corp. to operate a Samurai Sam's Teriyaki Grill restaurant in Vancouver, Washington. Their agreement allowed them to transfer the franchise only on Kahala's approval. Six years later, the Klutzes sold the restaurant to William Thorbecke and Regina Norby-Thorbecke for $170,000. The Thorbeckes signed a promissory note to the Klutzes for $110,000 of the price. At the time, the Klutzes claimed that they also had the right to sell the franchise to the Thorbeckes. They advised the Thorbeckes, however, to operate the restaurant under the Klutzes' franchise agreement to avoid paying a $5,000 transfer fee to Kahala. When Kahala learned of the deal, the franchisor told the Thorbeckes to stop using the Samurai Sam's name and filed a suit in a Washington state court against the Klutzes. The Thorbeckes stopped paying on the note, and the Klutzes filed a claim against them for the unpaid amount. In defense, the Thorbeckes asserted breach of contract and fraud. Are the Thorbeckes' defenses effective against the Klutzes? Explain. [*Kahala Franchise Corp. v. Hit Enterprises, LLC,* 159 Wash.App. 1013 (2011)]

16–9 A Question of Ethics *Clarence Morgan, Jr., owned Easy Way Automotive, a car dealership in D'Lo, Mississippi. Easy Way sold a truck to Loyd Barnard, who signed a note for the amount of the price payable to Trustmark National Bank in six months. Before the note came due, Barnard returned the truck to Easy Way, which sold it to another buyer. Using some of the proceeds from the second sale, Easy Way sent a check to Trustmark to pay Barnard's note. Meanwhile, Barnard obtained another truck from Easy Way financed through another six-month note payable to Trustmark. After eight of these deals, some of which involved more than one truck, an Easy Way check to Trustmark was dishonored. In a suit in a Mississippi state court, Trustmark sought to recover the amounts of two of the notes from Barnard. Trustmark had not secured titles to two of the trucks covered by the notes, however, and this complicated Barnard's efforts to reclaim the vehicles from the later buyers.* [Trustmark National Bank v. Barnard, *930 So.2d 1281 (Miss.App. 2006)]*

1. On what basis might Barnard be liable on the Trustmark notes? Would he be primarily or secondarily liable? Could this liability be discharged on the theory that Barnard's right of recourse had been impaired when Trustmark did not secure titles to the trucks covered by the notes? Explain.
2. Easy Way's account had been subject to other recent overdrafts, and a week after the check to Trustmark was returned for insufficient funds, Morgan committed suicide. At the same time, Barnard was unable to obtain a mortgage because the unpaid notes affected his credit rating. How do the circumstances of this case underscore the importance of practicing business ethics?

16–10 Video Question To watch this chapter's video, *Negotiable Instruments,* go to **www.cengagebrain.com**. Register the access code that came with your new book or log in to your existing account. Select the link for the "Business Law Digital Video Library Online Access" or "Business Law CourseMate." Click on "Complete Video List," view Video 30, and then answer the following questions:

1. Who is the maker of the promissory note discussed in the video?
2. Is the note in the video payable on demand or at a definite time?
3. Does the note contain an unconditional promise or order to pay?
4. If the note does not meet the requirements of negotiability, can Onyx assign the note (assignment was discussed in Chapter 11) to the bank in exchange for cash?

Chapter 17

Checks and Banking in the Digital Age

Learning Objectives

After reading this chapter, you should be able to answer the following questions:

1. What type of check does a bank agree in advance to accept when the check is presented for payment?
2. When may a bank properly dishonor a customer's check without the bank being liable to the customer?
3. What duties does the Uniform Commercial Code impose on a bank's customers with regard to forged and altered checks? What are the consequences if a customer is negligent in performing those duties?
4. What are the four most common types of electronic fund transfers?
5. What laws apply to e-money transactions and online banking services?

The Learning Objectives above are designed to help improve your understanding of the chapter.

Checks are the most common type of negotiable instruments regulated by the Uniform Commercial Code (UCC). Checks are convenient to use because they serve as a substitute for cash. To be sure, most students today tend to use debit cards rather than checks for many retail transactions. Debit cards now account for more retail payments than checks. Nonetheless, commercial checks remain an integral part of the U.S. economic system.

Articles 3 and 4 of the UCC govern issues relating to checks. Article 4 of the UCC governs bank deposits and collections as well as bank-customer relationships. Article 4 also regulates the relationships of banks with one another as they process checks for payment, and it establishes a framework for deposit and checking agreements between a bank and its customers. A check therefore may fall within the scope of Article 3 and yet be subject to the provisions of Article 4 while in the course of collection. If a conflict between Article 3 and Article 4 arises, Article 4 controls [UCC 4–102(a)].

Checks

A **check** is a special type of draft that is drawn on a bank, ordering the bank to pay a fixed amount of money on demand [UCC 3–104(f)]. Article 4 defines a bank as "a person engaged in the business of banking, including a savings bank, savings and loan association, credit union or trust company" [UCC 4–105(1)]. If any other institution (such as a brokerage firm) handles a check for payment or for collection, the check is not covered by Article 4.

Recall from the preceding chapter that a person who writes a check is called the *drawer*. The drawer is a depositor in the bank on which the check is drawn. The person to whom the check is payable is the *payee*. The bank or financial institution on which the check is drawn is the *drawee*. When Anita Cruzak writes a check from her checking account to pay her college tuition, she is the drawer, her bank is the drawee, and her college is the payee. We now look at some special types of checks.

• *Exhibit* **17–1 A Cashier's Check**

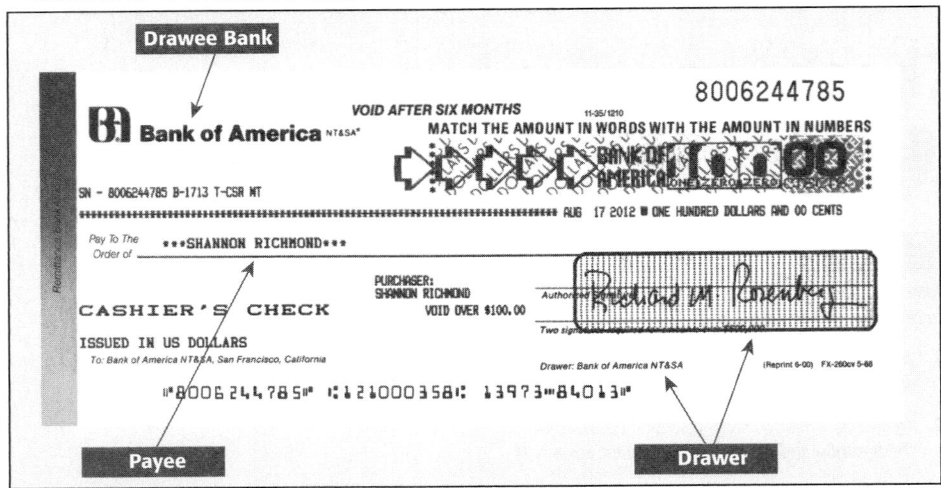

*The abbreviation *NT&SA* stands for National Trust and Savings Association. The Bank of America NT&SA is a subsidiary of Bank of America Corporation, which is engaged in financial services, insurance, investment management, and other businesses.

Cashier's Checks

Checks usually are three-party instruments, but on certain types of checks, the bank can serve as both the drawer and the drawee. For example, when a bank draws a check on itself, the check is called a **cashier's check** and is a negotiable instrument on issue (see Exhibit 17–1 above) [UCC 3–104(g)]. Normally, a cashier's check indicates a specific payee. In effect, with a cashier's check, the bank assumes responsibility for paying the check, thus making the check more readily acceptable as a substitute for cash.

EXAMPLE 17.1 Kramer needs to pay a moving company $8,000 for moving his household goods to a new home in another state. The moving company requests payment in the form of a cashier's check. Kramer goes to a bank (he does not need to have an account at the bank) and purchases a cashier's check, payable to the moving company, in the amount of $8,000. Kramer has to pay the bank the $8,000 for the check, plus a small service fee. He then gives the check to the moving company. •

Cashier's checks are sometimes used in the business community as nearly the equivalent of cash. Except in very limited circumstances, the issuing bank must honor its cashier's checks when they are presented for payment. If a bank wrongfully dishonors a cashier's check, a holder can recover from the bank all expenses incurred, interest, and consequential damages [UCC 3–411]. This same rule applies if a bank wrongfully dishonors a certified check (to be discussed shortly) or a teller's check. (A *teller's check* is a check drawn by a bank on another bank or, when drawn on a nonbank, payable at or through a bank [UCC 3–104(h)]. For instance, when a credit union issues a check to withdraw funds from its account at another financial institution, and the teller at the credit union signs the check, it is a teller's check.)

Rather than being treated as the equivalent of cash, should a cashier's check be treated as a note with all of the applicable defenses? That was the question in the following case.

Case 17.1 MidAmerica Bank, FSB v. Charter One Bank

Illinois Supreme Court, 232 Ill.2d 560, 905 N.E.2d 839 (2009).

FACTS Mary Christelle was the mother of David Hernandez, president of Essential Technologies of Illinois (ETI). Christelle bought a $50,000 cashier's check from Charter One Bank payable to ETI. ETI deposited the check into its account with MidAmerica Bank, FSB. Four days later, Christelle asked Charter One to *stop payment* (see the discussion on page 319). Charter One agreed and refused to honor the check. MidAmerica returned the check to ETI. Within two weeks, ETI's account had a negative balance of $52,000. MidAmerica closed the account and filed a suit in an Illinois state court against Charter One, alleging that the defendant wrongfully dishonored the cashier's check. Charter One argued that a cashier's check should be treated as a note subject to the defense of fraud. The court ruled in MidAmerica's favor, but a state intermediate appellate court reversed the ruling. MidAmerica appealed.

ISSUE Can a bank obtain payment on a cashier's check over the drawee bank's stop-payment order?

Case 17.1—Continued

DECISION Yes. The Illinois Supreme Court reversed the lower court's decision, awarded MidAmerica the amount of the check, and remanded the case for a determination of interest and fees.

REASON A bank's refusal to pay a cashier's check based on its customer's request to stop payment is wrongful under UCC 3–411. A customer has no right to stop payment on a cashier's check under UCC 4–403, which permits payment to be stopped only on items drawn "on the customer's account." A cashier's check is drawn on the issuing bank, not on the customer's account. Thus, Christelle had no right to stop payment after she gave the check to ETI. Charter One argued that the check should be treated as a note, and the court agreed. The court reasoned that the drawer of a cashier's check has the same liability as the maker of a note "because a bank issuing a cashier's check is both the drawer and drawee of the check." But "the UCC provides that cashier's checks are drafts, not notes." Besides, the bank cannot assert fraud as a defense because it did not know of any fraud when it dishonored the check.

WHY IS THIS CASE IMPORTANT? *The UCC has been amended periodically since it was first issued in 1949. In particular, Article 3 was significantly revised in 1990 when many sections were rewritten and renumbered. The reasoning in this case underscores that through all of the changes, the treatment of cashier's checks as "cash equivalents" in the world of commerce has never varied, and none of the amendments to Article 3 have been intended to alter that status.*

Traveler's Checks

A **traveler's check** is an instrument that is payable on demand, drawn on or payable at or through a financial institution (such as a bank), and designated as a traveler's check. The issuing institution is directly obligated to accept and pay its traveler's check according to the check's terms. Traveler's checks are designed as a safe substitute for cash when a person is on vacation or traveling and are issued for a fixed amount, such as $20, $50, or $100. The purchaser is required to sign the check at the time it is bought and again at the time it is used [UCC 3–104(i)]. Most banks today purchase and issue American Express traveler's checks for their customers (see Exhibit 17–2 below).

Certified Checks

A **certified check** is a check that has been *accepted* in writing by the bank on which it is drawn [UCC 3–409(d)]. When a drawee bank *certifies* (accepts) a check, it immediately charges the drawer's account with the amount of the check and transfers those funds to its own certified check account. In effect, the bank is agreeing in advance to accept that check when it is presented for payment and to make payment from those funds reserved in the certified check account. Essentially, certification prevents the bank from denying liability. It is a promise that sufficient funds are on deposit *and have been set aside* to cover the check.

To certify a check, the bank writes or stamps the word *certified* on the face of the check and typically writes the amount that it will pay.[1] Either the drawer or the holder (payee) of a check can request certification, but the drawee bank is not required to certify a check. (Note, though, that a

1. If the certification does not state an amount, and the amount is later increased and the instrument negotiated to a holder in due course (HDC), the obligation of the certifying bank is the amount of the instrument when it was taken by the HDC [UCC 3–413(b)].

• ***Exhibit* 17–2 A Traveler's Check**

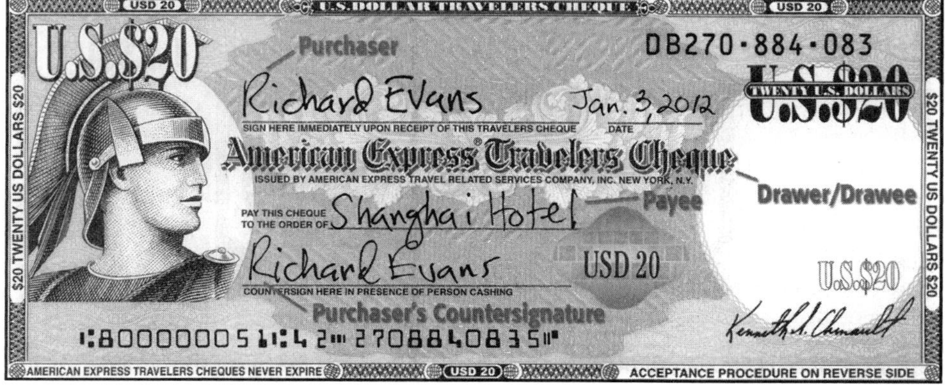

bank's refusal to certify a check is not a dishonor of the check [UCC 3–409(d)].) Once a check is certified, the drawer and any prior indorsers are completely discharged from liability on the check [UCC 3–414(c), 3–415(d)]. Only the certifying bank is required to pay the instrument.

The Bank-Customer Relationship

The bank-customer relationship begins when the customer opens a checking account and deposits funds that the bank will use to pay for checks written by the customer. Essentially, three types of relationships come into being, as discussed next.

Creditor-Debtor Relationship

A creditor-debtor relationship is created between a customer and a bank when, for example, the customer makes cash deposits into a checking account. When a customer makes a deposit, the customer becomes a creditor, and the bank a debtor, for the amount deposited.

Agency Relationship

An agency relationship also arises between the customer and the bank when the customer writes a check on his or her account. In effect, the customer is ordering the bank to pay the amount specified on the check to the holder when the holder presents the check to the bank for payment. In this situation, the bank becomes the customer's agent and is obligated to honor the customer's request. Similarly, if the customer deposits a check into her or his account, the bank, as the customer's agent, is obligated to collect payment on the check from the bank on which the check was drawn. To transfer checkbook funds among different banks, each bank acts as the agent of collection for its customer [UCC 4–201(a)].

Contractual Relationship

Whenever a bank-customer relationship is established, certain contractual rights and duties arise. The specific rights and duties of the bank and its customer depend on the nature of the transaction. The respective rights and duties of banks and their customers are discussed in detail in the following pages.

Bank's Duty to Honor Checks

When a banking institution provides checking services, it agrees to honor the checks written by its customers, with the usual stipulation that the account must have sufficient funds available to pay each check [UCC 4–401(a)]. When a drawee bank *wrongfully* fails to honor a check, it is liable to its customer for damages resulting from its refusal to pay [UCC 4–402(b)]. The customer does not have to prove that the bank breached its contractual commitment or was negligent.

The customer's agreement with the bank includes a general obligation to keep sufficient funds on deposit to cover all checks written. The customer is liable to the payee or to the holder of a check in a civil suit if a check is dishonored for insufficient funds. If intent to defraud can be proved, the customer can also be subject to criminal prosecution for writing a bad check.

When the bank properly dishonors a check for insufficient funds, it has no liability to the customer. The bank may rightfully refuse payment on a customer's check in other circumstances as well. We look here at the rights and duties of both the bank and its customers in relation to specific situations.

Overdrafts

When the bank receives an item properly payable from its customer's checking account but the account contains insufficient funds to cover the amount of the check, the bank has two options. It can either (1) dishonor the item or (2) pay the item and charge the customer's account, thus creating an **overdraft**, providing that the customer has authorized the payment and the payment does not violate any bank-customer agreement [UCC 4–401(a)].[2] The bank can subtract the difference (plus a service charge) from the customer's next deposit or other customer funds because the check carries with it an enforceable implied promise to reimburse the bank.

A bank can expressly agree with a customer to accept overdrafts through what is sometimes called an "overdraft protection agreement." If such an agreement is formed, any failure of the bank to honor a check because it would create an overdraft breaches this agreement and is treated as a wrongful dishonor [UCC 4–402(a)].

Postdated Checks

A bank may also charge a postdated check against a customer's account, unless the customer notifies the bank, in a timely manner, not to pay the check until the stated date. The notice of postdating must be given in time to allow the bank to act on the notice before committing itself to pay on the check. The UCC states that the bank should treat a notice of postdating the same as a stop-payment order—to be discussed shortly. If the bank fails to act on the customer's notice and charges the customer's account before the date on the postdated check, the bank may be liable for any damages incurred by the customer [UCC 4–401(c)].[3]

2. With a joint account, the bank cannot hold the nonsigning customer liable for payment of an overdraft unless that person benefited from its proceeds [UCC 4–401(b)].

3. As noted in Chapter 16, postdating does not affect the negotiability of a check. Under the automated check-collection system now in use, a check usually is paid without respect to its date. Thus, today banks typically ignore the dates on checks (and treat them as demand instruments) unless they have received notice from a customer that a check was postdated.

Stale Checks

Commercial banking practice regards a check that is presented for payment more than six months from its date as a **stale check.** A bank is not obligated to pay an uncertified check presented more than six months from its date [UCC 4–404]. When receiving a stale check for payment, the bank has the option of paying or not paying the check. The bank may consult the customer before paying the check. If a bank pays a stale check in good faith without consulting the customer, however, the bank has the right to charge the customer's account for the amount of the check.

Stop-Payment Orders

A **stop-payment order** is an order by a customer to his or her bank not to pay or certify a certain check. Only a customer or a person authorized to draw on the account can order the bank not to pay the check when it is presented for payment [UCC 4–403(a)].[4] A customer has no right to stop payment on a check that has been certified or accepted by a bank, however. The customer must issue the stop-payment order within a reasonable time and in a reasonable manner to permit the bank to act on it [UCC 4–403(a)]. Although a stop-payment order can be given orally, usually by phone, it is binding on the bank for only fourteen calendar days unless confirmed in writing.[5] A written stop-payment order (the bank typically provides a preprinted form for the customer) or an oral order confirmed in writing is effective for six months, at which time it must be renewed in writing [UCC 4–403(b)].

BANK'S LIABILITY FOR WRONGFUL PAYMENT If the bank pays the check in spite of a stop-payment order, the bank will be obligated to recredit the customer's account. In addition, if the bank's payment over a stop-payment order causes subsequent checks written on the drawer's account to "bounce," the bank will be liable for the resultant costs the drawer incurs.

The bank is liable only for the amount of the actual damages suffered by the drawer, however [UCC 4–403(c)]. **EXAMPLE 17.2** Mako Murano orders six bamboo palms from a local nursery at $50 each and gives the nursery a check for $300. Later that day, the nursery tells Murano that it will not deliver the palms as arranged. Murano immediately calls his bank and stops payment on the check. If the bank nonetheless honors the check, the bank will be liable to Murano for the full $300. The result would be different, however, if the nursery had delivered five palms. In that situation, Murano would owe the nursery $250 for the delivered palms, and his actual losses would be only $50. Consequently, the bank would be liable to Murano for only $50. •

CUSTOMER'S LIABILITY FOR WRONGFUL STOP-PAYMENT ORDER A stop-payment order has its risks for a customer. The customer-drawer must have a *valid legal ground* for issuing such an order. Otherwise, the holder can sue the drawer for payment. Moreover, defenses sufficient to refuse payment against a payee may not be valid grounds to prevent payment against a subsequent holder in due course [UCC 3–305, 3–306]. A person who wrongfully stops payment on a check is liable to the payee for the amount of the check and can also be liable for consequential damages incurred by the payee.

Death or Incompetence of a Customer

Neither the death nor the incompetence of a customer revokes a bank's authority to pay an item until the bank is informed of the situation and has had a reasonable amount of time to act on the notice. Thus, if a bank is unaware that the customer who wrote a check has been declared incompetent or has died, the bank can pay the item without incurring liability [UCC 4–405]. Even when a bank knows of the death of its customer, for ten days after the *date of death,* it can pay or certify checks drawn on or before the date of death. An exception to this rule is made if a person claiming an interest in that account, such as an heir, orders the bank to stop payment. Without this provision, banks would constantly be required to verify the continued life and competence of their drawers.

Checks Bearing Forged Drawers' Signatures

When a bank pays a check on which the drawer's signature is forged, generally the bank is liable. A bank may be able to recover at least some of the loss from the customer, however, if the customer's negligence contributed to the making of the forgery. A bank may also obtain partial recovery from the forger of the check (if he or she can be found) or from the holder who presented the check for payment (if the holder knew that the signature was forged).

THE GENERAL RULE A forged signature on a check has no legal effect as the signature of a drawer [UCC 3–403(a)]. For this reason, banks require a signature card from each customer who opens a checking account. Signature cards allow the bank to verify whether the signatures on its customers' checks are genuine.

The general rule is that the bank must recredit the customer's account when it pays a check with a forged signature. (Note that banks today normally verify signatures only on checks that exceed a certain threshold, such as $2,500 or some higher amount. Even though a bank sometimes incurs liability costs when it has paid forged checks, the costs involved in verifying every check's signature would be much higher.)

4. For a deceased customer, any person claiming a legitimate interest in the account may issue a stop-payment order [UCC 4–405].

5. Some states do not recognize oral stop-payment orders; they must be in writing.

Note that a bank may contractually shift to the customer the risk of forged checks created by the use of facsimile or other nonmanual signatures. For instance, the contract might stipulate that the customer is solely responsible for maintaining security over any device affixing a signature.

CUSTOMER NEGLIGENCE When the customer's negligence substantially contributes to the forgery, the bank normally will not be obligated to recredit the customer's account for the amount of the check [UCC 3–406]. The customer's liability may be reduced, however, by the amount of loss caused by negligence on the part of the bank (or other "person") paying the instrument or taking it for value if the negligence substantially contributed to the loss [UCC 3–406(b)].

EXAMPLE 17.3 Gemco Corporation uses special check-writing equipment to write its payroll and business checks. Gemco discovers that one of its employees used the equipment to write himself a check for $10,000 and that the bank subsequently honored it. Gemco asks the bank to recredit $10,000 to its account for improperly paying the forged check. If the bank can show that Gemco failed to take reasonable care in controlling access to the check-writing equipment, the bank will not be required to recredit Gemco's account for the amount of the forged check. If Gemco can show that negligence on the part of the bank contributed substantially to the loss, however, then Gemco's liability may be reduced proportionately. •

In the following case, an employee opened a bogus bank account and fraudulently deposited his employer's checks in it for years. The court had to determine if the bank should have requested written authorization from the company before opening the account.

Case 17.2 Auto-Owners Insurance Co. v. Bank One

Supreme Court of Indiana, 879 N.E.2d 1086 (2008).

FACTS Kenneth Wulf worked in the claims department of Auto-Owners Insurance Company for ten years. When the department received a check, a staff member would note it in the file and send it on to headquarters. Wulf opened a checking account at Bank One in the name of "Auto-Owners, Kenneth B. Wulf." Over a period of eight years, he deposited $546,000 worth of checks that he had stolen from Auto-Owners and had indorsed with a stamp that read "Auto-Owners Insurance Deposit Only." When the scam was finally discovered, Auto-Owners sued Bank One, contending that it had failed to exercise ordinary care in opening the account because it had not asked for documentation to show that Wulf was authorized to open an account in the name of Auto-Owners. The lower courts rejected that argument and granted summary judgment for Bank One. Auto-Owners appealed.

ISSUE Did the bank's failure to request proof from Wulf that he was authorized to deposit checks made payable to Auto-Owners substantially contribute to the company's loss?

DECISION No. The state supreme court affirmed the decision of the lower courts, finding that Bank One's conduct did not "substantially contribute" to the losses suffered by Auto-Owners.

REASON The court reasoned that UCC 3–405(b) makes no mention of a bank's responsibilities when opening an account for a new customer. Rather, subsection (b) requires ordinary care from a bank in the "paying" or "taking" of an instrument. Therefore, the bank did not breach any duty to the insurance company by opening Wulf's checking account. In such cases, the courts consider all of the facts surrounding the transactions that occurred. Here, the major reasons for the losses suffered by Auto-Owners were its weak internal monitoring of its own files and the lack of controls in the handling of company checks. The bank did not worsen the situation by allowing Wulf to have a checking account.

FOR CRITICAL ANALYSIS—Management Consideration *What reasonable steps could Auto-Owners have taken to prevent such internal fraud?*

Timely Examination of Bank Statements Required. Banks typically either mail customers monthly statements detailing activity in their checking accounts or make these statements available in some other way—for example, online or via an automated teller machine (ATM). In the past, banks routinely included the canceled checks themselves (or photocopies of the canceled checks), with the statement sent to the customer.

Today, most banks simply provide the customer with information (check number, amount, and date of payment) on the statement that will allow the customer to reasonably identify the checks that the bank has paid [UCC 4–406(a), (b)]. If the bank retains the canceled checks, it must keep the checks—or legible copies of the checks—for seven years [UCC 4–406(b)]. The customer can obtain a copy of a canceled check during this period of time.

The customer has a duty to promptly examine bank statements (and canceled checks or photocopies, if they are included) with reasonable care and to report any alterations or forged signatures [UCC 4–406(c)]. This includes forged signatures of indorsers, if discovered (to be discussed shortly). If the customer fails to fulfill this duty and the bank suffers a loss as a result, the customer will be liable for the loss [UCC 4–406(d)].

Consequences of Failing to Detect Forgeries. Sometimes, the same wrongdoer has forged the customer's signature on a series of checks. In that situation, the customer, to recover for all the forged items, must discover and report the *first* forged check to the bank within thirty calendar days of the receipt of the bank statement [UCC 4–406(d)(2)]. Failure to notify the bank within this period of time discharges the bank's liability for *all* of the forged checks that it pays prior to notification.

CASE EXAMPLE 17.4 Joseph Montanez, an employee and bookkeeper for Espresso Roma Corporation, used stolen computer software and blank checks to generate company checks on his home computer. The series of forged checks spanned a period of more than two years and totaled more than $330,000. When the bank statements containing the forged checks arrived in the mail, Montanez sorted through the statements and removed the checks so that the forgeries would go undetected. Eventually, Espresso Roma discovered the forgeries and asked the bank to recredit its account. The bank refused, and litigation ensued. The court held that the bank was not liable for the forged checks because Espresso Roma had failed to report the first forgeries within the UCC's time period of thirty days.[6] •

WHEN THE BANK IS ALSO NEGLIGENT In one situation, a bank customer can escape liability, at least in part, for failing to notify the bank of forged or altered checks promptly or within the required thirty-day period. That situation occurs when the customer can prove that the bank was also negligent—that is, the bank failed to exercise ordinary care. Then the bank will also be liable, and the loss will be allocated between the bank and the customer on the basis of comparative negligence [UCC 4–406(e)]. In other words, even though a customer may have been negligent, the bank may still have to recredit the customer's account for a portion of the loss if the bank failed to exercise ordinary care.

The UCC defines *ordinary care* as the "observance of reasonable commercial standards, prevailing in the area in which [a] person is located, with respect to the business in which that person is engaged" [UCC 3–103(a)(7)]. As mentioned earlier, it is customary in the banking industry to manually examine signatures only on checks over a certain amount (such as $2,500 or some higher amount). Thus, if a bank, in accordance with prevailing banking standards, fails to examine a signature on a particular check, the bank has not necessarily breached its duty to exercise ordinary care.

One-Year Time Limit. Regardless of the degree of care exercised by the customer or the bank, the UCC places an absolute time limit on the liability of a bank for paying a check with a customer's forged signature. A customer who fails to report her or his forged signature within one year from the date that the statement was made available for inspection loses the legal right to have the bank recredit her or his account [UCC 4–406(f)]. The parties can also agree in their contract to a lower time limit, but the UCC stipulates that the bank has no liability on forged instruments after one year.

CASE EXAMPLE 17.5 Wanda Williamson, a clerk at Visiting Nurses Association of Telfair County, Inc. (VNA), was responsible for making VNA bank deposits, but she was not a signatory on the association's account. Over a four-year period, Williamson embezzled more than $250,000 from VNA by forging its indorsement on checks, cashing them at the bank, and keeping a portion of the proceeds. Williamson was eventually arrested and convicted. VNA then filed a lawsuit against the bank claiming that it had been negligent in allowing Williamson to cash the checks. The court dismissed the case because VNA had failed to report the forged indorsements within the prescribed time period. Not only did UCC 4–406(f) preclude the action, but the bank's contract with VNA had also included a clause stating that customers had to report a forgery within sixty days. Thus, the bank was not liable.[7] •

Other Parties from Whom the Bank May Recover. As noted earlier, a forged signature on a check has no legal effect as the signature of a drawer. A forged signature, however, is effective as the signature of the unauthorized signer [UCC 3–403(a)]. Therefore, when a bank pays a check on which the drawer's signature is forged, the bank has a right to recover from the party who forged the signature. The bank may also have a right to recover from a party (its customer or a collecting bank—to be discussed later in this chapter) who transferred a check bearing a forged drawer's signature and received payment. This right is limited, however, in that the bank cannot recover from a person who took the check in good faith and for value or who in good faith changed position in reliance on the payment or acceptance [UCC 3–418(c)].

Checks Bearing Forged Indorsements

A bank that pays a customer's check bearing a forged indorsement must recredit the customer's account or be liable to the customer-drawer for breach of contract. **EXAMPLE 17.6** Simon issues a $500 check "to the order of Antonio." Juan steals the check, forges Antonio's indorsement, and cashes the check. When the check reaches Simon's bank, the bank pays it and debits Simon's account. The bank must recredit the $500 to Simon's account because it failed to carry out Simon's order to pay "to the order of Antonio" [UCC 4–401(a)]. Of course,

6. *Espresso Roma Corp. v. Bank of America, N.A.*, 100 Cal.App.4th 525, 124 Cal.Rptr.2d 549 (2002).

7. *Security State Bank v. Visiting Nurses Association of Telfair County, Inc.*, 568 S.E.2d 491 (Ga.App. 2002).

Simon's bank can in turn recover—for breach of warranty (see Chapter 16)—from the bank that cashed the check when Juan presented it [UCC 4–207(a)(2)]. •

Eventually, the loss usually falls on the first party to take the instrument bearing the forged indorsement because, as discussed in Chapter 16, a forged indorsement does not transfer title. Thus, whoever takes an instrument with a forged indorsement cannot become a holder.

In any event, the customer has a duty to report forged indorsements promptly. Failure to report forged indorsements within a three-year period after the forged items have been made available to the customer relieves the bank of liability [UCC 4–111].

Altered Checks

The customer's instruction to the bank is to pay the exact amount on the face of the check to the holder. The bank has a duty to examine each check before making final payment. If it fails to detect an alteration, it is liable to its customer for the loss because it did not pay as the customer ordered. The loss is the difference between the original amount of the check and the amount actually paid [UCC 4–401(d)(1)]. **EXAMPLE 17.7** A check written for $11 is raised to $111. The customer's account will be charged $11 (the amount the customer ordered the bank to pay). The bank normally will be responsible for the $100. •

CUSTOMER NEGLIGENCE As in a situation involving a forged drawer's signature, a customer's negligence can shift the loss when payment is made on an altered check (unless the bank was also negligent). For example, a person may carelessly write a check leaving large gaps around the numbers and words where additional numbers and words can be inserted (see Exhibit 17–3 below).

Similarly, a person who signs a check and leaves the dollar amount for someone else to fill in is barred from protesting when the bank unknowingly and in good faith pays whatever amount is shown [UCC 4–401(d)(2)]. Finally, if the bank can trace its loss on successive altered checks to the customer's failure to discover the initial alteration, then the bank can reduce its liability for reimbursing the customer's account [UCC 4–406].

In every situation involving a forged drawer's signature or an alteration, a bank must observe reasonable commercial standards of care in paying on a customer's checks [UCC 4–406(e)]. The customer's negligence can be used as a defense only if the bank has exercised ordinary care.

OTHER PARTIES FROM WHOM THE BANK MAY RECOVER The bank is entitled to recover the amount of loss from the transferor who, by presenting the check for payment, warrants that the check has not been materially altered (warranty liability was discussed in Chapter 16). This rule has two exceptions, though. If the bank is the drawer (as it is on a cashier's check and a teller's check), it cannot recover from the presenting party if the party is a holder in due course (HDC) acting in good faith [UCC 3–417(a)(2), 4–208(a)(2)]. The reason is that an instrument's drawer is in a better position than an HDC to know whether the instrument has been altered.

Similarly, an HDC who presents a certified check for payment in good faith will not be held liable under warranty principles if the check was altered before the HDC acquired it [UCC 3–417(a)(2), 4–207(a)(2)]. **EXAMPLE 17.8** Jordan draws a check for $500 payable to David. David alters the amount to $5,000. The drawee bank, First National, certifies the check for $5,000. David negotiates the check to Ethan, an HDC. The drawee bank pays Ethan $5,000. On discovering the mistake, the bank cannot recover from Ethan the $4,500 paid by mistake, even though the bank was not in a superior position to

• ***Exhibit* 17–3 A Poorly Filled-Out Check**

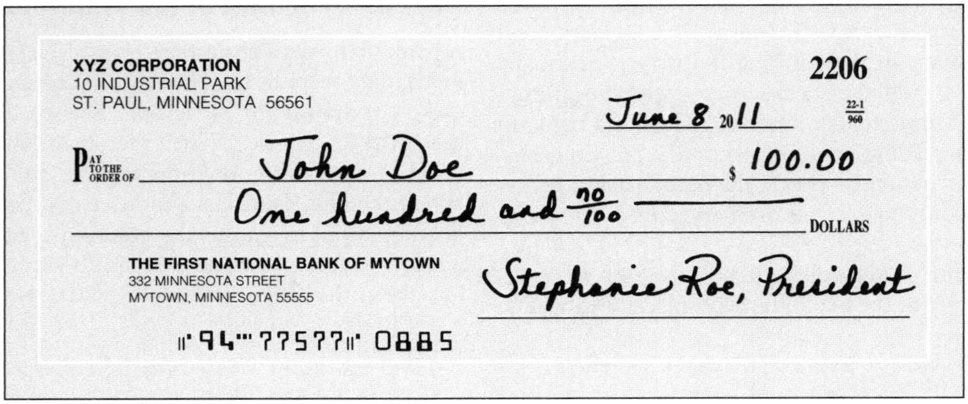

XYZ CORPORATION
10 INDUSTRIAL PARK
ST. PAUL, MINNESOTA 56561

2206

June 8 20 11

22-1
960

PAY TO THE ORDER OF John Doe $ 100.00

One hundred and no/100 DOLLARS

THE FIRST NATIONAL BANK OF MYTOWN
332 MINNESOTA STREET
MYTOWN, MINNESOTA 55555

Stephanie Roe, President

⑈94⑈ 77577⑈ 0885

detect the alteration. This is in accord with the purpose of certification, which is to obtain the definite obligation of a bank to honor a definite instrument. •

Bank's Duty to Accept Deposits

A bank has a duty to its customer to accept the customer's deposits of cash and checks. When checks are deposited, the bank must make the funds represented by those checks available within certain time frames. A bank also has a duty to collect payment on any checks payable or indorsed to its customers and deposited by them into their accounts. Cash deposits made in U.S. currency are received into customers' accounts without being subject to further collection procedures.

Availability Schedule for Deposited Checks

The Expedited Funds Availability Act of 1987[8] and Regulation CC,[9] which was issued by the Federal Reserve Board of Governors (the *Federal Reserve System* will be discussed shortly) to implement the act, require that any local check deposited must be available for withdrawal by check or as cash within one business day from the date of deposit. A check is classified as a local check if the first bank to receive the check for payment and the bank on which the check is drawn are located in the same check-processing region (check-processing regions are designated by the Federal Reserve Board of Governors). For nonlocal checks, the funds must be available for withdrawal within not more than five business days. The Expedited Funds Availability Act requires the following:

1. That funds be available on the next business day for cash deposits and wire transfers, government checks, the first $100 of a day's check deposits, cashier's checks, certified checks, and checks for which the depositary and payor banks are branches of the same institution (*depositary* and *payor banks* will be discussed shortly).
2. That the first $100 of any deposit be available for cash withdrawal on the opening of the next business day after deposit. If a local check is deposited, the next $400 is to be available for withdrawal by no later than 5:00 P.M. the next business day. If, for example, you deposit a local check for $500 on Monday, you can withdraw $100 in cash at the opening of the business day on Tuesday, and an additional $400 must be available for withdrawal by no later than 5:00 P.M. on Wednesday.

A different availability schedule applies to deposits made at *nonproprietary* automated teller machines (ATMs). These are ATMs that are not owned or operated by the bank receiving the deposits. Basically, a five-day hold is permitted on all deposits, including cash deposits, made at nonproprietary ATMs. Other exceptions also exist. A depository institution has eight days to make funds available in new accounts (those open less than thirty days) and has an extra four days on deposits that exceed $5,000 (except deposits of government and cashier's checks).

8. 12 U.S.C. Sections 4001–4010.

9. 12 C.F.R. Sections 229.1–229.42.

The Traditional Collection Process

Usually, deposited checks involve parties that do business at different banks, but sometimes checks are written between customers of the same bank. Either situation brings into play the bank collection process as it operates within the statutory framework of Article 4 of the UCC. Note that the check-collection process described in the following subsections will continue to be modified as the banking industry implements Check 21 (see page 325).

DESIGNATIONS OF BANKS INVOLVED IN THE COLLECTION PROCESS The first bank to receive a check for payment is the **depositary bank.**[10] For example, when a person deposits an IRS tax-refund check into a personal checking account at the local bank, that bank is the depositary bank. The bank on which a check is drawn (the drawee bank) is called the **payor bank.** Any bank except the payor bank that handles a check during some phase of the collection process is a **collecting bank.** Any bank except the payor bank or the depositary bank to which an item is transferred in the course of this collection process is called an **intermediary bank.**

During the collection process, any bank can take on one or more of the various roles of depositary, payor, collecting, and intermediary bank. **EXAMPLE 17.9** A buyer in New York writes a check on her New York bank and sends it to a seller in San Francisco. The seller deposits the check in her San Francisco bank account. The seller's bank is both a *depositary bank* and a *collecting bank*. The buyer's bank in New York is the *payor bank*. As the check travels from San Francisco to New York, any collecting bank handling the item in the collection process (other than the depositary bank and the payor bank) is also called an *intermediary bank*. Exhibit 17–4 on the following page illustrates how various banks function in the collection process in the context of this example. •

CHECK COLLECTION BETWEEN CUSTOMERS OF THE SAME BANK An item that is payable by the depositary bank (also

10. All definitions in this section are found in UCC 4–105. The terms *depositary* and *depository* have different meanings in the banking context. A depository bank is a *physical place* (a bank or other institution) in which deposits or funds are held or stored.

• ***Exhibit* 17–4 The Check-Collection Process**

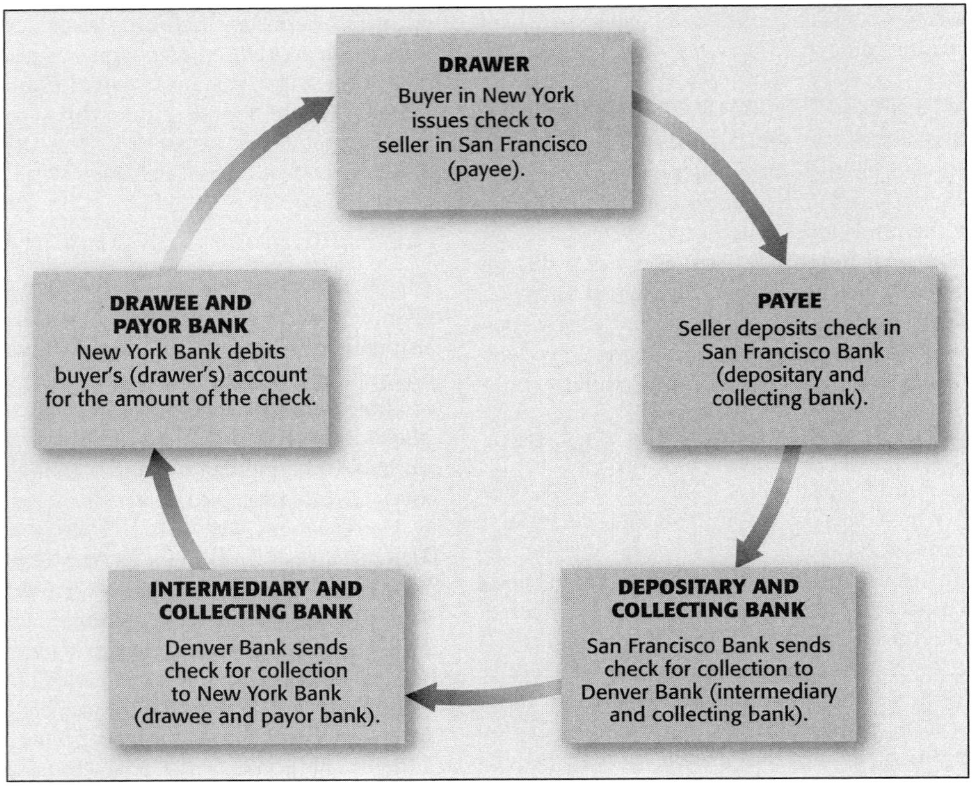

DRAWER
Buyer in New York issues check to seller in San Francisco (payee).

PAYEE
Seller deposits check in San Francisco Bank (depositary and collecting bank).

DEPOSITARY AND COLLECTING BANK
San Francisco Bank sends check for collection to Denver Bank (intermediary and collecting bank).

INTERMEDIARY AND COLLECTING BANK
Denver Bank sends check for collection to New York Bank (drawee and payor bank).

DRAWEE AND PAYOR BANK
New York Bank debits buyer's (drawer's) account for the amount of the check.

the payor bank) that receives it is called an "on-us item." Usually, a bank issues a "provisional credit" for on-us items within the same day. If the bank does not dishonor the check by the opening of the second banking day following its receipt, the check is considered paid [UCC 4–215(e)(2)].

CHECK COLLECTION BETWEEN CUSTOMERS OF DIFFERENT BANKS Once a depositary bank receives a check, it must arrange to present it either directly or through intermediary banks to the appropriate payor bank. Each bank in the collection chain must pass the check on before midnight of the next banking day following its receipt [UCC 4–202(b)].[11] A "banking day" is any part of a day on which the bank is open to carry on substantially all of its banking functions. Thus, if only a bank's drive-through facilities are open, a check deposited on Saturday will not trigger the bank's midnight deadline until the following Monday. When the check reaches the payor bank, that bank is liable for the face amount of the check, unless the payor bank dishonors the check or returns it by midnight on the next banking day following receipt [UCC 4–302].[12]

Because of this deadline and because banks need to maintain an even work flow in the many items they handle daily, the UCC permits what is called *deferred posting*. According to UCC 4–108, "a bank may fix an afternoon hour of 2:00 P.M. or later as a cutoff hour for the handling of money and items and the making of entries on its books." Any checks received after that hour "may be treated as being received at the opening of the next banking day." Thus, if a bank's "cutoff hour" is 3:00 P.M., a check received by a payor bank at 4:00 P.M. on Monday will be deferred for posting until Tuesday. In this situation, the payor bank's deadline will be midnight Wednesday.

The provisional credit mentioned at left on this page also applies to checks presented to one bank for collection from another. The number of banks in the collection chain lengthens the time before the credit becomes final and the check is considered paid, as illustrated in the following case.

11. A bank may take a "reasonably longer time" in certain circumstances, such as when the bank's computer system is down due to a power failure, but the bank must show that its action is still timely [UCC 4–202(b)].

12. Most checks are cleared by a computerized process, and communication and computer facilities may fail because of electrical outages, or other conditions. A bank may be "excused" from liability for failing to meet its midnight deadline if such conditions arise and the bank has exercised "such diligence as the circumstances require" [UCC 4–109(d)].

Case 17.3 Cumis Mutual Insurance Society, Inc. v. Rosol

Superior Court of New Jersey, Appellate Division, __ A.3d __ (2011).

FACTS Mizek Rosol, a resident of New Jersey, received an e-mail message from someone he did not know offering to pay him a 10 percent fee if he would receive checks, deposit them, and transfer the funds to others. He agreed and began to receive checks. Rosol opened a new account at Polish & Slavic Federal Credit Union (PSFCU) and deposited a cashier's check for $9,800 issued by a credit union in Florida. Three days later, he deposited a check for $45,000 drawn on a Canadian bank. Within a week, PSFCU told him that payment on the first check had been "stopped," but it did not disclose that the check was fraudulent. PSFCU issued a provisional credit to Rosol's account for the amount of the Canadian check. A PSFCU employee told Rosol that "these monies were collected and in his account." Rosol transferred $36,240 to a party in Japan and $4,500 to someone in Great Britain. Ten days later, PSFCU told Rosol that the Canadian check had been dishonored and demanded that he repay the transferred funds. He refused. PSFCU filed a claim with its insurer, Cumis Mutual Insurance Society, Inc. Cumis paid the claim and filed a suit in a New Jersey state court against Rosol to recover the amount. The court issued a summary judgment in Cumis's favor. Rosol appealed.

ISSUE Were the funds that Rosol deposited from the Canadian check provisional at the time he transferred them to Japan and Great Britain?

DECISION Yes. A state intermediate appellate court reversed the lower court's judgment and remanded the case because "there were genuine issues of material fact precluding summary judgment." If PSFCU reasonably led Rosol to believe that the Canadian check had been finally credited to his account, the credit union could not recover the transferred funds.

REASON The appellate court explained that UCC 2–401(a) governed the relationship between PSFCU and Rosol. Under that statute, a credit to the account of "the owner" of a check is provisional until the final settlement of the check. The credit to Rosol's account for the checks was thus provisional between the time of their deposit and the time of their dishonor. During that period, PSFCU had a "right of recoupment" for the funds that Rosol had transferred. But Rosol contended that he would not have transferred those funds if PSFCU had told him that the first check was fraudulent—not just "stopped." The court reasoned that "the state of his knowledge" about the first check could bear on the question of whether he had acted reasonably in relying on what he was told about the second check.

FOR CRITICAL ANALYSIS—Ethical Consideration *In what ways was Rosol's apparent motive similar to the most common reason that ethical problems occur in business?*

How the Federal Reserve System Clears Checks

The **Federal Reserve System** is a network of twelve district banks, which are located around the country and headed by the Federal Reserve Board of Governors. Most banks in the United States have Federal Reserve accounts. The Federal Reserve System has greatly simplified the check-collection process by acting as a **clearinghouse**—a system or a place where banks exchange checks and drafts drawn on each other and settle daily balances.

EXAMPLE 17.10 Pamela Moy of Philadelphia writes a check to Jeanne Sutton in San Francisco. When Sutton receives the check in the mail, she deposits it in her bank. Her bank then deposits the check in the Federal Reserve Bank of San Francisco, which transfers it to the Federal Reserve Bank of Philadelphia. That Federal Reserve bank then sends the check to Moy's bank, which deducts the amount of the check from Moy's account. ●

Check Clearing in the 21st Century Act

In the traditional collection process, paper checks were processed manually and physically transported before they could be cleared. Although the UCC allowed banks to use *electronic presentment* (that is, encoding check information and using computers to transmit and process for payment), this method was not widely adopted because it required agreements among individual banks [UCC 3–501(b)(2), 4–110].

To streamline the costly and time-consuming process and improve the overall efficiency of the nation's payment system, Congress passed the Check Clearing in the 21st Century Act (Check 21).[13] Check 21 changed the situation by creating a new negotiable instrument called a substitute check. A **substitute check** is a paper reproduction of the front and back of an original check that contains all of the same information required on checks for automated processing. Although Check 21 does not require banks to change their current check-collection practices, the creation of substitute checks facilitates the use of electronic check processing.

Banks create a substitute check from a digital image of an original check. Those financial institutions that exchange digital images of checks do not have to send the original paper checks. They can simply transmit the information electronically and replace the original checks with the substitute checks. Banks that do not exchange checks electronically are

13. 12 U.S.C. Sections 5001–5018.

required to accept substitute checks in the same way that they accept original checks. Because the original check can be destroyed after a substitute check is created, the financial system can prevent the check from being paid twice and reduce the expense of paper storage and retrieval. As Check 21 has been implemented, the time required to process checks has been reduced substantially.

Electronic Fund Transfers

The application of computer technology to banking, in the form of electronic fund transfer systems, has helped to relieve banking institutions of the burden of having to move mountains of paperwork to process fund transfers. An **electronic fund transfer (EFT)** is a transfer of funds through the use of an electronic terminal, a telephone, a computer, or magnetic tape. The law governing EFTs depends on the type of transfer involved. Consumer fund transfers are governed by the Electronic Fund Transfer Act (EFTA) of 1978.[14] Commercial fund transfers are governed by Article 4A of the UCC. Although electronic banking offers numerous benefits, it also poses difficulties on occasion, such as fewer records are available to prove or disprove that a transaction took place and the possibilities for tampering with private banking information have increased.

Types of EFT Systems

Most banks today offer EFT services to their customers. The most common types of EFT systems include:

1. *Automated teller machines* (ATMs)—The machines are connected online to the bank's computers. A customer inserts a plastic card (called an *ATM* or *debit card*) issued by the bank and keys in a *personal identification number* (PIN) to access her or his accounts and conduct banking transactions.
2. *Point-of-sale systems*—Online terminals allow consumers to transfer funds to merchants to pay for purchases using a debit card.
3. *Direct deposits and withdrawals*—Customers can authorize the bank to allow another party—such as the government or an employer—to make direct deposits into their accounts. Similarly, customers can request the bank to make automatic payments to a third party at regular, recurrent intervals from the customers' funds.
4. *Internet payment systems*—Many financial institutions permit their customers to access the institution's computer system via the Internet and direct a transfer of funds between accounts or pay a particular bill.

14. 15 U.S.C. Sections 1693–1693r.

Consumer Fund Transfers

The Electronic Fund Transfer Act (EFTA) provides a basic framework for the rights, liabilities, and responsibilities of users of EFT systems. Additionally, the act gave the Federal Reserve Board authority to issue rules and regulations to help implement the act's provisions. The Federal Reserve Board's implemental regulation is called **Regulation E.**

The EFTA governs financial institutions that offer electronic fund transfers involving consumer accounts. The types of accounts covered include checking accounts, savings accounts, and any other asset accounts established for personal, family, or household purposes. Telephone transfers are covered by the EFTA only if they are made in accordance with a prearranged plan under which periodic or recurring transfers are contemplated.

Disclosure Requirements The EFTA is essentially a disclosure law benefiting consumers. The act requires financial institutions to inform consumers of their rights and responsibilities, including those listed here, with respect to EFT systems.

1. If a customer's debit card is lost or stolen and used without his or her permission, the customer shall be required to pay no more than $50. The customer, however, must notify the bank of the loss or theft within two days of learning about it. Otherwise, the liability increases to $500. The customer may be liable for more than $500 if he or she does not report the unauthorized use within sixty days after it appears on the customer's statement. (If a customer voluntarily gives her or his debit card to another, who then uses it improperly, the protections just mentioned do not apply.)
2. The customer must discover any error on the monthly statement within sixty days and must notify the bank. The bank then has ten days to investigate and must report its conclusions to the customer in writing. If the bank takes longer than ten days, it must return the disputed amount to the customer's account until it finds the error. If there is no error, the customer has to return the disputed funds to the bank.
3. The bank must furnish receipts for transactions made through computer terminals, but it is not obligated to do so for telephone transfers.
4. The bank must provide a monthly statement for every month in which there is an electronic transfer of funds. Otherwise, the bank must provide statements every quarter. The statement must show the amount and date of the transfer, the names of the retailers or other third parties involved, the location or identification of the terminal, and the fees. Additionally, the statement must give an address and a phone number for inquiries and error notices.
5. Any preauthorized payment for utility bills and insurance premiums can be stopped three days before the scheduled transfer if the customer notifies the financial institution orally or in writing. (The institution may require the

customer to provide written confirmation within fourteen days of an oral notification.)

UNAUTHORIZED ELECTRONIC FUND TRANSFERS Because of the vulnerability of EFT systems to fraudulent activities, the EFTA clearly defined what constitutes an unauthorized transfer. Under the act, a transfer is unauthorized if (1) it is initiated by a person other than the consumer who has no actual authority to initiate the transfer; (2) the consumer receives no benefit from it; and (3) the consumer did not furnish the person "with the card, code, or other means of access" to her or his account. Unauthorized access to an EFT system constitutes a federal felony, and those convicted may be fined up to $10,000 and sentenced to as long as ten years in prison.

VIOLATIONS AND DAMAGES Banks must strictly comply with the terms of the EFTA and are liable for any failure to adhere to its provisions. For a bank's violation of the EFTA, a consumer may recover both actual damages (including attorneys' fees and costs) and punitive damages of not less than $100 and not more than $1,000. (Unlike actual damages, *punitive damages* are assessed to punish a defendant or to deter similar wrongdoers.) Failure to investigate an error in good faith makes the bank liable for treble damages (three times the amount of damages). Even when a customer has sustained no actual damage, the bank may be liable for legal costs and punitive damages if it fails to follow the proper procedures outlined by the EFTA in regard to error resolution.

Commercial Transfers

Funds are also transferred electronically "by wire" between commercial parties. In fact, the dollar volume of payments by wire transfer is more than $1 trillion a day—an amount that far exceeds the dollar volume of payments made by other means. The two major wire payment systems are the Federal Reserve's wire transfer network (Fedwire) and the New York Clearing House Interbank Payments Systems (CHIPS).

Commercial wire transfers are governed by Article 4A of the UCC, which has been adopted by most states. **EXAMPLE 17.11** Jellux, Inc., owes $5 million to Perot Corporation. Instead of sending Perot a check or some other instrument that would enable Perot to obtain payment, Jellux instructs its bank, East Bank, to credit $5 million to Perot's account in West Bank. East Bank debits Jellux's East Bank account and wires $5 million to Perot's West Bank account. In more complex transactions, additional banks would be involved. •

E-Money and Online Banking

New forms of electronic payments (e-payments) have the potential to replace *physical* cash—coins and paper currency—with *virtual* cash in the form of electronic impulses. This is the unique promise of **digital cash,** which consists of funds stored on microchips and on other computer devices. Online banking has also become commonplace in today's world. In a few minutes, anybody with the proper software can access his or her account, transfer funds, write "checks," pay bills, monitor investments, and often even buy and sell stocks.

Various forms of electronic money, or **e-money,** are emerging. The simplest kind of e-money system uses **stored-value cards.** These are plastic cards embossed with magnetic strips containing magnetically encoded data. In some applications, a stored-value card can be used only to purchase specific goods and services offered by the card issuer. **Smart cards** are plastic cards containing computer microchips that can hold more information than a magnetic strip can. A smart card carries and processes security programming. This capability gives smart cards a technical advantage over stored-value cards. The microprocessors on smart cards can also authenticate the validity of transactions. Retailers can program electronic cash registers to confirm the authenticity of a smart card by examining a unique digital signature stored on its microchip. (Digital signatures were discussed in Chapter 8.)

Online Banking Services

Most customers use three kinds of online banking services: bill consolidation and payment, transferring funds among accounts, and applying for loans. Customers typically have to appear in person to finalize the terms of a loan, however. Generally, customers are not yet able to deposit and withdraw funds online, although smart cards may eventually allow people to do so (withdrawing funds and depositing them onto the card as needed).

Since the late 1990s, several banks have operated exclusively on the Internet. These "virtual banks" have no physical branch offices. Because few people are equipped to send funds to virtual banks via smart-card technology, the virtual banks have accepted deposits through physical delivery systems, such as the U.S. Postal Service and FedEx.

Privacy Protection

At the present time, it is not clear which, if any, laws apply to the security of e-money payment information and e-money issuers' financial records. The Federal Reserve has decided not to impose Regulation E, which governs certain electronic fund transfers, on e-money transactions. Federal laws prohibiting unauthorized access to electronic communications might apply, however. For instance, the Electronic Communications Privacy Act of 1986[15] prohibits any person from knowingly divulging to any other person the contents of an electronic communication while that communication is in transmission or in electronic storage.

15. 18 U.S.C. Sections 2510–2521.

E-MONEY ISSUERS' FINANCIAL RECORDS Under the Right to Financial Privacy Act of 1978,[16] before a financial institution may give financial information about you to a federal agency, you must explicitly consent. If you do not, a federal agency wishing to access your financial records must obtain a warrant. A digital cash issuer may be subject to this act if that issuer is deemed to be (1) a bank, by virtue of its holding customer funds, or (2) any entity that issues a physical card similar to a credit or debit card.

CONSUMER FINANCIAL DATA In 1999, Congress passed the Financial Services Modernization Act,[17] also known as the Gramm-Leach-Bliley Act, in an attempt to delineate how financial institutions can treat customer data. In general, the act and its rules[18] place restrictions and obligations on financial institutions to protect consumer data and privacy. Every financial institution must provide its customers with information on its privacy policies and practices. No financial institution can disclose nonpublic personal information about a consumer to an unaffiliated third party unless the act's disclosure and opt-out requirements are met.

16. 12 U.S.C. Sections 3401 *et seq.*
17. 12 U.S.C. Sections 24a, 248b, 1820a, 1828b, 1831v–1831y, 1848a, 2908, 4809; 15 U.S.C. Sections 80b-10a, 6701, 6711–6717, 6731–6735, 6751–6766, 6781, 6801–6809, 6821–6827, 6901–6910; and others.
18. 12 C.F.R. Part 40.

Reviewing . . . Checks and Banking in the Digital Age

RPM Pizza, Inc., issued a check for $96,000 to Systems Marketing for an advertising campaign. A few days later, RPM decided not to go through with the deal and placed a written stop-payment order on the check. RPM and Systems had no further contact for many months. Three weeks after the stop-payment order expired, however, Toby Rierson, an employee at Systems, cashed the check. Bank One Cambridge, RPM's bank, paid the check with funds from RPM's account. Because the check was more than six months old, it was stale. Thus, according to standard banking procedures as well as Bank One's own policies, the signature on the check should have been specially verified, but it was not. RPM filed a suit in a federal district court against Bank One to recover the amount of the check. Using the information presented in the chapter, answer the following questions.

1. How long is a written stop-payment order effective? What else could RPM have done to prevent this check from being cashed?
2. What would happen if it turned out that RPM did not have a legitimate reason for stopping payment on the check?
3. What are a bank's obligations with respect to stale checks?
4. Would a court be likely to hold the bank liable for the amount of the check because it failed to verify the signature on the check? Why or why not?

Terms and Concepts

cashier's check 316
certified check 317
check 315
clearinghouse 325
collecting bank 323
depositary bank 323
digital cash 327
electronic fund transfer (EFT) 326
e-money 327
Federal Reserve System 325
intermediary bank 323
overdraft 318
payor bank 323
Regulation E 326
smart card 327
stale check 319
stop-payment order 319
stored-value card 327
substitute check 325
traveler's check 317

Chapter Summary: Checks and Banking in the Digital Age

Checks (See pages 315–318.)	1. *Cashier's check*—A check drawn by a bank on itself (the bank is both the drawer and the drawee) and purchased by a customer. In effect, the bank assumes responsibility for paying the check, thus making the check nearly the equivalent of cash.

Chapter Summary: Checks and Banking in the Digital Age—Continued

Checks—Continued	2. *Traveler's check*—An instrument on which a financial institution is both the drawer and the drawee. The purchaser must provide his or her signature as a countersignature for a traveler's check to become a negotiable instrument. 3. *Certified check*—A check for which the drawee bank certifies in writing that it has set aside funds from the drawer's account to ensure payment of the check on presentation. On certification, the drawer and all prior indorsers are completely discharged from liability on the check.
The Bank-Customer Relationship (See page 318.)	1. *Creditor-debtor relationship*—The bank and its customer have a creditor-debtor relationship (the bank is the debtor because it holds the customer's funds on deposit). 2. *Agency relationship*—Because a bank must act in accordance with the customer's orders in regard to the customer's deposited money, an agency relationship also arises—the bank is the agent for the customer, who is the principal. 3. *Contractual relationship*—The bank's relationship with its customer is also contractual. Both the bank and the customer assume certain contractual duties when a customer opens a bank account.
Bank's Duty to Honor Checks (See pages 318–323.)	Generally, a bank has a duty to honor its customers' checks, provided that the customers have sufficient funds on deposit to cover the checks [UCC 4–401(a)]. The bank is liable to its customers for actual damages proved to be due to wrongful dishonor. The bank's duty to honor its customers' checks is not absolute.
Bank's Duty to Accept Deposits (See pages 323–326.)	A bank has a duty to accept deposits made by its customers into their accounts. Funds represented by checks deposited must be made available to customers according to a schedule mandated by the Expedited Funds Availability Act of 1987 and Regulation CC. A bank also has a duty to collect payment on any checks deposited by its customers. When checks deposited by customers are drawn on other banks, the check-collection process comes into play. 1. *Definitions of banks*—UCC 4–105 provides the following definitions of banks involved in the collection process: a. Depositary bank—The first bank to accept a check for payment. b. Payor bank—The bank on which a check is drawn. c. Collecting bank—Any bank except the payor bank that handles a check during the collection process. d. Intermediary bank—Any bank except the payor bank or the depositary bank to which an item is transferred in the course of the collection process. 2. *Check collection between customers of the same bank*—A check payable by the depositary bank that receives it is an "on-us item." If the bank does not dishonor the check by the opening of the second banking day following its receipt, the check is considered paid [UCC 4–215(e)(2)]. 3. *Check collection between customers of different banks*—Each bank in the collection process must pass the check on to the next appropriate bank before midnight of the next banking day following its receipt [UCC 4–108, 4–202(b), 4–302]. 4. *How the Federal Reserve System clears checks*—The Federal Reserve System facilitates the check-clearing process by serving as a clearinghouse for checks. 5. *Check Clearing in the 21st Century Act (Check 21)*—Check 21 changes the traditional paper check-collection process by creating a new negotiable instrument called a substitute check, thus gradually reducing the number of paper checks and the length of float time. Additionally, banks will eventually have less time to hold funds from deposited checks before making them available, allowing account holders quicker access to those funds.
Electronic Fund Transfers (See pages 326–327.)	1. *Types of EFT systems*— a. Automated teller machines (ATMs). b. Point-of-sale systems. c. Direct deposits and withdrawals. d. Internet payment systems. 2. *Consumer fund transfers*—Consumer fund transfers are governed by the Electronic Fund Transfer Act (EFTA) of 1978. The EFTA is basically a disclosure law that sets forth the rights and duties of the bank and the customer with respect to EFT systems. Banks must comply strictly with EFTA requirements.

Continued

Chapter Summary: Checks and Banking in the Digital Age—Continued

Electronic Fund Transfers—Continued	3. *Commercial transfers*—Article 4A of the UCC, which has been adopted by almost all of the states, governs fund transfers not subject to the EFTA or other federal or state statutes.
E-Money and Online Banking (See pages 327–328.)	1. *New forms of e-payments*—These include stored-value cards and smart cards. 2. *Current online banking services*— a. Bill consolidation and payment. b. Transferring funds among accounts. c. Applying for loans. 3. *Privacy protection*—It is not clear which laws apply to the security of e-money payment information and e-money issuers' financial records. The Financial Services Modernization Act (the Gramm-Leach-Bliley Act) outlines how financial institutions can treat consumer data in general. The Right to Financial Privacy Act may also apply.

ExamPrep

ISSUE SPOTTERS

—Check your answers to these questions against the answers provided in Appendix G.

1 Lyn writes a check for $900 to Mac, who indorses the check in blank and transfers it to Nan. She presents the check to Omega Bank, the drawee bank, for payment. Omega does not honor the check. Is Lyn liable to Nan? Could Lyn be subject to criminal prosecution? Why or why not?

2 Roni writes a check for $700 to Sela. Sela indorses the check in blank and transfers it to Titus, who alters the check to read $7,000 and presents it to Union Bank, the drawee, for payment. The bank cashes it. Roni discovers the alteration and sues the bank. How much, if anything, can Roni recover? From whom can the bank recover this amount?

BEFORE THE TEST

Go to **www.cengagebrain.com**, enter the ISBN 9781111530624, and click on "Find" to locate this textbook's Web site. Then, click on "Access Now" under "Study Tools," and select Chapter 17 at the top. There, you will find an Interactive Quiz that you can take to assess your mastery of the concepts in this chapter, as well as Flashcards and a Glossary of important terms.

For Review

1 What type of check does a bank agree in advance to accept when the check is presented for payment?
2 When may a bank properly dishonor a customer's check without the bank being liable to the customer?
3 What duties does the Uniform Commercial Code impose on a bank's customers with regard to forged and altered checks? What are the consequences if a customer is negligent in performing those duties?
4 What are the four most common types of electronic fund transfers?
5 What laws apply to e-money transactions and online banking services?

Questions and Case Problems

17–1 Forged Checks. Roy Supply, Inc., and R.M.R. Drywall, Inc., had checking accounts at Wells Fargo Bank. Both accounts required all checks to carry two signatures—that of Edward Roy and that of Twila June Moore, both of whom were executive officers of both companies. Between January 2007 and March 2009, the bank honored hundreds of checks on which Roy's signature was forged by Moore. On January 31, 2010, Roy and the two corporations notified the bank of the forgeries and then filed a suit in a California state court against the bank, alleging negligence. Who is liable for the amounts of the forged checks? Why?

17–2 Online Banking. iBank operates exclusively on the Web with no physical branch offices. Although some of iBank's business is transacted with smart-card technology, most of its business with its customers is conducted through the mail. iBank offers free checking, no-fee money market accounts, mortgage refinancing, and other services. With what regulation covering banks might iBank find it difficult to comply, and what is the difficulty?

17–3 Bank's Duty to Honor Checks. On January 5, Brian drafts a check for $3,000 drawn on Southern Marine Bank and payable to his assistant, Shanta. Brian puts last year's date on the check by mistake. On January 7, before Shanta has had a chance to go to the bank, Brian is killed in an automobile accident. Southern Marine Bank is aware of Brian's death. On January 10, Shanta presents the check to the bank, and the bank honors the check by payment to Shanta. Later, Brian's widow, Joyce, claims that because the bank knew of Brian's death and also because the check was by date over one year old, the bank acted wrongfully when it paid Shanta. Joyce, as executor of Brian's estate and sole heir by his will, demands that Southern Marine Bank recredit Brian's estate for the check paid to Shanta. Discuss fully Southern Marine's liability in light of Joyce's demand.

17–4 Customer Negligence. Gary goes grocery shopping and carelessly leaves his checkbook in his shopping cart. His checkbook, with two blank checks remaining, is stolen by Dolores. On May 5, Dolores forges Gary's name on a check for $10 and cashes the check at Gary's bank, Citizens Bank of Middletown. Gary has not reported the loss of his blank checks to his bank. On June 1, Gary receives his monthly bank statement and copies of canceled checks from Citizens Bank, including the forged check, but he does not examine the canceled checks. On June 20, Dolores forges Gary's last check. This check is for $1,000 and is cashed at Eastern City Bank, a bank with which Dolores has previously done business. Eastern City Bank puts the check through the collection process, and Citizens Bank honors it. On July 1, on receipt of his bank statement and canceled checks covering June transactions, Gary discovers both forgeries and immediately notifies Citizens Bank. Dolores cannot be found. Gary claims that Citizens Bank must recredit his account for both checks, as his signature was forged. Discuss fully Gary's claim.

17–5 Forged Indorsements. In 1994, Brian and Penny Grieme bought a house in Mandan, North Dakota. They borrowed for the purchase through a loan program financed by the North Dakota Housing Finance Agency (NDHFA). The Griemes obtained insurance for the house from Center Mutual Insurance Co. When a hailstorm damaged the house in 2001, Center Mutual determined that the loss was $4,378 and issued a check for that amount, drawn on Bremer Bank, N.A. The check's payees included Brian Grieme and the NDHFA. Grieme presented the check for payment to Wells Fargo Bank of Tempe, Arizona. The back of the check bore his signature and in hand-printed block letters the words "ND Housing Finance." The check was processed for collection and paid, and the canceled check was returned to Center Mutual. By the time the insurer learned that NDHFA's indorsement had been forged, the Griemes had canceled their policy, defaulted on their loan, and filed for bankruptcy. The NDHFA filed a suit in a North Dakota state court against Center Mutual for the amount of the check. Who is most likely to suffer the loss in this case? Why? [*State ex rel. North Dakota Housing Finance Agency v. Center Mutual Insurance Co.*, 720 N.W.2d 425 (N.Dak. 2006)]

17–6 Bank's Duty to Honor Checks. Sheila Bartell was arrested and subject to various charges related to burglary, the possession for sale of methamphetamine, and other crimes. She pleaded guilty in a California state court to some charges in exchange for the dismissal of others and an agreement to reimburse the victims. The victims included "Rita E.," who reported that her checkbook had been stolen and her signature forged on three checks totaling $590. Wells Fargo Bank had "covered" the checks and credited her account, however, so the court ordered Bartell to pay the bank. Bartell appealed, arguing that the bank was not entitled to restitution. What principles apply when a person forges a drawer's signature on a check? Is the bank entitled to recover from the defendant? Explain. [*People v. Bartell*, 170 Cal. App.4th 1258, 88 Cal.Rptr.3d 844 (3 Dist. 2009)]

17–7 Bank's Duty of Care. Arnett Gertrude, a widow with no children, lived with her sister and her nephew Jack Scriber. When Gertrude was diagnosed with cancer, she added Scriber to her checking account as an authorized signatory and gave him power of attorney. Shortly before Gertrude died, Scriber wrote checks on the account to withdraw nearly all of the $600,000 in the account and transferred the funds into his account. After her death, the administrator of Gertrude's estate discovered the withdrawals. The administrator sued the bank for aiding Scriber in converting Gertrude's funds. The bank's defense was that Scriber had power of attorney over Gertrude's finances and had the power to write checks on the account, so the bank had to honor the checks that Scriber had written. The estate argued that the bank breached its duty to Gertrude to guard against such obvious misappropriation. The trial court held for the bank. Did the bank breach its duty to Gertrude? Discuss why or why not. [*Caudill v. Salyersville National Bank*, ___ S.W.3d ___ (Ky.App. 2010)]

17–8 Case Problem with Sample Answer Debbie Brooks and Martha Tingstrom lived together. Tingstrom handled their finances. For five years, Brooks did not look at any statements concerning her accounts. When she finally reviewed the statements, she discovered that Tingstrom had taken $85,500 from her through her checking account with Transamerica Financial Advisors. Tingstrom had forged Brooks's name on six checks paid between one and two years earlier. Another year passed before Brooks filed a suit in a Louisiana state court against Transamerica. Brooks alleged that the bank had paid the unauthorized checks without obtaining proper identification and approval from her, the account holder. The defendant contended that Brooks was too late. Who is most likely to suffer the loss for the checks paid with Brooks's forged signature? Why? [*Brooks v. Transamerica Financial Advisors*, 57 So.3d 1153 (La.App. 2 Cir. 2011)]

—For a sample answer to Problem 17–8, go to Appendix F at the end of this text.

17–9 A Question of Ethics *From the 1960s, James Johnson served as Bradley Union's personal caretaker and* *assistant, and was authorized by Union to handle his banking transactions. Louise Johnson, James's wife, wrote checks on Union's checking account to pay his bills, normally signing the checks "Brad Union." Branch Banking & Trust Co. (BB&T) managed Union's account. In December 2000, on the basis of Union's deteriorating mental and physical condition, a North Carolina state court declared him incompetent. Douglas Maxwell was appointed as Union's guardian. Maxwell "froze" Union's checking account and asked BB&T for copies of the canceled checks, which were provided by July 2001. Maxwell believed that Union's signature on the checks had been forged. In August 2002, Maxwell contacted BB&T, which refused to recredit Union's account. Maxwell filed a suit on Union's behalf in a North Carolina state court against BB&T. [*Union v. Branch Banking & Trust Co.*, 176 N.C.App. 711, 627 S.E.2d 276 (2006)]*

1 Before Maxwell's appointment, BB&T sent monthly statements and canceled checks to Union, and Johnson reviewed them, but no unauthorized signatures were ever reported. On whom can liability be imposed in the case of a forged drawer's signature on a check? What are the limits set by Section 4–406(f) of the Uniform Commercial Code? Should Johnson's position, Union's incompetence, or Maxwell's appointment affect the application of these principles? Explain.
2 Why was this suit brought against BB&T? Is BB&T liable? If not, who is? Why? Regardless of any violations of the law, did anyone act unethically in this case? If so, who and why?

17–10 **Critical Thinking Legal Question** Since the 1990 revision of Article 4, a bank is no longer required to include the customer's canceled checks when it sends monthly statements to the customer. A bank may simply itemize the checks (by number, date, and amount); it may provide photocopies of the checks as well but is not required to do so. What implications do the revised rules have for bank customers in terms of liability for unauthorized signatures and indorsements?

Unit Five

Unit Case Study with Dissenting Opinion: *Prestridge v. Bank of Jena*

In Chapters 16 and 17, we reviewed some of the laws that govern checks and the banking system, explaining the rights, duties, and liabilities of banks and their customers. We discussed those concepts as they apply under Articles 3 and 4 of the Uniform Commercial Code (UCC).

In this Unit Case Study with Dissenting Opinion, *we examine* Prestridge v. Bank of Jena,[1] *a decision focusing on the parties' obligations under the UCC with respect to a series of forged checks. A bank is generally liable if it pays a check over the forged signature of its customer, but to enforce this liability, the customer must report a forgery within thirty days of receiving his or her account statement on which the check amount appears. How do these principles apply when neither the bank nor the customer verifies the signatures on the checks?*

1. 924 So.2d 1266 (La.App. 3 Cir. 2006).

CASE BACKGROUND

In October 2002, sisters Glynda and Vera Prestridge opened a checking account at Bank of Jena in Libuse, Rapides Parish, Louisiana. Each sister signed a signature card. Vera's name was included on the account only so that she could access it, if necessary, while Glynda and her husband were traveling. Vera did not make a deposit into the account, write a check on it, or receive correspondence regarding it.

Over the next seven months, Marye Prestridge, Glynda's daughter-in-law, obtained blank checks on the account. Marye forged Glynda's name on the checks to steal more than $60,000 from the account. In April 2003, Glynda discovered that the balance was significantly lower than she expected. She learned of Marye's withdrawals and froze the account, but was able to recover only $5,700. Marye and Glynda's son Larry were soon divorced.

Glynda and Vera filed a suit in a Louisiana state court against the bank, claiming that it should reimburse them for the missing funds because it had been negligent in paying on the forged checks. The court awarded the plaintiffs $37,450, the amount that Marye took before January 22. The court ruled that after that date, the plaintiffs were negligent in not checking their account statements. Both parties appealed to a state intermediate appellate court.

MAJORITY OPINION

GENOVESE, **Judge.**

* * * *

On appeal, both parties have asserted the provisions of La.R.S. 10:4-406 [Louisiana's version of UCC 4–406] in support of their respective positions. Bank of Jena asserts that the Plaintiffs should be precluded from recovery because they also failed to exercise reasonable care after the forgeries had been committed. Bank of Jena argues that Glynda had a duty to examine the monthly account statements sent to her, and that she failed * * * to examine them * * * before April 2003. The Plaintiffs, however, assert that Bank of Jena improperly paid on the instruments because it failed to verify the signatures on any of the checks at the time they were paid.

* * * *

Our review of the evidence supports a determination that Bank of Jena made statements available to the Plaintiffs by sending Glynda the account information monthly. Further, the record supports a finding that * * * Glynda had not examined the statements that were sent to her * * * .

* * * *

In support of their [argument] that Bank of Jena failed to exercise ordinary care, and that apportionment of fault is therefore appropriate, the Plaintiffs point out that the signatures which appear on the signature lines of the forged checks clearly do not match Glynda's signature as it appears on the signature card that she signed with Bank of Jena when she opened the account. * * * The Plaintiffs contend that this failure to verify Glynda's signature was below the level of ordinary care and substantially contributed to their loss.

* * * *

Our review of the record in the instant case [the case now before the court] reveals that Bank of Jena had adopted an automated means of clearing its checks, by sending them to Computer Services, Inc ("CSI") [which] clears checks for Bank of Jena as well as more than five hundred other banks nationally. * * * CSI * * * electronically photographed the checks and kept the original paper checks for ninety days before destroying them. * * * Bank of Jena never sees the paper check[s] and can only view the checks electronically.

* * * *

Continued

After review, we do not find that overall the record supports a determination that the Plaintiffs have proven that Bank of Jena failed to adhere to a reasonable commercial standard, prevailing in the area, when paying on the instruments at issue. * * * Other area community banks use data processing companies like CSI to process their checks using a similar check-clearing process. Accordingly, because the Plaintiffs have not proven that Bank of Jena failed overall to exercise ordinary care, * * * the loss due to the forgeries should not be allocated between the parties.

* * * *

* * * *La.R.S. 10:4-406(d)(2) allow[s] Plaintiffs a thirty-day period from the issuance of their monthly account statement to identify any forged instrument and notify the bank accordingly.* * * * Therefore, Bank of Jena is liable unto Plaintiffs for paying on fraudulent instruments up through December 22, 2002, which is thirty days after * * * the first bank statement [was] issued. The trial court judgment is affirmed in that regard, but amended to allow Plaintiffs to recover only for forged instruments up through thirty days after the first bank statement, i.e., December 22, 2002, and no further. [Emphasis added.]

* * * Because we cannot determine from the record the exact amount of the forgeries up through December 22, 2002, we remand this matter to the trial court for a hearing to determine said amount * * *.

* * * *

For the foregoing reasons, the judgment of the trial court in favor of the Plaintiffs, Glynda Prestridge and Vera Prestridge, is affirmed in part as amended, reversed in part, and remanded to the trial court * * *.

DISSENTING OPINION

AMY, **J. [Judge], dissenting.**

I respectfully dissent from the majority opinion. Chiefly, I disagree that the plaintiffs are entitled to any recovery given the present circumstances.

The evidence supports a determination that Bank of Jena made monthly statements available to the plaintiffs * * *.

* * * La.R.S. 10:4-406(c) * * * states that "the customer must exercise reasonable promptness in examining the statement * * * to determine whether any payment was not authorized because of an alteration of an item or because a purported signature by or on behalf of the customer was not authorized." It further provides that, if an authorized payment should have been discovered, "the customer must promptly notify the bank of the relevant facts." As the plaintiffs failed to do so within the period of "reasonable promptness," required by La.R.S. 10:4-406(c) * * *, the plaintiffs cannot recover for the initial forgeries.

With regard to subsequent forgeries, La.R.S. 10:4-406 provides:

> (d) If the bank proves that the customer failed, with respect to an item, to comply with the duties imposed on the customer by Subsection (c), the customer is precluded from asserting against the bank: * * *
>
> (2) the customer's unauthorized signature or alteration by the same wrongdoer on any other item paid in good faith by the bank if the payment was made before the bank received notice from the customer of the unauthorized signature or alteration and after the customer had been afforded a reasonable period of time, not exceeding thirty days, in which to examine the item or statement of account and notify the bank.

Again, the plaintiffs failed to notify the bank of the irregularities within this time frame.

In short, I conclude that the trial court erred in allowing the plaintiffs to recover any funds paid by the Bank of Jena on the checks forged by Marye Prestridge.

QUESTIONS FOR ANALYSIS

1. **Law.** How did the majority in this case respond to the question stated at the beginning of this feature? What was the reasoning behind the response?
2. **Law.** Did the dissent agree with the majority's application of UCC 4–406? With what part of the majority's ruling did the dissent disagree? Why?
3. **Ethics.** Should a bank that uses outsourced check-collection procedures be absolved of responsibility for verifying the signatures of its customers on items drawn on the bank?
4. **Technological Dimensions.** How has electronic banking affected the relationship between a bank and its customer?
5. **Implications for the Business Owner.** What is the significance of the outcome in this case to a business?

Unit Six

Debtor-Creditor Relationships

Unit Contents

18 Security Interests in Personal Property

19 Creditors' Rights and Bankruptcy

20 Mortgages and Foreclosures after the Recession

Chapter 18

Security Interests in Personal Property

Learning Objectives

After reading this chapter, you should be able to answer the following questions:

1. What is a security interest? Who is a secured party? What is a security agreement? What is a financing statement?
2. What three requirements must be met to create an enforceable security interest?
3. What is the most common method of perfecting a security interest under Article 9?
4. If two secured parties have perfected security interests in the collateral of the debtor, which party has priority to the collateral on the debtor's default?
5. What rights does a secured creditor have on the debtor's default?

The Learning Objectives above are designed to help improve your understanding of the chapter.

Whenever the payment of a debt is guaranteed, or *secured,* by personal property owned by the debtor or in which the debtor has a legal interest, the transaction becomes known as a **secured transaction.** The concept of the secured transaction is as basic to modern business practice as the concept of credit. When buying or leasing goods, debtors frequently pay some portion of the price now and promise to pay the remainder in the future. Logically, sellers and lenders do not want to risk nonpayment, so they usually will not sell goods or lend funds unless the payment is somehow guaranteed. Indeed, business as we know it could not exist without laws permitting and governing secured transactions.

Article 9 of the Uniform Commercial Code (UCC) governs secured transactions in personal property. Personal property includes accounts, agricultural liens, *chattel paper* (any writing evidencing a debt secured by personal property), *fixtures* (certain property that is attached to land—see Chapter 28), instruments, and other types of intangible property, such as patents. Article 9 does not cover other creditor devices, such as liens and real estate mortgages, which will be discussed in Chapters 19 and 20. In this chapter, we first look at the terminology of secured transactions. We then discuss how the rights and duties of creditors and debtors are created and enforced under Article 9. As will become evident, the law of secured transactions tends to favor the rights of creditors, but it also offers debtors some protections, though to a lesser extent.

The Terminology of Secured Transactions

The UCC's terminology has been uniformly adopted in all documents used in situations involving secured transactions. A brief summary of the UCC's definitions of terms relating to secured transactions follows.

1. A **secured party** is any creditor who has a *security interest* in the *debtor's collateral.* This creditor can be a seller, a lender, a cosigner, or even a buyer of accounts or chattel paper [UCC 9–102(a)(72)].

2. A **debtor** is the "person" who *owes payment* or other performance of a secured obligation [UCC 9–102(a)(28)].
3. A **security interest** is the *interest* in the collateral (such as personal property or fixtures) that *secures payment or performance of an obligation* [UCC 1–201(37)].
4. A **security agreement** is an *agreement* that *creates* or provides for a *security interest* [UCC 9–102(a)(73)].
5. **Collateral** is the *subject* of the *security interest* [UCC 9–102(a)(12)].
6. A **financing statement**—referred to as the UCC-1 form—is the *instrument normally filed* to give *public notice* to *third parties* of the *secured party's security interest* [UCC 9–102(a)(39)].

These basic definitions form the concept under which a debtor-creditor relationship becomes a secured transaction relationship (see Exhibit 18–1 below).

Creating a Security Interest

A creditor has two main concerns if the debtor **defaults** (fails to pay the debt as promised): (1) Can the debt be satisfied through the possession and (usually) sale of the collateral? (2) Will the creditor have priority over any other creditors or buyers who may have rights in the same collateral? These two concerns are met through the creation and perfection of a security interest. We begin by examining how a security interest is created.

To become a secured party, the creditor must obtain a security interest in the collateral of the debtor. Three requirements must be met for a creditor to have an enforceable security interest:

1. Unless the creditor has possession of the collateral, there must be a written or authenticated security agreement that clearly describes the collateral subject to the security interest and is signed or authenticated by the debtor.
2. The secured party must give something of value to the debtor.
3. The debtor must have "rights" in the collateral.

Once these requirements have been met, the creditor's rights are said to attach to the collateral. **Attachment** gives the creditor an enforceable security interest in the collateral [UCC 9–203].[1]

Written or Authenticated Security Agreement

When the collateral is *not* in the possession of the secured party, the security agreement must be either written or authenticated, and it must describe the collateral. Here, *authentication* means to sign, execute, or adopt any symbol on an electronic record that verifies the person signing has the intent to adopt or accept the record [UCC 9–102(a)(7)(69)]. The reason authentication is acceptable is to provide for electronic filing (the filing process will be discussed later).

A security agreement must contain a description of the collateral that reasonably identifies it. Generally, such phrases as "all the debtor's personal property" or "all the debtor's assets" would *not* constitute a sufficient description [UCC 9–108(c)].

Secured Party Must Give Value

The secured party must give something of value to the debtor. Some examples of value include a binding commitment to extend credit or consideration to support a simple contract [UCC 1–204]. Normally, the value given by a secured party is in the form of a direct loan or a commitment to sell goods on credit.

1. Note that in the context of judicial liens, to be discussed in Chapter 19, the term *attachment* has a different meaning. In that context, it refers to a court-ordered seizure and taking into custody of property prior to the securing of a court judgment for a past-due debt.

• ***Exhibit* 18–1 Secured Transactions—Concept and Terminology**
In a security agreement, a debtor and a creditor agree that the creditor will have a security interest in collateral in which the debtor has rights. In essence, the collateral secures the loan and ensures the creditor of payment should the debtor default.

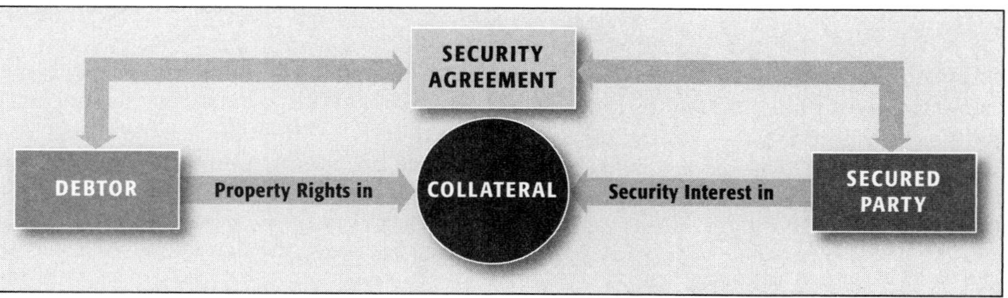

Debtor Must Have Rights in the Collateral

The debtor must have rights in the collateral—that is, the debtor must have a current or a future ownership interest in or right to obtain possession of that collateral. For instance, a retail seller-debtor can give a secured party a security interest not only in existing inventory owned by the retailer but also in *future* inventory to be acquired by the retailer.

One common misconception about having rights in the collateral is that the debtor must have title. This is not a requirement. A beneficial interest in a *trust* (trusts will be discussed in Chapter 29), when the trustee holds title to the trust property, can be the subject of a security interest for a loan that a creditor makes to the beneficiary.

Perfecting a Security Interest

Perfection is the legal process by which secured parties protect themselves against the claims of third parties who may wish to have their debts satisfied out of the same collateral. Whether a secured party's security interest is perfected or unperfected can have serious consequences for the secured party if, for example, the debtor defaults on the debt or files for bankruptcy. What if the debtor has borrowed from two different creditors, using the same property as collateral for both loans? If the debtor defaults on both loans, which of the two creditors has first rights to the collateral? In this situation, the creditor with a perfected security interest will prevail.

Usually, perfection is accomplished by filing a financing statement with the office of the appropriate government official. In some circumstances, however, a security interest becomes perfected without the filing of a financing statement. Where or how a security interest is perfected sometimes depends on the type of collateral. Collateral is generally divided into two classifications: *tangible collateral* (collateral that can be seen, felt, and touched) and *intangible collateral* (collateral that consists of or generates rights).

Exhibit 18–2 on the facing page summarizes the various classifications of collateral and the methods of perfecting a security interest in collateral falling within each of these classifications.[2]

Perfection by Filing

The most common means of perfection is by filing a *financing statement*—a document that gives public notice to third parties of the secured party's security interest—with the office of the appropriate government official. The security agreement itself can also be filed to perfect the security interest. The financing statement must provide the names of the debtor and the secured party, and must indicate the collateral covered by the financing statement. A uniform financing statement form is now used in all states [see UCC 9–521].

Communication of the financing statement to the appropriate filing office, together with the correct filing fee, or the acceptance of the financing statement by the filing officer constitutes a filing [UCC 9–516(a)]. The word *communication* means that the filing can be accomplished electronically [UCC 9–102(a)(18)]. Once completed, filings are indexed in the name of the debtor so that they can be located by subsequent searchers. A financing statement may be filed even before a security agreement is made or a security interest attaches [UCC 9–502(d)].

The Debtor's Name The UCC requires that a financing statement be filed under the name of the debtor [UCC 9–502(a)(1)]. Slight variations in names normally will not be considered misleading if a search of the filing office's records, using a standard computer search engine routinely used by that office, would disclose the filings [UCC 9–506(c)].[3] If the debtor is identified by the correct name at the time of the filing of a financing statement, the secured party's interest retains its priority even if the debtor later changes his or her name. Because most states use electronic filing systems, UCC 9–503 sets out some detailed rules for determining when the debtor's name as it appears on a financing statement is sufficient.

Specific Types of Debtors. For corporations, which are organizations that have registered with the state, the debtor's name on the financing statement must be "the name of the debtor indicated on the public record of the debtor's jurisdiction of organization" [UCC 9–503(a)(1)]. If the debtor is a trust or a trustee with respect to property held in trust, the filed financing statement must disclose this information and must provide the trust's name as specified in its official documents [UCC 9–503(a)(3)]. For all others, the filed financing statement must disclose "the individual or organizational name of the debtor" [UCC 9–503(a)(4)(A)]. As used here, the word *organization* includes unincorporated associations, such as clubs and some churches, as well as joint ventures and general partnerships. If an organizational debtor does not have a group name, the names of the individuals in the group must be listed.

Trade Names. Providing only the debtor's trade name (or a fictitious name) in a financing statement is *not* sufficient for perfection [UCC 9–503(c)]. **EXAMPLE 18.1** A loan is being made to a sole proprietorship owned by Peter Jones. The trade, or

2. There are additional classifications, such as agricultural liens, investment property, and commercial tort claims. For definitions of these types of collateral, see UCC 9–102(a)(5), (a)(13), and (a)(49).

3. If the name listed in the financing statement is so inaccurate that a search using the standard search engine will not disclose the debtor's name, then the financing statement is deemed seriously misleading under UCC 9–506. See also UCC 9–507, which governs the effectiveness of financing statements found to be seriously misleading.

• ***Exhibit* 18–2 Selected Types of Collateral and Their Methods of Perfection**

TANGIBLE COLLATERAL All things that are movable at the time the security interest attaches (such as livestock) or that are attached to the land, including timber to be cut and growing crops.		**METHOD OF PERFECTION**
Consumer Goods [UCC 9–301, 9–303, 9–309(1), 9–310(a), 9–313(a)]	Goods used or bought primarily for personal, family, or household purposes—for example, household furniture [UCC 9–102(a)(23)].	For purchase-money security interest, attachment (that is, the creation of a security interest) is sufficient; for boats, motor vehicles, and trailers, filing or compliance with a certificate-of-title statute is required; for other consumer goods, general rules of filing or possession apply.
Equipment [UCC 9–301, 9–310(a), 9–313(a)]	Goods bought for or used primarily in business (and not part of inventory or farm products)—for example, a delivery truck [UCC 9–102(a)(33)].	Filing or (rarely) possession by secured party.
Inventory [UCC 9–301, 9–310(a), 9–313(a)]	Goods held by a person for sale or under a contract of service or lease; raw materials held for production and work in progress [UCC 9–102(a)(48)].	Filing or (rarely) possession by secured party.
INTANGIBLE COLLATERAL Nonphysical property that exists only in connection with something else.		**METHOD OF PERFECTION**
Chattel Paper [UCC 9–301, 9–310(a), 9–312(a), 9–313(a), 9–314(a)]	A writing or electronic record that evidences both a monetary obligation and a security interest in goods and software used in goods—for example, a security agreement or a security agreement and promissory note.	Filing or possession or control by secured party.
Instruments [UCC 9–301, 9–309(4), 9–310(a), 9–312(a) and (e), 9–313(a)]	A negotiable instrument, such as a check, note, certificate of deposit, or draft, or other writing that evidences a right to the payment of money and is not a security agreement or lease but rather a type that can ordinarily be transferred (after indorsement, if necessary) by delivery [UCC 9–102(a)(47)].	Except for temporary perfected status, filing or possession. For the sale of promissory notes, perfection can be by attachment (automatically on the creation of the security interest).
Accounts [UCC 9–301, 9–309(2) and (5), 9–310(a)]	Any right to receive payment for property (real or personal), including intellectual licensed property, services, insurance policies, and certain other receivables.	Filing required except for certain assignments that can be perfected by attachment (automatically on the creation of the security interest).
Deposit Accounts [UCC 9–104, 9–304, 9–312(b), 9–314(a)]	Any demand, time, savings, passbook, or similar account maintained with a bank [UCC 9–102(a)(29)].	Perfection by control, such as when the secured party is the bank in which the account is maintained or when the parties have agreed that the secured party can direct the disposition of funds in a particular account.

fictitious, name is Pete's Plumbing. A financing statement filed in the trade name Pete's Plumbing would not be sufficient because it does not identify Peter Jones as the actual debtor. As will be discussed in Chapter 23, a sole proprietorship (such as Pete's Plumbing) is not a legal entity distinct from the person who owns it. • The reason for this rule is to ensure that the debtor's name on a financing statement is one that prospective lenders can locate and recognize in future searches.

Description of the Collateral Both the security agreement and the financing statement must describe the collateral in which the secured party has a security interest. The security agreement must describe the collateral because no security interest in goods can exist unless the parties agree on which goods are subject to the security interest. The financing statement must also describe the collateral because the purpose of filing the statement is to give public notice of the fact that certain goods of the debtor are subject to a security interest. For land-related security interests, a legal description of the realty is also required [UCC 9–502(b)].

Sometimes, the descriptions in the two documents vary, with the description in the security agreement being more precise than the description in the financing statement, which is allowed to be more general. **EXAMPLE 18.2** A security agreement for a commercial loan to a manufacturer may list all of the manufacturer's equipment subject to the loan by serial number. The financing statement for the equipment may simply state "all equipment owned or hereafter acquired." •

The UCC permits broad, general descriptions in the financing statement, such as "all assets" or "all personal property." Generally, whenever the description in a financing statement accurately describes the agreement between the secured party and the debtor, the description is sufficient [UCC 9–504].

WHERE TO FILE In most states, a financing statement must be filed centrally in the appropriate state office, such as the office of the secretary of state, in the state where the debtor is located. Filing in the county where the collateral is located is required only when the collateral consists of timber to be cut, fixtures, or items to be extracted—such as oil, coal, gas, and minerals [UCC 9–301(3) and (4), 9–502(b)].

The state office in which a financing statement should be filed depends on the *debtor's location,* not the location of the collateral [UCC 9–301]. The debtor's location is determined as follows [UCC 9–307]:

1. For *individual debtors,* it is the state of the debtor's principal residence.
2. For an organization that is registered with the state, such as a corporation or limited liability company, it is the state in which the organization is registered. Thus, if a debtor is incorporated in Maryland and has its chief executive office in New York, a secured party would file the financing statement in Maryland—the state of the debtor's organizational formation.
3. For all other entities, it is the state in which the business is located or, if the debtor has more than one office, the place from which the debtor manages its business operations and affairs (the office of its chief executive).

CONSEQUENCES OF AN IMPROPER FILING Any improper filing renders the security interest unperfected and reduces the secured party's claim in bankruptcy to that of an unsecured creditor. For instance, if the debtor's name on the financing statement is seriously misleading or if the collateral is not sufficiently described in the financing statement, the filing may not be effective.

CASE EXAMPLE 18.3 Corona Fruits & Veggies, Inc., sublet farmland to Armando Munoz Juarez, a strawberry farmer, and loaned funds to Juarez for payroll and production expenses. The sublease and other documents set out Juarez's full name, but Juarez generally went by the name "Munoz" and signed the sublease "Armando Munoz." Corona filed financing statements that identified the debtor as "Armando Munoz." In December, Juarez contracted to sell strawberries to Frozsun Foods, Inc., which advanced funds secured by a financing statement that identified the debtor as "Armando Juarez." By the next July, Juarez owed Corona $230,482.52 and Frozsun $19,648.52. When Juarez did not repay his debt, Corona took possession of the farmland, harvested and sold the strawberries, and kept the proceeds. Corona and Frozsun then filed a suit against Juarez to collect the rest. At trial, Frozsun presented evidence that it had conducted a debtor name search for "Juarez" and had not discovered Corona's financing statement. The court concluded that the "Armando Munoz" debtor name in Corona's financing statement was seriously misleading. Frozsun's interest thus took priority because its financing statement was recorded properly.[4] •

The UCC financing statement includes a section for listing an "Additional Debtor." When there is more than one additional debtor, is it appropriate to include the names on an attached list and refer to the list in the "Additional Debtor" section? Is it misleading to attach the list and not refer to it? The court in the following case considered these questions.

4. *Corona Fruits and Veggies, Inc. v. Frozsun Foods, Inc.,* 143 Cal.App.4th 319, 48 Cal.Rptr.3d 868 (2006).

Case 18.1 In re Camtech Precision Manufacturing, Inc.

United States Bankruptcy Court, Southern District of Florida, 443 Bankr. 190 (2011).

FACTS Camtech Precision Manufacturing, Inc., makes precision parts and assemblies for aerospace and defense customers. Camtech is a subsidiary of R&J National Enterprises, Inc. (R&J). R&J had a nearly $4 million line of credit with Regions Bank in 2010. Regions Bank filed a series of financing statements with the appropriate state offices in Florida and New York to perfect security interests in the assets of R&J and its related companies. All of the statements were filed on the Uniform Commercial Code financing statement form used in all states. The forms listed R&J as the debtor in the "Debtor" box and Avstar Aircraft Accessories, Inc., another R&J subsidiary, as an additional debtor in the "Additional Debtor" box. Nothing in either box indicated that there were more debtors. Attached to each form, however, was a sheet of plain paper that listed Camtech Precision Manufacturing, Inc., and Avstar Fuel Systems, Inc., as additional debtors. In 2010, R&J and the others filed a petition in a federal bankruptcy court to declare bankruptcy (discussed in Chapter 19). A committee of the companies' unsecured creditors asked the court to rule that Regions Bank's statements failed to perfect the bank's security interest in the assets of Camtech and Avstar Fuel.

ISSUE Were the financing statements seriously misleading because they did not mention or refer to the additional debtors (including Camtech) that were listed on an attached page?

Case 18.1—Continued

DECISION Yes. The bankruptcy court found that Regions Bank's financing statements were seriously misleading and ineffective to perfect security interests in the assets of Camtech and Avstar Fuel.

REASON Florida and New York have approved the use of a standard UCC form for listing additional debtors. Regions Bank did not use this form, but merely listed Camtech and Avstar Fuel as additional debtors on a single sheet of plain paper attached to each financing statement. Minor errors in a financing statement do not undercut its effectiveness. Appending a list of additional debtors without a reference in the "Additional Debtor" box on the financing statement, however, was "an error and an omission that made the financing statements seriously misleading." Searches of the two states' records failed to reveal any financing statement that identified Regions Bank as a secured creditor of Camtech or Avstar Fuel. This failure rendered Regions Bank's financing statements ineffective to perfect its security interests in the assets of Camtech and Avstar Fuel. With respect to these assets, the bank's claim was reduced to that of an unsecured creditor.

WHAT IF THE FACTS WERE DIFFERENT? *Suppose that searches of the Florida and New York records had revealed that Regions Bank was a secured creditor of Camtech and Avstar Fuel. Would the result have been different in this case? Explain.*

Perfection without Filing

In two types of situations, security interests can be perfected without filing a financing statement. The first occurs when the collateral is transferred into the possession of the secured party. The second occurs when the security interest is one of a limited number under the UCC that can be perfected on attachment (without a filing and without having to possess the goods) [UCC 9–309]. The phrase *perfected on attachment* means that these security interests are automatically perfected at the time of their creation. Two of the more common security interests that are perfected on attachment are a *purchase-money security interest* in consumer goods (defined and explained shortly) and an assignment of a beneficial interest in a decedent's estate [UCC 9–309(1), (13)].

PERFECTION BY POSSESSION In the past, one of the most common means of obtaining financing was to **pledge** certain collateral as security for the debt and transfer the collateral into the creditor's possession. When the debt was paid, the collateral was returned to the debtor. Although the debtor usually entered into a written security agreement, an oral security agreement was also enforceable as long as the secured party possessed the collateral.

Article 9 of the UCC retained the common law pledge and the principle that the security agreement need not be in writing to be enforceable if the collateral is transferred to the secured party [UCC 9–310, 9–312(b), 9–313]. **EXAMPLE 18.4** Sheila needs cash to pay for a medical procedure. She gets a loan for $4,000 from Trent. As security on the loan, she gives him a promissory note on which she is the payee. Even though the agreement to hold the note as collateral was oral, Trent has a perfected security interest and does not need to file a financing statement. No other creditor of Sheila's can attempt to recover the promissory note from Trent in payment for other debts. •

For most collateral, possession by the secured party is impractical because it denies the debtor the right to use or derive income from the property to pay off the debt. **EXAMPLE 18.5** Jed, a farmer, takes out a loan to finance the purchase of a large corn harvester and uses the equipment as collateral. Clearly, the purpose of the purchase would be defeated if Jed transferred the collateral into the creditor's possession, because he would not be able to use the equipment to harvest his corn. • Certain items, however, such as stocks, bonds, negotiable instruments, and jewelry, are commonly transferred into the creditor's possession when they are used as collateral for loans.

PERFECTION BY ATTACHMENT—THE PURCHASE-MONEY SECURITY INTEREST IN CONSUMER GOODS Under the UCC, fourteen types of security interests are perfected automatically at the time they are created [UCC 9–309]. The most common of these is the **purchase-money security interest (PMSI)** in *consumer goods* (items bought primarily for personal, family, or household purposes). A PMSI in consumer goods is created when a person buys goods and the seller or lender agrees to extend credit for part or all of the purchase price of the goods. The entity that extends the credit and obtains the PMSI can be either the seller (a store, for example) or a financial institution that lends the buyer the funds with which to purchase the goods [UCC 9–102(a)(2)].

Automatic Perfection. A PMSI in consumer goods is perfected automatically at the time of a credit sale—that is, at the time the PMSI is created. The seller in this situation does not need to do anything more to perfect her or his interest.

EXAMPLE 18.6 Jamie wants to purchase a new 3D television from ABC Television, Inc. The purchase price is $2,500. Not being able to pay the entire amount in cash, Jamie signs a purchase agreement to pay $1,000 down and $100 per month until the balance, plus interest, is fully paid. ABC is to retain a security interest in the television until full payment has been made. Because the security interest was created as part of the purchase agreement, it is a PMSI in consumer goods. ABC does not need to do anything else to perfect its security interest. •

Exceptions to the Rule of Automatic Perfection. There are exceptions to the rule of automatic perfection. First, certain types of security interests that are subject to other federal or state laws may require additional steps to be perfected [UCC 9–311]. For instance, most states have certificate-of-title statutes that establish perfection requirements for specific goods, such as automobiles, trailers, boats, mobile homes, and farm tractors. If a consumer in these jurisdictions purchases a boat, for example, the secured party will need to file a certificate of title with the appropriate state official to perfect the PMSI. A second exception involves PMSIs in nonconsumer goods, such as livestock or a business's inventory, which are not automatically perfected (these types of PMSIs will be discussed later in this chapter in the context of priorities).

Effective Time Duration of Perfection

A financing statement is effective for five years from the date of filing [UCC 9–515]. If a **continuation statement** is filed within six months *prior to* the expiration date, the effectiveness of the original statement is continued for another five years, starting with the expiration date of the first five-year period [UCC 9–515(d), (e)]. The effectiveness of the statement can be continued in the same manner indefinitely. Any attempt to file a continuation statement outside the six-month window will render the continuation ineffective, and the perfection will lapse at the end of the five-year period.

If a financing statement lapses, the security interest that had been perfected by the filing now becomes unperfected. A purchaser for value can acquire the collateral as if the security interest had never been perfected [UCC 9–515(c)].

The Scope of a Security Interest

As previously stated, a security interest can cover property in which the debtor has ownership or possessory rights in the present or in the future. Therefore, security agreements can cover the proceeds from the sale of collateral, after-acquired property, and future advances, as discussed next.

Proceeds

Proceeds are whatever cash or property is received when collateral is sold or disposed of in some other way [UCC 9–102(a)(64)]. A security interest in the collateral gives the secured party a security interest in the proceeds acquired from the sale of that collateral.

EXAMPLE 18.7 People's Bank has a perfected security interest in the inventory of a retail seller of heavy farm machinery. The retailer sells a tractor out of this inventory to Jacob Dunn, a farmer, who is by definition a *buyer in the ordinary course of business* (see page 344). Dunn agrees, in a security agreement, to make monthly payments to the retailer for a period of twenty-four months. If the retailer goes into default on the loan from the bank, the bank is entitled to the remaining payments Dunn owes to the retailer as proceeds. •

A security interest in proceeds perfects automatically on the *perfection* of the secured party's security interest in the original collateral and remains perfected for twenty days after the debtor receives the proceeds. One way to extend the twenty-day automatic perfection period is to provide for extended coverage in the original security agreement [UCC 9–315(c), (d)]. This is typically done when the collateral is the type that is likely to be sold, such as a retailer's inventory—for example, of computers or cell phones. The UCC also permits a security interest in identifiable cash proceeds to remain perfected after twenty days [UCC 9–315(d)(2)].

After-Acquired Property

After-acquired property is property that the debtor acquired after the execution of the security agreement. The security agreement may provide for a security interest in after-acquired property, such as a debtor's inventory [UCC 9–204(1)]. Generally, the debtor will purchase new inventory to replace the inventory sold. The secured party wants this newly acquired inventory to be subject to the original security interest. Thus, the after-acquired property clause continues the secured party's claim to any inventory acquired thereafter. (This is not to say that the original security interest will take priority over the rights of all other creditors with regard to this after-acquired inventory, as will be discussed later.)

EXAMPLE 18.8 Amato buys factory equipment from Bronson on credit, giving as security an interest in all of her equipment—both what she is buying and what she already owns. The security interest with Bronson contains an after-acquired property clause. Six months later, Amato pays cash to another seller of factory equipment for more equipment. Six months after that, Amato goes out of business before she has paid off her debt to Bronson. Bronson has a security interest in all of Amato's equipment, even the equipment bought from the other seller. •

Future Advances

Often, a debtor will arrange with a bank to have a *continuing line of credit* under which the debtor can borrow funds intermittently. Advances against lines of credit can be subject to a properly perfected security interest in certain collateral. The security agreement may provide that any future advances made against that line of credit are also subject to the security interest in the same collateral [UCC 9–204(c)]. Future advances do not have to be of the same type or otherwise related to the original advance to benefit from this type of **cross-collateralization.** Cross-collateralization occurs when an asset that is not the subject of a loan is used to secure that loan.

EXAMPLE 18.9 Stroh is the owner of a small manufacturing plant with equipment valued at $1 million. He has an immediate need for $50,000 of working capital, so he obtains a loan from Midwestern Bank and signs a security agreement, putting up all of his equipment as security. The bank properly perfects its security interest. The security agreement provides that Stroh can borrow up to $500,000 in the future, using the same equipment as collateral for any future advances. In this situation, Midwestern Bank does not have to execute a new security agreement and perfect a security interest in the collateral each time an advance is made, up to a cumulative total of $500,000. For priority purposes, each advance is perfected as of the date of the *original* perfection. •

The Floating-Lien Concept

A security agreement that provides for a security interest in proceeds, in after-acquired property, or in collateral subject to future advances by the secured party (or in all three) is often characterized as a **floating lien.** This type of security interest continues in the collateral or proceeds even if the collateral is sold, exchanged, or disposed of in some other way.

A FLOATING LIEN IN INVENTORY Floating liens commonly arise in the financing of inventories. A creditor is not interested in specific pieces of inventory, which are constantly changing, so the lien "floats" from one item to another, as the inventory changes.

EXAMPLE 18.10 Cascade Sports, Inc., is an Oregon corporation that operates as a cross-country ski dealer and has a line of credit with Portland First Bank to finance its inventory of cross-country skis. Cascade and Portland First enter into a security agreement that provides for coverage of proceeds, after-acquired inventory, present inventory, and future advances. Portland First perfects its security interest in the inventory by filing centrally with the office of the secretary of state in Oregon. One day, Cascade sells a new pair of the latest cross-country skis and receives a used pair in trade. That same day, Cascade purchases two new pairs of cross-country skis from a local manufacturer for cash. Later that day, to meet its payroll, Cascade borrows $8,000 from Portland First Bank under the security agreement.

Portland First gets a perfected security interest in the used pair of skis under the proceeds clause, has a perfected security interest in the two new pairs of skis purchased from the local manufacturer under the after-acquired property clause, and has the new amount of funds advanced to Cascade secured on all of the above collateral by the future-advances clause. All of this is accomplished under the original perfected security interest. The various items in the inventory have changed, but Portland First still has a perfected security interest in Cascade's inventory. Hence, it has a floating lien in the inventory. •

A FLOATING LIEN IN A SHIFTING STOCK OF GOODS The concept of the floating lien can also apply to a shifting stock of goods. The lien can start with raw materials; follow them as they become finished goods and inventories; and continue as the goods are sold and are turned into accounts receivable, chattel paper, or cash.

Priorities

When more than one party claims an interest in the same collateral, which has priority? The UCC sets out detailed rules to answer this question. Although in many situations the party who has a perfected security interest will have priority, there are exceptions.

General Rules of Priority

The basic rule is that when more than one security interest has been perfected in the same collateral, the first security interest to be perfected (or filed) has priority over any security interests that are perfected later. If only one of the conflicting security interests has been perfected, then that security interest has priority. If none of the security interests have been perfected, then the first security interest that attaches has priority. The UCC's rules of priority can be summarized as follows:

1. *A perfected security interest has priority over unsecured creditors and unperfected security interests.* When two or more parties have claims to the same collateral, a perfected secured party's interest has priority over the interests of most other parties [UCC 9–322(a)(2)]. This includes priority to the proceeds from a sale of collateral resulting from a bankruptcy (giving the perfected secured party rights superior to that of the bankruptcy trustee, which will be discussed in Chapter 19).
2. *Conflicting perfected security interests.* When two or more secured parties have perfected security interests in the same collateral, the first to perfect (by filing or taking possession of the collateral) generally has priority [UCC 9–322(a)(1)].
3. *Conflicting unperfected security interests.* When two conflicting security interests are unperfected, the first to attach (be created) has priority [UCC 9–322(a)(3)]. This is sometimes called the "first-in-time" rule.

In the following case, the court had to determine which of two conflicting security interests in a mobile home took priority.

Case 18.2 Citizens National Bank of Jessamine County v. Washington Mutual Bank

Court of Appeals of Kentucky, 309 S.W.3d 792 (2010).

FACTS Rose Day transferred land and a mobile home to Anthony and Kim Reynolds. The deed was duly recorded at the appropriate county office. The deed description did not mention the mobile home, but it was clear from the record that the Reynoldses were purchasing both from Day. The Reynoldses executed a mortgage conveying a security interest in the property to Washington Mutual Bank. There was no mention of the mobile home in the mortgage. Furthermore, the Reynoldses did not obtain a title certificate to the mobile home in their names. Because the mobile home was therefore not legally affixed to the real property, its character did not change from personal property to real property. Several years later, the Reynoldses obtained a second mortgage from Citizens National Bank of Jessamine County. Again, there was no description of the mobile home in the mortgage. When the Reynoldses subsequently defaulted on both loans, Washington Mutual filed a complaint, claiming lien priority on both the real estate and the mobile home. Citizens was listed as an interested party and was served with the complaint. After being served, Citizens and the Reynoldses executed a title lien statement regarding the mobile home, which was recorded in the county clerk's office. The trial court ruled that the filing of the complaint and notice of the lawsuit by Washington Mutual created a priority claim in the mobile home. Citizens appealed that decision. The sole issue to be decided in the appeal was the priority of competing liens in the mobile home.

ISSUE Did Citizens' security interest in the mobile home take priority over Washington Mutual's?

DECISION Yes. The state appellate court reversed the trial court's decision. Washington Mutual's filing of a complaint and a notice of a pending lawsuit did not create a priority lien on the mobile home but applied only to the interest in the real estate. Citizens' security interest in the mobile home had priority because it was perfected when Citizens recorded the title lien.

REASON The UCC explicitly "provides that the sole means of perfecting a security interest in personal property for which a certificate of title is issued is by placing a notation of the lien on the certificate of title." The court reasoned that Citizens (and the Reynoldses) had so perfected its lien, but Washington Mutual had not. "It is fundamental that unperfected security interests are subordinate to perfected security interests." It was irrelevant that Citizens had knowledge that Washington Mutual had filed a notice of a claim to both the real property and the mobile home. "Because Washington Mutual failed to perfect its lien under the mandates of the [UCC], its interest in the Reynoldses' manufactured [mobile] home must necessarily give way to Citizens' perfected claim."

WHAT IF THE FACTS WERE DIFFERENT? *Suppose that the mobile home had been affixed to the land and was regarded as real property. In that situation, which of the two security interests would take priority? Discuss.*

Exceptions to the General Rule

Under some circumstances, on the debtor's default, the perfection of a security interest will not protect a secured party against certain other third parties having claims to the collateral. For example, the UCC provides that in some instances a PMSI, properly perfected,[5] will prevail over another security interest in after-acquired collateral, even though the other was perfected first. We discuss several significant exceptions to the general rules of priority in the following subsections.

BUYERS IN THE ORDINARY COURSE OF BUSINESS Under the UCC, a person who buys "in the ordinary course of business" takes the goods free from any security interest created by the seller *even if the security interest is perfected and the buyer knows of its existence* [UCC 9–320(a)]. In other words, a buyer in the ordinary course will have priority even if a previously perfected security interest exists as to the goods. The rationale for this rule is obvious: if buyers could not obtain the goods free and clear of any security interest the merchant had created—for example, in inventory—the free flow of goods in the marketplace would be hindered.

A *buyer in the ordinary course of business* is a person who in good faith, and without knowledge that the sale violates the rights of another in the goods, buys goods in the ordinary course from a person in the business of selling goods of that kind [UCC 1–201(9)]. Note that the buyer can know about the existence of a perfected security interest, so long as he or she does not know that buying the goods violates the rights of any third party.

PMSI IN GOODS OTHER THAN INVENTORY AND LIVESTOCK An important exception to the first-in-time rule involves certain types of collateral, such as equipment, that is *not* inventory (or livestock) and in which one of the secured parties has a perfected PMSI [UCC 9–324(a)].

EXAMPLE 18.11 Sandoval borrows funds from West Bank, signing a security agreement in which she puts up all of her present and after-acquired equipment as security. On May 1, West Bank perfects this security interest (which is not a PMSI).

5. Recall that, with some exceptions (such as motor vehicles), a PMSI in *consumer goods* is automatically perfected—no filing is necessary. A PMSI that is not in consumer goods must still be perfected, however.

On July 1, Sandoval purchases a new piece of equipment from Zylex Company on credit, signing a security agreement. The delivery date for the new equipment is August 1.

Zylex thus has a PMSI in the new equipment (that is not part of its inventory), but the PMSI is not in consumer goods and thus is not automatically perfected. If Sandoval defaults on her payments to both West Bank and Zylex, which of them has priority with regard to the new piece of equipment? Generally, West Bank would have priority because its interest perfected first in time. In this situation, however, Zylex has a PMSI, and provided that Zylex perfected its interest in the equipment within twenty days after Sandoval took possession on August 1, Zylex has priority. •

PMSI IN INVENTORY Another important exception to the first-in-time rule has to do with security interests in inventory [UCC 9–324(b)]. **CASE EXAMPLE 18.12** Rebel Rents, Inc., was a California firm that offered a variety of equipment for sale or lease. In September 2000, Rebel bought certain equipment from Snorkel International, Inc., to use as inventory. Textron Financial Corporation agreed to finance the purchase, for which Rebel granted Textron a security interest in the equipment and its proceeds. In December 2000, General Electric Capital Corporation (GECC) agreed to loan Rebel up to $25 million, for which Rebel granted GECC a security interest in substantially all of Rebel's assets, including its inventory and proceeds.

On January 5, 2001, GECC filed a financing statement with the California secretary of state to perfect its interest. Textron filed its financing statement on January 16. Rebel filed a bankruptcy petition with a federal bankruptcy court in September 2002. Between that date and September 2003, Rebel obtained $430,661 from leasing the Snorkel equipment. Pursuant to an order of the court, Rebel surrendered the Snorkel equipment to Textron. Textron asserted that because of its security interest, it was also owed the income from the recent leases. The court, however, ruled that GECC's security interest had priority over Textron's interest in Rebel's income because of the date of perfection. Textron's security interest attached on September 14, 2000, but was not perfected until January 16, 2001. GECC's financing statement was filed on January 5—eleven days before Textron's financing statement was filed.[6] •

BUYERS OF THE COLLATERAL The UCC recognizes that there are certain types of buyers whose interest in purchased goods could conflict with those of a perfected secured party on the debtor's default. These include buyers in the ordinary course of business (as discussed), as well as buyers of farm products, instruments, documents, or securities. The UCC sets down special rules of priority for these types of buyers.

6. *In re Rebel Rents, Inc.*, 307 Bankr. 171 (C.D.Cal. 2004).

See Exhibit 18–3 on the following page for a review of the rules on the priority of claims to a debtor's collateral.

Rights and Duties of Debtors and Creditors

The security agreement itself determines most of the rights and duties of the debtor and the secured party. The UCC, however, imposes some rights and duties that are applicable in the absence of a valid security agreement that states the contrary.

Information Requests

At the time of filing, a secured party has the option of furnishing a *copy* of the financing statement being filed to the filing officer and requesting that the filing officer make a note of the file number, the date, and the hour of the original filing on the copy [UCC 9–523(a)]. The filing officer must send this copy to the person designated by the secured party or to the debtor, if the debtor makes the request. Under UCC 9–523(c) and (d), a filing officer must also give information to a person who is contemplating obtaining a security interest from a prospective debtor. The filing officer must issue a certificate that provides information on possible perfected financing statements with respect to the named debtor.

Release, Assignment, and Amendment

A secured party can release all or part of any collateral described in the financing statement, thereby terminating its security interest in that collateral. The release is recorded by filing a uniform amendment form [UCC 9–512, 9–521(b)]. A secured party can also assign all or part of the security interest to a third party (the assignee). The assignee becomes the secured party of record if the assignment is filed by use of a uniform amendment form [UCC 9–514, 9–521(a)].

If the debtor and the secured party agree, they can amend the financing statement—to add new collateral, for instance—by filing a uniform amendment form that indicates the file number of the initial financing statement [UCC 9–512(a)]. The amendment does not extend the time period of perfection, but if collateral is added, the perfection date (for priority purposes) for the new collateral begins on the date the amendment is filed [UCC 9–512(b), (c)].

Confirmation or Accounting Request by Debtor

The debtor may believe that the amount of the unpaid debt or the listing of the collateral subject to the security interest is inaccurate. The debtor has the right to request a confirmation of the unpaid debt or listing of collateral [UCC 9–210]. The debtor is entitled to one request without charge every six months.

• ***Exhibit* 18–3 Priority of Claims to a Debtor's Collateral**

PARTIES	PRIORITY
Perfected Secured Party versus Unsecured Parties and Creditors	A perfected secured party's interest has priority over the interests of most other parties, including unsecured creditors, unperfected secured parties, subsequent lien creditors, trustees in bankruptcy, and buyers who do not purchase the collateral in the ordinary course of business.
Perfected Secured Party versus Perfected Secured Party	Between two perfected secured parties in the same collateral, the general rule is that the first in time of perfection is the first in right to the collateral [UCC 9–322(a)(1)].
Perfected Secured Party versus Perfected PMSI	A PMSI, even if second in time of perfection, has priority providing that the following conditions are met: 1. *Other collateral*—A PMSI has priority, providing it is perfected within twenty days after the debtor takes possession [UCC 9–324(a)]. 2. *Inventory*—A PMSI has priority if it is perfected and proper written or authenticated notice is given to the other security-interest holder *on* or *before* the time the debtor takes possession [UCC 9–324(b)]. 3. *Software*—Applies to a PMSI in software only if used in goods subject to a PMSI. If the goods are inventory, priority is determined the same as for inventory. If they are not, priority is determined as for goods other than inventory [UCC 9–103(c), 9–324(f)].
Perfected Secured Party versus Purchaser of Debtor's Collateral	1. *Buyer of goods in the ordinary course of the seller's business*—Buyer prevails over a secured party's security interest, even if perfected and even if the buyer knows of the security interest [UCC 9–320(a)]. 2. *Buyer of consumer goods purchased outside the ordinary course of business*—Buyer prevails over a secured party's interest, even if perfected by attachment, providing the buyer purchased as follows: a. For value. b. Without actual knowledge of the security interest. c. For use as a consumer good. d. Prior to the secured party's perfection by *filing* [UCC 9–320(b)]. 3. *Buyer of chattel paper*—Buyer prevails if the buyer: a. Gave new value in making the purchase. b. Took possession in the ordinary course of the buyer's business. c. Took without knowledge of the security interest [UCC 9–330]. 4. *Buyer of instruments, documents, or securities*—Buyer who is a holder in due course, a holder to whom negotiable documents have been duly negotiated, or a bona fide purchaser of securities has priority over a previously perfected security interest [UCC 9–330(d), 9–331(a)]. 5. *Buyer of farm products*—Buyer from a farmer takes free and clear of perfected security interests unless, where permitted, a secured party files centrally an effective financing statement (EFS) or the buyer receives proper notice of the security interest before the sale.
Unperfected Secured Party versus Unsecured Creditor	An unperfected secured party prevails over unsecured creditors and creditors who have obtained judgments against the debtor but who have not begun the legal process to collect on those judgments [UCC 9–201(a)].

The secured party must comply with the debtor's confirmation request by authenticating and sending to the debtor an accounting within fourteen days after the request is received. Otherwise, the secured party will be held liable for any loss suffered by the debtor, plus $500 [UCC 9–210, 9–625(f)].

Termination Statement

When the debtor has fully paid the debt, if the secured party perfected the security interest by filing, the debtor is entitled to have a termination statement filed. Such a statement demonstrates to the public that the filed perfected security interest has been terminated [UCC 9–513].

Whenever consumer goods are involved, the secured party *must* file a termination statement (or, alternatively, a release) within one month of the final payment or within twenty days of receiving the debtor's authenticated demand, whichever is earlier [UCC 9–513(b)].

When the collateral is other than consumer goods, on an authenticated demand by the debtor, the secured party must either send a termination statement to the debtor or file such a statement within twenty days [UCC 9–513(c)]. Otherwise, the secured party is not required to file or send a termination statement. Whenever a secured party fails to file or send the termination statement as requested, the debtor can recover $500 plus any additional loss suffered [UCC 9–625(e)(4), (f)].

Default

Article 9 defines the rights, duties, and remedies of the secured party and of the debtor on the debtor's default. Should the secured party fail to comply with her or his duties, the debtor is afforded particular rights and remedies.

The topic of default is one of great concern to secured lenders and to the lawyers who draft security agreements. What constitutes default is not always clear. In fact, Article 9 does not define the term. Consequently, parties are encouraged in practice—and by the UCC—to include in their security agreements certain standards to be applied in determining when default has actually occurred. In so doing, the parties can stipulate the conditions that will constitute a default [UCC 9–601, 9–603]. Often, these critical terms are shaped by the creditor in an attempt to provide the maximum protection possible. The ultimate terms, however, may not go beyond the limitations imposed by the good faith requirement and the unconscionability provisions of the UCC.

Any breach of the terms of the security agreement can constitute default. Nevertheless, default occurs most commonly when the debtor fails to meet the scheduled payments that the parties have agreed on or when the debtor becomes bankrupt.

Basic Remedies

The rights and remedies set out in UCC 9–601(a) and (b) are *cumulative* [UCC 9–601(c)]. Therefore, if a creditor is unsuccessful in enforcing rights by one method, he or she can pursue another method. Generally, a secured party's remedies can be divided into the two basic categories discussed next.

REPOSSESSION OF THE COLLATERAL—THE SELF-HELP REMEDY On the debtor's default, a secured party can take peaceful possession of the collateral without the use of judicial process [UCC 9–609(b)]. This provision is often referred to as the "self-help" provision of Article 9. The UCC does not define *peaceful possession,* however. The general rule is that the collateral has been taken peacefully if the secured party can take possession without committing (1) trespass onto land, (2) assault and/or battery, or (3) breaking and entering. On taking possession, the secured party may either retain the collateral for satisfaction of the debt [UCC 9–620] or resell the goods and apply the proceeds toward the debt [UCC 9–610].

JUDICIAL REMEDIES Alternatively, a secured party can relinquish the security interest and use any judicial remedy available, such as obtaining a judgment on the underlying debt, followed by execution and levy. (**Execution** is the implementation of a court's decree or judgment. **Levy** is the obtaining of funds by legal process through the seizure and sale of nonexempt property, usually done after a writ of execution has been issued.) Execution and levy are rarely undertaken unless the collateral is no longer in existence or has declined so much in value that it is worth substantially less than the amount of the debt and the debtor has other assets available that may be legally seized to satisfy the debt [UCC 9–601(a)].[7]

Disposition of Collateral

Once default has occurred and the secured party has obtained possession of the collateral, the secured party has several options. The secured party can (1) retain the collateral in full or partial satisfaction of the debt, or (2) sell, lease, license, or otherwise dispose of the collateral in any commercially reasonable manner and apply the proceeds toward satisfaction of the debt [UCC 9–602(7), 9–603, 9–610(a), 9–613, 9–620]. Any sale is always subject to procedures established by state law.

RETENTION OF COLLATERAL BY THE SECURED PARTY The UCC acknowledges that parties are sometimes better off if they do not sell the collateral. Therefore, a secured party may retain the collateral unless it consists of consumer goods and the debtor has paid 60 percent or more of the purchase price in a PMSI or debt in a non-PMSI—as will be discussed shortly [UCC 9–620(e)].

This general right, however, is subject to several conditions. The secured party must notify the debtor of its proposal to retain the collateral. Notice is required unless the debtor has signed a statement renouncing or modifying her or his rights *after default* [UCC 9–620(a), 9–621]. If the collateral is consumer goods, the secured party does not need to give any other notice. In all other situations, the secured party must send notice to any other secured party from whom the secured party has received written or authenticated notice of a claim of interest in the collateral. The secured party must also send notice to any other **junior lienholder** (one holding a lien that is subordinate to one or more other liens on the same property) who has filed a statutory lien (such as a *mechanic's lien*—see Chapter 19) or a security interest in the collateral ten days before the debtor consented to the retention [UCC 9–621].

If, within twenty days after the notice is sent, the secured party receives an objection sent by a person entitled to receive notification, the secured party must sell or otherwise dispose of the collateral (disposition procedures will be discussed shortly). If no written objection is received, the secured party may retain the collateral in full or partial satisfaction of the debtor's obligation [UCC 9–620(a), 9–621].

---

7. Some assets are exempt from creditors' claims—see Chapter 19.

CONSUMER GOODS When the collateral is consumer goods and the debtor has paid 60 percent or more of the purchase price or loan amount, the secured party must sell or otherwise dispose of the repossessed collateral within ninety days [UCC 9–620(e), (f)]. Failure to comply opens the secured party to an action for conversion or other liability under UCC 9–625(b) and (c) unless the consumer-debtor signed a written statement *after default* renouncing or modifying the right to demand the sale of the goods [UCC 9–624].

DISPOSITION PROCEDURES A secured party who does not choose to retain the collateral or who is required to sell it must resort to the disposition procedures prescribed in the UCC. The UCC allows substantial flexibility with regard to disposition. A secured party may sell, lease, license, or otherwise dispose of any or all of the collateral in its present condition or following any commercially reasonable preparation or processing [UCC 9–610(a)].

The collateral can be disposed of at public or private proceedings, but every aspect of the disposition's method, manner, time, and place must be commercially reasonable [UCC 9–610(b)]. The secured party must notify the debtor and other specified parties in writing ahead of time about the sale or disposition of the collateral. Notification is not required if the collateral is perishable, will decline rapidly in value, or is a type customarily sold on a recognized market [UCC 9–611(b), (c)]. The debtor may waive the right to receive this notice, but only after default [UCC 9–624(a)].

The secured party may purchase the collateral at a public sale, but not at a private sale—unless the collateral is of a kind customarily sold on a recognized market or is the subject of widely distributed standard price quotations [UCC 9–610(c)]. If the secured party does not dispose of the collateral in a commercially reasonable manner and the price paid for the collateral is affected, a court can reduce the amount of any deficiency that the debtor owes to the secured party [UCC 9–626(a)(3)].

Under the UCC, the secured party must meet a high standard when disposing of collateral. Although obtaining a satisfactory price is the purpose of requiring the secured party to resell collateral in a commercially reasonable way, price is only one aspect, as the following case makes clear.

Case 18.3 Hicklin v. Onyx Acceptance Corp.

Delaware Supreme Court, 970 A.2d 244 (2009).
courts.delaware.gov[a]

FACTS Shannon Hicklin bought a 1993 Ford Explorer under an installment sales contract. When she fell three payments behind–still owing $5,741.65–Onyx Acceptance Corporation repossessed the car. The car was sold for $1,500 at a private auction held by ABC Washington-Dulles, LLC. After deducting the costs of repossession and sale, there was a deficiency under the contract of $5,018.88. Onyx filed a suit in a Delaware state court to collect this amount from Hicklin. To establish that the sale was commercially reasonable, Onyx offered proof only of the price. The court found that the fair market value of the car at the time of the sale was $2,335 and held that the sale was commercially reasonable solely because the auction price was more than 50 percent of this estimated market value at the time of the auction. The court granted Onyx a deficiency judgment, which a state intermediate appellate court affirmed. Hicklin appealed.

ISSUE Does the price obtained on a sale of collateral prove, without more, that the sale was commercially reasonable?

a. In the left-hand column, click on "Supreme Court." On that page, in the "Opinions" pull-down menu, select "Supreme Court." In the result, in the "Year" pull-down menu, select "2009." In the "Search For:" box, type "Hicklin" and click on "Search." Click on the case name to access the opinion. The Delaware Judiciary maintains this Web site.

DECISION No. The Delaware Supreme Court reversed the lower court's judgment and remanded the case.

REASON The appellate court explained that under UCC 9–610(a), Onyx could prove that its sale was commercially reasonable in one of two ways. It could show that every aspect of the sale was conducted in a commercially reasonable manner or, under UCC 9–627(b)(3), that the sale conformed with the reasonable commercial practices among dealers in the type of property that was the subject of the disposition. Onyx did not meet either of these standards. Because every aspect of a sale must be commercially reasonable, Onyx's showing only that the private auction sale grossed more than 50 percent of the value of the collateral was not enough. Onyx did not provide any proof of the details of the auction–its procedure, publicity, attendance, or convenience of location. Nor did Onyx offer any proof that the sale conformed to the accepted practices in its trade.

FOR CRITICAL ANALYSIS—Ethical Consideration *Why does UCC 9–627(b)(3) require that a sale be conducted in conformity with the reasonable commercial practices among dealers in the type of property that was the subject of the disposition?*

Proceeds from the Disposition Proceeds from the disposition of collateral after default on the underlying debt are distributed in the following order:

1. Reasonable expenses incurred by the secured party in repossessing, storing, and reselling the collateral.
2. Balance of the debt owed to the secured party.
3. Junior lienholders who have made written or authenticated demands.
4. Unless the collateral consists of accounts, payment intangibles, promissory notes, or chattel paper, any surplus goes to the debtor [UCC 9–608(a); 9–615(a), (e)].

Noncash Proceeds Whenever the secured party receives noncash proceeds from the disposition of collateral after default, the secured party must make a value determination and apply this value in a commercially reasonable manner [UCC 9–608(a)(3), 9–615(c)].

Deficiency Judgment Often, after proper disposition of the collateral, the secured party has not collected all that the debtor still owes. Unless otherwise agreed, the debtor is liable for any deficiency, and the creditor can obtain a **deficiency judgment** from a court to collect the deficiency.[8] Note, however, that if the underlying transaction was, for example, a sale of accounts or of chattel paper, the debtor is entitled to any surplus or is liable for any deficiency only if the security agreement so provides [UCC 9–615(d), (e)].

Redemption Rights At any time before the secured party disposes of the collateral or enters into a contract for its disposition, or before the debtor's obligation has been discharged through the secured party's retention of the collateral, the debtor or any other secured party can exercise the right of *redemption* of the collateral. The debtor or other secured party can do this by tendering performance of all obligations secured by the collateral and by paying the expenses reasonably incurred by the secured party in retaking and maintaining the collateral [UCC 9–623].

8. As noted previously, the amount of the deficiency judgment may be reduced if the secured party failed to act in a commercially reasonable manner in disposing of the collateral.

Reviewing . . . Security Interests in Personal Property

Paul Barton owned a small property-management company, doing business as Brighton Homes. In October, Barton went on a spending spree. First, he bought a Bose surround-sound system for his home from KDM Electronics. The next day, he purchased a Wilderness Systems kayak from Outdoor Outfitters, and the day after that he bought a new Toyota 4-Runner financed through Bridgeport Auto. Two weeks later, Barton purchased six new iMac computers for his office, also from KDM Electronics. Barton bought all of these items under installment sales contracts. Six months later, Barton's property-management business was failing, and he could not make the payments due on any of these purchases and thus defaulted on the loans. Using the information presented in the chapter, answer the following questions.

1 For which of Barton's purchases (the surround-sound system, the kayak, the 4-Runner, and the six iMacs) would the creditor need to file a financing statement to perfect its security interest?
2 Suppose that Barton's contract for the office computers mentioned only the name Brighton Homes. What would be the consequences if KDM Electronics filed a financing statement that listed only Brighton Homes as the debtor's name?
3 Which of these purchases would qualify as a PMSI in consumer goods?
4 Suppose that after KDM Electronics repossesses the surround-sound system, it decides to keep the system rather than sell it. Can KDM do this under Article 9? Why or why not?

Terms and Concepts

after-acquired property 342
attachment 337
collateral 337
continuation statement 342
cross-collateralization 343
debtor 337
default 337
deficiency judgment 349
execution 347
financing statement 337
floating lien 343
junior lienholder 347
levy 347
perfection 338
pledge 341
proceeds 342
purchase-money security interest (PMSI) 341
secured party 336
secured transaction 336
security agreement 337
security interest 337

Chapter Summary: Security Interests in Personal Property

Creating a Security Interest (See pages 337–338.)	1. Unless the creditor has possession of the collateral, there must be a written or authenticated security agreement that is signed or authenticated by the debtor and describes the collateral subject to the security interest. 2. The secured party must give value to the debtor. 3. The debtor must have rights in the collateral—some ownership interest in or right to obtain possession of the specified collateral.
Perfecting a Security Interest (See pages 338–342.)	1. *Perfection by filing*—The most common method of perfection is by filing a financing statement containing the names of the secured party and the debtor and indicating the collateral covered by the financing statement. a. Communication of the financing statement to the appropriate filing office, together with the correct filing fee, constitutes a filing. b. The financing statement must be filed under the name of the debtor. Fictitious (trade) names normally are not sufficient. c. The classification of collateral determines whether filing is necessary and, if it is, where to file (see Exhibit 18–2 on page 339). 2. *Perfection without filing*— a. By transfer of collateral—The debtor can transfer possession of the collateral to the secured party. A *pledge* is an example of this type of transfer. b. By attachment, such as the attachment of a purchase-money security interest (PMSI) in consumer goods—If the secured party has a PMSI in consumer goods (goods bought or used by the debtor for personal, family, or household purposes), the secured party's security interest is perfected automatically. In all, fourteen types of security interests can be perfected by attachment.
The Scope of a Security Interest (See pages 342–343.)	A security agreement can cover the following types of property: 1. *Collateral in the present possession or control of the debtor.* 2. *Proceeds from a sale, exchange, or disposition of secured collateral.* 3. *After-acquired property*—A security agreement may provide that property acquired after the execution of the security agreement will also be secured by the agreement. This provision is often included in security agreements covering a debtor's inventory. 4. *Future advances*—A security agreement may provide that any future advances made against a line of credit will be subject to the initial security interest in the same collateral.
Priorities (See pages 343–345.)	See Exhibit 18–3 on page 346.
Rights and Duties of Debtors and Creditors (See pages 345–347.)	1. *Information request*—On request by any person, the filing officer must send a statement listing the file number, the date, and the hour of the filing of financing statements and other documents covering collateral of a particular debtor. 2. *Release, assignment, and amendment*—A secured party may (a) release part or all of the collateral described in a filed financing statement, thus ending the creditor's security interest; (b) assign part or all of the security interest to another party; and (c) amend a filed financing statement. 3. *Confirmation or accounting request by debtor*—The debtor has the right to request a confirmation of his or her view of the unpaid debt or listing of collateral. The secured party must authenticate and send to the debtor an accounting within fourteen days after the request is received. 4. *Termination statement*—When a debt is paid, the secured party generally must send a *termination statement* to the debtor or file such a statement with the filing officer to whom the original financing statement was given. If the financing statement covers consumer goods, the termination statement must be filed by the secured party within one month after the debt is paid.
Default (See pages 347–349.)	On the debtor's default, the secured party may do either of the following: 1. Take possession (peacefully or by court order) of the collateral covered by the security agreement and then pursue one of two alternatives: a. Retain the collateral (unless the secured party has a PMSI in consumer goods and the debtor has paid 60 percent or more of the selling price or loan). The secured party may be required to give notice to the

Chapter Summary: Security Interests in Personal Property—Continued

Default—Continued	debtor and to other secured parties or lienholders with an interest in the collateral. If any of the notified parties objects within twenty days, the creditor must dispose of the collateral. b. Dispose of the collateral in accordance with the requirements of UCC 9–602(7), 9–603, 9–610(a), and 9–613. The disposition must be carried out in a commercially reasonable manner. Unless the collateral is perishable or will rapidly decline in value, notice of the disposition must be given to the debtor and other specified parties. The proceeds are applied as follows: (1) Reasonable expenses incurred by the secured party in repossessing, storing, and reselling the collateral. (2) The balance of the debt owed to the secured party. (3) Junior lienholders who have made written or authenticated demands. (4) Surplus to the debtor (unless the collateral consists of accounts, payment intangibles, promissory notes, or chattel paper). 2. Relinquish the security interest and use any judicial remedy available, such as proceeding to judgment on the underlying debt, followed by execution and levy on the nonexempt assets of the debtor.

ExamPrep

ISSUE SPOTTERS

—Check your answers to these questions against the answers provided in Appendix G.

1 Nero needs $500 to buy textbooks and other supplies. Olivia agrees to loan Nero $500, accepting as collateral Nero's computer. They put their agreement in writing. How can Olivia let other creditors know of her interest in the computer?

2 Liberty Bank loans $5,000 to Michelle to buy a car, which is used as collateral to secure the loan. Michelle has paid less than 50 percent of the loan, when she defaults. Liberty could repossess and keep the car, but the bank does not want it. What are the alternatives?

BEFORE THE TEST

Go to **www.cengagebrain.com**, enter the ISBN 9781111530624, and click on "Find" to locate this textbook's Web site. Then, click on "Access Now" under "Study Tools," and select Chapter 18 at the top. There, you will find an Interactive Quiz that you can take to assess your mastery of the concepts in this chapter, as well as Flashcards and a Glossary of important terms.

For Review

1 What is a security interest? Who is a secured party? What is a security agreement? What is a financing statement?

2 What three requirements must be met to create an enforceable security interest?

3 What is the most common method of perfecting a security interest under Article 9?

4 If two secured parties have perfected security interests in the collateral of the debtor, which party has priority to the collateral on the debtor's default?

5 What rights does a secured creditor have on the debtor's default?

Questions and Case Problems

18–1 Priority Disputes. Redford is a seller of electric generators. He purchases a large quantity of generators from a manufacturer, Mallon Corp., by making a down payment and signing an agreement to pay the balance over a period of time. The agreement gives Mallon Corp. a security interest in the generators and the proceeds. Mallon Corp. properly files a financing statement on its security interest. Redford receives the generators and immediately sells one of them to Garfield on an installment contract with payment to be made in twelve equal installments. At the time of the sale, Garfield knows of Mallon's security interest. Two months later, Redford goes into default on his payments to Mallon. Discuss Mallon's rights against purchaser Garfield in this situation.

18–2 **Question with Sample Answer** Marsh has a prize horse named Arabian Knight. Marsh is in need of working capital. She borrows $5,000 from Mendez, who takes possession of Arabian Knight as security for the loan. No written agreement is signed. Discuss whether, in the absence of a written agreement, Mendez has a security interest in Arabian Knight. If Mendez does have a security interest, is it a perfected security interest? Explain.

—For a sample answer to Question 18–2, go to Appendix E at the end of this text.

18–3 **The Scope of a Security Interest.** Edward owned a retail sporting goods shop. A new ski resort was being constructed in his area, and to take advantage of the potential business, Edward decided to expand his operations. He borrowed a large sum from his bank, which took a security interest in his present inventory and any after-acquired inventory as collateral for the loan. The bank properly perfected the security interest by filing a financing statement. Edward's business was profitable, so he doubled his inventory. A year later, just a few months after the ski resort had opened, an avalanche destroyed the ski slope and lodge. Edward's business consequently took a turn for the worse, and he defaulted on his debt to the bank. The bank then sought possession of his entire inventory, even though the inventory was now twice as large as it had been when the loan was made. Edward claimed that the bank had rights to only half of his inventory. Is Edward correct? Explain.

18–4 **Priorities.** EX Services, Inc., was an excavating business. Union Bank made loans to EX, subject to a perfected security interest in its equipment and other assets, including "after-acquired property." In late 2006, EX leased heavy construction equipment from Mac's Machinery. The lease agreements required monthly payments, which EX often made late or missed. After eighteen months, Mac's demanded that EX either return the equipment or buy it. While attempting to obtain financing for the purchase, EX continued to make monthly payments. In November 2009, Mac's, which had not filed a financing statement to cover the transaction, demanded full payment of the amount due. Before paying the price, EX went out of business and surrendered its assets to Union, which prepared to sell them. Mac's objected and filed a lawsuit against Union to recover the equipment, claiming that the bank's security interest had not attached to the equipment because EX had not paid for it. Who has priority to the equipment, and why?

18–5 **Case Problem with Sample Answer** Primesouth Bank issued a loan to Okefenokee Aircraft, Inc. (OAI), to buy a plane. OAI executed a note in favor of Primesouth in the amount of $161,306.25, plus interest. The plane secured the note. When OAI defaulted, Primesouth repossessed the plane. Instead of disposing of the collateral and seeking a deficiency judgment, however, the bank retained possession of the plane and filed a suit in a Georgia state court against OAI to enforce the note. OAI did not deny defaulting on the note or dispute the amount due. Instead, OAI argued that Primesouth Bank was not acting in a commercially reasonable manner. According to OAI, the creditor must sell the collateral and apply the proceeds against the debt. What is a secured creditor's obligation in these circumstances? Can the creditor retain the collateral and seek a judgment for the amount of the underlying debt, or is a sale required? Discuss. [*Okefenokee Aircraft, Inc. v. Primesouth Bank,* 296 Ga.App. 872, 676 S.E.2d 394 (2009)]

—For a sample answer to Problem 18–5, go to Appendix F at the end of this text.

18–6 **Purchase-Money Security Interest.** In 2007, James Cavazos purchased a new Mercedes vehicle from a dealer and gave JPMorgan Chase Bank (Chase) a purchase-money security interest (PMSI) in the car. The state recorded Chase's lien on the original certificate of title. Cavazos then forged a release of the lien against the title and received a certified copy of the original title. In reliance of that title, NXCESS Motor Cars, Inc., bought the car. It sold the car to Xavier Valeri, who granted a PMSI to U.S. Bank. NXCESS warranted that the title was free of all liens. When a new title was issued, Chase learned of Cavazos's forgery. It sued Cavazos, Valeri, and U.S. Bank for conversion (see Chapter 4). It demanded possession of the vehicle and that Cavazos repay the loan. Valeri and U.S. Bank contended that they were buyers in the ordinary course of business and had good title to the Mercedes because the state provided a title free of liens and claims. Cavazos is liable on the loan, but who has the right to possess the car? Which purchase-money security interest dominates? Explain your answers. [*NXCESS Motor Cars, Inc. v. JPMorgan Chase Bank, N.A.* 317 S.W.3d 462 (Tex.App.—Houston 2010)]

18–7 **Disposition of Collateral.** PRA Aviation, LLC, borrowed $3 million from Center Capital Corp. to buy a Gates Learjet 55B. Center perfected a security interest in the plane. PRA defaulted on the loan less than two years later and surrendered the jet. Center hired Business Air International, an aircraft broker, to sell it. Business Air reviewed the market, design, and mechanical condition of similar aircraft to arrive at a value estimate of $1.45 million. Business Air marketed the jet in trade publications, on the Internet, and by direct advertising to select customers for $1.59 million. There were three offers. The high bid was $1.35 million subject to an inspection. Center offered $1.3 million for a "cash deal, as is, where is, kick the tires, start the engines" deal. The buyer agreed. Center filed a suit in a federal district court against PRA to collect the deficiency. PRA argued that the jet should have sold for $2.4 million to $2.9 million, considering the asking prices for newer aircraft. Was the sale commercially reasonable? Explain. [*Center Capital Corp. v. PRA Aviation, LLC,* __ F.Supp.2d __ (E.D.Pa. 2011)]

18–8 **A Question of Ethics** *In 1995, Mark Denton cosigned a $101,250 loan that the First Interstate Bank (FIB) in Missoula, Montana, issued to Denton's friend Eric Anderson. Denton's business assets—a mini-warehouse operation—secured the loan. On his own, Anderson obtained a $260,000 U.S. Small Business Administration (SBA) loan from FIB at the same time. The purpose of* *both loans was to buy logging equipment with which Anderson could start a business. In 1997, the business failed. As a consequence, FIB repossessed and sold the equipment and applied the proceeds to the SBA loan. FIB then asked Denton to pay the other loan's outstanding balance ($98,460) plus interest. When Denton refused, FIB initiated proceedings to obtain his business assets. Denton filed a suit in a Montana state court against FIB, claiming, in part, that Anderson's equipment was the collateral for the loan that FIB was attempting to collect from Denton. [*Denton v. First Interstate Bank of Commerce, *2006 MT 193, 333 Mont. 169, 142 P.3d 797 (2006)]*

1 Denton's assets served as the security for Anderson's loan because Anderson had nothing to offer. When the loan was obtained, Dean Gillmore, FIB's loan officer, explained to them that if Anderson defaulted, the proceeds from the sale of the logging equipment would be applied to the SBA loan first. Under these circumstances, is it fair to hold Denton liable for the unpaid balance of Anderson's loan? Why or why not?

2 Denton argued that the loan contract was unconscionable and constituted a "contract of adhesion." What makes a contract unconscionable? Did the transaction between the parties in this case qualify? What is a "contract of adhesion"? Was this deal unenforceable on that basis? Explain.

18–9 **Critical Thinking Legal Question** Review the three requirements for an enforceable security interest. Why is each of these requirements necessary?

18–10 **Video Question** To watch this chapter's video, *Secured Transactions*, go to **www.cengagebrain.com**. Register the access code that came with your new book or log in to your existing account. Select the link for the "Business Law Digital Video Library Online Access" or "Business Law CourseMate." Click on "Complete Video List," view Video 33, and then answer the following questions:

1 This chapter lists three requirements for creating a security interest. In the video, which requirement does Laura assert has not been met?

2 What, if anything, must the bank have done to perfect its interest in the editing equipment?

3 If the bank exercises its self-help remedy to repossess Onyx's editing equipment, does Laura have any chance of getting it back? Explain.

4 Assume that the bank had a perfected security interest and repossessed the editing equipment. Also assume that the purchase price (and the loan amount) for the equipment was $100,000, of which Onyx has paid $65,000. Discuss the rights and duties of the bank with regard to the collateral in this situation.

Chapter 19

Creditors' Rights and Bankruptcy

Learning Objectives

After reading this chapter, you should be able to answer the following questions:

1. What is a prejudgment attachment? What is a writ of execution? How does a creditor use these remedies?
2. What is garnishment? When might a creditor undertake a garnishment proceeding?
3. In a bankruptcy proceeding, what constitutes the debtor's estate in property? What property is exempt from the estate under federal bankruptcy law?
4. What is the difference between an exception to discharge and an objection to discharge?
5. In a Chapter 11 reorganization, what is the role of the debtor in possession?

The Learning Objectives above are designed to help improve your understanding of the chapter.

Normally, creditors have no problem collecting the debts owed to them. When disputes arise over the amount owed, however, or when the debtor simply cannot or will not pay, what happens? What remedies are available to creditors when debtors default (fail to pay as promised)?

In this chapter, we first focus on some basic laws that assist the creditor and debtor in resolving their dispute without resorting to bankruptcy or mortgage foreclosure (see Chapter 20). We then examine the process of bankruptcy, which is the last resort in resolving creditor-debtor problems. We look at the different types of relief available to debtors under federal bankruptcy law, as amended in 2005, and discuss the basic bankruptcy procedures required for each type of relief.

Laws Assisting Creditors

Both the common law and statutory laws create various rights and remedies for creditors. Here, we discuss some of these rights and remedies.

Liens

A **lien** is an encumbrance on (claim against) property to satisfy a debt or protect a claim for the payment of a debt. Creditors' liens may arise under statutory law or under the common law. Statutory liens include *mechanic's liens,* whereas *artisan's liens* were recognized at common law. *Judicial liens* arise when a creditor attempts to collect on a debt before or after a judgment is entered by a court.

Liens can be an important tool for creditors because they generally take priority over other claims, except those of creditors who have a *perfected security interest* in the same property. (As Chapter 18 explained, a *security interest* is an interest in a debtor's personal property—called *collateral*—that a creditor takes to secure payment of an obligation. *Perfection,* which is generally accomplished by filing a financing statement with a state official, is the legal process by which a creditor protects its security interest from the claims of others.) In fact, unless a statute provides otherwise, the holders of mechanic's and artisan's liens normally take priority even over creditors who have a perfected security interest in the property.

For liens other than mechanic's and artisan's liens, priority depends on whether the lien was obtained before the other creditor perfected its security interest. If the lien was obtained first, the lienholder has priority, but if the security interest was perfected first, the party with the perfected security interest has priority.

MECHANIC'S LIEN When a person contracts for labor, services, or materials to be furnished for the purpose of making improvements on real property (land and things attached to the land, such as buildings and trees—see Chapter 28) but does not immediately pay for the improvements, the creditor can file a **mechanic's lien** on the property. This creates a special type of debtor-creditor relationship in which the real estate itself becomes security for the debt.

EXAMPLE 19.1 A painter agrees to paint a homeowner's house for an agreed-on price to cover labor and materials. If the homeowner refuses to pay for the work or pays only a portion of the charges, a mechanic's lien against the property can be created. The painter is the lienholder, and the real property is encumbered (burdened) with a mechanic's lien for the amount owed. If the homeowner does not pay the lien, the property can be sold to satisfy the debt. Notice of the foreclosure (the process by which the creditor deprives the debtor of his or her property) and sale must be given to the debtor in advance, however. •

State law governs the procedures that must be followed to create a mechanic's lien. Generally, the lienholder must file a written notice of lien against the particular property involved. The notice must be filed within a specific time period, normally measured from the last date on which materials or labor were provided (usually within 60 to 120 days). If the property owner fails to pay the debt, the lienholder is entitled to foreclose on the real estate for which the work or materials were provided and to sell it to satisfy the amount of the debt.

In the following case, a contractor attempted to foreclose on a piece of property under a mechanic's lien. The property owner claimed to be unaware of any work done by the contractor. Could this prevent the foreclosure?

Case 19.1 BHP Land Services, Inc. v. Seymour

Superior Court of Connecticut, __ A.3d __ (2011).

FACTS Jean Seymour lived in Barkhamsted, Connecticut, but she also owned a house, a horse barn, and several acres of land in Enfield. Jean's daughter, Jennifer, lived on the Enfield property, which she called the RoundTuit Ranch. Jennifer boarded, trained, and sold horses on the ranch. Jean paid the property taxes and the mortgage but did not participate in the RoundTuit business. Jennifer did not pay rent, but she paid the costs of the business, including snow plowing and house repairs. Jennifer hired BHP Land Services, Inc., to remove tree stumps and grade two acres for $2,450 per acre. When the work was done, Jennifer paid the bill. The next year, she hired BHP to do similar work on another nine acres at the same price per acre. When Jennifer did not pay the bill, BHP filed a suit in a Connecticut state court against Jean, who responded that she had never authorized the work.

ISSUE Was BHP entitled to foreclose under a mechanic's lien even though it was the property owner's (Jean's) daughter who had hired BHP to do the work?

DECISION Yes. The court issued a judgment in BHP's favor for $26,250, "which was the . . . price for the work done." The court set the matter to be scheduled for a hearing to determine the terms of the foreclosure and its fees and costs.

REASON The court held that a contractor who renders services for the improvement of the land can place a mechanic's lien on real estate if the owner of the land–"or someone having authority"–has agreed to the services. The court reasoned that Jean had given Jennifer the "unfettered authority" to operate the ranch on the Enfield property "as she saw fit." This authority included overseeing improvements that enhanced the property to Jean's benefit, such as BHP's clearing work. The court noted that Jennifer and Jean had appeared before a local agency in regard to the clearing project and that Jean had represented to the agency that Jennifer could act as her agent. Thus, Jennifer had the authority to agree to BHP's work on the property without any further authorization from Jean.

FOR CRITICAL ANALYSIS—Legal Consideration *When no actual contract exists, under what theory may a court step in to prevent a property owner from being unjustly enriched by the work, labor, or services of a contractor?*

ARTISAN'S LIEN An **artisan's lien** is a security device created at common law through which a creditor can recover payment from a debtor for labor and materials furnished for the repair or improvement of personal property. In contrast to a mechanic's lien, an artisan's lien is *possessory*. This means that the lienholder ordinarily must have retained possession of the property and have expressly or impliedly agreed to provide the services on a cash, not a credit, basis. The lien remains in existence as long as the lienholder maintains possession, and the lien is terminated once possession is voluntarily surrendered—unless the surrender is only temporary.

EXAMPLE 19.2 Selena leaves her diamond ring at the jeweler's to be repaired and to have her initials engraved on the band. In the absence of an agreement, the jeweler can keep the ring until she pays for the services. Should Selena fail to pay, the jeweler has a lien on her ring for the amount of the bill and normally can sell the ring in satisfaction of the lien. •

Modern statutes permit the holder of an artisan's lien to foreclose and sell the property subject to the lien to satisfy payment of the debt. As with a mechanic's lien, the holder of an artisan's lien is required to give notice to the owner of the property prior to foreclosure and sale. The sale proceeds are used to pay the debt and the costs of the legal proceedings, and the surplus, if any, is paid to the former owner.

JUDICIAL LIENS When a debt is past due, a creditor can bring a legal action against the debtor to collect the debt. If the creditor is successful in the action, the court awards the creditor a judgment against the debtor (usually for the amount of the debt plus any interest and legal costs incurred in obtaining the judgment). Frequently, however, the creditor is unable to collect the awarded amount.

To help ensure that a judgment in the creditor's favor will be collectible, the creditor is permitted to request that certain nonexempt property of the debtor be seized to satisfy the debt. (Under state or federal statutes, certain property is exempt from attachment by creditors. Additionally, many judgments are uncollectible because of bankruptcy exemptions.) A court's order to seize the debtor's property is known as a *writ of attachment* if it is issued before a judgment in the creditor's favor. If the order is issued after a judgment, it is referred to as a *writ of execution*.

Writ of Attachment. In the context of judicial liens, **attachment** is a court-ordered seizure and taking into custody of property prior to the securing of a judgment for a past-due debt. Attachment rights are created by state statutes. Normally, attachment is a *prejudgment* remedy occurring either at the time a lawsuit is filed or immediately afterward. To attach before judgment, a creditor must comply with the specific state's statutory restrictions and requirements. The due process clause of the Fourteenth Amendment to the U.S. Constitution also applies and requires that the debtor be given notice and an opportunity to be heard (see Chapter 1).

The creditor must have an enforceable right to payment of the debt under law and must follow certain procedures. Otherwise, the creditor can be liable for damages for wrongful attachment. She or he must file with the court an *affidavit* (a written or printed statement, made under oath or sworn to) stating that the debtor is in default and indicating the statutory grounds under which attachment is sought. The creditor must also post a bond to cover at least the court costs, the value of the loss of use of the good suffered by the debtor, and the value of the property attached. When the court is satisfied that all the requirements have been met, it issues a **writ of attachment,** which directs the sheriff or another public officer to seize nonexempt property. If the creditor prevails at trial, the seized property can be sold to satisfy the judgment.

Writ of Execution. If the creditor wins at trial and the debtor will not or cannot pay the judgment, the creditor is entitled to go back to the court and request a **writ of execution.** This writ is a court order directing the sheriff to seize (levy) and sell any of the debtor's nonexempt real or personal property that is within the court's geographic jurisdiction (usually the county in which the courthouse is located). The proceeds of the sale are used to pay the judgment, accrued interest, and the costs of the sale. Any excess is paid to the debtor. The debtor can pay the judgment and redeem the nonexempt property any time before the sale takes place.

Garnishment

An order for **garnishment** permits a creditor to collect a debt by seizing property of the debtor that is being held by a third party. In a garnishment proceeding, the third party—the person or entity that the court is ordering to garnish an individual's property—is called the *garnishee*. Typically, a garnishee is the debtor's employer, and the creditor is seeking a judgment so that part of the debtor's usual paycheck will be paid to the creditor.

In some situations, however, the garnishee is a third party that holds funds belonging to the debtor (such as a bank) or has possession of, or exercises control over, other types of property belonging to the debtor. A creditor can garnish almost all types of property—including tax refunds, pensions, and trust funds—so long as the property is not exempt from garnishment and is in the possession of a third party.

CASE EXAMPLE 19.3 Helen Griffin failed to pay a debt she owed to Indiana Surgical Specialists. Indiana Surgical filed a lawsuit to collect, and Griffin did not answer the complaint or appear in court. The court issued a default judgment in favor of Indiana Surgical and a garnishment order to withhold the appropriate amount from Griffin's earnings until her debt was paid. At the time, Griffin was working as a subcontractor driving for a courier service. She claimed that her wages could not be garnished because she was an independent contractor, and not an employee (see Chapter 21 for a discussion of independent-contractor status). Ultimately, an Indiana intermediate appellate court held that payments for the services of an independent contractor fall within the definition of earnings and can be garnished.[1] •

GARNISHMENT PROCEEDINGS Because state law governs garnishment actions, the procedures differ from state to state. Garnishment can be a prejudgment remedy, requiring a hearing before a court, but it is most often a postjudgment remedy. In some states, the creditor needs to obtain only one order of garnishment, which then applies continuously to the debtor's wages until the entire debt is paid. In other states, the creditor must go back to court for a separate order of garnishment for each pay period.

LAWS LIMITING THE AMOUNT OF WAGES SUBJECT TO GARNISHMENT Both federal and state laws limit the amount that can be taken from a debtor's weekly take-home pay through garnishment proceedings.[2] Federal law provides a minimal framework to protect debtors from suffering unduly when paying judgment debts.[3] State laws also provide dollar exemptions, and these amounts are often larger than those provided by federal law. Under federal law, an employer cannot dismiss an employee because his or her wages are being garnished.

Creditors' Composition Agreements

Creditors may contract with the debtor for discharge of the debtor's liquidated debts (debts that are definite, or fixed, in amount) on payment of a sum less than that owed. These agreements are called **creditors' composition agreements**, or simply *composition agreements,* and usually are held to be enforceable.

Suretyship and Guaranty

When a third person promises to pay a debt owed by another in the event the debtor does not pay, either a *suretyship* or a *guaranty* relationship is created. Suretyship and guaranty provide creditors with the right to seek payment from the third party if the primary debtor defaults on her or his obligations. Exhibit 19–1 below illustrates the relationship between a suretyship or guaranty party and the creditor. At common law, there were significant differences in the liability of a surety and a guarantor, as discussed in the following subsections. Today,

1. *Indiana Surgical Specialists v. Griffin,* 867 N.E.2d 260 (Ind.App. 2007).
2. Some states (for example, Texas) do not permit garnishment of wages by private parties except under a child-support order.
3. For example, the federal Consumer Credit Protection Act of 1968, 15 U.S.C. Sections 1601–1693r, provides that a debtor can retain either 75 percent of disposable earnings per week or a sum equivalent to thirty hours of work paid at federal minimum-wage rates, whichever is greater.

• ***Exhibit* 19–1 Suretyship and Guaranty Parties**

In a suretyship or guaranty arrangement, a third party promises to be responsible for a debtor's obligations. A third party who agrees to be responsible for the debt even if the primary debtor does not default is known as a surety; a third party who agrees to be *secondarily* responsible for the debt—that is, responsible only if the primary debtor defaults—is known as a guarantor. A promise of guaranty (a collateral, or secondary, promise) normally must be in writing to be enforceable.

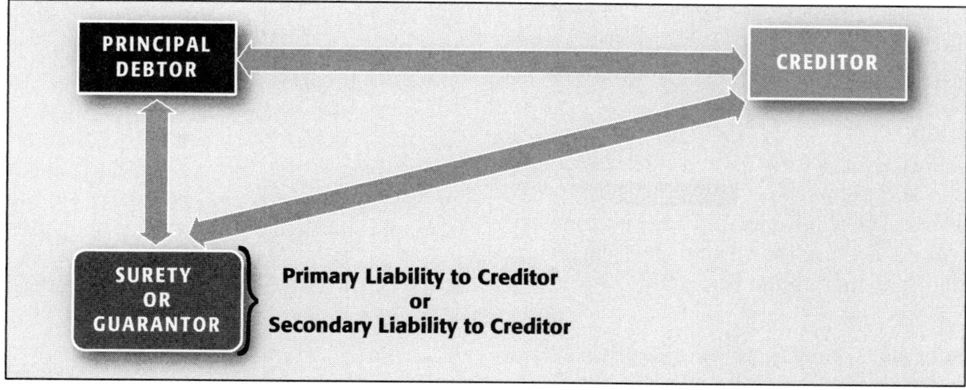

however, the distinctions outlined here have been abolished in some states.

SURETY A contract of strict **suretyship** is a promise made by a third person to be responsible for the debtor's obligation. It is an express contract between the **surety** (the third party) and the creditor. The surety in the strictest sense is primarily liable for the debt of the principal. The creditor need not exhaust all legal remedies against the principal debtor before holding the surety responsible for payment. The creditor can demand payment from the surety from the moment the debt is due.

EXAMPLE 19.4 Roberto Delmar wants to borrow from the bank to buy a used car. Because Roberto is still in college, the bank will not lend him the funds unless his father, José Delmar, who has dealt with the bank before, will cosign the note (add his signature to the note, thereby becoming a surety and thus jointly liable for payment of the debt). When José Delmar cosigns the note, he becomes primarily liable to the bank. On the note's due date, the bank can seek payment from either Roberto or José Delmar, or both jointly. •

GUARANTY With a suretyship arrangement, the surety is *primarily* liable for the debtor's obligation. With a guaranty arrangement, the **guarantor**—the third person making the guaranty—is *secondarily* liable. The guarantor can be required to pay the obligation *only after the principal debtor defaults,* and default usually takes place only after the creditor has made an attempt to collect from the debtor.

EXAMPLE 19.5 BX Enterprises, a small corporation, needs to borrow funds to meet its payroll. The bank is skeptical about the creditworthiness of BX and requires Dawson, its president, who is a wealthy businessperson and the owner of 70 percent of BX Enterprises, to sign an agreement making himself personally liable for payment if BX does not pay off the loan. As a guarantor of the loan, Dawson cannot be held liable until BX Enterprises is in default. •

Under the Statute of Frauds, a guaranty contract between the guarantor and the creditor must be in writing to be enforceable unless the *main purpose rule* applies.[4] At common law, a suretyship agreement did not need to be in writing to be enforceable, and oral surety agreements were sufficient. Today, however, some states require a writing (or electronic record) to enforce a suretyship.

Normally, a guaranty contract that is in a signed writing is presumed to be valid and enforceable. **CASE EXAMPLE 19.6** Nam Koo Kim created Majestic Group Korea, Ltd., to open a restaurant. Majestic borrowed $1.5 million from Overseas Private Investment Corporation to finance the restaurant. Kim and his wife, Hee Sun, issued personal guaranties for the loan. When Majestic defaulted on the debt, Overseas sued Kim and his wife seeking payment from them personally. Hee Sun claimed that she did not understand her full liability under the guaranty at the time that she signed it. A New York appellate court found that the guaranty had clearly specified that Hee Sun was personally guaranteeing full payment on the loan. Because there was no fraud, duress, or other wrongdoing by a party to the contract, the court held that Hee Sun's signature on the guaranty was binding and enforceable.[5] •

ACTIONS THAT RELEASE THE SURETY AND THE GUARANTOR Basically, the same actions will release a surety or a guarantor from an obligation. If a material modification is made in the terms of the original contract between the principal debtor and the creditor—without the consent of the surety or guarantor—the surety or guarantor's obligation will be discharged. (The extent to which the surety or guarantor is discharged depends on whether he or she was compensated and to what extent he or she suffered a loss from the modification.)

Similarly, if a debt is secured by collateral and the creditor surrenders the collateral to the debtor or impairs the collateral without the consent of the surety or guarantor, these acts can reduce the obligation of the surety or guarantor.

Naturally, any payment of the principal obligation by the debtor or by another person on the debtor's behalf will discharge the surety or guarantor from the obligation. Even if the creditor refused to accept payment of the principal debt when it was tendered, the obligation of the surety or guarantor can be discharged.

DEFENSES OF THE SURETY AND THE GUARANTOR Generally, the surety or guarantor can also assert any of the defenses available to a principal debtor to avoid liability on the obligation to the creditor. A few exceptions do exist, however. The surety or guarantor cannot assert the principal debtor's incapacity or bankruptcy as a defense, nor can the surety assert the statute of limitations as a defense.

Obviously, a surety or guarantor may also have her or his own defenses—for example, her or his own incapacity or bankruptcy. If the creditor fraudulently induced the surety to guarantee the debt of the debtor, the surety can assert fraud as a defense. In most states, the creditor has a legal duty to inform the surety, before the formation of the suretyship contract, of material facts known by the creditor that would substantially increase the surety's risk. Failure to so inform may constitute fraud and renders the suretyship obligation voidable.

RIGHTS OF THE SURETY AND THE GUARANTOR Usually, when the surety or guarantor pays the debt owed to the

4. Briefly, the main purpose rule, or exception, provides that if the main purpose of the guaranty agreement is to benefit the guarantor, then the contract need not be in writing to be enforceable (see Chapter 10).

5. *Overseas Private Investment Corp. v. Kim,* 69 A.D.3d 1185, 895 N.Y.S.2d 217 (N.Y.A.D. 2010).

creditor, the surety or guarantor is entitled to certain rights. Because the rights of the surety and guarantor are basically the same, the following discussion applies to both.

The Right of Subrogation. The surety has the legal **right of subrogation.** Simply stated, this means that any right the creditor had against the debtor now becomes the right of the surety. Included are creditor rights in bankruptcy, rights to collateral possessed by the creditor, and rights to judgments secured by the creditor. In short, the surety now stands in the shoes of the creditor and may pursue any remedies that were available to the creditor against the debtor.

The Right of Reimbursement. The surety has a **right of reimbursement** from the debtor. Basically, the surety is entitled to receive from the debtor all outlays made on behalf of the suretyship arrangement. Such outlays can include expenses incurred, as well as the actual amount of the debt paid to the creditor.

The Right of Contribution. Two or more sureties are called **co-sureties.** When one surety pays more than her or his proportionate share on a debtor's default, that surety is entitled to recover the amount paid above her or his obligation from the other co-sureties. This is the **right of contribution.** Generally, a co-surety's liability either is determined by agreement between the co-sureties or, in the absence of an agreement, is specified in the suretyship contract itself.

EXAMPLE 19.7 Two co-sureties are obligated under a suretyship contract to guarantee the debt of a debtor. Together, the sureties' maximum liability is $25,000. As specified in the suretyship contract, Surety A's maximum liability is $15,000, and surety B's is $10,000. The debtor owes $10,000 and is in default. Surety A pays the creditor the entire $10,000. In the absence of any agreement between the two co-sureties, Surety A can recover $4,000 from Surety B ($10,000/$25,000 × $10,000 = $4,000). •

Protection for Debtors

The law protects debtors as well as creditors. Certain property of the debtor, for example, is exempt under state law from creditors' actions. Of course, bankruptcy laws, which will be discussed shortly, are designed specifically to assist debtors in need of help.

In most states, certain types of real and personal property are exempt from execution or attachment. State exemption statutes usually include both real and personal property.

Exempted Real Property

Probably the most familiar exemption for real property is the **homestead exemption.** Each state permits the debtor to retain the family home, either in its entirety or up to a specified dollar amount, free from the claims of unsecured creditors or trustees in bankruptcy. (Note that federal bankruptcy law now places a cap on the amount of equity that debtors filing bankruptcy can claim is exempt under their state's homestead exemption—see page 365.)

EXAMPLE 19.8 Beere owes Veltman $40,000. The debt is the subject of a lawsuit, and the court awards Veltman a judgment of $40,000 against Beere. Beere's home is valued at $50,000, and the homestead exemption is $25,000. There are no outstanding mortgages or other liens on his home. To satisfy the judgment debt, Beere's family home is sold at public auction for $45,000. The proceeds of the sale are distributed as follows:

1. Beere is given $25,000 as his homestead exemption.
2. Veltman is paid $20,000 toward the judgment debt, leaving a $20,000 deficiency judgment (that is, "leftover debt") that can be satisfied from any other nonexempt property (personal or real) that Beere may own, if permitted by state law. •

In a few states, statutes allow the homestead exemption only if the judgment debtor has a family. If a judgment debtor does not have a family, a creditor may be entitled to collect the full amount realized from the sale of the debtor's home. In addition, the homestead exemption interacts with other areas of law and can sometimes operate to cancel out a portion of a lien on a debtor's real property.

CASE EXAMPLE 19.9 Antonio Stanley purchased a modular home from Yates Mobile Services Corporation. When Stanley failed to pay the purchase price of the home, Yates obtained a judicial lien against Stanley's property in the amount of $165,138.05. Stanley then filed for bankruptcy and asserted the homestead exemption. The court found that Stanley was entitled to avoid the lien to the extent that it impaired his exemption. Using a bankruptcy law formula, the court determined that the total impairment was $143,639.05 and that Stanley could avoid paying this amount to Yates. Thus, Yates was left with a judicial lien on Stanley's home in the amount of $21,499.[6] •

Exempted Personal Property

Personal property that is most often exempt from satisfaction of judgment debts includes the following:

1. Household furniture up to a specified dollar amount.
2. Clothing and certain personal possessions, such as family pictures or a Bible.
3. A vehicle (or vehicles) for transportation (at least up to a specified dollar amount).
4. Certain classified animals, usually livestock but including pets.
5. Equipment that the debtor uses in a business or trade, such as tools or professional instruments, up to a specified dollar amount.

6. *In re Stanley*, 2010 WL 2103441 (M.D.N.C. 2010).

Bankruptcy Law

Bankruptcy law in the United States has two goals—to protect a debtor by giving him or her a fresh start, free from creditors' claims, and to provide a fair means of distributing a debtor's assets to creditors. Bankruptcy law is federal law, but state laws on secured transactions, liens, judgments, and exemptions also play a role in federal bankruptcy proceedings.

Bankruptcy law (called the Bankruptcy Code, or simply, the Code) prior to 2005 was based on the Bankruptcy Reform Act of 1978, as amended. In 2005, Congress enacted bankruptcy reform legislation that significantly overhauled certain provisions of the Bankruptcy Code for the first time in twenty-five years.[7] One of the major goals of this legislation was to require more consumers to pay as many of their debts as they possibly could, instead of having those debts fully extinguished in bankruptcy.

Bankruptcy Courts

Bankruptcy proceedings are held in federal bankruptcy courts, which are under the authority of U.S. district courts, and rulings by bankruptcy courts can be appealed to the district courts. A bankruptcy court holds proceedings that are required to administer the estate of the debtor in bankruptcy. (The *estate* consists of the debtor's assets, as will be discussed shortly.) A bankruptcy court can conduct a jury trial if the appropriate district court has authorized it and if the parties to the bankruptcy consent to a jury trial.

Types of Bankruptcy Relief

The Bankruptcy Code is contained in Title 11 of the *United States Code* (U.S.C.) and has eight "chapters." Chapters 1, 3, and 5 of the Code include general definitional provisions, as well as provisions governing case administration, creditors, the debtor, and the estate. These three chapters of the Code normally apply to all types of bankruptcies.

Four chapters of the Code set forth the most important types of relief that debtors can seek.

1. Chapter 7 provides for *liquidation* proceedings—that is, the selling of all nonexempt assets and the distribution of the proceeds to the debtor's creditors.
2. Chapter 11 governs reorganizations.
3. Chapter 12 (for family farmers and family fishermen) and Chapter 13 (for individuals) provide for adjustment of the debts of parties with regular incomes.[8]

7. The full title of the act is the Bankruptcy Abuse Prevention and Consumer Protection Act of 2005, Pub. L. No. 109-8, 119 Stat. 23 (April 20, 2005).

8. There are no Chapters 2, 4, 6, 8, or 10 in Title 11. Such "gaps" are not uncommon in the *United States Code*. They occur because, when a statute is enacted, chapter numbers (or other subdivisional unit numbers) are sometimes reserved for future use. A gap may also appear if a law has been repealed.

Note that a debtor (except for a municipality) need not be insolvent[9] to file for bankruptcy relief under the Code. Anyone obligated to a creditor can declare bankruptcy.

Special Requirements for Consumer-Debtors

A **consumer-debtor** is a debtor whose debts result primarily from the purchase of goods for personal, family, or household use. To ensure that a consumer-debtor is aware of the types of relief available, the Code requires that the clerk of the court give all consumer-debtors written notice of the general purpose, benefits, and costs of each chapter under which they might proceed. In addition, the clerk must provide consumer-debtors with information on the types of services available from credit counseling agencies. In practice, most of these steps are handled by an attorney, not by court clerks.

Chapter 7—Liquidation

Liquidation under Chapter 7 of the Bankruptcy Code is probably the most familiar type of bankruptcy proceeding and is often referred to as an *ordinary,* or *straight, bankruptcy*. Put simply, a debtor in a liquidation bankruptcy turns all assets over to a *bankruptcy trustee,* a person appointed by the court to manage the debtor's funds. The trustee sells the nonexempt assets and distributes the proceeds to creditors. With certain exceptions, the remaining debts are then **discharged** (extinguished), and the debtor is released from the obligation to pay the debts.

Any "person"—defined as including individuals, partnerships, and corporations[10]—may be a debtor in a liquidation proceeding. A husband and wife may file jointly for bankruptcy under a single petition. Insurance companies, banks, railroads, savings and loan associations, investment companies licensed by the Small Business Administration, and credit unions *cannot* be debtors in a liquidation bankruptcy, however. Other chapters of the Code or other federal or state statutes apply to them.

A straight bankruptcy can be commenced by the filing of either a voluntary or an involuntary **petition in bankruptcy**—the document that is filed with a bankruptcy court to initiate bankruptcy proceedings. If a debtor files the petition, the bankruptcy is voluntary. If one or more creditors file a petition to force the debtor into bankruptcy, the bankruptcy

9. The inability to pay debts as they come due is known as *equitable* insolvency. A *balance-sheet* insolvency, which exists when a debtor's liabilities exceed assets, is not used as the test for filing for relief. Thus, it is possible for debtors to petition voluntarily for bankruptcy even though their assets far exceed their liabilities. This situation may occur when a debtor's cash-flow problems become severe.

10. The definition of *corporation* includes unincorporated companies and associations. It also covers labor unions.

is involuntary. We discuss both voluntary and involuntary bankruptcy proceedings under Chapter 7 in the following subsections.

Voluntary Bankruptcy

To bring a voluntary petition in bankruptcy, the debtor files official forms designated for that purpose in the bankruptcy court. Current bankruptcy law specifies that before debtors can file a petition, they must receive credit counseling from an approved nonprofit agency within the 180-day period preceding the date of filing. Debtors filing a Chapter 7 petition must include a certificate proving that they have received individual or group counseling from an approved agency within the last 180 days (roughly six months).

A consumer-debtor who is filing for liquidation bankruptcy must confirm the accuracy of the petition's contents. The debtor must also state in the petition, at the time of filing, that he or she understands the relief available under other chapters of the Code and has chosen to proceed under Chapter 7. Attorneys representing consumer-debtors must file an affidavit stating that they have informed the debtors of the relief available under each chapter of the Code. In addition, the attorneys must reasonably attempt to verify the accuracy of the consumer-debtors' petitions and schedules (described below). Failure to do so is considered perjury.

CHAPTER 7 SCHEDULES The voluntary petition must contain the following schedules:

1. A list of both secured and unsecured creditors, their addresses, and the amount of debt owed to each. (A *secured* creditor is one who received an interest in collateral—personal property of the debtor—as security for payment of the debt.)
2. A statement of the financial affairs of the debtor.
3. A list of all property owned by the debtor, including property that the debtor claims is exempt.
4. A list of current income and expenses.
5. A certificate of credit counseling (as discussed previously).
6. Proof of payments received from employers within sixty days prior to the filing of the petition.
7. A statement of the amount of monthly income, itemized to show how the amount is calculated.
8. A copy of the debtor's federal income tax return for the most recent year ending immediately before the filing of the petition.

The official forms must be completed accurately, sworn to under oath, and signed by the debtor. To conceal assets or knowingly supply false information on these schedules is a crime under the bankruptcy laws.

With the exception of tax returns, failure to file the required schedules within forty-five days after the filing of the petition (unless an extension of up to forty-five days is granted) will result in an automatic dismissal of the petition. The debtor has up to seven days before the date of the first creditors' meeting to provide a copy of the most recent tax returns to the trustee.

TAX RETURNS DURING BANKRUPTCY In addition, a debtor may be required to file a tax return at the end of each tax year while the case is pending and to provide a copy to the court. This may be done at the request of the court or of the **U.S. trustee**—a government official who performs administrative tasks that a bankruptcy judge would otherwise have to perform, including supervising the work of the bankruptcy trustee. Any *party in interest* (a party, such as a creditor, who has a valid interest in the outcome of the proceedings) may make this request as well. Debtors may also be required to file tax returns during Chapter 11 and 13 bankruptcies.

SUBSTANTIAL ABUSE AND THE MEANS TEST In the past, a bankruptcy court could dismiss a Chapter 7 petition for relief (discharge of debts) if the use of Chapter 7 would constitute a "substantial abuse" of bankruptcy law. Today, the law provides a *means test* to determine a debtor's eligibility for Chapter 7. The purpose of the test is to keep upper-income people from abusing the bankruptcy process by filing for Chapter 7, as was thought to have happened in the past. The test forces more people to file for Chapter 13 bankruptcy rather than have their debts discharged under Chapter 7.

The Basic Formula. A debtor wishing to file for bankruptcy must complete the means test to determine whether she or he qualifies for Chapter 7. The debtor's average monthly income in recent months is compared with the median income in the geographic area in which the person lives. (The U.S. Trustee Program provides these data at its Web site.) If the debtor's income is below the median income, the debtor usually is allowed to file for Chapter 7 bankruptcy, as there is no presumption of bankruptcy abuse.

Applying the Means Test to Future Disposable Income. If the debtor's income is above the median income, then further calculations must be made to determine whether the person will have sufficient disposable income in the future to repay at least some of his or her unsecured debts. *Disposable income* is calculated by subtracting living expenses and secured debt payments, such as mortgage payments, from monthly income.

In making this calculation, the debtor's recent monthly income is presumed to continue for the next sixty months. Living expenses are the amounts allowed under formulas used by the Internal Revenue Service (IRS). The IRS allowances include modest allocations for food, clothing, housing, utilities, transportation (including a car payment), health care, and other necessities. (The U.S. Trustee Program's Web site also provides these amounts.) The allowances do not include expenditures for items such as cell phones and cable television service.

Once future disposable income has been estimated, that amount is used to determine whether the debtor will have income that could be applied to unsecured debts. To a large extent, this process follows the prior law on substantial abuse. The court may also consider the debtor's bad faith or other circumstances indicating abuse.

ADDITIONAL GROUNDS FOR DISMISSAL As noted, a debtor's voluntary petition for Chapter 7 relief may be dismissed for substantial abuse or for failing to provide the necessary documents (such as schedules and tax returns) within the specified time. In addition, a motion to dismiss a Chapter 7 filing might be granted in two other situations. First, if the debtor has been convicted of a violent crime or a drug-trafficking offense, the victim can file a motion to dismiss the voluntary petition. Second, if the debtor fails to pay postpetition domestic-support obligations (which include child and spousal support), the court may dismiss the debtor's petition.

ORDER FOR RELIEF If the voluntary petition for bankruptcy is found to be proper, the filing of the petition will itself constitute an **order for relief.** (An order for relief is a court's grant of assistance to a petitioner.) Once a consumer-debtor's voluntary petition has been filed, the trustee and creditors must be given notice of the order for relief by mail not more than twenty days after entry of the order.

Involuntary Bankruptcy

An involuntary bankruptcy occurs when the debtor's creditors force the debtor into bankruptcy proceedings.[11] For an involuntary action to be filed, the following requirements must be met: If the debtor has twelve or more creditors, three or more of these creditors having unsecured claims totaling at least $14,425 must join in the petition. If a debtor has fewer than twelve creditors, one or more creditors having a claim totaling $14,425 or more may file.[12]

If the debtor challenges the involuntary petition, a hearing will be held, and the bankruptcy court will enter an order for relief if it finds either of the following:

1. The debtor is not paying debts as they come due.
2. A general receiver, assignee, or custodian took possession of, or was appointed to take charge of, substantially all of the debtor's property within 120 days before the filing of the petition.

If the court grants an order for relief, the debtor will be required to supply the same information in the bankruptcy schedules as in a voluntary bankruptcy.

An involuntary petition should not be used as an everyday debt-collection device, and the Code provides penalties for the filing of frivolous petitions against debtors. Petitioning creditors may be required to pay the costs and attorneys' fees incurred by the debtor in defending against the petition. If the petition was filed in bad faith, damages can be awarded for injury to the debtor's reputation.

Automatic Stay

The moment a petition, either voluntary or involuntary, is filed, an **automatic stay,** or suspension, of almost all actions by creditors against the debtor or the debtor's property normally goes into effect. In other words, once a petition has been filed, creditors cannot contact the debtor by phone or mail or start any legal proceedings to recover debts or to repossess property. (In some circumstances, a secured creditor or other party in interest may petition the bankruptcy court for relief from the automatic stay, as will be discussed shortly.)

The Code provides that if a creditor *knowingly* violates the automatic stay (a willful violation), any injured party, including the debtor, is entitled to recover actual damages, costs, and attorneys' fees, and may be awarded punitive damages as well. Until the bankruptcy proceeding is closed or dismissed, the automatic stay prohibits a creditor from taking any act to collect, assess, or recover a claim against the debtor that arose before the filing of the petition.

THE ADEQUATE PROTECTION DOCTRINE Underlying the Code's automatic-stay provision for a secured creditor is a concept known as *adequate protection.* The *adequate protection doctrine,* among other things, protects secured creditors from losing their security as a result of the automatic stay. The bankruptcy court can provide adequate protection by requiring the debtor or trustee to make periodic cash payments or a one-time cash payment (or to provide additional collateral or replacement liens) to the extent that the stay may actually cause the value of the property to decrease.

EXCEPTIONS TO THE AUTOMATIC STAY The Code provides several exceptions to the automatic stay. Collection efforts can continue for domestic-support obligations, which include any debt owed to or recoverable by a spouse, a former spouse, a child of the debtor, that child's parent or

11. An involuntary case cannot be filed against a charitable institution or a farmer (an individual or business that receives more than 50 percent of gross income from farming operations).
12. 11 U.S.C. Section 303. The amounts stated are in accordance with those computed on April 1, 2010.

guardian, or a governmental unit. In addition, proceedings against the debtor related to divorce, child custody or visitation, domestic violence, and support enforcement are not stayed. Also excepted are investigations by a securities regulatory agency (see Chapter 26) and certain statutory liens for property taxes.

LIMITATIONS ON THE AUTOMATIC STAY A secured creditor or other party in interest can petition the bankruptcy court for relief from the automatic stay. If a creditor or other party requests relief from the stay, the stay will automatically terminate sixty days after the request, unless the court grants an extension or the parties agree otherwise. Also, the automatic stay on secured debts, such as a financed automobile, will terminate thirty days after the petition is filed if the debtor filed a bankruptcy petition that was dismissed within the prior year. Any party in interest can request that the court extend the stay by showing that the filing is in good faith.

If the debtor had two or more bankruptcy petitions dismissed during the prior year, the Code presumes bad faith, and the automatic stay does *not* go into effect until the court determines that the petition was filed in good faith. In addition, the automatic stay on secured property terminates forty-five days after the creditors' meeting (to be discussed shortly) unless the debtor redeems or reaffirms certain debts (*reaffirmation* will be discussed later in this chapter). In other words, the debtor cannot keep the secured property, even if she or he continues to make payments on it, without reinstating the rights of the secured party to collect on the debt.

Bankruptcy Estate

On the commencement of a liquidation proceeding under Chapter 7, a *bankruptcy estate* (sometimes called an *estate in property*) is created. This task is performed by the bankruptcy trustee, as described next. The estate consists of all the debtor's interests in property currently held, wherever located. It also includes *community property*—that is, property jointly owned by a husband and wife in certain states—property transferred in a transaction voidable by the trustee, proceeds and profits from the property of the estate, and certain after-acquired property. Interests in certain property—such as gifts, inheritances, property settlements (from a divorce), and life insurance death proceeds—to which the debtor becomes entitled *within 180 days after filing* may also become part of the estate. Withholdings for employee benefit plan contributions are excluded from the estate.

Generally, though, the filing of a bankruptcy petition fixes a dividing line: property acquired prior to the filing of the petition becomes property of the estate, and property acquired after the filing of the petition (except as just noted) remains the debtor's.

The Bankruptcy Trustee

Promptly after the order for relief in the liquidation proceeding has been entered, a *bankruptcy trustee* is appointed. The basic duty of the bankruptcy trustee is to collect and reduce to cash the property in the bankruptcy estate that is not exempt. (Exemptions will be discussed later in the chapter.) The trustee is held accountable for administering the debtor's estate to preserve the interests of both the debtor and unsecured creditors. To enable the trustee to accomplish this duty, the Code gives the trustee certain powers, stated in both general and specific terms. These powers must be exercised within two years of the order for relief.

DUTIES FOR MEANS TESTING The trustee is required to promptly review all materials filed by the debtor to determine if there is substantial abuse. Within ten days after the first meeting of the creditors (held soon after the order for relief is granted, as discussed later), the trustee must file a statement indicating whether the case is presumed to be an abuse under the means test. When there is a presumption of abuse, the trustee must either file a motion to dismiss the petition (or convert it to a Chapter 13 case) or file a statement setting forth the reasons why a motion would not be appropriate.

THE TRUSTEE'S POWERS The trustee has the power to require persons holding the debtor's property at the time the petition is filed to deliver the property to the trustee.[13] To enable the trustee to implement this power, the Code provides that the trustee has rights *equivalent* to those of certain other parties, such as a creditor who has a judicial lien. This power of a trustee, which is equivalent to that of a lien creditor, is known as *strong-arm power.*

In addition, the trustee has specific *powers of avoidance*—that is, the trustee can set aside (avoid) a sale or other transfer of the debtor's property, taking it back as a part of the debtor's estate. These powers include voidable rights available to the debtor, preferences, and fraudulent transfers by the debtor. Each is discussed in more detail below. In addition, a trustee can avoid certain statutory liens (creditors' claims against the debtor's property).

The debtor shares most of the trustee's avoidance powers. Thus, if the trustee does not take action to enforce one of the rights just mentioned, the debtor in a liquidation bankruptcy can enforce that right.

VOIDABLE RIGHTS A trustee steps into the shoes of the debtor. Thus, any reason that a debtor can use to obtain the

13. Usually, though, the trustee takes constructive, rather than actual, possession of the debtor's property. For example, to obtain control of a debtor's business inventory, a trustee might change the locks on the doors to the business and hire a security guard.

return of her or his property can be used by the trustee as well. These grounds include fraud, duress, incapacity, and mutual mistake.

EXAMPLE 19.10 Ben sells his boat to Tara. Tara gives Ben a check, knowing that she has insufficient funds in her bank account to cover the check. Tara has committed fraud. Ben has the right to avoid that transfer and recover the boat from Tara. If Ben files for bankruptcy relief under Chapter 7, the trustee can exercise the same right to recover the boat from Tara, and the boat becomes a part of the debtor's estate. •

PREFERENCES A debtor is not permitted to transfer property or to make a payment that favors—or gives a **preference** to—one creditor over others. The trustee is allowed to recover payments made both voluntarily and involuntarily to one creditor in preference over another.

To have made a preferential payment that can be recovered, an *insolvent* debtor must have transferred property, for a *preexisting* debt, within *ninety days* prior to the filing of the bankruptcy petition. The transfer must have given the creditor more than the creditor would have received as a result of the bankruptcy proceedings. The Code presumes that a debtor is insolvent during the ninety-day period before filing a petition.

If a **preferred creditor** (one who has received a preferential transfer from the debtor) has sold the property to an innocent third party, the trustee cannot recover the property from the innocent party. The trustee generally can force the preferred creditor to pay the value of the property, however.

Preferences to Insiders. Sometimes, the creditor receiving the preference is an *insider*—an individual, a partner, a partnership, a corporation, or an officer or a director of a corporation (or a relative of one of these) who has a close relationship with the debtor. In this situation, the avoidance power of the trustee is extended to transfers made within *one year* before filing. (If the transfer was fraudulent, as will be discussed shortly, the trustee can avoid transfers made within *two years* before filing.) Note, however, that if the transfer occurred before the ninety-day period, the trustee is required to prove that the debtor was insolvent at the time it occurred or that the transfer was made to or for the benefit of an insider.

What Constitutes a Preference? Not all transfers are preferences. To be a preference, the transfer must be made for something other than current consideration. Most courts generally assume that payment for services rendered *within fifteen days* before the payment is not a preference. If a creditor receives payment in the ordinary course of business from an individual or business debtor, such as payment of last month's cell phone bill, the bankruptcy trustee cannot recover the payment. To be recoverable, a preference must be a transfer for an antecedent (preexisting) debt, such as a year-old landscaping bill. In addition, the Code permits a consumer-debtor to transfer any property to a creditor up to a total value of $5,850 without the transfer's constituting a preference. Payment of domestic-support debts does not constitute a preference.

FRAUDULENT TRANSFERS The trustee may avoid fraudulent transfers or obligations if they (1) were made within two years of the filing of the petition or (2) were made with actual intent to hinder, delay, or defraud a creditor. For example, a debtor who is thinking about petitioning for bankruptcy sells her gold jewelry, worth $10,000, to a friend for $500. The friend agrees that in the future he will "sell" the collection back to the debtor for the same amount. This is a fraudulent transfer that the trustee can undo.

Transfers made for less than reasonably equivalent consideration are also vulnerable if the debtor thereby became insolvent or was left engaged in business with an unreasonably small amount of capital. When a fraudulent transfer is made outside the Code's two-year limit, creditors may seek alternative relief under state laws. Some state laws may allow creditors to recover for transfers made up to three years before the filing of a petition. Courts have even held that severance payments—that is, compensation paid to an employee who is fired—can constitute a fraudulent transfer under the Code.[14]

Exemptions

As just described, the trustee takes control over the debtor's property in a Chapter 7 bankruptcy, but an individual debtor is entitled to exempt (exclude) certain property from the bankruptcy. The Bankruptcy Code exempts the following property:[15]

1. Up to $21,625 in equity in the debtor's residence and burial plot (the homestead exemption).
2. Interest in a motor vehicle up to $3,450.
3. Interest, up to $550 for a particular item, in household goods and furnishings, wearing apparel, appliances, books, animals, crops, and musical instruments (the aggregate total of all items is limited to $11,525).
4. Interest in jewelry up to $1,450.
5. Interest in any other property up to $1,150, plus any unused part of the $21,625 homestead exemption up to $10,825.
6. Interest in any tools of the debtor's trade up to $2,175.
7. A life insurance contract owned by the debtor (other than a credit life insurance contract).

14. See, for example, *In the Matter of TransTexas Gas Corp.*, 597 F.3d 298 (5th Cir. 2010).

15. The dollar amounts stated in the Bankruptcy Code are adjusted automatically every three years on April 1 based on changes in the Consumer Price Index. The adjusted amounts are rounded to the nearest $25. The amounts stated are in accordance with those computed on April 1, 2010.

8. Certain interests in accrued dividends and interest under, or loan value of, life insurance contracts owned by the debtor, not to exceed $11,525.
9. Professionally prescribed health aids.
10. The right to receive Social Security and certain welfare benefits, alimony and support, certain retirement funds and pensions, and education savings accounts held for specific periods of time.
11. The right to receive certain personal-injury and other awards up to $21,625.

Individual states have the power to pass legislation precluding debtors from using the federal exemptions within the state. A majority of the states have done this. In those states, debtors may use only state, not federal, exemptions. In the rest of the states, an individual debtor (or a husband and wife filing jointly) may choose either the exemptions provided under state law or the federal exemptions.

The Homestead Exemption

The 2005 reforms significantly changed the law for those debtors seeking to use state homestead exemption statutes (see page 359). In six states, including Florida and Texas, these exemptions allowed debtors petitioning for bankruptcy to shield *unlimited* amounts of equity in their homes from creditors. The Bankruptcy Code now places limits on the amount that can be claimed as exempt in bankruptcy. In addition, a debtor must have lived in a state for two years before filing the bankruptcy petition to use the state homestead exemption.

In general, if the debtor acquired the home within three and a half years preceding the date of filing, the maximum equity exempted is $146,450, even if state law would permit a higher amount. Note, however, that a debtor who has violated securities laws, been convicted of a felony, or engaged in certain other intentional misconduct may not be able to claim the exemption.

Creditors' Meeting and Claims

Within a reasonable time after the order for relief has been granted (not less than twenty days or more than forty days), the trustee must call a meeting of the creditors listed in the schedules filed by the debtor. The bankruptcy judge does not attend this meeting. The debtor is required to attend (unless excused by the court) and to submit to examination under oath by the creditors and the trustee. At the meeting, the debtor is questioned under oath to ensure that he or she is aware of the potential consequences of bankruptcy and of relief available under the different chapters of the Bankruptcy Code.

To be entitled to receive a portion of the debtor's estate, each creditor normally files a *proof of claim* with the bankruptcy court clerk within ninety days of the creditors' meeting.[16] The proof of claim lists the creditor's name and address, as well as the amount that the creditor asserts is owed to the creditor by the debtor. A creditor need not file a proof of claim if the debtor's schedules list the creditor's claim as liquidated (exactly determined) and the creditor does not dispute the amount of the claim. A proof of claim is necessary if there is any dispute concerning the claim.

Distribution of Property

In the next step in a Chapter 7 bankruptcy, the trustee distributes the bankruptcy estate to the creditors, following specific rules provided in the Code for the distribution of the debtor's property. These rules are discussed next and illustrated in Exhibit 19–2 on the next page.

In the distribution of the debtor's estate, secured creditors take priority over unsecured creditors. Within thirty days of filing a liquidation petition or before the date of the first meeting of the creditors (whichever is first), a consumer-debtor must file with the clerk a statement of intention with respect to the secured collateral. The statement must indicate whether the debtor will retain the collateral or surrender it to the secured party. Also, if applicable, the debtor must specify whether the collateral will be claimed as exempt property and whether the debtor intends to redeem the property or reaffirm the debt secured by the collateral. The trustee is obligated to enforce the debtor's statement within forty-five days after it is filed.

In a bankruptcy case in which the debtor has no assets (called a "no-asset case"), creditors are notified of the debtor's petition for bankruptcy but are instructed not to file a claim. In no-asset cases, the unsecured creditors will receive no payment, and most, if not all, of these debts will be discharged.

DISTRIBUTION TO SECURED CREDITORS As discussed earlier, secured creditors are creditors who received an interest in collateral to secure a debtor's payment or performance. If the collateral is surrendered to the secured party, the secured creditor can enforce the security interest either by accepting the property in full satisfaction of the debt or by selling the collateral and using the proceeds to pay off the debt. Thus, the secured party has priority over unsecured parties as to the proceeds from the disposition of the collateral. Should the collateral be insufficient to cover the secured debt owed, the secured creditor becomes an unsecured creditor for the difference.

DISTRIBUTION TO UNSECURED CREDITORS Bankruptcy law establishes an order of priority for classes of debts owed to *unsecured* creditors, and they are paid in the order of their priority. Each class must be fully paid before the next class is

16. This ninety-day rule applies in Chapter 12 and Chapter 13 bankruptcies as well.

• *Exhibit* **19–2 Collection and Distribution of Property in Most Voluntary Bankruptcies**
This exhibit illustrates the property that might be collected in a debtor's voluntary bankruptcy and how it might be distributed to creditors. Involuntary bankruptcies and some voluntary bankruptcies could include additional types of property and other creditors.

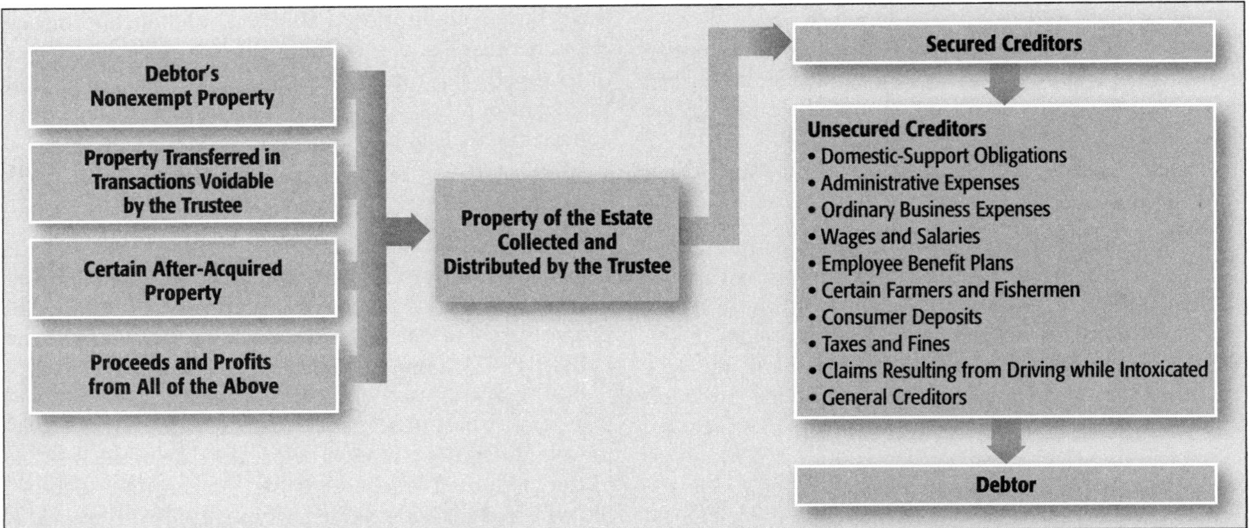

entitled to any of the remaining proceeds. If there are insufficient proceeds to pay fully all the creditors in a class, the proceeds are distributed *proportionately* to the creditors in that class, and classes lower in priority receive nothing.

In almost all Chapter 7 bankruptcies, the funds will be insufficient to pay all creditors. Note that claims for domestic-support obligations, such as child support and alimony, have the highest priority among unsecured claims, so these debts must be paid first. If any amount remains after the priority classes of creditors have been satisfied, it is turned over to the debtor.

Discharge

From the debtor's point of view, the primary purpose of liquidation is to obtain a fresh start through a discharge of debts. Certain debts, however, are not dischargeable in bankruptcy. Also, certain debtors may not qualify to have all debts discharged in bankruptcy. These situations are discussed next.

Exceptions to Discharge Discharge of a debt may be denied because of the nature of the claim or the conduct of the debtor. A court will not discharge claims that are based on a debtor's willful or malicious conduct or fraud, or claims related to property or funds that the debtor obtained by false pretenses, embezzlement, or larceny. Any monetary judgment against the debtor for driving while intoxicated cannot be discharged in bankruptcy. When a debtor fails to list a creditor on the bankruptcy schedules, that creditor's claims are not dischargeable because the creditor was not notified of the bankruptcy.

Claims that are not dischargeable in a liquidation bankruptcy include amounts due to the government for taxes, fines, or penalties, and any amounts borrowed to pay these debts.[17] Domestic-support obligations and property settlements arising from a divorce or separation cannot be discharged. Certain student loans or educational debts are not dischargeable (unless payment of the loans imposes an "undue hardship" on the debtor and the debtor's dependents), nor are amounts due on a retirement account loan. Consumer debts for purchasing luxury items worth more than $600 and cash advances totaling more than $875 generally are not dischargeable.

Objections to Discharge In addition, a bankruptcy court may deny the discharge based on the debtor's conduct. In such a situation, the assets of the debtor are still distributed to the creditors, but the debtor remains liable for the unpaid portion of all claims. Grounds for a denial of discharge of the debtor include the following:

1. The debtor's concealment or destruction of property with the intent to hinder, delay, or defraud a creditor.
2. The debtor's fraudulent concealment or destruction of financial records.
3. The grant of a discharge to the debtor within eight years before the petition was filed.
4. The debtor's failure to complete the required consumer education course.

17. Taxes accruing within three years prior to bankruptcy are nondischargeable, including federal and state income taxes, employment taxes, taxes on gross receipts, property taxes, excise taxes, customs duties, and any other taxes for which the government claims the debtor is liable in some capacity. See 11 U.S.C. Sections 507(a)(8), 523(a)(1).

5. Proceedings in which the debtor could be found guilty of a felony (basically, a court may not discharge any debt until the completion of felony proceedings against the debtor).

Effect of a Discharge The primary effect of a discharge is to void, or set aside, any judgment on a discharged debt and prohibit any action to collect a discharged debt. A discharge does not affect the liability of a co-debtor.

On petition by the trustee or a creditor, the bankruptcy court can, within one year, revoke the discharge decree if it is discovered that the debtor acted fraudulently or dishonestly during the bankruptcy proceedings. The revocation renders the discharge void, allowing creditors not satisfied by the distribution of the debtor's estate to proceed with their claims against the debtor.

Reaffirmation of Debt

An agreement to pay a debt dischargeable in bankruptcy is called a **reaffirmation agreement.** A debtor may wish to pay a debt—for example, a debt owed to a family member, physician, bank, or some other creditor—even though the debt could be discharged in bankruptcy.

Procedures To be enforceable, a reaffirmation agreement must be made before the debtor is granted a discharge. The agreement must be signed and filed with the court. Court approval is required unless the debtor is represented by an attorney during the negotiation of the reaffirmation and submits the proper documents and certifications. Even when the debtor is represented by an attorney, court approval may be required if it appears that the reaffirmation will result in undue hardship on the debtor. When court approval is required, a separate hearing will take place. The court will approve the reaffirmation only if it finds that the agreement will not result in undue hardship to the debtor and that the reaffirmation is consistent with the debtor's best interests.

Required Disclosures To discourage creditors from engaging in abusive reaffirmation practices, the law provides specific language for disclosures that must be given to debtors entering into reaffirmation agreements. Among other things, these disclosures explain that the debtor is not required to reaffirm any debt, but that liens on secured property, such as mortgages and cars, will remain in effect even if the debt is not reaffirmed.

The reaffirmation agreement must disclose the amount of the debt reaffirmed, the rate of interest, the date payments begin, and the right to rescind. The disclosures also caution the debtor: "Only agree to reaffirm a debt if it is in your best interest. Be sure you can afford the payments you agree to make." The original disclosure documents must be signed by the debtor, certified by the debtor's attorney, and filed with the court at the same time as the reaffirmation agreement. A reaffirmation agreement that is not accompanied by the original signed disclosures will not be effective.

Sometimes, creditors and credit reporting agencies have engaged in another form of abuse—failing to remove discharged debts from consumers' credit reports. See this chapter's *Adapting the Law to the Online Environment* feature on the following page for a discussion of this issue.

Chapter 11–Reorganization

The type of bankruptcy proceeding most commonly used by corporate debtors is the Chapter 11 *reorganization.* In a reorganization, the creditors and the debtor formulate a plan under which the debtor pays a portion of the debts and is discharged of the remainder. The debtor is allowed to continue in business. Although this type of bankruptcy is generally a corporate reorganization, any debtor (except a stockbroker or a commodities broker) who is eligible for Chapter 7 relief is eligible for relief under Chapter 11. Railroads are also eligible.

In 1994, Congress established a "fast-track" Chapter 11 procedure for small-business debtors whose liabilities do not exceed $2.19 million and who do not own or manage real estate. The fast track enables a debtor to avoid the appointment of a creditors' committee and also shortens the filing periods and relaxes certain other requirements. Because the process is shorter and simpler, it is less costly.

The same principles that govern the filing of a liquidation (Chapter 7) petition apply to reorganization (Chapter 11) proceedings. The case may be brought either voluntarily or involuntarily. The automatic-stay provisions and adequate protection doctrine apply in reorganizations as well. An exception from the automatic stay is triggered if the debtor files for bankruptcy again within two years and new grounds for dismissal (such as substantial abuse) or conversion of the case are established.

Workouts

In some instances, to avoid bankruptcy proceedings, creditors may prefer private, negotiated adjustments of creditor-debtor relations, also known as **workouts.** Often, these out-of-court workouts are much more flexible and thus more conducive to a speedy settlement. Speed is critical because delay is one of the most costly elements in any bankruptcy proceeding. Another advantage of workouts is that they avoid the various administrative costs of bankruptcy proceedings.

Creditors' Best Interests

After a petition for Chapter 11 bankruptcy has been filed, a bankruptcy court, after notice and a hearing, can dismiss or suspend all proceedings at any time if dismissal or suspension would better serve the interests of the creditors. The Bankruptcy Code also allows a court, after notice and a hearing, to dismiss

Adapting the Law to the Online Environment

The Debt That Never Goes Away—It's Discharged in Bankruptcy but Still on the Debtor's Credit Report

Bankruptcy, especially under Chapter 7, allows a judge to discharge certain debts. When these debts are discharged, they are no longer supposed to appear on the debtor's online credit report.

For Dan Rathavongsa, a factory worker in Raleigh, North Carolina, however, the discharged debt did not go away. A bankruptcy judge discharged a $9,523 debt that he owed to Capital One Financial. Nonetheless, Capital One continued to report Rathavongsa's debt to the various credit bureaus as a "live" balance. When Rathavongsa tried to obtain a mortgage for a new house a year after the debt had been discharged, the would-be lender told him that he would have to either pay the Capital One debt or prove that the debt had been discharged. When Capital One refused to revise his credit report, Rathavongsa gave in and paid Capital One for a debt he no longer legally owed.

Discharged Debts Attract Buyers

Capital One is not alone. Many credit-card companies and other creditors have been keeping debts active even after they have been discharged by a bankruptcy court. Consequently, some aggressive entrepreneurs have founded companies with names such as Max Recovery and eCast Settlement that purchase discharged debt obligations at pennies on the dollar. Then, they pursue the debtors and pressure them to pay the debts, even though the debts have already been discharged in bankruptcy. Some of these companies have been successful enough to become publicly traded on a stock exchange.

The billions of dollars' worth of debts that have been discharged in bankruptcy should have a zero-dollar value, yet the fact that there are buyers for these debts indicates that some consumers have been paying them. Indeed, as the number of bankruptcies rose as a result of the recent economic recession that swept the country in 2008 and 2009, the price of discharged Chapter 7 debt actually increased. Certainly, one reason why consumers have paid debts that they did not owe is because they found themselves in the same situation as Rathavongsa—their credit reports still listed the debt as active.

A Federal Judge Issues an Order That Changes the Reporting of Discharged Debt

That situation may change now, however, thanks to an order issued by one federal district court. A class-action lawsuit was brought against the three major credit-reporting agencies—Equifax, Experian, and TransUnion—all of which have a major online presence. The plaintiffs included consumers from across the country. They claimed that the agencies violated the federal Fair Credit Reporting Act by failing to follow reasonable procedures to ensure the accurate reporting of debts discharged in Chapter 7 bankruptcies. The court agreed and ordered the agencies to revise their procedures.[a] Ultimately, damages were awarded to the class of plaintiffs in the amount of $45 million, and in 2011, the court granted the plaintiffs more than $11 million in attorneys' fees.[b]

Previously, the credit bureaus would remove debts incurred before bankruptcy only if the creditors updated their accounts—which often was not done. Today, the credit agencies are required to automatically report all prebankruptcy debt as "discharged," unless the debt is nondischargeable. Although the purchasers of discharged debt may still attempt to pressure consumers into paying debts that they do not owe, the change in the credit bureaus' procedures gives consumers help in their efforts to rebuild their lives after bankruptcy.

FOR CRITICAL ANALYSIS

About five years ago, one could buy debt that had been discharged in bankruptcy for less than five cents on the dollar. Why do you think the price increased to seven cents on the dollar?

a. *White v. Experian Information Solutions, Inc.*, No. 05-CV-1-70 DOC (C.D.Cal. 2008).
b. *White v. Experian Information Solutions, Inc.*, 2011 WL 2971836 (C.D.Cal. 2011).

a case under reorganization "for cause." Cause includes the absence of a reasonable likelihood of rehabilitation, the inability to effect a plan, and an unreasonable delay by the debtor that is prejudicial to (may harm the interests of) creditors.[18]

Debtor in Possession

On entry of the order for relief, the debtor generally continues to operate the business as a **debtor in possession (DIP).** The court, however, may appoint a trustee (often referred to as a *receiver*) to operate the debtor's business if gross mismanagement of the business is shown or if appointing a trustee is in the best interests of the estate.

The DIP's role is similar to that of a trustee in a liquidation. The DIP is entitled to avoid preferential payments made to creditors and fraudulent transfers of assets. The DIP has the power to decide whether to cancel or assume obligations under prepetition executory contracts (those that are not yet performed) or unexpired leases. Cancellation of executory contracts or unexpired leases can be a substantial benefit to a Chapter 11 debtor. The DIP can also exercise a trustee's strong-arm powers (see page 363). **EXAMPLE 19.11** Five years ago, before a national recession, APT Corporation leased an office building for a twenty-year term. Now, APT can no longer afford to pay the

18. See 11 U.S.C. Section 1112(b). Debtors are not prohibited from filing successive petitions, however. A debtor whose petition is dismissed, for example, can file a new Chapter 11 petition (which may be granted unless it is filed in bad faith).

rent due under the lease and has filed for Chapter 11 reorganization. In this situation, the DIP can cancel the lease so that APT will not be required to continue paying the substantial rent for the building for fifteen more years. ●

Creditors' Committees

As soon as practicable after the entry of the order for relief, a creditors' committee of unsecured creditors is appointed.[19] This committee often is composed of the biggest suppliers to the business. The committee may consult with the trustee or the DIP concerning the administration of the case or the formulation of the plan. Additional creditors' committees may be appointed to represent special interest creditors.

Generally, no orders affecting the estate will be entered without the consent of the committee or a hearing in which the judge is informed of the committee's position. As mentioned earlier, businesses with debts of less than $2.19 million that do not own or manage real estate can avoid creditors' committees. In these cases, orders can be entered without a committee's consent.

The Reorganization Plan

A reorganization plan to rehabilitate the debtor is a plan to conserve and administer the debtor's assets in the hope of an eventual return to successful operation and solvency. The plan must be fair and equitable and must do the following:

1. Designate classes of claims and interests.
2. Specify the treatment to be afforded the classes. (The plan must provide the same treatment for all claims in a particular class.)
3. Provide an adequate means for execution. (Individual debtors are required to utilize postpetition assets as necessary to execute the plan.)
4. Provide for payment of tax claims over a five-year period.

Filing the Plan Only the debtor may file a plan within the first 120 days after the date of the order for relief. This period may be extended, but not beyond eighteen months from the date of the order for relief. If the debtor does not meet the 120-day deadline or obtain an extension, and if the debtor fails to procure the required creditor consent (discussed below) within 180 days, any party may propose a plan. The plan need not provide for full repayment to unsecured creditors. Instead, creditors receive a percentage of each dollar owed to them by the debtor. If a small-business debtor chooses to avoid a creditors' committee, the time for the debtor's filing is 180 days.

Acceptance and Confirmation of the Plan Once the plan has been developed, it is submitted to each class of creditors for acceptance. For the plan to be adopted, each class that is adversely affected by the plan must accept it. A class has accepted the plan when a majority of the creditors, representing two-thirds of the amount of the total claim, vote to approve it. Confirmation is conditioned on the debtor's certification that all postpetition domestic-support obligations have been paid in full.

Even when all classes of creditors accept the plan, the court may refuse to confirm it if it is not "in the best interests of the creditors." The plan can also be modified on the request of the debtor, the trustee, the U.S. trustee, or a holder of an unsecured claim. If an unsecured creditor objects to the plan, specific rules apply to the value of property to be distributed under the plan. Tax claims must be paid over a five-year period.

Even if only one class of creditors has accepted the plan, the court may still confirm the plan under the Code's so-called **cram-down provision.** In other words, the court may confirm the plan over the objections of a class of creditors. Before the court can exercise this right of cram-down confirmation, it must be demonstrated that the plan does not discriminate unfairly against any creditors and is fair and equitable.

Discharge The plan is binding on confirmation. The law provides, however, that confirmation of a plan does not discharge an individual debtor. *For individual debtors, the plan must be completed before discharge will be granted,* unless the court orders otherwise. For all other debtors, the court may order discharge at any time after the plan is confirmed. At this time, the debtor is given a reorganization discharge from all claims not protected under the plan. This discharge does not apply to any claims that would be denied discharge under liquidation.

Bankruptcy Relief under Chapter 12 and Chapter 13

In addition to bankruptcy relief through liquidation (Chapter 7) and reorganization (Chapter 11), the Code also provides for family-farmer and family-fisherman debt adjustments (Chapter 12) and individuals' repayment plans (Chapter 13).

Chapter 12—Family Farmers and Fishermen

In 1986, to help relieve economic pressure on small farmers, Congress created Chapter 12 of the Bankruptcy Code. In 2005, Congress extended this protection to family fishermen, modified its provisions somewhat, and made it a permanent chapter in the Bankruptcy Code. For purposes of Chapter 12, a *family farmer* is one whose gross income is at least 50 percent farm dependent and whose debts are at least 50 percent farm related.[20] The total debt must not exceed $3,792,650. A

19. If the debtor has filed a reorganization plan accepted by the creditors, the trustee may decide not to call a meeting of the creditors.

20. Note that the Bankruptcy Code defines a *family farmer* and a *farmer* differently. To be a farmer, a person or business must receive 50 percent of gross income from a farming operation that the person or business owns or operates.

partnership or a close corporation (see Chapters 23 and 24) that is at least 50 percent owned by the farm family can also qualify as a family farmer.[21]

A *family fisherman* is one whose gross income is at least 50 percent dependent on commercial fishing operations and whose debts are at least 80 percent related to commercial fishing. The total debt for a family fisherman must not exceed $1,757,475. As with family farmers, a partnership or close corporation can also qualify.

Filing the Petition The procedure for filing a family-farmer or family-fisherman bankruptcy plan is very similar to the procedure for filing a repayment plan under Chapter 13. The debtor must file a plan not later than ninety days after the order for relief. The filing of the petition acts as an automatic stay against creditors' and co-obligors' actions against the estate. A farmer or fisherman who has already filed a reorganization or repayment plan may convert the plan to a Chapter 12 plan. The debtor may also convert a Chapter 12 plan to a liquidation plan.

Content and Confirmation of the Plan The content of a plan under Chapter 12 can be modified by the debtor but, except for cause, must be confirmed or denied within forty-five days of the filing of the plan.

Court confirmation of the plan is the same as for a repayment plan. In summary, the plan must provide for payment of secured debts at the value of the collateral. If the secured debt exceeds the value of the collateral, the remaining debt is unsecured. For unsecured debtors, the plan must be confirmed if either the value of the property to be distributed under the plan equals the amount of the claim or the plan provides that all of the debtor's disposable income to be received in a three-year period (or longer, by court approval) will be applied to making payments. Completion of payments under the plan discharges all debts provided for by the plan.

Chapter 13—Individuals' Repayment Plan

Chapter 13 of the Bankruptcy Code provides for the "Adjustment of Debts of an Individual with Regular Income." Individuals (not partnerships or corporations) with regular income who owe fixed (liquidated) unsecured debts of less than $360,475 or fixed secured debts of less than $1,081,400 may take advantage of bankruptcy repayment plans. Among those eligible are salaried employees; sole proprietors; and individuals who live on welfare, Social Security benefits, fixed pensions, or investment income. Many small-business debtors have a choice of filing under either Chapter 11 or Chapter 13. Repayment plans offer some advantages because they are typically less expensive and less complicated than reorganization or liquidation proceedings.

Filing the Petition A Chapter 13 repayment plan case can be initiated only by the filing of a voluntary petition by the debtor or by the conversion of a Chapter 7 petition (because of a finding of substantial abuse under the means test, for example). Certain liquidation and reorganization cases may be converted to Chapter 13 with the consent of the debtor.[22] A trustee, who will make payments under the plan, must be appointed. On the filing of a repayment plan petition, the automatic stay previously discussed takes effect. Although the stay applies to all or part of the debtor's consumer debt, it does not apply to any business debt incurred by the debtor or to any domestic-support obligations.

Good Faith Requirement The Bankruptcy Code imposes the requirement of good faith on a debtor at both the time of the filing of the petition and the time of the filing of the plan. The Code does not define good faith, but if the circumstances as a whole indicate bad faith, a court can dismiss a debtor's Chapter 13 petition.

CASE EXAMPLE 19.12 Roger and Pauline Buis operated an air show business under the name Otto Airshows with a helicopter decorated as "Otto the Clown." After the Buises accused a competitor of safety lapses, the competitor won a defamation lawsuit against the Buises and Otto Airshows. The Buises then stopped doing business as Otto Airshows and formed a new firm, Prop and Rotor Aviation, Inc., to which they leased the Otto equipment. Within a month, they filed a bankruptcy petition under Chapter 13. The plan and the schedules did not mention the lawsuit, the equipment lease, and several other items. The court therefore dismissed the Buises' petition due to bad faith. The debtors had not included all of their assets and liabilities on their initial petition, and they had timed its filing to avoid payment on the defamation judgment.[23] •

The Repayment Plan A plan of rehabilitation by repayment must provide for the following:

1. The turning over to the trustee of such future earnings or income of the debtor as is necessary for execution of the plan.
2. Full payment through deferred cash payments of all claims entitled to priority, such as taxes.[24]

21. For a corporation or partnership to qualify under Chapter 12, at least 80 percent of the value of the firm's assets must consist of assets related to the farming operation.

22. A Chapter 13 repayment plan may be converted to a Chapter 7 liquidation either at the request of the debtor or, under certain circumstances, "for cause" by a creditor. A Chapter 13 case may be converted to a Chapter 11 case after a hearing.

23. *In re Buis*, 337 Bankr. 243 (N.D.Fla. 2006).

24. As with a Chapter 11 reorganization plan, full repayment of all claims is not always required.

3. Identical treatment of all claims within a particular class. (The Code permits the debtor to list co-debtors, such as guarantors or sureties, as a separate class.)

The repayment plan may provide for payment of all obligations in full or for payment of a lesser amount. The debtor must begin making payments under the proposed plan within thirty days after the plan has been filed and must continue to make "timely" payments from her or his disposable income. If the debtor fails to make timely payments or to commence payments within the thirty-day period, the court can convert the case to a liquidation bankruptcy or dismiss the petition.

The length of the payment plan can be three or five years, depending on the debtor's family income. If the debtor's family income is greater than the median family income in the relevant geographic area under the means test, the term of the proposed plan must be five years.[25] The term may not exceed five years.

In putting together a repayment plan, a debtor must apply the means test to identify the amount of disposable income that will be available to repay creditors. The debtor is allowed to deduct certain expenses from monthly income to arrive at this amount. Can a debtor who owns a car outright claim the costs of car ownership as an expense? That was the issue in the following case.

25. See 11 U.S.C. Section 1322(d) for details.

Case 19.2 Ransom v. FIA Card Services, N.A.

Supreme Court of the United States, __ U.S. __, 131 S.Ct. 716, 178 L.Ed.2d 603 (2011).
www.supremecourt.gov[a]

FACTS Jason Ransom filed a petition in a federal bankruptcy court to declare bankruptcy under Chapter 13. Among his assets, Ransom reported a Toyota Camry that he owned free of any debt. In listing monthly expenses for the means test, he claimed a deduction of $471 for car ownership and a separate deduction of $388 for car-operating costs. Based on his means-test calculations, Ransom proposed a five-year plan that would repay about 25 percent of his unsecured debt. He listed FIA Card Services, N.A., as an unsecured creditor. FIA objected to Ransom's plan, arguing that he should not have claimed the car-ownership allowance because he did not make payments on his car. The court agreed with FIA and issued a decision in its favor. A Bankruptcy Appellate Panel and the U.S. Court of Appeals for the Ninth Circuit affirmed the decision. Ransom appealed to the United States Supreme Court.

ISSUE Can a debtor in bankruptcy claim the car-ownership deduction when the debtor owns the car outright and does not make payments?

a. In the "Supreme Court Documents" column, in the "Opinions" pull-down menu, select "Bound Volumes." On the next page, in the "For Search Term:" box, type "Ransom" and click on "Search." In the result, click on the name of the case to access the opinion. The United States Supreme Court maintains this Web site.

DECISION No. The United States Supreme Court affirmed the lower court's decision. The ultimate result was that confirmation of Ransom's repayment plan was denied. (Confirmation of repayment plans will be discussed in the next section.)

REASON The United States Supreme Court referred to the tables of standardized expense amounts that a debtor could claim as reasonable living expenses and thus shield from creditors. The Bankruptcy Code limits a debtor's expense amounts to those that are "applicable" or appropriate. A deduction is appropriate only if the debtor will incur that expense during the life of the Chapter 13 plan. Because Ransom owned the car free and clear, the "Ownership Costs" category was not "applicable" to him. As a result, he could not claim such an expense.

FOR CRITICAL ANALYSIS—Economic Consideration *Should debtors with older vehicles be allowed to take an additional deduction for operating expenses? Explain.*

CONFIRMATION OF THE PLAN After the plan is filed, the court holds a confirmation hearing, at which interested parties (such as creditors) may object to the plan. The hearing must be held at least twenty days, but no more than forty-five days, after the meeting of the creditors. The debtor must have filed all prepetition tax returns and paid all postpetition domestic-support obligations before a court will confirm any plan. The court will confirm a plan with respect to each claim of a secured creditor under any of the following circumstances:

1. If the secured creditors have accepted the plan.
2. If the plan provides that secured creditors retain their liens until there is payment in full or until the debtor receives a discharge.
3. If the debtor surrenders the property securing the claims to the creditors.

DISCHARGE After the completion of all payments, the court grants a discharge of all debts provided for by the repayment plan. Except for allowed claims not provided for by the plan, certain long-term debts provided for by the plan, certain tax claims, payments on retirement accounts, and claims for domestic-support obligations, all other debts are dischargeable. Under current law, debts related to injury or property damage caused while driving under the influence of alcohol or drugs are nondischargeable.

In the following case, a debtor had proposed to discharge some of his student loan debt in a Chapter 13 repayment plan. Certain student loan debts can be discharged under Chapter 13, but only if the court finds that payment of the debt would constitute an "undue hardship" for the debtor. Due to an oversight by the creditor and an error by the bankruptcy court, the plan was approved and subsequently confirmed without the required finding of "undue hardship." The United States Supreme Court had to decide whether these problems rendered the discharge of the debt void.

Case 19.3 United Student Aid Funds, Inc. v. Espinosa

Supreme Court of the United States, ___ U.S. ___, 130 S.Ct. 1367, 176 L.Ed.2d 158 (2010).
www.supremecourt.gov[a]

FACTS Francisco Espinosa filed a petition for an individual repayment plan under Chapter 13 of the Bankruptcy Code. The plan proposed that Espinosa would repay only the principal of his student loan debt and that the interest on the loan would be discharged once the principal was repaid. Under Chapter 13, a student loan cannot be discharged unless the bankruptcy court finds that payment of the debt would constitute an undue hardship for the debtor. Notwithstanding this requirement, no undue hardship hearing was requested by the debtor, by the court, or by the creditor, United Student Aid Funds (United). The creditor received notice of the plan but did not object to it—nor did the creditor file an appeal after the bankruptcy court subsequently confirmed the plan. Years later, however, United filed a motion under Federal Rule of Civil Procedure 60(b)(4) asking the bankruptcy court to rule that its order confirming the plan was void because the order was issued in violation of the laws and rules governing bankruptcy. The court denied United's petition and ordered the creditor to cease its collection efforts. The creditor appealed to the U.S. District Court for the District of Arizona, and the district court reversed the bankruptcy court's ruling. On further appeal, the U.S. Court of Appeals for the Ninth Circuit reversed the district court's judgment. United appealed to the United States Supreme Court.

ISSUE If a bankruptcy court committed a legal error by confirming a debtor's repayment plan to discharge student loan debt without the required finding of undue hardship, but the creditor did not object, is the court's judgment void?

DECISION No. The United States Supreme Court affirmed the judgment of the U.S. Court of Appeals for the Ninth Circuit. The bankruptcy court's order confirming Espinosa's Chapter 13 repayment plan was not void, and the student loan debt was thus discharged.

REASON The United States Supreme Court pointed out that the Bankruptcy Court's order confirming Espinosa's proposed plan was a final judgment from which United did not appeal. Federal Rule of Civil Procedure 60(b)(4) does authorize the court to relieve a party from a final judgment if that judgment is void, but a judgment is not void simply because it is or may have been erroneous. Moreover, a motion under this rule is not a substitute for a timely appeal. "The Bankruptcy Court's failure to find undue hardship before confirming Espinosa's plan was a legal error. But the order remains enforceable and binding on United because United had notice of the error and failed to object or timely appeal."

FOR CRITICAL ANALYSIS—Ethical Consideration *At one point, United argued that if the Court failed to declare the bankruptcy court's order void, it would encourage dishonest debtors to abuse the Chapter 13 process. How might such abuse occur, and should the possibility of such abuse affect the Court's decision?*

a. In the "Supreme Court Documents" column, in the "Opinions" pull-down menu, select "Bound Volumes." On the next page, in the "For Search Term:" box, type "Espinosa" and click on "Search." In the result, click on the name of the case to access the opinion. The United States Supreme Court maintains this Web site.

Reviewing . . . Creditors' Rights and Bankruptcy

Three months ago, Janet Hart's husband of twenty years died of cancer. Although he had medical insurance, he left Janet with outstanding medical bills of more than $50,000. Janet has worked at the local library for the past ten years, earning $1,500 per month. Since her husband's death, Janet also has received $1,500 in Social Security benefits and $1,100 in life insurance proceeds every month, giving her a monthly income of $4,300. After she pays the mortgage payment of $1,500 and the amounts due on other debts each month, Janet barely has enough left to buy groceries for her family (she has two teenaged daughters at home). She decides to file for Chapter 7 bankruptcy, hoping for a fresh start. Using the information provided in the chapter, answer the following questions.

1 What must Janet do before filing a petition for relief under Chapter 7?
2 How much time does Janet have after filing the bankruptcy petition to submit the required schedules? What happens if Janet does not meet the deadline?
3 Assume that Janet files a petition under Chapter 7. Further assume that the median family income in the state in which Janet lives is $49,300. What steps would a court take to determine whether Janet's petition is presumed to be "substantial abuse" under the means test?
4 Suppose that the court determines that no presumption of substantial abuse applies in Janet's case. Nevertheless, the court finds that Janet does have the ability to pay at least a portion of the medical bills out of her disposable income. What would the court likely order in that situation?

Terms and Concepts

artisan's lien 356
attachment 356
automatic stay 362
consumer-debtor 360
co-surety 359
cram-down provision 369
creditors' composition agreement 357
debtor in possession (DIP) 368
discharge 360
garnishment 356
guarantor 358
homestead exemption 359
lien 354
liquidation 360
mechanic's lien 355
order for relief 362
petition in bankruptcy 360
preference 364
preferred creditor 364
reaffirmation agreement 367
right of contribution 359
right of reimbursement 359
right of subrogation 359
surety 358
suretyship 358
U.S. trustee 361
workout 367
writ of attachment 356
writ of execution 356

Chapter Summary: Creditors' Rights and Bankruptcy

LAWS ASSISTING CREDITORS	
Liens (See pages 354–356.)	1. *Mechanic's lien*—A nonpossessory, filed lien on an owner's real estate for labor, services, or materials furnished to or used to make improvements on the realty. 2. *Artisan's lien*—A possessory lien on an owner's personal property for labor performed or value added. 3. *Judicial liens*— a. Writ of attachment—A court-ordered seizure of property prior to a court's final determination of the creditor's rights to the property. Attachment is available only on the creditor's posting of a bond and strict compliance with the applicable state statutes. b. Writ of execution—A court order directing the sheriff to seize (levy) and sell a debtor's nonexempt real or personal property to satisfy a court's judgment in the creditor's favor.
Garnishment (See pages 356–357.)	A collection remedy that allows the creditor to attach a debtor's funds (such as wages owed or bank accounts) and property that are held by a third person.
Creditors' Composition Agreements (See page 357.)	A contract between a debtor and his or her creditors by which the debtor's debts are discharged by payment of a sum less than the amount that is actually owed.
Suretyship and Guaranty (See pages 357–359.)	Under contract, a third person agrees to be primarily or secondarily liable for the debt owed by the principal debtor. A creditor can turn to this third person for satisfaction of the debt.

Continued

Chapter Summary: Creditors' Rights and Bankruptcy—Continued

LAWS ASSISTING DEBTORS			
Exemptions (See page 359.)	Certain property of a debtor is exempt from creditors' actions under state laws. Each state permits a debtor to retain the family home, either in its entirety or up to a specified dollar amount, free from the claims of unsecured creditors or trustees in bankruptcy (homestead exemption).		
BANKRUPTCY—A COMPARISON OF CHAPTERS 7, 11, 12, AND 13			
Issue	**Chapter 7**	**Chapter 11**	**Chapters 12 and 13**
Purpose	Liquidation.	Reorganization.	Adjustment.
Who Can Petition	Debtor (voluntary) or creditors (involuntary).	Debtor (voluntary) or creditors (involuntary).	Debtor (voluntary) only.
Who Can Be a Debtor	Any "person" (including partnerships and corporations) except railroads, insurance companies, banks, savings and loan institutions, investment companies licensed by the U.S. Small Business Administration, and credit unions. Farmers and charitable institutions cannot be involuntarily petitioned.	Any debtor eligible for Chapter 7 relief; railroads are also eligible.	*Chapter 12*—Any family farmer (one whose gross income is at least 50 percent farm dependent and whose debts are at least 50 percent farm related) or family fisherman (one whose gross income is at least 50 percent dependent on and whose debts are at least 80 percent related to commercial fishing) or any partnership or close corporation at least 50 percent owned by a family farmer or fisherman, when total debt does not exceed \$3,792,650 for a family farmer and \$1,757,475 for a family fisherman. *Chapter 13*—Any individual (not partnerships or corporations) with regular income who owes fixed (liquidated) unsecured debts of less than \$360,475 or fixed secured debts of less than \$1,081,400.
Procedure Leading to Discharge	Nonexempt property is sold with proceeds to be distributed (in order) to priority groups. Dischargeable debts are terminated.	Plan is submitted. If it is approved and followed, debts are discharged.	Plan is submitted and must be approved if the value of the property to be distributed equals the amount of the claims or if the debtor turns over disposable income for a three- or five-year period. If the plan is followed, debts are discharged.
Advantages	On liquidation and distribution, most debts are discharged, and the debtor has an opportunity for a fresh start.	Debtor continues in business. Creditors can either accept the plan, or it can be "crammed down" on them. The plan allows for the reorganization and liquidation of debts over the plan period.	Debtor continues in business or possession of assets. If the plan is approved, most debts are discharged after a three-year period.

ExamPrep

ISSUE SPOTTERS

—Check your answers to these questions against the answers provided in Appendix G.

1 Joe contracts with Larry of Midwest Roofing to fix Joe's roof. Joe pays half of the contract price in advance. Larry and Midwest complete the job, but Joe refuses to pay the rest of the price. What can Larry and Midwest do?

2 Ogden is a vice president of Plumbing Service, Inc. (PSI). On May 1, Ogden loans PSI $10,000. On June 1, the firm repays the loan. On July 1, PSI files for bankruptcy. Quentin is appointed trustee. Can Quentin recover the $10,000 paid to Ogden on June 1? Explain.

BEFORE THE TEST

Go to **www.cengagebrain.com**, enter the ISBN number "9781111530624," and click on "Find" to locate this textbook's Web site. Then, click on "Access Now" under "Study Tools," and select Chapter 19 at the top. There you will find an Interactive Quiz that you can take to assess your mastery of the concepts in this chapter, as well as Flashcards and a Glossary of important terms.

For Review

1 What is a prejudgment attachment? What is a writ of execution? How does a creditor use these remedies?

2 What is garnishment? When might a creditor undertake a garnishment proceeding?

3 In a bankruptcy proceeding, what constitutes the debtor's estate in property? What property is exempt from the estate under federal bankruptcy law?

4 What is the difference between an exception to discharge and an objection to discharge?

5 In a Chapter 11 reorganization, what is the role of the debtor in possession?

Questions and Case Problems

19–1 Mechanic's Lien. Grant is the owner of a relatively old home valued at $45,000. He notices that the bathtubs and fixtures in both bathrooms are leaking and need to be replaced. He contracts with Jane's Plumbing to replace the bathtubs and fixtures. Jane replaces them, and on June 1 she submits her bill of $4,000 to Grant. Because of financial difficulties, Grant does not pay the bill. Grant's only asset is his home, but his state's homestead exemption is $40,000. Discuss fully Jane's remedies in this situation.

19–2 Voluntary versus Involuntary Bankruptcy. Burke has been a rancher all her life, raising cattle and crops. Her ranch is valued at $500,000, almost all of which is exempt under state law. Burke has eight creditors and a total indebtedness of $70,000. Two of her largest creditors are Oman ($30,000 owed) and Sneed ($25,000 owed). The other six creditors have claims of less than $5,000 each. A drought has ruined all of Burke's crops and forced her to sell many of her cattle at a loss. She cannot pay off her creditors.

1 Under the Bankruptcy Code, can Burke, with a $500,000 ranch, voluntarily petition herself into bankruptcy? Explain.

2 Could either Oman or Sneed force Burke into involuntary bankruptcy? Explain.

19–3 Preferences. Peaslee is not known for his business sense. He started a greenhouse and nursery business two years ago, and because of his lack of experience, he soon was in debt to a number of creditors. On February 1, Peaslee borrowed $5,000 from his father to pay some of these creditors. On May 1, Peaslee paid back the $5,000, depleting his entire working capital. One creditor, the Cool Springs Nursery Supply Corp., extended credit to Peaslee on numerous purchases. Cool Springs pressured Peaslee for payment, and on July 1, Peaslee paid Cool Springs half the amount owed. On September 1, Peaslee voluntarily petitioned himself into bankruptcy. The trustee in bankruptcy claimed that both Peaslee's father and Cool Springs must turn over to the debtor's estate the amounts Peaslee paid to them. Discuss fully the trustee's claims.

19–4 Bankruptcy. Cathy Coleman took out loans to complete her college education. After graduation, Coleman was irregularly employed as a teacher before filing a petition in a federal bankruptcy court under Chapter 13. The court confirmed a five-year plan under which Coleman was required to commit all of her disposable income to paying the student loans. Less than a year later, she was laid off. Still owing more than $100,000 to Educational Credit Management Corp., Coleman asked the court to discharge the debt on the ground that it would be undue hardship for her to pay it. Under Chapter 13, when is a debtor normally entitled to a discharge? Are student loans dischargeable? If not, is "undue hardship" a legitimate ground for an exception? With respect to a debtor, what is the goal of bankruptcy? With these facts and principles in mind, what argument could be made in support of Coleman's request? [*In re Coleman,* 560 F.3d 1000 (9th Cir. 2009)]

19–5 Discharge in Bankruptcy. Caroline McAfee loaned $400,000 to Carter Oaks Crossing. Joseph Harman, president of Carter Oaks Crossing, signed a promissory note providing that the company would repay the amount with interest in installments beginning in 1999 and ending by 2006. Harman signed a personal guaranty for the note. Carter Oaks Crossing defaulted on the note, so McAfee sued Harman for payment under the guaranty. Harman moved for summary judgment on the ground that McAfee's claim against him had been discharged in his Chapter 7 bankruptcy case, filed after 1999 but before the default on the note. The guaranty was not listed among Harman's debts in the bankruptcy filing. Would the obligation under the guaranty have been discharged in bankruptcy, as Harman claimed? Why or why not? [*Harman v. McAfee,* 302 Ga.App. 698, 691 S.E.2d 586 (2010)]

19–6 Liens. Autolign Manufacturing Group, Inc., was a plastic injection molder that made parts for the auto industry. Because of a fire at its plant, Autolign subcontracted its work to several other companies to produce parts for its customers. Autolign provided the subcontractors with molds it owned so that they could produce the exact parts needed. After the subcontractors produced the parts, Autolign sold them to automakers. Shortly afterward, Autolign ceased operations. The subcontractors sued Autolign for breach of contract, claiming that they were never paid for the parts that they had produced for Autolign. The subcontractors asserted a statutory "molder's lien" on the molds in their possession. A molder's lien is similar to an artisan's lien in that it is possessory, but it was established by a Michigan statute rather than common law. One of Autolign's creditors, Wamco 34, Ltd., argued that the molds were its property because the molds were used to secure repayment of a debt that Autolign owed to Wamco. The trial court held that Wamco was a secured creditor and that its interest had priority over the plaintiffs' lien in the molds. The subcontractors appealed. Which party had the superior claim? Explain your answer. [*Delta Engineered Plastics, LLC v. Autolign Manufacturing Group, Inc.,* 286 Mich.App. 115, 777 N.W.2d 502 (2010)]

19–7 Case Problem with Sample Answer Bill and Betty Ma owned one-half of a two-unit residential building in San Francisco, California. Betty and her mother lived in one of the units, and Bill lived in China. Mei-Fang Zhang (and others) obtained a judgment in a federal district court against Bill Ma (and others, including Wei-Man Raymond Tse) based on a claim that they had been the victims of a foreign currency trading scam operated by Bill Ma and others. The judgment was more than $1 million. Zhang asked the court for a writ of execution, directing the sheriff to seize and sell the Mas' building. California state law allows a $100,000 homestead exemption free from the claims of creditors, if the debtor or the debtor's spouse lives in the home. A greater exemption of $175,000 is allowed if either of these persons lives in the home *and* is disabled and "unable to engage in gainful employment." Bill Ma argued that he was "unable to engage in gainful employment as a waiter or a driver" because of "gout and dizziness" and claimed a homestead exemption of $175,000. To how much of an exemption is Bill entitled? Why? How will the proceeds from the sale be distributed? [*Zhang v. Tse,* __ F.Supp.2d __ (N.D.Cal. 2011)]

—To view a sample answer for Problem 19–7, go to Appendix F at the end of this text.

19–8 Discharge in Bankruptcy. Monica Sexton filed a petition in a federal bankruptcy court under Chapter 13. One of her creditors was Friedman's Jewelers of Savannah, Georgia. Her schedules misclassified Friedman's claim as $800 of unsecured debt. Within days, Friedman's filed proof of a secured claim for $300 and an unsecured claim for $462.26. Eventually, Friedman's was sent payments of about $300 by check. None of these checks was cashed, however, because Friedman's had filed its own bankruptcy petition under Chapter 11. As a result, Bankruptcy Receivables Management (BRM) had bought Friedman's unpaid accounts, and the checks had not been forwarded to BRM. In the meantime, Sexton had received a discharge on the completion of her plan, but BRM was not notified. BRM wrote to Sexton's attorney to ask about the status of her case, but received no response. BRM then wrote to Sexton, demanding that she surrender the collateral on its claim. Sexton asked the court to impose sanctions on BRM for violating the discharge order. Was Sexton's debt to Friedman's dischargeable? What is the effect of a discharge? Should BRM be sanctioned? Discuss. [*In re Sexton,* __ Bankr. __ (E.D.N.C. 2011)]

19–9 A Question of Ethics *73-75 Main Avenue, LLC, agreed to lease a portion of the commercial property at 73 Main Avenue, Norwalk, Connecticut, to PP Door Enterprise, Inc. Nan Zhang, as manager of PP Door, signed the lease agreement. The lessor required the principal officers of PP Door to execute personal guaranties. In addition, the principal officers agreed to provide the lessor with credit information. Apparently, both the lessor and the principals of PP Door signed the lease and guaranty agreements that were sent to PP Door's office. When PP Door failed to make monthly payments, 73-75 Main Avenue filed a suit against PP Door and its owner, Ping Ying Li. At trial, Li testified that she was the sole owner of PP Door but denied that Zhang was its manager. She also denied signing the guaranty agreement. She claimed that she had signed the credit authorization form because Zhang had told her he was too young to have good credit. Li claimed to have no knowledge of the lease agreement. She did admit, however, that she had paid the rent. She claimed that Zhang had been in a car* *accident and had asked her to help pay his bills, including the rent at 73 Main Avenue. Li further testified that she did not see the name PP Door on the storefront of the leased location.* [73-75 Main Avenue, LLC v. PP Door Enterprise, Inc., *120 Conn.App. 150, 991 A.2d 650 (2010)*]

1 Li argued that she was not liable on the lease agreement because Zhang was not authorized to bind her to the lease. Do the facts support Li? Why or why not?

2 Li claimed that the guaranty for rent was not enforceable against her. Why might the court agree?

19–10 VIDEO **Video Question** To watch this chapter's video, *Field of Dreams,* go to **www.cengagebrain.com**. Register the access code that came with your new book or log in to your existing account. Select the link for the "Business Law Digital Video Library Online Access" or "Business Law CourseMate." Click on "Complete Video List," view Video 73, and then answer the following questions:

1 Before this scene, the movie makes clear that Ray (Kevin Costner) is unable to pay his bills, but he has not filed a voluntary petition for bankruptcy. What would be required for Ray's creditors to force him into an involuntary bankruptcy?

2 If Ray did file a voluntary petition for a Chapter 7 bankruptcy, what exemptions might protect him from "losing everything" and being evicted, as the man indicated in this scene? How much equity in the farm home could Ray claim as exempt if he filed the petition?

3 What are the requirements for Ray to qualify as a family farmer under Chapter 12 of the Bankruptcy Code?

4 How would the results of a Chapter 12 bankruptcy differ from those of a Chapter 7 bankruptcy for Ray?

Chapter 20

Mortgages and Foreclosures after the Recession

Learning Objectives

After reading this chapter, you should be able to answer the following questions:

1. What is a subprime mortgage? How does it differ from a standard fixed-rate mortgage?
2. When is private mortgage insurance required? Which party does it protect?
3. Does the Truth-in-Lending Act (TILA) apply to all mortgages? How do the TILA provisions protect borrowers and curb abusive practices by mortgage lenders?
4. What is a short sale?
5. In a mortgage foreclosure, what legal rights do mortgage holders have if the sale proceeds are insufficient to pay the underlying debt?

The Learning Objectives above are designed to help improve your understanding of the chapter.

During the early years of the twenty-first century, the United States experienced one of the biggest real estate bubbles in its history as housing prices in many areas increased at unprecedented rates. The bubble started to shrink in 2006 and was still deflating in 2012. As a result of the collapse of the housing market and the financial crisis that accompanied it, the United States and much of the rest of the world suffered through what is now called the Great Recession.

Although several years have passed since the housing crisis and recession began, the real estate market is still in turmoil. Many people lost their homes to foreclosure because they could not make the payments on their *mortgages*—the loans that borrowers obtain to purchase homes. Others can afford the payments but choose not to pay because they owe more on the properties than those properties are worth.

As the problems drag on, it has become apparent that the entire mortgage process during the bubble years was fraught with fraud. In June 2011, for example, Bank of America announced that it would pay as much as $20 billion to settle claims involving mortgage-backed securities the bank had sold as safe investments. In fact, the securities were actually based on mortgages granted to borrowers who had little, if any, ability to repay their loans (see Chapter 26 for more on securities fraud). Other major mortgage companies, including Citigroup, JPMorgan Chase, and Wells Fargo, faced similar fraud claims. In the meantime, complaints about fraud in the mortgage foreclosure process by both borrowers and lenders have risen—in fact, they were up 31 percent in the first quarter of 2011.[1]

This chapter examines the rights and obligations that apply to homeowners and their lenders. It begins with a discussion of mortgages, which lenders provide to enable borrowers to purchase real property (*real property* will be discussed in Chapter 28). Next, we examine the laws that protect borrowers when they obtain mortgages. The chapter concludes with a discussion of the options that lenders and homeowners have when homeowners cannot continue to make their mortgage payments.

1. This figure is according to the Financial Crimes Enforcement Network, a U.S. Treasury bureau that tracks illegal financial activity.

Mortgages

When individuals purchase real property, they typically borrow funds from a financial institution for part or all of the purchase price. A **mortgage** is a written instrument that gives the creditor (the *mortgagee*) an interest in, or lien on, the property being acquired by the debtor (the *mortgagor*) as security for the debt's payment. Here, we look first at the different types of mortgages, including some new varieties that helped to inflate the housing bubble. Then we consider some of the ways that creditors protect their interest in the property and examine some of the more important provisions in a typical mortgage document.

Types of Mortgages

Mortgage loans are contracts, and as such, they come in a variety of forms. Lenders offer various types of mortgages to meet the needs of different borrowers. In recent decades, the expansion of home ownership became a political goal, and lenders were encouraged to become more creative in devising new types of mortgages. In many instances, these new mortgages were aimed at borrowers who could not qualify for traditional mortgages and lacked the funds to make a **down payment** (the part of the purchase price that is paid up front).

In general, these mortgages, which include some adjustable-rate mortgages, interest-only mortgages, and balloon mortgages, feature a low initial interest rate. Often, the borrower hopes to refinance—pay off the original mortgage and obtain a new one at more favorable terms—within a few years. When the housing bubble burst and house prices began to decline, however, refinancing became more difficult than many borrowers had anticipated.

Fixed-Rate Mortgages *Fixed-rate mortgages* are the simplest mortgage loans. A **fixed-rate mortgage** is a standard mortgage with a fixed, or unchanging, rate of interest. Payments on the loan remain the same for the duration of the mortgage, which ranges from fifteen to forty years. Lenders determine the interest rate based on a variety of factors, including the borrower's credit history, credit score, income, and debts. Today, for a borrower to qualify for a standard fixed-rate mortgage loan, lenders typically require that the monthly mortgage payment (including principal, interest, taxes, and insurance) not exceed 28 percent of the person's gross income.

Adjustable-Rate Mortgages The rate of interest paid by the borrower changes periodically with an **adjustable-rate mortgage (ARM).** Typically, the initial interest rate for an ARM is set at a relatively low fixed rate for a specified period, such as a year or three years. After that time, the interest rate adjusts annually or by some other period, such as biannually or monthly. ARMs generally are described in terms of the initial fixed period and the adjustment period. For example, if the interest rate is fixed for three years and then adjusts annually, the mortgage is called a 3/1 ARM, whereas if the rate adjusts annually after five years, the mortgage is a 5/1 ARM.

The interest rate adjustment is calculated by adding a certain number of percentage points (called the margin) to an index rate (one of various government interest rates). The margin and index rate are specified in the mortgage loan documents. **EXAMPLE 20.1** Greta and Marcus obtain a 3/1 ARM to purchase a home. After three years, when the first adjustment is to be made, the index rate is 6 percent. If the margin specified in the loan documents is 3 percentage points, the fully indexed interest rate for the ARM would be 9 percent. • Most ARMs, however, have lifetime interest rate caps that limit the amount that the rate can rise over the duration of the loan.

Some ARMs also have caps that stipulate the maximum increase that can occur at any particular adjustment period. **EXAMPLE 20.2** In the Greta and Marcus example above, if the initial interest rate was 5 percent and the loan stipulated that the rate could rise no more than 3 percentage points in one adjustment period, the interest rate after three years would increase to 8 percent, not 9 percent, because of the cap. • Note that the interest rate could be adjusted downward as well as upward. If the index rate was 1 percent, the adjusted rate would potentially fall to 4 percent, although some ARMs also limit the amount that the rate can fall.

Interest-Only (IO) Mortgages With an **interest-only (IO) mortgage,** the borrower can choose to pay only the interest portion of the monthly payments and forgo paying any of the principal for a specified period of time. (IO loans can be for fixed-rate or adjustable-rate mortgages.) This IO payment usually is available for three to ten years. After the IO payment option is exhausted, the borrower's payment increases to include payments on the principal.

Subprime Mortgages During the late 1990s and the first decade of the 2000s, *subprime lending* increased significantly. A **subprime mortgage** is a loan made to a borrower who does not qualify for a standard mortgage. Often, such borrowers have poor credit scores or high current *debt-to-income ratios*—that is, the total amount owed as a percentage of current after-tax income. Subprime mortgages are riskier than traditional mortgages and have a higher default rate. Consequently, lenders charge a higher interest rate for subprime loans. Subprime mortgages can be fixed-rate, adjustable-rate, or IO loans. Subprime lending allows many people who could not otherwise purchase real property to do so, but at a higher risk to the lender.

CONSTRUCTION LOANS A **construction loan** is similar to a mortgage in many ways—for example, this type of loan comes in all varieties, including fixed-rate and adjustable-rate loans. Rather than purchasing an existing home, the borrower uses the funds from a construction loan to build a new home. Construction loans are often set up with a schedule of "draws." **EXAMPLE 20.3** Joel and Jen borrow funds to purchase real estate and build a home. The first draw of funds pays for the land. Subsequent draws occur when the foundation is laid, when the framing for the structure is finished, when the exterior is completed, and finally when the interior is completed and the contractor turns the house over to the couple for occupancy. •

BALLOON MORTGAGES Similar to an ARM, a **balloon mortgage** starts with low payments for a specified period, usually seven to ten years. At the end of that period, a large balloon payment for the entire balance of the mortgage loan is due. Because the balloon payment is often very large, many borrowers refinance when this payment is due. A potential disadvantage is that the lender will set the interest rate of the refinanced loan at whatever the market dictates at that time. As a result, the payments may be higher than they would have been if the buyer had initially obtained a fixed-rate mortgage instead of a balloon mortgage.

HYBRID AND REVERSE MORTGAGES A variety of other less common mortgages are also available. One example is a **hybrid mortgage** (also called a *two-step mortgage*), which starts as a fixed-rate mortgage and then converts into an ARM.

With a **reverse mortgage,** instead of borrowing from a bank to buy a home, existing homeowners receive funds for the equity, or value, in their home. The mortgage does not need to be repaid until the home is sold or the owner dies. Reverse mortgages are geared toward older borrowers (over the age of sixty-two) who have substantial equity in their homes. By converting a portion of that equity into cash, the homeowners can supplement their retirement income.

Home Equity Loans

Home equity refers to the portion of a home's value that is "paid off." **EXAMPLE 20.4** If Susanna has a home valued at $200,000 and owes the bank $120,000 on her mortgage, she has 40 percent equity in her house ($80,000/$200,000 = 40 percent). With a **home equity loan,** a bank accepts the borrower's equity as *collateral,* which can be seized if the loan is not repaid on time. If Susanna takes out a $30,000 home equity loan, the amount is added to the amount of her mortgage ($30,000 + $120,000 = $150,000), so she now has only $50,000 (25 percent) equity in her $200,000 home. •

Borrowers often take out home equity loans to obtain funds to renovate the property itself. Others obtain home equity loans to pay off debt, such as credit-card debt, that carries a higher interest rate than they will pay on the home equity loan. This strategy can lead to problems, however, if the borrower cannot keep up the payments. Many Americans who lost their homes during the Great Recession were able to pay their original mortgage loans, but not their home equity loans. From the lender's perspective, a home equity loan is riskier than a mortgage loan because home equity loans are *subordinated,* which means that they take a lower priority in any proceeding that occurs if the homeowner fails to make the payments on the primary mortgage.

Creditor Protection

When creditors grant mortgages, they are advancing a significant amount of funds for a number of years. Consequently, creditors take a number of steps to protect their interest. One precaution is to require debtors to obtain private mortgage insurance if they do not make a down payment of at least 20 percent of the purchase price. For example, if a borrower makes a down payment of only 5 percent of the purchase price, the creditor might require insurance covering 15 percent of the cost. Then, if the debtor defaults, the creditor repossesses the house and receives reimbursement from the insurer for the covered portion of the loan.

In addition, the creditor will record the mortgage with the appropriate office in the county where the property is located. Recording ensures that the creditor is officially on record as holding an interest in the property. A lender that fails to record a mortgage could find itself in the position of an unsecured creditor.

Mortgages normally are lengthy documents that include a number of provisions. Many of these provisions are aimed at protecting the creditor's investment.

STATUTE OF FRAUDS Because a mortgage involves a transfer of real property, it must be in writing to comply with the Statute of Frauds (see page 183 in Chapter 10). Most mortgages today are highly formal documents with similar formats, but a mortgage is not required to follow any particular form. Indeed, as long as the mortgage satisfies the Statute of Frauds, it generally will be effective.

IMPORTANT MORTGAGE PROVISIONS Mortgage documents ordinarily contain all or most of the following terms:

1. *The terms of the underlying loan.* These include the loan amount, the interest rate, the period of repayment, and other important financial terms, such as the margin and index rate for an ARM. Many lenders include a **prepayment penalty clause,** which requires the borrower to pay a penalty if the mortgage is repaid in full within a certain period. A prepayment penalty helps to protect the lender should

the borrower refinance within a short time after obtaining a mortgage.

2. *Provisions relating to the maintenance of the property.* Because the mortgage conveys an interest in the property to the lender, the lender will require the borrower to maintain the property in such a way that the lender's investment is protected.
3. *A statement obligating the borrower to maintain* **homeowners' insurance** *(also known as* hazard insurance) *on the property.* This type of insurance protects the lender's interest in the event of a loss due to certain hazards, such as fire or storm damage.
4. *A list of the nonloan financial obligations to be borne by the borrower.* For example, the borrower typically is required to pay all property taxes, assessments, and other claims against the property.
5. *A provision requiring that the borrower pay certain obligations.* For example, a borrower may be required to pay some or all of the taxes, insurance, assessments, or other expenses associated with the property in advance or through the lender. In this way, the lender is assured that the funds for these expenses will be available when the bills come due.

Although a record number of homeowners have failed to keep up with their mortgage payments in recent years, courts have continued to enforce the terms of plainly written financing documents. In today's environment, borrowers cannot avoid the clear meaning of terms in financing documents, even when the effect may be harsh.

Real Estate Financing Law

During the real estate boom in the first years of the 2000s, some lenders were less than honest with borrowers about the loan terms the latter were signing. As a result, many individuals failed to understand how much the monthly payments on ARMs, interest-only mortgages, and other exotic types of loans might increase.

In addition, fees and penalties often were not properly disclosed. In an effort to provide more protection for borrowers, Congress and the Federal Reserve Board have instituted a number of new requirements, mostly in the form of required disclosures. Here, we examine some of the more important statutes that provide protection for borrowers. First, though, we look at some of the practices that led to the enactment of these statutes.

Predatory Lending and Other Improper Practices

The general term *predatory lending* is often used to describe situations in which borrowers are the victims of loan terms or lending procedures that are excessive, deceptive, or not properly disclosed. Predatory lending typically occurs during the loan origination process. It includes a number of practices ranging from failure to disclose terms to providing misleading information to outright dishonesty.

Two specific types of improper practices are often at the core of a violation. *Steering and targeting* occurs when the lender manipulates a borrower into accepting a loan product that benefits the lender but is not the best loan for the borrower. For instance, a lender may steer a borrower toward an ARM, even though the buyer qualifies for a fixed-rate mortgage. *Loan flipping* occurs when a lender convinces a homeowner to refinance soon after obtaining a mortgage. Such early refinancing rarely benefits the homeowner and may, in fact, result in prepayment penalties.

The Truth-in-Lending Act (TILA)

The Truth-in-Lending Act (TILA) of 1968[2] requires lenders to disclose the terms of a loan in clear, readily understandable language so that borrowers can make rational choices. With respect to real estate transactions, the TILA applies only to residential loans.

REQUIRED DISCLOSURES The major terms that must be disclosed under the TILA include the loan principal; the interest rate at which the loan is made; the **annual percentage rate,** or **APR** (the actual cost of the loan on a yearly basis); and all fees and costs associated with the loan. The TILA requires that these disclosures be made on standardized forms and based on uniform formulas of calculation.

Certain types of loans—including ARMs, reverse mortgages, open-ended home equity loans, and high-interest loans—have specially tailored disclosure requirements. The Mortgage Disclosure Improvement Act of 2008[3] amended the TILA to strengthen the disclosures required for ARMs, which, as mentioned earlier, played a leading role in the recent real estate meltdown.

PROHIBITIONS AND REQUIREMENTS The TILA prohibits certain lender abuses and creates certain borrower rights. Among the prohibited practices is the charging of prepayment penalties on most subprime mortgages and home equity loans.

The TILA also addresses other unfair, abusive, or deceptive home mortgage–lending practices. For example, lenders may not coerce an **appraiser** (an individual who specializes in determining the value of specified real or personal property)

2. 15 U.S.C. Sections 1601–1693r.

3. The Mortgage Disclosure Improvement Act is contained in Sections 2501 through 2503 of the Housing and Economic Recovery Act of 2008, Pub. L. No. 110-289, enacted on July 30, 2008. Congress then amended its provisions as part of the Emergency Economic Stabilization Act of 2008 (also known as the Bailout Bill), Pub. L. No. 110-343, enacted on October 3, 2008.

into misstating the value of a property on which a loan is to be issued. Also, a loan cannot be advertised as a fixed-rate loan if, in fact, its rate or payment amounts will change.

Right to Rescind. A mortgage cannot be finalized until at least seven days after a borrower has received the TILA paperwork. Even if all required disclosures are provided, the TILA gives the borrower the right to rescind (cancel) a mortgage within three business days. According to the 2008 amendments, Sunday is the only day of the week that is not a business day. If the lender fails to provide material TILA disclosures, including the three-day right to rescind, the rescission period lasts up to three years.

Written Representations. The TILA requirements apply to the written materials the lender provides, not to any oral representations. If a lender provides the required TILA disclosures, a borrower who fails to read the relevant documents cannot claim fraud, even if the lender orally misrepresented the terms of the loan.

CASE EXAMPLE 20.5 Patricia Ostolaza and José Diaz owned a home on which they had two mortgage loans and a home equity line of credit provided by Bank of America. Anthony Falcone called them and said that he could refinance their mortgages in a manner that would reduce their monthly payments. Falcone said that he represented Bank of America when in fact he represented Countrywide Home Loans, Inc. At the closing of the new loan, the homeowners were given all of the relevant documents, including the TILA disclosure statement. The documents accurately stated the monthly payment under the new loan, which was higher than the couple's original payments. The homeowners later filed a lawsuit against Falcone and Countrywide Bank, alleging fraud. The trial court dismissed the suit, and the appellate court upheld the dismissal because the homeowners had been given the opportunity to read all of the relevant documents, but had not done so.[4] ●

Protection for High-Cost Mortgage Loan Recipients

In the last twenty years, lenders have provided many high-cost and high-fee mortgage products to people who could not easily obtain credit under other loan programs. These loans are commonly known as HOEPA loans, named after the Home Ownership and Equity Protection Act (HOEPA) of 1994,[5] which amended the TILA to create this special category of loans. The rules pertaining to HOEPA loans are contained in Section 32 of *Regulation Z,* enacted by the Federal Reserve Board to implement the TILA.

A loan can qualify for protection under HOEPA either because it carries a high rate of interest or because it entails high fees for the borrower. HOEPA applies if the APR disclosed for the loan exceeds the interest rates of **Treasury securities** (or bonds) of comparable maturity by more than 8 percentage points for a first mortgage and 10 percentage points for a second mortgage. HOEPA can also apply when the total fees paid by the consumer exceed 8 percent of the loan amount or a set dollar amount (based on changes in the Consumer Price Index), whichever is larger.

SPECIAL CONSUMER PROTECTIONS If a loan qualifies for HOEPA protection, the consumer must receive several disclosures in addition to those required by the TILA. The lender must disclose the APR, the regular payment amount, and any required balloon payments. For loans with a variable rate of interest, the lender must disclose that the rate and monthly payments may increase and state the potential maximum monthly payment. These disclosures must be provided at least three business days before the loan is finalized.

In addition, the lender must provide a written notice stating that the consumer need not complete the loan simply because he or she received the disclosures or signed the loan application. Borrowers must also be informed that they could lose their home (and all funds invested in it) if they default on the loan.

HOEPA also prohibits lenders from engaging in certain practices, such as requiring balloon payments for loans with terms of five years or less. Loans that result in negative amortization are also prohibited. **Negative amortization** occurs when the monthly payments are insufficient to cover the interest due on the loan. The difference is then added to the principal, so the balance owed on the loan increases over time.

REMEDIES AND LIABILITIES For HOEPA violations, consumers can obtain damages in an amount equal to all finance charges and fees paid if the lender's failure to disclose is deemed material. Any failure to comply with HOEPA provisions also extends the borrower's right to rescind the loan for up to three years.

Whether a particular loan is covered by HOEPA and thus is entitled to the statute's significant protections can have important ramifications because it can determine whether a borrower can recover on a lender's failure to comply with HOEPA's provisions and the amount of the recovery. In the following case, a consumer attempted to recover from a lender for alleged violations of the TILA and HOEPA.

4. *Ostolaza-Diaz v. Countrywide Bank, N.A.*, 2010 WL 95145 (4th Cir. 2010).
5. 15 U.S.C. Sections 1637 and 1647.

Case 20.1 In re Kitts

United States Bankruptcy Court, District of Utah, 447 Bankr. 330 (2011).

FACTS Facing the loss of his family's home in Park City, Utah, to creditors, Brian Kitts sought to refinance the debt. He entered into two mortgage loan agreements for $1.35 million and $39,603.47, respectively, with Winterfox, LLC. As part of the deal, Kitts paid $87,500 in "loan origination fees." Kitts defaulted on the loans and filed a petition in a federal bankruptcy court to declare bankruptcy. He also filed a complaint against Winterfox to recover damages for alleged violations of the federal Truth-in-Lending Act (TILA). The bankruptcy court dismissed the action, but on appeal, a federal district court ruled that Winterfox had failed to make certain required disclosures. The district court remanded the case for "further fact finding concerning damages" for violation of the TILA, as well as for Kitts's request for attorneys' fees.

ISSUE Was Kitts entitled to recover damages and attorneys' fees because Winterfox charged him $87,500 in finance charges in violation of HOEPA and TILA provisions?

DECISION Yes. The bankruptcy court concluded that HOEPA covered the Winterfox loans, which were high-cost mortgages on which the debtor had not been provided any disclosures. Kitts was awarded statutory TILA damages of $4,000, compensatory damages of $87,500 under HOEPA for the finance charges paid in connection with the loans, and $150,000 for attorneys' fees.

REASON The parties did not dispute that Winterfox had charged $87,500 in fees. The dispute was whether those fees qualified as "finance charges paid by the consumer" under TILA, even though the funds were paid from the loan proceeds rather than coming out of the debtor's pocket. The court reasoned that because Kitts was obligated to pay the fees, they qualified as finance charges paid by the debtor. Thus, Winterfox violated the TILA by failing to provide disclosures on these high-cost loans, and Kitts was entitled to the statutory damages under the TILA. The court further reasoned that Winterfox's failure to provide notice of the required disclosures (under TILA) constituted a material failure to comply with HOEPA. Under HOEPA, the plaintiff is entitled to compensatory damages, so the court awarded damages in the amount of the fees paid ($87,500), plus reasonable attorneys' fees ($150,000, which is 750 hours at $200 per hour).

FOR CRITICAL ANALYSIS—Legal Consideration *The TILA, HOEPA, and other consumer-protection laws exist to protect purchasers from "unscrupulous" lenders or sellers. As consumers become better informed about these issues, will these laws still be needed? Discuss.*

Protection for Higher-Priced Mortgage Loans

In 2008, the Federal Reserve Board enacted an amendment to Regulation Z that created a second category of expensive loans, called Higher-Priced Mortgage Loans (HPMLs). Only mortgages secured by a consumer's principal home qualify to receive the HPML designation.

REQUIREMENTS TO QUALIFY To be an HPML, a mortgage must have an APR that exceeds the *average prime offer rate* for a comparable transaction by 1.5 percentage points or more if the loan is a first lien on a dwelling. (The **average prime offer rate** is the rate offered to the best-qualified borrowers as established by a survey of lenders.) If the loan is secured by a subordinate lien on a home, then the APR must exceed the average prime offer rate by 3.5 percentage points or more in order to be considered an HPML.

Mortgages excluded from coverage include those for the initial construction of a home, temporary or *bridge loans* that are one year or shorter in duration, home equity lines of credit, and reverse mortgages. (**Bridge loans** are short-term loans that allow a buyer to make a down payment on a new home before selling her or his current home.)

SPECIAL PROTECTIONS FOR CONSUMERS As with a HOEPA loan, consumers receiving an HPML receive additional protections. First, lenders cannot make an HPML based on the value of the consumer's home without verifying the consumer's ability to repay the loan. This verification is typically accomplished through review of the consumer's financial records such as tax returns, bank account statements, and payroll records. The creditor must also verify the consumer's other credit obligations.

Second, prepayment penalties are severely restricted for HPMLs. Prepayment penalties are allowed only if they are limited to two years, and they will not even apply if the source of the prepayment funds is a refinancing by the creditor or the creditor's affiliate. Additionally, lenders must establish *escrow accounts* for borrowers' payments for homeowners' insurance and property taxes for all first mortgages. (An escrow account holds funds to be paid to a third party.) Finally, lenders cannot structure a loan specifically to evade the HPML protections.

Foreclosures

If a homeowner **defaults,** or fails to make mortgage payments, the lender has the right to foreclose on the mortgaged property. **Foreclosure** is a process that allows a lender to legally repossess and auction off the property that is securing a loan.[6]

Foreclosure is expensive and time consuming, however, and generally benefits neither the borrower, who loses his or her home, nor the lender, which faces the prospect of a loss on its loans. Therefore, various methods to avoid foreclosure have been developed. We look first at some of these methods and then turn to the foreclosure process itself.

How to Avoid Foreclosure

In the past, especially during the Great Depression of the 1930s, a number of alternatives to foreclosure were developed. More recently, as foreclosures have become more common than at any time since the Great Depression, Congress has intervened to aid in the modification of mortgage loans.

FORBEARANCE AND WORKOUT AGREEMENTS The first preforeclosure option a borrower has is called forbearance. **Forbearance** is the postponement, for a limited time, of part or all of the payments on a loan in jeopardy of foreclosure. Such payment waivers had their origins in the Great Depression. A lender grants forbearance when it expects that, during the forbearance period, the borrower can solve the problem by securing a new job, selling the property, or finding another acceptable solution.

When a borrower fails to make payments as required, the lender may attempt to negotiate a workout. As noted in Chapter 19, a *workout* is a voluntary process to cure the default in some fashion. The parties may even create a formal **workout agreement**—a written document that describes the rights and responsibilities of the parties as they try to resolve the default without proceeding to foreclosure. In such an agreement, the lender will likely agree to delay seeking foreclosure or other legal rights. In exchange, the borrower may agree to provide to the lender financial information on which a workout might be constructed.

Whether a workout is possible or preferable to foreclosure depends on many factors, including the value of the property, the amount of the unpaid principal, the market in which the property will be sold, the relationship of the lender and the borrower, and the financial condition of the borrower.

HOUSING AND URBAN DEVELOPMENT ASSISTANCE A lender may be able to work with the borrower to obtain an interest-free loan from the U.S. Department of Housing and Urban Development (HUD) to bring the mortgage current. HUD assistance may be available if the loan is at least four months (but not more than twelve months) delinquent, if the property is not in foreclosure, and if the borrower is able to make full mortgage payments. When the lender files a claim, HUD pays the lender the amount necessary to make the mortgage current. The borrower executes a note to HUD, and a lien for the second loan is placed on the property. The promissory note is interest free and comes due if the property is sold.

SHORT SALES When a borrower is unable to make mortgage payments, the lender may agree to a **short sale**—that is, a sale of the property for less than the balance due on the mortgage loan. The borrower must obtain the lender's permission for the short sale, and typically she or he has to show some hardship, such as the loss of a job, a decline in the value of the home, a divorce, or a death in the household. The lender receives the proceeds of the sale, and the borrower still owes the balance of the debt to the lender, unless the lender specifically agrees to forgive the remaining debt. In 2007, Congress passed the Mortgage Forgiveness Debt Relief Act,[7] which eliminated income taxes on the forgiven debt. (Ordinarily, forgiven debt must be reported as income that is subject to federal income tax.)

A short sale can offer several advantages. Although the borrower's credit rating is affected, the negative impact is less than it would be with a foreclosure, which generally remains on the borrower's credit report for seven years.[8] The short sale process also avoids the expense of foreclosure for the lender and the trauma of being evicted from the home for the homeowner. But because the lender often has approval rights in a short sale, the sale process can take much longer than a standard real estate transaction. In addition, although the parties' losses are mitigated, the borrower still loses her or his home.

SALE AND LEASEBACK In some situations, the homeowner may be able to sell the property to an investor who is looking for an income property. The owner sells the property to the investor and then leases it back at an amount that is less than the monthly mortgage payment. The owner-seller uses the proceeds of the sale to pay off the mortgage and still has the use and possession of the property. In some circumstances, this strategy can also be used to raise capital when there is no risk of loss of the property.

HOME AFFORDABLE MODIFICATION PROGRAM In 2009, the U.S. Treasury Department launched the Home Affordable

6. Lenders other than those holding a first mortgage on a property may also foreclose. For example, a roofing company holding a mechanic's lien for the unpaid cost of a new roof can foreclose on the property.

7. Pub. L. No. 110-142, December 7, 2007.

8. Credit reporting agencies also claim that a foreclosure looks much worse on a credit report than a bankruptcy.

Modification Program (HAMP) to encourage private lenders to modify mortgages so as to lower the monthly payments of borrowers who are in default. The program may share in the costs of modifying the loan and provides incentives to lenders based on successful loan modification. A series of steps must be taken to determine debtor eligibility, the appropriate method for reducing the mortgage burden, and the possibility of forbearance of part of the mortgage loan.

Determination If a Homeowner Qualifies. HAMP modifications are not available for every mortgage. To qualify, the loan must have originated on or before January 1, 2009, the home must be occupied by the owner, and the unpaid balance may not exceed $729,750 for a single-unit property.[9] The homeowner must be facing financial hardship and be either more than sixty days late on mortgage payments or at risk of imminent default. Homeowners are required to verify their hardship through appropriate documentation.

In addition, the home must be the homeowner's primary residence. Investor-owned homes, vacant homes, and condemned properties are not eligible under the program. Borrowers in active litigation related to their mortgage may take advantage of the program without waiving their legal rights.

Steps Taken to Alleviate the Mortgage Burden. The purpose of HAMP is not to force lenders to forgive all high-risk mortgages, but rather to reduce monthly mortgage payments to a level that the homeowner can reasonably pay. The goal is to reduce the debtor's mortgage payment to 31 percent of his or her gross monthly income.

The loan is then restructured by adding any delinquencies (such as accrued interest, past-due taxes, or unpaid insurance premiums) to the principal amount. This increases the number of payments but eliminates the delinquencies by spreading them over the life of the loan. Once the loan is restructured, lenders try to incrementally lower the mortgage interest rate to a level at which the payments are less than 31 percent of the debtor's income. If the lender cannot reach the 31 percent target by lowering the interest rate to 2 percent, then the lender can **reamortize** the loan (change the way the payments are configured), extending the schedule of payments for up to forty years.

Borrowers who qualify under HAMP then begin a ninety-day trial period to determine their ability to make three modified monthly mortgage payments. If they succeed, the lender offers them permanent modifications.

VOLUNTARY CONVEYANCE Under some circumstances, the parties might benefit from a **deed in lieu of foreclosure**, by which the property is conveyed (transferred) to the lender in satisfaction of the mortgage. A property that is worth close to the outstanding loan principal and on which no other loans have been taken might be the subject of such a conveyance.

Although the lender faces the risk that it may ultimately sell the property for less than the loan amount, the lender avoids the time, risk, and expense of foreclosure litigation. The borrower who gives the property to the lender without a fight also avoids the foreclosure process and may preserve a better credit rating than if he or she had been forced to give up the property involuntarily.

FRIENDLY FORECLOSURE Another way for the parties to avoid a contested foreclosure is to engage in a friendly foreclosure. In such a transaction, the borrower in default agrees to submit to the court's jurisdiction, to waive any defenses as well as the right to appeal, and to cooperate with the lender. This process takes longer than a voluntary conveyance, but all of the parties have greater certainty as to the finality of the transaction with respect to others who might have a financial interest in the property.

PREPACKAGED BANKRUPTCY Bankruptcy allows a borrower to escape payment of some debts (see Chapter 19). A prepackaged bankruptcy allows a debtor to negotiate terms with all of her or his creditors in advance. The package of agreements is then submitted to the bankruptcy court for approval. This approach to bankruptcy will likely save considerable time and expense for all parties involved, although the creditors are also likely to receive less than full payment on their particular debts.

The Foreclosure Procedure

If all efforts to find another solution fail, the lender will proceed to foreclosure—a process that dates back to English law. A formal foreclosure is necessary to extinguish the borrower's *equitable right of redemption* (discussed later). Generally, two types of foreclosure are used in the United States: **judicial foreclosure** and **power of sale foreclosure.** In a judicial foreclosure, which is available in all states, a court supervises the process. In a power of sale foreclosure, the lender is allowed to foreclose on and sell the property without judicial supervision.

Only a few states permit power of sale foreclosures because borrowers have less protection when a court does not supervise the process. In these states, lenders must strictly comply with the terms of the state statute governing power of sale foreclosures. The following case turned on whether two banks that had foreclosed on certain properties had the right to do so under the power of sale foreclosure law of Massachusetts.

9. Higher limits are allowed for properties with two to four units.

Case 20.2 U.S. Bank National Association v. Ibanez

Supreme Judicial Court of Massachusetts, 458 Mass. 637, 941 N.E.2d 40 (2011).

FACTS Mortgage, Inc., issued Antonio Ibanez a $103,500 home loan, and Option One Mortgage issued Mark and Tammy LaRace a $129,000 home loan. Each of the loans subsequently changed hands several times through various banks, as is common in the mortgage-lending industry. Both Ibanez and the LaRaces defaulted on their mortgages. U.S. Bank National Association foreclosed on the Ibanez mortgage, and Wells Fargo foreclosed on the LaRace mortgage. Both banks published notices of the foreclosure sales in a newspaper, as required by statute, and then bought the homes at the foreclosure auctions. Both banks purchased the properties for significantly less than the purported market value. At the time of the foreclosures, each bank represented that it was the "owner (assignee) and holder" of the mortgage. The banks filed separate lawsuits in a Massachusetts state court seeking a declaration that the banks now owned the properties. Neither bank, however, produced any signed documents showing that the mortgage had been properly assigned to it before the foreclosure sale. U.S. Bank received a written assignment of the mortgage more than a year after the foreclosure sale, and Wells Fargo received an assignment ten months after the sale. The court held that the banks, which were not the original mortgagees, had failed to show that they were holders of the mortgages at the time of the foreclosures. The banks appealed, and the cases were consolidated for appeal.

ISSUE Did U.S. Bank and Wells Fargo strictly comply with the statutory requirement that they prove they were entitled to exercise a power of sale foreclosure?

DECISION No. The Supreme Judicial Court of Massachusetts affirmed the lower court's ruling in favor of Ibanez and the LaRaces. U.S. Bank had failed to show that the Ibanez mortgage was among the mortgages assigned by the trust agreement. Wells Fargo had failed to demonstrate that it was the holder of the LaRace mortgage. Thus, the banks did not have the authority to foreclose, and the foreclosure sales were invalid.

REASON Although the state's power of sale statute provides a mortgage holder with substantial power to foreclose without immediate judicial oversight, the mortgage holder must strictly follow the statutory requirements. One of these requirements concerns who is entitled to foreclose. Only "the mortgagee or his [or her] executors, administrators, successors or assigns" can exercise the statutory power of sale. For the plaintiffs (the banks) to obtain the judicial declaration of clear title that they sought, they had to prove their compliance with this requirement. U.S. Bank argued that it was assigned the mortgage under a trust agreement that covered multiple mortgages, but it did not submit a copy of this agreement to the court.[a] The court reasoned that U.S. Bank therefore had failed to show that it had the authority to foreclose on the Ibanez mortgage. With regard to the LaRace mortgage, Wells Fargo did submit an assignment document (a mortgage loan schedule) to the court, but that document did not adequately specify the LaRace mortgage as one of the mortgages to be assigned. Moreover, Wells Fargo did not offer any evidence that the party purportedly assigning the mortgage in that document actually held it. Thus, both the foreclosure sales were invalid. The banks did not demonstrate that they were the holders of the Ibanez and LaRace mortgages at the time that they foreclosed these properties. Therefore, they also failed to demonstrate that they had acquired title to these properties by purchasing them at the foreclosure sale.

FOR CRITICAL ANALYSIS—Economic Consideration *After the court's ruling, the price of Wells Fargo's stock dropped by about 3.4 percent. Why would a court's decision regarding a few mortgages affect the company's stock price?*

a. In recent years, due to the large numbers of foreclosures, banks and mortgage companies have increasingly transferred some of their mortgages in default into mortgage-backed trusts, or pools.

ACCELERATION CLAUSES In a strict foreclosure, the lender may seek only the amount of the missed payments, not the entire loan amount. Therefore, lenders often include an *acceleration clause* in their loan documents. An **acceleration clause** allows the lender to call the entire loan due—even if only one payment is late or missed. Thus, with an acceleration clause, the lender can foreclose only once on the entire amount of the loan rather than having to foreclose on smaller amounts over a period of time as each payment is missed.

NOTICE OF DEFAULT AND OF SALE To initiate a foreclosure, a lender must record a **notice of default** with the appropriate county office. The borrower is then on notice of a possible foreclosure and can take steps to pay the loan and cure the default. If the loan is not paid within a reasonable time (usually three months), the borrower will receive a **notice of sale.** In addition, the notice of sale usually is posted on the property, recorded with the county, and published in a newspaper.

The property is then sold in an auction on the courthouse steps at the time and location indicated in the notice of sale. The buyer generally has to pay cash within twenty-four hours for the property. If the procedures are not followed precisely, the parties may have to resort to litigation to establish clear ownership of the property. The following case illustrates how the notice requirements work.

Case 20.3 Mitchell v. Valteau

Court of Appeal of Louisiana, Fourth Circuit, 30 So.3d 1108 (2010).
www.la4th.org/Opinions.aspx[a]

FACTS In 2001, Dr. Pamela Mitchell borrowed $143,724 to purchase a house and lot. The loan was secured by a mortgage on the property. The mortgage provided for the sale of the property in the event of a default. In 2006, Mitchell defaulted on her mortgage payments. The lending bank commenced a foreclosure proceeding, and the trial court ordered the issuance of a writ of seizure and sale. On January 23, 2007, Mitchell was served personally with a notice of seizure and the date of the sheriff's sale. Subsequently, the lending bank and Mitchell entered into a repayment agreement that postponed the seizure and sale. Mitchell made two payments and then was unable to comply with the payment terms of the new agreement. The trial court ordered that the original petition be amended and that an amended writ of seizure be issued, which the sheriff completed. The sheriff was unable to serve Mitchell at her residence on seven occasions, however. Therefore, the court appointed a receiver who accepted the service of process on Mitchell's behalf. On January 3, 2008, the property was sold at a sheriff's sale. Several months later, Mitchell filed a petition to annul the judicial sale and to ask for damages for wrongful seizure against the sheriff, Paul Valteau, as well as the lending bank and others. The bank filed a motion for summary judgment, which the trial court granted. Mitchell appealed.

a. From the search mode choices, select "Search Cases by Published Date." When that page opens, select "Click for Calendar." Using the arrow at the top of the calendar, go to January 2010, select "27," and then click on "Search." Scroll through the list at the bottom of the page to the case title and click on "Download" to access the opinion. The Louisiana court system maintains this Web site.

ISSUE Is a debtor who received the notice of seizure and sale in a foreclosure proceeding, and then entered into a repayment agreement with the lender, entitled to receive a second notice of sale if she defaults again?

DECISION No. The state appellate court affirmed the lower court's decision in favor of the bank. Mitchell was not entitled to another notice of seizure and sale under Louisiana law.

REASON Mitchell claimed that even though she had been served with the initial notice of seizure, the sheriff should have served her with the amended notice of seizure. After examining Louisiana law and other cases, the reviewing court concluded that there was "no Louisiana authority for requiring a creditor to provide a debtor with notice of a rescheduled judicial sale." Further, it was clear from the repayment agreement that the seizure and sale proceedings would be placed on hold only during the time the repayment agreement was in place. "The agreement also provided for the resumption of the foreclosure in the event of a default in its terms, which Dr. Mitchell acknowledged occurred. There was no obligation to serve Dr. Mitchell with another notice of seizure."

FOR CRITICAL ANALYSIS—Ethical Consideration *What is the underlying purpose for requiring lenders to serve a written notice of seizure of property? Was the court's holding fair to Mitchell? Why or why not?*

Deficiency Judgments If any equity remains after the foreclosed property is sold, the borrower is often able to keep the difference between the sale price and the mortgage amount. If the sale amount is not enough to cover the loan amount, the lender (in the majority of states) can ask a court for a **deficiency judgment.** (A judgment against the borrower for the amount of debt remaining unpaid after the collateral is sold). A deficiency judgment requires the borrower to make up the difference to the lender over time. Note that some states do not allow deficiency judgments for mortgaged residential real estate.

Redemption Rights

Borrowers in every state have the right to purchase the property after default by paying the full amount of the debt, plus any interest and costs that have accrued, before the foreclosure sale. This is referred to as the buyer's **equitable right of redemption.** Equitable redemption allows a defaulting borrower to gain title and regain possession of a property.[10] The idea behind equitable redemption is that it is only fair, or equitable, for the borrower to have a chance to regain possession after default. Although many critics question the utility of this right, all states still allow for an equitable right of redemption.

Some states have passed laws that entitle a borrower to repurchase property even *after* a judicial foreclosure.[11] This is called a **statutory right of redemption,** and it may be exercised even if the property was purchased at auction by a third party. Generally, the borrower may exercise this right for up to one year from the time the house is sold at a foreclosure sale.[12]

10. Note that a foreclosure proceeding is the legal means by which a lender terminates the borrower's equitable right of redemption.
11. This right of redemption is not available after a power of sale foreclosure.
12. Some states do not allow a borrower to waive the statutory right of redemption. This means that a buyer at auction must wait one year to obtain title to, and possession of, a foreclosed property.

The borrower[13] must pay the price at which the house was sold at the foreclosure sale (the redemption price), plus taxes, interest, and assessments, as opposed to the balance owed on the foreclosed loan.

13. Some states also allow the spouse of a defaulting borrower or creditors holding liens on the property to purchase the property under the statutory right of redemption.

Some states allow the borrower to retain possession of the property after the foreclosure sale until the statutory redemption period ends. If the borrower does not exercise the right of redemption, the new buyer receives title to and possession of the property. The statutes creating this right were enacted to drive up sale prices at foreclosure auctions on the theory that third parties would offer prices too high for defaulting borrowers to afford. Instead, in many states, the statutory right of redemption has created a strong disincentive for potential buyers to tie up their funds in an uncertain transaction.

Reviewing . . . Mortgages and Foreclosures after the Recession

Al and Betty Smith's home is valued at $200,000. They have paid off their mortgage and own the house outright—that is, they have 100 percent home equity. They lost most of their savings when the stock market declined during the Great Recession. Now they want to start a new business and need funds, so they decide to obtain a home equity loan. They borrow $150,000 for ten years at an interest rate of 12 percent. On the date they take out the loan, a ten-year Treasury bond is yielding 3 percent. The Smiths pay a total of $10,000 in fees to Alpha Bank. The Smiths are not given any notice that they can lose their home if they do not meet their obligations under the loan. Two weeks after completing the loan, the Smiths change their minds and want to rescind the loan.

1 Is the Smiths' loan covered by the Truth-in-Lending Act as amended by the Home Ownership and Equity Protection Act? Why or why not?
2 Do the Smiths have a right to rescind the loan two weeks after the fact, or are they too late? Explain.
3 Assume now that Alpha Bank gave the Smiths all of the required notices before the loan was completed. If all other facts remain the same, do the Smiths have a right to rescind? Discuss your answer.
4 Suppose now that the Smiths never rescind the loan and that they default four years later while still owing Alpha Bank $120,000. The bank forecloses and raises only $110,000 when the house is sold at auction. If the state where the Smiths live follows the rule in most states, can Alpha Bank seek the remaining $10,000 from the Smiths?

Terms and Concepts

acceleration clause 386
adjustable-rate mortgage (ARM) 379
annual percentage rate (APR) 381
appraiser 381
average prime offer rate 383
balloon mortgage 380
bridge loan 383
construction loan 380
deed in lieu of foreclosure 385
default 384
deficiency judgment 387
down payment 379
equitable right of redemption 387
fixed-rate mortgage 379
forbearance 384
foreclosure 384
home equity loan 380
homeowners' insurance 381
hybrid mortgage 380
interest-only (IO) mortgage 379
judicial foreclosure 385
mortgage 379
negative amortization 382
notice of default 386
notice of sale 386
power of sale foreclosure 385
prepayment penalty clause 380
reamortize 385
reverse mortgage 380
short sale 384
statutory right of redemption 387
subprime mortgage 379
Treasury securities 382
workout agreement 384

Chapter Summary: Mortgages and Foreclosures after the Recession

Mortgages (See pages 379–381.)	1. *Types of mortgages*—A mortgage loan is a contract between a creditor (mortgagee) and a borrower (mortgagor). A down payment is the part of the purchase price that is paid up front. There are many types of mortgages, including: a. Fixed-rate mortgages, which are standard mortgages with a fixed rate of interest and payments that stay the same for the duration of the loan. b. Adjustable-rate mortgages (ARMs), in which the interest rate changes periodically, usually starting low and increasing over time. c. Interest-only mortgages, which allow borrowers to pay only the interest portion of the monthly payments for a limited time, after which the size of the payment increases. d. Subprime mortgages, which carry higher rates of interest because they are made to borrowers who do not qualify for standard mortgages. e. Construction loans, which finance the building of a new house and are often set up to release funds at particular stages of the project. 2. *Creditor protection*—When creditors grant mortgages, they take a number of steps to protect their interests. They may require private mortgage insurance if borrowers do not make a down payment of at least 20 percent of the home's purchase price. A creditor also usually records the mortgage with the county in which the property is located to notify all others of its interest in the property. Several provisions typically included in the mortgage contract also protect the lender's interests. These include prepayment penalty clauses and clauses requiring the borrower to maintain homeowners' insurance.
Real Estate Financing Law (See pages 381–383.)	1. *Predatory lending*—This term describes situations in which borrowers are the victims of loan terms or lending procedures that are excessive, deceptive, or not properly disclosed. a. Steering and targeting occurs when a lender manipulates a borrower into a loan that benefits the lender but is not the best loan for the borrower. b. Loan flipping occurs when a lender convinces a borrower to refinance soon after a mortgage term begins. 2. *Truth-in-Lending Act (TILA)*—This federal statute requires mortgage lenders to disclose the terms of a loan in clear, readily understandable language on standardized forms. a. Terms that must be disclosed include the loan principal, the interest rate at which the loan is made, the annual percentage rate, and all fees and costs. b. The TILA prohibits certain unfair lender practices, such as charging prepayment penalties on most subprime mortgages and home equity loans and coercing an appraiser into misstating the value of property. c. A borrower has the right to rescind a mortgage within three business days. If a lender does not provide the required disclosures, the rescission period runs for three years. 3. *High-cost mortgages*—The Home Ownership and Equity Protection Act (HOEPA) of 1994 created a special category of high-cost and high-fee mortgage products. Rules for the loans are in Regulation Z. a. HOEPA rules apply to loans that carry a high rate of interest or entail high fees. b. In addition to the TILA disclosures, HOEPA requires lenders to make several other disclosures. These include the APR; the regular payment amount; any balloon payments; that the home may be lost if the borrower defaults; that the rate and payment amounts of variable-rate loans may increase; and what the maximum increase could be. HOEPA also prohibits short-term loans requiring balloon payments and loans that result in negative amortization. c. On a lender's material failure to disclose, a consumer may receive damages equal to all finance charges and fees paid. If a lender fails to comply with HOEPA, the borrower's right to rescind is extended to three years. 4. *Higher-priced mortgages*—A 2008 amendment to Regulation Z gave protection to consumers of a second category of expensive loans called Higher-Priced Mortgage Loans (HPMLs). To qualify as an HPML, a mortgage must have an APR that exceeds the average prime offer rate by a certain amount for a comparable transaction.
Foreclosures (See pages 384–388.)	If a borrower defaults, or fails to pay a loan, the lender can foreclose on the mortgaged property. The foreclosure process allows a lender to repossess and auction the property. A foreclosure can be expensive and remains on a borrower's credit report for seven years. 1. *Ways to avoid foreclosure proceedings*— a. A forbearance and workout agreement.

Continued

Chapter Summary: Mortgages and Foreclosures after the Recession—Continued

Foreclosures—Continued	b. An interest-free loan from the U.S. Department of Housing and Urban Development. c. A short sale. d. A sale to an investor and leaseback to the former owner. e. A modification of monthly payments under the Home Affordable Modification Program. f. A deed in lieu of foreclosure. g. A friendly foreclosure. h. A prepackaged bankruptcy. 2. *Foreclosure procedures*— a. In a judicial foreclosure, which is available in all states, a court supervises the process. b. In a power of sale foreclosure, which is permitted in only a few states, the lender can foreclose on and sell the property without judicial supervision. c. An acceleration clause allows a lender to call an entire loan due, even if only one payment is late or missed. d. To initiate a foreclosure, a lender records a notice of default with the county. If the amount due on the loan is not paid, the borrower receives a notice of sale, which also usually appears in a newspaper and is posted on the property. e. If the sale proceeds do not cover the amount of the loan, the lender can ask a court for a deficiency judgment. Some states do not permit deficiency judgments for mortgaged residential property. 3. *Redemption rights*— a. Equitable right of redemption—In all of the states, borrowers have the right to purchase the property after default by paying the full amount of the debt, plus any interest and costs that have accrued, before the foreclosure sale. b. Statutory right of redemption—Some states allow borrowers to repurchase property even *after* a judicial foreclosure.

ExamPrep

ISSUE SPOTTERS

—Check your answers to these questions against the answers provided in Appendix G.

1 Ruth Ann borrows $175,000 from Sunny Valley Bank to buy a home. Federal law regulates primarily the terms of the mortgage that must be disclosed in writing in clear, readily understandable language. What are the major terms that must be disclosed under the Truth-in-Lending Act?

2 Tanner borrows $150,000 from Southeast Credit Union to buy a home, which secures the loan. Two years into the term, Tanner stops making payments on the loan. After six months without payments, Southeast informs Tanner that he is in default and that it will proceed to foreclosure. What is foreclosure, and what is the usual procedure?

BEFORE THE TEST

Go to **www.cengagebrain.com**, enter the ISBN 9781111530624, and click on "Find" to locate this textbook's Web site. Then, click on "Access Now" under "Study Tools," and select Chapter 20 at the top. There, you will find an Interactive Quiz that you can take to assess your mastery of the concepts in this chapter, as well as Flashcards and a Glossary of important terms.

For Review

1 What is a subprime mortgage? How does it differ from a standard fixed-rate mortgage?

2 When is private mortgage insurance required? Which party does it protect?

3 Does the Truth-in-Lending Act (TILA) apply to all mortgages? How do the TILA provisions protect borrowers and curb abusive practices by mortgage lenders?

4 What is a short sale?

5 In a mortgage foreclosure, what legal rights do mortgage holders have if the sale proceeds are insufficient to pay the underlying debt?

Questions and Case Problems

20–1 Disclosure Requirements. Rancho Mortgage, Inc., is planning a new advertising campaign designed to attract homebuyers in a difficult economic environment. Rancho wants to promote its new loan product, which offers a fixed interest rate for the first five years and then switches to a variable rate of interest. Rancho believes that Spanish-speaking homebuyers have been underserved in recent years, and it wants to direct its ads to that market. What must Rancho say (and not say) in its advertising campaigns about the structure of the loan product, and in what language? What language should Rancho use in its Truth-in-Lending disclosures? Why?

20–2 Real Estate Financing. Jane Lane refinanced her mortgage with Central Equity, Inc. Central Equity split the transaction into two separate loan documents with separate Truth-in-Lending disclosure statements and settlement statements. Two years later, Lane sought to exercise her right to rescission under the Home Ownership and Equity Protection Act (HOEPA), but Central Equity refused. Central Equity responded that the original transactions comprised two separate loan transactions and because neither loan imposed sufficient fees and costs to trigger HOEPA, its protections did not apply. Lane claims that if the costs and fees were combined into a single transaction (which Lane expected the loan to be), they would surpass the HOEPA threshold and trigger its protections. In turn, because Central Equity did not provide the necessary disclosures under HOEPA, Lane argues that she can properly rescind under its provisions. Is Lane correct? Does loan splitting allow the lender to count each loan transaction with a borrower separately for HOEPA purposes? Why or why not?

20–3 Lender's Options. In 2008, Frank relocated and purchased a home in a beautiful mountain town. The home was five years old, and Frank purchased it for $450,000. He paid $90,000 as a down payment and financed the remaining $360,000 of the purchase price with a loan from Bank of Town. Frank signed mortgage documents that gave Bank of Town a mortgage interest in the home. Frank made payments on the loan for three years. But the housing market declined significantly, and Frank's home is now valued at only $265,000. The balance due on his loan is $354,000. In addition to the decline in housing prices, the economy has slowed, and the booming business that Frank started when he bought the home has experienced a decrease in revenues. It seems inevitable that Frank will not be able to make his mortgage payments. Discuss Bank of Town's options in this situation.

20–4 Home Ownership and Equity Protection Act. Michael and Edith Jones owned a home that went into foreclosure. During this time, they were contacted by a representative of Rees-Max, whose notice read: "There are only a few months to go in your redemption period! Your options to save the equity in your home are fading. Call me immediately for a no-bull, no-obligation assessment of your situation. Even if you have been 'promised' by a mortgage broker or investor that they will help, CALL ME . . . ." The Joneses contacted Rees-Max, and they entered into a sale and leaseback transaction. Rees-Max would purchase the property from the Joneses, the Joneses would lease the property for a few months, and then the Joneses would purchase the property back from Rees-Max on a contract. The property was appraised at $278,000 and purchased by Rees-Max for $214,000, with more than $30,000 in fees. The Joneses disputed these fees, and Rees-Max moved to evict them. The agreement did not use the terms *debt, security,* or *mortgage,* and the documents stated that no security interest was granted. Does this transaction constitute a mortgage that would receive protection under the Truth-in-Lending Act and the Home Ownership and Equity Protection Act? Why or why not? [*Jones v. Rees-Max, LLC,* 514 F.Supp.2d 1139 (D.Minn. 2007)]

20–5 Right of Rescission. George and Mona Antanuos obtained a mortgage loan secured with rental property from the First National Bank of Arizona. At the closing, they received from the bank a "Notice of Right to Cancel," informing them of their three-day rescission period under the Truth-in-Lending Act (TILA). The following day, according to the Antanuoses, they informed the lender via fax that they wished to exercise their right to rescind. The lender refused to rescind the agreement. George and Mona sued the bank. In federal court, the Antanuoses did not dispute that a consumer's right to rescind under the TILA applies only to the consumer's original dwelling and that they had used their commercial property as a security interest. Instead, the Antanuoses argued that the bank was prohibited from denying them the rescission right because they relied to their detriment on the bank's disclosure, which would have been required under the TILA. Would the court be convinced? Explain. [*Antanuos v. First National Bank of Arizona,* 508 F.Supp.2d 466 (E.D.Va. 2007)]

20–6 Mortgage Foreclosure. In January 2003, Gary Ryder and Washington Mutual Bank, F.A., executed a note in which Ryder promised to pay $2,450,000, plus interest at a rate that could vary from month to month. The amount of the first payment was $10,933. The note was to be paid in full by February 1, 2033. A mortgage on Ryder's real property at 345 Round Hill Road in Greenwich, Connecticut, in favor of the bank secured his obligations under the note. The note and mortgage required that he pay the taxes on the property, which he did not do in 2004 and 2005. The bank notified him that he was in default and, when he failed to act, paid $50,095.92 in taxes, penalties, interest, and fees. Other disputes arose between the parties, and Ryder filed a suit in a federal district court against the bank, alleging, in part, breach of contract. He charged, among other things, that some of his timely payments were not processed and were subjected to incorrect late fees, forcing him to make excessive payments and ultimately resulting in "non-payment by Ryder." The bank filed a counterclaim, seeking to foreclose on the mortgage. What should a creditor be required to prove to foreclose on mortgaged property? What would be a debtor's most effective defense? Which party in this case is likely to prevail on the bank's counterclaim? Why? [*Ryder v. Washington Mutual Bank, F.A.*, 501 F.Supp.2d 311 (D.Conn. 2007)]

20–7 **Case Problem with Sample Answer** After the debtors experienced a series of bankruptcies and foreclosures, Wells Fargo Home Mortgage, the mortgagee, foreclosed on the debtors' home and purchased it for $33,500. The debtors then filed a complaint against Wells Fargo and certain related entities, claiming wrongful foreclosure and breach of contract. The debtors sought damages, specific performance, and other remedies. The dispute grew out of a loan note for $51,300 that the debtors had executed with Southern Atlantic Financial Services, Inc. In exchange for that loan, the debtors gave Southern Atlantic a security interest in their home. Southern Atlantic transferred its interest in the property and the note to GE Capital Mortgage Services, Inc. On September 30, 2000, Wells Fargo Home Mortgage started servicing this loan for GE. Wells Fargo acquired the loan from GE on December 1, 2004. When the debtors did not make all of the required payments, Wells Fargo sought relief from a stay to file a foreclosure because the debtors were in arrears on the mortgage. The parties agreed that Wells Fargo could have relief from the stay if the debtors failed to make all future payments. Claiming default, Wells Fargo then filed a foreclosure and bought the property at the sale. The debtors filed a complaint alleging that the price paid was shockingly insufficient and constituted wrongful foreclosure and a breach of fiduciary duty. Under what circumstances is a foreclosure sale unfair? Does a foreclosure sale have to realize the market price for the property? The amount owed on the note? Discuss. [*In re Sharpe*, 425 Bankr. 620 (N.D.Ala. 2010)]

—To view a sample answer for Problem 20–7, go to Appendix F at the end of this text.

20–8 **Foreclosure on Mortgage and Liens.** LaSalle Bank loaned $8 million to Cypress Creek to build an apartment complex. The loan was secured by a mortgage. Cypress Creek hired contractors to provide concrete work, plumbing, carpentry, and other construction services. Cypress Creek went bankrupt, owing LaSalle $3 million. The contractors recorded *mechanic's liens* (see page 355 in Chapter 19) when they did not get paid for their work. The property was sold to LaSalle at a sheriff's sale for $1.3 million. The contractors claimed that they should be paid the amounts they were owed out of the $1.3 million and that the mechanic's liens should be satisfied before any funds were distributed to LaSalle for its mortgage. The trial court distributed the $1.3 million primarily to LaSalle, with only a small fraction going to the contractors. Do the liens come before the mortgage in priority of payment? Discuss. [*LaSalle Bank National Association v. Cypress Creek, 1, LP*, 242 Ill.2d 231, 950 N.E.2d 1109 2011)]

20–9 **A Question of Ethics** *Peter Sutton owned a home that was subject to two mortgages, but his only source of income was a $1,080 monthly Social Security benefit. In an effort to reduce his mortgage payments, which exceeded $1,400 per month, he sought a refinancing loan through an Apex Mortgage Services mortgage broker. According to Sutton, the broker led him to believe that he could receive, from Countrywide Home Loans, Inc., a refinancing loan with payments of $428 per month. The broker, however, ultimately arranged for Sutton to receive an adjustable-rate loan from Countrywide. The loan required monthly payments that started at more than $1,000 per month and were subject to further increases. Sutton also alleged that the broker reported his monthly income as four times the actual amount and failed to inform Sutton about the existence of a prepayment penalty. Sutton signed forms stating that he agreed to the terms of the loan arranged by the broker. He claimed, however, that he did not understand the terms of the loan until after the closing. As compensation for brokering Sutton's loan, Countrywide paid Apex $7,270, which included a yield-spread premium of $4,710. (A yield-spread premium is a form of compensation paid to a broker by a lender for providing a borrower with a loan that carries an interest rate above the lender's par rate.) Sutton sued the broker and lender claiming violations of federal law.* [Sutton v. Countrywide Home Loans, Inc., ___ *F.3d* ___ *(11th Cir. 2009)]*

1 Who is ethically responsible for Sutton's predicament? To what extent does Sutton have a duty to read and understand what he signs? Discuss.
2 Sutton argued that because the broker provided services that were of no value to Sutton, the broker should not receive the yield-spread premium. Do you agree? Why or why not?
3 Did Countrywide, the lender, have any ethical obligation to monitor the activities of the broker? Would the result have been different if Countrywide had intervened before the documents were signed? Explain.

Unit Six

Unit Case Study with Dissenting Opinion: *Central Virginia Community College v. Katz*

We discussed bankruptcy law in Chapter 19. The Constitution, in Article I, grants Congress the authority to enact "uniform Laws on the subject of Bankruptcies throughout the United States."

Under this clause, in the Bankruptcy Code, Congress has empowered a bankruptcy trustee to recover from a creditor a debtor's preferential transfer—a transfer of property or a payment made within ninety days of the filing of a bankruptcy petition.

The question before the United States Supreme Court in Central Virginia Community College v. Katz,[1] *the case that we examine in this* Unit Case Study with Dissenting Opinion *is whether a state can refuse, on an assertion of sovereign immunity, to comply with a federal bankruptcy court's order to return a debtor's preferential transfer.*

1. 546 U.S. 356, 126 S.Ct. 990, 163 L.Ed.2d 945 (2006).

CASE BACKGROUND

Wallace's Book Stores, Inc. (WBI), Wallace's Book Company (WBC), and their subsidiaries were at one time among the nation's largest suppliers of new and used textbooks and college bookstore supplies throughout North America. They provided textbook buy-back and wholesale textbook distribution services, as well as textbooks, trade books, miscellaneous course books, materials, and other goods, to colleges and universities on an open account basis.

In 2001, WBI, WBC, and sixty-seven of WBI's subsidiaries filed a petition in a federal bankruptcy court under Chapter 11 of the Bankruptcy Code. Under their "Plan of Liquidation," Bernard Katz was appointed "Liquidating Supervisor," or trustee, and was vested with a variety of responsibilities that included a duty to avoid preferential transfers.

During the ninety-day period immediately preceding the date of the petition, Central Virginia Community College and other Virginia state institutions of higher learning had received transfers that Katz sought to recover. The institutions filed a motion to dismiss this request on the basis of their sovereign immunity. The court denied the motion. On appeal, a federal district court affirmed this decision, as did the U.S. Court of Appeals for the Sixth Circuit. The institutions appealed to the United States Supreme Court.

MAJORITY OPINION

Justice *STEVENS* delivered the opinion of the Court.

* * * *

* * * [In bankruptcy proceedings, the] term "discharge" historically had a dual meaning; it referred to both release of debts and release of the debtor from prison.

Well into the 18th century, imprisonment for debt was still ubiquitous [widespread] in * * * the American Colonies. Bankruptcy and insolvency laws remained as much concerned with ensuring full satisfaction of creditors (and, relatedly, preventing debtors' flight to parts unknown) as with securing new beginnings for debtors.

Common as imprisonment itself was, the American Colonies, and later the several States, had wildly divergent schemes for discharging debtors and their debts. At least four jurisdictions offered relief through private Acts of their legislatures. Those Acts released debtors from prison upon surrender of their property, and many coupled the release from prison with a discharge of debts. Other jurisdictions enacted general laws providing for release from prison and, in a few places, discharge of debt. Others still granted release from prison, but only in exchange for indentured servitude. Some jurisdictions provided no relief at all for the debtor. [And a debtor might be discharged in one state only to be imprisoned in another.]

* * * *

* * * The absence of extensive debate [during the Constitutional Convention] over the text of the Bankruptcy Clause * * * indicates that there was general agreement on the importance of authorizing a uniform federal response * * *.

* * * *

The text of Article I, Section 8, [clause] 4, of the Constitution * * * provides that Congress shall have the power to establish "uniform Laws on the subject of Bankruptcies throughout the United States." Although the interest in avoiding unjust imprisonment for debt and making federal discharges in bankruptcy enforceable in every State was a primary motivation for the adoption of that provision, its coverage encompasses the entire "subject of Bankruptcies."

* * * *

Continued

* * * *Those who crafted the Bankruptcy Clause would have understood it to give Congress the power to authorize courts to avoid preferential transfers and to recover the transferred property.* Petitioners do not dispute that that authority has been a core aspect of the administration of bankrupt estates since at least the 18th century. [Emphasis added.]

* * * *

Insofar as orders * * * [of] the bankruptcy courts * * * implicate States' sovereign immunity from suit, the States agreed in the plan of the [Constitutional] Convention not to assert that immunity. So much is evidenced not only by the history of the Bankruptcy Clause, * * * but also by legislation considered and enacted in the immediate wake of the Constitution's ratification.

* * * *

* * * [The Bankruptcy Act of 1800] specifically granted federal courts the authority to issue writs of *habeas corpus* effective to release debtors from state prisons.

This grant of *habeas* power is remarkable not least because it would be another 67 years, after ratification of the Fourteenth Amendment, before the writ would be made generally available to state prisoners. * * * Yet there appears to be no record of any objection to the bankruptcy legislation or its grant of *habeas* power to federal courts based on an infringement of sovereign immunity.

* * * *The Framers, in adopting the Bankruptcy Clause, plainly intended to give Congress the power to redress the rampant injustice resulting from States' refusal to respect one another's discharge orders.* As demonstrated by * * * Congress' enactment of a provision granting federal courts the authority to release debtors from state prisons, the power to enact bankruptcy legislation was understood to carry with it the power to subordinate state sovereignty * * *. [Emphasis added.]

* * * *

The judgment of the Court of Appeals for the Sixth Circuit is affirmed.

DISSENTING OPINION

Justice *THOMAS*, * * * dissenting.

* * * *

The majority maintains that the States' consent to suit can be ascertained from the history of the Bankruptcy Clause. But history confirms that the adoption of the Constitution merely established federal power to legislate in the area of bankruptcy law, and did not manifest an additional intention to waive the States' sovereign immunity against suit. Accordingly, I respectfully dissent.

* * * *

* * * It is inherent in the nature of sovereignty not to be amenable to the suit of an individual without [the sovereign's] consent. This * * * exemption * * * is * * * enjoyed by the government of every State in the Union.

* * * *

The majority finds a surrender of the States' immunity from suit in Article I of the Constitution, which authorizes Congress "to establish * * * uniform Laws on the subject of Bankruptcies throughout the United States." But nothing in the text of the Bankruptcy Clause suggests an abrogation or limitation of the States' sovereign immunity.

It is difficult to discern an intention to abrogate state sovereign immunity through the Bankruptcy Clause when no such intention has been found in any of the other clauses in Article I.

* * * *

For example, Article I also empowers Congress * * * to protect * * * patents. [This provision], no less than the Bankruptcy Clause, [was] motivated by the Framers' desire for nationally uniform legislation. * * * Nonetheless, we have refused, in addressing patent law, to give the need for uniformity the weight the majority today assigns it in the context of bankruptcy, instead recognizing that this need is a factor which belongs to the Article I patent-power calculus, rather than to any determination of whether a state plea of sovereign immunity deprives a patentee of property without due process of law.

QUESTIONS FOR ANALYSIS

1. **Law.** What did the majority conclude in this case? What was the majority's reasoning in support of this conclusion?
2. **Law.** What was the dissent's argument? On what points did the dissent base its contention?
3. **Ethics.** From an ethical perspective, why should a trustee be allowed to recover a debtor's transfer of property or a payment of money to a creditor over the creditor's objection? What might be an ethical basis for permitting the creditor to keep the property or the money transferred?
4. **Economic Dimensions.** How might the result in this case affect a state's decision to grant or deny credit to potential debtors?
5. **Implications for the Business Owner.** How might the holding in this case influence the decision of an individual or a business firm to conduct business with a state?

Unit Seven

Employment Relations

Unit Contents

21 Agency Relationships

22 Employment, Immigration, and Labor Law

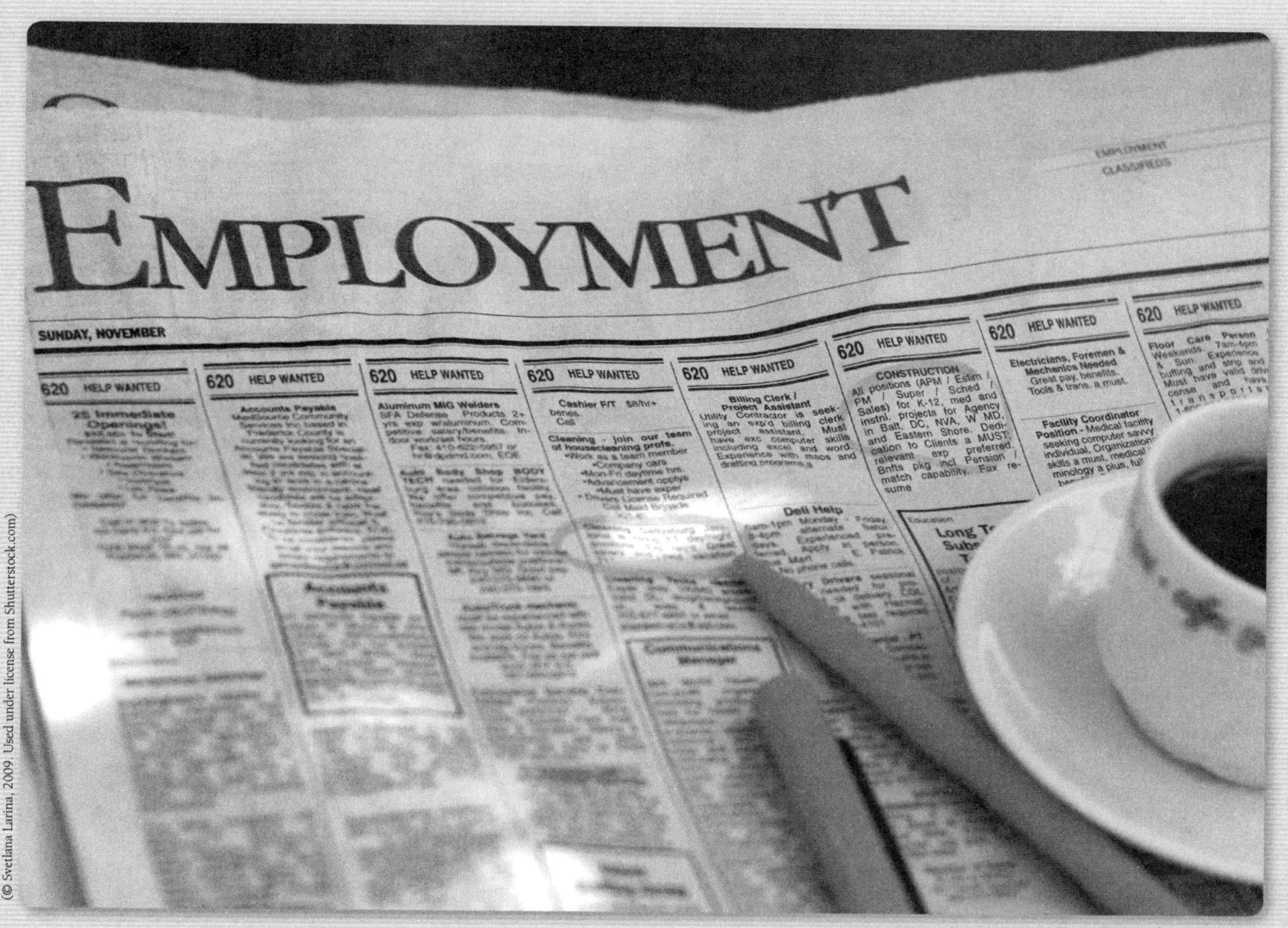

Chapter 21

Agency Relationships

Learning Objectives

After reading this chapter, you should be able to answer the following questions:

1. What is the difference between an employee and an independent contractor?
2. How do agency relationships arise?
3. What duties do agents and principals owe to each other?
4. When is a principal liable for the agent's actions with respect to third parties? When is the agent liable?
5. What are some of the ways in which an agency relationship can be terminated?

The Learning Objectives above are designed to help improve your understanding of the chapter.

One of the most common, important, and pervasive legal relationships is that of **agency.** In an agency relationship between two parties, one of the parties, called the *agent,* agrees to represent or act for the other, called the *principal.* The principal has the right to control the agent's conduct in matters entrusted to the agent, and the agent must exercise his or her powers "for the benefit of the principal only." By using agents, a principal can conduct multiple business operations simultaneously in various locations. Thus, for example, contracts that bind the principal can be made at different places with different persons at the same time.

Agency relationships permeate the business world. Indeed, agency law is essential to the existence and operation of a corporate entity, because only through its agents can a corporation function and enter into contracts. A familiar example of an agent is a corporate officer who serves in a representative capacity for the owners of the corporation. In this capacity, the officer has the authority to bind the principal (the corporation) to a contract.

Agency Relationships

Section 1(1) of the *Restatement (Third) of Agency*[1] defines agency as "the fiduciary relation which results from the manifestation of consent by one person to another that the other shall act in his [or her] behalf and subject to his [or her] control, and consent by the other so to act." In other words, in a principal-agent relationship, the parties have agreed that the agent will act *on behalf and instead of* the principal in negotiating and transacting business with third parties.

The term **fiduciary** is at the heart of agency law. The term can be used both as a noun and as an adjective. When used as a noun, it refers to a person having a duty created by her or his undertaking to act primarily for another's benefit in matters connected with the undertaking. When used as

1. The *Restatement (Third) of Agency* is an authoritative summary of the law of agency and is often referred to by judges and other legal professionals.

an adjective, as in "fiduciary relationship," it means that the relationship involves trust and confidence.

Agency relationships commonly exist between employers and employees. Agency relationships may sometimes also exist between employers and independent contractors who are hired to perform special tasks or services.

Employer-Employee Relationships

Normally, all employees who deal with third parties are deemed to be agents. A salesperson in a department store, for instance, is an agent of the store's owner (the principal) and acts on the owner's behalf. Any sale of goods made by the salesperson to a customer is binding on the principal. Similarly, most representations of fact made by the salesperson with respect to the goods sold are binding on the principal.

Because employees who deal with third parties are generally deemed to be agents of their employers, agency law and employment law overlap considerably. Agency relationships, though, as will become apparent, can exist outside an employer-employee relationship and thus have a broader reach than employment laws do. Additionally, bear in mind that agency law is based on the common law. In the employment realm, many common law doctrines have been displaced by statutory law and government regulations relating to employment relationships.

Employment laws (state and federal) apply only to the employer-employee relationship. Statutes governing Social Security, withholding taxes, workers' compensation, unemployment compensation, workplace safety, employment discrimination, and the like (see Chapter 22) are applicable only if employer-employee status exists. *These laws do not apply to an independent contractor.*

Employer–Independent Contractor Relationships

Independent contractors are not employees because, by definition, those who hire them have no control over the details of their physical performance. Section 2 of the *Restatement (Third) of Agency* defines an **independent contractor** as follows:

> [An independent contractor is] a person who contracts with another to do something for him [or her] but who is not controlled by the other nor subject to the other's right to control with respect to his [or her] physical conduct in the performance of the undertaking. *He [or she] may or may not be an agent.* [Emphasis added.]

Building contractors and subcontractors are independent contractors; a property owner does not control the acts of either of these professionals. Truck drivers who own their equipment and hire themselves out on a per-job basis are independent contractors, but truck drivers who drive company trucks on a regular basis are usually employees.

The relationship between a person or firm and an independent contractor may or may not involve an agency relationship. To illustrate: An owner of real estate who hires a real estate broker to negotiate a sale of his or her property not only has contracted with an independent contractor (the real estate broker) but also has established an agency relationship for the specific purpose of assisting in the sale of the property. Another example is an insurance agent, who is both an independent contractor and an agent of the insurance company for which she or he sells policies. (Note that an insurance *broker,* in contrast, normally is an agent of the person obtaining insurance and not of the insurance company.)

Determining Employee Status

The courts are frequently asked to determine whether a particular worker is an employee or an independent contractor. How a court decides this issue can have a significant effect on the rights and liabilities of the parties. Employers are required to pay certain taxes, such as Social Security and unemployment taxes, for employees but not for independent contractors. (See this chapter's *Management Perspective* feature on the following page for more details on this topic.)

CRITERIA USED BY THE COURTS In determining whether a worker has the status of an employee or an independent contractor, the courts often consider the following questions:

1. How much control can the employer exercise over the details of the work? (If an employer can exercise considerable control over the details of the work, this would indicate employee status. This is perhaps the most important factor weighed by the courts in determining employee status.)
2. Is the worker engaged in an occupation or business distinct from that of the employer? (If so, this points to independent-contractor status, not employee status.)
3. Is the work usually done under the employer's direction or by a specialist without supervision? (If the work is usually done under the employer's direction, this would indicate employee status.)
4. Does the employer supply the tools at the place of work? (If so, this would indicate employee status.)
5. For how long is the person employed? (If the person is employed for a long period of time, this would indicate employee status.)
6. What is the method of payment—by time period or at the completion of the job? (Payment by time period, such as once every two weeks or once a month, would indicate employee status.)
7. What degree of skill is required of the worker? (If little skill is required, this may indicate employee status.)

MANAGEMENT PERSPECTIVE • Independent-Contractor Negligence

Management Faces a Legal Issue

Managers often hire independent contractors. They do so for a variety of reasons, such as reducing paperwork and avoiding certain tax liabilities. More important, business managers wish to avoid negligence lawsuits. As a general rule, employers are not liable for torts (wrongs) that an independent contractor commits against third parties. If an employer exercises significant control over the work activity of an independent contractor, however, that contractor may be considered an employee, and the employer may be held liable for the contractor's torts.

What the Courts Say

In one case, a trucking company that hired independent contractors to make deliveries was sued after a motorist was killed in a collision with one of the company's independent-contractor drivers. At trial, the trucking company prevailed. The plaintiff argued that the company had failed to investigate the background, qualifications, or experience of the driver. The appellate court, however, pointed out that an employer of an independent contractor has no control over the manner in which the work is done. The plaintiff failed to offer any proof as to why the company should have investigated the driver.[a]

In another case, a tenant whose hand was injured sued the building's owner. An independent contractor, hired by the owner to perform repair work on the outside of the building, had attempted to close the tenant's balcony door, and the tenant's hand got caught, causing her injury. The appellate court ultimately held that the building's owner and its managing agent could not be held liable for the independent contractor's alleged negligence. As in the previous case, the court noted that the employer (the building's owner) had no right to control the manner in which the independent contractor did his work. The tenant suffered harm because of the independent contractor's actions, not because the premises were in disrepair.[b]

Finally, another issue that sometimes arises is a business owner's liability for injuries to employees of independent contractors that the owner has hired. In one case, two employees of an independent subcontractor suffered electrical burns while working on a construction project. They sued the business owner of the project, among others. The defendants prevailed at trial, and on appeal, the court agreed.[c]

Implications for Managers

To minimize the possibility of being held liable for an independent contractor's negligence, managers should check the qualifications of all contractors before hiring them. A thorough investigation of a contractor's background is especially important when the work may present a danger to the public (as in delivering explosives). It is also wise to require a written contract in which the contractor assumes liability for any harm caused to third parties by the contractor's negligence. Managers should insist that independent contractors carry liability insurance and ensure that the liability insurance policy is current. Additionally, business managers should refrain from doing anything that would lead a third party to believe that an independent contractor is an employee. And, of course, they cannot maintain control over an independent contractor's actions.

a. *Stander v. Dispoz-O-Products, Inc.*, 973 So.2d 603 (Fla.App. 2008).

b. *Stagno v. 143-50 Hoover Owners Corp.*, 48 A.D.3d 548, 853 N.Y.S.2d 85 (2008).

c. *Dalton v. 933 Peachtree, LP*, 291 Ga.App. 123, 661 S.E.2d 156 (2008).

Sometimes, workers may benefit from having employee status—for tax purposes and to be protected under certain employment laws, for example. As mentioned earlier, federal statutes governing employment discrimination apply only when an employer-employee relationship exists. Protection under employment-discrimination statutes provides a significant incentive for workers to claim that they are employees rather than independent contractors.

CASE EXAMPLE 21.1 A Puerto Rican television station, WIPR, contracted with a woman to co-host a television show profiling cities in Puerto Rico. The woman signed a new contract for each episode, each of which required her to work a certain number of days. She was under no other commitment to work for WIPR and was free to pursue other opportunities during the weeks between filming. WIPR did not withhold any taxes from the lump-sum amount it paid her for each contract. When the woman became pregnant, WIPR stopped contracting with her. She filed a lawsuit claiming that WIPR was discriminating against her in violation of federal employment-discrimination laws, but the court found in favor of WIPR. Because the parties had structured their relationship through the use of repeated fixed-length contracts and had described the woman as an independent contractor on tax documents, she could not maintain an employment-discrimination suit.[2] •

Whether a worker is an employee or an independent contractor can also affect the employer's liability for the worker's actions. In the following case, the court had to determine the status of a taxi driver whose passengers were injured in a collision.

2. *Alberty-Vélez v. Corporación de Puerto Rico para la Difusión Pública*, 361 F.3d 1 (1st Cir. 2004).

Case 21.1 Lopez v. El Palmar Taxi, Inc.

Court of Appeals of Georgia, 297 Ga.App. 121, 676 S.E.2d 460 (2009).

FACTS El Palmar Taxi, Inc., requires its drivers to supply their own cabs, which must display El Palmar's logo. The drivers pay gas, maintenance, and insurance costs, and a fee to El Palmar. They are expected to follow certain rules–dress neatly, for example–and to comply with the law, including licensing regulations, but they can work when they want for as long as they want. El Palmar might dispatch a driver to pick up a fare, or the driver can look for a fare. Mario Julaju drove a taxi under a contract with El Palmar that described him as an independent contractor. El Palmar sent Julaju to pick up Maria Lopez and her children. During the ride, Julaju's cab collided with a truck. To recover for their injuries, the Lopezes filed a suit in a Georgia state court against El Palmar. The employer argued that it was not liable because Julaju was an independent contractor. The court ruled in El Palmar's favor. The plaintiffs appealed.

ISSUE Is a taxi driver who is not subject to the control of the taxi company considered an independent contractor?

DECISION Yes. A state intermediate appellate court affirmed this part of the lower court's decision. A taxi driver who is not subject to the control of the taxi company is an independent contractor. The appellate court reversed the judgment in El Palmar's favor on other grounds, however, and remanded the case for trial.

REASON An employer normally is not responsible for the actions of an independent contractor with whom the employer contracts. The test to determine if a worker is an independent contractor is whether the employer has the right to control the time, manner, and method of the work. In this case, the only restriction imposed on Julaju was to comply with the law. El Palmar did not own the cab that Julaju was driving at the time of the collision, nor did it exercise control over the time, manner, or method of his work. Julaju could work any time for as long as he wanted. He was not required to accept fares from the company. The cab displayed the El Palmar logo and El Palmar might dispatch him to pick up a passenger, but these factors alone do not create an employer-employee relationship.

WHY IS THIS CASE IMPORTANT? *When an employment contract clearly designates one party as an independent contractor, the relationship between the parties is presumed to be that of employer and independent contractor. But this is only a presumption. Evidence can be introduced to show that the employer exercised sufficient control to establish the other party as an employee. Or, as this case makes clear, the evidence can underscore that the parties' relationship is that of employer and independent contractor.*

CRITERIA USED BY THE IRS The Internal Revenue Service (IRS) has established its own criteria for determining whether a worker is an independent contractor or an employee. Although the IRS once considered twenty factors in determining a worker's status, guidelines today encourage IRS examiners to focus on just one of those factors—the degree of control the business exercises over the worker.

The IRS tends to closely scrutinize a firm's classification of its workers because employers can avoid certain tax liabilities by hiring independent contractors instead of employees. Even when a firm classifies a worker as an independent contractor, the IRS may decide that the worker is actually an employee. In that situation, the employer will be responsible for paying any applicable Social Security, withholding, and unemployment taxes.

EMPLOYEE STATUS AND "WORKS FOR HIRE" Under the Copyright Act of 1976, any copyrighted work created by an employee within the scope of her or his employment at the request of the employer is a "work for hire," and the *employer* owns the copyright to the work. When an employer hires an independent contractor—a freelance artist, writer, or computer programmer, for example—the independent contractor owns the copyright *unless* the parties agree in writing that the work is a "work for hire" and the work falls into one of nine specific categories, including audiovisual and other works.

CASE EXAMPLE 21.2 Artisan House, Inc., hired a professional photographer, Steven H. Lindner, owner of SHL Imaging, Inc., to take pictures of its products for the creation of color slides to be used by Artisan's sales force. Lindner controlled his own work and carefully chose the lighting and angles used in the photographs. When Lindner later discovered that Artisan had published the photographs in a catalogue and brochures without his permission, he had SHL register the photographs with the copyright office and file a lawsuit for copyright infringement. Artisan claimed that its publication of the photographs was authorized because they were works for hire. The court, however, decided that SHL was an independent contractor and owned the copyright to the photographs. SHL had only given Artisan permission (a license) to provide the photographs to its sales reps, not to reproduce them in other publications. Because Artisan had used the photographs in an unauthorized manner, the court ruled that Artisan was liable for copyright infringement.[3] ●

3. *SHL Imaging, Inc. v. Artisan House, Inc.*, 117 F.Supp.2d 301 (S.D.N.Y. 2000).

How Agency Relationships Are Formed

Agency relationships normally are consensual—that is, they come about by voluntary consent and agreement between the parties. Generally, the agreement need not be in writing,[4] and consideration is not required.

A person must have contractual capacity to be a principal.[5] Those who cannot legally enter into contracts directly should not be allowed to do so indirectly through an agent. Any person can be an agent, though, regardless of whether he or she has the capacity to enter a contract (including minors).

An agency relationship can be created for any legal purpose. An agency relationship that is created for an illegal purpose or that is contrary to public policy is unenforceable. **EXAMPLE 21.3** Sharp (as principal) contracts with McKenzie (as agent) to sell illegal narcotics. This agency relationship is unenforceable because selling illegal narcotics is a felony and is contrary to public policy. ● It is also illegal for physicians and other licensed professionals to employ unlicensed agents to perform professional actions.

Generally, an agency relationship can arise in four ways: by agreement of the parties, by ratification, by estoppel, or by operation of law.

Agency by Agreement of the Parties

Most agency relationships are based on an express or implied agreement that the agent will act for the principal and that the principal agrees to have the agent so act. An agency agreement can take the form of an express written contract or be created by an oral agreement. **EXAMPLE 21.4** Reese asks Cary, a gardener, to contract with others for the care of his lawn on a regular basis. Cary agrees. An agency relationship is established between Reese and Cary for the lawn care. ●

An agency agreement can also be implied by conduct. **EXAMPLE 21.5** A hotel expressly allows only Boris Koontz to park cars, but Boris has no employment contract there. The hotel's manager tells Boris when to work, as well as where and how to park the cars. The hotel's conduct amounts to a manifestation of its willingness to have Boris park its customers' cars, and Boris can infer from the hotel's conduct that he has authority to act as a parking valet. It can be inferred that Boris is an agent-employee of the hotel, his purpose being to provide valet parking services for hotel guests. ●

In the following case, the court had to decide whether an agency relationship arose when a man who was being hospitalized asked his wife to sign the admissions papers for him.

4. The following are two main exceptions to the statement that agency agreements need not be in writing: (1) Whenever agency authority empowers the agent to enter into a contract that the Statute of Frauds requires to be in writing, the agent's authority from the principal must likewise be in writing (this is called the *equal dignity rule,* to be discussed later in this chapter). (2) A power of attorney, which confers authority to an agent, must be in writing.

5. Note that some states allow a minor to be a principal, but any resulting contracts will be voidable by the minor.

Case 21.2 Laurel Creek Health Care Center v. Bishop

Court of Appeals of Kentucky, ___ S.W.3d ___ (2010).

FACTS Gilbert Bishop was admitted to Laurel Creek Health Care Center suffering from various physical ailments. During an examination, Bishop told Laurel Creek staff that he could not use his hands well enough to write or hold a pencil, but he was otherwise found to be mentally competent. Bishop's sister, Rachel Combs, testified that when she arrived at the facility she offered to sign the admissions forms, but Laurel Creek employees told her that it was their policy to have a patient's spouse sign the admissions papers if the patient was unable to do so. Combs also testified that Bishop asked her to get his wife, Anna, so that she could sign his admissions papers. Combs then brought Anna to the hospital, and Anna signed the admissions paperwork, which contained a provision for mandatory arbitration. Subsequently, Bishop went into cardiopulmonary arrest and died. Following his death, Bishop's family brought an action in a Kentucky state court against Laurel Creek for negligence. Laurel Creek requested that the trial court order the parties to proceed to arbitration in accordance with the mandatory arbitration provision contained in the admissions paperwork signed by Anna. The trial court denied the request on the ground that Anna was not Bishop's agent and had no legal authority to make decisions for him. Laurel Creek appealed.

ISSUE Did Anna Bishop become her husband's agent by agreeing to sign the hospital admission papers on his behalf?

DECISION Yes. The Kentucky Court of Appeals reversed the lower court's judgment and remanded the case for further proceedings consistent with its opinion. An actual agency relationship between Bishop and his wife, Anna, had been formed, and the trial court had erred when it found otherwise.

REASON The court reasoned that to establish an agency relationship under the *Restatement (Third) of Agency,* a principal must voluntarily

Case 21.2–Continued

consent to be affected by the agent's actions, and the agent's actions must express consent to act on the principal's behalf. The court noted that "according to his sister, Rachel, Gilbert [Bishop] specifically asked that his wife be brought to the nursing home so that she could sign the admissions documents for him, and [his wife] acted upon that delegation of authority and signed the admissions papers." It is also required that the agent's actions affect the principal's legal relations. Clearly here, the court concluded, Gilbert's wife's actions "affected Gilbert's relations with Laurel Creek, a third party." Therefore, "Gilbert had created an agency relationship upon which Laurel Creek justifiably relied."

FOR CRITICAL ANALYSIS—Legal Consideration *Laurel Creek argued that even if there was no actual agency relationship, an implied agency relationship existed. Is this argument valid? Why or why not?*

Agency by Ratification

On occasion, a person who is in fact not an agent (or who is an agent acting outside the scope of her or his authority) may make a contract on behalf of another (a principal). If the principal affirms that contract by word or by action, an agency relationship is created by **ratification.** Ratification involves a question of intent, and intent can be expressed by either words or conduct. The basic requirements for ratification will be discussed later in this chapter.

Agency by Estoppel

When a principal causes a third person to believe that another person is his or her agent, and the third person deals with the supposed agent, the principal is "estopped to deny" the agency relationship. In such a situation, the principal's actions create the *appearance* of an agency that does not in fact exist. The third person must prove that she or he *reasonably* believed that an agency relationship existed, though.[6] Facts and circumstances must show that an ordinary, prudent person familiar with business practice and custom would have been justified in concluding that the agent had authority.

CASE EXAMPLE 21.6 Marsha and Jerry Wiedmaier owned Wiedmaier, Inc., a corporation that operated a truck stop. Their son, Michael, did not own any interest in the corporation but had worked at the truck stop as a fuel operator. Michael decided to form his own business called Extreme Diecast, LLC. To obtain a line of credit with Motorsport Marketing, Inc., a company that sells racing memorabilia, Michael asked his mother to sign the credit application form. After Marsha had signed as "Secretary-Owner" of Wiedmaier, Inc., Michael added his name to the list of corporate owners and faxed it to Motorsport. Later, when Michael stopped making payments on the merchandise he had ordered, Motorsport sued Wiedmaier for the unpaid balance. The court ruled that Michael was an apparent agent of Wiedmaier, Inc., because the credit application had caused Motorsport to reasonably believe that Michael was acting as Wiedmaier's agent in ordering merchandise.[7] •

Note that the acts or declarations of a purported *agent* in and of themselves do not create an agency by estoppel. Rather, it is the deeds or statements *of the principal* that create an agency by estoppel. In other words, in Case Example 21.6, if Marsha Wiedmaier had not signed the credit application on behalf of the principal-corporation, then Motorsport would not have been reasonable in believing that Michael was Wiedmaier's agent.

Agency by Operation of Law

The courts may find an agency relationship in the absence of a formal agreement in other situations as well. This can occur in family relationships, such as when one spouse purchases certain basic necessaries and charges them to the other spouse's charge account. The courts will often rule that a spouse is liable to pay for the necessaries, either because of a social policy of promoting the general welfare of the spouse or because of a legal duty to supply necessaries to family members.

Agency by operation of law may also occur in emergency situations, when the agent's failure to act outside the scope of his or her authority would cause the principal substantial loss. If the agent is unable to contact the principal, the courts will often grant this emergency power. For instance, a railroad engineer may contract on behalf of her or his employer for medical care for an injured motorist hit by the train.

Duties of Agents and Principals

Once the principal-agent relationship has been created, both parties have duties that govern their conduct. As discussed previously, an agency relationship is *fiduciary*—one of trust. In a fiduciary relationship, each party owes the other the duty to act with the utmost good faith. We now examine the various duties of agents and principals.

6. These concepts also apply when a person who is in fact an agent undertakes an action that is beyond the scope of her or his authority, as will be discussed later in this chapter.

7. *Motorsport Marketing, Inc. v. Wiedmaier, Inc.*, 195 S.W.3d 492 (Mo.App. 2006).

In general, for every duty of the principal, the agent has a corresponding right, and vice versa. When one party to the agency relationship violates his or her duty to the other party, the remedies available to the nonbreaching party arise out of contract and tort law. These remedies include monetary damages, termination of the agency relationship, an injunction, and required accountings.

Agent's Duties to the Principal

Generally, the agent owes the principal five duties—performance, notification, loyalty, obedience, and accounting.

PERFORMANCE An implied condition in every agency contract is the agent's agreement to use reasonable diligence and skill in performing the work. When an agent fails entirely to perform her or his duties, liability for breach of contract normally will result. The degree of skill or care required of an agent is usually that expected of a reasonable person under similar circumstances. Generally, this is interpreted to mean ordinary care. If an agent has represented himself or herself as possessing special skills, however, the agent is expected to exercise the degree of skill or skills claimed. Failure to do so constitutes a breach of the agent's duty.

Not all agency relationships are based on contract. In some situations, an agent acts gratuitously—that is, not for monetary compensation. A gratuitous agent cannot be liable for breach of contract, as there is no contract. He or she is subject only to tort liability. Once a gratuitous agent has begun to act in an agency capacity, he or she has the duty to continue to perform in that capacity in an acceptable manner and is subject to the same standards of care and duty to perform as other agents.

NOTIFICATION An agent is required to notify the principal of all matters that come to her or his attention concerning the subject matter of the agency. This is the duty of notification, or the duty to inform. **EXAMPLE 21.7** Lang, an artist, is about to negotiate a contract to sell a series of paintings to Barber's Art Gallery for $25,000. Lang's agent learns that Barber is insolvent and will be unable to pay for the paintings. The agent has a duty to inform Lang of this fact because it is relevant to the subject matter of the agency, which is the sale of Lang's paintings. •

Generally, the law assumes that the principal knows of any information acquired by the agent that is relevant to the agency—regardless of whether the agent actually passes on this information to the principal. It is a basic tenet of agency law that notice to the agent is notice to the principal.

LOYALTY Loyalty is one of the most fundamental duties in a fiduciary relationship. Basically, the agent has the duty to act *solely for the benefit of his or her principal* and not in the interest of the agent or a third party. For example, an agent cannot represent two principals in the same transaction unless both know of the dual capacity and consent to it. The duty of loyalty also means that any information or knowledge acquired through the agency relationship is considered confidential. It would be a breach of loyalty to disclose such information either during the agency relationship or after its termination. Typical examples of confidential information are trade secrets and customer lists compiled by the principal.

In short, the agent's loyalty must be undivided. The agent's actions must be strictly for the benefit of the principal and must not result in any secret profit for the agent. **CASE EXAMPLE 21.8** Don Cousins contracts with Leo Hodgins, a real estate agent, to negotiate the purchase of an office building as an investment. While working for Cousins, Hodgins discovers that the property owner will sell the building only as a package deal with another parcel. If Hodgins then forms a new company with his brother to buy the two properties and resell the building to Cousins, he has breached his fiduciary duties. As a real estate agent, Hodgins has a duty to communicate all offers to his principal and not to secretly purchase the property and then resell it to his principal. Hodgins is required to act in Cousins's best interests and can become the purchaser in this situation only with Cousins's knowledge and approval.[8] •

OBEDIENCE When acting on behalf of a principal, an agent has a duty to follow all lawful and clearly stated instructions of the principal. Any deviation from such instructions is a violation of this duty. During emergency situations, however, when the principal cannot be consulted, the agent may deviate from the instructions without violating this duty. Whenever instructions are not clearly stated, the agent can fulfill the duty of obedience by acting in good faith and in a manner reasonable under the circumstances.

ACCOUNTING Unless an agent and a principal agree otherwise, the agent has the duty to keep and make available to the principal an account of all property and funds received and paid out on behalf of the principal. This includes gifts from third parties in connection with the agency. For example, a gift from a customer to a salesperson for prompt deliveries made by the salesperson's firm, in the absence of a company policy to the contrary, belongs to the firm. The agent has a duty to maintain separate accounts for the principal's funds and for the agent's personal funds, and the agent must not intermingle these accounts.

Principal's Duties to the Agent

The principal also owes certain duties to the agent. These duties relate to compensation, reimbursement and indemnification, cooperation, and safe working conditions.

8. *Cousins v. Realty Ventures, Inc.*, 844 So.2d 860 (La.App. 5 Cir. 2003).

COMPENSATION In general, when a principal requests certain services from an agent, the agent reasonably expects payment. The principal therefore has a duty to pay the agent for services rendered. For example, when an accountant or an attorney is asked to act as an agent, an agreement to compensate the agent for such service is implied. The principal also has a duty to pay that compensation in a timely manner. Except in a gratuitous agency relationship, in which an agent does not act for payment in return, the principal must pay the agreed-on value for an agent's services. If no amount has been expressly agreed on, the principal owes the agent the customary compensation for such services.

REIMBURSEMENT AND INDEMNIFICATION Whenever an agent disburses funds to fulfill the request of the principal or to pay for necessary expenses in the course of reasonable performance of his or her agency duties, the principal has the duty to reimburse the agent for these payments. Agents cannot recover for expenses incurred through their own misconduct or negligence, though.

Subject to the terms of the agency agreement, the principal has the duty to compensate, or *indemnify,* an agent for liabilities incurred because of authorized and lawful acts and transactions. For instance, if the principal fails to perform a contract formed by the agent with a third party and the third party then sues the agent, the principal is obligated to compensate the agent for any costs incurred in defending against the lawsuit.

Additionally, the principal must indemnify (pay) the agent for the value of benefits that the agent confers on the principal. The amount of indemnification usually is specified in the agency contract. If it is not, the courts will look to the nature of the business and the type of loss to determine the amount. Note that this rule applies to acts by gratuitous agents as well. If the finder of a dog that becomes sick takes the dog to a veterinarian and pays the required fees for the veterinarian's services, the gratuitous agent is entitled to be reimbursed for those fees by the dog's owner.

COOPERATION A principal has a duty to cooperate with the agent and to assist the agent in performing her or his duties. The principal must do nothing to prevent such performance.

When a principal grants an agent an exclusive territory, for example, the principal creates an *exclusive agency* and cannot compete with the agent or appoint or allow another agent to so compete. If the principal does so, she or he will be exposed to liability for the agent's lost sales or profits. **EXAMPLE 21.9** Akers (the principal) creates an exclusive agency by granting Johnson (the agent) an exclusive territory within which Johnson may sell Akers's products. If Akers begins to sell the products himself within Johnson's territory or permits another agent to do so, Akers has violated the exclusive agency and can be held liable for Johnson's lost sales or profits. •

SAFE WORKING CONDITIONS Under the common law, a principal is required to provide safe working premises, equipment, and conditions for all agents and employees. The principal has a duty to inspect the working conditions and to warn agents and employees about any unsafe areas. When the agent is an employee, the employer's liability is frequently covered by state workers' compensation insurance, and federal and state statutes often require the employer to meet certain safety standards (to be discussed in Chapter 22).

Agent's Authority

An agent's authority to act can be either actual (express or implied) or apparent. If an agent contracts outside the scope of his or her authority, the principal may still become liable by ratifying the contract.

Express Authority

Express authority is authority declared in clear, direct, and definite terms. Express authority can be given orally or in writing.

EQUAL DIGNITY RULE In most states, the **equal dignity rule** requires that if the contract being executed is or must be in writing, then the agent's authority must also be in writing. Failure to comply with the equal dignity rule can make a contract voidable *at the option of the principal.* The law regards the contract at that point as a mere offer. If the principal decides to accept the offer, acceptance must be ratified, or affirmed, in writing.

EXAMPLE 21.10 Lee (the principal) orally asks Parkinson (the agent) to sell a ranch that Lee owns. Parkinson finds a buyer and signs a sales contract (a contract for an interest in realty must be in writing) on behalf of Lee to sell the ranch. The buyer cannot enforce the contract unless Lee subsequently ratifies Parkinson's agency status *in writing.* Once Parkinson's agency status is ratified, either party can enforce rights under the contract. •

Modern business practice allows an exception to the equal dignity rule. An executive officer of a corporation normally is not required to obtain written authority from the corporation to conduct *ordinary* business transactions. The equal dignity rule does not apply when an agent acts in the presence of a principal or when the agent's act of signing is merely perfunctory (automatic). Thus, if Dickens (the principal) negotiates a contract but is called out of town the day it is to be signed and orally authorizes Santini to sign the contract, the oral authorization is sufficient.

POWER OF ATTORNEY A **power of attorney** confers express authority to an agent.[9] The power of attorney normally is a written document and is usually notarized. (A document is notarized when a **notary public**—a public official authorized

9. An agent who holds the power of attorney is called an *attorney-in-fact* for the principal. The holder does not have to be an attorney-at-law (and often is not).

to attest to the authenticity of signatures—signs and dates the document and imprints it with his or her seal of authority.) Most states have statutory provisions for creating a power of attorney.

A power of attorney can be special (permitting the agent to do specified acts only), or it can be general (permitting the agent to transact all business for the principal). Because a general power of attorney grants extensive authority to an agent to act on behalf of the principal in many ways, it should be used with great caution. Ordinarily, a power of attorney terminates on the incapacity or death of the person giving the power.[10]

Implied Authority

Actual authority may also be implied. An agent has the *implied authority* to do what is reasonably necessary to carry out express authority and accomplish the objectives of the agency. Authority can also be implied by custom or inferred from the position the agent occupies.

EXAMPLE 21.11 Mueller is employed by Al's Supermarket to manage one of its stores. Al's has not expressly stated that Mueller has authority to contract with third persons. In this situation, though, authority to manage a business implies authority to do what is reasonably required (as is customary or can be inferred from a manager's position) to operate the business. This includes forming contracts to hire employees, to buy merchandise and equipment, and to advertise the products sold in the store. •

In general, implied authority is authority customarily associated with the position occupied by the agent or authority that can be inferred from the express authority given to the agent to perform fully his or her duties. For example, an agent has authority to solicit orders for goods sold by the principal. The agent, however, does not carry any goods with him or her when soliciting orders, and thus generally would not have the authority to collect payments for the goods. The test is whether it was reasonable for the agent to believe that she or he had the authority to enter into the contract in question.

Apparent Authority

Actual authority (express or implied) arises from what the principal manifests *to the agent*. An agent has **apparent authority** when the principal, by either words or actions, causes a *third party* reasonably to believe that an agent has authority to act, even though the agent has no express or implied authority.

PATTERN OF CONDUCT Apparent authority usually comes into existence through a principal's pattern of conduct over time. **CASE EXAMPLE 21.12** Francis Azur was the president of ATM Corporation of America, and Michelle Vanek was his personal assistant. Vanek's responsibilities included opening Azur's personal bills, preparing and presenting checks for him to sign, balancing his checking and savings accounts, and reviewing his credit-card and bank statements. Vanek also had access to Azur's credit-card number so that she could make purchases for him. Over a period of seven years, Vanek withdrew unauthorized cash advances from Azur's credit-card account with Chase Bank, USA. The fraudulent charges were reflected on at least sixty-five monthly billing statements sent by Chase to Azur, and Vanek paid the bills by writing checks and forging Azur's signature or by making online payments from Azur's checking account. In all, Vanek misappropriated more than $1 million from Azur. When Azur discovered Vanek's fraudulent scheme, he terminated her employment and closed the Chase account. Azur then sued Chase, seeking reimbursement of the fraudulent charges under the Truth-in-Lending Act, or TILA (which protects cardholders from liability for the fraudulent use of their credit cards). Because Vanek had apparent authority to use Azur's credit card, however, the court dismissed Azur's claim, and he was unable to recover for the loss.[11] •

APPARENT AUTHORITY AND ESTOPPEL The doctrine of agency by estoppel (see page 401) may be applied in situations in which a principal has given a third party reason to believe that an agent has authority to act. If the third party changes position to his or her detriment in good faith reliance on the principal's representations, the principal may be estopped (prevented) from denying that the agent had authority.

Ratification

As already mentioned, ratification occurs when the principal affirms an agent's *unauthorized* act. When ratification occurs, the principal is bound to the agent's act, and the act is treated as if it had been authorized by the principal *from the outset*. Ratification can be either express or implied.

If the principal does not ratify the contract, the principal is not bound, and the third party's agreement with the agent is viewed as merely an unaccepted offer. Because the third party's agreement is an unaccepted offer, the third party can revoke the offer at any time, without liability, before the principal ratifies the contract.

The requirements for ratification can be summarized as follows:

1. The agent must have acted on behalf of an identified principal who subsequently ratifies the action.

10. A *durable* power of attorney, however, continues to be effective despite the principal's incapacity. An elderly person, for example, might grant a durable power of attorney to provide for the handling of property and investments or specific health-care needs should she or he become incompetent.

11. *Azur v. Chase Bank, USA*, 601 F.3d 212 (3d Cir. 2010).

2. The principal must know of all material facts involved in the transaction. If a principal ratifies a contract without knowing all of the facts, the principal can rescind (cancel) the contract.
3. The principal must affirm the agent's act in its entirety.
4. The principal must have the legal capacity to authorize the transaction at the time the agent engages in the act and at the time the principal ratifies. The third party must also have the legal capacity to engage in the transaction.
5. The principal's affirmation must occur before the third party withdraws from the transaction.
6. The principal must observe the same formalities when approving the act done by the agent as would have been required to authorize it initially.

Liability in Agency Relationships

Frequently, a question arises as to which party, the principal or the agent, should be held liable for contracts formed by the agent or for torts or crimes committed by the agent. We look here at these aspects of agency law.

Liability for Contracts

Liability for contracts formed by an agent depends on how the principal is classified and on whether the actions of the agent were authorized or unauthorized. Principals are classified as disclosed, partially disclosed, or undisclosed.[12]

A **disclosed principal** is a principal whose identity is known by the third party at the time the contract is made by the agent. A **partially disclosed principal** is a principal whose identity is not known by the third party, but the third party knows that the agent is or may be acting for a principal at the time the contract is made.

EXAMPLE 21.13 Sarah has contracted with a real estate agent to sell certain property. She wishes to keep her identity a secret, but the agent makes it perfectly clear to potential buyers of the property that the agent is acting in an agency capacity. In this situation, Sarah is a partially disclosed principal. •

An **undisclosed principal** is a principal whose identity is totally unknown by the third party, and the third party has no knowledge that the agent is acting in an agency capacity at the time the contract is made.

Authorized Acts If an agent acts within the scope of her or his authority, normally the principal is obligated to perform the contract regardless of whether the principal was disclosed, partially disclosed, or undisclosed. Whether the agent may also be held liable under the contract, however, depends on the disclosed, partially disclosed, or undisclosed status of the principal.

Disclosed or Partially Disclosed Principal. A disclosed or partially disclosed principal is liable to a third party for a contract made by an agent who is acting within the scope of her or his authority. If the principal is disclosed, an agent has no contractual liability for the nonperformance of the principal or the third party. If the principal is partially disclosed, in most states the agent is also treated as a party to the contract, and the third party can hold the agent liable for contractual nonperformance.[13]

CASE EXAMPLE 21.14 Walgreens leased commercial property at a mall owned by Kedzie Plaza Associates to operate a drugstore. A property management company, Taxman Corporation, signed the lease on behalf of the principal, Kedzie. The lease required the landlord to keep the sidewalks free of snow and ice, so Taxman, on behalf of Kedzie, contracted with another company to remove ice and snow from the sidewalks surrounding the Walgreens store. When a Walgreens employee slipped on ice outside the store and was injured, she sued Taxman, among others, for negligence. Because the principal's identity (Kedzie) was fully disclosed in the snow-removal contract, however, the court ruled that the agent, Taxman, could not be held liable. Taxman did not assume a contractual obligation to remove the snow but merely retained a contractor to do so on behalf of the owner.[14] •

Undisclosed Principal. When neither the fact of agency nor the identity of the principal is disclosed, the undisclosed principal is bound to perform just as if the principal had been fully disclosed at the time the contract was made. The agent is also liable as a party to the contract.

When a principal's identity is undisclosed and the agent is forced to pay the third party, the agent is entitled to be indemnified (compensated) by the principal. The principal had a duty to perform, even though his or her identity was undisclosed, and failure to do so will make the principal ultimately liable. Once the undisclosed principal's identity is revealed, the third party generally can elect to hold either the principal or the agent liable on the contract.

Conversely, the undisclosed principal can require the third party to fulfill the contract, *unless* (1) the undisclosed principal was expressly excluded as a party in the contract; (2) the contract is a negotiable instrument signed by the agent with no indication of signing in a representative capacity; or (3) the performance of the agent is personal to the contract, allowing the third party to refuse the principal's performance.

In the following case, three parties involved in an auto sales transaction were embroiled in a dispute over who was liable when the car's engine caught fire.

12. *Restatement (Third) of Agency,* Section 1.04(2).

13. *Restatement (Third) of Agency,* Section 6.02.

14. *McBride v. Taxman Corp.,* 327 Ill.App.3d 992, 765 N.E.2d 51 (2002).

Case 21.3 Williams v. Pike

Court of Appeal of Louisiana, Second Circuit, 58 So.3d 525 (2011).
www.lacoa2.org[a]

FACTS Bobby Williams bought a car for $3,000 at Sherman Henderson's auto repair business in Monroe, Louisiana. Although the car's owner was Joe Pike, the owner of Justice Wrecker Service, Henderson negotiated the sale, accepted Williams's payment, and gave him two receipts. Williams drove the car to Memphis, Tennessee, where his daughter was a student. Three days after the sale, the car began to emit smoke and flames from under the hood. Williams extinguished the blaze and contacted Henderson. The next day, Williams's daughter had the vehicle towed at her expense to her apartment's parking lot, from which it was soon stolen. Williams filed a suit in a Louisiana state court against Pike and Henderson. The court awarded Williams $2,000, plus the costs of the suit, adding that if Williams had returned the car, it would have awarded him the entire price. Pike and Henderson appealed.

ISSUE Can the buyer of a defective car hold both the agent and principal liable when the agent sold that car for the undisclosed principal?

a. At the top, click on "Opinions." On the next page, in the "Search:" box, type "Williams v. Pike," and click on "Search." In the result, click on the case number to access the opinion. The Court of Appeal of Louisiana for the Second Circuit maintains this Web site.

DECISION Yes. A state intermediate appellate court affirmed the ruling of the lower court, including its judgment and the assessment of costs against both defendants. The appellate court added the costs of the appeal to the amount. Both Pike and Henderson–the undisclosed principal and his agent–were liable to Williams.

REASON The court noted that a state permit to sell the car had been issued to Pike, and it showed that Joe Pike was the owner. The car was displayed for sale at Henderson's business, however, and he actually sold it. The court reasoned that this made Pike the principal and Henderson his agent. The fact that their agency relationship was not made clear to Williams made Pike an undisclosed principal. Williams could thus choose to hold either Pike or Henderson liable for the condition of the car, which constituted a breach of implied warranty because the car did not fulfill the purpose for which it was intended. The loss of the use of the car, the "inconvenience" caused by the defect, the price, and the cost of the tow were among the factors that supported the award.

WHAT IF THE FACTS WERE DIFFERENT? *Suppose that Henderson had fully disclosed the fact of his agency relationship and the identity of his principal. Would the result have been different? Why or why not?*

UNAUTHORIZED ACTS If an agent has no authority but nevertheless contracts with a third party, the principal cannot be held liable on the contract. It does not matter whether the principal was disclosed, partially disclosed, or undisclosed. The *agent* is liable, however. **EXAMPLE 21.15** Scranton signs a contract for the purchase of a truck, purportedly acting as an agent under authority granted by Johnson. In fact, Johnson has not given Scranton any such authority. Johnson refuses to pay for the truck, claiming that Scranton had no authority to purchase it. The seller of the truck is entitled to hold Scranton liable for payment. •

If the principal is disclosed or partially disclosed, the agent is liable to the third party as long as the third party relied on the agency status. The agent's liability here is based on the breach of an *implied warranty of authority* (an agent impliedly warrants that he or she has the authority to enter a contract on behalf of the principal), not on breach of the contract itself.[15] If the third party knows at the time the contract is made that the agent does not have authority—or if the agent expresses to the third party *uncertainty* as to the extent of her or his authority—then the agent is not personally liable.

15. The agent is not liable on the contract because the agent was never intended personally to be a party to the contract.

LIABILITY FOR E-AGENTS Although in the past standard agency principles applied only to *human* agents, today these same principles are being applied to electronic agents. An electronic agent, or **e-agent,** is a semiautonomous computer program that is capable of executing specific tasks. E-agents used in e-commerce include software that can search through many databases and retrieve only information that is relevant for the user.

The Uniform Electronic Transactions Act (UETA), which was discussed in Chapter 8 and has been adopted by most states, contains several provisions relating to the principal's liability for the actions of e-agents. Section 15 of the UETA states that e-agents may enter into binding agreements on behalf of their principals. Presumably, then—at least in those states that have adopted the act—the principal will be bound by the terms in a contract entered into by an e-agent. Thus, when you place an order over the Internet, the company (principal) whose system took the order via an e-agent cannot claim that it did not receive your order.

The UETA also stipulates that if an e-agent does not provide an opportunity to prevent errors at the time of the transaction, the other party to the transaction can avoid the transaction. For instance, if an e-agent fails to provide an on-screen confirmation of a purchase or sale, the other party can avoid the effect of any errors.

Liability for Torts and Crimes

Obviously, any person, including an agent, is liable for her or his own torts and crimes. Whether a principal can also be held liable for an agent's torts and crimes depends on several factors, which we examine here. In some situations, a principal may be held liable not only for the torts of an agent but also for the torts committed by an independent contractor.

PRINCIPAL'S TORTIOUS CONDUCT A principal conducting an activity through an agent may be liable for harm resulting from the principal's own negligence or recklessness. Thus, a principal may be liable for giving improper instructions, authorizing the use of improper materials or tools, or establishing improper rules that resulted in the agent's committing a tort. **EXAMPLE 21.16** Jack knows that Suki cannot drive because her license has been suspended, but nevertheless, he tells her to use the company truck to deliver some equipment to a customer. If someone is injured as a result, Jack (the principal) will be liable for his own negligence in giving improper instructions to Suki. •

PRINCIPAL'S AUTHORIZATION OF AGENT'S TORTIOUS CONDUCT A principal who authorizes an agent to commit a tort may be liable to persons or property injured thereby, because the act is considered to be the principal's. **EXAMPLE 21.17** Selkow directs his agent, Warren, to cut the corn on specific acreage, which neither of them has the right to do. The harvest is therefore a trespass (a tort), and Selkow is liable to the owner of the corn. •

Note also that an agent acting at the principal's direction can be liable as a *tortfeasor* (one who commits a wrong, or tort), along with the principal, for committing the tortious act even if the agent was unaware of the wrongfulness of the act. Assume in the above example that Warren, the agent, did not know that Selkow had no right to harvest the corn. Warren can be held liable to the owner of the field for damages, along with Selkow, the principal.

LIABILITY FOR AGENT'S MISREPRESENTATION A principal is exposed to tort liability whenever a third person sustains a loss due to the agent's misrepresentation. The principal's liability depends on whether the agent was actually or apparently authorized to make representations and whether the representations were made within the scope of the agency. The principal is always directly responsible for an agent's misrepresentation made within the scope of the agent's authority.

EXAMPLE 21.18 Bassett is a demonstrator for Moore's products. Moore sends Bassett to a home show to demonstrate the products and to answer questions from consumers. Moore has given Bassett authority to make statements about the products. If Bassett makes only true representations, all is fine; but if he makes false claims, Moore will be liable for any injuries or damages sustained by third parties in reliance on Bassett's false representations. •

LIABILITY FOR AGENT'S NEGLIGENCE As mentioned, an agent is liable for his or her own torts. A principal may also be liable for harm an agent caused to a third party under the doctrine of ***respondeat superior***,[16] a Latin term meaning "let the master respond." It imposes **vicarious liability**, or indirect liability, on the employer—that is, liability without regard to the personal fault of the employer—for torts committed by an employee in the course or scope of employment.

Determining the Scope of Employment. The key to determining whether a principal may be liable for the torts of an agent under the doctrine of *respondeat superior* is whether the torts are committed within the scope of the agency or employment. The *Restatement (Second) of Agency*, Section 229, indicates the factors that today's courts will consider in determining whether a particular act occurred within the course and scope of employment. These factors are as follows:

1. Whether the employee's act was authorized by the employer.
2. The time, place, and purpose of the act.
3. Whether the act was one commonly performed by employees on behalf of their employers.
4. The extent to which the employer's interest was advanced by the act.
5. The extent to which the private interests of the employee were involved.
6. Whether the employer furnished the means or instrumentality (for example, a truck or a machine) by which the injury was inflicted.
7. Whether the employer had reason to know that the employee would do the act in question and whether the employee had ever done it before.
8. Whether the act involved the commission of a serious crime.

The Distinction between a "Detour" and a "Frolic." A useful insight into the "scope of employment" concept may be gained from the judge's classic distinction between a "detour" and a "frolic" in the case of *Joel v. Morison*.[17] In this case, the English court held that if a servant merely took a detour from his master's business, the master will be responsible. If, however, the servant was on a "frolic of his own" and not in any way "on his master's business," the master will not be liable.

EXAMPLE 21.19 Mandel, a traveling salesperson, while driving his employer's vehicle to call on a customer, decides to stop at the post office—which is one block off his route—to mail a personal letter. As Mandel approaches the post office,

16. Pronounced ree-*spahn*-dee-uht soo-*peer*-ee-your.
17. 6 Car. & P. 501, 172 Eng. Reprint 1338 (1834).

he negligently runs into a parked vehicle owned by Chan. In this situation, because Mandel's detour from the employer's business is not substantial, he is still acting within the scope of employment, and the employer is liable. The result would be different, though, if Mandel had decided to pick up a few friends for cocktails in another city and in the process had negligently run into Chan's vehicle. In that circumstance, the departure from the employer's business would be substantial, and the employer normally would not be liable to Chan for damages. Mandel would be considered to have been on a "frolic" of his own. •

Employee Travel Time. An employee going to and from work or to and from meals is usually considered outside the scope of employment. If travel is part of a person's position, however, such as a traveling salesperson or a regional representative of a company, then travel time is normally considered within the scope of employment. Thus, the duration of the business trip, including the return trip home, is within the scope of employment unless there is a significant departure from the employer's business.

Notice of Dangerous Conditions. The employer is charged with knowledge of any dangerous conditions discovered by an employee and pertinent to the employment situation. **EXAMPLE 21.20** Chad, a maintenance employee in Martin's apartment building, notices a lead pipe protruding from the ground in the building's courtyard. The employee neglects either to fix the pipe or to inform the employer of the danger. John falls on the pipe and is injured. The employer is charged with knowledge of the dangerous condition regardless of whether or not Chad actually informed the employer. That knowledge is imputed to the employer by virtue of the employment relationship. •

LIABILITY FOR AGENT'S INTENTIONAL TORTS Most intentional torts that employees commit have no relation to their employment; thus, their employers will not be held liable. Nevertheless, under the doctrine of *respondeat superior,* the employer can be liable for intentional torts of the employee that are committed within the course and scope of employment, just as the employer is liable for negligence. For instance, an employer is liable when an employee (such as a "bouncer" at a nightclub or a security guard at a department store) commits the tort of assault and battery or false imprisonment while acting within the scope of employment.

In addition, an employer who knows or should know that an employee has a propensity for committing tortious acts is liable for the employee's acts even if they would not ordinarily be considered within the scope of employment. For example, if the employer hires a bouncer knowing that he has a history of arrests for assault and battery, the employer may be liable if the employee viciously attacks a patron in the parking lot after hours.

An employer may also be liable for permitting an employee to engage in reckless actions that can injure others. **EXAMPLE 21.21** An employer observes an employee smoking while filling containerized trucks with highly flammable liquids. Failure to stop the employee will cause the employer to be liable for any injuries that result if a truck explodes. •

LIABILITY FOR INDEPENDENT CONTRACTOR'S TORTS Generally, an employer is not liable for physical harm caused to a third person by the negligent act of an independent contractor in the performance of the contract. This is because the employer does not have the right to control the details of an independent contractor's performance. Exceptions to this rule are made in certain situations, though, such as when unusually hazardous activities are involved. Typical examples of such activities include blasting operations, the transportation of highly volatile chemicals, or the use of poisonous gases. In these situations, an employer cannot be shielded from liability merely by using an independent contractor. Strict liability is imposed on the employer-principal as a matter of law. Also, in some states, strict liability may be imposed by statute.

LIABILITY FOR AGENT'S CRIMES An agent is liable for his or her own crimes. A principal or employer is not liable for an agent's crime even if the crime was committed within the scope of authority or employment—unless the principal participated by conspiracy or other action. In some jurisdictions, under specific statutes, a principal may be liable for an agent's violation, in the course and scope of employment, of regulations, such as those governing sanitation, prices, weights, and the sale of liquor.

How Agency Relationships Are Terminated

Agency law is similar to contract law in that both an agency and a contract can be terminated by an act of the parties or by operation of law. Once the relationship between the principal and the agent has ended, the agent no longer has the right (*actual* authority) to bind the principal. For an agent's *apparent* authority to be terminated, though, third persons may also need to be notified that the agency has been terminated.

Termination by Act of the Parties

An agency may be terminated by act of the parties in any of the following ways:

1. *Lapse of time.* When an agency agreement specifies the time period during which the agency relationship will exist, the agency ends when that time period expires. If no definite time is stated, then the agency continues for a reasonable

time and can be terminated at will by either party. What constitutes a "reasonable time" depends, of course, on the circumstances and the nature of the agency relationship.

2. *Purpose achieved.* If an agent is employed to accomplish a particular objective, such as the purchase of breeding stock for a cattle rancher, the agency automatically ends after the cattle have been purchased. If more than one agent is employed to accomplish the same purpose, such as the sale of real estate, the first agent to complete the sale automatically terminates the agency relationship for all the others.
3. *Occurrence of a specific event.* When an agency relationship is to terminate on the happening of a certain event, the agency automatically ends when the event occurs. If Posner appoints Rubik to handle her business affairs while she is away, the agency terminates when Posner returns.
4. *Mutual agreement.* The parties to an agency can cancel (rescind) their contract by mutually agreeing to terminate the agency relationship, whether the agency contract is in writing or whether it is for a specific duration.
5. *Termination by one party.* As a general rule, either party can terminate the agency relationship (the act of termination is called *revocation* if done by the principal and *renunciation* if done by the agent). Although both parties have the *power* to terminate the agency, they may not possess the *right* to terminate and therefore may be liable for breach of contract, or *wrongful termination.*

WRONGFUL TERMINATION Wrongful termination can subject the canceling party to a suit for breach of contract. **EXAMPLE 21.22** Rawlins has a one-year employment contract with Munro to act as an agent in return for $65,000. Although Munro has the *power* to discharge Rawlins before the contract period expires, if he does so, he can be sued for breaching the contract because he had no *right* to terminate the agency. •

NOTICE OF TERMINATION When an agency has been terminated by act of the parties, it is the principal's duty to inform any third parties who know of the existence of the agency that it has been terminated (although notice of the termination may be given by others). Although an agent's actual authority ends when the agency is terminated, an agent's *apparent authority* continues until the third party receives notice (from any source) that such authority has been terminated. If the principal knows that a third party has dealt with the agent, the principal is expected to notify that person *directly.* For third parties who have heard about the agency but have not yet dealt with the agent, *constructive notice* is sufficient.[18]

No particular form is required for notice of agency termination to be effective. The principal can personally notify the agent, or the agent can learn of the termination through some other means. **EXAMPLE 21.23** Manning bids on a shipment of steel, and Stone is hired as an agent to arrange transportation of the shipment. When Stone learns that Manning has lost the bid, Stone's authority to make the transportation arrangement terminates. • If the agent's authority is written, however, it normally must be revoked in writing.

Termination by Operation of Law

Termination of an agency by operation of law occurs in the circumstances discussed here. Note that when an agency terminates by operation of law, there is no duty to notify third persons.

DEATH OR INSANITY The general rule is that the death or mental incompetence of either the principal or the agent automatically and immediately terminates an ordinary agency relationship. Knowledge of the death is not required. **EXAMPLE 21.24** Geer sends Pyron to China to purchase a rare painting. Before Pyron makes the purchase, Geer dies. Pyron's agent status is terminated at the moment of Geer's death, even though Pyron does not know that Geer has died. • Some states, however, have enacted statutes changing this common law rule to make knowledge of the principal's death a requirement for agency termination.

IMPOSSIBILITY When the specific subject matter of an agency is destroyed or lost, the agency terminates. **EXAMPLE 21.25** Bullard employs Gonzalez to sell Bullard's house. Prior to any sale, the house is destroyed by fire. In this situation, Gonzalez's agency and authority to sell Bullard's house terminate. • Similarly, when it is impossible for the agent to perform the agency lawfully because of a change in the law, the agency terminates.

CHANGED CIRCUMSTANCES When an event occurs that has such an unusual effect on the subject matter of the agency that the agent can reasonably infer that the principal will not want the agency to continue, the agency terminates. **EXAMPLE 21.26** Roberts hires Mullen to sell a tract of land for $20,000. Subsequently, Mullen learns that there is oil under the land and that the land is worth $1 million. The agency and Mullen's authority to sell the land for $20,000 are terminated. •

BANKRUPTCY If either the principal or the agent petitions for bankruptcy, the agency is *usually* terminated. In certain circumstances, as when the agent's financial status is irrelevant to the purpose of the agency, the agency relationship may continue. Insolvency—that is, the inability to pay debts when they become due or the situation in which liabilities exceed assets—as distinguished from bankruptcy, does not necessarily terminate the relationship.

---

18. *Constructive notice* is information or knowledge of a fact imputed by law to a person if he or she could have discovered the fact by proper diligence. Constructive notice is often accomplished by newspaper publication.

WAR When the principal's country and the agent's country are at war with each other, the agency is terminated. In this situation, the agency is automatically suspended or terminated because there is no way to enforce the legal rights and obligations of the parties.

Reviewing . . . Agency Relationships

Lynne Meyer, on her way to a business meeting and in a hurry, stopped at a Buy-Mart store for a new pair of nylons to wear to the meeting. There was a long line at one of the checkout counters, but a cashier, Valerie Watts, opened another counter and began loading the cash drawer. Meyer told Watts that she was in a hurry and asked Watts to work faster. Watts, however, only slowed her pace. At this point, Meyer hit Watts. It is not clear from the record whether Meyer hit Watts intentionally or, in an attempt to retrieve the nylons, hit her inadvertently. In response, Watts grabbed Meyer by the hair and hit her repeatedly in the back of the head, while Meyer screamed for help. Management personnel separated the two women and questioned them about the incident. Watts was immediately fired for violating the store's no-fighting policy. Meyer subsequently sued Buy-Mart, alleging that the store was liable for the tort (assault and battery) committed by its employee. Using the information presented in the chapter, answer the following questions.

1 Under what doctrine discussed in this chapter might Buy-Mart be held liable for the tort committed by Watts?
2 What is the key factor in determining whether Buy-Mart is liable under this doctrine?
3 How is Buy-Mart's potential liability affected depending on whether Watts's behavior constituted an intentional tort or a tort of negligence?
4 Suppose that when Watts applied for the job at Buy-Mart, she disclosed in her application that she had previously been convicted of felony assault and battery. Nevertheless, Buy-Mart hired Watts as a cashier. How might this fact affect Buy-Mart's liability for Watts's actions?

Terms and Concepts

agency 396
apparent authority 404
disclosed principal 405
e-agent 406
equal dignity rule 403
fiduciary 396
independent contractor 397
notary public 404
partially disclosed principal 405
power of attorney 403
ratification 401
respondeat superior 407
undisclosed principal 405
vicarious liability 407

Chapter Summary: Agency Relationships

Agency Relationships (See pages 396–399.)	In a *principal-agent* relationship, an agent acts on behalf of and instead of the principal in dealing with third parties. An employee who deals with third parties is normally an agent. An independent contractor is not an employee, and the employer has no control over the details of physical performance. An independent contractor may or may not be an agent.
How Agency Relationships Are Formed (See pages 400–401.)	Agency relationships may be formed by agreement of the parties, by ratification, by estoppel, and by operation of law.
Duties of Agents and Principals (See pages 401–403.)	1. *Duties of the agent*– a. Performance–The agent must use reasonable diligence and skill in performing her or his duties or use the special skills that the agent has represented to the principal that the agent possesses. b. Notification–The agent is required to notify the principal of all matters that come to his or her attention concerning the subject matter of the agency. c. Loyalty–The agent has a duty to act solely for the benefit of the principal and not in the interest of the agent or a third party. d. Obedience–The agent must follow all lawful and clearly stated instructions of the principal. e. Accounting–The agent has a duty to make available to the principal records of all property and funds received and paid out on behalf of the principal.

Chapter Summary: Agency Relationships—Continued

Duties of Agents and Principals—Continued	2. *Duties of the principal*— a. Compensation—Except in a gratuitous agency relationship, the principal must pay the agreed-on value (or reasonable value) for an agent's services. b. Reimbursement and indemnification—The principal must reimburse the agent for all funds disbursed at the request of the principal and for all funds that the agent disburses for necessary expenses in the course of reasonable performance of his or her agency duties. c. Cooperation—A principal must cooperate with and assist an agent in performing her or his duties. d. Safe working conditions—A principal must provide safe working conditions for the agent-employee.
Agent's Authority (See pages 403–405.)	1. *Express authority*—Can be oral or in writing. Authorization must be in writing if the agent is to execute a contract that must be in writing. 2. *Implied authority*—Authority customarily associated with the position of the agent or authority that is deemed necessary for the agent to carry out expressly authorized tasks. 3. *Apparent authority*—Exists when the principal, by word or action, causes a third party reasonably to believe that an agent has authority to act, even though the agent has no express or implied authority. 4. *Ratification*—The affirmation by the principal of an agent's unauthorized action or promise. For the ratification to be effective, the principal must be aware of all material facts.
Liability in Agency Relationships (See pages 405–408.)	1. *Liability for contracts*—If the principal's identity is disclosed or partially disclosed at the time the agent forms a contract with a third party, the principal is liable to the third party under the contract if the agent acted within the scope of his or her authority. If the principal's identity is undisclosed at the time of contract formation, the agent is personally liable to the third party, but if the agent acted within the scope of his or her authority, the principal is also bound by the contract. 2. *Liability for agent's negligence*—Under the doctrine of *respondeat superior,* the principal is liable for any harm caused to another through the agent's torts if the agent was acting within the scope of her or his employment at the time the harmful act occurred. 3. *Liability for agent's intentional torts*—Usually, employers are not liable for the intentional torts that their agents commit, *unless:* a. The acts are committed within the scope of employment, and thus the doctrine of *respondeat superior* applies. b. The employer knows or should know that the employee has a propensity for committing tortious acts. c. The employer allowed an employee to engage in reckless acts that caused injury to another. 4. *Liability for independent contractor's torts*—A principal is not liable for harm caused by an independent contractor's negligence, unless hazardous activities are involved (in this situation, the principal is strictly liable for any resulting harm) or other exceptions apply. 5. *Liability for agent's crimes*—An agent is responsible for his or her own crimes, even if the crimes were committed while the agent was acting within the scope of authority or employment. A principal will be liable for an agent's crime only if the principal participated by conspiracy or other action or (in some jurisdictions) if the agent violated certain government regulations in the course of employment.
How Agency Relationships Are Terminated (See pages 408–410.)	1. *By act of the parties*—Notice to third parties is required when an agency is terminated by act of the parties. Direct notice is required for those who have previously dealt with the agency; constructive notice will suffice for all other third parties. See pages 408 and 409 for a list of the ways that an agency may be terminated by act of the parties. 2. *By operation of law*—Notice to third parties is not required when an agency is terminated by operation of law. Ways that an agency can be terminated by operation of law include death or insanity, impossibility, changed circumstances, bankruptcy, and war.

ExamPrep

ISSUE SPOTTERS

—Check your answers to these questions against the answers provided in Appendix G.

1 Vivian, owner of Wonder Goods Company, employs Xena as an administrative assistant. In Vivian's absence, and without authority, Xena represents herself as Vivian and signs a promissory note in Vivian's name. In what circumstance is Vivian liable on the note?

2 Davis contracts with Estee to buy a certain horse on her behalf. Estee asks Davis not to reveal her identity. Davis makes a deal with Farmland Stables, the owner of the horse, and makes a down payment. Estee does not pay the rest of the price. Farmland Stables sues Davis for breach of contract. Can Davis hold Estee liable for whatever damages he has to pay? Why or why not?

BEFORE THE TEST

Go to **www.cengagebrain.com**, enter the ISBN 9781111530624, and click on "Find" to locate this textbook's Web site. Then, click on "Access Now" under "Study Tools," and select Chapter 21 at the top. There, you will find an Interactive Quiz that you can take to assess your mastery of the concepts in this chapter, as well as Flashcards and a Glossary of important terms.

For Review

1. What is the difference between an employee and an independent contractor?
2. How do agency relationships arise?
3. What duties do agents and principals owe to each other?
4. When is a principal liable for the agent's actions with respect to third parties? When is the agent liable?
5. What are some of the ways in which an agency relationship can be terminated?

Questions and Case Problems

21–1 Ratification by Principal. Springer was a political candidate running for Congress. He was operating on a tight budget and instructed his campaign staff not to purchase any campaign materials without his explicit authorization. In spite of these instructions, one of his campaign workers ordered Dubychek Printing Co. to print some promotional materials for Springer's campaign. When the printed materials arrived, Springer did not return them but instead used them during his campaign. When Springer failed to pay for the materials, Dubychek sued for recovery of the price. Springer contended that he was not liable on the sales contract because he had not authorized his agent to purchase the printing services. Dubychek argued that the campaign worker was Springer's agent and that the worker had authority to make the printing contract. Additionally, Dubychek claimed that even if the purchase was unauthorized, Springer's use of the materials constituted ratification of his agent's unauthorized purchase. Is Dubychek correct? Explain.

21–2 Question with Sample Answer Paul Gett is a well-known, wealthy financial expert living in the city of Torris. Adam Wade, Gett's friend, tells Timothy Brown that he is Gett's agent for the purchase of rare coins. Wade even shows Brown a local newspaper clipping mentioning Gett's interest in coin collecting. Brown, knowing of Wade's friendship with Gett, contracts with Wade to sell a rare coin valued at $25,000 to Gett. Wade takes the coin and disappears with it. On the payment due date, Brown seeks to collect from Gett, claiming that Wade's agency made Gett liable. Gett does not deny that Wade was a friend, but he claims that Wade was never his agent. Discuss fully whether an agency was in existence at the time the contract for the rare coin was made.

—For a sample answer to Question 21–2, go to Appendix E at the end of this text.

21–3 Liability for Independent Contractor's Torts. Dean Brothers Corp. owns and operates a steel drum manufacturing plant. Lowell Wyden, the plant superintendent, hired Best Security Patrol, Inc. (BSP), a security company, to guard Dean property and "deter thieves and vandals." Some BSP security guards, as Wyden knew, carried firearms. Pete Sidell, a BSP security guard, was not certified as an armed guard but nevertheless took his gun, in a briefcase, to work. While working at the Dean plant on October 31, 2011, Sidell fired his gun at Tyrone Gaines, in the belief that Gaines was an intruder. The bullet struck and killed Gaines. Gaines's mother filed a lawsuit claiming that her son's death was the result of BSP's negligence, for which Dean was responsible. What is the plaintiff's best argument that Dean is responsible for BSP's actions? What is Dean's best defense? Explain.

21–4 Case Problem with Sample Answer Homeowners Jim and Lisa Criss hired Kevin and Cathie Pappas, doing business as Outside Creations, to undertake a landscaping project. Kevin signed the parties' contract as "Outside Creations Rep." The Crisses' payments on the contract were by checks payable to Kevin, who deposited them in his personal account—there was no Outside Creations account. Later, alleging breach, the Crisses filed a suit in a Georgia state court against the Pappases. The defendants contended that they could not be liable because the contract was not with them personally. They claimed that they were the agents of Forever Green Landscaping and Irrigation, Inc., which had been operating under the name "Outside Creations" at the time of the contract and had since filed for bankruptcy. The Crisses pointed out that the name "Forever Green" was not in the contract. Can the Pappases be liable on this contract? Why or why not? [*Pappas v. Criss*, 296 Ga.App. 803, 676 S.E.2d 21 (2009)]

—For a sample answer to Problem 21–4, go to Appendix F at the end of this text.

21–5 Agency by Ratification. Wesley Hall, an independent contractor managing property for Acree Investments, Ltd., lost control of a fire he had set to clear ten acres of Acree land. The runaway fire burned seventy-eight acres of Earl Barrs's property. Russell Acree, one of the owners of Acree Investments, had previously owned the ten acres, but he had put it into the company and he was no longer the principal owner. Hall had worked for Russell Acree in the past and had told the state forestry department that he was burning the land for Acree. Barrs sued Russell Acree for the acts of his agent, Hall. In his suit, Barrs noted that Hall had been an employee of Russell Acree, Hall had talked about burning the land "for Acree," Russell Acree had apologized to Barrs for the fire, and Acree Investments had not been identified as the principal property owner until Barrs had filed his lawsuit. Barrs argued that those facts were sufficient to create an agency by ratification to impose liability on Russell Acree. Was Barrs's agency by ratification claim valid? Why or why not? [*Barrs v. Acree*, 302 Ga.App. 521, 691 S.E.2d 575 (2010)]

21–6 Liability Based on Actual or Apparent Authority. Summerall Electric Co. and other subcontractors were hired by National Church Services, Inc. (NCS), which was the general contractor on a construction project for the Church of God at Southaven (the Church). As work progressed, payments from NCS to the subcontractors became later and later until they eventually stopped. The Church had paid NCS in full for the entire project beforehand, but apparently, NCS had mismanaged the project. When payments from NCS stopped, the subcontractors filed mechanic's liens (see Chapter 19) for the value of the work they had performed but for which they had not been paid. The subcontractors sued the Church, contending that NCS was its agent based on either actual authority or apparent authority, and thus the Church was liable for the payments. Was NCS an agent for the Church based on actual or apparent authority, thereby making the Church liable to the subcontractors? Discuss your reasons. [Summerall Electric Co. v. Church of God at Southaven, 25 So.3d 1090 (App.Miss. 2010)]

21–7 Employment Relationships. William Moore owned and operated Moore Enterprises, a wholesale tire business, in Idaho. While in high school, William's son, Jonathan, worked as a Moore employee. Later, Jonathan started his own business, called Morecedes Tire. Morecedes regrooved tires and sold them to businesses, including Moore. Moore made payments for the tires not to Jonathan, but to Morecedes Tire, without tax withholding. A decade after Jonathan started Morecedes, William offered him work with Moore for $12 per hour. Jonathan accepted but retained Morecedes Tire. On the first day, William told Jonathan to load some tires on a trailer. While Jonathan was unhooking the trailer, a jack handle struck him. He suffered several broken bones in his face and a detached retina. He was never paid for the work. He filed a workers' compensation claim. Under Idaho's laws, an individual must be an employee—not an independent contractor—to obtain workers' compensation. What criteria do the courts use to determine employee status? How do they apply to Jonathan? Discuss. [*Moore v. Moore*, __ P.3d __ (Idaho 2011)]

21–8 Disclosed Principal. Mario Sclafani (doing business as Martinucci Desserts USA, Inc.), wanted to place small refrigeration units containing point-of-purchase imported Italian desserts in New York City restaurants. Felix Storch, Inc., makes commercial refrigeration units. Sclafani ordered custom units for $18,000. Felix faxed a credit application to Sclafani. The application was faxed back with Sclafani's business banking information, credit references, and a signature that appeared to be Sclafani's beneath a personal guaranty clause. Felix made and delivered the units. The imported dessert business failed, and the units were not paid for. Felix filed a suit in a New York state court against Sclafani to collect. Sclafani denied that he had seen the credit application or signed it and testified that he referred all credit questions to "the girls in the office." Among these parties, who is the principal? Who are the agents? Who is liable on the contract? Explain. [*Felix Storch, Inc. v. Martinucci Desserts USA, Inc.*, 30 Misc.3d 1217, 924 N.Y.S.2d 308 (2011)]

21–9 A Question of Ethics *Emergency One, Inc. (EO), makes fire and rescue vehicles. Western Fire Truck, Inc., contracted with EO to be its exclusive dealer in Colorado and Wyoming through December 2003. James Costello, a Western salesperson, was authorized to order EO vehicles for his customers. Without informing Western, Costello e-mailed EO about Western's difficulties in obtaining cash to fund its operations. He asked about the viability of Western's contract and his possible employment with EO. On EO's request, and in disregard of Western's instructions, Costello sent some payments for EO vehicles directly to EO. In addition, Costello, with EO's help, sent a competing bid to a potential Western customer. EO's representative e-mailed Costello, "You have my permission to kick [Western's] ass." In April 2002, EO terminated its contract with Western, which, after reviewing Costello's e-mail, fired Costello. Western filed a suit in a Colorado state court against Costello and EO, alleging, among other things, that Costello breached his duty as an agent and that EO aided and abetted the breach. [*Western Fire Truck, Inc. v. Emergency One, Inc., *134 P.3d 570 (Colo.App. 2006)]*

1. Was there an agency relationship between Western and Costello? Western required monthly reports from its sales staff, but Costello did not report regularly. Does this indicate that Costello was not Western's agent? In determining whether an agency relationship exists, is the *right* to control or the *fact* of control more important? Explain.
2. Did Costello owe Western a duty? If so, what was the duty? Did Costello breach it? How?
3. A Colorado state statute allows a court to award punitive damages in "circumstances of fraud, malice, or willful and wanton conduct." Did any of these circumstances exist in this case? Should punitive damages be assessed against either defendant? Why or why not?

21–10 Critical Thinking Legal Question What policy is served by the law that employers do not have copyright ownership in works created by independent contractors (unless there is a written "work for hire" agreement)?

Chapter 22

Employment, Immigration, and Labor Law

Learning Objectives

After reading this chapter, you should be able to answer the following questions:

1. Under the Family and Medical Leave Act of 1993, in what circumstances may an employee take family or medical leave?
2. Generally, what kind of conduct is prohibited by Title VII of the Civil Rights Act of 1964, as amended?
3. What federal acts prohibit discrimination based on age and discrimination based on disability?
4. What are the two most important federal statutes governing immigration and employment today?
5. What federal statute gave employees the right to organize unions and engage in collective bargaining?

The Learning Objectives above are designed to help improve your understanding of the chapter.

Until the early 1900s, most employer-employee relationships were governed by the common law. Today, however, common law doctrines have to a large extent been displaced by statutory law. Although employers still generally are free to hire and fire workers at will under the common law *employment-at-will* doctrine, for example, an employer may not do so if the action would violate the employee's contractual or statutory rights. In many other ways as well, the workplace now is regulated by numerous statutes and administrative agency regulations.

Some of this statutory law originated during the Great Depression in the 1930s, when both state and federal governments began to regulate employment relationships. Legislation enacted during the 1930s and subsequent decades has established many protections for employees including the right to form labor unions and bargain with management for improved working conditions, salaries, and benefits. The ultimate weapon of labor is, of course, the strike. Strikes and lockouts (the employer's counterpart to the worker's right to strike) are still utilized by unions today. In 2011, for example, the owners of the National Football League (NFL) teams imposed a lockout during their dispute with NFL players over salaries and other issues (discussed on page 435).

In this chapter, we look at the most significant laws regulating employment relationships. We also discuss other important laws regulating the workplace—those that prohibit employment discrimination.

Employment at Will

Traditionally, employment relationships have generally been governed by the common law doctrine of **employment at will.** Under the employment-at-will doctrine, either party may terminate the employment relationship at any time and for any reason, unless doing so would violate the provisions of an employment contract. The majority of U.S. workers continue to have the legal status of "employees at will." In other words, this common law doctrine is still in widespread use, and only one state (Montana) does not apply the doctrine.

Nonetheless, as mentioned in the chapter introduction, federal and state statutes governing employment relationships prevent this doctrine from being applied in a number of circumstances. Today, an employer is not permitted to fire an employee if doing so would violate a federal or state employment statute, such as one prohibiting employment termination for discriminatory reasons (discussed later in this chapter).

Note that the distinction made under agency law (discussed in Chapter 21) between employee status and independent-contractor status is important here. The employment laws that are discussed in this chapter apply only to the employer-employee relationship, *not to independent contractors.*

Exceptions to the Employment-at-Will Doctrine

Because of the harsh effects of the employment-at-will doctrine for employees, the courts have carved out various exceptions to the doctrine. These exceptions are based on contract theory, tort theory, and public policy.

EXCEPTIONS BASED ON CONTRACT THEORY Some courts have held that an *implied* employment contract exists between an employer and an employee. If an employee is fired outside the terms of the implied contract, he or she may succeed in an action for breach of contract even though no written employment contract exists. **EXAMPLE 22.1** BDI Enterprise's employment manual and personnel bulletin both state that, as a matter of policy, workers will be dismissed only for good cause. If an employee reasonably expects BDI to follow this policy, a court may find that there is an implied contract based on the terms stated in the manual and bulletin. • Generally, in determining whether an employment manual created an implied contractual obligation, the courts focus on the employee's reasonable expectations.

An employer's oral promises to employees regarding discharge policy may also be considered part of an implied contract. If the employer fires a worker in a manner contrary to what was promised, a court may hold that the employer has violated the implied contract and is liable for damages. Most state courts will judge a claim of breach of an implied employment contract by traditional contract standards.

Courts in a few states have gone further and held that all employment contracts contain an implied covenant of good faith. This means that both sides promise to abide by the contract in good faith. If an employer fires an employee for an arbitrary or unjustified reason, the employee can claim that the covenant of good faith was breached and the contract violated.

EXCEPTIONS BASED ON TORT THEORY In a few situations, the discharge of an employee may give rise to an action for wrongful discharge under tort theories. Abusive discharge procedures may result in a suit for intentional infliction of emotional distress or defamation. In addition, some courts have permitted workers to sue their employers under the tort theory of fraud. **EXAMPLE 22.2** Goldfinch, Inc., induces a prospective employee to leave a lucrative job and move to another state by offering "a long-term job with a thriving business." In fact, Goldfinch is not only having significant financial problems but is also planning a merger that will result in the elimination of the position offered to the prospective employee. If the employee takes the job in reliance on Goldfinch's representations and is fired shortly thereafter, the employee may be able to bring an action against the employer for fraud. •

EXCEPTIONS BASED ON PUBLIC POLICY The most common exception to the employment-at-will doctrine is made on the basis of public policy. Courts may apply this exception when an employer fires a worker for reasons that violate a fundamental public policy of the jurisdiction. Generally, the public policy involved must be expressed clearly in the statutory law governing the jurisdiction.

An exception may also be made when an employee "blows the whistle" on an employer's wrongdoing. **Whistleblowing** occurs when an employee tells government authorities, upper-level managers, or the media that her or his employer is engaged in some unsafe or illegal activity. Whistleblowers on occasion have been protected from wrongful discharge for reasons of public policy.

CASE EXAMPLE 22.3 Rebecca Wendeln was the staff coordinator at a nursing home. One of the patients was wheelchair-bound and could be moved only by two persons using a special belt. When Wendeln discovered that the patient had been improperly moved and was injured as a result, she reported the incident to state authorities, as she was required to do by state law. Wendeln's supervisor angrily confronted her about the report, and she was fired shortly after that. Wendeln filed a lawsuit. The court held that although Wendeln was an employee at will, she was protected in this instance from retaliatory firing because a very clear mandate of public policy had been violated.[1] • Normally, however, whistleblowers seek protection from retaliatory discharge under federal and state statutory laws, such as the Whistleblower Protection Act of 1989.[2]

Wrongful Discharge

Whenever an employer discharges an employee in violation of an employment contract or a statute protecting employees, the employee may bring an action for **wrongful discharge.** Even if an employer's actions do not violate any provisions in an employment contract or a statute, the employer may still be subject to liability under a common law doctrine, such as a tort theory or agency. Note that in today's business world, an employment contract may be established or modified via

1. *Wendeln v. The Beatrice Manor, Inc.*, 271 Neb. 373, 712 N.W.2d 226 (2006).
2. 5 U.S.C. Section 1201.

MANAGEMENT PERSPECTIVE • Can Parties Create and Modify Employment Contracts via E-Mail?

Management Faces a Legal Issue

E-mail is used in nearly every aspect of the employment environment–from workplace communications to contracts with employees. Under the one-year rule of the Statute of Frauds, most employment contracts must be in writing. But electronic communications, including e-mail, instant messages, text messages, and even Twitter, can be used as evidence to show that a contract existed or that the parties modified their contract. A legal issue that managers are facing today involves how they negotiate and modify employment contracts. Specifically, what constitutes a signed writing has changed.

What the Courts Say

Consider an example. Robert Moroni negotiated a deal to provide consulting services for Medco Health Solutions, Inc., a third party administrator of prescription-drug plans. Medco's agent, Brian Griffin, sent Moroni an e-mail setting forth the details of the parties' agreement. Moroni e-mailed a counteroffer suggesting that he would work on Medco's projects two days a week for thirteen months, in exchange for $17,000 a month ($204,000 annually), plus travel expenses. Medco accepted via e-mail, and Moroni began performing the contract. When Medco refused to pay him, Moroni sued for breach of contract. Medco argued that no enforceable contract existed and that the e-mail showed only an agreement to agree. The court, however, ruled that the e-mail amounted to an agreement to the essential terms of an employment contract.[a]

In another case, Arthur Stevens sold his public relations firm in New York to Publicis, S.A.,[b] a French global communications company. The sale involved two contracts: a stock purchase agreement and an employment contract. The employment contract allowed Stevens to stay on as chief executive officer (CEO) of the new company for three years and contained an integration clause requiring any modification to be in a signed writing. Within six months of the sale, however, the new company had lost $900,000 and was not meeting revenue and profit targets. Stevens was removed as CEO and given the option of leaving the firm or staying to develop new business. An agent of Publicis, Bob Bloom, then e-mailed Stevens another option, giving him specific information on the responsibilities he could assume. Within a day, Stevens e-mailed a response, "I accept your proposal with total enthusiasm and excitement," and said that he was "psyched" about his new position. Nevertheless, Stevens later sued Publicis, claiming that it had breached the terms of his original employment contract by not keeping him on as CEO.

The court, however, held that in the e-mail exchanges with Bloom, Stevens had accepted the proposed modification of his employment contract in a signed writing. Because the e-mail modification was binding, Stevens could not sue Publicis.[c]

Implications for Managers

E-mail has become practically the only method of business communications today. Managers and business owners must now assume that any contract changes and decisions made via e-mail may be binding. Consequently, managers need to track and monitor their e-mails very carefully to ensure that they understand how their communications could potentially modify an employment contract or change the company's position within a business contract. Organizing e-mails into relevant files will help managers keep track of what was said and when. As communications technology continues to evolve online and through mobile devices, such as BlackBerrys, iPhones, and iPads, business managers will need to develop additional policies and strategies for their negotiations with prospective employees, suppliers, and partners.

a. *Moroni v. Medco Health Solutions, Inc.*, 2008 WL 3539476 (E.D.Mich. 2008).

b. *S.A.* are the initials for *Société Anonyme*, which is the French equivalent to a corporation in the United States.

c. *Stevens v. Publicis, S.A.*, 50 A.D.3d 253, 854 N.Y.S.2d 690 (1 Dept. 2008). See also *Naldi v. Grunberg*, 80 A.D.3d 1, 908 N.Y.S.2d 639 (1 Dept. 2010).

e-mail exchanges, as discussed in this chapter's *Management Perspective* feature above.

Wage and Hour Laws

In the 1930s, Congress enacted several laws regulating the wages and working hours of employees. In 1931, Congress passed the Davis-Bacon Act,[3] which requires contractors and subcontractors working on federal government construction projects to pay "prevailing wages" to their employees. In 1936, the Walsh-Healey Act[4] was passed. This act requires that a minimum wage, as well as overtime pay at 1.5 times regular pay rates, be paid to employees of manufacturers or suppliers entering into contracts with agencies of the federal government.

In 1938, Congress passed the Fair Labor Standards Act (FLSA).[5] This act extended wage and hour requirements to cover all employers engaged in interstate commerce or in the production of goods for interstate commerce, plus selected types of other businesses. More than 130 million American workers are protected (or covered) by the FLSA, which is enforced by the Wage and Hour Division of the U.S. Department of Labor.

3. 40 U.S.C. Sections 276a–276a-5.

4. 41 U.S.C. Sections 35–45.

5. 29 U.S.C. Sections 201–260.

Here, we examine the FLSA's provisions in regard to child labor, minimum wages, and maximum hours.

Child Labor

The FLSA prohibits oppressive child labor. Children under fourteen years of age are allowed to do certain types of work, such as deliver newspapers, work for their parents, and work in the entertainment and (with some exceptions) agricultural areas. Children who are fourteen or fifteen years of age are allowed to work, but not in hazardous occupations. There are also numerous restrictions on how many hours per day (particularly on school days) and per week they can work.

Working times and hours are not restricted for persons between the ages of sixteen and eighteen, but they cannot be employed in hazardous jobs or in jobs detrimental to their health and well-being. None of these restrictions apply to persons over the age of eighteen.

Minimum Wage Requirements

The FLSA provides that a **minimum wage** of $7.25 per hour must be paid to employees in covered industries. Congress periodically revises this federal minimum wage. Additionally, many states have minimum wage laws. When the state minimum wage is greater than the federal minimum wage, the employee is entitled to the higher wage.

When an employee receives tips while on the job, an employer is required to pay only $2.13 an hour in direct wages—but only if that amount, plus the tips received, equals at least the federal minimum wage (because under the FLSA every covered employee is required to be paid $7.25 per hour). If an employee's tips combined with the employer's direct wages of at least $2.13 an hour do not equal the federal minimum hourly wage, the employer must make up the difference. If employers are paying at least the federal minimum hourly wage, the FLSA does not prevent them from taking employee tips and making another arrangement for tip distribution. Under the FLSA, employers who customarily furnish food or lodging to employees can deduct the reasonable cost of those services from the employees' wages.

Overtime Provisions and Exemptions

Under the FLSA, employees who work more than forty hours per week normally must be paid 1.5 times their regular pay for all hours over forty. Note that the FLSA overtime provisions apply only after an employee has worked more than forty hours per *week*. Thus, employees who work for ten hours a day, four days per week, are not entitled to overtime pay because they do not work more than forty hours per week.

Certain employees—usually executive, administrative, and professional employees, as well as outside salespersons and computer programmers—are exempt from the FLSA's overtime provisions. Employers are not required to pay overtime wages to exempt employees. Employers can voluntarily pay overtime to ineligible employees but cannot waive or reduce the overtime requirements of the FLSA.

An executive employee is one whose primary duty is management. An employee's primary duty is determined by what he or she does that is of principal value to the employer, not by how much time the employee spends doing particular tasks. **CASE EXAMPLE 22.4** Kevin Keevican, a manager at a Starbucks store, worked seventy hours a week for $650 to $800, a 10 to 20 percent bonus, and paid sick leave. Keevican (and other former managers) filed a claim against Starbucks for unpaid overtime, claiming that he had spent 70 to 80 percent of his time waiting on customers and thus was not an executive employee. The court, however, found that Keevican was "the single highest-ranking employee" in his particular store and was responsible on site for that store's day-to-day overall operations. Because his primary duty was managerial, Starbucks was not required to pay overtime.[6] •

In the following case, the issue before the court was whether an employee of a pharmaceutical company was exempt from the overtime requirements of the FLSA as an administrative employee.

6. *Mims v. Starbucks Corp.*, 2007 WL 10369 (S.D.Tex. 2007).

Case 22.1 Smith v. Johnson and Johnson

United States Court of Appeals, Third Circuit, 593 F.3d 280 (2010).
www.ca3.uscourts.gov[a]

FACTS Patty Lee Smith was a senior professional sales representative for McNeil Pediatrics, a wholly owned subsidiary of Johnson and Johnson (J&J). Smith's position required her to visit prescribing doctors to describe the benefits of J&J's pharmaceutical drug Concerta. Smith, however, did not sell Concerta (a controlled substance) directly to the doctors, as such sales are prohibited by law. J&J gave Smith a list of target doctors and told her to complete an average of ten visits per day, visiting every doctor on her target list at least once each quarter. To schedule visits with reluctant doctors, Smith had to be inventive and cultivate relationships with the doctor's

a. In the "Opinions and Oral Arguments" box, select "Opinion Archives." When that page opens, select "February" in the listing under "2010 Decisions." Scroll down the list of "Precedential" cases in the left-hand column and click on the highlighted case title to access the opinion. The U.S. Court of Appeals for the Third Circuit maintains this Web site.

Case 22.1–Continues next page ➡

Case 22.1–Continued

staff—an endeavor in which she found that coffee and doughnuts were useful tools. J&J left the itinerary and order of Smith's visits to her discretion. J&J gave her a budget, and she could use the funds to take the doctors to lunch or to sponsor seminars. In Smith's deposition, she stated that she was unsupervised about 95 percent of the time. According to Smith, "It was really up to me to run the territory the way I wanted to." Smith earned a base salary of $66,000 but was not paid overtime. Smith filed a suit in a federal district court under the Fair Labor Standards Act (FLSA), seeking overtime pay. J&J moved for summary judgment in its favor, arguing that Smith was exempt from the FLSA's overtime requirements because she was an administrative employee. The court granted the motion, and Smith appealed.

ISSUE Was Smith an administrative employee and thus exempt from the overtime requirements of the FLSA?

DECISION Yes. The U.S. Court of Appeals for the Third Circuit affirmed the judgment of the district court. Smith qualified as an administrative employee.

REASON To qualify under the administrative employee exemption, the employee must be paid on a salary basis and his or her primary duty must be directly related to the management or general business operations of the employer. In addition, the employee's primary duty must include the exercise of discretion and independent judgment with respect to matters of significance. The court noted that "while testifying at her deposition, Smith elaborated on the independent and managerial qualities that her position required. Her . . . position required her to form a strategic plan designed to maximize sales in her territory." The court reasoned that this satisfied the "directly related to the management or general business operations of the employer" requirement of the administrative employee exemption. Clearly, Smith had to engage in high-level planning and foresight, and she had to develop her own strategic plan. Furthermore, she exercised nearly all of her duties without direct oversight. The lack of oversight and the freedom to develop her own sales strategy indicated that Smith was an administrative employee who was not entitled to overtime pay.

FOR CRITICAL ANALYSIS—Ethical Consideration *Is it unfair to exempt certain employees to deprive them of overtime wages? Why or why not?*

Layoffs

During the latest economic recession in the United States, hundreds of thousands of workers lost their jobs as many businesses disappeared. Other companies struggling to keep afloat reduced costs by restructuring their operations and downsizing their workforces, which meant layoffs.

Mass layoffs of U.S. workers resulted in high unemployment rates. Later in this chapter, we will discuss unemployment insurance, which helps some workers manage financially until they can find another job. In this section, we discuss the laws pertaining to employee layoffs—an area that is increasingly the subject of litigation.

The Worker Adjustment and Retraining Notification (WARN) Act

Since 1988, federal law has required large employers to provide sixty days' notice before implementing a mass layoff or closing a plant that employs more than fifty full-time workers. The Worker Adjustment and Retraining Notification Act,[7] or WARN Act, applies to employers with at least one hundred full-time employees. It is intended to give workers advance notice so that they can start looking for a new job while they are still employed and to alert state agencies so that they can provide training and other resources for displaced workers.

The WARN Act defines the term *mass layoff* as a reduction in the workforce that, during any thirty-day period, results in an employment loss of either:

1. At least 33 percent of the full-time employees at a single job site and at least fifty employees; or
2. At least five hundred full-time employees.

An *employment loss* is defined as a layoff that exceeds six months or a reduction in hours of work of more than 50 percent during each month of any six-month period.

The WARN Act requires that advance notice of the layoff be sent to the affected workers *or* their representative (if the workers are members of a labor union), as well as to state and local government authorities. Even companies that anticipate filing for bankruptcy normally must provide notice under the WARN Act before implementing a mass layoff. If sued, an employer that orders a mass layoff or plant closing in violation of the WARN Act can be fined up to $500 for each day of the violation. Employees can recover back pay for each day of the violation (up to sixty days), plus reasonable attorneys' fees.

State Laws May Also Require Layoff Notices

Many states also have statutes requiring employers to provide notice before initiating mass layoffs, and these laws may have different and even stricter requirements than the WARN Act. In New York, for instance, companies with fifty or more employees must provide ninety days' notice before any layoff

7. 29 U.S.C. Sections 2101 *et seq.*

that affects twenty-five or more full-time employees. The law in Illinois applies to companies with seventy-five or more employees and requires sixty days' advance notice of any layoff that affects twenty-five or more full-time employees at one plant or 250 employees.

Family and Medical Leave

In 1993, Congress passed the Family and Medical Leave Act (FMLA)[8] to allow employees to take time off from work for family or medical reasons. A majority of the states also have legislation allowing for a leave from employment for family or medical reasons, and many employers maintain private family-leave plans for their workers. FMLA regulations recently created new categories of leave for military caregivers and for qualifying exigencies that arise due to military service.

Coverage and Application

The FMLA requires employers that have fifty or more employees to provide employees with up to twelve weeks of unpaid family or medical leave during any twelve-month period. The FMLA expressly covers private and public (government) employees who have worked for their employers for at least a year.[9] An employee may take *family leave* to care for a newborn baby, an adopted child, or a foster child.[10] An employee can take *medical leave* when the employee or the employee's spouse, child, or parent has a "serious health condition" requiring care.

In addition, an employee caring for a family member with a serious injury or illness incurred as a result of military duty can now take up to *twenty-six weeks of military caregiver leave* within a twelve-month period.[11] Also, an employee can take up to twelve weeks of *qualifying exigency* (emergency) *leave* to handle specified *nonmedical* emergencies when a spouse, parent, or child is on, or called to, active military duty.[12] For instance, when a spouse is deployed to Afghanistan, an employee may take exigency leave to arrange for child care or to deal with financial or legal matters.

When an employee takes FMLA leave, the employer must continue the worker's health-care coverage on the same terms as if the employee had continued to work. On returning from FMLA leave, most employees must be restored to their original position or to a comparable position (with nearly equivalent pay and benefits, for example). An important exception allows the employer to avoid reinstating a *key employee*—defined as an employee whose pay falls within the top 10 percent of the firm's workforce.

Violations

An employer that violates the FMLA can be required to provide various remedies, including the following:

1. Damages to compensate an employee for lost benefits, denied compensation, and actual monetary losses (such as the cost of providing for care of the family member) up to an amount equivalent to the employee's wages for twelve weeks (twenty-six weeks for military caregiver leave);
2. Job reinstatement; and
3. Promotion, if a promotion has been denied.

A successful plaintiff is entitled to court costs and attorneys' fees, and, if bad faith on the part of the employer is shown, can recover two times the amount of damages awarded by a judge or jury. Supervisors can also be held personally liable, as employers, for violations of the act. Employers generally are required to notify employees when an absence will be counted against leave authorized under the act. If an employer fails to provide such notice, and the employee consequently suffers some detriment because he or she did not receive notice, the employer may be sanctioned.

Worker Health and Safety

Under the common law, employees who were injured on the job had to file lawsuits against their employers to obtain recovery. Today, numerous state and federal statutes protect employees and their families from the risk of accidental injury, death, or disease resulting from their employment. This section discusses the primary federal statute governing health and safety in the workplace, along with state workers' compensation laws.

The Occupational Safety and Health Act

At the federal level, the primary legislation protecting employees' health and safety is the Occupational Safety and Health Act of 1970,[13] which is administered by the Occupational Safety and Health Administration (OSHA). The act imposes on employers a general duty to keep workplaces safe. To this end, OSHA has established specific safety standards that employers must follow depending on the industry. For instance, OSHA regulations require the use of safety guards on certain mechanical equipment and set maximum exposure

8. 29 U.S.C. Sections 2601, 2611–2619, 2651–2654.
9. Note that changes to the FMLA rules allow employees who have taken a break from their employment to qualify for FMLA leave if they worked a total of twelve months during the previous seven years. See 29 C.F.R. Section 825.110(b)(1-2).
10. The foster care must be state sanctioned before such an arrangement falls within the coverage of the FMLA.
11. 29 C.F.R. Section 825.200.
12. 29 C.F.R. Section 825.126.
13. 29 U.S.C. Sections 553, 651–678.

levels to substances in the workplace that may be harmful to a worker's health.

The act also requires that employers post certain notices in the workplace, perform prescribed record keeping, and submit specific reports. For instance, employers with eleven or more employees are required to keep occupational injury and illness records for each employee. Each record must be made available for inspection when requested by an OSHA compliance officer. Whenever a work-related injury or disease occurs, employers must make reports directly to OSHA. If an employee dies or three or more employees are hospitalized because of a work-related incident, the employer must notify OSHA within eight hours. A company that fails to do so will be fined and may also be prosecuted under state law. Following the incident, a complete inspection of the premises is mandatory.

OSHA compliance officers may enter and inspect the facilities of any establishment covered by the Occupational Safety and Health Act. Employees may also file complaints of violations. Under the act, an employer cannot discharge an employee who files a complaint or who, in good faith, refuses to work in a high-risk area if bodily harm or death might result.

State Workers' Compensation Laws

State **workers' compensation laws** establish an administrative procedure for compensating workers injured on the job. Instead of suing, an injured worker files a claim with the administrative agency or board that administers local workers' compensation claims.

Most workers' compensation statutes are similar. No state covers all employees. Typically, domestic workers, agricultural workers, temporary employees, and employees of common carriers (companies that provide transportation services to the public) are excluded, but minors are covered. Usually, the statutes allow employers to purchase insurance from a private insurer or a state fund to pay workers' compensation benefits in the event of a claim. Most states also allow employers to be *self-insured*—that is, employers that show an ability to pay claims do not need to buy insurance.

In general, the only requirements to recover benefits under state workers' compensation laws are:

1. The existence of an employment relationship; and
2. An *accidental* injury that *occurred on the job or in the course of employment,* regardless of fault. (If an injury occurs while an employee is commuting to or from work, it usually will not be considered to have occurred on the job or in the course of employment and hence will not be covered.)

An injured employee must notify her or his employer promptly (usually within thirty days of the accident). Generally, an employee must also file a workers' compensation claim with the appropriate state agency or board within a certain period (sixty days to two years) from the time the injury is first noticed, rather than from the time of the accident.

An employee's acceptance of workers' compensation benefits bars the employee from suing for injuries caused by the employer's negligence. By barring lawsuits for negligence, workers' compensation laws also prevent employers from raising common law defenses to negligence, such as contributory negligence, or assumption of risk. A worker may sue an employer who *intentionally* injures the worker, however.

Income Security

Federal and state governments participate in insurance programs designed to protect employees and their families by covering the financial impact of retirement, disability, death, hospitalization, and unemployment. The key federal law on this subject is the Social Security Act of 1935.[14]

Social Security

The Social Security Act provides for old-age (retirement), survivors', and disability insurance. The act is therefore often referred to as OASDI. Both employers and employees must "contribute" under the Federal Insurance Contributions Act (FICA)[15] to help pay for benefits that will partially make up for the employees' loss of income on retirement.

The basis for the employee's and the employer's contributions is the employee's annual wage base—the maximum amount of the employee's wages that is subject to the tax. The employer withholds the employee's FICA contribution from the employee's wages and then matches this contribution. (In 2012, employers were required to withhold 6.2 percent of each employee's wages, up to a maximum wage base of $110,000, and to match this contribution.)[16]

Retired workers are then eligible to receive monthly payments from the Social Security Administration, which administers the Social Security Act. Social Security benefits are fixed by statute but increase automatically with increases in the cost of living.

Medicare

Medicare, a federal government health-insurance program, is administered by the Social Security Administration for people sixty-five years of age and older and for some under the age of sixty-five who are disabled. It originally had two parts, one

14. 42 U.S.C. Sections 301–1397e.
15. 26 U.S.C. Sections 3101–3125.
16. Under the Tax Relief, Unemployment Insurance Reauthorization, and Job Creation Act of 2010, the amount employees pay into Social Security was temporarily reduced from 6.2 percent to 4.2 percent in 2011 only.

pertaining to hospital costs and the other to nonhospital medical costs, such as visits to physicians' offices. Medicare now offers additional coverage options and a prescription-drug plan. People who have Medicare hospital insurance can also obtain additional federal medical insurance if they pay small monthly premiums, which increase as the cost of medical care increases.

As with Social Security contributions, both the employer and the employee "contribute" to Medicare, but unlike Social Security, there is no cap on the amount of wages subject to the Medicare tax. In 2012, both the employer and the employee were required to pay 1.45 percent of *all* wages and salaries to finance Medicare.[17] Thus, for Social Security and Medicare together, in 2012 the employer and the employee each paid 7.65 percent of the first $110,000 of income (6.2 percent for Social Security + 1.45 percent for Medicare) for a combined total of 15.3 percent. In addition, all wages and salaries above $110,000 were taxed at a combined (employer and employee) rate of 2.9 percent for Medicare. Self-employed persons pay both the employer and the employee portions of the Social Security and Medicare taxes (15.3 percent of income up to $110,000 and 2.9 percent of income above that amount in 2012). In addition, starting in 2013, a Medicare tax of 3.8 percent will be applied to all investment income for those making more than $200,000.

Private Pension Plans

The major federal act regulating employee retirement plans is the Employee Retirement Income Security Act (ERISA) of 1974.[18] This act empowers a branch of the U.S. Department of Labor to enforce its provisions governing employers that have private pension funds for their employees. ERISA created the Pension Benefit Guaranty Corporation (PBGC), an independent federal agency, to provide timely and uninterrupted payment of voluntary private pension benefits. The pension plans pay annual insurance premiums (at set rates adjusted for inflation) to the PBGC, which then pays benefits to participants in the event that a plan is unable to do so. Under the Pension Protection Act of 2006,[19] the director of the PBGC is appointed by the president and confirmed by the U.S. Senate.

ERISA does not require an employer to establish a pension plan. When a plan exists, however, ERISA specifies standards for its management. A key provision of ERISA concerns vesting. **Vesting** gives an employee a legal right to receive pension benefits at some future date when he or she stops working. Before ERISA was enacted, some employees who had worked for companies for as long as thirty years received no pension benefits when their employment terminated, because those benefits had not vested. ERISA establishes complex vesting rules. Generally, however, all employee contributions to pension plans vest immediately, and employee rights to employer contributions to a plan vest after five years of employment.

In an attempt to prevent mismanagement of pension funds, ERISA has established rules on how they must be invested. Pension managers must be cautious in choosing investments and must diversify the plan's investments to minimize the risk of large losses. ERISA also imposes detailed record-keeping and reporting requirements.

Unemployment Compensation

To ease the financial impact of unemployment, the United States has a system of unemployment insurance. The Federal Unemployment Tax Act (FUTA) of 1935[20] created a state-administered system that provides unemployment compensation to eligible individuals. Under this system, employers pay into a fund, and the proceeds are paid out to qualified unemployed workers. The FUTA and state laws require employers that fall under the provisions of the act to pay unemployment taxes at regular intervals.

To be eligible for unemployment compensation, a worker must be willing and able to work. Workers who have been fired for misconduct or who have voluntarily left their jobs are not eligible for benefits. In the past, workers had to be actively seeking employment to continue receiving benefits. Due to the high unemployment rates after the Great Recession, however, President Barack Obama announced measures that allow jobless persons to retain their unemployment benefits while pursuing additional education and training (rather than seeking employment).

COBRA

For workers whose jobs have been terminated—and who are thus no longer eligible for group health-insurance plans—federal law also provides a right to continue their health-care coverage. The Consolidated Omnibus Budget Reconciliation Act (COBRA) of 1985[21] prohibits an employer from eliminating a worker's medical, optical, or dental insurance on the voluntary or involuntary termination of the worker's employment. Employers, with some exceptions, must provide information about COBRA's provisions to an employee who faces

17. Note that as a result of the Health Care and Education Reconciliation Act of 2010, not only are Medicare tax rates expected to rise, but also the applicable compensation base will expand to include more than just wage and salary income.

18. 29 U.S.C. Sections 1001 *et seq.*

19. The Pension Protection Act amended 26 U.S.C. Sections 430–432, 436, 4966, 4967, 6039I, 6050U, 6050V, 6695A, 6720B, 7443B; and 29 U.S.C. Sections 1082–1085, 1202a.

20. 26 U.S.C. Sections 3301–3310.

21. 29 U.S.C. Sections 1161–1169.

termination or a reduction of hours that would affect his or her eligibility for coverage under the plan. Only workers fired for gross misconduct are excluded from protection.

PROCEDURES A worker has sixty days (beginning with the date that the group coverage would stop) to decide whether to continue with the employer's group insurance plan. If the worker chooses to discontinue the coverage, the employer has no further obligation. If the worker opts to continue coverage, though, the employer is obligated to keep the policy active for up to eighteen months (or twenty-nine months if the worker is disabled). The coverage provided must be the same as that enjoyed by the worker prior to the termination or reduction of work. If family members were originally included, for instance, COBRA prohibits their exclusion.

PAYMENT The worker does not receive the insurance coverage for free. Generally, an employer can require the employee to pay all of the premiums, plus a 2 percent administrative charge. If the worker fails to pay the required amount (or if the employer completely eliminates its group benefit plan), the employer is relieved of further responsibility. An employer that does not comply with COBRA risks substantial penalties, such as a tax of up to 10 percent of the annual cost of the group plan or $500,000, whichever is less.

Employee Privacy Rights

In the last thirty years, concerns about the privacy rights of employees have arisen in response to the sometimes invasive tactics used by employers to monitor and screen workers. More than half of employers engage in some form of surveillance of their employees. Types of monitoring include reviewing employees' e-mail, blogs, instant messages, tweets, Internet use, and computer files; video recording of employee job performance; and recording and reviewing telephone conversations, voice mail, and text messages. Private employers generally can use specially designed software to track employees' Internet use and block access to certain Web sites without violating the First Amendment's protection of free speech (which applies only to government employers).

Tort law (see Chapter 4), state constitutions, and a number of state and federal statutes also provide for privacy rights. When determining whether an employer should be held liable for violating an employee's privacy rights, the courts generally weigh the employer's interests against the employee's reasonable expectation of privacy. Normally, if employees have been informed that their communications are being monitored, they cannot reasonably expect those interactions to be private. If employees are not informed that certain communications are being monitored, however, the employer may be held liable for invading their privacy.

The Electronic Communications Privacy Act

Employers must comply with the federal Electronic Communications Privacy Act (ECPA) of 1986.[22] The ECPA prohibits the intentional interception and disclosure of any wire or electronic communication. An exception is made when the employer provided the device (such as a smart phone or an iPad) or furnished the service (such as e-mail or Internet) in the ordinary course of business. An employer also may not intentionally access a stored electronic communication without authorization.

CASE EXAMPLE 22.5 Jeff Quon, a police sergeant for the city of Ontario, California, was issued a pager with wireless text-messaging services provided by Arch Wireless Operating Company. Although the city had a general policy that employees should not use work computers, Internet, and e-mail for personal matters, it did not expressly mention the pagers or text messaging. On several occasions, Quon paid the city overage charges for exceeding the limit on text messages. Without Quon's knowledge, his supervisors then requested transcripts of his stored text messages from Arch Wireless and read them to determine whether the texts were work related or personal. When Quon learned that his supervisors had read his personal (and sexually explicit) texts to his wife, he filed a lawsuit against the city and Arch Wireless for violating his privacy rights. Ultimately, the United States Supreme Court held that the search of Quon's text messages was reasonable. Because the police department had a written policy, which Quon admitted that he understood applied to the pagers, he had no reasonable expectation of privacy.[23] •

Drug Testing

In the interests of public safety, many employers, including government employers, require their employees to submit to drug testing. Government (public) employers are constrained in drug testing by the Fourth Amendment to the U.S. Constitution, which prohibits unreasonable searches and seizures (see Chapter 6). Drug testing of public employees is allowed by statute for transportation workers and normally is upheld by the courts when drug use in a particular job may threaten public safety. Also, when there is a reasonable basis for suspecting government employees of using drugs, courts often find that drug testing does not violate the Fourth Amendment.

The Fourth Amendment does not apply to drug testing conducted by private employers. Hence, the privacy rights and drug testing of private-sector employees are governed by state law, which varies widely. Many states allow drug testing by private employers but place restrictions on when and how the testing may be performed. A collective bargaining agreement may

22. 18 U.S.C. Sections 2510–2521.

23. *City of Ontario, California v. Quon,* __ U.S. __, 130 S.Ct. 2619, 177 L.Ed.2d 216 (2010).

also provide protection against drug testing (or authorize drug testing under certain conditions). The permissibility of a private employer's drug tests typically hinges on whether the testing was reasonable. Random drug tests and even "zero-tolerance" policies (that deny a "second chance" to employees who test positive for drugs) have been held to be reasonable.[24]

24. See, for example, *CITGO Asphalt Refining Co. v. Paper, Allied-Industrial, Chemical, and Energy Workers International Union Local No. 2-991*, 385 F.3d 809 (3d Cir. 2004).

Federal government employees have long been required to submit to background checks as a condition of employment. Many workers who work at U.S. government facilities, however, are employees of private contractors, not of the government. They generally have not been subject to background checks. When new standards required background checks for all federal workers, including contract employees, several contract workers brought a lawsuit asserting that their privacy rights had been violated.

Case 22.2 National Aeronautics and Space Administration v. Nelson

Supreme Court of the United States, __ U.S. __, 131 S.Ct. 746, 178 L.Ed.2d 667 (2011).
www.supremecourt.gov[a]

FACTS The National Aeronautics and Space Administration (NASA) is an independent federal agency charged with planning and conducting "space activities." One of NASA's facilities is the Jet Propulsion Laboratory (JPL) in Pasadena, California, which is staffed exclusively by contract employees. In 2007, under newly implemented standards, contract employees with long-term access to federal facilities were ordered to complete a standard background check—the National Agency Check with Inquiries (NACI). The NACI is designed to obtain information on such issues as counseling and treatment, as well as mental and financial stability. Robert Nelson and other JPL employees filed a lawsuit in a federal district court against NASA, claiming that the NACI violated their privacy rights. The court denied the plaintiffs' request to prohibit use of the NACI, but the U.S. Court of Appeals for the Ninth Circuit reversed this decision. NASA appealed to the United States Supreme Court, arguing that the Privacy Act of 1974 provides sufficient protection for employees' privacy. This act allows the government to retain information only for "relevant and necessary" purposes, requires written consent before the information may be disclosed, and imposes criminal liability for violations.

a. In the "Supreme Court Documents" column, in the "Opinions" pull-down menu, select "Bound Volumes." On the next page, in the "For Search Term:" box, type "NASA v. Nelson" and click on "Search." In the results, click on the name of the case to access the opinion. The United States Supreme Court maintains this Web site.

ISSUE Can the U.S. government require employees of private contractors, who work at federal facilities, to undergo NACI background checks without violating their privacy rights?

DECISION Yes. The United States Supreme Court reversed the judgment of the federal appellate court and remanded the case. The inquiries made by the NACI are reasonable and do not violate an individual's right to privacy. The Privacy Act protects against the disclosure of private information.

REASON The Court reasoned that even if it presumed that the government's inquiries implicated a constitutional right to privacy, that does not prevent the government from asking reasonable questions as part of an employment background check. Moreover, the Privacy Act provides safeguards against the public disclosure of an individual's private information without the individual's consent. The Court pointed out that the government has conducted employment investigations of applicants for the federal civil service for more than fifty years. With the guidelines implemented in 2007, a decision was made to extend this requirement to contract employees with long-term access to federal facilities. "Reasonable investigations of applicants and employees aid the Government in ensuring the security of its facilities and in employing a competent, reliable workforce."

WHAT IF THE FACTS WERE DIFFERENT? *Suppose that after the decision in this case, a JPL employee refused to cooperate in an NACI background check. What would be the most likely consequences?*

Employment Discrimination

Out of the 1960s civil rights movement to end racial and other forms of discrimination grew a body of law protecting employees against discrimination in the workplace. This protective legislation further eroded the employment-at-will doctrine, which was discussed on page 414. In the past several decades, judicial decisions, administrative agency actions, and legislation have restricted the ability of both employers and unions to discriminate against workers on the basis of race, color, religion, national origin, gender, age, or disability. A class of persons defined by one or more of these criteria is known as a **protected class.**

Several federal statutes prohibit **employment discrimination** against members of protected classes. The most important statute is Title VII of the Civil Rights Act of 1964.[25] Title VII prohibits discrimination on the basis of race, color, religion, national origin, or gender at any stage of employment. The Age Discrimination in Employment Act of 1967[26] and the Americans with Disabilities Act of 1990[27] prohibit discrimination on the basis of age and disability, respectively.

One of the most talked-about cases in 2011 was the Wal-Mart gender discrimination case. **CASE EXAMPLE 22.6** A group of female employees sued Wal-Mart, the nation's largest private employer, alleging that store managers who had discretion over pay and promotions were biased against women and disproportionately favored men. The United States Supreme Court ruled in favor of Wal-Mart, effectively blocking the class action (a lawsuit in which a small group of plaintiffs sues on behalf of a larger group). The Court held that the women could not maintain a class action because they had failed to prove a companywide policy of discrimination that had a common effect on all women covered by the class action.[28] • This important decision may limit the rights of employees to sue their employers for job discrimination in a class action, but it does not change the rights of individuals to sue for employment discrimination.

Title VII of the Civil Rights Act of 1964

Title VII of the Civil Rights Act of 1964 and its amendments prohibit job discrimination against employees, applicants, and union members on the basis of race, color, national origin, religion, or gender at any stage of employment. Title VII applies to employers with fifteen or more employees, labor unions with fifteen or more members, labor unions that operate hiring halls (to which members go regularly to be rationed jobs as they become available), employment agencies, and state and local governing units or agencies. A special section of the act prohibits discrimination in most federal government employment.

THE EQUAL EMPLOYMENT OPPORTUNITY COMMISSION

Compliance with Title VII is monitored by the Equal Employment Opportunity Commission (EEOC). A victim of alleged discrimination must file a claim with the EEOC before bringing a suit against the employer. The EEOC may investigate the dispute and attempt to obtain the parties' voluntary consent to an out-of-court settlement. If a voluntary agreement cannot be reached, the EEOC may then file a suit against the employer on the employee's behalf. If the EEOC decides not to investigate the claim, the victim may bring her or his own lawsuit against the employer.

The EEOC does not investigate every claim of employment discrimination, regardless of the merits of the claim. Generally, it investigates only "priority cases," such as cases involving retaliatory discharge (firing an employee in retaliation for submitting a claim to the EEOC) and cases involving types of discrimination that are of particular concern to the EEOC.

INTENTIONAL AND UNINTENTIONAL DISCRIMINATION

Title VII also prohibits both intentional and unintentional discrimination.

Intentional Discrimination. Intentional discrimination by an employer against an employee is known as **disparate-treatment discrimination.** Because intent may sometimes be difficult to prove, courts have established certain procedures for resolving disparate-treatment cases. Suppose that a woman applies for employment with a construction firm and is rejected. If she sues on the basis of disparate-treatment discrimination in hiring, she must show that (1) she is a member of a protected class, (2) she applied and was qualified for the job in question, (3) she was rejected by the employer, and (4) the employer continued to seek applicants for the position or filled the position with a person not in a protected class.

If the woman can meet these relatively easy requirements, she has made out a ***prima facie* case** of illegal discrimination. *Prima facie* is Latin for "at first sight." Legally, it refers to a fact that is presumed to be true unless contradicted by evidence. Making out a *prima facie* case of discrimination means that the plaintiff has met her initial burden of proof and will win in the absence of a legally acceptable employer defense. (Defenses will be discussed later in this chapter.) The burden then shifts to the employer-defendant, who must articulate a legal reason for not hiring the plaintiff. To prevail, the plaintiff must then show that the employer's reason is a *pretext* (not the true reason) and that discriminatory intent actually motivated the employer's decision.

Unintentional Discrimination. Employers often use interviews and testing procedures to choose from among a large number of applicants for job openings. Minimum educational requirements are also common. These practices and procedures may have an unintended discriminatory impact on a protected class.

Disparate-impact discrimination occurs when a protected group of people is adversely affected by an employer's practices, procedures, or tests, even though they do not appear to be discriminatory. In a disparate-impact discrimination case, the complaining party must first show statistically that the employer's practices, procedures, or tests are discriminatory in effect. Once the plaintiff has made out a *prima facie*

---

25. 42 U.S.C. Sections 2000e–2000e-17.

26. 29 U.S.C. Sections 621–634.

27. 42 U.S.C. Sections 12102–12118.

28. *Wal-Mart Stores, Inc. v. Dukes,* ___ U.S. ___, 131 S.Ct. 2541, 180 L.Ed.2d 374 (2011).

case, the burden of proof shifts to the employer to show that the practices or procedures in question were justified.

A plaintiff can prove a disparate impact by comparing the employer's workforce with the pool of qualified individuals available in the local labor market. The plaintiff must show that as a result of educational or other job requirements or hiring procedures, the percentage of nonwhites, women, or members of other protected classes in the employer's workforce does not reflect the percentage of that group in the pool of qualified applicants.

A plaintiff can also prove disparate-impact discrimination by comparing the selection rates of whites and nonwhites (or members of another protected class), regardless of the racial balance in the employer's workforce. The EEOC has devised a test, called the "four-fifths rule," to determine whether an employment examination is discriminatory on its face. Under this rule, a selection rate for protected classes that is less than four-fifths, or 80 percent, of the rate for the group with the highest rate will generally be regarded as evidence of disparate impact. **EXAMPLE 22.7** One hundred white applicants take an employment test, and fifty pass the test and are hired. One hundred minority applicants take the test, and twenty pass the test and are hired. Because twenty is less than four-fifths (80 percent) of fifty, the test would be considered discriminatory under the EEOC guidelines. •

DISCRIMINATION BASED ON RACE, COLOR, AND NATIONAL ORIGIN Title VII prohibits employers from discriminating against employees or job applicants on the basis of race, color, or national origin. Although there has been some uncertainty in the federal courts about what constitutes race versus national origin discrimination, race is interpreted broadly to include the ancestry or ethnic characteristics of a group of persons, such as Native Americans. The national origin provisions make it unlawful to discriminate against persons based on their birth in another country, such as Iraq or the Philippines, or their ancestry or culture, such as Hispanic.

If an employer's standards or policies for selecting or promoting employees have a discriminatory effect on employees or job applicants in these protected classes, then a presumption of illegal discrimination arises. To avoid liability, the employer must then show that its standards or policies have a substantial, demonstrable relationship to realistic qualifications for the job in question.

CASE EXAMPLE 22.8 Jiann Min Chang was an instructor at Alabama Agricultural and Mechanical University (AAMU). When AAMU terminated his employment, Chang filed a lawsuit claiming discrimination based on national origin. Chang established a *prima facie* case because he (1) was a member of a protected class, (2) was qualified for the job, (3) suffered an adverse employment action, and (4) was replaced by someone outside his protected class (a non-Asian instructor). When the burden of proof shifted to the employer, however, AAMU showed that Chang had argued with a university vice president and refused to comply with her instructions. The court ruled that the university had not renewed Chang's contract for a legitimate reason—insubordination—and therefore was not liable for unlawful discrimination.[29] •

Note that discrimination based on race can also take the form of *reverse discrimination,* or discrimination against "majority group" individuals, such as white males.

DISCRIMINATION BASED ON RELIGION Title VII of the Civil Rights Act of 1964 also prohibits government employers, private employers, and unions from discriminating against persons because of their religion. Employers cannot treat their employees more or less favorably based on their religious beliefs or practices and cannot require employees to participate in any religious activity (or forbid them from participating in one).

An employer must "reasonably accommodate" the religious practices of its employees, unless to do so would cause undue hardship to the employer's business. If an employee's religion prohibits him or her from working on a certain day of the week or at a certain type of job, for instance, the employer must make a reasonable attempt to accommodate these religious requirements. Employers must reasonably accommodate an employee's religious belief even if the belief is not based on the doctrines of a traditionally recognized religion, such as Christianity or Judaism, or a denomination, such as Baptist. The only requirement is that the belief be sincerely held by the employee.

DISCRIMINATION BASED ON GENDER Under Title VII, as well as other federal acts (including the Equal Pay Act of 1963, which we also discuss here), employers are forbidden from discriminating against employees on the basis of gender. Employers are prohibited from classifying jobs as male or female and from advertising in help-wanted columns that are designated male or female unless the employer can prove that the gender of the applicant is essential to the job. Employers also cannot have separate male and female seniority lists or refuse to promote employees based on gender.

Generally, to succeed in a suit for gender discrimination, a plaintiff must demonstrate that gender was a determining factor in the employer's decision to fire or refuse to hire or promote her or him. Typically, this involves looking at all of the surrounding circumstances.

CASE EXAMPLE 22.9 Turner Industries Group contracted to provide maintenance services and labor at a fertilizer plant owned by Agrium Conda Phosphate Industries. Wanda Collier worked for Turner at the plant. In 2008, Collier informed both

29. *Jiann Min Chang v. Alabama Agricultural and Mechanical University,* 2009 WL 3403180 (11th Cir. 2009).

her supervisor at Turner and her supervisor at Agrium, David Eastridge, that Jack Daniell, Agrium's head of maintenance, had berated her and treated her unfairly. Eastridge told Collier that Daniell was "old school," had a problem with Collier's gender, and was harder on women. He spoke with Daniell about Collier's allegations, but concluded that the dispute was based on factors other than gender. A month later, Daniell confronted Collier again, pushed her up against a wall, and berated her. Collier immediately reported this incident to her supervisors and filed formal complaints of gender discrimination at both Turner and Agrium. Turner offered to transfer her to another position, but she rejected the offer. A month later, Collier was fired. When she subsequently filed a gender discrimination suit in an Idaho district court, the court concluded that there was enough evidence that gender was a determining factor in Daniell's conduct to allow Collier's claims to go to a jury.[30] •

Pregnancy Discrimination. The Pregnancy Discrimination Act of 1978,[31] which amended Title VII, expanded the definition of gender discrimination to include discrimination based on pregnancy. Women affected by pregnancy, childbirth, or related medical conditions must be treated—for all employment-related purposes, including the receipt of benefits under employee benefit programs—the same as other persons not so affected but similar in ability to work.

Equal Pay Act. The Equal Pay Act of 1963, which amended the Fair Labor Standards Act of 1938, prohibits employers from gender-based wage discrimination. For the act's equal pay requirements to apply, the male and female employees must work at the same establishment doing similar work (a barber and a beautician, for example). To determine whether the Equal Pay Act has been violated, a court will look to the primary duties of the two jobs. It is the job content rather than the job description that controls in all cases. If a court finds that the wage differential is due to any factor other than gender, such as a seniority or merit system, then it does not violate the Equal Pay Act.

2009 Equal Pay Legislation. Forty-five years after the Equal Pay Act was enacted, there was still a significant gap between the wages earned by male and female employees. This continuing disparity prompted Congress to pass the Paycheck Fairness Act of 2009, which closed some of the loopholes in the Equal Pay Act. Because the courts had interpreted the defense of "any factor other than gender" so broadly, employers had been able to justify alleged wage discrimination simply by not using the word *gender* or *sex*. The Paycheck Fairness Act clarified employers' defenses and prohibited the use of gender-based differentials in assessing an employee's education, training, or experience. The act also provided additional remedies for wage discrimination, including compensatory and punitive damages, which are available as remedies for discrimination based on race and national origin.

In 2009, Congress also overturned a 2007 decision by the United States Supreme Court, which had required a plaintiff alleging wage discrimination to file a complaint within 180 days of the decision that set the discriminatory pay.[32] Congress rejected this limit when it enacted the Lilly Ledbetter Fair Pay Act of 2009.[33] The act made discriminatory wages actionable under federal law regardless of when the discrimination began. Each time a person is paid discriminatory wages, benefits, or other compensation, a cause of action arises (and the plaintiff has 180 days from that date to file a complaint). In other words, if a plaintiff continues to work for the employer while receiving discriminatory wages, the time period for filing a complaint is basically unlimited.

CONSTRUCTIVE DISCHARGE The majority of Title VII complaints involve unlawful discrimination in decisions to hire or fire employees. In some situations, however, employees who leave their jobs voluntarily can claim that they were "constructively discharged" by the employer.

Constructive discharge occurs when the employer causes the employee's working conditions to be so intolerable that a reasonable person in the employee's position would feel compelled to quit. The plaintiff must present objective proof of intolerable working conditions, which the employer knew or had reason to know about yet failed to correct within a reasonable time period. Courts generally also require the employee to show causation—that the employer's unlawful discrimination caused the working conditions to be intolerable. Put a different way, the employee's resignation must be a foreseeable result of the employer's discriminatory action.

EXAMPLE 22.10 Khalil's employer humiliates him in front of his co-workers by informing him that he is being demoted to an inferior position. Khalil's co-workers then continually insult and harass him about his national origin (he is from Iran). The employer is aware of this discriminatory treatment but does nothing to remedy the situation, despite repeated complaints from Khalil. After several months, Khalil quits his job and files a Title VII claim. In this situation, Khalil would likely have sufficient evidence to maintain an action for constructive discharge in violation of Title VII. • Although courts weigh the facts on a case-by-case basis, employee demotion is one of the most frequently cited reasons for a finding of constructive discharge, particularly when the employee was subjected to humiliation.

30. *Collier v. Turner Industries Group, LLC*, 2011 WL 2517020 (D. Idaho 2011).
31. 42 U.S.C. Section 2000e(k).

32. *Ledbetter v. Goodyear Tire Co.*, 550 U.S. 618, 127 S.Ct. 2162, 167 L.Ed.2d 982 (2007).
33. Pub. L. No. 111-2, 123 Stat. 5 (January 5, 2009), amending 42 U.S.C. Section 2000e-5[e].

Note that plaintiffs can use constructive discharge as the basis to establish *any* type of discrimination claims under Title VII but also claims of discrimination based on age or disability. When constructive discharge is claimed, the employee can pursue damages for loss of income, including back pay. These damages ordinarily are not available to an employee who left a job voluntarily.

SEXUAL HARASSMENT Title VII also protects employees against **sexual harassment** in the workplace. Sexual harassment can take two forms: *quid pro quo* harassment and hostile-environment harassment. *Quid pro quo* is a Latin phrase that is often translated to mean "something in exchange for something else." *Quid pro quo* harassment occurs when sexual favors are demanded in return for job opportunities, promotions, salary increases, and the like. According to the United States Supreme Court, hostile-environment harassment occurs when "the workplace is permeated with discriminatory intimidation, ridicule, and insult, that is sufficiently severe or pervasive to alter the conditions of the victim's employment and create an abusive working environment."[34]

The courts determine whether the sexually offensive conduct was sufficiently severe or pervasive as to create a hostile environment on a case-by-case basis. Typically, a single incident of sexually offensive conduct is not enough to create a hostile environment (although there have been exceptions when the conduct was particularly objectionable). Note also that if the employee who is alleging sexual harassment has signed an arbitration clause (see Chapter 2 on page 43), she or he will most likely be required to arbitrate the claim.[35]

Harassment by Supervisors. For an employer to be held liable for a supervisor's sexual harassment, the supervisor normally must have taken a tangible employment action against the employee. A **tangible employment action** is a significant change in employment status or benefits, such as when an employee is fired, refused a promotion, demoted, or reassigned to a position with significantly different responsibilities. Only a supervisor, or another person acting with the authority of the employer, can cause this sort of injury. A constructive discharge also qualifies as a tangible employment action.[36]

The *Ellerth/Faragher* Affirmative Defense. In 1998, the United States Supreme Court issued several important rulings that have had a lasting impact on cases alleging sexual harassment by supervisors.[37] The Court held that an employer (a city) was liable for a supervisor's harassment of employees even though the employer was unaware of the behavior. Although the city had a written policy against sexual harassment, it had not distributed the policy to its employees and had not established any complaint procedures for employees who felt that they had been sexually harassed. In another case, the Court held that an employer can be liable for a supervisor's sexual harassment even though the employee does not suffer adverse job consequences.

The Court's decisions in these cases established what has become known as the "*Ellerth/Faragher* affirmative defense" to charges of sexual harassment. The defense has two elements:

1. That the employer has taken reasonable care to prevent and promptly correct any sexually harassing behavior (by establishing effective antiharassment policies and complaint procedures, for example).
2. That the plaintiff-employee unreasonably failed to take advantage of any preventive or corrective opportunities provided by the employer to avoid harm.

An employer that can prove both elements will not be liable for a supervisor's harassment.

Retaliation by Employers. Employers sometimes retaliate against employees who complain about sexual harassment or other Title VII violations. Retaliation can take many forms. An employer might demote or fire the person, or otherwise change the terms, conditions, and benefits of his or her employment. Title VII prohibits retaliation, and employees can sue their employers. In a *retaliation claim,* an individual asserts that she or he has suffered a harm as a result of making a charge, testifying, or participating in a Title VII investigation or proceeding.

Plaintiffs do not have to prove that the challenged action adversely affected their workplace or employment. Instead, to prove retaliation, plaintiffs must show that the challenged action was one that would likely have dissuaded a reasonable worker from making or supporting a charge of discrimination. In 2009, the United States Supreme Court ruled that Title VII's retaliation protection extends to an employee who speaks out about discrimination not on her or his own initiative, but in answering questions during an employer's internal investigation of another employee's complaint.[38]

In the following case, an employee was fired after his fiancée filed a gender discrimination claim against their employer. The United States Supreme Court had to decide whether the employer's firing of this employee constituted unlawful retaliation under Title VII.

---

34. *Harris v. Forklift Systems,* 510 U.S. 17, 114 S.Ct. 367, 126 L.Ed.2d 295 (1993). See also *Billings v. Town of Grafton,* 515 F.3d 39 (1st Cir. 2008).

35. See, for example, *EEOC v. Cheesecake Factory, Inc.,* 2009 WL 1259359 (D.Ariz. 2009).

36. See, for example, *Pennsylvania State Police v. Suders,* 542 U.S. 129, 124 S.Ct. 2342, 159 L.Ed.2d 204 (2004).

37. *Burlington Industries, Inc. v. Ellerth,* 524 U.S. 742, 118 S.Ct. 2257, 141 L.Ed.2d 633 (1998); and *Faragher v. City of Boca Raton,* 524 U.S. 775, 118 S.Ct. 2275, 141 L.Ed.2d 662 (1998).

38. *Crawford v. Metropolitan Government of Nashville and Davidson County, Tennessee,* 555 U.S. 271, 129 S.Ct. 846, 172 L.Ed.2d 650 (2009).

Case 22.3 Thompson v. North American Stainless, LP

Supreme Court of the United States, ___ U.S. ___, 131 S.Ct. 863, 178 L.Ed.2d 694 (2011).
www.supremecourt.gov/opinions/10pdf/09-291.pdf[a]

FACTS Eric Thompson and his fiancée, Miriam Regalado, were employees of North American Stainless, LP (NAS). In February 2003, Regalado filed a gender discrimination claim against NAS with the Equal Employment Opportunity Commission (EEOC). Three weeks later, NAS fired Thompson. Thompson then filed a claim with the EEOC. After conciliation efforts proved unsuccessful, he sued NAS in a U.S. district court, alleging violations of Title VII of the Civil Rights Act of 1964. Thompson claimed that NAS had fired him in retaliation for Regalado's complaint to the EEOC. The district court granted summary judgment for NAS, concluding that Title VII "does not permit third-party retaliation claims." Thompson appealed. The U.S. Court of Appeals for the Sixth Circuit affirmed the district court's decision. Thompson appealed again, and the United States Supreme Court granted *certiorari.*

ISSUE Can an employee who was fired because his fiancée filed a gender discrimination claim against their employer sue that employer for retaliation in violation of Title VII?

DECISION Yes. The United States Supreme Court ruled that Title VII's antiretaliation provision covers a broad range of employer conduct, including third-party retaliation claims. The Court reversed the lower court's decision and remanded the case for a determination of the facts. If the facts were as Thompson alleged, then NAS's firing of Thompson had violated Title VII.

REASON The Court compared the language of Title VII's antiretaliation provision with the language of its antidiscrimination provision and concluded that the antiretaliation provision is worded more broadly. Accordingly, the Court reasoned that the antiretaliation provision must be construed to cover a broad range of employer conduct. The provision prohibits any employer action that "might [dissuade] a reasonable worker from making or supporting a charge of discrimination." In the Court's view, it was obvious that a reasonable worker (such as Miriam Regalado) might be dissuaded from engaging in protected activity if she knew that her fiancé would be fired as a result.

WHY IS THIS CASE IMPORTANT? *This case is important for business owners and managers because it illustrates the broad coverage of Title VII's antiretaliation provision. Any company that employs more than one member of a family must be very careful not to retaliate against one family member for legally protected actions taken by another family member. Many companies try to avoid potential problems by establishing a policy of not hiring relatives of employees. Such a policy would not have avoided the problems that arose in this case, however, because the employees were not married and thus were not "family."*

a. The United States Supreme Court provides this URL, which goes directly to a PDF file of this case opinion.

Harassment by Co-Workers and Nonemployees. When harassment by co-workers, rather than supervisors, creates a hostile working environment, an employee may still have a cause of action against the employer. Normally, though, the employer will be held liable only if the employer knew, or should have known, about the harassment and failed to take immediate remedial action.

Occasionally, a court may also hold an employer liable for harassment by *nonemployees* if the employer knew about the harassment and failed to take corrective action. **EXAMPLE 22.11** Gordon, who owns and manages a Great Bites restaurant, knows that one of his regular customers, Dean, repeatedly harasses Sharon, a waitress. If Gordon does nothing and permits the harassment to continue, he may be liable under Title VII even though Dean is not an employee of the restaurant. •

Same-Gender Harassment. In *Oncale v. Sundowner Offshore Services, Inc.*,[39] the United States Supreme Court held that Title VII protection extends to situations in which individuals are sexually harassed by members of the same gender. Proving that the harassment in same-gender cases is "based on sex" can be difficult, though. It is easier to establish a case of same-gender harassment when the harasser is homosexual.

CASE EXAMPLE 22.12 James Tepperwien was a security officer for three years at a nuclear power plant owned by Entergy Nuclear Operations. During that time, Tepperwien twice reported to his superiors that Vito Messina, another security officer who allegedly was gay, had sexually harassed him. After the first incident, Entergy made all the security officers read and sign its no-tolerance antiharassment policy. After the second incident, Messina was placed on administrative leave for ten weeks. After Messina returned to work, Tepperwien was disciplined for failing to report some missing equipment. He then filed another harassment complaint and quit his job, claiming that he had been constructively discharged and that Entergy had not taken sufficient steps to prevent further harassment.

The court noted that a male victim of same-gender harassment must show that he was harassed because he was male. The court found that Tepperwien had presented credible evidence that Messina was a homosexual and had made sexual

39. 523 U.S. 75, 118 S.Ct. 998, 140 L.Ed.2d 207 (1998).

advances toward other security officers. This evidence was sufficient to establish a *prima facie* case of hostile-environment sexual harassment, allowing the case to go to trial, but it was not enough to show the intolerable conditions required for a finding of constructive discharge.[40] ●

Although federal law (Title VII) does not prohibit discrimination or harassment based on a person's sexual orientation, a growing number of states have enacted laws that prohibit sexual orientation discrimination in private employment. Also, many companies have voluntarily established nondiscrimination policies that include sexual orientation.

REMEDIES UNDER TITLE VII Employer liability under Title VII may be extensive. If the plaintiff successfully proves that unlawful discrimination occurred, he or she may be awarded reinstatement, back pay, retroactive promotions, and damages. Compensatory damages are available only in cases of intentional discrimination. Punitive damages may be recovered against a private employer only if the employer acted with malice or reckless indifference to an individual's rights. The statute limits the total amount of compensatory and punitive damages that the plaintiff can recover from specific employers—ranging from $50,000 against employers with one hundred or fewer employees to $300,000 against employers with more than five hundred employees.

The Age Discrimination in Employment Act of 1967

Age discrimination is potentially the most widespread form of discrimination, because anyone—regardless of race, color, national origin, or gender—could be a victim at some point in life. The Age Discrimination in Employment Act (ADEA) of 1967, as amended, prohibits employment discrimination on the basis of age against individuals forty years of age or older. The act also prohibits mandatory retirement for nonmanagerial workers. For the act to apply, an employer must have twenty or more employees, and the employer's business activities must affect interstate commerce. The EEOC administers the ADEA, but the act also permits private causes of action against employers for age discrimination.

The ADEA includes a provision that extends protections against age discrimination to federal government employees. In 2008, the United States Supreme Court ruled that this provision encompasses not only claims of age discrimination, but also claims of retaliation for complaining about age discrimination, which are not specifically mentioned in the statute.[41] Thus, the ADEA protects federal and private-sector employees from retaliation based on age-related complaints.

PROCEDURES The burden-shifting procedure under the ADEA differs from the procedure under Title VII as a result of a United States Supreme Court decision in 2009, which dramatically changed the burden of proof in age discrimination cases.[42] As explained earlier, if the plaintiff in a Title VII case can show that the employer was motivated, at least in part, by unlawful discrimination, the burden of proof shifts to the employer to articulate a legitimate nondiscriminatory reason. Thus, in cases in which the employer has a "mixed motive" for discharging an employee, the employer has the burden of proving its reason was legitimate.

Under the ADEA, in contrast, a plaintiff must show that the unlawful discrimination was not just a reason but *the* reason for the adverse employment action. In other words, the employee has the burden of establishing "but for" causation—that is, that age discrimination was the reason for the adverse decision. Thus, to establish a *prima facie* case, the plaintiff must show that he or she (1) was a member of the protected age group, (2) was qualified for the position from which he or she was discharged, and (3) was discharged because of age discrimination. Then the burden shifts to the employer. If the employer offers a legitimate reason for its action, then the plaintiff must show that the stated reason is only a pretext and that the plaintiff's age was the real reason for the employer's decision.

STATE EMPLOYEES NOT COVERED Generally, the states are immune from lawsuits brought by private individuals in federal court—unless a state consents to the suit. This immunity stems from the United States Supreme Court's interpretation of the Eleventh Amendment (the text of this amendment is included in Appendix B).

State immunity under the Eleventh Amendment is not absolute, however. In some situations, such as when fundamental rights are at stake, Congress has the power to abolish state immunity to private suits through legislation that unequivocally shows Congress's intent to subject states to private suits.[43] As a general rule, though, the Court has found that state employers are immune from private suits brought by employees under the ADEA (for age discrimination, as noted above), the Americans with Disabilities Act[44] (for disability discrimination), and the Fair Labor Standards Act[45] (which

40. *Tepperwien v. Entergy Nuclear Operations, Inc.,* 606 F.Supp.2d 427 (S.D.N.Y. 2009).

41. *Gomez-Perez v. Potter,* 553 U.S. 474, 128 S.Ct. 1931, 170 L.Ed.2d 887 (2008).

42. *Gross v. FBL Financial Services,* ___ U.S. ___, 129 S.Ct. 2343, 174 L.Ed.2d 119 (2009).

43. *Tennessee v. Lane,* 541 U.S. 509, 124 S.Ct. 1978, 158 L.Ed.2d 820 (2004).

44. *Board of Trustees of the University of Alabama v. Garrett,* 531 U.S. 356, 121 S.Ct. 955, 148 L.Ed.2d 866 (2001).

45. *Alden v. Maine,* 527 U.S. 706, 119 S.Ct. 2240, 144 L.Ed.2d 636 (1999).

relates to wages and hours). In contrast, states are not immune from the requirements of the Family and Medical Leave Act.[46]

The Americans with Disabilities Act of 1990

The Americans with Disabilities Act (ADA) of 1990 was designed to eliminate discriminatory employment practices that prevent otherwise qualified workers with disabilities from fully participating in the national labor force. The ADA prohibits disability-based discrimination in workplaces with fifteen or more workers (with the exception of state government employers, who are generally immune under the Eleventh Amendment, as just discussed). Basically, the ADA requires that employers "reasonably accommodate" the needs of persons with disabilities unless to do so would cause the employer to suffer an "undue hardship." In 2008, Congress enacted the ADA Amendments Act,[47] which broadened the coverage of the ADA's protections, as will be discussed shortly.

Procedures and Remedies To prevail on a claim under the ADA, a plaintiff must show that he or she (1) has a disability, (2) is otherwise qualified for the employment in question, and (3) was excluded from the employment solely because of the disability. As in Title VII cases, a plaintiff must pursue her or his claim through the EEOC before filing an action in court for a violation of the ADA. The EEOC may decide to investigate and perhaps even sue the employer on behalf of the employee. If the EEOC decides not to sue, then the employee is entitled to sue in court.

Plaintiffs in lawsuits brought under the ADA may obtain many of the same remedies available under Title VII. These include reinstatement, back pay, a limited amount of compensatory and punitive damages (for intentional discrimination), and certain other forms of relief. Repeat violators may be ordered to pay fines of up to $100,000.

What Is a Disability? The ADA is broadly drafted to cover persons with a wide range of disabilities. Specifically, the ADA defines *disability* as "(1) a physical or mental impairment that substantially limits one or more of the major life activities of such individuals; (2) a record of such impairment; or (3) being regarded as having such an impairment." Health conditions that have been considered disabilities under the federal law include blindness, alcoholism, heart disease, cancer, muscular dystrophy, cerebral palsy, paraplegia, diabetes, acquired immune deficiency syndrome (AIDS), testing positive for the human immunodeficiency virus (HIV), and morbid obesity (defined as existing when an individual's weight is twice the normal weight for his or her height). The ADA excludes from coverage certain conditions, such as kleptomania (the obsessive desire to steal).

Although the ADA's definition of disability is broad, rulings by the United States Supreme Court from 1999 to 2007 interpreted that definition narrowly and made it harder for employees to establish a disability under the act. For instance, in 2002 the Court held that repetitive-stress injuries (such as carpal tunnel syndrome) ordinarily do not constitute a disability under the ADA.[48] After that, the courts began focusing on how the person functioned when using corrective devices or taking medication, not on how the person functioned without these measures.

In response to the Supreme Court's limiting decisions, Congress decided to amend the ADA in 2008. Basically, the amendments reverse the Court's restrictive interpretation of disability under the ADA and prohibit employers from considering mitigating measures or medications when determining if an individual has a disability. In other words, disability is now determined on a case-by-case basis.

Reasonable Accommodation The ADA does not require that employers accommodate the needs of job applicants or employees with disabilities who are not otherwise qualified for the work. If a job applicant or an employee with a disability, with reasonable accommodation, can perform essential job functions, however, the employer must make the accommodation. Required modifications may include installing ramps for a wheelchair, establishing more flexible working hours, creating or modifying job assignments, and creating or improving training materials and procedures. Generally, employers should give primary consideration to employees' preferences in deciding what accommodations should be made.

Employers who do not accommodate the needs of persons with disabilities must demonstrate that the accommodations would cause "undue hardship" in terms of being significantly difficult or expensive for the employer. Usually, the courts decide whether an accommodation constitutes an undue hardship on a case-by-case basis by looking at the employer's resources in relation to the specific accommodation.

Employers must modify their job-application process so that those with disabilities can compete for jobs with those who do not have disabilities. Employers are restricted in the kinds of questions they may ask on job-application forms and during preemployment interviews. Furthermore, they cannot require persons with disabilities to submit to preemployment physicals unless such exams are required of all other applicants. An employer can condition an offer of employment on the applicant's successfully passing a medical examination, but can

46. *Nevada Department of Human Resources v. Hibbs,* 538 U.S. 721, 123 S.Ct. 1972, 155 L.Ed.2d 953 (2003).

47. 42 U.S.C. Sections 12103 and 12205a.

48. *Toyota Motor Manufacturing, Kentucky, Inc. v. Williams,* 534 U.S. 184, 122 S.Ct. 681, 151 L.Ed.2d 615 (2002). This ruling was invalidated by the 2008 amendments to the ADA.

disqualify the applicant only if the exam reveals medical problems that would render the applicant unable to perform the job.

CASE EXAMPLE 22.13 When filling the position of delivery truck driver, a company cannot screen out all applicants who are unable to meet the U.S. Department of Transportation's hearing standard. The company would first have to prove that drivers who are deaf are not qualified to perform the essential job function of driving safely and pose a higher risk of accidents than drivers who are not deaf.[49] •

Defenses to Employment Discrimination

The first line of defense for an employer charged with employment discrimination is, of course, to assert that the plaintiff has failed to meet his or her initial burden of proving that discrimination occurred. Once a plaintiff succeeds in proving that discrimination occurred, the burden shifts to the employer to justify the discriminatory practice. Often, employers attempt to justify the discrimination by claiming that it was the result of a business necessity, a bona fide occupational qualification, or a seniority system. In some cases, as noted earlier, an effective antiharassment policy and prompt remedial action when harassment occurs may shield employers from liability for sexual harassment under Title VII.

BUSINESS NECESSITY An employer may defend against a claim of disparate-impact (unintentional) discrimination by asserting that a practice that has a discriminatory effect is a **business necessity.** **EXAMPLE 22.14** If requiring a high school diploma is shown to have a discriminatory effect, an employer might argue that a high school education is necessary for workers to perform the job at a required level of competence. If the employer can demonstrate to the court's satisfaction that a definite connection exists between a high school education and job performance, the employer normally will succeed in this business necessity defense. •

BONA FIDE OCCUPATIONAL QUALIFICATION Another defense applies when discrimination against a protected class is essential to a job—that is, when a particular trait is a **bona fide occupational qualification (BFOQ).** Race, however, can never be a BFOQ. Generally, courts have restricted the BFOQ defense to instances in which the employee's gender is essential to the job.

EXAMPLE 22.15 A women's clothing store might legitimately hire only female sales attendants if part of an attendant's job involves assisting clients in the store's dressing rooms. Similarly, the Federal Aviation Administration can legitimately impose age limits for airline pilots—but an airline cannot impose weight limits only on female flight attendants. •

49. *Bates v. United Parcel Service, Inc.*, 465 F.3d 1069 (9th Cir. 2006).

SENIORITY SYSTEMS An employer with a history of discrimination might have no members of protected classes in upper-level positions. Even if the employer now seeks to be unbiased, it may face a lawsuit in which the plaintiff asks a court to order that minorities be promoted ahead of schedule to compensate for past discrimination.

If no present intent to discriminate is shown, however, and if promotions or other job benefits are distributed according to a fair **seniority system** (in which workers with more years of service are promoted first or laid off last), the employer normally has a good defense against the suit. This defense may also apply to alleged discrimination under the ADA.

AFTER-ACQUIRED EVIDENCE OF EMPLOYEE MISCONDUCT In some situations, employers have attempted to avoid liability for employment discrimination on the basis of "after-acquired evidence"—that is, evidence that the employer discovers after a lawsuit is filed—of an employee's misconduct.

EXAMPLE 22.16 An employer fires a worker who then sues the employer for employment discrimination. During pretrial investigation, the employer learns that the employee made material misrepresentations on his employment application—misrepresentations that, had the employer known about them, would have served as grounds to fire the individual. •

After-acquired evidence of wrongdoing cannot be used to shield an employer entirely from liability for employment discrimination. It may, however, be used to limit the amount of damages for which the employer is liable.

Immigration Law

The United States had no laws restricting immigration until the late nineteenth century. Today, the most important laws governing immigration and employment are the Immigration Reform and Control Act (IRCA) of 1986[50] and the Immigration Act of 1990.[51] In recent years, immigration law has become an area of increasing concern for businesses as the number of immigrants—especially illegal immigrants—to the United States has grown. An estimated 12 million illegal immigrants now live in the United States. The great majority came to find jobs, but U.S. employers face serious penalties if they hire illegal immigrants. Thus, an understanding of immigration laws has become increasingly important for businesses.

Immigration Reform and Control Act

When the IRCA was enacted in 1986, it provided amnesty to certain groups of illegal aliens living in the United States at the time. It also established a system that sanctions employers

50. 29 U.S.C. Section 1802.

51. This act amended various provisions of the Immigration and Nationality Act of 1952, 8 U.S.C. Sections 1101 *et seq.*

that hire illegal immigrants who lack work authorization. The IRCA makes it illegal to hire, recruit, or refer for a fee someone not authorized to work in this country. Through Immigration and Customs Enforcement officers, the federal government conducts random compliance audits and engages in enforcement actions against employers that hire illegal immigrants.

I-9 EMPLOYMENT VERIFICATION To comply with current law (based on the 1986 act), an employer must perform **I-9 verifications** for new hires, including those hired as "contractors" or "day workers" if they work under the employer's direct supervision. Form I-9, Employment Eligibility Verification, which is available from U.S. Citizenship and Immigration Services,[52] must be completed within three days of a worker's commencement of employment. The three-day period is to allow the employer to check the form's accuracy and to review and verify documents establishing the prospective worker's identity and eligibility for employment in the United States.

The employer must attest, under penalty of perjury, that an employee produced documents establishing his or her identity and legal employability. Acceptable documents include a U.S. passport establishing the person's citizenship or a document authorizing a foreign citizen to work in the United States, such as a Permanent Resident Card or an Alien Registration Receipt (discussed at bottom right on this page).

Note that most legal actions alleging violations of I-9 rules are brought against employees. An employee must state that she or he is a U.S. citizen or otherwise authorized to work in the United States. If the employee enters false information on an I-9 form or presents false documentation, the employer can fire the worker, who then may be subject to deportation.

The IRCA prohibits "knowing" violations, including situations in which an employer "should have known" that the worker was unauthorized. Good faith is a defense under the statute, and employers are legally entitled to rely on a document authorizing a person to work that reasonably appears on its face to be genuine, even if it is later established to be counterfeit.

ENFORCEMENT U.S. Immigration and Customs Enforcement (ICE) is the largest investigative arm of the U.S. Department of Homeland Security. ICE has a general inspection program that conducts random compliance audits. Other audits may occur if the agency receives a written complaint alleging an employer's violations. Government inspections include a review of an employer's file of I-9 forms. The government does not need a subpoena or a warrant to conduct such an inspection.

If an investigation reveals a possible violation, ICE will bring an administrative action and issue a Notice of Intent to Fine, which sets out the charges against the employer. The employer has a right to a hearing on the enforcement action but must file a request within thirty days. This hearing is conducted before an *administrative law judge*, and the employer has a right to counsel and to *discovery* (see Chapter 2). The typical defense in such actions is good faith or substantial compliance with the documentation provisions.

52. U.S. Citizenship and Immigration Services is a federal agency that is part of the U.S. Department of Homeland Security.

PENALTIES An employer who violates the law by hiring an unauthorized alien is subject to substantial penalties. The employer may be fined up to $2,200 for each unauthorized employee for a first offense, $5,000 per employee for a second offense, and up to $11,000 for subsequent offenses. Criminal penalties, including additional fines and imprisonment for up to ten years, apply to employers who have engaged in a "pattern or practice of violations." A company may also be barred from future government contracts for violations. In determining the penalty, ICE considers the seriousness of the violation (such as intentional falsification of documents) and the employer's past compliance. ICE regulations also provide for mitigation or aggravation of the penalty under certain circumstances, such as whether the employer cooperated in the investigation or is a small business.

The Immigration Act of 1990

Often, U.S. businesses find that they cannot hire sufficient domestic workers with specialized skills. For this reason, U.S. immigration laws have long made provisions for businesses to hire foreign workers with special qualification. The Immigration Act of 1990 placed caps on the number of visas (entry permits) that can be issued to immigrants each year.

Most temporary visas are set aside for workers who can be characterized as "persons of extraordinary ability," members of the professions holding advanced degrees, or other skilled workers and professionals. To hire these individuals, employers must submit a petition to U.S. Citizenship and Immigration Services, which determines whether the job candidate meets the legal standards. Each visa is for a specific job, and the law limits the employee's ability to change jobs once in the United States.

I-551 ALIEN REGISTRATION RECEIPTS A company seeking to hire a noncitizen worker may do so if the worker is self-authorized. This means that the worker either is a lawful permanent resident or has a valid temporary Employment Authorization Document. A lawful permanent resident can prove his or her status to an employer by presenting an **I-551 Alien Registration Receipt**, known as a "green card," or a properly stamped foreign passport.

Many immigrant workers are not already self-authorized, and employers may obtain labor certification, or green cards, for the immigrants they wish to hire. To gain authorization for hiring a foreign worker, the employer must show that no

U.S. worker is qualified, willing, and able to take the job. The employer must also be able to show that the qualifications required for the job are a business necessity. Approximately fifty thousand new green cards are issued each year. A green card can be obtained only for a person who is being hired for a permanent, full-time position. (A separate authorization system provides for the temporary entry and hiring of nonimmigrant visa workers.)

THE H-1B VISA PROGRAM The most common and controversial visa program today is the H-1B visa system. To obtain an H-1B visa, the potential employee must be qualified in a "specialty occupation," meaning that the individual has highly specialized knowledge and has attained a bachelor's or higher degree or its equivalent. Individuals with H-1B visas can stay in the United States for three to six years and can work only for the sponsoring employer. The recipients of these visas include many high-tech workers, such as computer programmers and electronics specialists. A maximum of sixty-five thousand H-1B visas is set aside each year for new immigrants, and that limit is typically reached within the first few weeks of the year. Consequently, many businesses, such as Microsoft, continue to lobby Congress to expand the number of H-1B visas available to immigrants.

LABOR CERTIFICATION A common criticism of the H-1B visa system is that it depresses the wages of U.S. workers because H-1B workers may be willing to work for less. The law addresses this complaint by requiring employers to pay H-1B workers the prevailing wage. Before an employer can submit an H-1B application, it must file a Labor Certification application on Form ETA 9035. The employer must agree to provide a wage level at least equal to the wages offered to other individuals with similar experience and qualifications and attest that the hiring will not adversely affect other workers similarly employed. The employer must also inform U.S. workers of the intent to hire a foreign worker by posting the form. The U.S. Department of Labor reviews the applications and may reject them for omissions or inaccuracies.

H-2, O, L, AND E VISAS Other specialty temporary visas are available for other categories of employees. H-2 visas provide for workers performing agricultural labor of a seasonal nature. O visas provide entry for persons who have "extraordinary ability in the sciences, arts, education, business or athletics which has been demonstrated by sustained national or international acclaim." L visas allow a company's foreign managers or executives to work inside the United States. E visas permit the entry of certain foreign investors or entrepreneurs.

As the unemployment rate has remained stubbornly high since the recession, there has been growing public resentment toward illegal immigrants, who are perceived to be taking jobs away from U.S. citizens. Although immigration law has always been a federal matter, in 2010 the state of Arizona, which faces a large problem of unauthorized immigration along its border with Mexico, enacted its own immigration law (S.B. 1070). Essentially, S.B. 1070 requires a police officer who lawfully stops or detains someone and reasonably suspects that the person is an alien to make a reasonable attempt to determine the person's immigration status. The law would require immigrants to carry their alien registration documents at all times and would give police considerable discretion to question individuals regarding their immigration status.

Although fifteen other states proposed to enact legislation similar to Arizona's statute, the law immediately became highly controversial. Many contended that the law is unconstitutional because it would institutionalize racial profiling, which occurs when police target suspects because of their race or ethnicity. In this instance, the concern was that police would focus on stopping Hispanics, many of whom are U.S. citizens.

Before S.B. 1070 went into effect, the U.S. government filed a lawsuit in federal district court, seeking an injunction to block the implementation of the law. The government argued that the law violated the commerce clause and the supremacy clause and that it was preempted by the federal Immigration and Nationality Act.[53] (A valid federal statute takes precedence over, or preempts, a conflicting state law.) The district court agreed that the state law was preempted and granted the injunction, and the state of Arizona appealed.

In 2011, the U.S. Court of Appeals for the Ninth Circuit affirmed the district court's ruling.[54] Although the United States Supreme Court has not yet ruled on this issue, the appellate court's decision calls into question the legitimacy of state immigration laws. Nevertheless, Alabama and a few other states have passed legislation that uses slightly different language but is still aimed at stepping up enforcement against illegal immigrants in that state.

Labor Unions

In the 1930s, in addition to wage-hour laws, the government also enacted the first of several labor laws. These laws protect employees' rights to join labor unions, to bargain with management over the terms and conditions of employment, and to conduct strikes.

Federal Labor Laws

Federal labor laws governing union-employer relations have developed considerably since the first law was enacted in 1932. Initially, the laws were concerned with protecting the

53. 8 U.S.C. Sections 1101 *et seq.*

54. *United States v. Arizona,* 641 F.3d 339 (9th Cir. 2011).

rights and interests of workers. Subsequent legislation placed some restraints on unions and granted rights to employers. Coverage of federal labor laws is broad and extends to all employers whose business activity either involves or affects interstate commerce.

NORRIS-LAGUARDIA ACT In 1932, Congress protected peaceful strikes, picketing, and boycotts in the Norris-LaGuardia Act.[55] The statute restricted the power of federal courts to issue injunctions against unions engaged in peaceful strikes. In effect, this act established a national policy permitting employees to organize.

NATIONAL LABOR RELATIONS ACT One of the foremost statutes regulating labor is the National Labor Relations Act (NLRA) of 1935.[56] This act established the rights of employees to engage in collective bargaining and to strike. The act also specifically defined a number of employer practices as unfair to labor:

1. Interference with the efforts of employees to form, join, or assist labor organizations or with the efforts of employees to engage in concerted activities for their mutual aid or protection.
2. An employer's domination of a labor organization or contribution of financial or other support to it.
3. Discrimination in the hiring or awarding of tenure to employees based on union affiliation.
4. Discrimination against employees for filing charges under the act or giving testimony under the act.
5. Refusal to bargain collectively with the duly designated representative of the employees.

The National Labor Relations Board. The NLRA also created the National Labor Relations Board (NLRB) to oversee union elections and to prevent employers from engaging in unfair and illegal union activities and unfair labor practices. When a union or employee believes that an employer has violated federal labor law (or vice versa), a charge is filed with a regional office of the NLRB. The NLRB has the authority to investigate employees' charges of unfair labor practices and to file complaints against employers in response to these charges.

When violations are found, the NLRB may issue a *cease-and-desist order* compelling the employer to stop engaging in the unfair practices. Cease-and-desist orders can be enforced by a federal appellate court if necessary. After the NLRB rules on claims of unfair labor practices, its decision may be appealed to a federal court. Under the NLRA, employers and unions have a duty to bargain in good faith. Bargaining over certain subjects is mandatory, and a party's refusal to bargain over these subjects is an unfair labor practice that can be reported to the NLRB.

Workers Protected by the NLRA. To be protected under the NLRA, an individual must be an *employee,* as that term is defined in the statute. Courts have long held that job applicants fall within the definition (otherwise, the NLRA's ban on discrimination in hiring would mean nothing). Additionally, individuals who are hired by a union to organize a company are to be considered employees of the company for NLRA purposes. Some workers are specifically excluded from the NLRA. Railroad and airline workers are not covered by the NLRA but are covered by a separate act, the Railway Labor Act, which closely parallels the NLRA. Other types of workers, such as agricultural workers and domestic servants, are excluded from the NLRA and have no coverage under separate legislation.

LABOR-MANAGEMENT RELATIONS ACT The Labor-Management Relations Act (LMRA) of 1947 (also called the Taft-Hartley Act)[57] was passed to proscribe certain unfair union practices, such as the *closed shop.* A **closed shop** requires union membership by its workers as a condition of employment. Although the act made the closed shop illegal, it preserved the legality of the union shop. A **union shop** does not require membership as a prerequisite for employment but can, and usually does, require that workers join the union after a specified amount of time on the job.

The LMRA also prohibited unions from refusing to bargain with employers, engaging in certain types of picketing, and *featherbedding*—causing employers to hire more employees than necessary. The act also allowed individual states to pass their own **right-to-work laws,** which make it illegal for union membership to be required for *continued* employment in any establishment. Thus, union shops are technically illegal in the twenty-three states that have right-to-work laws.

Collective Bargaining

Once the NLRB certifies a union, that union becomes the *exclusive bargaining representative* of the workers. The central legal right of a union is to engage in collective bargaining on the members' behalf. **Collective bargaining** is the process by which labor and management negotiate the terms and conditions of employment, including wages, benefits, working conditions, and other matters. Although management is not necessarily required to bargain over a decision to close or relocate a particular facility, it must bargain over the economic consequences of such decisions. Decisions whether to grant severance pay (compensation for the termination of employment), for example, are appropriate for bargaining.

55. 29 U.S.C. Sections 101–110, 113–115.
56. 20 U.S.C. Section 151.
57. 29 U.S.C. Sections 141 *et seq.*

When a union is officially recognized, it may demand to bargain with the employer and negotiate new terms or conditions of employment. In collective bargaining, as in most other business negotiations, each side uses its economic power to pressure or persuade the other side to grant concessions.

Bargaining does not mean that one side must give in to the other or that compromises must be made. It does mean that a demand to bargain with the employer must be taken seriously and that both sides must bargain in "good faith." Good faith bargaining means that management, for instance, must be willing to meet with union representatives and consider the union's wishes when negotiating a contract.

Strikes

Even when labor and management have bargained in good faith, they may be unable to reach a final agreement. When extensive collective bargaining has been conducted and an impasse results, the union may call a strike against the employer to pressure it into making concessions. In a **strike,** the unionized workers leave their jobs and refuse to work. The workers also typically picket the workplace, walking or standing outside the facility with signs stating their complaints.

The right to strike is guaranteed by the NLRA, within limits, and strike activities, such as picketing, are protected by the free speech guarantee of the First Amendment to the U.S. Constitution.

A strike is an extreme action. Striking workers lose their rights to be paid, and management loses production and may lose customers when orders cannot be filled. Labor law regulates the circumstances and conduct of strikes. Most strikes take the form of "economic strikes," which are initiated because the union wants a better contract. **EXAMPLE 22.17** In 2010, the union representing workers at the Disneyland Hotel organized a hunger strike to draw attention to the prolonged contract dispute over health-care benefits and workloads. After two years of negotiations with the hotel, the workers still did not have a signed contract with health-care benefits. •

Lockouts

Lockouts are the employer's counterpart to the workers' right to strike. A **lockout** occurs when the employer shuts down to prevent employees from working. Lockouts usually are used when the employer believes that a strike is imminent. Lockouts may be a legal employer response.

Some lockouts are illegal, however. An employer may not use a lockout as a tool to break the union and pressure employees into decertification. Consequently, an employer must show some economic justification for instituting a lockout.

EXAMPLE 22.18 In 2011, the owners of the National Football League (NFL) teams imposed a lockout on the National Football League Players Association, the players' union, after negotiations on a new collective bargaining agreement broke down. At issue was the owners' proposal to decrease players' salaries and extend the season by two games. The owners claimed that the salary decrease was necessary because their profits from ticket sales had declined due to the struggling economy. When the lockout was imposed, the union requested decertification, which cleared the way for a group of players to file an antitrust lawsuit. Meanwhile, retired NFL players filed a complaint against the league seeking more medical benefits and better pensions. A settlement was reached before the start of the 2011 football season. The players accepted 3 percent less of the revenue generated (47 percent rather than 50 percent) in exchange for better working conditions and more retirement benefits. The owners agreed to keep the same number of games per season. •

Reviewing . . . Employment, Immigration, and Labor Law

Amaani Lyle, an African American woman, took a job as a scriptwriters' assistant at Warner Television Productions. She worked for the writers of *Weeds*, a popular, adult-oriented television series. One of her essential job duties was to type detailed notes for the scriptwriters during brainstorming sessions in which they discussed jokes, dialogue, and story lines. The writers then combed through Lyle's notes after the meetings for script material. During these meetings, the three male scriptwriters told lewd and vulgar jokes and made sexually explicit comments and gestures. They often talked about their personal sexual experiences and fantasies, and some of these conversations were then used in episodes of *Weeds*.

During the meetings, Lyle never complained that she found the writers' conduct offensive. After four months, she was fired because she could not type fast enough to keep up with the writers' conversations during the meetings. She filed a suit against Warner alleging sexual harassment and claiming that her termination was based on racial discrimination. Using the information presented in the chapter, answer the following questions.

1. Would Lyle's claim of racial discrimination be for intentional (disparate treatment) or unintentional (disparate impact) discrimination? Explain.
2. Can Lyle establish a *prima facie* case of racial discrimination? Why or why not?

3 Lyle was told when she was hired that typing speed was extremely important to her position. At the time, she maintained that she could type eighty words per minute, so she was not given a typing test. It later turned out that Lyle could type only fifty words per minute. What impact might typing speed have on Lyle's lawsuit?

4 Lyle's sexual-harassment claim is based on the hostile work environment created by the writers' sexually offensive conduct at meetings that she was required to attend. The writers, however, argue that their behavior was essential to the "creative process" of writing *Weeds,* a show that routinely contained sexual innuendos and adult humor. Which defense discussed in the chapter might Warner assert using this argument?

Terms and Concepts

bona fide occupational qualification (BFOQ) 431
business necessity 431
closed shop 434
collective bargaining 434
constructive discharge 426
disparate-impact discrimination 424
disparate-treatment discrimination 424
employment at will 414
employment discrimination 424
I-9 verification 432
I-551 Alien Registration Receipt 432
lockout 435
minimum wage 417
***prima facie* case 424**
protected class 423
right-to-work law 434
seniority system 431
sexual harassment 427
strike 435
tangible employment action 427
union shop 434
vesting 421
whistleblowing 415
workers' compensation laws 420
wrongful discharge 415

Chapter Summary: Employment, Immigration, and Labor Law

Employment at Will **(See pages 414–416.)**	1. *Employment-at-will doctrine*—Under this common law doctrine, either party may terminate the employment relationship at any time and for any reason ("at will"). This doctrine is still in widespread use throughout the United States, although federal and state statutes prevent it from being applied in certain circumstances. 2. *Exceptions to the employment-at-will doctrine*—To protect employees from some of the harsh results of the employment-at-will doctrine, courts have made exceptions to the doctrine on the basis of contract theory, tort theory, and public policy. Whistleblowers have occasionally received protection under the common law for reasons of public policy. 3. *Wrongful discharge*—Whenever an employer discharges an employee in violation of an employment contract or statutory law protecting employees, the employee may bring a suit for wrongful discharge.
Wage and Hour Laws **(See pages 416–418.)**	1. *Davis-Bacon Act (1931)*—Requires contractors and subcontractors working on federal government construction projects to pay their employees "prevailing wages." 2. *Walsh-Healey Act (1936)*—Requires firms that contract with federal agencies to pay their employees a minimum wage and overtime pay. 3. *Fair Labor Standards Act (1938)*—Extended wage and hour requirements to cover all employers whose activities affect interstate commerce, plus certain other businesses. The act has specific requirements in regard to child labor, minimum wages, and overtime.
Layoffs **(See pages 418–419.)**	1. *The Worker Adjustment and Retraining Notification (WARN) Act*—Applies to employers with at least one hundred full-time employees and requires that sixty days' advance notice of mass layoffs be given to affected employees or their representative (if workers are in a labor union). Employers who violate the WARN Act can be fined up to $500 for each day of the violation and may also have to pay damages and attorneys' fees to the laid-off employees affected by the failure to warn. 2. *State layoff notice requirements*—Many states have statutes requiring employers to provide notice before initiating mass layoffs, and these laws may have different and even stricter requirements than the WARN Act.
Family and Medical Leave **(See page 419.)**	The Family and Medical Leave Act (FMLA) requires employers with fifty or more employees to provide their employees with up to twelve weeks of unpaid leave (twenty-six weeks for military caregiver leave) during any twelve-month period. The FMLA authorizes leave for the following reasons:

Chapter Summary: Employment, Immigration, and Labor Law—Continued

Family and Medical Leave—Continued	1. *Family leave*—May be taken to care for a newborn baby, an adopted child, or a foster child. 2. *Medical leave*—May be taken when the employee or the employee's spouse, child, or parent has a serious health condition requiring care. 3. *Military caregiver leave*—May be taken when the employee is caring for a family member with a serious injury or illness incurred as a result of military duty. 4. *Qualifying exigency leave*—May be taken by an employee to handle specified nonmedical emergencies when a spouse, parent, or child is on, or is called to, active military duty.
Worker Health and Safety (See pages 419–420.)	1. *Occupational Safety and Health Act (1970)*—Requires employers to meet specific safety and health standards that are established and enforced by the Occupational Safety and Health Administration (OSHA). 2. *State workers' compensation laws*—Establish an administrative procedure for compensating workers who are injured in accidents that occur on the job, regardless of fault.
Income Security (See pages 420–422.)	1. *Social Security and Medicare*—The Social Security Act of 1935 provides for old-age (retirement), survivors', and disability insurance. Both employers and employees must make contributions under the Federal Insurance Contributions Act (FICA) to help pay for benefits that will partially make up for the employees' loss of income on retirement. The Social Security Administration also administers Medicare, a health-insurance program for older or disabled persons. 2. *Private pension plans*—The federal Employee Retirement Income Security Act (ERISA) of 1974 establishes standards for the management of employer-provided pension plans. 3. *Unemployment compensation*—The Federal Unemployment Tax Act of 1935 created a system that provides unemployment compensation to eligible individuals. Covered employers are taxed to help defray the costs of unemployment compensation. 4. *COBRA*—The Consolidated Omnibus Budget Reconciliation Act (COBRA) of 1985 requires employers to give employees, on termination of employment, the option of continuing their medical, optical, or dental insurance coverage for a certain period.
Employee Privacy Rights (See pages 422–423.)	A right to privacy has been inferred from the U.S. Constitution. State laws may also provide for privacy rights. Employer practices that are often challenged by employees as invasive of their privacy rights include monitoring of electronic communications and drug testing.
Title VII of the Civil Rights Act of 1964 (See pages 424–429.)	Title VII prohibits employment discrimination based on race, color, national origin, religion, or gender. 1. *Procedures*—Employees must file a claim with the Equal Employment Opportunity Commission (EEOC). The EEOC may sue the employer on the employee's behalf. If it does not, the employee may sue the employer directly. 2. *Types of discrimination*—Title VII prohibits both intentional (disparate-treatment) and unintentional (disparate-impact) discrimination. Disparate-impact discrimination occurs when an employer's practice, such as hiring only persons with a certain level of education, has the effect of discriminating against a class of persons protected by Title VII. Title VII also extends to discriminatory practices, such as various forms of harassment, in the online environment. 3. *Remedies for discrimination under Title VII*—If a plaintiff proves that unlawful discrimination occurred, he or she may be awarded reinstatement, back pay, and retroactive promotions. Damages (both compensatory and punitive) may be awarded for intentional discrimination
The Age Discrimination in Employment Act of 1967 (See pages 429–430.)	The Age Discrimination in Employment Act (ADEA) of 1967 prohibits employment discrimination on the basis of age against individuals forty years of age or older. Procedures for bringing a case under the ADEA are similar to those for bringing a case under Title VII.
The Americans with Disabilities Act of 1990 (See pages 430–431.)	The Americans with Disabilities Act (ADA) of 1990 prohibits employment discrimination against persons with disabilities who are otherwise qualified to perform the essential functions of the jobs for which they apply. 1. *Procedures and remedies*—To prevail on a claim under the ADA, the plaintiff must show that she or he has a disability, is otherwise qualified for the employment in question, and was excluded from the employment solely because of the disability. Procedures under the ADA are similar to those required in Title VII cases. Remedies are also similar to those under Title VII.

Continued

Chapter Summary: Employment, Immigration, and Labor Law—Continued

The Americans with Disabilities Act of 1990—Continued	2. *Definition of disability*—The ADA defines *disability* as a physical or mental impairment that substantially limits one or more major life activities, a record of such impairment, or being regarded as having such an impairment. 3. *Reasonable accommodation*—Employers are required to reasonably accommodate the needs of persons with disabilities. Reasonable accommodations may include altering job-application procedures, modifying the physical work environment, and permitting more flexible work schedules. Employers are not required to accommodate the needs of all workers with disabilities.
Defenses to Employment Discrimination (See page 431.)	If a plaintiff proves that employment discrimination occurred, employers may avoid liability by successfully asserting certain defenses. Employers may assert that the discrimination was required for reasons of business necessity, to meet a bona fide occupational qualification, or to maintain a legitimate seniority system. Evidence of prior employee misconduct acquired after the employee has been fired is not a defense to discrimination.
Immigration Law (See pages 431–433.)	1. *Immigration Reform and Control Act (1986)*—Prohibits employers from hiring illegal immigrants; administered by U.S. Citizenship and Immigration Services. Compliance audits and enforcement actions are conducted by U.S. Immigration and Customs Enforcement. 2. *Immigration Act (1990)*—Limits the number of legal immigrants entering the United States by capping the number of visas (entry permits) that are issued each year.
Labor Unions (See pages 433–435.)	1. *Federal labor laws*— a. Norris-LaGuardia Act (1932)—Protects peaceful strikes, picketing, and boycotts. b. National Labor Relations Act (1935)—Established the rights of employees to engage in collective bargaining and to strike; also defined specific employer practices as unfair to labor. The National Labor Relations Board (NLRB) was created to administer and enforce the act. c. Labor-Management Relations Act (1947)—Proscribes certain unfair union practices, such as the closed shop. 2. *Collective bargaining*—The process by which labor and management negotiate the terms and conditions of employment (such as wages, benefits, and working conditions). The central legal right of a labor union is to engage in collective bargaining on the members' behalf. 3. *Strikes and lockouts*—When collective bargaining reaches an impasse, union members may use their ultimate weapon in labor-management struggles—the strike. A strike occurs when unionized workers leave their jobs and refuse to work. Lockouts are the employer's counterpart to the workers' right to strike.

ExamPrep

ISSUE SPOTTERS

—Check your answers to these questions against the answers provided in Appendix G.

1 Onyx applies for work with Precision Design Company, which tells her that it requires union membership as a condition of employment. She applies for work with Quality Engineering, Inc., which does not require union membership as a condition of employment but requires employees to join a union after six months on the job. Are these conditions legal? Why or why not?

2 Koko, a person with a disability, applies for a job at Lively Sales Corporation for which she is well qualified, but she is rejected. Lively continues to seek applicants and eventually fills the position with a person who does not have a disability. Could Koko succeed in a suit against Lively for discrimination? Explain.

BEFORE THE TEST

Go to **www.cengagebrain.com**, enter the ISBN 9781111530624, and click on "Find" to locate this textbook's Web site. Then, click on "Access Now" under "Study Tools," and select Chapter 22 at the top. There, you will find an Interactive Quiz that you can take to assess your mastery of the concepts in this chapter, as well as Flashcards and a Glossary of important terms.

For Review

1 Under the Family and Medical Leave Act of 1993, in what circumstances may an employee take family or medical leave?
2 Generally, what kind of conduct is prohibited by Title VII of the Civil Rights Act of 1964, as amended?
3 What federal acts prohibit discrimination based on age and discrimination based on disability?
4 What are the two most important federal statutes governing immigration and employment today?
5 What federal statute gave employees the right to organize unions and engage in collective bargaining?

Questions and Case Problems

22–1 Wages and Hours. Calzoni Boating Co. is an interstate business engaged in manufacturing and selling boats. The company has five hundred nonunion employees. Representatives of these employees are requesting a four-day, ten-hours-per-day workweek, and Calzoni is concerned that this would require paying time and a half after eight hours per day. Which federal act is Calzoni thinking of that might require this? Will the act in fact require paying time and a half for all hours worked over eight hours per day if the employees' proposal is accepted? Explain.

22–2 Religious Discrimination. When Kayla Caldwell got a job as a cashier at a Costco store, she wore multiple pierced earrings and had four tattoos, but she had no facial piercings. Over the next two years, Caldwell engaged in various forms of body modification, including facial piercing and cutting. Then Costco revised its dress code to prohibit all facial jewelry, except earrings. Caldwell was told that she would have to remove her facial jewelry. She asked for a complete exemption from the code, asserting that she was a member of the Church of Body Modification and that eyebrow piercing was part of her religion. She was told to remove the jewelry, cover it, or go home. She went home and was later discharged for her absence. Based on these facts, will Caldwell be successful in a lawsuit against Costco for religious discrimination in violation of Title VII? Does an employer have an obligation to accommodate its employees' religious practices? If so, to what extent?

22–3 Illegal Aliens. Nicole Tipton and Sadik Seferi owned and operated a restaurant in Iowa. Acting on a tip from the local police, agents of Immigration and Customs Enforcement executed search warrants at the restaurant and at an apartment where some restaurant workers lived. The agents discovered six undocumented aliens working at the restaurant and living together. When the I-9 forms for the restaurant's employees were reviewed, none were found for the six aliens. They were paid in cash while other employees were paid by check. The jury found Tipton and Seferi guilty of hiring and harboring illegal aliens. Both were given prison terms. The defendants challenged the conviction, contending that they did not violate the law because they did not know that the workers were unauthorized aliens. Was that argument credible? Why or why not? [*United States v. Tipton,* 518 F.3d 591 (8th Cir. 2008)]

22–4 Fair Labor Standards Act. Misty Cumbie worked as a waitress at Vita Café in Portland, Oregon. The café was owned and operated by Woody Woo, Inc. Woody Woo paid its servers an hourly wage that was higher than the state's minimum wage, but the servers were required to contribute their tips into a "tip pool." Approximately one-third of the tip-pool funds went to the servers, and the rest was distributed to the kitchen staff that otherwise rarely received tips for their service. Cumbie sued Woody Woo, alleging that the tip-pooling arrangement violated the minimum wage provisions of the Fair Labor Standards Act (FLSA). The district court dismissed the suit for failure to state a claim. Cumbie appealed. Did Woody Woo's tip-pooling policy violate the FLSA rights of the servers? Explain your answer. [*Cumbie v. Woody Woo, Inc.,* 596 F.3d 577 (9th Cir. 2010)]

22–5 Discrimination Based on Gender. Brenda Lewis worked for two years at Heartland Inns of America, LLC, and gradually worked her way up the management ladder. Lewis, who described herself as a tomboy, was commended for her good work. When she moved to a different Heartland hotel, the director of operations, Barbara Cullinan, told one of the owners that Lewis was not a "good fit" for the front desk because she was not feminine enough. Cullinan told various people that the hotel wanted "pretty" girls at the front desk. Explaining to Lewis that her hiring had not been done properly, Cullinan said Lewis would need to perform another interview. Cullinan fired Lewis soon after the interview. The reason given in a letter was that Lewis was hostile during the interview process. Lewis sued Heartland for discrimination based on unlawful gender stereotyping. The district court dismissed the suit. Lewis appealed. Does her claim fall under Title VII's restriction on discrimination based on gender? Why or why not? [*Lewis v. Heartland Inns of America, LLC,* 591 F.3d 1033 (8th Cir. 2010)]

22–6 Workers' Compensation. As a safety measure, Dynea USA, Inc., required Tony Fairbanks, a millwright and company employee, to wear steel-toed boots. One afternoon, Fairbanks felt some discomfort on his left shin. At the end of the workday, he removed his boot, pulled his sock down, and saw a large red area below the top of the boot. Over the next two days, the red area became swollen and sore until Fairbanks had trouble walking. By the third day, the skin over the sore had broken. Within a week, Fairbanks was hospitalized with a methicillin-resistant *staphylococcus aureus* (MRSA) infection. Fairbanks notified Dynea and filed a workers' compensation claim. Dynea argued that the MRSA bacteria were on Fairbanks's skin before he came to work. What are the requirements to recover workers' compensation benefits? Does this claim qualify? Explain. [*In re Compensation of Fairbanks,* 241 Or.App. 311, 250 P.3d 389 (2011)]

22–7 **Case Problem with Sample Answer** Entek International, an Oregon-based company, hired Shane Dawson, a male homosexual, as a temporary production-line worker. Dawson worked with twenty-four other employees, all male. Certain individuals at work began making derogatory comments about Dawson's sexual orientation, calling him a "fag," a "homo," and a "worthless queer." Oregon law prohibits discrimination based on sexual orientation. Dawson asked his supervisor, Troy Guzon, to do something about the treatment he was receiving, but Guzon did not. In fact, Guzon also made derogatory comments about Dawson's sexual orientation. Dawson began to experience stress, and his work deteriorated. As a result of this situation, he went to the human resources department and filed a complaint. Two days later, he was fired. Dawson initiated a lawsuit, claiming that he had been fired in retaliation for filing a complaint, but the district court granted Entek a summary judgment. Dawson appealed. How should the federal appellate court rule? Has Dawson established a claim for retaliatory discharge? Should his case be allowed to go forward to a trial? Explain. [*Dawson v. Entek International,* 630 F.3d 928 (9th Cir. 2011)]

—For a sample answer to Problem 22–7, go to Appendix F at the end of this text.

22–8 **A Question of Ethics** *Titan Distribution, Inc., employed Quintak, Inc., to run its tire mounting and distribution operation in Des Moines, Iowa. Robert Chalfant worked for Quintak as a second-shift supervisor at Titan. He suffered a heart attack in 1992 and underwent heart bypass surgery in 1997. He also had arthritis. In July 2002, Titan decided to terminate Quintak. Chalfant applied to work at Titan. On his application, he described himself as having a disability. After a physical exam, Titan's doctor concluded that Chalfant could work in his current capacity, and he was notified that he would be hired. Despite the notice, Nadis Barucic, a Titan employee, wrote "not pass px" at the top of Chalfant's application, and he was not hired. He took a job with AMPCO Systems, a parking ramp management company. This work involved walking up to five miles a day and lifting more weight than he had at Titan. In September, Titan eliminated its second shift. Chalfant filed a suit in a federal district court against Titan, in part, under the Americans with Disabilities Act (ADA). Titan argued that the reason it had not hired Chalfant was not that he did not pass the physical, but no one—including Barucic—could explain why she had written "not pass px" on his application. Later, Titan claimed that Chalfant was not hired because the entire second shift was going to be eliminated.* [Chalfant v. Titan Distribution, Inc., *475 F.3d 982 (8th Cir. 2007)]*

1. What must Chalfant establish to make his case under the ADA? Can he meet these requirements? Explain.
2. In employment-discrimination cases, punitive damages can be appropriate when an employer acts with malice or reckless indifference to an employee's protected rights. Would an award of punitive damages to Chalfant be appropriate in this case? Discuss.

22–9 **Critical Thinking Legal Question** Why has the federal government limited the application of the statutes discussed in this chapter to firms with a specified number of employees, such as fifteen or twenty? Should these laws apply to all employers, regardless of size? Why or why not?

22–10 **Video Question** To watch this chapter's video, *Mary Tyler Moore,* go to **www.cengagebrain.com**. Register the access code that came with your new book or log in to your existing account. Select the link for the "Business Law Digital Video Library Online Access" or "Business Law CourseMate." Click on "Complete Video List," view Video 68, and then answer the following questions:

1. In the video, Mr. Grant (Ed Asner) asks Mary (Mary Tyler Moore) some personal questions during a job interview, including why she is not married and what religion she practices. He also tells her that he "figured he'd hire a man." Can Mary make out a *prima facie* case of gender or religious discrimination based on these questions? Why or why not?
2. Can Mary prove a *prima facie* case of age discrimination because Mr. Grant asked her age during the interview and then implied that she was "hedging" about her age? What would she need to prove under the Age Discrimination in Employment Act?
3. How does the fact that Mr. Grant hired Mary as an associate producer affect her ability to establish a case of employment discrimination?
4. Mr. Grant says that he will hire Mary to see if it works out, but he will fire her if he does not like her or if she does not like him at the end of a trial period. Can he do that? Explain. If he fired Mary a few weeks later, would this affect her ability to sue for employment discrimination? Why or why not?

Unit Seven Unit Case Study with Dissenting Opinion: *Media General Operations, Inc. v. National Labor Relations Board*

The National Labor Relations Act (NLRA), which was discussed in Chapter 22, ensures that employees are not discriminated against for engaging in collective action in the workplace. It protects the rights of employees to organize and engage in collective bargaining and related activities. This protection prevents employers from retaliating against workers for participating in "concerted activities" and provides a process for enforcing the rights that the NLRA guarantees.

In this Unit Case Study with Dissenting Opinion, *we review the case of* Media General Operations, Inc. v. National Labor Relations Board,[1] *which involved a worker who was fired for making a profane reference to a company executive during collective bargaining contract negotiations between the employer and the employees' union. Was the worker's derogatory remark a protected "concerted activity" under the NLRA or an unprotected "attack"?*

1. 560 F.3d 181 (4th Cir. 2009).

CASE BACKGROUND

Gregg McMillen was a journeyman pressman for *The Tampa Tribune,* a newspaper published by Media General Operations, Inc., which does business as *The Tampa Tribune.* The Graphic Communications Conference of the International Brotherhood of Teamsters, Local 180 represented McMillen and the other pressroom employees.

Negotiations between the union and the publisher over a contract to cover the employees had failed to yield results more than a year after the previous contract expired. Bill Barker, vice president of the Tribune, wrote to the pressroom workers, accusing the union of delaying the process. About two dozen employees, including McMillen, protested in a letter to Barker.

Barker responded with a letter that repeated his view. During a subsequent shift, McMillen walked into the pressroom office where Glenn Lerro, the pressroom foreman, and Joel Bridges, the assistant foreman, asked him whether he had seen the letter. He said no, referring to the company executive as "that f * * * ing idiot." He later apologized to Lerro for the remark. Three days later, he was fired for violating a workplace rule that bars the use of "threatening, abusive, or harassing language."

McMillen filed a charge with the National Labor Relations Board (NLRB), which concluded that McMillen's discharge violated the NLRA. On appeal, an administrative law judge (ALJ) found that McMillen's remark was not a protected act. The NLRB reversed this decision. The publisher appealed to the U.S. Court of Appeals for the Fourth Circuit.

MAJORITY OPINION

DUNCAN, **Circuit Judge:**

* * * *

* * * *Four factors * * * determine whether the Act's protection applies: (1) the place of the discussion; (2) the subject matter of the discussion; (3) the nature of the employee's outburst; and (4) whether the outburst was, in any way, provoked by an employer's unfair labor practice. If the balance is such that the conduct crosses the line from protected activity * * * to opprobrious [despicable] conduct, the worker loses the protection of the Act.* [Emphasis added.]

In the instant case, the ALJ found and the Board agreed that the first two factors weighed in favor of McMillen retaining the Act's protections. The discussion during which the derogatory remark was made took place away from the pressroom floor in an office that was used by pressroom supervisors and thus was at least semi-private. In addition, McMillen's comment occurred in the context of a discussion of Barker's letters, and those letters dealt with the ongoing contract negotiations between the Tribune and the Union. The Board also agreed with the ALJ that the fourth factor militated against extending the protection of the Act, since McMillen never claimed that he was responding to an unfair labor practice. Instead, his outburst was in response to a series of admittedly legal and truthful letters written by Barker.

Where the two adjudicators parted ways was on the significance of the third factor. The ALJ determined that the nature of the outburst was "so egregious [offensive]" that it removed McMillen's statement from the Act's protection. The Board disagreed. Analyzing the record, it found that the nature of the remark was only moderately prejudicial to McMillen's retention of the Act's protection. The Board based this determination on the fact that the remark was not made directly to Barker, that it was an isolated statement for which McMillen later apologized, and that it was neither a direct challenge to Barker's authority nor did it undermine employee discipline. Because of this different weighting of the third factor, the Board overturned the ALJ's conclusion and found that on the balance of the factors McMillen was entitled to the protection of the Act.

Continued

We disagree. The Board overreached as a matter of law in finding that the conduct in question was not so egregious as to forfeit the protection of the Act.

The lack of concurrence between Barker's lawful letter and McMillen's comment particularly disfavors protection. This was not a spontaneous outburst in response to an illegal threat but an *ad hominem* [appealing to people's emotions] attack made in the context of a discussion McMillen initiated with two supervisors. It was a response to an undisputedly legal letter issued in exercise of the company's rights. In addition, McMillen had not even read the letter in question, which further divorces his derogatory remark from the context of the ongoing labor dispute and thus makes the remark of a nature less eligible for protection. Insulting, obscene personal attacks by an employee against a supervisor need not be tolerated, even when they occur during otherwise protected activity.

It is also of particular significance * * * that McMillen made his derogatory remark in response to a series of *lawful* letters sent by his employer. Thus, the fourth factor of the * * * test weighs more than slightly against extending the Act's protection.

* * * McMillen's opprobrious *ad hominem* attack on a supervisor made at a point temporally remove[d] from and concerned only with lawful behavior by the employer falls outside the zone of protection.

* * * *

* * * We therefore reverse the judgment of the Board and reinstate the opinion of [the] ALJ.

DISSENTING OPINION

KING, **Circuit Judge, dissenting.**

* * * *

* * * The panel majority * * * seems to reject the Board's analysis of at least two * * * factors (factors one and three). The majority's analysis of these factors, however, is * * * problematic and unconvincing * * * . For example, the majority suggests that factor one, i.e., the place of the discussion, should weigh against the Act's protection because McMillen's comment was made in a "setting * * * physically * * * removed from the site of the ongoing collective bargaining negotiations." * * * The majority's apparent view—that only employee conduct occurring at the physical site of labor negotiations should be accorded protection—is not only grossly unfair, but also completely at odds with precedent. That is, the typical factor one assessment focuses on whether the employee conduct, because of the place where it occurred, somehow undermined workplace discipline. Here, the majority does not—and cannot—identify anything in this record supportive of the notion that McMillen's comment undermined workplace discipline.

The panel majority further suggests that factor three—the nature of the employee's outburst—should be given more than the "moderate" weight against protection assigned to it by the Board. More specifically, the majority * * * [indicates] that insulting, obscene personal attacks by an employee against a supervisor need not be tolerated * * * . [But] care must be exercised in evaluating employee language uttered in the course of engaging in activity protected by * * * the Act, and * * * an employee's exercise of rights under the Act must not be stifled by the threat of liability for the over enthusiastic use of rhetoric. Strikingly, * * * it has been held that calling an employer's president a "son-of-a-bitch" was not so outrageous as to justify discharge. In light of this and other precedent, it was entirely rational and consistent with the Act for the Board to rule that McMillen's comment should weigh only moderately against the Act's protection.

* * * The Board's disposition of this dispute was well within the parameters of its legal authority and binding precedent, and it is instead the panel majority that has reached beyond its bounds.

QUESTIONS FOR ANALYSIS

1. **Law.** What was the majority's decision in this case? On what was this decision based?
2. **Law.** What was the dissent's position with respect to the majority's reasoning and decision? If the majority of the court had agreed with the dissent, what would have resulted?
3. **Technology.** Would the decision in this case likely have been different if the employee had made the derogatory remark online?
4. **Cultural Dimensions.** What is the possible effect on an employee who is aware of the outcome in this case?
5. **Implications for the Investor.** What does the outcome in this case suggest to an employer engaged in collective bargaining negotiations with an employees' union?

Unit Eight

Business Organizations

Unit Contents

23 Sole Proprietorships, Partnerships, and Limited Liability Companies

24 Corporate Formation, Financing, and Termination

25 Corporate Directors, Officers, and Shareholders

26 Investor Protection, Insider Trading, and Corporate Governance

(Othermore/Creative Commons)

Chapter 23

Sole Proprietorships, Partnerships, and Limited Liability Companies

Learning Objectives

After reading this chapter, you should be able to answer the following questions:

1. What advantages and disadvantages are associated with the sole proprietorship?
2. What is meant by joint and several liability? Why is this often considered to be a disadvantage of doing business as a general partnership?
3. What advantages do limited liability partnerships offer to entrepreneurs that are not offered by general partnerships?
4. What are the key differences between the rights and liabilities of general partners and those of limited partners?
5. How are limited liability companies formed, and who decides how they will be managed and operated?

The Learning Objectives above are designed to help improve your understanding of the chapter.

(Othermore/Creative Commons)

An entrepreneur's primary motive for undertaking a business enterprise is to make profits. An **entrepreneur** is by definition one who initiates and assumes the financial risks of a new enterprise and undertakes to provide or control its management.

One of the questions faced by anyone who wishes to start a business is what form of business organization should be chosen for the business endeavor. In making this determination, the entrepreneur needs to consider a number of factors. Among the most important are (1) ease of creation, (2) the liability of the owners, (3) tax considerations, and (4) the need for capital. Keep these factors in mind as you read about the various business organizational forms available to entrepreneurs.

Traditionally, entrepreneurs have used three major forms to structure their business enterprises: the sole proprietorship, the partnership, and the corporation. In this chapter, we examine the forms of business most often used by small business enterprises, including two of these traditional forms—sole proprietorships and partnerships. In addition, we describe limited liability partnerships, limited partnerships, and limited liability companies—all of which offer businessowners special advantages particularly with respect to liability and taxation. In Chapters 24 and 25, we will discuss the third major traditional form of business—the corporation. Exhibit 25–3 on pages 496 and 497 summarizes and compares aspects of all the business organizations.

Sole Proprietorships

A **sole proprietorship** is the simplest form of business organization. In this form, the owner is the business. Thus, anyone who does business without creating a separate business organization has a sole proprietorship. More than two-thirds of all U.S. businesses are sole proprietorships. They are usually small enterprises—about 99 percent of the sole proprietorships in the United States have revenues of less than $1 million per year. Sole proprietors can own and manage any type of business, ranging from an informal, home-office undertaking to a large restaurant or construction firm. Today, a number of online businesses that sell goods and services nationwide are organized as sole proprietorships.

Advantages of the Sole Proprietorship

A major advantage of the sole proprietorship is that the proprietor owns the entire business and has a right to receive all of the profits (because he or she assumes all of the risk). In addition, it is often easier and less costly to start a sole proprietorship than to start any other kind of business, as few legal formalities are involved.[1] One does not need to file any documents with the government to start a sole proprietorship (though a state business license may be required to operate certain businesses).

This form of business organization also allows more flexibility than does a partnership or a corporation. The sole proprietor is free to make any decision she or he wishes concerning the business—including whom to hire, when to take a vacation, and what kind of business to pursue. In addition, the proprietor can sell or transfer all or part of the business to another party at any time and does not need approval from anyone else (as would be required from partners in a partnership or, normally, from shareholders in a corporation).

A sole proprietor pays only personal income taxes (including self-employment tax, which consists of Social Security and Medicare taxes) on the business's profits, which are reported as personal income on the proprietor's personal income tax return. Sole proprietors are also allowed to establish certain retirement accounts that are tax-exempt until the funds are withdrawn.

Disadvantages of the Sole Proprietorship

The major disadvantage of the sole proprietorship is that the proprietor alone bears the burden of any losses or liabilities incurred by the business enterprise. In other words, the sole proprietor has unlimited liability, or legal responsibility, for all obligations incurred in doing business. Any lawsuit against the business or its employees can lead to unlimited personal liability for the owner of a sole proprietorship. Creditors can go after the owner's personal assets to satisfy any business debts. This unlimited liability is a major factor to be considered in choosing a business form.

EXAMPLE 23.1 Sheila Fowler operates a golf shop business as a sole proprietorship. The shop is located near one of the best golf courses in the country. A professional golfer, Dean Maheesh, is seriously injured when a display of golf clubs, which one of Fowler's employees has failed to secure, falls on him. If Maheesh sues Fowler's shop (a sole proprietorship) and wins, Fowler's personal liability could easily exceed the limits of her insurance policy. In this situation, not only might Fowler lose her business, but she could also lose her house, her car, and any other personal assets that can be attached to pay the judgment. •

The sole proprietorship also has the disadvantage of lacking continuity on the death of the proprietor. When the owner dies, so does the business—it is automatically dissolved. Another disadvantage is that the proprietor's opportunity to raise capital is limited to personal funds and the funds of those who are willing to make loans.

Partnerships

A **partnership** arises from an agreement, express or implied, between two or more persons to carry on a business for profit. Partners are co-owners of a business and have joint control over its operation and the right to share in its profits.

Partnerships are governed both by common law concepts—in particular, those relating to agency (discussed in Chapter 21)—and by statutory law. The National Conference of Commissioners on Uniform State Laws has drafted the Uniform Partnership Act (UPA), which governs the operation of partnerships *in the absence of express agreement* and has done much to reduce controversies in the law relating to partnerships. In other words, the partners are free to establish rules for their partnership that differ from those stated in the UPA.

The UPA has undergone several major revisions since it was first issued in 1914. Except for Louisiana, every state has adopted the UPA. The majority of states have adopted the most recent version of the UPA, which was issued in 1994 and amended in 1997 to provide limited liability for partners in a limited liability partnership. We therefore base our discussion of the UPA in this chapter on the 1997 version of the act.

Agency Concepts and Partnership Law

When two or more persons agree to do business as partners, they enter into a special relationship with one another. To an extent, their relationship is similar to an agency relationship because each partner is deemed to be the agent of the other partners and of the partnership. The common law agency concepts you read about in Chapter 21 thus apply—specifically, the imputation of knowledge of, and responsibility for, acts done within the scope of the partnership relationship. In their relations with one another, partners, like agents, are bound by fiduciary ties.

In one important way, however, partnership law is distinct from agency law. In a partnership, two or more persons agree to contribute some or all of their funds or other assets, labor,

1. Although starting a sole proprietorship involves relatively few legal formalities compared with other business organizational forms, even small sole proprietorships may need to comply with certain zoning requirements, obtain appropriate licenses, and the like.

and skills to a business with the understanding that profits and losses will be shared. Thus, each partner has an ownership interest in the firm. In a nonpartnership agency relationship, the agent usually does not have an ownership interest in the business, nor is he or she obliged to bear a portion of the ordinary business losses.

When Does a Partnership Exist?

Conflicts sometimes arise over whether a business enterprise is legally a partnership, especially in the absence of a formal, written partnership agreement. The UPA defines a partnership as "an association of two or more persons to carry on as co-owners a business for profit" [UPA 101(6)]. Note that under the UPA a corporation is a "person" [UPA 101(10)]. The *intent* to associate is a key element of a partnership, and a person cannot join a partnership unless all of the other partners consent [UPA 401(i)].

In resolving disputes over whether partnership status exists, courts usually look for the following three essential elements, which are implicit in the UPA's definition of a partnership:

1. A sharing of profits and losses.
2. A joint ownership of the business.
3. An equal right to be involved in the management of the business.

Joint ownership of property, obviously, does not in and of itself create a partnership. In fact, the sharing of gross revenues and even profits from such ownership is usually not enough to create a partnership [UPA 202(c)(1), (2)]. **EXAMPLE 23.2** Chiang and Burke jointly own a piece of rural property. They lease the land to a farmer, with the understanding that—in lieu of set rental payments—they will receive a share of the profits from the farming operation conducted by the farmer. This arrangement normally would not make Chiang, Burke, and the farmer partners. •

Note, though, that although the sharing of profits from ownership of property does not prove the existence of a partnership, sharing *both profits and losses* usually does. **EXAMPLE 23.3** Two sisters, Zoe and Cienna, buy a restaurant together, open a joint bank account from which they pay for expenses and supplies, and share the net profits that the restaurant generates. Zoe manages the restaurant and Cienna handles the bookkeeping. After eight years, Cienna stops doing the bookkeeping and does no other work for the restaurant. Zoe, who is now operating the restaurant by herself, no longer wants to share the profits with Cienna. She offers to buy her sister out, but the two cannot agree on a fair price. When Cienna files a lawsuit, a question arises as to whether the two sisters were partners in the restaurant. In this situation, a court would find that a partnership existed because the sisters shared management responsibilities, had joint accounts, and shared the profits and the losses of the restaurant equally. •

Entity versus Aggregate Theory of Partnerships

At common law, a partnership was treated only as an aggregate of individuals and never as a separate legal entity. Thus, at common law a suit could never be brought by or against the firm in its own name. Instead, each individual partner had to sue or be sued.

Today, in contrast, a majority of the states follow the UPA and treat a partnership as an entity for most purposes. For example, a partnership usually can sue or be sued, collect judgments, and have all accounting procedures in the name of the partnership entity [UPA 201, 307(a)]. As an entity, a partnership may hold the title to real or personal property in its name rather than in the names of the individual partners. Additionally, federal procedural laws permit the partnership to be treated as an entity in suits in federal courts and bankruptcy proceedings.

For federal income tax purposes, however, the partnership is treated as an aggregate of the individual partners rather than a separate legal entity. The partnership is a pass-through entity and not a taxpaying entity. A **pass-through entity** is a business entity that has no tax liability because the entity's income is passed through to the owners, who pay taxes on it. Thus, the income or losses the partnership incurs are "passed through" the entity framework and attributed to the partners on their individual tax returns. The partnership itself has no tax liability and is responsible only for filing an **information return** with the Internal Revenue Service. In other words, the firm itself pays no taxes. A partner's profit from the partnership (whether distributed or not) is taxed as individual income to the individual partner.

Partnership Formation

As a general rule, an agreement to form a partnership can be *oral, written,* or *implied by conduct.* Some partnership agreements, however, must be in writing to be legally enforceable under the Statute of Frauds (see Chapter 10 for details). A written partnership agreement, called **articles of partnership,** can include almost any terms that the parties wish, unless they are illegal or contrary to public policy or statute [UPA 103]. The agreement usually specifies the name and location of the business, the duration of the partnership, the purpose of the business, each partner's share of the profits, how the partnership will be managed, and how assets will be distributed on dissolution, among other things.

Duration of the Partnership The partnership agreement can specify the duration of the partnership by stating that it will continue until a certain date or the completion of a particular project. A partnership that is specifically limited in duration is called a *partnership for a term.* Generally, withdrawing from a partnership for a term prematurely (prior to the expiration date) constitutes a breach of the agreement, and the responsible partner can be held liable for any resulting losses [UPA 602(b)(2)]. If no fixed duration is specified, the partnership is a *partnership at will.*

PARTNERSHIP BY ESTOPPEL Occasionally, persons who are not partners may nevertheless hold themselves out as partners and make representations that third parties rely on in dealing with them. In such a situation, a court may conclude that a *partnership by estoppel* exists. The law does not confer any partnership rights on these persons, but it may impose liability on them. This is also true when a partner represents, expressly or impliedly, that a nonpartner is a member of the firm [UPA 308].

CASE EXAMPLE 23.4 Gary Chavers operated Chavers Welding and Construction (CWC). His sons, Reggie and Mark, worked in the business as well. CWC contracted with Epsco, Inc., to provide payroll and employee services. Initially, Epsco collected payments for its services each week, but later Epsco extended credit to CWC, which the Chaverses had represented was a partnership. Eventually, when CWC's account was more than $80,000 delinquent, Epsco filed a lawsuit to recover payment. Gary filed for bankruptcy, and his obligation to Epsco was discharged. Reggie and Mark claimed that their father owned CWC as a sole proprietor and that they were not partners in the business. The court, however, held that the sons were liable for CWC's debts based on partnership by estoppel. Because the Chaverses had represented to Epsco that CWC was a partnership and Epsco had relied on this representation when extending credit, the sons could not claim that no partnership existed.[2] •

Rights of Partners

The rights of partners in a partnership relate to the following areas: management, interest in the partnership, compensation, inspection of books, accounting, and property. In the absence of provisions to the contrary in the partnership agreement, the law imposes the rights discussed here.

MANAGEMENT RIGHTS In a general partnership, all partners have equal rights in managing the partnership [UPA 401(f)]. Unless the partners agree otherwise, each partner has one vote in management matters *regardless of the proportional size of his or her interest in the firm.* Often, in a large partnership, partners agree to delegate daily management responsibilities to a management committee made up of one or more of the partners.

Decisions on ordinary matters connected with partnership business are made by majority rule, unless the agreement specifies otherwise. Decisions that significantly affect the nature of the partnership or that are not apparently for carrying on the ordinary course of the partnership business, or business of the kind, however, require the *unanimous* consent of the partners [UPA 301(2), 401(i), (j)]. Unanimous consent is typically required for such decisions as whether to admit new partners, amend the articles of partnership, engage in a new business, or undertake any act that would make further conduct of the partnership impossible.

INTEREST IN THE PARTNERSHIP Each partner is entitled to the proportion of business profits and losses that is designated in the partnership agreement. If the agreement does not apportion profits (indicate how the profits will be shared), the UPA provides that profits will be shared equally. If the agreement does not apportion losses, losses will be shared in the same ratio as profits [UPA 401(b)].

EXAMPLE 23.5 The partnership agreement for Rico and Brent provides for capital contributions of $60,000 from Rico and $40,000 from Brent, but it is silent as to how Rico and Brent will share profits or losses. In this situation, Rico and Brent will share both profits and losses equally. If their partnership agreement provided for profits to be shared in the same ratio as capital contributions, however, 60 percent of the profits would go to Rico, and 40 percent of the profits would go to Brent. If their partnership agreement was silent as to losses, losses would be shared in the same ratio as profits (60 percent and 40 percent, respectively). •

COMPENSATION Devoting time, skill, and energy to partnership business is a partner's duty and generally is not a compensable service. Rather, as mentioned, a partner's income from the partnership takes the form of a distribution of profits according to the partner's share in the business. Partners can, of course, agree otherwise. For instance, the managing partner of a law firm often receives a salary—in addition to her or his share of profits—for performing special administrative duties, such as managing the office or personnel.

INSPECTION OF BOOKS Partnership books and records must be kept at the firm's principal business office and be accessible to all partners. Each partner has the right to receive (and the corresponding duty to produce) full and complete information concerning the conduct of all aspects of partnership business [UPA 403]. Every partner is entitled to inspect all books and records on demand and to make copies of the materials.

ACCOUNTING OF PARTNERSHIP ASSETS OR PROFITS An accounting of partnership assets or profits is required to determine the value of each partner's share in the partnership. An accounting can be performed voluntarily, or it can be compelled by court order. Under UPA 405(b), a partner has the right to bring an action for an accounting during the term of

2. *Chavers v. Epsco, Inc.*, 352 Ark. 65, 98 S.W.3d 421 (2003).

the partnership, as well as on the partnership's dissolution and winding up (see page 451).

Property Rights Property acquired by a partnership is the property of the partnership and not of the partners individually [UPA 203]. Partnership property includes all property that was originally contributed to the partnership and anything later purchased by the partnership or in the partnership's name (except in rare circumstances) [UPA 204]. A partner may use or possess partnership property only on behalf of the partnership [UPA 401(g)]. A partner is *not* a co-owner of partnership property and has no right to sell, mortgage, or transfer partnership property to another. (A partner can assign her or his right to a share of the partnership profits to another to satisfy a debt, however.)

Duties and Liabilities of Partners

The duties and liabilities of partners are basically derived from agency law (discussed in Chapter 21). Each partner is an agent of every other partner and acts as both a principal and an agent in any business transaction within the scope of the partnership agreement. Each partner is also a general agent of the partnership in carrying out the usual business of the firm "or business of the kind carried on by the partnership" [UPA 301(1)]. Thus, every act of a partner concerning partnership business and "business of the kind," and every contract signed by that partner in the partnership's name, binds the firm.

One significant disadvantage associated with a traditional partnership is that partners are *personally* liable for the debts of the partnership. Moreover, the liability is essentially unlimited because the acts of one partner in the ordinary course of business subject the other partners to personal liability [UPA 305]. We examine here the fiduciary duties of partners, the authority of partners, and the liability of partners.

Fiduciary Duties The fiduciary duties a partner owes to the partnership and the other partners are the duty of loyalty and the duty of care [UPA 404(a)]. The duty of loyalty requires a partner to account to the partnership for "any property, profit, or benefit" derived by the partner from the partnership's business or the use of its property [UPA 404(b)]. A partner must also refrain from competing with the partnership in business or dealing with the firm as an adverse party. A partner's duty of care involves refraining from "grossly negligent or reckless conduct, intentional misconduct, or a knowing violation of law" [UPA 404(c)].

These duties may not be waived or eliminated in the partnership agreement, and in fulfilling them, each partner must act consistently with the obligation of good faith and fair dealing, which applies to all contracts, including partnership agreements [UPA 103(b), 404(d)]. The agreement can specify acts that the partners agree will violate a fiduciary duty.

Note that a partner may pursue his or her own interests without automatically violating these duties [UPA 404(e)]. The key is whether the partner has disclosed the interest to the other partners. **EXAMPLE 23.6** Jayne Trell, a partner at Jacoby & Meyers, owns a shopping mall. Trell may vote against a partnership proposal to open a competing mall, provided that she has fully disclosed her interest in the existing shopping mall to the other partners at the firm. ●

A partner can breach his or her duty of loyalty by self-dealing, misusing partnership property, disclosing trade secrets, or usurping a partnership business opportunity. The following case is a classic example.

Classic Case 23.1 Meinhard v. Salmon

Court of Appeals of New York, 249 N.Y. 458, 164 N.E. 545 (1928).
www.nycourts.gov/reporter/Index.htm[a]

FACTS Walter Salmon negotiated a twenty-year lease for the Hotel Bristol in New York City. To pay for the conversion of the building into shops and offices, Salmon entered into an agreement with Morton Meinhard to assume half of the cost. They agreed to share the profits and losses from the joint venture (a *joint venture* is similar to a partnership but typically is created for a single project, whereas a partnership usually involves an ongoing business), but Salmon was to have the sole power to manage the building. Less than four months before the end of the lease term, the building's owner, Elbridge Gerry, approached Salmon about a project to raze the converted structure, clear five adjacent lots, and construct a single building across the whole property. Salmon agreed and signed a new lease in the name of his own business, Midpoint Realty Company, without telling Meinhard. When Meinhard learned of the deal, he filed a suit in a New York state court against Salmon. From a judgment in Meinhard's favor, Salmon appealed.

ISSUE Did Salmon breach his fiduciary duty of loyalty to Meinhard by failing to inform him of another business opportunity and secretly taking advantage of it for himself?

DECISION Yes. The Court of Appeals of New York affirmed the lower court's decision. Salmon had breached his fiduciary duty by failing to inform Meinhard of the business opportunity. The appellate court therefore

a. In the links at the bottom of the page, click on "Archives." In the result, scroll to the name of the case and click on it to access the opinion. The New York State Law Reporting Bureau maintains this Web site.

Classic Case 23.1–Continued

granted Meinhard an interest "measured by the value of half of the entire lease."

REASON The court stated, "Joint adventurers, like copartners, owe to one another, while the enterprise continues, the duty of the finest loyalty." Salmon's conduct excluded Meinhard from any chance to compete and from any chance to enjoy the opportunity for benefit. As a partner, Salmon was bound by his "obligation to his copartners in such dealings not to separate his interest from theirs, but, if he acquires any benefit, to communicate it to them." Salmon was also the managing co-adventurer, and thus the court found that "for him and for those like him the rule of undivided loyalty is relentless and supreme."

WHAT IF THE FACTS WERE DIFFERENT? *Suppose that Salmon had disclosed Gerry's proposal to Meinhard, who had said that he was not interested. Would the result in this case have been different? Explain.*

IMPACT OF THIS CASE ON TODAY'S LAW *This landmark case involved a joint venture, not a partnership. At the time, a member of a joint venture had only the duty to refrain from actively subverting the rights of the other members. The decision in this case imposed the highest standard of loyalty on joint-venture members. The duty is now the same in both joint ventures and partnerships. The eloquent language in this case that describes the standard of loyalty is frequently quoted approvingly by courts in cases involving partnerships.*

AUTHORITY OF PARTNERS Under the UPA and agency law, a partner has the authority to bind a partnership in contract. A partner may also subject the partnership to tort liability under agency principles. When a partner is carrying on partnership business or business of the kind with third parties in the usual way, both the partner and the firm share liability.

If a partner acts within the scope of her or his authority, the partnership is legally bound to honor the partner's commitments to third parties. The partnership will not be liable, however, if the third parties know that the partner had no authority to commit the partnership. Agency concepts that we explored in Chapter 21 relating to actual (express and implied) authority, apparent authority, and ratification also apply to partnerships. The extent of implied authority is generally broader for partners than for ordinary agents, though.

JOINT LIABILITY OF PARTNERS Each partner in a partnership is jointly liable for the partnership's obligations. **Joint liability** means that a third party must sue all of the partners as a group, but each partner can be held liable for the full amount. Under the prior version of the UPA, which is still in effect in a few states, partners were subject to joint liability on partnership debts and contracts, but not on partnership debts arising from torts.

If, for instance, a third party sues a partner on a partnership contract, the partner has the right to demand that the other partners be sued with her or him. In fact, if the third party does not sue all of the partners, the assets of the partnership cannot be used to satisfy the judgment. With joint liability, the partnership's assets must be exhausted before creditors can reach the partners' individual assets.[3]

JOINT AND SEVERAL LIABILITY OF PARTNERS In the majority of states, under UPA 306(a), partners are jointly and severally (separately or individually) liable for all partnership obligations, including contracts, torts, and breaches of trust. **Joint and several liability** means that a third party may sue all of the partners together (jointly) or one or more of the partners separately (severally) at his or her option. All partners in a partnership can be held liable regardless of whether the partner participated in, knew about, or ratified the conduct that gave rise to the lawsuit. Normally, though, the partnership's assets must be exhausted before a creditor can enforce a judgment against a partner's separate assets [UPA 307(d)].

A judgment against one partner severally (separately) does not extinguish the others' liability. Those not sued in the first action normally may be sued subsequently, unless the court in the first action held that the partnership was in no way liable. If a plaintiff is successful in a suit against a partner or partners, he or she may collect on the judgment only against the assets of those partners named as defendants. A partner who commits a tort may be required to indemnify (reimburse) the partnership for any damages it pays—unless the tort was committed in the ordinary course of the partnership's business.

CASE EXAMPLE 23.7 Nicole Moren was a partner in Jax Restaurant. After work one day, Moren was called back to the restaurant to help in the kitchen. She brought her two-year-old-son, Remington, and sat him on the kitchen counter. While she was making pizzas, Remington reached into the dough press. His hand was crushed, causing permanent injuries. Through his father, Remington filed a suit against the partnership for negligence. The partnership filed a complaint against Moren, arguing that it was entitled to indemnity (compensation or reimbursement) from Moren for her negligence. The court held in favor of Moren and ordered the partnership to pay damages to Remington. Moren was not required to indemnify the partnership because her negligence occurred in the ordinary course of the partnership's business.[4] ●

3. For a case applying joint liability to partnerships, see *Shar's Cars, LLC v. Elder*, 97 P.3d 724 (Utah App. 2004).

4. *Moren v. Jax Restaurant*, 679 N.W.2d 165 (Minn.App. 2004).

Partner's Dissociation

Dissociation occurs when a partner ceases to be associated in the carrying on of the partnership business. Although a partner always has the *power* to dissociate from the firm, he or she may not have the *right* to dissociate. Dissociation normally entitles the partner to have his or her interest purchased by the partnership and terminates his or her actual authority to act for the partnership and to participate with the partners in running the business. Otherwise, the partnership continues to do business without the dissociating partner.[5]

EVENTS CAUSING DISSOCIATION Under UPA 601, a partner can be dissociated from a partnership in any of the following ways:

1. By the partner's voluntarily giving notice of an "express will to withdraw."
2. By the occurrence of an event agreed to in the partnership agreement.
3. By a unanimous vote of the other partners under certain circumstances, such as when a partner transfers substantially all of her or his interest in the partnership, or when it becomes unlawful to carry on partnership business with that partner.
4. By order of a court or arbitrator if the partner has engaged in wrongful conduct that affects the partnership business, breached the partnership agreement or violated a duty owed to the partnership or the other partners, or engaged in conduct that makes it "not reasonably practicable to carry on the business in partnership with the partner" [UPA 601(5)].
5. By the partner's declaring bankruptcy, assigning his or her interest in the partnership for the benefit of creditors, or becoming physically or mentally incapacitated, or by the partner's death. Note that although the bankruptcy or death of a partner represents that partner's "dissociation" from the partnership, it is not an *automatic* ground for the partnership's dissolution (*dissolution* will be discussed shortly).

WRONGFUL DISSOCIATION As mentioned, a partner has the power to dissociate from a partnership at any time, but if she or he lacks the right to dissociate, then the dissociation is considered wrongful under the law [UPA 602]. When a partner's dissociation is in breach of the partnership agreement, for instance, it is wrongful. **EXAMPLE 23.8** Jenson & Burke's partnership agreement states that it is a breach of the agreement for any partner to assign partnership property to a creditor without the consent of the others. If a partner, Janis, makes such an assignment, she has not only breached the agreement but has also wrongfully dissociated from the partnership. ● Similarly, if a partner refuses to perform duties required by the partnership agreement—such as accounting for profits earned from the use of partnership property—this breach can be treated as wrongful dissociation. A partner who wrongfully dissociates is liable to the partnership and to the other partners for damages caused by the dissociation.

EFFECTS OF DISSOCIATION Dissociation (rightful or wrongful) terminates some of the rights of the dissociated partner, requires that the partnership purchase his or her interest, and alters the liability of both parties to third parties. On a partner's dissociation, his or her right to participate in the management and conduct of the partnership business terminates [UPA 603]. The partner's duty of loyalty also ends. A partner's duty of care continues only with respect to events that occurred before dissociation, unless the partner participates in winding up the partnership's business (to be discussed shortly). **EXAMPLE 23.9** Amy Pearson, a partner who leaves an accounting firm, Bubb & Pearson, can immediately compete with the firm for new clients. She must exercise care in completing ongoing client transactions, however, and must account to the firm for any fees received from the old clients based on those transactions. ●

After a partner's dissociation, his or her interest in the partnership must be purchased according to the rules in UPA 701. The **buyout price** is based on the amount that would have been distributed to the partner if the partnership were wound up on the date of dissociation. Offset against the price are amounts owed by the partner to the partnership, including any damages for the partner's wrongful dissociation.

For two years after a partner dissociates from a continuing partnership, the partnership may be bound by the acts of the dissociated partner based on apparent authority [UPA 702]. In other words, the partnership may be liable to a third party with whom a dissociated partner enters into a transaction if the third party reasonably believed that the dissociated partner was still a partner. Similarly, a dissociated partner may be liable for partnership obligations entered into during a two-year period following dissociation [UPA 703].

Partnership Termination

The same events that cause dissociation can result in the end of the partnership if the remaining partners no longer wish to (or are unable to) continue the partnership business. The termination of a partnership is referred to as **dissolution,** which essentially means the commencement of the winding up process. **Winding up** is the process of collecting, liquidating, and distributing the partnership assets.[6]

5. Under the previous version of the UPA, when a partner dissociated from a partnership, the partnership was considered dissolved, its business had to be wound up, and the proceeds had to be distributed to creditors and among partners. The amendments to the UPA recognize that a partnership may not want to break up just because one partner has left the firm.

6. Although "winding down" would seem to describe more accurately the process of settling accounts and liquidating the assets of a partnership, "winding up" has been traditionally used in English and U.S. statutory and case law to denote this final stage of a partnership's existence.

DISSOLUTION Dissolution of a partnership generally can be brought about by acts of the partners, by operation of law, and by judicial decree [UPA 801]. Any partnership (including one for a fixed term) can be dissolved by the partners' agreement. Similarly, if the partnership agreement states that it will dissolve on a certain event, such as a partner's death or bankruptcy, then the occurrence of that event will dissolve the partnership. A partnership for a fixed term or a particular undertaking is dissolved by operation of law at the expiration of the term or on the completion of the undertaking. Under the UPA, a court may order dissolution when it becomes obviously impractical for the firm to continue—for example, if the business can only be operated at a loss [UPA 801(5)].

WINDING UP After dissolution, the partnership continues for the limited purpose of the winding up process. The partners cannot create new obligations on behalf of the partnership. They have authority only to complete transactions begun but not finished at the time of dissolution and to wind up the business of the partnership [UPA 803, 804(1)]. *Winding up* includes collecting and preserving partnership assets, discharging liabilities (paying debts), and accounting to each partner for the value of her or his interest in the partnership. Partners continue to have fiduciary duties to one another and to the firm during this process.

Both creditors of the partnership and creditors of the individual partners can make claims on the partnership's assets. In general, partnership creditors share proportionately with the partners' individual creditors in the assets of the partners' estates, which include their interests in the partnership. A partnership's assets are distributed according to the following priorities [UPA 807]:

1. Payment of debts, including those owed to partner and nonpartner creditors.
2. Return of capital contributions and distribution of profits to partners.

If the partnership's liabilities are greater than its assets, the partners bear the losses—in the absence of a contrary agreement—in the same proportion in which they shared the profits (rather than, for example, in proportion to their contributions to the partnership's capital).

Limited Liability Partnerships

The **limited liability partnership (LLP)** is a hybrid form of business designed mostly for professionals, such as attorneys and accountants, who normally do business as partners in a partnership. In fact, nearly all the big accounting firms are LLPs. The major advantage of the LLP is that it allows a partnership to continue as *a pass-through entity* for tax purposes, but limits the personal liability of the partners. A special form of LLP is the *family limited liability partnership* (FLLP), in which the majority of the partners are persons related to each other, essentially as spouses, parents, grandparents, siblings, cousins, nephews, or nieces.

LLPs must be formed and operated in compliance with state statutes, which often include provisions of the UPA. The appropriate form must be filed with a state agency, and the business's name must include either "Limited Liability Partnership" or "LLP" [UPA 1001, 1002]. In addition, an LLP must file an annual report with the state to remain qualified as an LLP in that state [UPA 1003]. In most states, it is relatively easy to convert a traditional partnership into an LLP because the firm's basic organizational structure remains the same. Additionally, all of the statutory and common law rules governing partnerships still apply (apart from those modified by the state's LLP statute).

The LLP allows professionals to avoid personal liability for the malpractice of other partners. A partner in an LLP is still liable for her or his own wrongful acts, such as negligence, however. Also liable is the partner who supervised the party who committed a wrongful act. This generally is true for all types of partners and partnerships, not just LLPs.

Although LLP statutes vary from state to state, generally each state statute limits the liability of partners in some way. For example, Delaware law protects each innocent partner from the "debts and obligations of the partnership arising from negligence, wrongful acts, or misconduct." The UPA more broadly exempts partners from personal liability for any partnership obligation, "whether arising in contract, tort, or otherwise" [UPA 306(c)].

Limited Partnerships

We now look at a business organizational form that limits the liability of *some* of its owners—the **limited partnership (LP).** LPs originated in medieval Europe and have been in existence in the United States since the early 1800s. In many ways, LPs are like the general partnerships discussed earlier in this chapter, but they differ from general partnerships in several ways. Hence, they are sometimes referred to as *special partnerships.*

An LP consists of at least one **general partner** and one or more **limited partners.** A general partner assumes responsibility for managing the partnership and so has full responsibility for the partnership and for all of its debts. A limited partner contributes funds or other property and owns an interest in the firm but does not undertake any management responsibilities and is not personally liable for partnership debts beyond the amount of his or her investment. A limited partner can forfeit limited liability by taking part in the management of the business.

Until 1976, the law governing limited partnerships in all states except Louisiana was the Uniform Limited Partnership Act (ULPA). Since 1976, most states and the District of Columbia have adopted the revised version of the ULPA, known as the Revised Uniform Limited Partnership Act (RULPA). Because the RULPA is the dominant law governing limited partnerships in the United States, we will refer to it in the following discussion of limited partnerships.

Formation of a Limited Partnership

In contrast to the informal, private, and voluntary agreement that usually suffices for a general partnership, the formation of a limited partnership is formal and public. The parties must follow specific statutory requirements and file a certificate with the state. A limited partnership must have at least one general partner and one limited partner, as mentioned previously. Additionally, the partners must sign a **certificate of limited partnership,** which requires information similar to that found in articles of incorporation (see Chapter 24), such as the name, mailing address, and capital contribution of each general and limited partner. The certificate usually is open to public inspection.

Liabilities of Partners in a Limited Partnership

General partners, unlike limited partners, are personally liable to the partnership's creditors. This policy can be circumvented in states that allow a corporation to be the general partner in a partnership. Because the corporation has limited liability by virtue of corporate laws, if a corporation is the general partner, no one in the limited partnership has personal liability.

In contrast to the personal liability of general partners, the liability of a limited partner is limited to the capital that she or he contributes or agrees to contribute to the partnership [RULPA 502]. Limited partners enjoy limited liability so long as they do not participate in management [RULPA 303]. A limited partner who participates in management will be just as liable as a general partner to any creditor who transacts business with the limited partnership and believes, based on the limited partner's conduct, that he or she is a general partner [RULPA 303]. How much actual review and advisement a limited partner can engage in before being exposed to liability is an unsettled question.

Dissociation and Dissolution

A general partner has the power to voluntarily dissociate, or withdraw, from a limited partnership unless the partnership agreement specifies otherwise. A limited partner theoretically can withdraw from the partnership by giving six months' notice unless the partnership agreement specifies a term, which most do. Also, some states have passed laws prohibiting the withdrawal of limited partners.

In a limited partnership, a general partner's voluntary dissociation from the firm normally will lead to dissolution *unless* all partners agree to continue the business. Similarly, the bankruptcy, retirement, death, or mental incompetence of a general partner will cause the dissociation of that partner and the dissolution of the limited partnership unless the other members agree to continue the firm [RULPA 801]. Bankruptcy of a limited partner, however, does not dissolve the partnership unless it causes the bankruptcy of the firm. Death or an assignment of the interest of a limited partner does not dissolve a limited partnership [RULPA 702, 704, 705]. A limited partnership can be dissolved by court decree [RULPA 802].

On dissolution, creditors' claims, including those of partners who are creditors, take first priority. After that, partners and former partners receive unpaid distributions of partnership assets and, except as otherwise agreed, amounts representing returns on their contributions and amounts proportionate to their shares of the distributions [RULPA 804].

The limited partners in the following case dissociated from their partnership by giving notice. The dissociation triggered the provisions of a partnership buy-sell agreement. The withdrawing partners and the partnership, however, read those provisions somewhat differently. Which interpretation the court accepted would determine whether the partnership had the obligation to buy the partners' interests.

Case 23.2 Craton Capital, LP v. Natural Pork Production II, LLP

Court of Appeals of Iowa, 797 N.W.2d 623 (2011).
www.iowacourts.gov/Court_of_Appeals[a]

FACTS Natural Pork Production II, LLP (NPP), an Iowa limited partnership, raises hogs. Under a partnership buy-sell agreement, NPP was obligated to buy a dissociating partner's interests (units) but could defer the purchase payment if, in the judgment of the managing partners, it would "adversely affect the working capital, cash flow or other financial means, condition or operation of the Partnership." Once this "Impairment Circumstance" was "no longer applicable," NPP was to make the purchase payment within thirty days. Craton Capital, LP, and Kruse Investment Company were among NPP's limited partners. When they notified NPP of their dissociation, a wave of similar notices from other partners followed. NPP declared an impairment circumstance. Craton and Kruse filed a suit in an Iowa state court against NPP, asking the court to order the partnership

a. In the left column, click on "Opinions." On the next page, click on "Opinions Archive." On the page that opens, enter the docket number "10-0680 " in the search box to access the opinion. The Iowa Judicial Branch maintains this Web site.

Case 23.2–Continued

to buy their units. NPP responded that the impairment circumstance still existed. Both parties filed motions for summary judgment on the issue of whether NPP was obligated to buy. The court issued a summary judgment in NPP's favor. Craton and Kruse appealed.

ISSUE Was NPP required to buy the dissociating partners' interests under the buy-sell agreement?

DECISION Yes. A state intermediate appellate court reversed the lower court's judgment in favor of NPP and remanded the case for the entry of a summary judgment in favor of Craton and Kruse.

REASON The "Dissociation Notice" provision of the partnership agreement stated that NPP *shall* buy a dissociating partner's units. This is mandatory. The only restriction is set out in the "impairment circumstance" provision. This provision applies when NPP is obligated to buy a dissociating partner's units and an impairment circumstance arises. Payment is then postponed, but the partnership is still obligated to buy the units. That is what occurred in this case. NPP argued that under the impairment circumstance provision, an obligation to buy a partner's units would never arise if it would materially impair or adversely affect the financial condition of the partnership. But this interpretation, the court reasoned, was not consistent with "the actual wording." The word "shall" is mandatory. Thus, once Craton and Kruse gave their dissociation notice, NPP was obligated to buy their units. The declaration of an impairment circumstance only deferred the purchase payment.

WHAT IF THE FACTS WERE DIFFERENT? *Suppose that Craton and Kruse had been general partners rather than limited partners. In that circumstance, what might their dissociation have meant for NPP?*

Limited Liability Companies

For many entrepreneurs and investors, the ideal business form would combine the tax advantages of the partnership form of business with the limited liability of the corporate enterprise. Although the limited partnership partially addresses these needs, the limited liability of limited partners is conditional: limited liability exists only so long as the limited partner does *not* participate in management.

This is one reason that every state has adopted legislation authorizing a form of business organization called the **limited liability company (LLC).** The LLC is a hybrid form of business enterprise that offers the limited liability of the corporation but the tax advantages of a partnership. Today, LLCs are a common form of business.

Like an LLP or LP, an LLC must be formed and operated in compliance with state law. About one-fourth of the states specifically require LLCs to have at least two owners, called **members.** In the rest of the states, although some LLC statutes are silent on this issue, one-member LLCs are usually permitted.

Formation of an LLC

To form an LLC, **articles of organization** must be filed with a state agency—usually the secretary of state's office. Typically, the articles are required to set forth such information as the name of the business, its principal address, the name and address of a registered agent, the names of the owners, and information on how the LLC will be managed. The business's name must include the words "Limited Liability Company" or the initials "LLC." In addition to requiring that articles of organization be filed, a few states require that a notice of the intention to form an LLC be published in a local newspaper.

Sometimes, the future members of an LLC may enter into contracts on the entity's behalf before the LLC is formally formed. As you will read in Chapter 24, a similar process often occurs with corporations. Persons forming a corporation may enter into contracts during the process of incorporation but before the corporation becomes a legal entity. These contracts are referred to as preincorporation contracts. Once the corporation is formed and adopts the preincorporation contract (by means of a *novation*, discussed in Chapter 11), it can then enforce the contract terms.

In dealing with the preorganization contracts of LLCs, courts may apply the well-established principles of corporate law relating to preincorporation contracts. **CASE EXAMPLE 23.10** 607 South Park, LLC, entered into a written agreement to sell a hotel to 607 Park View Associates, Ltd., whose general partner then assigned the rights to the hotel purchase to another company, 02 Development, LLC. At the time, 02 Development did not yet exist—it was legally created several months later. 607 South Park subsequently refused to sell the hotel to 02 Development, and 02 Development sued for breach of the purchase agreement. A California appellate court ruled that LLCs should be treated the same as corporations with respect to preorganization contracts. Although 02 Development did not exist when the agreement was executed, once it came into existence, it could enforce any preorganization contract made on its behalf.[7] •

Jurisdictional Requirements

One of the significant differences between LLCs and corporations has to do with federal jurisdictional requirements. Under the federal jurisdiction statute, a corporation is deemed to be a citizen of the state where it is incorporated and maintains its principal place of business. The statute does not mention the state citizenship of partnerships, LLCs, and other

7. *02 Development, LLC v. 607 South Park, LLC*, 159 Cal.App.4th 609, 71 Cal.Rptr.3d 608 (2008). For a case in which a state court applied another corporate law principle (piercing the corporate veil) to LLCs, see *ORX Resources, Inc. v. MBW Exploration, LLC*, 32 So.3d 931 (La.App. 2010).

unincorporated associations, but the courts have tended to regard these entities as citizens of every state in which their members are citizens.

The state citizenship of an LLC may come into play when a party sues the LLC based on diversity of citizenship. Remember from Chapter 2 that when parties to a lawsuit are from different states and the amount in controversy exceeds $75,000, a federal court can exercise diversity jurisdiction. *Total* diversity of citizenship must exist, however. **EXAMPLE 23.11** Jen Fong, a citizen of New York, wishes to bring a suit against Skycel, an LLC formed under the laws of Connecticut. One of Skycel's members also lives in New York. Fong will not be able to bring a suit against Skycel in federal court on the basis of diversity jurisdiction because the defendant LLC is also a citizen of New York. The same would be true if Fong was bringing a suit against multiple defendants and one of the defendants lived in New York. •

Advantages of the LLC

The LLC offers many advantages to businesspersons, which is why this form of business organization has become increasingly popular.

LIMITED LIABILITY A key advantage of the LLC is that the liability of members is limited to the amount of their investments. Although the LLC as an entity can be held liable for any loss or injury caused by the wrongful acts or omissions of its members, the members themselves generally are not personally liable.

TAXATION Another advantage is the flexibility of the LLC in regard to taxation. An LLC that has *two or more members* can choose to be taxed either as a partnership or as a corporation. As you will read in Chapter 24, a corporate entity must pay income taxes on its profits, and the shareholders pay personal income taxes on profits distributed as dividends. An LLC that wants to distribute profits to its members may prefer to be taxed as a partnership to avoid the "double taxation" that is characteristic of the corporate entity.

Unless an LLC indicates that it wishes to be taxed as a corporation, the IRS automatically taxes it as a partnership. This means that the LLC as an entity pays no taxes. Rather, as in a partnership, profits are "passed through" the LLC to the members who then personally pay taxes on the profits. If an LLC's members want to reinvest the profits in the business, however, rather than distribute the profits to members, they may prefer that the LLC be taxed as a corporation. Corporate income tax rates may be lower than personal tax rates. Part of the attractiveness of the LLC is this flexibility with respect to taxation.

For federal income tax purposes, one-member LLCs are automatically taxed as sole proprietorships unless they indicate that they wish to be taxed as corporations. With respect to state taxes, most states follow the IRS rules.

MANAGEMENT AND FOREIGN INVESTORS Still another advantage of the LLC for businesspersons is the flexibility it offers in terms of business operations and management—as will be discussed shortly. Finally, because foreign investors can participate in an LLC, the LLC form of business is attractive as a way to encourage investment.

Disadvantages of the LLC

The main disadvantage of the LLC is that state LLC statutes are not uniform. Therefore, businesses that operate in more than one state may not receive consistent treatment in these states. Generally, though, most states apply to a foreign LLC (an LLC formed in another state) the law of the state where the LLC was formed.

Difficulties can arise, nonetheless, when one state's court must interpret and apply another state's laws. In an attempt to create more uniformity among the states, in 1995 the National Conference of Commissioners on Uniform State Laws (NCCUSL) issued the Uniform Limited Liability Company Act (ULLCA), but less than one-fifth of the states adopted it. In 2006, the NCCUSL issued a revised version of this uniform law (the Re-ULLCA), which has been adopted in a few states.

The LLC Operating Agreement

The members of an LLC can decide how to operate the various aspects of the business by forming an **operating agreement** [ULLCA 103(a)]. Operating agreements typically contain provisions relating to management, how profits will be divided, the transfer of membership interests, whether the LLC will be dissolved on the death or departure of a member, and other important issues.

An operating agreement need not be in writing and indeed need not even be formed for an LLC to exist. Generally, though, LLC members should protect their interests by forming a written operating agreement. As with any business arrangement, disputes may arise over any number of issues. If there is no agreement covering the topic under dispute, such as how profits will be divided, the state LLC statute will govern the outcome. For example, most LLC statutes provide that if the members have not specified how profits will be divided, they will be divided equally among the members. Generally, when an issue is not covered by an operating agreement or by an LLC statute, the courts apply the principles of partnership law.

CASE EXAMPLE 23.12 Clifford Kuhn, Jr., and Joseph Tumminelli formed Touch of Class Limousine Service as an LLC. They did not create a written operating agreement but orally agreed that Kuhn would provide the financial backing and procure customers, and that Tumminelli would manage the company's day-to-day operations. Tumminelli embezzled $283,000 from the company after cashing customers' checks at Quick Cash, Inc., a local check-cashing service. Kuhn filed a lawsuit against Tumminelli, the banks, and others in a New Jersey state court to recover the embezzled funds. He argued that Quick Cash and the banks were liable because Tumminelli did not have the authority to cash the company's checks and convert the funds. The court, however, held that in the absence of a written operating agreement to the contrary, a member of an LLC, like a partner in a partnership, does have the authority to cash the firm's checks.[8] •

Management of an LLC

Basically, there are two options for managing an LLC. The members may decide in their operating agreement to be either a "member-managed" LLC or a "manager-managed" LLC. Most LLC statutes and the ULLCA provide that unless the articles of organization specify otherwise, an LLC is assumed to be member managed [ULLCA 203(a)(6)].

In a *member-managed* LLC, all of the members participate in management, and decisions are made by majority vote [ULLCA 404(a)]. In a *manager-managed* LLC, the members designate a group of persons to manage the firm. The management group may consist of only members, both members and nonmembers, or only nonmembers.

FIDUCIARY DUTIES Under the ULLCA, managers in a manager-managed LLC owe fiduciary duties to the LLC and its members, including the duty of loyalty and the duty of care [ULLCA 409(a), (h)], just as corporate directors and officers owe fiduciary duties to the corporation and its shareholders (see Chapter 25). Because not all states have adopted the ULLCA, though, some state statutes provide that managers owe fiduciary duties only to the LLC and not to the LLC's members individually. Although to whom the duty is owed may seem insignificant at first glance, it can have a dramatic effect on the outcome of litigation.

In Alabama, where the following case arose, managers owe fiduciary duties to the LLC and its members.

8. *Kuhn v. Tumminelli*, 366 N.J.Super. 431, 841 A.2d 496 (2004).

Case 23.3 Polk v. Polk

Court of Civil Appeals of Alabama, __ So.3d __ (2011).

FACTS Leslie Polk and his children, Yurii and Dusty Polk and Lezanne Proctor, formed Polk Plumbing, LLC, in Alabama. Leslie, Dusty, and Yurii performed commercial plumbing work, and Lezanne, an accountant, maintained the financial records and served as the office manager. After a couple of years, Yurii quit the firm. Eighteen months later, Leslie "fired" Dusty and Lezanne. He denied them access to the LLC's books and offices but continued to operate the business. Dusty and Lezanne filed a suit in an Alabama state court against Leslie, claiming breach of fiduciary duty. The court submitted the claim to a jury with the instruction that in Alabama employment relationships are "at will" (see Chapter 22). The court also told the jury that it could not consider the plaintiffs' "firing" as part of their claim. The jury awarded Dusty and Lezanne one dollar each in damages. They appealed, arguing that the judge's instructions to the jury were prejudicial—that is, that the instructions had substantially affected the outcome of the trial.

ISSUE Did the trial court properly instruct the jury on which evidence could be considered in Dusty and Lezanne's breach of fiduciary duty claim?

DECISION No. A state intermediate appellate court reversed the lower court's judgment on the claim for breach of fiduciary duty and remanded the case for a new trial. The lower court committed reversible error by instructing the jury that Dusty and Lezanne's employment as managers was at will and by failing to instruct the jury that it could consider their "firing" as evidence in support of their claim.

REASON The court reasoned that the lower court had committed reversible errors that had "probably injuriously affected substantial rights of Dusty and Lezanne." Dusty and Lezanne served as managers of the LLC. The operating agreement provided that managers served until replaced or recalled by a vote of the majority of the members. Therefore, their employment as managers was not at will. Because no vote had been taken to recall or replace Dusty and Lezanne, their father did not have the authority to terminate their employment. His attempted "firing" of them was in violation of the LLC's operating agreement. If the jury had considered all of this evidence, the amount of damages might have been higher.

WHAT IF THE FACTS WERE DIFFERENT? *Suppose that Leslie owned a majority of the shares in Polk Plumbing. Could his "firing" of Dusty and Lezanne still be considered as evidence of a breach of fiduciary duty? Explain.*

DECISION-MAKING PROCEDURES The members of an LLC can also set forth in their operating agreement provisions governing decision-making procedures. For instance, the agreement can include procedures for choosing or removing managers. Although most LLC statutes are silent on this issue, the ULLCA provides that members may choose and remove managers by majority vote [ULLCA 404(b)(3)].

Members may also specify in their agreement how voting rights will be apportioned. If they do not, LLC statutes in most states provide that voting rights are apportioned according to each member's capital contributions. Some states provide that, in the absence of an agreement to the contrary, each member has one vote.

Dissociation and Dissolution of an LLC

Recall that in the context of partnerships, *dissociation* occurs when a partner ceases to be associated in the carrying on of the business. The same concept applies to limited liability companies. A member of an LLC has the *power* to dissociate from the LLC at any time, but he or she may not have the *right* to dissociate. Under the ULLCA, the events that trigger a member's dissociation in an LLC are similar to the events causing a partner to be dissociated under the Uniform Partnership Act (UPA). These include voluntary withdrawal, expulsion by other members or by court order, bankruptcy, incompetence, and death. Generally, even if a member dies or otherwise dissociates from an LLC, the other members may continue to carry on LLC business, unless the operating agreement has contrary provisions.

DISSOCIATION When a member dissociates from an LLC, he or she loses the right to participate in management and the right to act as an agent for the LLC. His or her duty of loyalty to the LLC also terminates, and the duty of care continues only with respect to events that occurred before dissociation. Generally, the dissociated member also has a right to have his or her interest in the LLC bought by the other members of the LLC. The LLC's operating agreement may contain provisions establishing a buyout price, but if it does not, the member's interest is usually purchased at a fair value. In states that have adopted the ULLCA, the LLC must purchase the interest at "fair" value within 120 days after the dissociation.

If the member's dissociation violates the LLC's operating agreement, it is considered legally wrongful, and the dissociated member can be held liable for damages caused by the dissociation. **EXAMPLE 23.13** Chadwick and Barrel are members in an LLC. Chadwick manages the accounts, and Barrel, who has many connections in the community and is a skilled investor, brings in the business. If Barrel wrongfully dissociates from the LLC, the LLC's business will suffer, and Chadwick can hold Barrel liable for the loss of business resulting from her withdrawal. •

DISSOLUTION Regardless of whether a member's dissociation was wrongful or rightful, normally the dissociated member has no right to force the LLC to dissolve. The remaining members can opt to either continue or dissolve the business. Members can also stipulate in their operating agreement that certain events will cause dissolution, or they can agree that they have the power to dissolve the LLC by vote. As with partnerships, a court can order an LLC to be dissolved in certain circumstances, such as when the members have engaged in illegal or oppressive conduct, or when it is no longer feasible to carry on the business.

When an LLC is dissolved, any members who did not wrongfully dissociate may participate in the winding up process. To wind up the business, members must collect, liquidate, and distribute the LLC's assets. Members may preserve the assets for a reasonable time to optimize their return, and they continue to have the authority to perform reasonable acts in conjunction with winding up. In other words, the LLC will be bound by the reasonable acts of its members during the winding up process. Once all the LLC's assets have been sold, the proceeds are distributed to pay off debts to creditors first (including debts owed to members who are creditors of the LLC). The members' capital contributions are returned next, and any remaining amounts are then distributed to members in equal shares or according to their operating agreement.

Reviewing . . . Sole Proprietorships, Partnerships, and Limited Liability Companies

A bridge on a prominent public roadway in the city of Papagos, Arizona, was deteriorating and in need of repair. The city posted notices seeking proposals for an artistic bridge design and reconstruction. Davidson Masonry, LLC, which was owned and managed by Carl Davidson and his wife, Marilyn Rowe, submitted a bid for a decorative concrete project that incorporated artistic metalwork. They contacted Shana Lafayette, a local sculptor who specialized in large-scale metal forms, to help them design the bridge. The city selected their bridge design and awarded them the contract for a commission of $184,000. Davidson Masonry and Lafayette then entered into an agreement to work together on the bridge project. Davidson Masonry agreed to install and pay for concrete and structural work, and Lafayette agreed to install the metalwork at her expense. They agreed that overall profits would be split, with 25 percent going to Lafayette and 75 percent going to Davidson Masonry. Lafayette designed numerous metal sculptures of salmon that were incorporated into colorful decorative concrete forms designed by Rowe, while Davidson performed the structural engineering. Using the information presented in the chapter, answer the following questions.

1 Would Davidson Masonry automatically be taxed as a partnership or a corporation? Explain.
2 Is Davidson Masonry a member-managed or manager-managed LLC? Explain.
3 Suppose that during construction, Lafayette had entered into an agreement to rent space in a warehouse that was close to the bridge so that she could work on her sculptures near the site where they would be installed. She entered into the contract without the knowledge or consent of Davidson Masonry. In this situation, would a court be likely to hold that Davidson Masonry was bound by the contract that Lafayette entered? Why or why not?
4 Now suppose that Rowe has an argument with her husband and wants to withdraw from being a member of Davidson Masonry. What is the term for such a withdrawal, and what effect does it have on the LLC?

Terms and Concepts

articles of organization 453
articles of partnership 446
buyout price 450
certificate of limited partnership 452
dissociation 450
dissolution 450
entrepreneur 444
general partner 451
information return 446
joint and several liability 449
joint liability 449
limited liability company (LLC) 453
limited liability partnership (LLP) 451
limited partner 451
limited partnership (LP) 451
member 453
operating agreement 454
partnership 445
pass-through entity 446
sole proprietorship 444
winding up 450

Chapter Summary: Sole Proprietorships, Partnerships, and Limited Liability Companies

Sole Proprietorships (See pages 444–445.)	The simplest form of business organization; used by anyone who does business without creating a separate organization. The owner is the business. The owner pays personal income taxes on all profits and is personally liable for all business debts.
Partnerships (See pages 445–451.)	1. A partnership is created by agreement of the parties. 2. A partnership is treated as an entity except for limited purposes. 3. Each partner pays a proportionate share of income taxes on the net profits of the partnership, whether or not they are distributed. The partnership files only an information return with the Internal Revenue Service. 4. Each partner has an equal voice in management unless the partnership agreement provides otherwise. 5. In the absence of an agreement, partners share profits equally and share losses in the same ratio as they share profits. 6. Partners have unlimited personal liability for partnership debts. 7. A partnership can be terminated by agreement or can be dissolved by action of the partners, operation of law (subsequent illegality), or court decree.
Limited Liability Partnerships (LLPs) (See page 451.)	1. *Formation*—LLPs must be formed in compliance with state statutes. Typically, an LLP is formed by professionals who normally work together as partners in a partnership. Under most state LLP statutes, it is relatively easy to convert a traditional partnership into an LLP. 2. *Liability of partners*—LLP statutes vary, but under the UPA, professionals generally can avoid personal liability for acts committed by other partners. Partners in an LLP continue to be liable for their own wrongful acts and for the wrongful acts of those whom they supervise.
Limited Partnerships (See pages 451–453.)	1. *Formation*—A certificate of limited partnership must be filed with the designated state official. The certificate must include information about the business, similar to the information included in articles of incorporation. The partnership consists of one or more general partners and one or more limited partners.

Continued

Chapter Summary: Sole Proprietorships, Partnerships, and Limited Liability Companies—Continued

Limited Partnerships—Continued	2. *Rights and liabilities of partners*—With some exceptions, the rights of partners are the same as the rights of partners in a general partnership. General partners have unlimited liability for partnership obligations. Limited partners are liable only to the extent of their contributions. 3. *Limited partners and management*—Only general partners can participate in management. Limited partners have no voice in management. If they do participate in management activities, they risk having liability as a general partner. 4. *Dissociation and dissolution*—Generally, a limited partnership can be dissolved in much the same way as an ordinary partnership. A general partner has the power to voluntarily dissociate unless the parties' agreement specifies otherwise. Some states limit the power of limited partners to voluntarily withdraw from the firm. The death or assignment of the interest of a limited partner does not dissolve the partnership. Bankruptcy of a limited partner also will not dissolve the partnership unless it causes the bankruptcy of the firm.
Limited Liability Companies (LLCs) (See pages 453–456.)	1. *Formation*—Articles of organization must be filed with the appropriate state office—usually the office of the secretary of state—setting forth the name of the business, its principal address, the names of the owners (called members), and other relevant information. 2. *Advantages and disadvantages*—Advantages of the LLC include limited liability, the option to be taxed as a partnership or as a corporation, and flexibility in deciding how the business will be managed and operated. The main disadvantage is the lack of uniformity in state LLC statutes. 3. *Operating agreement*—When an LLC is formed, the members decide, in an operating agreement, how the business will be managed and what rules will apply to the organization. 4. *Management*—An LLC may be managed by members only, by some members and some nonmembers, or by nonmembers only. 5. *Dissociation and dissolution*—Members of an LLC have the power to dissociate from the LLC at any time, but they may not have the right to dissociate. Dissociation does not always result in the dissolution of an LLC. The remaining members can choose to continue the business. Dissociated members have a right to have their interest purchased by the other members. If the LLC is dissolved, the business must be wound up and the assets sold. Creditors are paid first, and then members' capital investments are returned. Any remaining proceeds are distributed to members.

ExamPrep

ISSUE SPOTTERS

—Check your answers to these questions against the answers provided in Appendix G.

1 Darnell and Eliana are partners in D&E Designs, an architectural firm. When Darnell dies, his widow claims that as Darnell's heir, she is entitled to take his place as Eliana's partner or to receive a share of the firm's assets. Is she right? Why or why not?

2 Gomer, Harry, and Ida are members of Jeweled Watches, LLC. What are their options with respect to the management of their firm?

BEFORE THE TEST

Go to **www.cengagebrain.com**, enter the ISBN 9781111530624, and click on "Find" to locate this textbook's Web site. Then, click on "Access Now" under "Study Tools," and select Chapter 23 at the top. There, you will find an Interactive Quiz that you can take to assess your mastery of the concepts in this chapter, as well as Flashcards and a Glossary of important terms.

For Review

1 What advantages and disadvantages are associated with the sole proprietorship?

2 What is meant by joint and several liability? Why is this often considered to be a disadvantage of doing business as a general partnership?

3 What advantages do limited liability partnerships offer to entrepreneurs that are not offered by general partnerships?
4 What are the key differences between the rights and liabilities of general partners and those of limited partners?
5 How are limited liability companies formed, and who decides how they will be managed and operated?

Questions and Case Problems

23–1 Limited Liability Companies. John, Lesa, and Tabir form a limited liability company. John contributes 60 percent of the capital, and Lesa and Tabir each contribute 20 percent. Nothing is decided about how profits will be divided. John assumes that he will be entitled to 60 percent of the profits, in accordance with his contribution. Lesa and Tabir, however, assume that the profits will be divided equally. A dispute over the question arises, and ultimately a court has to decide the issue. What law will the court apply? In most states, what will result? How could this dispute have been avoided in the first place? Discuss fully.

23–2 Question with Sample Answer Dorinda, Luis, and Elizabeth form a limited partnership. Dorinda is a general partner, and Luis and Elizabeth are limited partners. Consider each of the separate events below, and discuss fully which would constitute a dissolution of the limited partnership.

1 Luis assigns his partnership interest to Ashley.
2 Elizabeth is petitioned into involuntary bankruptcy.
3 Dorinda dies.

—For a sample answer to Question 23–2, go to Appendix E at the end of this text.

23–3 Partnership Formation. Daniel is the owner of a chain of shoe stores. He hires Rubya to be the manager of a new store, which is to open in Grand Rapids, Michigan. Daniel, by written contract, agrees to pay Rubya a monthly salary and 20 percent of the profits. Without Daniel's knowledge, Rubya represents himself to Classen as Daniel's partner, showing Classen the agreement to share profits. Classen extends credit to Rubya. Rubya defaults. Discuss whether Classen can hold Daniel liable as a partner.

23–4 Sole Proprietorship. Julie Anne Gaskill is an oral and maxillofacial surgeon in Bowling Green, Kentucky. Her medical practice is a sole proprietorship that consists of Gaskill as the sole surgeon and an office staff. She sees every patient, exercises all professional judgment and skill, and manages the business. When Gaskill and her spouse, John Robbins, initiated divorce proceedings in a Kentucky state court, her accountant estimated the value of the practice at $221,610, excluding goodwill. Robbins's accountant estimated the value at $669,075, including goodwill. (Goodwill is the ability or reputation of a business to draw customers, get them to return, and contribute to future profitability.) How can a sole proprietor's reputation, skill, and relationships with customers be valued? Could these qualities be divided into "personal" and "enterprise" goodwill, with some goodwill associated with the business and some solely due to the personal qualities of the proprietor? If so, what might comprise each type? Is this an effective method for valuing Gaskill's practice? Discuss. [*Gaskill v. Robbins*, 282 S.W.3d 306 (Ky. 2009)]

23–5 LLC Dissolution. Walter Van Houten and John King formed 1545 Ocean Avenue, LLC, with each managing 50 percent of the business. Its purpose was to renovate an existing building and build a new commercial building. Van Houten and King quarreled over many aspects of the work on the properties. King claimed that Van Houten paid contractors too much for the work performed. As the project neared completion, King demanded that the LLC be dissolved and that Van Houten agree to a buyout. Because the parties could not agree on a buyout, King sued for dissolution. The trial court prevented further work on the project while the dispute was settled. As the ground for dissolution, King cited the fights over management decisions. There was no claim of fraud or frustration of purpose. The trial court ordered that the LLC be dissolved. Van Houten appealed. Should either of the owners be forced to dissolve the LLC before completion of its purpose—that is, finishing the building projects? Discuss. [*In re 1545 Ocean Avenue, LLC,* 893 N.Y.S.2d 590 (N.Y.A.D. 2 Dept. 2010)]

23–6 Fiduciary Duties of Partners. Karl Horvath, Hein Rüsen, and Carl Thomas formed a partnership, HRT Enterprises, to buy a vacant manufacturing plant and an annex building on eleven acres in Detroit, Michigan. HRT leased the plant to companies owned by the partners, including Horvath's Canadian-American Steel. When Horvath's firm missed three payments under its lease, HRT evicted it from the plant. Horvath objected but remained an HRT partner. Later, Rüsen and Thomas leased the entire plant to their company, Merkur Steel. Merkur then sublet the premises to City Steel and Merkur Technical Services—both of which were owned (or substantially owned) by Rüsen and Thomas. The rent these companies paid to Merkur was higher than the rent Merkur paid to HRT, which meant that Merkur profited from the arrangement. Rüsen and Thomas did not tell Horvath about the subleases. When Horvath learned of the deals, he filed a suit in a Michigan state court against HRT and the other partners for an accounting of their actions. Did Rüsen and Thomas breach their fiduciary duty to HRT and Horvath? Discuss. [*Horvath v. HRT Enterprises*, 489 Mich. 992, 800 N.W.2d 595 (2011)]

23–7 Case Problem with Sample Answer James Williford, Patricia Mosser, Marquetta Smith, and Michael Floyd formed two member-managed limited liability companies—Bluewater Bay, LLC, and Bluewater Logistics, LLC (collectively Bluewater)—in Mississippi to bid on contracts related to the aftermath of Hurricane Katrina. Under Mississippi law, every member of a member-managed LLC is entitled to participate in managing the business. Under Bluewater's operating agreements, "a 75% Super Majority Vote of the members" could redeem any member's interest if the "member has either committed a felony or under any other circumstances that would jeopardize the company status" as a contractor. Bluewater had completed more than $5 million in contracts when Smith told Williford that he was "fired" and that she, Mosser, and Floyd were exercising their "super majority" right to buy him out. No reason was provided. Williford filed a suit in a Mississippi state court against Bluewater and the other members, who then told Williford that they had changed their minds about buying him out but that he was still fired. Did Smith, Mosser, and Floyd breach the state LLC statute, their fiduciary duties, or the Bluewater operating agreements? Discuss. [*Bluewater Logistics, LLC v. Williford,* 55 So.3d 148 (Miss. 2011)]

—To view a sample answer for Problem 23–7, go to Appendix F at the end of this text.

23–8 **A Question of Ethics** *Elliot Willensky and Beverly Moran formed a partnership to renovate and "flip" (resell) some property. According to their agreement, Moran would finance the purchase and renovation of the property, and Willensky would provide labor and oversight of the renovation work. Moran would be reimbursed from the profits of the sale, and the remainder of the profits would be divided evenly. Any losses would also be divided evenly. Moran paid $240,000 for a house and planned to spend $60,000 for its renovation. The parties agreed that the renovation would be completed in six months. Willensky lived in the house during the renovation. More than a year later, the project still was not completed, and the cost was much more than the $60,000 originally planned. Willensky often failed to communicate with Moran, and when she learned that her funds were nearly exhausted and the house nowhere near completion, she became worried. She told Willensky that he would have to pay rent and utility bills if he wished to continue to live in the house. Shortly thereafter, Willensky left for Florida due to a family emergency, saying that he would return as soon as he could. He never returned, however, and Moran lost touch with him. Moran took over the project and discovered that Willensky had left numerous bills unpaid, spent money on excessive or unnecessary items, and misappropriated funds for his personal use. After completing the project, paying all expenses relating to the renovation (in all, the renovation costs came to $311,222), and selling the property, Moran brought an action in a Tennessee state court to dissolve the partnership and to recover damages from Willensky for breach of contract and wrongful dissociation from the partnership.* [Moran v. Willensky, ___ *S.W.3d* ___ *(Tenn.Ct.App. 2010)]*

1. Moran alleged that Willensky had wrongfully dissociated from the partnership. When did this dissociation occur? Why was his dissociation wrongful?
2. Which of Willensky's actions simply represent unethical behavior or bad management, and which constitute a breach of the agreement?

23–9 **Critical Thinking Managerial Question** Sandra Lerner and Patricia Holmes were friends. One evening, while applying nail polish to Lerner, Holmes layered a raspberry color over black to produce a new color, which Lerner liked. Later, the two created other colors with names like "Bruise," "Smog," and "Oil Slick," and titled their concept "Urban Decay." Lerner and Holmes started a firm to produce and market the polishes but never discussed the sharing of profits and losses. They agreed to build the business and then sell it. Together, they did market research, worked on a logo and advertising, obtained capital, and hired employees. Then Lerner began working to edge Holmes out of the firm. Did Lerner violate her fiduciary duty? Why or why not?

Chapter 24

Corporate Formation, Financing, and Termination

Learning Objectives

After reading this chapter, you should be able to answer the following questions:

1. What steps are involved in bringing a corporation into existence?
2. In what circumstances might a court disregard the corporate entity (pierce the corporate veil) and hold the shareholders personally liable?
3. How are corporations financed?
4. What are the steps of a merger, a consolidation, or a share exchange procedure?
5. What are the two ways in which a corporation can be voluntarily dissolved?

The Learning Objectives above are designed to help improve your understanding of the chapter.

(Othermore/Creative Commons)

The corporation is a creature of statute. As an artificial being, it exists only in law and is neither tangible nor visible. Its existence generally depends on state law, although some corporations, especially public organizations, can be created under state or federal law.

Each state has its own body of corporate law, and these laws are not entirely uniform. The Model Business Corporation Act (MBCA) is a codification of modern corporation law that has been influential in the drafting and revision of state corporation statutes. Today, the majority of state statutes are guided by the revised version of the MBCA, which is often referred to as the Revised Model Business Corporation Act (RMBCA).[1] You should keep in mind, however, that there is considerable variation among the statutes of the states that have used the MBCA or the RMBCA as a basis for their statutes, and several states do not follow either act. Consequently, individual state corporation laws should be relied on rather than the MBCA or the RMBCA.

1. Excerpts from the Revised Model Business Corporation Act (RMBCA) are presented on the Web site that accompanies this text.

In this chapter, we examine the nature of the corporate form of business enterprise; the various classifications of corporations; and the formation, financing, and termination of today's corporations.

Corporate Nature and Classification

A **corporation** is a legal entity created and recognized by state law. It can consist of one or more *natural persons* (as opposed to the artificial *legal person* of the corporation) identified under a common name. A corporation can be owned by a single person, or it can have hundreds, thousands, or even millions of owners (shareholders). The corporation substitutes itself for its shareholders in conducting corporate business and in incurring liability, yet its authority to act and the liability for its actions are separate and apart from the individuals who own it.

The shareholder form of business organization emerged in Europe at the end of the seventeenth century. These organizations, called joint stock companies, frequently collapsed because their organizers absconded with the funds or proved to be incompetent. Because of this history of fraud and collapse, organizations resembling corporations were regarded with suspicion in the United States during its early years. Although several business corporations were formed after the Revolutionary War, the corporation did not come into common use for private business until the nineteenth century.

Corporate Personnel

In a corporation, the responsibility for the overall management of the firm is entrusted to a *board of directors,* whose members are elected by the shareholders. The board of directors hires *corporate officers* and other employees to run the daily business operations of the corporation.

When an individual purchases a share of stock in a corporation, that person becomes a shareholder and thus an owner of the corporation. Unlike the members of a partnership, the body of shareholders can change constantly without affecting the continued existence of the corporation. A shareholder can sue the corporation, and the corporation can sue a shareholder. Also, under certain circumstances, a shareholder can sue on behalf of a corporation. The rights and duties of corporate personnel will be examined in detail in Chapter 25.

The Constitutional Rights of Corporations

A corporation is recognized as a "person," and it has many of the same rights and privileges under state and federal law that U.S. citizens enjoy. The Bill of Rights guarantees persons certain protections, and corporations are considered persons in most instances. Under the First Amendment, corporations are entitled to freedom of speech, although commercial speech (such as advertising) and political speech (such as contributions to political causes or candidates) receive significantly less protection than noncommercial speech. A corporation has the same right of access to the courts as a natural person and can sue or be sued. It also has a right to due process (see Chapter 1), as well as freedom from unreasonable searches and seizures (see Chapter 6) and from double jeopardy.

Generally, though, a corporation is not entitled to claim the Fifth Amendment privilege against self-incrimination. Agents or officers of the corporation therefore cannot refuse to produce corporate records on the ground that doing so might incriminate them. Additionally, the privileges and immunities clause of the U.S. Constitution, which requires each state to treat citizens of other states equally with respect to certain rights, such as travel, does not apply to corporations.

The Limited Liability of Shareholders

One of the key advantages of the corporate form is the limited liability of its owners (shareholders). Corporate shareholders normally are not personally liable for the obligations of the corporation beyond the extent of their investments. In certain limited situations, however, a court can *pierce the corporate veil* (see page 470) and impose liability on shareholders for the corporation's obligations. Additionally, to enable the firm to obtain credit, shareholders in small companies sometimes voluntarily assume personal liability, as guarantors, for corporate obligations.

Corporate Earnings and Taxation

When a corporation earns profits, it can either pass them on to shareholders in the form of **dividends** or retain them as profits. These **retained earnings,** if invested properly, will yield higher corporate profits in the future and thus cause the price of the company's stock to rise. Individual shareholders can then reap the benefits of these retained earnings in the capital gains that they receive when they sell their stock.

Whether a corporation retains its profits or passes them on to the shareholders as dividends, those profits are subject to income tax by various levels of government. Failure to pay taxes can lead to severe consequences. The state can suspend the entity's corporate status until the taxes are paid or even dissolve the corporation for failing to pay taxes.

Another important aspect of corporate taxation is that corporate profits can be subject to double taxation. The company pays tax on its profits, and then if the profits are passed on to the shareholders as dividends, the shareholders must also pay income tax on them. The corporation normally does not receive a tax deduction for dividends it distributes to shareholders. This double-taxation feature is one of the major disadvantages of the corporate business form.

Some U.S. corporations use holding companies to reduce—or at least defer—their U.S. income taxes. At its simplest, a **holding company** (sometimes referred to as a *parent company*) is a company whose business activity consists of holding shares in another company. Typically, the holding company is established in a low-tax or no-tax offshore jurisdiction. Among the best known are the Cayman Islands, Dubai, Hong Kong, Luxembourg, Monaco, and Panama.

A taxation issue of increasing importance to corporations is whether they are required to collect state sales taxes on goods or services sold to consumers via the Internet. See this chapter's *Adapting the Law to the Online Environment* feature on the facing page for a discussion of this issue.

Torts and Criminal Acts

A corporation is liable for the torts committed by its agents or officers within the course and scope of their employment. This principle applies to a corporation exactly as it applies to the ordinary agency relationships discussed in Chapter 21. It follows the doctrine of *respondeat superior.*

Adapting the Law to the Online Environment

Economic Recession Fuels the "Amazon Tax" Debate

Governments at the state and federal levels have long debated whether states should be able to collect sales taxes on online sales to in-state customers. State governments claim that their inability to tax online sales has caused them to lose billions of dollars in sales tax revenue. The issue has taken on new urgency as the states search desperately for revenue in the wake of the economic recession that began in December 2007.

Supreme Court Precedent Requires Physical Presence

In 1992, the United States Supreme Court ruled that no individual state can compel an out-of-state business that lacks a substantial physical presence (such as a warehouse, office, or retail store) within that state to collect and remit state taxes.[a] The Court recognized that Congress has the power to pass legislation requiring out-of-state corporations to collect and remit state sales taxes, but Congress so far has chosen not to tax Internet transactions. In fact, Congress temporarily prohibited the states from taxing Internet sales, and that ban was extended until 2014.[b] Thus, only online retailers that also have a physical presence within a state must collect state taxes on any Web sales made to residents of that state. (Otherwise, state residents are required to self-report their purchases and pay use taxes to the state, which rarely happens.)

New York Changed Its Definition of Physical Presence

In an effort to collect taxes on Internet sales made by out-of-state corporations, New York changed its tax laws in 2008 to redefine *physical presence.* Under the new law, if an online retailer pays any party within the state to solicit business for its products, that retailer has a physical presence in the state and must collect state taxes.[c] For example, Amazon.com, America's largest online retailer, pays thousands of associates in New York to post ads that link to Amazon's Web site. Consequently, the law requires Amazon to collect tax on any sales to New York residents.

a. See *Quill Corp. v. North Dakota,* 504 U.S. 298, 112 S.Ct. 1904, 119 L.Ed.2d 91 (1992).
b. Internet Tax Freedom Act, Pub. L. No. 105-277; 47 U.S.C. Section 151 note (1998), extended to 2014 by Pub. L. No. 110-108.
c. New York Tax Law Section 1101(b)(8)(vi).

Both Amazon and Overstock.com, a Utah corporation, filed lawsuits in 2009 claiming that the new law was unconstitutional. A New York court dismissed Amazon's case, finding that the law provided a sufficient basis for requiring collection of New York taxes. As long as the seller has a substantial connection with the state, the taxes need not derive from in-state activity. The court also observed that "out-of-state sellers can shield themselves from a tax-collection obligation by altogether prohibiting in-state solicitation activities . . . on their behalf."[d] As a result, Amazon now collects and pays state sales taxes on shipments to New York. Overstock canceled agreements with its New York affiliates.

The "Amazon Tax"

Since then, a number of states have changed their law on physical presence in an effort to collect sales tax from online retailers and close substantial gaps in their state budgets. These new laws, which many call the "Amazon tax" because they are largely aimed at Amazon, affect all online sellers (including Overstock.com and Drugstore.com)—especially those that pay affiliates to direct traffic to their Web sites. California enacted such a law in 2011, and Amazon quickly announced that it had canceled agreements with its California affiliates. By 2012, the Amazon tax had caused Amazon to end its arrangements with affiliates in Colorado, Illinois, North Carolina, and Rhode Island as well. When California officials insisted that its law still applied to Amazon because of other contacts with the state, such as the presence of a firm that handles some of Amazon's advertising, Amazon announced that it would support a proposed ballot initiative to repeal the law in 2012.

FOR CRITICAL ANALYSIS

Should the fact that an out-of-state corporation pays affiliates in a state to direct consumers to its Web site be sufficient to require the corporation to collect taxes on Web sales to state residents? Why or why not?

d. *Amazon.com, LLC v. New York State Department of Taxation and Finance,* 23 Misc.3d 418, 877 N.Y.S.2d 842 (2009); affirmed at 81 A.D.3d 183, 913 N.Y.S.2d 129 (2010).

Recall from Chapter 6 that under modern criminal law, a corporation may be held liable for the criminal acts of its agents and employees, provided the punishment is one that can be applied to the corporation. Although corporations cannot be imprisoned, they can be fined. (Of course, corporate directors and officers can be imprisoned, and many have been in recent years.) In addition, under sentencing guidelines for crimes committed by corporate employees (white-collar crimes), corporate lawbreakers can face fines amounting to hundreds of millions of dollars.[2]

CASE EXAMPLE 24.1 Brian Gauthier was a truck driver who worked for Angelo Todesca Corporation. Gauthier drove the AT-56, a ten-wheel dump truck. Although Angelo's safety

2. Note that the Sarbanes-Oxley Act of 2002, discussed in Chapter 3, stiffened the penalties for certain types of corporate crime and ordered the U.S. Sentencing Commission to revise the sentencing guidelines accordingly.

manual required its trucks to be equipped with back-up alarms that automatically sounded when the trucks were put into reverse, the AT-56's alarm was missing. Angelo ordered a new alarm but allowed Gauthier to continue driving the AT-56. At a worksite, when Gauthier backed up the AT-56 to dump its load, he struck and killed a police officer who was directing traffic through the site and facing away from the truck. The state charged Angelo and Gauthier with the crime of vehicular homicide. Angelo argued that a "corporation" could not be guilty of vehicular homicide because it cannot "operate" a vehicle. The court ruled that if an employee commits a crime "while engaged in corporate business that the employee has been authorized to conduct," a corporation can be held liable for the crime. Hence, the court held that Angelo was liable for Gauthier's negligent operation of its truck, which resulted in a person's death.[3] •

Classification of Corporations

Corporations can be classified in several ways. The classification of a corporation normally depends on its location, purpose, and ownership characteristics, as described in the following subsections.

DOMESTIC, FOREIGN, AND ALIEN CORPORATIONS A corporation is referred to as a **domestic corporation** by its home state (the state in which it incorporates). A corporation formed in one state but doing business in another is referred to in the second state as a **foreign corporation.** A corporation formed in another country (say, Mexico) but doing business in the United States is referred to in the United States as an **alien corporation.**

A corporation does not have an automatic right to do business in a state other than its state of incorporation. In some instances, it must obtain a *certificate of authority* in any state in which it plans to do business. Once the certificate has been issued, the corporation generally can exercise in that state all of the powers conferred on it by its home state. If a foreign corporation does business in a state without obtaining a certificate of authority, the state can impose substantial fines and sanctions on the corporation, and sometimes even on its officers, directors, or agents. Note that most state statutes specify certain activities, such as soliciting orders via the Internet, that are not considered doing business within the state. Thus, a foreign corporation normally does not need a certificate of authority to sell goods or services via the Internet or by mail.

PUBLIC AND PRIVATE CORPORATIONS A public corporation is one formed by the government to meet some political or governmental purpose. Cities and towns that incorporate are common examples. In addition, many federal government organizations, such as the U.S. Postal Service, the Tennessee Valley Authority, and AMTRAK, are public corporations. Note that a public corporation is not the same as a *publicly held* corporation (often called a *public company*). A publicly held corporation is any corporation whose shares are publicly traded in securities markets, such as the New York Stock Exchange or the NASDAQ (an electronic stock exchange founded by the National Association of Securities Dealers).

In contrast to public corporations (*not* public companies), private corporations are created either wholly or in part for private benefit. Most corporations are private. Although they may serve a public purpose, as a public electric or gas utility does, they are owned by private persons rather than by the government.[4]

NONPROFIT CORPORATIONS Corporations formed for purposes other than making a profit are called *nonprofit* or *not-for-profit* corporations. Private hospitals, educational institutions, charities, and religious organizations, for example, are frequently organized as nonprofit corporations. The nonprofit corporation is a convenient form of organization that allows various groups to own property and to form contracts without exposing the individual members to personal liability.

CLOSE CORPORATIONS Most corporate enterprises in the United States fall into the category of close corporations. A **close corporation** is one whose shares are held by members of a family or by relatively few persons. Close corporations are also referred to as *closely held, family,* or *privately held* corporations. Usually, the members of the small group constituting a close corporation are personally known to one another. Because the number of shareholders is so small, there is no trading market for the shares.

In practice, a close corporation is often operated like a partnership. Some states have enacted special statutory provisions that apply to close corporations. These provisions expressly permit close corporations to depart significantly from certain formalities required by traditional corporation law.[5]

Additionally, a provision added to the RMBCA in 1991 gives close corporations a substantial amount of flexibility in determining the rules by which they will operate [RMBCA 7.32]. If all of a corporation's shareholders agree in writing, the corporation can operate without directors, bylaws, annual or special shareholders' or directors' meetings, stock certificates, or formal records of shareholders' or directors' decisions.[6]

---

3. *Commonwealth v. Angelo Todesca Corp.,* 446 Mass. 128, 842 N.E.2d 930 (2006).

4. The United States Supreme Court first recognized the property rights of private corporations and clarified the distinction between public and private corporations in the landmark case *Trustees of Dartmouth College v. Woodward,* 17 U.S. (4 Wheaton) 518, 4 L.Ed. 629 (1819).

5. For example, in some states (such as Maryland), a close corporation need not have a board of directors.

6. Shareholders cannot agree, however, to eliminate certain rights of shareholders, such as the right to inspect corporate books and records or the right to bring *derivative actions* (lawsuits on behalf of the corporation—see Chapter 25).

Management of Close Corporations. A close corporation has a single shareholder or a closely knit group of shareholders, who usually hold the positions of directors and officers. Management of a close corporation resembles that of a sole proprietorship or a partnership. As a corporation, however, the firm must meet all specific legal requirements set forth in state statutes.

To prevent a majority shareholder from dominating a close corporation, the corporation may require that more than a simple majority of the directors approve any action taken by the board. Typically, this would apply only to extraordinary actions, such as changing the amount of dividends or dismissing an employee-shareholder, and not to ordinary business decisions.

Transfer of Shares in Close Corporations. By definition, a close corporation has a small number of shareholders. Thus, the transfer of one shareholder's shares to someone else can cause serious management problems. The other shareholders may find themselves required to share control with someone they do not know or like.

EXAMPLE 24.2 Three brothers—Terry, Damon, and Henry Johnson—are the only shareholders of Johnson's Car Wash, Inc. Terry and Damon do not want Henry to sell his shares to an unknown third person. To avoid this situation, the corporation could restrict the transferability of shares to outside persons. Shareholders could be required to offer their shares to the corporation or the other shareholders before selling them to an outside purchaser. In fact, a few states have statutes that prohibit the transfer of close corporation shares unless certain persons—including shareholders, family members, and the corporation—are first given the opportunity to purchase the shares for the same price. ●

Control of a close corporation can also be stabilized through the use of a *shareholder agreement*. A shareholder agreement can provide that when one of the original shareholders dies, her or his shares of stock in the corporation will be divided in such a way that the proportionate holdings of the survivors, and thus their proportionate control, will be maintained. Courts are generally reluctant to interfere with private agreements, including shareholder agreements.

Misappropriation of Close Corporation Funds. Sometimes, a majority shareholder in a close corporation takes advantage of his or her position and misappropriates company funds. In such situations, the normal remedy for the injured minority shareholders is to have their shares appraised and to be paid the fair market value for them.

In the following case, a minority shareholder charged that the majority shareholders paid themselves excessive compensation in breach of their fiduciary duty.

Case 24.1 Rubin v. Murray

Appeals Court of Massachusetts, 79 Mass.App.Ct. 64, 943 N.E.2d 949 (2011).
www.massreports.com/OpinionArchive[a]

FACTS Olympic Adhesives, Inc., makes and sells industrial adhesives. John Murray, Stephen Hopkins, and Paul Ryan (the defendants) were the controlling shareholders of the company, as well as officers, directors, and employees. Merek Rubin was a minority shareholder. Murray, Hopkins, and Ryan were paid salaries. Under Olympic's profit-sharing plan, one-third of its net operating income was paid into a fund that was distributed to employees, including Murray, Hopkins, and Ryan. Twice a year, Murray, Hopkins, and Ryan also paid themselves additional compensation–a percentage of the net profits after profit sharing, allocated according to their stock ownership. Over a fifteen-year period, the percentage grew from 75 percent to between 92 and 98 percent. During this time, the additional compensation totaled nearly $15 million. Rubin filed a suit in a Massachusetts state court against Murray, Hopkins, and Ryan, alleging that they had paid themselves excessive compensation and deprived him of his share of Olympic's profits in violation of their fiduciary duty to him as a minority shareholder. The court ordered the defendants to repay Olympic nearly $6 million to be distributed among its shareholders. The defendants appealed.

ISSUE Did the majority shareholders in a close corporation breach their fiduciary duty to the minority shareholders by paying themselves a large percentage of the company's net profits twice a year?

DECISION Yes. A state intermediate appellate court affirmed the lower court's judgment. The trial judge had discretion to determine what constituted reasonable compensation for the defendants, and its findings were based on sufficient evidence. The compensation of the majority shareholders was excessive and deprived Rubin of his share of Olympic profits in breach of their fiduciary duty to him as a minority shareholder.

REASON The court reasoned that a salary should reasonably relate to a corporate officer's ability and the quantity and quality of services the officer renders. Profits resulting from an officer's performance may also affect the amount of compensation. In this case, the trial judge found that a reasonable amount of compensation for each officer would have been 4 percent

Case 24.1–Continues next page ➡

a. In the "Release date:" box, type "03/16/2011," and click on "submit." In the result, click on the appropriate link to view the opinion. The Reporter of Decisions for the Massachusetts Supreme Judicial Court and the Appeals Court maintains this Web site.

Case 24.1–Continued

to 7 percent of net sales, plus a "success premium" related to individual contributions, for a total of 10 percent of Olympic's average annual net sales. This amount was comparable to the average compensation for officers in similar firms. The appellate court also pointed out that Murray was vague when he attempted to explain the basis for distributing the profits among the defendants. Those amounts seemed to correspond only to the percentage of the officers' stock ownership, rather than to any aspect of their performance.

WHAT IF THE FACTS WERE DIFFERENT? *Suppose that Murray could have pinpointed a job-related basis for the distribution of the net profits among the defendants. Would the result have been different? Explain.*

S CORPORATIONS A close corporation that meets the qualifying requirements specified in Subchapter S of the Internal Revenue Code can operate as an **S corporation.** If a corporation has S corporation status, it can avoid the imposition of income taxes at the corporate level while retaining many of the advantages of a corporation, particularly limited liability. Among the numerous requirements for S corporation status, the following are the most important:

1. The corporation must be a domestic corporation.
2. The corporation must not be a member of an affiliated group of corporations.
3. The shareholders of the corporation must be individuals, estates, or certain trusts. Partnerships and nonqualifying trusts cannot be shareholders. Corporations can be shareholders under certain circumstances.
4. The corporation must have no more than one hundred shareholders.
5. The corporation must have only one class of stock, although all shareholders do not have to have the same voting rights.
6. No shareholder of the corporation may be a nonresident alien.

An S corporation is treated differently from a regular corporation for tax purposes. An S corporation is taxed like a partnership, so the corporate income passes through to the shareholders, who pay personal income tax on it. This treatment enables the S corporation to avoid the double taxation that is imposed on regular corporations. In addition, the shareholders' tax brackets may be lower than the tax bracket that the corporation would have been in if the tax had been imposed at the corporate level.

This tax saving is particularly attractive when the corporation wants to accumulate earnings for some future business purpose. If the corporation has losses, the S election allows the shareholders to use the losses to offset other taxable income. Nevertheless, because the limited liability company and the limited liability partnership (see Chapter 23) offer similar tax advantages and greater flexibility, the S corporation has lost some of its significance.

PROFESSIONAL CORPORATIONS Professionals such as physicians, lawyers, dentists, and accountants can incorporate. Professional corporations typically are identified by the letters *S.C.* (service corporation), *P.C.* (professional corporation), or *P.A.* (professional association).

In general, the laws governing the formation and operation of professional corporations are similar to those governing ordinary business corporations. There are some differences in terms of liability, however, because the shareholder-owners are professionals who are held to a higher standard of conduct. For liability purposes, some courts treat a professional corporation somewhat like a partnership and hold each professional liable for any malpractice committed within the scope of the business by the others in the firm. With the exception of malpractice or a breach of duty to clients or patients, a shareholder in a professional corporation generally cannot be held liable for the torts committed by other professionals at the firm.

Corporate Formation and Powers

Up to this point, we have discussed some of the general characteristics of corporations. We now examine the process by which corporations come into existence. Incorporating a business is much simpler today than it was twenty years ago, and many states allow businesses to incorporate via the Internet. If the owners of a partnership or sole proprietorship wish to expand the business, they may decide to incorporate because a corporation can obtain more capital by issuing shares of stock.

Promotional Activities

In the past, preliminary steps were taken to organize and promote the business prior to incorporating. Contracts were made with investors and others on behalf of the future corporation. Today, due to the relative ease of forming a corporation in most states, persons incorporating their business rarely, if ever, engage in preliminary promotional activities. Nevertheless, it is important for businesspersons to understand that they are personally liable for all preincorporation contracts made with investors, accountants, or others on behalf of the future corporation. This personal liability continues until the corporation assumes the preincorporation contracts by *novation* (see page 204 in Chapter 11).

EXAMPLE 24.3 Jade Sorrel contracts with an accountant, Ray Cooper, to provide tax advice for a proposed corporation,

Blackstone, Inc. Cooper provides the services to Sorrel, knowing that the corporation has not yet been formed. Once Blackstone, Inc., is formed, Cooper sends an invoice to the corporation and to Sorrel personally, but the bill is not paid. Because Sorrel is personally liable for the preincorporation contract, Cooper can file a lawsuit against Sorrel for breaching the contract for accounting services. Cooper cannot seek to hold Blackstone, Inc., liable unless he has entered into a novation contract with the corporation. •

Incorporation Procedures

Exact procedures for incorporation differ among states, but the basic steps are as follows: (1) select the state of incorporation, (2) secure the corporate name by confirming its availability, (3) prepare the articles of incorporation, and (4) file the articles of incorporation with the secretary of state accompanied by payment of the specified fees. These steps are discussed in more detail in the following subsections.

SELECT THE STATE OF INCORPORATION The first step in the incorporation process is to select a state in which to incorporate. Because state corporation laws differ, individuals may look for the states that offer the most advantageous tax or other provisions. Another consideration is the fee that a particular state charges to incorporate, as well as the annual fees and the fees for specific transactions (such as stock transfers).

Delaware has historically had the least restrictive laws and provisions that favor corporate management. Consequently, many corporations, including a number of the largest, have incorporated there. Delaware's statutes permit firms to incorporate in that state and conduct business and locate their operating headquarters elsewhere. Most other states now permit this as well. Note, though, that close corporations, particularly those of a professional nature, generally incorporate in the state where their principal shareholders live and work. For reasons of convenience and cost, businesses often choose to incorporate in the state in which the corporation's business will primarily be conducted.

SECURE THE CORPORATE NAME The choice of a corporate name is subject to state approval to ensure against duplication or deception. State statutes usually require that the secretary of state run a check on the proposed name in the state of incorporation. Some states require that the persons incorporating a firm, at their own expense, run a check on the proposed name, which can often be accomplished via Internet-based services. Once cleared, a name can be reserved for a short time, for a fee, pending the completion of the articles of incorporation. All corporate statutes require the corporation name to include the word *Corporation, Incorporated, Company,* or *Limited,* or abbreviations of these terms.

A new corporation's name cannot be the same as (or deceptively similar to) the name of an existing corporation doing business within the state. The name should also be one that can be used as the business's Internet domain name. **EXAMPLE 24.4** If an existing corporation is named Digital Synergy, Inc., you cannot choose the name Digital Synergy Company because that name is deceptively similar to the first. The state will be unlikely to allow the corporate name because it could impliedly transfer a part of the goodwill established by the first corporate user to the second corporation. In addition, you would not want to choose the name Digital Synergy Company because you would be unable to acquire an Internet domain name using even part of the name of the business. •

If those incorporating a firm contemplate doing business in other states—or over the Internet—they also need to check on existing corporate names in those states as well. Otherwise, if the firm does business under a name that is the same as or deceptively similar to an existing company's name, it may be liable for trade name infringement (see Chapter 5).

PREPARE THE ARTICLES OF INCORPORATION The primary document needed to incorporate a business is the **articles of incorporation.** The articles include basic information about the corporation and serve as a primary source of authority for its future organization and business functions. The person or persons who execute (sign) the articles are called *incorporators*. Generally, the articles of incorporation *must* include the following information [RMBCA 2.02]:

1. The name of the corporation.
2. The number of shares the corporation is authorized to issue.
3. The name and address of the corporation's initial registered agent.
4. The name and address of each incorporator.

In addition, the articles *may* set forth other information, such as the names and addresses of the initial board of directors, the duration and purpose of the corporation, a par value of shares of the corporation, and any other information pertinent to the rights and duties of the corporation's shareholders and directors. Articles of incorporation vary widely depending on the size and type of corporation and the jurisdiction. Frequently, the articles do not provide much detail about the firm's operations, which are spelled out in the company's **bylaws** (internal rules of management adopted by the corporation at its first organizational meeting).

Shares of the Corporation. The articles must specify the number of shares of stock authorized for issuance. For instance, a company might state that the aggregate number of shares that the corporation has the authority to issue is five thousand. Large corporations often state a par value of each share, such as twenty cents per share, and specify the various types or classes of stock authorized for issuance (see the discussion of *common* and *preferred stock* later in this chapter). Sometimes, the articles set forth the capital structure of the corporation and other relevant information concerning equity, shares, and credit.

Registered Office and Agent. The corporation must indicate the location and address of its registered office within the state. Usually, the registered office is also the principal office of the corporation. The corporation must also give the name and address of a specific person who has been designated as an *agent* and can receive legal documents (such as orders to appear in court) on behalf of the corporation.

Incorporators. Each incorporator must be listed by name and address. The incorporators need not have any interest at all in the corporation, and sometimes signing the articles is their only duty. Many states do not have residency or age requirements for incorporators. States vary on the required number of incorporators; it can be as few as one or as many as three. Incorporators frequently participate in the first organizational meeting of the corporation.

Duration and Purpose. A corporation has perpetual existence unless the articles state otherwise. The RMBCA does not require a specific statement of purpose to be included in the articles. A corporation can be formed for any lawful purpose. Some incorporators choose to include a general statement of purpose "to engage in any lawful act or activity," while others opt to specify the intended business activities ("to engage in the production and sale of agricultural products," for example). It is increasingly common for the articles to state that the corporation is organized for "any legal business," with no mention of specifics, to avoid the need for future amendments to the corporate articles.

Internal Organization. The articles can describe the internal management structure of the corporation, although this is usually included in the bylaws adopted after the corporation is formed. The articles of incorporation commence the corporation; the bylaws are formed after commencement by the board of directors. Bylaws cannot conflict with the corporation statute or the articles of incorporation [RMBCA 2.06].

Under the RMBCA, shareholders may amend or repeal the bylaws. The board of directors may also amend or repeal the bylaws unless the articles of incorporation or provisions of the corporation statute reserve this power to the shareholders exclusively [RMBCA 10.20]. Typical bylaw provisions describe such matters as voting requirements for shareholders, the election of the board of directors, the methods of replacing directors, and the manner and time of holding shareholders' and board meetings (these corporate activities will be discussed in Chapter 25).

File the Articles with the State Once the articles of incorporation have been prepared, signed, and authenticated by the incorporators, they are sent to the appropriate state official, usually the secretary of state, along with the required filing fee. In most states, the secretary of state then stamps the articles as "Filed" and returns a copy of the articles to the incorporators. Once this occurs, the corporation officially exists.

(Note that some states issue a *certificate of incorporation,* which is similar to articles of incorporation, representing the state's authorization for the corporation to conduct business. This procedure was typical under the unrevised MBCA.)

First Organizational Meeting to Adopt Bylaws

After incorporation, the first organizational meeting must be held. Usually, the most important function of this meeting is the adoption of bylaws—the internal rules of management for the corporation. If the articles of incorporation named the initial board of directors, then the directors, by majority vote, call the meeting to adopt the bylaws and complete the company's organization.

If the articles did not name the directors (as is typical), then the incorporators hold the meeting to elect the directors, adopt bylaws, and complete the routine business of incorporation (authorizing the issuance of shares and hiring employees, for example). The business transacted depends on the requirements of the state's corporation statute, the nature of the corporation, the provisions made in the articles, and the desires of the incorporators.

Improper Incorporation

The procedures for incorporation are very specific. If they are not followed precisely, others may be able to challenge the existence of the corporation. Errors in incorporation procedures can become important when, for example, a third party who is attempting to enforce a contract or bring a suit for a tort injury learns of them. If a corporation has substantially complied with all conditions precedent to incorporation, the corporation is said to have *de jure* (rightful and lawful) existence. In most states and under RMBCA 2.03(b), the secretary of state's filing of the articles of incorporation is conclusive proof that all mandatory statutory provisions have been met [RMBCA 2.03(b)].

Sometimes, the incorporators fail to comply with all statutory mandates. If the defect is minor, such as an incorrect address listed on the articles of incorporation, most courts will overlook the defect and find that a corporation *(de jure)* exists.

If the defect is substantial, however, such as a corporation's failure to hold an organizational meeting to adopt bylaws, the outcome will vary depending on the court. Some states, including Mississippi, New York, Ohio, and Oklahoma, still recognize the common law doctrine of *de facto* corporation.[7] In those states, the courts will treat a corporation as a legal corporation despite the defect in its formation if the following three requirements are met:

1. A state statute exists under which the corporation can be validly incorporated.
2. The parties have made a good faith attempt to comply with the statute.
3. The parties have already undertaken to do business as a corporation.

Many state courts, however, have interpreted their states' version of the RMBCA as abolishing the common law doctrine of *de facto* corporations. These states include Alaska, Arizona, the District of Columbia, Minnesota, New Mexico, Oregon, South Dakota, Tennessee, Utah, and Washington. In those states, if there is a substantial defect in complying with the incorporation statute, the corporation does not legally exist, and the incorporators are personally liable.

Corporation by Estoppel

If a business holds itself out to others as being a corporation but has made no attempt to incorporate, the firm may be estopped (prevented) from denying corporate status in a lawsuit by a third party. This doctrine of corporation by estoppel is most commonly applied when a third party contracts with an entity that claims to be a corporation but has not filed articles of incorporation—or contracts with a person claiming to be an agent of a corporation that does not in fact exist. When justice requires, courts in some states will treat an alleged corporation as if it were an actual corporation for the purpose of determining the rights and liabilities in particular circumstances.[8] Recognition of corporate status does not extend beyond the resolution of the problem at hand.

CASE EXAMPLE 24.5 In 2001, W. P. Media, Inc., and Alabama MBA, Inc., agreed to form Alabaster Wireless MBA, LLC, to provide wireless Internet services to consumers. W. P. Media was to create a wireless network and provide ongoing technical support. Alabama MBA was to contribute the capital. Hugh Brown signed the parties' contract on Alabama MBA's behalf as the chair of its board. At the time, however, Alabama MBA's articles of incorporation had not yet been filed. Brown filed the articles of incorporation in 2002. Later, Brown and Alabama MBA filed a suit in a state court, alleging that W. P. Media had breached their contract by not building the wireless network. The Supreme Court of Alabama held that because W. P. Media had treated Alabama MBA as a corporation, W. P. Media was estopped from denying Alabama MBA's corporate existence.[9] •

Corporate Powers

When a corporation is created, the express and implied powers necessary to achieve its purpose also come into existence.

EXPRESS POWERS The express powers of a corporation are found in its articles of incorporation, in the law of the state of incorporation, and in the state and federal constitutions.

Corporate bylaws also establish the express powers of the corporation. Because state corporation statutes frequently provide default rules that apply if the company's bylaws are silent on an issue, it is important that the bylaws set forth the specific operating rules of the corporation. In addition, after the bylaws are adopted, the corporation's board of directors will pass resolutions that also grant or restrict corporate powers.

The following order of priority is used when conflicts arise among documents involving corporations:

1. The U.S. Constitution
2. State constitutions
3. State statutes
4. The articles of incorporation
5. Bylaws
6. Resolutions of the board of directors

IMPLIED POWERS When a corporation is created, it acquires certain implied powers. Barring express constitutional, statutory, or other prohibitions, the corporation has the implied power to perform all acts reasonably appropriate and necessary to accomplish its corporate purposes. For this reason, a corporation has the implied power to borrow funds within certain limits, to lend funds, and to extend credit to those with whom it has a legal or contractual relationship.

To borrow funds, the corporation acts through its board of directors to authorize the loan. Most often, the president or chief executive officer of the corporation will execute the necessary papers on behalf of the corporation. In so doing,

7. See, for example, *In re Hausman,* 13 N.Y.3d 408, 921 N.E.2d 191, 893 N.Y.S.2d 499 (2009).
8. Some states have expressly rejected the common law theory of corporation by estoppel, finding that it is inconsistent with their statutory law, whereas other states have abolished only the doctrines of *de facto* and *de jure* corporations. See, for example, *Stone v. Jetmar Properties, LLC,* 733 N.W.2d 480 (Minn.App. 2007).
9. *Brown v. W. P. Media, Inc.,* 17 So.3d 1167 (Ala.Sup. 2009).

corporate officers have the implied power to bind the corporation in matters directly connected with the *ordinary* business affairs of the enterprise. There is a limit to what a corporate officer can do, though. A corporate officer does not have the authority to bind the corporation to an action that will greatly affect the corporate purpose or undertaking, such as the sale of substantial corporate assets.

ULTRA VIRES DOCTRINE The term ***ultra vires*** means "beyond the power." In corporate law, acts of a corporation that are beyond its express or implied powers are *ultra vires* acts. Under Section 3.04 of the RMBCA, the shareholders can seek an injunction from a court to prevent the corporation from engaging in *ultra vires* acts. The attorney general in the state of incorporation can also bring an action to obtain an injunction against the *ultra vires* transactions or to institute dissolution proceedings against the corporation on the basis of *ultra vires* acts. The corporation or its shareholders (on behalf of the corporation) can seek damages from the officers and directors who were responsible for the *ultra vires* acts.

In the past, most cases dealing with *ultra vires* acts involved contracts made for unauthorized purposes. Now, however, most private corporations are organized for "any legal business" and do not state a specific purpose, so the *ultra vires* doctrine has declined in importance in recent years. Today, cases that allege *ultra vires* acts usually involve nonprofit corporations or municipal (public) corporations.

CASE EXAMPLE 24.6 Four men formed a nonprofit corporation to create the Armenian Genocide Museum & Memorial (AGM&M). The bylaws appointed them as trustees (similar to corporate directors) for life. One of the trustees, Gerard L. Cafesjian, became the chair and president of AGM&M. Eventually, the relationship among the trustees deteriorated, and Cafesjian resigned. The corporation then brought a suit claiming that Cafesjian had engaged in numerous *ultra vires* acts, self-dealing, and mismanagement. Among other things, although the bylaws required an 80 percent affirmative vote of the trustees to take action, Cafesjian had taken many actions without the board's approval. He had also entered into contracts for real estate transactions in which he had a personal interest. Because Cafesjian had taken actions that exceeded his authority and had failed to follow the rules set forth in the bylaws for board meetings, the court ruled that the corporation could go forward with its suit.[10] ●

10. *Armenian Assembly of America, Inc. v. Cafesjian*, 692 F.Supp.2d 20 (D.C. 2010).

Piercing the Corporate Veil

Occasionally, the owners use a corporate entity to perpetrate a fraud, circumvent the law, or in some other way accomplish an illegitimate objective. In these situations, the court will ignore the corporate structure and **pierce the corporate veil** and expose the shareholders to personal liability. Generally, when the corporate privilege is abused for personal benefit or when the corporate business is treated so carelessly that the corporation and the controlling shareholder are no longer separate entities, the court will require the owner to assume personal liability to creditors for the corporation's debts.

In short, when the facts show that great injustice would result from the use of a corporation to avoid individual responsibility, a court will look behind the corporate structure to the individual shareholder.

FACTORS COURTS USE The following are some of the factors that frequently cause the courts to pierce the corporate veil:

1. A party is tricked or misled into dealing with the corporation rather than the individual.
2. The corporation is set up never to make a profit or always to be insolvent, or it is too "thinly" capitalized—that is, it has insufficient capital at the time of formation to meet its prospective debts or other potential liabilities.
3. Statutory corporate formalities, such as holding required corporation meetings, are not followed.
4. Personal and corporate interests are **commingled** (mixed together) to such an extent that the corporation has no separate identity.

A POTENTIAL PROBLEM FOR CLOSE CORPORATIONS The potential for corporate assets to be used for personal benefit is especially great in a close corporation, in which the shares are held by a single person or by only a few individuals, usually family members. In such a situation, the separate status of the corporate entity and the sole shareholder (or family-member shareholders) must be carefully preserved. Certain practices invite trouble for the one-person or family-owned corporation: the commingling of corporate and personal funds, the failure to hold board of directors' meetings and record the minutes, or the shareholders' continuous personal use of corporate property (for example, vehicles).

In the following case, a creditor asked the court to pierce the corporate veil and hold the sole shareholder-owner of the debtor corporation personally liable for a corporate debt.

Case 24.2 Schultz v. General Electric Healthcare Financial Services

Court of Appeals of Kentucky, __ S.W.3d __ (2010).

FACTS Thomas Schultz was the president and sole shareholder-owner of Intra-Med Services, Inc., a Kentucky corporation that performed medical diagnostic-imaging services. Several General Electric Companies (collectively, GE) leased certain medical equipment to Intra-Med. When Intra-Med failed to make the required lease payments, GE sued Intra-Med to recover the payments. In 2004, the court entered a judgment in favor of GE for more than $4.7 million. GE was able to collect approximately $700,000 of the judgment. GE then learned of documents from another lawsuit that revealed Schultz had used Intra-Med assets for his own purposes. He had bought property using Intra-Med funds, and when it was sold, he had kept the proceeds. GE intervened in the other lawsuit and filed a third party complaint against Schultz, seeking to pierce the corporate veil and hold him personally liable for the judgment against Intra-Med. GE requested a judgment in the amount of $1,150,000, allegedly the amount of Intra-Med funds that Schultz had used improperly. The trial court denied GE's request, stating that Schultz might have been entitled to some payments from Intra-Med because he had personally loaned the company $700,000. GE agreed to settle for $450,000, the difference between $1,150,000 and the claimed $700,000 loan. The court issued a judgment in GE's favor, and Schultz appealed.

ISSUE Should the court pierce the veil of the corporation because Schultz, the sole shareholder-owner, improperly used Intra-Med funds for his own purposes?

DECISION Yes. The Court of Appeals of Kentucky affirmed the trial court's judgment on the pleadings. The corporate veil of Intra-Med should be pierced to hold Schultz liable for the debt owed to GE.

REASON The trial court used the instrumentality theory to pierce the corporate veil. Under this theory, the corporation is merely an instrumentality of the shareholder. The appellate court agreed with the trial court's decision. "The admitted facts . . . support the finding that the corporate veil should be pierced under the instrumentality theory. Mr. Schultz treated the corporation as a mere instrumentality by using corporate funds for his own individual purposes to purchase real estate and [other property]. The admitted facts also demonstrate that Mr. Schultz harmed GE by using corporate funds as his own even after GE obtained a monetary judgment against Intra-Med." The court concluded that not piercing the corporate veil would subject GE to an unjust loss. "Piercing the corporate veil appears to be the only method for GE to recover its judgment."

FOR CRITICAL ANALYSIS—Economic Consideration *Schultz argued that even if the corporate veil should be pierced, the $450,000 judgment against him was too much and should be reduced. How might the court have responded to this argument?*

Corporate Financing

Part of the process of corporate formation involves corporate financing. Corporations are financed by the issuance and sale of corporate securities. **Securities** (stocks and bonds) evidence the right to participate in earnings and the distribution of corporate property or the obligation to pay funds.

Stocks, or *equity securities,* represent the purchase of ownership in the business firm. **Bonds** (debentures), or *debt securities,* represent the borrowing of funds by firms (and governments). Of course, not all debt is in the form of debt securities. For example, some debt is in the form of accounts payable and notes payable, which typically are short-term debts. Bonds are simply a way for the corporation to split up its long-term debt so that it can be more easily marketed.

Bonds

Bonds are issued by business firms and by governments at all levels as evidence of the funds they are borrowing from investors. Bonds normally have a designated *maturity date*—the date when the principal, or face, amount of the bond is returned to the investor. They are sometimes referred to as *fixed-income securities* because their owners (that is, the creditors) receive fixed-dollar interest payments, usually semiannually, during the period of time prior to maturity.

Because debt financing represents a legal obligation on the part of the corporation, various features and terms of a particular bond issue are specified in a lending agreement called a **bond indenture.** A corporate trustee, often a commercial bank trust department, represents the collective well-being of all bondholders in ensuring that the corporation meets the terms of the bond issue. The bond indenture specifies the maturity date of the bond and the pattern of interest payments until maturity.

Stocks

Issuing stocks is another way that corporations can obtain financing. The ways in which stocks differ from bonds are summarized in Exhibit 24–1 on the next page. Basically, as mentioned, stocks represent ownership in a business firm, whereas bonds represent borrowing by the firm.

• ***Exhibit* 24–1 How Do Stocks and Bonds Differ?**

STOCKS	BONDS
1. Stocks represent ownership.	1. Bonds represent debt.
2. Stocks (common) do not have a fixed dividend rate.	2. Interest on bonds must always be paid, whether or not any profit is earned.
3. Stockholders can elect the board of directors, which controls the corporation.	3. Bondholders usually have no voice in, or control over, management of the corporation.
4. Stocks do not have a maturity date; the corporation usually does not repay the stockholder.	4. Bonds have a maturity date, when the corporation is to repay the bondholder the face value of the bond.
5. All corporations issue or offer to sell stocks. This is the usual definition of a corporation.	5. Corporations do not necessarily issue bonds.
6. Stockholders have a claim against the property and income of a corporation after all creditors' claims have been met.	6. Bondholders have a claim against the property and income of a corporation that must be met *before* the claims of stockholders.

Exhibit 24–2 on the facing page summarizes the types of stocks issued by corporations. We look now at the two major types of stock—*common stock* and *preferred stock.*

Common Stock The true ownership of a corporation is represented by **common stock.** Common stock provides a proportionate interest in the corporation with regard to (1) control, (2) earnings, and (3) net assets. A shareholder's interest is generally in proportion to the number of shares he or she owns out of the total number of shares issued.

Voting rights in a corporation apply to the election of the firm's board of directors and to any proposed changes in the ownership structure of the firm. For example, a holder of common stock generally has the right to vote in a decision on a proposed merger, as mergers can change the proportion of ownership. State corporation law specifies the types of actions for which shareholder approval must be obtained.

Firms are not obligated to return a principal amount per share to each holder of common stock because no firm can ensure that the market price per share of its common stock will not decline over time. The issuing firm also does not have to guarantee a dividend; indeed, some corporations never pay dividends.

Holders of common stock are investors who assume a *residual* position in the overall financial structure of a business. In terms of receiving payment for their investments, they are last in line. They are entitled to the earnings that are left after preferred stockholders, bondholders, suppliers, employees, and other groups have been paid. Once those groups are paid, however, the owners of common stock may be entitled to *all* the remaining earnings as dividends. (The board of directors normally is not under any duty to declare the remaining earnings as dividends, however.)

Preferred Stock **Preferred stock** is stock with *preferences*. Usually, this means that holders of preferred stock have priority over holders of common stock as to dividends and as to payment on dissolution of the corporation. Holders of preferred stock may or may not have the right to vote.

Preferred stock is not included among the liabilities of a business because it is equity. Like other equity securities, preferred shares have no fixed maturity date on which the firm must pay them off. Although firms occasionally buy back preferred stock, they are not legally obligated to do so. Holders of preferred stock are investors who have assumed a rather cautious position in their relationship to the corporation. They have a stronger position than common shareholders with respect to dividends and claims on assets, but they will not share in the full prosperity of the firm if it grows successfully over time. Preferred stockholders do receive fixed dividends periodically, however, and they may benefit to some extent from changes in the market price of the shares.

The return and the risk for preferred stock lie somewhere between those for bonds and those for common stock. Preferred stock is more similar to bonds than to common stock, even though preferred stock appears in the ownership section of the firm's balance sheet. As a result, preferred stock is often categorized with corporate bonds as a fixed-income security, even though the legal status is not the same.

Venture Capital and Private Equity Capital

As discussed, corporations traditionally obtain financing through issuing and selling securities (stocks and bonds) in the capital market. In reality, however, many investors do not want to purchase stock in a business that lacks a track record, and banks are generally reluctant to extend loans to high-risk enterprises. Numerous corporations fail because they are undercapitalized.

• ***Exhibit* 24–2 Types of Stocks**

Common stock	Voting shares that represent ownership interest in a corporation. Common stock has the lowest priority with respect to payment of dividends and distribution of assets on the corporation's dissolution.
Preferred stock	Shares of stock that have priority over common-stock shares as to payment of dividends and distribution of assets on dissolution. Dividend payments are usually a fixed percentage of the face value of the share.
Cumulative preferred stock	Preferred shares on which required dividends not paid in a given year must be paid in a subsequent year before any common-stock dividends are paid.
Participating preferred stock	Preferred shares entitling the owner to receive the preferred-stock dividend and additional dividends if the corporation has paid dividends on common stock.
Convertible preferred stock	Preferred shares that, under certain conditions, can be converted into a specified number of common shares either in the issuing corporation or, sometimes, in another corporation.
Redeemable, or callable, preferred stock	Preferred shares issued with the express condition that the issuing corporation has the right to repurchase the shares as specified.

Therefore, to obtain sufficient financing, many entrepreneurs seek alternative financing.

VENTURE CAPITAL Start-up businesses and high-risk enterprises often obtain venture capital financing. **Venture capital** is capital provided by professional, outside investors (called *venture capitalists,* who usually are groups of wealthy investors and securities firms) to new business ventures. Venture capital investments are high risk—the investors must be willing to lose all of their invested funds—but offer the potential for well-above-average returns at some point in the future.

To obtain venture capital financing, the start-up business typically gives up a share of its ownership to the venture capitalists. In addition to funding, venture capitalists may provide managerial and technical expertise, and they nearly always are given some control over the new company's decisions. Many Internet-based companies, such as Google, were initially financed by venture capital.

PRIVATE EQUITY CAPITAL Private equity firms obtain their capital from wealthy investors in private markets. The firms use their **private equity capital** to invest in existing—often, publicly traded—corporations. Usually, they buy an entire corporation and then reorganize it. Sometimes, divisions of the purchased company are sold off to pay down debt. Ultimately, the private equity firm may sell shares in the reorganized (and perhaps more profitable) company to the public in an *initial public offering* (usually called an IPO). In this way, the private equity firm can make profits by selling its shares in the company to the public.

Mergers and Acquisitions

A corporation typically extends its operations by combining with another corporation through a merger, a consolidation, a share exchange, a purchase of assets, or a purchase of a controlling interest (stock) in the other corporation.

The terms *merger* and *consolidation* traditionally referred to two legally distinct proceedings. Today, however, the term *consolidation* generally is used as a generic term to refer to all types of combinations, including mergers and acquisitions. Whether a combination is a merger, a consolidation, or a share exchange, the rights and liabilities of shareholders, the corporation, and the corporation's creditors are the same.

Merger

A **merger** involves the legal combination of two or more corporations in such a way that only one of the corporations continues to exist. **EXAMPLE 24.7** Corporation A and Corporation B decide to merge. They agree that A will absorb B. Therefore, on merging, B ceases to exist as a separate entity, and A continues as the *surviving corporation.* Exhibit 24–3 below graphically illustrates this process. ●

After the merger, Corporation A is recognized as a single corporation, possessing all the rights, privileges, and powers of itself and Corporation B. It automatically acquires all of B's property and assets without the necessity of a formal transfer. Additionally, A becomes liable for all of B's debts and obligations. Finally, A's articles of incorporation are deemed amended to include any changes that are stated in the *articles of merger* (a document setting forth the terms and conditions of the merger that is filed with the secretary of state).

In a merger, the surviving corporation inherits the disappearing corporation's preexisting legal rights and obligations. If the disappearing corporation had a right of action against a third party under tort or property law, for example, the surviving corporation can bring a suit after the merger to recover the disappearing corporation's damages.

• ***Exhibit* 24–3 Merger**

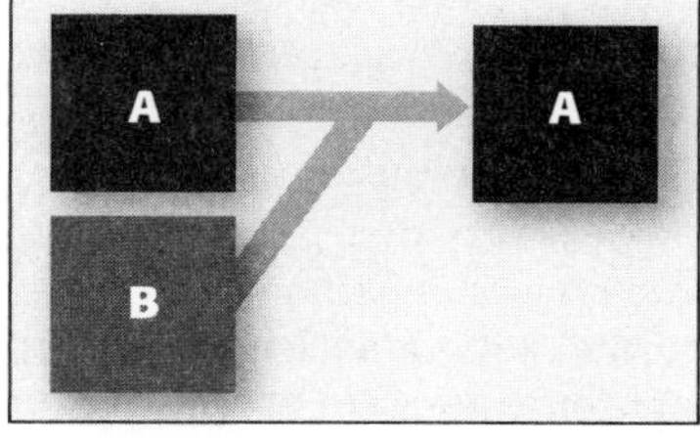

Consolidation

In a **consolidation,** two or more corporations combine in such a way that each corporation ceases to exist and a new one emerges. **EXAMPLE 24.8** Corporation A and Corporation B consolidate to form an entirely new organization, Corporation C. In the process, A and B both terminate, and C comes into existence as an entirely new entity. • Exhibit 24–4 below graphically illustrates this process.

• ***Exhibit* 24–4 Consolidation**

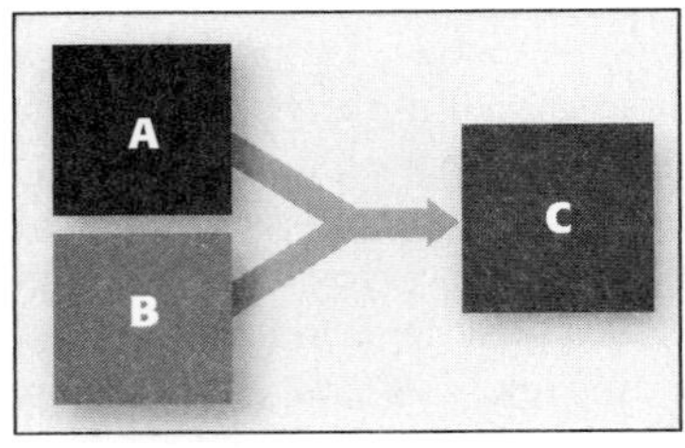

The results of a consolidation are essentially the same as the results of a merger. C is recognized as a new corporation and a single entity; A and B cease to exist. C inherits all of the rights, privileges, and powers previously held by A and B. Title to any property and assets owned by A and B passes to C without a formal transfer. C assumes liability for all of the debts and obligations owed by A and B. The *articles of consolidation,* which state the terms of the consolidation, take the place of A's and B's original corporate articles and are thereafter regarded as C's corporate articles.

When a merger or consolidation takes place, the surviving corporation or newly formed corporation will issue shares or pay some fair consideration to the shareholders of the corporation or corporations that cease to exist. True consolidations have become less common among for-profit corporations because it is often advantageous for one of the firms to survive. In contrast, nonprofit corporations and associations may prefer consolidation because it suggests a new beginning in which neither of the two initial entities is dominant.

Share Exchange

In a **share exchange,** some or all of the shares of one corporation are exchanged for some or all of the shares of another corporation, but both of these companies continue to exist. Share exchanges are often used to create *holding companies* (companies that own part or all of other companies' stock). For example, UAL Corporation is a large holding company that owns United Airlines. If one corporation owns *all* of the shares of another corporation, it is referred to as the *parent corporation,* and the wholly owned company is the *subsidiary corporation.*

Merger, Consolidation, or Share Exchange Procedures

As discussed earlier, each state has its own body of corporate law and these laws are not entirely uniform, although most states base their laws on the Revised Model Business Corporation Act (RMBCA).

Thus, all states have statutes authorizing mergers, consolidations, and share exchanges for domestic (in-state) and foreign (out-of-state) corporations. The procedures vary somewhat among jurisdictions, however. In some states, for example, a consolidation resulting in an entirely new corporation simply follows the initial incorporation procedures, whereas other business combinations must follow the procedures outlined below.

The RMBCA sets forth the following basic requirements [RMBCA 11.01–11.07]:

1. The board of directors of *each* corporation involved must approve the merger or consolidation plan.
2. The plan must specify any terms and conditions of the merger. It also must state how the value of the shares of each merging corporation will be determined and how they will be converted into shares or other securities, cash, property, or other interests in another corporation.
3. The majority of the shareholders of *each* corporation must vote to approve the plan at a shareholders' meeting. If any class of stock is entitled to vote as a separate group, the majority of each separate voting group must approve the plan. Although RMBCA 11.04(e) requires the approval of only a simple majority of the shareholders entitled to vote once a quorum is present, frequently a corporation's articles of incorporation or bylaws require a higher level of approval (Chapter 25 discusses *quorums* and other voting requirements). In addition, some state statutes require the approval of two-thirds of the outstanding shares of voting stock, and others require a four-fifths vote.
4. Once approved by the directors and the shareholders of both corporations, the surviving corporation files the plan (articles of merger, consolidation, or share exchange) with the appropriate official, usually the secretary of state.
5. When state formalities are satisfied, the state issues a certificate of merger to the surviving corporation or a certificate of consolidation to the newly consolidated corporation.

Short-Form Mergers

RMBCA 11.04 provides a simplified procedure for the merger of a substantially owned subsidiary corporation into its parent corporation. Under these provisions, a **short-form merger**—also referred to as a *parent-subsidiary merger*—can be accomplished *without* the approval of the shareholders of either corporation.

The short-form merger can be used only when the parent corporation owns at least 90 percent of the outstanding shares of each class of stock of the subsidiary corporation. Once the board of directors of the parent corporation approves the plan, it is filed with the state, and copies are sent to each shareholder of record in the subsidiary corporation.

Shareholder Approval

As mentioned, except in a short-form merger, the shareholders of both corporations must approve a merger or consolidation plan. Shareholders invest in a corporation with the expectation that the board of directors will manage the enterprise and make decisions on ordinary business matters. For *extraordinary* matters, normally both the board of directors and the shareholders must approve of the transaction.

Mergers and other combinations are extraordinary business matters, meaning that the board of directors must normally obtain the shareholders' approval and provide appraisal rights (discussed next). Amendments to the articles of incorporation and the dissolution of the corporation also generally require shareholder approval. Sometimes, a transaction can be structured in such a way that shareholder approval is not required, but if the shareholders challenge the transaction, a court might require shareholder approval. For this reason, the board of directors may request shareholder approval even when it might not be legally required.

Appraisal Rights

What if a shareholder disapproves of a merger or a consolidation but is outvoted by the other shareholders? The law recognizes that a dissenting shareholder should not be forced to become an unwilling shareholder in a corporation that is new or different from the one in which the shareholder originally invested. Dissenting shareholders therefore are given a statutory right to be paid the fair value of the shares they held on the date of the merger or consolidation. This right is referred to as the shareholder's **appraisal right.** So long as the transaction does not involve fraud or other illegal conduct, appraisal rights are the exclusive remedy for a shareholder who is dissatisfied with the price received for the stock.

Appraisal rights normally extend to regular mergers, consolidations, share exchanges, short-form mergers, and sales of substantially all of the corporate assets not in the ordinary course of business. Such rights can be particularly important in a short-form merger because the minority stockholders do not receive advance notice of the merger, the directors do not consider or approve it, and there is no vote. Appraisal rights are often the only recourse available to shareholders who object to parent-subsidiary mergers.

Each state establishes the procedures for asserting appraisal rights in that jurisdiction. Shareholders may lose their appraisal rights if they do not adhere precisely to the procedures prescribed by statute. When they lose the right to an appraisal, dissenting shareholders must go along with the transaction despite their objections.

Purchase of Assets

When a corporation acquires all or substantially all of the assets of another corporation by direct purchase, the purchasing, or *acquiring,* corporation simply extends its ownership and control over more assets. Because no change in the legal entity occurs, the acquiring corporation is not required to obtain shareholder approval for the purchase.[11] The U.S. Department of Justice and the Federal Trade Commission, however, have issued guidelines that significantly constrain and often prohibit mergers that could result from a purchase of assets, including takeover bids.

SALES OF CORPORATE ASSETS Note that the corporation that is *selling* all of its assets is substantially changing its business position and perhaps its ability to carry out its corporate purposes. For that reason, the corporation whose assets are being sold must obtain the approval of both the board of directors and the shareholders. In most states and under RMBCA 13.02, a dissenting shareholder of the selling corporation can demand appraisal rights.

SUCCESSOR LIABILITY IN PURCHASES OF ASSETS Generally, a corporation that purchases the assets of another corporation is not responsible for the liabilities of the selling corporation. Exceptions to this rule are made in certain circumstances, however. In any of the following situations, the acquiring corporation will be held to have assumed *both* the assets and the liabilities of the selling corporation:

1. When the purchasing corporation impliedly or expressly assumes the seller's liabilities.
2. When the sale transaction is actually a merger or consolidation of the two companies.
3. When the purchaser continues the seller's business and retains the same personnel (same shareholders, directors, and officers).
4. When the sale is fraudulently executed to escape liability.

The following case involved a sale of corporate assets. Although the parties agreed that the purchasing corporation was assuming the seller's liabilities, the parties disagreed as to whether the liabilities being assumed were limited to those that were existing and outstanding as of the closing date. That was the question before the court.

---

11. Shareholder approval may be required in a few situations. If the acquiring corporation plans to pay for the assets with its own corporate stock and not enough authorized unissued shares are available, the shareholders must vote to approve the issuance of additional shares by amendment of the corporate articles. Also, if the acquiring corporation is a company whose stock is traded on a national stock exchange and it will be issuing a significant number (at least 20 percent) of its outstanding shares, shareholder approval can be required.

Case 24.3 American Standard, Inc. v. OakFabco, Inc.

Court of Appeals of New York, 14 N.Y.3d 399, 901 N.Y.S.2d 572 (2010).
www.courts.state.ny.us/decisions/index.shtml[a]

FACTS American Standard, Inc., sold its Kewanee Boiler division to Kewanee Boiler Corporation, which is known as OakFabco, Inc. The parties' agreement stated that OakFabco would purchase Kewanee assets subject to Kewanee liabilities. The phrase *Kewanee liabilities* was defined as "all the debts, liabilities, obligations, and commitments (fixed or contingent) connected with or attributable to Kewanee existing and outstanding at the Closing Date." The boilers manufactured by Kewanee had been insulated with asbestos, and as a result, many tort claims had been made in the years following the purchase of the business. Some of those claims were brought by plaintiffs who had suffered injuries after the closing of the transaction, allegedly attributable to boilers manufactured and sold before the closing. American Standard brought an action against OakFabco, asking the court for a declaratory judgment on the issue of whether liabilities for such injuries were among the "Kewanee Liabilities" that OakFabco had assumed. The trial court entered a declaratory judgment holding that OakFabco had assumed the liabilities. An intermediate appellate court affirmed the trial court's ruling, and OakFabco appealed to the New York Court of Appeals.

ISSUE When a corporation purchases all of another corporation's assets and existing liabilities and debts, does that limit the purchasing corporation's liability for tort claims that arose after the closing date?

a. In the left-hand column, select "Court of Appeals." On the page that opens, click on "Court of Appeals Content Search." In the results, in the "Search by Official Reports Citation for Opinions" boxes, type "14" and "399," and click on "Find." Click on the resulting link to access this case. The New York State court system maintains this Web site.

DECISION No. The New York Court of Appeals affirmed the intermediate appellate court's decision. The court concluded that the contract expressed the intention that OakFabco was to assume the liabilities of the selling corporation, including claims that arose after the closing date.

REASON The transaction in question "was a purchase and sale of substantially all of the assets of the Kewanee Boiler business 'subject to all debts, liabilities, and obligations connected with or attributable to such business and operations.' Nothing in the nature of the transaction suggested that the parties intended OakFabco, which got all the assets, to escape any of the related obligations." OakFabco pointed to the fact that the definition of *Kewanee Liabilities* specified the debts, liabilities, obligations, and commitments existing and outstanding at the closing date. It argued that a tort claim could not be "existing and outstanding" before the tort plaintiff has been injured, because until then, it is not possible for a tort lawsuit to be brought. The court, however, found that no intention to adopt this meaning was made clear by any clause in the agreement. Rather, the language in the agreement "clearly meant that the buyer would deal with any problems customers had after the closing date with boilers that had been installed previously." Consequently, the liabilities assumed by OakFabco included claims bought by tort claimants injured after the closing date by boilers installed before that date.

FOR CRITICAL ANALYSIS—Legal Consideration *Generally, a corporation that purchases the assets of another is not automatically responsible for the liabilities of the selling corporation, with some exceptions. Which exception applied to this case? Explain.*

Purchase of Stock and Tender Offers

An alternative to the purchase of another corporation's assets is the purchase of a substantial number of the voting shares of its stock. This enables the acquiring corporation to control the **target corporation** (the corporation being acquired). The process of acquiring control over a corporation in this way is commonly referred to as a corporate **takeover.**

The acquiring corporation deals directly with the target company's shareholders in seeking to purchase the shares they hold. It does this by making a **tender offer** to all of the shareholders of the target corporation. The tender offer can be conditioned on receiving a specified number of shares by a certain date. The price offered generally is higher than the market price of the target corporation's stock prior to the announcement of the tender offer as a means of inducing shareholders to accept the offer.

EXAMPLE 24.9 In the 2009 merger of two Fortune 500 pharmaceutical companies, Pfizer, Inc., paid $68 billion to acquire its rival Wyeth. Wyeth shareholders reportedly received approximately $50.19 per share (part in cash and part in Pfizer stock), which amounted to a 15 percent premium over the market price of the stock. • Federal securities laws strictly control the terms, duration, and circumstances under which most tender offers are made. In addition, many states have passed antitakeover statutes.

A firm may respond to a tender offer in numerous ways. Sometimes, a target firm's board of directors will see a tender offer as favorable and will recommend to the shareholders that they accept it. To resist a takeover, a target company can make a *self-tender,* which is an offer to acquire stock from its own shareholders and thereby retain corporate control. A target corporation might also resort to other defenses. In one commonly used tactic, known as a "poison pill," a target company gives its shareholders rights to purchase additional shares at low prices when there is a takeover attempt. The use of poison pills is an attempt to prevent takeovers by making a takeover prohibitively expensive.

Termination

The termination of a corporation's existence has two phases—dissolution and winding up. **Dissolution** is the legal death of the artificial "person" of the corporation. *Winding up* is the process by which corporate assets are liquidated, or converted into cash, and distributed among creditors and shareholders.[12]

Voluntary Dissolution

Dissolution can be brought about voluntarily by the directors and the shareholders. State corporation statutes establish the procedures required to voluntarily dissolve a corporation. Basically, there are two possible methods: (1) by the shareholders' unanimous vote to initiate dissolution proceedings[13] or (2) by a proposal of the board of directors that is submitted to the shareholders at a shareholders' meeting.

When a corporation is dissolved voluntarily, the corporation must file *articles of dissolution* with the state and notify its creditors of the dissolution. The corporation must also establish a date (at least 120 days after the date of dissolution) by which all claims against the corporation must be received [RMBCA 14.06].

Involuntary Dissolution

Because corporations are creatures of statute, the state can also dissolve a corporation in certain circumstances. The secretary of state or the state attorney general can bring an action to dissolve a corporation that has failed to pay its annual taxes or to submit required annual reports, for example. A state court can also dissolve a corporation that has engaged in *ultra vires* acts (see page 470) or committed fraud or misrepresentation to the state during incorporation.

Sometimes, a shareholder or a group of shareholders petitions a court for corporate dissolution. A court may dissolve a corporation if the controlling shareholders or directors have engaged in fraudulent, illegal, or oppressive conduct.

CASE EXAMPLE 24.10 Mt. Princeton Trout Club, Inc. (MPTC), was formed to own land in Colorado and provide fishing and other recreational benefits to its shareholders. The articles of incorporation prohibited MPTC from selling or leasing any of the property and assets of the corporation without the approval of a majority of the directors. Despite this provision, MPTC officers entered into leases and contracts to sell corporate property without even notifying the directors. When a shareholder, Sam Colt, petitioned for dissolution, the court dissolved MPTC based on a finding that its officers had engaged in illegal, oppressive, and fraudulent conduct.[14] •

Shareholders may also petition a court for dissolution when the board of directors is deadlocked and the affairs of the corporation can no longer be conducted because of the deadlock.

Winding Up

When dissolution takes place by voluntary action, the members of the board of directors act as trustees of the corporate assets. As trustees, they are responsible for winding up the affairs of the corporation for the benefit of corporate creditors and shareholders. This makes the board members personally liable for any breach of their fiduciary trustee duties.

When the dissolution is involuntary—or if board members do not wish to act as trustees of the assets—the court will appoint a **receiver** to wind up the corporate affairs and liquidate corporate assets. Courts may also appoint a receiver when shareholders or creditors can show that the board of directors should not be permitted to act as trustees of the corporate assets.

12. Some prefer to call this phase *liquidation*, but we use the term *winding up* to mean all acts needed to bring the legal and financial affairs of the business to an end, including liquidating the assets and distributing them among creditors and shareholders.

13. Only some states allow shareholders to initiate corporate dissolution. See, for example, Delaware Code Section 275(c).

14. *Colt v. Mt. Princeton Trout Club, Inc.*, 78 P.3d 1115 (Colo.App. 2003).

Reviewing . . . Corporate Formation, Financing, and Termination

William Sharp was the sole shareholder and manager of Chickasaw Club, Inc., an S corporation that operated a popular nightclub of the same name in Columbus, Georgia. Sharp maintained a corporate checking account but paid the club's employees, suppliers, and entertainers in cash out of the club's proceeds. Sharp owned the property on which the club was located. He rented it to the club but made mortgage payments out of the club's proceeds and often paid other personal expenses with Chickasaw corporate funds. At 12:45 A.M. on July 31, 2005, eighteen-year-old Aubrey Lynn Pursley, who was already intoxicated, entered the Chickasaw Club. A city ordinance prohibited individuals under the age of twenty-one from entering nightclubs, but Chickasaw employees did not check Pursley's identification to verify her age. Pursley drank more alcohol at Chickasaw and was visibly intoxicated when she left the club at 3:00 A.M. with a beer in her hand. Shortly afterward, Pursley lost control of her car, struck a tree, and was killed. Joseph Dancause,

Continued

Pursley's stepfather, filed a tort lawsuit in a Georgia state court against Chickasaw Club, Inc., and William Sharp, seeking damages. Using the information presented in the chapter, answer the following questions.

1 Under what theory might the court in this case make an exception to the limited liability of shareholders and hold Sharp personally liable for the damages? What factors would be relevant to the court's decision?
2 Suppose that Chickasaw's articles of incorporation failed to describe the corporation's purpose or management structure as required by state law. Would the court be likely to rule that Sharp is personally liable to Dancause on that basis?
3 Suppose that the club extended credit to its regular patrons in an effort to maintain a loyal clientele, although neither the articles of incorporation nor the corporate bylaws authorized this practice. Would the corporation likely have the power to engage in this activity? Explain.
4 How would the court classify the Chickasaw Club corporation—domestic or foreign, public or private?

Terms and Concepts

alien corporation 464
appraisal right 475
articles of incorporation 467
bond 471
bond indenture 471
bylaws 467
close corporation 464
commingle 470
common stock 472
consolidation 474
corporation 461
dissolution 477
dividend 462
domestic corporation 464
foreign corporation 464
holding company 462
merger 473
pierce the corporate veil 470
preferred stock 472
private equity capital 473
receiver 477
retained earnings 462
S corporation 466
securities 471
share exchange 474
short-form merger 474
stock 471
takeover 476
target corporation 476
tender offer 476
ultra vires 470
venture capital 473

Chapter Summary: Corporate Formation, Financing, and Termination

Corporate Nature and Classification (See pages 461–466.)	A corporation is a legal entity distinct from its owners. Formal statutory requirements, which vary somewhat from state to state, must be followed in forming a corporation. 1. *Corporate personnel*—The shareholders own the corporation. They elect a board of directors to govern the corporation. The board of directors hires corporate officers and other employees to run the daily business of the firm. 2. *Corporate taxation*—The corporation pays income tax on net profits; shareholders pay income tax on the disbursed dividends that they receive from the corporation (double-taxation feature). 3. *Torts and criminal acts*—The corporation is liable for the torts committed by its agents or officers within the course and scope of their employment (under the doctrine of *respondeat superior*). In some circumstances, a corporation can be held liable (and be fined) for the criminal acts of its agents and employees. In certain situations, corporate officers may be held personally liable for corporate crimes. 4. *Domestic, foreign, and alien corporations*—A corporation is referred to as a *domestic corporation* within its home state (the state in which it incorporates). A corporation is referred to as a *foreign corporation* by any state that is not its home state. A corporation is referred to as an *alien corporation* if it originates in another country but does business in the United States. 5. *Public and private corporations*—A public corporation is one formed by a government (for example, cities, towns, and public projects). A private corporation is one formed wholly or in part for private benefit. Most corporations are private corporations. 6. *Nonprofit corporations*—Corporations formed without a profit-making purpose (for example, charitable, educational, and religious organizations and hospitals). 7. *Close corporations*—Corporations owned by a family or a relatively small number of individuals. Transfer of shares is usually restricted, and the corporation cannot make a public offering of its securities.

Chapter Summary: Corporate Formation, Financing, and Termination—Continued

Corporate Nature and Classification—Continued	8. *S corporations*—Small domestic corporations (with no more than one hundred shareholders) that, under Subchapter S of the Internal Revenue Code, are given special tax treatment. These corporations allow shareholders to enjoy the limited legal liability of the corporate form but avoid its double-taxation feature. 9. *Professional corporations*—Corporations formed by professionals (for example, physicians and lawyers) to obtain the benefits of incorporation (such as limited liability). In most situations, the professional corporation is treated like other corporations, but sometimes the courts will disregard the corporate form and treat the shareholders as partners.
Corporate Formation and Powers (See pages 466–471.)	1. *Promotional activities*—Preliminary promotional activities are rarely if ever taken today. A person who enters contracts with investors and others on behalf of the future corporation is personally liable on all preincorporation contracts. Liability remains until the corporation is formed and assumes the contract by novation. 2. *Incorporation procedures*—Exact procedures for incorporation differ among states, but the basic steps are as follows: (a) select a state of incorporation, (b) secure the corporate name by confirming its availability, (c) prepare the articles of incorporation, and (d) file the articles of incorporation with the secretary of state accompanied by payment of the specified fees. 3. *The first organizational meeting*—A meeting is held after incorporation. The usual purpose of this meeting is to adopt the bylaws, or internal rules of the corporation, but other business, such as election of the board of directors, may also take place. 4. *Improper incorporation*—If a corporation has been improperly incorporated, the courts will sometimes impute corporate status to the firm by holding that it is a *de jure* corporation (cannot be challenged by the state or third parties) or a *de facto* corporation (can be challenged by the state but not by third parties). If a firm is neither a *de jure* nor a *de facto* corporation but represents itself to be a corporation and is sued as such by a third party, it may be held to be a corporation by estoppel. 5. *Express powers*—The express powers of a corporation are granted by the following laws and documents (listed according to their priority): federal constitution, state constitutions, state statutes, articles of incorporation, bylaws, and resolutions of the board of directors. 6. *Implied powers*—Barring express constitutional, statutory, or other prohibitions, the corporation has the implied power to do all acts reasonably appropriate and necessary to accomplish its corporate purposes. 7. *Ultra vires doctrine*—Any act of a corporation that is beyond its express or implied powers to undertake is an *ultra vires* act and may lead to a lawsuit by the shareholders, corporation, or state attorney general to enjoin or recover damages for the *ultra vires* acts. 8. *Piercing the corporate veil*—To avoid injustice, courts may pierce the corporate veil and hold a shareholder or shareholders personally liable for a judgment against the corporation. This usually occurs only when the corporation was established to circumvent the law, when the corporate form is used for an illegitimate or fraudulent purpose, or when the controlling shareholder commingles his or her own interests with those of the corporation to such an extent that the corporation no longer has a separate identity.
Corporate Financing (See pages 471–473.)	1. *Bonds*—Corporate bonds are securities representing *corporate debt*—funds borrowed by a corporation. 2. *Stocks*—Stocks are equity securities issued by a corporation that represent the purchase of ownership in the business firm. Exhibit 24–1 on page 472 describes how stocks differ from bonds, and Exhibit 24–2 on page 473 describes the various types of stocks issued by corporations, including the two main types—common stock and preferred stock.
Mergers and Acquisitions (See pages 473–476.)	1. *Merger*—The legal combination of two or more corporations, with the result that the surviving corporation acquires all the assets and obligations of the other corporation, which then ceases to exist. 2. *Consolidation*—The legal combination of two or more corporations, with the result that each corporation ceases to exist and a new one emerges. The new corporation assumes all the assets and obligations of the former corporations. 3. *Share exchange*—Some or all of the shares of one corporation are exchanged for some or all of the shares of another corporation, but both corporations continue to exist.

Continued

Chapter Summary: Corporate Formation, Financing, and Termination—Continued

Mergers and Acquisitions—Continued	4. *Procedures*—Determined by state statutes. The basic requirements are listed on page 474. 5. *Short-form merger*—Possible when the parent corporation owns at least 90 percent of the outstanding shares of each class of stock of the subsidiary corporation. Shareholder approval is not required. The merger need be approved only by the board of directors of the parent corporation. 6. *Appraisal rights*—Rights of dissenting shareholders (given by state statute) to receive the *fair value* for their shares when a merger or consolidation takes place. 7. *Purchase of assets*—Occurs when one corporation acquires all or substantially all of the assets of another corporation. a. *Acquiring corporation*—The acquiring (purchasing) corporation is not required to obtain shareholder approval; the corporation is merely increasing its assets, and no fundamental business change occurs. b. *Acquired corporation*—The acquired (purchased) corporation is required to obtain the approval of both its directors and its shareholders for the sale of its assets, because the sale will substantially change the corporation's business position. 8. *Purchase of stock*— A purchase of stock occurs when one corporation acquires a substantial number of the voting shares of the stock of another (target) corporation. 9. *Tender offer*—A public offer to all shareholders of the target corporation to purchase its stock at a price that generally is higher than the market price of the target stock prior to the announcement of the tender offer. Federal and state securities laws strictly control the terms, duration, and circumstances under which most tender offers are made.
Termination (See page 477.)	The termination of a corporation involves the following two phases: 1. *Dissolution*—The legal death of the artificial "person" of the corporation. Dissolution can be brought about voluntarily by the directors and shareholders or involuntarily by the state or through a court order. 2. *Winding up (liquidation)*—The process by which corporate assets are converted into cash and distributed to creditors and shareholders according to specified rules of preference. May be supervised by members of the board of directors (when dissolution is voluntary) or by a receiver appointed by the court to wind up corporate affairs.

ExamPrep

ISSUE SPOTTERS

—Check your answers to these questions against the answers provided in Appendix G.

1 Name Brand, Inc., is a small business. Twelve members of a single family own all of its stock. Ordinarily, corporate income is taxed at the corporate and shareholder levels. How can Name Brand avoid this double taxation of income?

2 The incorporators of Precision Systems, Inc., want their new firm to have the authority to transact virtually all types of business. Can they grant this authority to their firm? Why or why not?

BEFORE THE TEST

Go to **www.cengagebrain.com**, enter the ISBN 9781111530624, and click on "Find" to locate this textbook's Web site. Then, click on "Access Now" under "Study Tools," and select Chapter 24 at the top. There, you will find an Interactive Quiz that you can take to assess your mastery of the concepts in this chapter, as well as Flashcards and a Glossary of important terms.

For Review

1 What steps are involved in bringing a corporation into existence?

2 In what circumstances might a court disregard the corporate entity (pierce the corporate veil) and hold the shareholders personally liable?

3 How are corporations financed?

4 What are the steps of a merger, a consolidation, or a share exchange procedure?
5 What are the two ways in which a corporation can be voluntarily dissolved?

Questions and Case Problems

24–1 Preincorporation. Cummings, Okawa, and Taft are recent college graduates who want to form a corporation to manufacture and sell personal computers. Peterson tells them he will set in motion the formation of their corporation. First, Peterson makes a contract with Owens for the purchase of a piece of land for $20,000. Owens does not know of the prospective corporate formation at the time the contract is signed. Second, Peterson makes a contract with Babcock to build a small plant on the property being purchased. Babcock's contract is conditional on the corporation's formation. Peterson secures all necessary subscription agreements and capitalization, and he files the articles of incorporation. Discuss whether the newly formed corporation, Peterson, or both are liable on the contracts with Owens and Babcock. Is the corporation automatically liable to Babcock on formation? Explain.

24–2 *Ultra Vires* Doctrine. Oya Paka and two business associates formed a corporation called Paka Corp. for the purpose of selling computer services. Oya, who owned 50 percent of the corporate shares, served as the corporation's president. Oya wished to obtain a personal loan from her bank for $250,000, but the bank required the note to be cosigned by a third party. Oya cosigned the note in the name of the corporation. Later, Oya defaulted on the note, and the bank sued the corporation for payment. The corporation asserted, as a defense, that Oya had exceeded her authority when she cosigned the note on behalf of the corporation. Had she? Explain.

24–3 Incorporation. Jonathan, Gary, and Ricardo are active members of a partnership called Swim City. The partnership manufactures, sells, and installs outdoor swimming pools in the states of Arkansas and Texas. The partners want to continue to be active in management and to expand the business into other states as well. They are also concerned about rather large recent judgments entered against swimming pool companies throughout the United States. Based on these facts only, discuss whether the partnership should incorporate.

24–4 Involuntary Dissolution. Charles Brooks began working as an independent supplier for Georgia-Pacific, LLC, when the paper products manufacturer acquired a mill in Crossett, Arkansas. Brooks soon organized Charles Brooks Co. in corporate form. Each of the parties' contracts provided, "there is absolutely no guarantee as to the amount of work to be performed." Charles Brooks Co. borrowed funds to buy new equipment. When Georgia-Pacific reduced the quantity of timber that it bought from the supplier, the firm was unable to pay its loans. In 2002, some of the new equipment was returned to the seller. The rest was sold, but the proceeds were not enough to eliminate the debt. The same year, the Arkansas secretary of state revoked Charles Brooks Co.'s corporate status for nonpayment of franchise taxes. In 2006, Charles Brooks Co. filed a suit in a federal district court against Georgia-Pacific, alleging breach of contract. Can the plaintiff maintain this suit? Explain. [*Charles Brooks Co. v. Georgia-Pacific, LLC,* 552 F.3d 718 (8th Cir. 2009)]

24–5 Case Problem with Sample Answer Tony Smith was the sole owner of Smith Services, Inc. Bear, Inc., operated Laker Express, a fueling station in London, Kentucky. Smith charged fuel to an account at Laker Express and owed approximately $35,000. There was no written agreement regarding who was liable in the event of default, but all invoices had been issued to Smith Services. Even though Smith Services ceased doing business and was dissolved, Smith continued his business as a sole proprietor after the corporate form had been abandoned. Laker Express sued Smith Services to collect on the debt, but there were no assets in the corporation. Laker Express sued Tony Smith personally and asked the court to pierce the corporate veil, claiming that Smith was engaged in fraud and was using the corporate form only to protect himself. The trial court dismissed the case, and Laker Express appealed. Should the court pierce the corporate veil and hold Smith personally liable for the unpaid corporate debt? Or should Laker Express have been more careful when dealing with clients? Explain. [*Bear, Inc. v. Smith,* 303 S.W.3d 137 (Ky.App. 2010)]

—For a sample answer to Problem 24–5, go to Appendix F at the end of this text.

24–6 Purchase of Assets. Grand Adventures Tour & Travel Publishing Corp. (GATT), a Texas corporation, provided travel services to *interliners* (airline employees). Duane Boyd was a GATT director when the firm hired him as an unpaid consultant to address its financial problems. Consequently, Boyd resigned his directorship and made loans to GATT for security interests in its assets. GATT defaulted on the loans. Boyd incorporated Interline Travel & Tour, Inc., and transferred all rights under his loans to GATT to Interline. At a public sale, Interline bought GATT's assets. Interline moved into GATT's office building, began to provide travel services to GATT's customers, and hired former GATT employees. Another GATT creditor, Call Center Technologies, Inc., filed a complaint in a federal district court to collect the unpaid amount on a contract with GATT from Interline. Is Interline liable? Why or why not? [*Call Center Technologies, Inc. v. Grand Adventures Tour & Travel Publishing Corp.,* 635 F.3d 48 (2d Cir. 2011)]

24–7 Close Corporations. Mark Burnett and Kamran Pourgol were the only shareholders in a corporation that built and sold a house in North Hempstead, New York. The town revoked the certificate of occupancy on the ground that the house exceeded the amount of square footage allowed by the building permit. The corporation agreed with the buyers to pay a certain amount to renovate the house to conform with the permit and to obtain a new certificate of occupancy. Burnett, however, bought the house and then filed a suit in a New York state court against Pourgol. Burnett charged that Pourgol had submitted incorrect plans to the town without Burnett's knowledge, had assumed responsibility for the error in square footage in discussions with the buyers, had knowingly misrepresented the extent of the renovations, and had failed to undertake any work to fix the house. Do the charges indicate misconduct? How might this situation have been avoided? Discuss. [*Burnett v. Pourgol,* 83 A.D.3d 756, 921 N.Y.S.2d 280 (2011)]

24–8  **A Question of Ethics** *Topps Co. makes baseball and other cards, including the Pokemon collection, and distributes Bazooka bubble gum and other confections. Arthur Shorin, the son of Joseph Shorin, one of Topps's founders and the inspiration for "Bazooka Joe" (a character in the comic strip wrapped around each piece of gum), worked for Topps for fifty years and had served as its board chair and chief executive officer since 1980. Shorin's son-in-law, Scott Silverstein, served as Topps's president and chief operating officer. When Topps's financial performance began to lag, the board considered selling the company. Michael Eisner (formerly head of Disney Studios) offered to pay $9.75 per share and to retain Topps's management in a merger with his company. Upper Deck Co., Topps's chief competitor in the sports-card business, offered $10.75 per share but did not offer to retain the managers. Topps demanded that Upper Deck not reveal its bid publicly, but Topps publicized the offer, without accurately representing Upper Deck's interest and disparaging its seriousness. Upper Deck asked Topps to allow it to tell its side of events and to make a tender offer to Topps's shareholders. Topps refused and scheduled a shareholder vote on the Eisner offer. Topps's shareholders filed a suit in a Delaware state court against their firm, asking the court to prevent the vote.* [In re Topps Co. Shareholders Litigation, *926 A.2d 58 (Del.Ch. 2007)*]

1. The shareholders contended that Topps's conduct had "tainted the vote." What factors support this contention? How might these factors affect the vote?
2. Why might Topps's board and management be opposed to either of the offers for the company? Is this opposition ethical? Should the court enjoin (prevent) the scheduled vote? Explain.

24–9  **Critical Thinking Legal Question** If you had started a business, under what circumstances would you be willing to give up a substantial percentage of its ownership to obtain venture capital financing?

24–10 **Video Question** To watch this chapter's video, *Corporation or LLC: Which Is Better?* go to **www.cengagebrain.com**. Register the access code that came with your new book or log in to your existing account. Select the link for the "Business Law Digital Video Library Online Access" or "Business Law CourseMate." Click on "Complete Video List," view Video 46, and then answer the following questions:

1. Compare the liability that Anna and Caleb would be exposed to as shareholders/owners of a corporation versus as members of a limited liability company (LLC).
2. How does the taxation of corporations differ from that of LLCs?
3. Given that Anna and Caleb conduct their business (Wizard Internet) over the Internet, can you think of any drawbacks to forming an LLC?
4. If you were in the position of Anna and Caleb, would you choose to create a corporation or an LLC? Why?

Chapter 25

Corporate Directors, Officers, and Shareholders

Learning Objectives

After reading this chapter, you should be able to answer the following questions:

1. What are the duties of corporate directors and officers?
2. What must directors do to avoid liability for honest mistakes of judgment and poor business decisions?
3. What is a voting proxy? What is cumulative voting?
4. If a group of shareholders perceives that the corporation has suffered a wrong and the directors refuse to take action, can the shareholders compel the directors to act? If so, how?
5. From what sources may dividends be paid legally? In what circumstances is a dividend illegal? What happens if a dividend is illegally paid?

The Learning Objectives above are designed to help improve your understanding of the chapter.

(Othermore/Creative Commons)

A corporation is not a "natural" person but a legal fiction. No one individual shareholder or director bears sole responsibility for the corporation and its actions. Rather, a corporation joins together the efforts and resources of a large number of individuals for the purpose of producing greater returns than those persons could have obtained individually.

Sometimes, actions that benefit the corporation as a whole do not coincide with the separate interests of the individuals making up the corporation. In such situations, it is important to know the rights and duties of all participants in the corporate enterprise. This chapter focuses on the rights and duties of directors, officers, and shareholders and the ways in which conflicts among them are resolved.

Roles of Directors and Officers

The board of directors is the ultimate authority in every corporation. Directors have responsibility for all policymaking decisions necessary to the management of all corporate affairs. The board selects and removes the corporate officers, determines the capital structure of the corporation, and declares dividends. Each director has one vote, and customarily the majority rules. The general areas of responsibility of the board of directors are shown in Exhibit 25–1 on the following page.

Directors are sometimes inappropriately characterized as *agents* because they act on behalf of the corporation. No *individual* director, however, can act as an agent to bind the corporation; and as a group, directors collectively control the corporation in a way that no agent is able to control a principal. In addition, although directors occupy positions of trust and control over the corporation, they are not *trustees* because they do not hold title to property for the use and benefit of others.

There are few legal requirements concerning directors' qualifications. Only a handful of states impose minimum age and residency requirements. A director may be a shareholder, but this is not necessary (unless the articles of incorporation or bylaws require ownership interest).

• *Exhibit* **25–1 Directors' Management Responsibilities**

AUTHORIZE MAJOR CORPORATE POLICY DECISIONS	SELECT AND REMOVE CORPORATE OFFICERS AND OTHER MANAGERIAL EMPLOYEES, AND DETERMINE THEIR COMPENSATION	MAKE CORPORATE FINANCIAL DECISIONS
Examples: • Oversee major contract negotiations and management-labor negotiations. • Initiate negotiations on the sale or lease of corporate assets outside the regular course of business. • Decide whether to pursue new product lines or business opportunities.	*Examples:* • Search for and hire corporate executives and determine the elements of their compensation packages, including stock options. • Supervise managerial employees and make decisions regarding their termination.	*Examples:* • Make decisions regarding the issuance of authorized shares and bonds. • Decide when to declare dividends that are to be paid to shareholders.

Election of Directors

Subject to statutory limitations, the number of directors is set forth in the corporation's articles or bylaws. Historically, the minimum number of directors has been three, but today many states permit fewer. Normally, the incorporators appoint the first board of directors at the time the corporation is created. The initial board serves until the first annual shareholders' meeting. Subsequent directors are elected by a majority vote of the shareholders.

A director usually serves for a term of one year—from annual meeting to annual meeting. Most state statutes permit longer and staggered terms. A common practice is to elect one-third of the board members each year for a three-year term. In this way, there is greater management continuity.

REMOVAL OF DIRECTORS A director can be removed *for cause*—that is, for failing to perform a required duty—either as specified in the articles or bylaws or by shareholder action. The board of directors may also have the power to remove a director for cause, subject to shareholder review. In most states, a director cannot be removed without cause unless the shareholders have reserved the right to do so at the time of his or her election.

VACANCIES ON THE BOARD OF DIRECTORS If a director dies or resigns or if a new position is created through amendment of the articles or bylaws, either the shareholders or the board itself can fill the vacant position, depending on state law or the provisions of the bylaws. Note, however, that even when an election appears to be authorized by the bylaws, a court can invalidate it if the directors were attempting to manipulate the election in order to reduce the shareholders' influence.

CASE EXAMPLE 25.1 The bylaws of Liquid Audio, a Delaware corporation, authorized a board of five directors. Two directors on the board were elected each year. Another company offered to buy all of Liquid Audio's stock, but the board of directors rejected this offer. An election was coming up, and the directors feared that the shareholders would elect new directors who would allow the sale. The directors, therefore, amended the bylaws to increase the number of directors to seven, thereby diminishing the shareholders' influence in the vote. The shareholders filed an action challenging the election. The Delaware Supreme Court ruled that the directors' action was illegal because they had attempted to diminish the shareholders' right to vote effectively in an election of directors.[1] •

Compensation of Directors

In the past, corporate directors rarely were compensated, but today they are often paid at least nominal sums and may receive more substantial compensation in large corporations because of the time, work, effort, and especially risk involved. Most states permit the corporate articles or bylaws to authorize compensation for directors. In fact, the Revised Model Business Corporation Act (RMBCA) states that unless the articles or bylaws provide otherwise, the directors may set their own compensation [RMBCA 8.11]. Directors also gain through indirect benefits, such as business contacts and prestige, and other rewards, such as stock options.

In many corporations, directors are also chief corporate officers (president or chief executive officer, for example) and receive compensation in their managerial positions. A director who is also an officer of the corporation is referred to as an **inside director**, whereas a director who does not hold a management position is an **outside director.** Typically, a corporation's board of directors includes both inside and outside directors.

Board of Directors' Meetings

The board of directors conducts business by holding formal meetings with recorded minutes. The dates of regular meetings are usually established in the articles or bylaws or by board resolution, and ordinarily no further notice is required.

1. *MM Companies v. Liquid Audio, Inc.*, 813 A.2d 1118 (Del.Sup. 2003).

Special meetings can be called, with notice sent to all directors. Today, most states allow directors to participate in board of directors' meetings from remote locations via telephone or Web conferencing, provided that all the directors can simultaneously hear one another during the meeting [RMBCA 8.20].

Unless the articles of incorporation or bylaws specify a greater number, a majority of the board of directors normally constitutes a quorum [RMBCA 8.24]. (A **quorum** is the minimum number of members of a body of officials or other group who must be present in order for business to be validly transacted.) Some state statutes specifically allow corporations to set a quorum as less than a majority but not less than one-third of the directors.[2]

Once a quorum is present, the directors transact business and vote on issues affecting the corporation. Each director present at the meeting has one vote.[3] Ordinary matters generally require a simple majority vote. Certain extraordinary issues may require a greater-than-majority vote.

Rights of Directors

A corporate director must have certain rights to function properly in that position and make informed policy decisions for the company. The *right to participation* means that directors are entitled to participate in all board of directors' meetings and have a right to be notified of these meetings. Because the dates of regular board meetings are usually specified in the bylaws, as noted earlier, no notice of these meetings is required. If special meetings are called, however, notice is required unless waived by the director.

A director also has the *right of inspection,* which means that each director can access the corporation's books and records, facilities, and premises. Inspection rights are essential for directors to make informed decisions and to exercise the necessary supervision over corporate officers and employees. This right of inspection is almost absolute and cannot be restricted (by the articles, bylaws, or any act of the board).

When a director becomes involved in litigation by virtue of her or his position or actions, the director may also have a right to indemnification (reimbursement) for legal costs, fees, and damages incurred. Most states allow corporations to indemnify and purchase liability insurance for corporate directors [RMBCA 8.51].

Committees of the Board of Directors

When a board of directors has a large number of members and must deal with myriad complex business issues, meetings can become unwieldy. Therefore, the boards of large, publicly held corporations typically create committees, appoint directors to serve on individual committees, and delegate certain tasks to these committees. Committees focus on individual subjects and increase the efficiency of the board. The most common types of committees include the following:

1. *Executive committee.* The board members often elect an executive committee to handle interim management decisions between board meetings. The committee is limited to making decisions about ordinary business matters and conducting preliminary investigations into proposals. It cannot declare dividends, authorize the issuance of shares, amend the bylaws, or initiate any actions that require shareholder approval.
2. *Audit committee.* The audit committee is responsible for the selection, compensation, and oversight of the independent public accountants that audit the corporation's financial records. The Sarbanes-Oxley Act of 2002 requires all publicly held corporations to have an audit committee (as will be discussed in Chapters 26 and 30).
3. *Nominating committee.* This committee chooses the candidates for the board of directors that management wishes to submit to the shareholders in the next election. The committee can nominate but cannot select directors to fill vacancies on the board [RMBCA 8.25].
4. *Compensation committee.* The compensation committee reviews and decides the salaries, bonuses, stock options, and other benefits that are given to the corporation's top executives. The committee may also determine the compensation of directors.
5. *Litigation committee.* This committee decides whether the corporation should pursue requests by shareholders to file a lawsuit against some party that has allegedly harmed the corporation. The committee members investigate the allegations and weigh the costs and benefits of litigation.

In addition to appointing committees, the board of directors can also delegate some of its functions to corporate officers. In doing so, the board is not relieved of its overall responsibility for directing the affairs of the corporation. Instead, corporate officers and managerial personnel are empowered to make decisions relating to ordinary, daily corporate activities within well-defined guidelines.

Corporate Officers and Executives

Corporate officers and other executive employees are hired by the board of directors. At a minimum, most corporations have a president, one or more vice presidents, a secretary, and a treasurer. In most states, an individual can hold more than one office, such as president and secretary, and can be both an officer and a director of the corporation. In addition to carrying out the duties articulated in the bylaws, corporate and

2. See, for example, Delaware Code Annotated Title 8, Section 141(b); and New York Business Corporation Law Section 707.
3. Except in Louisiana, which allows a director to authorize another person to cast a vote in his or her place under certain circumstances.

managerial officers act as agents of the corporation, and the ordinary rules of agency (discussed in Chapter 21) normally apply to their employment.

Corporate officers and other high-level managers are employees of the company, so their rights are defined by employment contracts. The board of directors normally can remove corporate officers at any time with or without cause and regardless of the terms of the employment contracts—although in so doing, the corporation may be liable for breach of contract.

The duties of corporate officers and directors are the same because both groups are involved in decision making and are in similar positions of control. We discuss those duties next.

Duties and Liabilities of Directors and Officers

Directors and officers are deemed fiduciaries of the corporation because their relationship with the corporation and its shareholders is one of trust and confidence. As fiduciaries, directors and officers owe ethical—and legal—duties to the corporation and to the shareholders as a whole. These fiduciary duties include the duty of care and the duty of loyalty. (Directors and officers also have a duty not to destroy evidence in the event of a lawsuit involving the corporation.)

Duty of Care

Directors and officers must exercise due care in performing their duties. The standard of *due care* has been variously described in judicial decisions and codified in many state corporation codes. Generally, a director or officer is expected to act in good faith, to exercise the care that an ordinarily prudent person would exercise in similar circumstances, and to act in what he or she considers to be the best interests of the corporation [RMBCA 8.30]. Directors and officers whose failure to exercise due care results in harm to the corporation or its shareholders can be held liable for negligence (unless the *business judgment rule* applies, as will be discussed shortly).

DUTY TO MAKE INFORMED AND REASONABLE DECISIONS Directors and officers are expected to be informed on corporate matters and to conduct a reasonable investigation of the situation before making a decision. This means that they must do what is necessary to keep adequately informed: attend meetings and presentations, ask for information from those who have it, read reports, and review other written materials. In other words, directors and officers must investigate, study, and discuss matters and evaluate alternatives before making a decision. They cannot decide on the spur of the moment without adequate research.

Although directors and officers are expected to act in accordance with their own knowledge and training, they are also normally entitled to rely on information given to them by certain other persons. Most states and Section 8.30(b) of the RMBCA allow a director to make decisions in reliance on information furnished by competent officers or employees, professionals such as attorneys and accountants, and committees of the board of directors (on which the director does not serve). The reliance must be in good faith, of course, to insulate a director from liability if the information later proves to be inaccurate or unreliable.

DUTY TO EXERCISE REASONABLE SUPERVISION Directors are also expected to exercise a reasonable amount of supervision when they delegate work to corporate officers and employees. **EXAMPLE 25.2** Dale, a corporate bank director, fails to attend any board of directors' meetings for five years. In addition, Dale never inspects any of the corporate books or records and generally fails to supervise the efforts of the bank president and the loan committee. Meanwhile, Brennan, the bank president, who is a corporate officer, makes various improper loans and permits large overdrafts. In this situation, Dale (the corporate director) can be held liable to the corporation for losses resulting from the unsupervised actions of the bank president and the loan committee. •

DISSENTING DIRECTORS Directors are expected to attend board of directors' meetings, and their votes should be entered into the minutes of the meetings. Sometimes, an individual director disagrees with the majority's vote (which becomes an act of the board of directors). Unless a dissent is entered, the director is presumed to have assented. If a decision later leads to the directors being held liable for mismanagement, dissenting directors are rarely held individually liable to the corporation. For this reason, a director who is absent from a given meeting sometimes registers a dissent with the secretary of the board regarding actions taken at the meeting.

The Business Judgment Rule

Directors and officers are expected to exercise due care and to use their best judgment in guiding corporate management, but they are not insurers of business success. Under the **business judgment rule,** a corporate director or officer will not be liable to the corporation or to its shareholders for honest mistakes of judgment and bad business decisions.

Courts give significant deference to the decisions of corporate directors and officers, and consider the reasonableness of a decision at the time it was made, without the benefit of hindsight.

Thus, corporate decision makers are not subjected to second-guessing by shareholders or others in the corporation. The business judgment rule will apply as long as the director or officer:

1. Took reasonable steps to become informed about the matter.
2. Had a rational basis for his or her decision.
3. Did not have a conflict of interest between his or her personal interest and that of the corporation.

In fact, unless there is evidence of bad faith, fraud, or a clear breach of fiduciary duties, most courts will apply the rule and protect directors and officers who make bad business decisions from liability for those choices. Consequently, if there is a reasonable basis for a business decision, a court is unlikely to interfere with that decision, even if the corporation suffers as a result. Note also that as a practical matter, corporate officers face liability more often than directors under this rule because they work at the corporation every day, whereas directors meet once a month or even less frequently.

Does the business judgment rule protect directors and officers from liability for all mistakes in judgment and bad decisions, except those that constitute gross negligence? Gross negligence is more than a mere failure to exercise ordinary care—it is an intentional failure to perform a duty in reckless disregard of the consequences. In the following case, the defendant argued that without a finding of gross negligence, the business judgment rule should apply.

Case 25.1 Henrichs v. Chugach Alaska Corp.

Supreme Court of Alaska, 250 P.3d 531 (2011).
government.westlaw.com/akcases[a]

FACTS The board of Chugach Alaska Corporation (CAC, a corporation of Alaska Natives) split into two factions–one led by Sheri Buretta, who had chaired the board for several years, and the other by director Robert Henrichs. A coalition of directors voted to remove Buretta and install Henrichs as the board's chair. During his term, Henrichs held mini-board meetings and made decisions with only his supporters present. He refused to comply with bylaws that required a special meeting of shareholders in response to a shareholder petition. In addition, he acted without board discussion or approval and ignored board rules in the conduct of meetings. He also personally mistreated directors, shareholders, and employees, as well as retaliated against directors who challenged his decisions by excluding them from the board and spending corporate funds to file meritless complaints against them with state authorities. After six months, the board voted to reinstall Buretta. CAC filed a suit in an Alaska state court against Henrichs, alleging a breach of fiduciary duty. A jury found Henrichs liable, and the court banned him from serving on CAC's board for five years. Henrichs appealed, claiming under the business judgment rule, he could not be found liable unless he had been "grossly negligent."

a. In the left column, in the "Search" section, click on "By Word." On the next page, in the "Search for:" box, type "Henrichs." In the result, click on the name of the case to view the opinion. The Alaska State Court Law Library maintains this Web site.

ISSUE Does the business judgment rule protect Henrichs who acted in breach of his fiduciary duties?

DECISION No. The Alaska Supreme Court affirmed the lower court's decision. The business judgment rule did not protect Henrichs. A director or officer can be held liable for a breach of fiduciary duty without a finding of gross negligence.

REASON Henrichs contended that, under the business judgment rule, he could not be found liable unless he had been grossly negligent. The court agreed that the business judgment rule affords some protection for corporate directors, but added, "We have never measured the degree of protection afforded by the business judgment rule in terms of gross negligence." If there is evidence of bad faith, breach of a fiduciary duty, or acts in violation of public policy, the rule will not protect a director who makes bad business decisions from liability for those choices. The jury and the lower court had found that Henrichs committed a breach of fiduciary duty. The conduct was "volitional"–that is, Henrichs chose to act as he did and knew that his actions exceeded the rules. The misconduct was serious and egregious (outstandingly bad). In light of these findings, the business judgment rule did not protect Henrichs.

FOR CRITICAL ANALYSIS—Ethical Consideration *Does misbehavior such as the conduct at the heart of this case constitute a breach of business ethics? Discuss.*

Duty of Loyalty

Loyalty can be defined as faithfulness to one's obligations and duties. In the corporate context, the duty of loyalty requires directors and officers to subordinate their personal interests to the welfare of the corporation. Directors cannot use corporate funds or confidential corporate information for personal advantage and must refrain from self-dealing.

For instance, a director should not oppose a tender offer (see Chapter 24) that is in the corporation's best interest simply because its acceptance may cost the director her or his position. Cases dealing with the duty of loyalty typically involve one or more of the following:

1. Competing with the corporation.
2. Usurping (taking advantage of) a corporate opportunity.
3. Having an interest that conflicts with the interest of the corporation.
4. Engaging in *insider trading* (using information that is not public to make a profit trading securities).
5. Authorizing a corporate transaction that is detrimental to minority shareholders.
6. Selling control over the corporation.

The following classic case illustrates the conflict that can arise between a corporate official's personal interest and his or her duty of loyalty.

***Classic* Case 25.2** **Guth v. Loft, Inc.**

Supreme Court of Delaware, 23 Del.Ch. 255, 5 A.2d 503 (1939).

FACTS In the 1920s, Loft Candy Company was a publicly held company with a $13 million candy-and-restaurant chain. At the time Charles Guth became Loft's president in 1930, Guth and his family owned Grace Company, which made syrups for soft drinks in a plant in Baltimore, Maryland. Coca-Cola Company supplied Loft with cola syrup. Unhappy with what he felt was Coca-Cola's high price, Guth entered into an agreement with Roy Megargel to acquire the trademark and formula for Pepsi-Cola and form Pepsi-Cola Corporation. Neither Guth nor Megargel could finance the new venture, however, and Grace Company was insolvent. Without the knowledge of Loft's board of directors, Guth used Loft's capital, credit, facilities, and employees to further the Pepsi enterprise. At Guth's direction, a Loft employee made the concentrate for the syrup, which was sent to Grace Company to add sugar and water. Loft charged Grace Company for the concentrate but allowed forty months' credit. Grace charged Pepsi for the syrup but also granted substantial credit. Grace sold the syrup to Pepsi's customers, including Loft, which paid on delivery or within thirty days. Loft also paid for Pepsi's advertising. Finally, losing profits at its stores as a result of switching from Coca-Cola, Loft filed a suit in a Delaware state court against Guth, Grace, and Pepsi, seeking their Pepsi stock and an accounting. The court entered a judgment in the plaintiff's favor. The defendants appealed to the Delaware Supreme Court.

ISSUE Did Guth violate his duty of loyalty to Loft, Inc., by acquiring the Pepsi-Cola trademark and formula for himself without the knowledge of Loft's board of directors?

DECISION Yes. The Delaware Supreme Court upheld the judgment of the lower court. The state supreme court was "convinced that the opportunity to acquire the Pepsi-Cola trademark and formula, goodwill and business belonged to [Loft], and that Guth, as its president, had no right to appropriate the opportunity to himself."

REASON The court pointed out that the officers and directors of a corporation stand in a fiduciary relation to that corporation and to its shareholders. Corporate officers and directors must protect the corporation's interest at all times. They must also "refrain from doing anything that works injury to the corporation." In other words, corporate officers and directors must provide undivided and unselfish loyalty to the corporation, and "there should be no conflict between duty and self-interest." Whenever an opportunity is presented to the corporation, officers and directors with knowledge of that opportunity cannot seize it for themselves. "The corporation may elect to claim all of the benefits of the transaction for itself, and the law will impress a trust in favor of the corporation upon the property, interest, and profits required." Guth clearly created a conflict between his self-interest and his duty to Loft—the corporation for which he was president and director. Guth illegally appropriated the Pepsi-Cola opportunity for himself and thereby placed himself in a competitive position with the company for which he worked.

WHAT IF THE FACTS WERE DIFFERENT? *Suppose that Loft's board of directors had approved Pepsi-Cola's use of its personnel and equipment. Would the court's decision have been different? Discuss.*

IMPACT OF THIS CASE ON TODAY'S LAW *This early Delaware decision was one of the first to set forth a test for determining when a corporate officer or director has breached the duty of loyalty. The test has two basic parts—whether the opportunity was reasonably related to the corporation's line of business, and whether the corporation was financially able to undertake the opportunity. The court also considered whether the corporation had an interest or expectancy in the opportunity and recognized that when the corporation had "no interest or expectancy, the officer or director is entitled to treat the opportunity as his own."*

Conflicts of Interest

Corporate directors often have many business affiliations, and a director may sit on the board of more than one corporation. Of course, directors are precluded from entering into or supporting businesses that operate in direct competition with corporations on whose boards they serve. Their fiduciary duty requires them to make a full disclosure of any potential conflicts of interest that might arise in any corporate transaction [RMBCA 8.60].

Sometimes, a corporation enters into a contract or engages in a transaction in which an officer or director has a personal interest. The director or officer must make a *full disclosure* of that interest and must abstain from voting on the proposed transaction.

EXAMPLE 25.3 Southwood Corporation needs office space. Lambert Alden, one of its five directors, owns the building adjoining the corporation's main office building. He negotiates a lease with Southwood for the space, making a full disclosure to Southwood and the other four board directors. The lease arrangement is fair and reasonable, and it is unanimously approved by the other four directors. In this situation, Alden has not breached his duty of loyalty to the corporation, and thus the contract is valid. If it were otherwise, directors would be prevented from ever transacting business with the corporations they serve. •

Liability of Directors and Officers

Directors and officers are exposed to liability on many fronts. Corporate directors and officers may be held liable for the crimes and torts committed by themselves or by corporate employees under their supervision, as discussed in Chapter 6 and Chapter 21, respectively. Additionally, if shareholders perceive that the corporate directors are not acting in the best interests of the corporation, they may sue the directors, in what is called a *shareholder's derivative suit,* on behalf of the corporation. (This type of action is discussed on page 494 in the context of shareholders' rights.) Directors and officers also can be held personally liable under a number of statutes, such as statutes enacted to protect consumers or the environment.

Roles of Shareholders

The acquisition of a share of stock makes a person an owner and shareholder in a corporation. Shareholders thus own the corporation. Although they have no legal title to corporate property, such as buildings and equipment, they do have an equitable (ownership) interest in the firm.

As a general rule, shareholders have no responsibility for the daily management of the corporation, even if they are ultimately responsible for choosing the board of directors, which does have such control. Ordinarily, corporate officers and directors owe no duty to individual shareholders unless some contract or special relationship exists between them in addition to the corporate relationship. Their duty is to act in the best interests of the corporation and its shareholder-owners as a whole. In turn, as you will read on pages 495 and 496, controlling shareholders owe a fiduciary duty to minority shareholders. Normally, there is no legal relationship between shareholders and creditors of the corporation. Shareholders can be creditors of the corporation, though, and they have the same rights of recovery against the corporation as any other creditor.

In this section, we look at the powers and voting rights of shareholders, which are generally established in the articles of incorporation and by the state's general corporation law.

Shareholders' Powers

Shareholders must approve fundamental changes affecting the corporation before the changes can be implemented. Hence, shareholders are empowered to amend the articles of incorporation (charter) and bylaws, approve a merger or the dissolution of the corporation, and approve the sale of all or substantially all of the corporation's assets. Some of these powers are subject to prior board approval.

Members of the board of directors are elected and removed by a vote of the shareholders. The first board of directors is either named in the articles of incorporation or chosen by the incorporators to serve until the first shareholders' meeting. From that time on, the selection and retention of directors are exclusively shareholder functions.

Directors usually serve their full terms. If the shareholders judge them unsatisfactory, they are simply not reelected. Shareholders have the inherent power, however, to remove a director from office for cause (such as for breach of duty or misconduct) by a majority vote.[4] As mentioned earlier, some state statutes (and some corporate articles) permit removal of directors without cause by the vote of a majority of the holders of outstanding shares entitled to vote.

Shareholders' Meetings

Shareholders' meetings must occur at least annually. In addition, special meetings can be called to deal with urgent matters.

NOTICE OF MEETINGS A corporation must notify its shareholders of the date, time, and place of an annual or special shareholders' meeting at least ten days, but not more than sixty days, before the meeting date [RMBCA 7.05].[5] Notice of a special meeting must include a statement of the purpose of the meeting, and business transacted at the meeting is limited to that purpose.

PROXIES It is usually not practical for owners of only a few shares of stock of publicly traded corporations to attend shareholders' meetings. Therefore, the law allows stockholders to either vote in person or appoint another person as their agent to vote their shares at the meeting. The signed appointment

4. A director can often demand court review of removal for cause.

5. A shareholder can waive the requirement of written notice by signing a waiver form. In some states, a shareholder who does not receive written notice, but who learns of the meeting and attends without protesting the lack of notice, is said to have waived notice by such conduct. State statutes and corporate bylaws typically set forth the time within which notice must be sent, what methods can be used, and what the notice must contain.

form or electronic transmission authorizing an agent to vote the shares is called a **proxy** (from the Latin *procurare,* meaning "to manage, take care of").

Management often solicits proxies, but any person can solicit proxies to concentrate voting power. Proxies have been used by a group of shareholders as a device for taking over a corporation (corporate takeovers were discussed in Chapter 24). Proxies normally are revocable—that is, they can be withdrawn—unless they are specifically designated as irrevocable. Under RMBCA 7.22(c), proxies last for eleven months, unless the proxy agreement provides for a longer period.

PROXY MATERIALS AND SHAREHOLDER PROPOSALS When shareholders want to change a company policy, they can put their idea up for a shareholder vote. They can do this by submitting a shareholder proposal to the board of directors and asking the board to include the proposal in the proxy materials that are sent to all shareholders before meetings.

The Securities and Exchange Commission (SEC), which regulates the purchase and sale of securities (see Chapter 26), has special provisions relating to proxies and shareholder proposals. SEC Rule 14a-8 provides that all shareholders who own stock worth at least $1,000 are eligible to submit proposals for inclusion in corporate proxy materials. The corporation is required to include information on whatever proposals will be considered at the shareholders' meeting along with proxy materials. Only those proposals that relate to significant policy considerations rather than ordinary business operations must be included.

For a discussion of how the SEC is adapting its rules regarding proxies to take advantage of today's communications technology, see this chapter's *Adapting the Law to the Online Environment* feature on the facing page.

Shareholder Voting

Shareholders exercise ownership control through the power of their votes. Corporate business matters are presented in the form of *resolutions,* which shareholders vote to approve or disapprove. Each common shareholder is entitled to one vote per share, although the voting techniques to be discussed shortly all enhance the power of the shareholder's vote. The articles of incorporation can exclude or limit voting rights, particularly for certain classes of shares. For example, owners of preferred shares are usually denied the right to vote [RMBCA 7.21]. If a state statute requires specific voting procedures, the corporation's articles or bylaws must be consistent with the statute.

QUORUM REQUIREMENTS For shareholders to conduct business at a meeting, a quorum must be present. Generally, a quorum exists when shareholders holding more than 50 percent of the outstanding shares are present. In some states, obtaining the unanimous written consent of shareholders is a permissible alternative to holding a shareholders' meeting [RMBCA 7.25].

Once a quorum is present, voting can proceed. A majority vote of the shares represented at the meeting usually is required to pass resolutions. **EXAMPLE 25.4** Novo Pictures, Inc., has 10,000 outstanding shares of voting stock. Its articles of incorporation set the quorum at 50 percent of outstanding shares and provide that a majority vote of the shares present is necessary to pass resolutions concerning ordinary matters. Therefore, for this firm, a quorum of shareholders representing 5,000 outstanding shares must be present at a shareholders' meeting to conduct business. If exactly 5,000 shares are represented at the meeting, a vote of at least 2,501 of those shares is needed to pass a resolution. If 6,000 shares are represented, a vote of 3,001 is required. •

At times, more than a simple majority vote is required either by a state statute or by the corporate articles. Extraordinary corporate matters, such as a merger, consolidation, or dissolution of the corporation (see Chapter 24), require a higher percentage of all corporate shares entitled to vote [RMBCA 7.27].

VOTING LISTS The corporation prepares voting lists prior to each meeting of the shareholders. Ordinarily, only persons whose names appear on the corporation's shareholder records as owners are entitled to vote.[6] The voting list contains the name and address of each shareholder as shown on the corporate records on a given cutoff, or record, date. (Under RMBCA 7.07, the record date may be as much as seventy days before the meeting.) The voting list also includes the number of voting shares held by each owner. The list is usually kept at the corporate headquarters and is available for shareholder inspection [RMBCA 7.20].

CUMULATIVE VOTING Most states permit, and some require, shareholders to elect directors by *cumulative voting,* which is a voting method designed to allow minority shareholders to be represented on the board of directors.[7] With cumulative voting, each shareholder is entitled to a total number of votes equal to the number of board members to be elected multiplied by the number of voting shares a shareholder owns. The shareholder can cast all of these votes for one candidate or split them among several nominees for director. All nominees stand for election at the same time. When cumulative voting is not required either by statute or under the articles, the entire board can be elected by a simple majority of shares at a shareholders' meeting.

---

6. When the legal owner is bankrupt, incompetent, deceased, or in some other way under a legal disability, his or her vote can be cast by a person designated by law to control and manage the owner's property.

7. See, for example, California Corporations Code Section 708. Under RMBCA 7.28, however, no cumulative voting rights exist unless the articles of incorporation so provide.

Adapting the Law to the Online Environment

Moving Company Information to the Internet

Anyone who has ever owned shares in a public company knows that such companies often are required to distribute voluminous documents relating to proxies to all shareholders. Traditionally, large packets of paper documents were sent to shareholders, but in 2007 the Securities and Exchange Commission (SEC) permitted publicly held companies to voluntarily distribute electronic proxy (e-proxy) materials. In 2009, the SEC's e-proxy rules became mandatory. Now, all public companies must post their proxy materials on the Internet, although they may still choose among several options–including paper documents sent by mail–for actually delivering the materials to shareholders.[a]

Notice and Access: E-Proxy Rules

Companies that want to distribute proxy materials only via the Internet can choose the notice and access delivery option. Under this model, the corporation posts the proxy materials on a Web site and notifies the shareholders that the proxy materials are available online.

The notice and access model involves the following steps:

1. The company posts the proxy materials on its publicly accessible Web site.
2. Subsequently, the company sends a (paper) notice to each shareholder at least forty calendar days before the date of the shareholders' meeting for which the proxy is being solicited.
3. No other materials can be sent along with the initial notice (unless the proxy is being combined with the meeting notice required by state law).
4. The notice must be written in plain English, and it must include a prominent statement of the following: the date, time, and location of the shareholders' meeting; the specific Web site at which shareholders can access the proxy materials; an explanation of how they can obtain paper copies of the proxy materials at no cost; and a clear and impartial description of each matter to be considered at the shareholders' meeting.
5. Next, the company must wait at least ten days before sending a "paper" proxy card to the shareholders. This ten-day waiting period provides shareholders with sufficient time to access the proxy materials online or to request paper copies.
6. If a shareholder requests paper proxy materials, the company must send them within three business days.
7. After receiving the initial paper notice, a shareholder can permanently elect to receive all future proxy materials on paper or by e-mail.

Other Delivery Options

Rather than using notice and access delivery, public companies can choose to deliver the full set of proxy materials to the shareholders in paper or electronic form, such as on a CD or DVD. They can also use a blend of these two options, as long as they also post the materials on a Web site. Many corporations choose one option for certain shareholders and another option for other shareholders, depending on the number of shares owned or whether the shareholders are domestic or foreign. The shareholder can always choose to receive paper documents rather than accessing materials online.

Some corporate executives want the SEC to go even further and allow corporations to disseminate important information to the public via CEO blogs. Thus far, however, the SEC has not allowed companies to distribute proxy materials (or disclose material information to the public as required before issuing shares–see Chapter 26) via blogs.

FOR CRITICAL ANALYSIS

Why might a company or other party choose to solicit proxies the old-fashioned way–by providing paper documents instead of Internet access–despite the added costs?

a. 17 C.F.R. Parts 240, 249, and 274.

Cumulative voting can best be understood through an example. **EXAMPLE 25.5** A corporation has 10,000 shares issued and outstanding. The minority shareholders hold 3,000 shares, and the majority shareholders hold the other 7,000 shares. Three members of the board are to be elected. The majority shareholders' nominees are Acevedo, Barkley, and Craycik. The minority shareholders' nominee is Drake. Can Drake be elected by the minority shareholders?

If cumulative voting is allowed, the answer is yes. Together, the minority shareholders have 9,000 votes (the number of directors to be elected times the number of shares held by the minority shareholders equals 3 times 3,000, which equals 9,000 votes). All of these votes can be cast to elect Drake. The majority shareholders have 21,000 votes (3 times 7,000 equals 21,000 votes), but these votes have to be distributed among their three nominees. The principle of cumulative voting is that no matter how the majority shareholders cast their 21,000 votes, they will not be able to elect all three directors if the minority shareholders cast all of their 9,000 votes for Drake, as illustrated in Exhibit 25–2 on the following page. •

OTHER VOTING TECHNIQUES Before a shareholders' meeting, a group of shareholders can agree in writing to vote their shares together in a specified manner. Such agreements, called *shareholder voting agreements,* usually are held to be

• *Exhibit* **25–2 Results of Cumulative Voting**

BALLOT	MAJORITY SHAREHOLDERS' VOTES			MINORITY SHAREHOLDERS' VOTES	DIRECTORS ELECTED
	Acevedo	Barkley	Craycik	Drake	
1	10,000	10,000	1,000	9,000	Acevedo/Barkley/Drake
2	9,001	9,000	2,999	9,000	Acevedo/Barkley/Drake
3	6,000	7,000	8,000	9,000	Barkley/Craycik/Drake

valid and enforceable. A shareholder can also appoint a voting agent and vote by proxy.

Although shareholders are free to make voting agreements among themselves and with management, corporate managers must be careful that such agreements do not constitute a breach of their fiduciary duties. Agreements regarding voting must be in the corporation's best interests, or the corporate officers and directors can be sued.

CASE EXAMPLE 25.6 Several shareholders of Cryo-Cell International, Inc., mounted a proxy contest in an effort to replace the board of directors. Another stockholder, Andrew Filipowski, agreed to support management in exchange for being included in management's slate of directors. The company's chief executive officer, Mercedes Walton, secretly promised Filipowski that if management's slate won, the board of directors would add another board seat to be filled by a Filipowski designee. After management won the election, Walton prepared to add Filipowski's designee to the board. When the dissident shareholders challenged the election's results, the court held that the board's actions and Walton's secret agreement constituted serious breaches of fiduciary duty that had tainted the election. The court therefore ordered a new election to be held.[8] •

Rights of Shareholders

Shareholders possess numerous rights. A significant right—the right to vote their shares—has already been discussed. We now look at some additional rights of shareholders.

Stock Certificates

A **stock certificate** is a certificate issued by a corporation that evidences ownership of a specified number of shares in the corporation. In jurisdictions that require the issuance of stock certificates, shareholders have the right to demand that the corporation issue certificates. In most states and under RMBCA 6.26, boards of directors may provide that shares of stock will be uncertificated—that is, no actual, physical stock certificates will be issued. When shares are uncertificated, the corporation may be required to send each shareholder a letter or some other form of notice that contains the same information that would normally appear on the face of stock certificates.

Stock is intangible personal property, and the ownership right exists independently of the certificate itself. If a stock certificate is lost or destroyed, ownership is not destroyed with it. A new certificate can be issued to replace one that has been lost or destroyed. Notice of shareholders' meetings, dividends, and operational and financial reports are all distributed according to the recorded ownership listed in the corporation's books, not on the basis of possession of the certificate.

Preemptive Rights

Sometimes, the articles of incorporation grant preemptive rights to shareholders [RMBCA 6.30]. With **preemptive rights,** a shareholder receives a preference over all other purchasers to subscribe to or purchase a prorated share of a new issue of stock. In other words, a shareholder who is given preemptive rights can purchase the same percentage of the new shares being issued as she or he already holds in the company. This allows each shareholder to maintain her or his proportionate control, voting power, or financial interest in the corporation. Generally, preemptive rights apply only to additional, newly issued stock sold for cash, and the preemptive rights must be exercised within a specified time period, which is usually thirty days.

EXAMPLE 25.7 Tran Corporation authorizes and issues 1,000 shares of stock. Lebow purchases 100 shares, making her the owner of 10 percent of the company's stock. Subsequently, Tran, by vote of its shareholders, authorizes the issuance of another 1,000 shares (by amending the articles of incorporation). This increases its capital stock to a total of 2,000 shares. If preemptive rights have been provided, Lebow can purchase one additional share of the new stock being issued for each share she already owns—or 100 additional shares. Thus, she can own 200 of the 2,000 shares outstanding, and she will maintain her relative position as a shareholder. If preemptive rights are not allowed, her proportionate control and voting power may be diluted from that of a 10 percent shareholder to that of a 5 percent shareholder because of the issuance of the additional 1,000 shares. •

Preemptive rights are most important in close corporations because each shareholder owns a relatively small number of

8. *Portnoy v. Cryo-Cell International, Inc.*, 940 A.2d 43 (Del.Ch. 2008).

shares but controls a substantial interest in the corporation. Without preemptive rights, it would be possible for a shareholder to lose his or her proportionate control over the firm.

Stock Warrants

Stock warrants are rights to buy stock at a stated price by a specified date that are created by the company. Usually, when preemptive rights exist and a corporation is issuing additional shares, it issues its shareholders stock warrants. Warrants are often publicly traded on securities exchanges.

Dividends

As mentioned in Chapter 24, a *dividend* is a distribution of corporate profits or income *ordered by the directors* and paid to the shareholders in proportion to their respective shares in the corporation. Dividends can be paid in cash, property, stock of the corporation that is paying the dividends, or stock of other corporations.[9]

State laws vary, but each state determines the general circumstances and legal requirements under which dividends are paid. State laws also control the sources of revenue to be used; only certain funds are legally available for paying dividends. Depending on state law, dividends may be paid from the following sources:

1. *Retained earnings.* All states allow dividends to be paid from the undistributed net profits earned by the corporation, including capital gains from the sale of fixed assets. As mentioned in Chapter 24, the undistributed net profits are called *retained earnings.*
2. *Net profits.* A few states allow dividends to be issued from current net profits without regard to deficits in prior years.
3. *Surplus.* A number of states allow dividends to be paid out of any kind of surplus.

ILLEGAL DIVIDENDS Sometimes, dividends are improperly paid from an unauthorized account, or their payment causes the corporation to become insolvent. Generally, shareholders must return illegal dividends only if they knew that the dividends were illegal when the payment was received (or if the dividends were paid when the corporation was insolvent). Whenever dividends are illegal or improper, the board of directors can be held personally liable for the amount of the payment.

DIRECTORS' FAILURE TO DECLARE A DIVIDEND When directors fail to declare a dividend, shareholders can ask a court to compel the directors to meet and to declare a dividend. To succeed, the shareholders must show that the directors have acted so unreasonably in withholding the dividend that their conduct is an abuse of their discretion.

Often, a corporation accumulates large cash reserves for a legitimate corporate purpose, such as expansion or research. The mere fact that the firm has sufficient earnings or surplus available to pay a dividend is not enough to compel directors to distribute funds that, in the board's opinion, should not be distributed. The courts are reluctant to interfere with corporate operations and will not compel directors to declare dividends unless abuse of discretion is clearly shown.

Inspection Rights

Shareholders in a corporation enjoy both common law and statutory inspection rights. The RMBCA provides that every shareholder is entitled to examine specified corporate records. The shareholder's right of inspection is limited, however, to the inspection and copying of corporate books and records for a *proper purpose,* provided the request is made in advance. The shareholder can inspect in person, or an attorney, accountant, or other authorized assistant can do so as the shareholder's agent.

The power of inspection is fraught with potential abuses, and the corporation is allowed to protect itself from them. For instance, a shareholder can properly be denied access to corporate records to prevent harassment or to protect trade secrets or other confidential corporate information. Some states require that a shareholder must have held his or her shares for a minimum period of time immediately preceding the demand to inspect or must hold a minimum number of outstanding shares. A shareholder who is denied the right of inspection can seek a court order to compel the inspection.

Transfer of Shares

Corporate stock represents an ownership right in intangible personal property. The law generally recognizes the right to transfer stock to another person unless there are valid restrictions on its transferability. Although stock certificates are negotiable and freely transferable by indorsement and delivery, transfer of stock in closely held corporations usually is restricted. These restrictions must be reasonable and may be set out in the bylaws or in a shareholder agreement. The existence of any restrictions on transferability must always be indicated on the face of the stock certificate.

When shares are transferred, a new entry is made in the corporate stock book to indicate the new owner. Until the corporation is notified and the entry is complete, all rights—including voting rights, the right to notice of shareholders' meetings, and the right to dividend distributions—remain with the current record owner.

9. Technically, dividends paid in stock are not dividends. They maintain each shareholder's proportionate interest in the corporation. On one occasion, a distillery declared and paid a "dividend" in bonded whiskey.

Rights on Dissolution

When a corporation is dissolved and its outstanding debts and the claims of its creditors have been satisfied, the remaining assets are distributed to the shareholders in proportion to the percentage of shares owned by each shareholder. Certain classes of preferred stock can be given priority. If no class of stock has been given preference in the distribution of assets on liquidation, then all of the stockholders share the remaining assets.

As noted in Chapter 24, in some situations, shareholders can petition a court to have the corporation dissolved. The RMBCA permits any shareholder to initiate a dissolution proceeding in any of the following circumstances [RMBCA 14.30]:

1. The directors are deadlocked in the management of corporate affairs. The shareholders are unable to break that deadlock, and irreparable injury to the corporation is being suffered or threatened.
2. The acts of the directors or those in control of the corporation are illegal, oppressive, or fraudulent.
3. Corporate assets are being misapplied or wasted.
4. The shareholders are deadlocked in voting power and have failed, for a specified period (usually two annual meetings), to elect successors to directors whose terms have expired or would have expired with the election of successors.

The Shareholder's Derivative Suit

When the corporation is harmed by the actions of a third party, the directors can bring a lawsuit in the name of the corporation against that party. If the corporate directors fail to bring a lawsuit, shareholders can do so "derivatively" in what is known as a **shareholder's derivative suit.** A shareholder cannot bring a derivative suit until ninety days after making a written demand on the corporation (the board of directors) to take suitable action [RMBCA 7.40]. Only if the directors refuse to take appropriate action can the derivative suit go forward.

The right of shareholders to bring a derivative action is especially important when the wrong suffered by the corporation results from the actions of corporate directors or officers. This is because the directors and officers would probably be unwilling to take any action against themselves. Nevertheless, a court will dismiss a derivative suit if the majority of directors or an independent panel determines in good faith that the lawsuit is not in the best interests of the corporation [RMBCA 7.44].

When shareholders bring a derivative suit, they are not pursuing rights or benefits for themselves personally but are acting as guardians of the corporate entity. Therefore, if the suit is successful, any damages recovered normally go into the corporation's treasury, not to the shareholders personally.[10]

EXAMPLE 25.8 Zeon Corporation is owned by two shareholders, each holding 50 percent of the corporate shares. One of the shareholders wants to sue the other for misusing corporate assets or usurping corporate opportunities. In this situation, the plaintiff-shareholder will have to bring a shareholder's derivative suit (not a suit in his or her own name) because the alleged harm was suffered by Zeon, not by the plaintiff personally. Any damages awarded will go to the corporation, not to the plaintiff-shareholder. •

The following case illustrates some of the hurdles that shareholders must overcome when undertaking a shareholder's derivative suit.

10. The shareholders may be entitled to reimbursement for reasonable expenses involved in the derivative suit, however, including attorneys' fees.

Case 25.3 Bezirdjian v. O'Reilly

Court of Appeal of California, First District, 183 Cal.App.4th 316, 107 Cal.Rptr.3d 384 (2010).
www.courts.ca.gov/1dca.htm[a]

FACTS Lawrence Bezirdjian was a shareholder of Chevron Corporation. In 2007, he filed a shareholder's derivative action against David O'Reilly and other members of Chevron's board of directors. The complaint included claims of breach of fiduciary duties, gross mismanagement, and waste of corporate assets in connection with illicit payments Chevron had allegedly made to Saddam Hussein in exchange for Iraqi oil from 2000 to 2003. In the complaint, Bezirdjian acknowledged that most of his factual allegations were derived from an article published by the *New York Times.* He also claimed that he was excused from making a prefiling demand on the board to institute this action because such a demand would be futile. Specifically, he stated that "the [board] cannot exercise independent objective judgment in deciding whether to bring this action or whether to vigorously prosecute this action because each of its members participated personally in the wrongdoing or are dependent upon other Defendants who did." The trial court stayed the action until Bezirdjian made a prefiling demand to give the board members an opportunity to decide whether to sue on behalf of the corporation. So the board formed a special committee of directors

a. Select "Case Information" in the middle of the page. On the search page, in the box under the heading "Search by Court of Appeal or Trial Court Case Number," enter "A124859." Then click on "Search by Case Number." On the page showing the search results, under "Case Summary," select the PDF for the "Court of Appeal Opinion" to access the case. The California Court of Appeal for the First District maintains this Web site.

Case 25.3—Continued

to consider and respond to this demand. The committee reported that it did not think it was in the best interests of Chevron or its stockholders to pursue the claims in the demand. The board decided not to sue. Subsequently, Bezirdjian submitted an amended shareholder's derivative complaint stating, among other things, that he had "made sufficient effort to get Chevron to bring this action and need do no more." The trial court granted Chevron's motion for judgment on the pleadings and dismissed the action. Bezirdjian appealed.

ISSUE Did Bezirdjian present enough evidence to rebut the presumption that the board of directors' decision not to litigate was made in good faith and thus protected by the business judgment rule?

DECISION No. The California appellate court affirmed the trial court's judgment. Bezirdjian failed to rebut the presumption that the board of directors' decision was made in good faith, and thus he could not go forward with the derivative action.

REASON Chevron was incorporated in Delaware, and therefore, Delaware corporate law applied to this lawsuit. According to that state's law, "The decision to bring a lawsuit or to refrain from litigating a claim on behalf of a corporation is a decision concerning the management of the corporation. Consequently, such decisions are part of the responsibilities of the board of directors." The court went on to apply the business judgment rule to the Chevron board's actions. "Because a conscious decision by a board of directors to refrain from acting may be a valid exercise of business judgment, where demand on a board has been made and refused, courts apply the business judgment rule in reviewing the board's refusal to act pursuant to a stockholder's demand to file a lawsuit." In this case, even though the allegations brought by Bezirdjian with respect to Chevron's alleged payments to Saddam Hussein suggested corporate wrongdoing, Bezirdjian had offered no specific facts that created a reasonable doubt as to the good faith of the board's investigation. He had thus failed to rebut the presumption created by the business judgment rule. In other words, "It was within the Board's power to refuse to undertake this lawsuit if it deemed the litigation would be contrary to the corporation's best interest."

FOR CRITICAL ANALYSIS—Ethical Consideration *Given that a shareholder's derivative suit is brought against the directors and not a party outside the corporation, is it fair to require that the shareholder first demand that the directors undertake the suit? Why or why not?*

Duties and Liabilities of Shareholders

One of the hallmarks of the corporate form of business organization is that shareholders are not personally liable for the debts of the corporation. If the corporation fails, shareholders can lose their investments, but generally that is the limit of their liability.

As discussed in Chapter 24, in certain instances of fraud, undercapitalization, or careless observance of corporate formalities, a court will pierce the corporate veil and hold the shareholders individually liable. These situations are the exception, however, not the rule. A shareholder can also be personally liable in certain other rare instances. One relates to illegal dividends, which were discussed previously. Another relates to *watered stock*. Finally, in certain instances, a majority shareholder who engages in oppressive conduct or attempts to exclude minority shareholders from receiving certain benefits can be held personally liable.

Watered Stock

When a corporation issues shares for less than their fair market value, the shares are referred to as **watered stock.**[11] Usually, the shareholder who receives watered stock must pay the difference to the corporation (the shareholder is personally liable). In some states, the shareholder who receives watered stock may be liable to creditors of the corporation for unpaid corporate debts.

EXAMPLE 25.9 During the formation of a corporation, Gomez, one of the incorporators, transfers his property, Sunset Beach, to the corporation for 10,000 shares of stock. The stock has a specific face value *(par value)* of $100 per share, and thus the total price of the 10,000 shares is $1 million. After the property is transferred and the shares are issued, Sunset Beach is carried on the corporate books at a value of $1 million. On appraisal, it is discovered that the market value of the property at the time of transfer was only $500,000. The shares issued to Gomez are therefore watered stock, and he is liable to the corporation for the difference between the value of the shares and the value of the property. •

Duties of Majority Shareholders

In some instances, a majority shareholder is regarded as having a fiduciary duty to the corporation and to the minority shareholders. This occurs when a single shareholder (or a few shareholders acting in concert) owns a sufficient number of shares to exercise *de facto* (actual) control over the corporation. In these situations, majority shareholders owe a fiduciary duty to the minority shareholders.

When a majority shareholder breaches her or his fiduciary duty to a minority shareholder, the minority shareholder can sue for damages. A breach of fiduciary duties by those who control a closely held corporation normally constitutes what is known as *oppressive conduct*. A common example of a

11. The phrase *watered stock* was originally used to describe cattle that were kept thirsty during a long drive and then were allowed to drink large quantities of water just before their sale. The increased weight of the "watered stock" allowed the seller to reap a higher profit.

breach of fiduciary duty occurs when the majority shareholders "freeze out" the minority shareholders and exclude them from certain benefits of participating in the firm.

CASE EXAMPLE 25.10 Brodie, Jordan, and Barbuto formed a close corporation to operate a machine shop. Each owned one-third of the shares in the company, and all three were directors. Brodie served as the corporate president for twelve years but thereafter met with the other shareholders only a few times a year. After disagreements arose, Brodie asked the company to purchase his shares, but his requests were refused. A few years later, Brodie died, and his wife inherited his shares in the company. Jordan and Barbuto refused to perform a valuation of the company, denied her access to the corporate information she requested, did not declare any dividends, and refused to elect her as a director. In this situation, a court found that the majority shareholders had violated their fiduciary duty to Brodie's wife.[12] •

Major Business Forms Compared

When deciding which form of business organization to choose, businesspersons normally consider several factors, including ease of creation, the liability of the owners, tax considerations, and the ability to raise capital. Each major form of business organization offers distinct advantages and disadvantages with respect to these and other factors.

Exhibit 25–3 below and on the facing page summarizes the essential advantages and disadvantages of each of the forms of business organization discussed in Chapters 23 through 25.

12. *Brodie v. Jordan*, 447 Mass. 866, 857 N.E.2d 1076 (2006).

• ***Exhibit* 25–3 Major Forms of Business Compared**

CHARACTERISTIC	SOLE PROPRIETORSHIP	PARTNERSHIP	CORPORATION
Method of Creation	Created at will by owner.	Created by agreement of the parties.	Authorized by the state under the state's corporation law.
Legal Position	Not a separate entity; owner is the business.	A traditional partnership is a separate legal entity in most states.	Always a legal entity separate and distinct from its owners—a legal fiction for the purposes of owning property and being a party to litigation.
Liability	Unlimited liability.	Unlimited liability.	Limited liability of shareholders—shareholders are not liable for the debts of the corporation.
Duration	Determined by owner; automatically dissolved on owner's death.	Terminated by agreement of the partners, but can continue to do business even when a partner dissociates from the partnership.	Can have perpetual existence.
Transferability of Interest	Interest can be transferred, but individual's proprietorship then ends.	Although partnership interest can be assigned, assignee does not have full rights of a partner.	Shares of stock can be transferred.
Management	Completely at owner's discretion.	Each partner has a direct and equal voice in management unless expressly agreed otherwise in the partnership agreement.	Shareholders elect directors, who set policy and appoint officers.
Taxation	Owner pays personal taxes on business income.	Each partner pays pro rata share of income taxes on net profits, whether or not they are distributed.	Double taxation—corporation pays income tax on net profits, with no deduction for dividends, and shareholders pay income tax on disbursed dividends they receive.
Organizational Fees, Annual License Fees, and Annual Reports	None or minimal.	None or minimal.	All required.
Transaction of Business in Other States	Generally no limitation.	Generally no limitation.[a]	Normally must qualify to do business and obtain certificate of authority.

a. A few states have enacted statutes requiring that foreign partnerships qualify to do business there.

• ***Exhibit* 25–3 Major Forms of Business Compared–Continued**

CHARACTERISTIC	LIMITED PARTNERSHIP	LIMITED LIABILITY COMPANY	LIMITED LIABILITY PARTNERSHIP
Method of Creation	Created by agreement to carry on a business for profit. At least one party must be a general partner and the other(s) limited partner(s). Certificate of limited partnership is filed. Charter must be issued by the state.	Created by an agreement of the member-owners of the company. Articles of organization are filed. Charter must be issued by the state.	Created by agreement of the partners. A statement of qualification for the limited liability partnership is filed.
Legal Position	Treated as a legal entity.	Treated as a legal entity.	Generally, treated same as a traditional partnership.
Liability	Unlimited liability of all general partners; limited partners are liable only to the extent of capital contributions.	Member-owners' liability is limited to the amount of capital contributions or investments.	Varies, but under the Uniform Partnership Act, liability of a partner for acts committed by other partners is limited.
Duration	By agreement in certificate, or by termination of the last general partner (retirement, death, and the like) or last limited partner.	Unless a single-member LLC, can have perpetual existence (same as a corporation).	Remains in existence until cancellation or revocation.
Transferability of Interest	Interest can be assigned (same as a traditional partnership), but if assignee becomes a member with consent of other partners, certificate must be amended.	Member interests are freely transferable.	Interest can be assigned same as in a traditional partnership.
Management	General partners have equal voice or by agreement. Limited partners may not retain limited liability if they actively participate in management.	Member-owners can fully participate in management or can designate a group of persons to manage on behalf of the members.	Same as a traditional partnership.
Taxation	Generally taxed as a partnership.	LLC is not taxed, and members are taxed personally on profits "passed through" the LLC.	Same as a traditional partnership.
Organizational Fees, Annual License Fees, and Annual Reports	Organizational fee required; usually not others.	Organizational fee required; others vary with states.	Fees are set by each state for filing statements of qualification, statements of foreign qualification, and annual reports.
Transaction of Business in Other States	Generally no limitations.	Generally no limitations, but may vary depending on state.	Must file a statement of foreign qualification before doing business in another state.

Reviewing . . . Corporate Directors, Officers, and Shareholders

David Brock is on the board of directors of Firm Body Fitness, Inc., which owns a string of fitness clubs in New Mexico. Brock owns 15 percent of the Firm Body stock, and he is also employed as a tanning technician at one of the fitness clubs. After the January financial report showed that Firm Body's tanning division was operating at a substantial net loss, the board of directors, led by Marty Levinson, discussed terminating the tanning operations. Brock successfully convinced a majority of the board that the tanning division was necessary to market the club's overall fitness package. By April, the tanning division's financial losses had risen. The board hired a business analyst who conducted surveys and determined that the tanning operations did not significantly increase membership. A shareholder, Diego Peñada, discovered that Brock owned stock in Sunglow, Inc., the company from which Firm Body purchased its tanning equipment. Peñada notified Levinson, who privately reprimanded Brock. Shortly afterwards, Brock and Mandy Vail, who owned 37 percent of the Firm Body stock and also held shares of Sunglow, voted to replace Levinson on the board of directors. Using the information presented in the chapter, answer the following questions.

1 What duties did Brock, as a director, owe to Firm Body?

Continued

2 Does the fact that Brock owned shares in Sunglow establish a conflict of interest? Why or why not?

3 Suppose that Firm Body brought an action against Brock claiming that he had breached the duty of loyalty by not disclosing his interest in Sunglow to the other directors. What theory might Brock use in his defense?

4 Now suppose that Firm Body did not bring an action against Brock. What type of lawsuit might Peñada be able to bring based on these facts?

Terms and Concepts

business judgment rule 486
inside director 484
outside director 484
preemptive right 492
proxy 490
quorum 485
shareholder's derivative suit 494
stock certificate 492
stock warrant 493
watered stock 495

Chapter Summary: Corporate Directors, Officers, and Shareholders

Roles of Directors and Officers (See pages 483–486.)	1. *Directors' qualifications*—Few qualifications are required; a director may be a shareholder but is not required to be. Directors are responsible for all policymaking decisions necessary to the management of all corporate affairs (see Exhibit 25–1 on page 484). 2. *Election and compensation of directors*—The first board of directors is usually appointed by the incorporators; thereafter, directors are elected by the shareholders. Directors usually serve a one-year term, although their terms can be longer or staggered. Compensation is usually specified in the corporate articles or bylaws. 3. *Board of directors' meetings*—The board of directors conducts business by holding formal meetings with recorded minutes. The date of regular meetings is usually established in the corporate articles or bylaws; special meetings can be called, with notice sent to all directors. Quorum requirements vary from state to state. Usually, a quorum is a majority of the directors. Voting normally must be done in person, and in ordinary matters only a majority vote is required. 4. *Rights of directors*—Directors' rights include the rights of participation, inspection, compensation, and indemnification. 5. *Directors' committees*—A board of directors may create committees of directors and delegate various responsibilities to them. Common types of committees are listed and described on page 485. 6. *Corporate officers and executives*—Corporate officers and other executive employees are normally hired by the board of directors and have the rights defined by their employment contracts. The duties of corporate officers are the same as those of directors.
Duties and Liabilities of Directors and Officers (See pages 486–489.)	1. *Duty of care*—Directors and officers are obligated to act in good faith, to use prudent business judgment in the conduct of corporate affairs, and to act in the corporation's best interests. If a director fails to exercise this duty of care, she or he can be answerable to the corporation and to the shareholders for breaching the duty. 2. *The business judgment rule*—This rule immunizes directors and officers from liability when they acted in good faith, acted in the best interests of the corporation, and exercised due care. For the rule to apply, the directors and officers must have made an informed, reasonable, and loyal decision. 3. *Duty of loyalty*—Directors and officers have a fiduciary duty to subordinate their own interests to those of the corporation in matters relating to the corporation. 4. *Conflicts of interest*—To fulfill their duty of loyalty, directors and officers must make a full disclosure of any potential conflicts between their personal interests and those of the corporation. 5. *Liability of directors and officers*—Corporate directors and officers are personally liable for their own torts and crimes. Additionally, they may be held personally liable for the torts and crimes committed by corporate personnel under their supervision (see Chapters 6 and 21).
Roles of Shareholders (See pages 489–492.)	1. *Shareholders' powers*—Shareholders' powers include the approval of all fundamental changes affecting the corporation and the election of the board of directors. 2. *Shareholders' meetings*—Shareholders' meetings must occur at least annually. Special meetings can be called when necessary. Notice of the date, time, and place of the meeting (and its purpose, if it is specially

Chapter Summary: Corporate Directors, Officers, and Shareholders—Continued

Roles of Shareholders—Continued	called) must be sent to shareholders. Shareholders may vote by proxy (authorizing someone else to vote their shares) and may submit proposals to be included in the company's proxy materials sent to shareholders before meetings. 3. *Shareholder voting*—Shareholder voting requirements and procedures are as follows: a. A minimum number of shareholders (a quorum—generally, more than 50 percent of shares held) must be present at a meeting for business to be conducted. Resolutions are passed (usually) by simple majority vote. b. The corporation must prepare voting lists of shareholders of record prior to each shareholders' meeting. c. Cumulative voting may or may not be required or permitted. Cumulative voting gives minority shareholders a better chance to be represented on the board of directors. d. A shareholder voting agreement (an agreement of shareholders to vote their shares together) is usually held to be valid and enforceable.
Rights of Shareholders (See pages 492–495.)	Shareholders have numerous rights, which may include the following: 1. The right to a stock certificate, preemptive rights, and the right to stock warrants (depending on the articles of incorporation). 2. The right to obtain a dividend (at the discretion of the directors). 3. Voting rights. 4. The right to inspect the corporate records. 5. The right to transfer shares (this right may be restricted in close corporations). 6. The right to a share of corporate assets when the corporation is dissolved. 7. The right to sue on behalf of the corporation (bring a shareholder's derivative suit) when the directors fail to do so.
Duties and Liabilities of Shareholders (See pages 495–496.)	1. Shareholders may be liable for the retention of illegal dividends and for the value of watered stock. 2. In certain situations, majority shareholders may be regarded as having a fiduciary duty to minority shareholders and will be liable if that duty is breached.

ExamPrep

ISSUE SPOTTERS

—Check your answers to these questions against the answers provided in Appendix G.

1 Wonder Corporation has an opportunity to buy stock in XL, Inc. The directors decide that instead of Wonder buying the stock, the directors will buy it. Yvon, a Wonder shareholder, learns of the purchase and wants to sue the directors on Wonder's behalf. Can she do it? Explain.

2 Nico is Omega Corporation's majority shareholder. He owns enough stock in Omega that if he were to sell it, the sale would be a transfer of control of the firm. Discuss whether Nico owes a duty to Omega or the minority shareholders in selling his shares.

BEFORE THE TEST

Go to **www.cengagebrain.com**, enter the ISBN 9781111530624, and click on "Find" to locate this textbook's Web site. Then, click on "Access Now" under "Study Tools," and select Chapter 25 at the top. There, you will find an Interactive Quiz that you can take to assess your mastery of the concepts in this chapter, as well as Flashcards and a Glossary of important terms.

For Review

1 What are the duties of corporate directors and officers?

2 What must directors do to avoid liability for honest mistakes of judgment and poor business decisions?

3 What is a voting proxy? What is cumulative voting?

4 If a group of shareholders perceives that the corporation has suffered a wrong and the directors refuse to take action, can the shareholders compel the directors to act? If so, how?

5 From what sources may dividends be paid legally? In what circumstances is a dividend illegal? What happens if a dividend is illegally paid?

Questions and Case Problems

25–1 Voting Techniques. Algonquin Corp. has issued and has outstanding 100,000 shares of common stock. Four stockholders own 60,000 of these shares, and for the past six years they have nominated a slate of candidates for membership on the board, all of whom have been elected. Sergio and twenty other shareholders, owning 20,000 shares, are dissatisfied with corporate management and want a representative on the board who shares their views. Explain under what circumstances Sergio and the twenty other shareholders can elect their representative to the board.

25–2 Liability of Directors. Starboard, Inc., has a board of directors consisting of three members (Ellsworth, Green, and Morino) and approximately five hundred shareholders. At a regular meeting of the board, the board selects Tyson as president of the corporation by a two-to-one vote, with Ellsworth dissenting. The minutes of the meeting do not register Ellsworth's dissenting vote. Later, during an audit, it is discovered that Tyson is a former convict and has openly embezzled $500,000 from Starboard. This loss is not covered by insurance. The corporation wants to hold directors Ellsworth, Green, and Morino liable. Ellsworth claims no liability. Discuss the personal liability of the directors to the corporation.

25–3 Rights of Shareholders. Lucia has acquired one share of common stock of a multimillion-dollar corporation with more than 500,000 shareholders. Lucia's ownership is so small that she is wondering what her rights are as a shareholder. For example, she wants to know whether owning this one share entitles her to (1) attend and vote at shareholders' meetings, (2) inspect the corporate books, and (3) receive yearly dividends. Discuss Lucia's rights in these three matters.

25–4 Fiduciary Duties and Liabilities. Harry Hoaas and Larry Griffiths were shareholders in Grand Casino, Inc., which owned and operated a casino in Watertown, South Dakota. Griffiths owned 51 percent of the stock and Hoaas 49 percent. Hoaas managed the casino, which Griffiths typically visited once a week. At the end of 1997, an accounting showed that the cash on hand was less than the amount posted in the casino's books. Later, more shortfalls were discovered. In October 1999, Griffiths did a complete audit. Hoaas was unable to account for $135,500 in missing cash. Griffiths then kept all of the casino's most recent profits, including Hoaas's $9,447.20 share, and, without telling Hoaas, sold the casino for $100,000 and kept all of the proceeds. Hoaas filed a suit in a South Dakota state court against Griffiths, asserting, among other things, a breach of fiduciary duty. Griffiths countered with evidence of Hoaas's misappropriation of corporate cash. What duties did these parties owe each other? Did either Griffiths or Hoaas, or both of them, breach those duties? How should their dispute be resolved? How should their finances be reconciled? Explain. [*Hoaas v. Griffiths,* 2006 SD 27, 714 N.W.2d 61 (2006)]

25–5 Role of Directors. The board of directors of a property management corporation in Oregon meets on a regular basis. The company paid the directors $6,000 each in the third quarter of 2003. It did not report the payments as part of its payroll and did not pay unemployment tax on the payments. The Oregon Employment Department contended that the company owed $700 in unemployment taxes on the payments to the directors. The company protested. The administrative law judge (ALJ) for the Employment Department held that the company owed the taxes because directors' fees are the same as wages for employment. The company appealed. The court of appeals affirmed the ALJ's ruling. The company appealed again. Are payments to directors the same as wages for tax purposes? Explain. [*Necanicum Investment Co. v. Employment Department,* 345 Or. 138, 190 P.3d 368 (2008)]

25–6  **Case Problem with Sample Answer** First Niles Financial, Inc., is a company whose sole business is to own and operate a bank, Home Federal Savings and Loan Association of Niles, Ohio. First Niles's directors include bank officers William Stephens, Daniel Csontos, and Lawrence Safarek; James Kramer, president of an air-conditioning company that services the bank; and Ralph Zuzolo, whose law firm serves the bank and whose title company participates in most of its real estate deals. First Niles's board put the bank up for sale. There were three bids. Farmers National Bank Corp. stated that it would not retain the board. Cortland Bancorp indicated that it would terminate the directors but consider them for future service. First Financial Corp. said nothing about the directors. The board did not pursue Farmers' offer, failed to respond timely to Cortland's request, and rejected First Financial's bid. Leonard Gantler and other First Niles shareholders filed a suit in a Delaware state court against Stephens and the others. What duties do directors and officers owe to a corporation and its shareholders? How might those duties have been breached here? Discuss. [*Gantler v. Stephens,* 965 A.2d 695 (Del.Sup. 2009)]

—For a sample answer to Problem 25–6, go to Appendix F at the end of this text.

25–7 Fiduciary Duty. Designer Surfaces, Inc., supplied countertops to homeowners who shopped at stores such as Lowe's or Costco. The homeowners paid the store, which then contracted with Designer to fabricate and install the countertops. Designer bought materials from Arizona Tile, LLC, on an open account. Designer's only known corporate officers were Howard Berger and John McCarthy. Designer became insolvent and could not pay Arizona Tile for all the materials it had purchased, including materials for which Designer had already received payment from the retail stores. Arizona Tile sued Designer and won a default judgment, but the company had no funds. Arizona Tile then sued Berger and McCarthy personally for diverting company funds that Designer had received in trust for payment to Arizona Tile. Arizona Tile argued that the use of the funds for other purposes was a breach of fiduciary duty. Berger and McCarthy argued that corporate law imposed neither a fiduciary duty on corporate officers nor personal liability for breach of a duty to suppliers of materials. Which argument is more credible and why? [*Arizona Tile, LLC v. Berger,* 223 Ariz. 491, 224 P.3d 988 (2010)]

25–8 Rights of Shareholders. Stanka Woods was the manager and sole member of Hair Ventures, LLC, which owned 3 million shares of stock in Biolustré, Inc. For several years, Woods and other Biolustré shareholders did not receive notices of shareholders' meetings or financial reports. Nevertheless, Woods learned that Biolustré planned to issue more stock, and her boyfriend, Daniel Davila, proposed that they meet with other shareholders to discuss the company's operations and oppose the issue. To obtain information regarding what was going on at Biolustré, Woods, through Hair Ventures, sent Biolustré a demand to examine its books and records. Biolustré did not respond. Hair Ventures filed a suit in a Texas state court against the corporation, seeking an order to compel it to comply. Biolustré asserted that Hair Ventures' request was not for a proper purpose. Does a shareholder have a right to inspect corporate books and records? If so, what are the limits? Do any of those limits apply in this case? Explain. [*Biolustré Inc. v. Hair Ventures, LLC,* __ S.W.3d __ (Tex.App.—San Antonio 2011)]

25–9 A Question of Ethics *New Orleans Paddlewheels, Inc. (NOP), is a Louisiana corporation formed in 1982, when James Smith, Sr., and Warren Reuther were its only shareholders, with each holding 50 percent of the stock. NOP is part of a sprawling enterprise of tourism and hospitality companies in New Orleans. The positions on the board of each company were split equally between the Smith and Reuther families. At Smith's request, his son James Smith, Jr. (JES), became involved in the businesses. In 1999, NOP's board elected JES as president, in charge of day-to-day operations, and Reuther as chief executive officer (CEO), in charge of marketing and development. Over the next few years, animosity developed between Reuther and JES. In October 2001, JES terminated Reuther as CEO and denied him access to the offices and books of NOP and the other companies, literally changing the locks on the doors. At the next meetings of the boards of NOP and the overall enterprise, deadlock ensued, with the directors voting along family lines on every issue. Complaining that the meetings were a "waste of time," JES began to run the entire enterprise by taking advantage of an unequal balance of power on the companies' executive committees. In NOP's subsequent bankruptcy proceeding, Reuther filed a motion for the appointment of a trustee to formulate a plan for the firm's reorganization, alleging, among other things, misconduct by NOP's management. [*In re New Orleans Paddlewheels, Inc.*, *350 Bankr. 667 (E.D.La. 2006)]*

1. Was Reuther legally entitled to have access to the books and records of NOP and the other companies? JES maintained, among other things, that NOP's books were "a mess." Was JES's denial of that access unethical? Explain.
2. How would you describe JES's attempt to gain control of NOP and the other companies? Were his actions deceptive and self-serving in the pursuit of personal gain or legitimate and reasonable in the pursuit of a business goal? Discuss.

Chapter 26

Investor Protection, Insider Trading, and Corporate Governance

Learning Objectives

After reading this chapter, you should be able to answer the following questions:

1. What is meant by the term *securities*?
2. What are the two major statutes regulating the securities industry?
3. What is insider trading? Why is it prohibited?
4. What are some of the features of state securities laws?
5. What certification requirements does the Sarbanes-Oxley Act impose on corporate executives?

The Learning Objectives above are designed to help improve your understanding of the chapter.

(Othermore/Creative Commons)

After the stock market crash of 1929, Congress enacted legislation to regulate securities markets. **Securities** generally are defined as any documents or records evidencing corporate ownership (stock) or debts (bonds). The goal of regulation was to provide investors with more information to help them make buying and selling decisions about securities and to prohibit deceptive, unfair, and manipulative practices.

Today, the sale and transfer of securities are heavily regulated by federal and state statutes and by government agencies, and even more regulations have been enacted since the Great Recession. For example, the Dodd-Frank Wall Street Reform and Consumer Protection Act,[1] which Congress passed in 2010, requires significant changes to the financial regulatory environment. As a result, the Securities and Exchange Commission (SEC)—the federal agency that has the primary responsibility for regulating the securities markets—developed rules to implement the provisions of that act. Despite all of these efforts to regulate the securities markets, people continue to break the rules. For instance, billionaire hedge-fund manager, Raj Rajaratnam, who was sentenced to eleven years in prison in 2011, perpetrated one of the largest and most lucrative insider-trading schemes in history.

This chapter discusses the nature of federal securities regulation and its effect on the business world. We first examine the major traditional laws governing securities offerings and trading. We then discuss corporate governance and the Sarbanes-Oxley Act,[2] which affects certain types of securities transactions. Finally, we look at the problem of online securities fraud.

The Securities Act of 1933

The Securities Act of 1933[3] governs initial sales of stock by businesses. The act was designed to prohibit various forms of fraud and to stabilize the securities industry by requiring that all essential information concerning the issuance of securities be made available to the investing public. Basically, the

1. Pub. L. No. 111-203, July 21, 2010, 124 Stat. 1376; 12 U.S.C. Sections 5301 *et seq.*
2. 15 U.S.C. Sections 7201 *et seq.*
3. 15 U.S.C. Sections 77–77aa.

purpose of this act is to require disclosure. The 1933 act provides that all securities transactions must be registered with the SEC or be exempt from registration requirements.

What Is a Security?

Section 2(1) of the Securities Act of 1933 contains a broad definition of securities, which generally include the following:[4]

1. Instruments and interests commonly known as securities, such as preferred and common stocks, treasury stocks, bonds, debentures, and stock warrants.
2. Any interests in securities, such as stock options, puts, calls, or other types of privilege on a security or on the right to purchase a security or a group of securities in a national security exchange.
3. Notes, instruments, or other evidence of indebtedness, including certificates of interest in a profit-sharing agreement and certificates of deposit.
4. Any fractional undivided interest in oil, gas, or other mineral rights.
5. Investment contracts, which include interests in limited partnerships and other investment schemes.

In interpreting the act, the United States Supreme Court has held that an **investment contract** is any transaction in which a person (1) invests (2) in a common enterprise (3) reasonably expecting profits (4) derived *primarily* or *substantially* from others' managerial or entrepreneurial efforts. Known as the *Howey* test, this definition continues to guide the determination of what types of contracts can be considered securities.[5]

For our purposes, it is probably convenient to think of securities in their most common forms—stocks and bonds issued by corporations. Keep in mind, though, that securities can take many forms, including interests in whiskey, cosmetics, worms, beavers, boats, vacuum cleaners, muskrats, and cemetery lots. Almost any stake in the ownership or debt of a company can be considered a security. Investment contracts in condominiums, franchises, limited partnerships in real estate, and oil or gas or other mineral rights have qualified as securities.

CASE EXAMPLE 26.1 Alpha Telcom sold, installed, and maintained pay-phone systems. As part of its pay-phone program, Alpha guaranteed buyers a 14 percent return on the amount of their purchase. Alpha was operating at a net loss, however, and continually borrowed funds to pay investors the fixed rate of return it had promised. Eventually, the company filed for bankruptcy, and the SEC brought an action alleging that Alpha had violated the Securities Act of 1933. In this situation, a federal court concluded that the pay-phone program was a security because it involved an investment contract.[6] ●

4. 15 U.S.C. Section 77b(1). Amendments in 1982 added stock options.

5. *SEC v. W.J. Howey Co.*, 328 U.S. 293, 66 S.Ct. 1100, 90 L.Ed. 1244 (1946).

Registration Statement

Section 5 of the Securities Act of 1933 broadly provides that a security must be *registered* before being offered to the public unless it qualifies for an exemption. The issuing corporation must file a *registration statement* with the SEC and must provide all investors with a *prospectus*. A **prospectus** is a written disclosure document that describes the security being sold, the financial operations of the issuing corporation, and the investment or risk attaching to the security. The prospectus also serves as a selling tool for the issuing corporation. The SEC now allows an issuer to deliver its prospectus to investors electronically via the Internet.[7] In principle, the registration statement and the prospectus supply sufficient information to enable unsophisticated investors to evaluate the financial risk involved.

CONTENTS OF THE REGISTRATION STATEMENT The registration statement must be written in plain English and fully describe the following:

1. The securities being offered for sale, including their relationship to the registrant's other capital securities.
2. The corporation's properties and business (including a financial statement certified by an independent public accounting firm).
3. The management of the corporation, including managerial compensation, stock options, pensions, and other benefits. Any interests of directors or officers in any material transactions with the corporation must be disclosed.
4. How the corporation intends to use the proceeds of the sale.
5. Any pending lawsuits or special risk factors.

All companies, both domestic and foreign, must file their registration statements electronically so that they can be posted on the SEC's EDGAR (Electronic Data Gathering, Analysis, and Retrieval) database. The EDGAR database includes material on initial public offerings, proxy statements, corporations' annual reports, registration statements, and other documents that have been filed with the SEC. Investors can access the database via the Internet (www.sec.gov/edgar.shtml) to obtain information that can be used to make investment decisions.

6. *SEC v. Alpha Telcom, Inc.*, 187 F.Supp.2d 1250 (2002). See also *SEC v. Edwards*, 540 U.S. 389, 124 S.Ct. 892, 157 L.Ed.2d 813 (2004), in which the United States Supreme Court held that an investment scheme offering contractual entitlement to a fixed rate of return can be an investment contract and therefore can be considered a security under federal law.

7. Basically, an electronic prospectus must meet the same requirements as a printed prospectus. The SEC has special rules that address situations in which the graphics, images, or audio files in a printed prospectus cannot be reproduced in an electronic form. 17 C.F.R. Section 232.304.

REGISTRATION PROCESS The registration statement does not become effective until after it has been reviewed and approved by the SEC. The 1933 act restricted the types of activities that an issuer can engage in at each stage in the registration process. During the *prefiling period* (before filing the registration statement), the issuer normally cannot either sell or offer to sell the securities. Once the registration statement has been filed, a waiting period begins while the SEC reviews the registration statement for completeness.[8]

During the *waiting period,* the securities can be offered for sale but cannot be sold by the issuing corporation. Only certain types of offers are allowed. All issuers can distribute a *preliminary prospectus,* which contains most of the information that will be included in the final prospectus but often does not include a price. Most issuers can also use a *free-writing prospectus* during this period (although some inexperienced issuers will need to file a preliminary prospectus first).[9] A **free-writing prospectus** is any type of written, electronic, or graphic offer that describes the issuer or its securities and includes a legend indicating that the investor may obtain the prospectus at the SEC's Web site.

Once the SEC has reviewed and approved the registration statement and the waiting period is over, the registration is effective, and the *posteffective period* begins. The issuer can now offer and sell the securities without restrictions. If the company issued a preliminary or free-writing prospectus to investors, it must provide those investors with a final prospectus either before or at the time they purchase the securities. The issuer can require investors to download the final prospectus from a Web site if it notifies them of the appropriate Internet address.

WELL-KNOWN SEASONED ISSUERS In 2005, the SEC revised the registration process and loosened some of the restrictions on large experienced issuers.[10] The rules created new categories of issuers depending on their size and presence in the market and provided a simplified registration process for these issuers. The large, well-known securities firms that issue most securities have the greatest flexibility. A *well-known seasoned issuer* (WKSI) is a firm that has issued at least $1 billion in securities in the previous three years or has at least $700 million of value of outstanding stock in the hands of the public. WKSIs can file registration statements the day they announce a new offering and are not required to wait for SEC review and approval. They can also use a free-writing prospectus at any time, even during the prefiling period.

Exempt Securities and Transactions

Certain types of securities are exempt from the registration requirements of the Securities Act of 1933. These securities—which generally can also be resold without being registered—are summarized in Exhibit 26–1 on the facing page under the "Exempt Securities" heading.[11] The exhibit also lists and describes certain transactions that are exempt from registration requirements under various SEC regulations.

The transaction exemptions are the most important because they are very broad and can enable an issuer to avoid the high cost and complicated procedures associated with registration. Because the coverage of the exemptions overlaps somewhat, an offering may qualify for more than one. Therefore, many sales of securities occur without registration. Even when a transaction is exempt from the registration requirements, the offering is still subject to the antifraud provisions of the 1933 act (as well as those of the 1934 act, to be discussed later in this chapter).

REGULATION A OFFERINGS Securities issued by an issuer that has offered less than $5 million in securities during any twelve-month period are exempt from registration.[12] Under Regulation A,[13] the issuer must file with the SEC a notice of the issue and an offering circular, which must also be provided to investors before the sale. This is a much simpler and less expensive process than the procedures associated with full registration. Companies are allowed to "test the waters" for potential interest before preparing the offering circular. To *test the waters* means to determine potential interest without actually selling any securities or requiring any commitment on the part of those who express interest. Small-business issuers (companies with annual revenues of less than $25 million) can also use an integrated registration and reporting system that uses simpler forms than the full registration system.

Some companies have sold their securities via the Internet using Regulation A. **EXAMPLE 26.2** The Spring Street Brewing Company became the first company to sell securities via an online initial public offering (IPO). Spring Street raised about $1.6 million—without having to pay any commissions to brokers or underwriters. ● Such online IPOs are particularly attractive to small companies and start-up ventures that may find it difficult to raise capital from institutional investors or through underwriters.

REGULATION D OFFERINGS The SEC's Regulation D contains several exemptions from registration requirements (Rules

8. The waiting period must last at least twenty days but always extends much longer because the SEC inevitably requires numerous changes and additions to the registration statement.
9. See SEC Rules 164 and 433.
10. Securities Offering Reform, codified at 17 C.F.R. Sections 200, 228, 229, 230, 239, 240, 243, 249, and 274.
11. 15 U.S.C. Section 77c.
12. 15 U.S.C. Section 77c(b).
13. 17 C.F.R. Sections 230.251–230.263.

• *Exhibit* **26–1 Exemptions for Securities Offerings under the 1933 Securities Act**

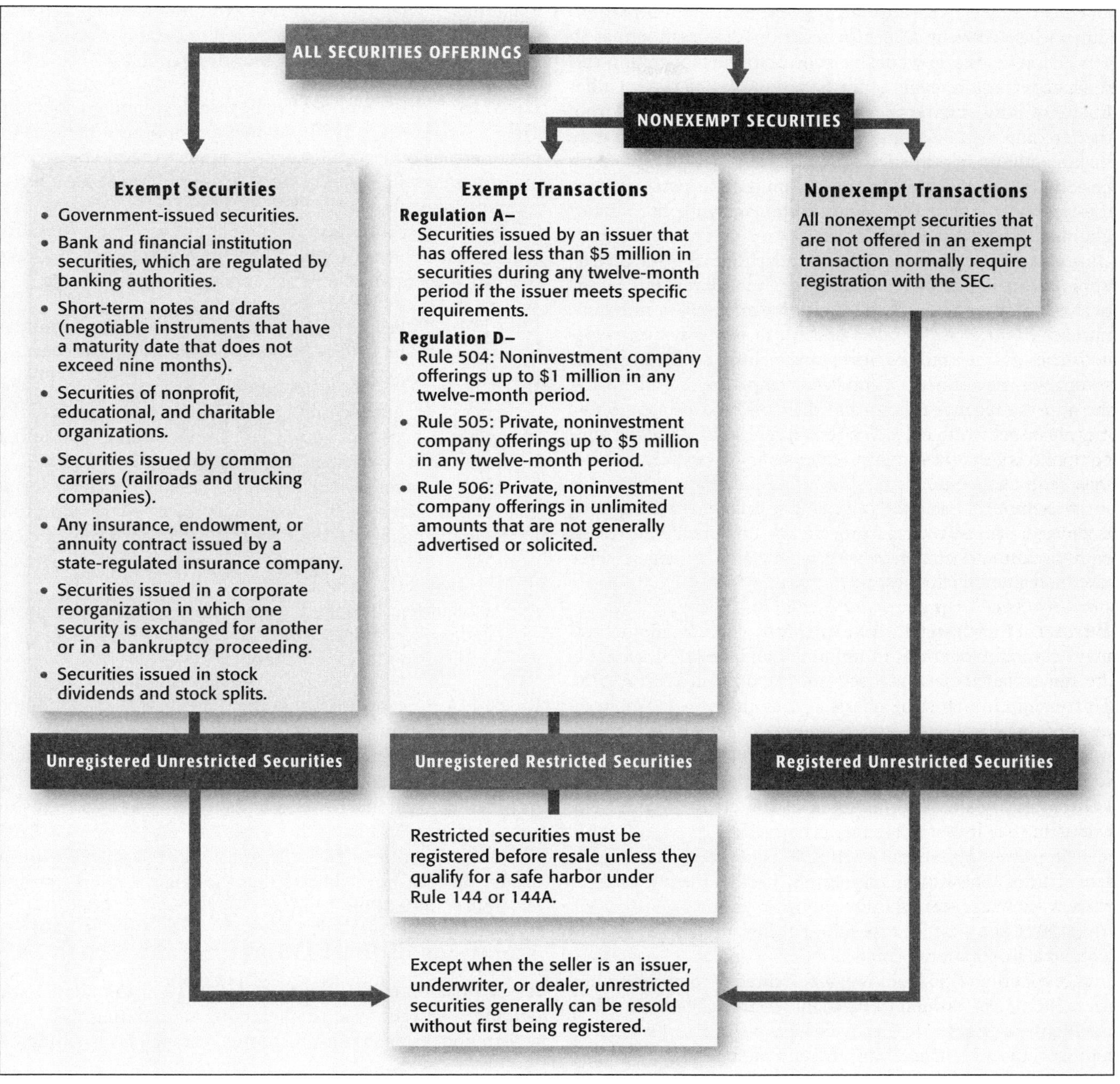

ALL SECURITIES OFFERINGS
NONEXEMPT SECURITIES
Exempt Securities
• Government-issued securities.
• Bank and financial institution securities, which are regulated by banking authorities.
• Short-term notes and drafts (negotiable instruments that have a maturity date that does not exceed nine months).
• Securities of nonprofit, educational, and charitable organizations.
• Securities issued by common carriers (railroads and trucking companies).
• Any insurance, endowment, or annuity contract issued by a state-regulated insurance company.
• Securities issued in a corporate reorganization in which one security is exchanged for another or in a bankruptcy proceeding.
• Securities issued in stock dividends and stock splits.
Exempt Transactions
Regulation A–
Securities issued by an issuer that has offered less than $5 million in securities during any twelve-month period if the issuer meets specific requirements.
Regulation D–
• Rule 504: Noninvestment company offerings up to $1 million in any twelve-month period.
• Rule 505: Private, noninvestment company offerings up to $5 million in any twelve-month period.
• Rule 506: Private, noninvestment company offerings in unlimited amounts that are not generally advertised or solicited.
Nonexempt Transactions
All nonexempt securities that are not offered in an exempt transaction normally require registration with the SEC.
Unregistered Unrestricted Securities
Unregistered Restricted Securities
Registered Unrestricted Securities
Restricted securities must be registered before resale unless they qualify for a safe harbor under Rule 144 or 144A.
Except when the seller is an issuer, underwriter, or dealer, unrestricted securities generally can be resold without first being registered.

504, 505, and 506) for offers that either involve a small dollar amount or are made in a limited manner. Rule 504 is the exemption used by most small businesses. It provides that noninvestment company offerings up to $1 million in any twelve-month period are exempt. Noninvestment companies are firms that are not engaged primarily in the business of investing or trading in securities. (In contrast, an **investment company** is a firm that buys a large portfolio of securities and professionally manages it on behalf of many smaller shareholders/owners. A **mutual fund** is a type of investment company.)

EXAMPLE 26.3 Zeta Enterprises is a limited partnership that develops commercial property. Zeta intends to offer $600,000 of its limited partnership interests for sale between June 1 and next May 31. Because an interest in a limited partnership meets the definition of a security (discussed earlier in this chapter), its sale would be subject to the registration and prospectus requirements of the Securities Act of 1933. Under Rule 504, however, the sales of Zeta's interests are exempt from these requirements because Zeta is a noninvestment company making an offering of less than $1 million in a twelve-month period. Therefore, Zeta can sell its limited partnership interests without filing a registration statement with the SEC or issuing a prospectus to any investor. •

Another exemption is available under Rule 505 for private, noninvestment company offerings up to $5 million in any twelve-month period. The offer may be made to an unlimited number of *accredited investors* and up to thirty-five unaccredited investors. **Accredited investors** include banks, insurance companies, investment companies, employee benefit plans, the issuer's executive officers and directors, and persons whose income or net worth exceeds a certain threshold. The SEC must be notified of the sales, and precautions must be taken because these restricted securities may be resold only by registration or in an exempt transaction. No general solicitation or advertising is allowed. The issuer must provide any unaccredited investors with disclosure documents that generally are the same as those used in registered offerings.

PRIVATE PLACEMENT EXEMPTION Private, noninvestment company offerings in unlimited amounts that generally are not solicited or advertised are exempt under Rule 506. This exemption is often referred to as the *private placement* exemption because it exempts "transactions not involving any public offering."[14] To qualify for the exemption, the issuer must believe that each unaccredited investor has sufficient knowledge or experience in financial matters to be capable of evaluating the investment's merits and risks.[15]

The private placement exemption is perhaps most important to firms that want to raise funds through the sale of securities without registering them.

EXAMPLE 26.4 Citco Corporation needs to raise capital to expand its operations. Citco decides to make a private $10 million offering of its common stock directly to two hundred accredited investors and thirty highly sophisticated, but unaccredited, investors. Citco provides all of these investors with a prospectus and material information about the firm, including its most recent financial statements. As long as Citco notifies the SEC of the sale, this offering will likely qualify for the private placement exemption. The offering is nonpublic and not generally advertised. There are fewer than thirty-five unaccredited investors, and each of them possesses sufficient knowledge and experience to evaluate the risks involved. The issuer has provided all purchasers with the material information. Thus, Citco will *not* be required to comply with the registration requirements of the Securities Act of 1933. •

RESALES Most securities can be resold without registration. The Securities Act of 1933 provides exemptions for resales by most persons other than issuers or underwriters. The average investor who sells shares of stock does not have to file a registration statement with the SEC. Resales of restricted securities, however, trigger the registration requirements unless the party selling them complies with Rule 144 or Rule 144A. These rules are sometimes referred to as "safe harbors."

Rule 144. Rule 144 exempts restricted securities from registration on resale if all of the following conditions are met:

1. There is adequate current public information about the issuer. ("Adequate current public information" refers to the reports that certain companies are required to file under the Securities Exchange Act of 1934.)
2. The person selling the securities has owned them for at least six months if the issuer is subject to the reporting requirements of the 1934 act.[16] If the issuer is not subject to the 1934 act's reporting requirements, the seller must have owned the securities for at least one year.
3. The securities are sold in certain limited amounts in unsolicited brokers' transactions.
4. The SEC is notified of the resale.[17]

Rule 144A. Securities that at the time of issue are not of the same class as securities listed on a national securities exchange or quoted in a U.S. automated interdealer quotation system may be resold under Rule 144A.[18] They may be sold only to a qualified institutional buyer (an institution, such as an insurance company or a bank that owns and invests at least $100 million in securities). The seller must take reasonable steps to ensure that the buyer knows that the seller is relying on the exemption under Rule 144A.

Violations of the 1933 Act

It is a violation of the Securities Act of 1933 to intentionally defraud investors by misrepresenting or omitting facts in a registration statement or prospectus. Liability is also imposed

14. 15 U.S.C. Section 77d(2).
15. 7 C.F.R. Section 230.506.
16. Before 2008, when amendments to Rule 144 became effective, the holding period was one year if the issuer was subject to the reporting requirements of the 1934 act. See the revised SEC Rules and Regulations at 72 Federal Rules 71546-01, 2007 WL 4368599, Release No. 33-8869. This reduced holding period allows nonpublic issuers to raise capital electronically from private and overseas sources more quickly.
17. 17 C.F.R. Section 230.144.
18. 17 C.F.R. Section 230.144A.

on those who are negligent for not discovering the fraud. Selling securities before the effective date of the registration statement or under an exemption for which the securities do not qualify results in liability.

REMEDIES Criminal violations are prosecuted by the U.S. Department of Justice. Violators may be fined up to $10,000, imprisoned for up to five years, or both. The SEC is authorized to seek civil sanctions against those who willfully violate the 1933 act. It can request an injunction to prevent further sales of the securities involved or ask the court to grant other relief, such as an order to a violator to refund profits. Parties who purchase securities and suffer harm as a result of false or omitted statements may also bring suits in a federal court to recover their losses and other damages.

DEFENSES There are three basic defenses to charges of violations under the 1933 act. A defendant can avoid liability by proving that (1) the statement or omission was not material, (2) the plaintiff knew about the misrepresentation at the time of purchasing the securities, or (3) the defendant exercised *due diligence* in preparing the registration and reasonably believed at the time that the statements were true and that there were no omissions of material facts. The due diligence defense is the most important because it can be asserted by any defendant except the issuer of the securities.

The following case involved allegations of omissions of material information from an issuing company's registration statement. The defendants contended that the omissions were not material.

Case 26.1 Litwin v. Blackstone Group, LP

United States Court of Appeals, Second Circuit, 634 F.3d 706 (2011).
www.ca2.uscourts.gov[a]

FACTS Blackstone Group, LP, manages investments. Its Corporate Private Equity Division accounts for nearly 40 percent of the assets under the company's management. In preparation for an initial public offering (IPO), Blackstone filed a registration statement with the Securities and Exchange Commission (SEC). At the time, the Corporate Private Equity Division's investments included FGIC Corporation and Freescale Semiconductor, Inc. FGIC insured investments in subprime mortgages. Before the IPO, FGIC's customers began to suffer large losses. By the time of the IPO, this situation was generating substantial losses for FGIC and, in turn, for Blackstone. Meanwhile, Freescale had recently lost an exclusive contract to make wireless 3G chipsets for Motorola, Inc. (its largest customer). Blackstone's registration statement did not mention the impact on its revenue of the investments in FGIC and Freescale. Martin Litwin and others who invested in the IPO filed a suit in a federal district court against Blackstone and its officers, alleging material omissions from the statement. Blackstone filed a motion to dismiss, which the court granted. The plaintiffs appealed.

ISSUE Was the fact that Blackstone had recently suffered substantial losses on two of its investments sufficient proof of material information that should have been disclosed in its registration statement?

DECISION Yes. The federal appellate court vacated the lower court's dismissal and remanded the case. The plaintiffs had provided sufficient allegations that Blackstone had omitted material information that it was required to disclose under securities law for the case to go to trial.

REASON Information is material if a reasonable investor would consider it significant in making an investment decision. A complaint can be dismissed on the ground that an omission is not material only if it would be "so obviously unimportant to a reasonable investor that reasonable minds could not differ on the question." In this case, the information concerned the extent to which known events and trends could reasonably be expected to affect Blackstone's investments and revenue. The plaintiffs alleged that Blackstone should have disclosed this information. In particular, a reasonable investor would want to know the expected effect on the corporate private equity sector's future revenue. Thus "the alleged . . . omissions relating to FGIC and Freescale were plausibly material."

FOR CRITICAL ANALYSIS—Legal Consideration *Litwin alleged that Blackstone had negligently omitted material information from the registration statement. What will he and the others have to show to prove their case?*

a. In the left column, click on "Decisions." On the next page, in the "Enter Docket #, Date, Party Name or find decisions that contain:" box, type "09-4426-cv" and click on "Search." In the result, click on the docket number to access the opinion (the case name is shown as *Landmen Partners, Inc. v. Blackstone Group, LP)*. The U.S. Court of Appeals for the Second Circuit maintains this Web site.

The Securities Exchange Act of 1934

The Securities Exchange Act of 1934 provides for the regulation and registration of securities exchanges, brokers, dealers, and national securities associations, such as the National Association of Securities Dealers (NASD). Unlike the 1933 act, which is a one-time disclosure law, the 1934 act provides for continuous periodic disclosures by publicly held corporations to enable the SEC to regulate subsequent trading. For a discussion of how the Securities Exchange Act applies in the online context, see the *Adapting the Law to the Online Environment* feature on the next page.

Adapting the Law to the Online Environment

Corporate Blogs and Tweets Must Comply with the Securities Exchange Act

In the fast-paced world of securities trading, there is great demand for the latest information about companies, earnings, and market conditions. Corporations are meeting this demand by establishing Web sites and blogs, and using other interactive online media, such as Twitter and online shareholder forums. Nearly 20 percent of Fortune 500 companies now sponsor blogs. Corporations that use the Internet to distribute information to investors, however, must make sure that they comply with SEC regulations. For purposes of federal securities laws, the SEC treats statements by employees on online media, such as blogs and Twitter, the same as any other company statements.

Beware of Tweets Containing Financial Information

Some corporate blogs include links to corporate employees' accounts on Twitter, LinkedIn, Tumblr, and similar sites so that readers can communicate directly with, and get updates from, the individual who posted the information.

For example, eBay, Inc., launched its corporate blog in 2008. A few months later, Richard Brewer-Hay, a seasoned blogger whom eBay hired to report online regarding the company, began tweeting about eBay's quarterly earnings and what took place at Silicon Valley technology conferences. Brewer-Hay's tweets gained him a following, but then eBay's lawyers required him to include a regulatory disclaimer with certain posts to avoid problems with the SEC. Many members of his audience were disappointed by the company's supervision, which curbed his spontaneity. Brewer-Hay became more reserved in his tweets on financial matters and often simply repeated eBay executives' statements verbatim.[a]

A 2008 SEC Release Provides Guidance

The reaction of eBay's lawyers to Brewer-Hay's tweets was prompted, in part, by an interpretive release issued by the SEC in August 2008. As noted earlier, the SEC generally embraces new technology and encourages companies to use it. In the release, the SEC noted that, in some circumstances, posting information on a company's Web site may be a "sufficient method of public disclosure."

The release also acknowledged that company-sponsored blogs, shareholders' electronic forums, and other interactive Web features can be a useful means of ongoing communications between companies and their shareholders and other stakeholders. The SEC cautioned, though, that all communications made by or on behalf of a company are subject to the antifraud provisions of federal securities laws. "While blogs or forums can be informal and conversational in nature, statements made there . . . will not be treated differently from other company statements." In addition, the release stated that companies cannot require investors to waive protections under federal securities laws as a condition of participating in a blog or forum. The release also warned companies that, in some situations, they can be liable for providing hyperlinks to third party information or inaccurate summaries of financial information on their Web sites.[b]

In 2011, an attorney for the SEC announced that the agency was going to allow disclosure of financial information through corporate blogs. The SEC will provide guidance to companies on when they can use their Web sites and blogs to disclose material information.

FOR CRITICAL ANALYSIS

Would Brewer-Hay's tweets about what had transpired at technology conferences require SEC disclosures? Why or why not?

a. Cari Tuna, "Corporate Blogs and 'Tweets' Must Keep SEC in Mind," *Wall Street Journal Online,* April 27, 2009: n.p. Web.

b. SEC Release Nos. 34–58288, IC–28351, File No. S7–23–08, Commission Guidance on the Use of Company Web Sites.

The Securities Exchange Act of 1934 applies to companies that have assets in excess of $10 million and five hundred or more shareholders. These corporations are referred to as Section 12 companies because they are required to register their securities under Section 12 of the 1934 act. Section 12 companies are required to file reports with the SEC annually and quarterly, and sometimes even monthly if specified events occur (such as a merger). Other provisions in the 1934 act require all securities brokers and dealers to be registered, to keep detailed records of their activities, and to file annual reports with the SEC.

The act also authorizes the SEC to engage in market surveillance to deter undesirable market practices such as fraud, market manipulation (attempts at illegally influencing stock prices), and misrepresentation. In addition, the act provides for the SEC's regulation of proxy solicitations for voting (discussed in Chapter 25).

Section 10(b), SEC Rule 10b-5, and Insider Trading

Section 10(b) is one of the more important sections of the Securities Exchange Act of 1934. This section prohibits the use of any manipulative or deceptive mechanism in violation of SEC rules and regulations. Among the rules that the SEC has promulgated pursuant to the 1934 act is **SEC Rule 10b-5,** which prohibits the commission of fraud in connection with the purchase or sale of any security.

APPLICABILITY OF SEC RULE 10B-5 SEC Rule 10b-5 applies to almost all trading of securities, whether on organized exchanges, in over-the-counter markets, or in private transactions. Generally, the rule covers just about any form of security, including, among other things, notes, bonds, agreements to form a corporation, and joint-venture agreements. The securities need not be registered under the 1933 act for the 1934 act to apply.

SEC Rule 10b-5 applies only when the requisites of federal jurisdiction—such as the use of stock exchange facilities or any means of interstate commerce—are present, but this requirement is easily met because almost every commercial transaction involves interstate contacts. In addition, the states have corporate securities laws, many of which include provisions similar to SEC Rule 10b-5.

INSIDER TRADING One of the major goals of Section 10(b) and SEC Rule 10b-5 is to prevent so-called **insider trading,** which occurs when persons buy or sell securities on the basis of *inside information* (information that is not available to the public). Corporate directors, officers, and others such as majority shareholders, for instance, often have advance inside information that can affect the future market value of the corporate stock. Obviously, if they act on this information, their positions give them a trading advantage over the general public and other shareholders. The 1934 Securities Exchange Act defines inside information and extends liability to those who take advantage of such information in their personal transactions when they know that the information is unavailable to those with whom they are dealing. Section 10(b) of the 1934 act and SEC Rule 10b-5 apply to anyone who has access to or receives information of a nonpublic nature on which trading is based—not just to corporate "insiders."

DISCLOSURE UNDER SEC RULE 10B-5 Any material omission or misrepresentation of material facts in connection with the purchase or sale of a security may violate not only the Securities Act of 1933 but also the antifraud provisions of Section 10(b) of the 1934 act and SEC Rule 10b-5. The key to liability (which can be civil or criminal) under Section 10(b) and SEC Rule 10b-5 is whether the insider's information is *material.*

The following are some examples of material facts calling for disclosure under SEC Rule 10b-5:

1. Fraudulent trading in the company stock by a broker-dealer.
2. A dividend change (whether up or down).
3. A contract for the sale of corporate assets.
4. A new discovery, a new process, or a new product.
5. A significant change in the firm's financial condition.
6. Potential litigation against the company.

Note that any one of these facts, by itself, is not *automatically* considered a material fact. Rather, it will be regarded as a material fact if it is significant enough that it would likely affect an investor's decision as to whether to purchase or sell the company's securities. **EXAMPLE 26.5** ANK, Inc., is the defendant in a class-action product liability suit that its attorney, Paula Frasier, believes that the company will lose. Frasier has advised ANK's directors, officers, and accountants that the company will likely have to pay a substantial damages award. ANK plans to make a $5 million offering of newly issued stock before the date when the trial is expected to end. ANK's potential liability and the financial consequences to the firm are material facts that must be disclosed because they are significant enough to affect an investor's decision as to whether to purchase the stock. •

The following is one of the classic cases interpreting materiality under SEC Rule 10b-5.

Classic Case 26.2 Securities and Exchange Commission v. Texas Gulf Sulphur Co.

United States Court of Appeals, Second Circuit, 401 F.2d 833 (1968).

FACTS In 1963, in an area where surveys had indicated potentially large mineral deposits, the Texas Gulf Sulphur Company (TGS) drilled a hole that appeared to yield a core with an exceedingly high mineral content, although further drilling would be necessary to establish whether there was enough ore to be mined commercially. TGS kept secret the results of the core sample. After learning of the ore discovery, officers and employees of the company made substantial purchases of TGS's stock. On April 11, 1964, an unauthorized report of the mineral find appeared in the newspapers. On the following day, April 12, TGS issued a press release that played down the discovery and stated that it was too early to tell whether the ore find would be significant. Later on, TGS announced a strike of at least 25 million tons of ore. The news led to a substantial increase in the price of TGS stock. The Securities and Exchange Commission (SEC) brought a suit in a federal district court against the officers and employees of TGS for violating the insider-trading prohibition of SEC Rule 10b-5. The officers and employees argued that the prohibition did not apply. They reasoned that the information on which they had traded was not material, as the find had not been commercially proved. The trial court held that most of the defendants had not violated SEC Rule 10b-5, and the SEC appealed.

Case 26.2—Continues next page ➥

Classic Case 26.2–Continued

ISSUE Did the officers and employees of TGS violate SEC Rule 10b-5 by buying the stock, even though they did not know the full extent and profit potential of the ore discovery at the time of their purchases?

DECISION Yes. The federal appellate court reversed the lower court's decision and remanded the case for further proceedings. All of the trading by insiders who knew of the mineral find before its true extent had been publicly announced had violated SEC Rule 10b-5.

REASON For SEC Rule 10b-5 purposes, the test of materiality is whether the information would affect the judgment of reasonable investors. Reasonable investors include speculative as well as conservative investors. "A major factor in determining whether the . . . discovery [of the ore] was a material fact is the importance attached to the drilling results by those who knew about it. . . . The timing by those who knew of it of their stock purchases and their purchases of short-term calls [rights to buy shares at a specified price within a specified time period]–purchases in some cases by individuals who had never before purchased calls or even TGS stock–virtually compels the inference that the insiders were influenced by the drilling results. . . . We hold, therefore, that all transactions in TGS stock or calls by individuals apprised of the drilling results . . . were made in violation of Rule 10b-5."

WHAT IF THE FACTS WERE DIFFERENT? *Suppose that further drilling revealed that there was not enough ore at this site for it to be mined commercially. Would the defendants still have been liable for violating SEC Rule 10b-5? Why or why not?*

IMPACT OF THIS CASE ON TODAY'S LAW *This landmark case affirmed the principle that the test of whether information is "material," for SEC Rule 10b-5 purposes, is whether it would affect the judgment of reasonable investors. The corporate insiders' purchases of stock indicated that they were influenced by the results and that the information about the results was material. The courts continue to cite this case when applying SEC Rule 10b-5 to other cases of alleged insider trading.*

The Private Securities Litigation Reform Act

One of the unintended effects of SEC Rule 10b-5 was to deter the disclosure of forward-looking information. To understand why, consider an example. **EXAMPLE 26.6** QT Company announces that its projected earnings in a future time period will be a certain amount, but the forecast turns out to be wrong. The earnings are in fact much lower, and the price of QT's stock is affected—negatively. The shareholders then bring a class-action suit against the company, alleging that the directors violated SEC Rule 10b-5 by disclosing misleading financial information. •

In an attempt to rectify this problem and promote disclosure, Congress passed the Private Securities Litigation Reform Act of 1995. The act provides a "safe harbor" for publicly held companies that make forward-looking statements, such as financial forecasts. Those who make such statements are protected against liability for securities fraud as long as the statements are accompanied by "meaningful cautionary statements identifying important factors that could cause actual results to differ materially from those in the forward-looking statement."[19]

After the 1995 act was passed, a number of securities class-action suits were filed in state courts to skirt its requirements. In response to this problem, Congress passed the Securities Litigation Uniform Standards Act of 1998 (SLUSA).[20] The act placed stringent limits on the ability of plaintiffs to bring class-action suits in state courts against firms whose securities are traded on national stock exchanges. SLUSA not only prevents the purchasers and sellers of securities from bringing class-action fraud claims under state securities laws, but also applies to investors who are fraudulently induced to hold on to their securities.[21]

Outsiders and SEC Rule 10b-5

The traditional insider-trading case involves true insiders—corporate officers, directors, and majority shareholders who have access to (and trade on) inside information. Increasingly, liability under Section 10(b) of the 1934 act and SEC Rule 10b-5 is being extended to certain "outsiders"—those persons who trade on inside information acquired indirectly.

Two theories have been developed under which outsiders may be held liable for insider trading: the *tipper/tippee theory* and the *misappropriation theory.*

Tipper/Tippee Theory.

Anyone who acquires inside information as a result of a corporate insider's breach of his or her fiduciary duty can be liable under SEC Rule 10b-5. This liability extends to **tippees** (those who receive "tips" from insiders) and even remote tippees (tippees of tippees). At the trial of Raj Rajaratnam (mentioned on page 502), for instance, prosecutors presented extensive wiretap evidence that Rajaratnam had received numerous tips from corporate insiders about such matters as company earnings and pending mergers.

19. 15 U.S.C. Sections 77z-2, 78u-5.

20. Pub. L. No. 105-353. This act amended many sections of Title 15 of the *United States Code.*

21. *Merrill Lynch, Pierce, Fenner & Smith, Inc. v. Dabit,* 547 U.S. 71, 126 S.Ct. 1503, 164 L.Ed.2d 179 (2006).

The key to liability under this theory is that the inside information must be obtained as a result of someone's breach of a fiduciary duty to the corporation whose shares are involved in the trading. The tippee is liable under this theory only if (1) there is a breach of a duty not to disclose inside information, (2) the disclosure is in exchange for personal benefit, and (3) the tippee knows (or should know) of this breach and benefits from it.

Misappropriation Theory. Liability for insider trading may also be established under the misappropriation theory. This theory holds that an individual who wrongfully obtains (misappropriates) inside information and trades on it for her or his personal gain should be held liable because, in essence, she or he stole information rightfully belonging to another.

The misappropriation theory has been controversial because it significantly extends the reach of SEC Rule 10b-5 to outsiders who ordinarily would *not* be deemed fiduciaries of the corporations in whose stock they trade. It is not always wrong to disclose material, nonpublic information about a company to another person. Nevertheless, a person who obtains the information and trades securities on it can be liable.

CASE EXAMPLE 26.7 Patricia Rocklage was the wife of Scott Rocklage, the chair and chief executive officer of Cubist Pharmaceuticals, Inc. Scott had sometimes disclosed material, nonpublic information about Cubist to Patricia, and she had always kept the information confidential. In December 2001, however, when Scott told Patricia that one of Cubist's key drugs had failed its clinical trial and reminded her not to tell anyone, Patricia refused to keep the information secret. She then warned her brother, William Beaver, who owned Cubist stock. William sold his 5,583 Cubist shares and tipped off his friend David Jones, who sold his 7,500 shares.

On January 16, 2002, Cubist publicly announced the trial results, and the price of its stock dropped. William and David had avoided losses of $99,527 and $133,222, respectively, by selling when they did. The SEC filed a lawsuit against Patricia, William, and David, alleging insider trading. The defendants claimed that because Patricia had told Scott that she was going to tell William about the failed trial, they had not "misappropriated" the information. The court, however, determined that Patricia had "engaged in deceptive devices," because she "tricked her husband into revealing confidential information to her so that she could, and did, assist her brother with the sale of his Cubist stock." The court therefore found all three defendants guilty of insider trading under the misappropriation theory.[22] •

22. *SEC v. Rocklage*, 470 F.3d 1 (1st Cir. 2006).

Insider Reporting and Trading—Section 16(b)

Section 16(b) of the 1934 act provides for the recapture by the corporation of all profits realized by an insider on any purchase and sale or sale and purchase of the corporation's stock within any six-month period.[23] It is irrelevant whether the insider actually uses inside information; *all such* **short-swing profits** *must be returned to the corporation.* In this context, *insiders* means officers, directors, and large stockholders of Section 12 corporations (those owning at least 10 percent of the class of equity securities registered under Section 12 of the 1934 act). To discourage such insiders from using nonpublic information about their companies for their personal benefit in the stock market, they must file reports with the SEC concerning their ownership and trading of the corporation's securities.

Section 16(b) applies not only to stock but also to warrants, options, and securities convertible into stock. In addition, the courts have fashioned complex rules for determining profits. Note that the SEC exempts a number of transactions under Rule 16b-3. For all of these reasons, corporate insiders are wise to seek specialized counsel before trading in the corporation's stock. Exhibit 26–2 on the next page compares the effects of SEC Rule 10b-5 and Section 16(b).

Regulation of Proxy Statements

Section 14(a) of the Securities Exchange Act of 1934 regulates the solicitation of proxies (see Chapter 25) from shareholders of Section 12 companies. The SEC regulates the content of proxy statements. Whoever solicits a proxy must fully and accurately disclose in the proxy statement all of the facts that are pertinent to the matter on which the shareholders are to vote. SEC Rule 14a-9 is similar to the antifraud provisions of SEC Rule 10b-5. Remedies for violations are extensive, ranging from injunctions to prevent a vote from being taken to monetary damages.

Violations of the 1934 Act

Violations of Section 10(b) of the Securities Exchange Act of 1934 and SEC Rule 10b-5, including insider trading, may be subject to criminal or civil liability. For either criminal or civil sanctions to be imposed, however, *scienter* must exist—that is, the violator must have had an intent to defraud or knowledge of her or his misconduct (see Chapter 10). *Scienter* can be proved by showing that the defendant made false statements or wrongfully failed to disclose material facts.

23. A person who expects the price of a particular stock to decline can realize profits by "selling short"—selling at a high price and repurchasing later at a lower price to cover the "short sale."

• ***Exhibit* 26–2 Comparison of SEC Rule 10b-5 and Section 16(b)**

AREA OF COMPARISON	SEC RULE 10b-5	SECTION 16(b)
What is the subject matter of the transaction?	Any security (does not have to be registered).	Any security (does not have to be registered).
What transactions are covered?	Purchase or sale.	Short-swing purchase and sale or short-swing sale and purchase.
Who is subject to liability?	Almost anyone with inside information under a duty to disclose—including officers, directors, controlling shareholders, and tippees.	Officers, directors, and certain shareholders who own 10 percent or more.
Is omission or misrepresentation necessary for liability?	Yes.	No.
Are there any exempt transactions?	No.	Yes, there are a number of exemptions.
Who may bring an action?	A person transacting with an insider, the SEC, or a purchaser or seller damaged by a wrongful act.	A corporation or a shareholder by derivative action.

Violations of Section 16(b) include the sale by insiders of stock acquired less than six months before the sale (or less than six months after the sale if selling short). These violations are subject to civil sanctions. Liability under Section 16(b) is strict liability. Neither *scienter* nor negligence is required.

In the following case, the defendants were accused of securities fraud in violation of Section 10(b) and SEC Rule 10b-5. At issue was whether they had acted with *scienter*.

Case 26.3 Gebhart v. Securities and Exchange Commission

United States Court of Appeals, Ninth Circuit, 595 F.3d 1034 (2010).
www.ca9.uscourts.gov/opinions[a]

FACTS Alvin Gebhart worked at Mutual of New York (MONY), where he sold annuities and mutual funds. Jack Archer, a fellow MONY salesperson, told Gebhart about Community Service Group (CSG)—a business venture that purchased mobile home parks, converted them to resident ownership, and assisted residents in purchasing them. MHP Conversions, LLC, which was created to facilitate the conversion process, issued promissory notes that were sold to individual investors to raise funds for CSG's purchase of the parks. Each note stated that it would "ultimately be secured by a deed of trust" on the particular park to be purchased with the funds. In 1996, Gebhart moved from MONY to Mutual Service Corporation (MSC), a broker-dealer and member of the National Association of Securities Dealers (NASD). His wife, Donna Gebhart, joined him at MSC. Over the next several years, the Gebharts, on Archer's recommendation, sold nearly $2.4 million in MHP promissory notes to forty-five of their clients, who bought the notes based on the Gebharts' positive statements about the investment. It became obvious later that these statements were false. The Gebharts had failed to disclose that their statements were based on information provided by Archer rather than their own, independent investigation. At the time of MHP's collapse, the Gebharts' clients had more than $1.5 million invested in outstanding MHP notes. The Gebharts were fired, and in 2002, the NASD filed a complaint against them for securities fraud. An NASD hearing panel found that the Gebharts had acted in good faith and rejected the fraud charges, but the NASD National Adjudicatory Council (NAC) reversed. The NAC found that the Gebharts had committed fraud, imposed a lifetime bar on Alvin Gebhart, and imposed a one-year suspension and a $15,000 fine on Donna Gebhart. The Securities and Exchange Commission (SEC) upheld the NAC's ruling, and the Gebharts petitioned a federal appellate court to review the SEC's decision.

a. On the page that opens, select the "Advanced Search" mode and enter "08-74943" in the "by Case No.:" box. Then click on "Search." In the search results, click on the case title to access the opinion. The U.S. Court of Appeals for the Ninth Circuit maintains this Web site.

ISSUE Was there sufficient evidence that the Gebharts had acted with *scienter*?

DECISION Yes. The U.S. Court of Appeals for the Ninth Circuit upheld the SEC's decision. The Gebharts had acted with *scienter* and had thus committed securities fraud in violation of Section 10(b) and Rule 10b-5.

REASON The court pointed out that to establish a violation of Section 10(b) and Rule 10b-5, the SEC had to show that the Gebharts had made misstatements or omissions of material facts with *scienter*. "*Scienter* . . .

Case 26.3–Continued

is a subjective inquiry. It turns on the defendant's actual state of mind. Thus, although we may consider the objective unreasonableness of the defendant's conduct to raise an inference of *scienter,* the ultimate question is whether the defendant knew his or her statements were false, or was consciously reckless as to their truth or falsity." The court found that the Gebharts were consciously aware of the risk that their statements were false. They failed to perform any meaningful investigation into MHP promissory notes. Thus, their assertions of good faith were not plausible. The SEC had correctly determined that the Gebharts "knew they had no direct knowledge of the truth or falsity" of their statements.

FOR CRITICAL ANALYSIS—Legal Consideration *At one point in the opinion (not included in this excerpt), the court noted "there is no evidence in the record that the Gebharts ever intended to defraud anyone." Why, then, did the court conclude that the Gebharts had acted with* scienter*?*

Criminal Penalties For violations of Section 10(b) and Rule 10b-5, an individual may be fined up to $5 million, imprisoned for up to twenty years, or both. A partnership or a corporation may be fined up to $25 million. Under Section 807 of the Sarbanes-Oxley Act of 2002, for a *willful* violation of the 1934 act the violator may, in addition to being subject to a fine, be imprisoned for up to twenty-five years.

For a defendant to be convicted in a criminal prosecution under the securities laws, there can be no reasonable doubt that the defendant knew he or she was acting wrongfully—a jury is not allowed merely to speculate that the defendant may have acted willfully.

CASE EXAMPLE 26.8 Martha Stewart, founder of a well-known media and homemaking empire, was charged with intentionally deceiving investors based on public statements she made. In 2001, Stewart's stockbroker allegedly had informed Stewart that the head of ImClone Systems, Inc., was selling his shares in that company. Stewart then sold her ImClone shares. The next day, ImClone announced that the U.S. Food and Drug Administration had failed to approve Erbitux, the company's greatly anticipated medication. After the government began investigating Stewart's ImClone trades, she publicly stated that she had previously instructed her stockbroker to sell her ImClone stock if the price fell to $60 per share. The government then filed a lawsuit, claiming that Stewart's statement showed she had the intent to deceive investors. The court, however, acquitted Stewart on this charge because "to find the essential element of criminal intent beyond a reasonable doubt, a rational juror would have to speculate."[24] •

Civil Sanctions The SEC can also bring suit in a federal district court against anyone violating or aiding in a violation of the 1934 act or SEC rules by purchasing or selling a security while in the possession of material nonpublic information.[25] The violation must occur on or through the facilities of a national securities exchange or from or through a broker or dealer. The court may assess a penalty for as much as triple the profits gained or the loss avoided by the guilty party.[26] The Insider Trading and Securities Fraud Enforcement Act of 1988 enlarged the class of persons who may be subject to civil liability for insider trading and gave the SEC authority to give monetary rewards to informants.[27]

Private parties may also sue violators of Section 10(b) and Rule 10b-5. A private party may obtain rescission (cancellation) of a contract to buy securities or damages to the extent of the violator's illegal profits. Those found liable have a right to seek contribution from those who share responsibility for the violations, including accountants, attorneys, and corporations. For violations of Section 16(b), a corporation can bring an action to recover the short-swing profits.

State Securities Laws

Today, every state has its own corporate securities laws, or blue sky laws, that regulate the offer and sale of securities within its borders. (The phrase *blue sky laws* dates to a decision by the United States Supreme Court in which the Court declared that the purpose of such laws was to prevent "speculative schemes which have no more basis than so many feet of 'blue sky.'")[28] Article 8 of the Uniform Commercial Code, which has been adopted by all of the states, also imposes various requirements relating to the purchase and sale of securities.

Requirements under State Securities Laws

Typically, state laws have disclosure requirements and antifraud provisions, many of which are patterned after Section 10(b) of the Securities Exchange Act of 1934 and SEC Rule 10b-5. State laws also provide for the registration of securities offered or issued for sale within the state and impose disclosure

24. *United States v. Stewart,* 305 F.Supp.2d 368 (S.D.N.Y. 2004).

25. The Insider Trading Sanctions Act of 1984, 15 U.S.C. Section 78u(d)(2)(A).

26. *Profit or loss* is defined as "the difference between the purchase or sale price of the security and the value of that security as measured by the trading price of the security at a reasonable period of time after public dissemination of the nonpublic information." 15 U.S.C. Section 78u(d)(2)(C).

27. 15 U.S.C. Section 78u-1.

28. *Hall v. Geiger-Jones Co.,* 242 U.S. 539, 37 S.Ct. 217, 61 L.Ed. 480 (1917).

requirements. Methods of registration, required disclosures, and exemptions from registration vary among states. Unless an exemption from registration is applicable, issuers must register or qualify their stock with the appropriate state official, often called a *corporations commissioner.* Additionally, most state securities laws regulate securities brokers and dealers.

Concurrent Regulation

State securities laws apply mainly to intrastate transactions. Since the adoption of the 1933 and 1934 federal securities acts, the state and federal governments have regulated securities concurrently. Issuers must comply with both federal and state securities laws, and exemptions from federal law are not exemptions from state laws.

The dual federal and state system has not always worked well, particularly during the early 1990s, when the securities markets underwent considerable expansion. In response, Congress passed the National Securities Markets Improvement Act of 1996, which eliminated some of the duplicate regulations and gave the SEC exclusive power to regulate most national securities activities. The National Conference of Commissioners on Uniform State Laws then substantially revised the Uniform Securities Act to coordinate state and federal securities regulation and enforcement efforts. The new version was offered to the states for adoption in 2002. Seventeen states have adopted the Uniform Securities Act, and other states are considering its adoption.[29]

Corporate Governance

Corporate governance can be narrowly defined as the relationship between a corporation and its shareholders. Some argue for a broader definition—that corporate governance specifies the rights and responsibilities among different participants in the corporation, such as the board of directors, managers, shareholders, and other stakeholders, and spells out the rules and procedures for making decisions on corporate affairs. Regardless of the way it is defined, effective corporate governance requires more than just compliance with laws and regulations.

Effective corporate governance is essential in large corporations because corporate ownership (by shareholders) is separated from corporate control (by officers and managers). Under these circumstances, officers and managers may attempt to advance their own interests at the expense of the shareholders. The well-publicized corporate scandals in the first decade of the 2000s clearly illustrate the reasons for concern about managerial opportunism.

Attempts at Aligning the Interests of Officers with Those of Shareholders

Some corporations have sought to align the financial interests of their officers with those of the company's shareholders by providing the officers with **stock options,** which enable them to purchase shares of the corporation's stock at a set price. When the market price rises above that level, the officers can sell their shares for a profit. Because a stock's market price generally increases as the corporation prospers, the options give the officers a financial stake in the corporation's well-being and supposedly encourage them to work hard for the benefit of the shareholders.

Options have turned out to be an imperfect device for providing effective governance, however. Executives in some companies have been tempted to "cook" the company's books in order to keep share prices higher so that they could sell their stock for a profit. Executives in other corporations have experienced no losses when share prices dropped. Instead, their options were "repriced" so that they did not suffer from the share price decline and could still profit from future increases above the lowered share price. Thus, although stock options theoretically can motivate officers to protect shareholder interests, stock option plans have often become a way for officers to take advantage of shareholders.

With stock options generally failing to work as planned and numerous headline-making scandals occurring within major corporations, there has been an outcry for more "outside" directors (those with no formal employment affiliation with the company). The theory is that independent directors will more closely monitor the actions of corporate officers. Hence, today we see more boards with outside directors. Note, though, that outside directors may not be truly independent of corporate officers; they may be friends or business associates of the leading officers.

The Goal Is to Promote Accountability

Corporate governance standards are designed to address problems (such as those briefly discussed above) and to motivate officers to make decisions that promote the financial interests of the company's shareholders. Generally, corporate governance entails corporate decision-making structures that monitor employees (particularly officers) to ensure that they are acting for the benefit of the shareholders. Thus, corporate governance involves, at a minimum:

1. The audited reporting of financial progress at the corporation, so managers can be evaluated.

---

29. At the time this book went to press, the Uniform Securities Act had been adopted in Georgia, Hawaii, Idaho, Indiana, Iowa, Kansas, Maine, Michigan, Minnesota, Mississippi, Missouri, New Mexico, Oklahoma, South Carolina, South Dakota, Vermont, and Wisconsin, as well as in the U.S. Virgin Islands. Adoption legislation was pending in Indiana and Washington State. You can find current information on state adoptions at www.nccusl.com.

2. Legal protections for shareholders, so violators of the law, who attempt to take advantage of shareholders, can be punished for misbehavior and victims may recover damages for any associated losses.

Effective corporate governance can have considerable practical significance because corporate decision makers necessarily become more accountable for their actions to shareholders. Firms that are more accountable to shareholders typically report higher profits, higher sales growth, higher firm value, and other economic advantages. Thus, a corporation with better corporate governance and greater accountability to investors may also have a higher valuation than a corporation that is less concerned about governance.

Governance and Corporate Law

State corporation statutes set up the legal framework for corporate governance. Under the corporate law of Delaware, where most major companies incorporate, all corporations must have certain structures of corporate governance in place. The most important structure, of course, is the board of directors because the board makes the major decisions about the future of the corporation.

Some argue that shareholder democracy is the key to improving corporate governance. If shareholders could have more say on major corporate decisions, they presumably could have more control over the corporation. Essential to shareholder democracy is the election of the board of directors, usually at the corporation's annual meeting.

Although shareholders vote for directors, they often find it difficult to elect their nominees because organizing enough shareholders to sway an election can be very costly. In 2010, the SEC announced that it would work to modernize shareholder voting and proxy rules to reduce these costs and give shareholders direct access to other shareholders through the company's facilities for communicating with shareholders. The SEC's goal is to make the contest more even between the shareholders' candidates and the company's nominees.

THE BOARD OF DIRECTORS Under corporate law, a corporation must have a board of directors elected by the shareholders. Almost anyone can become a director, though some organizations, such as the New York Stock Exchange, require certain standards of service for directors of their listed corporations.

Directors are responsible for ensuring that the corporation's officers are operating wisely and in the exclusive interest of shareholders. The directors receive reports from the officers and give them managerial directions. In reality, though, corporate directors devote a relatively small amount of time to monitoring officers.

Ideally, shareholders would monitor the directors' supervision of the officers. In practice, however, it can be difficult for shareholders to monitor directors and hold them responsible for corporate failings. Although the directors can be sued for failing to do their jobs effectively, directors are rarely held personally liable.

THE AUDIT COMMITTEE A crucial committee of the board of directors is the *audit committee,* which oversees the corporation's accounting and financial reporting processes, including both internal and outside auditors. Unless the committee members have sufficient expertise and are willing to spend the time to carefully examine the corporation's accounts, however, the audit committee may be ineffective.

The audit committee also oversees the corporation's "internal controls," which are the measures taken to ensure that reported results are accurate. They are carried out largely by the company's internal auditing staff. As an example, these controls help to determine whether a corporation's debts are collectible. If the debts are not collectible, it is up to the audit committee to make sure that the corporation's financial officers do not simply pretend that payment will eventually be made.

THE COMPENSATION COMMITTEE Another important committee of the board of directors is the *compensation committee.* This committee monitors and determines the compensation the company's officers are paid. As part of this process, the committee is responsible for assessing the officers' performance and for designing a compensation system that will better align the officers' interests with those of shareholders.

The Sarbanes-Oxley Act

In 2002, following a series of corporate scandals, Congress passed the Sarbanes-Oxley Act. The act separately addresses certain issues relating to corporate governance. Generally, the act attempts to increase corporate accountability by imposing strict disclosure requirements and harsh penalties for violations of securities laws. Among other things, the act requires chief corporate executives to take responsibility for the accuracy of financial statements and reports that are filed with the SEC.

Additionally, the act requires that certain financial and stock-transaction reports be filed with the SEC earlier than was required under the previous rules. The act also created a new entity, called the Public Company Accounting Oversight Board, which regulates and oversees public accounting firms. Other provisions of the act establish private civil actions and expand the SEC's remedies in administrative and civil actions.

Because of the importance of this act for corporate leaders and for those dealing with securities transactions, we present excerpts and explanatory comments in Appendix D at the end of this text. We also highlight some of its key provisions relating to corporate accountability in Exhibit 26–3 below.

MORE INTERNAL CONTROLS AND ACCOUNTABILITY The Sarbanes-Oxley Act includes some traditional securities law provisions but also introduces direct *federal* corporate governance requirements for public companies (companies whose shares are traded in the public securities markets). The law addresses many of the corporate governance procedures just discussed and creates new requirements in an attempt to make the system work more effectively. The requirements deal with independent monitoring of company officers by both the board of directors and auditors.

Sections 302 and 404 of Sarbanes-Oxley require high-level managers (the most senior officers) to establish and maintain an effective system of internal controls. Moreover, senior management must reassess the system's effectiveness annually. Some companies already had strong and effective internal control systems in place before the passage of the act, but others had to take expensive steps to bring their internal controls up to the new federal standard. These include "disclosure controls and procedures" to ensure that company financial reports are accurate and timely. Assessment must involve the documenting of financial results and accounting policies before reporting the results. After the act was passed, hundreds of companies reported that they had identified and corrected shortcomings in their internal control systems.

The act initially required all public companies to have an independent auditor file a report with the SEC on management's assessment of internal controls. Congress, however, enacted an exemption for smaller companies in 2010 in an

• ***Exhibit* 26–3 Some Key Provisions of the Sarbanes-Oxley Act Relating to Corporate Accountability**

Certification Requirements—Under Section 906 of the Sarbanes-Oxley Act, the chief executive officers (CEOs) and chief financial officers (CFOs) of most major companies listed on public stock exchanges must certify financial statements that are filed with the SEC. CEOs and CFOs have to certify that filed financial reports "fully comply" with SEC requirements and that all of the information reported "fairly represents in all material respects, the financial conditions and results of operations of the issuer."

Under Section 302 of the act, CEOs and CFOs of reporting companies are required to certify that a signing officer reviewed each quarterly and annual filing with the SEC and that it contains no untrue statements of material fact. Also, the signing officer or officers must certify that they have established an internal control system to identify all material information and that any deficiencies in the system were disclosed to the auditors.

Effectiveness of Internal Controls on Financial Reporting—Under Section 404(a), all public companies are required to assess the effectiveness of their internal control over financial reporting. Section 404(b) requires independent auditors to report on management's assessment of internal controls, but companies with a public float of less than $75 million are exempted from this requirement.

Loans to Directors and Officers—Section 402 prohibits any reporting company, as well as any private company that is filing an initial public offering, from making personal loans to directors and executive officers (with a few limited exceptions, such as for certain consumer and housing loans).

Protection for Whistleblowers—Section 806 protects "whistleblowers"—employees who report ("blow the whistle" on) securities violations by their employers—from being fired or in any way discriminated against by their employers.

Blackout Periods—Section 306 prohibits certain types of securities transactions during "blackout periods"—periods during which the issuer's ability to purchase, sell, or otherwise transfer funds in individual account plans (such as pension funds) is suspended.

Enhanced Penalties for—

- *Violations of Section 906 Certification Requirements*—A CEO or CFO who certifies a financial report or statement filed with the SEC knowing that the report or statement does not fulfill all of the requirements of Section 906 will be subject to criminal penalties of up to $1 million in fines, ten years in prison, or both. *Willful* violators of the certification requirements may be subject to $5 million in fines, twenty years in prison, or both.
- *Violations of the Securities Exchange Act of 1934*—Penalties for securities fraud under the 1934 act were also increased (as discussed earlier in this chapter). Individual violators may be fined up to $5 million, imprisoned for up to twenty years, or both. *Willful* violators may be imprisoned for up to twenty-five years in addition to being fined.
- *Destruction or Alteration of Documents*—Anyone who alters, destroys, or conceals documents or otherwise obstructs any official proceeding will be subject to fines, imprisonment for up to twenty years, or both.
- *Other Forms of White-Collar Crime*—The act stiffened the penalties for certain criminal violations, such as federal mail and wire fraud, and ordered the U.S. Sentencing Commission to revise the sentencing guidelines for white-collar crimes (see Chapter 6).

Statute of Limitations for Securities Fraud—Section 804 provides that a private right of action for securities fraud may be brought no later than two years after the discovery of the violation or five years after the violation, whichever is earlier.

effort to reduce compliance costs. Public companies with a market capitalization, or public float, of less than $75 million no longer need to have an auditor report on management's assessment of internal controls.

Certification and Monitoring Requirements Section 906 requires that chief executive officers and chief financial officers certify that the information in the corporate financial statements "fairly represents in all material respects, the financial conditions and results of operations of the issuer." These corporate officers are subject to both civil and criminal penalties for violation of this section. This requirement makes officers directly accountable for the accuracy of their financial reporting and avoids any "ignorance defense" if shortcomings are later discovered.

Sarbanes-Oxley also includes requirements to improve directors' monitoring of officers' activities. All members of the corporate audit committee for public companies must be outside directors. The New York Stock Exchange (NYSE) has a similar rule that also extends to the board's compensation committee. The audit committee must have a written charter that sets out its duties and provides for performance appraisal. At least one "financial expert" must serve on the audit committee, which must hold executive meetings without company officers being present. The audit committee must establish procedures to encourage "whistleblowers" to report violations. In addition to reviewing the internal controls, the committee also monitors the actions of the outside auditor.

Online Securities Fraud and Ponzi Schemes

A major problem facing the SEC today is how to enforce the antifraud provisions of the securities laws in the online environment. In 1999, in the first cases involving illegal online securities offerings, the SEC filed a suit against three individuals for illegally offering securities on an Internet auction site. In essence, all three indicated that their companies would go public soon and attempted to sell unregistered securities via the Web auction site. All of these actions were in violation of Sections 5, 17(a)(1), and 17(a)(3) of the 1933 Securities Act. Since then, the SEC has brought a variety of Internet-related fraud cases and regularly issues interpretive releases to explain how securities laws apply in the online environment.

Online Investment Scams

An ongoing problem is how to curb online investment scams. As discussed in Chapter 6, the Internet has created a new vehicle for criminals to use to commit fraud and has provided them with new ways of targeting innocent investors. The criminally inclined can use spam, online newsletters and bulletin boards, chat rooms, blogs, and tweets to spread false information and perpetrate fraud. For a relatively small cost, criminals can even build sophisticated Web pages to facilitate their investment scams.

Fraudulent E-Mails There are countless variations of online investment scams, most of which promise spectacular returns for small investments. A person might receive spam e-mail, for example, that falsely claims a home business can "turn $5 into $60,000 in just three to six weeks." Another popular investment scam claims "your stimulus package has arrived" and promises you can make $100,000 a year using your home computer. Although most people today are dubious of the bogus claims made in spam messages, such offers can be more attractive during times of economic recession. Often, investment scams are simply the electronic version of pyramid schemes in which the participants attempt to profit solely by recruiting new participants.

Online Investment Newsletters and Forums Hundreds of online investment newsletters provide free information on stocks. Legitimate online newsletters can help investors gather valuable information, but some of these newsletters are used for fraud. The law allows companies to pay people who write these newsletters to tout their securities, but the newsletters are required to disclose who paid for the advertising. Many fraudsters either fail to disclose or lie about who paid them. Thus, an investor reading an online newsletter may believe that the information is unbiased, when in fact the fraudsters will directly profit by convincing investors to buy or sell particular stocks.

The same deceptive tactics can be used on online bulletin boards (such as newsgroups and usenet groups), blogs, and social networking sites, including Twitter. While hiding their true identity, fraudsters may falsely pump up a company or reveal some "inside" information about a new product or lucrative contract to convince people to invest. By using multiple aliases on an online forum, a single person can easily create the illusion of widespread interest in a small stock.

Hacking into Online Stock Accounts

Millions of people now buy and sell investments online through online brokerage companies such as E*Trade and TD Ameritrade. Sophisticated hackers have learned to use online investing to their advantage. By installing keystroke-monitoring software on computer terminals in public places, such as hotels, libraries, and airports, hackers can gain access to online account information. All they have to do is wait for a person to access an online trading account and then monitor the next several dozen keystrokes to determine the customer's account number and password. Once they have the log-in information, they can access the customer's account and liquidate her or his existing stock holdings.

The hackers then use the customer's funds to purchase thinly traded, microcap securities, also known as penny stocks. The goal is to boost the price of a stock that the hacker has already purchased at a lower price. Then, when the stock price goes up, the hacker sells all the stock and wires the funds to either an offshore account or a dummy corporation, making it difficult for the SEC to trace the transactions and prosecute the offender.

EXAMPLE 26.9 Aleksey Kamardin, a twenty-one-year-old Florida college student, purchased 55,000 shares of stock in Fuego Entertainment using an E*Trade account in his own name. Kamardin then hacked into other customers' accounts at E*Trade and other brokerage companies, and used their funds to purchase a total of 458,000 shares of Fuego stock. When the stock price rose from $0.88 per share to $1.28 per share, Kamardin sold all of his shares, making a profit of $9,164.28 in about three hours. Kamardin did this with other thinly traded stocks as well, allegedly making $82,960 in about five weeks. The SEC filed charges against him, and he was later ordered to return the profits, plus interest. •

Ponzi Schemes

In recent years, the SEC has filed an increasing number of enforcement actions against perpetrators of *Ponzi schemes* (see page 50). In these scams, the fraudster promises high returns to investors and then uses their funds to pay previous investors. In 2009, Bernard Madoff was convicted of bilking investors out of more than $65 billion in the largest Ponzi scheme to date.

OFFSHORE FRAUD Ponzi schemes sometimes target U.S. residents and convince them to invest in offshore companies or banks. **EXAMPLE 26.10** Texas billionaire R. Allen Stanford, of the Stanford Financial Group, was indicted for allegedly orchestrating a $7 billion scheme to defraud more than five thousand investors. For about ten years, Stanford advised clients to buy certificates of deposit with improbably high interest rates from his Antigua-based Stanford International Bank. Some early investors were paid returns from the funds provided by later investors, but Stanford allegedly used $1.6 billion of the funds for personal expenditures. He also falsified financial statements that were filed with the SEC and reportedly paid more than $100,000 in bribes to an Antigua official to ensure that the bank would not be audited. •

"RISK-FREE" FRAUD Another type of fraud scheme offers risk-free or low-risk investments to lure investors. **EXAMPLE 26.11** For several years, Michael C. Regan used his firm to fraudulently obtain at least $15.9 million from dozens of investors by selling securities in his River Stream Fund. Regan told investors that he had a proven track record of successful securities trading and showed them falsified financial documents with artificially high account balances. In reality, Regan was not a registered investment adviser and had suffered substantial investment losses. Regan promised investors returns averaging 20 percent with minimal risk to their principal and claimed to be using an investment strategy based on "short-term price trends." He used less than half of the funds entrusted to him for trading purposes and personally spent at least $2.4 million. In 2009, the SEC filed a complaint and Regan agreed to settle the case and return more than $8.7 million of the wrongfully acquired funds. •

Reviewing . . . Investor Protection, Insider Trading, and Corporate Governance

Dale Emerson served as the chief financial officer for Reliant Electric Company, a distributor of electricity serving portions of Montana and North Dakota. Reliant was in the final stages of planning a takeover of Dakota Gasworks, Inc., a natural gas distributor that operated solely within North Dakota. Emerson went on a weekend fishing trip with his uncle, Ernest Wallace. Emerson mentioned to Wallace that he had been putting in a lot of extra hours at the office planning a takeover of Dakota Gasworks. When he returned from the fishing trip, Wallace purchased $20,000 worth of Reliant stock. Three weeks later, Reliant made a tender offer to Dakota Gasworks stockholders and purchased 57 percent of Dakota Gasworks stock. Over the next two weeks, the price of Reliant stock rose 72 percent before leveling out. Wallace then sold his Reliant stock for a gross profit of $14,400. Using the information presented in the chapter, answer the following questions.

1. Would registration with the SEC be required for Dakota Gasworks securities? Why or why not?
2. Did Emerson violate Section 10(b) of the Securities Exchange Act of 1934 and SEC Rule 10b-5? Why or why not?
3. What theory or theories might a court use to hold Wallace liable for insider trading?
4. Under the Sarbanes-Oxley Act of 2002, who would be required to certify the accuracy of financial statements filed with the SEC?

Terms and Concepts

accredited investor 506
corporate governance 514
free-writing prospectus 504
insider trading 509
investment company 505
investment contract 503
mutual fund 505
prospectus 503
SEC Rule 10b-5 508
security 502
short-swing profits 511
stock option 514
tippee 510

Chapter Summary: Investor Protection, Insider Trading, and Corporate Governance

The Securities Act of 1933 (See pages 502–507.)	Prohibits fraud and stabilizes the securities industry by requiring disclosure of all essential information relating to the issuance of securities to the investing public. 1. *Registration requirements*—Securities, unless exempt, must be registered with the SEC before being offered to the public. The registration statement must include detailed financial information about the issuing corporation; the intended use of the proceeds of the securities being issued; and certain disclosures, such as interests of directors or officers and pending lawsuits. 2. *Prospectus*—The issuer must provide investors with a prospectus that describes the security being sold, the issuing corporation, and the risk attaching to the security. 3. *Exemptions*—The SEC has exempted certain offerings from the requirements of the Securities Act of 1933. Exemptions may be determined on the basis of the size of the issue, whether the offering is private or public, and whether advertising is involved. Exemptions are summarized in Exhibit 26–1 on page 505.
The Securities Exchange Act of 1934 (See pages 507–513.)	Provides for the regulation and registration of securities exchanges, brokers, dealers, and national securities associations (such as the NASD). Maintains a continuous disclosure system for all corporations with securities on the securities exchanges and for those companies that have assets in excess of $10 million and five hundred or more shareholders (Section 12 companies). 1. *SEC Rule 10b-5 [under Section 10(b) of the 1934 act]*— a. Applies to almost all trading of securities—a firm's securities do not have to be registered under the 1933 act for the 1934 act to apply. b. Applies only when the requisites of federal jurisdiction (such as use of the mails, stock exchange facilities, or any facility of interstate commerce) are present. c. Applies to insider trading by corporate officers, directors, majority shareholders, and any persons receiving inside information (information not available to the public) who base their trading on this information. d. Liability for violations can be civil or criminal. e. May be violated by failing to disclose "material facts" that must be disclosed under this rule. f. Liability may be based on the tipper/tippee or the misappropriation theory. 2. *Insider trading [under Section 16(b) of the 1934 act]*—To prevent corporate insiders from taking advantage of inside information, the 1934 act requires officers, directors, and shareholders owning 10 percent or more of the issued stock of a corporation to turn over to the corporation all short-term profits (called short-swing profits) realized from the purchase and sale or sale and purchase of corporate stock within any six-month period. 3. *Regulation of proxies*—The SEC regulates the content of proxy statements sent to shareholders of Section 12 companies. Section 14(a) is essentially a disclosure law, with provisions similar to the antifraud provisions of SEC Rule 10b-5.
State Securities Laws (See pages 513–514.)	All states have corporate securities laws *(blue sky laws)* that regulate the offer and sale of securities within state borders; these laws are designed to prevent "speculative schemes which have no more basis than so many feet of 'blue sky.'" States regulate securities concurrently with the federal government. The Uniform Securities Act of 2002, which has been adopted by several states and is being considered by several others, is designed to promote coordination and reduce duplication between state and federal securities regulation.

Continued

Chapter Summary: Investor Protection, Insider Trading, and Corporate Governance—Continued

Corporate Governance (See pages 514–517.)	1. *Definition*—Corporate governance is the system by which business corporations are governed, including policies and procedures for making decisions on corporate affairs. 2. *The need for corporate governance*—Corporate governance is necessary in large corporations because corporate ownership (by the shareholders) is separated from corporate control (by officers and managers). This separation of corporate ownership and control can often result in conflicting interests. Corporate governance standards address such issues. 3. *Sarbanes-Oxley Act*—This act attempts to increase corporate accountability by imposing strict disclosure requirements and harsh penalties for violations of securities laws.
Online Securities Fraud and Ponzi Schemes (See pages 517–518.)	A major problem facing the SEC today is how to enforce the antifraud provisions of the securities laws in the online environment. Internet-related forms of securities fraud include numerous types of investment scams, Ponzi schemes, and hacking into online trading accounts.

ExamPrep

ISSUE SPOTTERS

—Check your answers to these questions against the answers provided in Appendix G.

1 When a corporation wishes to issue certain securities, it must provide sufficient information for an unsophisticated investor to evaluate the financial risk involved. Specifically, the law imposes liability for making a false statement or omission that is "material." What sort of information would an investor consider material?

2 Lee is an officer of Magma Oil, Inc. Lee knows that a Magma geologist has just discovered a new deposit of oil. Can Lee take advantage of this information to buy and sell Magma stock? Why or why not?

BEFORE THE TEST

Go to **www.cengagebrain.com**, enter the ISBN 9781111530624, and click on "Find" to locate this textbook's Web site. Then, click on "Access Now" under "Study Tools," and select Chapter 26 at the top. There, you will find an Interactive Quiz that you can take to assess your mastery of the concepts in this chapter, as well as Flashcards and a Glossary of important terms.

For Review

1 What is meant by the term *securities?*
2 What are the two major statutes regulating the securities industry?
3 What is insider trading? Why is it prohibited?
4 What are some of the features of state securities laws?
5 What certification requirements does the Sarbanes-Oxley Act impose on corporate executives?

Questions and Case Problems

26–1 Registration Requirements. Langley Brothers, Inc., a corporation incorporated and doing business in Kansas, decides to sell common stock worth $1 million to the public. The stock will be sold only within the state of Kansas. Joseph Langley, the chairman of the board, says the offering need not be registered with the Securities and Exchange Commission. His brother, Harry, disagrees. Who is right? Explain.

26–2 Insider Trading. David Gain was chief executive officer (CEO) of Forest Media Corp., which became interested in acquiring RS Communications, Inc., in 2010. To initiate negotiations, Gain met with RS's CEO, Gill Raz, on Friday, July 12. Two days later, Gain phoned his brother Mark, who, on Monday, bought 3,800 shares of RS stock. Mark discussed the deal with their father, Jordan, who bought 20,000 RS shares on Thursday. On July 25, the day before the RS bid was due, Gain phoned his parents' home, and Mark bought another 3,200 RS shares. The same routine was followed over the next few days, with Gain periodically phoning Mark or Jordan, both of whom continued to buy RS shares. Forest's bid was refused, but on August 5, RS announced its merger with another company. The price of RS stock rose 30 percent, increasing the value of Mark and Jordan's shares by $664,024 and $412,875, respectively. Did Gain engage in insider trading? What is required to impose sanctions for this offense? Could a court hold Gain liable? Why or why not?

26–3 Registration Requirements. Huron Corp. has 300,000 common shares outstanding. The owners of these outstanding shares live in several different states. Huron has decided to split the 300,000 shares two for one. Will Huron Corp. have to file a registration statement and prospectus on the 300,000 new shares to be issued as a result of the split? Explain.

26–4 Securities Violations. In 1997, WTS Transnational, Inc., required financing to develop a prototype of an unpatented fingerprint-verification system. At the time, WTS had no revenue, $655,000 in liabilities, and only $10,000 in assets. Thomas Cavanagh and Frank Nicolois, who operated an investment banking company called U.S. Milestone (USM), arranged the financing using Curbstone Acquisition Corp. Curbstone had no assets but had registered approximately 3.5 million shares of stock with the Securities and Exchange Commission (SEC). Under the terms of the deal, Curbstone acquired WTS, and the resulting entity was named Electro-Optical Systems Corp. (EOSC). New EOSC shares were issued to all of the WTS shareholders. Only Cavanagh and others affiliated with USM could sell EOSC stock to the public, however. Over the next few months, these individuals issued false press releases, made small deceptive purchases of EOSC shares at high prices, distributed hundreds of thousands of shares to friends and relatives, and sold their own shares at inflated prices through third party companies they owned. When the SEC began to investigate, the share price fell to its actual value, and innocent investors lost more than $15 million. Were any securities laws violated in this case? If so, what might be an appropriate remedy? [*SEC v. Cavanagh,* 445 F.3d 105 (2d Cir. 2006)]

26–5 Case Problem with Sample Answer Orphan Medical, Inc., was a pharmaceutical company that focused on central nervous system disorders. Its major product was the drug Xyrem. In June 2004, Orphan merged with Jazz, and Orphan shareholders received $10.75 per share for their stock. Before the merger was final, Orphan completed a phase of testing of Xyrem that indicated that the U.S. Food and Drug Administration (FDA) would allow the drug to go to the next stage of testing, which was necessary for the drug to be widely marketed. If that happened, the value of the drug and Orphan would go up, and the stock would have been worth more than $10.75. Little Gem Life Sciences, LLC, was an Orphan shareholder that received $10.75 a share. It sued, claiming violations of federal securities laws because shareholders were not told, during the merger process, that the current stage of FDA tests had been successful. Little Gem claimed that if the information had been public, the stock price would have been higher. The district court dismissed the suit, holding that it did not meet the standards required by the Private Securities Litigation Reform Act. Little Gem appealed. Did Orphan's directors have a duty to reveal all relevant drug-testing information to shareholders? Why or why not? [*Little Gem Life Sciences, LLC v. Orphan Medical, Inc.,* 537 F.3d 913 (8th Cir. 2008)]

—For a sample answer to Problem 26–5, go to Appendix F at the end of this text.

26–6 Violations of the 1934 Act. To comply with accounting principles, a company that engages in software development must either "expense" the cost (record it immediately on the company's financial statement) or "capitalize" it (record it as a cost incurred in increments over time). If the project is in the pre- or post-development stage, the cost must be expensed. Otherwise it may be capitalized. Capitalizing a cost makes a company look more profitable in the short term. Digimarc Corp., which provides secure personal identification documents such as drivers' licenses using digital watermark technology, announced that it had improperly capitalized software development costs over at least the previous eighteen months. The errors resulted in $2.7 million in overstated earnings, requiring a restatement of prior financial statements. Zucco Partners, LLC, which had bought Digimarc stock within the relevant period, filed a suit in a federal district court against the firm. Zucco claimed that it could show that there had been disagreements within Digimarc over its accounting. Is this sufficient to establish a violation of SEC Rule 10b-5? Why or why not? [*Zucco Partners, LLC v. Digimarc Corp.,* 552 F.3d 981 (9th Cir. 2009)]

26–7 Insider Trading. Jabil Circuit, Inc., is a publicly traded electronics and technology company headquartered in St. Petersburg, Florida. In 2008, a group of shareholders who owned Jabil stock from 2001 to 2007 sued the company and its auditors, directors, and officers for insider trading. Stock options were a part of Jabil's compensation for executives. In some situations, stock options were backdated to a point in time when the stock price was lower, so that the options were worth more to certain company executives. Backdating is not illegal so long as it is reported, but Jabil did not report the fact that backdating had occurred. Thus, expenses were underreported and net income was overstated by millions of dollars. The shareholders claimed that by rigging the stock price by backdating, the executives had engaged in insider trading and could pick favorable purchase prices and that there was a general practice of selling stock before unfavorable news about the company was reported to the public. The shareholders, however, had no specific information about these stock trades or when (or even if) a particular executive was aware of any accounting errors during the time of any backdating purchases. Were the shareholders' allegations sufficient enough to assert that insider trading had occurred under Rule 10b-5? Why or why not? [*Edward J. Goodman Life Income Trust v. Jabil Circuit, Inc.,* 594 F.3d 783 (11th Cir. 2010)]

26–8 Violations of the 1934 Act. Matrixx Initiatives, Inc., makes and sells over-the-counter pharmaceutical products. Its core brand is Zicam, which accounts for 70 percent of its sales. Matrixx received reports that some consumers had lost their sense of smell (a condition called *anosmia*) after using Zicam Cold Remedy. Four product liability suits were filed against Matrixx, seeking damages for anosmia. In public statements relating to revenues and product safety, however, Matrixx did not reveal this information. James Siracusano and other Matrixx investors filed a suit in a federal district court against the company and its executives under Section 10(b) of the Securities Exchange Act of 1934 and SEC Rule 10b-5, claiming that the statements were misleading because they did not disclose the information regarding the product liability suits. Matrixx argued that to be material, information must consist of a statistically significant number of adverse events that require disclosure. Because Siracusano's claim did not allege that Matrixx knew of a statistically significant number of adverse events, the company contended that the claim should be dismissed. What is the standard for materiality in this context? Should Siracusano's claim be dismissed? Explain. [*Matrixx Initiatives, Inc. v. Siracusano*, __ U.S. __, 131 S.Ct. 1309, 179 L.Ed.2d 398 (2011)]

26–9 **A Question of Ethics** *Melvin Lyttle told John Montana and Paul Knight about a "Trading Program" that purportedly would buy and sell securities in deals that were fully insured, as well as monitored and controlled by the Federal Reserve Board. Without checking the details or even verifying whether the Program existed, Montana and Knight, with Lyttle's help, began to sell interests in the Program to investors. For a minimum investment of $1 million, the investors were promised extraordinary rates of return—from 10 percent to as much as 100 percent per week—without risk. They were told, among other things, that the Program would "utilize banks that can ensure full bank integrity of The Transaction whose undertaking[s] are in complete harmony with international banking rules and protocol and who [sic] guarantee maximum security of a Funder's Capital Placement Amount." Nothing was required but the investors' funds and their silence—the Program was to be kept secret. Over a four-month period in 1999, Montana raised approximately $23 million from twenty-two investors. The promised gains did not accrue, however. Instead, Montana, Lyttle, and Knight depleted the investors' funds in high-risk trades or spent the funds on themselves. [*SEC v. Montana*, *464 F.Supp.2d 772 (S.D.Ind. 2006)]*

1. The Securities and Exchange Commission (SEC) filed a suit in a federal district court against Montana and the others, seeking an injunction, civil penalties, and disgorgement with interest. The SEC alleged, among other things, violations of Section 10(b) of the Securities Exchange Act of 1934 and SEC Rule 10b-5. What is required to establish a violation of these laws? Explain how and why the facts in this case meet, or fail to meet, these requirements.
2. It is often remarked, "There's a sucker born every minute!" Does that phrase describe the Program's investors? Ultimately, about half of the investors recouped the amount they invested. Should the others be considered at least partly responsible for their own losses? Why or why not?

26–10 **Video Question** To watch this chapter's video, *Jack's Restaurant, Scene 1*, go to **www.cengagebrain.com**. Register the access code that came with your new book or log in to your existing account. Select the link for the "Business Law Digital Video Library Online Access" or "Business Law CourseMate." Click on "Complete Video List," view Video 76, and then answer the following questions:

1. Assuming that the companies involved in the merger are Section 12 companies, what statutory provisions prohibit Susan from trading company stock based on her inside knowledge of the merger with GTS?
2. Did Susan breach a fiduciary duty to the corporation by telling the bartender about the proposed merger? Does the fact that she may be laid off by the company after the merger affect her duties? Explain.
3. Under what legal theory might it be illegal for the bartender to buy shares in the company based on the information that he got from Susan? Analyze the owner's potential liability. Is there enough evidence of *scienter* in this scenario for the Securities and Exchange Commission to file criminal charges against Susan if the bartender buys the stock? Discuss.

Unit Eight Unit Case Study with Dissenting Opinion: *Notz v. Everett Smith Group, Ltd.*

This Unit Case Study with Dissenting Opinion *examines* Notz v. Everett Smith Group, Ltd.,[1] *in which a minority shareholder was allegedly excluded from some of the benefits of participating in the corporation. The shareholder claimed that the majority shareholder and the board of directors, which was controlled by the majority shareholder, had breached their fiduciary duties to the minority shareholder and to the firm (see Chapter 25 on the fiduciary duties of majority shareholders and directors).*

The court had to decide, among other things, whether the minority shareholder could bring a suit directly to recover personally from the directors or whether he was limited to bringing a shareholder's derivative suit on behalf of the corporation (see the discussion of the options of shareholders with respect to appraisal rights in Chapter 24, as well as the discussion of shareholders' derivative suits in Chapter 25).

1. 316 Wis.2d 640, 764 N.W.2d 904 (2009).

CASE BACKGROUND

Albert Trostel & Sons (ATS) began as a tannery in Milwaukee, Wisconsin, in the 1800s. Over the decades, ATS acquired subsidiaries and expanded into the production of rubber and plastics. Everett Smith came to work for ATS in 1938, later became its president, and eventually gained control of the company. Smith formed Everett Smith Group, Ltd., which owned 88.9 percent of ATS by 2003. Edward Notz owned 5.5 percent, and others owned the rest. All of the members of ATS's board of directors were either officers or directors of the Smith Group.

In 2004, ATS had an opportunity to acquire Dickten & Masch, a competing thermoplastics maker. The ATS board chose not to act. Instead, the Smith Group, which had no direct holdings in the plastics field, acquired Dickten & Masch. Within months, the Smith Group's new affiliate bought the assets of ATS's plastics subsidiary, Trostel Specialty Elastomers Group, Inc. (Trostel SEG), from ATS.

Notz filed a suit in a Wisconsin state court against the Smith Group, alleging breach of fiduciary duty for stripping ATS of its most important assets and diverting the corporate opportunity to buy Dickten & Masch. The court dismissed the claim, and a state intermediate appellate court affirmed. Notz appealed to the Wisconsin Supreme Court.

MAJORITY OPINION

N. Patrick *CROOKS*, J. [Justice]:

* * * *

Notz's claims of breach of fiduciary duty are primarily based on the series of transactions in which the Smith Group acquired two plastics companies. The allegations are that the Smith Group, as ATS's majority shareholder, rejected the opportunity ATS had to buy Dickten & Masch; the Smith Group subsequently bought Dickten & Masch itself; and the Smith Group, in its capacity as majority shareholder, orchestrated the sale of ATS's valuable plastics group, Trostel SEG, to its own new acquisition.

The question is whether those allegations support direct claims for breach of fiduciary duty to a minority shareholder. * * * The Smith Group argues that * * * these are derivative claims; Notz argues that * * * these are direct claims.

* * * *Though each shareholder has an individual right to be treated fairly by the board of directors, when the injury from such actions is primarily to the corporation, there can be no direct claim by minority shareholders.* [Emphasis added.]

* * * It is true the fiduciary duty of a director is owed to the individual stockholders as well as to the corporation. Directors in this state may not use their position of trust to further their private interests. Thus, where some individual right of a stockholder is being impaired by the improper acts of a director, the stockholder can bring a direct suit on his own behalf because it is his individual right that is being violated. However, a right of action that belongs to the corporation cannot be pursued as a direct claim by an individual stockholder. * * * *Even where the injury to the corporation results in harm to a shareholder, it won't transform an action from a derivative to a direct one* * * *. That such primary and direct injury to a corporation may have a subsequent impact on the value of the stockholders' shares is clear, but that is not enough to create a right to bring a direct, rather than derivative, action. Where the injury to the corporation is the primary injury, and any injury to stockholders secondary, it is the derivative action alone that can be brought and maintained. That is the general rule, and, if it were to be abandoned, there would be no reason left for the concept of derivative actions for the redress of wrongs to a corporation. [Emphasis added.]

Continued

* * * *

Notz alleges self-dealing on the part of the majority shareholder, but * * * a shareholder-director's self-dealing [does not] transform an action that primarily injures the corporation into one that primarily injures a shareholder.

We agree with the Smith Group that breach of fiduciary duty claims, based on the lost opportunity to purchase one company and the sale of a subsidiary with great growth potential, are [derivative claims]. Our analysis * * * centers on a determination of whether the primary injury is to the corporation or to the shareholder. * * * An injury primarily * * * to an individual shareholder [is] one which affects a shareholder's rights in a manner distinct from the effect upon other shareholders. We agree with the court of appeals that the allegations here are essentially that the Smith Group stripped ATS of its most important assets and engaged in various acts of self-dealing, and that those are allegations of injury primarily to ATS. * * * All of the shareholders of ATS were affected equally by the loss of the opportunity to acquire Dickten & Masch and by the sale of Trostel SEG, the plastics division.

* * * *

* * * We agree with the court of appeals that the claims of harm alleged—the loss of a corporate opportunity and the sale of a subsidiary with high growth potential—caused harm primarily to the corporation, and thus we affirm the dismissal of Notz's direct claim of breach of fiduciary duty as to those allegations.

DISSENTING OPINION

Ann Walsh *BRADLEY*, J. [Justice] (* * * dissenting * * *).

* * * *

* * * I disagree with the majority * * * that Notz's claim for breach of fiduciary duty arising out of corporate usurpation is a derivative rather than a direct claim and that it thus must be dismissed.

Instead, * * * I conclude that Notz states a direct claim for breach of fiduciary duty arising out of the defendants' usurpation of a corporate opportunity.

* * * *

* * * Officers and directors owe a fiduciary duty to shareholders to act in good faith and to treat each shareholder fairly. The directors and officers of a corporation owe a fiduciary duty to not use their positions for their own personal advantage * * * to the detriment of the interests of the stockholders of the corporation.

That same fiduciary duty is also owed by majority shareholders to minority shareholders.

Officers, directors, and controlling shareholders breach their fiduciary duties when they treat minority shareholders differently, and inequitably, or when they use their position of trust to further their private interests. If through that control a sale of the corporate property is made and the property acquired by the majority, the minority may not be excluded from a fair participation in the fruits of the sale.

* * * *

[The majority's] conclusion is antithetical to the facts. It is true that all shareholders suffered a common injury in that the value of their investment in ATS depreciated. Nonetheless, Notz suffered an additional injury that was unique to the minority shareholders. The Smith Group who planned and executed these transactions received a net gain, but Notz suffered a net loss. * * * Notz's injury was distinct from the injury to the controlling shareholder—unlike the defendants, Notz was denied continued participation in a thriving growth industry.

QUESTIONS FOR ANALYSIS

1. **Law.** What did the majority rule with respect to the dispute before the court? On what reasoning did the majority base its ruling?
2. **Law.** What was the dissent's interpretation of the facts in this case? How would the dissent have applied the law to these facts? Why?
3. **Ethics.** From an ethical perspective, should ATS's directors have made different decisions on the choices that came before the board? Discuss.
4. **Economic Dimensions.** Could a shareholder in the position of the minority shareholder in this case seek a judicial dissolution? If so, what would be the likely result?
5. **Implications for the Shareholder.** Can a shareholder pursue a derivative claim on behalf of a corporation? If so, what steps must the shareholder take? Why might a shareholder be reluctant to take these steps?

Unit Nine

Property and Its Protection

Unit Contents

27 Personal Property and Bailments

28 Real Property and Landlord-Tenant Law

29 Insurance, Wills, and Trusts

Chapter 27

Personal Property and Bailments

Learning Objectives

After reading this chapter, you should be able to answer the following questions:

1. What is real property? What is personal property?
2. What is the difference between a joint tenancy and a tenancy in common?
3. What are the three elements necessary for an effective gift?
4. What are the three elements of a bailment?
5. What are the basic rights and duties of a bailee? What are the rights and duties of a bailor?

The Learning Objectives above are designed to help improve your understanding of the chapter.

Property consists of the legally protected rights and interests a person has in anything with an ascertainable value that is subject to ownership. Property would have little value—and the word would have little meaning—if the law did not define the right to use it, to sell or dispose of it, and to prevent trespass on it.

Property is divided into real property and personal property. **Real property** (sometimes called *realty* or *real estate*) means the land and everything permanently attached to it. Everything else is **personal property,** or *personalty.* Attorneys sometimes refer to personal property as **chattel,** a term used under the common law to denote all forms of personal property. Personal property can be tangible or intangible. *Tangible* personal property, such as a television set or a car, has physical substance. *Intangible* personal property represents some set of rights and interests but has no real physical existence. Stocks and bonds, patents, and copyrights are examples of intangible personal property.

Property Ownership

Ownership of property—both real and personal property—can be viewed as a bundle of rights, including the right to possess the property and to dispose of it by sale, gift, lease, or other means. As discussed in Chapter 13, the right of ownership in property is often referred to as *title*.

Fee Simple

A person who holds the entire bundle of rights to property is said to be the owner in **fee simple.** The owner in fee simple is entitled to use, possess, or dispose of the property as he or she chooses during his or her lifetime, and on this owner's death, the interests in the property descend to his or her heirs. We will return to this form of property ownership in Chapter 28, in the context of ownership rights in real property.

Concurrent Ownership

Persons who share ownership rights simultaneously in a particular piece of property are said to be *concurrent* owners. There are two principal types of **concurrent ownership:** *tenancy in common* and *joint tenancy.* Additionally, in some states, married persons can hold property together as *community property.*

TENANCY IN COMMON The term **tenancy in common** refers to a form of co-ownership in which each of two or more persons owns an *undivided* interest in the property. The interest is undivided because each tenant has rights in the *whole* property. On the death of a tenant in common, that tenant's interest in the property passes to her or his heirs.

EXAMPLE 27.1 Sofia and Greg own a rare stamp collection together as tenants in common. This means that Sofia and Greg each have rights in the *entire* collection. (If Sofia owned some of the stamps and Greg owned others, then the interest would be *divided.*) In the event that Sofia dies before Greg, a one-half interest in the stamp collection will become the property of Sofia's heirs. If Sofia sells her interest to Jorge before she dies, Jorge and Greg will be co-owners as tenants in common. If Jorge dies, his interest in the personal property will pass to his heirs, and they in turn will own the property with Greg as tenants in common. •

JOINT TENANCY In a **joint tenancy,** each of two or more persons owns an undivided interest in the property, but a deceased joint tenant's interest passes to the surviving joint tenant or tenants.[1] The rights of a surviving joint tenant to inherit a deceased joint tenant's ownership interest—which are referred to as *survivorship rights*—distinguish the joint tenancy from the tenancy in common. A joint tenancy can be terminated before a joint tenant's death by gift or by sale; in this situation, the person who receives the property as a gift or who purchases the property becomes a tenant in common, not a joint tenant.

EXAMPLE 27.2 In Example 27.1, suppose that Sofia and Greg held their stamp collection in a joint tenancy. In that situation, if Sofia died before Greg, the entire collection would become the property of Greg. Sofia's heirs would receive absolutely no interest in the collection. If Sofia, while living, sold her interest to Jorge, however, the sale would terminate the joint tenancy, and Jorge and Greg would become owners as tenants in common. •

Generally, it is presumed that a co-tenancy is a tenancy in common unless there is a clear intention to establish a joint tenancy. Thus, language such as "to Jerrold and Eva as joint tenants with right of survivorship, and not as tenants in common," would be necessary to create a joint tenancy.

1. See, for example, *In re Estate of Grote,* 766 N.W.2d 82 (Minn.App. 2009).

COMMUNITY PROPERTY A married couple is allowed to own property as **community property** in a limited number of states.[2] If property is held as community property, each spouse technically owns an undivided one-half interest in property acquired during the marriage. Generally, community property does *not* include property acquired before the marriage or property acquired by gift or inheritance as separate property during the marriage. After a divorce, community property is divided equally in some states and according to the discretion of the court in other states.

Acquiring Ownership of Personal Property

The most common way of acquiring personal property is by purchasing it. We have already discussed the purchase and sale of personal property (goods) in Chapters 13 through 15. Often, property is acquired by will or inheritance, a topic we will cover in Chapter 29. Here, we look at additional ways in which ownership of personal property can be acquired, including acquisition by possession, production, gifts, accession, and confusion.

Possession

Sometimes, a person can become the owner of personal property merely by possessing it. One example of acquiring ownership by possession is the capture of wild animals. Wild animals belong to no one in their natural state, and the first person to take possession of a wild animal normally owns it. A hunter who kills a deer, for instance, has assumed ownership of it (unless he or she acted in violation of the law).

Those who find lost or abandoned property can also acquire ownership rights through mere possession of the property, as will be discussed later in the chapter. (Ownership rights in real property can also be acquired through possession, such as adverse possession—see Chapter 28.)

Production

Production—the fruits of labor—is another means of acquiring ownership of personal property. For instance, writers, inventors, and manufacturers all produce personal property and thereby acquire title to it. (In some situations, though, as when a researcher is hired to invent a new product or technique, the researcher-producer may not own what is produced—see Chapter 21.)

2. These states include Alaska, Arizona, California, Idaho, Louisiana, Nevada, New Mexico, Texas, Washington, and Wisconsin. Puerto Rico allows property to be owned as community property as well.

Gifts

A **gift** is another fairly common means of acquiring and transferring ownership of real and personal property. A gift is essentially a *voluntary* transfer of property ownership for which no consideration is given. As discussed in Chapter 9, the presence of consideration is what distinguishes a contract from a gift.

For a gift to be effective, three requirements must be met: (1) donative intent on the part of the *donor* (the one giving the gift), (2) delivery, and (3) acceptance by the *donee* (the one receiving the gift). We examine each of these requirements here, as well as the requirements of a gift made in contemplation of imminent death. Until these three requirements are met, no effective gift has been made. **EXAMPLE 27.3** Denzel's aunt tells him that she *intends* to give him a new Mercedes-Benz for his next birthday. This is simply a promise to make a gift. It is not considered a gift until the Mercedes-Benz is delivered and accepted. •

DONATIVE INTENT When a gift is challenged in court, the court will determine whether donative intent exists by looking at the language of the donor and the surrounding circumstances. A court may look at the relationship between the parties and the size of the gift in relation to the donor's other assets. When a person has given away a large portion of her or his assets, the court will scrutinize the transaction closely to determine the donor's mental capacity and look for indications of fraud or duress.

In the following case, the court examined the intent and capacity of a woman who gave more than $50,000 to her dog's veterinarian.

Case 27.1 Goodman v. Atwood

Appeals Court of Massachusetts, 78 Mass.App.Ct. 655, 940 N.E.2d 514 (2011).

FACTS Jean Knowles Goodman, who was eighty-five years old, gave Dr. Steven Atwood several checks over a period of three months that totaled $56,100. Atwood was a veterinarian who had cared for Goodman's dogs for nearly twenty years. Atwood and Goodman had become friends, and he had regularly visited her house to care for her dogs and socialize with her. Shortly after writing the last check, Goodman was hospitalized and diagnosed with dementia (loss of brain function) and alcohol dependency. A guardian was appointed for Goodman. The guardian filed a lawsuit against Atwood to invalidate the gifts, claiming that Goodman had lacked mental capacity and donative intent. At trial, a psychiatrist who had examined Goodman testified on behalf of Atwood that while Goodman lacked the capacity to care for herself, she would have understood that she was giving away her funds. The trial judge ruled that Goodman had the capacity and intent to make the gifts to Atwood. The guardian appealed.

ISSUE Was there sufficient proof that Goodman had donative intent to make the gifts to Atwood, even though she was later found to be mentally incompetent?

DECISION Yes. The state appellate court affirmed the lower court's judgment in favor of Atwood, the defendant.

REASON The plaintiff in civil actions bears the burden of proving the essential elements of a claim—in this case, the lack of capacity and intent. The court found that the trial judge had used the proper standard of evidence and had kept the burden of proof on the plaintiff. There was sufficient evidence of the donor's capacity and intent to support the trial judge's findings. "The plaintiff's own witness conceded the possibility that the donor experienced periods of mental awareness in addition to her lucidity regarding financial affairs." The appellate court acknowledged "that a reasonable and conscientious finder of fact could have reached a different conclusion." Nonetheless, it is not the task of an appellate court "to substitute our judgment for that of the fact finder, and on this record we do not conclude that a mistake has clearly been made."

WHAT IF THE FACTS WERE DIFFERENT? ***If this had been a jury trial, and the jury had concluded that Goodman lacked mental capacity and intent at the time she made the gifts to Atwood, would the appellate court still have affirmed the decision? Why or why not?***

DELIVERY The gift must be delivered to the donee. Delivery may be accomplished by means of a third person who is the agent of either the donor or the donee. Naturally, no delivery is necessary if the gift is already in the hands of the donee (provided there is donative intent and acceptance). Delivery is obvious in most instances, but some objects cannot be relinquished physically. Then the question of delivery depends on the surrounding circumstances.

Constructive Delivery. When the object itself cannot be physically delivered, a symbolic, or constructive, delivery will be sufficient. **Constructive delivery** does not confer actual possession of the object in question, only the right to take actual possession. Thus, constructive delivery is a general term used to describe an action that the law holds to be the equivalent of real delivery.

EXAMPLE 27.4 Angela wants to make a gift of various rare coins that she has stored in a safe-deposit box at a bank. She certainly cannot deliver the box itself to the donee, and she does not want to take the coins out of the bank. In this situation, she can simply deliver the key to the box to the donee and authorize the donee's access to the box and its contents. This action constitutes a constructive delivery of the contents of the box. •

The delivery of intangible property—such as stocks, bonds, insurance policies, and contracts, for example—must always be accomplished by symbolic, or constructive, delivery. This is because the documents represent rights and are not, in themselves, the true property.

Relinquishing Dominion and Control. An effective delivery also requires giving up complete control and **dominion** (ownership rights) over the subject matter of the gift. The outcome of disputes often turns on whether control has actually been relinquished. The Internal Revenue Service scrutinizes transactions between relatives, especially when one claims to have given income-producing property to another who is in a lower marginal tax bracket. Unless complete control over the property has been relinquished, the "donor"—not the family member who received the "gift"—will have to pay taxes on the income from that property.

In the following classic case, the court focused on the requirement that a donor must relinquish complete control and dominion over property given to the donee before a gift can be effectively delivered.

Classic Case 27.2 In re Estate of Piper

Missouri Court of Appeals, 676 S.W.2d 897 (1984).

FACTS Gladys Piper died intestate (without a will) in 1982. At her death, she owned miscellaneous personal property worth $5,000 and had in her purse $200 in cash and two diamond rings, known as the Andy Piper rings. The contents of her purse were taken by her niece Wanda Brown, allegedly to preserve them for the estate. Clara Kaufmann, a friend of Piper's, filed a claim against the estate for $4,800. From October 1974 until Piper's death, Kaufmann had taken Piper to the doctor, beauty shop, and grocery store; had written her checks to pay her bills; and had helped her care for her home. Kaufmann maintained that Piper had promised to pay her for these services and had given her the diamond rings as a gift. A Missouri state trial court denied her request for payment. The court found that her services had been voluntary. Kaufmann then filed a petition for delivery of personal property–the rings–which was granted by the trial court. Brown, other heirs, and the administrator of Piper's estate appealed.

ISSUE Had Piper made an effective gift of the rings to Kaufmann?

DECISION No. The state appellate court reversed the judgment of the trial court on the ground that Piper had never delivered the rings to Kaufmann.

REASON Kaufmann claimed that the rings belonged to her by reason of a "consummated gift long prior to the death of Gladys Piper." Two witnesses testified at the trial that Piper had told them that she was going to wear the rings until she died but that the rings belonged to Kaufmann. The appellate court, however, found "no evidence of any actual delivery." The court pointed out that the essentials of a gift are (1) a present intention to make a gift on the part of the donor, (2) a delivery of the property by the donor to the donee, and (3) an acceptance by the donee. Here, the evidence showed only an intent to make a gift. Because there was no delivery–either actual or constructive–a valid gift was not made. For Piper to have made a gift, she would have had to execute her intention by the complete and unconditional delivery of the property or the delivery of a proper written instrument evidencing the gift. As this did not occur, the court found that there had been no gift.

WHAT IF THE FACTS WERE DIFFERENT? *Suppose that Gladys Piper had told Clara Kaufmann that she was giving the rings to Clara but wished to keep them in her possession for a few more days. Would this have affected the court's decision in this case? Explain.*

IMPACT OF THIS CASE ON TODAY'S LAW *This case clearly illustrates the delivery requirement when making a gift. Assuming that Piper did, indeed, intend for Kaufmann to have the rings, it was unfortunate that Kaufmann had no right to receive them after Piper's death. Yet the alternative could lead to perhaps even more unfairness. The policy behind the delivery requirement is to protect alleged donors and their heirs from fraudulent claims based solely on parol evidence. If not for this policy, an alleged donee could easily claim that a gift was made when, in fact, it was not.*

ACCEPTANCE The final requirement of a valid gift is acceptance by the donee. This rarely presents any problem, as most donees readily accept their gifts. The courts generally assume acceptance unless the circumstances indicate otherwise.

GIFTS *INTER VIVOS* AND GIFTS *CAUSA MORTIS* A gift made during one's lifetime is termed a **gift *inter vivos*. Gifts *causa mortis*** (so-called *deathbed gifts*), in contrast, are made in contemplation of imminent death. A gift *causa mortis* does not become absolute until the donor dies from the contemplated illness, and it is automatically revoked if the donor recovers from that illness. The gift is also revoked if the prospective donee dies before the donor. To be effective, a gift *causa mortis* must also meet the three requirements discussed earlier—donative intent, delivery, and acceptance by the donee.

EXAMPLE 27.5 Yang, who is about to undergo surgery to remove a cancerous tumor, delivers an envelope to Chao, a close business associate. The envelope contains a letter saying, "I realize my days are numbered, and I want to give you this check for $1 million in the event of my death from this operation." Chao cashes the check. The surgeon performs the operation and removes the tumor. Yang fully recovers. Several months later, Yang dies from a heart attack that is totally unrelated to the operation. If Yang's personal representative (the party charged with administering Yang's estate) tries to recover the $1 million, she normally will succeed. The gift *causa mortis* to Chao is automatically revoked if Yang recovers. The *specific event* that was contemplated in making the gift was death from a particular operation. Because Yang's death was not the result of this event, the gift is revoked, and the $1 million passes to Yang's estate. Similarly, even if Yang had died during the operation, the gift would have been revoked if Chao had died a few minutes earlier. In that event, the $1 million would have passed to Yang's estate, and not to Chao's heirs. •

Accession

Accession means "something added." Accession occurs when someone adds value to an item of personal property by the use of either labor or materials. Generally, there is no dispute about who owns the property after the accession occurs, especially when the accession is accomplished with the owner's consent. **EXAMPLE 27.6** Hoshi buys all the materials necessary to customize his Corvette. He hires Zach, a customizing specialist, to come to his house to perform the work. Hoshi pays Zach for the value of the labor, obviously retaining title to the property. •

If the improvement was made wrongfully—without the permission of the owner—the owner retains title to the property and normally does not have to pay for the improvement. This is true even if the accession increased the value of the property substantially. **EXAMPLE 27.7** Patti steals a car and puts expensive new tires on it. If the rightful owner later recovers the car, he obviously will not be required to compensate Patti, a car thief, for the value of the new tires. •

If the accession is performed in good faith—and the improvement was made due to an honest mistake of judgment—the owner normally still retains title to the property but usually must pay for the improvement. In rare instances, when the improvement greatly increases the value of the property or changes its identity, the court may rule that ownership has passed to the improver. In those rare situations, the improver must compensate the original owner for the value of the property before the accession occurred.

Confusion

Confusion is the commingling (mixing together) of goods to such an extent that one person's personal property cannot be distinguished from another's. Confusion frequently occurs with *fungible goods,* such as grain or oil, which consist of identical units.

If confusion occurs as a result of agreement, an honest mistake, or the act of some third party, the owners share ownership as tenants in common and will share any loss in proportion to their ownership interests in the property. **EXAMPLE 27.8** Five farmers in a small Iowa community enter into a cooperative arrangement. Each fall, the farmers harvest the same amount of number 2–grade yellow corn and store it in silos that are held by the cooperative. Each farmer thus owns one-fifth of the total corn in the silos. If a fire burns down one of the silos, each farmer will bear one-fifth of the loss. • When goods are confused due to an intentional wrongful act, then the innocent party ordinarily acquires title to the whole.

Mislaid, Lost, and Abandoned Property

As already mentioned, one of the methods of acquiring ownership of property is to possess it. Simply finding something and holding on to it, however, does not necessarily give the finder any legal rights in the property. Different rules apply, depending on whether the property was mislaid, lost, or abandoned.

Mislaid Property

Property that has voluntarily been placed somewhere by the owner and then inadvertently forgotten is **mislaid property.** A person who finds mislaid property does not obtain title to the goods. Instead, the owner of the place where the property was mislaid becomes the caretaker of the property because it is highly likely that the true owner will return.[3] **EXAMPLE 27.9** Austin goes to a movie theater. While paying for popcorn at the concessions stand, he sets his iPad on the counter and then leaves it there. The iPad is mislaid property, and the theater owner is entrusted with the duty of reasonable care for it. •

Lost Property

Property that is *involuntarily* left is **lost property.** A finder of the property can claim title to the property against the whole world—*except the true owner.*[4] The well-known children's adage "Finders keepers, losers weepers" is actually written

3. The finder of mislaid property is an involuntary bailee (to be discussed later in this chapter).
4. For a classic English case establishing this principle, see *Armory v. Delamirie,* 93 Eng.Rep. 664 (K.B. [King's Bench] 1722).

into law—provided that the loser (the rightful owner) cannot be found. If the true owner is identified and demands that the lost property be returned, the finder must return it. In contrast, if a third party attempts to take possession of the lost property, the finder will have a better title than the third party.

EXAMPLE 27.10 Khalia works in a large library at night. As she crosses the courtyard on her way home, she finds a gold bracelet set with what seem to be precious stones. She takes the bracelet to a jeweler to have it appraised. While pretending to weigh the bracelet, the jeweler's employee removes several of the stones. If Khalia brings an action to recover the stones from the jeweler, she normally will win because she found lost property and holds title against everyone *except the true owner.* •

CONVERSION OF LOST PROPERTY When a finder of lost property knows the true owner and fails to return the property to that person, the finder has committed the tort of conversion (the wrongful taking of another's property—see Chapter 4).

EXAMPLE 27.11 In Example 27.10, suppose that Khalia knows that the gold bracelet she found belongs to Geneva. If Khalia does not return Geneva's bracelet, she can be held liable for conversion. • Many states require the finder to make a reasonably diligent search to locate the true owner of lost property.

ESTRAY STATUTES Many states have **estray statutes,** which encourage and facilitate the return of property to its true owner and then reward the finder for honesty if the property remains unclaimed. These laws provide an incentive for finders to report their discoveries by making it possible for them, after the passage of a specified period of time, to acquire legal title to the property they have found. Generally, the item must be lost property, not merely mislaid property, for estray statutes to apply. Estray statutes usually require the finder or the county clerk to advertise the property in an attempt to help the owner recover what has been lost.

CASE EXAMPLE 27.12 Drug smugglers often enter the United States illegally from Canada via a frozen river that flows through Van Buren, Maine. When two railroad employees, walking near the railroad tracks in Van Buren, found a duffel bag that contained $165,580 in cash, they reported their find to U.S. Customs agents, who took custody of the bag and cash. The next day, a drug-sniffing dog gave a positive alert on the bag for the scent of drugs. The U.S. government filed a lawsuit claiming title to the property under forfeiture laws, which provide that cash and property involved in illegal drug transactions are forfeited to the government. The two employees argued that they were entitled to the $165,580 under Maine's estray statute. The statute required finders to (1) provide written notice to the town clerk within seven days after finding the property, (2) post a public notice in the town, and (3) advertise in the town's newspaper for one month. Because the employees had not fulfilled these requirements, the court ruled that they had not acquired title to the property. Thus, the federal government had a right to seize the cash.[5] •

Abandoned Property

Property that has been discarded by the true owner, who has no intention of reclaiming title to it, is **abandoned property.** Someone who finds abandoned property acquires title to it that is good against the whole world, *including the original owner.* The owner of lost property who eventually gives up any further attempt to find it is frequently held to have abandoned the property. If a person finds abandoned property while trespassing on the property of another, title vests in the owner of the land, not in the finder.

EXAMPLE 27.13 As Aleka is driving on the freeway, her valuable scarf blows out the window. She retraces her route and searches for the scarf but cannot find it. She finally gives up her search and proceeds to her destination five hundred miles away. When Frye later finds the scarf, he acquires title to it that is good even against Aleka. By completely giving up her search, Aleka abandoned the scarf just as effectively as if she had intentionally discarded it. •

Bailments

Many routine personal and business transactions involve bailments. A **bailment** is formed by the delivery of personal property, without transfer of title, by one person, called a **bailor,** to another, called a **bailee,** usually under an agreement for a particular purpose—for example, to loan, lease, store, repair, or transport the property. The distinguishing characteristic of a bailment compared with a sale or a gift is that there is no passage of title and no intent to transfer title. On completion of the purpose, the bailee is obligated to return the bailed property in the same or better condition to the bailor or a third person or to dispose of it as directed.

Bailments usually are created by agreement, but not necessarily by contract, because in many bailments not all of the elements of a contract (such as mutual assent and consideration) are present. **EXAMPLE 27.14** If Amy lends her bicycle to a friend, a bailment is created, but not by contract, because there is no consideration. Many commercial bailments, such as the delivery of clothing to the cleaners for dry cleaning, are based on contract, though. •

Elements of a Bailment

Not all transactions involving the delivery of property from one person to another create a bailment. For such a transfer to become a bailment, the following three elements must be present:

5. *United States v. One Hundred Sixty-Five Thousand Five Hundred Eighty Dollars ($165,580) in U.S. Currency,* 502 F.Supp.2d 114 (D.Me. 2007).

1. Personal property.
2. Delivery of possession (without title).
3. Agreement that the property will be returned to the bailor or otherwise disposed of according to its owner's directions.

PERSONAL PROPERTY REQUIREMENT Only personal property, not real property or persons, can be the subject of a bailment. Although bailments commonly involve *tangible items*—jewelry, cattle, automobiles, and the like—*intangible personal* property, such as promissory notes and shares of corporate stock, may also be bailed.

DELIVERY OF POSSESSION *Delivery of possession* means the transfer of possession of the property to the bailee. For delivery to occur, the bailee must be given *exclusive possession and control* over the property, and the bailee must *knowingly* accept the personal property.[6] In other words, the bailee must *intend* to exercise control over it.

If either delivery of possession or knowing acceptance is lacking, there is no bailment relationship. **EXAMPLE 27.15** Olga goes to a five-star restaurant and checks her coat at the door. In the pocket of the coat is a diamond necklace worth $20,000. In accepting the coat, the bailee does not *knowingly* also accept the necklace. Thus, a bailment of the coat exists—because the restaurant has exclusive possession and control over the coat and knowingly accepted it—but not a bailment of the necklace. •

Physical versus Constructive Delivery. Either *physical* or *constructive* delivery will result in the bailee's exclusive possession of and control over the property. As discussed earlier in the context of gifts, constructive delivery is a substitute, or symbolic, delivery. What is delivered to the bailee is not the actual property bailed (such as a car) but something so related to the property (such as the car keys) that the requirement of delivery is satisfied.

Involuntary Bailments. In certain situations, a bailment is found despite the apparent lack of the requisite elements of control and knowledge. One example of such a situation occurs when the bailee acquires the property accidentally or by mistake—as in finding someone else's lost or mislaid property. A bailment is created even though the bailor did not voluntarily deliver the property to the bailee. Such bailments are called *constructive* or *involuntary* bailments.

EXAMPLE 27.16 Several corporate managers are asked to attend an urgent meeting at the law firm of Jacobs & Matheson. One of the corporate officers, Kyle Gustafson, inadvertently leaves his briefcase at the firm at the conclusion of the meeting. In this situation, a court could find that an involuntary bailment was created, even though Gustafson did not voluntarily deliver the briefcase and the law firm did not intentionally accept it. If an involuntary bailment existed, the firm would be responsible for taking care of the briefcase and returning it to Gustafson. •

6. We are dealing here with *voluntary bailments*. This does not apply to *involuntary bailments*.

BAILMENT AGREEMENT A bailment agreement can be express or implied. Although a written contract is not required for bailments of less than one year—that is, the Statute of Frauds does not apply—see Chapter 10—it is a good idea to have one, especially when valuable property is involved.

The bailment agreement expressly or impliedly provides for the return of the bailed property to the bailor or to a third person, or for the disposal of the property by the bailee. The agreement presupposes that the bailee will return the identical goods originally given by the bailor. In certain types of bailments, though, such as bailments of fungible goods, the property returned need only be equivalent property.

EXAMPLE 27.17 If Holman stores his grain (fungible goods) in Kwan's warehouse, a bailment is created. At the end of the storage period, however, Kwan is not obligated to return to Holman exactly the same grain that he stored. As long as Kwan's warehouse returns grain of the same *type, grade,* and *quantity,* the warehouse—the bailee—has performed its obligation. •

Ordinary Bailments

Bailments are either *ordinary* or *special (extraordinary)*. There are three types of ordinary bailments. They are distinguished according *to which party receives a benefit from the bailment.* This factor will dictate the rights and liabilities of the parties, and the courts use it to determine the standard of care required of the bailee in possession of the personal property. The three types of ordinary bailments are as follows:

1. *Bailment for the sole benefit of the bailor.* This is a gratuitous bailment (a bailment without consideration) for the convenience and benefit of the bailor. Basically, the bailee is caring for the bailor's property as a favor. **EXAMPLE 27.18** Allen asks his friend, Sumi, to store his car in her garage while he is away. If Sumi agrees to do so, then this is a gratuitous bailment because the bailment of the car is for the sole benefit of the bailor (Allen). •
2. *Bailment for the sole benefit of the bailee.* This type of bailment typically occurs when one person lends an item to another person (the bailee) solely for the bailee's convenience and benefit. **EXAMPLE 27.19** Allen asks to borrow Sumi's boat so that he can go sailing over the weekend. The bailment of the boat is for Allen's (the bailee's) sole benefit. •
3. *Bailment for the mutual benefit of the bailee and the bailor.* This is the most common kind of bailment and involves some form of compensation for storing items or holding

property while it is being serviced. It is a contractual bailment and may be referred to as a *bailment for hire* or *a commercial bailment.* **EXAMPLE 27.20** Allen leaves his car at a service station for an oil change. Because the service station will be paid to change Allen's oil, this is a mutual-benefit bailment. • Many lease arrangements in which the lease involves goods (leases were discussed in Chapters 13 through 15) also fall into this category of bailment once the lessee takes possession.

Rights of the Bailee Certain rights are implicit in the bailment agreement. Generally, the bailee has the right to take possession of the property, to utilize the property for accomplishing the purpose of the bailment, to receive some form of compensation, and to limit her or his liability for the bailed goods. These rights of the bailee are present (with some limitations) in varying degrees in all bailment transactions.

Right of Possession. A hallmark of the bailment agreement is that the bailee acquires the *right to control and possess the property temporarily.* The bailee's right of possession permits the bailee to recover damages from any third person for damage or loss of the property. **EXAMPLE 27.21** No-Spot Dry Cleaners sends all suede leather garments to Cleanall Company for special processing. If Cleanall loses or damages any leather goods, No-Spot has the right to recover against Cleanall. • If the bailed property is stolen, the bailee has a legal right to regain possession of it or to recover damages.

Right to Use Bailed Property. Depending on the type of bailment and the terms of the bailment agreement, a bailee may also have a right to use the bailed property. When no provision is made, the extent of use depends on how necessary it is for the goods to be at the bailee's disposal for the ordinary purpose of the bailment to be carried out. **EXAMPLE 27.22** If you borrow a friend's car to drive to the airport, you, as the bailee, would obviously be expected to use the car. In a bailment involving the long-term storage of a car, however, the bailee is not expected to use the car because the ordinary purpose of a storage bailment does not include use of the property. •

Right of Compensation. Except in a gratuitous bailment, a bailee has a right to be compensated as provided for in the bailment agreement. The bailee also has a right to be reimbursed for costs incurred and services rendered in the keeping of the bailed property—even in a gratuitous bailment. **EXAMPLE 27.23** Margo loses her pet dog, and Justine finds it. Justine takes Margo's dog to her home and feeds it. Even though she takes good care of the dog, it becomes ill, and she takes it to a veterinarian. Justine pays the bill for the veterinarian's services and the medicine. Justine normally will be entitled to be reimbursed by Margo for all reasonable costs incurred in the keeping of Margo's dog. •

To enforce the right of compensation, the bailee has a right to place a *possessory lien* on the specific bailed property until he or she has been fully compensated. A lien on bailed property is referred to as a **bailee's lien,** or artisan's lien (discussed in Chapter 19). If the bailor refuses to pay or cannot pay the charges (compensation), in most states the bailee is entitled to foreclose on the lien and sell the property to recover the amount owed.

Right to Limit Liability. In ordinary bailments, bailees have the right to limit their liability, provided that the limitations are called to the attention of the bailor and are not against public policy. It is essential that the bailor be informed of the limitation in some way.

Even when the bailor knows of the limitation, courts consider certain types of disclaimers of liability to be against public policy and therefore illegal. The courts carefully scrutinize *exculpatory clauses,* or clauses that limit a person's liability for her or his own wrongful acts, and in bailments they are often held to be illegal. This is particularly true in bailments for the mutual benefit of the bailor and the bailee. **EXAMPLE 27.24** A receipt from a parking garage expressly disclaims liability for any damage to parked cars, regardless of the cause. Because the bailee has attempted to exclude liability for the bailee's own negligence, including the parking attendant's negligence, the clause will likely be deemed unenforceable because it is against public policy. •

Duties of the Bailee The bailee has two basic responsibilities: (1) to take appropriate care of the property and (2) to surrender the property to the bailor or dispose of it in accordance with the bailor's instructions at the end of the bailment.

The Duty of Care. The bailee must exercise reasonable care in preserving the bailed property (the duty of care was discussed in Chapter 4). What constitutes reasonable care in a bailment situation normally depends on the nature and specific circumstances of the bailment.

The courts determine the appropriate standard of care on the basis of the type of bailment involved. In a bailment for the sole benefit of the bailor, the bailee need exercise only a slight degree of care. In a bailment for the sole benefit of the bailee, however, the bailee must exercise great care. In a mutual-benefit bailment, courts normally impose a reasonable standard of care—that is, the bailee must exercise the degree of care that a reasonable and prudent person would exercise in the same circumstances. Exhibit 27–1 on the following page illustrates these concepts. A bailee's failure to exercise appropriate care in handling the bailor's property results in tort liability.

Duty to Return Bailed Property. At the end of the bailment, the bailee normally must hand over the original property to either the bailor or someone the bailor designates, or must otherwise dispose of it as directed. This is usually a *contractual*

• ***Exhibit* 27–1 Degree of Care Required of a Bailee**

Bailment for the Sole Benefit of the Bailor	Mutual-Benefit Bailment	Bailment for the Sole Benefit of the Bailee
DEGREE OF CARE →		
SLIGHT	REASONABLE	GREAT

duty arising from the bailment agreement (contract). Failure to give up possession at the time the bailment ends is a breach of contract and could result in the tort of conversion or an action based on bailee negligence.

If the bailed property has been lost or is returned damaged, a court will presume that the bailee was negligent. The bailee's obligation is excused, however, if the property was destroyed, lost, or stolen through no fault of the bailee (or claimed by a third party with a superior claim).

Because the bailee has a duty to return the bailed goods to the bailor, a bailee may be liable for conversion or misdelivery if the goods being held or delivered are given to the wrong person. Hence, a bailee must be satisfied that the person (other than the bailor) to whom the goods are being delivered is the actual owner or has authority from the owner to take possession of the goods.

A bailee's alleged negligence was at the heart of the following case.

Case 27.3 LaPlace v. Briere

New Jersey Superior Court, Appellate Division, 404 N.J.Super. 585, 962 A.2d 1139 (2009).
www.lawlibrary.rutgers.edu/search.shtml[a]

FACTS Michael LaPlace boarded his horses, including a trained Quarter Horse named Park Me In First, at Pierre Briere's stable in New Jersey. Charlene Bridgwood also boarded a horse at the stable. About a dozen years earlier, LaPlace had boarded horses at the farm owned by Bridgwood's husband. To exercise a horse, its handler often uses a technique known as *lunging*—that is, having the horse walk, trot, or canter in a circle while it is secured to a lunge line held by the handler, who stands in the center of the circle. Bridgwood had often lunged the horses, including those owned by LaPlace. In 2006, after a snowy night while LaPlace and Briere were at a horse show, Bridgwood offered to help Briere's shorthanded staff by lunging the horses, even though she was not an employee of the stable. During the exercise, Park Me In First suddenly reared up on his hind legs. He then collapsed with blood pumping from his nose and died. The veterinarian could not determine the cause of death without performing a necropsy (autopsy). Briere and Bridgwood offered to pay for the procedure, but none was performed because LaPlace did not authorize it until after the horse's remains had been removed. LaPlace filed a suit in a New Jersey state court against Briere, claiming negligence. The court issued a summary judgment in the defendant's favor. LaPlace appealed.

ISSUE Without proof of negligence, can a bailee (Briere) be absolved of liability on a claim for the loss of bailed goods (Park Me In First)?

DECISION Yes. The state intermediate appellate court affirmed the lower court's judgment. Briere could not be held liable on that claim for the death of Park Me In First.

REASON A bailee has a duty to take reasonable care of bailed property and is liable for any loss caused by a failure to do so. If the property is damaged in the care of the bailee, a presumption of negligence arises. But this presumption may be rebutted by proof that the loss was not caused by the bailee's negligence or that he or she exercised due care. In this case, LaPlace's horse, Park Me In First, died in Briere's care during its bailment, giving rise to a presumption of negligence. Briere showed, however, that at the time the horse died, Bridgwood, who was experienced in handling horses, was exercising the horse in an ordinary manner. This proof is "devoid of any evidence of negligence causing the death of the horse, and thus rebuts the presumption of negligence." LaPlace did not offer any additional proof of negligence, and "determining the cause of death was uniquely within the control of plaintiff," whose permission was required for a necropsy.

FOR CRITICAL ANALYSIS—Legal Consideration *As a bailee, was Briere liable in conversion for the death of Park Me In First? Explain. (Hint: Did Briere wrongfully possess or use the horse without permission and without just cause?)*

a. In the "Search the N.J. Courts Decisions" section, in the "Please enter your search term(s) below:" box, type "LaPlace" and click on "Search!" In the result, click on the name of the case to access the opinion. Rutgers University maintains this Web site.

Duties of the Bailor The duties of a bailor are essentially the same as the rights of a bailee. A bailor has a duty to compensate the bailee either as agreed or as reimbursement for costs incurred by the bailee in keeping the bailed property. A bailor also has an all-encompassing duty to provide the bailee with goods or chattels that are free from known defects that could cause injury to the bailee.

Bailor's Duty to Reveal Defects. The bailor's duty to reveal defects to the bailee translates into two rules:

1. In a *mutual-benefit bailment,* the bailor must notify the bailee of all known defects and any hidden defects that the bailor knows of or could have discovered with reasonable diligence and proper inspection.
2. In a *bailment for the sole benefit of the bailee,* the bailor must notify the bailee of any known defects.

The bailor's duty to reveal defects is based on a negligence theory of tort law. A bailor who fails to give the appropriate notice is liable to the bailee and to any other person who might reasonably be expected to come into contact with the defective article.

EXAMPLE 27.25 Rentco (the bailor) rents a tractor to Hal Iverson. Unknown to Rentco, the brake mechanism on the tractor is defective at the time the bailment is made. Iverson uses the defective tractor without knowledge of the brake problem and is injured, along with two other field workers, when the tractor rolls out of control down an incline after failing to stop. In this situation, Rentco is liable for the injuries sustained by Iverson and the other workers because it negligently failed to discover the defect and notify Iverson. •

Warranty Liability for Defective Goods. A bailor can also incur *warranty liability* based on contract law (see Chapter 15) for injuries resulting from the bailment of defective articles. Property leased by a bailor must be *fit for the intended purpose of the bailment.* Warranties of fitness arise by law in sales contracts and leases, and judges have extended these warranties to situations in which the bailees are compensated for the bailment (such as when one leaves a car with a parking attendant). Article 2A of the Uniform Commercial Code (UCC) extends the implied warranties of merchantability and fitness for a particular purpose to bailments whenever the bailments include rights to use the bailed goods.[7]

Special Types of Bailments

Although many bailments are the ordinary bailments that we have just discussed, a business is also likely to engage in some special types of bailment transactions. These include bailments in which the bailee's duty of care is *extraordinary*—that is, the bailee's liability for loss or damage to the property is absolute—as is generally true in bailments involving common carriers and hotel operators. Warehouse companies have the same duty of care as ordinary bailees, but, like carriers, they are subject to extensive regulation under federal and state laws, including Article 7 of the UCC.

Common Carriers *Common carriers* are publicly licensed to provide transportation services to the general public. They are distinguished from private carriers, which operate transportation facilities for a select clientele. A private carrier is not required to provide service to every person or company making a request. A common carrier, however, must arrange carriage for all who apply, within certain limitations.[8]

The delivery of goods to a common carrier creates a bailment relationship between the shipper (bailor) and the common carrier (bailee). Unlike ordinary bailees, the common carrier is held to a standard of care based on *strict liability,* rather than reasonable care, in protecting the bailed personal property. This means that the common carrier is absolutely liable, regardless of due care, for all loss or damage to goods except damage caused by one of the following common law exceptions: (1) an act of God, (2) an act of a public enemy, (3) an order of a public authority, (4) an act of the shipper, or (5) the inherent nature of the goods.

Common carriers cannot contract away their liability for damaged goods. Subject to government regulations, however, they are permitted to limit their dollar liability to an amount stated on the shipment contract or rate filing.[9]

Warehouse Companies *Warehousing* is the business of providing storage of property for compensation.[10] Like ordinary bailees, warehouse companies are liable for loss or damage to property resulting from negligence. A warehouse company, though, is a professional bailee and is therefore expected to exercise a high degree of care to protect and preserve the goods. A warehouse company can limit the dollar amount of its liability, but the bailor must be given the option of paying an increased storage rate for an increase in the liability limit.

7. UCC 2A–212, 2A–213.

8. A common carrier is not required to take any and all property anywhere in all instances. Public regulatory agencies govern common carriers, and carriers can be restricted to geographic areas. They can also be limited to carrying certain kinds of goods or to providing only special types of transportation equipment.

9. Federal laws require common carriers to offer shippers the opportunity to obtain higher dollar limits for loss by paying a higher fee for the transport. See *Treiber & Straub, Inc. v. United Parcel Service, Inc.*, 474 F.3d 379 (7th Cir. 2007).

10. UCC 7–102(h) refers to the person engaged in the storing of goods for hire as a *warehouseman.*

Unlike ordinary bailees, a warehouse company can issue *documents of title*—in particular, *warehouse receipts*—and is subject to extensive government regulation, including Article 7 of the UCC.[11] A warehouse receipt describes the bailed property and the terms of the bailment contract. It can be negotiable or nonnegotiable, depending on how it is written. It is negotiable if its terms provide that the warehouse company will deliver the goods "to the bearer" of the receipt or "to the order of" a person named on the receipt.[12] The warehouse receipt represents the goods (that is, it indicates title) and hence has value and utility in financing commercial transactions.

EXAMPLE 27.26 Ossip delivers 6,500 cases of canned corn to Chaney, the owner of a warehouse. Chaney issues a negotiable warehouse receipt payable "to bearer" and gives it to Ossip. Ossip sells and delivers the warehouse receipt to Better Foods, Inc. Better Foods is now the owner of the corn and has the right to obtain the cases by simply presenting the warehouse receipt to Chaney. •

11. A *document of title* is defined in UCC 1–201(15) as any "document which in the regular course of business or financing is treated as adequately evidencing that the person in possession of it is entitled to receive, hold, and dispose of the document and the goods it covers." A *warehouse receipt* is a document of title issued by a person engaged for hire in the business of storing goods.

12. UCC 7–104.

HOTEL OPERATORS At common law, hotel owners were strictly liable for the loss of any cash or property that guests brought into their rooms. Today, only those who provide lodging to the public for compensation as a *regular* business are covered under this rule of strict liability. Moreover, the rule applies only to those who are guests, as opposed to lodgers, who are persons that permanently reside at the hotel or motel.

In many states, hotel operators can avoid strict liability for loss of guests' cash and valuables by (1) providing a safe in which to keep them and (2) notifying guests that a safe is available. In addition, statutes often limit the liability of hotel operators with regard to articles that are not kept in the safe and may limit the availability of damages in the absence of hotel operator negligence. Most statutes require that the hotel operator post these limitations or otherwise notify the guest. Such postings, or notices, are frequently found on the doors of the rooms in hotels.

EXAMPLE 27.27 Joyce stays for a night at the Harbor Hotel. When she returns from eating breakfast in the hotel's restaurant, she discovers that her suitcase has been stolen and sees that the lock on the door between her room and the room next door was forced open. Joyce claims that the hotel is liable for her loss. Because the hotel was not negligent, however, it normally is not liable under state law. •

Reviewing . . . Personal Property and Bailments

Vanessa Denai owned forty acres of land in rural Louisiana with a 1,600-square-foot house on it and a metal barn near the house. Denai later met Lance Finney, who had been seeking a small plot of rural property to rent. After several meetings, Denai invited Finney to live on a corner of her land in exchange for Finney's assistance in cutting wood and tending her property. Denai agreed to store Finney's sailboat in her barn. With Denai's consent, Finney constructed a concrete and oak foundation on Denai's property and purchased a 190-square-foot dome from Dome Baja for $3,395. The dome was shipped by Doty Express, a transportation company licensed to serve the public. When it arrived, Finney installed the dome frame and fabric exterior so that the dome was detachable from the foundation. A year after Finney installed the dome, Denai wrote Finney a note stating, "I've decided to give you four acres of land surrounding your dome as drawn on this map." This gift violated no local land-use restrictions. Using the information presented in the chapter, answer the following questions.

1 Is the dome real property or personal property? Explain.
2 Is Denai's gift of land to Finney a gift *causa mortis* or a gift *inter vivos*? What is the difference?
3 What type of bailment relationship was created when Denai agreed to store Finney's boat? What degree of care was Denai required to exercise in storing the boat?
4 What standard of care applied to the shipment of the dome by Doty Express?

Terms and Concepts

abandoned property 531
accession 530
bailee 531
bailee's lien 533
bailment 531
bailor 531
chattel 526
community property 527
concurrent ownership 527

confusion 530
constructive delivery 528
dominion 529
estray statute 531
fee simple 526
gift 528
gift *causa mortis* 529
gift *inter vivos* 529
joint tenancy 527
lost property 530
mislaid property 530
personal property 526
property 526
real property 526
tenancy in common 527

Chapter Summary: Personal Property and Bailments

PERSONAL PROPERTY	
Definition of Personal Property (See page 526.)	Personal property (personalty) includes all property not classified as real property (realty). Personal property can be tangible (such as a TV or a car) or intangible (such as stocks or bonds). Personal property may be referred to legally as *chattel*—a term used under the common law to denote all forms of personal property.
Property Ownership (See pages 526–527.)	1. *Fee simple*—Owners of property in fee simple have the fullest ownership rights in property. They have the right to use, possess, or dispose of the property as they choose during their lifetimes and to pass on the property to their heirs at death. 2. *Tenancy in common*—Co-ownership in which two or more persons own an undivided interest in property. On one tenant's death, that tenant's property interest passes to his or her heirs. 3. *Joint tenancy*—Co-ownership in which two or more persons own an undivided interest in property. On the death of a joint tenant, that tenant's property interest transfers to the remaining tenant(s), *not* to the heirs of the deceased. 4. *Community property*—A form of co-ownership between a husband and wife in which each spouse technically owns an undivided one-half interest in property acquired during the marriage. This type of ownership exists in only some states.
Acquiring Ownership of Personal Property (See pages 527–530.)	The most common way of acquiring ownership in personal property is by purchasing it. Another way in which personal property is often acquired is by will or inheritance (see Chapter 29). The following are additional methods of acquiring personal property: 1. *Possession*—Ownership may be acquired by possession if no other person has ownership title (for example, capturing wild animals or finding abandoned property). 2. *Production*—Any product or item produced by an individual (with minor exceptions) becomes the property of that individual. 3. *Gifts*—A gift is effective when the following conditions exist: a. There is evidence of *intent* to make a gift of the property in question. b. The gift is *delivered* (physically or constructively) to the donee or the donee's agent. c. The gift is *accepted* by the donee. 4. *Accession*—When someone adds value to an item of personal property by the use of labor or materials, the added value generally becomes the property of the owner of the original property (although the owner sometimes must pay for good faith accessions). In rare situations, good faith accessions that substantially increase the property's value or change the identity of the property may cause title to pass to the improver. 5. *Confusion*—If a person wrongfully and willfully commingles fungible goods with those of another in order to render them indistinguishable, the innocent party acquires title to the whole. Otherwise, the owners become tenants in common of the commingled goods.
Mislaid, Lost, and Abandoned Property (See pages 530–531.)	The finder of property acquires different rights depending on whether the property was mislaid, lost, or abandoned. If the property is placed somewhere voluntarily by the owner and then inadvertently forgotten, it is considered mislaid property, and the finder will not acquire title. If it is involuntarily left and forgotten, it is considered lost property, and the finder can claim title to the property against the whole world *except the true owner*. If an owner discards property and has no intention of claiming it in the future, it is considered abandoned property, and the finder acquires absolute title to it (even against the original owner).

Continued

Chapter Summary: Personal Property and Bailments—Continued

BAILMENTS	
Elements of a Bailment (See pages 531–532.)	1. *Personal property*—Bailments involve only personal property. 2. *Delivery of possession*—For an effective bailment to exist, the bailee (the one receiving the property) must be given exclusive possession and control over the property, and in a voluntary bailment, the bailee must knowingly accept the personal property. 3. *The bailment agreement*—Expressly or impliedly provides for the return of the bailed property to the bailor or a third party, or for the disposal of the bailed property by the bailee.
Ordinary Bailments (See pages 532–535.)	1. *Types of bailments*— a. Bailment for the sole benefit of the bailor—A gratuitous bailment undertaken for the sole benefit of the bailor (for example, as a favor to the bailor). b. Bailment for the sole benefit of the bailee—A gratuitous loan of an article to a person (the bailee) solely for the bailee's benefit. c. Mutual-benefit (contractual) bailment—The most common kind of bailment; involves compensation between the bailee and bailor for the service provided. 2. *Rights of a bailee (duties of a bailor)*— a. The right of possession—Allows a bailee to sue any third persons who damage, lose, or convert the bailed property. b. The right to be compensated and reimbursed for expenses—In the event of nonpayment, the bailee has the right to place a possessory (bailee's) lien on the bailed property. c. The right to limit liability—An ordinary bailee can limit his or her liability for loss or damage, provided proper notice is given and the limitation is not against public policy. In special bailments, limitations on liability for negligence or on types of losses usually are not allowed, but limitations on the monetary amount of liability are permitted. 3. *Duties of a bailee (rights of a bailor)*— a. A bailee must exercise appropriate care over property entrusted to her or him. What constitutes appropriate care normally depends on the nature and circumstances of the bailment. See Exhibit 27–1 on page 534. b. Bailed goods in a bailee's possession must be either returned to the bailor or disposed of according to the bailor's directions. A bailee's failure to return the bailed property creates a presumption of negligence and constitutes a breach of contract or the tort of conversion of goods.
Special Types of Bailments (See pages 535–536.)	1. *Common carriers*—Carriers that are publicly licensed to provide transportation services to the general public. A common carrier is held to a standard of care based on *strict liability* unless the bailed property is lost or destroyed due to (a) an act of God, (b) an act of a public enemy, (c) an order of a public authority, (d) an act of the shipper, or (e) the inherent nature of the goods. 2. *Warehouse companies*—Professional bailees differ from ordinary bailees in that they (a) can issue documents of title (warehouse receipts) and (b) are subject to state and federal statutes, including Article 7 of the UCC (as are common carriers). They must exercise a high degree of care over the bailed property and are liable for loss of or damage to property if they fail to do so. 3. *Hotel operators*—Those who provide lodging to the public for compensation as a *regular* business. The common law strict liability standard to which hotel operators were once held is limited today by state statutes, which vary from state to state.

ExamPrep

ISSUE SPOTTERS

—Check your answers to these questions against the answers provided in Appendix G.

1 Quintana Corporation sends important documents to Regal Nursery, Inc., via Speedy Messenger Service. While the documents are in Speedy's care, a third party causes an accident to Speedy's delivery vehicle that results in the loss of the documents. Does Speedy have a right to recover from the third party for the loss of the documents? Why or why not?

2 Rosa de la Mar Corporation ships a load of goods via Southeast Delivery Company. The load of goods is lost in a hurricane in Florida. Who suffers the loss? Explain your answer.

BEFORE THE TEST

Go to **www.cengagebrain.com**, enter the ISBN 9781111530624, and click on "Find" to locate this textbook's Web site. Then, click on "Access Now" under "Study Tools," and select Chapter 27 at the top. There, you will find an Interactive Quiz that you can take to assess your mastery of the concepts in this chapter, as well as Flashcards and a Glossary of important terms.

For Review

1 What is real property? What is personal property?
2 What is the difference between a joint tenancy and a tenancy in common?
3 What are the three elements necessary for an effective gift?
4 What are the three elements of a bailment?
5 What are the basic rights and duties of a bailee? What are the rights and duties of a bailor?

Questions and Case Problems

27–1 Duties of the Bailee. Discuss the standard of care traditionally required of the bailee for the bailed property in each of the following situations, and determine whether the bailee breached that duty.

1 Ricardo borrows Steve's lawn mower because his own lawn mower needs repair. Ricardo mows his front yard. To mow the backyard, he needs to move some hoses and lawn furniture. He leaves the mower in front of his house while doing so. When he returns to the front yard, he discovers that the mower has been stolen.

2 Alicia owns a valuable speedboat. She is going on vacation and asks her neighbor, Maureen, to store the boat in one stall of Maureen's double garage. Maureen consents, and the boat is moved into the garage. Maureen needs some grocery items for dinner and drives to the store. She leaves the garage door open while she is gone, as is her custom, and the speedboat is stolen during that time.

27–2 Gifts. Jaspal has a severe heart attack and is taken to the hospital. He is aware that he is not expected to live. Because he is a bachelor with no close relatives nearby, Jaspal gives his car keys to his close friend, Friedrich, telling Friedrich that he is expected to die and that the car is Friedrich's. Jaspal survives the heart attack, but two months later he dies from pneumonia. Sam, Jaspal's uncle and the executor of his estate, wants Friedrich to return the car. Friedrich refuses, claiming that the car was given to him by Jaspal as a gift. Discuss whether Friedrich will be required to return the car to Jaspal's estate.

27–3 Question with Sample Answer Curtis is an executive on a business trip to the West Coast. He has driven his car on this trip and checks into the Hotel Ritz. The hotel has a guarded underground parking lot. Curtis gives his car keys to the parking lot attendant but fails to notify the attendant that his wife's $10,000 fur coat is in a box in the trunk. The next day, on checking out, he discovers that his car has been stolen. Curtis wants to hold the hotel liable for both the car and the coat. Discuss the probable success of his claim.

—For a sample answer to Question 27–3, go to Appendix E at the end of this text.

27–4 Property Ownership. Vincent Slavin was a partner at Cantor Fitzgerald Securities in the World Trade Center (WTC) in New York City. In 1998, Slavin and Anna Baez became engaged and began living together. They placed both of their names on three accounts at Chase Manhattan Bank according to the bank's terms, which provided that "accounts with multiple owners are joint, payable to either owner or the survivor." Slavin arranged for the direct deposit of his salary and commissions into one of the accounts. On September 11, 2001, Slavin died when two planes piloted by terrorists crashed into the WTC towers, causing their collapse. At the time, the balance in the three accounts was $656,944.36. On September 14, Cantor Fitzgerald deposited an additional $58,264.73 into the direct-deposit account. Baez soon withdrew the entire amount from all of the accounts. Mary Jelnek, Slavin's mother, filed a suit in a New York state court against Baez to determine the ownership of the funds that had been in the accounts. In what form of ownership were the accounts held? Who is entitled to which of the funds, and why? [*Matter of Slavin*, 3 Misc.3d 725, 777 N.Y.S.2d 871 (2004)]

27–5 Case Problem with Sample Answer In July 2003, Chester Dellinger and his son Michael opened a joint bank account with Advancial Federal Credit Union in Dallas, Texas. Both of them signed the "Account Application," which designated Chester as a "member" and Michael as a "joint owner." Both of them received a copy of the "Account Agreement, Disclosures and Privacy Policy," which provided that "a multiple party account includes rights of survivorship." Chester died in February 2005. His will designated Michael as the executor of the estate, most of which was to be divided equally between Michael and his brother, Joseph, Chester's other son. Michael determined the value of the estate to be about $117,000. He did not include the Advancial account balance, which was about $234,000. Joseph filed a suit in a Texas state court against Michael, contending that the funds in the Advancial account should be included in the estate. Michael filed a motion for summary judgment. Who owned the Advancial account when Chester was alive? Who owned it after he died? What should the court rule? Explain. [*In re Estate of Dellinger,* 224 S.W.3d 434 (Tex.App.—Dallas 2007)]

—For a sample answer to Problem 27–5, go to Appendix F at the end of this text.

27–6 Gifts. John Wasniewski opened a brokerage account with Quick and Reilly, Inc., in his son James's name. Twelve years later, when the balance was $52,085, the account was closed. The funds were then transferred into a joint account in the names of James's father and brother. Only after the transfer, when James received a tax form for the prior account's final year, did James learn of this new account. He filed a suit in a Connecticut state court against Quick and Reilly, alleging breach of contract and seeking to recover the account's principal and interest. What are the elements of a valid gift? Did John's initial opening of the account with Quick and Reilly constitute a gift to James? What is the likely result in this case, and why? [*Wasniewski v. Quick and Reilly, Inc.,* 292 Conn. 98, 971 A.2d 8 (2009)]

27–7 Bailment Obligation. Don Gray, who ran an aircraft paint shop, was hired to repaint an airplane owned by Bob Moreland. When Moreland left the plane for the paint job, a bailment was created. The price agreed upon was $9,470. When Moreland picked up the airplane, he was disappointed in the quality of the work and pointed out numerous defects. Gray had signed the airplane logbooks, indicating that the work was complete. Moreland flew the plane to another shop, which redid the paint job and estimated the cost of repairing the damage caused by Gray to be about $7,000. Moreland refused to pay Gray, who then sued for the work he had performed on Moreland's plane. Moreland made a counterclaim. The jury awarded Moreland damages of $9,385, plus attorneys' fees of $12,420. Gray appealed, contending that when Moreland took possession of the airplane after the job was completed, he had accepted the work. Moreland had no right to take it to another shop without giving Gray a chance to repair any defects. Is that argument correct? Why or why not? [*Gray v. Moreland,* 2010 Ark.App. 207 (2010)]

27–8 A Question of Ethics *Marcella Lashmett was engaged in the business of farming in Illinois. Her daughter Christine Montgomery was also a farmer. Christine often borrowed Marcella's farm equipment. More than once, Christine used the equipment as a trade-in on the purchase of new equipment titled in Christine's name alone. After each transaction, Christine paid Marcella an agreed-to sum of money, and Marcella filed a gift tax return. Marcella died on December 19, 1999. Her heirs included Christine and Marcella's other daughter, Cheryl Thomas. Marcella's will gave whatever farm equipment remained on her death to Christine. If Christine chose to sell or trade any of the items, however, the proceeds were to be split equally with Cheryl. The will designated Christine to handle the disposition of the estate, but she did nothing. Eventually, Cheryl filed a petition with an Illinois state court, which appointed her to administer the will. Cheryl then filed a suit against her sister to discover what assets their mother had owned. [*In re Estate of Lashmett, *369 Ill.App.3d 1013, 874 N.E.2d 65 (2007)]*

1 Cheryl learned that three months before Marcella's death, Christine had used Marcella's tractor as a trade-in on the purchase of a new tractor. The trade-in credit had been $55,296.28. Marcella had been paid nothing, and no gift tax return had been filed. Christine claimed, among other things, that the old tractor had been a gift. What is a "gift"? What are the elements of a gift? What do the facts suggest on this claim? Discuss.
2 Christine also claimed that she had tried to pay Marcella $20,000 on the trade-in of the tractor but that her mother had refused to accept it. Christine showed a check made out to Marcella for that amount and marked "void." Would you rule in Christine's favor on this claim? Why or why not?

27–9 Critical Thinking Legal Question Suppose that a certificate of deposit (CD) owned by two joint tenants (with the right of survivorship) is given by one of the joint tenants as security for a loan (without the other joint tenant's knowledge). Further suppose that the joint tenant dies after defaulting on the loan. Who has superior rights in the CD, the creditor or the other surviving joint tenant? Explain.

27–10 Video Question To watch this chapter's video, *Personal Property and Bailments,* go to **www.cengagebrain.com**. Register the access code that came with your new book or log in to your existing account. Select the link for the "Business Law Digital Video Library Online Access" or "Business Law CourseMate." Click on "Complete Video List," view Video 53, and then answer the following questions:

1 What type of bailment is discussed in the video?
2 What were Vinny's duties with regard to the rug-cleaning machine? What standard of care should apply?
3 Did Vinny exercise the appropriate degree of care? Why or why not? How would a court decide this issue?

Chapter 28

Real Property and Landlord-Tenant Law

Learning Objectives

After reading this chapter, you should be able to answer the following questions:

1. What can a person who holds property in fee simple absolute do with the property?
2. What are the requirements for acquiring property by adverse possession?
3. What limitations may be imposed on the rights of property owners?
4. What is a leasehold estate? What types of leasehold estates, or tenancies, can be created when real property is leased?
5. What are the respective duties of the landlord and the tenant concerning the use and maintenance of leased property?

The Learning Objectives above are designed to help improve your understanding of the chapter.

(©Joe Gough, 2009. Used under license from Shutterstock)

From earliest times, property has provided a means for survival. Primitive peoples lived off the fruits of the land, eating the vegetation and wildlife. Later, as the vegetation was cultivated and the wildlife domesticated, property provided farmland and pasture. Throughout history, property has continued to be an indicator of family wealth and social position. Indeed, an individual's right to his or her property has become one of the most prized rights of legal residency or citizenship.

In this chapter, we first examine the nature of real property. We then look at the various ways in which real property can be owned and how ownership rights in real property are transferred from one person to another. We conclude the chapter with a discussion of leased property and landlord-tenant relationships.

The Nature of Real Property

Real property consists of land and the buildings, plants, and trees that are on it. Real property also includes subsurface and airspace rights, as well as personal property that has become permanently attached to real property. Whereas personal property is movable, real property—also called *real estate* or *realty*—is immovable.

Land

Land includes the soil on the surface of the earth and the natural or artificial structures that are attached to it. It further includes all the waters contained on or under the surface and much, but not necessarily all, of the airspace above it. The exterior boundaries of land extend down to the center of the earth and up to the farthest reaches of the atmosphere (subject to certain qualifications).

Airspace and Subsurface Rights

The owner of real property has rights to the airspace above the land, as well as to the soil and minerals underneath it. Limitations on either airspace rights or subsurface rights normally must be indicated on the document that transfers title at the time of purchase. When no such limitations, or *encumbrances,* are noted, a purchaser generally can expect to have an unlimited right to possession of the property.

AIRSPACE RIGHTS Disputes concerning airspace rights may involve the right of commercial and private planes to fly over property and the right of individuals and governments to seed clouds and produce rain artificially. Flights over private land normally do not violate property rights unless the flights are so low and so frequent that they directly interfere with the owner's enjoyment and use of the land. Leaning walls or buildings and projecting eave spouts or roofs may also violate the airspace rights of an adjoining property owner.

SUBSURFACE RIGHTS In many states, land ownership may be separated, in that the surface of a piece of land and the subsurface may have different owners. Subsurface rights can be extremely valuable, as these rights include the ownership of minerals, oil, and natural gas. Subsurface rights would be of little value, however, if the owner could not use the surface to exercise those rights. Hence, a subsurface owner has a right (called a *profit,* to be discussed later in this chapter) to go onto the surface of the land to, for example, discover and mine minerals.

When ownership is separated into surface and subsurface rights, each owner can pass title to what she or he owns without the consent of the other owner. Of course, conflicts can arise between the surface owner's use of the property and the subsurface owner's need to extract minerals, oil, or natural gas. In that situation, one party's interest may become subservient (secondary) to the other party's interest either by statute or by case law. If the owners of the subsurface rights excavate (dig), they are absolutely liable if their excavation causes the surface to collapse. Many states have statutes that also make the excavators liable for any damage to structures on the land. Typically, these statutes provide precise requirements for excavations of various depths.

Plant Life and Vegetation

Plant life, both natural and cultivated, is also considered to be real property. In many instances, the natural vegetation, such as trees, adds greatly to the value of the realty. When a parcel of land is sold and the land has growing crops on it, the sale includes the crops, unless otherwise specified in the sales contract. When crops are sold by themselves, however, they are considered to be personal property or goods. Consequently, the sale of crops is a sale of goods and thus is governed by the Uniform Commercial Code (UCC) rather than by real property law.[1]

Fixtures

Certain personal property can become so closely associated with the real property to which it is attached that the law views it as real property. Such property is known as a **fixture**—an item *affixed* to realty. A fixture is attached to the real property by roots; embedded in it; permanently situated on it; or permanently attached by means of cement, plaster, bolts, nails, or screws. The fixture can be physically attached to real property, be attached to another fixture, or even be without any actual physical attachment to the land (such as a statue). As long as the owner intends the property to be a fixture, normally it will be a fixture.

Fixtures are included in the sale of land if the sales contract does not provide otherwise. The sale of a house includes the land and the house and the garage on the land, as well as the cabinets, plumbing, and windows. Because these are permanently affixed to the property, they are considered to be a part of it. Certain items, such as drapes and window-unit air conditioners, are difficult to classify. Thus, a contract for the sale of a house or commercial realty should indicate which items of this sort are included in the sale.

The following case illustrates the importance of intent in determining whether property is a fixture.

1. See UCC 2–107(2), discussed in Chapters 13 and 14.

Case 28.1 APL Limited v. State of Washington Department of Revenue

Court of Appeals of Washington, 154 Wash.App. 1020 (2010).

FACTS The Port of Seattle entered into a thirty-year lease with APL Limited and others (collectively, APL) for premises at Terminal 5 for loading and unloading shipping-container ships. The Port had substantially rebuilt Terminal 5 and had constructed and installed loading cranes. These cranes run on steel crane rails that are set one hundred feet apart, embedded in a concrete apron, and supported by specially designed steel-reinforced concrete piers engineered specifically to support the cranes. The cranes themselves are steel structures 198 feet tall, 85 feet wide, and more than 370 feet long—each weighing more than eight hundred tons. They are hard-wired to a dedicated high-voltage electrical system that includes a power substation built specifically for Terminal 5 to power the cranes. The cranes are attached to the power substation by cables that are more than two inches thick. The cranes have been in use continuously on Terminal 5 since their construction more than twenty years ago. APL sued the state for a refund of sales tax paid on the rent for the cranes, claiming that the cranes were fixtures. The state argued that the cranes were personal property and, as such, subject to sales tax. The trial court granted the state's motion for summary judgment, and APL appealed.

Case 28.1–Continued

ISSUE Was there some evidence that the Port of Seattle installed the loading cranes at Terminal 5 with the intent that they would be permanently attached as fixtures?

DECISION Yes. The state appellate court reversed the trial court's ruling.

REASON After examining the record of the trial court, the reviewing court determined that a critical aspect of the case was missing. It concerned whether the parties, in constructing the cranes and annexing (attaching) them to the real property, intended to make a permanent accession—that is, a permanent addition to the real property. "The determinative factor for whether a chattel [personal property] annexed to real property becomes part of the real property [is] the intent with which the chattel was annexed to the land. . . . When the owner and the person that annexes the chattel are one and the same, a rebuttable presumption arises that the owner's intention was for the chattel to become part of the realty." Because the trial court recognized that it had not examined the facts regarding the Port's intent to annex the cranes, the granting of summary judgment was inappropriate.

FOR CRITICAL ANALYSIS—Economic Consideration *Why did it matter to the parties in this lawsuit whether the cranes were fixtures or not?*

Ownership Interests in Real Property

Ownership of property is an abstract concept that cannot exist independently of the legal system. No one can actually possess or *hold* a piece of land, the airspace above it, the earth below it, and all the water contained on it. The legal system therefore recognizes certain rights and duties that constitute ownership interests in real property.

Recall from Chapter 27 that property ownership is often viewed as a bundle of rights. One who possesses the entire bundle of rights is said to hold the property in *fee simple,* which is the most complete form of ownership. When only some of the rights in the bundle are transferred to another person, the effect is to limit the ownership rights of both the transferor of the rights and the recipient.

Ownership in Fee Simple

In a **fee simple absolute,** the owner has the greatest aggregation of rights, privileges, and power possible. The owner can give the property away or dispose of the property by *deed* (the instrument used to transfer property, as will be discussed later in this chapter) or by will. When there is no will, the fee simple ownership interest passes to the owner's legal heirs on her or his death. A fee simple is potentially infinite in duration and is assigned forever to a person and her or his heirs without limitation or condition. The owner has the rights of *exclusive* possession and use of the property.

The rights that accompany a fee simple include the right to use the land for whatever purpose the owner sees fit. Of course, other laws, including applicable zoning, noise, and environmental laws, may limit the owner's ability to use the property in certain ways. A person who uses his or her property in a manner that unreasonably interferes with others' right to use or enjoy their own property can be liable for the tort of nuisance.

CASE EXAMPLE 28.1 Nancy and James Biglane owned and lived in a building in Natchez, Mississippi. Next door to the Biglanes' property was a popular bar called the Under the Hill Saloon that featured live music. During the summer, the Saloon, which had no air-conditioning, opened its windows and doors, and live music echoed up and down the street. Although the Biglanes installed extra insulation, thicker windows, and air-conditioning units in their building, the noise from the Saloon kept them awake at night. Eventually, the Biglanes sued the owners of the Saloon for nuisance. The court held that the noise from the bar unreasonably interfered with the Biglanes' right to enjoy their property and enjoined (prevented) the Saloon from opening its windows and doors while playing music.[2] ●

Life Estates

A **life estate** is an estate that lasts for the life of some specified individual. A **conveyance,** or transfer of real property, "to A for his life" creates a life estate. In a life estate, the life tenant's ownership rights cease to exist on the life tenant's death.[3] The life tenant has the right to use the land, provided that he or she commits no waste (injury to the land). In other words, the life tenant cannot use the land in a manner that would adversely affect its value. The life tenant is entitled to any rents generated by the land and can harvest crops from the land. If mines and oil wells are already on the land, the life tenant can extract minerals and oil and is entitled to the royalties, but he or she cannot exploit the land by creating new wells or mines.

---

2. *Biglane v. Under the Hill Corp.,* 949 So.2d 9 (Miss.Sup.Ct. 2007).
3. Because a life tenant's rights in the property cease at death, life estates frequently are used to avoid probate proceedings—see Chapter 29. The person who owns the property deeds it to the person who would eventually inherit the property and reserves a life estate for herself or himself. That way, the property owner can live there until death, and the property then passes to the intended heir without the need for legal proceedings.

The life tenant can create liens, *easements* (discussed next), and leases, but none can extend beyond the life of the tenant. In addition, with few exceptions, the owner of a life estate has an exclusive right to possession during her or his life.

Along with these rights, the life tenant also has some duties—to keep the property in repair and to pay property taxes. In short, the owner of the life estate has the same rights as a fee simple owner except that the life tenant must maintain the value of the property during her or his tenancy.

Nonpossessory Interests

In contrast to the types of property interests just described, some interests in land do not include any rights to possess the property. These interests are therefore known as **nonpossessory interests.** They include easements, profits, and licenses.

An **easement** is the right of a person to make limited use of another person's real property without taking anything from the property. An easement, for instance, can be the right to walk or drive across another's property. In contrast, a **profit**[4] is the right to go onto land owned by another and take away some part of the land itself or some product of the land. **EXAMPLE 28.2** Akmed owns Sandy View. Akmed gives Carmen the right to go there to remove all the sand and gravel that she needs for her cement business. Carmen has a profit. •

Easements and profits can be classified as either *appurtenant* or *in gross*. Because easements and profits are similar and the same rules apply to both, we discuss them together.

EASEMENT OR PROFIT APPURTENANT An easement or profit *appurtenant* arises when the owner of one piece of land has a right to go onto (or remove something from) an adjacent piece of land owned by another. The land that is benefited by the easement is called the *dominant estate,* and the land that is burdened is called the *servient estate.* Because easements appurtenant are intended to *benefit the land,* they run (are conveyed) with the land when it is transferred. **EXAMPLE 28.3** Acosta has a right to drive his car across Green's land, which is adjacent to Acosta's land. This right-of-way over Green's property is an easement appurtenant to Acosta's property and can be used only by Acosta. If Acosta sells his land, the easement runs with the land to benefit the new owner. •

EASEMENT OR PROFIT IN GROSS In an easement or profit *in gross,* the right to use or take things from another's land is given to one who does not own an adjacent tract of land. These easements are intended to *benefit a particular person or business,* not a particular piece of land, and cannot be transferred. **EXAMPLE 28.4** Avery owns a parcel of land with a marble quarry. Avery conveys (transfers) to Classic Stone Corporation the right to come onto her land and remove up to five hundred pounds of marble per day. Classic Stone owns a profit in gross and cannot transfer this right to another. • Similarly, when a utility company is granted an easement to run its power lines across another's property, it obtains an easement in gross.

CREATION OF AN EASEMENT OR PROFIT Most easements and profits are created by an express grant in a contract, deed (see page 546), or will (see Chapter 29). This allows the parties to include terms defining the extent and length of time of use. In some situations, an easement or profit can also be created without an express agreement.

An easement or profit may arise by *implication* when the circumstances surrounding the division of a parcel of property imply its existence. **EXAMPLE 28.5** Barrow divides a parcel of land that has only one well for drinking water. If Barrow conveys the half without a well to Jarad, a profit by implication arises because Jarad needs drinking water. •

An easement may also be created by *necessity*. An easement by necessity does not require a division of property for its existence. A person who rents an apartment, for example, has an easement by necessity in the private road leading up to it.

An easement arises by *prescription* when one person exercises an easement, such as a right-of-way, on another person's land without the landowner's consent, and the use is apparent and continues for the length of time required by the applicable statute of limitations. (In much the same way, title to property may be obtained by *adverse possession*—see page 547.)

TERMINATION OF AN EASEMENT OR PROFIT An easement or profit can be terminated or extinguished in several ways. The simplest way is to deed it back to the owner of the land that is burdened by it. Another way is to abandon it and create evidence of intent to relinquish the right to use it. Mere nonuse will not extinguish an easement or profit *unless the nonuse is accompanied by an overt act showing the intent to abandon.* Also, if the owner of an easement or profit becomes the owner of the property burdened by it, then it is merged into the property.

LICENSE In the context of real property, a **license** is the revocable right of a person to come onto another person's land. It is a personal privilege that arises from the consent of the owner of the land and can be revoked by the owner. A ticket to attend a movie at a theater is an example of a license.

EXAMPLE 28.6 The owner of a Broadway theater issues Alena a ticket to see a play. If Alena is refused entry into the theater because she is improperly dressed, she has no right to force her way into the theater. The ticket is only a revocable license and not a conveyance of an interest in property. •

In essence, a license grants a person the authority to enter the land of another and perform a specified act or series of acts

4. The term *profit,* as used here, does not refer to the profits made by a business firm. Rather, it means a gain or an advantage.

without obtaining any permanent interest in the land. When a person with a license exceeds the authority granted and undertakes some action on the property that is not permitted, the property owner can sue that person for trespass (discussed in Chapter 4).

CASE EXAMPLE 28.7 A Catholic church granted Prince Realty Management, LLC, a three-month license to use a three-foot strip of its property adjacent to Prince's property. The license authorized Prince to "put up plywood panels," creating a temporary fence to protect Prince's property during the construction of a new building, and then restore the boundary line between the properties with a new brick fence. During the license's term, Prince installed steel piles and beams on the licensed property. When Prince ignored the church's demands that these structures be removed, the church sued Prince for trespass. The court held that because the license allowed only temporary structures and Prince had exceeded its authority by installing steel piles and beams, the church was entitled to damages.[5] •

Transfer of Ownership

Ownership interests in real property are frequently transferred (conveyed) by sale, and the terms of the transfer are specified in a real estate sales contract. Often, real estate brokers or agents who are licensed by the state assist the buyers and sellers during the sales transaction. Real property ownership can also be transferred by gift, by will or inheritance, by possession, or by *eminent domain.* When ownership rights in real property are transferred, the type of interest being transferred and the conditions of the transfer normally are set forth in a *deed* executed by the person who is conveying the property.

Real Estate Sales Contracts

In some ways, a sale of real estate is similar to a sale of goods because it involves a transfer of ownership, often with specific warranties. A sale of real estate, however, is generally a more complicated transaction that involves certain formalities that are not required in a sale of goods. Usually, after lengthy negotiations (involving offers, counteroffers, and responses), the parties enter into a detailed contract setting forth their agreement. A contract for a sale of land includes such terms as the purchase price, the type of deed the buyer will receive, the condition of the premises, and any items that will be included.

Unless the buyer pays cash for the property, he or she must obtain financing through a mortgage loan. (As discussed in Chapter 20, a *mortgage* is a loan made by an individual or institution, such as a banking institution or trust company, for which the property is given as security.) Real estate sales contracts are often contingent on the buyer's ability to obtain financing at or below a specified rate of interest. The contract may also be contingent on the buyer's sale of other real property, the seller's acquisition of title insurance, or the completion of a survey of the property and its passing one or more inspections. Normally, the buyer is responsible for having the premises inspected for physical or mechanical defects and for insect infestation.

CLOSING DATE AND ESCROW The contract usually fixes a date for performance, or **closing,** which is frequently four to twelve weeks after the contract is signed. On this day, the seller conveys the property to the buyer by delivering the deed to the buyer in exchange for payment of the purchase price. Deposits toward the purchase price normally are held in a special account, called an **escrow account,** until all of the conditions of sale have been met. Once the closing takes place, the funds remaining in the escrow account (after payments have been made to the escrow agency, title insurance company, and any lien holders) are transferred to the seller. The *escrow agent,* which may be a title company, bank, or special escrow company, acts as a neutral party in the sales transaction and facilitates the sale by allowing the buyer and seller to close the transaction without having to exchange documents and funds.

IMPLIED WARRANTIES IN THE SALE OF NEW HOMES Most states recognize a warranty—the **implied warranty of habitability** (see also page 550)—in the sale of new homes. The seller of a new house warrants that it will be fit for human habitation even if the deed or contract of sale does not include such a warranty.

Essentially, the seller is warranting that the house is in reasonable working order and is of reasonably sound construction. Thus, under this warranty, the seller of a new home is in effect a guarantor of its fitness. In some states, the warranty protects not only the first purchaser but any subsequent purchaser as well.

SELLER'S DUTY TO DISCLOSE HIDDEN DEFECTS In most jurisdictions, courts impose on sellers a duty to disclose any known defect that materially affects the value of the property and that the buyer could not reasonably discover. Failure to disclose such a material defect gives the buyer a right to rescind the contract and to sue for damages based on fraud or misrepresentation.

A dispute may arise over whether the seller knew of the defect before the sale, and there is normally a limit to the time within which the buyer can bring a suit against the seller based on the defect. For instance, in Louisiana, the prescribed limit for a suit against a seller who knew, or can be presumed to have known, of the defect is one year from the day that the buyer discovered it. If the seller did not know of the defect, the limit is one year from the date of the sale.

5. *Roman Catholic Church of Our Lady of Sorrows v. Prince Realty Management, LLC,* 47 A.D.3d 909, 850 N.Y.S.2d 569 (2008).

CASE EXAMPLE 28.8 Matthew Humphrey paid $44,000 for a house in Louisiana and partially renovated it. He then sold the house to Terry and Tabitha Whitehead for $67,000. A few months after the Whiteheads moved in, they discovered rotten wood behind the tile in the bathroom and experienced problems with the fireplace and the plumbing. Two years later, the Whiteheads filed a suit against Humphrey seeking to rescind the sale. They argued that the plumbing problems were a latent defect that the seller had failed to disclose. Evidence revealed that prior to the sale, the parties were made aware of issues regarding the sewer system and that corrective actions were taken. At the time of the sale, the toilets flushed, and neither side realized that the latent defects had not been resolved. The court ruled that rescission was not warranted for the sewer problems because the Whiteheads had waited too long after their discovery to file a claim against Humphrey. The court did order Humphrey to pay damages for the repairs to the fireplace and for replacing some of the rotten wood, however, because Humphrey knew about these defects at the time of the sale.[6] •

Deeds

Possession and title to land are passed from person to person by means of a **deed**—the instrument of conveyance of real property. A deed is a writing signed by an owner of real property that transfers title to another. Deeds must meet certain requirements, but unlike a contract, a deed does not have to be supported by legally sufficient consideration. Gifts of real property are common, and they require deeds even though there is no consideration for the gift. To be valid, a deed must include the following:

1. The names of the *grantor* (the giver or seller) and the *grantee* (the donee or buyer).
2. Words evidencing an intent to convey the property (for example, "I hereby bargain, sell, grant, or give").
3. A legally sufficient description of the land.
4. The grantor's (and usually her or his spouse's) signature.
5. Delivery of the deed.

WARRANTY DEEDS Different types of deeds provide different degrees of protection against defects of title. A **warranty deed** makes the greatest number of warranties and thus provides the greatest protection against defects of title. In most states, special language is required to create a general warranty deed.

Warranty deeds commonly include a number of *covenants,* or promises, that the grantor makes to the grantee. These covenants include a covenant that the grantor has the title to, and the power to convey, the property; a covenant of quiet enjoyment (a warranty that the buyer will not be disturbed in her or his possession of the land); and a covenant that transfer of the property is made without knowledge of adverse claims of third parties.

Generally, the warranty deed makes the grantor liable for all defects of title by the grantor and previous titleholders. **EXAMPLE 28.9** Julio sells a two-acre lot and office building by warranty deed. Subsequently, a third person shows up who has better title than Julio had and forces the buyer off the property. Here, the covenant of quiet enjoyment has been breached. The buyer can sue Julio to recover the purchase price of the land, plus any other damages incurred as a result. •

SPECIAL WARRANTY DEEDS In contrast to a warranty deed, a **special warranty deed,** which is also referred to as a *limited warranty deed,* warrants only that the grantor or seller held good title during his or her ownership of the property. In other words, the grantor is not warranting that there were no defects of title when the property was held by previous owners.

If the special warranty deed discloses all liens or other encumbrances, the seller will not be liable to the buyer if a third person subsequently interferes with the buyer's ownership. If the third person's claim arises out of, or is related to, some act of the seller, however, the seller will be liable to the buyer for damages.

GRANT AND SHERIFF'S DEEDS With a grant deed, the grantor simply states, "I grant the property to you." By state statute, grant deeds carry with them an implied warranty that the grantor owns the property and has not previously transferred it to someone else or encumbered it, except as set out in the deed. A sheriff's deed is a document giving ownership rights to a buyer of property at a sheriff's sale—a sale held by a sheriff when a property owner has failed to pay a court judgment. Typically, the property was subject to mortgage or tax payments, and the owner defaulted.

QUITCLAIM DEEDS A **quitclaim deed** offers the least amount of protection against defects of title. Basically, a quitclaim deed conveys to the grantee whatever interest the grantor had. Thus, if the grantor had no interest, then the grantee receives no interest. Naturally, if the grantor had a defective title or no title at all, a conveyance by warranty deed or special warranty deed would not cure the defects. Such deeds, however, will give the buyer a cause of action to sue the seller.

A quitclaim deed can and often does serve as a release of the grantor's interest in a particular parcel of property. **EXAMPLE 28.10** After ten years of marriage, Sandi and Jim are getting a divorce. During the marriage, Sandi purchased a parcel of waterfront property next to her grandparents' home in Louisiana. Jim helped make some improvements to the property, but he is not sure what ownership interests, if any, he has in the property because Sandi used her own funds (acquired before the marriage) to purchase the lot. Jim agrees to quitclaim the property to Sandi as part of the divorce settlement, releasing any interest he might have in that piece of property. •

6. *Whitehead v. Humphrey,* 954 So.2d 859 (La.App. 2007).

RECORDING STATUTES Every jurisdiction has **recording statutes,** which allow deeds to be recorded for a fee. The grantee normally pays this fee because he or she is the one who will be protected by recording the deed.

Recording a deed gives notice to the public that a certain person is now the owner of a particular parcel of real estate. Thus, prospective buyers can check the public records to see whether there have been earlier transactions creating interests or rights in specific parcels of real property. Putting everyone on notice as to the identity of the true owner is intended to prevent the previous owners from fraudulently conveying the land to other purchasers. Deeds are recorded in the county where the property is located. Many state statutes require that the grantor sign the deed in the presence of two witnesses before it can be recorded.

Will or Inheritance

Property that is transferred on an owner's death is passed either by will or by state inheritance laws. If the owner of land dies with a will, the land passes in accordance with the terms of the will. If the owner dies without a will, state inheritance statutes prescribe how and to whom the property will pass. Transfers of property by will or inheritance will be examined in Chapter 29.

Adverse Possession

Adverse possession is a means of obtaining title to land without delivery of a deed. Essentially, when one person possesses the property of another for a certain statutory period of time (three to thirty years, with ten years being most common), that person, called the *adverse possessor,* acquires title to the land and cannot be removed from it by the original owner. The adverse possessor may ultimately obtain a perfect title just as if there had been a conveyance by deed.

REQUIREMENTS For property to be held adversely, four elements must be satisfied:

1. Possession must be *actual and exclusive*—that is, the possessor must take sole physical occupancy of the property.
2. The possession must be *open, visible, and notorious,* not secret or clandestine. The possessor must occupy the land for all the world to see.
3. Possession must be *continuous and peaceable for the required period of time.* This requirement means that the possessor must not be interrupted in the occupancy by the true owner or by the courts.
4. Possession must be *hostile and adverse.* In other words, the possessor must claim the property as against the whole world. He or she cannot be living on the property with the permission of the owner.

PURPOSE There are a number of public-policy reasons for the adverse possession doctrine. These include society's interest in resolving boundary disputes, determining title when title to property is in question, and ensuring that real property remains in the stream of commerce. More fundamentally, policies behind the doctrine include rewarding possessors for putting land to productive use and punishing owners who sit on their rights too long and do not take action when they see adverse possession.

In the following case, the question before the court was whether a landowner had obtained title to a portion of adjacent land by adverse possession.

Case 28.2 Scarborough v. Rollins

Court of Appeals of Mississippi, 44 So.3d 381 (2010).

FACTS Charles Scarborough and Mildred Rollins were adjoining landowners, sharing one common boundary. Based on Rollins's survey of the property, Rollins believed that she owned a portion of a gravel road located to the south of the apartment buildings she owned. In contrast, Scarborough believed that the gravel road was located totally on his property and that he owned some property north of the gravel road toward Rollins's apartment buildings. In July 2006, Scarborough filed a complaint seeking to quiet and confirm his title to the property. Rollins filed a counterclaim seeking to quiet and confirm her title. The court entered judgment for Rollins. Scarborough appealed.

ISSUE Did Rollins prove that she owned a portion of the gravel road by adverse possession?

DECISION Yes. The Court of Appeals of Mississippi affirmed the lower court's judgment and assessed all costs of the appeal to Scarborough.

REASON In his appeal, Scarborough asserted that Rollins had failed to prove by clear and convincing evidence that her possession of the disputed area had been hostile, open, notorious, visible, continuing, exclusive, and peaceful. Rather, Scarborough asserted that both he and Rollins had used the disputed land, thus exercising joint use of the land and preventing a claim of adverse possession by Rollins. The reviewing court determined otherwise. There was sufficient evidence to show that Rollins had paid taxes on the property in dispute. Moreover, Rollins and the previous

Case 28.2—Continues next page ➡

Case 28.2—Continued

owners of the disputed land had used and enjoyed peaceful possession of the property for more than thirty-five years. It generally was known that the apartment complex owned the yard up to the end of the gravel road—the property in dispute. Furthermore, until Scarborough brought the lawsuit, no one had claimed use of any part of the property. Rollins's claim of adverse possession provided her with title to the land.

WHAT IF THE FACTS WERE DIFFERENT? *Suppose that Rollins had not paid any taxes on the disputed land and that Scarborough had done so. Would the result have been different? Explain.*

Eminent Domain

Even ownership in fee simple absolute is limited by a superior ownership. Just as in medieval England the king was the ultimate landowner, so in the United States the government has an ultimate ownership right in all land. This right, known as **eminent domain,** is sometimes referred to as the condemnation power of government to take land for public use. It gives the government the right to acquire possession of real property in the manner directed by the U.S. Constitution and the laws of the state whenever the public interest requires it. Property may be taken only for public use, not for private benefit.

EXAMPLE 28.11 When a new public highway is to be built, the government must decide where to build it and how much land to condemn. After the government determines that a particular parcel of land is necessary for public use, it will first offer to buy the property. If the owner refuses the offer, the government brings a judicial (condemnation) proceeding to obtain title to the land. Then, in another proceeding, the court determines the *fair value* of the land, which usually is approximately equal to its market value. •

When the government uses its power of eminent domain to acquire land owned by a private party, a **taking** occurs. Under the *takings clause* of the Fifth Amendment to the U.S. Constitution, the government must pay "just compensation" to the property owner. State constitutions contain similar provisions.

In 2005, the United States Supreme Court ruled that the power of eminent domain may be used to further economic development.[7] Since that decision, a number of state legislatures have passed laws limiting the power of the government to use eminent domain, particularly for urban redevelopment projects that benefit private developers.

The following case involved condemnation actions brought by a town to acquire rights-of-way for a natural gas pipeline to be constructed through the town. The issue was whether the pipeline was for public use, even though it was not built to furnish natural gas to the residents of that town.

7. *Kelo v. City of New London, Connecticut,* 545 U.S. 528, 125 S.Ct. 2655, 162 L.Ed.2d 439 (2005).

Case 28.3 Town of Midland v. Morris

Court of Appeals of North Carolina, 704 S.E.2d 329 (2011).

FACTS The Transcontinental Pipeline transports and distributes natural gas from the Gulf of Mexico to the northeastern United States. The city of Monroe, North Carolina, decided to supply its citizens and the surrounding area with natural gas by constructing a direct connection between its natural gas distribution system and the Transcontinental Pipeline. To construct the connecting pipeline, Monroe needed to acquire the rights to property along a forty-two-mile route. To do this, Monroe entered into an agreement with the town of Midland under which Midland would acquire the property (either by voluntary transfer or by eminent domain) and grant an easement to Monroe. In exchange, Midland would have the right to install a tap on the pipeline and receive discounted natural gas services. In 2008, Midland began the process of acquiring the property necessary for construction of the pipeline. When negotiations for voluntary acquisitions of the rights-of-way failed, Midland exercised its eminent domain authority to condemn the needed property. Midland filed fifteen condemnation actions, which the property owners (including Harry Morris) challenged. The trial court ruled in favor of Midland, and the property owners appealed. The property owners claimed, among other things, that Midland's condemnation of the property was not for public use or benefit because Midland had no concrete plans to furnish natural gas services from the pipeline to the city and its citizens.

ISSUE Was Midland's condemnation of property to construct a natural gas pipeline for public use (even though the city had no immediate plan to actually furnish gas to its residents)?

DECISION Yes. The state appellate court affirmed the lower court's decision that Midland had lawfully exercised its eminent domain power.

REASON The court chose to interpret the relevant state statutes broadly rather than narrowly. A narrow interpretation would have limited the city's power to establish a public utility to situations in which the city had a concrete plan to furnish services. Under the court's broader interpretation, the city had the power to establish a public utility when the city had a plan to develop the infrastructure and capability but no

Case 28.3–Continued

immediate plan to actually furnish the services. The agreement with Monroe gave Midland control over a tap on the pipeline and the right to receive a specific amount of natural gas per day at a discounted cost. Even though Midland may never tap into the pipeline, the court found that the condemnation satisfied the public use test because it gave the citizens of Midland a right to a definite use of the condemned property. Furthermore, the court reasoned that the availability of natural gas benefited the public by contributing to the general welfare and prosperity of the public at large. "Midland's tap on the Pipeline, and its potential to provide natural gas service, likely will spur growth, as well as provide Midland with an advantage in industrial recruitment. These opportunities must be seen as public benefits accruing to the citizens of Midland, such that Midland's condemnations are for the public benefit."

FOR CRITICAL ANALYSIS—Ethical Consideration *Is it fair that a city can exercise its eminent domain power to take property even though the property will not be used immediately to benefit the city's residents? Why or why not?*

Leasehold Estates

A **leasehold estate** is created when a real property owner or lessor (landlord) agrees to convey the right to possess and use the property to a lessee (tenant) for a certain period of time. In every leasehold estate, the tenant has a *qualified* right to exclusive possession (qualified by the right of the landlord to enter on the premises to ensure that waste is not being committed). The *temporary* nature of possession, under a lease, is what distinguishes a tenant from a purchaser, who acquires title to the property. The tenant can use the land—for example, by harvesting crops—but cannot injure it by such activities as cutting down timber for sale or extracting oil.

Fixed-Term Tenancy

A **fixed-term tenancy,** also called a *tenancy for years,* is created by an express contract by which property is leased for a specified period of time, such as a day, a month, a year, or a period of years. Signing a one-year lease to occupy an apartment, for instance, creates a fixed-term tenancy. Note that the term need not be specified by date and can be conditioned on the occurrence of an event, such as leasing a cabin for the summer or an apartment during Mardi Gras. At the end of the period specified in the lease, the lease ends (without notice), and possession of the property returns to the lessor. If the tenant dies during the period of the lease, the lease interest passes to the tenant's heirs as personal property. Often, leases include renewal or extension provisions.

Periodic Tenancy

A **periodic tenancy** is created by a lease that does not specify how long it is to last but does specify that rent is to be paid at certain intervals. This type of tenancy is automatically renewed for another rental period unless properly terminated. **EXAMPLE 28.12** Kayla enters into a lease with Capital Properties. The lease states, "Rent is due on the tenth day of every month." This provision creates a periodic tenancy from month to month. • This type of tenancy can also extend from week to week or from year to year.

Under the common law, to terminate a periodic tenancy, the landlord or tenant must give at least one period's notice to the other party. If the tenancy extends from month to month, for example, one month's notice must be given prior to the last month's rent payment. State statutes may require a different period for notice of termination in a periodic tenancy, however.

Tenancy at Will

With a **tenancy at will,** either party can terminate the tenancy without notice. This type of tenancy can arise if a landlord rents property to a tenant "for as long as both agree" or allows a person to live on the premises without paying rent. Tenancies at will are rare today because most state statutes require a landlord to provide some period of notice to terminate a tenancy (as previously noted). States may also require a landowner to have sufficient cause (reason) to end a residential tenancy. Certain events, such as the death of either party or the voluntary commission of waste by the tenant, automatically terminate a tenancy at will.

Tenancy at Sufferance

The mere possession of land without right is called a **tenancy at sufferance.** A tenancy at sufferance is not a true tenancy because it is created when a tenant *wrongfully* retains possession of property. Whenever a tenancy for years or a periodic tenancy ends and the tenant continues to retain possession of the premises without the owner's permission, a tenancy at sufferance is created.

When a commercial or residential tenant wrongfully retains possession, the landlord is entitled to damages. Typically, the damages are based on the fair market rental value of the premises after the expiration of the lease. If the landlord has increased the rent for the premises, and the tenant does not agree to pay the higher rent and does not vacate the premises, then the proper standard of damages may be an issue. A court has to determine whether another tenant was willing to pay the higher rent during the time the existing tenant retained possession. If the landlord cannot show that another tenant was ready to rent the property at the higher rent, the proper standard of damages is the existing rental rate (rather than the higher rate).

Landlord-Tenant Relationships

A landlord-tenant relationship is established by a lease contract. As mentioned, a lease contract arises when a property owner (landlord) agrees to give another party (the tenant) the exclusive right to possess the property—usually for a price and for a specified term. In most states, statutes require leases for terms exceeding one year to be in writing. The lease should describe the property and indicate the length of the term, the amount of the rent, and how and when it is to be paid.

State or local law often dictates permissible lease terms. For example, a statute or ordinance might prohibit the leasing of a structure that is in a certain physical condition or is not in compliance with local building codes. In 1972, in an effort to create more uniformity in the law governing landlord-tenant relationships, the National Conference of Commissioners on Uniform State Laws issued the Uniform Residential Landlord and Tenant Act (URLTA). Twenty-one states have adopted variations of the URLTA.

In the past forty years, landlord-tenant relationships, which were traditionally governed by contract law, have become much more complex, as has the law governing them. We look now at the respective rights and duties of landlords and tenants.

Rights and Duties

The rights and duties of landlords and tenants generally pertain to four broad areas of concern—the possession, use, maintenance, and, of course, rent of leased property.

POSSESSION A landlord is obligated to give a tenant possession of the property that the tenant has agreed to lease. After obtaining possession, the tenant retains the property exclusively until the lease expires, unless the lease states otherwise.

The covenant of quiet enjoyment mentioned previously also applies to leased premises. Under this covenant, the landlord promises that during the lease term, neither the landlord nor anyone having a superior title to the property will disturb the tenant's use and enjoyment of the property. This covenant forms the essence of the landlord-tenant relationship, and if it is breached, the tenant can terminate the lease and sue for damages.

If the landlord deprives the tenant of possession of the leased property or interferes with the tenant's use or enjoyment of it, an eviction occurs. An **eviction** arises, for instance, when the landlord changes the lock and refuses to give the tenant a new key. A **constructive eviction** occurs when the landlord wrongfully performs or fails to perform any of the duties the lease requires, thereby making the tenant's further use and enjoyment of the property exceedingly difficult or impossible. Examples of constructive eviction include a landlord's failure to provide heat in the winter, electricity, or other essential utilities.

USE AND MAINTENANCE OF THE PREMISES If the parties do not limit by agreement the uses to which the property may be put, the tenant may make any use of it, as long as the use is legal and reasonably relates to the purpose for which the property is adapted or ordinarily used and does not injure the landlord's interest.

The tenant is responsible for any damage to the premises that he or she causes, intentionally or negligently, and may be held liable for the cost of returning the property to the physical condition it was in at the lease's inception. Also, the tenant is not entitled to create a *nuisance* by substantially interfering with others' quiet enjoyment of their property rights. Unless the parties have agreed otherwise, the tenant is not responsible for ordinary wear and tear and the property's consequent depreciation in value.

In some jurisdictions, landlords of residential property are required by statute to maintain the premises in good repair. Landlords must also comply with any applicable state statutes and city ordinances regarding maintenance and repair of buildings.

IMPLIED WARRANTY OF HABITABILITY The implied warranty of habitability, which was discussed earlier in this chapter in the context of the sale of new homes, also applies to residential leases. It requires a landlord who leases residential property to ensure that the premises are habitable—that is, safe and suitable for people to live in. Also, the landlord must make repairs to maintain the premises in that condition for the lease's duration. Generally, this warranty applies to major, or substantial, physical defects that the landlord knows or should know about and has had a reasonable time to repair—for example, a large hole in the roof.

RENT Rent is the tenant's payment to the landlord for the tenant's occupancy or use of the landlord's real property. Usually, the tenant must pay the rent even if she or he refuses to occupy the property or moves out, as long as the refusal or the move is unjustified and the lease is in force. Under the common law, if the leased premises were destroyed by fire or flood, the tenant still had to pay rent. Today, however, if an apartment building burns down, most states' laws do not require tenants to continue to pay rent.

In some situations, such as when a landlord breaches the implied warranty of habitability, a tenant may be allowed to withhold rent as a remedy. When rent withholding is authorized under a statute, the tenant must usually put the amount withheld into an escrow account. This account is held in the name of the depositor (the tenant) and an escrow agent (usually the court or a government agency), and the funds are returnable to the depositor if the third person (the landlord) fails to make the premises habitable.

Transferring Rights to Leased Property

Either the landlord or the tenant may wish to transfer her or his rights to the leased property during the term of the lease. If a landlord transfers complete title to the leased property to another, the tenant becomes the tenant of the new owner. The new owner may collect subsequent rent but must abide by the terms of the existing lease.

ASSIGNMENT The tenant's transfer of his or her entire interest in the leased property to a third person is an *assignment of the lease.* Many leases require that an assignment have the landlord's written consent. An assignment that lacks consent can be avoided (nullified) by the landlord. State statutes may specify that the landlord may not unreasonably withhold consent, though. Also, a landlord who knowingly accepts rent from the assignee may be held to have waived the consent requirement.

When an assignment is valid, the assignee acquires all of the tenant's rights under the lease. An assignment, however, does not release the original tenant (the assignor) from the obligation to pay rent should the assignee default. Also, if the assignee exercises an option under the original lease to extend the term, the assigning tenant remains liable for the rent during the extension, unless the landlord agrees otherwise.

SUBLEASES The tenant's transfer of all or part of the premises for a period shorter than the lease term is a **sublease.** Many leases also require the landlord's written consent for a sublease. If the landlord's consent is required, a sublease without such permission is ineffective. Also, like an assignment, a sublease does not release the tenant from her or his obligations under the lease.

EXAMPLE 28.13 Derek, a student, leases an apartment for a two-year period. Although Derek had planned on attending summer school, he decides to accept a job offer in Europe for the summer months instead. Derek therefore obtains his landlord's consent to sublease the apartment to Ava. Ava is bound by the same terms of the lease as Derek, and the landlord can hold Derek liable if Ava violates the lease terms. •

Reviewing . . . Real Property and Landlord-Tenant Law

Vern Shoepke purchased a two-story home from Walter and Eliza Bruster in the town of Roche, Maine. The warranty deed did not specify what covenants would be included in the conveyance. The property was adjacent to a public park that included a popular Frisbee golf course. (Frisbee golf is a sport similar to golf but using Frisbees.) Wayakichi Creek ran along the north end of the park and along Shoepke's property. The deed allowed Roche citizens the right to walk across a five-foot-wide section of the lot beside Wayakichi Creek as part of a two-mile public trail system. Teenagers regularly threw Frisbee golf discs from the walking path behind Shoepke's property over his yard to the adjacent park. Shoepke habitually shouted and cursed at the teenagers, demanding that they not throw the discs over his yard. Two months after moving into his Roche home, Shoepke leased the second floor to Lauren Slater for nine months. (The lease agreement did not specify that Shoepke's consent would be required to sublease the second floor.) After three months of tenancy, Slater sublet the second floor to a local artist, Javier Indalecio. Over the remaining six months, Indalecio's use of oil paints damaged the carpeting in Shoepke's home. Using the information presented in the chapter, answer the following questions.

1. What is the term for the right of Roche citizens to walk across Shoepke's land on the trail?
2. What covenants would most courts infer were included in the warranty deed that was used in the property transfer from the Brusters to Shoepke?
3. Can Shoepke hold Slater financially responsible for the damage to the carpeting caused by Indalecio?
4. Suppose that Slater—to offset her liability for the carpet damage caused by Indalecio—files a counterclaim against Shoepke for breach of the covenant of quiet enjoyment. Could the fact that teenagers continually throw Frisbees over the leased property arguably be a breach of the covenant of quiet enjoyment? Why or why not?

Terms and Concepts

adverse possession 547
closing 545
constructive eviction 550
conveyance 543
deed 546
easement 544
eminent domain 548
escrow account 545
eviction 550
fee simple absolute 543
fixed-term tenancy 549
fixture 542
implied warranty of habitability 545
leasehold estate 549
license 544

life estate 543
nonpossessory interest 544
periodic tenancy 549
profit 544
quitclaim deed 546
recording statutes 547
special warranty deed 546
sublease 551
taking 548
tenancy at sufferance 549
tenancy at will 549
warranty deed 546

Chapter Summary: Real Property and Landlord-Tenant Law

The Nature of Real Property (See pages 541–543.)	Real property (also called real estate or realty) is immovable. It includes land, subsurface and airspace rights, plant life and vegetation, and fixtures.
Ownership Interests in Real Property (See pages 543–545.)	1. *Fee simple absolute*—The most complete form of ownership. 2. *Life estate*—An estate that lasts for the life of a specified individual, during which time the individual is entitled to possess, use, and benefit from the estate. The life tenant's ownership rights in the life estate cease to exist on her or his death. 3. *Nonpossessory interest*—An interest that involves the right to use real property but not to possess it. Easements, profits, and licenses are nonpossessory interests.
Transfer of Ownership (See pages 545–549.)	1. *By deed*—When real property is sold or transferred as a gift, title to the property is conveyed by means of a deed. A deed must meet specific legal requirements. A *warranty deed* provides the most extensive protection against defects of title. A *quitclaim deed* conveys to the grantee only whatever interest the grantor had in the property. A deed may be recorded in the manner prescribed by *recording statutes* in the appropriate jurisdiction to give third parties notice of the owner's interest. 2. *By will or inheritance*—If the owner dies after having made a valid will, the land passes as specified in the will. If the owner dies without having made a will, the heirs inherit according to state inheritance statutes. 3. *By adverse possession*—When a person possesses the property of another for a statutory period of time (ten years is the most common), that person acquires title to the property, provided the possession is actual and exclusive, open and visible, continuous and peaceable, and hostile and adverse (without the permission of the owner). 4. *By eminent domain*—The government can take land for public use, with just compensation, when the public interest requires the taking.
Leasehold Estates (See pages 549–550.)	A leasehold estate is an interest in real property that is held for only a limited period of time, as specified in the lease agreement. Types of tenancies include the following: 1. *Fixed-term tenancy*—Tenancy for a period of time stated by express contract. 2. *Periodic tenancy*—Tenancy for a period determined by the frequency of rent payments; automatically renewed unless proper notice is given. 3. *Tenancy at will*—Tenancy for as long as both parties agree; no notice of termination is required. 4. *Tenancy at sufferance*—Possession of land without legal right.
Landlord-Tenant Relationships (See pages 550–551.)	1. *Lease agreement*—The landlord-tenant relationship is created by a lease agreement. State or local laws may dictate whether the lease must be in writing and what lease terms are permissible. 2. *Rights and duties*—The rights and duties that arise under a lease agreement generally pertain to the following areas: a. Possession—The tenant has an exclusive right to possess the leased premises. Under the covenant of quiet enjoyment, the landlord promises that during the lease term neither the landlord nor anyone having superior title to the property will disturb the tenant's use and enjoyment of the property. b. Use and maintenance of the premises—Unless the parties agree otherwise, the tenant may make any legal use of the property. The tenant is responsible for any damage that he or she causes. The landlord must comply with laws that set specific standards for the maintenance of real property. The implied warranty of habitability requires that a landlord furnish and maintain residential premises in a habitable condition (that is, in a condition safe and suitable for human life). c. Rent—The tenant must pay the rent as long as the lease is in force, unless the tenant justifiably refuses to occupy the property or withholds the rent because of the landlord's failure to maintain the premises properly.

Chapter Summary: Real Property and Landlord-Tenant Law—Continued

Landlord-Tenant Relationships—Continued	3. *Transferring rights to leased property*— a. If the landlord transfers complete title to the leased property, the tenant becomes the tenant of the new owner. The new owner may then collect the rent but must abide by the existing lease. b. Generally, in the absence of an agreement to the contrary, tenants may assign their rights (but not their duties) under a lease contract to a third person. Tenants may also sublease leased property to a third person, but the original tenant is not relieved of any obligations to the landlord under the lease. In either situation, the landlord's consent may be required, but statutes may prohibit the landlord from unreasonably withholding consent.

ExamPrep

ISSUE SPOTTERS

—Check your answers to these questions against the answers provided in Appendix G.

1 Bernie sells his house to Consuela under a warranty deed. Later, Delmira appears, holding a better title to the house than Consuela has. Delmira wants Consuela off the property. What can Consuela do?

2 Grey owns a commercial building in fee simple. Grey transfers temporary possession of the building to Haven Corporation (HC). Can HC transfer possession for even less time to Idyll Company? Explain.

BEFORE THE TEST

Go to **www.cengagebrain.com**, enter the ISBN 9781111530624, and click on "Find" to locate this textbook's Web site. Then, click on "Access Now" under "Study Tools," and select Chapter 28 at the top. There, you will find an Interactive Quiz that you can take to assess your mastery of the concepts in this chapter, as well as Flashcards and a Glossary of important terms.

For Review

1 What can a person who holds property in fee simple absolute do with the property?
2 What are the requirements for acquiring property by adverse possession?
3 What limitations may be imposed on the rights of property owners?
4 What is a leasehold estate? What types of leasehold estates, or tenancies, can be created when real property is leased?
5 What are the respective duties of the landlord and the tenant concerning the use and maintenance of leased property?

Questions and Case Problems

28–1 Property Ownership. Twenty-two years ago, Lorenz was a wanderer. At that time, he decided to settle down on an unoccupied, three-acre parcel of land that he did not own. People in the area told him that they had no idea who owned the property. Lorenz built a house on the land, got married, and raised three children while living there. He fenced in the land, installed a gate with a sign above it that read "Lorenz's Homestead," and removed trespassers. Lorenz is now confronted by Joe Reese, who has a deed in his name as owner of the property. Reese, claiming ownership of the land, orders Lorenz and his family off the property. Discuss who has the better "title" to the property.

28–2 Deeds. Wiley and Gemma are neighbors. Wiley's lot is extremely large, and his present and future use of it will not involve the entire area. Gemma wants to build a single-car garage and driveway along the present lot boundary. Because the placement of her existing structures makes it impossible for her to comply with an ordinance requiring buildings to be set back fifteen feet from an adjoining property line, Gemma cannot build the garage. Gemma contracts to purchase ten feet of Wiley's property along their boundary line for $3,000. Wiley is willing to sell but will give Gemma only a quitclaim deed, whereas Gemma wants a warranty deed. Discuss the differences between these deeds as they would affect the rights of the parties if the title to this ten feet of land later proves to be defective.

28–3 Eviction. James owns a three-story building. He leases the ground floor to Juan's Mexican restaurant. The lease is to run for a five-year period and contains an express covenant of quiet enjoyment. One year later, James leases the top two stories to the Upbeat Club, a discotheque. The club's hours run from 5:00 P.M. to 1:00 A.M. The noise from the Upbeat Club is so loud that it is driving customers away from Juan's restaurant. Juan has notified James of the interference and has called the police on a number of occasions. James refuses to talk to the owners of the Upbeat Club or to do anything to remedy the situation. Juan abandons the premises. James files suit for breach of the lease agreement and for the rental payments still due under the lease. Juan claims that he was constructively evicted and files a countersuit for damages. Discuss who will be held liable.

28–4 Ownership in Fee Simple. Thomas and Teresa Cline built a house on a 76-acre parcel of real estate next to Roy Berg's home and property in Augusta County, Virginia. The homes were about 1,800 feet apart but in view of each other. After several disagreements between the parties, Berg equipped an 11-foot tripod with motion sensors and floodlights that intermittently illuminated the Clines' home. Berg also installed surveillance cameras that tracked some of the movement on the Clines' property. The cameras transmitted on an open frequency, which could be received by any television within range. The Clines asked Berg to turn off, or at least redirect, the lights. When he refused, they erected a fence for 200 feet along the parties' common property line. The 32-foot-high fence consisted of 20 utility poles spaced 10 feet apart with plastic wrap stretched between the poles. This effectively blocked the lights and cameras. Berg filed a suit against the Clines in a Virginia state court, complaining that the fence interfered unreasonably with his use and enjoyment of his property. He asked the court to order the Clines to take the fence down. What are the limits on an owner's use of property? How should the court rule in this case? Why? [*Cline v. Berg,* 273 Va. 142, 639 S.E.2d 231 (2007)]

28–5 Commercial Lease Terms. Gi Hwa Park entered into a lease with Landmark HHH, LLC, for retail space in the Plaza at Landmark, a shopping center in Virginia. The lease required that the landlord keep the roof "in good repair" and that the tenant obtain insurance on her inventory and absolve the landlord from any losses to the extent of the insurance proceeds. Park opened a store—The Four Seasons—in the space, specializing in imported men's suits and accessories. Within a month of the opening and continuing for nearly eight years, water intermittently leaked through the roof, causing damage. Landmark eventually had a new roof installed, but water continued to leak into The Four Seasons. On a night of record rainfall, the store suffered substantial water damage, and Park was forced to close the store. On what basis might Park seek to recover from Landmark? What might Landmark assert in response? Which party's argument is more likely to succeed, and why? [*Landmark HHH, LLC v. Gi Hwa Park,* 277 Va. 50, 671 S.E.2d 143 (2009)]

28–6 Case Problem with Sample Answer In 1974, Alana Mansell built a large shed, which she used as a three-car garage, on the back of her property. This building encroached on a neighbor's property by fourteen feet; however, the neighbor knew of the encroachment and informally approved it. But the neighbor did not transfer ownership of the property to Mansell. In 2001, Betty Hunter bought Mansell's neighbor's property. The survey done at that time indicated the encroachment. In 2003, Hunter's attorney notified Mansell about the encroachment, but nothing was done. In 2006, Mansell installed a concrete foundation under the garage, which had previously been dirt. Mansell also sought a declaratory judgment that she was the fee simple owner of the area under the garage that encroached on Hunter's property, arguing that the possession of the property from 1974 to 2001 gave her ownership by adverse possession. Hunter filed a counterclaim, demanding removal of the encroaching structure. The trial court held that the property belonged to Hunter, but did not order removal of the garage. Hunter and Mansell appealed. Would the open occupation of the property for nearly thirty years give Mansell title by adverse possession? Explain your answer. [*Hunter v. Mansell,* ___ P.3d ___ (Colo.App. 2010)]

—For a sample answer to Problem 28–6, go to Appendix F at the end of this text.

28–7 A Question of Ethics *In 1999, Stephen and Linda Kailin bought the Monona Center, a mall in Madison, Wisconsin, from Perry Armstrong for $760,000. The contract provided, "Seller represents to Buyer that as of the date of acceptance Seller had no notice or knowledge of conditions affecting the Property or transaction" other than certain items disclosed at the time of the offer. Armstrong told the Kailins of the Center's eight tenants, their lease expiration dates, and the monthly and annual rent due under each lease. One of the lessees, Ring's All-American Karate, occupied about a third of the Center's space under a five-year lease. Because of Ring's financial difficulties, Armstrong had agreed to reduce its rent for nine months in 1997. By the time of the sale to the Kailins, Ring owed $13,910 in unpaid rent, but Armstrong did not tell the Kailins, who did not ask. Ring continued to fail to pay rent and finally vacated the Center. The Kailins filed a suit in a Wisconsin state court against Armstrong and others, alleging, among other things, misrepresentation. [*Kailin v. Armstrong, *2002 WI App. 70, 252 Wis.2d 676, 643 N.W.2d 132 (2002)]*

1 Did Armstrong have a duty to disclose Ring's delinquency and default to the Kailins? Explain.
2 What obligation, if any, did Ring have to the Kailins or Armstrong after failing to pay the rent and eventually defaulting on the lease? Why?

28–8 Critical Thinking Managerial Question Garza Construction Co. erects a silo (a grain storage facility) on Reeve's ranch. Garza also lends Reeve funds to pay for the silo under an agreement providing that the silo is not to become part of the land until Reeve completes the loan payments. Before the silo is paid for, Metropolitan State Bank, the mortgage holder on Reeve's land, forecloses on the property. Metropolitan contends that the silo is a fixture to the realty and that the bank is therefore entitled to the proceeds from its sale. Garza argues that the silo is personal property and that the proceeds should therefore go to Garza. Is the silo a fixture? Why or why not?

Chapter 29

Insurance, Wills, and Trusts

Learning Objectives

After reading this chapter, you should be able to answer the following questions:

1. What is an insurable interest? When must an insurable interest exist—at the time the insurance policy is obtained, at the time the loss occurs, or both?
2. Is an insurance broker the agent of the insurance applicant or the agent of the insurer?
3. What are the basic requirements for executing a will? How may a will be revoked?
4. What is the difference between a *per stirpes* distribution and a *per capita* distribution of an estate to the grandchildren of the deceased?
5. What are the four essential elements of a trust? What is the difference between an express trust and an implied trust?

The Learning Objectives above are designed to help improve your understanding of the chapter.

Most individuals insure both real and personal property (as well as their lives). The first part of this chapter focuses on insurance, which is a foremost concern of all property owners. We then examine how property is transferred on the death of its owner. Certainly, the laws of succession of property are a necessary corollary to the concept of private ownership of property. Our laws require that on death, title to the property of the decedent (one who has recently died) must be delivered in full somewhere. In this chapter, we see that this can be done by will, through trusts, or through state laws prescribing distribution of property among heirs or next of kin.

Insurance

Many precautions may be taken to protect against the hazards of life. For instance, an individual may wear a seat belt to protect against injuries from automobile accidents or install smoke detectors to guard against injury from fire. Of course, no one can predict whether an accident or a fire will ever occur, but individuals and businesses must establish plans to protect their personal and financial interests should some event threaten to undermine their security.

Insurance is a contract by which the insurance company (the insurer) promises to pay an amount or to give something of value to another (either the insured or the beneficiary) in the event that the insured is injured, dies, or sustains damage to her or his property as a result of particular, stated contingencies. Basically, insurance is an arrangement for *transferring and allocating risk.* In many instances, **risk** can be described as a prediction concerning potential loss based on known and unknown factors. Insurance, however, involves much more than a game of chance.

Risk management normally involves the transfer of certain risks from the individual to the insurance company by a contractual agreement. The insurance contract and its provisions will be examined shortly. First, however, we look at the different types of insurance that can be obtained, insurance terminology, and the concept of insurable interest.

Classifications of Insurance

Insurance is classified according to the nature of the risk involved. For instance, fire insurance, casualty insurance, life insurance, and title insurance apply to different types of risk. Furthermore, policies of these types protect different persons and interests. This is reasonable because the types of losses that are expected and that are foreseeable or unforeseeable vary with the nature of the activity. Exhibit 29–1 below presents a list of selected insurance classifications.

• *Exhibit* **29–1 Selected Insurance Classifications**

TYPE OF INSURANCE	COVERAGE
Accident	Covers expenses, losses, and suffering incurred by the insured because of accidents causing physical injury and any consequent disability; sometimes includes a specified payment to heirs of the insured if death results from an accident.
All-risk	Covers all losses that the insured may incur except those that are specifically excluded. Typical exclusions are war, pollution, earthquakes, and floods.
Automobile	May cover damage to automobiles resulting from specified hazards or occurrences (such as fire, vandalism, theft, or collision); normally provides protection against liability for personal injuries and property damage resulting from the operation of the vehicle.
Casualty	Protects against losses incurred by the insured as a result of being held liable for personal injuries or property damage sustained by others.
Decreasing-term life	Provides life insurance; requires uniform payments over the life (term) of the policy, but with a decreasing face value (amount of coverage).
Disability	Replaces a portion of the insured's monthly income from employment in the event that illness or injury causes a short- or long-term disability. Some states require employers to provide short-term disability insurance. Benefits typically last a set period of time, such as six months for short-term coverage or five years for long-term coverage.
Employer's liability	Insures an employer against liability for injuries or losses sustained by employees during the course of their employment; covers claims not covered under workers' compensation insurance.
Fire	Covers losses incurred by the insured as a result of fire.
Floater	Covers movable property, as long as the property is within the territorial boundaries specified in the contract.
Health	Covers expenses incurred by the insured as a result of physical injury or illness and other expenses relating to health and life maintenance.
Homeowners'	Protects homeowners against some or all risks of loss to their residences and the residences' contents or liability arising from the use of the property.
Key-person	Protects a business in the event of the death or disability of a key employee.
Liability	Protects against liability imposed on the insured as a result of injuries to the person or property of another.
Life	Covers the death of the policyholder. On the death of the insured, the insurer pays the amount specified in the policy to the insured's beneficiary.
Major medical	Protects the insured against major hospital, medical, or surgical expenses.
Malpractice	Protects professionals (physicians, lawyers, and others) against malpractice claims brought against them by their patients or clients; a form of liability insurance.
Mortgage	Covers a mortgage loan. The insurer pays the balance of the mortgage to the creditor on the death or disability of the debtor.
Term life	Provides life insurance for a specified period of time (term) with no cash surrender value; usually renewable.
Title	Protects against any defects in title to real property and any losses incurred as a result of existing claims against or liens on the property at the time of purchase.

Insurance Terminology

An insurance contract is called a **policy**, the consideration paid to the insurer is called a **premium**, and the insurance company is sometimes called an **underwriter.** The parties to an insurance policy are the *insurer* (the insurance company) and the insured (the person covered by its provisions or the holder of the policy).

Insurance contracts usually are obtained through an *agent*, who ordinarily works for the insurance company, or through a *broker*, who is ordinarily an *independent contractor.* When a broker deals with an applicant for insurance, the broker is, in effect, the applicant's agent and not an agent of the insurance company. In contrast, an insurance agent is an agent of the insurance company, not of the applicant. Thus, the agent owes fiduciary duties to the insurer (the insurance company), but not to the person who is applying for insurance. As a general rule, the insurance company is bound by the acts of its insurance agents when they act within the agency relationship (discussed in Chapter 21). In most situations, state law determines the status of all parties writing or obtaining insurance.

Insurable Interest

A person can insure anything in which she or he has an **insurable interest.** In regard to real and personal property, an insurable interest exists when the insured derives a pecuniary benefit (a benefit consisting of or relating to money) from the preservation and continued existence of the property. Put another way, one has an insurable interest in property when one would sustain a financial loss from its destruction. Without an insurable interest, there is no enforceable contract, and a transaction to purchase insurance coverage would have to be treated as a wager.

LIFE INSURANCE In regard to life insurance, a person must have a reasonable expectation of benefit from the continued life of another in order to have an insurable interest in that person's life. The insurable interest must exist *at the time the policy is obtained.* The benefit may be pecuniary (as with so-called *key-person insurance,* which insures the lives of important employees, usually in small companies), or it may be founded on the relationship between the parties (by blood or affinity).

PROPERTY INSURANCE For property insurance, the insurable interest must exist at the time the loss occurs but need not exist when the policy is purchased. The existence of an insurable interest is a primary concern in determining liability under an insurance policy.

CASE EXAMPLE 29.1 ABM Industries, Inc., an engineering, lighting, and janitorial service contractor, leased office and storage space in the World Trade Center (WTC) in New York City in 2001. ABM also ran the buildings' heating, ventilation, and air-condition systems, and maintained all of the WTC's common areas. At the time, ABM employed more than eight hundred workers at the WTC. Zurich American Insurance Company insured ABM against losses resulting from "business interruption" caused by direct physical loss or damage "to property owned, controlled, used, leased or intended for use" by ABM. After the terrorist attacks on September 11, 2001, ABM filed a claim with Zurich to recover for the loss of all income derived from ABM's WTC operations. Zurich argued that ABM's recovery should be limited to the income lost as a result of the destruction of ABM's office and storage space and supplies. A federal appellate court, however, ruled that ABM was entitled to compensation for the loss of all of its WTC operations. The court reasoned that the "policy's scope expressly includes real or personal property that the insured 'used,' 'controlled,' or 'intended for use.'" Because ABM's income depended on "the common areas and leased premises in the WTC complex," it had an insurable interest in that property at the time of the loss.[1] •

The Insurance Contract

An insurance contract is governed by the general principles of contract law, although the insurance industry is heavily regulated by each state. Here, we discuss the application for insurance, the date when the contract takes effect, and some of the important provisions typically found in insurance contracts. We will also discuss the cancellation of an insurance policy and defenses that insurance companies can raise against payment on a policy.

APPLICATION The filled-in application form for insurance is usually attached to the policy and made a part of the insurance contract. Thus, an insurance applicant is bound by any false statements that appear in the application (subject to certain exceptions). Because the insurance company evaluates the risk factors based on the information included in the insurance application, misstatements or misrepresentations can void a policy, especially if the insurance company can show that it would not have extended insurance if it had known the true facts.

EFFECTIVE DATE The effective date of an insurance contract—that is, the date on which the insurance coverage begins—is important. In some situations, the insurance applicant is not protected until a formal written policy is issued. For instance, if the parties agree that the policy will be issued and delivered at a later time, the contract is not effective until the policy is issued and delivered. Thus, any loss sustained between the time of application and the delivery of the policy is not

1. *Zurich American Insurance Co. v. ABM Industries, Inc.,* 397 F.3d 158 (2d Cir. 2005).

covered. Also, when a person hires a broker to obtain insurance, the broker is merely the agent of the applicant. Therefore, if the broker fails to procure a policy, the applicant normally is not insured.

In other situations, the applicant is protected between the time the application is received and the time the insurance company either accepts or rejects it. A person who seeks insurance from an insurance company's agent is usually protected from the moment the application is made, provided—for life insurance—that some form of premium has been paid. Usually, the agent will write a memorandum, or **binder**, indicating that a policy is pending and stating its essential terms.

Parties may agree that a life insurance policy will be binding at the time the insured pays the first premium, or the policy may be expressly contingent on the applicant's passing a physical examination. If the applicant pays the premium but dies before having the physical examination, then in order to collect, the applicant's estate normally must show that the applicant *would have passed* the examination had he or she not died.

COINSURANCE CLAUSES Often, when taking out fire insurance policies, property owners insure their property for less than full value because most fires do not result in a total loss. To encourage owners to insure their property for an amount as close to full value as possible, fire insurance policies commonly include a coinsurance clause. Typically, a *coinsurance clause* provides that if the owner insures the property up to a specified percentage—usually 80 percent—of its value, she or he will recover any loss up to the face amount of the policy. If the insurance is for less than the fixed percentage, the owner is responsible for a proportionate share of the loss.

Coinsurance applies only in instances of partial loss. The amount of the recovery is calculated by using the following formula:

$$\text{Loss} \times \left(\frac{\text{Amount of Insurance Coverage}}{\text{Coinsurance Percentage} \times \text{Property Value}} \right) = \text{Amount of Recovery}$$

EXAMPLE 29.2 The owner of property valued at $200,000 takes out a policy in the amount of $100,000. If the owner then suffers a loss of $80,000, the recovery will be $50,000. The owner will be responsible for (coinsure) the balance of the loss, or $30,000.

$$\$80{,}000 \times \left(\frac{\$100{,}000}{0.8 \times \$200{,}000} \right) = \$50{,}000$$

If the owner had taken out a policy in the amount of 80 percent of the value of the property, or $160,000, then according to the same formula, the owner would have recovered the full amount of the loss (the face amount of the policy). •

INCONTESTABILITY CLAUSES Statutes commonly require that a policy for life or health insurance provide that after the policy has been in force for a specified length of time—often two or three years—the insurer cannot contest statements made in the application. This is known as an **incontestability clause.** Once a policy becomes incontestable, the insurer cannot later avoid a claim on the basis of, for example, fraud on the part of the insured, unless the clause provides an exception for that circumstance.

Some other important provisions and clauses contained in insurance contracts are listed and defined in Exhibit 29–2 below.

INTERPRETING PROVISIONS The courts are aware that most people do not have the special training necessary to understand the intricate terminology used in insurance poli-

• ***Exhibit* 29–2 Selected Insurance Contract Provisions and Clauses**

Antilapse clause	An antilapse clause provides that the policy will not automatically lapse if no payment is made on the date due. Ordinarily, under such a provision, the insured has a *grace period* of thirty or thirty-one days within which to pay an overdue premium before the policy is canceled.
Appraisal clause	Insurance policies frequently provide that if the parties cannot agree on the amount of a loss covered under the policy or the value of the property lost, an appraisal, or estimate, by an impartial and qualified third party can be demanded.
Arbitration clause	Many insurance policies include clauses that call for arbitration of disputes that may arise between the insurer and the insured concerning the settlement of claims.
Incontestability clause	An incontestability clause provides that after a policy has been in force for a specified length of time—usually two or three years—the insurer cannot contest statements made in the application.
Multiple insurance	Many insurance policies include a clause providing that if the insured has multiple insurance policies that cover the same property and the amount of coverage exceeds the loss, the loss will be shared proportionately by the insurance companies.

cies. Therefore, when disputes arise, the courts will interpret the words used in an insurance contract according to their ordinary meanings in light of the nature of the coverage involved.

When there is an ambiguity in the policy, the provision generally is interpreted against the insurance company. Also, when it is unclear whether an insurance contract actually exists because the written policy has not been delivered, the uncertainty normally is resolved against the insurance company. The court presumes that the policy is in effect unless the company can show otherwise. Similarly, an insurer must make sure that the insured is adequately notified of any change in coverage under an existing policy.

Disputes over insurance often focus on the application of an exclusion in the policy, as the following case illustrates.

Case 29.1 Valero v. Florida Insurance Guaranty Association, Inc.

District Court of Appeal of Florida, Fourth District, 59 So.3d 1166 (2011).
www.4dca.org/opinions/2011op.shtml[a]

FACTS Alberto and Karelli Mila were insured under a homeowners' liability policy. The policy, in "exclusion k," stated that coverage did not apply to "bodily injury arising out of sexual molestation, corporal punishment or physical or mental abuse." Verushka Valero, on behalf of her child, filed a suit in a Florida state court against the Milas, charging them with negligent supervision of a perpetrator who had sexually molested Valero's child. The Milas filed a claim with their insurer to provide a defense against the charges. The insurer had become insolvent, so the claim was submitted to the Florida Insurance Guaranty Association, Inc. (FIGA). FIGA is a nonprofit corporation created by the Florida legislature to evaluate and resolve claims when insurance companies become insolvent (a similar insurance guaranty association exists in nearly every state). FIGA refused to pay the Milas' claim and asked the court to rule that it had no obligation under the policy to provide such a defense. The court issued a summary judgment in FIGA's favor. Valero and the Milas appealed, arguing that exclusion k was ambiguous.

ISSUE Was the term of the Milas' insurance policy that excluded coverage for "bodily injury arising out of sexual molestation" ambiguous as to whether it covered acts by someone under their supervision?

a. In the "March" section, click on "03-02-2011." In the result, click on the case title to view the opinion. The District Court of Appeal of Florida maintains this Web site.

DECISION No. A state intermediate appellate court affirmed the lower court's judgment. The exclusion applied to preclude coverage in this case.

REASON The Milas pointed out that a different exclusion, exclusion l, used the phrase "by any person" and exclusion k did not. According to the Milas, this meant that it was not clear whether exclusion k applied only to acts caused by an insured. The court read the entire list of twelve exclusions together and concluded that the phrase in exclusion l was "superfluous." Even if the phrase "by any person" had been used in exclusion k, coverage might still have been denied, as in this case. Valero and the Milas also cited decisions from other jurisdictions to support their argument. The court found these decisions to be "not helpful" because they considered exclusions in isolation, not in the context of other exclusions.

WHAT IF THE FACTS WERE DIFFERENT? *Suppose that exclusion k, instead of exclusion l, had used the phrase "by any person." Would the result have been different? Explain.*

Cancellation The insured can cancel a policy at any time, and the insurer can cancel under certain circumstances. When an insurance company can cancel its insurance contract, the policy or a state statute usually requires that the insurer give advance written notice of the cancellation to the insured. The same requirement applies when only part of a policy is canceled. Any premium paid in advance may be refundable on the policy's cancellation. The insured may also be entitled to a life insurance policy's cash surrender value.

The insurer may cancel an insurance policy for various reasons, depending on the type of insurance. For example, automobile insurance can be canceled for nonpayment of premiums or suspension of the insured's driver's license. Property insurance can be canceled for nonpayment of premiums or for other reasons, including the insured's fraud or misrepresentation, conviction for a crime that increases the hazard insured against, or gross negligence that increases the risk assumed by the insurer. Life and health policies can be canceled because of false statements made by the insured in the application, but the cancellation must take place before the effective date of an incontestability clause. An insurer cannot cancel—or refuse to renew—a policy for discriminatory reasons or other reasons that violate public policy, or because the insured has appeared as a witness in a case against the company.

Good Faith Obligations Both parties to an insurance contract are responsible for the obligations they assume under the contract (contract law was discussed in Chapters 7 through 12). In addition, both the insured and the insurer have an implied duty to act in good faith.

Good faith requires the party who is applying for insurance to reveal everything necessary for the insurer to evaluate the risk. In other words, the applicant must disclose all material facts, including all facts that an insurer would consider in determining whether to charge a higher premium or to refuse to issue a policy altogether. Once the insurance policy is issued, the insured has three basic duties under the contract: (1) to pay the premiums as stated in the contract, (2) to notify the insurer within a reasonable time if an event occurs that gives rise to a claim, and (3) to cooperate with the insurer during any investigation or litigation. Many insurance companies today require that an applicant give the company permission to access other information, such as private medical records and credit ratings, for the purpose of evaluating the risk.

After the insurer has accepted the risk and some event occurs that gives rise to a claim, the insurer has a duty to investigate to determine the facts. When a policy provides insurance against third party claims, the insurer is obligated to make reasonable efforts to settle such a claim. If a settlement cannot be reached, then regardless of the claim's merit, the insurer must defend any suit against the insured. Usually, a policy provides that in this situation the insured must cooperate in the defense and attend hearings and trials if necessary.

Bad Faith Actions Although the law of insurance generally follows contract law, most states now recognize a "bad faith" tort action against insurers. Thus, if an insurer in bad faith denies coverage of a claim, the insured may recover in tort in an amount exceeding the policy's coverage limits and may also recover punitive damages. Some courts have held insurers liable for bad faith refusals to settle claims for reasonable amounts within the policy limits.

Defenses against Payment An insurance company can raise any of the defenses that would be valid in an ordinary action on a contract, as well as some defenses that do not apply in ordinary contract actions.

1. If the insurance company can show that the policy was procured by fraud or misrepresentation, it may have a valid defense for not paying on a claim. (The insurance company may also have the right to disaffirm or rescind the insurance contract.)
2. An absolute defense exists if the insurer can show that the insured lacked an insurable interest—thus rendering the policy void from the beginning.
3. Improper actions, such as those that are against public policy or that are otherwise illegal, can also give the insurance company a defense against the payment of a claim or allow it to rescind the contract.

An insurance company can be prevented, or estopped, from asserting some defenses that are normally available, however. For instance, an insurance company generally cannot escape payment on the death of an insured on the ground that the person's age was stated incorrectly on the application. Also, incontestability clauses prevent the insurer from asserting certain defenses.

Wills

Not only do the owners of property want to protect it during their lifetime through insurance coverage, but they also wish to transfer it to their loved ones at the time of their death. A **will** is the final declaration of how a person desires to have her or his property disposed of after death. It is a formal instrument that must follow exactly the requirements of state law to be effective. A will is referred to as a *testamentary disposition* of property, and one who dies after having made a valid will is said to have died **testate.**

A will can serve other purposes besides the distribution of property. It can appoint a guardian for minor children or incapacitated adults. It can also appoint a personal representative to settle the affairs of the deceased. Exhibit 29–3 on the facing page presents excerpts from the will of Michael Jackson, the "King of Pop," who died in 2009 at the age of fifty. Jackson held a substantial amount of tangible and intangible property, including the publishing rights to most of The Beatles' music catalogue. The will is a "pour-over" will, meaning that it transfers all of his property (that is not already held in the name of the trust) into the Michael Jackson Family Trust (*trusts* will be discussed later in the chapter). Jackson's will also appoints his mother, Katherine Jackson, as the guardian of his three minor children.

A person who dies without having created a valid will is said to have died **intestate.** In this situation, state **intestacy laws** prescribe the distribution of the property among heirs or next of kin. If no heirs or kin can be found, title to the property will be transferred to the state.

Terminology of Wills

A person who makes out a will is known as a **testator** (from the Latin *testari,* "to make a will"). The court responsible for administering any legal problems surrounding a will is called a *probate court,* as mentioned in Chapter 2. When a person dies, a personal representative administers the estate and settles finally all of the decedent's (deceased person's) affairs. An **executor** is a personal representative named in the will; an **administrator** is a personal representative appointed by the court for a decedent who dies without a will. The court will also appoint an administrator if the will does not name an executor or if the named person lacks the capacity to serve as an executor.

• ***Exhibit* 29–3 Excerpts from Michael Jackson's Will**

LAST WILL OF MICHAEL JOSEPH JACKSON

I, MICHAEL JOSEPH JACKSON, a resident of the State of California, declare this to be my last Will, and do hereby revoke all former wills and codicils made by me.

I. I declare that I am not married. My marriage to DEBORAH JEAN ROWE JACKSON has been dissolved. I have three children now living, PRINCE MICHAEL JACKSON, JR., PARIS MICHAEL KATHERINE JACKSON and PRINCE MICHAEL JOSEPH JACKSON, II. I have no other children, living or deceased.

II. It is my intention by this Will to dispose of all property which I am entitled to dispose of by will. I specifically refrain from exercising all powers of appointment that I may possess at the time of my death.

III. I give my entire estate to the Trustee or Trustees then acting under that certain Amended and Restated Declaration of Trust executed on March 22, 2002 by me as Trustee and Trustor which is called the MICHAEL JACKSON FAMILY TRUST, giving effect to any amendments thereto made prior to my death. All such assets shall be held, managed and distributed as a part of said Trust according to its terms and not as a separate testamentary trust.

If for any reason this gift is not operative or is invalid, or if the aforesaid Trust fails or has been revoked, I give my residuary estate to the Trustee or Trustees named to act in the MICHAEL JACKSON FAMILY TRUST, as Amended and Restated on March 22, 2002, and I direct said Trustee or Trustees to divide, administer, hold and distribute the trust estate pursuant to the provisions of said Trust * * *.

* * * *

IV. I direct that all federal estate taxes and state inheritance or succession taxes payable upon or resulting from or by reason of my death (herein "Death Taxes") attributable to property which is part of the trust estate of the MICHAEL JACKSON FAMILY TRUST, including property which passes to said trust from my probate estate shall be paid by the Trustee of said trust in accordance with its terms. Death Taxes attributable to property passing outside this Will, other than property constituting the trust estate of the trust mentioned in the preceding sentence, shall be charged against the taker of said property.

V. I appoint JOHN BRANCA, JOHN McCLAIN and BARRY SIEGEL as co-Executors of this Will. In the event of any of their deaths, resignations, inability, failure or refusal to serve or continue to serve as a co-Executor, the other shall serve and no replacement need be named. The co-Executors serving at any time after my death may name one or more replacements to serve in the event that none of the three named individuals is willing or able to serve at any time.

The term "my executors" as used in this Will shall include any duly acting personal representative or representatives of my estate. No individual acting as such need post a bond.

I hereby give to my Executors, full power and authority at any time or times to sell, lease, mortgage, pledge, exchange or otherwise dispose of the property, whether real or personal comprising my estate, upon such terms as my Executors shall deem best, to continue any business enterprises, to purchase assets from my estate, to continue in force and pay any insurance policy * * *.

VI. Except as otherwise provided in this Will or in the Trust referred to in Article III hereof, I have intentionally omitted to provide for my heirs. I have intentionally omitted to provide for my former wife, DEBORAH JEAN ROWE JACKSON.

* * * *

VIII. If any of my children are minors at the time of my death, I nominate my mother, KATHERINE JACKSON as guardian of the persons and estates of such minor children. If KATHERINE JACKSON fails to survive me, or is unable or unwilling to act as guardian, I nominate DIANA ROSS as guardian of the persons and estates of such minor children.

* * * *

A gift of real estate by will is generally called a **devise**, and a gift of personal property by will is called a **bequest**, or **legacy.** The recipient of a gift by will is a **devisee** or a **legatee**, depending on whether the gift was a devise or a legacy.

Types of Gifts

Gifts by will can be specific, general, or residuary. A specific devise or bequest (legacy) describes particular property (such as "Eastwood Estate" or "my gold pocket watch") that can be distinguished from all the rest of the testator's property. A *general* devise or bequest (legacy) uses less restrictive terminology. For instance, "I devise all my lands" is a general devise. A general bequest often specifies a sum of money instead of a particular item of property, such as a watch or an automobile. "I give to my nephew, Carleton, $30,000," for example, is a general bequest.

If the assets of an estate are insufficient to pay in full all general bequests provided for in the will, an *abatement* takes place, meaning the legatees receive reduced benefits. **EXAMPLE 29.3** Yusuf's will leaves $15,000 each to his children,

Tamara and Kwame. On Yusuf's death, only $10,000 is available to honor these bequests. By abatement, each child will receive $5,000. • If bequests are more complicated, abatement may be more complex. The testator's intent, as expressed in the will, controls.

Sometimes, a will provides that any assets remaining after the estate's debts have been paid and specific gifts have been made—called the *residuary* (or *residuum*)—are to be distributed in a specific way, such as to the testator's spouse or descendants. Such a clause, called a *residuary clause,* is often used when the exact amount to be distributed cannot be determined until all of the other gifts and payouts have been made. If the testator has not indicated what party or parties should receive the residuary of the estate, the residuary passes according to state laws of intestacy.

Requirements for a Valid Will

A will must comply with statutory formalities designed to ensure that the testator understood his or her actions at the time the will was made. These formalities are intended to help prevent fraud. Unless they are followed, the will is declared void, and the decedent's property is distributed according to the laws of intestacy of that state.

Although the required formalities vary among jurisdictions, most states uphold certain basic requirements for executing a will. In 1969, to promote more uniformity among the states, the National Conference of Commissioners on Uniform State Laws issued the Uniform Probate Code (UPC). Almost half of the states have enacted some part of the UPC and incorporated it into their own probate codes. Several states have adopted amendments to the UPC that were issued in 2008. We now look at the basic requirements for a valid will, including references to the UPC where appropriate.

TESTAMENTARY CAPACITY AND INTENT For a will to be valid, the testator must have testamentary capacity—that is, the testator must be of legal age and sound mind *at the time the will is made*. The legal age for executing a will varies, but in most states and under the UPC, the minimum age is eighteen years [UPC 2–501]. Thus, the will of a twenty-one-year-old decedent written when the person was sixteen is invalid if, under state law, the legal age for executing a will is eighteen.

The "Sound-Mind" Requirement. The concept of "being of sound mind" refers to the testator's ability to formulate and to comprehend a personal plan for the disposition of property. Generally, a testator must (1) intend the document to be his or her last will and testament, (2) comprehend the kind and character of the property being distributed, and (3) comprehend and remember the "natural objects of his or her bounty" (usually, family members and persons for whom the testator has affection).

Intent. A valid will is one that represents the maker's intention to transfer and distribute her or his property. When it can be shown that the decedent's plan of distribution was the result of fraud or of undue influence, the will is declared invalid. A court may sometimes infer undue influence when the named beneficiary was in a position to influence the making of the will. If the testator ignored blood relatives and named as a beneficiary a nonrelative who was in constant close contact with the testator, for instance, a court might infer undue influence.

EXAMPLE 29.4 Frieda is a nurse who was responsible for caring for Julie, the testator, during the last years of her life. After Julie's death, her family discovers that her will names Frieda as a beneficiary and excludes all family members. If Julie's family challenges the validity of the will on the basis of undue influence, the court might infer that Frieda unduly influenced Julie and declare the will invalid. •

In the following case, a testator's children and grandchildren claimed that his third wife had unduly influenced him to create a new will that did not provide for them. After a jury trial, the court declared the will invalid. An appellate court had to determine if there was sufficient evidence of undue influence to support the jury's verdict.

Case 29.2 In re Estate of Johnson

Court of Appeals of Texas, San Antonio, 340 S.W.3d 769 (2011).

FACTS Belton Kleberg Johnson was a descendant of the founders of the King Ranch, a famous ranch in Texas that dates back to the 1850s. He was married three times and had three children from his first marriage, as well as eight grandchildren. Johnson was a long-term alcoholic who had received both in-patient and out-patient treatment at alcohol rehabilitation facilities during his life. Johnson executed a will in 1991, when he was married to his second wife. That will provided for her during her lifetime and left the remainder of his estate in a trust for his grandchildren and children. When his second wife died in 1994, he changed the will to give each grandchild $1 million and to give the remainder to five charities. His children were provided for in a separate trust. Johnson met his third wife, Laura, shortly after the death of his second wife, and they were married in 1996. In 1997, Johnson executed a will that left $1 million to each grandchild and the remainder to Laura. In 1999, Johnson executed a new will that left

Case 29.2–Continued

his entire estate in trust to Laura for her life and then to a foundation that she controlled. After Johnson died in 2001, his attorney submitted the will from 1999 to probate. Johnson's children and grandchildren (the plaintiffs) challenged the will in court. A jury concluded that the will was invalid as a result of undue influence by Laura. She appealed, claiming that there was insufficient evidence to support the jury's finding.

ISSUE Was Johnson's 1999 will—which left his sizeable estate to his third wife, Laura, and excluded his children and grandchildren—a result of undue influence?

DECISION Yes. The state appellate court affirmed the lower court's judgment in favor of the plaintiffs. The court concluded that the evidence was legally and factually sufficient to support the jury's finding of undue influence.

REASON To prevail on an undue influence claim in Texas, the plaintiff must prove that (1) undue influence was exerted, (2) the influence overpowered the mind of the testator, and (3) the will would not have been executed but for the undue influence. The court reasoned that "the exertion of undue influence is usually a subtle thing, and by its very nature usually involves an extended course of dealings and circumstances." In this case, the evidence showed that Johnson was an alcoholic, and psychological and medical tests indicated that the alcohol had had an adverse effect on his mental state. Several experts testified that he had permanent cognitive defects and memory problems that would have caused him to be more susceptible to undue influence. Laura denied Johnson's drinking problem in court, although Johnson himself had admitted that it was ongoing when he was hospitalized in 2000, a year before his death. Evidence also suggested that Laura had exerted substantial control over many aspects of Johnson's life. She had refused to sign a prenuptial agreement, for example, and was involved in his estate planning. She had also made negative remarks about his children and grandchildren. Furthermore, evidence established that Johnson was quite proud of his heritage and wanted to provide for his descendants, as well as for the charities named in the earlier will.

WHAT IF THE FACTS WERE DIFFERENT? *Suppose that Johnson, in his 1999 will, had specifically mentioned that it was his intention that his children and grandchildren would not receive any portion of his estate. Would that have changed the outcome? Why or why not?*

WRITING Generally, a will must be in writing. The writing itself can be informal as long as it substantially complies with the statutory requirements. In some states, a will can be handwritten in crayon or ink. It can be written on a sheet or scrap of paper, on a paper bag, or on a piece of cloth. A will that is completely in the handwriting of the testator is called a **holographic will** (sometimes referred to as an *olographic will*).

In some instances, a court may find an oral will valid. A **nuncupative will** is an oral will made before witnesses. It is not permitted in most states. Where authorized by statute, such wills are generally valid only if made during the last illness of the testator and are therefore sometimes referred to as *deathbed wills.* Normally, only personal property can be transferred by a nuncupative will. Statutes frequently permit members of the military to make nuncupative wills when on active duty.

SIGNATURE A fundamental requirement is that the testator's signature must appear on the will, generally at the end. Each jurisdiction dictates by statute and court decision what constitutes a signature. Initials, an X or other mark, and words such as "Mom" have all been upheld as valid when it was shown that the testators *intended* them to be signatures.

WITNESS A will normally must be attested (sworn to) by two, and sometimes three, witnesses. The number of witnesses, their qualifications, and the manner in which the witnessing must be done are generally set out in a statute. A witness can be required to be disinterested—that is, not a beneficiary under the will. The UPC, however, provides that a will is valid even if it is attested by an interested witness [UPC 2–505]. There are no age requirements for witnesses, but they must be mentally competent.

The purpose of the witnesses is to verify that the testator actually executed (signed) the will and had the requisite intent and capacity at the time. A witness does not have to read the contents of the will. Usually, the testator and all witnesses must sign in the sight or the presence of one another, but there are exceptions.[2] The UPC does not require all parties to sign in the presence of one another and deems it sufficient if the testator acknowledges her or his signature to the witnesses [UPC 2–502].

PUBLICATION A will is *published* by an oral declaration by the maker to the witnesses that the document they are about to sign is his or her "last will and testament." Publication is becoming an unnecessary formality in most states, and it is not required under the UPC.

Revocation of Wills

An executed will is revocable by the maker at any time during the maker's lifetime. The maker may revoke a will by a physical

2. See, for example, *Slack v. Truitt,* 368 Md. 2, 791 A.2d 129 (2000). Also, note that the 2008 amendments to the UPC provide an alternative to traditional witnesses—the signature may be acknowledged by the testator before a notary public [amended UPC 2–502].

act, such as tearing up the will, or by a subsequent writing. Wills can also be revoked by operation of law. Revocation can be partial or complete, and it must follow certain strict formalities.

Revocation by a Physical Act of the Maker A testator may revoke a will by *intentionally* burning, tearing, canceling, obliterating, or otherwise destroying it, or by having someone else do so in the presence of the maker and at the maker's direction.[3] In some states, partial revocation by physical act of the maker is recognized. Thus, those portions of a will lined out or torn away are dropped, and the remaining parts of the will are valid. In no circumstances, however, can a provision be crossed out and an additional or substitute provision written in. Such altered portions require reexecution (re-signing) and reattestation (rewitnessing).

To revoke a will by physical act, it is necessary to follow the mandates of a state statute exactly. When a state statute prescribes the specific methods for revoking a will by physical act, only those methods can be used to revoke the will.

Revocation by a Subsequent Writing A will may also be wholly or partially revoked by a **codicil**, a written instrument separate from the will that amends or revokes provisions in the will. A codicil eliminates the necessity of redrafting an entire will merely to add to it or amend it. A codicil can also be used to revoke an entire will. The codicil must be executed with the same formalities required for a will, and it must refer expressly to the will. In effect, it updates a will because the will is "incorporated by reference" into the codicil.

A new will (second will) can be executed that may or may not revoke the first or a prior will, depending on the language used. To revoke a prior will, the second will must use language specifically revoking other wills, such as "This will hereby revokes all prior wills." If the second will is otherwise valid and properly executed, it will revoke all prior wills. If the express *declaration of revocation* is missing, then both wills are read together. If there are any discrepancies between the wills, the second will controls.

Revocation by Operation of Law Revocation by *operation of law* occurs when marriage, divorce or annulment, or the birth of a child takes place after a will has been executed. In most states, when a testator marries after executing a will that does not include the new spouse, on the testator's death the spouse can still receive the amount he or she would have taken had the testator died intestate—that is, without a will (how an intestate's property is distributed under state laws will be discussed shortly). In effect, the will is revoked to the point of providing the spouse with an intestate share. The rest of the estate is passed under the will [UPC 2–301, 2–508]. If, however, the new spouse is otherwise provided for in the will (or by transfer of property outside the will), he or she will not be given an intestate amount.

At common law and under the UPC, divorce does not necessarily revoke the entire will.[4] A divorce or an annulment occurring after a will has been executed revokes those dispositions of property made under the will to the former spouse [UPC 2–508]. Note also that a married person who makes a will generally cannot avoid leaving a certain portion of the estate to the surviving spouse (unless there is a valid prenuptial agreement—see Chapter 10). In most states, this is called an elective share, or a forced share, and it is often one-third of the estate or an amount equal to a spouse's share under intestacy laws.

If a child is born after a will has been executed and if it appears that the deceased parent would have made a provision for the child, that child may be entitled to a portion of the estate. Most state laws allow a child to receive some portion of a parent's estate even if no provision is made in the parent's will. This is true unless it is clear from the will's terms that the testator intended to disinherit the child. Under the UPC, the rule is the same.

Probate Procedures

To **probate** a will means to establish its validity and to carry the administration of the estate through a court process. Probate laws vary from state to state. Typically, the procedure depends on the size of the decedent's estate.

Informal Probate For smaller estates, most state statutes provide for the distribution of assets without formal probate proceedings. Faster and less expensive methods are then used. Property can be transferred by *affidavit* (a written statement taken before a person who has authority to affirm it), and problems or questions can be handled during an administrative hearing. Some state statutes allow title to cars, savings and checking accounts, and certain other property to be transferred simply by filling out forms.

A majority of states also provide for *family settlement agreements,* which are private agreements among the beneficiaries. Once a will is admitted to probate, the family members can agree to settle among themselves the distribution of the decedent's assets. Although a family settlement agreement speeds the settlement process, a court order is still needed to protect the estate from future creditors and to clear title to the assets involved. The use of these and other types of

3. The destruction cannot be inadvertent. The maker's intent to revoke must be shown. Consequently, when a will has been burned or torn accidentally, the maker should normally have a new document created to avoid any suggestion that the maker intended to revoke the will.

4. Note that the 2008 amendments to the UPC, which have been adopted by only a few states, do provide for automatic revocation of testamentary devises on divorce [amended UPC 2–804].

summary procedures in estate administration can save time and expenses.

FORMAL PROBATE For larger estates, formal probate proceedings normally are undertaken, and the probate court supervises every aspect of the settlement of the decedent's estate. Additionally, in some situations—such as when a guardian for minor children must be appointed—more formal probate procedures cannot be avoided. Formal probate proceedings may take several months or several years to complete, depending on the size and complexity of the estate and whether the will is contested. As a result, a sizable portion of the decedent's assets (as much as 10 percent) may go toward payment of court costs and fees charged by attorneys and personal representatives.

PROPERTY TRANSFERS OUTSIDE THE PROBATE PROCESS In the ordinary situation, a person can employ various **will substitutes** to avoid the cost of probate—for example, living trusts (which will be discussed later in this chapter), life insurance policies or individual retirement accounts (IRAs) with named beneficiaries, or joint-tenancy arrangements.[5] Not all alternatives to formal probate administration are suitable to every estate, however.

Intestacy Laws

As mentioned, each state regulates by statute how property will be distributed when a person dies intestate (without a valid will). Intestacy laws attempt to carry out the likely intent and wishes of the decedent. These laws assume that deceased persons would have intended that their natural heirs (spouses, children, grandchildren, or other family members) inherit their property. Therefore, intestacy statutes set out rules and priorities under which these heirs inherit the property. If no heirs exist, the state will assume ownership of the property. The rules of descent vary widely from state to state.

SURVIVING SPOUSE AND CHILDREN Usually, state statutes provide that first the debts of the decedent must be satisfied out of the estate. Then, the remaining assets pass to the surviving spouse and to the children. A surviving spouse usually receives only a share of the estate—one-half if there is also a surviving child and one-third if there are two or more children. Only if no children or grandchildren survive the decedent will a surviving spouse be entitled to the entire estate.

EXAMPLE 29.5 Allen dies intestate and is survived by his wife, Beth, and his children, Duane and Tara. Allen's property passes according to intestacy laws. After his outstanding debts are paid, Beth will receive the homestead (either in fee simple or as a life estate) and ordinarily a one-third interest in all other property. The remaining real and personal property will pass to Duane and Tara in equal portions. •

Under most state intestacy laws and under the UPC, in-laws do not share in an estate. If a child dies before his or her parents, the child's spouse will not receive an inheritance on the parents' death. For instance, if Duane died before his father (Allen), Duane's spouse would not inherit Duane's share of Allen's estate.

When there is no surviving spouse or child, the order of inheritance is grandchildren, then brothers and sisters, and, in some states, parents of the decedent. These relatives are usually called *lineal descendants*. If there are no lineal descendants, then *collateral heirs*—nieces, nephews, aunts, and uncles of the decedent—make up the next group to share. If there are no survivors in any of these groups, most statutes provide for the property to be distributed among the next of kin of the collateral heirs.

STEP, ADOPTED, AND ILLEGITIMATE CHILDREN Under intestacy laws, stepchildren are not considered kin. Legally adopted children, however, are recognized as lawful heirs of their adoptive parents (as are children who are in the process of being adopted at the time of death). Statutes vary from state to state in regard to the inheritance rights of illegitimate children (children born out of wedlock). Generally, an illegitimate child is treated as the child of the mother and can inherit from her and her relatives. Traditionally, the child usually was not regarded as the legal child of the father for inheritance purposes—unless paternity was established through some legal proceeding.

Given the dramatic increase in the number of children born out of wedlock in society today, many states have relaxed their laws of inheritance. A majority of states now consider a child born of any union that has the characteristics of a formal marriage relationship (such as unmarried parents who cohabit) to be legitimate. Under the revised UPC, a child is the child of his or her natural (biological) parents, regardless of their marital status, as long as the natural parent has openly treated the child as her or his child [UPC 2–114]. Although illegitimate children may have inheritance rights in most states, their rights are not necessarily identical to those of legitimate children.

GRANDCHILDREN Usually, a will provides for how the decedent's estate will be distributed to descendants of deceased children—that is, to the decedent's grandchildren. If a will does not include such a provision—or if a person dies intestate—the question arises as to what share the grandchildren of the decedent will receive. Each state designates one of two methods of distributing the assets of intestate decedents.

One method of dividing an intestate's estate is ***per stirpes***. Under this method, within a class or group of distributees (for example, grandchildren), the children of any one descendant

5. Recall from Chapters 27 and 28 that in a joint tenancy, when one joint tenant dies, the other joint tenant or tenants automatically inherit the deceased tenant's share of the property.

take the share that their deceased parent *would have been* entitled to inherit.

EXAMPLE 29.6 Michael, a widower, has two children, Scott and Jonathan. Scott has two children (Becky and Holly), and Jonathan has one child (Paul). Scott and Jonathan die before their father, and then Michael dies. If Michael's estate is distributed *per stirpes,* Becky and Holly each receive one-fourth of the estate (dividing Scott's one-half share). Paul receives one-half of the estate (taking Jonathan's one-half share). Exhibit 29–4 below illustrates the *per stirpes* method of distribution. •

An estate may also be distributed on a ***per capita*** basis, which means that each person in a class or group takes an equal share of the estate. If Michael's estate is distributed *per capita,* Becky, Holly, and Paul each receive a one-third share. Exhibit 29–5 on the facing page illustrates the *per capita* method of distribution.

Trusts

A **trust** is any arrangement through which property is transferred from one person to a trustee to be administered for the transferor's or another party's benefit. It can also be defined as a right of property, real or personal, held by one party for the benefit of another. A trust can be created for any purpose that is not illegal or against public policy. Its essential elements are as follows:

1. A designated beneficiary.
2. A designated trustee.
3. A fund sufficiently identified to enable title to pass to the trustee.
4. Actual delivery by the *settlor* or *grantor* (the person creating the trust) to the trustee with the intention of passing title.

Numerous types of trusts can be established. In this section, we look at some of the types of trusts and their characteristics.

Express Trusts

An express trust is created or declared in explicit terms, usually in writing. There are many types of express trusts, each with its own special characteristics.

LIVING TRUSTS A living trust—or ***inter vivos* trust** (*inter vivos* is Latin for "between or among the living")—is a trust created by a grantor during her or his lifetime. Living trusts have become a popular estate-planning option because at the grantor's death, assets held in a living trust can pass to the heirs without going through probate. Note, however, that living trusts do not shelter assets from estate taxes, and the grantor may still have to pay income taxes on trust earnings—depending on whether the trust is revocable or irrevocable.

Revocable Living Trusts. Living trusts can be revocable or irrevocable. In a *revocable* living trust, which is the most common type, the grantor retains control over the trust property during her or his lifetime. The grantor deeds the property to the trust but retains the power to amend, alter, or revoke the trust during her or his lifetime. The grantor may also serve as a trustee or co-trustee and can arrange to receive income earned by the trust assets during her or his lifetime. Because the grantor is in control of the funds, she or he is required to pay income taxes on the trust earnings. Unless the trust is revoked, the principal of the trust is transferred to the trust beneficiary on the grantor's death.

EXAMPLE 29.7 James Cortez owns and operates a large farm. After his wife dies, James decides to create a living trust for the benefit of his three children, Alicia, Emma, and Jayden. He contacts his attorney, who prepares the documents creating the trust, executes a deed conveying the farm to the trust, and transfers the farm's bank accounts into the name of the trust. The trust designates James as the trustee and names his son Jayden as the *successor trustee,* who will take over the

• ***Exhibit* 29–4 *Per Stirpes* Distribution**

Under this method of distribution, an heir takes the share that his or her deceased parent would have been entitled to inherit, had the parent lived. This may mean that a class of distributees—the grandchildren in this example—will not inherit in equal portions. Note that Becky and Holly receive only one-fourth of Michael's estate while Paul inherits one-half.

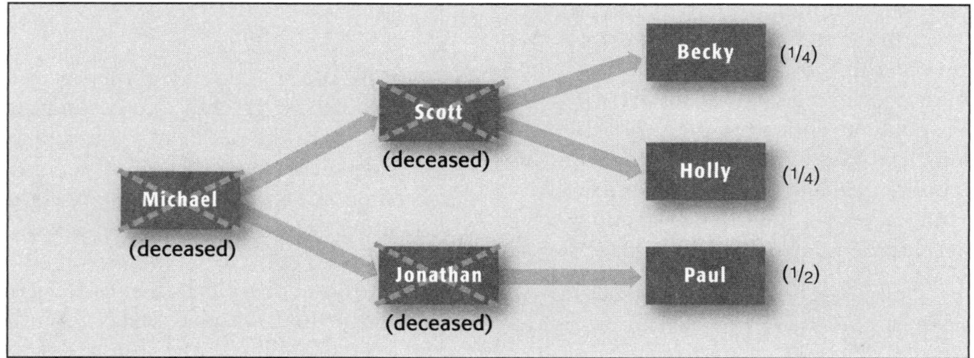

• *Exhibit* **29–5** ***Per Capita*** **Distribution**
Under this method of distribution, all heirs in a certain class—in this example, the grandchildren—inherit equally. Note that Becky and Holly in this situation each inherit one-third, as does Paul.

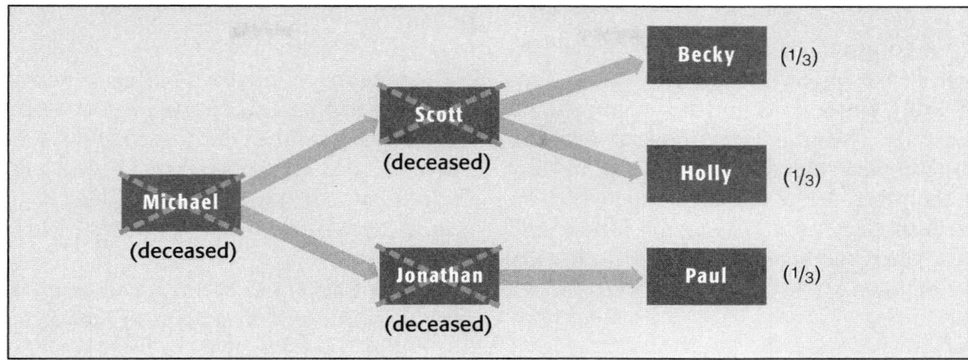

management of the trust when James dies or becomes incapacitated. Each of the children will receive income from the trust while James is alive, and when James dies, the farm will pass to them without having to go through probate. By holding the property in a revocable living trust, James still has control over the farm during his life. This trust arrangement is illustrated in Exhibit 29–6 below. •

Irrevocable Living Trusts. In an *irrevocable* living trust, in contrast, the grantor permanently gives up control over the property to the trustee. The grantor executes a trust deed, and legal title to the trust property passes to the named trustee. The trustee has a duty to administer the property as directed by the grantor for the benefit and in the interest of the beneficiaries. The trustee must preserve the trust property; make it productive; and, if required by the terms of the trust agreement, pay income to the beneficiaries, all in accordance with the terms of the trust. Because the grantor has, in effect, given over the property for the benefit of the beneficiaries, he or she is no longer responsible for paying income taxes on the trust earnings.

TESTAMENTARY TRUSTS A **testamentary trust** is created by will and comes into existence on the settlor's death. Although a testamentary trust has a trustee who maintains legal title to the trust property, the trustee's actions are subject to judicial approval. This trustee can be named in the will or be appointed by the court. Thus, a testamentary trust does not fail because a trustee has not been named in the will. The legal responsibilities of the trustee are the same as in an *inter vivos* trust.

If a court finds that the will setting up a testamentary trust is invalid, then the trust will also be invalid. The property that was supposed to be in the trust will then pass according to intestacy laws, not according to the terms of the trust.

CHARITABLE TRUSTS A **charitable trust** is an express trust designed for the benefit of a segment of the public or the public in general. It differs from other types of trusts in that the identities of the beneficiaries are uncertain and it can be established to last indefinitely. Usually, to be deemed a charitable trust, a trust must be created for charitable, educational, religious, or scientific purposes.

SPENDTHRIFT TRUSTS A **spendthrift trust** is created to provide for the maintenance of a beneficiary by preventing him or her from being careless with the bestowed funds. Unlike the beneficiaries of other trusts, the beneficiary in a spendthrift trust is not permitted to transfer or assign his or her right to the trust's principal or future payments from the trust (*assignments* were discussed in Chapter 11). Essentially, the beneficiary can withdraw only a certain portion of the

• *Exhibit* **29–6 A Revocable Living Trust Arrangement**

total amount to which he or she is entitled at any one time. The majority of states allow spendthrift trust provisions that prohibit creditors from attaching such trusts.

TOTTEN TRUSTS A **Totten trust**[6] is created when one person deposits funds in her or his own name with instructions that on the settlor's death, whatever is in that account should go to a specific beneficiary. This trust is revocable at will until the depositor dies or completes the gift during her or his lifetime (by delivering the funds to the intended beneficiary, for example). The beneficiary has no access to the funds until the depositor's death, when the beneficiary obtains property rights to the balance on hand.

Implied Trusts

Sometimes, a trust will be imposed (implied) by law, even in the absence of an express trust. Implied trusts include resulting trusts and constructive trusts.

RESULTING TRUSTS A **resulting trust** arises from the conduct of the parties. The trust results, or is created, when circumstances raise an inference that the party holding legal title to the property does so for the benefit of another. **EXAMPLE 29.8** Garrison wants to put one acre of land she owns on the market for sale. Because she is going out of the country for two years and will not be able to deed the property to a buyer during that period, Garrison conveys (transfers) the property to her good friend Oswald. Oswald can then attempt to sell the property while Garrison is gone. Because the intent of the transaction in which Garrison conveyed the property to Oswald is neither a sale nor a gift, the property will be held in trust (a resulting trust) by Oswald for the benefit of Garrison. Therefore, on Garrison's return, Oswald will be required either to deed back the property to Garrison or, if the property has been sold, to turn over the proceeds (held in trust) to her. ●

CONSTRUCTIVE TRUSTS A **constructive trust** is an equitable trust imposed by a court in the interests of fairness and justice. In a constructive trust, the owner is declared to be a trustee for the parties who are, in equity, actually entitled to the benefits that flow from the trust. If someone wrongfully holds legal title to property—because the property was obtained through fraud or in breach of a legal duty, for example—a court may impose a constructive trust. Courts often impose constructive trusts when someone who is in a confidential or fiduciary relationship with another person, such as a guardian to a ward, has breached a duty to that person.

In the following case, bank accounts and other financial assets with a value of about $500,000 were at the heart of a dispute over the imposition of a constructive trust.

6. This type of trust derives its unusual name from *In re Totten,* 179 N.Y. 112, 71 N.E. 748 (1904).

Case 29.3 Garrigus v. Viarengo

Appellate Court of Connecticut, 112 Conn.App. 655, 963 A.2d 1065 (2009).
www.jud.state.ct.us/index.html[a]

FACTS Stella Jankowski added her niece Genevieve Viarengo as a joint owner on several savings and checking accounts, certificates of deposit, and savings bonds. In executing a will, Jankowski told her attorney John Wabiszczewicz that she wanted her estate divided equally among her ten nieces, nephews, and cousins. She named Viarengo and Richard Golebiewski as coexecutors. Wabiszczewicz was not aware of the jointly held accounts and neither Jankowski nor Viarengo mentioned them. Jankowski died in 2001. Within days, Viarengo emptied Jankowski's safe and removed her financial records. Despite requests from Golebiewski and Wabiszczewicz, Viarengo did not reveal the contents of the safe or the records. Jankowski's estate–jewelry; a home in Waterbury, Connecticut; and the jointly held accounts–totaled about $600,000. The jointly owned assets were valued at about $500,000. Viarengo claimed that those accounts were hers. Diane Garrigus and other relatives filed a suit in a Connecticut state court against Viarengo. The court imposed a constructive trust. Viarengo appealed.

ISSUE Can a court impose a constructive trust in the absence of a confidential relationship?

DECISION Yes. A state intermediate appellate court affirmed the lower court's judgment.

REASON A constructive trust is imposed against a party who obtains property by fraud or other misconduct. Here, the court found that Viarengo committed fraud in obtaining the assets that she had held jointly with Jankowski and would be unjustly enriched if she were allowed to retain them. Jankowski wanted the assets divided among her ten nieces, nephews, and cousins, and Viarengo did not do that. Viarengo argued that to impose a constructive trust, the court had to find a confidential

a. In the left-hand column, in the "Opinions" pullout menu, select "Appellate Court." On that page, in the "Search the Archives:" section, click on "Appellate Court Archive." In the result, click on "2009." On that page, scroll to the "Published in Connecticut Law Journal – 2/17/09:" section and click on the number of the case to access the opinion. The State of Connecticut Judicial Branch maintains this Web site.

Case 29.3–Continued

relationship between Jankowski and herself, as well as fraud. But "our case law does not support that position." The imposition of a constructive trust requires proof of fraud or other wrongdoing, including abuse of confidential relations. "If fraud is established by clear and convincing evidence, which it was in this case, there is no additional requirement to prove the existence of a confidential relationship."

FOR CRITICAL ANALYSIS—Legal Consideration *What are the elements of fraud? Which facts in this case support the court's finding of fraud?*

The Trustee

The *trustee* is the person holding the trust property. Anyone legally capable of holding title to, and dealing in, property can be a trustee. If the settlor of a trust fails to name a trustee, or if a named trustee cannot or will not serve, the trust does not fail—an appropriate court can appoint a trustee.

TRUSTEE'S DUTIES A trustee must act with honesty, good faith, and prudence in administering the trust and must exercise a high degree of loyalty toward the trust beneficiary. The general standard of care is the degree of care a prudent person would exercise in his or her personal affairs.[7] The duty of loyalty requires that the trustee act in the exclusive interest of the beneficiary.

Among specific duties, a trustee must keep clear and accurate accounts of the trust's administration and furnish complete and correct information to the beneficiary. A trustee must keep trust assets separate from her or his own assets. A trustee has a duty to pay to an income beneficiary the net income of the trust assets at reasonable intervals. A trustee also has a duty to distribute the risk of loss from investments by reasonable diversification and to dispose of assets that do not represent prudent investments. Depending on the particular circumstances, prudent investment choices might include federal, state, or municipal bonds; corporate bonds; and shares of preferred or common stock.

TRUSTEE'S POWERS When a settlor creates a trust, he or she may set forth the trustee's powers and performance. State law governs in the absence of specific terms in the trust, and the states often restrict the trustee's investment of trust funds.

7. Revised Uniform Principal and Income Act, Section 2(a)(3); *Restatement (Third) of Trusts* (Prudent Investor Rule) Section 227. This rule is in force in the majority of states by statute and in a small number of states under the common law.

Typically, statutes confine trustees to investments in conservative debt securities such as government, utility, and railroad bonds. Frequently, though, a settlor grants a trustee discretionary investment power. In that circumstance, any statute may be considered only advisory, with the trustee's decisions subject in most states to the prudent person rule. Of course, a trustee is responsible for carrying out the purposes of the trust. If the trustee fails to comply with the terms of the trust or the controlling statute, he or she is personally liable for any loss.

ALLOCATIONS BETWEEN PRINCIPAL AND INCOME Often, a settlor will provide one beneficiary with a life estate and another beneficiary with the remainder interest in a trust. A farmer, for example, may create a testamentary trust providing that the farm's income be paid to her surviving spouse and that on the surviving spouse's death, the farm be given to their children. In this example, the surviving spouse has a *life estate* in the farm's income, and the children have a *remainder interest* in the farm (the principal). When a trust is set up in this manner, questions may arise among the income and principal beneficiaries as to how the receipts and expenses for the farm's management and the trust's administration should be allocated between income and principal.

When a trust instrument does not provide instructions, a trustee must refer to applicable state law. The general rule is that ordinary receipts and expenses are chargeable to the income beneficiary, whereas extraordinary receipts and expenses are allocated to the principal beneficiaries.[8] For example, the receipt of rent from trust realty would be ordinary, as would the expense of paying the property's taxes. The cost of long-term improvements and proceeds from the property's sale, however, would be extraordinary.

8. Revised Uniform Principal and Income Act, Sections 3, 6, 8, and 13; *Restatement (Second) of Trusts,* Section 233.

Reviewing . . . Insurance, Wills, and Trusts

In June 2011, Bernard Ramish set up a $48,000 trust fund through West Plains Credit Union to provide tuition for his nephew, Nathan Covacek, to attend Tri-State Polytechnic Institute. The trust was established under Ramish's control and went into effect that August. In December, Ramish suffered a brain aneurysm that caused frequent, severe headaches but no other symptoms. In August 2012, Ramish developed heat stroke and collapsed on the golf course at La Prima Country Club. After recuperating at the clubhouse, Ramish quickly wrote his will on the back of a wine list. It stated, "My last will and

Continued

testament: Upon my death, I give all of my personal property to my friend Bernard Eshom and my home to Lizzie Johansen." He signed the will at the bottom in the presence of five men in the La Prima clubhouse, and all five men signed as witnesses. A week later, Ramish suffered a second aneurysm and died in his sleep. He was survived by his mother, Dorris Ramish; his nephew, Nathan Covacek; his son-in-law, Bruce Lupin; and his granddaughter, Tori Lupin. Using the information presented in the chapter, answer the following questions.

1 Does Ramish's testament on the back of the wine list meet the requirements for a valid will?
2 Suppose that after Ramish's first aneurysm in 2011, Covacek contacted an insurance company to obtain a life insurance policy on Ramish's life. Would Covacek have had an insurable interest in his uncle's life? Why or why not?
3 What would the order of inheritance have been if Ramish had died intestate?
4 What will most likely happen to the trust fund established for Covacek on Ramish's death?

Terms and Concepts

administrator 560
bequest 561
binder 558
charitable trust 567
codicil 564
constructive trust 568
devise 561
devisee 561
executor 560
holographic will 563
incontestability clause 558
insurable interest 557
insurance 555
***inter vivos* trust 566**
intestacy laws 560
intestate 560
legacy 561
legatee 561
nuncupative will 563
***per capita* 566**
***per stirpes* 565**
policy 557
premium 557
probate 564
resulting trust 568
risk 555
risk management 555
spendthrift trust 567
testamentary trust 567
testate 560
testator 560
Totten trust 568
trust 566
underwriter 557
will 560
will substitutes 565

Chapter Summary: Insurance, Wills, and Trusts

INSURANCE	
Classifications (See page 556.)	See Exhibit 29–1 on page 556.
Terminology (See page 557.)	1. *Policy*—The insurance contract. 2. *Premium*—The consideration paid to the insurer for a policy. 3. *Underwriter*—The insurance company. 4. *Parties*—Include the insurer (the insurance company), the insured (the person covered by insurance), an agent (a representative of the insurance company) or a broker (ordinarily an independent contractor), and a beneficiary (a person to receive proceeds under the policy).
Insurable Interest (See page 557.)	An insurable interest exists whenever an individual or entity benefits from the preservation of the health or life of the insured or the property to be insured. For life insurance, an insurable interest must exist at the time the policy is issued. For property insurance, an insurable interest must exist at the time of the loss.
The Insurance Contract (See pages 557–560.)	1. *Laws governing*—The general principles of contract law are applied. The insurance industry is also heavily regulated by the states. 2. *Application*—An insurance applicant is bound by any false statements that appear in the application (subject to certain exceptions), which is part of the insurance contract. Misstatements or misrepresentations may be grounds for voiding the policy. 3. *Effective date*—Coverage on an insurance policy can begin when a *binder* (a written memorandum indicating that a formal policy is pending and stating its essential terms) is written; when the policy is issued; at the time of contract formation; or depending on the terms of the contract, when certain conditions are met.

Chapter Summary: Insurance, Wills, and Trusts—Continued

The Insurance Contract—Continued	4. *Provisions and clauses*—See Exhibit 29–2 on page 558. Words will be given their ordinary meanings, and any ambiguity in the policy will be interpreted against the insurance company. When the written policy has not been delivered and it is unclear whether an insurance contract actually exists, the uncertainty will be resolved against the insurance company. The court will presume that the policy is in effect unless the company can show otherwise. 5. *Defenses against payment to the insured*—Defenses include misrepresentation or fraud by the applicant.
	WILLS
Terminology (See pages 560–562.)	1. *Intestate*—One who dies without a valid will. 2. *Testator*—A person who makes out a will. 3. *Personal representative*—A person appointed in a will or by a court to settle the affairs of a decedent. A personal representative named in the will is an executor. A personal representative appointed by the court for an intestate decedent is an *administrator*. 4. *Devise*—A gift of real estate by will; may be general or specific. The recipient of a devise is a *devisee*. 5. *Bequest, or legacy*—A gift of personal property by will; may be general or specific. The recipient of a bequest (legacy) is a *legatee*.
Requirements for a Valid Will (See pages 562–563.)	1. The testator must have testamentary capacity (be of legal age and sound mind at the time the will is made). 2. A will must be in writing (except for nuncupative wills). A holographic will is completely in the handwriting of the testator. 3. A will must be signed by the testator. What constitutes a signature varies from jurisdiction to jurisdiction. 4. A nonholographic will (an attested will) must be witnessed in the manner prescribed by state statute. 5. A will may have to be *published*—that is, the testator may be required to announce to witnesses that this is his or her "last will and testament"; not required under the Uniform Probate Code.
Revocation of Wills (See pages 563–564.)	1. *By physical act of the maker*—Tearing up, canceling, obliterating, or deliberately destroying part or all of a will. 2. *By subsequent writing*— a. Codicil—A formal, separate document to amend or revoke an existing will. b. Second will or new will—A new, properly executed will expressly revoking the existing will. 3. *By operation of law*— a. Marriage—Generally revokes part of a will written before the marriage. b. Divorce or annulment—Revokes dispositions of property made under a will to a former spouse. c. Subsequently born child—It is *inferred* that the child is entitled to receive the portion of the estate granted under intestacy distribution laws.
Probate Procedures (See pages 564–565.)	To probate a will means to establish its validity and to carry the administration of the estate through a court process. Probate laws vary from state to state. Probate procedures may be informal or formal, depending on the size of the estate and other factors, such as whether a guardian for minor children must be appointed.
Intestacy Laws (See pages 565–566.)	1. Intestacy laws vary widely from state to state. Usually, the law provides that the surviving spouse and children inherit the property of the decedent (after the decedent's debts are paid). The spouse usually inherits the entire estate if there are no children, one-half of the estate if there is one child, and one-third of the estate if there are two or more children. 2. If there is no surviving spouse or child, then, in order, lineal descendants (grandchildren, brothers and sisters, and—in some states—parents of the decedent) inherit. If there are no lineal descendants, then collateral heirs (nieces, nephews, aunts, and uncles of the decedent) inherit.
	TRUSTS
Definition (See page 566.)	A trust is any arrangement through which property is transferred from one person to a trustee to be administered for another party's benefit. The essential elements of a trust are (1) a designated beneficiary, (2) a designated trustee, (3) a fund sufficiently identified to enable title to pass to the trustee, and (4) actual delivery to the trustee with the intention of passing title.

Continued

Chapter Summary: Insurance, Wills, and Trusts—Continued

Express Trusts (See pages 566–568.)	Express trusts are created by explicit terms, usually in writing, and include the following: 1. *Living (inter vivos) trust*—A trust created by a grantor during her or his lifetime. 2. *Testamentary trust*—A trust that is created by will and comes into existence on the death of the grantor. 3. *Charitable trust*—A trust designed for the benefit of a public group or the public in general. 4. *Spendthrift trust*—A trust created to provide for the maintenance of a beneficiary and to protect him or her from spending all the funds to which he or she is entitled. The beneficiary is allowed to withdraw only a certain amount at any one time. 5. *Totten trust*—A trust created when one person deposits funds in his or her own name as a trustee for another.
Implied Trusts (See pages 568–569.)	Implied trusts, which are imposed by law in the interests of fairness and justice, include the following: 1. *Resulting trust*—Arises from the conduct of the parties when an apparent intention to create a trust is present. 2. *Constructive trust*—Arises by operation of law when a person wrongfully takes title to property. A court may require the owner to hold the property in trust for those who, in equity, are entitled to enjoy the beneficial interest therein.

ExamPrep

ISSUE SPOTTERS

—Check your answers to these questions against the answers provided in Appendix G.

1 Sheila makes out a will, leaving her property in equal thirds to Toby and Umeko, her children, and Velda, her niece. Two years later, Sheila is adjudged mentally incompetent, and that same year, she dies. Can Toby and Umeko have Sheila's will revoked on the ground that she did not have the capacity to make a will? Why or why not?

2 Ralph dies without having made a will. He is survived by many relatives—a spouse, children, adopted children, sisters, brothers, uncles, aunts, cousins, nephews, and nieces. What determines who gets what?

BEFORE THE TEST

Go to **www.cengagebrain.com**, enter the ISBN 9781111530624, and click on "Find" to locate this textbook's Web site. Then, click on "Access Now" under "Study Tools," and select Chapter 29 at the top. There, you will find an Interactive Quiz that you can take to assess your mastery of the concepts in this chapter, as well as Flashcards and a Glossary of important terms.

For Review

1 What is an insurable interest? When must an insurable interest exist—at the time the insurance policy is obtained, at the time the loss occurs, or both?

2 Is an insurance broker the agent of the insurance applicant or the agent of the insurer?

3 What are the basic requirements for executing a will? How may a will be revoked?

4 What is the difference between a *per stirpes* distribution and a *per capita* distribution of an estate to the grandchildren of the deceased?

5 What are the four essential elements of a trust? What is the difference between an express trust and an implied trust?

Questions and Case Problems

29–1 Timing of Insurance Coverage. On October 10, Joleen Vora applied for a $50,000 life insurance policy with Magnum Life Insurance Co.; she named her husband, Jay, as the beneficiary. Joleen paid the insurance company the first year's policy premium on making the application. Two days later, before she had a chance to take the physical examination required by the insurance company and before the policy was issued, Joleen was killed in an automobile accident. Jay submitted a claim to the insurance company for the $50,000. Can Jay collect? Explain.

29–2 Wills and Intestacy Laws. Benjamin is a widower who has two married children, Edward and Patricia. Patricia has two children, Perry and Paul. Edward has no children. Benjamin dies, and his will leaves all his property equally to his children, Edward and Patricia, and provides that should a child predecease him, the grandchildren are to take *per stirpes.* The will was witnessed by Patricia and by Benjamin's lawyer and was signed by Benjamin in their presence. Patricia has predeceased Benjamin. Edward claims the will is invalid.

1 Discuss whether the will is valid.

2 Discuss the distribution of Benjamin's estate if the will is invalid.

3 Discuss the distribution of Benjamin's estate if the will is valid.

29–3 Insurer's Defenses. Patrick contracts with an Ajax Insurance Co. agent for a $50,000 ordinary life insurance policy. The application form is filled in to show Patrick's age as thirty-two. In addition, the application form asks whether Patrick has ever had any heart ailments or problems. Patrick answers no, forgetting that as a young child he was diagnosed as having a slight heart murmur. A policy is issued. Three years later, Patrick becomes seriously ill and dies. A review of the policy discloses that Patrick was actually thirty-three at the time of the application and the issuance of the policy and that he erred in answering the question about a history of heart ailments. Discuss whether Ajax can void the policy and escape liability on Patrick's death.

29–4 Intestacy Laws. A Florida statute provides that the right of election of a surviving spouse can be waived by written agreement: "A waiver of 'all rights,' or equivalent language, in the property or estate of a present or prospective spouse . . . is a waiver of all rights to elective share." The day before Mary Ann Taylor married Louis Taylor in Florida, they entered into a prenuptial agreement. The agreement stated that all property belonging to each spouse would "forever remain his or her personal estate," "said property shall remain forever free of claim by the other," and the parties would retain "full rights and authority" over their property as they would have as "if not married." After Louis's death, his only child, Joshua Taylor, filed a petition in a Florida state court for a determination of the beneficiaries of Louis's estate. How much of the estate can Mary Ann elect to receive? Explain. [*Taylor v. Taylor,* 1 So.3d 348 (Fla.App. 2009)]

29–5 Duty to Cooperate. Dr. James Bubenik, a dentist practicing in Missouri, had two patients die within six months while under sedation. Bubenik had medical malpractice insurance with Medical Protective Co. (MPC). The families of both patients sued Bubenik for malpractice. MPC noted to Bubenik that a clause in his policy stated that the "Insured shall at all times fully cooperate with the Company in any claim hereunder and shall attend and assist in the preparation and trial of any such claim." During the litigation, however, Bubenik refused to submit to depositions, answer interrogatories, or testify at trial, invoking the Fifth Amendment privilege against self-incrimination. He also refused to communicate with MPC and entered into an agreement with the plaintiffs stating that he would assist them in pursuing judgment against MPC. MPC requested a declaratory judgment from the court. The insurance company contended that it had no duty to defend Bubenik or counter the claims brought against him because of his refusal to cooperate. Did Bubenik's constitutional right to invoke the Fifth Amendment trump the insurance policy's duty-to-cooperate clause? Why or why not? [*Medical Protective Co. v. Bubenik,* 594 F.3d 1047 (8th Cir. 2010)]

29–6 Wills. Elnora Maxey became the guardian of Sean Hall after his parents died. In 1996, Maxey died, and she left the two houses in her estate to Hall. Julia Jordan became Hall's new guardian, and when she died, her husband, John Jordan, became his guardian. In 1998, when Hall was eighteen years old, he died intestate, and Jordan was appointed as the administrator of Hall's estate. The two houses had remained in Maxey's estate, but Jordan had paid the mortgage and tax payments on the houses for Hall's estate because Hall had inherited the houses. Anthony Cooper, a relative of Maxey, petitioned the probate court to be appointed executor of Maxey's estate, stating that there was now no heir. The court granted the request. Jordan was not aware of the proceedings. Cooper then sold both houses in a sweetheart deal for $20,000 each to Quan Smith, without informing Jordan. The property was then resold to JSD Properties, LLC, for $190,000. Learning of the sale, Jordan sued, contending that Cooper had breached his fiduciary duty and had lied to the court since Maxey's will had clearly left the houses to Hall. Does Jordan have the right to demand that JSD return the property? What factors would be considered in making this decision? [*Witcher v. JSD Properties, LLC,* 286 Ga. 717, 690 S.E.2d 855 (2010)]

29–7 Case Problem with Sample Answer Leo and Mary Deters owned Deters Tower Service, Inc., in Iowa. Deters Tower serviced television and radio towers and antennas in a multistate area. The firm obtained a commercial general liability policy issued by USF Insurance Co. to provide coverage for its officers, including Leo. One afternoon, Leo and two Deters Tower employees were working on a TV tower in Council Bluffs when they fell from the tower to their deaths. The workers' families filed a negligence suit against Leo's estate. As the estate's representative, Mary filed a claim with USF to defend against the suit and pay any resulting claim. The insurer investigated the matter and refused to pay the claim. Mary filed a suit against USF, alleging bad faith. USF did not provide a reasonable basis for refusing the claim. What are the duties of an insurer in these circumstances? If USF were held liable for bad faith, what might Mary recover? [*Deters v. USF Insurance Co.,* 797 N.W.2d 621 (Iowa App. 2011)]

—For a sample answer to Problem 29–7, go to Appendix F at the end of this text.

29–8 Intent Requirement. In 2007, Susie Walker executed a will that left her entire estate to her grandson. When her grandson died suddenly, Walker executed a new will that named her great-grandson as the sole beneficiary of her estate and specifically disinherited her son, Tommy. Walker died in 2009, and the executor named in the will, Tommy's ex-wife, submitted the will to probate. Tommy filed objections alleging that the will was invalid because Susie had lacked testamentary capacity (intent) and claiming that the will was the product of undue influence and fraud. Tommy argued that his ex-wife—who had been living with his mother when the will was executed and who accompanied her to the attorney's office—had unduly influenced Susie. But the ex-wife inherited nothing under the will, and several witnesses testified that Susie had been mentally competent when she had executed it. What does a plaintiff who contests a will have to prove to show that the testator lacked the required intent? Can Tommy prove undue influence based on the facts given? [*In re Estate of Walker*, 80 A.D.3d 865, 914 N.Y.S.2d 379 (N.Y.A.D. 3 Dept. 2011)]

29–9 **A Question of Ethics** *Vickie Lynn Smith, an actress and model also known as Anna Nicole Smith, met J. Howard Marshall II in 1991. During their courtship, J. Howard lavished gifts and large sums of money on Anna Nicole, and they married on June 27, 1994. J. Howard died on August 4, 1995. According to Anna Nicole, J. Howard intended to provide for her financial security through a trust, but under the terms of his will, all of his assets were transferred to a trust for the benefit of E. Pierce Marshall, one of J. Howard's sons. While J. Howard's estate was subject to probate proceedings in a Texas state court, Anna Nicole filed for bankruptcy in a federal bankruptcy court. Pierce filed a claim in the bankruptcy proceeding, alleging that Anna Nicole had defamed him when her lawyers told the media that Pierce had engaged in forgery and fraud to gain control of his father's assets. Anna Nicole filed a counterclaim, alleging that Pierce prevented the transfer of his father's assets to a trust for her by, among other things, imprisoning J. Howard against his wishes, surrounding him with security guards to prevent contact with her, and transferring property against his wishes.* [Marshall v. Marshall, *547 U.S. 293, 126 S.Ct. 1735, 164 L.Ed.2d 480 (2006)]*

1. What is the purpose underlying the requirements for a valid will? Which of these requirements might be at issue in this case? How should it apply here? Why?
2. State courts generally have jurisdiction over the probate of a will and the administration of an estate. Does the Texas state court thus have the sole authority to adjudicate all of the claims in this case? Why or why not?
3. How should Pierce's claim against Anna Nicole and her counterclaim be resolved?
4. Anna Nicole executed her will in 2001. The beneficiary—Daniel, her son, who was not J. Howard's child—died in 2006, shortly after Anna Nicole gave birth to a daughter, Dannielynn. In 2007, before executing a new will, Anna Nicole died. What happens if a will's beneficiary dies before the testator? What happens if a child is born after a will is executed?

29–10 **Critical Thinking Legal Question** Statistics show that the extent of risk assumed by insurance companies varies depending on the gender of the insured. Many people contend that laws prohibiting gender-based insurance rates are thus fundamentally unfair. Why might gender discrimination be fair when it comes to insurance premiums when it is clearly unfair (and illegal) in housing or employment?

Unit Nine Unit Case Study with Dissenting Opinion: *Kovarik v. Kovarik*

When a couple divorces, the division of the marital estate—all of the property that the parties accumulated during their marriage—often leads to disputes. Questions of ownership frequently arise in divorce proceedings: Who owned what property, and how did she or he acquire it? If property was allegedly acquired by gift, did the transfer satisfy the requirements for a valid gift?

Those questions arose in Kovarik v. Kovarik,[1] *which we examine in this* Unit Case Study with Dissenting Opinion. *During a divorce, a dispute arose over whether the couple's marital estate included several certificates of deposit (discussed in Chapter 16) worth about $60,000 in which one spouse allegedly had an interest. The acquisition, division, and transfer of ownership of personal property were discussed in Chapter 27, and other types of property transfers were covered in Chapter 28.*

1. 2009 ND 82, 765 N.W.2d 511 (2009).

CASE BACKGROUND

Jennifer Stahl and Bradly Kovarik were married in North Dakota in July 2001. A few months later, Bradly's parents, Dennis and Marlene, liquidated their farm business and equipment, and invested the proceeds in certificates of deposit (CDs). Four of the CDs were in the names of Kovarik and his sister, Wanda Morstad, but were retained by their parents.

Jennifer and Bradly separated in August 2007. Jennifer filed for divorce in a North Dakota state court. In a list of their marital property, she included the four CDs. Bradly denied any interest in those items.

At the trial, Bradly testified that he learned about the CDs from his sister, who cashed one without giving him any of the proceeds after Jennifer filed for divorce. At their mother's request, his sister also negotiated the other three CDs before the divorce trial. The court did not include the CDs in valuing and distributing the Kovariks' marital estate. Jennifer appealed to the North Dakota Supreme Court, arguing that Bradly's interest in the CDs should have been included.

MAJORITY OPINION

SANDSTROM, **Justice:**

* * * *

A [trial] court's decisions regarding the division of marital property are findings of fact and may be reversed on appeal only if clearly erroneous. A finding of fact is clearly erroneous if it is induced by an erroneous view of the law, if there is no evidence to support it, or if, after reviewing the entirety of the evidence, this Court is left with a definite and firm conviction a mistake has been made. A [trial] court's findings of fact are presumed correct, and we view the evidence in the light most favorable to its findings.

Division of marital property upon divorce must be equitable. Although the division does not have to be equal, a substantial disparity must be explained. *All of the real and personal property accumulated by the parties, regardless of source, must be included in the marital estate.* [Emphasis added.]

* * * *

A * * * court may consider property to be part of the marital estate, if supported by evidence, even if a party claims it is owned by a nonparty. The principles applicable to *inter vivos* gifts in general apply as well to purported gifts of certificates of deposit. A valid gift made during the donor's lifetime must satisfy certain requirements—donative intent, delivery, actual or constructive, and acceptance by donee. A donor's intent is a question of fact. The actual or constructive delivery must be of a nature sufficient to divest the owner of all dominion [control] over the property and to invest the donee therewith.

Bradly Kovarik's parents testified that after liquidating their farm and equipment * * * , they placed four certificates of deposit in Bradly Kovarik's and his sister's names—"Wanda Morstad or Bradly Kovarik." They also testified they did not intend to give Bradly Kovarik and Morstad any present interest in the certificates. Moreover, Bradly Kovarik's father testified that the certificates, prior to having been cashed out, had been locked in a safe in their home and neither Bradly Kovarik nor his sister could just come and take the certificates.

Bradly Kovarik testified he had no knowledge of the certificates' existence until his sister told him she cashed one out and used some of the proceeds for home repairs. He also testified he did not receive any of the remaining proceeds. Wanda Morstad

Continued

testified she did not expect the certificates of deposit to belong to her. When requested, she assisted her parents in cashing out the certificates, which she did with respect to the remaining three certificates.

The [trial] court found Bradly Kovarik's parents did not intend to gift the certificates to him and his sister. The court further found the certificates were never delivered to either Bradly Kovarik or his sister but were retained in their parents' possession. The record does not reflect donative intent or delivery of the certificates to Bradly Kovarik, either actual or constructive. *In the absence of a donative intent and delivery, the [trial] court's finding that there was no valid gift is not clearly erroneous.* [Emphasis added.]

* * * *

We hold the [trial] court's property distribution and property valuation is not clearly erroneous, and affirm.

DISSENTING OPINION

***MARING*, Justice, dissenting:**

I respectfully dissent from * * * the Majority opinion because the [trial] court * * * erred in concluding Bradly Kovarik's parents never gave him the certificates of deposit.

* * * *

First, the [trial] court found Bradly Kovarik's parents did not intend to give the certificates of deposit to Bradly Kovarik or his sister. This finding is not supported by the record. Bradly Kovarik admits that he and his sister were the co-owners of the certificates of deposit. Bradly Kovarik's sister also testified * * * that she was the co-owner of the certificates of deposit with her brother.

* * * *

Dennis Kovarik's testimony establishes that he knew Bradly Kovarik was a joint owner of the certificates of deposit * * *. Marlene Kovarik's testimony establishes that Bradly Kovarik was the joint owner of the certificates of deposit.

These admissions by Bradly Kovarik and his family that he owned the certificates of deposits are supported by the law. The parties do not dispute that Bradly Kovarik's name was on the certificate of deposit together with his sister's name or that neither of his parents' names were on the certificates of deposit. It is presumed that a certificate of deposit belongs to the person whose name appears on the certificate. * * * Bradly Kovarik's parents gave up their exclusive dominion and control over their assets when they placed the money in certificates of deposit in their children's names.

* * * *

The [trial] court found the certificates of deposit were never delivered to Bradly Kovarik or his sister because the parents kept possession of the certificates of deposit. This finding is not supported by the record.

* * * *

* * * Bradly Kovarik's parents divested themselves of the control of the certificates of deposit by first solely placing their children's names on the certificates of deposit and then delivering the certificates of deposit to Wanda Morstad to be cashed.

* * * *

In conclusion, I dissent because the certificates of deposit were completed gifts to Bradly Kovarik and must be included in the marital estate.

QUESTIONS FOR ANALYSIS

1. **Law.** How does the majority respond to the appellant's argument in this case? What is the majority's reasoning?
2. **Law.** How does the dissent analyze the issue before the court?
3. **Ethics.** According to Marlene Kovarik, the CDs were obtained in her children's names in an effort to avoid the parents' tax obligations, rather than to give the funds to the children. Is this ethical? Explain.
4. **Social Dimensions.** If the Kovariks had invested their funds in real estate in their children's names, instead of CDs, would the result in this case have been the same? Why or why not?
5. **Implications for the Estate Planner.** How might Marlene and Dennis Kovarik have avoided the question that Jennifer raised here? Discuss.

Unit Ten

Special Topics

Unit Contents

30 Liability of Accountants and Other Professionals

31 International Law in a Global Economy

(Moody75/Creative Commons)

Chapter 30

Liability of Accountants and Other Professionals

Learning Objectives

After reading this chapter, you should be able to answer the following questions:

1. Under what common law theories may professionals be liable to clients?
2. What are the rules concerning an auditor's liability to third parties?
3. How might an accountant violate federal securities laws?
4. What crimes might an accountant commit under the Internal Revenue Code?
5. What constrains professionals to keep communications with their clients confidential?

The Learning Objectives above are designed to help improve your understanding of the chapter.

(Moody75/Creative Commons)

Accountants, attorneys, physicians, and other professionals have found themselves increasingly subject to liability in the past decade or so. This more extensive liability has resulted in large part from a greater public awareness of the fact that professionals are required to deliver competent services and are obligated to adhere to standards of performance commonly accepted within their professions.

Certainly, the dizzying collapse of Enron Corporation and the failure of other major companies, including WorldCom, Inc., in recent years called attention to the importance of abiding by professional accounting standards. As a result of its failure to do so, Arthur Andersen, LLP, one of the world's leading public accounting firms, ceased to exist, and some 85,000 employees lost their jobs. Although the Sarbanes-Oxley Act of 2002 imposed stricter regulation and oversight on the public accounting industry, accounting fraud scandals have continued to arise. Numerous corporations and former corporations—from American International Group (AIG), the world's largest insurance company, to HealthSouth, Goldman Sachs, Lehman Brothers, Tyco International, and India-based Satyam Computer Services—have been accused of engaging in accounting fraud. These companies may have reported fictitious revenues, concealed liabilities and debts, or artificially inflated their assets.

Considering the many potential sources of legal liability that they face, accountants, attorneys, and other professionals should be very aware of their legal obligations. In this chapter, we look at the potential common law liability of professionals and then examine the potential liability of accountants under securities laws and the Internal Revenue Code. The chapter concludes with a brief examination of the relationship of professionals, particularly accountants and attorneys, with their clients.

Potential Common Law Liability to Clients

Under the common law, professionals may be liable to clients for breach of contract, negligence, or fraud.

Liability for Breach of Contract

Accountants and other professionals face liability under the common law for any breach of contract. A professional owes a duty to his or her client to honor the terms of their contract and to perform the contract within the stated time period. If the professional fails to perform as agreed in the contract, then he or she has breached the contract, and the client has the right to recover damages from the professional.

Damages may include expenses incurred by the client in securing another professional to provide the contracted-for services, penalties imposed on the client for failure to meet time deadlines, and any other reasonable and foreseeable losses that arise from the professional's breach.

Liability for Negligence

Accountants and other professionals may also be held liable under the common law for negligence in the performance of their services. The elements that must be proved to establish negligence on the part of a professional are as follows:

1. A duty of care existed.
2. That duty of care was breached.
3. The plaintiff suffered an injury.
4. The injury was proximately caused by the defendant's breach of the duty of care.

All professionals are subject to standards of conduct established by codes of professional ethics, by state statutes, and by judicial decisions. They are also governed by the contracts they enter into with their clients. In their performance of contracts, professionals must exercise the established standards of care, knowledge, and judgment generally accepted by members of their professional group. Here, we look at the duty of care owed by two groups of professionals that frequently perform services for business firms: accountants and attorneys.

ACCOUNTANT'S DUTY OF CARE Accountants play a major role in a business's financial system. Accountants have the necessary expertise and experience to establish and maintain accurate financial records; design, control, and audit record-keeping systems; prepare reliable statements that reflect an individual's or a business's financial status; and give tax advice and prepare tax returns.

GAAP and GAAS. In the performance of their services, accountants must comply with **generally accepted accounting principles (GAAP)** and **generally accepted auditing standards (GAAS).** The Financial Accounting Standards Board (FASB, usually pronounced "faz-bee") determines what accounting conventions, rules, and procedures constitute GAAP at a given point in time. GAAS are standards concerning an auditor's professional qualities and the judgment that he or she exercises in performing an audit and report. GAAS are established by the American Institute of Certified Public Accountants. As long as an accountant conforms to GAAP and acts in good faith, he or she normally will not be held liable to the client for incorrect judgment.

As a general rule, an accountant is not required to discover every impropriety, **defalcation**[1] (embezzlement), or fraud, in her or his client's books. If, however, the impropriety, defalcation, or fraud has gone undiscovered because of the accountant's negligence or failure to perform an express or implied duty, the accountant will be liable for any resulting losses suffered by the client. Therefore, an accountant who uncovers suspicious financial transactions and fails to investigate the matter fully or to inform the client of the discovery can be held liable to the client for the resulting loss.

A violation of GAAP and GAAS is considered *prima facie* evidence of negligence on the part of the accountant. Compliance with GAAP and GAAS, however, does not *necessarily* relieve an accountant from potential legal liability. An accountant may be held to a higher standard of conduct established by state statute and by judicial decisions.

Global Accounting Rules. In 2008, the Securities and Exchange Commission (SEC) unanimously approved a plan to require U.S. companies to use a set of global accounting rules established by the London-based International Accounting Standards Board. These rules, known as **International Financial Reporting Standards (IFRS),** will eventually be required for all of the financial reports that U.S. companies must file with the SEC. Under the plan, the use of GAAP will be phased out, with final approval of rules implementing the IFRS scheduled for 2011 or 2012.[2] To ease the transition, the SEC has set up a multiyear timetable for converting to the IFRS. The largest multinational companies are required to use the global rules by 2014, and the smallest publicly reporting companies must make the shift by 2016. The IFRS are simpler and more straightforward than GAAP and focus more on overriding principles than on specific rules.

Many countries already use the IFRS, so their adoption by the SEC will make it easier to compare the financial statements of U.S. and foreign companies. Nevertheless, the shift to the global rules has some drawbacks. It will be both costly and time consuming. Companies will have to upgrade their

1. This term, pronounced deh-fal-*kay*-shun, is derived from the Latin *de* ("off") and *falx* ("sickle"—a tool for cutting grain or tall grass). In law, the term refers to the act of a defaulter or of an embezzler. As used here, it means embezzlement.
2. Although the original deadline to implement the international rules was June 2011, that deadline was pushed back, and the new rules may not be adopted until 2012.

communications and software systems; study and implement the new rules; and train their employees, accountants, and tax attorneys. Another concern is that although the IFRS are simpler, they may not be better than GAAP. Because the global rules are broader and less detailed, they give companies more leeway in reporting, so less financial information may be disclosed. There are also indications that use of the IFRS can lead to wide variances in reported profits and tends to boost earnings above what they would have been under GAAP.

Audits, Qualified Opinions, and Disclaimers. One of the more important tasks that an accountant may perform for a business is an audit. An *audit* is a systematic inspection, by analyses and tests, of a business's financial records.

The purpose of an audit is to provide the auditor with evidence to support an opinion on the reliability of the business's financial statements. A normal audit is not intended to uncover fraud or other misconduct. Nevertheless, an accountant may be liable for failing to detect misconduct if a normal audit would have revealed it. Also, if the auditor agreed to examine the records for evidence of fraud or other obvious misconduct and then failed to detect it, he or she may be liable. After performing an audit, the auditor issues an opinion letter stating whether, in his or her opinion, the financial statements fairly present the business's financial position.

In issuing an opinion letter, an auditor may *qualify* the opinion or include a disclaimer. An opinion that disclaims any liability for false or misleading financial statements is too general, however. A qualified opinion or a disclaimer must be specific and identify the reason for the qualification or disclaimer. **EXAMPLE 30.1** Richard Zehr performs an audit of Lacey Corporation. In the opinion letter, Zehr qualifies his opinion by stating that there is uncertainty about how a lawsuit against the firm will be resolved. In this situation, Zehr will not be liable if the outcome of the suit is unfavorable for the firm. Zehr could still be liable, however, for failing to discover other problems that an audit in compliance with GAAS and GAAP would have revealed. ● In a disclaimer, the auditor basically is stating that she or he does not have sufficient information to issue an opinion. Again, the auditor must identify the problem and indicate what information is lacking.

Unaudited Financial Statements. Sometimes, accountants are hired to prepare unaudited financial statements. (A financial statement is considered unaudited if incomplete auditing procedures have been used in its preparation or if insufficient procedures have been used to justify an opinion.) Accountants may be subject to liability for failing, in accordance with standard accounting procedures, to designate a balance sheet as "unaudited." An accountant will also be held liable for failure to disclose to a client the facts or circumstances that give reason to believe that misstatements have been made or that a fraud has been committed.

Defenses to Negligence. If an accountant is found guilty of negligence, the client can collect damages for losses that arose from the accountant's negligence. An accountant facing a claim of negligence, however, has several possible defenses, including the following:

1. The accountant was not negligent.
2. If the accountant was negligent, this negligence was not the proximate cause of the client's losses.
3. The client was also negligent (depending on whether state law allows contributory negligence as a defense).

CASE EXAMPLE 30.2 Coopers & Lybrand, LLP, provided accounting services for Oregon Steel Mills (OSM), Inc. Coopers advised OSM to report a certain transaction as a $12.3 million gain on its financial statements. Later, when OSM planned to make a public offering of its stock, the SEC reviewed its financial statements, concluded that the accounting treatment of the transaction was incorrect, and required OSM to correct its statements. Because of the delay, the public offering did not occur on May 2, when OSM's stock was selling for $16 per share, but on June 13, when, due to unrelated factors, the price was $13.50. OSM filed a lawsuit against Coopers claiming that the negligent accounting resulted in the stock's being sold at a lower price. The court held, however, that although the accountant's negligence had delayed the stock offering, the negligence was not the proximate cause of the decline in the stock price. Thus, Coopers could not be held liable for damages based on the price decline.[3] ●

ATTORNEY'S DUTY OF CARE The conduct of attorneys is governed by rules established by each state and by the American Bar Association's Code of Professional Responsibility and Model Rules of Professional Conduct. All attorneys owe a duty to provide competent and diligent representation. Attorneys are required to be familiar with well-settled principles of law applicable to a case and to discover law that can be found through a reasonable amount of research. The lawyer must also investigate and discover facts that could materially affect the client's legal rights.

In judging an attorney's performance, the standard used will normally be that of a reasonably competent general practitioner of ordinary skill, experience, and capacity. If the attorney holds himself or herself out as having expertise in a particular area of law, the standard is that of a reasonably competent specialist of ordinary skill, experience, and capacity in that area of the law. If an attorney claims to have expertise in a particular area of law (for example, intellectual property), then the attorney's standard of care in that area is higher than the standards for attorneys without such expertise.

3. *Oregon Steel Mills, Inc. v. Coopers & Lybrand, LLP,* 336 Or. 329, 83 P.3d 322 (2004).

Misconduct. Generally, a state's rules of professional conduct for attorneys provide that committing a criminal act that reflects adversely on the person's "honesty or trustworthiness, or fitness as a lawyer in other respects" is professional misconduct. The rules often further provide that a lawyer should not engage in conduct involving "dishonesty, fraud, deceit, or misrepresentation." Under these rules, state authorities can discipline attorneys for many types of misconduct.

CASE EXAMPLE 30.3 Michael Inglimo, who was licensed to practice law in Wisconsin, occasionally used marijuana with a person who later became his client in a criminal case. After the trial, the client claimed that Inglimo had been high on drugs during the trial and had not adequately represented him. Two years later, Inglimo was convicted for misdemeanor possession of marijuana. State authorities also discovered that Inglimo had written several checks for personal expenses out of his client trust account, commingled client funds, and engaged in other trust account violations. The state initiated disciplinary proceedings and asked the court to suspend Inglimo's license to practice for three years. Inglimo argued that he should not be suspended because his misconduct was related to his past use of controlled substances and he no longer used drugs. The court, however, concluded that the suspension was necessary to protect the public in light of Inglimo's "disturbing pattern of disregard" for his professional obligations.[4] ●

Liability for Malpractice. When an attorney fails to exercise reasonable care and professional judgment, she or he breaches the duty of care and can be held liable for **malpractice** (professional negligence).

In malpractice cases—as in all cases involving allegations of negligence—the plaintiff must prove that the attorney's breach of the duty of care actually caused the plaintiff to suffer some injury. **EXAMPLE 30.4** Attorney Karen Boehmer negligently allows the statute of limitations to lapse on the claim of Dayna Curl, a client. Boehmer can be held liable for malpractice because Curl can no longer pursue her claim and has lost a potential award of damages. ●

Allegations of malpractice gave rise to the following case.

4. *In re Disciplinary Proceedings against Inglimo,* 2007 WI 126, 305 Wis.2d 71, 740 N.W.2d 125 (2007).

Case 30.1 Kelley v. Buckley

Court of Appeals of Ohio, Eighth District, 193 Ohio App.3d 11, 2011 Ohio 1362 (2011).
www.sconet.state.oh.us/rod[a]

FACTS Attorneys Michael Kelley and James Ferraro founded Kelley & Ferraro, LLP (K&F), a large Ohio law firm that specialized in asbestos litigation. Each of the two partners earned $11 million in the eighth year of the firm's existence. Two days into the ninth year, Kelley died of a heart attack. His wife, Lynn Kelley, contacted lawyer Brent Buckley of Buckley King, LPA, in Cleveland. Brent had drafted the K&F partnership agreement. The agreement provided that on Michael's death, Lynn was to be paid 40 percent of the firm's gross revenues. Buckley King had recently been retained by Ferraro to represent his interests in any dispute with Michael's estate, however, and Buckley himself advised Lynn, the executor of the estate, to settle with Ferraro quickly. Despite Lynn's repeated requests, Buckley did not give her a copy of the partnership agreement. Meanwhile, she became embroiled in litigation with lawyer John Sivinski, who had worked for K&F and claimed a share of Michael's profits. Buckley King represented Ferraro and K&F in this dispute and withheld copies of an employment contract between K&F and Sivinski. When Lynn eventually obtained a copy of Sivinski's contract, it revealed that his claim against the estate was fraudulent. She then filed a suit in an Ohio state court against Brent Buckley and Buckley King, alleging malpractice. The court issued a summary judgment in favor of Buckley and the firm. Lynn appealed.

a. Click on "8th Appellate District Opinions." On the next page, select "In the Year 2011" from the "Decided:" menu; type "2011-Ohio-1362" in the "WebCite No:" box; and click on "Submit." In the result, click on the name of the case to access the opinion. The Ohio Supreme Court and judicial system maintain this Web site.

ISSUE Did Lynn Kelley present sufficient evidence that attorney Buckley had committed malpractice to allow her claim to go forward to trial?

DECISION Yes. A state intermediate appellate court reversed the summary judgment in the defendants' favor and remanded the case for additional discovery and a trial. The court also awarded Lynn the costs of the appeal.

REASON The court reasoned that there were genuine issues of material fact relating to all of Lynn's claims. For example, she claimed that the defendants had breached a duty of care owed to Michael when they negotiated the original partnership agreement. They argued that Michael had limited the scope of their representation when he allegedly told Buckley over the phone that he was handling the negotiations and choosing the business entity and that Buckley should follow his instructions. The court, however, reasoned that any oral statements supposedly made by the late Michael Kelley were hearsay evidence that was not admissible for the purpose of showing he limited the attorney's representation. The court also reasoned that there were genuine issues of fact concerning Lynn's allegation that the defendants had drafted Sivinski's contract and could have ended his suit by producing a copy. The defendants denied that they had created the contract. They also contended that Lynn had consented to their representation of Ferraro and K&F in her claims against them, but she denied this. The defendants argued that Lynn had failed to show

Case 30.1—Continues next page ➥

Case 30.1–Continued

that her allegations of malpractice caused her to suffer any damages. She asserted, however, that their failure to give her a copy of the partnership agreement and their advice to settle with Ferraro quickly had caused her emotional distress.

WHAT IF THE FACTS WERE DIFFERENT? *Suppose that Buckley and the Buckley King firm were held legally liable on all of Lynn's claims for malpractice. What acts of ethical misconduct might this indicate?*

Liability for Fraud

An accountant may be found liable for either actual fraud or constructive fraud. Recall from Chapter 10 that fraud, or misrepresentation, involves the following elements:

1. A misrepresentation of a material fact has occurred.
2. There is an intent to deceive.
3. The innocent party has justifiably relied on the misrepresentation.
4. To obtain damages, the innocent party must have been injured.

A professional may be held liable for *actual fraud* when he or she intentionally misstates a material fact to mislead a client and the client is injured as a result of her or his justifiable reliance on the misstated fact. A material fact is one that a reasonable person would consider important in deciding whether to act.

In contrast, a professional may be held liable for *constructive* fraud whether or not he or she acted with fraudulent intent. **EXAMPLE 30.5** Paula, an accountant, is conducting an audit of National Computing Company (NCC). Paula accepts the explanations of Ron, an NCC officer, regarding certain financial irregularities, despite evidence that contradicts those explanations and indicates that the irregularities may be illegal. Paula's conduct could be characterized as an intentional failure to perform a duty in reckless disregard of the consequences of such failure. This would constitute gross negligence and could be held to be constructive fraud. • Both actual and constructive fraud are potential sources of legal liability for an accountant or other professional.

For fraudulent conduct, an accountant may also suffer penalties imposed by a state board of accountancy, as the following case illustrates.

Case 30.2 Walsh v. State

Nebraska Supreme Court, 276 Neb. 1034, 759 N.W.2d 100 (2009).

FACTS Stephen Teiper wrote a letter to the Nebraska Board of Public Accountancy to accuse his brother-in-law, Michael Walsh, a certified public accountant (CPA), of impersonating Teiper on the phone to obtain financial information from Teiper's insurance company. The board filed a complaint against Walsh for a violation of its rules. At a hearing, Walsh admitted that he had impersonated Teiper, but argued that Teiper had provided his personal information to Walsh for this purpose. The board found that Walsh had committed a "discreditable act" and concluded that his conduct was reprehensible and reflected adversely on his fitness to engage in the practice of public accountancy. As sanctions, the board reprimanded Walsh, placed him on probation for three months, and ordered him to attend four hours of continuing education in ethics. The board also ordered him to pay the costs of the hearing. Walsh petitioned a Nebraska state court, which affirmed the orders. Walsh appealed.

ISSUE Is there a sufficient connection between the practice of public accountancy and Walsh's conduct to allow the board to discipline him?

DECISION Yes. The Nebraska Supreme Court affirmed the lower court's decision. Walsh's actions reflected adversely on the accountancy profession, which demands a high level of honesty and integrity.

REASON A CPA cannot impersonate another person and "make false statements," or otherwise commit fraud, without "tainting" the CPA's reputation and the reputation of the accountancy profession. Like attorneys and other professionals, CPAs are held to "a high degree of moral and ethical integrity" because laypersons depend on their "honesty, integrity, sound professional judgment, and compliance with government regulations." The Nebraska Board of Public Accountancy has the authority to issue rules to "establish and maintain a high standard of integrity and dignity in the profession of public accountancy." Under these rules, a CPA "shall not commit an act that reflects adversely" on his or her fitness to practice the profession. The board can discipline CPAs who do not follow these standards and can impose various sanctions, including those levied on Walsh.

FOR CRITICAL ANALYSIS—Ethical Consideration *Was the specific reason for Walsh's impersonation significant to the result in this case? Why or why not?*

Potential Liability to Third Parties

Traditionally, an accountant or other professional did not owe any duty to a third person with whom she or he had no direct contractual relationship—that is, to any person not in *privity of contract.* A professional's duty was only to her or his client. Violations of statutory laws, fraud, and other intentional or reckless acts of wrongdoing were the only exceptions to this general rule.

Today, numerous third parties—including investors, shareholders, creditors, corporate managers and directors, and regulatory agencies—rely on professional opinions, such as those of auditors, when making decisions. In view of this extensive reliance, many courts have all but abandoned the privity requirement in regard to accountants' liability to third parties.

In this section, we focus primarily on the potential liability of auditors to third parties. Understanding an auditor's common law liability to third parties is critical because often, when a business fails, its independent auditor (accountant) is one of the few potentially *solvent* (able to pay expenses and debts) defendants. The majority of courts now hold that auditors can be held liable to third parties for negligence, but the standard for the imposition of this liability varies. There generally are three different views of accountants' liability to third parties, each of which we discuss below.

The *Ultramares* Rule

The traditional rule regarding an accountant's liability to third parties was enunciated by Chief Judge Benjamin Cardozo in *Ultramares Corp. v. Touche,* a case decided in 1931.[5] **CASE EXAMPLE 30.6** Fred Stern & Company hired the public accounting firm of Touche, Niven & Company to review Stern's financial records and prepare a balance sheet for the year ending December 31, 1923.[6] Touche prepared the balance sheet and supplied Stern with thirty-two certified copies. According to the certified balance sheet, Stern had a net worth (assets less liabilities) of $1,070,715.26. In reality, however, Stern's liabilities exceeded its assets—the company's records had been falsified by insiders at Stern to reflect a positive net worth (assets exceed liabilities). In reliance on the certified balance sheets, Ultramares Corporation loaned substantial amounts to Stern. After Stern was declared bankrupt, Ultramares brought an action against Touche for negligence in an attempt to recover damages. •

THE REQUIREMENT OF PRIVITY The New York Court of Appeals (that state's highest court) refused to impose liability on the Touche accountants and concluded that they owed a duty of care only to those persons for whose "primary benefit" the statements were intended. In this case, Stern was the only person for whose primary benefit the statements were intended. The court held that in the absence of privity or a relationship "so close as to approach that of privity," a party could not recover from an accountant. The court's requirement of privity has since been referred to as the *Ultramares* rule, or the New York rule.

CASE EXAMPLE 30.7 Toro Company supplied equipment and credit to Summit Power Equipment Distributors and required Summit to submit audited reports so that Toro could evaluate the distributor's financial condition. Summit supplied Toro with reports prepared by accountants at Krouse, Kern & Company, which allegedly contained mistakes and omissions regarding Summit's financial condition. Toro extended and renewed large amounts of credit to Summit in reliance on the audited reports, but Summit was unable to repay these amounts. Toro brought a negligence action against the accounting firm and proved that accountants at Krouse knew that its reports would be used by Summit to induce Toro to extend credit. Nevertheless, under the *Ultramares* rule, the court refused to hold the accounting firm liable because the firm was not in privity with Toro.[7] •

MODIFIED TO ALLOW "NEAR PRIVITY" The *Ultramares* rule was restated and somewhat modified in *Credit Alliance Corp. v. Arthur Andersen & Co.*[8] In that case, the court held that if a third party has a sufficiently close relationship or *nexus* (link or connection) with an accountant, then the *Ultramares* privity requirement may be satisfied even if no accountant-client relationship is established. The rule enunciated in the *Credit Alliance* case is often referred to as the "near privity" rule. Only a minority of states have adopted this rule of accountants' liability to third parties.

The *Restatement* Rule

The *Ultramares* rule has been severely criticized because much of the work performed by auditors is intended for use by persons who are not parties to the contract. Thus, it is asserted that the auditors owe a duty to these third parties. Consequently, there has been an erosion of the *Ultramares* rule, and accountants have increasingly been exposed to potential liability to third parties. The majority of courts have adopted the position taken by the *Restatement (Third) of Torts,* which states that accountants are subject to liability for negligence not only to their clients but also to foreseen, or *known,* users—or classes of users—of their reports or financial statements.

5. 255 N.Y. 170, 174 N.E. 441 (1931).

6. Banks, creditors, stockholders, purchasers, or sellers often rely on a balance sheet as a basis for making decisions relating to a company's business.

7. *Toro Co. v. Krouse, Kern & Co.,* 827 F.2d 155 (7th Cir. 1987).

8. 65 N.Y.2d 536, 483 N.E.2d 110 (1985). A "relationship sufficiently intimate to be equated with privity" is enough for a third party to sue another's accountant for negligence.

Under Section 552(2) of the *Restatement (Third) of Torts,* an accountant's liability extends to

1. Persons for whose benefit and guidance the accountant intends to supply the information or knows that the recipient intends to supply it, and
2. Persons whom the accountant intends the information to influence or knows that the recipient so intends.

EXAMPLE 30.8 Steve, an accountant, prepares a financial statement for Tech Software, Inc., a client, knowing that the client will submit that statement to First National Bank to secure a loan. If Steve makes negligent misstatements or omissions in the statement, he may be held liable by the bank because he knew that the bank would rely on his work product when deciding whether to make the loan. •

The "Reasonably Foreseeable Users" Rule

A small minority of courts hold accountants liable to any users whose reliance on an accountant's statements or reports was *reasonably foreseeable.* This standard has been criticized as extending liability too far and exposing accountants to massive liability.

The majority of courts have concluded that the *Restatement's* approach is more reasonable because it allows accountants to control their exposure to liability. Liability is "fixed by the accountants' particular knowledge at the moment the audit is published," not by the foreseeability of the harm that might occur to a third party after the report is released.

Like accountants, attorneys may be held liable under the common law to third parties who rely on legal opinions to their detriment. Generally, an attorney is not liable to a nonclient unless there is fraud (or malicious conduct) by the attorney. The liability principles stated in Section 552 of the *Restatement (Third) of Torts,* however, may apply to attorneys as well as to accountants.

Should an attorney's duty of care extend to third party beneficiaries (see Chapter 11) whose rights were harmed by the attorney's malpractice? That question was before the court in the following case.

Case 30.3 Perez[a] v. Stern

Nebraska Supreme Court, 279 Neb. 187, 777 N.W.2d 545 (2010).

FACTS Domingo Martinez died after he was struck by a car in a hit-and-run accident on July 8, 2001. Reyna Guido, the mother of his two minor children and the personal representative of his estate, retained an attorney, Sandra Stern, to file a wrongful death lawsuit. On July 8, 2003, Stern filed a wrongful death complaint in the district court. Stern, however, never perfected service of the complaint, and because the complaint was not served within six months of filing, the case was dismissed by operation of law. On February 6, 2007, Guido sued Stern for malpractice on behalf of herself, the children, and the estate. Guido alleged that the wrongful death claim expired as a result of Stern's failure to timely perfect service of the complaint. Stern moved for summary judgment on the ground that the malpractice claims were barred by the two-year statute of limitations for professional negligence. Before the court ruled on the motion, Guido voluntarily dismissed her individual claim, but maintained claims as personal representative of the estate and on behalf of the children. The trial court found that the estate's claim against Stern was barred by the statute of limitations. The court granted summary judgment in favor of Stern and dismissed the complaint. Guido appealed, claiming that the district court erred in determining that the children had no independent standing to sue Stern and that Stern owed no independent duty to the minor children to protect their rights and interests. Guido also argued that the statute of limitations was tolled (suspended) during the children's minority.

a. Esteban Perez is one of the two minor children whose father was killed in the car accident. Esteban's natural mother, Reyna Guido, brought the case on his behalf.

ISSUE Should an attorney's duty of care in a wrongful death case extend to the minor children of the deceased whose rights were harmed by the attorney's malpractice?

DECISION Yes. The Supreme Court of Nebraska reversed the lower court's summary judgment in favor of Stern and remanded the case for further proceedings. The statute of limitations had not expired with respect to the children because the statute was suspended during their minority.

REASON The question was whether Stern owed an independent duty to the children, who were Martinez's next of kin, to prosecute the underlying wrongful death claim in a timely manner. The reviewing court pointed out that a lawyer's duty generally does not extend to third parties. "Courts have repeatedly emphasized that the starting point for analyzing an attorney's duty to a third party is determining whether the third party was a direct and intended beneficiary of the attorney services." In this situation, Stern did owe a duty to Martinez's minor children—who were direct and intended beneficiaries—to represent their interests competently. "To hold otherwise would deny a legal recourse to the children for whose benefit Stern was hired in the first place." The court concluded that the children had standing to sue Stern for neglecting that duty. The claim was not barred by the statute of limitations because in Nebraska (and in most states), the statute was suspended while the children were minors.

WHAT IF THE FACTS WERE DIFFERENT? *If the children had suffered no harm as a result of the attorney's malpractice, would the outcome of this case have been different? Why or why not?*

The Sarbanes-Oxley Act

In 2002, Congress enacted the Sarbanes-Oxley Act. The act imposes a number of strict requirements on both domestic and foreign public accounting firms that provide auditing services to companies ("issuers") whose securities are sold to public investors. The act defines the term *issuer* as a company that has securities that are registered under Section 12 of the Securities Exchange Act of 1934, that is required to file reports under Section 15(d) of the 1934 act, or that files—or has filed—a registration statement that has not yet become effective under the Securities Act of 1933 (see Chapter 26).

The Public Company Accounting Oversight Board

Among other things, the Sarbanes-Oxley Act increased the degree of government oversight of public accounting practices by creating the Public Company Accounting Oversight Board, which reports to the Securities and Exchange Commission. The board consists of a chair and four other members. The purpose of the board is to oversee the audit of public companies that are subject to securities laws. The goal is to protect public investors and to ensure that public accounting firms comply with the provisions of the Sarbanes-Oxley Act.

Applicability to Public Accounting Firms

Titles I and II of the act set forth the key provisions relating to the duties of the oversight board and the requirements relating to *public accounting firms*—defined by the act as firms and associated persons that are "engaged in the practice of public accounting or preparing or issuing audit reports." These provisions are summarized in Exhibit 30–1 below. (Provisions relating to corporate fraud and the responsibilities of corporate officers and directors were listed in Exhibit 26–3 on page 516.)

• *Exhibit* 30–1 Key Provisions of the Sarbanes-Oxley Act Relating to Public Accounting Firms

AUDITOR INDEPENDENCE

To help ensure that auditors remain independent of the firms that they audit, Title II of the Sarbanes-Oxley Act does the following:

- Makes it unlawful for Registered Public Accounting Firms (RPAFs) to perform both audit and nonaudit services for the same company at the same time. Nonaudit services include the following:
    1. Bookkeeping or other services related to the accounting records or financial statements of the audit client.
    2. Financial information systems design and implementation.
    3. Appraisal or valuation services.
    4. Fairness opinions.
    5. Management functions.
    6. Broker or dealer, investment adviser, or investment banking services.
- Requires preapproval for most auditing services from the issuer's (the corporation's) audit committee.
- Requires audit partner rotation by prohibiting RPAFs from providing audit services to an issuer if either the lead audit partner or the audit partner responsible for reviewing the audit has provided such services to that corporation in each of the prior five years.
- Requires RPAFs to make timely reports to the audit committees of the corporations. The report must indicate all critical accounting policies and practices to be used; all alternative treatments of financial information within generally accepted accounting principles that have been discussed with the corporation's management officials, the ramifications of the use of such alternative treatments, and the treatment preferred by the auditor; and other material written communications between the auditor and the corporation's management.
- Makes it unlawful for an RPAF to provide auditing services to an issuer if the corporation's chief executive officer, chief financial officer, chief accounting officer, or controller was previously employed by the auditor and participated in any capacity in the audit of the corporation during the one-year period preceding the date that the audit began.

DOCUMENT RETENTION AND DESTRUCTION

- The Sarbanes-Oxley Act provides that anyone who destroys, alters, or falsifies records with the intent to obstruct or influence a federal investigation or in relation to bankruptcy proceedings can be criminally prosecuted and sentenced to a fine, imprisonment for up to twenty years, or both.
- The act also requires accountants who audit or review publicly traded companies to retain all working papers related to the audit or review for a period of five years (now amended to seven years). Violators can be sentenced to a fine, imprisonment for up to ten years, or both.

Requirements for Maintaining Working Papers

Performing an audit for a client involves an accumulation of **working papers**—the various documents used and developed during the audit. These include notes, computations, memoranda, copies, and other papers that make up the work product of an accountant's services to a client. Under the common law, which in this instance has been codified in a number of states, working papers remain the accountant's property. It is important for accountants to retain such records in the event that they need to defend against lawsuits for negligence or other actions in which their competence is challenged. The client also has a right to access an accountant's working papers because they reflect the client's financial situation. On a client's request, an accountant must return to the client any of the client's records or journals, and failure to do so may result in liability.

Section 802(a)(1) of the Sarbanes-Oxley Act provides that accountants must maintain working papers relating to an audit or review for five years—subsequently increased to seven years—from the end of the fiscal period in which the audit or review was concluded. A knowing violation of this requirement will subject the accountant to a fine, imprisonment for up to ten years, or both.

Potential Statutory Liability of Accountants under Securities Laws

Both civil and criminal liability may be imposed on accountants under the Securities Act of 1933, the Securities Exchange Act of 1934, and the Private Securities Litigation Reform Act of 1995.[9]

Liability under the Securities Act of 1933

The Securities Act of 1933 requires registration statements to be filed with the Securities and Exchange Commission (SEC) prior to an offering of securities (see Chapter 26).[10] Accountants frequently prepare and certify the issuer's financial statements that are included in the registration statement.

LIABILITY UNDER SECTION 11 Section 11 of the Securities Act of 1933 imposes civil liability on accountants for misstatements and omissions of material facts in registration statements. An accountant may be liable if he or she prepared any financial statements included in the registration statement that "contained an untrue statement of a material fact or omitted to state a material fact required to be stated therein or necessary to make the statements therein not misleading."[11]

Under Section 11, an accountant's liability for a misstatement or omission of a material fact in a registration statement extends to anyone who acquires a security covered by the registration statement. A purchaser of a security need only demonstrate that she or he has suffered a loss on the security. Proof of reliance on the materially false statement or misleading omission ordinarily is not required. Nor is there a requirement of privity between the accountant and the security purchasers.

The Due Diligence Standard. Section 11 imposes a duty on accountants to use **due diligence** in preparing the financial statements included in the filed registration statements. After a purchaser has proved a loss on the security, the accountant has the burden of showing that he or she exercised due diligence in preparing the financial statements. To avoid liability, the accountant must show that he or she had, "after reasonable investigation, reasonable grounds to believe and did believe, at the time such part of the registration statement became effective, that the statements therein were true and that there was no omission of a material fact required to be stated therein or necessary to make the statements therein not misleading."[12] Failure to follow GAAP and GAAS is also proof of a lack of due diligence.

In particular, the due diligence standard places a burden on accountants to verify information furnished by a corporation's officers and directors. The burden of proving due diligence requires an accountant to demonstrate that she or he is free from negligence or fraud. Merely asking questions is not always sufficient to satisfy the requirement. Accountants can be held liable for failing to detect danger signals in documents furnished by corporate officers that, under GAAS, require further investigation under the circumstances.[13]

Defenses to Liability. Besides proving that he or she has acted with due diligence, an accountant can raise the following defenses to Section 11 liability:

1. There were no misstatements or omissions.
2. The misstatements or omissions were not of material facts.
3. The misstatements or omissions had no causal connection to the plaintiff's loss.
4. The plaintiff-purchaser invested in the securities knowing of the misstatements or omissions.

9. Civil and criminal liability may also be imposed on accountants and other professionals under other statutes, including the Racketeer Influenced and Corrupt Organizations Act (RICO). RICO was discussed in Chapter 6.
10. Many securities and transactions are expressly exempted from the 1933 act.
11. 15 U.S.C. Section 77k(a).
12. 15 U.S.C. Section 77k(b)(3).
13. See *In re Cardinal Health, Inc. Securities Litigation,* 426 F.Supp.2d 688 (S.D. Ohio 2006); and *In re WorldCom, Inc. Securities Litigation,* 352 F.Supp.2d 472 (S.D.N.Y. 2005).

LIABILITY UNDER SECTION 12(2) Section 12(2) of the Securities Act of 1933 imposes civil liability for fraud in relation to offerings or sales of securities.[14] Liability is based on communication to an investor, whether orally or in the written prospectus,[15] of an untrue statement or omission of a material fact.

PENALTIES AND SANCTIONS FOR VIOLATIONS Those who purchase securities and suffer harm as a result of a false or omitted statement, or some other violation, may bring a suit in a federal court to recover their losses and other damages. The U.S. Department of Justice brings criminal actions against those who commit willful violations. The penalties include fines of up to $10,000, imprisonment for up to five years, or both. The SEC is authorized to seek an injunction against a willful violator to prevent further violations. The SEC can also ask a court to grant other relief, such as an order to a violator to refund profits derived from an illegal transaction.

Liability under the Securities Exchange Act of 1934

Under Sections 18 and 10(b) of the Securities Exchange Act of 1934 and SEC Rule 10b-5, an accountant may be found liable for fraud. A plaintiff has a substantially heavier burden of proof under the 1934 act than under the 1933 act, because under the 1934 act an accountant does not have to prove due diligence to escape liability.

LIABILITY UNDER SECTION 18 Section 18 of the 1934 act imposes civil liability on an accountant who makes or causes to be made in any application, report, or document a statement that at the time and in light of the circumstances was false or misleading with respect to any material fact.[16]

Section 18 liability is narrow in that it applies only to applications, reports, documents, and registration statements filed with the SEC. This remedy is further limited in that it applies only to sellers and purchasers. Under Section 18, a seller or purchaser must prove one of the following:

1. That the false or misleading statement affected the price of the security.
2. That the purchaser or seller relied on the false or misleading statement in making the purchase or sale and was not aware of the inaccuracy of the statement.

An accountant will not be liable for violating Section 18 if he or she acted in good faith in preparing the financial statement. To demonstrate good faith, an accountant must show that he or she had no knowledge that the financial statement was false and misleading. Acting in good faith also requires that the accountant lacked any intent to deceive, manipulate, defraud, or seek unfair advantage over another party. (Note that "mere" negligence in preparing a financial statement does not lead to liability under the 1934 act. This differs from the 1933 act, under which an accountant is liable for *all* negligent acts.)

In addition to the good faith defense, accountants can escape liability by proving that the buyer or seller of the security in question knew the financial statement was false and misleading. Sellers and purchasers must bring a cause of action "within one year after the discovery of the facts constituting the cause of action and within three years after such cause of action accrued."[17] A court also has the discretion to assess reasonable costs, including attorneys' fees, against accountants who violate this section.

LIABILITY UNDER SECTION 10(B) AND RULE 10B-5 Accountants additionally face potential legal liability under the antifraud provisions contained in the Securities Exchange Act of 1934 and SEC Rule 10b-5. The scope of these antifraud provisions is very broad and allows private parties to bring civil actions against violators.

Section 10(b) makes it unlawful for any person, including accountants, to use, in connection with the purchase or sale of any security, any manipulative or deceptive device or contrivance in contravention of SEC rules and regulations.[18] Rule 10b-5 further makes it unlawful for any person, by use of any means or instrumentality of interstate commerce, to do the following:

1. Employ any device, scheme, or artifice (pretense) to defraud.
2. Make any untrue statement of a material fact or omit to state a material fact necessary to make the statements made, in light of the circumstances, not misleading.
3. Engage in any act, practice, or course of business that operates or would operate as a fraud or deceit on any person, in connection with the purchase or sale of any security.[19]

Accountants may be held liable only to sellers or purchasers of securities under Section 10(b) and Rule 10b-5. Privity is not necessary for a recovery. An accountant may be found liable not only for fraudulent misstatements of material facts in written material filed with the SEC, but also for any fraudulent oral statements or omissions made in connection with the purchase or sale of any security.

For a plaintiff to succeed in recovering damages under these antifraud provisions, however, he or she must prove intent (*scienter*) to commit the fraudulent or deceptive act. Ordinary negligence is not enough.

14. 15 U.S.C. Section 77l.
15. As discussed in Chapter 26, a *prospectus* contains financial disclosures about the corporation for the benefit of potential investors.
16. 15 U.S.C. Section 78r(a).
17. 15 U.S.C. Section 78r(c).
18. 15 U.S.C. Section 78j(b)
19. 17 C.F.R. Section 240.10b-5.

The Private Securities Litigation Reform Act of 1995

The Private Securities Litigation Reform Act of 1995 made some changes to the potential liability of accountants and other professionals in securities fraud cases. Among other things, the act imposed a new statutory obligation on accountants. An auditor must use adequate procedures in an audit to detect any illegal acts of the company being audited. If something illegal is detected, the auditor must disclose it to the company's board of directors, the audit committee, or the SEC, depending on the circumstances.[20]

The 1995 act also provides that, in most situations, a party is liable only for the proportion of damages for which he or she is responsible.[21] An accountant who participates in, but is unaware of, illegal conduct may not be liable for the entire loss caused by the illegality.

EXAMPLE 30.9 Nina, an accountant, helps the president and owner of Midstate Trucking Company draft financial statements that misrepresent Midstate's financial condition, but Nina is not actually aware of the fraud. Nina might be held liable, but the amount of her liability could be proportionately less than the entire loss. •

If an accountant knowingly aids and abets a primary violator, the SEC can seek an injunction or monetary damages. **EXAMPLE 30.10** Smith & Jones, an accounting firm, performs an audit for ABC Sales Company that is so inadequate as to constitute gross negligence. ABC uses the materials provided by Smith & Jones as part of a scheme to defraud investors. When the scheme is uncovered, the SEC can bring an action against Smith & Jones for aiding and abetting on the ground that the firm knew or should have known of the material misrepresentations that were in its audit and on which investors were likely to rely. •

Potential Criminal Liability

An accountant may be found criminally liable for violations of the Securities Act of 1933, the Securities Exchange Act of 1934, the Internal Revenue Code, and both state and federal criminal codes. Under both the 1933 act and the 1934 act, accountants may be subject to criminal penalties for *willful* violations—imprisonment for up to five years and/or a fine of up to $10,000 under the 1933 act and imprisonment for up to ten years and a fine of $100,000 under the 1934 act. Under the Sarbanes-Oxley Act of 2002, for a securities filing that is accompanied by an accountant's false or misleading certified audit statement, the accountant may be fined up to $5 million, imprisoned for up to twenty years, or both.

The Internal Revenue Code makes aiding or assisting in the preparation of a false tax return a felony punishable by a fine of $100,000 ($500,000 in the case of a corporation) and imprisonment for up to three years.[22] This provision applies to anyone who prepares tax returns for others for compensation, and not just to accountants.[23] A penalty of $250 per tax return is levied on tax preparers for negligent understatement of the client's tax liability. For willful understatement of tax liability or reckless or intentional disregard of rules or regulations, a penalty of $1,000 is imposed.[24]

A tax preparer may also be subject to penalties for failing to furnish the taxpayer with a copy of the return, failing to sign the return, or failing to furnish the appropriate tax identification numbers.[25] In addition, those who prepare tax returns for others may be fined $1,000 per document for aiding and abetting another's understatement of tax liability (the penalty is increased to $10,000 in corporate cases).[26] The tax preparer's liability is limited to one penalty per taxpayer per tax year.

In most states, criminal penalties may be imposed for such actions as knowingly certifying false or fraudulent reports; falsifying, altering, or destroying books of account; and obtaining property or credit through the use of false financial statements.

Confidentiality and Privilege

Professionals are restrained by the ethical tenets of their professions to keep all communications with their clients confidential.

Attorney-Client Relationships

The confidentiality of attorney-client communications is protected by law, which confers a privilege on such communications. This privilege is granted because of the need for full disclosure to the attorney of the facts of a client's case. To encourage frankness, confidential attorney-client communications relating to representation are normally held in strictest confidence and protected by law. The attorney and her or his employees may not discuss the client's case with anyone—even under court order—without the client's permission. The client holds the privilege, and only the client may waive it—by disclosing privileged information to someone outside the privilege, for example.

Note, however, that since the Sarbanes-Oxley Act was enacted in 2002, the SEC has implemented new rules requiring attorneys who become aware that a client has violated securities laws to report the violation to the SEC. Reporting a client's misconduct could be a breach of the attorney-client privilege, however, an issue that has caused controversy in the legal community.

20. 15 U.S.C. Section 78j-1.
21. 15 U.S.C. Section 78u-4(g).
22. 26 U.S.C. Section 7206(2).
23. 26 U.S.C. Section 7701(a)(36).
24. 26 U.S.C. Section 6694.
25. 26 U.S.C. Section 6695.
26. 26 U.S.C. Section 6701.

Accountant-Client Relationships

In a few states, accountant-client communications are privileged by state statute. In these states, accountant-client communications may not be revealed even in court or in court-sanctioned proceedings without the client's permission. The majority of states, however, abide by the common law, which provides that, if a court so orders, an accountant must disclose information about his or her client to the court. Physicians and other professionals may similarly be compelled to disclose in court information given to them in confidence by patients or clients.

Communications between professionals and their clients—other than those between an attorney and her or his client—are not privileged under federal law. In cases involving federal law, state-provided rights to confidentiality of accountant-client communications are not recognized. Thus, in those cases, in response to a court order, an accountant must provide the information sought.

Reviewing . . . Liability of Accountants and Other Professionals

Superior Wholesale Corporation planned to purchase Regal Furniture, Inc., and wished to determine Regal's net worth. Superior hired Lynette Shuebke, of the accounting firm Shuebke Delgado, to review an audit that had been prepared by Norman Chase, the accountant for Regal. Shuebke advised Superior that Chase had performed a high-quality audit and that Regal's inventory on the audit dates was stated accurately on the general ledger. As a result of these representations, Superior went forward with its purchase of Regal. After the purchase, Superior discovered that the audit by Chase had been materially inaccurate and misleading, primarily because the inventory had been grossly overstated on the balance sheet. Later, a former Regal employee who had begun working for Superior exposed an e-mail exchange between Chase and former Regal chief executive officer Buddy Gantry. The exchange revealed that Chase had cooperated in overstating the inventory and understating Regal's tax liability. Using the information presented in the chapter, answer the following questions.

1. If Shuebke's review was conducted in good faith and conformed to generally accepted accounting principles, could Superior hold Shuebke Delgado liable for negligently failing to detect material omissions in Chase's audit? Why or why not?
2. According to the rule adopted by the majority of courts to determine accountants' liability to third parties, could Chase be liable to Superior? Explain.
3. Generally, what requirements must be met before Superior can recover damages under Section 10(b) of the Securities Exchange Act of 1934 and SEC Rule 10b-5? Can Superior meet these requirements?
4. Suppose that a court determined that Chase had aided Regal in willfully understating its tax liability. What is the maximum penalty that could be imposed on Chase?

Terms and Concepts

defalcation 579
due diligence 586
generally accepted accounting principles (GAAP) 579
generally accepted auditing standards (GAAS) 579
International Financial Reporting Standards (IFRS) 579
malpractice 581
working papers 586

Chapter Summary: Liability of Accountants and Other Professionals

COMMON LAW LIABILITY	
Potential Common Law Liability to Clients (See pages 578–582.)	1. *Breach of contract*—An accountant or other professional who fails to perform according to his or her contractual obligations can be held liable for breach of contract and resulting damages. 2. *Negligence*—An accountant, attorney, or other professional, in performance of her or his duties, must use the care, knowledge, and judgment generally used by professionals in the same or similar circumstances. Failure to do so is negligence. An accountant's violation of generally accepted accounting principles and generally accepted auditing standards is *prima facie* evidence of negligence. 3. *Fraud*—Intentionally misrepresenting a material fact to a client, when the client relies on the misrepresentation, is actual fraud. Gross negligence in performance of duties is constructive fraud.

Continued

Chapter Summary: Liability of Accountants and Other Professionals—Continued

Potential Liability to Third Parties (See pages 583–584.)	An accountant may be liable for negligence to any third person the accountant knows or should have known will benefit from the accountant's work. The standard for imposing this liability varies, but generally courts follow one of the following rules: 1. *The Ultramares rule*—Liability will be imposed only if the accountant is in privity, or near privity, with the third party. 2. *The Restatement rule*—Liability will be imposed only if the third party's reliance is foreseen, or known, or if the third party is among a class of foreseen, or known, users. The majority of courts have adopted this rule. 3. *The "reasonably foreseeable user" rule*—Liability will be imposed if the third party's use was reasonably foreseeable.
STATUTORY LIABILITY	
The Sarbanes-Oxley Act (See pages 585–586.)	1. *Purpose*—This act imposed requirements on public accounting firms that provide auditing services to companies whose securities are sold to public investors. 2. *Government oversight*—Among other things, the act created the Public Company Accounting Oversight Board to provide government oversight over public accounting practices. 3. *Working papers*—The act requires accountants to maintain working papers relating to an audit or review for seven years from the end of the fiscal period in which the audit or review was concluded. 4. *Other requirements*—See Exhibit 30–1 on page 585.
Securities Act of 1933, Section 11 (See page 586.)	An accountant who makes a false statement or omits a material fact in audited financial statements required for registration of securities under the law may be liable to anyone who acquires securities covered by the registration statement. The accountant's defense is basically the use of due diligence and the reasonable belief that the work was complete and correct. The burden of proof is on the accountant. Willful violations of this act may be subject to criminal penalties.
Securities Act of 1933, Section 12(2) (See page 587.)	An accountant may be liable for aiding and abetting the seller or offeror of securities when a prospectus or communication presented to an investor contained an untrue statement or omission of a material fact. To be liable, the accountant must have known, or at least should have known, that an untrue statement or omission of material fact existed in the offer to sell the security.
Securities Exchange Act of 1934, Sections 10(b) and 18 (See pages 587–588.)	Accountants may be held liable for false and misleading applications, reports, and documents required under the act. The burden is on the plaintiff, and the accountant has numerous defenses, including good faith and lack of knowledge that what was submitted was false.
Potential Criminal Liability (See page 588.)	1. Willful violations of the Securities Act of 1933 and the Securities Exchange Act of 1934 may be subject to criminal penalties. 2. Aiding or assisting in the preparation of a false tax return is a felony. Aiding and abetting an individual's understatement of tax liability is a separate crime. 3. Tax preparers who negligently or willfully understate a client's tax liability or who recklessly or intentionally disregard Internal Revenue rules or regulations are subject to criminal penalties. 4. Tax preparers who fail to provide a taxpayer with a copy of the return, fail to sign the return, or fail to furnish the appropriate tax identification numbers may also be subject to criminal penalties.

ExamPrep

ISSUE SPOTTERS

—Check your answers to these questions against the answers provided in Appendix G.

1 Dave, an accountant, prepares a financial statement for Excel Company, a client, knowing that Excel will use the statement to obtain a loan from First National Bank. Dave makes negligent omissions in the statement that result in a loss to the bank. Can the bank successfully sue Dave? Why or why not?

2 Nora, an accountant, prepares a financial statement as part of a registration statement that Omega, Inc., files with the Securities and Exchange Commission before making a public offering of securities. The statement contains a misstatement of material fact that is not attributable to Nora's fraud or negligence. Pat relies on the misstatement, buys some of the securities, and suffers a loss. Can Nora be held liable to Pat? Explain.

BEFORE THE TEST

Go to **www.cengagebrain.com**, enter the ISBN 9781111530624, and click on "Find" to locate this textbook's Web site. Then, click on "Access Now" under "Study Tools," and select Chapter 30 at the top. There, you will find an Interactive Quiz that you can take to assess your mastery of the concepts in this chapter, as well as Flashcards and a Glossary of important terms.

For Review

1 Under what common law theories may professionals be liable to clients?
2 What are the rules concerning an auditor's liability to third parties?
3 How might an accountant violate federal securities laws?
4 What crimes might an accountant commit under the Internal Revenue Code?
5 What constrains professionals to keep communications with their clients confidential?

Questions and Case Problems

30–1 The *Ultramares* Rule. Larkin, Inc., retains Howard Perkins to manage its books and prepare its financial statements. Perkins, a certified public accountant, lives in Indiana and practices there. After twenty years, Perkins has become a bit bored with generally accepted accounting principles (GAAP) and has adopted more creative accounting methods. Now, though, Perkins has a problem, as he is being sued by Molly Tucker, one of Larkin's creditors. Tucker alleges that Perkins either knew or should have known that Larkin's financial statements would be distributed to various individuals. Furthermore, she asserts that these financial statements were negligently prepared and seriously inaccurate. What are the consequences of Perkins's failure to follow GAAP? Under the traditional *Ultramares* rule, can Tucker recover damages from Perkins? Explain.

30–2 Question with Sample Answer The accounting firm of Goldman, Walters, Johnson & Co. prepared financial statements for Lucy's Fashions, Inc. After reviewing the various financial statements, Happydays State Bank agreed to loan Lucy's Fashions $35,000 for expansion. When Lucy's Fashions declared bankruptcy under Chapter 11 six months later, Happydays State Bank promptly filed an action against Goldman, Walters, Johnson & Co., alleging negligent preparation of financial statements. Assuming that the court has abandoned the *Ultramares* approach, what is the result? What are the policy reasons for holding accountants liable to third parties with whom they are not in privity?

—For a sample answer to Question 30–2, go to Appendix E at the end of this text.

30–3 Accountant's Liability under Rule 10b-5. In early 2010, Bennett, Inc., offered a substantial number of new common shares to the public. Harvey Helms had a long-standing interest in Bennett because his grandfather had once been president of the company. On receiving a prospectus prepared and distributed by Bennett, Helms was dismayed by the pessimism it embodied. Helms decided to delay purchasing stock in the company. Later, Helms asserted that the prospectus prepared by the accountants was overly pessimistic and contained materially misleading statements. Discuss fully how successful Helms would be in bringing a cause of action under Rule 10b-5 against the accountants of Bennett, Inc.

30–4 Confidentiality and Privilege. Napster, Inc., offered a service that allowed its users to browse digital music files on other users' computers and download selections for free. Music industry principals filed a suit in a federal district court against Napster, alleging copyright infringement. The court ordered Napster to remove from its service files that were identified as infringing. Napster failed to comply and was shut down in July 2001. In October, Bertelsmann AG, a German corporation, loaned Napster $85 million to fund its anticipated transition to a licensed digital music distribution system. The terms allowed Napster to spend the loan on "general, administrative and overhead expenses." In an e-mail, Hank Barry, Napster's chief executive officer, referred to a "side deal" under which Napster could use up to $10 million of the loan to pay litigation expenses. Napster failed to launch the new system before declaring bankruptcy in June 2002. Some of the plaintiffs filed a suit in a federal district court against Bertelsmann, charging that by its loan, it prolonged Napster's infringement. The plaintiffs asked the court to order the disclosure of all attorney-client communications related to the loan. What principle could Bertelsmann assert to protect these communications? What is the purpose of this protection? Should this principle protect a client who consults an attorney for advice that will help the client commit fraud? Should the court grant the plaintiffs' request? Discuss. [*In re Napster, Inc. Copyright Litigation,* 479 F.3d 1078 (9th Cir. 2007)]

30–5 Case Problem with Sample Answer A West Virginia bank ran its asset value from $100 million to $1 billion over seven years by aggressively marketing subprime loans. The Office of the Comptroller of the Currency, a federal regulator, audited the bank and discovered that the books had been falsified for several years and that the bank was insolvent. The Comptroller closed the bank and brought criminal charges against its managers. The Comptroller fined Grant Thornton, the bank's accounting firm, $300,000 for recklessly failing to meet generally accepted auditing standards during the years it audited the bank. The Comptroller claimed Thornton violated federal law by "participating in . . . unsafe and unsound banking practice." Thornton appealed, contending that it was not involved in bank operations to that extent based on its audit function. What would be the key to determining if the accounting firm could be held liable for that violation of federal law? [*Grant Thornton, LLP v. Office of the Comptroller of the Currency,* 514 F.3d 1328 (D.C.Cir. 2008)]

—For a sample answer to Problem 30–5, go to Appendix F at the end of this text.

30–6 Professional's Liability. Soon after Teresa DeYoung's husband died, her mother-in-law also died, leaving an inheritance of more than $400,000 for DeYoung's children. DeYoung hired John Ruggerio, an attorney, to ensure that her children would receive it. Ruggerio advised her to invest the funds in his real estate business. She declined. A few months later, $300,000 of the inheritance was sent to Ruggerio. Without telling DeYoung, he deposited the $300,000 in his account and began to use the funds in his real estate business. Nine months later, $109,000 of the inheritance was sent to Ruggerio. He paid this to DeYoung. She asked about the remaining amount. Ruggerio lied to hide his theft. Unable to access these funds, DeYoung's children changed their college plans to attend less expensive institutions. Nearly three years later, DeYoung learned the truth. Can she bring a suit against Ruggerio? If so, on what ground? If not, why not? Did Ruggerio violate any standard of professional ethics? Discuss. [*DeYoung v. Ruggerio,* 2009 VT 9, 971 A.2d 627 (2009)]

30–7 Professional Malpractice. Jeffery Guerrero hired James McDonald, a certified public accountant, to represent him and his business in an appeal to the Internal Revenue Service. The appeal was about audits that showed Guerrero owed more taxes. When the appeal failed, McDonald assisted in preparing materials for an appeal to the Tax Court, which was also not successful. Guerrero then sued McDonald for professional negligence in the preparation of his evidence for the court. Specifically, Guerrero claimed that McDonald had failed to adequately prepare witnesses and to present all the arguments that could have been made on his behalf so he could have won the case. Guerrero contended that McDonald was liable for all of the additional taxes he was required to pay. Is Guerrero's claim likely to result in liability on McDonald's part? What factors would the court consider? [*Guerrero v. McDonald,* 302 Ga.App. 164, 690 S.E.2d 486 (2010)]

30–8 A Question of Ethics *Portland Shellfish Co. processes live shellfish in Maine. As one of the firm's two owners, Frank Wetmore held 300 voting and 150 nonvoting shares of the stock. Donna Holden held the other 300 voting shares. Donna's husband, Jeff, managed the company's daily operations, including production, procurement, and sales. The board of directors consisted of Frank and Jeff. In 2001, disagreements arose over the company's management. The Holdens invoked the "Shareholders' Agreement," which provided that "[i]n the event of a deadlock, the directors shall hire an accountant at [MacDonald, Page, Schatz, Fletcher & Co., LLC] to determine the value of the outstanding shares. . . . [E]ach shareholder shall have the right to buy out the other shareholder(s)' interest." MacDonald Page estimated the stock's "fair market value" to be $1.09 million. Donna offered to buy Frank's shares at a price equal to his proportionate share. Frank countered by offering $1.25 million for Donna's shares. Donna rejected Frank's offer and insisted that he sell his shares to her or she would sue. In the face of this threat, Frank sold his shares to Donna for $750,705. Believing the stock to be worth more than twice MacDonald Page's estimate, Frank filed a suit in a federal district court against the accountant. [*Wetmore v. MacDonald, Page, Schatz, Fletcher & Co., LLC, *476 F.3d 1 (1st Cir. 2007)]*

1 Frank claimed that in valuing the stock, the accountant disregarded "commonly accepted and reliable methods of valuation in favor of less reliable methods." He alleged negligence, among other things. MacDonald Page filed a motion to dismiss the complaint. What are the elements that establish negligence? Which is the most critical element in this case?
2 MacDonald Page evaluated the company's stock by identifying its "fair market value," defined as "[t]he price at which the property would change hands between a willing buyer and a willing seller, neither being under a compulsion to buy or sell and both having reasonable knowledge of relevant facts." The accountant knew that the shareholders would use its estimate to determine the price that one would pay to the other. Under these circumstances, was Frank's injury foreseeable? Explain.
3 What factor might have influenced Frank to sell his shares to Donna even if he thought that MacDonald Page's "fair market value" figure was less than half what it should have been? Does this factor represent an unfair, or unethical, advantage? Why or why not?

30–9 Critical Thinking Legal Question In cases involving third parties who have suffered losses in reliance on negligent misrepresentations in accountants' financial reports, the courts apply different standards to assess liability. Some courts impose liability only when there is privity between the accountant and the party seeking recovery. Other courts impose liability under a foreseeability rule. What are the implications of imposing liability on accountants for losses suffered by third parties on the basis of foreseeability rather than privity?

30–10 Video Question To watch this chapter's video, *Accountant's Liability,* go to **www.cengagebrain.com**. Register the access code that came with your new book or log in to your existing account. Select the link for the "Business Law Digital Video Library Online Access" or "Business Law CourseMate." Click on "Complete Video List," view Video 54, and then answer the following questions:

1 Should Ray prepare a financial statement that values a list of assets provided by the advertising firm without verifying that the firm actually owns these assets?
2 Discuss whether Ray is in privity with the company interested in buying Laura's advertising firm.
3 Under the *Ultramares* rule, to whom does Ray owe a duty?
4 Assume that Laura did not tell Ray that she intended to give the financial statement to the potential acquirer. Would this fact change Ray's liability under the *Ultramares* rule? Explain.

Chapter 31

International Law in a Global Economy

Learning Objectives

After reading this chapter, you should be able to answer the following questions:

1. What is the principle of comity, and why do courts deciding disputes involving a foreign law or judicial decree apply this principle?
2. What is the act of state doctrine? In what circumstances is this doctrine applied?
3. Under the Foreign Sovereign Immunities Act of 1976, on what bases might a foreign state be considered subject to the jurisdiction of U.S. courts?
4. What types of provisions, or clauses, are often included in international sales contracts?
5. Do U.S. laws prohibiting employment discrimination apply in all circumstances to U.S. employees working for U.S. employers abroad?

The Learning Objectives above are designed to help improve your understanding of the chapter.

(Moody75/Creative Commons)

International business transactions are not unique to the modern world. What is new in our day is the dramatic growth in world trade and the emergence of a global business community. Because exchanges of goods, services, and ideas on a global level are now routine, students of business law and the legal environment should be familiar with the laws pertaining to international business transactions. Future businesspersons should also be aware that in response to the latest economic recession, the U.S. government has undertaken an initiative to encourage exports of goods and services to foreign markets by U.S. companies. Accordingly, we examine this recent initiative in this chapter.

Laws affecting the international legal environment of business include both international law and national law. **International law** can be defined as a body of law—formed as a result of international customs, treaties, and organizations—that governs relations among or between nations. International law may be public, creating standards for the nations themselves; or it may be private, establishing international standards for private transactions that cross national borders. *National law* is the law of a particular nation, such as Brazil, Germany, Japan, or the United States.

In this chapter, we examine how both international law and national law frame business operations in the global context. We also look at some selected areas relating to business activities in a global context, including international sales contracts, civil dispute resolution, letters of credit, and investment protection. We conclude the chapter with a discussion of the application of certain U.S. laws in an international setting.

International Law—Sources and Principles

The major difference between international law and national law is that government authorities can enforce national law. What government, however, can enforce international law? By definition, a *nation* is a sovereign entity—meaning that there is no higher authority to which that nation must submit. If a nation violates an international law and persuasive tactics fail, other countries or international organizations have no recourse except to take coercive actions—from severance of diplomatic relations and boycotts to, as a last resort, war—against the violating nation.

In essence, international law attempts to reconcile the need of each country to be the final authority over its own affairs with the desire of nations to benefit economically from trade and harmonious relations with one another. Sovereign nations can, and do, voluntarily agree to be governed in certain respects by international law for the purpose of facilitating international trade and commerce, as well as civilized discourse. As a result, a body of international law has evolved.

Sources of International Law

Basically, there are three sources of international law: international customs, treaties and international agreements, and international organizations. We look at each of these sources here.

International Customs One important source of international law consists of the international customs that have evolved among nations in their relations with one another. Article 38(1) of the Statute of the International Court of Justice refers to an international custom as "evidence of a general practice accepted as law." The legal principles and doctrines that you will read about shortly are rooted in international customs and traditions that have evolved over time in the international arena.

Treaties and International Agreements Treaties and other explicit agreements between or among foreign nations provide another important source of international law. A **treaty** is an agreement or contract between two or more nations that must be authorized and ratified by the supreme power of each nation. Under Article II, Section 2, of the U.S. Constitution, the president has the power "by and with the Advice and Consent of the Senate, to make Treaties, provided two-thirds of the Senators present concur."

A *bilateral* agreement, as the term implies, is an agreement formed by two nations to govern their commercial exchanges or other relations with one another. A *multilateral* agreement is formed by several nations. For example, regional trade associations such as the Andean Common Market, the Association of Southeast Asian Nations, and the European Union are the result of multilateral trade agreements.

International Organizations In international law, the term **international organization** generally refers to an organization that is composed mainly of officials of member nations and usually established by treaty. The United States is a member of more than one hundred multilateral and bilateral organizations, including at least twenty through the United Nations. These organizations adopt resolutions, declarations, and other types of standards that often require nations to behave in a particular manner. The General Assembly of the United Nations, for example, has adopted numerous nonbinding resolutions and declarations that embody principles of international law. Disputes involving these resolutions and declarations may be brought before the International Court of Justice. That court, however, normally has authority to settle legal disputes only when nations voluntarily submit to its jurisdiction.

The United Nations Commission on International Trade Law has made considerable progress in establishing uniformity in international law as it relates to trade and commerce. One of the commission's most significant creations to date is the 1980 Convention on Contracts for the International Sale of Goods (CISG). As discussed in Chapter 13, the CISG is similar to Article 2 of the Uniform Commercial Code. It is designed to settle disputes between parties to sales contracts if the parties have not agreed otherwise in their contracts. The CISG governs only sales contracts between trading partners in nations that have ratified the CISG, however.

International Principles and Doctrines

Over time, a number of legal principles and doctrines have evolved and have been employed by the courts of various nations to resolve or reduce conflicts that involve a foreign element. The three important legal principles discussed next are based primarily on courtesy and respect, and are applied in the interests of maintaining harmonious relations among nations.

The Principle of Comity Under the principle of **comity,** one nation will defer to and give effect to the laws and judicial decrees of another country, as long as they are consistent with the law and public policy of the accommodating nation.

CASE EXAMPLE 31.1 Karen Goldberg's husband was killed in a terrorist bombing in Israel. She filed a lawsuit in a federal court in New York against UBS AG, a Switzerland-based global financial services company with many offices in the United States. Goldberg claimed that UBS was liable under the U.S. Anti-Terrorism Act for aiding and abetting the murder of her husband because it provided financial services to the international terrorist organizations responsible for his murder. UBS argued that the case should be transferred to a court in Israel, which would offer a remedy "substantially the same" as the one available in the United States. The court refused to transfer the case, however, because that would require an Israeli court to take evidence and judge the emotional damage suffered by Goldberg, "raising distinct concerns of comity and enforceability." U.S. courts hesitate to impose U.S. law on foreign courts when such law is "an unwarranted intrusion" on the policies governing a foreign nation's judicial system.[1] •

1. *Goldberg v. UBS AG,* 690 F.Supp.2d 92 (E.D.N.Y. 2010).

One way to understand the principle of comity (and the *act of state doctrine,* which will be discussed shortly) is to consider the relationships among the states in our federal form of government. Each state honors (gives "full faith and credit" to) the contracts, property deeds, wills, and other legal obligations formed in other states, as well as judicial decisions with respect to such obligations. On a worldwide basis, nations similarly attempt to honor judgments rendered in other countries when it is feasible to do so. Of course, in the United States the states are constitutionally required to honor other states' actions, whereas internationally, nations are not *required* to honor the actions of other nations.

THE ACT OF STATE DOCTRINE The **act of state doctrine** provides that the judicial branch of one country will not examine the validity of public acts committed by a recognized foreign government within its own territory.

A government controls the natural resources, such as oil reserves, within its territory. It can decide to exploit the resources or preserve them, or to establish a balance between exploitation and preservation. Does the act of state doctrine apply to such decisions even though they may affect market prices in other countries? That was the question in the following case.

Case 31.1 Spectrum Stores, Inc. v. Citgo Petroleum Corp.

United States Court of Appeals, Fifth District, 632 F.3d 938 (2011).
www.ca5.uscourts.gov[a]

FACTS Spectrum Stores, Inc., and other U.S. gasoline retailers (the plaintiffs) filed a suit against Citgo Petroleum Corporation and other oil production companies in a federal district court. The plaintiffs alleged that the defendants had conspired to fix the prices of crude oil and refined petroleum products in the United States, primarily by limiting the production of crude oil. Citgo is owned by the national oil company of Venezuela, and most of the other defendants are owned entirely or in part by Venezuela or Saudi Arabia. Both nations are members of the Organization of Petroleum Exporting Countries (OPEC), which was formed by several oil-rich nations "to ensure the stabilization of oil markets in order to secure an efficient, economic and regular supply of petroleum." Spectrum sought damages, an injunction, and other relief. The court dismissed the suit, and Spectrum appealed.

ISSUE Does the act of state doctrine prevent a federal court from considering claims that companies owned by foreign governments had illegally conspired to fix oil prices in the United States?

a. In the left column, in the "Opinions" section, click on "Opinions Page." On the next page, in the "Search for opinions where:" section, in the "and/or Docket number is:" box, type "09-20084" and click on "Search." In the result, click on the docket number to access the opinion. (The title listed is "In Re: Refined Petro, et al.) The U.S. Court of Appeals for the Fifth Circuit maintains this Web site.

DECISION Yes. The U.S. Court of Appeals for the Fifth Circuit affirmed the lower court's dismissal. The act of state doctrine barred consideration of Spectrum's claims.

REASON The court reasoned that under the act of state doctrine, a U.S. court will not rule on the validity of a foreign government's acts within its own territory. It is the sovereign right of each nation to decide how to exploit its own resources. Granting relief to Spectrum would effectively have ordered foreign governments to dismantle their chosen means of exploiting the resources within their own territories. Such a decision would also have had the effect of "embarrassing" the diplomacy carried out by the executive and legislative branches of the U.S. government. In other words, a ruling in this case would have interfered with the political branches' policy of affecting the global supply of oil by engaging with the OPEC nations in diplomacy rather than litigation.

FOR CRITICAL ANALYSIS—Legal Consideration *If the judicial branch does not have the authority to rule on matters of foreign policy, which branch of government does? Explain.*

When a Foreign Government Takes Private Property. The act of state doctrine can have important consequences for individuals and firms doing business with, and investing in, other countries. This doctrine is frequently employed in cases involving **expropriation,** which occurs when a government seizes a privately owned business or privately owned goods for a proper public purpose and awards just compensation. When a government seizes private property for an illegal purpose and without just compensation, the taking is referred to as a **confiscation.** The line between these two forms of taking is sometimes blurred because of differing interpretations of what is illegal and what constitutes just compensation.

EXAMPLE 31.2 Flaherty, Inc., a U.S. company, owns a mine in Brazil. The government of Brazil seizes the mine for public use and claims that the profits Flaherty has already realized from the mine constitute just compensation. Flaherty disagrees, but the act of state doctrine may prevent that company's recovery in a U.S. court. ● Note that in a case alleging that a foreign government has wrongfully taken the plaintiff's property, the defendant government has the burden of proving that the taking was an expropriation, not a confiscation.

Doctrine May Immunize a Foreign Government's Actions. When applicable, both the act of state doctrine and the doctrine of *sovereign immunity*, which we discuss next, tend to shield foreign nations from the jurisdiction of U.S. courts. As a result, firms or individuals who own property overseas generally have little legal protection against government actions in the countries where they operate.

THE DOCTRINE OF SOVEREIGN IMMUNITY When certain conditions are satisfied, the doctrine of **sovereign immunity** immunizes foreign nations from the jurisdiction of U.S. courts. In 1976, Congress codified this rule in the Foreign Sovereign Immunities Act (FSIA).[2] The FSIA exclusively governs the circumstances in which an action may be brought in the United States against a foreign nation, including attempts to attach a foreign nation's property. Because the law is jurisdictional in nature, a plaintiff has the burden of showing that a defendant is not entitled to sovereign immunity.

Section 1605 of the FSIA sets forth the major exceptions to the jurisdictional immunity of a foreign state. A foreign state is not immune from the jurisdiction of U.S. courts in the following situations:

1. When the foreign state has waived its immunity either explicitly or by implication.
2. When the foreign state has engaged in commercial activity within the United States or in commercial activity outside the United States that has "a direct effect in the United States."[3]
3. When the foreign state has committed a tort in the United States or has violated certain international laws.

In applying the FSIA, questions frequently arise as to whether an entity is a "foreign state" and what constitutes a "commercial activity." Under Section 1603 of the FSIA, a *foreign state* includes both a political subdivision of a foreign state and an instrumentality of a foreign state. Section 1603 broadly defines a *commercial activity* as a regular course of commercial conduct, transaction, or act that is carried out by a foreign state within the United States. Section 1603, however, does not describe the particulars of what constitutes a commercial activity. Thus, the courts are left to decide whether a particular activity is governmental or commercial in nature.

Doing Business Internationally

A U.S. domestic firm can engage in international business transactions in a number of ways. The simplest way is for U.S. firms to **export** their goods and services to markets abroad.

2. 28 U.S.C. Sections 1602–1611.
3. See, for example, *O'Bryan v. Holy See*, 556 F.3d 361 (6th Cir. 2009).

Alternatively, a U.S. firm can establish foreign production facilities so as to be closer to the foreign market or markets in which its products are sold. The advantages may include lower labor costs, fewer government regulations, and lower taxes and trade barriers. A domestic firm can also obtain revenues by licensing its technology to an existing foreign company.

Exporting

Exporting can take two forms: direct exporting and indirect exporting. In *direct exporting*, a U.S. company signs a sales contract with a foreign purchaser that provides for the conditions of shipment and payment for the goods. (How payments are made in international transactions will be discussed later in this chapter.) If sufficient business develops in a foreign country, a U.S. corporation may set up a specialized marketing organization in that foreign market by appointing a foreign agent or a foreign distributor. This is called *indirect exporting*.

When a U.S. firm desires to limit its involvement in an international market, it will typically establish an *agency relationship* with a foreign firm (see Chapter 21). The foreign firm then acts as the U.S. firm's agent and can enter into contracts in the foreign location on behalf of the principal (the U.S. company).

DISTRIBUTORSHIPS When a foreign country represents a substantial market, a U.S. firm may wish to appoint a distributor located in that country. The U.S. firm and the distributor enter into a **distribution agreement,** which is a contract between the seller and the distributor setting out the terms and conditions of the distributorship. These terms and conditions—for example, price, currency of payment, availability of supplies, and method of payment—primarily involve contract law. Disputes concerning distribution agreements may involve jurisdictional or other issues, as well as contract law, which will be discussed later in this chapter.

THE NATIONAL EXPORT INITIATIVE Although the United States is one of the world's major exporters, exports make up a much smaller share of annual output in the United States than they do in our most important trading partners. This is because the United States has not promoted exports as actively as many other nations have.

In an effort to increase U.S. exports, in 2010 the Obama administration created the National Export Initiative (NEI) with a goal of doubling U.S. exports by 2015. Some commentators believe that another goal of the NEI is to reduce outsourcing—the practice of having manufacturing or other activities performed in lower-wage countries such as China and India. Especially in view of the stubbornly high U.S. unemployment rate, there is increasing concern that U.S. jobs are being shipped overseas.

Export Promotion. An important component of the NEI is the Export Promotion Cabinet, which consists of officials from sixteen government agencies and departments. All cabinet members must submit detailed plans to the president, outlining the steps that they will take to increase U.S. exports.

The U.S. Commerce Department plays a leading role in the NEI, and hundreds of its trade experts serve as advocates to help some twenty thousand U.S. companies increase their export sales. In addition, the Commerce Department and other cabinet members will work to promote U.S. exports in the high-growth developing markets of Brazil, China, and India. The members will also identify market opportunities in fast-growing sectors, such as environmental goods and services, biotechnology, and renewable energy.

Increased Export Financing. Under the NEI, the Export-Import Bank of the United States is increasing the financing that it makes available to small and medium-sized businesses by 50 percent. In the initial phase, the bank added hundreds of new small-business clients that sell a wide variety of products, from sophisticated polymers to date palm trees and nanotechnology-based cosmetics. In addition, the administration has proposed that $30 billion be used to boost lending to small businesses, especially for export purposes.

Manufacturing Abroad

An alternative to direct or indirect exporting is the establishment of foreign manufacturing facilities. Typically, U.S. firms establish manufacturing plants abroad if they believe that doing so will reduce their costs—particularly for labor, shipping, and raw materials—and enable them to compete more effectively in foreign markets. Foreign firms have done the same in the United States. Sony, Nissan, and other Japanese manufacturers have established U.S. plants to avoid import duties that the U.S. Congress may impose on Japanese products entering this country.

LICENSING A U.S. firm may license a foreign manufacturing company to use its copyrighted, patented, or trademarked intellectual property or trade secrets. Like any other licensing agreement (see Chapter 5), a licensing agreement with a foreign-based firm calls for a payment of royalties on some basis—such as so many cents per unit produced or a certain percentage of profits from units sold in a particular geographic territory.

EXAMPLE 31.3 The Coca-Cola Bottling Company licenses firms worldwide to employ (and keep confidential) its secret formula for the syrup used in its soft drink. In return, the foreign firms licensed to make the syrup pay Coca-Cola a percentage of the income earned from the sale of the soft drink. • Once a firm's trademark is known worldwide, the firm may experience increased demand for other products it manufactures or sells—obviously an important consideration.

SUBSIDIARIES Another way to expand into a foreign market is to establish a wholly owned subsidiary firm in a foreign country. When a wholly owned subsidiary is established, the parent company, which remains in the United States, retains complete ownership of all the facilities in the foreign country, as well as complete authority and control over all phases of the operation.

A U.S. firm can also expand into international markets through a joint venture. In a joint venture, the U.S. company owns only part of the operation. The rest is owned either by local owners in the foreign country or by another foreign entity. All of the firms involved in a joint venture share responsibilities, as well as profits and liabilities.

Regulation of Specific Business Activities

Doing business abroad can affect the economies, foreign policies, domestic policies, and other national interests of the countries involved. For this reason, nations impose laws to restrict or facilitate international business. Controls may also be imposed by international agreements. Here, we discuss how different types of international activities are regulated.

Investment Protections

Firms that invest in foreign nations face the risk that the foreign government may take possession of the investment property. Expropriation, as already mentioned, occurs when property is taken and the owner is paid just compensation for what is taken.

Expropriation generally does not violate observed principles of international law. Such principles are normally violated, however, when a government confiscates property without compensation (or without adequate compensation). Few remedies are available for confiscation of property by a foreign government. Claims are often resolved by lump-sum settlements after negotiations between the United States and the taking nation.

To counter the deterrent effect that the possibility of confiscation may have on potential investors, many countries guarantee that foreign investors will be compensated if their property is taken. A guaranty can take the form of statutory laws or provisions in international treaties. As further protection for foreign investments, some countries provide insurance for their citizens' investments abroad.

Export Controls

The U.S. Constitution provides in Article I, Section 9, that "No Tax or Duty shall be laid on Articles exported from any State." Thus, Congress cannot impose any export taxes. Congress can, however, use a variety of other devices to control exports. Congress may set export quotas on various items, such as grain being sold abroad. Under the Export Administration Act of 1979,[4] the flow of technologically advanced products and technical data can be restricted.

While restricting certain exports, the United States (and other nations) also uses devices such as export incentives and subsidies to stimulate other exports and thereby aid domestic businesses. Under the Export Trading Company Act of 1982,[5] U.S. banks are encouraged to invest in export trading companies, which are formed when exporting firms join together to export a line of goods. The Export-Import Bank of the United States provides financial assistance, consisting primarily of credit guaranties given to commercial banks that in turn lend funds to U.S. exporting companies.

Import Controls

All nations have restrictions on imports, and the United States is no exception. Restrictions include strict prohibitions, quotas, and tariffs. Under the Trading with the Enemy Act of 1917,[6] for instance, no goods may be imported from nations that have been designated enemies of the United States.

Other laws prohibit the importation of illegal drugs, books that urge insurrection against the United States, and agricultural products that pose dangers to domestic crops or animals. The import of goods that infringe U.S. patents is also prohibited. The International Trade Commission investigates allegations that imported goods infringe U.S. patents and imposes penalties if necessary.

4. 50 U.S.C. Sections 2401–2420.
5. 15 U.S.C. Sections 4001, 4003.
6. 12 U.S.C. Section 95a.

Quotas and Tariffs Limits on the amounts of goods that can be imported are known as **quotas.** At one time, the United States had legal quotas on the number of automobiles that could be imported from Japan. Today, Japan "voluntarily" restricts the number of automobiles exported to the United States. **Tariffs** are taxes on imports. A tariff usually is a percentage of the value of the import, but it can be a flat rate per unit (for example, per barrel of oil). Tariffs raise the prices of goods, causing some consumers to purchase more domestically manufactured goods and fewer imported goods.

Sometimes, countries impose tariffs on goods from a particular nation in retaliation for political acts. **EXAMPLE 31.4** In 2009, Mexico imposed tariffs of 10 to 20 percent on ninety products exported from the United States in retaliation for the Obama administration's cancellation of a cross-border trucking program. The program had been instituted to comply with a provision in the North American Free Trade Agreement (discussed shortly) that was intended to eventually grant Mexican trucks full access to U.S. highways. U.S truck drivers opposed the program, however, and consumer protection groups claimed that the Mexican trucks posed safety issues. Because the Mexican tariffs were imposed annually on $2.4 billion of U.S. goods, in 2011 President Barack Obama negotiated a deal that allowed Mexican truckers to enter the United States. In exchange, Mexico agreed to suspend half of the tariffs immediately and the remainder when the first Mexican hauler complied with the new U.S. requirements. • The agreement officially ended the ban on Mexican trucks crossing the U.S. border.

In the following case, an importer provided invoices that understated the value of its imports and resulted in lower tariffs than would have been paid on the full value of the goods. Was this fraud or negligence?

Case 31.2 United States v. Inn Foods, Inc.

United States Court of Appeals, Federal Circuit, 560 F.3d 1338 (2009).
www.cafc.uscourts.gov[a]

FACTS Between 1987 and 1990, Inn Foods, Inc., imported frozen produce from six Mexican growers who agreed to issue invoices that understated the value of the produce. For each understated invoice, Inn Foods sent an order confirmation that estimated the produce's actual market value. Inn Foods later remitted the difference to the growers. Through this double-invoicing system, Inn Foods undervalued its purchases by approximately $3.5 million and paid lower tariff taxes as a result. During an investigation by U.S. Customs and Border Protection, Inn Foods' accounting supervisor denied the existence of the double invoices. The federal government filed an action in the U.S. Court of International Trade against Inn Foods. The court held the defendant liable for fraud and assessed the amount of the unpaid taxes—$624,602.55—plus an additional penalty of $7.5 million. Inn Foods appealed, claiming that it had acted negligently, not fraudulently.

a. In the links at the bottom of the page, click on "Opinions & Orders." On that page, in the "Search By:" box, type "Inn Foods" and click on "Search." In the result, click on the link to access the opinion. The U.S. Court of Appeals for the Federal Circuit maintains this Web site.

ISSUE Does an importer's use of a double-invoicing system constitute proof of an intent to defraud the government of import duties?

DECISION Yes. The U.S. Court of Appeals for the Federal Circuit affirmed the lower court's judgment.

REASON The court reasoned that the evidence showed Inn Foods "knowingly entered goods by means of a material false statement." Each

Case 31.2–Continued

grower sent Inn Foods a copy of an undervalued invoice. The company knew that these invoices were "grossly undervalued and false"–the growers set out the details of the specific undervaluation in correspondence to Inn Foods. On receipt, Inn Foods adjusted the prices to reflect their true estimated value. The company entered the higher amount into its accounting system, sent a confirmation to the grower with the higher price, and paid the grower based on the confirmed price. But Inn Foods knew the false invoices would be used to import goods into the United States. The company used the undervalued invoices to declare the value of the produce to U.S. Customs and Border Protection for import. Moreover, Inn Foods concealed the existence of the double invoices during the government's investigation.

FOR CRITICAL ANALYSIS—Ethical Consideration *After Inn Foods learned of the investigation, the company included a disclaimer on some shipments stating that the declared value "is strictly for customs clearance" while the company determines the "true transaction value." Does this disclaimer legally or ethically absolve the importer of intent to defraud?*

ANTIDUMPING DUTIES The United States has laws specifically directed at what it sees as unfair international trade practices. **Dumping,** for example, is the sale of imported goods at "less than fair value." "Fair value" is usually determined by the price of those goods in the exporting country. Foreign firms that engage in dumping in the United States hope to undersell U.S. businesses to obtain a larger share of the U.S. market. To prevent this, an extra tariff—known as an *antidumping duty*—may be assessed on the imports.

Minimizing Trade Barriers

Restrictions on imports are also known as *trade barriers.* The elimination of trade barriers is sometimes seen as essential to the world's economic well-being. Most of the world's leading trading nations are members of the World Trade Organization (WTO), which was established in 1995. To minimize trade barriers among nations, each member country of the WTO is required to grant **normal trade relations (NTR) status** (formerly known as most-favored-nation status) to other member countries. This means each member is obligated to treat other members at least as well as it treats the country that receives its most favorable treatment with regard to imports or exports. Various regional trade agreements and associations also help to minimize trade barriers between nations.

THE EUROPEAN UNION (EU) The European Union (EU) arose out the 1957 Treaty of Rome, which created the Common Market, a free trade zone comprising the nations of Belgium, France, Italy, Luxembourg, the Netherlands, and West Germany. Today, the EU is a single integrated trading unit made up of twenty-seven European nations.

The EU has gone a long way toward creating a new body of law to govern all of the member nations—although some of its efforts to create uniform laws have been confounded by nationalism. The council and the commission issue regulations, or directives, that define EU law in various areas, such as environmental law, product liability, anticompetitive practices, and corporations. The directives normally are binding on all member countries.

THE NORTH AMERICAN FREE TRADE AGREEMENT The North American Free Trade Agreement (NAFTA) created a regional trading unit consisting of Canada, Mexico, and the United States. The goal of NAFTA is to eliminate tariffs among these three countries on substantially all goods by reducing the tariffs incrementally over a period of time. NAFTA gives the three countries a competitive advantage by retaining tariffs on goods imported from countries outside the NAFTA trading unit.

Additionally, NAFTA provides for the elimination of barriers that traditionally have prevented the cross-border movement of services, such as financial and transportation services. NAFTA also attempts to eliminate citizenship requirements for the licensing of accountants, attorneys, physicians, and other professionals.

THE CENTRAL AMERICA–DOMINICAN REPUBLIC–UNITED STATES FREE TRADE AGREEMENT The Central America–Dominican Republic–United States Free Trade Agreement (CAFTA-DR) was formed by Costa Rica, the Dominican Republic, El Salvador, Guatemala, Honduras, Nicaragua, and the United States. Its purpose is to reduce tariffs and improve market access among all of the signatory nations, including the United States. Legislatures from all seven countries have approved the CAFTA-DR, despite significant opposition in certain nations.

Bribing Foreign Officials

Giving cash or in-kind benefits to foreign government officials to obtain business contracts and other favors is often considered normal practice. To reduce such bribery by representatives of U.S. corporations, Congress enacted the Foreign Corrupt Practices Act in 1977.[7] This act and its implications for American businesspersons engaged in international business transactions were discussed in Chapter 6.

7. 15 U.S.C. Sections 78m–78ff.

Commercial Contracts in an International Setting

Like all commercial contracts, an international contract should be in writing. For an example of an actual international sales contract from Starbucks Coffee Company, refer back to the appendix at the end of Chapter 13.

Contract Clauses

Language and legal differences among nations can create special problems for parties to international contracts when disputes arise. To avoid these problems, parties should include special provisions in the contract that designate the language of the contract, where any disputes will be resolved, and the substantive law that will be applied in settling any disputes. Parties to international contracts should also indicate in their contracts what acts or events will excuse the parties from performance under the contract and whether disputes under the contract will be arbitrated or litigated.

CHOICE OF LANGUAGE A deal struck between a U.S. company and a company in another country normally involves two languages. Typically, many phrases in one language are not readily translatable into another. Consequently, the complex contractual terms involved may not be understood by one party in the other party's language. To make sure that no disputes arise out of this language problem, an international sales contract should have a **choice-of-language clause** designating the official language by which the contract will be interpreted in the event of disagreement.

CHOICE OF FORUM When a dispute arises, litigation may be pursued in courts of different nations. There are no universally accepted rules as to which court has jurisdiction over a particular subject matter or parties to a dispute. Consequently, parties to an international transaction should always include in the contract a **forum-selection clause** indicating what court, jurisdiction, or tribunal will decide any disputes arising under the contract. It is especially important to indicate the specific court that will have jurisdiction. The forum does not necessarily have to be within the geographic boundaries of the home nation of either party.

CASE EXAMPLE 31.5 Garware Polyester, Ltd., based in Mumbai, India, developed and made plastics and high-tech polyester film. Intermax Trading Corporation, based in New York, acted as Garware's North American sales agent and sold its products on a commission basis. Garware and Intermax had executed a series of agency agreements under which the courts of Mumbai, India, would have exclusive jurisdiction over any disputes relating to their agreement. When Intermax fell behind in its payments to Garware, Garware filed a lawsuit in a U.S. court to collect the balance due, claiming that the forum-selection clause did not apply to sales of warehoused goods. The court, however, sided with Intermax. Because the forum-selection clause was valid and enforceable, Garware had to bring its complaints against Intermax in a court in India.[8] •

CHOICE OF LAW A contractual provision designating the applicable law—such as the law of Germany or the United Kingdom or California—is called a **choice-of-law clause**. Every international contract typically includes a choice-of-law clause. At common law (and in European civil law systems), parties are allowed to choose the law that will govern their contractual relationship, provided that the law chosen is the law of a jurisdiction that has a substantial relationship to the parties and to the international business transaction.

Under Section 1–105 of the Uniform Commercial Code, parties may choose the law that will govern the contract as long as the choice is "reasonable." Article 6 of the United Nations Convention on Contracts for the International Sale of Goods (discussed in Chapter 13 on page 241), however, imposes no limitation on the parties' choice of what law will govern the contract. The 1986 Hague Convention on the Law Applicable to Contracts for the International Sale of Goods—often referred to as the Choice-of-Law Convention—allows unlimited autonomy in the choice of law. The Hague Convention indicates that whenever a contract does not specify a choice of law, the governing law is that of the country in which the *seller's* place of business is located.

FORCE MAJEURE CLAUSE Every contract, particularly those involving international transactions, should have a ***force majeure* clause.** *Force majeure* is a French term meaning "impossible or irresistible force"—sometimes loosely identified as "an act of God." In international business contracts, *force majeure* clauses commonly stipulate that in addition to acts of God, a number of other eventualities (such as government orders or embargoes, for example) may excuse a party from liability for nonperformance.

Civil Dispute Resolution

International contracts frequently include arbitration clauses. By means of such clauses, the parties agree in advance to be bound by the decision of a specified third party in the event of a dispute, as discussed in Chapter 2. (For an example of an arbitration clause in an international contract, refer to the appendix at the end of Chapter 13.) The United Nations Convention on the Recognition and Enforcement of Foreign Arbitral Awards (often referred to as the New York Convention) assists in the enforcement of arbitration clauses, as do provisions in specific

8. *Garware Polyester, Ltd. v. Intermax Trading Corp.*, ___ F.Supp.2d ___ (S.D.N.Y. 2001); see also *Laasko v. Xerox Corp.*, 566 F.Supp.2d 1018 (C.D.Cal. 2008).

treaties among nations. The New York Convention has been implemented in nearly one hundred countries, including the United States.

If a sales contract does not include an arbitration clause, litigation may occur. If the contract contains forum-selection and choice-of-law clauses, the lawsuit will be heard by a court in the specified forum and decided according to that forum's law. If no forum and choice of law have been specified, however, legal proceedings will be more complex and attended by much more uncertainty. For instance, litigation may take place in two or more countries, with each country applying its own choice-of-law rules to determine the substantive law that will be applied to the particular transactions. Even if a plaintiff wins a favorable judgment in a lawsuit litigated in the plaintiff's country, there is no way to predict whether courts in the defendant's country will enforce the judgment.

Payment Methods for International Transactions

Currency differences between nations and the geographic distance between parties to international sales contracts add a degree of complexity to international sales that does not exist in the domestic market. Because international contracts involve greater financial risks, special care should be taken in drafting these contracts to specify both the currency in which payment is to be made and the method of payment.

Monetary Systems

Although our national currency, the U.S. dollar, is one of the primary forms of international currency, any U.S. firm undertaking business transactions abroad must be prepared to deal with one or more other currencies. After all, a Japanese firm may want to be paid in Japanese yen for goods and services sold outside Japan. Both firms therefore must rely on the convertibility of currencies.

Currencies are convertible when they can be freely exchanged one for the other at some specified market rate in a **foreign exchange market.** Foreign exchange markets make up a worldwide system for the buying and selling of foreign currencies. The foreign exchange rate is simply the price of a unit of one country's currency in terms of another country's currency. For example, if today's exchange rate is one hundred Japanese yen for one dollar, that means that anybody with one hundred yen can obtain one dollar, and vice versa. Like other prices, the exchange rate is set by the forces of supply and demand.

Frequently, a U.S. company can rely on its domestic bank to take care of all international transfers of funds. Commercial banks often transfer funds internationally through their **correspondent banks** in other countries. **EXAMPLE 31.6** A customer of Citibank wishes to pay a bill in euros to a company in Paris. Citibank can draw a bank check payable in euros on its account in Crédit Agricole, a Paris correspondent bank, and then send the check to the French company to which its customer owes the funds. Alternatively, Citibank's customer can request a wire transfer of the funds to the French company. Citibank instructs Crédit Agricole by wire to pay the necessary amount in euros. •

Letters of Credit

Because buyers and sellers engaged in international business transactions are frequently separated by thousands of miles, special precautions are often taken to ensure performance under the contract. Sellers want to avoid delivering goods for which they might not be paid. Buyers desire the assurance that sellers will not be paid until there is evidence that the goods have been shipped. Thus, **letters of credit** are frequently used to facilitate international business transactions.

PARTIES TO A LETTER OF CREDIT In a simple letter-of-credit transaction, the *issuer* (a bank) agrees to issue a letter of credit and to ascertain whether the *beneficiary* (seller) performs certain acts. In return, the *account party* (buyer) promises to reimburse the issuer for the amount paid to the beneficiary. The transaction may also involve an *advising bank* that transmits information and a *paying bank* that expedites payment under the letter of credit. See Exhibit 31–1 on the following page for an illustration of a letter-of-credit transaction.

Under a letter of credit, the issuer is bound to pay the beneficiary (seller) when the beneficiary has complied with the terms and conditions of the letter of credit. The beneficiary looks to the issuer, not to the account party (buyer), when it presents the documents required by the letter of credit. Typically, the letter of credit will require that the beneficiary deliver a *bill of lading* to the issuing bank to prove that shipment has been made. A letter of credit assures the beneficiary (seller) of payment and at the same time assures the account party (buyer) that payment will not be made until the beneficiary has complied with the terms and conditions of the letter of credit.

THE VALUE OF A LETTER OF CREDIT The basic principle behind letters of credit is that payment is made against the documents presented by the beneficiary and not against the facts that the documents purport to reflect. Thus, in a letter-of-credit transaction, the issuer does not police the underlying contract. A letter of credit is independent of the underlying contract between the buyer and the seller. Eliminating the need for banks (issuers) to inquire into whether actual contractual conditions have been satisfied greatly reduces the costs of letters of credit. Moreover, the use of a letter of credit protects both buyers and sellers.

• ***Exhibit* 31–1 A Letter-of-Credit Transaction**

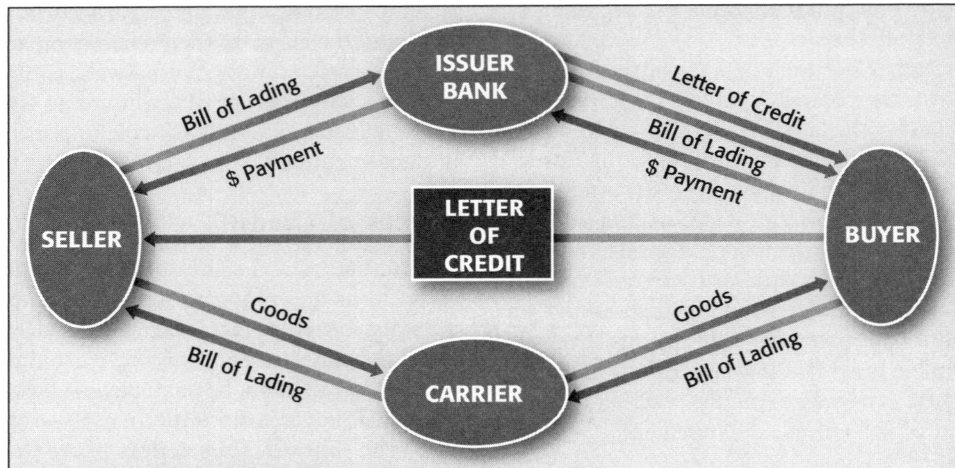

CHRONOLOGY OF EVENTS

1. Buyer contracts with issuer bank to issue a letter of credit; this sets forth the bank's obligation to pay on the letter of credit and buyer's obligation to pay the bank.
2. Letter of credit is sent to seller informing seller that on compliance with the terms of the letter of credit (such as presentment of necessary documents–in this example, a bill of lading), the bank will issue payment for the goods.
3. Seller delivers goods to carrier and receives a bill of lading.
4. Seller delivers the bill of lading to issuer bank and, if the document is proper, receives payment.
5. Issuer bank delivers the bill of lading to buyer.
6. Buyer delivers the bill of lading to carrier.
7. Carrier delivers the goods to buyer.
8. Buyer settles with issuer bank.

U.S. Laws in a Global Context

The internationalization of business raises questions about the extraterritorial application of a nation's laws—that is, the effect of the country's laws outside its boundaries. To what extent do U.S. domestic laws apply to other nations' businesses? To what extent do U.S. domestic laws apply to U.S. firms doing business abroad? Here, we discuss the extraterritorial application of certain U.S. laws, including tort laws and laws prohibiting employment discrimination.

International Tort Claims

The international application of tort liability is growing in significance and controversy. An increasing number of U.S. plaintiffs are suing foreign (or U.S.) entities for torts that these entities have allegedly committed overseas. Often, these cases involve human rights violations by foreign governments. The Alien Tort Claims Act (ATCA),[9] adopted in 1789, allows even foreign citizens to bring civil suits in U.S. courts for injuries caused by violations of international law or a treaty of the United States.

Since 1980, plaintiffs have increasingly used the ATCA to bring actions against companies operating in other countries. ATCA actions have been brought against companies doing business in nations such as Colombia, Ecuador, Egypt, Guatemala, India, Indonesia, Nigeria, and Saudi Arabia. Some of these cases have involved alleged environmental destruction. In addition, mineral companies in Southeast Asia have been sued for collaborating with oppressive government regimes.

The following case involved claims against hundreds of corporations that allegedly "aided and abetted" the government of South Africa in maintaining its apartheid (racially discriminatory) regime.

9. 28 U.S.C. Section 1350.

Case 31.3 Khulumani v. Barclay National Bank, Ltd.

United States Court of Appeals, Second Circuit, 504 F.3d 254 (2007).

FACTS The Khulumani plaintiffs, along with other plaintiff groups, filed class-action claims on behalf of victims of apartheid-related atrocities, human rights violations, crimes against humanity, and unfair and discriminatory forced-labor practices. The plaintiffs brought this action in federal district court under the Alien Tort Claims Act (ATCA) against a number of corporations, including Bank of America, Barclay National Bank, Citigroup, Credit Suisse Group, General Electric, and IBM. The district court dismissed the plaintiffs' complaints in their entirety. The court held that the plaintiffs had failed to establish subject-matter jurisdiction under the ATCA. The plaintiffs appealed to the U.S. Court of Appeals for the Second Circuit.

ISSUE Can the plaintiffs bring a claim against U.S. and foreign companies under the ATCA for "aiding and abetting" human rights violations?

DECISION Yes. The U.S. Court of Appeals for the Second Circuit vacated the district court's dismissal of the plaintiffs' claims and remanded the case for further proceedings. According to the reviewing court, a plaintiff may plead a theory of aiding and abetting liability under the ATCA.

REASON The court stated that the district court "erred in holding that aiding and abetting violations of a customary international law cannot provide a basis for ATCA jurisdiction." The court reasoned that the United States Supreme Court has instructed courts in this nation to exercise caution and carefully evaluate international norms and potential adverse foreign policy consequences in deciding whether to hear ATCA claims. Thus, "the determination whether a norm is sufficiently definite to support a cause of action should (indeed, inevitably must) involve an element of judgment about the practical consequences of making that cause available to litigants in the federal courts." The court rejected the defendants' argument that an adjudication of the case by the U.S. court "would offend amicable working relationships with a foreign country."

FOR CRITICAL ANALYSIS—Ethical Consideration *Should the companies cited as defendants in this case have refused all business dealings with South Africa during the era of apartheid when the country's white government severely limited the rights of the majority black African population?*

Antidiscrimination Laws

Laws in the United States prohibit discrimination on the basis of race, color, national origin, religion, gender, age, and disability, as discussed in Chapter 22. These laws, as they affect employment relationships, generally apply extraterritorially. U.S. employees working abroad for U.S. employers are protected under the Age Discrimination in Employment Act of 1967. The Americans with Disabilities Act of 1990, which requires employers to accommodate the needs of workers with disabilities, also applies to U.S. nationals working abroad for U.S. firms.

In addition, the major law regulating employment discrimination—Title VII of the Civil Rights Act of 1964—also applies extraterritorially to all U.S. employees working for U.S. employers abroad. U.S. employers must abide by U.S. discrimination laws unless to do so would violate the laws of the country where their workplaces are located. This "foreign laws exception" prevents employers from being subjected to conflicting laws.

Reviewing . . . International Law in a Global Economy

Robco, Inc., was a Florida arms dealer. The armed forces of Honduras contracted to purchase weapons from Robco over a six-year period. After the government was replaced and a democracy installed, the Honduran government sought to reduce the size of its military, and its relationship with Robco deteriorated. Honduras refused to honor the contract by purchasing the inventory of arms, which Robco could sell only at a much lower price. Robco filed a suit in a federal district court in the United States to recover damages for this breach of contract by the government of Honduras. Using the information provided in the chapter, answer the following questions.

1. Should the Foreign Sovereign Immunities Act preclude this lawsuit? Why or why not?
2. Does the act of state doctrine bar Robco from seeking to enforce the contract? Explain.
3. Suppose that before this lawsuit, the new government of Honduras had enacted a law making it illegal to purchase weapons from foreign arms dealers. What doctrine might lead a U.S. court to dismiss Robco's case in that situation?
4. Now suppose that the U.S. court hears the case and awards damages to Robco, but the government of Honduras has no assets in the United States that can be used to satisfy the judgment. Under which doctrine might Robco be able to collect the damages by asking another nation's court to enforce the U.S. judgment?

Terms and Concepts

act of state doctrine 595
choice-of-language clause 600
choice-of-law clause 600
comity 594
confiscation 595
correspondent bank 601
distribution agreement 596
dumping 599
export 596
expropriation 595
force majeure clause 600
foreign exchange market 601
forum-selection clause 600
international law 593
international organization 594
letter of credit 601
normal trade relations (NTR) status 599
quota 598
sovereign immunity 596
tariff 598
treaty 594

Chapter Summary: International Law in a Global Economy

International Principles and Doctrines (See pages 594–596.)	1. *The principle of comity*—Under this principle, nations give effect to the laws and judicial decrees of other nations for reasons of courtesy and international harmony. 2. *The act of state doctrine*—A doctrine under which U.S. courts avoid passing judgment on the validity of public acts committed by a recognized foreign government within its own territory. 3. *The doctrine of sovereign immunity*—When certain conditions are satisfied, foreign nations are immune from U.S. jurisdiction under the Foreign Sovereign Immunities Act of 1976. Exceptions are made when a foreign state (a) has waived its immunity either explicitly or by implication, (b) has engaged in commercial activity within the United States, or (c) has committed a tort within the United States.
Doing Business Internationally (See pages 596–597.)	U.S. domestic firms may engage in international business transactions in several ways including (a) exporting, which may involve foreign agents or distributors, and (b) manufacturing abroad through licensing arrangements, wholly owned subsidiaries, or joint ventures.
Regulation of Specific Business Activities (See pages 597–599.)	In the interests of their economies, foreign policies, domestic policies, or other national priorities, nations impose laws that restrict or facilitate international business. Such laws regulate foreign investments, exporting, and importing. The World Trade Organization attempts to minimize trade barriers among nations, as do regional trade agreements and associations, including the European Union and the North American Free Trade Agreement.
Commercial Contracts in an International Setting (See pages 600–601.)	International business contracts often include choice-of-language, forum-selection, and choice-of-law clauses to reduce the uncertainties associated with interpreting the language of the agreement and dealing with legal differences. Most domestic and international contracts include *force majeure* clauses. They commonly stipulate that acts of God and certain other events may excuse a party from liability for nonperformance of the contract. Arbitration clauses are also frequently found in international contracts.
Payment Methods for International Transactions (See pages 601–602.)	1. *Currency conversion*—Because nations have different monetary systems, payment on international contracts requires currency conversion at a rate specified in a foreign exchange market. 2. *Correspondent banking*—Correspondent banks facilitate the transfer of funds from a buyer in one country to a seller in another. 3. *Letters of credit*—Letters of credit facilitate international transactions by ensuring payment to sellers and assuring buyers that payment will not be made until the sellers have complied with the terms of the letters of credit. Typically, compliance occurs when a bill of lading is delivered to the issuing bank.
U.S. Laws in a Global Context (See pages 602–603.)	1. *Tort laws*—U.S. tort laws may be applied beyond the borders of the United States under the Alien Tort Claims Act. 2. *Antidiscrimination laws*—The major U.S. laws prohibiting employment discrimination, including Title VII of the Civil Rights Act of 1964, the Age Discrimination in Employment Act of 1967, and the Americans with Disabilities Act of 1990, cover U.S. employees working abroad for U.S. firms—*unless* to apply the U.S. laws would violate the laws of the host country.

ExamPrep

ISSUE SPOTTERS

—Check your answers to these questions against the answers provided in Appendix G.

1 Café Rojo, Ltd., an Ecuadoran firm, agrees to sell coffee beans to Dark Roast Coffee Company, a U.S. firm. Dark Roast accepts the beans but refuses to pay. Café Rojo sues Dark Roast in an Ecuadoran court and is awarded damages, but Dark Roast's assets are in the United States. Under what circumstances would a U.S. court enforce the judgment of the Ecuadoran court?

2 Gems International, Ltd., is a foreign firm that has a 12 percent share of the U.S. market for diamonds. To capture a larger share, Gems offers its products at a below-cost discount to U.S. buyers (and inflates the prices in its own country to make up the difference). How can this attempt to undersell U.S. businesses be defeated?

BEFORE THE TEST

Go to **www.cengagebrain.com**, enter the ISBN 9781111530624, and click on "Find" to locate this textbook's Web site. Then, click on "Access Now" under "Study Tools," and select Chapter 31 at the top. There, you will find an Interactive Quiz that you can take to assess your mastery of the concepts in this chapter, as well as Flashcards and a Glossary of important terms.

For Review

1 What is the principle of comity, and why do courts deciding disputes involving a foreign law or judicial decree apply this principle?

2 What is the act of state doctrine? In what circumstances is this doctrine applied?

3 Under the Foreign Sovereign Immunities Act of 1976, on what bases might a foreign state be considered subject to the jurisdiction of U.S. courts?

4 What types of provisions, or clauses, are often included in international sales contracts?

5 Do U.S. laws prohibiting employment discrimination apply in all circumstances to U.S. employees working for U.S. employers abroad?

Questions and Case Problems

31–1 **Letters of Credit.** The Swiss Credit Bank issued a letter of credit in favor of Antex Industries to cover the sale of 92,000 electronic integrated circuits manufactured by Electronic Arrays. The letter of credit specified that the chips would be transported to Tokyo by ship. Antex shipped the circuits by air. Payment on the letter of credit was dishonored because the shipment by air did not fulfill the precise terms of the letter of credit. Should a court compel payment? Explain.

31–2 **Dumping.** The U.S. pineapple industry alleged that producers of canned pineapple from the Philippines were selling their canned pineapple in the United States for less than its fair market value (dumping). The Philippine producers also exported other products, such as pineapple juice and juice concentrate, which used separate parts of the same fresh pineapple, so they shared raw material costs, according to the producers' own financial records. To determine fair value and antidumping duties, the plaintiffs argued that a court should calculate the Philippine producers' cost of production and allocate a portion of the shared fruit costs to the canned fruit. The result of this allocation showed that more than 90 percent of the canned fruit sales were below the cost of production. Is this a reasonable approach to determining the production costs and fair market value of canned pineapple in the United States? Why or why not?

31–3 **Dumping.** A newspaper printing press system is more than one hundred feet long, stands four or five stories tall, and weighs 2 million pounds. Only about ten of the systems are sold each year in the United States. Because of the size and cost, a newspaper may update its system, rather than replace it, by buying "additions." By the 1990s, Goss International Corp. was the only domestic maker of the equipment in the United States and represented the entire U.S. market. Tokyo Kikai Seisakusho (TKSC), a Japanese corporation, makes the systems in Japan. In the 1990s, TKSC began to compete in the U.S. market, forcing Goss to cut its prices below cost. TKSC's tactics included offering its customers "secret" rebates on prices that were ultimately substantially less than the products' actual market value in Japan. According to TKSC office memos, the goal was to "win completely this survival game" against Goss, the "enemy." Goss filed a suit in a federal district court against

TKSC and others, alleging illegal dumping. At what point does a foreign firm's attempt to compete with a domestic manufacturer in the United States become illegal dumping? Was that point reached in this case? Discuss. [*Goss International Corp. v. Man Roland Druckmaschinen Aktiengesellschaft,* 434 F.3d 1081 (8th Cir. 2006)]

31–4 Comity. Jan Voda, M.D., a resident of Oklahoma City, Oklahoma, owns three U.S. patents related to guiding catheters for use in interventional cardiology, as well as corresponding foreign patents issued by the European Patent Office, Canada, France, Germany, and Great Britain. Voda filed a suit in a federal district court against Cordis Corp., a U.S. firm, alleging infringement of the U.S. patents under U.S. patent law and of the corresponding foreign patents under the patent law of the various foreign countries. Cordis admitted, "The XB catheters have been sold domestically and internationally since 1994. The XB catheters were manufactured in Miami Lakes, Florida, from 1993 to 2001 and have been manufactured in Juarez, Mexico, since 2001." Cordis argued, however, that Voda could not assert infringement claims under foreign patent law because the court did not have jurisdiction over such claims. Which of the important international legal principles discussed in this chapter would be most likely to apply in this case? How should the court apply it? Explain. [*Voda v. Cordis Corp.,* 476 F.3d 887 (Fed.Cir. 2007)]

31–5 Case Problem with Sample Answer When Ferdinand Marcos was president of the Republic of the Philippines, he put assets into a company called Arelma. Its holdings are in New York. A group of plaintiffs, referred to as the Pimentel class, brought a class-action suit in a U.S. district court for human rights violations by Marcos. They won a judgment of $2 billion and sought to attach Arelma's assets to help pay the judgment. At the same time, the Republic of the Philippines established a commission to recover property wrongfully taken by Marcos. A court in the Philippines was determining whether Marcos's property, including Arelma, should be forfeited to the Republic or to other parties. The Philippine government, in opposition to the Pimentel judgment, moved to dismiss the U.S. court proceedings. The district court refused, and the U.S. Court of Appeals for the Ninth Circuit agreed that the Pimentel class should take the assets. The Republic of the Philippines appealed. What are the key international legal issues? [*Republic of the Philippines v. Pimentel,* 553 U.S. 851, 128 S.Ct. 2180, 171 L.Ed.2d 131 (2008)]

—For a sample answer to Problem 31–5, go to Appendix F at the end of this text.

31–6 Dumping. The fuel for nuclear power plants is low enriched uranium (LEU). LEU consists of feed uranium enriched by energy to a certain assay—its percentage of the isotope necessary for a nuclear reaction. The amount of energy is described by an industry standard as a "separative work unit" (SWU). A nuclear utility may buy LEU from an enricher, or the utility may provide an enricher with feed uranium and pay for the SWUs necessary to produce LEU. Under an SWU contract, the LEU returned to the utility may not be exactly the uranium the utility provided. This is because feed uranium is fungible and trades like a commodity (such as wheat or corn), and profitable enrichment requires the constant processing of undifferentiated stock. LEU imported from foreign enrichers, including Eurodif, S.A., was purportedly being sold in the United States for "less than fair value." Does this constitute dumping? Explain. If so, what could be done to prevent it? [*United States v. Eurodif, S.A.,* 555 U.S. 305, 129 S.Ct. 878, 172 L.Ed.2d 679 (2009)]

31–7 International Agreements and Jurisdiction. The plaintiffs in this case were descendants of Holocaust victims who had lived in various countries in Europe. Before the Holocaust, the plaintiffs' ancestors had purchased insurance policies from Assicurazioni Generali, S.P.A., an Italian insurance company. When Generali refused to pay benefits under the policies, the plaintiffs, who were U.S. citizens and the beneficiaries of these policies, sued for breach of the insurance contracts. Due to certain agreements among nations after World War II, such lawsuits could not be filed for many years. In 2000, however, the United States agreed that Germany could establish a foundation—the International Commission on Holocaust-Era Insurance Claims, or ICHEIC—that would compensate victims who had suffered losses at the hands of the Germans during the war. Whenever a German company was sued in a U.S. court based on a Holocaust-era claim, the U.S. government would inform the court that the matter should be referred to the ICHEIC as the exclusive forum and remedy for the resolution. There was no such agreement with Italy, however. The plaintiffs sued the Italy-based Generali in a U.S. district court. The court dismissed the suit, and the plaintiffs appealed. Did the plaintiffs have to take their claim to the ICHEIC rather than sue in a U.S. court? Why or why not? [*In re Assicurazioni Generali, S.P.A.,* 592 F.3d 113 (2d Cir. 2010)]

31–8 Sovereign Immunity. Bell Helicopter Textron, Inc., designs, makes, and sells helicopters with distinctive and famous trade dress that identifies them as Bell aircraft. Bell also owns the helicopters' design patents. Bell's Model 206 Series includes the Jet Ranger. Thirty-six years after Bell developed the Jet Ranger, the Islamic Republic of Iran began to make and sell counterfeit Model 206 Series helicopters and parts. Iran's counterfeit versions—the Shahed 278 and the Shahed 285—use Bell's *trade dress* (see Chapter 5). The Shahed aircraft was promoted at an international air show in Iran to aircraft customers. Bell filed a suit in a federal district court against Iran, alleging violations of trademark and patent laws. Is Iran—a foreign nation—exempt in these circumstances from the jurisdiction of U.S. courts? Explain. [*Bell Helicopter Textron, Inc. v. Islamic Republic of Iran,* 764 F.Supp.2d 122 (D.D.C. 2011)]

31–9 A Question of Ethics *On December 21, 1988, Pan Am Flight 103 exploded 31,000 feet in the air over Lockerbie, Scotland, killing all 259 passengers and crew on board and 11 people on the ground. Among those killed was Roger Hurst, a U.S. citizen. An investigation determined that a portable radio-cassette player packed in a brown Samsonite suitcase smuggled onto the plane was the source of the explosion. The explosive device* *was constructed with a digital timer specially made for, and bought by, Libya. Abdel Basset Ali Al-Megrahi, a Libyan government official and an employee of the Libyan Arab Airline (LAA), was convicted by the Scottish High Court of Justiciary on criminal charges that he planned and executed the bombing in association with members of the Jamahiriya Security Organization (JSO)—an agency of the Libyan government that performs security and intelligence functions—or the Libyan military. Members of the victims' families filed a suit in a U.S. federal district court against the JSO, the LAA, Al-Megrahi, and others. The plaintiffs claimed violations of U.S. federal law, including the Anti-Terrorism Act, and state law, including the intentional infliction of emotional distress. [*Hurst v. Socialist People's Libyan Arab Jamahiriya, *474 F.Supp.2d 19 (D.D.C. 2007)]*

1 Under what doctrine, codified in which federal statute, might the defendants claim to be immune from the jurisdiction of a U.S. court? Should this law include an exception for "state-sponsored terrorism"? Why or why not?
2 The defendants agreed to pay $2.7 billion, or $10 million per victim, to settle all claims for "compensatory death damages." The families of eleven victims, including Hurst, were excluded from the settlement because they were "not wrongful death beneficiaries under applicable state law." These plaintiffs continued the suit. The defendants filed a motion to dismiss. Should the motion be granted on the ground that the settlement bars the plaintiffs' claims? Explain.

31–10  **Video Question** To watch this chapter's video, *International: Letter of Credit,* go to **www.cengagebrain.com**. Register the access code that came with your new book or log in to your existing account. Select the link for the "Business Law Digital Video Library Online Access" or "Business Law CourseMate." Click on "Complete Video List," view Video 55, and then answer the following questions:

1 Do banks always require the same documents to be presented in letter-of-credit transactions? If not, who dictates what documents will be required in the letter of credit?
2 At what point does the seller receive payment in a letter-of-credit transaction?
3 What assurances does a letter of credit provide to the buyer and the seller involved in the transaction?

Unit Ten

Unit Case Study with Dissenting Opinion: *Dole Food Co. v. Patrickson*

Chapter 31 discusses the Foreign Sovereign Immunities Act of 1976 (FSIA). Under the FSIA, foreign states, or nations, can claim certain rights in suits against them in U.S. courts, including in some circumstances immunity from the litigation. A corporate entity that is an "instrumentality" of a foreign state, as defined in the FSIA, may also avail itself of some of these rights. (Corporations and their characteristics were covered in Chapters 24 and 25.)

In this Unit Case Study with Dissenting Opinion, *we review* Dole Food Co. v. Patrickson,[1] *a case focusing on the definition of "instrumentality." The specific question was whether a corporate subsidiary can claim to be an instrumentality of a foreign state if the state does not own a majority of the shares of the subsidiary's stock, but does own a majority of the shares of the corporate parent.*

1. 538 U.S. 468, 123 S.Ct. 1655, 155 L.Ed.2d 843 (2004). This opinion may be accessed online at www.law.cornell.edu/supct/search. Enter "Dole Food Company" in the "Search for:" box, and select "All Decisions." Scroll to the name of the case and click on it to access the opinion.

CASE BACKGROUND

In 1851, Dole Food Company was founded in Hawaii. Dole is the world's largest producer and seller of fresh fruit, fresh vegetables, and fresh-cut flowers and markets a growing line of packaged foods. The firm does business in more than 90 countries, employing globally more than 33,000 full-time permanent employees and 24,000 full-time seasonal or temporary employees.

In 1997, Gerardo Patrickson and other farmworkers who worked in banana fields in Costa Rica, Ecuador, Guatemala, and Panama filed a suit in a Hawaii state court against Dole and others, seeking damages for injuries from exposure to dibromochloropropane, a chemical used as an agricultural pesticide. Dole impleaded[2] two Israeli firms—Dead Sea Bromine Company and Bromine Compounds, Ltd. (the Dead Sea companies)—that allegedly made the pesticides.

2. To *implead* is to bring a new party into a suit between others, with the allegation that the new party is liable for part of the claim to the party that impleaded it.

The Dead Sea companies asked a U.S. district court to hear the suit on the ground that they were instrumentalities of a foreign state as defined in the FSIA. The court denied this request, but held that it had jurisdiction on other grounds and dismissed the suit. The workers appealed to the U.S. Court of Appeals for the Ninth Circuit, which reversed the dismissal but agreed that the Dead Sea companies were not instrumentalities of a foreign state as defined in the FSIA. The Dead Sea companies appealed to the United States Supreme Court.

MAJORITY OPINION

Justice *KENNEDY*, delivered the opinion of the Court.

* * * *

The State of Israel did not have direct ownership of shares in either of the Dead Sea Companies at any time pertinent to this suit. Rather, these companies were, at various times, separated from the State of Israel by one or more intermediate corporate tiers. For example, from 1984–1985, Israel wholly owned a company called Israeli Chemicals, Ltd.; which owned a majority of shares in another company called Dead Sea Works, Ltd.; which owned a majority of shares in Dead Sea Bromine Co., Ltd.; which owned a majority of shares in Bromine Compounds, Ltd.

* * * *

* * * The Dead Sea Companies urge us to ignore corporate formalities and use the colloquial [everyday] sense of that term. They ask whether, in common parlance, Israel would be said to own the Dead Sea Companies. *We reject this analysis. In issues of corporate law, structure often matters.* It is evident from the [FSIA's] text that Congress was aware of settled principles of corporate law and legislated within that context. The language of [Section] 1603(b)(2) refers to ownership of "shares," showing that *Congress intended statutory coverage to turn on formal corporate ownership.* Likewise, [Section] 1603(b)(1), another component of the definition of instrumentality, refers to a "separate legal person, corporate or otherwise." [Emphasis added.]

A basic tenet [rule] of American corporate law is that the corporation and its shareholders are distinct entities. An individual shareholder, by virtue of his ownership of shares, does not own the corporation's assets and, as a result, does not own subsidiary corporations in which the corporation holds an interest. A corporate parent which owns the shares of a subsidiary does not, for that reason alone, own or have legal title to the assets of the subsidiary; and, it follows with even greater force, *the parent does not own or have legal title to the subsidiaries of the subsidiary.*

The fact that the shareholder is a foreign state does not change the analysis. [Emphasis added.]

Applying these principles, it follows that Israel did not own a majority of shares in the Dead Sea Companies. The State of Israel owned a majority of shares, at various times, in companies one or more corporate tiers above the Dead Sea Companies, but at no time did Israel own a majority of shares in the Dead Sea Companies. Those companies were subsidiaries of other corporations.

* * * *

The Dead Sea Companies say that the State of Israel exercised considerable control over their operations, notwithstanding Israel's indirect relationship to those companies. They appear to think that, in determining instrumentality status under the Act, control may be substituted for an ownership interest. Control and ownership, however, are distinct concepts. The terms of [Section] 1603(b)(2) are explicit and straightforward. Majority ownership by a foreign state, not control, is the benchmark of instrumentality status.

* * * *

The judgment of the Court of Appeals * * * is affirmed * * * .

DISSENTING OPINION

Justice *BREYER*, * * * dissenting * * * .

* * * Unlike the majority, I believe that the statutory phrase "other ownership interest * * * owned by a foreign state" covers a Foreign Nation's legal interest in a Corporate Subsidiary, where that interest consists of the Foreign Nation's ownership of a Corporate Parent that owns the shares of the Subsidiary.

* * * *

As far as [the FSIA] is concerned, decisions about how to incorporate, how to structure corporate entities, or whether to act through a single corporate layer or through several corporate layers are matters purely of form, not of substance. The need for federal court determination of a sovereign immunity claim is no less important where subsidiaries are involved. The need for [the FSIA's] protections is no less compelling. The risk of adverse foreign policy consequences is no less great.

That is why I doubt the majority's claim that its reading of the text of the FSIA is "[t]he better reading," leading to "[t]he better rule." The majority's rule is not better for a foreign nation, say, Mexico or Honduras, which may use a tiered corporate structure to manage and control important areas of national interest, such as natural resources, and, as a result, will find its ability to use the [U.S.] federal courts to adjudicate matters of national importance and potential sensitivity restricted. Congress is most unlikely to characterize as "better" a rule tied to legal formalities that undercuts its basic jurisdictional objectives. And working lawyers will now have to factor into complex corporate restructuring equations * * * a risk that the government might lose its previously available access to federal court.

Given these consequences, from what perspective can the Court's unnecessarily technical reading of this part of the statute produce a "better rule"? To hold, as the Court does today, that for purposes of the FSIA "other ownership interest" does not include the interest that a Foreign Nation has in a tiered Corporate Subsidiary would be not merely to depart from the primary rule that words are to be taken in their ordinary sense, but to narrow the operation of the statute to an extent that would seriously imperil the accomplishment of its purpose.

QUESTIONS FOR ANALYSIS

1. **Law.** What did the majority rule in this case, and why?
2. **Law.** Why did the dissent disagree with the majority's ruling?
3. **Social Consideration.** Why did the majority conclude that "[m]ajority ownership by a foreign state, not control, is the benchmark of instrumentality status"?
4. **Ethical Dimensions.** Under what circumstances might a court "pierce the corporate veil" to hold a corporation's owner liable? Should the United States Supreme Court have applied these principles in this case to hold that the Dead Sea companies were instrumentalities of the state under the FSIA? Why or why not?
5. **Implications for the Investor.** How might the holding in this case affect investments in foreign "instrumentalities"?

Appendix A

How to Brief Cases and Analyze Case Problems

How to Brief Cases

To fully understand the law with respect to business, you need to be able to read and understand court decisions. To make this task easier, you can use a method of case analysis that is called *briefing*. There is a fairly standard procedure that you can follow when you "brief" any court case. You must first read the case opinion carefully. When you feel you understand the case, you can prepare a brief of it.

Although the format of the brief may vary, typically it will present the essentials of the case under headings such as the following:

1. **Citation.** Give the full citation for the case, including the name of the case, the date it was decided, and the court that decided it.
2. **Facts.** Briefly indicate (a) the reasons for the lawsuit; (b) the identity and arguments of the plaintiff(s) and defendant(s), respectively; and (c) the lower court's decision—if appropriate.
3. **Issue.** Concisely phrase, in the form of a question, the essential issue before the court. (If more than one issue is involved, you may have two—or even more—questions here.)
4. **Decision.** Indicate here—with a "yes" or "no," if possible—the court's answer to the question (or questions) in the *Issue* section above.
5. **Reason.** Summarize as briefly as possible the reasons given by the court for its decision (or decisions) and the case or statutory law relied on by the court in arriving at its decision.

An Example of a Briefed Sample Court Case

As an example of the format used in briefing cases, we present here a briefed version of the sample court case that was presented in the appendix to Chapter 1 in Exhibit 1A–3 on pages 26–27.

FEHR v. ALGARD
Superior Court of New Jersey, Appellate Division,
__ A.3d __, 2011 WL 13670 (2011).

FACTS Cathy Algard owns Sterling Harbor Motel & Marina, Inc. (SHM). SHM sponsored the Sterling Harbor Duke of Fluke Tournament in Wildwood, New Jersey. Prizes included the "single heaviest fluke prize" for the contestant who caught the heaviest live flounder and the "five heaviest fluke prize" for the boat catching the five flounder with the greatest combined weight. On behalf of Edward Fehr's boat, the *Gina Ariella,* Jack Aydelotte presented the heaviest live flounder. He also submitted five other fish for the five-fluke award. The judges ruled that two of the five flounder had not been caught during the contest and disqualified the *Gina Ariella.* Fehr filed a suit in a New Jersey state court against Algard, alleging breach of contract. The court issued a summary judgment in Fehr's favor, crowned him the "Duke of Fluke," and awarded him damages. Algard appealed.

ISSUE Can a contestant's award be withheld if that person did not comply with all of the contest's rules?

DECISION Yes. A state appellate court reversed the judgment of the lower court and remanded the case to give Algard an opportunity to prove that Aydelotte's deception warranted disqualification of the *Gina Ariella.*

REASON The state appellate court explained that the tournament—like the offer of a prize in any contest—becomes a binding contract in favor of a contestant who complies with the rules. The question was whether Fehr complied and was therefore entitled to the award. Fehr argued that he presented the heaviest live flounder and Algard's failure to award him the prize was a breach of contract. Algard pointed out that Aydelotte signed an entry form that proclaimed "anyone who is found to have provided false information is subject to immediate disqualification." The court stated, "The order of plaintiff's submissions for prizes should not allow the first fish to be considered for an award, if, in fact, he then tried to weigh-in day old fish." The court added, however, that "if the judges are found to have acted in bad faith and exceeded the rules in making a decision, plaintiff may prevail."

Review of Sample Court Case

Next, we provide a review of the briefed version to indicate the kind of information that is contained in each section.

CITATION The name of the case is *Fehr v. Algard.* Fehr is the plaintiff, and Algard is the defendant. The Superior Court of New Jersey, Appellate Division, decided this case in 2011. The citation states that this case can be found in the online Westlaw database at 2011 WL 13670.

FACTS The *Facts* section identifies the plaintiff and the defendant, describes the events leading up to this suit, the allegations made by the plaintiff in the initial suit, and (because this case is a decision of a state intermediate appellate court) the lower court's ruling and the party appealing. The appellant's contention on appeal is also sometimes included here.

ISSUE The *Issue* section presents the central issue (or issues) decided by the court. In this case, the Superior Court of New Jersey, Appellate Division, considers whether a contestant who may not have complied with all of the rules of the contest can still receive an award.

DECISION The *Decision* section includes the court's ruling on the issues before it. The decision reflects the opinion of the judge or justice hearing the case. Decisions by appellate courts are frequently phrased in reference to the lower court's decision. That is, the appellate court may "affirm" the lower court's ruling or "reverse" it. Here, the court determined that a contestant should not be considered for an award if he did not comply with all of the rules. The rules stated that a contestant would be disqualified for providing false information. On that basis, the contest judges could legitimately reject a contestant's submission for an award. The appellate court reversed the ruling of the lower court, which had been in the contestant's favor.

REASON The *Reason* section includes references to the relevant laws and legal principles that were applied in arriving at the conclusion in the case before the court. This section also explains the court's application of the law to the facts in the case. In this case, the court applied the principles of contract law to the contract between the contest's sponsors and the contestants.

Analyzing Case Problems

In addition to learning how to brief cases, students of business law and the legal environment also find it helpful to know how to analyze case problems. Part of the study of business law and the legal environment usually involves analyzing case problems, such as those included in selected chapters of this text.

For each case problem in this book, we provide the relevant background and facts of the lawsuit and the issue before the court. When you are assigned one of these problems, your job will be to determine how the court should decide the issue, and why. In other words, you will need to engage in legal analysis and reasoning. Here, we offer some suggestions on how to make this task less daunting. We begin by presenting a sample problem:

> While Janet Lawson, a famous pianist, was shopping in Quality Market, she slipped and fell on a wet floor in one of the aisles. The floor had recently been mopped by one of the store's employees, but there were no signs warning customers that the floor in that area was wet. As a result of the fall, Lawson injured her right arm and was unable to perform piano concerts for the next six months. Had she been able to perform the scheduled concerts, she would have earned approximately $60,000 over that period of time. Lawson sued Quality Market for this amount, plus another $10,000 in medical expenses. She claimed that the store's failure to warn customers of the wet floor constituted negligence and therefore the market was liable for her injuries. Will the court agree with Lawson? Discuss.

Understand the Facts

This may sound obvious, but before you can analyze or apply the relevant law to a specific set of facts, you must have a clear understanding of those facts. In other words, you should read through the case problem carefully—more than once, if necessary—to make sure you understand the identity of the plaintiff(s) and defendant(s) and the progression of events that led to the lawsuit.

In the sample case problem just given, the identity of the parties is fairly obvious. Janet Lawson is the one bringing the suit—therefore, she is the plaintiff. She is bringing the suit against Quality Market, so it is the defendant. Some of the case problems you may work on have multiple plaintiffs or defendants. Often, it is helpful to use abbreviations for the parties. A plaintiff, for example, may be denoted by a *pi* symbol (π), and a defendant by a *delta* (Δ) or triangle.

The events leading to the lawsuit are also fairly straightforward. Lawson slipped and fell on a wet floor, and she contends that Quality Market should be liable for her injuries because it was negligent in not posting a sign warning customers of the wet floor.

When you are working on case problems, realize that the facts should be accepted as they are given. For example, in our sample problem, it should be accepted that the floor was wet and that there was no sign. In other words, avoid making conjectures, such as "Maybe the floor wasn't too wet," or "Maybe an employee was getting a sign to put up," or "Maybe someone stole the sign." Questioning the facts as they are presented will only create confusion in your analysis.

Legal Analysis and Reasoning

Once you understand the facts given in the case problem, you can begin to analyze the case. The IRAC method is a helpful tool to use in the legal analysis and reasoning process. IRAC is an acronym for Issue, Rule, Application, Conclusion. Applying this method to our sample problem would involve the following steps:

1. First, you need to decide what legal **issue** is involved in the case. In our sample case, the basic issue is whether Quality Market's failure to warn customers of the wet floor constituted negligence. As discussed in Chapter 4, negligence is a *tort*—a civil wrong. In a tort lawsuit, the plaintiff seeks to be compensated for another's wrongful act. A defendant will be deemed negligent if he or she breached a duty of care owed to the plaintiff and the breach of that duty caused the plaintiff to suffer harm.
2. Once you have identified the issue, the next step is to determine what **rule of law** applies to the issue. To make this determination, carefully review the text of the chapter in which the relevant rule of law for the problem appears. Our sample case problem involves the tort of negligence, which is covered in Chapter 4. The applicable rule of law is the tort law principle that business owners owe a duty to exercise reasonable care to protect their customers ("business invitees"). Reasonable care, in this context, includes either removing—or warning customers of—*foreseeable* risks about which the owner *knew* or *should have known*. Business owners need not warn customers of "open and obvious" risks, however. If a business owner breaches this duty of care (fails to exercise the appropriate degree of care toward customers), and the breach of duty causes a customer to be injured, the business owner will be liable to the customer for the customer's injuries.
3. The next—and usually the most difficult—step in analyzing case problems is the **application** of the relevant rule of law to the

specific facts of the case you are studying. In our sample problem, applying the tort law principle just discussed presents few difficulties. An employee of the store had mopped the floor in the aisle where Lawson slipped and fell, but no sign was present indicating that the floor was wet. That a customer might fall on a wet floor is clearly a foreseeable risk. Therefore, the failure to warn customers about the wet floor was a breach of the duty of care owed by the business owner to the store's customers.

4. Once you have completed Step 3 in the IRAC method, you should be ready to draw your **conclusion.** In our sample problem, Quality Market is liable to Lawson for her injuries because the market's breach of its duty of care caused Lawson's injuries.

The fact patterns in the case problems presented in this text are not always as simple as those in our sample problem. Often, for example, a case has more than one plaintiff or defendant. A case may also involve more than one issue and have more than one applicable rule of law. Furthermore, in some case problems the facts may indicate that the general rule of law should not apply. For example, suppose that a store employee advised Lawson not to walk on the floor in the aisle because it was wet, but Lawson decided to walk on it anyway. This fact could alter the outcome of the case because the store could then raise the defense of assumption of risk (see Chapter 4). Nonetheless, a careful review of the chapter should always provide you with the knowledge you need to analyze the problem thoroughly and arrive at accurate conclusions.

Appendix B

The Constitution of the United States

Preamble

We the People of the United States, in Order to form a more perfect Union, establish Justice, insure domestic Tranquility, provide for the common defence, promote the general Welfare, and secure the Blessings of Liberty to ourselves and our Posterity, do ordain and establish this Constitution for the United States of America.

Article I

Section 1. All legislative Powers herein granted shall be vested in a Congress of the United States, which shall consist of a Senate and House of Representatives.

Section 2. The House of Representatives shall be composed of Members chosen every second Year by the People of the several States, and the Electors in each State shall have the Qualifications requisite for Electors of the most numerous Branch of the State Legislature.

No Person shall be a Representative who shall not have attained to the Age of twenty five Years, and been seven Years a Citizen of the United States, and who shall not, when elected, be an Inhabitant of that State in which he shall be chosen.

Representatives and direct Taxes shall be apportioned among the several States which may be included within this Union, according to their respective Numbers, which shall be determined by adding to the whole Number of free Persons, including those bound to Service for a Term of Years, and excluding Indians not taxed, three fifths of all other Persons. The actual Enumeration shall be made within three Years after the first Meeting of the Congress of the United States, and within every subsequent Term of ten Years, in such Manner as they shall by Law direct. The Number of Representatives shall not exceed one for every thirty Thousand, but each State shall have at Least one Representative; and until such enumeration shall be made, the State of New Hampshire shall be entitled to chuse three, Massachusetts eight, Rhode Island and Providence Plantations one, Connecticut five, New York six, New Jersey four, Pennsylvania eight, Delaware one, Maryland six, Virginia ten, North Carolina five, South Carolina five, and Georgia three.

When vacancies happen in the Representation from any State, the Executive Authority thereof shall issue Writs of Election to fill such Vacancies.

The House of Representatives shall chuse their Speaker and other Officers; and shall have the sole Power of Impeachment.

Section 3. The Senate of the United States shall be composed of two Senators from each State, chosen by the Legislature thereof, for six Years; and each Senator shall have one Vote.

Immediately after they shall be assembled in Consequence of the first Election, they shall be divided as equally as may be into three Classes. The Seats of the Senators of the first Class shall be vacated at the Expiration of the second Year, of the second Class at the Expiration of the fourth Year, and of the third Class at the Expiration of the sixth Year, so that one third may be chosen every second Year; and if Vacancies happen by Resignation, or otherwise, during the Recess of the Legislature of any State, the Executive thereof may make temporary Appointments until the next Meeting of the Legislature, which shall then fill such Vacancies.

No Person shall be a Senator who shall not have attained to the Age of thirty Years, and been nine Years a Citizen of the United States, and who shall not, when elected, be an Inhabitant of that State for which he shall be chosen.

The Vice President of the United States shall be President of the Senate, but shall have no Vote, unless they be equally divided.

The Senate shall chuse their other Officers, and also a President pro tempore, in the Absence of the Vice President, or when he shall exercise the Office of President of the United States.

The Senate shall have the sole Power to try all Impeachments. When sitting for that Purpose, they shall be on Oath or Affirmation. When the President of the United States is tried, the Chief Justice shall preside: And no Person shall be convicted without the Concurrence of two thirds of the Members present.

Judgment in Cases of Impeachment shall not extend further than to removal from Office, and disqualification to hold and enjoy any Office of honor, Trust, or Profit under the United States: but the Party convicted shall nevertheless be liable and subject to Indictment, Trial, Judgment, and Punishment, according to Law.

Section 4. The Times, Places and Manner of holding Elections for Senators and Representatives, shall be prescribed in each State by the Legislature thereof; but the Congress may at any time by Law make or alter such Regulations, except as to the Places of chusing Senators.

The Congress shall assemble at least once in every Year, and such Meeting shall be on the first Monday in December, unless they shall by Law appoint a different Day.

Section 5. Each House shall be the Judge of the Elections, Returns, and Qualifications of its own Members, and a Majority of each shall constitute a Quorum to do Business; but a smaller Number may adjourn from day to day, and may be authorized to compel the Attendance of absent Members, in such Manner, and under such Penalties as each House may provide.

Each House may determine the Rules of its Proceedings, punish its Members for disorderly Behavior, and, with the Concurrence of two thirds, expel a Member.

Each House shall keep a Journal of its Proceedings, and from time to time publish the same, excepting such Parts as may in their Judgment require Secrecy; and the Yeas and Nays of the Members of either House on any question shall, at the Desire of one fifth of those Present, be entered on the Journal.

Neither House, during the Session of Congress, shall, without the Consent of the other, adjourn for more than three days, nor to any other Place than that in which the two Houses shall be sitting.

Section 6. The Senators and Representatives shall receive a Compensation for their Services, to be ascertained by Law, and paid out of the Treasury of the United States. They shall in all Cases, except Treason, Felony and Breach of the Peace, be privileged from Arrest during their Attendance at the Session of their respective Houses, and in going to and returning from the same; and for any Speech or Debate in either House, they shall not be questioned in any other Place.

No Senator or Representative shall, during the Time for which he was elected, be appointed to any civil Office under the Authority of the United States, which shall have been created, or the Emoluments whereof shall have been increased during such time; and no Person holding any Office under the United States, shall be a Member of either House during his Continuance in Office.

Section 7. All Bills for raising Revenue shall originate in the House of Representatives; but the Senate may propose or concur with Amendments as on other Bills.

Every Bill which shall have passed the House of Representatives and the Senate, shall, before it become a Law, be presented to the President of the United States; If he approve he shall sign it, but if not he shall return it, with his Objections to the House in which it shall have originated, who shall enter the Objections at large on their Journal, and proceed to reconsider it. If after such Reconsideration two thirds of that House shall agree to pass the Bill, it shall be sent together with the Objections, to the other House, by which it shall likewise be reconsidered, and if approved by two thirds of that House, it shall become a Law. But in all such Cases the Votes of both Houses shall be determined by Yeas and Nays, and the Names of the Persons voting for and against the Bill shall be entered on the Journal of each House respectively. If any Bill shall not be returned by the President within ten Days (Sundays excepted) after it shall have been presented to him, the Same shall be a Law, in like Manner as if he had signed it, unless the Congress by their Adjournment prevent its Return in which Case it shall not be a Law.

Every Order, Resolution, or Vote, to which the Concurrence of the Senate and House of Representatives may be necessary (except on a question of Adjournment) shall be presented to the President of the United States; and before the Same shall take Effect, shall be approved by him, or being disapproved by him, shall be repassed by two thirds of the Senate and House of Representatives, according to the Rules and Limitations prescribed in the Case of a Bill.

Section 8. The Congress shall have Power To lay and collect Taxes, Duties, Imposts and Excises, to pay the Debts and provide for the common Defence and general Welfare of the United States; but all Duties, Imposts and Excises shall be uniform throughout the United States;

To borrow Money on the credit of the United States;

To regulate Commerce with foreign Nations, and among the several States, and with the Indian Tribes;

To establish an uniform Rule of Naturalization, and uniform Laws on the subject of Bankruptcies throughout the United States;

To coin Money, regulate the Value thereof, and of foreign Coin, and fix the Standard of Weights and Measures;

To provide for the Punishment of counterfeiting the Securities and current Coin of the United States;

To establish Post Offices and post Roads;

To promote the Progress of Science and useful Arts, by securing for limited Times to Authors and Inventors the exclusive Right to their respective Writings and Discoveries;

To constitute Tribunals inferior to the supreme Court;

To define and punish Piracies and Felonies committed on the high Seas, and Offenses against the Law of Nations;

To declare War, grant Letters of Marque and Reprisal, and make Rules concerning Captures on Land and Water;

To raise and support Armies, but no Appropriation of Money to that Use shall be for a longer Term than two Years;

To provide and maintain a Navy;

To make Rules for the Government and Regulation of the land and naval Forces;

To provide for calling forth the Militia to execute the Laws of the Union, suppress Insurrections and repel Invasions;

To provide for organizing, arming, and disciplining, the Militia, and for governing such Part of them as may be employed in the Service of the United States, reserving to the States respectively, the Appointment of the Officers, and the Authority of training the Militia according to the discipline prescribed by Congress;

To exercise exclusive Legislation in all Cases whatsoever, over such District (not exceeding ten Miles square) as may, by Cession of particular States, and the Acceptance of Congress, become the Seat of the Government of the United States, and to exercise like Authority over all Places purchased by the Consent of the Legislature of the State in which the Same shall be, for the Erection of Forts, Magazines, Arsenals, dock-Yards, and other needful Buildings;—And

To make all Laws which shall be necessary and proper for carrying into Execution the foregoing Powers, and all other Powers vested by this Constitution in the Government of the United States, or in any Department or Officer thereof.

Section 9. The Migration or Importation of such Persons as any of the States now existing shall think proper to admit, shall not be prohibited by the Congress prior to the Year one thousand eight hundred and eight, but a Tax or duty may be imposed on such Importation, not exceeding ten dollars for each Person.

The privilege of the Writ of Habeas Corpus shall not be suspended, unless when in Cases of Rebellion or Invasion the public Safety may require it.

No Bill of Attainder or ex post facto Law shall be passed.

No Capitation, or other direct, Tax shall be laid, unless in Proportion to the Census or Enumeration herein before directed to be taken.

No Tax or Duty shall be laid on Articles exported from any State.

No Preference shall be given by any Regulation of Commerce or Revenue to the Ports of one State over those of another: nor shall Vessels bound to, or from, one State be obliged to enter, clear, or pay Duties in another.

No Money shall be drawn from the Treasury, but in Consequence of Appropriations made by Law; and a regular Statement and Account of the Receipts and Expenditures of all public Money shall be published from time to time.

No Title of Nobility shall be granted by the United States: And no Person holding any Office of Profit or Trust under them, shall, without the Consent of the Congress, accept of any present, Emolument, Office, or Title, of any kind whatever, from any King, Prince, or foreign State.

Section 10. No State shall enter into any Treaty, Alliance, or Confederation; grant Letters of Marque and Reprisal; coin Money; emit Bills of Credit; make any Thing but gold and silver Coin a Tender in Payment of Debts; pass any Bill of Attainder, ex post facto Law, or Law impairing the Obligation of Contracts, or grant any Title of Nobility.

No State shall, without the Consent of the Congress, lay any Imposts or Duties on Imports or Exports, except what may be absolutely necessary for executing its inspection Laws: and the net Produce of all Duties and Imposts, laid by any State on Imports or Exports, shall be for the Use of the Treasury of the United States; and all such Laws shall be subject to the Revision and Controul of the Congress.

No State shall, without the Consent of Congress, lay any Duty of Tonnage, keep Troops, or Ships of War in time of Peace, enter into any Agreement or Compact with another State, or with a foreign Power, or engage in War, unless actually invaded, or in such imminent Danger as will not admit of delay.

Article II

Section 1. The executive Power shall be vested in a President of the United States of America. He shall hold his Office during the Term of four Years, and, together with the Vice President, chosen for the same Term, be elected, as follows:

Each State shall appoint, in such Manner as the Legislature thereof may direct, a Number of Electors, equal to the whole Number of Senators and Representatives to which the State may be entitled in the Congress; but no Senator or Representative, or Person holding an Office of Trust or Profit under the United States, shall be appointed an Elector.

The Electors shall meet in their respective States, and vote by Ballot for two Persons, of whom one at least shall not be an Inhabitant of the same State with themselves. And they shall make a List of all the Persons voted for, and of the Number of Votes for each; which List they shall sign and certify, and transmit sealed to the Seat of the Government of the United States, directed to the President of the Senate. The President of the Senate shall, in the Presence of the Senate and House of Representatives, open all the Certificates, and the Votes shall then be counted. The Person having the greatest Number of Votes shall be the President, if such Number be a Majority of the whole Number of Electors appointed; and if there be more than one who have such Majority, and have an equal Number of Votes, then the House of Representatives shall immediately chuse by Ballot one of them for President; and if no Person have a Majority, then from the five highest on the List the said House shall in like Manner chuse the President. But in chusing the President, the Votes shall be taken by States, the Representation from each State having one Vote; A quorum for this Purpose shall consist of a Member or Members from two thirds of the States, and a Majority of all the States shall be necessary to a Choice. In every Case, after the Choice of the President, the Person having the greater Number of Votes of the Electors shall be the Vice President. But if there should remain two or more who have equal Votes, the Senate shall chuse from them by Ballot the Vice President.

The Congress may determine the Time of chusing the Electors, and the Day on which they shall give their Votes; which Day shall be the same throughout the United States.

No person except a natural born Citizen, or a Citizen of the United States, at the time of the Adoption of this Constitution, shall be eligible to the Office of President; neither shall any Person be eligible to that Office who shall not have attained to the Age of thirty five Years, and been fourteen Years a Resident within the United States.

In Case of the Removal of the President from Office, or of his Death, Resignation or Inability to discharge the Powers and Duties of the said Office, the same shall devolve on the Vice President, and the Congress may by Law provide for the Case of Removal, Death, Resignation or Inability, both of the President and Vice President, declaring what Officer shall then act as President, and such Officer shall act accordingly, until the Disability be removed, or a President shall be elected.

The President shall, at stated Times, receive for his Services, a Compensation, which shall neither be increased nor diminished during the Period for which he shall have been elected, and he shall not receive within that Period any other Emolument from the United States, or any of them.

Before he enter on the Execution of his Office, he shall take the following Oath or Affirmation: "I do solemnly swear (or affirm) that I will faithfully execute the Office of President of the United States, and will to the best of my Ability, preserve, protect and defend the Constitution of the United States."

Section 2. The President shall be Commander in Chief of the Army and Navy of the United States, and of the Militia of the several States, when called into the actual Service of the United States; he may require the Opinion, in writing, of the principal Officer in each of the executive Departments, upon any Subject relating to the Duties of their respective Offices, and he shall have Power to grant Reprieves and Pardons for Offenses against the United States, except in Cases of Impeachment.

He shall have Power, by and with the Advice and Consent of the Senate to make Treaties, provided two thirds of the Senators present concur; and he shall nominate, and by and with the Advice and Consent of the Senate, shall appoint Ambassadors, other public Ministers and Consuls, Judges of the supreme Court, and all other Officers of the United States, whose Appointments are not herein otherwise provided for, and which shall be established by Law; but the Congress may by Law vest the Appointment of such inferior Officers, as they think proper, in the President alone, in the Courts of Law, or in the Heads of Departments.

The President shall have Power to fill up all Vacancies that may happen during the Recess of the Senate, by granting Commissions which shall expire at the End of their next Session.

Section 3. He shall from time to time give to the Congress Information of the State of the Union, and recommend to their Consideration such Measures as he shall judge necessary and expedient; he may, on extraordinary Occasions, convene both Houses, or either of them, and in Case of Disagreement between them, with Respect to the Time of Adjournment, he may adjourn them to such Time as he shall think proper; he shall receive Ambassadors and other public Ministers; he shall take Care that the Laws be faithfully executed, and shall Commission all the Officers of the United States.

Section 4. The President, Vice President and all civil Officers of the United States, shall be removed from Office on Impeachment for, and Conviction of, Treason, Bribery, or other high Crimes and Misdemeanors.

Article III

Section 1. The judicial Power of the United States, shall be vested in one supreme Court, and in such inferior Courts as the

Congress may from time to time ordain and establish. The Judges, both of the supreme and inferior Courts, shall hold their Offices during good Behaviour, and shall, at stated Times, receive for their Services a Compensation, which shall not be diminished during their Continuance in Office.

Section 2. The judicial Power shall extend to all Cases, in Law and Equity, arising under this Constitution, the Laws of the United States, and Treaties made, or which shall be made, under their Authority;—to all Cases affecting Ambassadors, other public Ministers and Consuls;—to all Cases of admiralty and maritime Jurisdiction;—to Controversies to which the United States shall be a Party;—to Controversies between two or more States;—between a State and Citizens of another State;—between Citizens of different States;—between Citizens of the same State claiming Lands under Grants of different States, and between a State, or the Citizens thereof, and foreign States, Citizens or Subjects.

In all Cases affecting Ambassadors, other public Ministers and Consuls, and those in which a State shall be a Party, the supreme Court shall have original Jurisdiction. In all the other Cases before mentioned, the supreme Court shall have appellate Jurisdiction, both as to Law and Fact, with such Exceptions, and under such Regulations as the Congress shall make.

The Trial of all Crimes, except in Cases of Impeachment, shall be by Jury; and such Trial shall be held in the State where the said Crimes shall have been committed; but when not committed within any State, the Trial shall be at such Place or Places as the Congress may by Law have directed.

Section 3. Treason against the United States, shall consist only in levying War against them, or, in adhering to their Enemies, giving them Aid and Comfort. No Person shall be convicted of Treason unless on the Testimony of two Witnesses to the same overt Act, or on Confession in open Court.

The Congress shall have Power to declare the Punishment of Treason, but no Attainder of Treason shall work Corruption of Blood, or Forfeiture except during the Life of the Person attainted.

Article IV

Section 1. Full Faith and Credit shall be given in each State to the public Acts, Records, and judicial Proceedings of every other State. And the Congress may by general Laws prescribe the Manner in which such Acts, Records and Proceedings shall be proved, and the Effect thereof.

Section 2. The Citizens of each State shall be entitled to all Privileges and Immunities of Citizens in the several States.

A Person charged in any State with Treason, Felony, or other Crime, who shall flee from Justice, and be found in another State, shall on Demand of the executive Authority of the State from which he fled, be delivered up, to be removed to the State having Jurisdiction of the Crime.

No Person held to Service or Labour in one State, under the Laws thereof, escaping into another, shall, in Consequence of any Law or Regulation therein, be discharged from such Service or Labour, but shall be delivered up on Claim of the Party to whom such Service or Labour may be due.

Section 3. New States may be admitted by the Congress into this Union; but no new State shall be formed or erected within the Jurisdiction of any other State; nor any State be formed by the Junction of two or more States, or Parts of States, without the Consent of the Legislatures of the States concerned as well as of the Congress.

The Congress shall have Power to dispose of and make all needful Rules and Regulations respecting the Territory or other Property belonging to the United States; and nothing in this Constitution shall be so construed as to Prejudice any Claims of the United States, or of any particular State.

Section 4. The United States shall guarantee to every State in this Union a Republican Form of Government, and shall protect each of them against Invasion; and on Application of the Legislature, or of the Executive (when the Legislature cannot be convened) against domestic Violence.

Article V

The Congress, whenever two thirds of both Houses shall deem it necessary, shall propose Amendments to this Constitution, or, on the Application of the Legislatures of two thirds of the several States, shall call a Convention for proposing Amendments, which, in either Case, shall be valid to all Intents and Purposes, as part of this Constitution, when ratified by the Legislatures of three fourths of the several States, or by Conventions in three fourths thereof, as the one or the other Mode of Ratification may be proposed by the Congress; Provided that no Amendment which may be made prior to the Year One thousand eight hundred and eight shall in any Manner affect the first and fourth Clauses in the Ninth Section of the first Article; and that no State, without its Consent, shall be deprived of its equal Suffrage in the Senate.

Article VI

All Debts contracted and Engagements entered into, before the Adoption of this Constitution shall be as valid against the United States under this Constitution, as under the Confederation.

This Constitution, and the Laws of the United States which shall be made in Pursuance thereof; and all Treaties made, or which shall be made, under the Authority of the United States, shall be the supreme Law of the Land; and the Judges in every State shall be bound thereby, any Thing in the Constitution or Laws of any State to the Contrary notwithstanding.

The Senators and Representatives before mentioned, and the Members of the several State Legislatures, and all executive and judicial Officers, both of the United States and of the several States, shall be bound by Oath or Affirmation, to support this Constitution; but no religious Test shall ever be required as a Qualification to any Office or public Trust under the United States.

Article VII

The Ratification of the Conventions of nine States shall be sufficient for the Establishment of this Constitution between the States so ratifying the Same.

Amendment I [1791]

Congress shall make no law respecting an establishment of religion, or prohibiting the free exercise thereof; or abridging the freedom of speech, or of the press; or the right of the people peaceably to assembly, and to petition the Government for a redress of grievances.

Amendment II [1791]

A well regulated Militia, being necessary to the security of a free State, the right of the people to keep and bear Arms, shall not be infringed.

Amendment III [1791]

No Soldier shall, in time of peace be quartered in any house, without the consent of the Owner, nor in time of war, but in a manner to be prescribed by law.

Amendment IV [1791]

The right of the people to be secure in their persons, houses, papers, and effects, against unreasonable searches and seizures, shall not be violated, and no Warrants shall issue, but upon probable cause, supported by Oath or affirmation, and particularly describing the place to be searched, and the persons or things to be seized.

Amendment V [1791]

No person shall be held to answer for a capital, or otherwise infamous crime, unless on a presentment or indictment of a Grand Jury, except in cases arising in the land or naval forces, or in the Militia, when in actual service in time of War or public danger; nor shall any person be subject for the same offence to be twice put in jeopardy of life or limb; nor shall be compelled in any criminal case to be a witness against himself, nor be deprived of life, liberty, or property, without due process of law; nor shall private property be taken for public use, without just compensation.

Amendment VI [1791]

In all criminal prosecutions, the accused shall enjoy the right to a speedy and public trial, by an impartial jury of the State and district wherein the crime shall have been committed, which district shall have been previously ascertained by law, and to be informed of the nature and cause of the accusation; to be confronted with the witnesses against him; to have compulsory process for obtaining witnesses in his favor, and to have the Assistance of Counsel for his defence.

Amendment VII [1791]

In Suits at common law, where the value in controversy shall exceed twenty dollars, the right of trial by jury shall be preserved, and no fact tried by jury, shall be otherwise re-examined in any Court of the United States, than according to the rules of the common law.

Amendment VIII [1791]

Excessive bail shall not be required, nor excessive fines imposed, nor cruel and unusual punishments inflicted.

Amendment IX [1791]

The enumeration in the Constitution, of certain rights, shall not be construed to deny or disparage others retained by the people.

Amendment X [1791]

The powers not delegated to the United States by the Constitution, nor prohibited by it to the States, are reserved to the States respectively, or to the people.

Amendment XI [1798]

The Judicial power of the United States shall not be construed to extend to any suit in law or equity, commenced or prosecuted against one of the United States by Citizens of another State, or by Citizens or Subjects of any Foreign State.

Amendment XII [1804]

The Electors shall meet in their respective states, and vote by ballot for President and Vice-President, one of whom, at least, shall not be an inhabitant of the same state with themselves; they shall name in their ballots the person voted for as President, and in distinct ballots the person voted for as Vice-President, and they shall make distinct lists of all persons voted for as President, and of all persons voted for as Vice-President, and of the number of votes for each, which lists they shall sign and certify, and transmit sealed to the seat of the government of the United States, directed to the President of the Senate;—The President of the Senate shall, in the presence of the Senate and House of Representatives, open all the certificates and the votes shall then be counted;—The person having the greatest number of votes for President, shall be the President, if such number be a majority of the whole number of Electors appointed; and if no person have such majority, then from the persons having the highest numbers not exceeding three on the list of those voted for as President, the House of Representatives shall choose immediately, by ballot, the President. But in choosing the President, the votes shall be taken by states, the representation from each state having one vote; a quorum for this purpose shall consist of a member or members from two-thirds of the states, and a majority of all states shall be necessary to a choice. And if the House of Representatives shall not choose a President whenever the right of choice shall devolve upon them, before the fourth day of March next following, then the Vice-President shall act as President, as in the case of the death or other constitutional disability of the President.—The person having the greatest number of votes as Vice-President, shall be the Vice-President, if such number be a majority of the whole number of Electors appointed, and if no person have a majority, then from the two highest numbers on the list, the Senate shall choose the Vice-President; a quorum for the purpose shall consist of two-thirds of the whole number of Senators, and a majority of the whole number shall be necessary to a choice. But no person constitutionally ineligible to the office of President shall be eligible to that of Vice-President of the United States.

Amendment XIII [1865]

Section 1. Neither slavery nor involuntary servitude, except as a punishment for crime whereof the party shall have been duly convicted, shall exist within the United States, or any place subject to their jurisdiction.

Section 2. Congress shall have power to enforce this article by appropriate legislation.

Amendment XIV [1868]

Section 1. All persons born or naturalized in the United States, and subject to the jurisdiction thereof, are citizens of the United States and of the State wherein they reside. No State shall make or enforce any law which shall abridge the privileges or immunities of citizens of the United States; nor shall any State deprive any person of life, liberty, or property, without due process of law; nor deny to any person within its jurisdiction the equal protection of the laws.

Section 2. Representatives shall be apportioned among the several States according to their respective numbers, counting the whole number of persons in each State, excluding Indians not taxed. But when the right to vote at any election for the choice of electors for President and Vice President of the United States, Representatives in Congress, the Executive and Judicial officers of a State, or the members of the Legislature thereof, is denied to any of the male inhabitants of such State, being twenty-one years of age, and citizens of the United States, or in any way abridged, except for participation in rebellion, or other crime, the basis of representation therein shall be reduced in the proportion which the number of such male citizens shall bear to the whole number of male citizens twenty-one years of age in such State.

Section 3. No person shall be a Senator or Representative in Congress, or elector of President and Vice President, or hold any office, civil or military, under the United States, or under any State, who having previously taken an oath, as a member of Congress, or as an officer of the United States, or as a member of any State legislature, or as an executive or judicial officer of any State, to support the Constitution of the United States, shall have engaged in insurrection or rebellion against the same, or given aid or comfort to the enemies thereof. But Congress may by a vote of two-thirds of each House, remove such disability.

Section 4. The validity of the public debt of the United States, authorized by law, including debts incurred for payment of pensions and bounties for services in suppressing insurrection or rebellion, shall not be questioned. But neither the United States nor any State shall assume or pay any debt or obligation incurred in aid of insurrection or rebellion against the United States, or any claim for the loss or emancipation of any slave; but all such debts, obligations and claims shall be held illegal and void.

Section 5. The Congress shall have power to enforce, by appropriate legislation, the provisions of this article.

Amendment XV [1870]

Section 1. The right of citizens of the United States to vote shall not be denied or abridged by the United States or by any State on account of race, color, or previous condition of servitude.

Section 2. The Congress shall have power to enforce this article by appropriate legislation.

Amendment XVI [1913]

The Congress shall have power to lay and collect taxes on incomes, from whatever source derived, without apportionment among the several States, and without regard to any census or enumeration.

Amendment XVII [1913]

Section 1. The Senate of the United States shall be composed of two Senators from each State, elected by the people thereof, for six years; and each Senator shall have one vote. The electors in each State shall have the qualifications requisite for electors of the most numerous branch of the State legislatures.

Section 2. When vacancies happen in the representation of any State in the Senate, the executive authority of such State shall issue writs of election to fill such vacancies: Provided, That the legislature of any State may empower the executive thereof to make temporary appointments until the people fill the vacancies by election as the legislature may direct.

Section 3. This amendment shall not be so construed as to affect the election or term of any Senator chosen before it becomes valid as part of the Constitution.

Amendment XVIII [1919]

Section 1. After one year from the ratification of this article the manufacture, sale, or transportation of intoxicating liquors within, the importation thereof into, or the exportation thereof from the United States and all territory subject to the jurisdiction thereof for beverage purposes is hereby prohibited.

Section 2. The Congress and the several States shall have concurrent power to enforce this article by appropriate legislation.

Section 3. This article shall be inoperative unless it shall have been ratified as an amendment to the Constitution by the legislatures of the several States, as provided in the Constitution, within seven years from the date of the submission hereof to the States by the Congress.

Amendment XIX [1920]

Section 1. The right of citizens of the United States to vote shall not be denied or abridged by the United States or by any State on account of sex.

Section 2. Congress shall have power to enforce this article by appropriate legislation.

Amendment XX [1933]

Section 1. The terms of the President and Vice President shall end at noon on the 20th day of January, and the terms of Senators and Representatives at noon on the 3d day of January, of the years in which such terms would have ended if this article had not been ratified; and the terms of their successors shall then begin.

Section 2. The Congress shall assemble at least once in every year, and such meeting shall begin at noon on the 3d day of January, unless they shall by law appoint a different day.

Section 3. If, at the time fixed for the beginning of the term of the President, the President elect shall have died, the Vice President elect shall become President. If the President shall not have been chosen before the time fixed for the beginning of his term, or if the President elect shall have failed to qualify, then the Vice President elect shall act as President until a President shall have qualified; and the Congress may by law provide for the case wherein neither a President elect nor a Vice President elect shall have qualified, declaring who shall then act as President, or the manner in which one who is to act shall be selected, and such person shall act accordingly until a President or Vice President shall have qualified.

Section 4. The Congress may by law provide for the case of the death of any of the persons from whom the House of Representatives may choose a President whenever the right of choice shall have devolved upon them, and for the case of the death of any of the persons from whom the Senate may choose a Vice President whenever the right of choice shall have devolved upon them.

Section 5. Sections 1 and 2 shall take effect on the 15th day of October following the ratification of this article.

Section 6. This article shall be inoperative unless it shall have been ratified as an amendment to the Constitution by the legislatures of three-fourths of the several States within seven years from the date of its submission.

Amendment XXI [1933]

Section 1. The eighteenth article of amendment to the Constitution of the United States is hereby repealed.

Section 2. The transportation or importation into any State, Territory, or possession of the United States for delivery or use therein of intoxicating liquors, in violation of the laws thereof, is hereby prohibited.

Section 3. This article shall be inoperative unless it shall have been ratified as an amendment to the Constitution by conventions in the several States, as provided in the Constitution, within seven years from the date of the submission hereof to the States by the Congress.

Amendment XXII [1951]

Section 1. No person shall be elected to the office of the President more than twice, and no person who has held the office of President, or acted as President, for more than two years of a term to which some other person was elected President shall be elected to the office of President more than once. But this Article shall not apply to any person holding the office of President when this Article was proposed by the Congress, and shall not prevent any person who may be holding the office of President, or acting as President, during the term within which this Article becomes operative from holding the office of President or acting as President during the remainder of such term.

Section 2. This article shall be inoperative unless it shall have been ratified as an amendment to the Constitution by the legislatures of three-fourths of the several States within seven years from the date of its submission to the States by the Congress.

Amendment XXIII [1961]

Section 1. The District constituting the seat of Government of the United States shall appoint in such manner as the Congress may direct:

A number of electors of President and Vice President equal to the whole number of Senators and Representatives in Congress to which the District would be entitled if it were a State, but in no event more than the least populous state; they shall be in addition to those appointed by the states, but they shall be considered, for the purposes of the election of President and Vice President, to be electors appointed by a state; and they shall meet in the District and perform such duties as provided by the twelfth article of amendment.

Section 2. The Congress shall have power to enforce this article by appropriate legislation.

Amendment XXIV [1964]

Section 1. The right of citizens of the United States to vote in any primary or other election for President or Vice President, for electors for President or Vice President, or for Senator or Representative in Congress, shall not be denied or abridged by the United States, or any State by reason of failure to pay any poll tax or other tax.

Section 2. The Congress shall have power to enforce this article by appropriate legislation.

Amendment XXV [1967]

Section 1. In case of the removal of the President from office or of his death or resignation, the Vice President shall become President.

Section 2. Whenever there is a vacancy in the office of the Vice President, the President shall nominate a Vice President who shall take office upon confirmation by a majority vote of both Houses of Congress.

Section 3. Whenever the President transmits to the President pro tempore of the Senate and the Speaker of the House of Representatives his written declaration that he is unable to discharge the powers and duties of his office, and until he transmits to them a written declaration to the contrary, such powers and duties shall be discharged by the Vice President as Acting President.

Section 4. Whenever the Vice President and a majority of either the principal officers of the executive departments or of such other body as Congress may by law provide, transmit to the President pro tempore of the Senate and the Speaker of the House of Representatives their written declaration that the President is unable to discharge the powers and duties of his office, the Vice President shall immediately assume the powers and duties of the office as Acting President.

Thereafter, when the President transmits to the President pro tempore of the Senate and the Speaker of the House of Representatives his written declaration that no inability exists, he shall resume the powers and duties of his office unless the Vice President and a majority of either the principal officers of the executive department or of such other body as Congress may by law provide, transmit within four days to the President pro tempore of the Senate and the Speaker of the House of Representatives their written declaration that the President is unable to discharge the powers and duties of his office. Thereupon Congress shall decide the issue, assembling within forty-eight hours for that purpose if not in session. If the Congress, within twenty-one days after receipt of the latter written declaration, or, if Congress is not in session, within twenty-one days after Congress is required to assemble, determines by two-thirds vote of both Houses that the President is unable to discharge the powers and duties of his office, the Vice President shall continue to discharge the same as Acting President; otherwise, the President shall resume the powers and duties of his office.

Amendment XXVI [1971]

Section 1. The right of citizens of the United States, who are eighteen years of age or older, to vote shall not be denied or abridged by the United States or by any State on account of age.

Section 2. The Congress shall have power to enforce this article by appropriate legislation.

Amendment XXVII [1992]

No law, varying the compensation for the services of the Senators and Representatives, shall take effect, until an election of Representatives shall have intervened.

Appendix C

The Uniform Commercial Code (Excerpts)

(Adopted in fifty-two jurisdictions; all fifty States, although Louisiana has adopted only Articles 1, 3, 4, 7, 8, and 9; the District of Columbia; and the Virgin Islands.)

The Uniform Commercial Code consists of the following articles:

1. **General Provisions**
2. **Sales**

2A. **Leases**

3. **Negotiable Instruments**
4. **Bank Deposits and Collections**

4A. **Fund Transfers**

5. **Letters of Credit**
6. **Repealer of Article 6–Bulk Transfers and [Revised] Article 6–Bulk Sales**
7. **Warehouse Receipts, Bills of Lading and Other Documents of Title**
8. **Investment Securities**
9. **Secured Transactions**
10. **Effective Date and Repealer**
11. **Effective Date and Transition Provisions**

Article 1 GENERAL PROVISIONS

Part 1 General Provisions

§ 1-101. Short Titles.

(a) This [Act] may be cited as Uniform Commercial Code.

(b) This article may be cited as Uniform Commercial Code-Uniform Provisions.

§ 1-102. Scope of Article.

This article applies to a transaction to the extent that it is governed by another article of [the Uniform Commercial Code].

§ 1-103. Construction of [Uniform Commercial Code] to Promote Its Purpose and Policies; Applicability of Supplemental Principles of Law.

(a) [The Uniform Commercial Code] must be liberally construed and applied to promote its underlying purposes and policies, which are:

(1) to simplify, clarify, and modernize the law governing commercial transactions;

(2) to permit the continued expansion of commercial practices through custom, usage, and agreement of the parties; and

(3) to make uniform the law among the various jurisdictions.

(b) Unless displaced by the particular provisions of [the Uniform Commercial Code], the principles of law and equity, including the law merchant and the law relative to capacity to contract, principal and agent, estoppel, fraud, misrepresentation, duress, coercion, mistake, bankruptcy, and other validating or invalidating cause, supplement its provisions.

§ 1-104. Construction Against Implicit Repeal.

This Act being a general act intended as a unified coverage of its subject matter, no part of it shall be deemed to be impliedly repealed by subsequent legislation if such construction can reasonably be avoided.

§ 1-105. Severability.

If any provision or clause of [the Uniform Commercial Code] or its application to any person or circumstance is held invalid, the invalidity does not affect other provisions or applications of [the Uniform Commercial Code] which can be given effect without the invalid provision or application, and to this end the provisions of [the Uniform Commercial Code] are severable.

§ 1-106. Use of Singular and Plural; Gender.

In [the Uniform Commercial Code], unless the statutory context otherwise requires:

(1) words in the singular number include the plural, and those in the plural include the singular; and

(2) words of any gender also refer to any other gender.

§ 1-107. Section Captions.

Section captions are part of [the Uniform Commercial Code].

§ 1-108. Relation to Electronic Signatures in Global and National Commerce Act.

This article modifies, limits, and supersedes the Federal Electronic Signatures in Global and National Commerce Act, 15 U.S.C. Sections 7001 *et seq.*, except that nothing in this article modifies, limits, or supersedes section 7001(c) of that act or authorizes electronic delivery of any of the notices described in section 7003(b) of that Act.

Part 2 General Definitions and Principles of Interpretation

§ 1-201. General Definitions.

Subject to additional definitions contained in the subsequent Articles of this Act which are applicable to specific Articles or Parts thereof, and unless the context otherwise requires, in this Act:

(1) "Action", in the sense of a judicial proceeding, includes recoupment, counterclaim, set-off, suit in equity, and any other proceedings in which rights are determined.

(2) "Aggrieved party" means a party entitled to resort to a remedy.

(3) "Agreement", as distinguished from "contract", means the bargain of the parties in fact, as found in their language or by implication from other circumstances, including course of performance, course of dealing, or usage of trade as provided in Section 1-303.

(4) "Bank" means a person engaged in the business of banking and includes a savings bank, savings and loan association, credit union, and trust company.

(5) "Bearer" means a person in control of a negotiable electronic document of title or a person in possession of a negotiable instrument, negotiable tangible document of title, or certificated security that is payable to bearer or indorsed in blank.

(6) "Bill of lading" means a document of title evidencing the receipt of goods for shipment issued by a person engaged in the business of directly or indirectly transporting or forwarding goods. The term does not include a warehouse receipt.

(7) "Branch" includes a separately incorporated foreign branch of a bank.

(8) "Burden of establishing" a fact means the burden of persuading the trier of fact that the existence of the fact is more probable than its nonexistence.

(9) "Buyer in ordinary course of business" means a person that buys goods in good faith, without knowledge that the sale violates the rights of another person in the goods, and in the ordinary course from a person, other than a pawnbroker, in the business of selling goods of that kind. A person buys goods in the ordinary course if the sale to the person comports with the usual or customary practices in the kind of business in which the seller is engaged or with the seller's own usual or customary practices. A person that sells oil, gas, or other minerals at the wellhead or minehead is a person in the business of selling goods of that kind. A buyer in ordinary course of business may buy for cash, by exchange of other property, or on secured or unsecured credit, and may acquire goods or documents of title under a pre-existing contract for sale. Only a buyer that takes possession of the goods or has a right to recover the goods from the seller under Article 2 may be a buyer in ordinary course of business. A person that acquires goods in a transfer in bulk or as security for or in total or partial satisfaction of a money debt is not a buyer in ordinary course of business.

(10) "Conspicuous", with reference to a term, means so written, displayed, or presented that a reasonable person against which it is to operate ought to have noticed it. Whether a term is "conspicuous" or not is a decision for the court. Conspicuous terms include the following:

(A) a heading in capitals equal to or greater in size than the surrounding text, or in contrasting type, font, or color to the surrounding text of the same or lesser size; and

(B) language in the body of a record or display in larger type than the surrounding text, or in contrasting type, font, or color to the surrounding text of the same size, or set off from surrounding text of the same size by symbols or other marks that call attention to the language.

(11) "Consumer" means an individual who enters into a transaction primarily for personal, family, or household purposes.

(12) "Contract", as distinguished from "agreement", means the total legal obligation that results from the parties' agreement as determined by [the Uniform Commercial Code] as supplemented by any other laws.

(13) "Creditor" includes a general creditor, a secured creditor, a lien creditor and any representative of creditors, including an assignee for the benefit of creditors, a trustee in bankruptcy, a receiver in equity and an executor or administrator of an insolvent debtor's or assignor's estate.

(14) "Defendant" includes a person in the position of defendant in a counterclaim, cross-action, or third-party claim.

(15) "Delivery" with respect to an electronic document of title means voluntary transfer of control and with respect to an instrument, a tangible document of title, or chattel paper means voluntary transfer of possession.

(16) "Document of title" means a record (i) that in regular course of business or financing is treated as adequately evidencing that the person in possession or control of the record is entitled to receive, control, hold, and dispose of the record and the goods the record covers and (ii) that purports to be issued by or addressed to a bailee and to cover goods in the bailee's possession which are either identified or are fungible portions of an identified mass. The term includes a bill of lading, transport document, dock warrant, dock receipt, warehouse receipt, and order for delivery of goods. An electronic document of title means a document of title evidenced by a record consisting of information stored in an electronic medium. A tangible document of title means a document of title evidenced by a record consisting of information that is inscribed on a tangible medium.

(17) "Fault" means a default, breach, or wrongful act or omission.

(18) "Fungible goods" means:

(A) goods of which any unit, by nature or usage of trade, is the equivalent of any other like unit; or

(B) goods that by agreement are treated as equivalent.

(19) "Genuine" means free of forgery or counterfeiting.

(20) "Good faith," except as otherwise provided in Article 5, means honesty in fact and the observance of reasonable commercial standards of fair dealing.

(21) "Holder" means:

(A) the person in possession of a negotiable instrument that is payable either to bearer or to an identified person that is the person in possession;

(B) the person in possession of a negotiable tangible document of title if the goods are deliverable either to bearer or to the order of the person in possession; or

(C) the person in control of a negotiable electronic document of title.

(22) "Insolvency proceeding" includes an assignment for the benefit of creditors or other proceeding intended to liquidate or rehabilitate the estate of the person involved.

(23) "Insolvent" means:

(A) having generally ceased to pay debts in the ordinary course of business other than as a result of bona fide dispute;

(B) being unable to pay debts as they become due; or

(C) being insolvent within the meaning of federal bankruptcy law.

(24) "Money" means a medium of exchange currently authorized or adopted by a domestic or foreign government. The term includes a monetary unit of account established by an intergovernmental organization or by agreement between two or more countries.

(25) "Organization" means a person other than an individual.

(26) "Party", as distinguished from "third party", means a person that has engaged in a transaction or made an agreement subject to [the Uniform Commercial Code].

(27) "Person" means an individual, corporation, business trust, estate, trust, partnership, limited liability company, association, joint venture, government, governmental subdivision, agency, or instrumentality, public corporation, or any other legal or commercial entity.

(28) "Present value" means the amount as of a date certain of one or more sums payable in the future, discounted to the date certain by use of either an interest rate specified by the parties if that rate is not manifestly unreasonable at the time the transaction is entered into or, if an interest rate is not so specified, a commercially reasonable rate that takes into account the facts and circumstances at the time the transaction is entered into.

(29) "Purchase" means taking by sale, lease, discount, negotiation, mortgage, pledge, lien, security interest, issue or reissue, gift, or any other voluntary transaction creating an interest in property.

(30) "Purchaser" means a person that takes by purchase.

(31) "Record" means information that is inscribed on a tangible medium or that is stored in an electronic or other medium and is retrievable in perceivable form.

(32) "Remedy" means any remedial right to which an aggrieved party is entitled with or without resort to a tribunal.

(33) "Representative" means a person empowered to act for another, including an agent, an officer of a corporation or association, and a trustee, executor, or administrator of an estate.

(34) "Right" includes remedy.

(35) "Security interest" means an interest in personal property or fixtures which secures payment or performance of an obligation. "Security interest" includes any interest of a consignor and a buyer of accounts, chattel paper, a payment intangible, or a promissory note in a transaction that is subject to Article 9. "Security interest" does not include the special property interest of a buyer of goods on identification of those goods to a contract for sale under Section 2-401, but a buyer may also acquire a "security interest" by complying with Article 9. Except as otherwise provided in Section 2-505, the right of a seller or lessor of goods under Article 2 or 2A to retain or acquire possession of the goods is not a "security interest", but a seller or lessor may also acquire a "security interest" by complying with Article 9. The retention or reservation of title by a seller of goods notwithstanding shipment or delivery to the buyer under Section 2-401 is limited in effect to a reservation of a "security interest." Whether a transaction in the form of a lease creates a "security interest" is determined pursuant to Section 1-203.

(36) "Send" in connection with a writing, record, or notice means:

(A) to deposit in the mail or deliver for transmission by any other usual means of communication with postage or cost of transmission provided for and properly addressed and, in the case of an instrument, to an address specified thereon or otherwise agreed, or if there be none to any address reasonable under the circumstances; or

(B) in any other way to cause to be received any record or notice within the time it would have arrived if properly sent.

(37) "Signed" includes using any symbol executed or adopted with present intention to adopt or accept a writing.

(38) "State" means a State of the United States, the District of Columbia, Puerto Rico, the United States Virgin Islands, or any territory or insular possession subject to the jurisdiction of the United States.

(39) "Surety" includes a guarantor or other secondary obligor.

(40) "Term" means a portion of an agreement that relates to a particular matter.

(41) "Unauthorized signature" means a signature made without actual, implied, or apparent authority. The term includes a forgery.

(42) "Warehouse receipt" means a document of title issued by a person engaged in the business of storing goods for hire.

(43) "Writing" includes printing, typewriting, or any other intentional reduction to tangible form. "Written" has a corresponding meaning.

As amended in 2003.

* * * *

§ 1-205. Reasonable Time; Seasonableness.

(a) Whether a time for taking an action required by [the Uniform Commercial Code] is reasonable depends on the nature, purpose, and circumstances of the action.

(b) An action is taken seasonably if it is taken at or within the time agreed or, if no time is agreed, at or within a reasonable time.

* * * *

Part 3 Territorial Applicability and General Rules

* * * *

§ 1-303. Course of Performance, Course of Dealing, and Usage of Trade.

(a) A "course of performance" is a sequence of conduct between the parties to a particular transaction that exists if:

(1) the agreement of the parties with respect to the transaction involves repeated occasions for performance by a party; and

(2) the other party, with knowledge of the nature of the performance and opportunity for objection to it, accepts the performance or acquiesces in it without objection.

(b) A "course of dealing" is a sequence of conduct concerning previous transactions between the parties to a particular transaction that is fairly to be regarded as establishing a common basis of understanding for interpreting their expressions and other conduct.

(c) A "usage of trade" is any practice or method of dealing having such regularity of observance in a place, vocation, or trade as to justify an expectation that it will be observed with respect to the transaction in question. The existence and scope of such a usage must be proved as facts. If it is established that such a usage is embodied in a trade code or similar record, the interpretation of the record is a question of law.

(d) A course of performance or course of dealing between the parties or usage of trade in the vocation or trade in which they are engaged or of which they are or should be aware is relevant in ascertaining the meaning of the parties' agreement, may give particular meaning to specific terms of the agreement, and may supplement or qualify the terms of the agreement. A usage of trade applicable in the place in which part of the performance under the agreement is to occur may be so utilized as to that part of the performance.

(e) Except as otherwise provided in subsection (f), the express terms of an agreement and any applicable course of performance, course of dealing, or usage of trade must be construed whenever reasonable as consistent with each other. If such a construction is unreasonable:

(1) express terms prevail over course of performance, course of dealing, and usage of trade;

(2) course of performance prevails over course of dealing and usage of trade; and

(3) course of dealing prevails over usage of trade.

(f) Subject to Section 2-209 and Section 2A-208, a course of performance is relevant to show a waiver or modification of any term inconsistent with the course of performance.

(g) Evidence of a relevant usage of trade offered by one party is not admissible unless that party has given the other party notice that the court finds sufficient to prevent unfair surprise to the other party.

§ 1–304. Obligation of Good Faith.

Every contract or duty within [the Uniform Commercial Code] imposes an obligation of good faith in its performance and enforcement.

* * * *

§ 1–309. Option to Accelerate at Will.

A term providing that one party or that party's successor in interest may accelerate payment or performance or require collateral or additional collateral "at will" or when the party "deems itself insecure," or words of similar import, means that the party has power to do so only if that party in good faith believes that the prospect of payment or performance is impaired. The burden of establishing lack of good faith is on the party against which the power has been exercised.

§ 1–310. Subordinated Obligations.

An obligation may be issued as subordinated to performance of another obligation of the person obligated, or a creditor may subordinate its right to performance of an obligation by agreement with either the person obligated or another creditor of the person obligated. Subordination does not create a security interest as against either the common debtor or a subordinated creditor.

Article 2 SALES

Part 1 Short Title, General Construction and Subject Matter

§ 2–101. Short Title.

This Article shall be known and may be cited as Uniform Commercial Code—Sales.

§ 2–102. Scope; Certain Security and Other Transactions Excluded From This Article.

Unless the context otherwise requires, this Article applies to transactions in goods; it does not apply to any transaction which although in the form of an unconditional contract to sell or present sale is intended to operate only as a security transaction nor does this Article impair or repeal any statute regulating sales to consumers, farmers or other specified classes of buyers.

§ 2–103. Definitions and Index of Definitions.

(1) In this Article unless the context otherwise requires

(a) "Buyer" means a person who buys or contracts to buy goods.

(b) "Good faith" in the case of a merchant means honesty in fact and the observance of reasonable commercial standards of fair dealing in the trade.

(c) "Receipt" of goods means taking physical possession of them.

(d) "Seller" means a person who sells or contracts to sell goods.

(2) Other definitions applying to this Article or to specified Parts thereof, and the sections in which they appear are:

"Acceptance". Section 2–606.
"Banker's credit". Section 2–325.
"Between merchants". Section 2–104.
"Cancellation". Section 2–106(4).
"Commercial unit". Section 2–105.
"Confirmed credit". Section 2–325.
"Conforming to contract". Section 2–106.
"Contract for sale". Section 2–106.
"Cover". Section 2–712.
"Entrusting". Section 2–403.
"Financing agency". Section 2–104.
"Future goods". Section 2–105.
"Goods". Section 2–105.
"Identification". Section 2–501.
"Installment contract". Section 2–612.
"Letter of Credit". Section 2–325.
"Lot". Section 2–105.
"Merchant". Section 2–104.
"Overseas". Section 2–323.
"Person in position of seller". Section 2–707.
"Present sale". Section 2–106.
"Sale". Section 2–106.
"Sale on approval". Section 2–326.
"Sale or return". Section 2–326.
"Termination". Section 2–106.

(3) The following definitions in other Articles apply to this Article:

"Check". Section 3–104.
"Consignee". Section 7–102.
"Consignor". Section 7–102.
"Consumer goods". Section 9–109.
"Dishonor". Section 3–507.
"Draft". Section 3–104.

(4) In addition Article 1 contains general definitions and principles of construction and interpretation applicable throughout this Article.

As amended in 1994 and 1999.

§ 2–104. Definitions: "Merchant"; "Between Merchants"; "Financing Agency".

(1) "Merchant" means a person who deals in goods of the kind or otherwise by his occupation holds himself out as having knowledge or skill peculiar to the practices or goods involved in the transaction or to whom such knowledge or skill may be attributed by his employment of an agent or broker or other intermediary who by his occupation holds himself out as having such knowledge or skill.

(2) "Financing agency" means a bank, finance company or other person who in the ordinary course of business makes advances against goods or documents of title or who by arrangement with either the seller or the buyer intervenes in ordinary course to make or collect payment due or claimed under the contract for sale, as by purchasing or paying the seller's draft or making advances against it or by merely taking it for collection whether or not documents of title accompany the draft. "Financing agency" includes also a bank or other person who similarly intervenes between persons who are in the position of seller and buyer in respect to the goods (Section 2–707).

(3) "Between merchants" means in any transaction with respect to which both parties are chargeable with the knowledge or skill of merchants.

§ 2–105. Definitions: Transferability; "Goods"; "Future" Goods; "Lot"; "Commercial Unit".

(1) "Goods" means all things (including specially manufactured goods) which are movable at the time of identification to the contract for sale other than the money in which the price is to be paid, investment securities (Article 8) and things in action. "Goods" also includes the unborn young of animals and growing crops and other identified things attached to realty as described in the section on goods to be severed from realty (Section 2–107).

(2) Goods must be both existing and identified before any interest in them can pass. Goods which are not both existing and identified are "future" goods. A purported present sale of future goods or of any interest therein operates as a contract to sell.

(3) There may be a sale of a part interest in existing identified goods.

(4) An undivided share in an identified bulk of fungible goods is sufficiently identified to be sold although the quantity of the bulk is not determined. Any agreed proportion of such a bulk or any quantity thereof agreed upon by number, weight or other measure may to the extent of the seller's interest in the bulk be sold to the buyer who then becomes an owner in common.

(5) "Lot" means a parcel or a single article which is the subject matter of a separate sale or delivery, whether or not it is sufficient to perform the contract.

(6) "Commercial unit" means such a unit of goods as by commercial usage is a single whole for purposes of sale and division of which materially impairs its character or value on the market or in use. A commercial unit may be a single article (as a machine) or a set of articles (as a suite of furniture or an assortment of sizes) or a quantity (as a bale, gross, or carload) or any other unit treated in use or in the relevant market as a single whole.

§ 2–106. Definitions: "Contract"; "Agreement"; "Contract for Sale"; "Sale"; "Present Sale"; "Conforming" to Contract; "Termination"; "Cancellation".

(1) In this Article unless the context otherwise requires "contract" and "agreement" are limited to those relating to the present or future sale of goods. "Contract for sale" includes both a present sale of goods and a contract to sell goods at a future time. A "sale" consists in the passing of title from the seller to the buyer for a price (Section 2–401). A "present sale" means a sale which is accomplished by the making of the contract.

(2) Goods or conduct including any part of a performance are "conforming" or conform to the contract when they are in accordance with the obligations under the contract.

(3) "Termination" occurs when either party pursuant to a power created by agreement or law puts an end to the contract otherwise than for its breach. On "termination" all obligations which are still executory on both sides are discharged but any right based on prior breach or performance survives.

(4) "Cancellation" occurs when either party puts an end to the contract for breach by the other and its effect is the same as that of "termination" except that the cancelling party also retains any remedy for breach of the whole contract or any unperformed balance.

§ 2–107. Goods to Be Severed From Realty: Recording.

(1) A contract for the sale of minerals or the like (including oil and gas) or a structure or its materials to be removed from realty is a contract for the sale of goods within this Article if they are to be severed by the seller but until severance a purported present sale thereof which is not effective as a transfer of an interest in land is effective only as a contract to sell.

(2) A contract for the sale apart from the land of growing crops or other things attached to realty and capable of severance without material harm thereto but not described in subsection (1) or of timber to be cut is a contract for the sale of goods within this Article whether the subject matter is to be severed by the buyer or by the seller even though it forms part of the realty at the time of contracting, and the parties can by identification effect a present sale before severance.

(3) The provisions of this section are subject to any third party rights provided by the law relating to realty records, and the contract for sale may be executed and recorded as a document transferring an interest in land and shall then constitute notice to third parties of the buyer's rights under the contract for sale.

As amended in 1972.

Part 2 Form, Formation and Readjustment of Contract

§ 2–201. Formal Requirements; Statute of Frauds.

(1) Except as otherwise provided in this section a contract for the sale of goods for the price of $500 or more is not enforceable by way of action or defense unless there is some writing sufficient to indicate that a contract for sale has been made between the parties and signed by the party against whom enforcement is sought or by his authorized agent or broker. A writing is not insufficient because it omits or incorrectly states a term agreed upon but the contract is not enforceable under this paragraph beyond the quantity of goods shown in such writing.

(2) Between merchants if within a reasonable time a writing in confirmation of the contract and sufficient against the sender is received and the party receiving it has reason to know its contents, its satisfies the requirements of subsection (1) against such party unless written notice of objection to its contents is given within ten days after it is received.

(3) A contract which does not satisfy the requirements of subsection (1) but which is valid in other respects is enforceable

(a) if the goods are to be specially manufactured for the buyer and are not suitable for sale to others in the ordinary course of the seller's business and the seller, before notice of repudiation is received and under circumstances which reasonably indicate that the goods are for the buyer, has made either a substantial beginning of their manufacture or commitments for their procurement; or

(b) if the party against whom enforcement is sought admits in his pleading, testimony or otherwise in court that a contract for sale was made, but the contract is not enforceable under this provision beyond the quantity of goods admitted; or

(c) with respect to goods for which payment has been made and accepted or which have been received and accepted (Sec. 2–606).

§ 2–202. Final Written Expression: Parol or Extrinsic Evidence.

Terms with respect to which the confirmatory memoranda of the parties agree or which are otherwise set forth in a writing intended by the parties as a final expression of their agreement with respect to such terms as are included therein may not be contradicted by evidence of any prior agreement or of a contemporaneous oral agreement but may be explained or supplemented

(a) by course of dealing or usage of trade (Section 1–205) or by course of performance (Section 2–208); and

(b) by evidence of consistent additional terms unless the court finds the writing to have been intended also as a complete and exclusive statement of the terms of the agreement.

§ 2–203. Seals Inoperative.

The affixing of a seal to a writing evidencing a contract for sale or an offer to buy or sell goods does not constitute the writing a sealed instrument and the law with respect to sealed instruments does not apply to such a contract or offer.

§ 2–204. Formation in General.

(1) A contract for sale of goods may be made in any manner sufficient to show agreement, including conduct by both parties which recognizes the existence of such a contract.

(2) An agreement sufficient to constitute a contract for sale may be found even though the moment of its making is undetermined.

(3) Even though one or more terms are left open a contract for sale does not fail for indefiniteness if the parties have intended to make a contract and there is a reasonably certain basis for giving an appropriate remedy.

§ 2–205. Firm Offers.

An offer by a merchant to buy or sell goods in a signed writing which by its terms gives assurance that it will be held open is not revocable, for lack of consideration, during the time stated or if no time is stated for a reasonable time, but in no event may such period of irrevocability exceed three months; but any such term of assurance on a form supplied by the offeree must be separately signed by the offeror.

§ 2–206. Offer and Acceptance in Formation of Contract.

(1) Unless other unambiguously indicated by the language or circumstances

(a) an offer to make a contract shall be construed as inviting acceptance in any manner and by any medium reasonable in the circumstances;

(b) an order or other offer to buy goods for prompt or current shipment shall be construed as inviting acceptance either by a prompt promise to ship or by the prompt or current shipment of conforming or nonconforming goods, but such a shipment of non-conforming goods does not constitute an acceptance if the seller seasonably notifies the buyer that the shipment is offered only as an accommodation to the buyer.

(2) Where the beginning of a requested performance is a reasonable mode of acceptance an offeror who is not notified of acceptance within a reasonable time may treat the offer as having lapsed before acceptance.

§ 2–207. Additional Terms in Acceptance or Confirmation.

(1) A definite and seasonable expression of acceptance or a written confirmation which is sent within a reasonable time operates as an acceptance even though it states terms additional to or different from those offered or agreed upon, unless acceptance is expressly made conditional on assent to the additional or different terms.

(2) The additional terms are to be construed as proposals for addition to the contract. Between merchants such terms become part of the contract unless:

(a) the offer expressly limits acceptance to the terms of the offer;

(b) they materially alter it; or

(c) notification of objection to them has already been given or is given within a reasonable time after notice of them is received.

(3) Conduct by both parties which recognizes the existence of a contract is sufficient to establish a contract for sale although the writings of the parties do not otherwise establish a contract. In such case the terms of the particular contract consist of those terms on which the writings of the parties agree, together with any supplementary terms incorporated under any other provisions of this Act.

§ 2–208. Course of Performance or Practical Construction.

(1) Where the contract for sale involves repeated occasions for performance by either party with knowledge of the nature of the performance and opportunity for objection to it by the other, any course of performance accepted or acquiesced in without objection shall be relevant to determine the meaning of the agreement.

(2) The express terms of the agreement and any such course of performance, as well as any course of dealing and usage of trade, shall be construed whenever reasonable as consistent with each other; but when such construction is unreasonable, express terms shall control course of performance and course of performance shall control both course of dealing and usage of trade (Section 1–303).

(3) Subject to the provisions of the next section on modification and waiver, such course of performance shall be relevant to show a waiver or modification of any term inconsistent with such course of performance.

§ 2–209. Modification, Rescission and Waiver.

(1) An agreement modifying a contract within this Article needs no consideration to be binding.

(2) A signed agreement which excludes modification or rescission except by a signed writing cannot be otherwise modified or rescinded, but except as between merchants such a requirement on a form supplied by the merchant must be separately signed by the other party.

(3) The requirements of the statute of frauds section of this Article (Section 2–201) must be satisfied if the contract as modified is within its provisions.

(4) Although an attempt at modification or rescission does not satisfy the requirements of subsection (2) or (3) it can operate as a waiver.

(5) A party who has made a waiver affecting an executory portion of the contract may retract the waiver by reasonable notification received by the other party that strict performance will be required of any term waived, unless the retraction would be unjust in view of a material change of position in reliance on the waiver.

§ 2–210. Delegation of Performance; Assignment of Rights.

(1) A party may perform his duty through a delegate unless otherwise agreed or unless the other party has a substantial interest in having his original promisor perform or control the acts required by the contract. No delegation of performance relieves the party delegating of any duty to perform or any liability for breach.

(2) Except as otherwise provided in Section 9–406, unless otherwise agreed, all rights of either seller or buyer can be assigned except where the assignment would materially change the duty of the other party, or increase materially the burden or risk imposed on him by his contract, or impair materially his chance of obtaining return performance. A right to damages for breach of the whole contract or a right arising out of the assignor's due performance of his entire obligation can be assigned despite agreement otherwise.

(3) The creation, attachment, perfection, or enforcement of a security interest in the seller's interest under a contract is not a transfer that materially changes the duty of or increases materially the burden or risk imposed on the buyer or impairs materially the buyer's chance of obtaining return performance within the purview of subsection (2) unless, and then only to the extent that, enforcement actually results in a delegation of material performance of the seller. Even in that event, the creation, attachment, perfection, and enforcement of the security interest remain effective, but (i) the seller is liable to the buyer for damages caused by the delegation to the extent that the damages could not reasonably by prevented by the buyer, and (ii) a court having jurisdiction may grant other appropriate relief, including cancellation of the contract for sale or an injunction against enforcement of the security interest or consummation of the enforcement.

(4) Unless the circumstances indicate the contrary a prohibition of assignment of "the contract" is to be construed as barring only the delegation to the assignee of the assignor's performance.

(5) An assignment of "the contract" or of "all my rights under the contract" or an assignment in similar general terms is an assignment of rights and unless the language or the circumstances (as in an assignment for security) indicate the contrary, it is a delegation of performance of the duties of the assignor and its acceptance by the assignee constitutes a promise by him to perform those duties. This promise is enforceable by either the assignor or the other party to the original contract.

(6) The other party may treat any assignment which delegates performance as creating reasonable grounds for insecurity and may without prejudice to his rights against the assignor demand assurances from the assignee (Section 2–609).

As amended in 1999.

Part 3 General Obligation and Construction of Contract

§ 2–301. General Obligations of Parties.

The obligation of the seller is to transfer and deliver and that of the buyer is to accept and pay in accordance with the contract.

§ 2–302. Unconscionable Contract or Clause.

(1) If the court as a matter of law finds the contract or any clause of the contract to have been unconscionable at the time it was made the court may refuse to enforce the contract, or it may enforce the remainder of the contract without the unconscionable clause, or it may so limit the application of any unconscionable clause as to avoid any unconscionable result.

(2) When it is claimed or appears to the court that the contract or any clause thereof may be unconscionable the parties shall be afforded a reasonable opportunity to present evidence as to its commercial setting, purpose and effect to aid the court in making the determination.

§ 2–303. Allocations or Division of Risks.

Where this Article allocates a risk or a burden as between the parties "unless otherwise agreed", the agreement may not only shift the allocation but may also divide the risk or burden.

§ 2–304. Price Payable in Money, Goods, Realty, or Otherwise.

(1) The price can be made payable in money or otherwise. If it is payable in whole or in part in goods each party is a seller of the goods which he is to transfer.

(2) Even though all or part of the price is payable in an interest in realty the transfer of the goods and the seller's obligations with reference to them are subject to this Article, but not the transfer of the interest in realty or the transferor's obligations in connection therewith.

§ 2–305. Open Price Term.

(1) The parties if they so intend can conclude a contract for sale even though the price is not settled. In such a case the price is a reasonable price at the time for delivery if

(a) nothing is said as to price; or

(b) the price is left to be agreed by the parties and they fail to agree; or

(c) the price is to be fixed in terms of some agreed market or other standard as set or recorded by a third person or agency and it is not so set or recorded.

(2) A price to be fixed by the seller or by the buyer means a price for him to fix in good faith.

(3) When a price left to be fixed otherwise than by agreement of the parties fails to be fixed through fault of one party the other may at his option treat the contract as cancelled or himself fix a reasonable price.

(4) Where, however, the parties intend not to be bound unless the price be fixed or agreed and it is not fixed or agreed there is no contract. In such a case the buyer must return any goods already received or if unable so to do must pay their reasonable value at the time of delivery and the seller must return any portion of the price paid on account.

§ 2–306. Output, Requirements and Exclusive Dealings.

(1) A term which measures the quantity by the output of the seller or the requirements of the buyer means such actual output or requirements as may occur in good faith, except that no quantity unreasonably disproportionate to any stated estimate or in the absence of a stated estimate to any normal or otherwise comparable prior output or requirements may be tendered or demanded.

(2) A lawful agreement by either the seller or the buyer for exclusive dealing in the kind of goods concerned imposes unless otherwise agreed an obligation by the seller to use best efforts to supply the goods and by the buyer to use best efforts to promote their sale.

§ 2–307. Delivery in Single Lot or Several Lots.

Unless otherwise agreed all goods called for by a contract for sale must be tendered in a single delivery and payment is due only on such tender but where the circumstances give either party the right to make or demand delivery in lots the price if it can be apportioned may be demanded for each lot.

§ 2–308. Absence of Specified Place for Delivery.

Unless otherwise agreed

(a) the place for delivery of goods is the seller's place of business or if he has none his residence; but

(b) in a contract for sale of identified goods which to the knowledge of the parties at the time of contracting are in some other place, that place is the place for their delivery; and

(c) documents of title may be delivered through customary banking channels.

§ 2–309. Absence of Specific Time Provisions; Notice of Termination.

(1) The time for shipment or delivery or any other action under a contract if not provided in this Article or agreed upon shall be a reasonable time.

(2) Where the contract provides for successive performances but is indefinite in duration it is valid for a reasonable time but unless otherwise agreed may be terminated at any time by either party.

(3) Termination of a contract by one party except on the happening of an agreed event requires that reasonable notification be received by the other party and an agreement dispensing with notification is invalid if its operation would be unconscionable.

§ 2–310. Open Time for Payment or Running of Credit; Authority to Ship Under Reservation.

Unless otherwise agreed

(a) payment is due at the time and place at which the buyer is to receive the goods even though the place of shipment is the place of delivery; and

(b) if the seller is authorized to send the goods he may ship them under reservation, and may tender the documents of title, but the buyer may inspect the goods after their arrival before payment is due unless such inspection is inconsistent with the terms of the contract (Section 2–513); and

(c) if delivery is authorized and made by way of documents of title otherwise than by subsection (b) then payment is due at the time and place at which the buyer is to receive the documents regardless of where the goods are to be received; and

(d) where the seller is required or authorized to ship the goods on credit the credit period runs from the time of shipment but post-dating the invoice or delaying its dispatch will correspondingly delay the starting of the credit period.

§ 2–311. Options and Cooperation Respecting Performance.

(1) An agreement for sale which is otherwise sufficiently definite (subsection (3) of Section 2–204) to be a contract is not made invalid by the fact that it leaves particulars of performance to be specified by one of the parties. Any such specification must be made in good faith and within limits set by commercial reasonableness.

(2) Unless otherwise agreed specifications relating to assortment of the goods are at the buyer's option and except as otherwise provided in subsections (1)(c) and (3) of Section 2–319 specifications or arrangements relating to shipment are at the seller's option.

(3) Where such specification would materially affect the other party's performance but is not seasonably made or where one party's cooperation is necessary to the agreed performance of the other but is not seasonably forthcoming, the other party in addition to all other remedies

(a) is excused for any resulting delay in his own performance; and

(b) may also either proceed to perform in any reasonable manner or after the time for a material part of his own performance treat the failure to specify or to cooperate as a breach by failure to deliver or accept the goods.

§ 2–312. Warranty of Title and Against Infringement; Buyer's Obligation Against Infringement.

(1) Subject to subsection (2) there is in a contract for sale a warranty by the seller that

(a) the title conveyed shall be good, and its transfer rightful; and

(b) the goods shall be delivered free from any security interest or other lien or encumbrance of which the buyer at the time of contracting has no knowledge.

(2) A warranty under subsection (1) will be excluded or modified only by specific language or by circumstances which give the buyer reason to know that the person selling does not claim title in himself or that he is purporting to sell only such right or title as he or a third person may have.

(3) Unless otherwise agreed a seller who is a merchant regularly dealing in goods of the kind warrants that the goods shall be delivered free of the rightful claim of any third person by way of infringement or the like but a buyer who furnishes specifications to the seller must hold the seller harmless against any such claim which arises out of compliance with the specifications.

§ 2–313. Express Warranties by Affirmation, Promise, Description, Sample.

(1) Express warranties by the seller are created as follows:

(a) Any affirmation of fact or promise made by the seller to the buyer which relates to the goods and becomes part of the basis of the bargain creates an express warranty that the goods shall conform to the affirmation or promise.

(b) Any description of the goods which is made part of the basis of the bargain creates an express warranty that the goods shall conform to the description.

(c) Any sample or model which is made part of the basis of the bargain creates an express warranty that the whole of the goods shall conform to the sample or model.

(2) It is not necessary to the creation of an express warranty that the seller use formal words such as "warrant" or "guarantee" or that he have a specific intention to make a warranty, but an affirmation merely of the value of the goods or a statement purporting to be merely the seller's opinion or commendation of the goods does not create a warranty.

§ 2–314. Implied Warranty: Merchantability; Usage of Trade.

(1) Unless excluded or modified (Section 2–316), a warranty that the goods shall be merchantable is implied in a contract for their sale if the seller is a merchant with respect to goods of that kind. Under this section the serving for value of food or drink to be consumed either on the premises or elsewhere is a sale.

(2) Goods to be merchantable must be at least such as

(a) pass without objection in the trade under the contract description; and

(b) in the case of fungible goods, are of fair average quality within the description; and

(c) are fit for the ordinary purposes for which such goods are used; and

(d) run, within the variations permitted by the agreement, of even kind, quality and quantity within each unit and among all units involved; and

(e) are adequately contained, packaged, and labeled as the agreement may require; and

(f) conform to the promises or affirmations of fact made on the container or label if any.

(3) Unless excluded or modified (Section 2–316) other implied warranties may arise from course of dealing or usage of trade.

§ 2–315. Implied Warranty: Fitness for Particular Purpose.

Where the seller at the time of contracting has reason to know any particular purpose for which the goods are required and that the buyer is relying on the seller's skill or judgment to select or furnish suitable goods, there is unless excluded or modified under the next section an implied warranty that the goods shall be fit for such purpose.

§ 2–316. Exclusion or Modification of Warranties.

(1) Words or conduct relevant to the creation of an express warranty and words or conduct tending to negate or limit warranty shall be construed wherever reasonable as consistent with each other; but subject to the provisions of this Article on parol or extrinsic evidence (Section 2–202) negation or limitation is inoperative to the extent that such construction is unreasonable.

(2) Subject to subsection (3), to exclude or modify the implied warranty of merchantability or any part of it the language must mention merchantability and in case of a writing must be conspicuous, and to exclude or modify any implied warranty of fitness the exclusion must be by a writing and conspicuous. Language to exclude all implied warranties of fitness is sufficient if it states, for example, that "There are no warranties which extend beyond the description on the face hereof."

(3) Notwithstanding subsection (2)

(a) unless the circumstances indicate otherwise, all implied warranties are excluded by expressions like "as is", "with all faults" or other language which in common understanding calls the buyer's attention to the exclusion of warranties and makes plain that there is no implied warranty; and

(b) when the buyer before entering into the contract has examined the goods or the sample or model as fully as he desired or has refused to examine the goods there is no implied warranty with regard to defects which an examination ought in the circumstances to have revealed to him; and

(c) an implied warranty can also be excluded or modified by course of dealing or course of performance or usage of trade.

(4) Remedies for breach of warranty can be limited in accordance with the provisions of this Article on liquidation or limitation of damages and on contractual modification of remedy (Sections 2–718 and 2–719).

§ 2–317. Cumulation and Conflict of Warranties Express or Implied.

Warranties whether express or implied shall be construed as consistent with each other and as cumulative, but if such construction is unreasonable the intention of the parties shall determine which warranty is dominant. In ascertaining that intention the following rules apply:

(a) Exact or technical specifications displace an inconsistent sample or model or general language of description.

(b) A sample from an existing bulk displaces inconsistent general language of description.

(c) Express warranties displace inconsistent implied warranties other than an implied warranty of fitness for a particular purpose.

§ 2–318. Third Party Beneficiaries of Warranties Express or Implied.

Note: If this Act is introduced in the Congress of the United States this section should be omitted. (States to select one alternative.)

Alternative A

A seller's warranty whether express or implied extends to any natural person who is in the family or household of his buyer or who is a guest in his home if it is reasonable to expect that such person may use, consume or be affected by the goods and who is injured in person by breach of the warranty. A seller may not exclude or limit the operation of this section.

Alternative B

A seller's warranty whether express or implied extends to any natural person who may reasonably be expected to use, consume or be affected by the goods and who is injured in person by breach of the warranty. A seller may not exclude or limit the operation of this section.

Alternative C

A seller's warranty whether express or implied extends to any person who may reasonably be expected to use, consume or be affected by the goods and who is injured by breach of the warranty. A seller may not exclude or limit the operation of this section with respect to injury to the person of an individual to whom the warranty extends.

As amended 1966.

§ 2–319. F.O.B. and F.A.S. Terms.

(1) Unless otherwise agreed the term F.O.B. (which means "free on board") at a named place, even though used only in connection with the stated price, is a delivery term under which

(a) when the term is F.O.B. the place of shipment, the seller must at that place ship the goods in the manner provided in this Article (Section 2–504) and bear the expense and risk of putting them into the possession of the carrier; or

(b) when the term is F.O.B. the place of destination, the seller must at his own expense and risk transport the goods to that place and there tender delivery of them in the manner provided in this Article (Section 2–503);

(c) when under either (a) or (b) the term is also F.O.B. vessel, car or other vehicle, the seller must in addition at his own expense and risk load the goods on board. If the term is F.O.B. vessel the buyer must name the vessel and in an appropriate case the seller must comply with the provisions of this Article on the form of bill of lading (Section 2–323).

(2) Unless otherwise agreed the term F.A.S. vessel (which means "free alongside") at a named port, even though used only in connection with the stated price, is a delivery term under which the seller must

(a) at his own expense and risk deliver the goods alongside the vessel in the manner usual in that port or on a dock designated and provided by the buyer; and

(b) obtain and tender a receipt for the goods in exchange for which the carrier is under a duty to issue a bill of lading.

(3) Unless otherwise agreed in any case falling within subsection (1)(a) or (c) or subsection (2) the buyer must seasonably give any

needed instructions for making delivery, including when the term is F.A.S. or F.O.B. the loading berth of the vessel and in an appropriate case its name and sailing date. The seller may treat the failure of needed instructions as a failure of cooperation under this Article (Section 2–311). He may also at his option move the goods in any reasonable manner preparatory to delivery or shipment.

(4) Under the term F.O.B. vessel or F.A.S. unless otherwise agreed the buyer must make payment against tender of the required documents and the seller may not tender nor the buyer demand delivery of the goods in substitution for the documents.

§ 2–320. C.I.F. and C. & F. Terms.

(1) The term C.I.F. means that the price includes in a lump sum the cost of the goods and the insurance and freight to the named destination. The term C. & F. or C.F. means that the price so includes cost and freight to the named destination.

(2) Unless otherwise agreed and even though used only in connection with the stated price and destination, the term C.I.F. destination or its equivalent requires the seller at his own expense and risk to

(a) put the goods into the possession of a carrier at the port for shipment and obtain a negotiable bill or bills of lading covering the entire transportation to the named destination; and

(b) load the goods and obtain a receipt from the carrier (which may be contained in the bill of lading) showing that the freight has been paid or provided for; and

(c) obtain a policy or certificate of insurance, including any war risk insurance, of a kind and on terms then current at the port of shipment in the usual amount, in the currency of the contract, shown to cover the same goods covered by the bill of lading and providing for payment of loss to the order of the buyer or for the account of whom it may concern; but the seller may add to the price the amount of the premium for any such war risk insurance; and

(d) prepare an invoice of the goods and procure any other documents required to effect shipment or to comply with the contract; and

(e) forward and tender with commercial promptness all the documents in due form and with any indorsement necessary to perfect the buyer's rights.

(3) Unless otherwise agreed the term C. & F. or its equivalent has the same effect and imposes upon the seller the same obligations and risks as a C.I.F. term except the obligation as to insurance.

(4) Under the term C.I.F. or C. & F. unless otherwise agreed the buyer must make payment against tender of the required documents and the seller may not tender nor the buyer demand delivery of the goods in substitution for the documents.

§ 2–321. C.I.F. or C. & F.: "Net Landed Weights"; "Payment on Arrival"; Warranty of Condition on Arrival.

Under a contract containing a term C.I.F. or C. & F.

(1) Where the price is based on or is to be adjusted according to "net landed weights", "delivered weights", "out turn" quantity or quality or the like, unless otherwise agreed the seller must reasonably estimate the price. The payment due on tender of the documents called for by the contract is the amount so estimated, but after final adjustment of the price a settlement must be made with commercial promptness.

(2) An agreement described in subsection (1) or any warranty of quality or condition of the goods on arrival places upon the seller the risk of ordinary deterioration, shrinkage and the like in transportation but has no effect on the place or time of identification to the contract for sale or delivery or on the passing of the risk of loss.

(3) Unless otherwise agreed where the contract provides for payment on or after arrival of the goods the seller must before payment allow such preliminary inspection as is feasible; but if the goods are lost delivery of the documents and payment are due when the goods should have arrived.

§ 2–322. Delivery "Ex-Ship".

(1) Unless otherwise agreed a term for delivery of goods "ex-ship" (which means from the carrying vessel) or in equivalent language is not restricted to a particular ship and requires delivery from a ship which has reached a place at the named port of destination where goods of the kind are usually discharged.

(2) Under such a term unless otherwise agreed

(a) the seller must discharge all liens arising out of the carriage and furnish the buyer with a direction which puts the carrier under a duty to deliver the goods; and

(b) the risk of loss does not pass to the buyer until the goods leave the ship's tackle or are otherwise properly unloaded.

§ 2–323. Form of Bill of Lading Required in Overseas Shipment; "Overseas".

(1) Where the contract contemplates overseas shipment and contains a term C.I.F. or C. & F. or F.O.B. vessel, the seller unless otherwise agreed must obtain a negotiable bill of lading stating that the goods have been loaded on board or, in the case of a term C.I.F. or C. & F., received for shipment.

(2) Where in a case within subsection (1) a bill of lading has been issued in a set of parts, unless otherwise agreed if the documents are not to be sent from abroad the buyer may demand tender of the full set; otherwise only one part of the bill of lading need be tendered. Even if the agreement expressly requires a full set

(a) due tender of a single part is acceptable within the provisions of this Article on cure of improper delivery (subsection (1) of Section 2–508); and

(b) even though the full set is demanded, if the documents are sent from abroad the person tendering an incomplete set may nevertheless require payment upon furnishing an indemnity which the buyer in good faith deems adequate.

(3) A shipment by water or by air or a contract contemplating such shipment is "overseas" insofar as by usage of trade or agreement it is subject to the commercial, financing or shipping practices characteristic of international deep water commerce.

§ 2–324. "No Arrival, No Sale" Term.

Under a term "no arrival, no sale" or terms of like meaning, unless otherwise agreed,

(a) the seller must properly ship conforming goods and if they arrive by any means he must tender them on arrival but he assumes no obligation that the goods will arrive unless he has caused the non-arrival; and

(b) where without fault of the seller the goods are in part lost or have so deteriorated as no longer to conform to the contract or arrive after the contract time, the buyer may proceed as if there had been casualty to identified goods (Section 2–613).

§ 2–325. "Letter of Credit" Term; "Confirmed Credit".

(1) Failure of the buyer seasonably to furnish an agreed letter of credit is a breach of the contract for sale.

(2) The delivery to seller of a proper letter of credit suspends the buyer's obligation to pay. If the letter of credit is dishonored, the seller may on seasonable notification to the buyer require payment directly from him.

(3) Unless otherwise agreed the term "letter of credit" or "banker's credit" in a contract for sale means an irrevocable credit issued by a financing agency of good repute and, where the shipment is overseas, of good international repute. The term "confirmed credit" means that the credit must also carry the direct obligation of such an agency which does business in the seller's financial market.

§ 2–326. Sale on Approval and Sale or Return; Rights of Creditors.

(1) Unless otherwise agreed, if delivered goods may be returned by the buyer even though they conform to the contract, the transaction is

(a) a "sale on approval" if the goods are delivered primarily for use, and

(b) a "sale or return" if the goods are delivered primarily for resale.

(2) Goods held on approval are not subject to the claims of the buyer's creditors until acceptance; goods held on sale or return are subject to such claims while in the buyer's possession.

(3) Any "or return" term of a contract for sale is to be treated as a separate contract for sale within the statute of frauds section of this Article (Section 2–201) and as contradicting the sale aspect of the contract within the provisions of this Article or on parol or extrinsic evidence (Section 2–202).

As amended in 1999.

§ 2–327. Special Incidents of Sale on Approval and Sale or Return.

(1) Under a sale on approval unless otherwise agreed

(a) although the goods are identified to the contract the risk of loss and the title do not pass to the buyer until acceptance; and

(b) use of the goods consistent with the purpose of trial is not acceptance but failure seasonably to notify the seller of election to return the goods is acceptance, and if the goods conform to the contract acceptance of any part is acceptance of the whole; and

(c) after due notification of election to return, the return is at the seller's risk and expense but a merchant buyer must follow any reasonable instructions.

(2) Under a sale or return unless otherwise agreed

(a) the option to return extends to the whole or any commercial unit of the goods while in substantially their original condition, but must be exercised seasonably; and

(b) the return is at the buyer's risk and expense.

§ 2–328. Sale by Auction.

(1) In a sale by auction if goods are put up in lots each lot is the subject of a separate sale.

(2) A sale by auction is complete when the auctioneer so announces by the fall of the hammer or in other customary manner. Where a bid is made while the hammer is falling in acceptance of a prior bid the auctioneer may in his discretion reopen the bidding or declare the goods sold under the bid on which the hammer was falling.

(3) Such a sale is with reserve unless the goods are in explicit terms put up without reserve. In an auction with reserve the auctioneer may withdraw the goods at any time until he announces completion of the sale. In an auction without reserve, after the auctioneer calls for bids on an article or lot, that article or lot cannot be withdrawn unless no bid is made within a reasonable time. In either case a bidder may retract his bid until the auctioneer's announcement of completion of the sale, but a bidder's retraction does not revive any previous bid.

(4) If the auctioneer knowingly receives a bid on the seller's behalf or the seller makes or procures such as bid, and notice has not been given that liberty for such bidding is reserved, the buyer may at his option avoid the sale or take the goods at the price of the last good faith bid prior to the completion of the sale. This subsection shall not apply to any bid at a forced sale.

Part 4 Title, Creditors and Good Faith Purchasers

§ 2–401. Passing of Title; Reservation for Security; Limited Application of This Section.

Each provision of this Article with regard to the rights, obligations and remedies of the seller, the buyer, purchasers or other third parties applies irrespective of title to the goods except where the provision refers to such title. Insofar as situations are not covered by the other provisions of this Article and matters concerning title became material the following rules apply:

(1) Title to goods cannot pass under a contract for sale prior to their identification to the contract (Section 2–501), and unless otherwise explicitly agreed the buyer acquires by their identification a special property as limited by this Act. Any retention or reservation by the seller of the title (property) in goods shipped or delivered to the buyer is limited in effect to a reservation of a security interest. Subject to these provisions and to the provisions of the Article on Secured Transactions (Article 9), title to goods passes from the seller to the buyer in any manner and on any conditions explicitly agreed on by the parties.

(2) Unless otherwise explicitly agreed title passes to the buyer at the time and place at which the seller completes his performance with reference to the physical delivery of the goods, despite any reservation of a security interest and even though a document of title is to be delivered at a different time or place; and in particular and despite any reservation of a security interest by the bill of lading

(a) if the contract requires or authorizes the seller to send the goods to the buyer but does not require him to deliver them at destination, title passes to the buyer at the time and place of shipment; but

(b) if the contract requires delivery at destination, title passes on tender there.

(3) Unless otherwise explicitly agreed where delivery is to be made without moving the goods,

(a) if the seller is to deliver a document of title, title passes at the time when and the place where he delivers such documents; or

(b) if the goods are at the time of contracting already identified and no documents are to be delivered, title passes at the time and place of contracting.

(4) A rejection or other refusal by the buyer to receive or retain the goods, whether or not justified, or a justified revocation of acceptance revests title to the goods in the seller. Such revesting occurs by operation of law and is not a "sale".

§ 2–402. Rights of Seller's Creditors Against Sold Goods.

(1) Except as provided in subsections (2) and (3), rights of unsecured creditors of the seller with respect to goods which have been identified to a contract for sale are subject to the buyer's rights to recover the goods under this Article (Sections 2–502 and 2–716).

(2) A creditor of the seller may treat a sale or an identification of goods to a contract for sale as void if as against him a retention of possession by the seller is fraudulent under any rule of law of the state where the goods are situated, except that retention of possession in good faith and current course of trade by a merchant-seller for a commercially reasonable time after a sale or identification is not fraudulent.

(3) Nothing in this Article shall be deemed to impair the rights of creditors of the seller

(a) under the provisions of the Article on Secured Transactions (Article 9); or

(b) where identification to the contract or delivery is made not in current course of trade but in satisfaction of or as security for a pre-existing claim for money, security or the like and is made under circumstances which under any rule of law of the state where the goods are situated would apart from this Article constitute the transaction a fraudulent transfer or voidable preference.

§ 2–403. Power to Transfer; Good Faith Purchase of Goods; "Entrusting".

(1) A purchaser of goods acquires all title which his transferor had or had power to transfer except that a purchaser of a limited interest acquires rights only to the extent of the interest purchased. A person with voidable title has power to transfer a good title to a good faith purchaser for value. When goods have been delivered under a transaction of purchase the purchaser has such power even though

(a) the transferor was deceived as to the identity of the purchaser, or

(b) the delivery was in exchange for a check which is later dishonored, or

(c) it was agreed that the transaction was to be a "cash sale", or

(d) the delivery was procured through fraud punishable as larcenous under the criminal law.

(2) Any entrusting of possession of goods to a merchant who deals in goods of that kind gives him power to transfer all rights of the entruster to a buyer in ordinary course of business.

(3) "Entrusting" includes any delivery and any acquiescence in retention of possession regardless of any condition expressed between the parties to the delivery or acquiescence and regardless of whether the procurement of the entrusting or the possessor's disposition of the goods have been such as to be larcenous under the criminal law.

(4) The rights of other purchasers of goods and of lien creditors are governed by the Articles on Secured Transactions (Article 9), Bulk Transfers (Article 6) and Documents of Title (Article 7).

As amended in 1988.

Part 5 Performance

§ 2–501. Insurable Interest in Goods; Manner of Identification of Goods.

(1) The buyer obtains a special property and an insurable interest in goods by identification of existing goods as goods to which the contract refers even though the goods so identified are non-conforming and he has an option to return or reject them. Such identification can be made at any time and in any manner explicitly agreed to by the parties. In the absence of explicit agreement identification occurs

(a) when the contract is made if it is for the sale of goods already existing and identified;

(b) if the contract is for the sale of future goods other than those described in paragraph (c), when goods are shipped, marked or otherwise designated by the seller as goods to which the contract refers;

(c) when the crops are planted or otherwise become growing crops or the young are conceived if the contract is for the sale of unborn young to be born within twelve months after contracting or for the sale of crops to be harvested within twelve months or the next normal harvest season after contracting whichever is longer.

(2) The seller retains an insurable interest in goods so long as title to or any security interest in the goods remains in him and where the identification is by the seller alone he may until default or insolvency or notification to the buyer that the identification is final substitute other goods for those identified.

(3) Nothing in this section impairs any insurable interest recognized under any other statute or rule of law.

§ 2–502. Buyer's Right to Goods on Seller's Insolvency.

(1) Subject to subsections (2) and (3) and even though the goods have not been shipped a buyer who has paid a part or all of the price of goods in which he has a special property under the provisions of the immediately preceding section may on making and keeping good a tender of any unpaid portion of their price recover them from the seller if:

(a) in the case of goods bought for personal, family, or household purposes, the seller repudiates or fails to deliver as required by the contract; or

(b) in all cases, the seller becomes insolvent within ten days after receipt of the first installment on their price.

(2) The buyer's right to recover the goods under subsection (1)(a) vests upon acquisition of a special property, even if the seller had not then repudiated or failed to deliver.

(3) If the identification creating his special property has been made by the buyer he acquires the right to recover the goods only if they conform to the contract for sale.

As amended in 1999.

§ 2–503. Manner of Seller's Tender of Delivery.

(1) Tender of delivery requires that the seller put and hold conforming goods at the buyer's disposition and give the buyer any notification reasonably necessary to enable him to take delivery. The manner, time and place for tender are determined by the agreement and this Article, and in particular

(a) tender must be at a reasonable hour, and if it is of goods they must be kept available for the period reasonably necessary to enable the buyer to take possession; but

(b) unless otherwise agreed the buyer must furnish facilities reasonably suited to the receipt of the goods.

(2) Where the case is within the next section respecting shipment tender requires that the seller comply with its provisions.

(3) Where the seller is required to deliver at a particular destination tender requires that he comply with subsection (1) and also in any appropriate case tender documents as described in subsections (4) and (5) of this section.

(4) Where goods are in the possession of a bailee and are to be delivered without being moved

(a) tender requires that the seller either tender a negotiable document of title covering such goods or procure acknowledgment by the bailee of the buyer's right to possession of the goods; but

(b) tender to the buyer of a non-negotiable document of title or of a written direction to the bailee to deliver is sufficient tender unless the buyer seasonably objects, and receipt by the bailee of notification of the buyer's rights fixes those rights as against the bailee and all third persons; but risk of loss of the goods and of any failure by the bailee to honor the non-negotiable document of title or to obey the direction remains on the seller until the buyer has had a reasonable time to present the document or direction, and a refusal by the bailee to honor the document or to obey the direction defeats the tender.

(5) Where the contract requires the seller to deliver documents

(a) he must tender all such documents in correct form, except as provided in this Article with respect to bills of lading in a set (subsection (2) of Section 2–323); and

(b) tender through customary banking channels is sufficient and dishonor of a draft accompanying the documents constitutes non-acceptance or rejection.

§ 2–504. Shipment by Seller.

Where the seller is required or authorized to send the goods to the buyer and the contract does not require him to deliver them at a particular destination, then unless otherwise agreed he must

(a) put the goods in the possession of such a carrier and make such a contract for their transportation as may be reasonable having regard to the nature of the goods and other circumstances of the case; and

(b) obtain and promptly deliver or tender in due form any document necessary to enable the buyer to obtain possession of the goods or otherwise required by the agreement or by usage of trade; and

(c) promptly notify the buyer of the shipment.

Failure to notify the buyer under paragraph (c) or to make a proper contract under paragraph (a) is a ground for rejection only if material delay or loss ensues.

§ 2–505. Seller's Shipment under Reservation.

(1) Where the seller has identified goods to the contract by or before shipment:

(a) his procurement of a negotiable bill of lading to his own order or otherwise reserves in him a security interest in the goods. His procurement of the bill to the order of a financing agency or of the buyer indicates in addition only the seller's expectation of transferring that interest to the person named.

(b) a non-negotiable bill of lading to himself or his nominee reserves possession of the goods as security but except in a case of conditional delivery (subsection (2) of Section 2–507) a non-negotiable bill of lading naming the buyer as consignee reserves no security interest even though the seller retains possession of the bill of lading.

(2) When shipment by the seller with reservation of a security interest is in violation of the contract for sale it constitutes an improper contract for transportation within the preceding section but impairs neither the rights given to the buyer by shipment and identification of the goods to the contract nor the seller's powers as a holder of a negotiable document.

§ 2–506. Rights of Financing Agency.

(1) A financing agency by paying or purchasing for value a draft which relates to a shipment of goods acquires to the extent of the payment or purchase and in addition to its own rights under the draft and any document of title securing it any rights of the shipper in the goods including the right to stop delivery and the shipper's right to have the draft honored by the buyer.

(2) The right to reimbursement of a financing agency which has in good faith honored or purchased the draft under commitment to or authority from the buyer is not impaired by subsequent discovery of defects with reference to any relevant document which was apparently regular on its face.

§ 2–507. Effect of Seller's Tender; Delivery on Condition.

(1) Tender of delivery is a condition to the buyer's duty to accept the goods and, unless otherwise agreed, to his duty to pay for them. Tender entitles the seller to acceptance of the goods and to payment according to the contract.

(2) Where payment is due and demanded on the delivery to the buyer of goods or documents of title, his right as against the seller to retain or dispose of them is conditional upon his making the payment due.

§ 2–508. Cure by Seller of Improper Tender or Delivery; Replacement.

(1) Where any tender or delivery by the seller is rejected because non-conforming and the time for performance has not yet expired, the seller may seasonably notify the buyer of his intention to cure and may then within the contract time make a conforming delivery.

(2) Where the buyer rejects a non-conforming tender which the seller had reasonable grounds to believe would be acceptable with or without money allowance the seller may if he seasonably notifies the buyer have a further reasonable time to substitute a conforming tender.

§ 2–509. Risk of Loss in the Absence of Breach.

(1) Where the contract requires or authorizes the seller to ship the goods by carrier

(a) if it does not require him to deliver them at a particular destination, the risk of loss passes to the buyer when the goods are duly delivered to the carrier even though the shipment is under reservation (Section 2–505); but

(b) if it does require him to deliver them at a particular destination and the goods are there duly tendered while in the possession of the carrier, the risk of loss passes to the buyer when the goods are there duly so tendered as to enable the buyer to take delivery.

(2) Where the goods are held by a bailee to be delivered without being moved, the risk of loss passes to the buyer

(a) on his receipt of a negotiable document of title covering the goods; or

(b) on acknowledgment by the bailee of the buyer's right to possession of the goods; or

(c) after his receipt of a non-negotiable document of title or other written direction to deliver, as provided in subsection (4)(b) of Section 2–503.

(3) In any case not within subsection (1) or (2), the risk of loss passes to the buyer on his receipt of the goods if the seller is a merchant; otherwise the risk passes to the buyer on tender of delivery.

(4) The provisions of this section are subject to contrary agreement of the parties and to the provisions of this Article on sale on approval (Section 2–327) and on effect of breach on risk of loss (Section 2–510).

§ 2–510. Effect of Breach on Risk of Loss.

(1) Where a tender or delivery of goods so fails to conform to the contract as to give a right of rejection the risk of their loss remains on the seller until cure or acceptance.

(2) Where the buyer rightfully revokes acceptance he may to the extent of any deficiency in his effective insurance coverage treat the risk of loss as having rested on the seller from the beginning.

(3) Where the buyer as to conforming goods already identified to the contract for sale repudiates or is otherwise in breach before risk of their loss has passed to him, the seller may to the extent of any deficiency in his effective insurance coverage treat the risk of loss as resting on the buyer for a commercially reasonable time.

§ 2–511. Tender of Payment by Buyer; Payment by Check.

(1) Unless otherwise agreed tender of payment is a condition to the seller's duty to tender and complete any delivery.

(2) Tender of payment is sufficient when made by any means or in any manner current in the ordinary course of business unless the seller demands payment in legal tender and gives any extension of time reasonably necessary to procure it.

(3) Subject to the provisions of this Act on the effect of an instrument on an obligation (Section 3–310), payment by check is conditional and is defeated as between the parties by dishonor of the check on due presentment.

As amended in 1994.

§ 2–512. Payment by Buyer Before Inspection.

(1) Where the contract requires payment before inspection nonconformity of the goods does not excuse the buyer from so making payment unless

(a) the non-conformity appears without inspection; or

(b) despite tender of the required documents the circumstances would justify injunction against honor under this Act (Section 5–109(b)).

(2) Payment pursuant to subsection (1) does not constitute an acceptance of goods or impair the buyer's right to inspect or any of his remedies.

As amended in 1995.

§ 2–513. Buyer's Right to Inspection of Goods.

(1) Unless otherwise agreed and subject to subsection (3), where goods are tendered or delivered or identified to the contract for sale, the buyer has a right before payment or acceptance to inspect them at any reasonable place and time and in any reasonable manner. When the seller is required or authorized to send the goods to the buyer, the inspection may be after their arrival.

(2) Expenses of inspection must be borne by the buyer but may be recovered from the seller if the goods do not conform and are rejected.

(3) Unless otherwise agreed and subject to the provisions of this Article on C.I.F. contracts (subsection (3) of Section 2–321), the buyer is not entitled to inspect the goods before payment of the price when the contract provides

(a) for delivery "C.O.D." or on other like terms; or

(b) for payment against documents of title, except where such payment is due only after the goods are to become available for inspection.

(4) A place or method of inspection fixed by the parties is presumed to be exclusive but unless otherwise expressly agreed it does not postpone identification or shift the place for delivery or for passing the risk of loss. If compliance becomes impossible, inspection shall be as provided in this section unless the place or method fixed was clearly intended as an indispensable condition failure of which avoids the contract.

§ 2–514. When Documents Deliverable on Acceptance; When on Payment.

Unless otherwise agreed documents against which a draft is drawn are to be delivered to the drawee on acceptance of the draft if it is payable more than three days after presentment; otherwise, only on payment.

§ 2–515. Preserving Evidence of Goods in Dispute.

In furtherance of the adjustment of any claim or dispute

(a) either party on reasonable notification to the other and for the purpose of ascertaining the facts and preserving evidence has the right to inspect, test and sample the goods including such of them as may be in the possession or control of the other; and

(b) the parties may agree to a third party inspection or survey to determine the conformity or condition of the goods and may agree that the findings shall be binding upon them in any subsequent litigation or adjustment.

Part 6 Breach, Repudiation and Excuse

§ 2–601. Buyer's Rights on Improper Delivery.

Subject to the provisions of this Article on breach in installment contracts (Section 2–612) and unless otherwise agreed under the sections on contractual limitations of remedy (Sections 2–718 and 2–719), if the goods or the tender of delivery fail in any respect to conform to the contract, the buyer may

(a) reject the whole; or

(b) accept the whole; or

(c) accept any commercial unit or units and reject the rest.

§ 2–602. Manner and Effect of Rightful Rejection.

(1) Rejection of goods must be within a reasonable time after their delivery or tender. It is ineffective unless the buyer seasonably notifies the seller.

(2) Subject to the provisions of the two following sections on rejected goods (Sections 2–603 and 2–604),

(a) after rejection any exercise of ownership by the buyer with respect to any commercial unit is wrongful as against the seller; and

(b) if the buyer has before rejection taken physical possession of goods in which he does not have a security interest under the provisions of this Article (subsection (3) of Section 2–711), he is under a duty after rejection to hold them with reasonable care at the seller's disposition for a time sufficient to permit the seller to remove them; but

(c) the buyer has no further obligations with regard to goods rightfully rejected.

(3) The seller's rights with respect to goods wrongfully rejected are governed by the provisions of this Article on Seller's remedies in general (Section 2–703).

§ 2–603. Merchant Buyer's Duties as to Rightfully Rejected Goods.

(1) Subject to any security interest in the buyer (subsection (3) of Section 2–711), when the seller has no agent or place of business at the market of rejection a merchant buyer is under a duty after rejection of goods in his possession or control to follow any reasonable instructions received from the seller with respect to the goods and in the absence of such instructions to make reasonable efforts to sell them for the seller's account if they are perishable or threaten to decline in value speedily. Instructions are not reasonable if on demand indemnity for expenses is not forthcoming.

(2) When the buyer sells goods under subsection (1), he is entitled to reimbursement from the seller or out of the proceeds for reasonable expenses of caring for and selling them, and if the expenses include no selling commission then to such commission as is usual in the trade or if there is none to a reasonable sum not exceeding ten per cent on the gross proceeds.

(3) In complying with this section the buyer is held only to good faith and good faith conduct hereunder is neither acceptance nor conversion nor the basis of an action for damages.

§ 2–604. Buyer's Options as to Salvage of Rightfully Rejected Goods.

Subject to the provisions of the immediately preceding section on perishables if the seller gives no instructions within a reasonable time after notification of rejection the buyer may store the rejected goods for the seller's account or reship them to him or resell them for the seller's account with reimbursement as provided in the preceding section. Such action is not acceptance or conversion.

§ 2–605. Waiver of Buyer's Objections by Failure to Particularize.

(1) The buyer's failure to state in connection with rejection a particular defect which is ascertainable by reasonable inspection precludes him from relying on the unstated defect to justify rejection or to establish breach

(a) where the seller could have cured it if stated seasonably; or

(b) between merchants when the seller has after rejection made a request in writing for a full and final written statement of all defects on which the buyer proposes to rely.

(2) Payment against documents made without reservation of rights precludes recovery of the payment for defects apparent on the face of the documents.

§ 2–606. What Constitutes Acceptance of Goods.

(1) Acceptance of goods occurs when the buyer

(a) after a reasonable opportunity to inspect the goods signifies to the seller that the goods are conforming or that he will take or retain them in spite of their nonconformity; or

(b) fails to make an effective rejection (subsection (1) of Section 2–602), but such acceptance does not occur until the buyer has had a reasonable opportunity to inspect them; or

(c) does any act inconsistent with the seller's ownership; but if such act is wrongful as against the seller it is an acceptance only if ratified by him.

(2) Acceptance of a part of any commercial unit is acceptance of that entire unit.

§ 2–607. Effect of Acceptance; Notice of Breach; Burden of Establishing Breach After Acceptance; Notice of Claim or Litigation to Person Answerable Over.

(1) The buyer must pay at the contract rate for any goods accepted.

(2) Acceptance of goods by the buyer precludes rejection of the goods accepted and if made with knowledge of a non-conformity cannot be revoked because of it unless the acceptance was on the reasonable assumption that the non-conformity would be seasonably cured but acceptance does not of itself impair any other remedy provided by this Article for non-conformity.

(3) Where a tender has been accepted

(a) the buyer must within a reasonable time after he discovers or should have discovered any breach notify the seller of breach or be barred from any remedy; and

(b) if the claim is one for infringement or the like (subsection (3) of Section 2–312) and the buyer is sued as a result of such a breach he must so notify the seller within a reasonable time after he receives notice of the litigation or be barred from any remedy over for liability established by the litigation.

(4) The burden is on the buyer to establish any breach with respect to the goods accepted.

(5) Where the buyer is sued for breach of a warranty or other obligation for which his seller is answerable over

(a) he may give his seller written notice of the litigation. If the notice states that the seller may come in and defend and that if the seller does not do so he will be bound in any action against him by his buyer by any determination of fact common to the two litigations, then unless the seller after seasonable receipt of the notice does come in and defend he is so bound.

(b) if the claim is one for infringement or the like (subsection (3) of Section 2–312) the original seller may demand in writing that his buyer turn over to him control of the litigation including settlement or else be barred from any remedy over and if he also agrees to bear all expense and to satisfy any adverse judgment, then unless the buyer after seasonable receipt of the demand does turn over control the buyer is so barred.

(6) The provisions of subsections (3), (4) and (5) apply to any obligation of a buyer to hold the seller harmless against infringement or the like (subsection (3) of Section 2–312).

§ 2–608. Revocation of Acceptance in Whole or in Part.

(1) The buyer may revoke his acceptance of a lot or commercial unit whose non-conformity substantially impairs its value to him if he has accepted it

(a) on the reasonable assumption that its nonconformity would be cured and it has not been seasonably cured; or

(b) without discovery of such non-conformity if his acceptance was reasonably induced either by the difficulty of discovery before acceptance or by the seller's assurances.

(2) Revocation of acceptance must occur within a reasonable time after the buyer discovers or should have discovered the ground for it and before any substantial change in condition of the goods which is not caused by their own defects. It is not effective until the buyer notifies the seller of it.

(3) A buyer who so revokes has the same rights and duties with regard to the goods involved as if he had rejected them.

§ 2–609. Right to Adequate Assurance of Performance.

(1) A contract for sale imposes an obligation on each party that the other's expectation of receiving due performance will not be impaired. When reasonable grounds for insecurity arise with respect to the performance of either party the other may in writing demand adequate assurance of due performance and until he receives such assurance may if commercially reasonable suspend any performance for which he has not already received the agreed return.

(2) Between merchants the reasonableness of grounds for insecurity and the adequacy of any assurance offered shall be determined according to commercial standards.

(3) Acceptance of any improper delivery or payment does not prejudice the party's right to demand adequate assurance of future performance.

(4) After receipt of a justified demand failure to provide within a reasonable time not exceeding thirty days such assurance of due performance as is adequate under the circumstances of the particular case is a repudiation of the contract.

§ 2–610. Anticipatory Repudiation.

When either party repudiates the contract with respect to a performance not yet due the loss of which will substantially impair the value of the contract to the other, the aggrieved party may

(a) for a commercially reasonable time await performance by the repudiating party; or

(b) resort to any remedy for breach (Section 2–703 or Section 2–711), even though he has notified the repudiating party that he would await the latter's performance and has urged retraction; and

(c) in either case suspend his own performance or proceed in accordance with the provisions of this Article on the seller's right to identify goods to the contract notwithstanding breach or to salvage unfinished goods (Section 2–704).

§ 2–611. Retraction of Anticipatory Repudiation.

(1) Until the repudiating party's next performance is due he can retract his repudiation unless the aggrieved party has since the repudiation cancelled or materially changed his position or otherwise indicated that he considers the repudiation final.

(2) Retraction may be by any method which clearly indicates to the aggrieved party that the repudiating party intends to perform, but must include any assurance justifiably demanded under the provisions of this Article (Section 2–609).

(3) Retraction reinstates the repudiating party's rights under the contract with due excuse and allowance to the aggrieved party for any delay occasioned by the repudiation.

§ 2–612. "Installment Contract"; Breach.

(1) An "installment contract" is one which requires or authorizes the delivery of goods in separate lots to be separately accepted, even though the contract contains a clause "each delivery is a separate contract" or its equivalent.

(2) The buyer may reject any installment which is non-conforming if the non-conformity substantially impairs the value of that installment and cannot be cured or if the non-conformity is a defect in the required documents; but if the non-conformity does not fall within subsection (3) and the seller gives adequate assurance of its cure the buyer must accept that installment.

(3) Whenever non-conformity or default with respect to one or more installments substantially impairs the value of the whole contract there is a breach of the whole. But the aggrieved party reinstates the contract if he accepts a non-conforming installment without seasonably notifying of cancellation or if he brings an action with respect only to past installments or demands performance as to future installments.

§ 2–613. Casualty to Identified Goods.

Where the contract requires for its performance goods identified when the contract is made, and the goods suffer casualty without fault of either party before the risk of loss passes to the buyer, or in a proper case under a "no arrival, no sale" term (Section 2–324) then

(a) if the loss is total the contract is avoided; and

(b) if the loss is partial or the goods have so deteriorated as no longer to conform to the contract the buyer may nevertheless demand inspection and at his option either treat the contract as voided or accept the goods with due allowance from the contract price for the deterioration or the deficiency in quantity but without further right against the seller.

§ 2–614. Substituted Performance.

(1) Where without fault of either party the agreed berthing, loading, or unloading facilities fail or an agreed type of carrier becomes unavailable or the agreed manner of delivery otherwise becomes commercially impracticable but a commercially reasonable substitute is available, such substitute performance must be tendered and accepted.

(2) If the agreed means or manner of payment fails because of domestic or foreign governmental regulation, the seller may withhold or stop delivery unless the buyer provides a means or manner of payment which is commercially a substantial equivalent. If delivery has already been taken, payment by the means or in the manner provided by the regulation discharges the buyer's obligation unless the regulation is discriminatory, oppressive or predatory.

§ 2–615. Excuse by Failure of Presupposed Conditions.

Except so far as a seller may have assumed a greater obligation and subject to the preceding section on substituted performance:

(a) Delay in delivery or non-delivery in whole or in part by a seller who complies with paragraphs (b) and (c) is not a breach of his duty under a contract for sale if performance as agreed has been made impracticable by the occurrence of a contingency the nonoccurrence of which was a basic assumption on which the contract was made or by compliance in good faith with any applicable foreign or domestic governmental regulation or order whether or not it later proves to be invalid.

(b) Where the causes mentioned in paragraph (a) affect only a part of the seller's capacity to perform, he must allocate production and deliveries among his customers but may at his option include regular customers not then under contract as well as his own requirements for further manufacture. He may so allocate in any manner which is fair and reasonable.

(c) The seller must notify the buyer seasonably that there will be delay or non-delivery and, when allocation is required under paragraph (b), of the estimated quota thus made available for the buyer.

§ 2–616. Procedure on Notice Claiming Excuse.

(1) Where the buyer receives notification of a material or indefinite delay or an allocation justified under the preceding section he may by written notification to the seller as to any delivery concerned, and where the prospective deficiency substantially impairs the value of the whole contract under the provisions of this Article relating to breach of installment contracts (Section 2–612), then also as to the whole,

(a) terminate and thereby discharge any unexecuted portion of the contract; or

(b) modify the contract by agreeing to take his available quota in substitution.

(2) If after receipt of such notification from the seller the buyer fails so to modify the contract within a reasonable time not exceeding thirty days the contract lapses with respect to any deliveries affected.

(3) The provisions of this section may not be negated by agreement except in so far as the seller has assumed a greater obligation under the preceding section.

Part 7 Remedies

§ 2–701. Remedies for Breach of Collateral Contracts Not Impaired.

Remedies for breach of any obligation or promise collateral or ancillary to a contract for sale are not impaired by the provisions of this Article.

§ 2–702. Seller's Remedies on Discovery of Buyer's Insolvency.

(1) Where the seller discovers the buyer to be insolvent he may refuse delivery except for cash including payment for all goods theretofore delivered under the contract, and stop delivery under this Article (Section 2–705).

(2) Where the seller discovers that the buyer has received goods on credit while insolvent he may reclaim the goods upon demand made within ten days after the receipt, but if misrepresentation of solvency has been made to the particular seller in writing within three months before delivery the ten day limitation does not apply. Except as provided in this subsection the seller may not base a right to reclaim goods on the buyer's fraudulent or innocent misrepresentation of solvency or of intent to pay.

(3) The seller's right to reclaim under subsection (2) is subject to the rights of a buyer in ordinary course or other good faith purchaser under this Article (Section 2–403). Successful reclamation of goods excludes all other remedies with respect to them.

§ 2–703. Seller's Remedies in General.

Where the buyer wrongfully rejects or revokes acceptance of goods or fails to make a payment due on or before delivery or repudiates with respect to a part or the whole, then with respect to any goods directly affected and, if the breach is of the whole contract (Section 2–612), then also with respect to the whole undelivered balance, the aggrieved seller may

(a) withhold delivery of such goods;

(b) stop delivery by any bailee as hereafter provided (Section 2–705);

(c) proceed under the next section respecting goods still unidentified to the contract;

(d) resell and recover damages as hereafter provided (Section 2–706);

(e) recover damages for non-acceptance (Section 2–708) or in a proper case the price (Section 2–709);

(f) cancel.

§ 2–704. Seller's Right to Identify Goods to the Contract Notwithstanding Breach or to Salvage Unfinished Goods.

(1) An aggrieved seller under the preceding section may

(a) identify to the contract conforming goods not already identified if at the time he learned of the breach they are in his possession or control;

(b) treat as the subject of resale goods which have demonstrably been intended for the particular contract even though those goods are unfinished.

(2) Where the goods are unfinished an aggrieved seller may in the exercise of reasonable commercial judgment for the purposes of avoiding loss and of effective realization either complete the manufacture and wholly identify the goods to the contract or cease manufacture and resell for scrap or salvage value or proceed in any other reasonable manner.

§ 2–705. Seller's Stoppage of Delivery in Transit or Otherwise.

(1) The seller may stop delivery of goods in the possession of a carrier or other bailee when he discovers the buyer to be insolvent (Section 2–702) and may stop delivery of carload, truckload, planeload or larger shipments of express or freight when the buyer repudiates or fails to make a payment due before delivery or if for any other reason the seller has a right to withhold or reclaim the goods.

(2) As against such buyer the seller may stop delivery until

(a) receipt of the goods by the buyer; or

(b) acknowledgment to the buyer by any bailee of the goods except a carrier that the bailee holds the goods for the buyer; or

(c) such acknowledgment to the buyer by a carrier by reshipment or as warehouseman; or

(d) negotiation to the buyer of any negotiable document of title covering the goods.

(3) (a) To stop delivery the seller must so notify as to enable the bailee by reasonable diligence to prevent delivery of the goods.

(b) After such notification the bailee must hold and deliver the goods according to the directions of the seller but the seller is liable to the bailee for any ensuing charges or damages.

(c) If a negotiable document of title has been issued for goods the bailee is not obliged to obey a notification to stop until surrender of the document.

(d) A carrier who has issued a non-negotiable bill of lading is not obliged to obey a notification to stop received from a person other than the consignor.

§ 2–706. Seller's Resale Including Contract for Resale.

(1) Under the conditions stated in Section 2–703 on seller's remedies, the seller may resell the goods concerned or the undelivered balance thereof. Where the resale is made in good faith and in a commercially reasonable manner the seller may recover the difference between the resale price and the contract price together with any incidental damages allowed under the provisions of this Article (Section 2–710), but less expenses saved in consequence of the buyer's breach.

(2) Except as otherwise provided in subsection (3) or unless otherwise agreed resale may be at public or private sale including sale by way of one or more contracts to sell or of identification to an existing contract of the seller. Sale may be as a unit or in parcels and at any time and place and on any terms but every aspect of the sale including the method, manner, time, place and terms must be commercially reasonable. The resale must be reasonably identified as referring to the broken contract, but it is not necessary that the goods be in existence or that any or all of them have been identified to the contract before the breach.

(3) Where the resale is at private sale the seller must give the buyer reasonable notification of his intention to resell.

(4) Where the resale is at public sale

(a) only identified goods can be sold except where there is a recognized market for a public sale of futures in goods of the kind; and

(b) it must be made at a usual place or market for public sale if one is reasonably available and except in the case of goods which are perishable or threaten to decline in value speedily the seller must give the buyer reasonable notice of the time and place of the resale; and

(c) if the goods are not to be within the view of those attending the sale the notification of sale must state the place where the goods are located and provide for their reasonable inspection by prospective bidders; and

(d) the seller may buy.

(5) A purchaser who buys in good faith at a resale takes the goods free of any rights of the original buyer even though the seller fails to comply with one or more of the requirements of this section.

(6) The seller is not accountable to the buyer for any profit made on any resale. A person in the position of a seller (Section 2–707) or a buyer who has rightfully rejected or justifiably revoked acceptance must account for any excess over the amount of his security interest, as hereinafter defined (subsection (3) of Section 2–711).

§ 2–707. "Person in the Position of a Seller".

(1) A "person in the position of a seller" includes as against a principal an agent who has paid or become responsible for the price of goods on behalf of his principal or anyone who otherwise holds a security interest or other right in goods similar to that of a seller.

(2) A person in the position of a seller may as provided in this Article withhold or stop delivery (Section 2–705) and resell (Section 2–706) and recover incidental damages (Section 2–710).

§ 2–708. Seller's Damages for Non-Acceptance or Repudiation.

(1) Subject to subsection (2) and to the provisions of this Article with respect to proof of market price (Section 2–723), the measure of damages for non-acceptance or repudiation by the buyer is the difference between the market price at the time and place for tender and the unpaid contract price together with any incidental damages provided in this Article (Section 2–710), but less expenses saved in consequence of the buyer's breach.

(2) If the measure of damages provided in subsection (1) is inadequate to put the seller in as good a position as performance would have done then the measure of damages is the profit (including reasonable overhead) which the seller would have made from full performance by the buyer, together with any incidental damages provided in this Article (Section 2–710), due allowance for costs reasonably incurred and due credit for payments or proceeds of resale.

§ 2–709. Action for the Price.

(1) When the buyer fails to pay the price as it becomes due the seller may recover, together with any incidental damages under the next section, the price

(a) of goods accepted or of conforming goods lost or damaged within a commercially reasonable time after risk of their loss has passed to the buyer; and

(b) of goods identified to the contract if the seller is unable after reasonable effort to resell them at a reasonable price or the circumstances reasonably indicate that such effort will be unavailing.

(2) Where the seller sues for the price he must hold for the buyer any goods which have been identified to the contract and are still in his control except that if resale becomes possible he may resell them at any time prior to the collection of the judgment. The net proceeds of any such resale must be credited to the buyer and payment of the judgment entitles him to any goods not resold.

(3) After the buyer has wrongfully rejected or revoked acceptance of the goods or has failed to make a payment due or has repudiated (Section 2–610), a seller who is held not entitled to the price under this section shall nevertheless be awarded damages for non-acceptance under the preceding section.

§ 2–710. Seller's Incidental Damages.

Incidental damages to an aggrieved seller include any commercially reasonable charges, expenses or commissions incurred in stopping delivery, in the transportation, care and custody of goods after the buyer's breach, in connection with return or resale of the goods or otherwise resulting from the breach.

§ 2–711. Buyer's Remedies in General; Buyer's Security Interest in Rejected Goods.

(1) Where the seller fails to make delivery or repudiates or the buyer rightfully rejects or justifiably revokes acceptance then with respect to any goods involved, and with respect to the whole if the breach goes to the whole contract (Section 2–612), the buyer may cancel and whether or not he has done so may in addition to recovering so much of the price as has been paid

(a) "cover" and have damages under the next section as to all the goods affected whether or not they have been identified to the contract; or

(b) recover damages for non-delivery as provided in this Article (Section 2–713).

(2) Where the seller fails to deliver or repudiates the buyer may also

(a) if the goods have been identified recover them as provided in this Article (Section 2–502); or

(b) in a proper case obtain specific performance or replevy the goods as provided in this Article (Section 2–716).

(3) On rightful rejection or justifiable revocation of acceptance a buyer has a security interest in goods in his possession or control for any payments made on their price and any expenses reasonably incurred in their inspection, receipt, transportation, care and custody and may hold such goods and resell them in like manner as an aggrieved seller (Section 2–706).

§ 2–712. "Cover"; Buyer's Procurement of Substitute Goods.

(1) After a breach within the preceding section the buyer may "cover" by making in good faith and without unreasonable delay any reason-

able purchase of or contract to purchase goods in substitution for those due from the seller.

(2) The buyer may recover from the seller as damages the difference between the cost of cover and the contract price together with any incidental or consequential damages as hereinafter defined (Section 2–715), but less expenses saved in consequence of the seller's breach.

(3) Failure of the buyer to effect cover within this section does not bar him from any other remedy.

§ 2–713. Buyer's Damages for Non-Delivery or Repudiation.

(1) Subject to the provisions of this Article with respect to proof of market price (Section 2–723), the measure of damages for non-delivery or repudiation by the seller is the difference between the market price at the time when the buyer learned of the breach and the contract price together with any incidental and consequential damages provided in this Article (Section 2–715), but less expenses saved in consequence of the seller's breach.

(2) Market price is to be determined as of the place for tender or, in cases of rejection after arrival or revocation of acceptance, as of the place of arrival.

§ 2–714. Buyer's Damages for Breach in Regard to Accepted Goods.

(1) Where the buyer has accepted goods and given notification (subsection (3) of Section 2–607) he may recover as damages for any non-conformity of tender the loss resulting in the ordinary course of events from the seller's breach as determined in any manner which is reasonable.

(2) The measure of damages for breach of warranty is the difference at the time and place of acceptance between the value of the goods accepted and the value they would have had if they had been as warranted, unless special circumstances show proximate damages of a different amount.

(3) In a proper case any incidental and consequential damages under the next section may also be recovered.

§ 2–715. Buyer's Incidental and Consequential Damages.

(1) Incidental damages resulting from the seller's breach include expenses reasonably incurred in inspection, receipt, transportation and care and custody of goods rightfully rejected, any commercially reasonable charges, expenses or commissions in connection with effecting cover and any other reasonable expense incident to the delay or other breach.

(2) Consequential damages resulting from the seller's breach include

(a) any loss resulting from general or particular requirements and needs of which the seller at the time of contracting had reason to know and which could not reasonably be prevented by cover or otherwise; and

(b) injury to person or property proximately resulting from any breach of warranty.

§ 2–716. Buyer's Right to Specific Performance or Replevin.

(1) Specific performance may be decreed where the goods are unique or in other proper circumstances.

(2) The decree for specific performance may include such terms and conditions as to payment of the price, damages, or other relief as the court may deem just.

(3) The buyer has a right of replevin for goods identified to the contract if after reasonable effort he is unable to effect cover for such goods or the circumstances reasonably indicate that such effort will be unavailing or if the goods have been shipped under reservation and satisfaction of the security interest in them has been made or tendered. In the case of goods bought for personal, family, or household purposes, the buyer's right of replevin vests upon acquisition of a special property, even if the seller had not then repudiated or failed to deliver.

As amended in 1999.

§ 2–717. Deduction of Damages From the Price.

The buyer on notifying the seller of his intention to do so may deduct all or any part of the damages resulting from any breach of the contract from any part of the price still due under the same contract.

§ 2–718. Liquidation or Limitation of Damages; Deposits.

(1) Damages for breach by either party may be liquidated in the agreement but only at an amount which is reasonable in the light of the anticipated or actual harm caused by the breach, the difficulties of proof of loss, and the inconvenience or nonfeasibility of otherwise obtaining an adequate remedy. A term fixing unreasonably large liquidated damages is void as a penalty.

(2) Where the seller justifiably withholds delivery of goods because of the buyer's breach, the buyer is entitled to restitution of any amount by which the sum of his payments exceeds

(a) the amount to which the seller is entitled by virtue of terms liquidating the seller's damages in accordance with subsection (1), or

(b) in the absence of such terms, twenty per cent of the value of the total performance for which the buyer is obligated under the contract or $500, whichever is smaller.

(3) The buyer's right to restitution under subsection (2) is subject to offset to the extent that the seller establishes

(a) a right to recover damages under the provisions of this Article other than subsection (1), and

(b) the amount or value of any benefits received by the buyer directly or indirectly by reason of the contract.

(4) Where a seller has received payment in goods their reasonable value or the proceeds of their resale shall be treated as payments for the purposes of subsection (2); but if the seller has notice of the buyer's breach before reselling goods received in part performance, his resale is subject to the conditions laid down in this Article on resale by an aggrieved seller (Section 2–706).

§ 2–719. Contractual Modification or Limitation of Remedy.

(1) Subject to the provisions of subsections (2) and (3) of this section and of the preceding section on liquidation and limitation of damages,

(a) the agreement may provide for remedies in addition to or in substitution for those provided in this Article and may limit or alter the measure of damages recoverable under this Article, as by limiting the buyer's remedies to return of the goods and repayment of the price or to repair and replacement of nonconforming goods or parts; and

(b) resort to a remedy as provided is optional unless the remedy is expressly agreed to be exclusive, in which case it is the sole remedy.

(2) Where circumstances cause an exclusive or limited remedy to fail of its essential purpose, remedy may be had as provided in this Act.

(3) Consequential damages may be limited or excluded unless the limitation or exclusion is unconscionable. Limitation of consequential damages for injury to the person in the case of consumer goods is *prima facie* unconscionable but limitation of damages where the loss is commercial is not.

§ 2–720. Effect of "Cancellation" or "Rescission" on Claims for Antecedent Breach.

Unless the contrary intention clearly appears, expressions of "cancellation" or "rescission" of the contract or the like shall not be construed as a renunciation or discharge of any claim in damages for an antecedent breach.

§ 2–721. Remedies for Fraud.

Remedies for material misrepresentation or fraud include all remedies available under this Article for non-fraudulent breach. Neither rescission or a claim for rescission of the contract for sale nor rejection or return of the goods shall bar or be deemed inconsistent with a claim for damages or other remedy.

§ 2–722. Who Can Sue Third Parties for Injury to Goods.

Where a third party so deals with goods which have been identified to a contract for sale as to cause actionable injury to a party to that contract

(a) a right of action against the third party is in either party to the contract for sale who has title to or a security interest or a special property or an insurable interest in the goods; and if the goods have been destroyed or converted a right of action is also in the party who either bore the risk of loss under the contract for sale or has since the injury assumed that risk as against the other;

(b) if at the time of the injury the party plaintiff did not bear the risk of loss as against the other party to the contract for sale and there is no arrangement between them for disposition of the recovery, his suit or settlement is, subject to his own interest, as a fiduciary for the other party to the contract;

(c) either party may with the consent of the other sue for the benefit of whom it may concern.

§ 2–723. Proof of Market Price: Time and Place.

(1) If an action based on anticipatory repudiation comes to trial before the time for performance with respect to some or all of the goods, any damages based on market price (Section 2–708 or Section 2–713) shall be determined according to the price of such goods prevailing at the time when the aggrieved party learned of the repudiation.

(2) If evidence of a price prevailing at the times or places described in this Article is not readily available the price prevailing within any reasonable time before or after the time described or at any other place which in commercial judgment or under usage of trade would serve as a reasonable substitute for the one described may be used, making any proper allowance for the cost of transporting the goods to or from such other place.

(3) Evidence of a relevant price prevailing at a time or place other than the one described in this Article offered by one party is not admissible unless and until he has given the other party such notice as the court finds sufficient to prevent unfair surprise.

§ 2–724. Admissibility of Market Quotations.

Whenever the prevailing price or value of any goods regularly bought and sold in any established commodity market is in issue, reports in official publications or trade journals or in newspapers or periodicals of general circulation published as the reports of such market shall be admissible in evidence. The circumstances of the preparation of such a report may be shown to affect its weight but not its admissibility.

§ 2–725. Statute of Limitations in Contracts for Sale.

(1) An action for breach of any contract for sale must be commenced within four years after the cause of action has accrued. By the original agreement the parties may reduce the period of limitation to not less than one year but may not extend it.

(2) A cause of action accrues when the breach occurs, regardless of the aggrieved party's lack of knowledge of the breach. A breach of warranty occurs when tender of delivery is made, except that where a warranty explicitly extends to future performance of the goods and discovery of the breach must await the time of such performance the cause of action accrues when the breach is or should have been discovered.

(3) Where an action commenced within the time limited by subsection (1) is so terminated as to leave available a remedy by another action for the same breach such other action may be commenced after the expiration of the time limited and within six months after the termination of the first action unless the termination resulted from voluntary discontinuance or from dismissal for failure or neglect to prosecute.

(4) This section does not alter the law on tolling of the statute of limitations nor does it apply to causes of action which have accrued before this Act becomes effective.

Article 2A
LEASES

Part 1 General Provisions

§ 2A–101. Short Title.

This Article shall be known and may be cited as the Uniform Commercial Code—Leases.

§ 2A–102. Scope.

This Article applies to any transaction, regardless of form, that creates a lease.

§ 2A–103. Definitions and Index of Definitions.

(1) In this Article unless the context otherwise requires:

(a) "Buyer in ordinary course of business" means a person who in good faith and without knowledge that the sale to him [or her] is in violation of the ownership rights or security interest or leasehold interest of a third party in the goods buys in ordinary course from a person in the business of selling goods of that kind but does not include a pawnbroker. "Buying" may be for cash or by exchange of other property or on secured or unsecured credit and includes receiving goods or documents of title under a pre-existing contract for sale but does not include a transfer in bulk or as security for or in total or partial satisfaction of a money debt.

(b) "Cancellation" occurs when either party puts an end to the lease contract for default by the other party.

(c) "Commercial unit" means such a unit of goods as by commercial usage is a single whole for purposes of lease and division of which materially impairs its character or value on the market or in use. A commercial unit may be a single article, as a machine, or a set of articles, as a suite of furniture or a line of machinery, or a quantity, as a gross or carload, or any other unit treated in use or in the relevant market as a single whole.

(d) "Conforming" goods or performance under a lease contract means goods or performance that are in accordance with the obligations under the lease contract.

(e) "Consumer lease" means a lease that a lessor regularly engaged in the business of leasing or selling makes to a lessee who is an individual and who takes under the lease primarily for a personal, family, or household purpose [, if the total payments to be made under the lease contract, excluding payments for options to renew or buy, do not exceed $_______].

(f) "Fault" means wrongful act, omission, breach, or default.

(g) "Finance lease" means a lease with respect to which:

(i) the lessor does not select, manufacture or supply the goods;

(ii) the lessor acquires the goods or the right to possession and use of the goods in connection with the lease; and

(iii) one of the following occurs:

(A) the lessee receives a copy of the contract by which the lessor acquired the goods or the right to possession and use of the goods before signing the lease contract;

(B) the lessee's approval of the contract by which the lessor acquired the goods or the right to possession and use of the goods is a condition to effectiveness of the lease contract;

(C) the lessee, before signing the lease contract, receives an accurate and complete statement designating the promises and warranties, and any disclaimers of warranties, limitations or modifications of remedies, or liquidated damages, including those of a third party, such as the manufacturer of the goods, provided to the lessor by the person supplying the goods in connection with or as part of the contract by which the lessor acquired the goods or the right to possession and use of the goods; or

(D) if the lease is not a consumer lease, the lessor, before the lessee signs the lease contract, informs the lessee in writing (a) of the identity of the person supplying the goods to the lessor, unless the lessee has selected that person and directed the lessor to acquire the goods or the right to possession and use of the goods from that person, (b) that the lessee is entitled under this Article to any promises and warranties, including those of any third party, provided to the lessor by the person supplying the goods in connection with or as part of the contract by which the lessor acquired the goods or the right to possession and use of the goods, and (c) that the lessee may communicate with the person supplying the goods to the lessor and receive an accurate and complete statement of those promises and warranties, including any disclaimers and limitations of them or of remedies.

(h) "Goods" means all things that are movable at the time of identification to the lease contract, or are fixtures (Section 2A–309), but the term does not include money, documents, instruments, accounts, chattel paper, general intangibles, or minerals or the like, including oil and gas, before extraction. The term also includes the unborn young of animals.

(i) "Installment lease contract" means a lease contract that authorizes or requires the delivery of goods in separate lots to be separately accepted, even though the lease contract contains a clause "each delivery is a separate lease" or its equivalent.

(j) "Lease" means a transfer of the right to possession and use of goods for a term in return for consideration, but a sale, including a sale on approval or a sale or return, or retention or creation of a security interest is not a lease. Unless the context clearly indicates otherwise, the term includes a sublease.

(k) "Lease agreement" means the bargain, with respect to the lease, of the lessor and the lessee in fact as found in their language or by implication from other circumstances including course of dealing or usage of trade or course of performance as provided in this Article. Unless the context clearly indicates otherwise, the term includes a sublease agreement.

(l) "Lease contract" means the total legal obligation that results from the lease agreement as affected by this Article and any other applicable rules of law. Unless the context clearly indicates otherwise, the term includes a sublease contract.

(m) "Leasehold interest" means the interest of the lessor or the lessee under a lease contract.

(n) "Lessee" means a person who acquires the right to possession and use of goods under a lease. Unless the context clearly indicates otherwise, the term includes a sublessee.

(o) "Lessee in ordinary course of business" means a person who in good faith and without knowledge that the lease to him [or her] is in violation of the ownership rights or security interest or leasehold interest of a third party in the goods, leases in ordinary course from a person in the business of selling or leasing goods of that kind but does not include a pawnbroker. "Leasing" may be for cash or by exchange of other property or on secured or unsecured credit and includes receiving goods or documents of title under a pre-existing lease contract but does not include a transfer in bulk or as security for or in total or partial satisfaction of a money debt.

(p) "Lessor" means a person who transfers the right to possession and use of goods under a lease. Unless the context clearly indicates otherwise, the term includes a sublessor.

(q) "Lessor's residual interest" means the lessor's interest in the goods after expiration, termination, or cancellation of the lease contract.

(r) "Lien" means a charge against or interest in goods to secure payment of a debt or performance of an obligation, but the term does not include a security interest.

(s) "Lot" means a parcel or a single article that is the subject matter of a separate lease or delivery, whether or not it is sufficient to perform the lease contract.

(t) "Merchant lessee" means a lessee that is a merchant with respect to goods of the kind subject to the lease.

(u) "Present value" means the amount as of a date certain of one or more sums payable in the future, discounted to the date certain. The discount is determined by the interest rate specified by the parties if the rate was not manifestly unreasonable at the time the transaction was entered into; otherwise, the discount is determined by a commercially reasonable rate that takes into account the facts and circumstances of each case at the time the transaction was entered into.

(v) "Purchase" includes taking by sale, lease, mortgage, security interest, pledge, gift, or any other voluntary transaction creating an interest in goods.

(w) "Sublease" means a lease of goods the right to possession and use of which was acquired by the lessor as a lessee under an existing lease.

(x) "Supplier" means a person from whom a lessor buys or leases goods to be leased under a finance lease.

(y) "Supply contract" means a contract under which a lessor buys or leases goods to be leased.

(z) "Termination" occurs when either party pursuant to a power created by agreement or law puts an end to the lease contract otherwise than for default.

(2) Other definitions applying to this Article and the sections in which they appear are:

"Accessions". Section 2A–310(1).

"Construction mortgage". Section 2A–309(1)(d).

"Encumbrance". Section 2A–309(1)(e).

"Fixtures". Section 2A–309(1)(a).

"Fixture filing". Section 2A–309(1)(b).

"Purchase money lease". Section 2A–309(1)(c).

(3) The following definitions in other Articles apply to this Article:

"Accounts". Section 9–106.

"Between merchants". Section 2–104(3).

"Buyer". Section 2–103(1)(a).

"Chattel paper". Section 9–105(1)(b).

"Consumer goods". Section 9–109(1).

"Document". Section 9–105(1)(f).

"Entrusting". Section 2–403(3).

"General intangibles". Section 9–106.

"Good faith". Section 2–103(1)(b).

"Instrument". Section 9–105(1)(i).

"Merchant". Section 2–104(1).

"Mortgage". Section 9–105(1)(j).

"Pursuant to commitment". Section 9–105(1)(k).

"Receipt". Section 2–103(1)(c).

"Sale". Section 2–106(1).

"Sale on approval". Section 2–326.

"Sale or return". Section 2–326.

"Seller". Section 2–103(1)(d).

(4) In addition Article 1 contains general definitions and principles of construction and interpretation applicable throughout this Article.

As amended in 1990 and 1999.

§ 2A–104. Leases Subject to Other Law.

(1) A lease, although subject to this Article, is also subject to any applicable:

(a) certificate of title statute of this State: (list any certificate of title statutes covering automobiles, trailers, mobile homes, boats, farm tractors, and the like);

(b) certificate of title statute of another jurisdiction (Section 2A–105); or

(c) consumer protection statute of this State, or final consumer protection decision of a court of this State existing on the effective date of this Article.

(2) In case of conflict between this Article, other than Sections 2A–105, 2A–304(3), and 2A–305(3), and a statute or decision referred to in subsection (1), the statute or decision controls.

(3) Failure to comply with an applicable law has only the effect specified therein.

As amended in 1990.

§ 2A–105. Territorial Application of Article to Goods Covered by Certificate of Title.

Subject to the provisions of Sections 2A–304(3) and 2A–305(3), with respect to goods covered by a certificate of title issued under a statute of this State or of another jurisdiction, compliance and the effect of compliance or noncompliance with a certificate of title statute are governed by the law (including the conflict of laws rules) of the jurisdiction issuing the certificate until the earlier of (a) surrender of the certificate, or (b) four months after the goods are removed from that jurisdiction and thereafter until a new certificate of title is issued by another jurisdiction.

§ 2A–106. Limitation on Power of Parties to Consumer Lease to Choose Applicable Law and Judicial Forum.

(1) If the law chosen by the parties to a consumer lease is that of a jurisdiction other than a jurisdiction in which the lessee resides at the time the lease agreement becomes enforceable or within 30 days thereafter or in which the goods are to be used, the choice is not enforceable.

(2) If the judicial forum chosen by the parties to a consumer lease is a forum that would not otherwise have jurisdiction over the lessee, the choice is not enforceable.

§ 2A–107. Waiver or Renunciation of Claim or Right After Default.

Any claim or right arising out of an alleged default or breach of warranty may be discharged in whole or in part without consideration by a written waiver or renunciation signed and delivered by the aggrieved party.

§ 2A–108. Unconscionability.

(1) If the court as a matter of law finds a lease contract or any clause of a lease contract to have been unconscionable at the time it was made the court may refuse to enforce the lease contract, or it may enforce the remainder of the lease contract without the unconscionable clause, or it may so limit the application of any unconscionable clause as to avoid any unconscionable result.

(2) With respect to a consumer lease, if the court as a matter of law finds that a lease contract or any clause of a lease contract has been induced by unconscionable conduct or that unconscionable conduct has occurred in the collection of a claim arising from a lease contract, the court may grant appropriate relief.

(3) Before making a finding of unconscionability under subsection (1) or (2), the court, on its own motion or that of a party, shall afford the parties a reasonable opportunity to present evidence as to the setting, purpose, and effect of the lease contract or clause thereof, or of the conduct.

(4) In an action in which the lessee claims unconscionability with respect to a consumer lease:

(a) If the court finds unconscionability under subsection (1) or (2), the court shall award reasonable attorney's fees to the lessee.

(b) If the court does not find unconscionability and the lessee claiming unconscionability has brought or maintained an action he [or she] knew to be groundless, the court shall award reasonable attorney's fees to the party against whom the claim is made.

(c) In determining attorney's fees, the amount of the recovery on behalf of the claimant under subsections (1) and (2) is not controlling.

§ 2A–109. Option to Accelerate at Will.

(1) A term providing that one party or his [or her] successor in interest may accelerate payment or performance or require collateral or additional collateral "at will" or "when he [or she] deems himself [or herself] insecure" or in words of similar import must be construed to mean that he [or she] has power to do so only if he [or she] in good faith believes that the prospect of payment or performance is impaired.

(2) With respect to a consumer lease, the burden of establishing good faith under subsection (1) is on the party who exercised the power; otherwise the burden of establishing lack of good faith is on the party against whom the power has been exercised.

Part 2 Formation and Construction of Lease Contract

§ 2A–201. Statute of Frauds.

(1) A lease contract is not enforceable by way of action or defense unless:

(a) the total payments to be made under the lease contract, excluding payments for options to renew or buy, are less than $1,000; or

(b) there is a writing, signed by the party against whom enforcement is sought or by that party's authorized agent, sufficient to indicate that a lease contract has been made between the parties and to describe the goods leased and the lease term.

(2) Any description of leased goods or of the lease term is sufficient and satisfies subsection (1)(b), whether or not it is specific, if it reasonably identifies what is described.

(3) A writing is not insufficient because it omits or incorrectly states a term agreed upon, but the lease contract is not enforceable under subsection (1)(b) beyond the lease term and the quantity of goods shown in the writing.

(4) A lease contract that does not satisfy the requirements of subsection (1), but which is valid in other respects, is enforceable:

(a) if the goods are to be specially manufactured or obtained for the lessee and are not suitable for lease or sale to others in the ordinary course of the lessor's business, and the lessor, before notice of repudiation is received and under circumstances that reasonably indicate that the goods are for the lessee, has made either a substantial beginning of their manufacture or commitments for their procurement;

(b) if the party against whom enforcement is sought admits in that party's pleading, testimony or otherwise in court that a lease contract was made, but the lease contract is not enforceable under this provision beyond the quantity of goods admitted; or

(c) with respect to goods that have been received and accepted by the lessee.

(5) The lease term under a lease contract referred to in subsection (4) is:

(a) if there is a writing signed by the party against whom enforcement is sought or by that party's authorized agent specifying the lease term, the term so specified;

(b) if the party against whom enforcement is sought admits in that party's pleading, testimony, or otherwise in court a lease term, the term so admitted; or

(c) a reasonable lease term.

§ 2A–202. Final Written Expression: Parol or Extrinsic Evidence.

Terms with respect to which the confirmatory memoranda of the parties agree or which are otherwise set forth in a writing intended by the parties as a final expression of their agreement with respect to such terms as are included therein may not be contradicted by evidence of any prior agreement or of a contemporaneous oral agreement but may be explained or supplemented:

(a) by course of dealing or usage of trade or by course of performance; and

(b) by evidence of consistent additional terms unless the court finds the writing to have been intended also as a complete and exclusive statement of the terms of the agreement.

§ 2A–203. Seals Inoperative.

The affixing of a seal to a writing evidencing a lease contract or an offer to enter into a lease contract does not render the writing a sealed instrument and the law with respect to sealed instruments does not apply to the lease contract or offer.

§ 2A–204. Formation in General.

(1) A lease contract may be made in any manner sufficient to show agreement, including conduct by both parties which recognizes the existence of a lease contract.

(2) An agreement sufficient to constitute a lease contract may be found although the moment of its making is undetermined.

(3) Although one or more terms are left open, a lease contract does not fail for indefiniteness if the parties have intended to make a lease contract and there is a reasonably certain basis for giving an appropriate remedy.

§ 2A–205. Firm Offers.

An offer by a merchant to lease goods to or from another person in a signed writing that by its terms gives assurance it will be held open is not revocable, for lack of consideration, during the time stated or, if no time is stated, for a reasonable time, but in no event may the period of irrevocability exceed 3 months. Any such term of assurance on a form supplied by the offeree must be separately signed by the offeror.

§ 2A–206. Offer and Acceptance in Formation of Lease Contract.

(1) Unless otherwise unambiguously indicated by the language or circumstances, an offer to make a lease contract must be construed as inviting acceptance in any manner and by any medium reasonable in the circumstances.

(2) If the beginning of a requested performance is a reasonable mode of acceptance, an offeror who is not notified of acceptance within a reasonable time may treat the offer as having lapsed before acceptance.

§ 2A–207. Course of Performance or Practical Construction.

(1) If a lease contract involves repeated occasions for performance by either party with knowledge of the nature of the performance

and opportunity for objection to it by the other, any course of performance accepted or acquiesced in without objection is relevant to determine the meaning of the lease agreement.

(2) The express terms of a lease agreement and any course of performance, as well as any course of dealing and usage of trade, must be construed whenever reasonable as consistent with each other; but if that construction is unreasonable, express terms control course of performance, course of performance controls both course of dealing and usage of trade, and course of dealing controls usage of trade.

(3) Subject to the provisions of Section 2A–208 on modification and waiver, course of performance is relevant to show a waiver or modification of any term inconsistent with the course of performance.

§ 2A–208. Modification, Rescission and Waiver.

(1) An agreement modifying a lease contract needs no consideration to be binding.

(2) A signed lease agreement that excludes modification or rescission except by a signed writing may not be otherwise modified or rescinded, but, except as between merchants, such a requirement on a form supplied by a merchant must be separately signed by the other party.

(3) Although an attempt at modification or rescission does not satisfy the requirements of subsection (2), it may operate as a waiver.

(4) A party who has made a waiver affecting an executory portion of a lease contract may retract the waiver by reasonable notification received by the other party that strict performance will be required of any term waived, unless the retraction would be unjust in view of a material change of position in reliance on the waiver.

§ 2A–209. Lessee under Finance Lease as Beneficiary of Supply Contract.

(1) The benefit of the supplier's promises to the lessor under the supply contract and of all warranties, whether express or implied, including those of any third party provided in connection with or as part of the supply contract, extends to the lessee to the extent of the lessee's leasehold interest under a finance lease related to the supply contract, but is subject to the terms warranty and of the supply contract and all defenses or claims arising therefrom.

(2) The extension of the benefit of supplier's promises and of warranties to the lessee (Section 2A–209(1)) does not: (i) modify the rights and obligations of the parties to the supply contract, whether arising therefrom or otherwise, or (ii) impose any duty or liability under the supply contract on the lessee.

(3) Any modification or rescission of the supply contract by the supplier and the lessor is effective between the supplier and the lessee unless, before the modification or rescission, the supplier has received notice that the lessee has entered into a finance lease related to the supply contract. If the modification or rescission is effective between the supplier and the lessee, the lessor is deemed to have assumed, in addition to the obligations of the lessor to the lessee under the lease contract, promises of the supplier to the lessor and warranties that were so modified or rescinded as they existed and were available to the lessee before modification or rescission.

(4) In addition to the extension of the benefit of the supplier's promises and of warranties to the lessee under subsection (1), the lessee retains all rights that the lessee may have against the supplier which arise from an agreement between the lessee and the supplier or under other law.

As amended in 1990.

§ 2A–210. Express Warranties.

(1) Express warranties by the lessor are created as follows:

(a) Any affirmation of fact or promise made by the lessor to the lessee which relates to the goods and becomes part of the basis of the bargain creates an express warranty that the goods will conform to the affirmation or promise.

(b) Any description of the goods which is made part of

the basis of the bargain creates an express warranty that the goods will conform to the description.

(c) Any sample or model that is made part of the basis of the bargain creates an express warranty that the whole of the goods will conform to the sample or model.

(2) It is not necessary to the creation of an express warranty that the lessor use formal words, such as "warrant" or "guarantee," or that the lessor have a specific intention to make a warranty, but an affirmation merely of the value of the goods or a statement purporting to be merely the lessor's opinion or commendation of the goods does not create a warranty.

§ 2A–211. Warranties Against Interference and Against Infringement; Lessee's Obligation Against Infringement.

(1) There is in a lease contract a warranty that for the lease term no person holds a claim to or interest in the goods that arose from an act or omission of the lessor, other than a claim by way of infringement or the like, which will interfere with the lessee's enjoyment of its leasehold interest.

(2) Except in a finance lease there is in a lease contract by a lessor who is a merchant regularly dealing in goods of the kind a warranty that the goods are delivered free of the rightful claim of any person by way of infringement or the like.

(3) A lessee who furnishes specifications to a lessor or a supplier shall hold the lessor and the supplier harmless against any claim by way of infringement or the like that arises out of compliance with the specifications.

§ 2A–212. Implied Warranty of Merchantability.

(1) Except in a finance lease, a warranty that the goods will be merchantable is implied in a lease contract if the lessor is a merchant with respect to goods of that kind.

(2) Goods to be merchantable must be at least such as

(a) pass without objection in the trade under the description in the lease agreement;

(b) in the case of fungible goods, are of fair average quality within the description;

(c) are fit for the ordinary purposes for which goods of that type are used;

(d) run, within the variation permitted by the lease agreement, of even kind, quality, and quantity within each unit and among all units involved;

(e) are adequately contained, packaged, and labeled as the lease agreement may require; and

(f) conform to any promises or affirmations of fact made on the container or label.

(3) Other implied warranties may arise from course of dealing or usage of trade.

§ 2A–213. Implied Warranty of Fitness for Particular Purpose.

Except in a finance of lease, if the lessor at the time the lease contract is made has reason to know of any particular purpose for which the goods are required and that the lessee is relying on the lessor's skill or judgment to select or furnish suitable goods, there is in the lease contract an implied warranty that the goods will be fit for that purpose.

§ 2A–214. Exclusion or Modification of Warranties.

(1) Words or conduct relevant to the creation of an express warranty and words or conduct tending to negate or limit a warranty must be construed wherever reasonable as consistent with each other; but, subject to the provisions of Section 2A–202 on parol or extrinsic evidence, negation or limitation is inoperative to the extent that the construction is unreasonable.

(2) Subject to subsection (3), to exclude or modify the implied warranty of merchantability or any part of it the language must mention "merchantability", be by a writing, and be conspicuous. Subject to subsection (3), to exclude or modify any implied warranty of fitness the exclusion must be by a writing and be conspicuous. Language to exclude all implied warranties of fitness is sufficient if it is in writing, is conspicuous and states, for example, "There is no warranty that the goods will be fit for a particular purpose".

(3) Notwithstanding subsection (2), but subject to subsection (4),

(a) unless the circumstances indicate otherwise, all implied warranties are excluded by expressions like "as is" or "with all faults" or by other language that in common understanding calls the lessee's attention to the exclusion of warranties and makes plain that there is no implied warranty, if in writing and conspicuous;

(b) if the lessee before entering into the lease contract has examined the goods or the sample or model as fully as desired or has refused to examine the goods, there is no implied warranty with regard to defects that an examination ought in the circumstances to have revealed; and

(c) an implied warranty may also be excluded or modified by course of dealing, course of performance, or usage of trade.

(4) To exclude or modify a warranty against interference or against infringement (Section 2A–211) or any part of it, the language must be specific, be by a writing, and be conspicuous, unless the circumstances, including course of performance, course of dealing, or usage of trade, give the lessee reason to know that the goods are being leased subject to a claim or interest of any person.

§ 2A–215. Cumulation and Conflict of Warranties Express or Implied.

Warranties, whether express or implied, must be construed as consistent with each other and as cumulative, but if that construction is unreasonable, the intention of the parties determines which warranty is dominant. In ascertaining that intention the following rules apply:

(a) Exact or technical specifications displace an inconsistent sample or model or general language of description.

(b) A sample from an existing bulk displaces inconsistent general language of description.

(c) Express warranties displace inconsistent implied warranties other than an implied warranty of fitness for a particular purpose.

§ 2A–216. Third-Party Beneficiaries of Express and Implied Warranties.

Alternative A

A warranty to or for the benefit of a lessee under this Article, whether express or implied, extends to any natural person who is in the family or household of the lessee or who is a guest in the lessee's home if it is reasonable to expect that such person may use, consume, or be affected by the goods and who is injured in person by breach of the warranty. This section does not displace principles of law and equity that extend a warranty to or for the benefit of a lessee to other persons. The operation of this section may not be excluded, modified, or limited, but an exclusion, modification, or limitation of the warranty, including any with respect to rights and remedies, effective against the lessee is also effective against any beneficiary designated under this section.

Alternative B

A warranty to or for the benefit of a lessee under this Article, whether express or implied, extends to any natural person who may reasonably be expected to use, consume, or be affected by the goods and who is injured in person by breach of the warranty. This section does not displace principles of law and equity that extend a warranty to or for the benefit of a lessee to other persons. The operation of this section may not be excluded, modified, or limited, but an exclusion, modification, or limitation of the warranty, including any with respect to rights and remedies, effective against the lessee is also effective against the beneficiary designated under this section.

Alternative C

A warranty to or for the benefit of a lessee under this Article, whether express or implied, extends to any person who may reasonably be expected to use, consume, or be affected by the goods and who is injured by breach of the warranty. The operation of this section may not be excluded, modified, or limited with respect to injury to the person of an individual to whom the warranty extends, but an exclusion, modification, or limitation of the warranty, including any with respect to rights and remedies, effective against the lessee is also effective against the beneficiary designated under this section.

§ 2A–217. Identification.

Identification of goods as goods to which a lease contract refers may be made at any time and in any manner explicitly agreed to by the parties. In the absence of explicit agreement, identification occurs:

(a) when the lease contract is made if the lease contract is for a lease of goods that are existing and identified;

(b) when the goods are shipped, marked, or otherwise designated by the lessor as goods to which the lease contract refers, if the lease contract is for a lease of goods that are not existing and identified; or

(c) when the young are conceived, if the lease contract is for a lease of unborn young of animals.

§ 2A–218. Insurance and Proceeds.

(1) A lessee obtains an insurable interest when existing goods are identified to the lease contract even though the goods identified are nonconforming and the lessee has an option to reject them.

(2) If a lessee has an insurable interest only by reason of the lessor's identification of the goods, the lessor, until default or insolvency or notification to the lessee that identification is final, may substitute other goods for those identified.

(3) Notwithstanding a lessee's insurable interest under subsections (1) and (2), the lessor retains an insurable interest until an option to buy has been exercised by the lessee and risk of loss has passed to the lessee.

(4) Nothing in this section impairs any insurable interest recognized under any other statute or rule of law.

(5) The parties by agreement may determine that one or more parties have an obligation to obtain and pay for insurance covering the goods and by agreement may determine the beneficiary of the proceeds of the insurance.

§ 2A–219. Risk of Loss.

(1) Except in the case of a finance lease, risk of loss is retained by the lessor and does not pass to the lessee. In the case of a finance lease, risk of loss passes to the lessee.

(2) Subject to the provisions of this Article on the effect of default on risk of loss (Section 2A–220), if risk of loss is to pass to the lessee and the time of passage is not stated, the following rules apply:

(a) If the lease contract requires or authorizes the goods to be shipped by carrier

(i) and it does not require delivery at a particular destination, the risk of loss passes to the lessee when the goods are duly delivered to the carrier; but

(ii) if it does require delivery at a particular destination and the goods are there duly tendered while in the possession of the carrier, the risk of loss passes to the lessee when the goods are there duly so tendered as to enable the lessee to take delivery.

(b) If the goods are held by a bailee to be delivered without being moved, the risk of loss passes to the lessee on acknowledgment by the bailee of the lessee's right to possession of the goods.

(c) In any case not within subsection (a) or (b), the risk of loss passes to the lessee on the lessee's receipt of the goods if the lessor, or, in the case of a finance lease, the supplier, is a merchant; otherwise the risk passes to the lessee on tender of delivery.

§ 2A–220. Effect of Default on Risk of Loss.

(1) Where risk of loss is to pass to the lessee and the time of passage is not stated:

(a) If a tender or delivery of goods so fails to conform to the lease contract as to give a right of rejection, the risk of their loss remains with the lessor, or, in the case of a finance lease, the supplier, until cure or acceptance.

(b) If the lessee rightfully revokes acceptance, he [or she], to the extent of any deficiency in his [or her] effective insurance coverage, may treat the risk of loss as having remained with the lessor from the beginning.

(2) Whether or not risk of loss is to pass to the lessee, if the lessee as to conforming goods already identified to a lease contract repudiates or is otherwise in default under the lease contract, the lessor, or, in the case of a finance lease, the supplier, to the extent of any deficiency in his [or her] effective insurance coverage may treat the risk of loss as resting on the lessee for a commercially reasonable time.

§ 2A–221. Casualty to Identified Goods.

If a lease contract requires goods identified when the lease contract is made, and the goods suffer casualty without fault of the lessee, the lessor or the supplier before delivery, or the goods suffer casualty before risk of loss passes to the lessee pursuant to the lease agreement or Section 2A–219, then:

(a) if the loss is total, the lease contract is avoided; and

(b) if the loss is partial or the goods have so deteriorated as to no longer conform to the lease contract, the lessee may nevertheless demand inspection and at his [or her] option either treat the lease contract as avoided or, except in a finance lease that is not a consumer lease, accept the goods with due allowance from the rent payable for the balance of the lease term for the deterioration or the deficiency in quantity but without further right against the lessor.

Part 3 Effect of Lease Contract

§ 2A–301. Enforceability of Lease Contract.

Except as otherwise provided in this Article, a lease contract is effective and enforceable according to its terms between the parties, against purchasers of the goods and against creditors of the parties.

§ 2A–302. Title to and Possession of Goods.

Except as otherwise provided in this Article, each provision of this Article applies whether the lessor or a third party has title to the goods, and whether the lessor, the lessee, or a third party has possession of the goods, notwithstanding any statute or rule of law that possession or the absence of possession is fraudulent.

§ 2A–303. Alienability of Party's Interest Under Lease Contract or of Lessor's Residual Interest in Goods; Delegation of Performance; Transfer of Rights.

(1) As used in this section, "creation of a security interest" includes the sale of a lease contract that is subject to Article 9, Secured Transactions, by reason of Section 9–109(a)(3).

(2) Except as provided in subsections (3) and Section 9–407, a provision in a lease agreement which (i) prohibits the voluntary or involuntary transfer, including a transfer by sale, sublease, creation or enforcement of a security interest, or attachment, levy, or other judicial process, of an interest of a party under the lease contract or of the lessor's residual interest in the goods, or (ii) makes such a transfer an event of default, gives rise to the rights and remedies provided in subsection (4), but a transfer that is prohibited or is an event of default under the lease agreement is otherwise effective.

(3) A provision in a lease agreement which (i) prohibits a transfer of a right to damages for default with respect to the whole lease contract or of a right to payment arising out of the transferor's due performance of the transferor's entire obligation, or (ii) makes such a transfer an event of default, is not enforceable, and such a transfer is not a transfer that materially impairs the propsect of obtaining return performance by, materially changes the duty of, or materially increases the burden or risk imposed on, the other party to the lease contract within the purview of subsection (4).

(4) Subject to subsection (3) and Section 9–407:

(a) if a transfer is made which is made an event of default under a lease agreement, the party to the lease contract not making the transfer, unless that party waives the default or otherwise agrees, has the rights and remedies described in Section 2A–501(2);

(b) if paragraph (a) is not applicable and if a transfer is made that (i) is prohibited under a lease agreement or (ii) materially impairs the prospect of obtaining return performance by, materially changes the duty of, or materially increases the burden or risk imposed on, the other party to the lease contract, unless the party not making the transfer agrees at any time to the transfer in the lease contract or otherwise, then, except as limited by contract,

(i) the transferor is liable to the party not making the transfer for damages caused by the transfer to the extent that the damages could not reasonably be prevented by the party not making the transfer and (ii) a court having jurisdiction may grant other appropriate relief, including cancellation of the lease contract or an injunction against the transfer.

(5) A transfer of "the lease" or of "all my rights under the lease", or a transfer in similar general terms, is a transfer of rights and, unless the language or the circumstances, as in a transfer for security, indicate the contrary, the transfer is a delegation of duties by the transferor to the transferee. Acceptance by the transferee constitutes a promise by the transferee to perform those duties. The promise is enforceable by either the transferor or the other party to the lease contract.

(6) Unless otherwise agreed by the lessor and the lessee, a delegation of performance does not relieve the transferor as against the other party of any duty to perform or of any liability for default.

(7) In a consumer lease, to prohibit the transfer of an interest of a party under the lease contract or to make a transfer an event of default, the language must be specific, by a writing, and conspicuous.

As amended in 1990 and 1999.

§ 2A-304. Subsequent Lease of Goods by Lessor.

(1) Subject to Section 2A–303, a subsequent lessee from a lessor of goods under an existing lease contract obtains, to the extent of the leasehold interest transferred, the leasehold interest in the goods that the lessor had or had power to transfer, and except as provided in subsection (2) and Section 2A–527(4), takes subject to the existing lease contract. A lessor with voidable title has power to transfer a good leasehold interest to a good faith subsequent lessee for value, but only to the extent set forth in the preceding sentence. If goods have been delivered under a transaction of purchase the lessor has that power even though:

(a) the lessor's transferor was deceived as to the identity of the lessor;

(b) the delivery was in exchange for a check which is later dishonored;

(c) it was agreed that the transaction was to be a "cash sale"; or

(d) the delivery was procured through fraud punishable as larcenous under the criminal law.

(2) A subsequent lessee in the ordinary course of business from a lessor who is a merchant dealing in goods of that kind to whom the goods were entrusted by the existing lessee of that lessor before the interest of the subsequent lessee became enforceable against that lessor obtains, to the extent of the leasehold interest transferred, all of that lessor's and the existing lessee's rights to the goods, and takes free of the existing lease contract.

(3) A subsequent lessee from the lessor of goods that are subject to an existing lease contract and are covered by a certificate of title issued under a statute of this State or of another jurisdiction takes no greater rights than those provided both by this section and by the certificate of title statute.

As amended in 1990.

§ 2A-305. Sale or Sublease of Goods by Lessee.

(1) Subject to the provisions of Section 2A–303, a buyer or sublessee from the lessee of goods under an existing lease contract obtains, to the extent of the interest transferred, the leasehold interest in the goods that the lessee had or had power to transfer, and except as provided in subsection (2) and Section 2A–511(4), takes subject to the existing lease contract. A lessee with a voidable leasehold interest has power to transfer a good leasehold interest to a good faith buyer for value or a good faith sublessee for value, but only to the extent set forth in the preceding sentence. When goods have been delivered under a transaction of lease the lessee has that power even though:

(a) the lessor was deceived as to the identity of the lessee;

(b) the delivery was in exchange for a check which is later dishonored; or

(c) the delivery was procured through fraud punishable as larcenous under the criminal law.

(2) A buyer in the ordinary course of business or a sublessee in the ordinary course of business from a lessee who is a merchant dealing in goods of that kind to whom the goods were entrusted by the lessor obtains, to the extent of the interest transferred, all of the lessor's and lessee's rights to the goods, and takes free of the existing lease contract.

(3) A buyer or sublessee from the lessee of goods that are subject to an existing lease contract and are covered by a certificate of title issued under a statute of this State or of another jurisdiction takes no greater rights than those provided both by this section and by the certificate of title statute.

§ 2A-306. Priority of Certain Liens Arising by Operation of Law.

If a person in the ordinary course of his [or her] business furnishes services or materials with respect to goods subject to a lease contract, a lien upon those goods in the possession of that person given by statute or rule of law for those materials or services takes priority over any interest of the lessor or lessee under the lease contract or this Article unless the lien is created by statute and the statute provides otherwise or unless the lien is created by rule of law and the rule of law provides otherwise.

§ 2A-307. Priority of Liens Arising by Attachment or Levy on, Security Interests in, and Other Claims to Goods.

(1) Except as otherwise provided in Section 2A–306, a creditor of a lessee takes subject to the lease contract.

(2) Except as otherwise provided in subsection (3) and in Sections 2A–306 and 2A–308, a creditor of a lessor takes subject to the lease contract unless the creditor holds a lien that attached to the goods before the lease contract became enforceable.

(3) Except as otherwise provided in Sections 9–317, 9–321, and 9–323, a lessee takes a leasehold interest subject to a security interest held by a creditor of the lessor.

As amended in 1990 and 1999.

§ 2A-308. Special Rights of Creditors.

(1) A creditor of a lessor in possession of goods subject to a lease contract may treat the lease contract as void if as against the creditor retention of possession by the lessor is fraudulent under any statute or rule of law, but retention of possession in good faith and current course of trade by the lessor for a commercially reasonable time after the lease contract becomes enforceable is not fraudulent.

(2) Nothing in this Article impairs the rights of creditors of a lessor if the lease contract (a) becomes enforceable, not in current course of trade but in satisfaction of or as security for a pre-existing

claim for money, security, or the like, and (b) is made under circumstances which under any statute or rule of law apart from this Article would constitute the transaction a fraudulent transfer or voidable preference.

(3) A creditor of a seller may treat a sale or an identification of goods to a contract for sale as void if as against the creditor retention of possession by the seller is fraudulent under any statute or rule of law, but retention of possession of the goods pursuant to a lease contract entered into by the seller as lessee and the buyer as lessor in connection with the sale or identification of the goods is not fraudulent if the buyer bought for value and in good faith.

§ 2A–309. Lessor's and Lessee's Rights When Goods Become Fixtures.

(1) In this section:

(a) goods are "fixtures" when they become so related to particular real estate that an interest in them arises under real estate law;

(b) a "fixture filing" is the filing, in the office where a mortgage on the real estate would be filed or recorded, of a financing statement covering goods that are or are to become fixtures and conforming to the requirements of Section 9–502(a) and (b);

(c) a lease is a "purchase money lease" unless the lessee has possession or use of the goods or the right to possession or use of the goods before the lease agreement is enforceable;

(d) a mortgage is a "construction mortgage" to the extent it secures an obligation incurred for the construction of an improvement on land including the acquisition cost of the land, if the recorded writing so indicates; and

(e) "encumbrance" includes real estate mortgages and other liens on real estate and all other rights in real estate that are not ownership interests.

(2) Under this Article a lease may be of goods that are fixtures or may continue in goods that become fixtures, but no lease exists under this Article of ordinary building materials incorporated into an improvement on land.

(3) This Article does not prevent creation of a lease of fixtures pursuant to real estate law.

(4) The perfected interest of a lessor of fixtures has priority over a conflicting interest of an encumbrancer or owner of the real estate if:

(a) the lease is a purchase money lease, the conflicting interest of the encumbrancer or owner arises before the goods become fixtures, the interest of the lessor is perfected by a fixture filing before the goods become fixtures or within ten days thereafter, and the lessee has an interest of record in the real estate or is in possession of the real estate; or

(b) the interest of the lessor is perfected by a fixture filing before the interest of the encumbrancer or owner is of record, the lessor's interest has priority over any conflicting interest of a predecessor in title of the encumbrancer or owner, and the lessee has an interest of record in the real estate or is in possession of the real estate.

(5) The interest of a lessor of fixtures, whether or not perfected, has priority over the conflicting interest of an encumbrancer or owner of the real estate if:

(a) the fixtures are readily removable factory or office machines, readily removable equipment that is not primarily used or leased for use in the operation of the real estate, or readily removable replacements of domestic appliances that are goods subject to a consumer lease, and before the goods become fixtures the lease contract is enforceable; or

(b) the conflicting interest is a lien on the real estate obtained by legal or equitable proceedings after the lease contract is enforceable; or

(c) the encumbrancer or owner has consented in writing to the lease or has disclaimed an interest in the goods as fixtures; or

(d) the lessee has a right to remove the goods as against the encumbrancer or owner. If the lessee's right to remove terminates, the priority of the interest of the lessor continues for a reasonable time.

(6) Notwithstanding paragraph (4)(a) but otherwise subject to subsections (4) and (5), the interest of a lessor of fixtures, including the lessor's residual interest, is subordinate to the conflicting interest of an encumbrancer of the real estate under a construction mortgage recorded before the goods become fixtures if the goods become fixtures before the completion of the construction. To the extent given to refinance a construction mortgage, the conflicting interest of an encumbrancer of the real estate under a mortgage has this priority to the same extent as the encumbrancer of the real estate under the construction mortgage.

(7) In cases not within the preceding subsections, priority between the interest of a lessor of fixtures, including the lessor's residual interest, and the conflicting interest of an encumbrancer or owner of the real estate who is not the lessee is determined by the priority rules governing conflicting interests in real estate.

(8) If the interest of a lessor of fixtures, including the lessor's residual interest, has priority over all conflicting interests of all owners and encumbrancers of the real estate, the lessor or the lessee may (i) on default, expiration, termination, or cancellation of the lease agreement but subject to the agreement and this Article, or (ii) if necessary to enforce other rights and remedies of the lessor or lessee under this Article, remove the goods from the real estate, free and clear of all conflicting interests of all owners and encumbrancers of the real estate, but the lessor or lessee must reimburse any encumbrancer or owner of the real estate who is not the lessee and who has not otherwise agreed for the cost of repair of any physical injury, but not for any diminution in value of the real estate caused by the absence of the goods removed or by any necessity of replacing them. A person entitled to reimbursement may refuse permission to remove until the party seeking removal gives adequate security for the performance of this obligation.

(9) Even though the lease agreement does not create a security interest, the interest of a lessor of fixtures, including the lessor's residual interest, is perfected by filing a financing statement as a fixture filing for leased goods that are or are to become fixtures in accordance with the relevant provisions of the Article on Secured Transactions (Article 9).

As amended in 1990 and 1999.

§ 2A–310. Lessor's and Lessee's Rights When Goods Become Accessions.

(1) Goods are "accessions" when they are installed in or affixed to other goods.

(2) The interest of a lessor or a lessee under a lease contract entered into before the goods became accessions is superior to all interests in the whole except as stated in subsection (4).

(3) The interest of a lessor or a lessee under a lease contract entered into at the time or after the goods became accessions is superior to all subsequently acquired interests in the whole except as stated in subsection (4) but is subordinate to interests in the whole existing at the time the lease contract was made unless the holders of such interests in the whole have in writing consented to the lease or disclaimed an interest in the goods as part of the whole.

(4) The interest of a lessor or a lessee under a lease contract described in subsection (2) or (3) is subordinate to the interest of

(a) a buyer in the ordinary course of business or a lessee in the ordinary course of business of any interest in the whole acquired after the goods became accessions; or

(b) a creditor with a security interest in the whole perfected before the lease contract was made to the extent that the creditor makes subsequent advances without knowledge of the lease contract.

(5) When under subsections (2) or (3) and (4) a lessor or a lessee of accessions holds an interest that is superior to all interests in the whole, the lessor or the lessee may (a) on default, expiration, termination, or cancellation of the lease contract by the other party but subject to the provisions of the lease contract and this Article, or (b) if necessary to enforce his [or her] other rights and remedies under this Article, remove the goods from the whole, free and clear of all interests in the whole, but he [or she] must reimburse any holder of an interest in the whole who is not the lessee and who has not otherwise agreed for the cost of repair of any physical injury but not for any diminution in value of the whole caused by the absence of the goods removed or by any necessity for replacing them. A person entitled to reimbursement may refuse permission to remove until the party seeking removal gives adequate security for the performance of this obligation.

§ 2A-311. Priority Subject to Subordination.

Nothing in this Article prevents subordination by agreement by any person entitled to priority.

As added in 1990.

Part 4 Performance of Lease Contract: Repudiated, Substituted and Excused

§ 2A-401. Insecurity: Adequate Assurance of Performance.

(1) A lease contract imposes an obligation on each party that the other's expectation of receiving due performance will not be impaired.

(2) If reasonable grounds for insecurity arise with respect to the performance of either party, the insecure party may demand in writing adequate assurance of due performance. Until the insecure party receives that assurance, if commercially reasonable the insecure party may suspend any performance for which he [or she] has not already received the agreed return.

(3) A repudiation of the lease contract occurs if assurance of due performance adequate under the circumstances of the particular case is not provided to the insecure party within a reasonable time, not to exceed 30 days after receipt of a demand by the other party.

(4) Between merchants, the reasonableness of grounds for insecurity and the adequacy of any assurance offered must be determined according to commercial standards.

(5) Acceptance of any nonconforming delivery or payment does not prejudice the aggrieved party's right to demand adequate assurance of future performance.

§ 2A-402. Anticipatory Repudiation.

If either party repudiates a lease contract with respect to a performance not yet due under the lease contract, the loss of which performance will substantially impair the value of the lease contract to the other, the aggrieved party may:

(a) for a commercially reasonable time, await retraction of repudiation and performance by the repudiating party;

(b) make demand pursuant to Section 2A–401 and await assurance of future performance adequate under the circumstances of the particular case; or

(c) resort to any right or remedy upon default under the lease contract or this Article, even though the aggrieved party has notified the repudiating party that the aggrieved party would await the repudiating party's performance and assurance and has urged retraction. In addition, whether or not the aggrieved party is pursuing one of the foregoing remedies, the aggrieved party may suspend performance or, if the aggrieved party is the lessor, proceed in accordance with the provisions of this Article on the lessor's right to identify goods to the lease contract notwithstanding default or to salvage unfinished goods (Section 2A–524).

§ 2A-403. Retraction of Anticipatory Repudiation.

(1) Until the repudiating party's next performance is due, the repudiating party can retract the repudiation unless, since the repudiation, the aggrieved party has cancelled the lease contract or materially changed the aggrieved party's position or otherwise indicated that the aggrieved party considers the repudiation final.

(2) Retraction may be by any method that clearly indicates to the aggrieved party that the repudiating party intends to perform under the lease contract and includes any assurance demanded under Section 2A–401.

(3) Retraction reinstates a repudiating party's rights under a lease contract with due excuse and allowance to the aggrieved party for any delay occasioned by the repudiation.

§ 2A-404. Substituted Performance.

(1) If without fault of the lessee, the lessor and the supplier, the agreed berthing, loading, or unloading facilities fail or the agreed type of carrier becomes unavailable or the agreed manner of delivery otherwise becomes commercially impracticable, but a commercially reasonable substitute is available, the substitute performance must be tendered and accepted.

(2) If the agreed means or manner of payment fails because of domestic or foreign governmental regulation:

(a) the lessor may withhold or stop delivery or cause the supplier to withhold or stop delivery unless the lessee provides a means or manner of payment that is commercially a substantial equivalent; and

(b) if delivery has already been taken, payment by the means or in the manner provided by the regulation discharges the lessee's obligation unless the regulation is discriminatory, oppressive, or predatory.

§ 2A-405. Excused Performance.

Subject to Section 2A–404 on substituted performance, the following rules apply:

(a) Delay in delivery or nondelivery in whole or in part by a lessor or a supplier who complies with paragraphs (b) and (c) is not a default under the lease contract if performance as agreed has been made impracticable by the occurrence of a contingency the nonoccurrence of which was a basic assumption on which the lease contract was made or by compliance in good faith with any applicable foreign or domestic governmental regulation or order, whether or not the regulation or order later proves to be invalid.

(b) If the causes mentioned in paragraph (a) affect only part of the lessor's or the supplier's capacity to perform, he [or she] shall allocate production and deliveries among his [or her] customers but at his [or her] option may include regular customers not then under contract for sale or lease as well as his [or her] own requirements for further manufacture. He [or she] may so allocate in any manner that is fair and reasonable.

(c) The lessor seasonably shall notify the lessee and in the case of a finance lease the supplier seasonably shall notify the lessor and the lessee, if known, that there will be delay or nondelivery and, if allocation is required under paragraph (b), of the estimated quota thus made available for the lessee.

§ 2A–406. Procedure on Excused Performance.

(1) If the lessee receives notification of a material or indefinite delay or an allocation justified under Section 2A–405, the lessee may by written notification to the lessor as to any goods involved, and with respect to all of the goods if under an installment lease contract the value of the whole lease contract is substantially impaired (Section 2A–510):

(a) terminate the lease contract (Section 2A–505(2)); or

(b) except in a finance lease that is not a consumer lease, modify the lease contract by accepting the available quota in substitution, with due allowance from the rent payable for the balance of the lease term for the deficiency but without further right against the lessor.

(2) If, after receipt of a notification from the lessor under Section 2A–405, the lessee fails so to modify the lease agreement within a reasonable time not exceeding 30 days, the lease contract lapses with respect to any deliveries affected.

§ 2A–407. Irrevocable Promises: Finance Leases.

(1) In the case of a finance lease that is not a consumer lease the lessee's promises under the lease contract become irrevocable and independent upon the lessee's acceptance of the goods.

(2) A promise that has become irrevocable and independent under subsection (1):

(a) is effective and enforceable between the parties, and by or against third parties including assignees of the parties, and

(b) is not subject to cancellation, termination, modification, repudiation, excuse, or substitution without the consent of the party to whom the promise runs.

(3) This section does not affect the validity under any other law of a covenant in any lease contract making the lessee's promises irrevocable and independent upon the lessee's acceptance of the goods.

As amended in 1990.

Part 5 Default

A. In General

§ 2A–501. Default: Procedure.

(1) Whether the lessor or the lessee is in default under a lease contract is determined by the lease agreement and this Article.

(2) If the lessor or the lessee is in default under the lease contract, the party seeking enforcement has rights and remedies as provided in this Article and, except as limited by this Article, as provided in the lease agreement.

(3) If the lessor or the lessee is in default under the lease contract, the party seeking enforcement may reduce the party's claim to judgment, or otherwise enforce the lease contract by self-help or any available judicial procedure or nonjudicial procedure, including administrative proceeding, arbitration, or the like, in accordance with this Article.

(4) Except as otherwise provided in Section 1–106(1) or this Article or the lease agreement, the rights and remedies referred to in subsections (2) and (3) are cumulative.

(5) If the lease agreement covers both real property and goods, the party seeking enforcement may proceed under this Part as to the goods, or under other applicable law as to both the real property and the goods in accordance with that party's rights and remedies in respect of the real property, in which case this Part does not apply.

As amended in 1990.

§ 2A–502. Notice After Default.

Except as otherwise provided in this Article or the lease agreement, the lessor or lessee in default under the lease contract is not entitled to notice of default or notice of enforcement from the other party to the lease agreement.

§ 2A–503. Modification or Impairment of Rights and Remedies.

(1) Except as otherwise provided in this Article, the lease agreement may include rights and remedies for default in addition to or in substitution for those provided in this Article and may limit or alter the measure of damages recoverable under this Article.

(2) Resort to a remedy provided under this Article or in the lease agreement is optional unless the remedy is expressly agreed to be exclusive. If circumstances cause an exclusive or limited remedy to fail of its essential purpose, or provision for an exclusive remedy is unconscionable, remedy may be had as provided in this Article.

(3) Consequential damages may be liquidated under Section 2A–504, or may otherwise be limited, altered, or excluded unless the limitation, alteration, or exclusion is unconscionable. Limitation, alteration, or exclusion of consequential damages for injury to the person in the case of consumer goods is *prima facie* unconscionable but limitation, alteration, or exclusion of damages where the loss is commercial is not *prima facie* unconscionable.

(4) Rights and remedies on default by the lessor or the lessee with respect to any obligation or promise collateral or ancillary to the lease contract are not impaired by this Article.

As amended in 1990.

§ 2A–504. Liquidation of Damages.

(1) Damages payable by either party for default, or any other act or omission, including indemnity for loss or diminution of anticipated tax benefits or loss or damage to lessor's residual interest, may be liquidated in the lease agreement but only at an amount or by a formula that is reasonable in light of the then anticipated harm caused by the default or other act or omission.

(2) If the lease agreement provides for liquidation of damages, and such provision does not comply with subsection (1), or such provision

is an exclusive or limited remedy that circumstances cause to fail of its essential purpose, remedy may be had as provided in this Article.

(3) If the lessor justifiably withholds or stops delivery of goods because of the lessee's default or insolvency (Section 2A–525 or 2A–526), the lessee is entitled to restitution of any amount by which the sum of his [or her] payments exceeds:

(a) the amount to which the lessor is entitled by virtue of terms liquidating the lessor's damages in accordance with subsection (1); or

(b) in the absence of those terms, 20 percent of the then present value of the total rent the lessee was obligated to pay for the balance of the lease term, or, in the case of a consumer lease, the lesser of such amount or $500.

(4) A lessee's right to restitution under subsection (3) is subject to offset to the extent the lessor establishes:

(a) a right to recover damages under the provisions of this Article other than subsection (1); and

(b) the amount or value of any benefits received by the lessee directly or indirectly by reason of the lease contract.

§ 2A–505. Cancellation and Termination and Effect of Cancellation, Termination, Rescission, or Fraud on Rights and Remedies.

(1) On cancellation of the lease contract, all obligations that are still executory on both sides are discharged, but any right based on prior default or performance survives, and the cancelling party also retains any remedy for default of the whole lease contract or any unperformed balance.

(2) On termination of the lease contract, all obligations that are still executory on both sides are discharged but any right based on prior default or performance survives.

(3) Unless the contrary intention clearly appears, expressions of "cancellation," "rescission," or the like of the lease contract may not be construed as a renunciation or discharge of any claim in damages for an antecedent default.

(4) Rights and remedies for material misrepresentation or fraud include all rights and remedies available under this Article for default.

(5) Neither rescission nor a claim for rescission of the lease contract nor rejection or return of the goods may bar or be deemed inconsistent with a claim for damages or other right or remedy.

§ 2A–506. Statute of Limitations.

(1) An action for default under a lease contract, including breach of warranty or indemnity, must be commenced within 4 years after the cause of action accrued. By the original lease contract the parties may reduce the period of limitation to not less than one year.

(2) A cause of action for default accrues when the act or omission on which the default or breach of warranty is based is or should have been discovered by the aggrieved party, or when the default occurs, whichever is later. A cause of action for indemnity accrues when the act or omission on which the claim for indemnity is based is or should have been discovered by the indemnified party, whichever is later.

(3) If an action commenced within the time limited by subsection (1) is so terminated as to leave available a remedy by another action for the same default or breach of warranty or indemnity, the other action may be commenced after the expiration of the time limited and within 6 months after the termination of the first action unless the termination resulted from voluntary discontinuance or from dismissal for failure or neglect to prosecute.

(4) This section does not alter the law on tolling of the statute of limitations nor does it apply to causes of action that have accrued before this Article becomes effective.

§ 2A–507. Proof of Market Rent: Time and Place.

(1) Damages based on market rent (Section 2A–519 or 2A–528) are determined according to the rent for the use of the goods concerned for a lease term identical to the remaining lease term of the original lease agreement and prevailing at the times specified in Sections 2A–519 and 2A–528.

(2) If evidence of rent for the use of the goods concerned for a lease term identical to the remaining lease term of the original lease agreement and prevailing at the times or places described in this Article is not readily available, the rent prevailing within any reasonable time before or after the time described or at any other place or for a different lease term which in commercial judgment or under usage of trade would serve as a reasonable substitute for the one described may be used, making any proper allowance for the difference, including the cost of transporting the goods to or from the other place.

(3) Evidence of a relevant rent prevailing at a time or place or for a lease term other than the one described in this Article offered by one party is not admissible unless and until he [or she] has given the other party notice the court finds sufficient to prevent unfair surprise.

(4) If the prevailing rent or value of any goods regularly leased in any established market is in issue, reports in official publications or trade journals or in newspapers or periodicals of general circulation published as the reports of that market are admissible in evidence. The circumstances of the preparation of the report may be shown to affect its weight but not its admissibility.

As amended in 1990.

B. Default by Lessor

§ 2A–508. Lessee's Remedies.

(1) If a lessor fails to deliver the goods in conformity to the lease contract (Section 2A–509) or repudiates the lease contract (Section 2A–402), or a lessee rightfully rejects the goods (Section 2A–509) or justifiably revokes acceptance of the goods (Section 2A–517), then with respect to any goods involved, and with respect to all of the goods if under an installment lease contract the value of the whole lease contract is substantially impaired (Section 2A–510), the lessor is in default under the lease contract and the lessee may:

(a) cancel the lease contract (Section 2A–505(1));

(b) recover so much of the rent and security as has been paid and is just under the circumstances;

(c) cover and recover damages as to all goods affected whether or not they have been identified to the lease contract (Sections 2A–518 and 2A–520), or recover damages for nondelivery (Sections 2A–519 and 2A–520);

(d) exercise any other rights or pursue any other remedies provided in the lease contract.

(2) If a lessor fails to deliver the goods in conformity to the lease contract or repudiates the lease contract, the lessee may also:

(a) if the goods have been identified, recover them (Section 2A–522); or

(b) in a proper case, obtain specific performance or replevy the goods (Section 2A–521).

(3) If a lessor is otherwise in default under a lease contract, the lessee may exercise the rights and pursue the remedies provided in the lease contract, which may include a right to cancel the lease, and in Section 2A–519(3).

(4) If a lessor has breached a warranty, whether express or implied, the lessee may recover damages (Section 2A–519(4)).

(5) On rightful rejection or justifiable revocation of acceptance, a lessee has a security interest in goods in the lessee's possession or control for any rent and security that has been paid and any expenses reasonably incurred in their inspection, receipt, transportation, and care and custody and may hold those goods and dispose of them in good faith and in a commercially reasonable manner, subject to Section 2A–527(5).

(6) Subject to the provisions of Section 2A–407, a lessee, on notifying the lessor of the lessee's intention to do so, may deduct all or any part of the damages resulting from any default under the lease contract from any part of the rent still due under the same lease contract.

As amended in 1990.

§ 2A–509. Lessee's Rights on Improper Delivery; Rightful Rejection.

(1) Subject to the provisions of Section 2A–510 on default in installment lease contracts, if the goods or the tender or delivery fail in any respect to conform to the lease contract, the lessee may reject or accept the goods or accept any commercial unit or units and reject the rest of the goods.

(2) Rejection of goods is ineffective unless it is within a reasonable time after tender or delivery of the goods and the lessee seasonably notifies the lessor.

§ 2A–510. Installment Lease Contracts: Rejection and Default.

(1) Under an installment lease contract a lessee may reject any delivery that is nonconforming if the nonconformity substantially impairs the value of that delivery and cannot be cured or the nonconformity is a defect in the required documents; but if the nonconformity does not fall within subsection (2) and the lessor or the supplier gives adequate assurance of its cure, the lessee must accept that delivery.

(2) Whenever nonconformity or default with respect to one or more deliveries substantially impairs the value of the installment lease contract as a whole there is a default with respect to the whole. But, the aggrieved party reinstates the installment lease contract as a whole if the aggrieved party accepts a nonconforming delivery without seasonably notifying of cancellation or brings an action with respect only to past deliveries or demands performance as to future deliveries.

§ 2A–511. Merchant Lessee's Duties as to Rightfully Rejected Goods.

(1) Subject to any security interest of a lessee (Section 2A–508(5)), if a lessor or a supplier has no agent or place of business at the market of rejection, a merchant lessee, after rejection of goods in his [or her] possession or control, shall follow any reasonable instructions received from the lessor or the supplier with respect to the goods. In the absence of those instructions, a merchant lessee shall make reasonable efforts to sell, lease, or otherwise dispose of the goods for the lessor's account if they threaten to decline in value speedily. Instructions are not reasonable if on demand indemnity for expenses is not forthcoming.

(2) If a merchant lessee (subsection (1)) or any other lessee (Section 2A–512) disposes of goods, he [or she] is entitled to reimbursement either from the lessor or the supplier or out of the proceeds for reasonable expenses of caring for and disposing of the goods and, if the expenses include no disposition commission, to such commission as is usual in the trade, or if there is none, to a reasonable sum not exceeding 10 percent of the gross proceeds.

(3) In complying with this section or Section 2A–512, the lessee is held only to good faith. Good faith conduct hereunder is neither acceptance or conversion nor the basis of an action for damages.

(4) A purchaser who purchases in good faith from a lessee pursuant to this section or Section 2A–512 takes the goods free of any rights of the lessor and the supplier even though the lessee fails to comply with one or more of the requirements of this Article.

§ 2A–512. Lessee's Duties as to Rightfully Rejected Goods.

(1) Except as otherwise provided with respect to goods that threaten to decline in value speedily (Section 2A–511) and subject to any security interest of a lessee (Section 2A–508(5)):

(a) the lessee, after rejection of goods in the lessee's possession, shall hold them with reasonable care at the lessor's or the supplier's disposition for a reasonable time after the lessee's seasonable notification of rejection;

(b) if the lessor or the supplier gives no instructions within a reasonable time after notification of rejection, the lessee may store the rejected goods for the lessor's or the supplier's account or ship them to the lessor or the supplier or dispose of them for the lessor's or the supplier's account with reimbursement in the manner provided in Section 2A–511; but

(c) the lessee has no further obligations with regard to goods rightfully rejected.

(2) Action by the lessee pursuant to subsection (1) is not acceptance or conversion.

§ 2A–513. Cure by Lessor of Improper Tender or Delivery; Replacement.

(1) If any tender or delivery by the lessor or the supplier is rejected because nonconforming and the time for performance has not yet expired, the lessor or the supplier may seasonably notify the lessee of the lessor's or the supplier's intention to cure and may then make a conforming delivery within the time provided in the lease contract.

(2) If the lessee rejects a nonconforming tender that the lessor or the supplier had reasonable grounds to believe would be acceptable with or without money allowance, the lessor or the supplier may have a further reasonable time to substitute a conforming tender if he [or she] seasonably notifies the lessee.

§ 2A–514. Waiver of Lessee's Objections.

(1) In rejecting goods, a lessee's failure to state a particular defect that is ascertainable by reasonable inspection precludes the lessee from relying on the defect to justify rejection or to establish default:

(a) if, stated seasonably, the lessor or the supplier could have cured it (Section 2A–513); or

(b) between merchants if the lessor or the supplier after rejection has made a request in writing for a full and final written statement of all defects on which the lessee proposes to rely.

(2) A lessee's failure to reserve rights when paying rent or other consideration against documents precludes recovery of the payment for defects apparent on the face of the documents.

§ 2A–515. Acceptance of Goods.

(1) Acceptance of goods occurs after the lessee has had a reasonable opportunity to inspect the goods and

(a) the lessee signifies or acts with respect to the goods in a manner that signifies to the lessor or the supplier that the goods are conforming or that the lessee will take or retain them in spite of their nonconformity; or

(b) the lessee fails to make an effective rejection of the goods (Section 2A–509(2)).

(2) Acceptance of a part of any commercial unit is acceptance of that entire unit.

§ 2A–516. Effect of Acceptance of Goods; Notice of Default; Burden of Establishing Default after Acceptance; Notice of Claim or Litigation to Person Answerable Over.

(1) A lessee must pay rent for any goods accepted in accordance with the lease contract, with due allowance for goods rightfully rejected or not delivered.

(2) A lessee's acceptance of goods precludes rejection of the goods accepted. In the case of a finance lease, if made with knowledge of a nonconformity, acceptance cannot be revoked because of it. In any other case, if made with knowledge of a nonconformity, acceptance cannot be revoked because of it unless the acceptance was on the reasonable assumption that the nonconformity would be seasonably cured. Acceptance does not of itself impair any other remedy provided by this Article or the lease agreement for nonconformity.

(3) If a tender has been accepted:

(a) within a reasonable time after the lessee discovers or should have discovered any default, the lessee shall notify the lessor and the supplier, if any, or be barred from any remedy against the party notified;

(b) except in the case of a consumer lease, within a reasonable time after the lessee receives notice of litigation for infringement or the like (Section 2A–211) the lessee shall notify the lessor or be barred from any remedy over for liability established by the litigation; and

(c) the burden is on the lessee to establish any default.

(4) If a lessee is sued for breach of a warranty or other obligation for which a lessor or a supplier is answerable over the following apply:

(a) The lessee may give the lessor or the supplier, or both, written notice of the litigation. If the notice states that the person notified may come in and defend and that if the person notified does not do so that person will be bound in any action against that person by the lessee by any determination of fact common to the two litigations, then unless the person notified after seasonable receipt of the notice does come in and defend that person is so bound.

(b) The lessor or the supplier may demand in writing that the lessee turn over control of the litigation including settlement if the claim is one for infringement or the like (Section 2A–211) or else be barred from any remedy over. If the demand states that the lessor or the supplier agrees to bear all expense and to satisfy any adverse judgment, then unless the lessee after seasonable receipt of the demand does turn over control the lessee is so barred.

(5) Subsections (3) and (4) apply to any obligation of a lessee to hold the lessor or the supplier harmless against infringement or the like (Section 2A–211).

As amended in 1990.

§ 2A–517. Revocation of Acceptance of Goods.

(1) A lessee may revoke acceptance of a lot or commercial unit whose nonconformity substantially impairs its value to the lessee if the lessee has accepted it:

(a) except in the case of a finance lease, on the reasonable assumption that its nonconformity would be cured and it has not been seasonably cured; or

(b) without discovery of the nonconformity if the lessee's acceptance was reasonably induced either by the lessor's assurances or, except in the case of a finance lease, by the difficulty of discovery before acceptance.

(2) Except in the case of a finance lease that is not a consumer lease, a lessee may revoke acceptance of a lot or commercial unit if the lessor defaults under the lease contract and the default substantially impairs the value of that lot or commercial unit to the lessee.

(3) If the lease agreement so provides, the lessee may revoke acceptance of a lot or commercial unit because of other defaults by the lessor.

(4) Revocation of acceptance must occur within a reasonable time after the lessee discovers or should have discovered the ground for it and before any substantial change in condition of the goods which is not caused by the nonconformity. Revocation is not effective until the lessee notifies the lessor.

(5) A lessee who so revokes has the same rights and duties with regard to the goods involved as if the lessee had rejected them.

As amended in 1990.

§ 2A–518. Cover; Substitute Goods.

(1) After a default by a lessor under the lease contract of the type described in Section 2A–508(1), or, if agreed, after other default by the lessor, the lessee may cover by making any purchase or lease of or contract to purchase or lease goods in substitution for those due from the lessor.

(2) Except as otherwise provided with respect to damages liquidated in the lease agreement (Section 2A–504) or otherwise determined pursuant to agreement of the parties (Sections 1–102(3) and 2A–503), if a lessee's cover is by lease agreement substantially similar to the original lease agreement and the new lease agreement is made in good faith and in a commercially reasonable manner, the lessee may recover from the lessor as damages (i) the present value, as of the date of the commencement of the term of the new lease agreement, of the rent under the new lease agreement applicable to that period of the new lease term which is comparable to the then remaining term of the original lease agreement minus the present value as of the same date of the total rent for the then remaining lease term of the original lease agreement, and (ii) any incidental or consequential damages, less expenses saved in consequence of the lessor's default.

(3) If a lessee's cover is by lease agreement that for any reason does not qualify for treatment under subsection (2), or is by purchase or otherwise, the lessee may recover from the lessor as if the lessee had elected not to cover and Section 2A–519 governs.

As amended in 1990.

§ 2A–519. Lessee's Damages for Non-Delivery, Repudiation, Default, and Breach of Warranty in Regard to Accepted Goods.

(1) Except as otherwise provided with respect to damages liquidated in the lease agreement (Section 2A–504) or otherwise determined pursuant to agreement of the parties (Sections 1–102(3) and 2A–503), if a lessee elects not to cover or a lessee elects to cover and the cover is by lease agreement that for any reason does not qualify for treatment under Section 2A–518(2), or is by purchase or otherwise, the measure of damages for non-delivery or repudiation by the lessor or for rejection or revocation of acceptance by the lessee is the present value, as of the date of the default, of the then market rent minus the present value as of the same date of the original rent, computed for the remaining lease term of the original lease agreement, together with incidental and consequential damages, less expenses saved in consequence of the lessor's default.

(2) Market rent is to be determined as of the place for tender or, in cases of rejection after arrival or revocation of acceptance, as of the place of arrival.

(3) Except as otherwise agreed, if the lessee has accepted goods and given notification (Section 2A–516(3)), the measure of damages for non-conforming tender or delivery or other default by a lessor is the loss resulting in the ordinary course of events from the lessor's default as determined in any manner that is reasonable together with incidental and consequential damages, less expenses saved in consequence of the lessor's default.

(4) Except as otherwise agreed, the measure of damages for breach of warranty is the present value at the time and place of acceptance of the difference between the value of the use of the goods accepted and the value if they had been as warranted for the lease term, unless special circumstances show proximate damages of a different amount, together with incidental and consequential damages, less expenses saved in consequence of the lessor's default or breach of warranty.

As amended in 1990.

§ 2A–520. Lessee's Incidental and Consequential Damages.

(1) Incidental damages resulting from a lessor's default include expenses reasonably incurred in inspection, receipt, transportation, and care and custody of goods rightfully rejected or goods the acceptance of which is justifiably revoked, any commercially reasonable charges, expenses or commissions in connection with effecting cover, and any other reasonable expense incident to the default.

(2) Consequential damages resulting from a lessor's default include:

(a) any loss resulting from general or particular requirements and needs of which the lessor at the time of contracting had reason to know and which could not reasonably be prevented by cover or otherwise; and

(b) injury to person or property proximately resulting from any breach of warranty.

§ 2A–521. Lessee's Right to Specific Performance or Replevin.

(1) Specific performance may be decreed if the goods are unique or in other proper circumstances.

(2) A decree for specific performance may include any terms and conditions as to payment of the rent, damages, or other relief that the court deems just.

(3) A lessee has a right of replevin, detinue, sequestration, claim and delivery, or the like for goods identified to the lease contract if after reasonable effort the lessee is unable to effect cover for those goods or the circumstances reasonably indicate that the effort will be unavailing.

§ 2A–522. Lessee's Right to Goods on Lessor's Insolvency.

(1) Subject to subsection (2) and even though the goods have not been shipped, a lessee who has paid a part or all of the rent and security for goods identified to a lease contract (Section 2A–217) on making and keeping good a tender of any unpaid portion of the rent and security due under the lease contract may recover the goods identified from the lessor if the lessor becomes insolvent within 10 days after receipt of the first installment of rent and security.

(2) A lessee acquires the right to recover goods identified to a lease contract only if they conform to the lease contract.

C. Default by Lessee

§ 2A–523. Lessor's Remedies.

(1) If a lessee wrongfully rejects or revokes acceptance of goods or fails to make a payment when due or repudiates with respect to a part or the whole, then, with respect to any goods involved, and with respect to all of the goods if under an installment lease contract the value of the whole lease contract is substantially impaired (Section 2A–510), the lessee is in default under the lease contract and the lessor may:

(a) cancel the lease contract (Section 2A–505(1));

(b) proceed respecting goods not identified to the lease contract (Section 2A–524);

(c) withhold delivery of the goods and take possession of goods previously delivered (Section 2A–525);

(d) stop delivery of the goods by any bailee (Section 2A–526);

(e) dispose of the goods and recover damages (Section 2A–527), or retain the goods and recover damages (Section 2A–528), or in a proper case recover rent (Section 2A–529)

(f) exercise any other rights or pursue any other remedies provided in the lease contract.

(2) If a lessor does not fully exercise a right or obtain a remedy to which the lessor is entitled under subsection (1), the lessor may recover the loss resulting in the ordinary course of events from the lessee's default as determined in any reasonable manner, together with incidental damages, less expenses saved in consequence of the lessee's default.

(3) If a lessee is otherwise in default under a lease contract, the lessor may exercise the rights and pursue the remedies provided in the lease contract, which may include a right to cancel the lease. In addition, unless otherwise provided in the lease contract:

(a) if the default substantially impairs the value of the lease contract to the lessor, the lessor may exercise the rights and pursue the remedies provided in subsections (1) or (2); or

(b) if the default does not substantially impair the value of the lease contract to the lessor, the lessor may recover as provided in subsection (2).

As amended in 1990.

§ 2A–524. Lessor's Right to Identify Goods to Lease Contract.

(1) After default by the lessee under the lease contract of the type described in Section 2A–523(1) or 2A–523(3)(a) or, if agreed, after other default by the lessee, the lessor may:

(a) identify to the lease contract conforming goods not already identified if at the time the lessor learned of the default they were in the lessor's or the supplier's possession or control; and

(b) dispose of goods (Section 2A–527(1)) that demonstrably have been intended for the particular lease contract even though those goods are unfinished.

(2) If the goods are unfinished, in the exercise of reasonable commercial judgment for the purposes of avoiding loss and of effective realization, an aggrieved lessor or the supplier may either complete manufacture and wholly identify the goods to the lease contract or cease manufacture and lease, sell, or otherwise dispose of the goods for scrap or salvage value or proceed in any other reasonable manner.

As amended in 1990.

§ 2A–525. Lessor's Right to Possession of Goods.

(1) If a lessor discovers the lessee to be insolvent, the lessor may refuse to deliver the goods.

(2) After a default by the lessee under the lease contract of the type described in Section 2A–523(1) or 2A–523(3)(a) or, if agreed, after other default by the lessee, the lessor has the right to take possession of the goods. If the lease contract so provides, the lessor may require the lessee to assemble the goods and make them available to the lessor at a place to be designated by the lessor which is reasonably convenient to both parties. Without removal, the lessor may render unusable any goods employed in trade or business, and may dispose of goods on the lessee's premises (Section 2A–527).

(3) The lessor may proceed under subsection (2) without judicial process if that can be done without breach of the peace or the lessor may proceed by action.

As amended in 1990.

§ 2A–526. Lessor's Stoppage of Delivery in Transit or Otherwise.

(1) A lessor may stop delivery of goods in the possession of a carrier or other bailee if the lessor discovers the lessee to be insolvent and may stop delivery of carload, truckload, planeload, or larger shipments of express or freight if the lessee repudiates or fails to make a payment due before delivery, whether for rent, security or otherwise under the lease contract, or for any other reason the lessor has a right to withhold or take possession of the goods.

(2) In pursuing its remedies under subsection (1), the lessor may stop delivery until

(a) receipt of the goods by the lessee;

(b) acknowledgment to the lessee by any bailee of the goods, except a carrier, that the bailee holds the goods for the lessee; or

(c) such an acknowledgment to the lessee by a carrier via reshipment or as warehouseman.

(3) (a) To stop delivery, a lessor shall so notify as to enable the bailee by reasonable diligence to prevent delivery of the goods.

(b) After notification, the bailee shall hold and deliver the goods according to the directions of the lessor, but the lessor is liable to the bailee for any ensuing charges or damages.

(c) A carrier who has issued a nonnegotiable bill of lading is not obliged to obey a notification to stop received from a person other than the consignor.

§ 2A–527. Lessor's Rights to Dispose of Goods.

(1) After a default by a lessee under the lease contract of the type described in Section 2A–523(1) or 2A–523(3)(a) or after the lessor refuses to deliver or takes possession of goods (Section 2A–525 or 2A–526), or, if agreed, after other default by a lessee, the lessor may dispose of the goods concerned or the undelivered balance thereof by lease, sale, or otherwise.

(2) Except as otherwise provided with respect to damages liquidated in the lease agreement (Section 2A–504) or otherwise determined pursuant to agreement of the parties (Sections 1–102(3) and 2A–503), if the disposition is by lease agreement substantially similar to the original lease agreement and the new lease agreement is made in good faith and in a commercially reasonable manner, the lessor may recover from the lessee as damages (i) accrued and unpaid rent as of the date of the commencement of the term of the new lease agreement, (ii) the present value, as of the same date, of the total rent for the then remaining lease term of the original lease agreement minus the present value, as of the same date, of the rent under the new lease agreement applicable to that period of the new lease term which is comparable to the then remaining term of the original lease agreement, and (iii) any incidental damages allowed under Section 2A–530, less expenses saved in consequence of the lessee's default.

(3) If the lessor's disposition is by lease agreement that for any reason does not qualify for treatment under subsection (2), or is by sale or otherwise, the lessor may recover from the lessee as if the lessor had elected not to dispose of the goods and Section 2A–528 governs.

(4) A subsequent buyer or lessee who buys or leases from the lessor in good faith for value as a result of a disposition under this section takes the goods free of the original lease contract and any rights of the original lessee even though the lessor fails to comply with one or more of the requirements of this Article.

(5) The lessor is not accountable to the lessee for any profit made on any disposition. A lessee who has rightfully rejected or justifiably revoked acceptance shall account to the lessor for any excess over the amount of the lessee's security interest (Section 2A–508(5)).

As amended in 1990.

§ 2A–528. Lessor's Damages for Non-acceptance, Failure to Pay, Repudiation, or Other Default.

(1) Except as otherwise provided with respect to damages liquidated in the lease agreement (Section 2A–504) or otherwise determined pursuant to agreement of the parties (Section 1–102(3) and 2A–503), if a lessor elects to retain the goods or a lessor elects to dispose of the goods and the disposition is by lease agreement that for any reason does not qualify for treatment under Section 2A–527(2), or is by sale or otherwise, the lessor may recover from the lessee as damages for a default of the type described in Section 2A–523(1) or 2A–523(3)(a), or if agreed, for other default of the lessee, (i) accrued and unpaid rent as of the date of the default if the lessee has never taken possession of the goods, or, if the lessee has taken possession of the goods, as of the date the lessor repossesses the goods or an earlier date on which the lessee makes a tender of the goods to the lessor, (ii) the present value as of the date determined under clause (i) of the total rent for the then remaining lease term of the original lease agreement minus the present value as of the same date of the market rent as the place where the goods are located computed for the same lease term, and (iii) any incidental damages allowed under Section 2A–530, less expenses saved in consequence of the lessee's default.

(2) If the measure of damages provided in subsection (1) is inadequate to put a lessor in as good a position as performance would have, the measure of damages is the present value of the profit, including reasonable overhead, the lessor would have made from full performance by the lessee, together with any incidental damages allowed under Section 2A–530, due allowance for costs reasonably incurred and due credit for payments or proceeds of disposition.

As amended in 1990.

§ 2A–529. Lessor's Action for the Rent.

(1) After default by the lessee under the lease contract of the type described in Section 2A–523(1) or 2A–523(3)(a) or, if agreed, after other default by the lessee, if the lessor complies with subsection (2), the lessor may recover from the lessee as damages:

(a) for goods accepted by the lessee and not repossessed by or tendered to the lessor, and for conforming goods lost or damaged within a commercially reasonable time after risk of loss passes to the lessee (Section 2A–219), (i) accrued and unpaid rent as of the date of entry of judgment in favor of the lessor (ii) the present value as of the same date of the rent for the then remaining lease term of the lease agreement, and (iii) any incidental damages allowed under Section 2A–530, less expenses saved in consequence of the lessee's default; and

(b) for goods identified to the lease contract if the lessor is unable after reasonable effort to dispose of them at a reasonable price or the circumstances reasonably indicate that effort will be unavailing, (i) accrued and unpaid rent as of the date of entry of judgment in favor of the lessor, (ii) the present value as of the same date of the rent for the then remaining lease term of the lease agreement, and (iii) any incidental damages allowed under Section 2A–530, less expenses saved in consequence of the lessee's default.

(2) Except as provided in subsection (3), the lessor shall hold for the lessee for the remaining lease term of the lease agreement any goods that have been identified to the lease contract and are in the lessor's control.

(3) The lessor may dispose of the goods at any time before collection of the judgment for damages obtained pursuant to subsection (1). If the disposition is before the end of the remaining lease term of the lease agreement, the lessor's recovery against the lessee for damages is governed by Section 2A–527 or Section 2A–528, and the lessor will cause an appropriate credit to be provided against a judgment for damages to the extent that the amount of the judgment exceeds the recovery available pursuant to Section 2A–527 or 2A–528.

(4) Payment of the judgment for damages obtained pursuant to subsection (1) entitles the lessee to the use and possession of the goods not then disposed of for the remaining lease term of and in accordance with the lease agreement.

(5) After default by the lessee under the lease contract of the type described in Section 2A–523(1) or Section 2A–523(3)(a) or, if agreed, after other default by the lessee, a lessor who is held not entitled to rent under this section must nevertheless be awarded damages for non-acceptance under Sections 2A–527 and 2A–528.

As amended in 1990.

§ 2A–530. Lessor's Incidental Damages.

Incidental damages to an aggrieved lessor include any commercially reasonable charges, expenses, or commissions incurred in stopping delivery, in the transportation, care and custody of goods after the lessee's default, in connection with return or disposition of the goods, or otherwise resulting from the default.

§ 2A–531. Standing to Sue Third Parties for Injury to Goods.

(1) If a third party so deals with goods that have been identified to a lease contract as to cause actionable injury to a party to the lease contract (a) the lessor has a right of action against the third party, and (b) the lessee also has a right of action against the third party if the lessee:

(i) has a security interest in the goods;

(ii) has an insurable interest in the goods; or

(iii) bears the risk of loss under the lease contract or has since the injury assumed that risk as against the lessor and the goods have been converted or destroyed.

(2) If at the time of the injury the party plaintiff did not bear the risk of loss as against the other party to the lease contract and there is no arrangement between them for disposition of the recovery, his [or her] suit or settlement, subject to his [or her] own interest, is as a fiduciary for the other party to the lease contract.

(3) Either party with the consent of the other may sue for the benefit of whom it may concern.

§ 2A–532. Lessor's Rights to Residual Interest.

In addition to any other recovery permitted by this Article or other law, the lessor may recover from the lessee an amount that will fully compensate the lessor for any loss of or damage to the lessor's residual interest in the goods caused by the default of the lessee.

As added in 1990.

Revised Article 3 NEGOTIABLE INSTRUMENTS

Part 1 General Provisions and Definitions

§ 3–101. Short Title.

This Article may be cited as Uniform Commercial Code–Negotiable Instruments.

§ 3–102. Subject Matter.

(a) This Article applies to negotiable instruments. It does not apply to money, to payment orders governed by Article 4A, or to securities governed by Article 8.

(b) If there is conflict between this Article and Article 4 or 9, Articles 4 and 9 govern.

(c) Regulations of the Board of Governors of the Federal Reserve System and operating circulars of the Federal Reserve Banks supersede any inconsistent provision of this Article to the extent of the inconsistency.

§ 3–103. Definitions.

(a) In this Article:

(1) "Acceptor" means a drawee who has accepted a draft.

(2) "Drawee" means a person ordered in a draft to make payment.

(3) "Drawer" means a person who signs or is identified in a draft as a person ordering payment.

(4) "Good faith" means honesty in fact and the observance of reasonable commercial standards of fair dealing.

(5) "Maker" means a person who signs or is identified in a note as a person undertaking to pay.

(6) "Order" means a written instruction to pay money signed by the person giving the instruction. The instruction may be addressed to any person, including the person giving the instruction, or to one or more persons jointly or in the alternative but not in succession. An authorization to pay is not an order unless the person authorized to pay is also instructed to pay.

(7) "Ordinary care" in the case of a person engaged in business means observance of reasonable commercial standards, prevailing in the area in which the person is located, with respect to the business in which the person is engaged. In the case of a bank that takes an instrument for processing for collection or payment by automated means, reasonable commercial standards do not require the bank to examine the instrument if the failure to examine does not violate the bank's prescribed procedures and the bank's procedures do not vary unreasonably from general banking usage not disapproved by this Article or Article 4.

(8) "Party" means a party to an instrument.

(9) "Promise" means a written undertaking to pay money signed by the person undertaking to pay. An acknowledgment of an obligation by the obligor is not a promise unless the obligor also undertakes to pay the obligation.

(10) "Prove" with respect to a fact means to meet the burden of establishing the fact (Section 1–201(8)).

(11) "Remitter" means a person who purchases an instrument from its issuer if the instrument is payable to an identified person other than the purchaser.

(b) [Other definitions' section references deleted.]

(c) [Other definitions' section references deleted.]

(d) In addition, Article 1 contains general definitions and principles of construction and interpretation applicable throughout this Article.

§ 3–104. Negotiable Instrument.

(a) Except as provided in subsections (c) and (d), "negotiable instrument" means an unconditional promise or order to pay a fixed amount of money, with or without interest or other charges described in the promise or order, if it:

(1) is payable to bearer or to order at the time it is issued or first comes into possession of a holder;

(2) is payable on demand or at a definite time; and

(3) does not state any other undertaking or instruction by the person promising or ordering payment to do any act in addition to the payment of money, but the promise or order may contain (i) an undertaking or power to give, maintain, or protect collateral to secure payment, (ii) an authorization or power to the holder to confess judgment or realize on or dispose of collateral, or (iii) a waiver of the benefit of any law intended for the advantage or protection of an obligor.

(b) "Instrument" means a negotiable instrument.

(c) An order that meets all of the requirements of subsection (a), except paragraph (1), and otherwise falls within the definition of "check" in subsection (f) is a negotiable instrument and a check.

(d) A promise or order other than a check is not an instrument if, at the time it is issued or first comes into possession of a holder, it contains a conspicuous statement, however expressed, to the effect that the promise or order is not negotiable or is not an instrument governed by this Article.

(e) An instrument is a "note" if it is a promise and is a "draft" if it is an order. If an instrument falls within the definition of both "note" and "draft," a person entitled to enforce the instrument may treat it as either.

(f) "Check" means (i) a draft, other than a documentary draft, payable on demand and drawn on a bank or (ii) a cashier's check or teller's check. An instrument may be a check even though it is described on its face by another term, such as "money order."

(g) "Cashier's check" means a draft with respect to which the drawer and drawee are the same bank or branches of the same bank.

(h) "Teller's check" means a draft drawn by a bank (i) on another bank, or (ii) payable at or through a bank.

(i) "Traveler's check" means an instrument that (i) is payable on demand, (ii) is drawn on or payable at or through a bank, (iii) is designated by the term "traveler's check" or by a substantially similar term, and (iv) requires, as a condition to payment, a countersignature by a person whose specimen signature appears on the instrument.

(j) "Certificate of deposit" means an instrument containing an acknowledgment by a bank that a sum of money has been received by the bank and a promise by the bank to repay the sum of money. A certificate of deposit is a note of the bank.

§ 3–105. Issue of Instrument.

(a) "Issue" means the first delivery of an instrument by the maker or drawer, whether to a holder or nonholder, for the purpose of giving rights on the instrument to any person.

(b) An unissued instrument, or an unissued incomplete instrument that is completed, is binding on the maker or drawer, but nonissuance is a defense. An instrument that is conditionally issued or is issued for a special purpose is binding on the maker or drawer, but failure of the condition or special purpose to be fulfilled is a defense.

(c) "Issuer" applies to issued and unissued instruments and means a maker or drawer of an instrument.

§ 3–106. Unconditional Promise or Order.

(a) Except as provided in this section, for the purposes of Section 3–104(a), a promise or order is unconditional unless it states (i) an express condition to payment, (ii) that the promise or order is subject to or governed by another writing, or (iii) that rights or obligations with respect to the promise or order are stated in another writing. A reference to another writing does not of itself make the promise or order conditional.

(b) A promise or order is not made conditional (i) by a reference to another writing for a statement of rights with respect to collateral, prepayment, or acceleration, or (ii) because payment is limited to resort to a particular fund or source.

(c) If a promise or order requires, as a condition to payment, a countersignature by a person whose specimen signature appears on the promise or order, the condition does not make the promise or order conditional for the purposes of Section 3–104(a). If the person whose specimen signature appears on an instrument fails to countersign the instrument, the failure to countersign is a defense to the obligation of the issuer, but the failure does not prevent a transferee of the instrument from becoming a holder of the instrument.

(d) If a promise or order at the time it is issued or first comes into possession of a holder contains a statement, required by applicable statutory or administrative law, to the effect that the rights of a holder or transferee are subject to claims or defenses that the issuer could assert against the original payee, the promise or order is not thereby made conditional for the purposes of Section 3–104(a); but if the promise or order is an instrument, there cannot be a holder in due course of the instrument.

§ 3–107. Instrument Payable in Foreign Money.

Unless the instrument otherwise provides, an instrument that states the amount payable in foreign money may be paid in the foreign money or in an equivalent amount in dollars calculated by using the current bank-offered spot rate at the place of payment for the purchase of dollars on the day on which the instrument is paid.

§ 3–108. Payable on Demand or at Definite Time.

(a) A promise or order is "payable on demand" if it (i) states that it is payable on demand or at sight, or otherwise indicates that it is payable at the will of the holder, or (ii) does not state any time of payment.

(b) A promise or order is "payable at a definite time" if it is payable on elapse of a definite period of time after sight or acceptance or at a fixed date or dates or at a time or times readily ascertainable at the time the promise or order is issued, subject to rights of (i) prepayment, (ii) acceleration, (iii) extension at the option of the holder, or (iv) extension to a further definite time at the option of the maker or acceptor or automatically upon or after a specified act or event.

(c) If an instrument, payable at a fixed date, is also payable upon demand made before the fixed date, the instrument is payable on demand until the fixed date and, if demand for payment is not made before that date, becomes payable at a definite time on the fixed date.

§ 3–109. Payable to Bearer or to Order.

(a) A promise or order is payable to bearer if it:

(1) states that it is payable to bearer or to the order of bearer or otherwise indicates that the person in possession of the promise or order is entitled to payment;

(2) does not state a payee; or

(3) states that it is payable to or to the order of cash or otherwise indicates that it is not payable to an identified person.

(b) A promise or order that is not payable to bearer is payable to order if it is payable (i) to the order of an identified person or (ii) to an identified person or order. A promise or order that is payable to order is payable to the identified person.

(c) An instrument payable to bearer may become payable to an identified person if it is specially indorsed pursuant to Section 3–205(a). An instrument payable to an identified person may become payable to bearer if it is indorsed in blank pursuant to Section 3–205(b).

§ 3–110. Identification of Person to Whom Instrument Is Payable.

(a) The person to whom an instrument is initially payable is determined by the intent of the person, whether or not authorized, signing as, or in the name or behalf of, the issuer of the instrument. The instrument is payable to the person intended by the signer even if that person is identified in the instrument by a name or other identification that is not that of the intended person. If more than one person signs in the name or behalf of the issuer of an instrument and all the signers do not intend the same person as payee, the instrument is payable to any person intended by one or more of the signers.

(b) If the signature of the issuer of an instrument is made by automated means, such as a check-writing machine, the payee of the instrument is determined by the intent of the person who supplied the name or identification of the payee, whether or not authorized to do so.

(c) A person to whom an instrument is payable may be identified in any way, including by name, identifying number, office, or account number. For the purpose of determining the holder of an instrument, the following rules apply:

(1) If an instrument is payable to an account and the account is identified only by number, the instrument is payable to the person to whom the account is payable. If an instrument is payable to an account identified by number and by the name of a person, the instrument is payable to the named person, whether or not that person is the owner of the account identified by number.

(2) If an instrument is payable to:

(i) a trust, an estate, or a person described as trustee or representative of a trust or estate, the instrument is payable to the trustee, the representative, or a successor of either, whether or not the beneficiary or estate is also named;

(ii) a person described as agent or similar representative of a named or identified person, the instrument is payable to the represented person, the representative, or a successor of the representative;

(iii) a fund or organization that is not a legal entity, the instrument is payable to a representative of the members of the fund or organization; or

(iv) an office or to a person described as holding an office, the instrument is payable to the named person, the incumbent of the office, or a successor to the incumbent.

(d) If an instrument is payable to two or more persons alternatively, it is payable to any of them and may be negotiated, discharged, or enforced by any or all of them in possession of the instrument. If an instrument is payable to two or more persons not alternatively, it is payable to all of them and may be negotiated, discharged, or enforced only by all of them. If an instrument payable to two or more persons is ambiguous as to whether it is payable to the persons alternatively, the instrument is payable to the persons alternatively.

§ 3–111. Place of Payment.

Except as otherwise provided for items in Article 4, an instrument is payable at the place of payment stated in the instrument. If no place of payment is stated, an instrument is payable at the address of the drawee or maker stated in the instrument. If no address is stated, the place of payment is the place of business of the drawee or maker. If a drawee or maker has more than one place of business, the place of payment is any place of business of the drawee or maker chosen by the person entitled to enforce the instrument. If the drawee or maker has no place of business, the place of payment is the residence of the drawee or maker.

§ 3–112. Interest.

(a) Unless otherwise provided in the instrument, (i) an instrument is not payable with interest, and (ii) interest on an interest-bearing instrument is payable from the date of the instrument.

(b) Interest may be stated in an instrument as a fixed or variable amount of money or it may be expressed as a fixed or variable rate or rates. The amount or rate of interest may be stated or described in the instrument in any manner and may require reference to information not contained in the instrument. If an instrument provides for interest, but the amount of interest payable cannot be ascertained from the description, interest is payable at the judgment rate in effect at the place of payment of the instrument and at the time interest first accrues.

§ 3–113. Date of Instrument.

(a) An instrument may be antedated or postdated. The date stated determines the time of payment if the instrument is payable at a fixed period after date. Except as provided in Section 4–401(c), an instrument payable on demand is not payable before the date of the instrument.

(b) If an instrument is undated, its date is the date of its issue or, in the case of an unissued instrument, the date it first comes into possession of a holder.

§ 3–114. Contradictory Terms of Instrument.

If an instrument contains contradictory terms, typewritten terms prevail over printed terms, handwritten terms prevail over both, and words prevail over numbers.

§ 3–115. Incomplete Instrument.

(a) "Incomplete instrument" means a signed writing, whether or not issued by the signer, the contents of which show at the time of signing that it is incomplete but that the signer intended it to be completed by the addition of words or numbers.

(b) Subject to subsection (c), if an incomplete instrument is an instrument under Section 3–104, it may be enforced according to its terms if it is not completed, or according to its terms as augmented by completion. If an incomplete instrument is not an instrument under Section 3–104, but, after completion, the requirements of Section 3–104 are met, the instrument may be enforced according to its terms as augmented by completion.

(c) If words or numbers are added to an incomplete instrument without authority of the signer, there is an alteration of the incomplete instrument under Section 3–407.

(d) The burden of establishing that words or numbers were added to an incomplete instrument without authority of the signer is on the person asserting the lack of authority.

§ 3–116. Joint and Several Liability; Contribution.

(a) Except as otherwise provided in the instrument, two or more persons who have the same liability on an instrument as makers, drawers, acceptors, indorsers who indorse as joint payees, or anomalous indorsers are jointly and severally liable in the capacity in which they sign.

(b) Except as provided in Section 3–419(e) or by agreement of the affected parties, a party having joint and several liability who pays the instrument is entitled to receive from any party having the same joint and several liability contribution in accordance with applicable law.

(c) Discharge of one party having joint and several liability by a person entitled to enforce the instrument does not affect the right under subsection (b) of a party having the same joint and several liability to receive contribution from the party discharged.

§ 3–117. Other Agreements Affecting Instrument.

Subject to applicable law regarding exclusion of proof of contemporaneous or previous agreements, the obligation of a party to an instrument to pay the instrument may be modified, supplemented, or nullified by a separate agreement of the obligor and a person entitled to enforce the instrument, if the instrument is issued or the obligation is incurred in reliance on the agreement or as part of the same transaction giving rise to the agreement. To the extent an obligation is modified, supplemented, or nullified by an agreement under this section, the agreement is a defense to the obligation.

§ 3–118. Statute of Limitations.

(a) Except as provided in subsection (e), an action to enforce the obligation of a party to pay a note payable at a definite time must be commenced within six years after the due date or dates stated in the note or, if a due date is accelerated, within six years after the accelerated due date.

(b) Except as provided in subsection (d) or (e), if demand for payment is made to the maker of a note payable on demand, an action to enforce the obligation of a party to pay the note must be commenced within six years after the demand. If no demand for payment is made to the maker, an action to enforce the note is barred if neither principal nor interest on the note has been paid for a continuous period of 10 years.

(c) Except as provided in subsection (d), an action to enforce the obligation of a party to an unaccepted draft to pay the draft must be commenced within three years after dishonor of the draft or 10 years after the date of the draft, whichever period expires first.

(d) An action to enforce the obligation of the acceptor of a certified check or the issuer of a teller's check, cashier's check, or traveler's check must be commenced within three years after demand for payment is made to the acceptor or issuer, as the case may be.

(e) An action to enforce the obligation of a party to a certificate of deposit to pay the instrument must be commenced within six years after demand for payment is made to the maker, but if the instrument states a due date and the maker is not required to pay before that date, the six-year period begins when a demand for payment is in effect and the due date has passed.

(f) An action to enforce the obligation of a party to pay an accepted draft, other than a certified check, must be commenced (i) within six years after the due date or dates stated in the draft or acceptance if the obligation of the acceptor is payable at a definite time, or (ii) within six years after the date of the acceptance if the obligation of the acceptor is payable on demand.

(g) Unless governed by other law regarding claims for indemnity or contribution, an action (i) for conversion of an instrument, for money had and received, or like action based on conversion, (ii) for breach of warranty, or (iii) to enforce an obligation, duty, or right arising under this Article and not governed by this section must be commenced within three years after the [cause of action] accrues.

§ 3–119. Notice of Right to Defend Action.

In an action for breach of an obligation for which a third person is answerable over pursuant to this Article or Article 4, the defendant may give the third person written notice of the litigation, and the person notified may then give similar notice to any other person who is answerable over. If the notice states (i) that the person notified may come in and defend and (ii) that failure to do so will bind the person notified in an action later brought by the person giving the notice as to any determination of fact common to the two litigations, the person notified is so bound unless after seasonable receipt of the notice the person notified does come in and defend.

Part 2 Negotiation, Transfer, and Indorsement

§ 3–201. Negotiation.

(a) "Negotiation" means a transfer of possession, whether voluntary or involuntary, of an instrument by a person other than the issuer to a person who thereby becomes its holder.

(b) Except for negotiation by a remitter, if an instrument is payable to an identified person, negotiation requires transfer of possession of the instrument and its indorsement by the holder. If an instrument is payable to bearer, it may be negotiated by transfer of possession alone.

§ 3–202. Negotiation Subject to Rescission.

(a) Negotiation is effective even if obtained (i) from an infant, a corporation exceeding its powers, or a person without capacity, (ii) by fraud, duress, or mistake, or (iii) in breach of duty or as part of an illegal transaction.

(b) To the extent permitted by other law, negotiation may be rescinded or may be subject to other remedies, but those remedies may not be asserted against a subsequent holder in due course or a person paying the instrument in good faith and without knowledge of facts that are a basis for rescission or other remedy.

§ 3–203. Transfer of Instrument; Rights Acquired by Transfer.

(a) An instrument is transferred when it is delivered by a person other than its issuer for the purpose of giving to the person receiving delivery the right to enforce the instrument.

(b) Transfer of an instrument, whether or not the transfer is a negotiation, vests in the transferee any right of the transferor to enforce the instrument, including any right as a holder in due course, but the transferee cannot acquire rights of a holder in due course by a transfer, directly or indirectly, from a holder in due course if the transferee engaged in fraud or illegality affecting the instrument.

(c) Unless otherwise agreed, if an instrument is transferred for value and the transferee does not become a holder because of lack of indorsement by the transferor, the transferee has a specifically enforceable right to the unqualified indorsement of the transferor, but negotiation of the instrument does not occur until the indorsement is made.

(d) If a transferor purports to transfer less than the entire instrument, negotiation of the instrument does not occur. The transferee obtains no rights under this Article and has only the rights of a partial assignee.

§ 3–204. Indorsement.

(a) "Indorsement" means a signature, other than that of a signer as maker, drawer, or acceptor, that alone or accompanied by other words is made on an instrument for the purpose of (i) negotiating the instrument, (ii) restricting payment of the instrument, or (iii) incurring indorser's liability on the instrument, but regardless of the intent of the signer, a signature and its accompanying words is an indorsement unless the accompanying words, terms of the instrument, place of the signature, or other circumstances unambiguously indicate that the signature was made for a purpose other than indorsement. For the purpose of determining whether a signature is made on an instrument, a paper affixed to the instrument is a part of the instrument.

(b) "Indorser" means a person who makes an indorsement.

(c) For the purpose of determining whether the transferee of an instrument is a holder, an indorsement that transfers a security interest in the instrument is effective as an unqualified indorsement of the instrument.

(d) If an instrument is payable to a holder under a name that is not the name of the holder, indorsement may be made by the holder in the name stated in the instrument or in the holder's name or both, but signature in both names may be required by a person paying or taking the instrument for value or collection.

§ 3–205. Special Indorsement; Blank Indorsement; Anomalous Indorsement.

(a) If an indorsement is made by the holder of an instrument, whether payable to an identified person or payable to bearer, and the indorsement identifies a person to whom it makes the instrument payable, it is a "special indorsement." When specially indorsed, an instrument becomes payable to the identified person and may be negotiated only by the indorsement of that person. The principles stated in Section 3–110 apply to special indorsements.

(b) If an indorsement is made by the holder of an instrument and it is not a special indorsement, it is a "blank indorsement." When indorsed in blank, an instrument becomes payable to bearer and may be negotiated by transfer of possession alone until specially indorsed.

(c) The holder may convert a blank indorsement that consists only of a signature into a special indorsement by writing, above the signature of the indorser, words identifying the person to whom the instrument is made payable.

(d) "Anomalous indorsement" means an indorsement made by a person who is not the holder of the instrument. An anomalous indorsement does not affect the manner in which the instrument may be negotiated.

§ 3–206. Restrictive Indorsement.

(a) An indorsement limiting payment to a particular person or otherwise prohibiting further transfer or negotiation of the instrument is not effective to prevent further transfer or negotiation of the instrument.

(b) An indorsement stating a condition to the right of the indorsee to receive payment does not affect the right of the indorsee to enforce the instrument. A person paying the instrument or taking it for value or collection may disregard the condition, and the rights and liabilities of that person are not affected by whether the condition has been fulfilled.

(c) If an instrument bears an indorsement (i) described in Section 4–201(b), or (ii) in blank or to a particular bank using the words "for deposit," "for collection," or other words indicating a purpose of having the instrument collected by a bank for the indorser or for a particular account, the following rules apply:

(1) A person, other than a bank, who purchases the instrument when so indorsed converts the instrument unless the amount paid for the instrument is received by the indorser or applied consistently with the indorsement.

(2) A depositary bank that purchases the instrument or takes it for collection when so indorsed converts the instrument unless

the amount paid by the bank with respect to the instrument is received by the indorser or applied consistently with the indorsement.

(3) A payor bank that is also the depositary bank or that takes the instrument for immediate payment over the counter from a person other than a collecting bank converts the instrument unless the proceeds of the instrument are received by the indorser or applied consistently with the indorsement.

(4) Except as otherwise provided in paragraph (3), a payor bank or intermediary bank may disregard the indorsement and is not liable if the proceeds of the instrument are not received by the indorser or applied consistently with the indorsement.

(d) Except for an indorsement covered by subsection (c), if an instrument bears an indorsement using words to the effect that payment is to be made to the indorsee as agent, trustee, or other fiduciary for the benefit of the indorser or another person, the following rules apply:

(1) Unless there is notice of breach of fiduciary duty as provided in Section 3–307, a person who purchases the instrument from the indorsee or takes the instrument from the indorsee for collection or payment may pay the proceeds of payment or the value given for the instrument to the indorsee without regard to whether the indorsee violates a fiduciary duty to the indorser.

(2) A subsequent transferee of the instrument or person who pays the instrument is neither given notice nor otherwise affected by the restriction in the indorsement unless the transferee or payor knows that the fiduciary dealt with the instrument or its proceeds in breach of fiduciary duty.

(e) The presence on an instrument of an indorsement to which this section applies does not prevent a purchaser of the instrument from becoming a holder in due course of the instrument unless the purchaser is a converter under subsection (c) or has notice or knowledge of breach of fiduciary duty as stated in subsection (d).

(f) In an action to enforce the obligation of a party to pay the instrument, the obligor has a defense if payment would violate an indorsement to which this section applies and the payment is not permitted by this section.

§ 3–207. Reacquisition.

Reacquisition of an instrument occurs if it is transferred to a former holder, by negotiation or otherwise. A former holder who reacquires the instrument may cancel indorsements made after the reacquirer first became a holder of the instrument. If the cancellation causes the instrument to be payable to the reacquirer or to bearer, the reacquirer may negotiate the instrument. An indorser whose indorsement is canceled is discharged, and the discharge is effective against any subsequent holder.

Part 3 Enforcement of Instruments

§ 3–301. Person Entitled to Enforce Instrument.

"Person entitled to enforce" an instrument means (i) the holder of the instrument, (ii) a nonholder in possession of the instrument who has the rights of a holder, or (iii) a person not in possession of the instrument who is entitled to enforce the instrument pursuant to Section 3–309 or 3–418(d). A person may be a person entitled to enforce the instrument even though the person is not the owner of the instrument or is in wrongful possession of the instrument.

§ 3–302. Holder in Due Course.

(a) Subject to subsection (c) and Section 3–106(d), "holder in due course" means the holder of an instrument if:

(1) the instrument when issued or negotiated to the holder does not bear such apparent evidence of forgery or alteration or is not otherwise so irregular or incomplete as to call into question its authenticity; and

(2) the holder took the instrument (i) for value, (ii) in good faith, (iii) without notice that the instrument is overdue or has been dishonored or that there is an uncured default with respect to payment of another instrument issued as part of the same series, (iv) without notice that the instrument contains an unauthorized signature or has been altered, (v) without notice of any claim to the instrument described in Section 3–306, and (vi) without notice that any party has a defense or claim in recoupment described in Section 3–305(a).

(b) Notice of discharge of a party, other than discharge in an insolvency proceeding, is not notice of a defense under subsection (a), but discharge is effective against a person who became a holder in due course with notice of the discharge. Public filing or recording of a document does not of itself constitute notice of a defense, claim in recoupment, or claim to the instrument.

(c) Except to the extent a transferor or predecessor in interest has rights as a holder in due course, a person does not acquire rights of a holder in due course of an instrument taken (i) by legal process or by purchase in an execution, bankruptcy, or creditor's sale or similar proceeding, (ii) by purchase as part of a bulk transaction not in ordinary course of business of the transferor, or (iii) as the successor in interest to an estate or other organization.

(d) If, under Section 3–303(a)(1), the promise of performance that is the consideration for an instrument has been partially performed, the holder may assert rights as a holder in due course of the instrument only to the fraction of the amount payable under the instrument equal to the value of the partial performance divided by the value of the promised performance.

(e) If (i) the person entitled to enforce an instrument has only a security interest in the instrument and (ii) the person obliged to pay the instrument has a defense, claim in recoupment, or claim to the instrument that may be asserted against the person who granted the security interest, the person entitled to enforce the instrument may assert rights as a holder in due course only to an amount payable under the instrument which, at the time of enforcement of the instrument, does not exceed the amount of the unpaid obligation secured.

(f) To be effective, notice must be received at a time and in a manner that gives a reasonable opportunity to act on it.

(g) This section is subject to any law limiting status as a holder in due course in particular classes of transactions.

§ 3–303. Value and Consideration.

(a) An instrument is issued or transferred for value if:

(1) the instrument is issued or transferred for a promise of performance, to the extent the promise has been performed;

(2) the transferee acquires a security interest or other lien in the instrument other than a lien obtained by judicial proceeding;

(3) the instrument is issued or transferred as payment of, or as security for, an antecedent claim against any person, whether or not the claim is due;

(4) the instrument is issued or transferred in exchange for a negotiable instrument; or

(5) the instrument is issued or transferred in exchange for the incurring of an irrevocable obligation to a third party by the person taking the instrument.

(b) "Consideration" means any consideration sufficient to support a simple contract. The drawer or maker of an instrument has a defense if the instrument is issued without consideration. If an instrument is issued for a promise of performance, the issuer has a defense to the extent performance of the promise is due and the promise has not been performed. If an instrument is issued for value as stated in subsection (a), the instrument is also issued for consideration.

§ 3–304. Overdue Instrument.

(a) An instrument payable on demand becomes overdue at the earliest of the following times:

(1) on the day after the day demand for payment is duly made;

(2) if the instrument is a check, 90 days after its date; or

(3) if the instrument is not a check, when the instrument has been outstanding for a period of time after its date which is unreasonably long under the circumstances of the particular case in light of the nature of the instrument and usage of the trade.

(b) With respect to an instrument payable at a definite time the following rules apply:

(1) If the principal is payable in installments and a due date has not been accelerated, the instrument becomes overdue upon default under the instrument for nonpayment of an installment, and the instrument remains overdue until the default is cured.

(2) If the principal is not payable in installments and the due date has not been accelerated, the instrument becomes overdue on the day after the due date.

(3) If a due date with respect to principal has been accelerated, the instrument becomes overdue on the day after the accelerated due date.

(c) Unless the due date of principal has been accelerated, an instrument does not become overdue if there is default in payment of interest but no default in payment of principal.

§ 3–305. Defenses and Claims in Recoupment.

(a) Except as stated in subsection (b), the right to enforce the obligation of a party to pay an instrument is subject to the following:

(1) a defense of the obligor based on (i) infancy of the obligor to the extent it is a defense to a simple contract, (ii) duress, lack of legal capacity, or illegality of the transaction which, under other law, nullifies the obligation of the obligor, (iii) fraud that induced the obligor to sign the instrument with neither knowledge nor reasonable opportunity to learn of its character or its essential terms, or (iv) discharge of the obligor in insolvency proceedings;

(2) a defense of the obligor stated in another section of this Article or a defense of the obligor that would be available if the person entitled to enforce the instrument were enforcing a right to payment under a simple contract; and

(3) a claim in recoupment of the obligor against the original payee of the instrument if the claim arose from the transaction that gave rise to the instrument; but the claim of the obligor may be asserted against a transferee of the instrument only to reduce the amount owing on the instrument at the time the action is brought.

(b) The right of a holder in due course to enforce the obligation of a party to pay the instrument is subject to defenses of the obligor stated in subsection (a)(1), but is not subject to defenses of the obligor stated in subsection (a)(2) or claims in recoupment stated in subsection (a)(3) against a person other than the holder.

(c) Except as stated in subsection (d), in an action to enforce the obligation of a party to pay the instrument, the obligor may not assert against the person entitled to enforce the instrument a defense, claim in recoupment, or claim to the instrument (Section 3–306) of another person, but the other person's claim to the instrument may be asserted by the obligor if the other person is joined in the action and personally asserts the claim against the person entitled to enforce the instrument. An obligor is not obliged to pay the instrument if the person seeking enforcement of the instrument does not have rights of a holder in due course and the obligor proves that the instrument is a lost or stolen instrument.

(d) In an action to enforce the obligation of an accommodation party to pay an instrument, the accommodation party may assert against the person entitled to enforce the instrument any defense or claim in recoupment under subsection (a) that the accommodated party could assert against the person entitled to enforce the instrument, except the defenses of discharge in insolvency proceedings, infancy, and lack of legal capacity.

§ 3–306. Claims to an Instrument.

A person taking an instrument, other than a person having rights of a holder in due course, is subject to a claim of a property or possessory right in the instrument or its proceeds, including a claim to rescind a negotiation and to recover the instrument or its proceeds. A person having rights of a holder in due course takes free of the claim to the instrument.

§ 3–307. Notice of Breach of Fiduciary Duty.

(a) In this section:

(1) "Fiduciary" means an agent, trustee, partner, corporate officer or director, or other representative owing a fiduciary duty with respect to an instrument.

(2) "Represented person" means the principal, beneficiary, partnership, corporation, or other person to whom the duty stated in paragraph (1) is owed.

(b) If (i) an instrument is taken from a fiduciary for payment or collection or for value, (ii) the taker has knowledge of the fiduciary status of the fiduciary, and (iii) the represented person makes a claim to the instrument or its proceeds on the basis that the transaction of the fiduciary is a breach of fiduciary duty, the following rules apply:

(1) Notice of breach of fiduciary duty by the fiduciary is notice of the claim of the represented person.

(2) In the case of an instrument payable to the represented person or the fiduciary as such, the taker has notice of the breach of fiduciary duty if the instrument is (i) taken in payment of or as security for a debt known by the taker to be the personal debt of the fiduciary, (ii) taken in a transaction known by the taker to be for the personal benefit of the fiduciary, or (iii) deposited to an account other than an account of the fiduciary, as such, or an account of the represented person.

(3) If an instrument is issued by the represented person or the fiduciary as such, and made payable to the fiduciary personally, the taker does not have notice of the breach of fiduciary duty unless the taker knows of the breach of fiduciary duty.

(4) If an instrument is issued by the represented person or the fiduciary as such, to the taker as payee, the taker has notice of the breach of fiduciary duty if the instrument is (i) taken in payment of or as security for a debt known by the taker to be the personal debt of the fiduciary, (ii) taken in a transaction known by the taker to be for the personal benefit of the fiduciary, or (iii) deposited to an account other than an account of the fiduciary, as such, or an account of the represented person.

§ 3–308. Proof of Signatures and Status as Holder in Due Course.

(a) In an action with respect to an instrument, the authenticity of, and authority to make, each signature on the instrument is admitted unless specifically denied in the pleadings. If the validity of a signature is denied in the pleadings, the burden of establishing validity is on the person claiming validity, but the signature is presumed to be authentic and authorized unless the action is to enforce the liability of the purported signer and the signer is dead or incompetent at the time of trial of the issue of validity of the signature. If an action to enforce the instrument is brought against a person as the undisclosed principal of a person who signed the instrument as a party to the instrument, the plaintiff has the burden of establishing that the defendant is liable on the instrument as a represented person under Section 3–402(a).

(b) If the validity of signatures is admitted or proved and there is compliance with subsection (a), a plaintiff producing the instrument is entitled to payment if the plaintiff proves entitlement to enforce the instrument under Section 3–301, unless the defendant proves a defense or claim in recoupment. If a defense or claim in recoupment is proved, the right to payment of the plaintiff is subject to the defense or claim, except to the extent the plaintiff proves that the plaintiff has rights of a holder in due course which are not subject to the defense or claim.

§ 3–309. Enforcement of Lost, Destroyed, or Stolen Instrument.

(a) A person not in possession of an instrument is entitled to enforce the instrument if (i) the person was in possession of the instrument and entitled to enforce it when loss of possession occurred, (ii) the loss of possession was not the result of a transfer by the person or a lawful seizure, and (iii) the person cannot reasonably obtain possession of the instrument because the instrument was destroyed, its whereabouts cannot be determined, or it is in the wrongful possession of an unknown person or a person that cannot be found or is not amenable to service of process.

(b) A person seeking enforcement of an instrument under subsection (a) must prove the terms of the instrument and the person's right to enforce the instrument. If that proof is made, Section 3–308 applies to the case as if the person seeking enforcement had produced the instrument. The court may not enter judgment in favor of the person seeking enforcement unless it finds that the person required to pay the instrument is adequately protected against loss that might occur by reason of a claim by another person to enforce the instrument. Adequate protection may be provided by any reasonable means.

§ 3–310. Effect of Instrument on Obligation for Which Taken.

(a) Unless otherwise agreed, if a certified check, cashier's check, or teller's check is taken for an obligation, the obligation is discharged to the same extent discharge would result if an amount of money equal to the amount of the instrument were taken in payment of the obligation. Discharge of the obligation does not affect any liability that the obligor may have as an indorser of the instrument.

(b) Unless otherwise agreed and except as provided in subsection (a), if a note or an uncertified check is taken for an obligation, the obligation is suspended to the same extent the obligation would be discharged if an amount of money equal to the amount of the instrument were taken, and the following rules apply:

(1) In the case of an uncertified check, suspension of the obligation continues until dishonor of the check or until it is paid or certified. Payment or certification of the check results in discharge of the obligation to the extent of the amount of the check.

(2) In the case of a note, suspension of the obligation continues until dishonor of the note or until it is paid. Payment of the note results in discharge of the obligation to the extent of the payment.

(3) Except as provided in paragraph (4), if the check or note is dishonored and the obligee of the obligation for which the instrument was taken is the person entitled to enforce the instrument, the obligee may enforce either the instrument or the obligation. In the case of an instrument of a third person which is negotiated to the obligee by the obligor, discharge of the obligor on the instrument also discharges the obligation.

(4) If the person entitled to enforce the instrument taken for an obligation is a person other than the obligee, the obligee may not enforce the obligation to the extent the obligation is suspended. If the obligee is the person entitled to enforce the instrument but no longer has possession of it because it was lost, stolen, or destroyed, the obligation may not be enforced to the extent of the amount payable on the instrument, and to that extent the obligee's rights against the obligor are limited to enforcement of the instrument.

(c) If an instrument other than one described in subsection (a) or (b) is taken for an obligation, the effect is (i) that stated in subsection (a) if the instrument is one on which a bank is liable as maker or acceptor, or (ii) that stated in subsection (b) in any other case.

§ 3–311. Accord and Satisfaction by Use of Instrument.

(a) If a person against whom a claim is asserted proves that (i) that person in good faith tendered an instrument to the claimant as full satisfaction of the claim, (ii) the amount of the claim was unliquidated or subject to a bona fide dispute, and (iii) the claimant obtained payment of the instrument, the following subsections apply.

(b) Unless subsection (c) applies, the claim is discharged if the person against whom the claim is asserted proves that the instrument or an accompanying written communication contained a conspicuous statement to the effect that the instrument was tendered as full satisfaction of the claim.

(c) Subject to subsection (d), a claim is not discharged under subsection (b) if either of the following applies:

(1) The claimant, if an organization, proves that (i) within a reasonable time before the tender, the claimant sent a conspicuous statement to the person against whom the claim is asserted that communications concerning disputed debts, including an

instrument tendered as full satisfaction of a debt, are to be sent to a designated person, office, or place, and (ii) the instrument or accompanying communication was not received by that designated person, office, or place.

(2) The claimant, whether or not an organization, proves that within 90 days after payment of the instrument, the claimant tendered repayment of the amount of the instrument to the person against whom the claim is asserted. This paragraph does not apply if the claimant is an organization that sent a statement complying with paragraph (1)(i).

(d) A claim is discharged if the person against whom the claim is asserted proves that within a reasonable time before collection of the instrument was initiated, the claimant, or an agent of the claimant having direct responsibility with respect to the disputed obligation, knew that the instrument was tendered in full satisfaction of the claim.

§ 3–312. Lost, Destroyed, or Stolen Cashier's Check, Teller's Check, or Certified Check.

(a) In this section:

(1) "Check" means a cashier's check, teller's check, or certified check.

(2) "Claimant" means a person who claims the right to receive the amount of a cashier's check, teller's check, or certified check that was lost, destroyed, or stolen.

(3) "Declaration of loss" means a written statement, made under penalty of perjury, to the effect that (i) the declarer lost possession of a check, (ii) the declarer is the drawer or payee of the check, in the case of a certified check, or the remitter or payee of the check, in the case of a cashier's check or teller's check, (iii) the loss of possession was not the result of a transfer by the declarer or a lawful seizure, and (iv) the declarer cannot reasonably obtain possession of the check because the check was destroyed, its whereabouts cannot be determined, or it is in the wrongful possession of an unknown person or a person that cannot be found or is not amenable to service of process.

(4) "Obligated bank" means the issuer of a cashier's check or teller's check or the acceptor of a certified check.

(b) A claimant may assert a claim to the amount of a check by a communication to the obligated bank describing the check with reasonable certainty and requesting payment of the amount of the check, if (i) the claimant is the drawer or payee of a certified check or the remitter or payee of a cashier's check or teller's check, (ii) the communication contains or is accompanied by a declaration of loss of the claimant with respect to the check, (iii) the communication is received at a time and in a manner affording the bank a reasonable time to act on it before the check is paid, and (iv) the claimant provides reasonable identification if requested by the obligated bank. Delivery of a declaration of loss is a warranty of the truth of the statements made in the declaration. If a claim is asserted in compliance with this subsection, the following rules apply:

(1) The claim becomes enforceable at the later of (i) the time the claim is asserted, or (ii) the 90th day following the date of the check, in the case of a cashier's check or teller's check, or the 90th day following the date of the acceptance, in the case of a certified check.

(2) Until the claim becomes enforceable, it has no legal effect and the obligated bank may pay the check or, in the case of a teller's check, may permit the drawee to pay the check. Payment to a person entitled to enforce the check discharges all liability of the obligated bank with respect to the check.

(3) If the claim becomes enforceable before the check is presented for payment, the obligated bank is not obliged to pay the check.

(4) When the claim becomes enforceable, the obligated bank becomes obliged to pay the amount of the check to the claimant if payment of the check has not been made to a person entitled to enforce the check. Subject to Section 4–302(a)(1), payment to the claimant discharges all liability of the obligated bank with respect to the check.

(c) If the obligated bank pays the amount of a check to a claimant under subsection (b)(4) and the check is presented for payment by a person having rights of a holder in due course, the claimant is obliged to (i) refund the payment to the obligated bank if the check is paid, or (ii) pay the amount of the check to the person having rights of a holder in due course if the check is dishonored.

(d) If a claimant has the right to assert a claim under subsection (b) and is also a person entitled to enforce a cashier's check, teller's check, or certified check which is lost, destroyed, or stolen, the claimant may assert rights with respect to the check either under this section or Section 3–309.

Added in 1991.

Part 4 Liability of Parties

§ 3–401. Signature.

(a) A person is not liable on an instrument unless (i) the person signed the instrument, or (ii) the person is represented by an agent or representative who signed the instrument and the signature is binding on the represented person under Section 3–402.

(b) A signature may be made (i) manually or by means of a device or machine, and (ii) by the use of any name, including a trade or assumed name, or by a word, mark, or symbol executed or adopted by a person with present intention to authenticate a writing.

§ 3–402. Signature by Representative.

(a) If a person acting, or purporting to act, as a representative signs an instrument by signing either the name of the represented person or the name of the signer, the represented person is bound by the signature to the same extent the represented person would be bound if the signature were on a simple contract. If the represented person is bound, the signature of the representative is the "authorized signature of the represented person" and the represented person is liable on the instrument, whether or not identified in the instrument.

(b) If a representative signs the name of the representative to an instrument and the signature is an authorized signature of the represented person, the following rules apply:

(1) If the form of the signature shows unambiguously that the signature is made on behalf of the represented person who is identified in the instrument, the representative is not liable on the instrument.

(2) Subject to subsection (c), if (i) the form of the signature does not show unambiguously that the signature is made in a representative capacity or (ii) the represented person is not identified in the instrument, the representative is liable on the instrument to a holder in due course that took the instrument without notice

that the representative was not intended to be liable on the instrument. With respect to any other person, the representative is liable on the instrument unless the representative proves that the original parties did not intend the representative to be liable on the instrument.

(c) If a representative signs the name of the representative as drawer of a check without indication of the representative status and the check is payable from an account of the represented person who is identified on the check, the signer is not liable on the check if the signature is an authorized signature of the represented person.

§ 3–403. Unauthorized Signature.

(a) Unless otherwise provided in this Article or Article 4, an unauthorized signature is ineffective except as the signature of the unauthorized signer in favor of a person who in good faith pays the instrument or takes it for value. An unauthorized signature may be ratified for all purposes of this Article.

(b) If the signature of more than one person is required to constitute the authorized signature of an organization, the signature of the organization is unauthorized if one of the required signatures is lacking.

(c) The civil or criminal liability of a person who makes an unauthorized signature is not affected by any provision of this Article which makes the unauthorized signature effective for the purposes of this Article.

§ 3–404. Impostors; Fictitious Payees.

(a) If an impostor, by use of the mails or otherwise, induces the issuer of an instrument to issue the instrument to the impostor, or to a person acting in concert with the impostor, by impersonating the payee of the instrument or a person authorized to act for the payee, an indorsement of the instrument by any person in the name of the payee is effective as the indorsement of the payee in favor of a person who, in good faith, pays the instrument or takes it for value or for collection.

(b) If (i) a person whose intent determines to whom an instrument is payable (Section 3–110(a) or (b)) does not intend the person identified as payee to have any interest in the instrument, or (ii) the person identified as payee of an instrument is a fictitious person, the following rules apply until the instrument is negotiated by special indorsement:

(1) Any person in possession of the instrument is its holder.

(2) An indorsement by any person in the name of the payee stated in the instrument is effective as the indorsement of the payee in favor of a person who, in good faith, pays the instrument or takes it for value or for collection.

(c) Under subsection (a) or (b), an indorsement is made in the name of a payee if (i) it is made in a name substantially similar to that of the payee or (ii) the instrument, whether or not indorsed, is deposited in a depositary bank to an account in a name substantially similar to that of the payee.

(d) With respect to an instrument to which subsection (a) or (b) applies, if a person paying the instrument or taking it for value or for collection fails to exercise ordinary care in paying or taking the instrument and that failure substantially contributes to loss resulting from payment of the instrument, the person bearing the loss may recover from the person failing to exercise ordinary care to the extent the failure to exercise ordinary care contributed to the loss.

§ 3–405. Employer's Responsibility for Fraudulent Indorsement by Employee.

(a) In this section:

(1) "Employee" includes an independent contractor and employee of an independent contractor retained by the employer.

(2) "Fraudulent indorsement" means (i) in the case of an instrument payable to the employer, a forged indorsement purporting to be that of the employer, or (ii) in the case of an instrument with respect to which the employer is the issuer, a forged indorsement purporting to be that of the person identified as payee.

(3) "Responsibility" with respect to instruments means authority (i) to sign or indorse instruments on behalf of the employer, (ii) to process instruments received by the employer for bookkeeping purposes, for deposit to an account, or for other disposition, (iii) to prepare or process instruments for issue in the name of the employer, (iv) to supply information determining the names or addresses of payees of instruments to be issued in the name of the employer, (v) to control the disposition of instruments to be issued in the name of the employer, or (vi) to act otherwise with respect to instruments in a responsible capacity. "Responsibility" does not include authority that merely allows an employee to have access to instruments or blank or incomplete instrument forms that are being stored or transported or are part of incoming or outgoing mail, or similar access.

(b) For the purpose of determining the rights and liabilities of a person who, in good faith, pays an instrument or takes it for value or for collection, if an employer entrusted an employee with responsibility with respect to the instrument and the employee or a person acting in concert with the employee makes a fraudulent indorsement of the instrument, the indorsement is effective as the indorsement of the person to whom the instrument is payable if it is made in the name of that person. If the person paying the instrument or taking it for value or for collection fails to exercise ordinary care in paying or taking the instrument and that failure substantially contributes to loss resulting from the fraud, the person bearing the loss may recover from the person failing to exercise ordinary care to the extent the failure to exercise ordinary care contributed to the loss.

(c) Under subsection (b), an indorsement is made in the name of the person to whom an instrument is payable if (i) it is made in a name substantially similar to the name of that person or (ii) the instrument, whether or not indorsed, is deposited in a depositary bank to an account in a name substantially similar to the name of that person.

§ 3–406. Negligence Contributing to Forged Signature or Alteration of Instrument.

(a) A person whose failure to exercise ordinary care substantially contributes to an alteration of an instrument or to the making of a forged signature on an instrument is precluded from asserting the alteration or the forgery against a person who, in good faith, pays the instrument or takes it for value or for collection.

(b) Under subsection (a), if the person asserting the preclusion fails to exercise ordinary care in paying or taking the instrument and that failure substantially contributes to loss, the loss is allocated between the person precluded and the person asserting the preclusion according to the extent to which the failure of each to exercise ordinary care contributed to the loss.

(c) Under subsection (a), the burden of proving failure to exercise ordinary care is on the person asserting the preclusion. Under subsection (b), the burden of proving failure to exercise ordinary care is on the person precluded.

§ 3–407. Alteration.

(a) "Alteration" means (i) an unauthorized change in an instrument that purports to modify in any respect the obligation of a party, or (ii) an unauthorized addition of words or numbers or other change to an incomplete instrument relating to the obligation of a party.

(b) Except as provided in subsection (c), an alteration fraudulently made discharges a party whose obligation is affected by the alteration unless that party assents or is precluded from asserting the alteration. No other alteration discharges a party, and the instrument may be enforced according to its original terms.

(c) A payor bank or drawee paying a fraudulently altered instrument or a person taking it for value, in good faith and without notice of the alteration, may enforce rights with respect to the instrument (i) according to its original terms, or (ii) in the case of an incomplete instrument altered by unauthorized completion, according to its terms as completed.

§ 3–408. Drawee Not Liable on Unaccepted Draft.

A check or other draft does not of itself operate as an assignment of funds in the hands of the drawee available for its payment, and the drawee is not liable on the instrument until the drawee accepts it.

§ 3–409. Acceptance of Draft; Certified Check.

(a) "Acceptance" means the drawee's signed agreement to pay a draft as presented. It must be written on the draft and may consist of the drawee's signature alone. Acceptance may be made at any time and becomes effective when notification pursuant to instructions is given or the accepted draft is delivered for the purpose of giving rights on the acceptance to any person.

(b) A draft may be accepted although it has not been signed by the drawer, is otherwise incomplete, is overdue, or has been dishonored.

(c) If a draft is payable at a fixed period after sight and the acceptor fails to date the acceptance, the holder may complete the acceptance by supplying a date in good faith.

(d) "Certified check" means a check accepted by the bank on which it is drawn. Acceptance may be made as stated in subsection (a) or by a writing on the check which indicates that the check is certified. The drawee of a check has no obligation to certify the check, and refusal to certify is not dishonor of the check.

§ 3–410. Acceptance Varying Draft.

(a) If the terms of a drawee's acceptance vary from the terms of the draft as presented, the holder may refuse the acceptance and treat the draft as dishonored. In that case, the drawee may cancel the acceptance.

(b) The terms of a draft are not varied by an acceptance to pay at a particular bank or place in the United States, unless the acceptance states that the draft is to be paid only at that bank or place.

(c) If the holder assents to an acceptance varying the terms of a draft, the obligation of each drawer and indorser that does not expressly assent to the acceptance is discharged.

§ 3–411. Refusal to Pay Cashier's Checks, Teller's Checks, and Certified Checks.

(a) In this section, "obligated bank" means the acceptor of a certified check or the issuer of a cashier's check or teller's check bought from the issuer.

(b) If the obligated bank wrongfully (i) refuses to pay a cashier's check or certified check, (ii) stops payment of a teller's check, or (iii) refuses to pay a dishonored teller's check, the person asserting the right to enforce the check is entitled to compensation for expenses and loss of interest resulting from the nonpayment and may recover consequential damages if the obligated bank refuses to pay after receiving notice of particular circumstances giving rise to the damages.

(c) Expenses or consequential damages under subsection (b) are not recoverable if the refusal of the obligated bank to pay occurs because (i) the bank suspends payments, (ii) the obligated bank asserts a claim or defense of the bank that it has reasonable grounds to believe is available against the person entitled to enforce the instrument, (iii) the obligated bank has a reasonable doubt whether the person demanding payment is the person entitled to enforce the instrument, or (iv) payment is prohibited by law.

§ 3–412. Obligation of Issuer of Note or Cashier's Check.

The issuer of a note or cashier's check or other draft drawn on the drawer is obliged to pay the instrument (i) according to its terms at the time it was issued or, if not issued, at the time it first came into possession of a holder, or (ii) if the issuer signed an incomplete instrument, according to its terms when completed, to the extent stated in Sections 3–115 and 3–407. The obligation is owed to a person entitled to enforce the instrument or to an indorser who paid the instrument under Section 3–415.

§ 3–413. Obligation of Acceptor.

(a) The acceptor of a draft is obliged to pay the draft (i) according to its terms at the time it was accepted, even though the acceptance states that the draft is payable "as originally drawn" or equivalent terms, (ii) if the acceptance varies the terms of the draft, according to the terms of the draft as varied, or (iii) if the acceptance is of a draft that is an incomplete instrument, according to its terms when completed, to the extent stated in Sections 3–115 and 3–407. The obligation is owed to a person entitled to enforce the draft or to the drawer or an indorser who paid the draft under Section 3–414 or 3–415.

(b) If the certification of a check or other acceptance of a draft states the amount certified or accepted, the obligation of the acceptor is that amount. If (i) the certification or acceptance does not state an amount, (ii) the amount of the instrument is subsequently raised, and (iii) the instrument is then negotiated to a holder in due course, the obligation of the acceptor is the amount of the instrument at the time it was taken by the holder in due course.

§ 3–414. Obligation of Drawer.

(a) This section does not apply to cashier's checks or other drafts drawn on the drawer.

(b) If an unaccepted draft is dishonored, the drawer is obliged to pay the draft (i) according to its terms at the time it was issued or, if not issued, at the time it first came into possession of a holder, or (ii) if the drawer signed an incomplete instrument, according to its terms when completed, to the extent stated in Sections 3–115 and 3–407.

The obligation is owed to a person entitled to enforce the draft or to an indorser who paid the draft under Section 3–415.

(c) If a draft is accepted by a bank, the drawer is discharged, regardless of when or by whom acceptance was obtained.

(d) If a draft is accepted and the acceptor is not a bank, the obligation of the drawer to pay the draft if the draft is dishonored by the acceptor is the same as the obligation of an indorser under Section 3–415(a) and (c).

(e) If a draft states that it is drawn "without recourse" or otherwise disclaims liability of the drawer to pay the draft, the drawer is not liable under subsection (b) to pay the draft if the draft is not a check. A disclaimer of the liability stated in subsection (b) is not effective if the draft is a check.

(f) If (i) a check is not presented for payment or given to a depositary bank for collection within 30 days after its date, (ii) the drawee suspends payments after expiration of the 30-day period without paying the check, and (iii) because of the suspension of payments, the drawer is deprived of funds maintained with the drawee to cover payment of the check, the drawer to the extent deprived of funds may discharge its obligation to pay the check by assigning to the person entitled to enforce the check the rights of the drawer against the drawee with respect to the funds.

§ 3–415. Obligation of Indorser.

(a) Subject to subsections (b), (c), and (d) and to Section 3–419(d), if an instrument is dishonored, an indorser is obliged to pay the amount due on the instrument (i) according to the terms of the instrument at the time it was indorsed, or (ii) if the indorser indorsed an incomplete instrument, according to its terms when completed, to the extent stated in Sections 3–115 and 3–407. The obligation of the indorser is owed to a person entitled to enforce the instrument or to a subsequent indorser who paid the instrument under this section.

(b) If an indorsement states that it is made "without recourse" or otherwise disclaims liability of the indorser, the indorser is not liable under subsection (a) to pay the instrument.

(c) If notice of dishonor of an instrument is required by Section 3–503 and notice of dishonor complying with that section is not given to an indorser, the liability of the indorser under subsection (a) is discharged.

(d) If a draft is accepted by a bank after an indorsement is made, the liability of the indorser under subsection (a) is discharged.

(e) If an indorser of a check is liable under subsection (a) and the check is not presented for payment, or given to a depositary bank for collection, within 30 days after the day the indorsement was made, the liability of the indorser under subsection (a) is discharged.

As amended in 1993.

§ 3–416. Transfer Warranties.

(a) A person who transfers an instrument for consideration warrants to the transferee and, if the transfer is by indorsement, to any subsequent transferee that:

(1) the warrantor is a person entitled to enforce the instrument;

(2) all signatures on the instrument are authentic and authorized;

(3) the instrument has not been altered;

(4) the instrument is not subject to a defense or claim in recoupment of any party which can be asserted against the warrantor; and

(5) the warrantor has no knowledge of any insolvency proceeding commenced with respect to the maker or acceptor or, in the case of an unaccepted draft, the drawer.

(b) A person to whom the warranties under subsection (a) are made and who took the instrument in good faith may recover from the warrantor as damages for breach of warranty an amount equal to the loss suffered as a result of the breach, but not more than the amount of the instrument plus expenses and loss of interest incurred as a result of the breach.

(c) The warranties stated in subsection (a) cannot be disclaimed with respect to checks. Unless notice of a claim for breach of warranty is given to the warrantor within 30 days after the claimant has reason to know of the breach and the identity of the warrantor, the liability of the warrantor under subsection (b) is discharged to the extent of any loss caused by the delay in giving notice of the claim.

(d) A [cause of action] for breach of warranty under this section accrues when the claimant has reason to know of the breach.

§ 3–417. Presentment Warranties.

(a) If an unaccepted draft is presented to the drawee for payment or acceptance and the drawee pays or accepts the draft, (i) the person obtaining payment or acceptance, at the time of presentment, and (ii) a previous transferor of the draft, at the time of transfer, warrant to the drawee making payment or accepting the draft in good faith that:

(1) the warrantor is, or was, at the time the warrantor transferred the draft, a person entitled to enforce the draft or authorized to obtain payment or acceptance of the draft on behalf of a person entitled to enforce the draft;

(2) the draft has not been altered; and

(3) the warrantor has no knowledge that the signature of the drawer of the draft is unauthorized.

(b) A drawee making payment may recover from any warrantor damages for breach of warranty equal to the amount paid by the drawee less the amount the drawee received or is entitled to receive from the drawer because of the payment. In addition, the drawee is entitled to compensation for expenses and loss of interest resulting from the breach. The right of the drawee to recover damages under this subsection is not affected by any failure of the drawee to exercise ordinary care in making payment. If the drawee accepts the draft, breach of warranty is a defense to the obligation of the acceptor. If the acceptor makes payment with respect to the draft, the acceptor is entitled to recover from any warrantor for breach of warranty the amounts stated in this subsection.

(c) If a drawee asserts a claim for breach of warranty under subsection (a) based on an unauthorized indorsement of the draft or an alteration of the draft, the warrantor may defend by proving that the indorsement is effective under Section 3–404 or 3–405 or the drawer is precluded under Section 3–406 or 4–406 from asserting against the drawee the unauthorized indorsement or alteration.

(d) If (i) a dishonored draft is presented for payment to the drawer or an indorser or (ii) any other instrument is presented for payment to a party obliged to pay the instrument, and (iii) payment is received, the following rules apply:

(1) The person obtaining payment and a prior transferor of the instrument warrant to the person making payment in good faith that the warrantor is, or was, at the time the warrantor transferred the instrument, a person entitled to enforce the instrument or

authorized to obtain payment on behalf of a person entitled to enforce the instrument.

(2) The person making payment may recover from any warrantor for breach of warranty an amount equal to the amount paid plus expenses and loss of interest resulting from the breach.

(e) The warranties stated in subsections (a) and (d) cannot be disclaimed with respect to checks. Unless notice of a claim for breach of warranty is given to the warrantor within 30 days after the claimant has reason to know of the breach and the identity of the warrantor, the liability of the warrantor under subsection (b) or (d) is discharged to the extent of any loss caused by the delay in giving notice of the claim.

(f) A [cause of action] for breach of warranty under this section accrues when the claimant has reason to know of the breach.

§ 3–418. Payment or Acceptance by Mistake.

(a) Except as provided in subsection (c), if the drawee of a draft pays or accepts the draft and the drawee acted on the mistaken belief that (i) payment of the draft had not been stopped pursuant to Section 4–403 or (ii) the signature of the drawer of the draft was authorized, the drawee may recover the amount of the draft from the person to whom or for whose benefit payment was made or, in the case of acceptance, may revoke the acceptance. Rights of the drawee under this subsection are not affected by failure of the drawee to exercise ordinary care in paying or accepting the draft.

(b) Except as provided in subsection (c), if an instrument has been paid or accepted by mistake and the case is not covered by subsection (a), the person paying or accepting may, to the extent permitted by the law governing mistake and restitution, (i) recover the payment from the person to whom or for whose benefit payment was made or (ii) in the case of acceptance, may revoke the acceptance.

(c) The remedies provided by subsection (a) or (b) may not be asserted against a person who took the instrument in good faith and for value or who in good faith changed position in reliance on the payment or acceptance. This subsection does not limit remedies provided by Section 3–417 or 4–407.

(d) Notwithstanding Section 4–215, if an instrument is paid or accepted by mistake and the payor or acceptor recovers payment or revokes acceptance under subsection (a) or (b), the instrument is deemed not to have been paid or accepted and is treated as dishonored, and the person from whom payment is recovered has rights as a person entitled to enforce the dishonored instrument.

§ 3–419. Instruments Signed for Accommodation.

(a) If an instrument is issued for value given for the benefit of a party to the instrument ("accommodated party") and another party to the instrument ("accommodation party") signs the instrument for the purpose of incurring liability on the instrument without being a direct beneficiary of the value given for the instrument, the instrument is signed by the accommodation party "for accommodation."

(b) An accommodation party may sign the instrument as maker, drawer, acceptor, or indorser and, subject to subsection (d), is obliged to pay the instrument in the capacity in which the accommodation party signs. The obligation of an accommodation party may be enforced notwithstanding any statute of frauds and whether or not the accommodation party receives consideration for the accommodation.

(c) A person signing an instrument is presumed to be an accommodation party and there is notice that the instrument is signed for accommodation if the signature is an anomalous indorsement or is accompanied by words indicating that the signer is acting as surety or guarantor with respect to the obligation of another party to the instrument. Except as provided in Section 3–605, the obligation of an accommodation party to pay the instrument is not affected by the fact that the person enforcing the obligation had notice when the instrument was taken by that person that the accommodation party signed the instrument for accommodation.

(d) If the signature of a party to an instrument is accompanied by words indicating unambiguously that the party is guaranteeing collection rather than payment of the obligation of another party to the instrument, the signer is obliged to pay the amount due on the instrument to a person entitled to enforce the instrument only if (i) execution of judgment against the other party has been returned unsatisfied, (ii) the other party is insolvent or in an insolvency proceeding, (iii) the other party cannot be served with process, or (iv) it is otherwise apparent that payment cannot be obtained from the other party.

(e) An accommodation party who pays the instrument is entitled to reimbursement from the accommodated party and is entitled to enforce the instrument against the accommodated party. An accommodated party who pays the instrument has no right of recourse against, and is not entitled to contribution from, an accommodation party.

§ 3–420. Conversion of Instrument.

(a) The law applicable to conversion of personal property applies to instruments. An instrument is also converted if it is taken by transfer, other than a negotiation, from a person not entitled to enforce the instrument or a bank makes or obtains payment with respect to the instrument for a person not entitled to enforce the instrument or receive payment. An action for conversion of an instrument may not be brought by (i) the issuer or acceptor of the instrument or (ii) a payee or indorsee who did not receive delivery of the instrument either directly or through delivery to an agent or a co-payee.

(b) In an action under subsection (a), the measure of liability is presumed to be the amount payable on the instrument, but recovery may not exceed the amount of the plaintiff's interest in the instrument.

(c) A representative, other than a depositary bank, who has in good faith dealt with an instrument or its proceeds on behalf of one who was not the person entitled to enforce the instrument is not liable in conversion to that person beyond the amount of any proceeds that it has not paid out.

Part 5 Dishonor

§ 3–501. Presentment.

(a) "Presentment" means a demand made by or on behalf of a person entitled to enforce an instrument (i) to pay the instrument made to the drawee or a party obliged to pay the instrument or, in the case of a note or accepted draft payable at a bank, to the bank, or (ii) to accept a draft made to the drawee.

(b) The following rules are subject to Article 4, agreement of the parties, and clearing-house rules and the like:

(1) Presentment may be made at the place of payment of the instrument and must be made at the place of payment if the instrument is payable at a bank in the United States; may be made

by any commercially reasonable means, including an oral, written, or electronic communication; is effective when the demand for payment or acceptance is received by the person to whom presentment is made; and is effective if made to any one of two or more makers, acceptors, drawees, or other payors.

(2) Upon demand of the person to whom presentment is made, the person making presentment must (i) exhibit the instrument, (ii) give reasonable identification and, if presentment is made on behalf of another person, reasonable evidence of authority to do so, and (. . .) sign a receipt on the instrument for any payment made or surrender the instrument if full payment is made.

(3) Without dishonoring the instrument, the party to whom presentment is made may (i) return the instrument for lack of a necessary indorsement, or (ii) refuse payment or acceptance for failure of the presentment to comply with the terms of the instrument, an agreement of the parties, or other applicable law or rule.

(4) The party to whom presentment is made may treat presentment as occurring on the next business day after the day of presentment if the party to whom presentment is made has established a cut-off hour not earlier than 2 p.m. for the receipt and processing of instruments presented for payment or acceptance and presentment is made after the cut-off hour.

§ 3–502. Dishonor.

(a) Dishonor of a note is governed by the following rules:

(1) If the note is payable on demand, the note is dishonored if presentment is duly made to the maker and the note is not paid on the day of presentment.

(2) If the note is not payable on demand and is payable at or through a bank or the terms of the note require presentment, the note is dishonored if presentment is duly made and the note is not paid on the day it becomes payable or the day of presentment, whichever is later.

(3) If the note is not payable on demand and paragraph (2) does not apply, the note is dishonored if it is not paid on the day it becomes payable.

(b) Dishonor of an unaccepted draft other than a documentary draft is governed by the following rules:

(1) If a check is duly presented for payment to the payor bank otherwise than for immediate payment over the counter, the check is dishonored if the payor bank makes timely return of the check or sends timely notice of dishonor or nonpayment under Section 4–301 or 4–302, or becomes accountable for the amount of the check under Section 4–302.

(2) If a draft is payable on demand and paragraph (1) does not apply, the draft is dishonored if presentment for payment is duly made to the drawee and the draft is not paid on the day of presentment.

(3) If a draft is payable on a date stated in the draft, the draft is dishonored if (i) presentment for payment is duly made to the drawee and payment is not made on the day the draft becomes payable or the day of presentment, whichever is later, or (ii) presentment for acceptance is duly made before the day the draft becomes payable and the draft is not accepted on the day of presentment.

(4) If a draft is payable on elapse of a period of time after sight or acceptance, the draft is dishonored if presentment for acceptance is duly made and the draft is not accepted on the day of presentment.

(c) Dishonor of an unaccepted documentary draft occurs according to the rules stated in subsection (b)(2), (3), and (4), except that payment or acceptance may be delayed without dishonor until no later than the close of the third business day of the drawee following the day on which payment or acceptance is required by those paragraphs.

(d) Dishonor of an accepted draft is governed by the following rules:

(1) If the draft is payable on demand, the draft is dishonored if presentment for payment is duly made to the acceptor and the draft is not paid on the day of presentment.

(2) If the draft is not payable on demand, the draft is dishonored if presentment for payment is duly made to the acceptor and payment is not made on the day it becomes payable or the day of presentment, whichever is later.

(e) In any case in which presentment is otherwise required for dishonor under this section and presentment is excused under Section 3–504, dishonor occurs without presentment if the instrument is not duly accepted or paid.

(f) If a draft is dishonored because timely acceptance of the draft was not made and the person entitled to demand acceptance consents to a late acceptance, from the time of acceptance the draft is treated as never having been dishonored.

§ 3–503. Notice of Dishonor.

(a) The obligation of an indorser stated in Section 3–415(a) and the obligation of a drawer stated in Section 3–414(d) may not be enforced unless (i) the indorser or drawer is given notice of dishonor of the instrument complying with this section or (ii) notice of dishonor is excused under Section 3–504(b).

(b) Notice of dishonor may be given by any person; may be given by any commercially reasonable means, including an oral, written, or electronic communication; and is sufficient if it reasonably identifies the instrument and indicates that the instrument has been dishonored or has not been paid or accepted. Return of an instrument given to a bank for collection is sufficient notice of dishonor.

(c) Subject to Section 3–504(c), with respect to an instrument taken for collection by a collecting bank, notice of dishonor must be given (i) by the bank before midnight of the next banking day following the banking day on which the bank receives notice of dishonor of the instrument, or (ii) by any other person within 30 days following the day on which the person receives notice of dishonor. With respect to any other instrument, notice of dishonor must be given within 30 days following the day on which dishonor occurs.

§ 3–504. Excused Presentment and Notice of Dishonor.

(a) Presentment for payment or acceptance of an instrument is excused if (i) the person entitled to present the instrument cannot with reasonable diligence make presentment, (ii) the maker or acceptor has repudiated an obligation to pay the instrument or is dead or in insolvency proceedings, (iii) by the terms of the instrument presentment is not necessary to enforce the obligation of indorsers or the drawer, (iv) the drawer or indorser whose obligation is being enforced has waived presentment or otherwise has no reason to expect or right to require that the instrument be paid or accepted, or (v) the drawer instructed the drawee not to pay or accept the draft or the drawee was not obligated to the drawer to pay the draft.

(b) Notice of dishonor is excused if (i) by the terms of the instrument notice of dishonor is not necessary to enforce the obligation of a party to pay the instrument, or (ii) the party whose obligation is being enforced waived notice of dishonor. A waiver of presentment is also a waiver of notice of dishonor.

(c) Delay in giving notice of dishonor is excused if the delay was caused by circumstances beyond the control of the person giving the notice and the person giving the notice exercised reasonable diligence after the cause of the delay ceased to operate.

§ 3–505. Evidence of Dishonor.

(a) The following are admissible as evidence and create a presumption of dishonor and of any notice of dishonor stated:

(1) a document regular in form as provided in subsection (b) which purports to be a protest;

(2) a purported stamp or writing of the drawee, payor bank, or presenting bank on or accompanying the instrument stating that acceptance or payment has been refused unless reasons for the refusal are stated and the reasons are not consistent with dishonor;

(3) a book or record of the drawee, payor bank, or collecting bank, kept in the usual course of business which shows dishonor, even if there is no evidence of who made the entry.

(b) A protest is a certificate of dishonor made by a United States consul or vice consul, or a notary public or other person authorized to administer oaths by the law of the place where dishonor occurs. It may be made upon information satisfactory to that person. The protest must identify the instrument and certify either that presentment has been made or, if not made, the reason why it was not made, and that the instrument has been dishonored by nonacceptance or nonpayment. The protest may also certify that notice of dishonor has been given to some or all parties.

Part 6 Discharge and Payment

§ 3–601. Discharge and Effect of Discharge.

(a) The obligation of a party to pay the instrument is discharged as stated in this Article or by an act or agreement with the party which would discharge an obligation to pay money under a simple contract.

(b) Discharge of the obligation of a party is not effective against a person acquiring rights of a holder in due course of the instrument without notice of the discharge.

§ 3–602. Payment.

(a) Subject to subsection (b), an instrument is paid to the extent payment is made (i) by or on behalf of a party obliged to pay the instrument, and (ii) to a person entitled to enforce the instrument. To the extent of the payment, the obligation of the party obliged to pay the instrument is discharged even though payment is made with knowledge of a claim to the instrument under Section 3–306 by another person.

(b) The obligation of a party to pay the instrument is not discharged under subsection (a) if:

(1) a claim to the instrument under Section 3–306 is enforceable against the party receiving payment and (i) payment is made with knowledge by the payor that payment is prohibited by injunction or similar process of a court of competent jurisdiction, or (ii) in the case of an instrument other than a cashier's check, teller's check, or certified check, the party making payment accepted, from the person having a claim to the instrument, indemnity against loss resulting from refusal to pay the person entitled to enforce the instrument; or

(2) the person making payment knows that the instrument is a stolen instrument and pays a person it knows is in wrongful possession of the instrument.

§ 3–603. Tender of Payment.

(a) If tender of payment of an obligation to pay an instrument is made to a person entitled to enforce the instrument, the effect of tender is governed by principles of law applicable to tender of payment under a simple contract.

(b) If tender of payment of an obligation to pay an instrument is made to a person entitled to enforce the instrument and the tender is refused, there is discharge, to the extent of the amount of the tender, of the obligation of an indorser or accommodation party having a right of recourse with respect to the obligation to which the tender relates.

(c) If tender of payment of an amount due on an instrument is made to a person entitled to enforce the instrument, the obligation of the obligor to pay interest after the due date on the amount tendered is discharged. If presentment is required with respect to an instrument and the obligor is able and ready to pay on the due date at every place of payment stated in the instrument, the obligor is deemed to have made tender of payment on the due date to the person entitled to enforce the instrument.

§ 3–604. Discharge by Cancellation or Renunciation.

(a) A person entitled to enforce an instrument, with or without consideration, may discharge the obligation of a party to pay the instrument (i) by an intentional voluntary act, such as surrender of the instrument to the party, destruction, mutilation, or cancellation of the instrument, cancellation or striking out of the party's signature, or the addition of words to the instrument indicating discharge, or (ii) by agreeing not to sue or otherwise renouncing rights against the party by a signed writing.

(b) Cancellation or striking out of an indorsement pursuant to subsection (a) does not affect the status and rights of a party derived from the indorsement.

§ 3–605. Discharge of Indorsers and Accommodation Parties.

(a) In this section, the term "indorser" includes a drawer having the obligation described in Section 3–414(d).

(b) Discharge, under Section 3–604, of the obligation of a party to pay an instrument does not discharge the obligation of an indorser or accommodation party having a right of recourse against the discharged party.

(c) If a person entitled to enforce an instrument agrees, with or without consideration, to an extension of the due date of the obligation of a party to pay the instrument, the extension discharges an indorser or accommodation party having a right of recourse against the party whose obligation is extended to the extent the indorser or accommodation party proves that the extension caused loss to the indorser or accommodation party with respect to the right of recourse.

(d) If a person entitled to enforce an instrument agrees, with or without consideration, to a material modification of the obligation of a party other than an extension of the due date, the modification discharges the obligation of an indorser or accommodation party having a right of recourse against the person whose obligation is modified to the extent the modification causes loss to the indorser or accommodation party with respect to the right of recourse. The loss suffered by the indorser or accommodation party as a result of the modification is equal to the amount of the right of recourse unless the person enforcing the instrument proves that no loss was caused by the modification or that the loss caused by the modification was an amount less than the amount of the right of recourse.

(e) If the obligation of a party to pay an instrument is secured by an interest in collateral and a person entitled to enforce the instrument impairs the value of the interest in collateral, the obligation of an indorser or accommodation party having a right of recourse against the obligor is discharged to the extent of the impairment. The value of an interest in collateral is impaired to the extent (i) the value of the interest is reduced to an amount less than the amount of the right of recourse of the party asserting discharge, or (ii) the reduction in value of the interest causes an increase in the amount by which the amount of the right of recourse exceeds the value of the interest. The burden of proving impairment is on the party asserting discharge.

(f) If the obligation of a party is secured by an interest in collateral not provided by an accommodation party and a person entitled to enforce the instrument impairs the value of the interest in collateral, the obligation of any party who is jointly and severally liable with respect to the secured obligation is discharged to the extent the impairment causes the party asserting discharge to pay more than that party would have been obliged to pay, taking into account rights of contribution, if impairment had not occurred. If the party asserting discharge is an accommodation party not entitled to discharge under subsection (e), the party is deemed to have a right to contribution based on joint and several liability rather than a right to reimbursement. The burden of proving impairment is on the party asserting discharge.

(g) Under subsection (e) or (f), impairing value of an interest in collateral includes (i) failure to obtain or maintain perfection or recordation of the interest in collateral, (ii) release of collateral without substitution of collateral of equal value, (iii) failure to perform a duty to preserve the value of collateral owed, under Article 9 or other law, to a debtor or surety or other person secondarily liable, or (iv) failure to comply with applicable law in disposing of collateral.

(h) An accommodation party is not discharged under subsection (c), (d), or (e) unless the person entitled to enforce the instrument knows of the accommodation or has notice under Section 3–419(c) that the instrument was signed for accommodation.

(i) A party is not discharged under this section if (i) the party asserting discharge consents to the event or conduct that is the basis of the discharge, or (ii) the instrument or a separate agreement of the party provides for waiver of discharge under this section either specifically or by general language indicating that parties waive defenses based on suretyship or impairment of collateral.

ADDENDUM TO REVISED ARTICLE 3

Notes to Legislative Counsel

1. If revised Article 3 is adopted in your state, the reference in Section 2–511 to Section 3–802 should be changed to Section 3–310.

2. If revised Article 3 is adopted in your state and the Uniform Fiduciaries Act is also in effect in your state, you may want to consider amending Uniform Fiduciaries Act § 9 to conform to Section 3–307(b)(2)(iii) and (4)(iii). See Official Comment 3 to Section 3–307.

Revised Article 4
BANK DEPOSITS AND COLLECTIONS

Part 1 General Provisions and Definitions

§ 4–101. Short Title.

This Article may be cited as Uniform Commercial Code—Bank Deposits and Collections.

As amended in 1990.

§ 4–102. Applicability.

(a) To the extent that items within this Article are also within Articles 3 and 8, they are subject to those Articles. If there is conflict, this Article governs Article 3, but Article 8 governs this Article.

(b) The liability of a bank for action or non-action with respect to an item handled by it for purposes of presentment, payment, or collection is governed by the law of the place where the bank is located. In the case of action or non-action by or at a branch or separate office of a bank, its liability is governed by the law of the place where the branch or separate office is located.

§ 4–103. Variation by Agreement; Measure of Damages; Action Constituting Ordinary Care.

(a) The effect of the provisions of this Article may be varied by agreement, but the parties to the agreement cannot disclaim a bank's responsibility for its lack of good faith or failure to exercise ordinary care or limit the measure of damages for the lack or failure. However, the parties may determine by agreement the standards by which the bank's responsibility is to be measured if those standards are not manifestly unreasonable.

(b) Federal Reserve regulations and operating circulars, clearing-house rules, and the like have the effect of agreements under subsection (a), whether or not specifically assented to by all parties interested in items handled.

(c) Action or non-action approved by this Article or pursuant to Federal Reserve regulations or operating circulars is the exercise of ordinary care and, in the absence of special instructions, action or non-action consistent with clearing-house rules and the like or with a general banking usage not disapproved by this Article, is *prima facie* the exercise of ordinary care.

(d) The specification or approval of certain procedures by this Article is not disapproval of other procedures that may be reasonable under the circumstances.

(e) The measure of damages for failure to exercise ordinary care in handling an item is the amount of the item reduced by an amount that could not have been realized by the exercise of ordinary care. If there is also bad faith it includes any other damages the party suffered as a proximate consequence.

As amended in 1990.

§ 4–104. Definitions and Index of Definitions.

(a) In this Article, unless the context otherwise requires:

(1) "Account" means any deposit or credit account with a bank, including a demand, time, savings, passbook, share draft, or like account, other than an account evidenced by a certificate of deposit;

(2) "Afternoon" means the period of a day between noon and midnight;

(3) "Banking day" means the part of a day on which a bank is open to the public for carrying on substantially all of its banking functions;

(4) "Clearing house" means an association of banks or other payors regularly clearing items;

(5) "Customer" means a person having an account with a bank or for whom a bank has agreed to collect items, including a bank that maintains an account at another bank;

(6) "Documentary draft" means a draft to be presented for acceptance or payment if specified documents, certificated securities (Section 8–102) or instructions for uncertificated securities (Section 8–102), or other certificates, statements, or the like are to be received by the drawee or other payor before acceptance or payment of the draft;

(7) "Draft" means a draft as defined in Section 3–104 or an item, other than an instrument, that is an order;

(8) "Drawee" means a person ordered in a draft to make payment;

(9) "Item" means an instrument or a promise or order to pay money handled by a bank for collection or payment. The term does not include a payment order governed by Article 4A or a credit or debit card slip;

(10) "Midnight deadline" with respect to a bank is midnight on its next banking day following the banking day on which it receives the relevant item or notice or from which the time for taking action commences to run, whichever is later;

(11) "Settle" means to pay in cash, by clearing-house settlement, in a charge or credit or by remittance, or otherwise as agreed. A settlement may be either provisional or final;

(12) "Suspends payments" with respect to a bank means that it has been closed by order of the supervisory authorities, that a public officer has been appointed to take it over, or that it ceases or refuses to make payments in the ordinary course of business.

(b) [Other definitions' section references deleted.]

(c) [Other definitions' section references deleted.]

(d) In addition, Article 1 contains general definitions and principles of construction and interpretation applicable throughout this Article.

§ 4–105. "Bank"; "Depositary Bank"; "Payor Bank"; "Intermediary Bank"; "Collecting Bank"; "Presenting Bank".

In this Article:

(1) "Bank" means a person engaged in the business of banking, including a savings bank, savings and loan association, credit union, or trust company;

(2) "Depositary bank" means the first bank to take an item even though it is also the payor bank, unless the item is presented for immediate payment over the counter;

(3) "Payor bank" means a bank that is the drawee of a draft;

(4) "Intermediary bank" means a bank to which an item is transferred in course of collection except the depositary or payor bank;

(5) "Collecting bank" means a bank handling an item for collection except the payor bank;

(6) "Presenting bank" means a bank presenting an item except a payor bank.

§ 4–106. Payable Through or Payable at Bank: Collecting Bank.

(a) If an item states that it is "payable through" a bank identified in the item, (i) the item designates the bank as a collecting bank and does not by itself authorize the bank to pay the item, and (ii) the item may be presented for payment only by or through the bank.

Alternative A

(b) If an item states that it is "payable at" a bank identified in the item, the item is equivalent to a draft drawn on the bank.

Alternative B

(b) If an item states that it is "payable at" a bank identified in the item, (i) the item designates the bank as a collecting bank and does not by itself authorize the bank to pay the item, and (ii) the item may be presented for payment only by or through the bank.

(c) If a draft names a nonbank drawee and it is unclear whether a bank named in the draft is a co-drawee or a collecting bank, the bank is a collecting bank.

As added in 1990.

§ 4–107. Separate Office of Bank.

A branch or separate office of a bank is a separate bank for the purpose of computing the time within which and determining the place at or to which action may be taken or notices or orders shall be given under this Article and under Article 3.

As amended in 1962 and 1990.

§ 4–108. Time of Receipt of Items.

(a) For the purpose of allowing time to process items, prove balances, and make the necessary entries on its books to determine its position for the day, a bank may fix an afternoon hour of 2 p.m. or later as a cutoff hour for the handling of money and items and the making of entries on its books.

(b) An item or deposit of money received on any day after a cutoff hour so fixed or after the close of the banking day may be treated as being received at the opening of the next banking day.

As amended in 1990.

§ 4–109. Delays.

(a) Unless otherwise instructed, a collecting bank in a good faith effort to secure payment of a specific item drawn on a payor other than a bank, and with or without the approval of any person involved, may waive, modify, or extend time limits imposed or permitted by this [act] for a period not exceeding two additional banking days without discharge of drawers or indorsers or liability to its transferor or a prior party.

(b) Delay by a collecting bank or payor bank beyond time limits prescribed or permitted by this [act] or by instructions is excused if (i) the delay is caused by interruption of communication or computer facilities, suspension of payments by another bank, war, emergency conditions, failure of equipment, or other circumstances beyond the control of the bank, and (ii) the bank exercises such diligence as the circumstances require.

§ 4–110. Electronic Presentment.

(a) "Agreement for electronic presentment" means an agreement, clearing-house rule, or Federal Reserve regulation or operating circular, providing that presentment of an item may be made by transmission of an image of an item or information describing the item ("presentment notice") rather than delivery of the item itself. The agreement may provide for procedures governing retention, presentment, payment, dishonor, and other matters concerning items subject to the agreement.

(b) Presentment of an item pursuant to an agreement for presentment is made when the presentment notice is received.

(c) If presentment is made by presentment notice, a reference to "item" or "check" in this Article means the presentment notice unless the context otherwise indicates.

As added in 1990.

§ 4–111. Statute of Limitations.

An action to enforce an obligation, duty, or right arising under this Article must be commenced within three years after the [cause of action] accrues.

As added in 1990.

Part 2 Collection of Items: Depositary and Collecting Banks

§ 4–201. Status of Collecting Bank as Agent and Provisional Status of Credits; Applicability of Article; Item Indorsed "Pay Any Bank".

(a) Unless a contrary intent clearly appears and before the time that a settlement given by a collecting bank for an item is or becomes final, the bank, with respect to an item, is an agent or sub-agent of the owner of the item and any settlement given for the item is provisional. This provision applies regardless of the form of indorsement or lack of indorsement and even though credit given for the item is subject to immediate withdrawal as of right or is in fact withdrawn; but the continuance of ownership of an item by its owner and any rights of the owner to proceeds of the item are subject to rights of a collecting bank, such as those resulting from outstanding advances on the item and rights of recoupment or setoff. If an item is handled by banks for purposes of presentment, payment, collection, or return, the relevant provisions of this Article apply even though action of the parties clearly establishes that a particular bank has purchased the item and is the owner of it.

(b) After an item has been indorsed with the words "pay any bank" or the like, only a bank may acquire the rights of a holder until the item has been:

(1) returned to the customer initiating collection; or

(2) specially indorsed by a bank to a person who is not a bank.

As amended in 1990.

§ 4–202. Responsibility for Collection or Return; When Action Timely.

(a) A collecting bank must exercise ordinary care in:

(1) presenting an item or sending it for presentment;

(2) sending notice of dishonor or nonpayment or returning an item other than a documentary draft to the bank's transferor after learning that the item has not been paid or accepted, as the case may be;

(3) settling for an item when the bank receives final settlement; and

(4) notifying its transferor of any loss or delay in transit within a reasonable time after discovery thereof.

(b) A collecting bank exercises ordinary care under subsection (a) by taking proper action before its midnight deadline following receipt of an item, notice, or settlement. Taking proper action within a reasonably longer time may constitute the exercise of ordinary care, but the bank has the burden of establishing timeliness.

(c) Subject to subsection (a)(1), a bank is not liable for the insolvency, neglect, misconduct, mistake, or default of another bank or person or for loss or destruction of an item in the possession of others or in transit.

As amended in 1990.

§ 4–203. Effect of Instructions.

Subject to Article 3 concerning conversion of instruments (Section 3–420) and restrictive indorsements (Section 3–206), only a collecting bank's transferor can give instructions that affect the bank or constitute notice to it, and a collecting bank is not liable to prior parties for any action taken pursuant to the instructions or in accordance with any agreement with its transferor.

§ 4–204. Methods of Sending and Presenting; Sending Directly to Payor Bank.

(a) A collecting bank shall send items by a reasonably prompt method, taking into consideration relevant instructions, the nature of the item, the number of those items on hand, the cost of collection involved, and the method generally used by it or others to present those items.

(b) A collecting bank may send:

(1) an item directly to the payor bank;

(2) an item to a nonbank payor if authorized by its transferor; and

(3) an item other than documentary drafts to a nonbank payor, if authorized by Federal Reserve regulation or operating circular, clearing-house rule, or the like.

(c) Presentment may be made by a presenting bank at a place where the payor bank or other payor has requested that presentment be made.

As amended in 1990.

§ 4–205. Depositary Bank Holder of Unindorsed Item.

If a customer delivers an item to a depositary bank for collection:

(1) the depositary bank becomes a holder of the item at the time it receives the item for collection if the customer at the time of delivery was a holder of the item, whether or not the customer indorses the item, and, if the bank satisfies the other requirements of Section 3–302, it is a holder in due course; and

(2) the depositary bank warrants to collecting banks, the payor bank or other payor, and the drawer that the amount of the item was paid to the customer or deposited to the customer's account.

As amended in 1990.

§ 4–206. Transfer Between Banks.

Any agreed method that identifies the transferor bank is sufficient for the item's further transfer to another bank.

As amended in 1990.

§ 4–207. Transfer Warranties.

(a) A customer or collecting bank that transfers an item and receives a settlement or other consideration warrants to the transferee and to any subsequent collecting bank that:

(1) the warrantor is a person entitled to enforce the item;

(2) all signatures on the item are authentic and authorized;

(3) the item has not been altered;

(4) the item is not subject to a defense or claim in recoupment (Section 3–305(a)) of any party that can be asserted against the warrantor; and

(5) the warrantor has no knowledge of any insolvency proceeding commenced with respect to the maker or acceptor or, in the case of an unaccepted draft, the drawer.

(b) If an item is dishonored, a customer or collecting bank transferring the item and receiving settlement or other consideration is obliged to pay the amount due on the item (i) according to the terms of the item at the time it was transferred, or (ii) if the transfer was of an incomplete item, according to its terms when completed as stated in Sections 3–115 and 3–407. The obligation of a transferor is owed to the transferee and to any subsequent collecting bank that takes the item in good faith. A transferor cannot disclaim its obligation under this subsection by an indorsement stating that it is made "without recourse" or otherwise disclaiming liability.

(c) A person to whom the warranties under subsection (a) are made and who took the item in good faith may recover from the warrantor as damages for breach of warranty an amount equal to the loss suffered as a result of the breach, but not more than the amount of the item plus expenses and loss of interest incurred as a result of the breach.

(d) The warranties stated in subsection (a) cannot be disclaimed with respect to checks. Unless notice of a claim for breach of warranty is given to the warrantor within 30 days after the claimant has reason to know of the breach and the identity of the warrantor, the warrantor is discharged to the extent of any loss caused by the delay in giving notice of the claim.

(e) A cause of action for breach of warranty under this section accrues when the claimant has reason to know of the breach.

As amended in 1990.

§ 4–208. Presentment Warranties.

(a) If an unaccepted draft is presented to the drawee for payment or acceptance and the drawee pays or accepts the draft, (i) the person obtaining payment or acceptance, at the time of presentment, and (ii) a previous transferor of the draft, at the time of transfer, warrant to the drawee that pays or accepts the draft in good faith that:

(1) the warrantor is, or was, at the time the warrantor transferred the draft, a person entitled to enforce the draft or authorized to obtain payment or acceptance of the draft on behalf of a person entitled to enforce the draft;

(2) the draft has not been altered; and

(3) the warrantor has no knowledge that the signature of the purported drawer of the draft is unauthorized.

(b) A drawee making payment may recover from a warrantor damages for breach of warranty equal to the amount paid by the drawee less the amount the drawee received or is entitled to receive from the drawer because of the payment. In addition, the drawee is entitled to compensation for expenses and loss of interest resulting from the breach. The right of the drawee to recover damages under this subsection is not affected by any failure of the drawee to exercise ordinary care in making payment. If the drawee accepts the draft (i) breach of warranty is a defense to the obligation of the acceptor, and (ii) if the acceptor makes payment with respect to the draft, the acceptor is entitled to recover from a warrantor for breach of warranty the amounts stated in this subsection.

(c) If a drawee asserts a claim for breach of warranty under subsection (a) based on an unauthorized indorsement of the draft or an alteration of the draft, the warrantor may defend by proving that the indorsement is effective under Section 3–404 or 3–405 or the drawer is precluded under Section 3–406 or 4–406 from asserting against the drawee the unauthorized indorsement or alteration.

(d) If (i) a dishonored draft is presented for payment to the drawer or an indorser or (ii) any other item is presented for payment to a party obliged to pay the item, and the item is paid, the person obtaining payment and a prior transferor of the item warrant to the person making payment in good faith that the warrantor is, or was, at the time the warrantor transferred the item, a person entitled to enforce the item or authorized to obtain payment on behalf of a person entitled to enforce the item. The person making payment may recover from any warrantor for breach of warranty an amount equal to the amount paid plus expenses and loss of interest resulting from the breach.

(e) The warranties stated in subsections (a) and (d) cannot be disclaimed with respect to checks. Unless notice of a claim for breach of warranty is given to the warrantor within 30 days after the claimant has reason to know of the breach and the identity of the warrantor, the warrantor is discharged to the extent of any loss caused by the delay in giving notice of the claim.

(f) A cause of action for breach of warranty under this section accrues when the claimant has reason to know of the breach.

As amended in 1990.

§ 4–209. Encoding and Retention Warranties.

(a) A person who encodes information on or with respect to an item after issue warrants to any subsequent collecting bank and to the payor bank or other payor that the information is correctly encoded. If the customer of a depositary bank encodes, that bank also makes the warranty.

(b) A person who undertakes to retain an item pursuant to an agreement for electronic presentment warrants to any subsequent collecting bank and to the payor bank or other payor that retention and presentment of the item comply with the agreement. If a customer of a depositary bank undertakes to retain an item, that bank also makes this warranty.

(c) A person to whom warranties are made under this section and who took the item in good faith may recover from the warrantor as damages for breach of warranty an amount equal to the loss suffered as a result of the breach, plus expenses and loss of interest incurred as a result of the breach.

As added in 1990.

§ 4–210. Security Interest of Collecting Bank in Items, Accompanying Documents and Proceeds.

(a) A collecting bank has a security interest in an item and any accompanying documents or the proceeds of either:

(1) in case of an item deposited in an account, to the extent to which credit given for the item has been withdrawn or applied;

(2) in case of an item for which it has given credit available for withdrawal as of right, to the extent of the credit given, whether or not the credit is drawn upon or there is a right of charge-back; or

(3) if it makes an advance on or against the item.

(b) If credit given for several items received at one time or pursuant to a single agreement is withdrawn or applied in part, the security interest remains upon all the items, any accompanying documents or the proceeds of either. For the purpose of this section, credits first given are first withdrawn.

(c) Receipt by a collecting bank of a final settlement for an item is a realization on its security interest in the item, accompanying documents, and proceeds. So long as the bank does not receive final settlement for the item or give up possession of the item or accompanying documents for purposes other than collection, the security interest continues to that extent and is subject to Article 9, but:

(1) no security agreement is necessary to make the security interest enforceable (Section 9–203(1)(a));

(2) no filing is required to perfect the security interest; and

(3) the security interest has priority over conflicting perfected security interests in the item, accompanying documents, or proceeds.

As amended in 1990 and 1999.

§ 4–211. When Bank Gives Value for Purposes of Holder in Due Course.

For purposes of determining its status as a holder in due course, a bank has given value to the extent it has a security interest in an item, if the bank otherwise complies with the requirements of Section 3–302 on what constitutes a holder in due course.

As amended in 1990.

§ 4–212. Presentment by Notice of Item Not Payable by, Through, or at Bank; Liability of Drawer or Indorser.

(a) Unless otherwise instructed, a collecting bank may present an item not payable by, through, or at a bank by sending to the party to accept or pay a written notice that the bank holds the item for acceptance or payment. The notice must be sent in time to be received on or before the day when presentment is due and the bank must meet any requirement of the party to accept or pay under Section 3–501 by the close of the bank's next banking day after it knows of the requirement.

(b) If presentment is made by notice and payment, acceptance, or request for compliance with a requirement under Section 3–501 is not received by the close of business on the day after maturity or, in the case of demand items, by the close of business on the third banking day after notice was sent, the presenting bank may treat the item as dishonored and charge any drawer or indorser by sending it notice of the facts.

As amended in 1990.

§ 4–213. Medium and Time of Settlement by Bank.

(a) With respect to settlement by a bank, the medium and time of settlement may be prescribed by Federal Reserve regulations or circulars, clearing-house rules, and the like, or agreement. In the absence of such prescription:

(1) the medium of settlement is cash or credit to an account in a Federal Reserve bank of or specified by the person to receive settlement; and

(2) the time of settlement is:

(i) with respect to tender of settlement by cash, a cashier's check, or teller's check, when the cash or check is sent or delivered;

(ii) with respect to tender of settlement by credit in an account in a Federal Reserve Bank, when the credit is made;

(iii) with respect to tender of settlement by a credit or debit to an account in a bank, when the credit or debit is made or, in the case of tender of settlement by authority to charge an account, when the authority is sent or delivered; or

(iv) with respect to tender of settlement by a funds transfer, when payment is made pursuant to Section 4A–406(a) to the person receiving settlement.

(b) If the tender of settlement is not by a medium authorized by subsection (a) or the time of settlement is not fixed by subsection (a), no settlement occurs until the tender of settlement is accepted by the person receiving settlement.

(c) If settlement for an item is made by cashier's check or teller's check and the person receiving settlement, before its midnight deadline:

(1) presents or forwards the check for collection, settlement is final when the check is finally paid; or

(2) fails to present or forward the check for collection, settlement is final at the midnight deadline of the person receiving settlement.

(d) If settlement for an item is made by giving authority to charge the account of the bank giving settlement in the bank receiving settlement, settlement is final when the charge is made by the bank receiving settlement if there are funds available in the account for the amount of the item.

As amended in 1990.

§ 4–214. Right of Charge-Back or Refund; Liability of Collecting Bank: Return of Item.

(a) If a collecting bank has made provisional settlement with its customer for an item and fails by reason of dishonor, suspension of payments by a bank, or otherwise to receive settlement for the item which is or becomes final, the bank may revoke the settlement given by it, charge back the amount of any credit given for the item to its customer's account, or obtain refund from its customer, whether or not it is able to return the item, if by its midnight deadline or within a longer reasonable time after it learns the facts it returns the item or sends notification of the facts. If the return or notice is delayed beyond the bank's midnight deadline or a longer reasonable time after it learns the facts, the bank may revoke the settlement, charge back the credit, or obtain refund from its customer, but it is liable for any loss resulting from the delay. These rights to revoke, charge back, and obtain refund terminate if and when a settlement for the item received by the bank is or becomes final.

(b) A collecting bank returns an item when it is sent or delivered to the bank's customer or transferor or pursuant to its instructions.

(c) A depositary bank that is also the payor may charge back the amount of an item to its customer's account or obtain refund in accordance with the section governing return of an item received by a payor bank for credit on its books (Section 4–301).

(d) The right to charge back is not affected by:

(1) previous use of a credit given for the item; or

(2) failure by any bank to exercise ordinary care with respect to the item, but a bank so failing remains liable.

(e) A failure to charge back or claim refund does not affect other rights of the bank against the customer or any other party.

(f) If credit is given in dollars as the equivalent of the value of an item payable in foreign money, the dollar amount of any charge-back or refund must be calculated on the basis of the bank-offered spot rate for the foreign money prevailing on the day when the person entitled to the charge-back or refund learns that it will not receive payment in ordinary course.

As amended in 1990.

§ 4–215. Final Payment of Item by Payor Bank; When Provisional Debits and Credits Become Final; When Certain Credits Become Available for Withdrawal.

(a) An item is finally paid by a payor bank when the bank has first done any of the following:

(1) paid the item in cash;

(2) settled for the item without having a right to revoke the settlement under statute, clearing-house rule, or agreement; or

(3) made a provisional settlement for the item and failed to revoke the settlement in the time and manner permitted by statute, clearing-house rule, or agreement.

(b) If provisional settlement for an item does not become final, the item is not finally paid.

(c) If provisional settlement for an item between the presenting and payor banks is made through a clearing house or by debits or credits in an account between them, then to the extent that provisional debits or credits for the item are entered in accounts between the presenting and payor banks or between the presenting and successive prior collecting banks seriatim, they become final upon final payment of the item by the payor bank.

(d) If a collecting bank receives a settlement for an item which is or becomes final, the bank is accountable to its customer for the amount of the item and any provisional credit given for the item in an account with its customer becomes final.

(e) Subject to (i) applicable law stating a time for availability of funds and (ii) any right of the bank to apply the credit to an obligation of the customer, credit given by a bank for an item in a customer's account becomes available for withdrawal as of right:

(1) if the bank has received a provisional settlement for the item, when the settlement becomes final and the bank has had a reasonable time to receive return of the item and the item has not been received within that time;

(2) if the bank is both the depositary bank and the payor bank, and the item is finally paid, at the opening of the bank's second banking day following receipt of the item.

(f) Subject to applicable law stating a time for availability of funds and any right of a bank to apply a deposit to an obligation of the depositor, a deposit of money becomes available for withdrawal as of right at the opening of the bank's next banking day after receipt of the deposit.

As amended in 1990.

§ 4– 216. Insolvency and Preference.

(a) If an item is in or comes into the possession of a payor or collecting bank that suspends payment and the item has not been finally paid, the item must be returned by the receiver, trustee, or agent in charge of the closed bank to the presenting bank or the closed bank's customer.

(b) If a payor bank finally pays an item and suspends payments without making a settlement for the item with its customer or the presenting bank which settlement is or becomes final, the owner of the item has a preferred claim against the payor bank.

(c) If a payor bank gives or a collecting bank gives or receives a provisional settlement for an item and thereafter suspends payments, the suspension does not prevent or interfere with the settlement's becoming final if the finality occurs automatically upon the lapse of certain time or the happening of certain events.

(d) If a collecting bank receives from subsequent parties settlement for an item, which settlement is or becomes final and the bank suspends payments without making a settlement for the item with its customer which settlement is or becomes final, the owner of the item has a preferred claim against the collecting bank.

As amended in 1990.

Part 3 Collection of Items: Payor Banks

§ 4–301. Deferred Posting; Recovery of Payment by Return of Items; Time of Dishonor; Return of Items by Payor Bank.

(a) If a payor bank settles for a demand item other than a documentary draft presented otherwise than for immediate payment over the counter before midnight of the banking day of receipt, the payor bank may revoke the settlement and recover the settlement if, before it has made final payment and before its midnight deadline, it

(1) returns the item; or

(2) sends written notice of dishonor or nonpayment if the item is unavailable for return.

(b) If a demand item is received by a payor bank for credit on its books, it may return the item or send notice of dishonor and may revoke any credit given or recover the amount thereof withdrawn by its customer, if it acts within the time limit and in the manner specified in subsection (a).

(c) Unless previous notice of dishonor has been sent, an item is dishonored at the time when for purposes of dishonor it is returned or notice sent in accordance with this section.

(d) An item is returned:

(1) as to an item presented through a clearing house, when it is delivered to the presenting or last collecting bank or to the clearing house or is sent or delivered in accordance with clearing-house rules; or

(2) in all other cases, when it is sent or delivered to the bank's customer or transferor or pursuant to instructions.

As amended in 1990.

§ 4–302. Payor Bank's Responsibility for Late Return of Item.

(a) If an item is presented to and received by a payor bank, the bank is accountable for the amount of:

(1) a demand item, other than a documentary draft, whether properly payable or not, if the bank, in any case in which it is not also the depositary bank, retains the item beyond midnight of the banking day of receipt without settling for it or, whether or not it is also the depositary bank, does not pay or return the item or send notice of dishonor until after its midnight deadline; or

(2) any other properly payable item unless, within the time allowed for acceptance or payment of that item, the bank either accepts or pays the item or returns it and accompanying documents.

(b) The liability of a payor bank to pay an item pursuant to subsection (a) is subject to defenses based on breach of a presentment warranty (Section 4–208) or proof that the person seeking enforcement of the liability presented or transferred the item for the purpose of defrauding the payor bank.

As amended in 1990.

§ 4–303. When Items Subject to Notice, Stop-Payment Order, Legal Process, or Setoff; Order in Which Items May Be Charged or Certified.

(a) Any knowledge, notice, or stop-payment order received by, legal process served upon, or setoff exercised by a payor bank comes too late to terminate, suspend, or modify the bank's right or duty to pay an item or to charge its customer's account for the item if the knowledge, notice, stop-payment order, or legal process is received or served and a reasonable time for the bank to act thereon expires or the setoff is exercised after the earliest of the following:

(1) the bank accepts or certifies the item;

(2) the bank pays the item in cash;

(3) the bank settles for the item without having a right to revoke the settlement under statute, clearing-house rule, or agreement;

(4) the bank becomes accountable for the amount of the item under Section 4–302 dealing with the payor bank's responsibility for late return of items; or

(5) with respect to checks, a cutoff hour no earlier than one hour after the opening of the next banking day after the banking day on which the bank received the check and no later than the close of that next banking day or, if no cutoff hour is fixed, the close of the next banking day after the banking day on which the bank received the check.

(b) Subject to subsection (a), items may be accepted, paid, certified, or charged to the indicated account of its customer in any order.

As amended in 1990.

Part 4 Relationship Between Payor Bank and Its Customer

§ 4–401. When Bank May Charge Customer's Account.

(a) A bank may charge against the account of a customer an item that is properly payable from the account even though the charge creates an overdraft. An item is properly payable if it is authorized by the customer and is in accordance with any agreement between the customer and bank.

(b) A customer is not liable for the amount of an overdraft if the customer neither signed the item nor benefited from the proceeds of the item.

(c) A bank may charge against the account of a customer a check that is otherwise properly payable from the account, even though payment was made before the date of the check, unless the customer has given notice to the bank of the postdating describing the check with reasonable certainty. The notice is effective for the period stated in Section 4–403(b) for stop-payment orders, and must be received at such time and in such manner as to afford the bank a reasonable opportunity to act on it before the bank takes any action with respect to the check described in Section 4–303. If a bank charges against the account of a customer a check before the date stated in the notice of postdating, the bank is liable for damages for the loss resulting from its act. The loss may include damages for dishonor of subsequent items under Section 4–402.

(d) A bank that in good faith makes payment to a holder may charge the indicated account of its customer according to:

(1) the original terms of the altered item; or

(2) the terms of the completed item, even though the bank knows the item has been completed unless the bank has notice that the completion was improper.

As amended in 1990.

§ 4–402. Bank's Liability to Customer for Wrongful Dishonor; Time of Determining Insufficiency of Account.

(a) Except as otherwise provided in this Article, a payor bank wrongfully dishonors an item if it dishonors an item that is properly payable, but a bank may dishonor an item that would create an overdraft unless it has agreed to pay the overdraft.

(b) A payor bank is liable to its customer for damages proximately caused by the wrongful dishonor of an item. Liability is limited to actual damages proved and may include damages for an arrest or prosecution of the customer or other consequential damages. Whether any consequential damages are proximately caused by the wrongful dishonor is a question of fact to be determined in each case.

(c) A payor bank's determination of the customer's account balance on which a decision to dishonor for insufficiency of available funds is based may be made at any time between the time the item is received by the payor bank and the time that the payor bank returns the item or gives notice in lieu of return, and no more than one determination need be made. If, at the election of the payor bank, a subsequent balance determination is made for the purpose of reevaluating the bank's decision to dishonor the item, the account balance at that time is determinative of whether a dishonor for insufficiency of available funds is wrongful.

As amended in 1990.

§ 4–403. Customer's Right to Stop Payment; Burden of Proof of Loss.

(a) A customer or any person authorized to draw on the account if there is more than one person may stop payment of any item drawn on the customer's account or close the account by an order to the bank describing the item or account with reasonable certainty received at a time and in a manner that affords the bank a reasonable opportunity to act on it before any action by the bank with respect to the item described in Section 4–303. If the signature of more than one person is required to draw on an account, any of these persons may stop payment or close the account.

(b) A stop-payment order is effective for six months, but it lapses after 14 calendar days if the original order was oral and was not confirmed in writing within that period. A stop-payment order may be renewed for additional six-month periods by a writing given to the bank within a period during which the stop-payment order is effective.

(c) The burden of establishing the fact and amount of loss resulting from the payment of an item contrary to a stop-payment order or order to close an account is on the customer. The loss from payment of an item contrary to a stop-payment order may include damages for dishonor of subsequent items under Section 4–402.

As amended in 1990.

§ 4–404. Bank Not Obliged to Pay Check More Than Six Months Old.

A bank is under no obligation to a customer having a checking account to pay a check, other than a certified check, which is presented more than six months after its date, but it may charge its customer's account for a payment made thereafter in good faith.

§ 4–405. Death or Incompetence of Customer.

(a) A payor or collecting bank's authority to accept, pay, or collect an item or to account for proceeds of its collection, if otherwise effective, is not rendered ineffective by incompetence of a customer of either bank existing at the time the item is issued or its collection is undertaken if the bank does not know of an adjudication of incompetence. Neither death nor incompetence of a customer revokes the authority to accept, pay, collect, or account until the bank knows of the fact of death or of an adjudication of incompetence and has reasonable opportunity to act on it.

(b) Even with knowledge, a bank may for 10 days after the date of death pay or certify checks drawn on or before the date unless ordered to stop payment by a person claiming an interest in the account.

As amended in 1990.

§ 4–406. Customer's Duty to Discover and Report Unauthorized Signature or Alteration.

(a) A bank that sends or makes available to a customer a statement of account showing payment of items for the account shall either return or make available to the customer the items paid or provide information in the statement of account sufficient to allow the customer reasonably to identify the items paid. The statement of account provides sufficient information if the item is described by item number, amount, and date of payment.

(b) If the items are not returned to the customer, the person retaining the items shall either retain the items or, if the items are destroyed, maintain the capacity to furnish legible copies of the items until the expiration of seven years after receipt of the items. A customer may request an item from the bank that paid the item, and that bank must provide in a reasonable time either the item or, if the item has been destroyed or is not otherwise obtainable, a legible copy of the item.

(c) If a bank sends or makes available a statement of account or items pursuant to subsection (a), the customer must exercise reasonable promptness in examining the statement or the items to determine whether any payment was not authorized because of an alteration of an item or because a purported signature by or on behalf of the customer was not authorized. If, based on the statement or items provided, the customer should reasonably have discovered the unauthorized payment, the customer must promptly notify the bank of the relevant facts.

(d) If the bank proves that the customer failed, with respect to an item, to comply with the duties imposed on the customer by subsection (c), the customer is precluded from asserting against the bank:

(1) the customer's unauthorized signature or any alteration on the item, if the bank also proves that it suffered a loss by reason of the failure; and

(2) the customer's unauthorized signature or alteration by the same wrongdoer on any other item paid in good faith by the bank if the payment was made before the bank received notice from the customer of the unauthorized signature or alteration and after the customer had been afforded a reasonable period of time, not exceeding 30 days, in which to examine the item or statement of account and notify the bank.

(e) If subsection (d) applies and the customer proves that the bank failed to exercise ordinary care in paying the item and that the failure substantially contributed to loss, the loss is allocated between the customer precluded and the bank asserting the preclusion according to the extent to which the failure of the customer to comply with subsection (c) and the failure of the bank to exercise ordinary care contributed to the loss. If the customer proves that the bank did not pay the item in good faith, the preclusion under subsection (d) does not apply.

(f) Without regard to care or lack of care of either the customer or the bank, a customer who does not within one year after the statement or items are made available to the customer (subsection (a)) discover and report the customer's unauthorized signature on or any alteration on the item is precluded from asserting against the bank the unauthorized signature or alteration. If there is a preclusion under this subsection, the payor bank may not recover for breach or warranty under Section 4–208 with respect to the unauthorized signature or alteration to which the preclusion applies.

As amended in 1990.

§ 4–407. Payor Bank's Right to Subrogation on Improper Payment.

If a payor has paid an item over the order of the drawer or maker to stop payment, or after an account has been closed, or otherwise under circumstances giving a basis for objection by the drawer or maker, to prevent unjust enrichment and only to the extent necessary to prevent loss to the bank by reason of its payment of the item, the payor bank is subrogated to the rights

(1) of any holder in due course on the item against the drawer or maker;

(2) of the payee or any other holder of the item against the drawer or maker either on the item or under the transaction out of which the item arose; and

(3) of the drawer or maker against the payee or any other holder of the item with respect to the transaction out of which the item arose.

As amended in 1990.

Part 5 Collection of Documentary Drafts

§ 4–501. Handling of Documentary Drafts; Duty to Send for Presentment and to Notify Customer of Dishonor.

A bank that takes a documentary draft for collection shall present or send the draft and accompanying documents for presentment and, upon learning that the draft has not been paid or accepted in due course, shall seasonably notify its customer of the fact even though it may have discounted or bought the draft or extended credit available for withdrawal as of right.

As amended in 1990.

§ 4–502. Presentment of "On Arrival" Drafts.

If a draft or the relevant instructions require presentment "on arrival", "when goods arrive" or the like, the collecting bank need not present until in its judgment a reasonable time for arrival of the goods has expired. Refusal to pay or accept because the goods have not arrived is not dishonor; the bank must notify its transferor of the refusal but need not present the draft again until it is instructed to do so or learns of the arrival of the goods.

§ 4-503. Responsibility of Presenting Bank for Documents and Goods; Report of Reasons for Dishonor; Referee in Case of Need.

Unless otherwise instructed and except as provided in Article 5, a bank presenting a documentary draft:

(1) must deliver the documents to the drawee on acceptance of the draft if it is payable more than three days after presentment, otherwise, only on payment; and

(2) upon dishonor, either in the case of presentment for acceptance or presentment for payment, may seek and follow instructions from any referee in case of need designated in the draft or, if the presenting bank does not choose to utilize the referee's services, it must use diligence and good faith to ascertain the reason for dishonor, must notify its transferor of the dishonor and of the results of its effort to ascertain the reasons therefor, and must request instructions.

However, the presenting bank is under no obligation with respect to goods represented by the documents except to follow any reasonable instructions seasonably received; it has a right to reimbursement for any expense incurred in following instructions and to prepayment of or indemnity for those expenses.

As amended in 1990.

§ 4-504. Privilege of Presenting Bank to Deal With Goods; Security Interest for Expenses.

(a) A presenting bank that, following the dishonor of a documentary draft, has seasonably requested instructions but does not receive them within a reasonable time may store, sell, or otherwise deal with the goods in any reasonable manner.

(b) For its reasonable expenses incurred by action under subsection (a) the presenting bank has a lien upon the goods or their proceeds, which may be foreclosed in the same manner as an unpaid seller's lien.

As amended in 1990.

Article 4A FUNDS TRANSFERS

Part 1 Subject Matter and Definitions

§ 4A-101. Short Title.

This Article may be cited as Uniform Commercial Code—Funds Transfers.

§ 4A-102. Subject Matter.

Except as otherwise provided in Section 4A–108, this Article applies to funds transfers defined in Section 4A–104.

§ 4A-103. Payment Order–Definitions.

(a) In this Article:

(1) "Payment order" means an instruction of a sender to a receiving bank, transmitted orally, electronically, or in writing, to pay, or to cause another bank to pay, a fixed or determinable amount of money to a beneficiary if:

(i) the instruction does not state a condition to payment to the beneficiary other than time of payment,

(ii) the receiving bank is to be reimbursed by debiting an account of, or otherwise receiving payment from, the sender, and

(iii) the instruction is transmitted by the sender directly to the receiving bank or to an agent, funds-transfer system, or communication system for transmittal to the receiving bank.

(2) "Beneficiary" means the person to be paid by the beneficiary's bank.

(3) "Beneficiary's bank" means the bank identified in a payment order in which an account of the beneficiary is to be credited pursuant to the order or which otherwise is to make payment to the beneficiary if the order does not provide for payment to an account.

(4) "Receiving bank" means the bank to which the sender's instruction is addressed.

(5) "Sender" means the person giving the instruction to the receiving bank.

(b) If an instruction complying with subsection (a)(1) is to make more than one payment to a beneficiary, the instruction is a separate payment order with respect to each payment.

(c) A payment order is issued when it is sent to the receiving bank.

§ 4A-104. Funds Transfer–Definitions.

In this Article:

(a) "Funds transfer" means the series of transactions, beginning with the originator's payment order, made for the purpose of making payment to the beneficiary of the order. The term includes any payment order issued by the originator's bank or an intermediary bank intended to carry out the originator's payment order. A funds transfer is completed by acceptance by the beneficiary's bank of a payment order for the benefit of the beneficiary of the originator's payment order.

(b) "Intermediary bank" means a receiving bank other than the originator's bank or the beneficiary's bank.

(c) "Originator" means the sender of the first payment order in a funds transfer.

(d) "Originator's bank" means (i) the receiving bank to which the payment order of the originator is issued if the originator is not a bank, or (ii) the originator if the originator is a bank.

§ 4A-105. Other Definitions.

(a) In this Article:

(1) "Authorized account" means a deposit account of a customer in a bank designated by the customer as a source of payment of payment orders issued by the customer to the bank. If a customer does not so designate an account, any account of the customer is an authorized account if payment of a payment order from that account is not inconsistent with a restriction on the use of that account.

(2) "Bank" means a person engaged in the business of banking and includes a savings bank, savings and loan association, credit union, and trust company. A branch or separate office of a bank is a separate bank for purposes of this Article.

(3) "Customer" means a person, including a bank, having an account with a bank or from whom a bank has agreed to receive payment orders.

(4) "Funds-transfer business day" of a receiving bank means the part of a day during which the receiving bank is open for the receipt, processing, and transmittal of payment orders and cancellations and amendments of payment orders.

(5) "Funds-transfer system" means a wire transfer network, automated clearing house, or other communication system of a clearing house or other association of banks through which a payment order by a bank may be transmitted to the bank to which the order is addressed.

(6) "Good faith" means honesty in fact and the observance of reasonable commercial standards of fair dealing.

(7) "Prove" with respect to a fact means to meet the burden of establishing the fact (Section 1–201(8)).

(b) Other definitions applying to this Article and the sections in which they appear are:

"Acceptance"	Section 4A–209
"Beneficiary"	Section 4A–103
"Beneficiary's bank"	Section 4A–103
"Executed"	Section 4A–301
"Execution date"	Section 4A–301
"Funds transfer"	Section 4A–104
"Funds-transfer system rule"	Section 4A–501
"Intermediary bank"	Section 4A–104
"Originator"	Section 4A–104
"Originator's bank"	Section 4A–104
"Payment by beneficiary's bank to beneficiary"	Section 4A–405
"Payment by originator to beneficiary"	Section 4A–406
"Payment by sender to receiving bank"	Section 4A–403
"Payment date"	Section 4A–401
"Payment order"	Section 4A–103
"Receiving bank"	Section 4A–103
"Security procedure"	Section 4A–201
"Sender"	Section 4A–103

(c) The following definitions in Article 4 apply to this Article:

"Clearing house"	Section 4–104
"Item"	Section 4–104
"Suspends payments"	Section 4–104

(d) In addition, Article 1 contains general definitions and principles of construction and interpretation applicable throughout this Article.

§ 4A–106. Time Payment Order Is Received.

(a) The time of receipt of a payment order or communication cancelling or amending a payment order is determined by the rules applicable to receipt of a notice stated in Section 1–201(27). A receiving bank may fix a cut-off time or times on a funds-transfer business day for the receipt and processing of payment orders and communications cancelling or amending payment orders. Different cut-off times may apply to payment orders, cancellations, or amendments, or to different categories of payment orders, cancellations, or amendments. A cut-off time may apply to senders generally or different cut-off times may apply to different senders or categories of payment orders. If a payment order or communication cancelling or amending a payment order is received after the close of a funds-transfer business day or after the appropriate cut-off time on a funds-transfer business day, the receiving bank may treat the payment order or communication as received at the opening of the next funds-transfer business day.

(b) If this Article refers to an execution date or payment date or states a day on which a receiving bank is required to take action, and the date or day does not fall on a funds-transfer business day, the next day that is a funds-transfer business day is treated as the date or day stated, unless the contrary is stated in this Article.

§ 4A–107. Federal Reserve Regulations and Operating Circulars.

Regulations of the Board of Governors of the Federal Reserve System and operating circulars of the Federal Reserve Banks supersede any inconsistent provision of this Article to the extent of the inconsistency.

§ 4A–108. Exclusion of Consumer Transactions Governed by Federal Law.

This Article does not apply to a funds transfer any part of which is governed by the Electronic Fund Transfer Act of 1978 (Title XX, Public Law 95–630, 92 Stat. 3728, 15 U.S.C. § 1693 *et seq.*) as amended from time to time.

Part 2 Issue and Acceptance of Payment Order

§ 4A–201. Security Procedure.

"Security procedure" means a procedure established by agreement of a customer and a receiving bank for the purpose of (i) verifying that a payment order or communication amending or cancelling a payment order is that of the customer, or (ii) detecting error in the transmission or the content of the payment order or communication. A security procedure may require the use of algorithms or other codes, identifying words or numbers, encryption, callback procedures, or similar security devices. Comparison of a signature on a payment order or communication with an authorized specimen signature of the customer is not by itself a security procedure.

§ 4A–202. Authorized and Verified Payment Orders.

(a) A payment order received by the receiving bank is the authorized order of the person identified as sender if that person authorized the order or is otherwise bound by it under the law of agency.

(b) If a bank and its customer have agreed that the authenticity of payment orders issued to the bank in the name of the customer as sender will be verified pursuant to a security procedure, a payment order received by the receiving bank is effective as the order of the customer, whether or not authorized, if (i) the security procedure is a commercially reasonable method of providing security against unauthorized payment orders, and (ii) the bank proves that it accepted the payment order in good faith and in compliance with the security procedure and any written agreement or instruction of the customer restricting acceptance of payment orders issued in the name of the customer. The bank is not required to follow an instruction that violates a written agreement with the customer or notice of which is not received at a time and in a manner affording the bank a reasonable opportunity to act on it before the payment order is accepted.

(c) Commercial reasonableness of a security procedure is a question of law to be determined by considering the wishes of the customer expressed to the bank, the circumstances of the customer known to the bank, including the size, type, and frequency of payment orders normally issued by the customer to the bank, alternative security procedures offered to the customer, and security procedures in general use by customers and receiving banks similarly situated. A security procedure is deemed to be commercially reasonable if (i) the security procedure was chosen by the customer after the bank offered, and the customer refused, a security procedure that was commercially reasonable for that customer, and (ii) the customer expressly agreed in writing to be bound by any payment order, whether or not authorized, issued in its name and accepted by the bank in compliance with the security procedure chosen by the customer.

(d) The term "sender" in this Article includes the customer in whose name a payment order is issued if the order is the authorized order of the customer under subsection (a), or it is effective as the order of the customer under subsection (b).

(e) This section applies to amendments and cancellations of payment orders to the same extent it applies to payment orders.

(f) Except as provided in this section and in Section 4A–203(a)(1), rights and obligations arising under this section or Section 4A–203 may not be varied by agreement.

§ 4A–203. Unenforceability of Certain Verified Payment Orders.

(a) If an accepted payment order is not, under Section 4A–202(a), an authorized order of a customer identified as sender, but is effective as an order of the customer pursuant to Section 4A–202(b), the following rules apply:

(1) By express written agreement, the receiving bank may limit the extent to which it is entitled to enforce or retain payment of the payment order.

(2) The receiving bank is not entitled to enforce or retain payment of the payment order if the customer proves that the order was not caused, directly or indirectly, by a person (i) entrusted at any time with duties to act for the customer with respect to payment orders or the security procedure, or (ii) who obtained access to transmitting facilities of the customer or who obtained, from a source controlled by the customer and without authority of the receiving bank, information facilitating breach of the security procedure, regardless of how the information was obtained or whether the customer was at fault. Information includes any access device, computer software, or the like.

(b) This section applies to amendments of payment orders to the same extent it applies to payment orders.

§ 4A–204. Refund of Payment and Duty of Customer to Report with Respect to Unauthorized Payment Order.

(a) If a receiving bank accepts a payment order issued in the name of its customer as sender which is (i) not authorized and not effective as the order of the customer under Section 4A–202, or (ii) not enforceable, in whole or in part, against the customer under Section 4A–203, the bank shall refund any payment of the payment order received from the customer to the extent the bank is not entitled to enforce payment and shall pay interest on the refundable amount calculated from the date the bank received payment to the date of the refund. However, the customer is not entitled to interest from the bank on the amount to be refunded if the customer fails to exercise ordinary care to determine that the order was not authorized by the customer and to notify the bank of the relevant facts within a reasonable time not exceeding 90 days after the date the customer received notification from the bank that the order was accepted or that the customer's account was debited with respect to the order. The bank is not entitled to any recovery from the customer on account of a failure by the customer to give notification as stated in this section.

(b) Reasonable time under subsection (a) may be fixed by agreement as stated in Section 1–204(1), but the obligation of a receiving bank to refund payment as stated in subsection (a) may not otherwise be varied by agreement.

§ 4A–205. Erroneous Payment Orders.

(a) If an accepted payment order was transmitted pursuant to a security procedure for the detection of error and the payment order (i) erroneously instructed payment to a beneficiary not intended by the sender, (ii) erroneously instructed payment in an amount greater than the amount intended by the sender, or (iii) was an erroneously transmitted duplicate of a payment order previously sent by the sender, the following rules apply:

(1) If the sender proves that the sender or a person acting on behalf of the sender pursuant to Section 4A–206 complied with the security procedure and that the error would have been detected if the receiving bank had also complied, the sender is not obliged to pay the order to the extent stated in paragraphs (2) and (3).

(2) If the funds transfer is completed on the basis of an erroneous payment order described in clause (i) or (iii) of subsection (a), the sender is not obliged to pay the order and the receiving bank is entitled to recover from the beneficiary any amount paid to the beneficiary to the extent allowed by the law governing mistake and restitution.

(3) If the funds transfer is completed on the basis of a payment order described in clause (ii) of subsection (a), the sender is not obliged to pay the order to the extent the amount received by the beneficiary is greater than the amount intended by the sender. In that case, the receiving bank is entitled to recover from the beneficiary the excess amount received to the extent allowed by the law governing mistake and restitution.

(b) If (i) the sender of an erroneous payment order described in subsection (a) is not obliged to pay all or part of the order, and (ii) the sender receives notification from the receiving bank that the order was accepted by the bank or that the sender's account was debited with respect to the order, the sender has a duty to exercise ordinary care, on the basis of information available to the sender, to discover the error with respect to the order and to advise the bank of the relevant facts within a reasonable time, not exceeding 90 days, after the bank's notification was received by the sender. If the bank proves that the sender failed to perform that duty, the sender is liable to the bank for the loss the bank proves it incurred as a result of the failure, but the liability of the sender may not exceed the amount of the sender's order.

(c) This section applies to amendments to payment orders to the same extent it applies to payment orders.

§ 4A–206. Transmission of Payment Order through Funds-Transfer or Other Communication System.

(a) If a payment order addressed to a receiving bank is transmitted to a funds-transfer system or other third party communication system for transmittal to the bank, the system is deemed to be an agent of the sender for the purpose of transmitting the payment order to the bank. If there is a discrepancy between the terms of the payment order transmitted to the system and the terms of the payment order transmitted by the system to the bank, the terms of the payment order of the sender are those transmitted by the system. This section does not apply to a funds-transfer system of the Federal Reserve Banks.

(b) This section applies to cancellations and amendments to payment orders to the same extent it applies to payment orders.

§ 4A–207. Misdescription of Beneficiary.

(a) Subject to subsection (b), if, in a payment order received by the beneficiary's bank, the name, bank account number, or other identification of the beneficiary refers to a nonexistent or unidentifiable person or account, no person has rights as a beneficiary of the order and acceptance of the order cannot occur.

(b) If a payment order received by the beneficiary's bank identifies the beneficiary both by name and by an identifying or bank account number and the name and number identify different persons, the following rules apply:

(1) Except as otherwise provided in subsection (c), if the beneficiary's bank does not know that the name and number refer to different persons, it may rely on the number as the proper identification of the beneficiary of the order. The beneficiary's bank need not determine whether the name and number refer to the same person.

(2) If the beneficiary's bank pays the person identified by name or knows that the name and number identify different persons, no person has rights as beneficiary except the person paid by the beneficiary's bank if that person was entitled to receive payment from the originator of the funds transfer. If no person has rights as beneficiary, acceptance of the order cannot occur.

(c) If (i) a payment order described in subsection (b) is accepted, (ii) the originator's payment order described the beneficiary inconsistently by name and number, and (iii) the beneficiary's bank pays the person identified by number as permitted by subsection (b)(1), the following rules apply:

(1) If the originator is a bank, the originator is obliged to pay its order.

(2) If the originator is not a bank and proves that the person identified by number was not entitled to receive payment from the originator, the originator is not obliged to pay its order unless the originator's bank proves that the originator, before acceptance of the originator's order, had notice that payment of a payment order issued by the originator might be made by the beneficiary's bank on the basis of an identifying or bank account number even if it identifies a person different from the named beneficiary. Proof of notice may be made by any admissible evidence. The originator's bank satisfies the burden of proof if it proves that the originator, before the payment order was accepted, signed a writing stating the information to which the notice relates.

(d) In a case governed by subsection (b)(1), if the beneficiary's bank rightfully pays the person identified by number and that person was not entitled to receive payment from the originator, the amount paid may be recovered from that person to the extent allowed by the law governing mistake and restitution as follows:

(1) If the originator is obliged to pay its payment order as stated in subsection (c), the originator has the right to recover.

(2) If the originator is not a bank and is not obliged to pay its payment order, the originator's bank has the right to recover.

§ 4A–208. Misdescription of Intermediary Bank or Beneficiary's Bank.

(a) This subsection applies to a payment order identifying an intermediary bank or the beneficiary's bank only by an identifying number.

(1) The receiving bank may rely on the number as the proper identification of the intermediary or beneficiary's bank and need not determine whether the number identifies a bank.

(2) The sender is obliged to compensate the receiving bank for any loss and expenses incurred by the receiving bank as a result of its reliance on the number in executing or attempting to execute the order.

(b) This subsection applies to a payment order identifying an intermediary bank or the beneficiary's bank both by name and an identifying number if the name and number identify different persons.

(1) If the sender is a bank, the receiving bank may rely on the number as the proper identification of the intermediary or beneficiary's bank if the receiving bank, when it executes the sender's order, does not know that the name and number identify different persons. The receiving bank need not determine whether the name and number refer to the same person or whether the number refers to a bank. The sender is obliged to compensate the receiving bank for any loss and expenses incurred by the receiving bank as a result of its reliance on the number in executing or attempting to execute the order.

(2) If the sender is not a bank and the receiving bank proves that the sender, before the payment order was accepted, had notice that the receiving bank might rely on the number as the proper identification of the intermediary or beneficiary's bank even if it identifies a person different from the bank identified by name, the rights and obligations of the sender and the receiving bank are governed by subsection (b)(1), as though the sender were a bank. Proof of notice may be made by any admissible evidence. The receiving bank satisfies the burden of proof if it proves that the sender, before the payment order was accepted, signed a writing stating the information to which the notice relates.

(3) Regardless of whether the sender is a bank, the receiving bank may rely on the name as the proper identification of the intermediary or beneficiary's bank if the receiving bank, at the time it executes the sender's order, does not know that the name and number identify different persons. The receiving bank need not determine whether the name and number refer to the same person.

(4) If the receiving bank knows that the name and number identify different persons, reliance on either the name or the number in executing the sender's payment order is a breach of the obligation stated in Section 4A–302(a)(1).

§ 4A–209. Acceptance of Payment Order.

(a) Subject to subsection (d), a receiving bank other than the beneficiary's bank accepts a payment order when it executes the order.

(b) Subject to subsections (c) and (d), a beneficiary's bank accepts a payment order at the earliest of the following times:

(1) When the bank (i) pays the beneficiary as stated in Section 4A–405(a) or 4A–405(b), or (ii) notifies the beneficiary of receipt of the order or that the account of the beneficiary has been credited with respect to the order unless the notice indicates that the bank is rejecting the order or that funds with respect to the order may not be withdrawn or used until receipt of payment from the sender of the order;

(2) When the bank receives payment of the entire amount of the sender's order pursuant to Section 4A–403(a)(1) or 4A–403(a)(2); or

(3) The opening of the next funds-transfer business day of the bank following the payment date of the order if, at that time, the amount of the sender's order is fully covered by a withdrawable credit balance in an authorized account of the sender or the bank has otherwise received full payment from the sender, unless the order was rejected before that time or is rejected within (i) one hour after that time, or (ii) one hour after the opening of the next business day of the sender following the payment date if that time is later. If notice of rejection is received by the sender after the payment date and the authorized account of the sender does not bear interest, the bank is obliged to pay interest to the sender on the amount of the order for the number of days elapsing after the payment date to the day the sender receives notice or learns that the order was not accepted, counting that day as an elapsed day. If the withdrawable credit balance during that period falls below the amount of the order, the amount of interest payable is reduced accordingly.

(c) Acceptance of a payment order cannot occur before the order is received by the receiving bank. Acceptance does not occur under subsection (b)(2) or (b)(3) if the beneficiary of the payment order does not have an account with the receiving bank, the account has been closed, or the receiving bank is not permitted by law to receive credits for the beneficiary's account.

(d) A payment order issued to the originator's bank cannot be accepted until the payment date if the bank is the beneficiary's bank, or the execution date if the bank is not the beneficiary's bank. If the originator's bank executes the originator's payment order before the execution date or pays the beneficiary of the originator's payment order before the payment date and the payment order is subsequently cancelled pursuant to Section 4A–211(b), the bank may recover from the beneficiary any payment received to the extent allowed by the law governing mistake and restitution.

§ 4A–210. Rejection of Payment Order.

(a) A payment order is rejected by the receiving bank by a notice of rejection transmitted to the sender orally, electronically, or in writing. A notice of rejection need not use any particular words and is sufficient if it indicates that the receiving bank is rejecting the order or will not execute or pay the order. Rejection is effective when the notice is given if transmission is by a means that is reasonable in the circumstances. If notice of rejection is given by a means that is not reasonable, rejection is effective when the notice is received. If an agreement of the sender and receiving bank establishes the means to be used to reject a payment order, (i) any means complying with the agreement is reasonable and (ii) any means not complying is not reasonable unless no significant delay in receipt of the notice resulted from the use of the noncomplying means.

(b) This subsection applies if a receiving bank other than the beneficiary's bank fails to execute a payment order despite the existence on the execution date of a withdrawable credit balance in an authorized account of the sender sufficient to cover the order. If the sender does not receive notice of rejection of the order on the execution date and the authorized account of the sender does not bear interest, the bank is obliged to pay interest to the sender on the amount of the order for the number of days elapsing after the execution date to the earlier of the day the order is cancelled pursuant to Section 4A–211(d) or the day the sender receives notice or learns that the order was not executed, counting the final day of the period as an elapsed day. If the withdrawable credit balance during that period falls below the amount of the order, the amount of interest is reduced accordingly.

(c) If a receiving bank suspends payments, all unaccepted payment orders issued to it are are deemed rejected at the time the bank suspends payments.

(d) Acceptance of a payment order precludes a later rejection of the order. Rejection of a payment order precludes a later acceptance of the order.

§ 4A–211. Cancellation and Amendment of Payment Order.

(a) A communication of the sender of a payment order cancelling or amending the order may be transmitted to the receiving bank orally, electronically, or in writing. If a security procedure is in effect between the sender and the receiving bank, the communication is not effective to cancel or amend the order unless the communication is verified pursuant to the security procedure or the bank agrees to the cancellation or amendment.

(b) Subject to subsection (a), a communication by the sender cancelling or amending a payment order is effective to cancel or amend the order if notice of the communication is received at a time and in a manner affording the receiving bank a reasonable opportunity to act on the communication before the bank accepts the payment order.

(c) After a payment order has been accepted, cancellation or amendment of the order is not effective unless the receiving bank agrees or a funds-transfer system rule allows cancellation or amendment without agreement of the bank.

(1) With respect to a payment order accepted by a receiving bank other than the beneficiary's bank, cancellation or amendment is not effective unless a conforming cancellation or amendment of the payment order issued by the receiving bank is also made.

(2) With respect to a payment order accepted by the beneficiary's bank, cancellation or amendment is not effective unless the order was issued in execution of an unauthorized payment order, or because of a mistake by a sender in the funds transfer which resulted in the issuance of a payment order (i) that is a duplicate of a payment order previously issued by the sender, (ii) that orders payment to a beneficiary not entitled to receive payment from the originator, or (iii) that orders payment in an amount greater than the amount the beneficiary was entitled to receive from the originator. If the payment order is cancelled or amended, the beneficiary's bank is entitled to recover from the beneficiary any amount paid to the beneficiary to the extent allowed by the law governing mistake and restitution.

(d) An unaccepted payment order is cancelled by operation of law at the close of the fifth funds-transfer business day of the receiving bank after the execution date or payment date of the order.

(e) A cancelled payment order cannot be accepted. If an accepted payment order is cancelled, the acceptance is nullified and no person has any right or obligation based on the acceptance. Amendment of a payment order is deemed to be cancellation of the original order at the time of amendment and issue of a new payment order in the amended form at the same time.

(f) Unless otherwise provided in an agreement of the parties or in a funds-transfer system rule, if the receiving bank, after accepting a payment order, agrees to cancellation or amendment of the order by the sender or is bound by a funds-transfer system rule allowing cancellation or amendment without the bank's agreement, the sender, whether or not cancellation or amendment is effective, is liable to the bank for any loss and expenses, including reasonable attorney's fees, incurred by the bank as a result of the cancellation or amendment or attempted cancellation or amendment.

(g) A payment order is not revoked by the death or legal incapacity of the sender unless the receiving bank knows of the death or of an adjudication of incapacity by a court of competent jurisdiction and has reasonable opportunity to act before acceptance of the order.

(h) A funds-transfer system rule is not effective to the extent it conflicts with subsection (c)(2).

§ 4A–212. Liability and Duty of Receiving Bank Regarding Unaccepted Payment Order.

If a receiving bank fails to accept a payment order that it is obliged by express agreement to accept, the bank is liable for breach of the agreement to the extent provided in the agreement or in this Article, but does not otherwise have any duty to accept a payment order or, before acceptance, to take any action, or refrain from taking action, with respect to the order except as provided in this Article or by express agreement. Liability based on acceptance arises only when acceptance occurs as stated in Section 4A–209, and liability is limited to that provided in this Article. A receiving bank is not the agent of the sender or beneficiary of the payment order it accepts, or of any other party to the funds transfer, and the bank owes no duty to any party to the funds transfer except as provided in this Article or by express agreement.

Part 3 Execution of Sender's Payment Order by Receiving Bank

§ 4A–301. Execution and Execution Date.

(a) A payment order is "executed" by the receiving bank when it issues a payment order intended to carry out the payment order received by the bank. A payment order received by the beneficiary's bank can be accepted but cannot be executed.

(b) "Execution date" of a payment order means the day on which the receiving bank may properly issue a payment order in execution of the sender's order. The execution date may be determined by instruction of the sender but cannot be earlier than the day the order is received and, unless otherwise determined, is the day the order is received. If the sender's instruction states a payment date, the execution date is the payment date or an earlier date on which execution is reasonably necessary to allow payment to the beneficiary on the payment date.

§ 4A–302. Obligations of Receiving Bank in Execution of Payment Order.

(a) Except as provided in subsections (b) through (d), if the receiving bank accepts a payment order pursuant to Section 4A–209(a), the bank has the following obligations in executing the order:

(1) The receiving bank is obliged to issue, on the execution date, a payment order complying with the sender's order and to follow the sender's instructions concerning (i) any intermediary bank or funds-transfer system to be used in carrying out the funds transfer, or (ii) the means by which payment orders are to be transmitted in the funds transfer. If the originator's bank issues a payment order to an intermediary bank, the originator's bank is obliged to instruct the intermediary bank according to the instruction of the originator. An intermediary bank in the funds transfer is similarly bound by an instruction given to it by the sender of the payment order it accepts.

(2) If the sender's instruction states that the funds transfer is to be carried out telephonically or by wire transfer or otherwise indicates that the funds transfer is to be carried out by the most expeditious means, the receiving bank is obliged to transmit its payment order by the most expeditious available means, and to instruct any intermediary bank accordingly. If a sender's instruction states a payment date, the receiving bank is obliged to transmit its payment order at a time and by means reasonably necessary to allow payment to the beneficiary on the payment date or as soon thereafter as is feasible.

(b) Unless otherwise instructed, a receiving bank executing a payment order may (i) use any funds-transfer system if use of that system is reasonable in the circumstances, and (ii) issue a payment order to the beneficiary's bank or to an intermediary bank through which a payment order conforming to the sender's order can expeditiously be issued to the beneficiary's bank if the receiving bank exercises ordinary care in the selection of the intermediary bank. A receiving bank is not required to follow an instruction of the sender designating a funds-transfer system to be used in carrying out the funds transfer if the receiving bank, in good faith, determines that it is not feasible to follow the instruction or that following the instruction would unduly delay completion of the funds transfer.

(c) Unless subsection (a)(2) applies or the receiving bank is otherwise instructed, the bank may execute a payment order by transmitting its payment order by first class mail or by any means reasonable in the circumstances. If the receiving bank is instructed to execute the sender's order by transmitting its payment order by a particular means, the receiving bank may issue its payment order by the means stated or by any means as expeditious as the means stated.

(d) Unless instructed by the sender, (i) the receiving bank may not obtain payment of its charges for services and expenses in connection with the execution of the sender's order by issuing a payment order in an amount equal to the amount of the sender's order less the amount of the charges, and (ii) may not instruct a subsequent receiving bank to obtain payment of its charges in the same manner.

§ 4A–303. Erroneous Execution of Payment Order.

(a) A receiving bank that (i) executes the payment order of the sender by issuing a payment order in an amount greater than the amount of the sender's order, or (ii) issues a payment order in execution of the sender's order and then issues a duplicate order, is entitled to payment of the amount of the sender's order under Section 4A–402(c) if that subsection is otherwise satisfied. The bank is entitled to recover from the beneficiary of the erroneous order the excess payment received to the extent allowed by the law governing mistake and restitution.

(b) A receiving bank that executes the payment order of the sender by issuing a payment order in an amount less than the amount of the sender's order is entitled to payment of the amount of the sender's order under Section 4A–402(c) if (i) that subsection is otherwise satisfied and (ii) the bank corrects its mistake by issuing an additional payment order for the benefit of the beneficiary of the sender's order. If the error is not corrected, the issuer of the erroneous order is entitled to receive or retain payment from the sender of the order it accepted only to the extent of the amount of the erroneous order. This subsection does not apply if the receiving bank executes the sender's payment order by issuing a payment order in an amount less than the amount of the sender's order for the purpose of obtaining payment of its charges for services and expenses pursuant to instruction of the sender.

(c) If a receiving bank executes the payment order of the sender by issuing a payment order to a beneficiary different from the beneficiary of the sender's order and the funds transfer is completed on the basis of that error, the sender of the payment order that was erroneously executed and all previous senders in the funds transfer are not obliged to pay the payment orders they issued. The issuer of the erroneous order is entitled to recover from the beneficiary of the order the payment received to the extent allowed by the law governing mistake and restitution.

§ 4A–304. Duty of Sender to Report Erroneously Executed Payment Order.

If the sender of a payment order that is erroneously executed as stated in Section 4A–303 receives notification from the receiving bank that the order was executed or that the sender's account was debited with respect to the order, the sender has a duty to exercise ordinary care to determine, on the basis of information available to the sender, that the order was erroneously executed and to notify the bank of the relevant facts within a reasonable time not exceeding 90 days after the notification from the bank was received by the sender. If the sender fails to perform that duty, the bank is not obliged to pay interest on any amount refundable to the sender under Section 4A–402(d) for the period before the bank learns of the execution error. The bank is not entitled to any recovery from the sender on account of a failure by the sender to perform the duty stated in this section.

§ 4A–305. Liability for Late or Improper Execution or Failure to Execute Payment Order.

(a) If a funds transfer is completed but execution of a payment order by the receiving bank in breach of Section 4A–302 results in delay in payment to the beneficiary, the bank is obliged to pay interest to either the originator or the beneficiary of the funds transfer for the period of delay caused by the improper execution. Except as provided in subsection (c), additional damages are not recoverable.

(b) If execution of a payment order by a receiving bank in breach of Section 4A–302 results in (i) noncompletion of the funds transfer, (ii) failure to use an intermediary bank designated by the originator, or (iii) issuance of a payment order that does not comply with the terms of the payment order of the originator, the bank is liable to the originator for its expenses in the funds transfer and for incidental expenses and interest losses, to the extent not covered by subsection (a), resulting from the improper execution. Except as provided in subsection (c), additional damages are not recoverable.

(c) In addition to the amounts payable under subsections (a) and (b), damages, including consequential damages, are recoverable to the extent provided in an express written agreement of the receiving bank.

(d) If a receiving bank fails to execute a payment order it was obliged by express agreement to execute, the receiving bank is liable to the sender for its expenses in the transaction and for incidental expenses and interest losses resulting from the failure to execute. Additional damages, including consequential damages, are recoverable to the extent provided in an express written agreement of the receiving bank, but are not otherwise recoverable.

(e) Reasonable attorney's fees are recoverable if demand for compensation under subsection (a) or (b) is made and refused before an action is brought on the claim. If a claim is made for breach of an agreement under subsection (d) and the agreement does not provide for damages, reasonable attorney's fees are recoverable if demand for compensation under subsection (d) is made and refused before an action is brought on the claim.

(f) Except as stated in this section, the liability of a receiving bank under subsections (a) and (b) may not be varied by agreement.

Part 4 Payment

§ 4A–401. Payment Date.

"Payment date" of a payment order means the day on which the amount of the order is payable to the beneficiary by the beneficiary's bank. The payment date may be determined by instruction of the sender but cannot be earlier than the day the order is received by the beneficiary's bank and, unless otherwise determined, is the day the order is received by the beneficiary's bank.

§ 4A–402. Obligation of Sender to Pay Receiving Bank.

(a) This section is subject to Sections 4A–205 and 4A–207.

(b) With respect to a payment order issued to the beneficiary's bank, acceptance of the order by the bank obliges the sender to pay the bank the amount of the order, but payment is not due until the payment date of the order.

(c) This subsection is subject to subsection (e) and to Section 4A–303. With respect to a payment order issued to a receiving bank other than the beneficiary's bank, acceptance of the order by the receiving bank obliges the sender to pay the bank the amount of the sender's order. Payment by the sender is not due until the execution date of the sender's order. The obligation of that sender to pay its payment order is excused if the funds transfer is not completed by acceptance by the beneficiary's bank of a payment order instructing payment to the beneficiary of that sender's payment order.

(d) If the sender of a payment order pays the order and was not obliged to pay all or part of the amount paid, the bank receiving payment is obliged to refund payment to the extent the sender was not obliged to pay. Except as provided in Sections 4A–204 and 4A–304, interest is payable on the refundable amount from the date of payment.

(e) If a funds transfer is not completed as stated in subsection (c) and an intermediary bank is obliged to refund payment as stated in subsection (d) but is unable to do so because not permitted by applicable law or because the bank suspends payments, a sender in the funds transfer that executed a payment order in compliance with an instruction, as stated in Section 4A–302(a)(1), to route the funds transfer through that intermediary bank is entitled to receive or retain payment from the sender of the payment order that it accepted. The first sender in the funds transfer that issued an instruction requiring routing through that intermediary bank is subrogated to the right of the bank that paid the intermediary bank to refund as stated in subsection (d).

(f) The right of the sender of a payment order to be excused from the obligation to pay the order as stated in subsection (c) or to receive refund under subsection (d) may not be varied by agreement.

§ 4A–403. Payment by Sender to Receiving Bank.

(a) Payment of the sender's obligation under Section 4A–402 to pay the receiving bank occurs as follows:

(1) If the sender is a bank, payment occurs when the receiving bank receives final settlement of the obligation through a Federal Reserve Bank or through a funds-transfer system.

(2) If the sender is a bank and the sender (i) credited an account of the receiving bank with the sender, or (ii) caused an account of the receiving bank in another bank to be credited, payment occurs when the credit is withdrawn or, if not withdrawn, at midnight of the day on which the credit is withdrawable and the receiving bank learns of that fact.

(3) If the receiving bank debits an account of the sender with the receiving bank, payment occurs when the debit is made to the extent the debit is covered by a withdrawable credit balance in the account.

(b) If the sender and receiving bank are members of a funds-transfer system that nets obligations multilaterally among participants, the receiving bank receives final settlement when settlement is complete in accordance with the rules of the system. The obligation of the sender to pay the amount of a payment order transmitted through the funds-transfer system may be satisfied, to the extent permitted by the rules of the system, by setting off and applying against the sender's obligation the right of the sender to receive payment from the receiving bank of the amount of any other payment order transmitted to the sender by the receiving bank through the funds-transfer system. The aggregate balance of obligations owed by each sender to each receiving bank in the funds-transfer system may be satisfied, to the extent permitted by the rules of the system, by setting off and applying against that balance the aggregate balance of obligations owed to the sender by other members of the system. The aggregate balance is determined after the right of setoff stated in the second sentence of this subsection has been exercised.

(c) If two banks transmit payment orders to each other under an agreement that settlement of the obligations of each bank to the other under Section 4A–402 will be made at the end of the day or other period, the total amount owed with respect to all orders transmitted by one bank shall be set off against the total amount owed with respect to all orders transmitted by the other bank. To the extent of the setoff, each bank has made payment to the other.

(d) In a case not covered by subsection (a), the time when payment of the sender's obligation under Section 4A–402(b) or 4A–402(c) occurs is governed by applicable principles of law that determine when an obligation is satisfied.

§ 4A–404. Obligation of Beneficiary's Bank to Pay and Give Notice to Beneficiary.

(a) Subject to Sections 4A–211(e), 4A–405(d), and 4A–405(e), if a beneficiary's bank accepts a payment order, the bank is obliged to pay the amount of the order to the beneficiary of the order. Payment is due on the payment date of the order, but if acceptance occurs on the payment date after the close of the funds-transfer business day of the bank, payment is due on the next funds-transfer business day. If the bank refuses to pay after demand by the beneficiary and receipt of notice of particular circumstances that will give rise to consequential damages as a result of nonpayment, the beneficiary may recover damages resulting from the refusal to pay to the extent the bank had notice of the damages, unless the bank proves that it did not pay because of a reasonable doubt concerning the right of the beneficiary to payment.

(b) If a payment order accepted by the beneficiary's bank instructs payment to an account of the beneficiary, the bank is obliged to notify the beneficiary of receipt of the order before midnight of the next funds-transfer business day following the payment date. If the payment order does not instruct payment to an account of the beneficiary, the bank is required to notify the beneficiary only if notice is required by the order. Notice may be given by first class mail or any other means reasonable in the circumstances. If the bank fails to give the required notice, the bank is obliged to pay interest to the beneficiary on the amount of the payment order from the day notice should have been given until the day the beneficiary learned of receipt of the payment order by the bank. No other damages are recoverable. Reasonable attorney's fees are also recoverable if demand for interest is made and refused before an action is brought on the claim.

(c) The right of a beneficiary to receive payment and damages as stated in subsection (a) may not be varied by agreement or a funds-transfer system rule. The right of a beneficiary to be notified as stated in subsection (b) may be varied by agreement of the beneficiary or by a funds-transfer system rule if the beneficiary is notified of the rule before initiation of the funds transfer.

§ 4A–405. Payment by Beneficiary's Bank to Beneficiary.

(a) If the beneficiary's bank credits an account of the beneficiary of a payment order, payment of the bank's obligation under Section 4A–404(a) occurs when and to the extent (i) the beneficiary is notified of the right to withdraw the credit, (ii) the bank lawfully applies the credit to a debt of the beneficiary, or (iii) funds with respect to the order are otherwise made available to the beneficiary by the bank.

(b) If the beneficiary's bank does not credit an account of the beneficiary of a payment order, the time when payment of the bank's obligation under Section 4A–404(a) occurs is governed by principles of law that determine when an obligation is satisfied.

(c) Except as stated in subsections (d) and (e), if the beneficiary's bank pays the beneficiary of a payment order under a condition to payment or agreement of the beneficiary giving the bank the right to recover payment from the beneficiary if the bank does not receive payment of the order, the condition to payment or agreement is not enforceable.

(d) A funds-transfer system rule may provide that payments made to beneficiaries of funds transfers made through the system are provisional until receipt of payment by the beneficiary's bank of the payment order it accepted. A beneficiary's bank that makes a payment that is provisional under the rule is entitled to refund from the beneficiary if (i) the rule requires that both the beneficiary and the originator be given notice of the provisional nature of the payment before the funds transfer is initiated, (ii) the beneficiary, the beneficiary's bank, and the originator's bank agreed to be bound by the rule, and (iii) the beneficiary's bank did not receive payment of the payment order that it accepted. If the beneficiary is obliged to refund payment to the beneficiary's bank, acceptance of the payment order by the beneficiary's bank is nullified and no payment by the originator of the funds transfer to the beneficiary occurs under Section 4A–406.

(e) This subsection applies to a funds transfer that includes a payment order transmitted over a funds-transfer system that (i) nets obligations multilaterally among participants, and (ii) has in effect a loss-sharing agreement among participants for the purpose of providing funds necessary to complete settlement of the obligations of one or more participants that do not meet their settlement obligations. If the beneficiary's bank in the funds transfer accepts a payment order and the system fails to complete settlement pursuant to its rules with respect to any payment order in the funds transfer, (i) the acceptance by the beneficiary's bank is nullified and no person has any right or obligation based on the acceptance, (ii) the beneficiary's bank is entitled to recover payment from the beneficiary, (iii) no payment by the originator to the beneficiary occurs under Section 4A–406, and (iv) subject to Section 4A–402(e), each sender in the funds transfer is excused from its obligation to pay its payment order under Section 4A–402(c) because the funds transfer has not been completed.

§ 4A–406. Payment by Originator to Beneficiary; Discharge of Underlying Obligation.

(a) Subject to Sections 4A–211(e), 4A–405(d), and 4A–405(e), the originator of a funds transfer pays the beneficiary of the originator's payment order (i) at the time a payment order for the benefit of the beneficiary is accepted by the beneficiary's bank in the funds transfer and (ii) in an amount equal to the amount of the order accepted by the beneficiary's bank, but not more than the amount of the originator's order.

(b) If payment under subsection (a) is made to satisfy an obligation, the obligation is discharged to the same extent discharge would result from payment to the beneficiary of the same amount in money, unless (i) the payment under subsection (a) was made by a means prohibited by the contract of the beneficiary with respect to the obligation, (ii) the beneficiary, within a reasonable time after receiving notice of receipt of the order by the beneficiary's bank, notified the originator of the beneficiary's refusal of the payment, (iii) funds with respect to the order were not withdrawn by the beneficiary or applied to a debt of the beneficiary, and (iv) the beneficiary would suffer a loss that could reasonably have been avoided if payment had been made by a means complying with the contract. If payment by the originator does not result in discharge under this section, the originator is subrogated to the rights of the beneficiary to receive payment from the beneficiary's bank under Section 4A–404(a).

(c) For the purpose of determining whether discharge of an obligation occurs under subsection (b), if the beneficiary's bank accepts a payment order in an amount equal to the amount of the originator's payment order less charges of one or more receiving banks in the funds transfer, payment to the beneficiary is deemed to be in the amount of the originator's order unless upon demand by the beneficiary the originator does not pay the beneficiary the amount of the deducted charges.

(d) Rights of the originator or of the beneficiary of a funds transfer under this section may be varied only by agreement of the originator and the beneficiary.

Part 5 Miscellaneous Provisions

§ 4A–501. Variation by Agreement and Effect of Funds-Transfer System Rule.

(a) Except as otherwise provided in this Article, the rights and obligations of a party to a funds transfer may be varied by agreement of the affected party.

(b) "Funds-transfer system rule" means a rule of an association of banks (i) governing transmission of payment orders by means of a funds-transfer system of the association or rights and obligations with respect to those orders, or (ii) to the extent the rule governs rights and obligations between banks that are parties to a funds transfer in which a Federal Reserve Bank, acting as an intermediary bank, sends a payment order to the beneficiary's bank. Except as otherwise provided in this Article, a funds-transfer system rule governing rights and obligations between participating banks using the system may be effective even if the rule conflicts with this Article and indirectly affects another party to the funds transfer who does not consent to the rule. A funds-transfer system rule may also govern rights and obligations of parties other than participating banks using the system to the extent stated in Sections 4A–404(c), 4A–405(d), and 4A–507(c).

§ 4A–502. Creditor Process Served on Receiving Bank; Setoff by Beneficiary's Bank.

(a) As used in this section, "creditor process" means levy, attachment, garnishment, notice of lien, sequestration, or similar process issued by or on behalf of a creditor or other claimant with respect to an account.

(b) This subsection applies to creditor process with respect to an authorized account of the sender of a payment order if the creditor process is served on the receiving bank. For the purpose of determining rights with respect to the creditor process, if the receiving bank accepts the payment order the balance in the authorized account is deemed to be reduced by the amount of the payment order to the extent the bank did not otherwise receive payment of the order, unless the creditor process is served at a time and in a manner affording the bank a reasonable opportunity to act on it before the bank accepts the payment order.

(c) If a beneficiary's bank has received a payment order for payment to the beneficiary's account in the bank, the following rules apply:

(1) The bank may credit the beneficiary's account. The amount credited may be set off against an obligation owed by the beneficiary to the bank or may be applied to satisfy creditor process served on the bank with respect to the account.

(2) The bank may credit the beneficiary's account and allow withdrawal of the amount credited unless creditor process with respect to the account is served at a time and in a manner affording the bank a reasonable opportunity to act to prevent withdrawal.

(3) If creditor process with respect to the beneficiary's account has been served and the bank has had a reasonable opportunity to act on it, the bank may not reject the payment order except for a reason unrelated to the service of process.

(d) Creditor process with respect to a payment by the originator to the beneficiary pursuant to a funds transfer may be served only on the beneficiary's bank with respect to the debt owed by that bank to the beneficiary. Any other bank served with the creditor process is not obliged to act with respect to the process.

§ 4A–503. Injunction or Restraining Order with Respect to Funds Transfer.

For proper cause and in compliance with applicable law, a court may restrain (i) a person from issuing a payment order to initiate a funds transfer, (ii) an originator's bank from executing the payment order of the originator, or (iii) the beneficiary's bank from releasing funds to the beneficiary or the beneficiary from withdrawing the funds. A court may not otherwise restrain a person from issuing a payment order, paying or receiving payment of a payment order, or otherwise acting with respect to a funds transfer.

§ 4A–504. Order in Which Items and Payment Orders May Be Charged to Account; Order of Withdrawals from Account.

(a) If a receiving bank has received more than one payment order of the sender or one or more payment orders and other items that are payable from the sender's account, the bank may charge the sender's account with respect to the various orders and items in any sequence.

(b) In determining whether a credit to an account has been withdrawn by the holder of the account or applied to a debt of the holder of the account, credits first made to the account are first withdrawn or applied.

§ 4A–505. Preclusion of Objection to Debit of Customer's Account.

If a receiving bank has received payment from its customer with respect to a payment order issued in the name of the customer as sender and accepted by the bank, and the customer received notification reasonably identifying the order, the customer is precluded from asserting that the bank is not entitled to retain the payment unless the customer notifies the bank of the customer's objection to the payment within one year after the notification was received by the customer.

§ 4A–506. Rate of Interest.

(a) If, under this Article, a receiving bank is obliged to pay interest with respect to a payment order issued to the bank, the amount payable may be determined (i) by agreement of the sender and receiving bank, or (ii) by a funds-transfer system rule if the payment order is transmitted through a funds-transfer system.

(b) If the amount of interest is not determined by an agreement or rule as stated in subsection (a), the amount is calculated by multiplying the applicable Federal Funds rate by the amount on which interest is payable, and then multiplying the product by the number of days for which interest is payable. The applicable Federal Funds rate is the average of the Federal Funds rates published by the Federal Reserve Bank of New York for each of the days for which interest is payable divided by 360. The Federal Funds rate for any day on which a published rate is not available is the same as the published rate for the next preceding day for which there is a published rate. If a receiving bank that accepted a payment order is required to refund payment to the sender of the order because the funds transfer was not completed, but the failure to complete was not due to any fault by the bank, the interest payable is reduced by a percentage equal to the reserve requirement on deposits of the receiving bank.

§ 4A–507. Choice of Law.

(a) The following rules apply unless the affected parties otherwise agree or subsection (c) applies:

(1) The rights and obligations between the sender of a payment order and the receiving bank are governed by the law of the jurisdiction in which the receiving bank is located.

(2) The rights and obligations between the beneficiary's bank and the beneficiary are governed by the law of the jurisdiction in which the beneficiary's bank is located.

(3) The issue of when payment is made pursuant to a funds transfer by the originator to the beneficiary is governed by the law of the jurisdiction in which the beneficiary's bank is located.

(b) If the parties described in each paragraph of subsection (a) have made an agreement selecting the law of a particular jurisdiction to govern rights and obligations between each other, the law of that jurisdiction governs those rights and obligations, whether or not the payment order or the funds transfer bears a reasonable relation to that jurisdiction.

(c) A funds-transfer system rule may select the law of a particular jurisdiction to govern (i) rights and obligations between participating banks with respect to payment orders transmitted or processed through the system, or (ii) the rights and obligations of some or all parties to a funds transfer any part of which is carried out by means of the system. A choice of law made pursuant to clause (i) is binding on participating banks. A choice of law made pursuant to clause (ii) is binding on the originator, other sender, or a receiving bank having notice that the funds-transfer system might be used in the funds transfer and of the choice of law by the system when the originator, other sender, or receiving bank issued or accepted a payment order. The beneficiary of a funds transfer is bound by the choice of law if, when the funds transfer is initiated, the beneficiary has notice that the funds-transfer system might be used in the funds transfer and of the choice of law by the system. The law of a jurisdiction selected pursuant to this subsection may govern, whether or not that law bears a reasonable relation to the matter in issue.

(d) In the event of inconsistency between an agreement under subsection (b) and a choice-of-law rule under subsection (c), the agreement under subsection (b) prevails.

(e) If a funds transfer is made by use of more than one funds-transfer system and there is inconsistency between choice-of-law rules of the systems, the matter in issue is governed by the law of the selected jurisdiction that has the most significant relationship to the matter in issue.

Revised Article 9 SECURED TRANSACTIONS

Part 1 General Provisions

[Subpart 1. Short Title, Definitions, and General Concepts]

§ 9–101. Short Title.

This article may be cited as Uniform Commercial Code—Secured Transactions.

§ 9–102. Definitions and Index of Definitions.

(a) In this article:

(1) "Accession" means goods that are physically united with other goods in such a manner that the identity of the original goods is not lost.

(2) "Account", except as used in "account for", means a right to payment of a monetary obligation, whether or not earned by performance, (i) for property that has been or is to be sold, leased, licensed, assigned, or otherwise disposed of, (ii) for services rendered or to be rendered, (iii) for a policy of insurance issued or to be issued, (iv) for a secondary obligation incurred or to be incurred, (v) for energy provided or to be provided, (vi) for the use or hire of a vessel under a charter or other contract, (vii) arising out of the use of a credit or charge card or information contained on or for use with the card, or (viii) as winnings in a lottery or other game of chance operated or sponsored by a State, governmental unit of a State, or person licensed or authorized to operate the game by a State or governmental unit of a State. The

term includes health-care insurance receivables. The term does not include (i) rights to payment evidenced by chattel paper or an instrument, (ii) commercial tort claims, (iii) deposit accounts, (iv) investment property, (v) letter-of-credit rights or letters of credit, or (vi) rights to payment for money or funds advanced or sold, other than rights arising out of the use of a credit or charge card or information contained on or for use with the card.

(3) "Account debtor" means a person obligated on an account, chattel paper, or general intangible. The term does not include persons obligated to pay a negotiable instrument, even if the instrument constitutes part of chattel paper.

(4) "Accounting", except as used in "accounting for", means a record:

(A) authenticated by a secured party;

(B) indicating the aggregate unpaid secured obligations as of a date not more than 35 days earlier or 35 days later than the date of the record; and

(C) identifying the components of the obligations in reasonable detail.

(5) "Agricultural lien" means an interest, other than a security interest, in farm products:

(A) which secures payment or performance of an obligation for:

(i) goods or services furnished in connection with a debtor's farming operation; or

(ii) rent on real property leased by a debtor in connection with its farming operation;

(B) which is created by statute in favor of a person that:

(i) in the ordinary course of its business furnished goods or services to a debtor in connection with a debtor's farming operation; or

(ii) leased real property to a debtor in connection with the debtor's farming operation; and

(C) whose effectiveness does not depend on the person's possession of the personal property.

(6) "As-extracted collateral" means:

(A) oil, gas, or other minerals that are subject to a security interest that:

(i) is created by a debtor having an interest in the minerals before extraction; and

(ii) attaches to the minerals as extracted; or

(B) accounts arising out of the sale at the wellhead or minehead of oil, gas, or other minerals in which the debtor had an interest before extraction.

(7) "Authenticate" means:

(A) to sign; or

(B) to execute or otherwise adopt a symbol, or encrypt or similarly process a record in whole or in part, with the present intent of the authenticating person to identify the person and adopt or accept a record.

(8) "Bank" means an organization that is engaged in the business of banking. The term includes savings banks, savings and loan associations, credit unions, and trust companies.

(9) "Cash proceeds" means proceeds that are money, checks, deposit accounts, or the like.

(10) "Certificate of title" means a certificate of title with respect to which a statute provides for the security interest in question to be indicated on the certificate as a condition or result of the security interest's obtaining priority over the rights of a lien creditor with respect to the collateral.

(11) "Chattel paper" means a record or records that evidence both a monetary obligation and a security interest in specific goods, a security interest in specific goods and software used in the goods, a security interest in specific goods and license of software used in the goods, a lease of specific goods, or a lease of specific goods and license of software used in the goods. In this paragraph, "monetary obligation" means a monetary obligation secured by the goods or owed under a lease of the goods and includes a monetary obligation with respect to software used in the goods. The term does not include (i) charters or other contracts involving the use or hire of a vessel or (ii) records that evidence a right to payment arising out of the use of a credit or charge card or information contained on or for use with the card. If a transaction is evidenced by records that include an instrument or series of instruments, the group of records taken together constitutes chattel paper.

(12) "Collateral" means the property subject to a security interest or agricultural lien. The term includes:

(A) proceeds to which a security interest attaches;

(B) accounts, chattel paper, payment intangibles, and promissory notes that have been sold; and

(C) goods that are the subject of a consignment.

(13) "Commercial tort claim" means a claim arising in tort with respect to which:

(A) the claimant is an organization; or

(B) the claimant is an individual and the claim:

(i) arose in the course of the claimant's business or profession; and

(ii) does not include damages arising out of personal injury to or the death of an individual.

(14) "Commodity account" means an account maintained by a commodity intermediary in which a commodity contract is carried for a commodity customer.

(15) "Commodity contract" means a commodity futures contract, an option on a commodity futures contract, a commodity option, or another contract if the contract or option is:

(A) traded on or subject to the rules of a board of trade that has been designated as a contract market for such a contract pursuant to federal commodities laws; or

(B) traded on a foreign commodity board of trade, exchange, or market, and is carried on the books of a commodity intermediary for a commodity customer.

(16) "Commodity customer" means a person for which a commodity intermediary carries a commodity contract on its books.

(17) "Commodity intermediary" means a person that:

(A) is registered as a futures commission merchant under federal commodities law; or

(B) in the ordinary course of its business provides clearance or settlement services for a board of trade that has been designated as a contract market pursuant to federal commodities law.

(18) "Communicate" means:

(A) to send a written or other tangible record;

(B) to transmit a record by any means agreed upon by the persons sending and receiving the record; or

(C) in the case of transmission of a record to or by a filing office, to transmit a record by any means prescribed by filing-office rule.

(19) "Consignee" means a merchant to which goods are delivered in a consignment.

(20) "Consignment" means a transaction, regardless of its form, in which a person delivers goods to a merchant for the purpose of sale and:

(A) the merchant:

(i) deals in goods of that kind under a name other than the name of the person making delivery;

(ii) is not an auctioneer; and

(iii) is not generally known by its creditors to be substantially engaged in selling the goods of others;

(B) with respect to each delivery, the aggregate value of the goods is $1,000 or more at the time of delivery;

(C) the goods are not consumer goods immediately before delivery; and

(D) the transaction does not create a security interest that secures an obligation.

(21) "Consignor" means a person that delivers goods to a consignee in a consignment.

(22) "Consumer debtor" means a debtor in a consumer transaction.

(23) "Consumer goods" means goods that are used or bought for use primarily for personal, family, or household purposes.

(24) "Consumer-goods transaction" means a consumer transaction in which:

(A) an individual incurs an obligation primarily for personal, family, or household purposes; and

(B) a security interest in consumer goods secures the obligation.

(25) "Consumer obligor" means an obligor who is an individual and who incurred the obligation as part of a transaction entered into primarily for personal, family, or household purposes.

(26) "Consumer transaction" means a transaction in which (i) an individual incurs an obligation primarily for personal, family, or household purposes, (ii) a security interest secures the obligation, and (iii) the collateral is held or acquired primarily for personal, family, or household purposes. The term includes consumer-goods transactions.

(27) "Continuation statement" means an amendment of a financing statement which:

(A) identifies, by its file number, the initial financing statement to which it relates; and

(B) indicates that it is a continuation statement for, or that it is filed to continue the effectiveness of, the identified financing statement.

(28) "Debtor" means:

(A) a person having an interest, other than a security interest or other lien, in the collateral, whether or not the person is an obligor;

(B) a seller of accounts, chattel paper, payment intangibles, or promissory notes; or

(C) a consignee.

(29) "Deposit account" means a demand, time, savings, passbook, or similar account maintained with a bank. The term does not include investment property or accounts evidenced by an instrument.

(30) "Document" means a document of title or a receipt of the type described in Section 7–201(2).

(31) "Electronic chattel paper" means chattel paper evidenced by a record or records consisting of information stored in an electronic medium.

(32) "Encumbrance" means a right, other than an ownership interest, in real property. The term includes mortgages and other liens on real property.

(33) "Equipment" means goods other than inventory, farm products, or consumer goods.

(34) "Farm products" means goods, other than standing timber, with respect to which the debtor is engaged in a farming operation and which are:

(A) crops grown, growing, or to be grown, including:

(i) crops produced on trees, vines, and bushes; and

(ii) aquatic goods produced in aquacultural operations;

(B) livestock, born or unborn, including aquatic goods produced in aquacultural operations;

(C) supplies used or produced in a farming operation; or

(D) products of crops or livestock in their unmanufactured states.

(35) "Farming operation" means raising, cultivating, propagating, fattening, grazing, or any other farming, livestock, or aquacultural operation.

(36) "File number" means the number assigned to an initial financing statement pursuant to Section 9–519(a).

(37) "Filing office" means an office designated in Section 9–501 as the place to file a financing statement.

(38) "Filing-office rule" means a rule adopted pursuant to Section 9–526.

(39) "Financing statement" means a record or records composed of an initial financing statement and any filed record relating to the initial financing statement.

(40) "Fixture filing" means the filing of a financing statement covering goods that are or are to become fixtures and satisfying Section 9–502(a) and (b). The term includes the filing of a financing statement covering goods of a transmitting utility which are or are to become fixtures.

(41) "Fixtures" means goods that have become so related to particular real property that an interest in them arises under real property law.

(42) "General intangible" means any personal property, including things in action, other than accounts, chattel paper, commercial

tort claims, deposit accounts, documents, goods, instruments, investment property, letter-of-credit rights, letters of credit, money, and oil, gas, or other minerals before extraction. The term includes payment intangibles and software.

(43) "Good faith" means honesty in fact and the observance of reasonable commercial standards of fair dealing.

(44) "Goods" means all things that are movable when a security interest attaches. The term includes (i) fixtures, (ii) standing timber that is to be cut and removed under a conveyance or contract for sale, (iii) the unborn young of animals, (iv) crops grown, growing, or to be grown, even if the crops are produced on trees, vines, or bushes, and (v) manufactured homes. The term also includes a computer program embedded in goods and any supporting information provided in connection with a transaction relating to the program if (i) the program is associated with the goods in such a manner that it customarily is considered part of the goods, or (ii) by becoming the owner of the goods, a person acquires a right to use the program in connection with the goods. The term does not include a computer program embedded in goods that consist solely of the medium in which the program is embedded. The term also does not include accounts, chattel paper, commercial tort claims, deposit accounts, documents, general intangibles, instruments, investment property, letter-of-credit rights, letters of credit, money, or oil, gas, or other minerals before extraction.

(45) "Governmental unit" means a subdivision, agency, department, county, parish, municipality, or other unit of the government of the United States, a State, or a foreign country. The term includes an organization having a separate corporate existence if the organization is eligible to issue debt on which interest is exempt from income taxation under the laws of the United States.

(46) "Health-care-insurance receivable" means an interest in or claim under a policy of insurance which is a right to payment of a monetary obligation for health-care goods or services provided.

(47) "Instrument" means a negotiable instrument or any other writing that evidences a right to the payment of a monetary obligation, is not itself a security agreement or lease, and is of a type that in ordinary course of business is transferred by delivery with any necessary indorsement or assignment. The term does not include (i) investment property, (ii) letters of credit, or (iii) writings that evidence a right to payment arising out of the use of a credit or charge card or information contained on or for use with the card.

(48) "Inventory" means goods, other than farm products, which:

(A) are leased by a person as lessor;

(B) are held by a person for sale or lease or to be furnished under a contract of service;

(C) are furnished by a person under a contract of service; or

(D) consist of raw materials, work in process, or materials used or consumed in a business.

(49) "Investment property" means a security, whether certificated or uncertificated, security entitlement, securities account, commodity contract, or commodity account.

(50) "Jurisdiction of organization", with respect to a registered organization, means the jurisdiction under whose law the organization is organized.

(51) "Letter-of-credit right" means a right to payment or performance under a letter of credit, whether or not the beneficiary has demanded or is at the time entitled to demand payment or performance. The term does not include the right of a beneficiary to demand payment or performance under a letter of credit.

(52) "Lien creditor" means:

(A) a creditor that has acquired a lien on the property involved by attachment, levy, or the like;

(B) an assignee for benefit of creditors from the time of assignment;

(C) a trustee in bankruptcy from the date of the filing of the petition; or

(D) a receiver in equity from the time of appointment.

(53) "Manufactured home" means a structure, transportable in one or more sections, which, in the traveling mode, is eight body feet or more in width or 40 body feet or more in length, or, when erected on site, is 320 or more square feet, and which is built on a permanent chassis and designed to be used as a dwelling with or without a permanent foundation when connected to the required utilities, and includes the plumbing, heating, air-conditioning, and electrical systems contained therein. The term includes any structure that meets all of the requirements of this paragraph except the size requirements and with respect to which the manufacturer voluntarily files a certification required by the United States Secretary of Housing and Urban Development and complies with the standards established under Title 42 of the United States Code.

(54) "Manufactured-home transaction" means a secured transaction:

(A) that creates a purchase-money security interest in a manufactured home, other than a manufactured home held as inventory; or

(B) in which a manufactured home, other than a manufactured home held as inventory, is the primary collateral.

(55) "Mortgage" means a consensual interest in real property, including fixtures, which secures payment or performance of an obligation.

(56) "New debtor" means a person that becomes bound as debtor under Section 9–203(d) by a security agreement previously entered into by another person.

(57) "New value" means (i) money, (ii) money's worth in property, services, or new credit, or (iii) release by a transferee of an interest in property previously transferred to the transferee. The term does not include an obligation substituted for another obligation.

(58) "Noncash proceeds" means proceeds other than cash proceeds.

(59) "Obligor" means a person that, with respect to an obligation secured by a security interest in or an agricultural lien on the collateral, (i) owes payment or other performance of the obligation, (ii) has provided property other than the collateral to secure payment or other performance of the obligation, or (iii) is otherwise accountable in whole or in part for payment or other performance of the obligation. The term does not include issuers or nominated persons under a letter of credit.

(60) "Original debtor", except as used in Section 9–310(c), means a person that, as debtor, entered into a security agreement to which a new debtor has become bound under Section 9–203(d).

(61) "Payment intangible" means a general intangible under which the account debtor's principal obligation is a monetary obligation.

(62) "Person related to", with respect to an individual, means:

(A) the spouse of the individual;

(B) a brother, brother-in-law, sister, or sister-in-law of the individual;

(C) an ancestor or lineal descendant of the individual or the individual's spouse; or

(D) any other relative, by blood or marriage, of the individual or the individual's spouse who shares the same home with the individual.

(63) "Person related to", with respect to an organization, means:

(A) a person directly or indirectly controlling, controlled by, or under common control with the organization;

(B) an officer or director of, or a person performing similar functions with respect to, the organization;

(C) an officer or director of, or a person performing similar functions with respect to, a person described in subparagraph (A);

(D) the spouse of an individual described in subparagraph (A), (B), or (C); or

(E) an individual who is related by blood or marriage to an individual described in subparagraph (A), (B), (C), or (D) and shares the same home with the individual.

(64) "Proceeds", except as used in Section 9–609(b), means the following property:

(A) whatever is acquired upon the sale, lease, license, exchange, or other disposition of collateral;

(B) whatever is collected on, or distributed on account of, collateral;

(C) rights arising out of collateral;

(D) to the extent of the value of collateral, claims arising out of the loss, nonconformity, or interference with the use of, defects or infringement of rights in, or damage to, the collateral; or

(E) to the extent of the value of collateral and to the extent payable to the debtor or the secured party, insurance payable by reason of the loss or nonconformity of, defects or infringement of rights in, or damage to, the collateral.

(65) "Promissory note" means an instrument that evidences a promise to pay a monetary obligation, does not evidence an order to pay, and does not contain an acknowledgment by a bank that the bank has received for deposit a sum of money or funds.

(66) "Proposal" means a record authenticated by a secured party which includes the terms on which the secured party is willing to accept collateral in full or partial satisfaction of the obligation it secures pursuant to Sections 9–620, 9–621, and 9–622.

(67) "Public-finance transaction" means a secured transaction in connection with which:

(A) debt securities are issued;

(B) all or a portion of the securities issued have an initial stated maturity of at least 20 years; and

(C) the debtor, obligor, secured party, account debtor or other person obligated on collateral, assignor or assignee of a secured obligation, or assignor or assignee of a security interest is a State or a governmental unit of a State.

(68) "Pursuant to commitment", with respect to an advance made or other value given by a secured party, means pursuant to the secured party's obligation, whether or not a subsequent event of default or other event not within the secured party's control has relieved or may relieve the secured party from its obligation.

(69) "Record", except as used in "for record", "of record", "record or legal title", and "record owner", means information that is inscribed on a tangible medium or which is stored in an electronic or other medium and is retrievable in perceivable form.

(70) "Registered organization" means an organization organized solely under the law of a single State or the United States and as to which the State or the United States must maintain a public record showing the organization to have been organized.

(71) "Secondary obligor" means an obligor to the extent that:

(A) the obligor's obligation is secondary; or

(B) the obligor has a right of recourse with respect to an obligation secured by collateral against the debtor, another obligor, or property of either.

(72) "Secured party" means:

(A) a person in whose favor a security interest is created or provided for under a security agreement, whether or not any obligation to be secured is outstanding;

(B) a person that holds an agricultural lien;

(C) a consignor;

(D) a person to which accounts, chattel paper, payment intangibles, or promissory notes have been sold;

(E) a trustee, indenture trustee, agent, collateral agent, or other representative in whose favor a security interest or agricultural lien is created or provided for; or

(F) a person that holds a security interest arising under Section 2–401, 2–505, 2–711(3), 2A–508(5), 4–210, or 5–118.

(73) "Security agreement" means an agreement that creates or provides for a security interest.

(74) "Send", in connection with a record or notification, means:

(A) to deposit in the mail, deliver for transmission, or transmit by any other usual means of communication, with postage or cost of transmission provided for, addressed to any address reasonable under the circumstances; or

(B) to cause the record or notification to be received within the time that it would have been received if properly sent under subparagraph (A).

(75) "Software" means a computer program and any supporting information provided in connection with a transaction relating to the program. The term does not include a computer program that is included in the definition of goods.

(76) "State" means a State of the United States, the District of Columbia, Puerto Rico, the United States Virgin Islands, or any territory or insular possession subject to the jurisdiction of the United States.

(77) "Supporting obligation" means a letter-of-credit right or secondary obligation that supports the payment or performance of an account, chattel paper, a document, a general intangible, an instrument, or investment property.

(78) "Tangible chattel paper" means chattel paper evidenced by a record or records consisting of information that is inscribed on a tangible medium.

(79) "Termination statement" means an amendment of a financing statement which:

(A) identifies, by its file number, the initial financing statement to which it relates; and

(B) indicates either that it is a termination statement or that the identified financing statement is no longer effective.

(80) "Transmitting utility" means a person primarily engaged in the business of:

(A) operating a railroad, subway, street railway, or trolley bus;

(B) transmitting communications electrically, electromagnetically, or by light;

(C) transmitting goods by pipeline or sewer; or

(D) transmitting or producing and transmitting electricity, steam, gas, or water.

(b) The following definitions in other articles apply to this article:

"Applicant."	Section 5–102
"Beneficiary."	Section 5–102
"Broker."	Section 8–102
"Certificated security."	Section 8–102
"Check."	Section 3–104
"Clearing corporation."	Section 8–102
"Contract for sale."	Section 2–106
"Customer."	Section 4–104
"Entitlement holder."	Section 8–102
"Financial asset."	Section 8–102
"Holder in due course."	Section 3–302
"Issuer" (with respect to a letter of credit or letter-of-credit right).	Section 5–102
"Issuer" (with respect to a security).	Section 8–201
"Lease."	Section 2A–103
"Lease agreement."	Section 2A–103
"Lease contract."	Section 2A–103
"Leasehold interest."	Section 2A–103
"Lessee."	Section 2A–103
"Lessee in ordinary course of business."	Section 2A–103
"Lessor."	Section 2A–103
"Lessor's residual interest."	Section 2A–103
"Letter of credit."	Section 5–102
"Merchant."	Section 2–104
"Negotiable instrument."	Section 3–104
"Nominated person."	Section 5–102
"Note."	Section 3–104
"Proceeds of a letter of credit."	Section 5–114
"Prove."	Section 3–103
"Sale."	Section 2–106
"Securities account."	Section 8–501
"Securities intermediary."	Section 8–102
"Security."	Section 8–102
"Security certificate."	Section 8–102
"Security entitlement."	Section 8–102
"Uncertificated security."	Section 8–102

(c) Article 1 contains general definitions and principles of construction and interpretation applicable throughout this article.

Amended in 1999 and 2000.

§ 9–103. Purchase-Money Security Interest; Application of Payments; Burden of Establishing.

(a) In this section:

(1) "purchase-money collateral" means goods or software that secures a purchase-money obligation incurred with respect to that collateral; and

(2) "purchase-money obligation" means an obligation of an obligor incurred as all or part of the price of the collateral or for value given to enable the debtor to acquire rights in or the use of the collateral if the value is in fact so used.

(b) A security interest in goods is a purchase-money security interest:

(1) to the extent that the goods are purchase-money collateral with respect to that security interest;

(2) if the security interest is in inventory that is or was purchase-money collateral, also to the extent that the security interest secures a purchase-money obligation incurred with respect to other inventory in which the secured party holds or held a purchase-money security interest; and

(3) also to the extent that the security interest secures a purchase-money obligation incurred with respect to software in which the secured party holds or held a purchase-money security interest.

(c) A security interest in software is a purchase-money security interest to the extent that the security interest also secures a purchase-money obligation incurred with respect to goods in which the secured party holds or held a purchase-money security interest if:

(1) the debtor acquired its interest in the software in an integrated transaction in which it acquired an interest in the goods; and

(2) the debtor acquired its interest in the software for the principal purpose of using the software in the goods.

(d) The security interest of a consignor in goods that are the subject of a consignment is a purchase-money security interest in inventory.

(e) In a transaction other than a consumer-goods transaction, if the extent to which a security interest is a purchase-money security interest depends on the application of a payment to a particular obligation, the payment must be applied:

(1) in accordance with any reasonable method of application to which the parties agree;

(2) in the absence of the parties' agreement to a reasonable method, in accordance with any intention of the obligor manifested at or before the time of payment; or

(3) in the absence of an agreement to a reasonable method and a timely manifestation of the obligor's intention, in the following order:

(A) to obligations that are not secured; and

(B) if more than one obligation is secured, to obligations secured by purchase-money security interests in the order in which those obligations were incurred.

(f) In a transaction other than a consumer-goods transaction, a purchase-money security interest does not lose its status as such, even if:

(1) the purchase-money collateral also secures an obligation that is not a purchase-money obligation;

(2) collateral that is not purchase-money collateral also secures the purchase-money obligation; or

(3) the purchase-money obligation has been renewed, refinanced, consolidated, or restructured.

(g) In a transaction other than a consumer-goods transaction, a secured party claiming a purchase-money security interest has the burden of establishing the extent to which the security interest is a purchase-money security interest.

(h) The limitation of the rules in subsections (e), (f), and (g) to transactions other than consumer-goods transactions is intended to leave to the court the determination of the proper rules in consumer-goods transactions. The court may not infer from that limitation the nature of the proper rule in consumer-goods transactions and may continue to apply established approaches.

§ 9–104. Control of Deposit Account.

(a) A secured party has control of a deposit account if:

(1) the secured party is the bank with which the deposit account is maintained;

(2) the debtor, secured party, and bank have agreed in an authenticated record that the bank will comply with instructions originated by the secured party directing disposition of the funds in the deposit account without further consent by the debtor; or

(3) the secured party becomes the bank's customer with respect to the deposit account.

(b) A secured party that has satisfied subsection (a) has control, even if the debtor retains the right to direct the disposition of funds from the deposit account.

§ 9–105. Control of Electronic Chattel Paper.

A secured party has control of electronic chattel paper if the record or records comprising the chattel paper are created, stored, and assigned in such a manner that:

(1) a single authoritative copy of the record or records exists which is unique, identifiable and, except as otherwise provided in paragraphs (4), (5), and (6), unalterable;

(2) the authoritative copy identifies the secured party as the assignee of the record or records;

(3) the authoritative copy is communicated to and maintained by the secured party or its designated custodian;

(4) copies or revisions that add or change an identified assignee of the authoritative copy can be made only with the participation of the secured party;

(5) each copy of the authoritative copy and any copy of a copy is readily identifiable as a copy that is not the authoritative copy; and

(6) any revision of the authoritative copy is readily identifiable as an authorized or unauthorized revision.

§ 9–106. Control of Investment Property.

(a) A person has control of a certificated security, uncertificated security, or security entitlement as provided in Section 8–106.

(b) A secured party has control of a commodity contract if:

(1) the secured party is the commodity intermediary with which the commodity contract is carried; or

(2) the commodity customer, secured party, and commodity intermediary have agreed that the commodity intermediary will apply any value distributed on account of the commodity contract as directed by the secured party without further consent by the commodity customer.

(c) A secured party having control of all security entitlements or commodity contracts carried in a securities account or commodity account has control over the securities account or commodity account.

§ 9–107. Control of Letter-of-Credit Right.

A secured party has control of a letter-of-credit right to the extent of any right to payment or performance by the issuer or any nominated person if the issuer or nominated person has consented to an assignment of proceeds of the letter of credit under Section 5–114(c) or otherwise applicable law or practice.

§ 9–108. Sufficiency of Description.

(a) Except as otherwise provided in subsections (c), (d), and (e), a description of personal or real property is sufficient, whether or not it is specific, if it reasonably identifies what is described.

(b) Except as otherwise provided in subsection (d), a description of collateral reasonably identifies the collateral if it identifies the collateral by:

(1) specific listing;

(2) category;

(3) except as otherwise provided in subsection (e), a type of collateral defined in [the Uniform Commercial Code];

(4) quantity;

(5) computational or allocational formula or procedure; or

(6) except as otherwise provided in subsection (c), any other method, if the identity of the collateral is objectively determinable.

(c) A description of collateral as "all the debtor's assets" or "all the debtor's personal property" or using words of similar import does not reasonably identify the collateral.

(d) Except as otherwise provided in subsection (e), a description of a security entitlement, securities account, or commodity account is sufficient if it describes:

(1) the collateral by those terms or as investment property; or

(2) the underlying financial asset or commodity contract.

(e) A description only by type of collateral defined in [the Uniform Commercial Code] is an insufficient description of:

(1) a commercial tort claim; or

(2) in a consumer transaction, consumer goods, a security entitlement, a securities account, or a commodity account.

[Subpart 2. Applicability of Article]

§ 9–109. Scope.

(a) Except as otherwise provided in subsections (c) and (d), this article applies to:

(1) a transaction, regardless of its form, that creates a security interest in personal property or fixtures by contract;

(2) an agricultural lien;

(3) a sale of accounts, chattel paper, payment intangibles, or promissory notes;

(4) a consignment;

(5) a security interest arising under Section 2–401, 2–505, 2–711(3), or 2A–508(5), as provided in Section 9–110; and

(6) a security interest arising under Section 4–210 or 5–118.

(b) The application of this article to a security interest in a secured obligation is not affected by the fact that the obligation is itself secured by a transaction or interest to which this article does not apply.

(c) This article does not apply to the extent that:

(1) a statute, regulation, or treaty of the United States preempts this article;

(2) another statute of this State expressly governs the creation, perfection, priority, or enforcement of a security interest created by this State or a governmental unit of this State;

(3) a statute of another State, a foreign country, or a governmental unit of another State or a foreign country, other than a statute generally applicable to security interests, expressly governs creation, perfection, priority, or enforcement of a security interest created by the State, country, or governmental unit; or

(4) the rights of a transferee beneficiary or nominated person under a letter of credit are independent and superior under Section 5–114.

(d) This article does not apply to:

(1) a landlord's lien, other than an agricultural lien;

(2) a lien, other than an agricultural lien, given by statute or other rule of law for services or materials, but Section 9–333 applies with respect to priority of the lien;

(3) an assignment of a claim for wages, salary, or other compensation of an employee;

(4) a sale of accounts, chattel paper, payment intangibles, or promissory notes as part of a sale of the business out of which they arose;

(5) an assignment of accounts, chattel paper, payment intangibles, or promissory notes which is for the purpose of collection only;

(6) an assignment of a right to payment under a contract to an assignee that is also obligated to perform under the contract;

(7) an assignment of a single account, payment intangible, or promissory note to an assignee in full or partial satisfaction of a preexisting indebtedness;

(8) a transfer of an interest in or an assignment of a claim under a policy of insurance, other than an assignment by or to a health-care provider of a health-care-insurance receivable and any subsequent assignment of the right to payment, but Sections 9–315 and 9–322 apply with respect to proceeds and priorities in proceeds;

(9) an assignment of a right represented by a judgment, other than a judgment taken on a right to payment that was collateral;

(10) a right of recoupment or set-off, but:

(A) Section 9–340 applies with respect to the effectiveness of rights of recoupment or set-off against deposit accounts; and

(B) Section 9–404 applies with respect to defenses or claims of an account debtor;

(11) the creation or transfer of an interest in or lien on real property, including a lease or rents thereunder, except to the extent that provision is made for:

(A) liens on real property in Sections 9–203 and 9–308;

(B) fixtures in Section 9–334;

(C) fixture filings in Sections 9–501, 9–502, 9–512, 9–516, and 9–519; and

(D) security agreements covering personal and real property in Section 9–604;

(12) an assignment of a claim arising in tort, other than a commercial tort claim, but Sections 9–315 and 9–322 apply with respect to proceeds and priorities in proceeds; or

(13) an assignment of a deposit account in a consumer transaction, but Sections 9–315 and 9–322 apply with respect to proceeds and priorities in proceeds.

§ 9–110. Security Interests Arising under Article 2 or 2A.

A security interest arising under Section 2–401, 2–505, 2–711(3), or 2A–508(5) is subject to this article. However, until the debtor obtains possession of the goods:

(1) the security interest is enforceable, even if Section 9–203(b)(3) has not been satisfied;

(2) filing is not required to perfect the security interest;

(3) the rights of the secured party after default by the debtor are governed by Article 2 or 2A; and

(4) the security interest has priority over a conflicting security interest created by the debtor.

Part 2 Effectiveness of Security Agreement; Attachment of Security Interest; Rights of Parties to Security Agreement

[Subpart 1. Effectiveness and Attachment]

§ 9–201. General Effectiveness of Security Agreement.

(a) Except as otherwise provided in [the Uniform Commercial Code], a security agreement is effective according to its terms between the parties, against purchasers of the collateral, and against creditors.

(b) A transaction subject to this article is subject to any applicable rule of law which establishes a different rule for consumers and [insert reference to (i) any other statute or regulation that regulates the rates, charges, agreements, and practices for loans, credit sales, or other extensions of credit and (ii) any consumer-protection statute or regulation].

(c) In case of conflict between this article and a rule of law, statute, or regulation described in subsection (b), the rule of law, statute, or regulation controls. Failure to comply with a statute or regulation described in subsection (b) has only the effect the statute or regulation specifies.

(d) This article does not:

(1) validate any rate, charge, agreement, or practice that violates a rule of law, statute, or regulation described in subsection (b); or

(2) extend the application of the rule of law, statute, or regulation to a transaction not otherwise subject to it.

§ 9–202. Title to Collateral Immaterial.

Except as otherwise provided with respect to consignments or sales of accounts, chattel paper, payment intangibles, or promissory notes, the provisions of this article with regard to rights and obligations apply whether title to collateral is in the secured party or the debtor.

§ 9–203. Attachment and Enforceability of Security Interest; Proceeds; Supporting Obligations; Formal Requisites.

(a) A security interest attaches to collateral when it becomes enforceable against the debtor with respect to the collateral, unless an agreement expressly postpones the time of attachment.

(b) Except as otherwise provided in subsections (c) through (i), a security interest is enforceable against the debtor and third parties with respect to the collateral only if:

(1) value has been given;

(2) the debtor has rights in the collateral or the power to transfer rights in the collateral to a secured party; and

(3) one of the following conditions is met:

(A) the debtor has authenticated a security agreement that provides a description of the collateral and, if the security interest covers timber to be cut, a description of the land concerned;

(B) the collateral is not a certificated security and is in the possession of the secured party under Section 9–313 pursuant to the debtor's security agreement;

(C) the collateral is a certificated security in registered form and the security certificate has been delivered to the secured party under Section 8–301 pursuant to the debtor's security agreement; or

(D) the collateral is deposit accounts, electronic chattel paper, investment property, or letter-of-credit rights, and the secured party has control under Section 9–104, 9–105, 9–106, or 9–107 pursuant to the debtor's security agreement.

(c) Subsection (b) is subject to Section 4–210 on the security interest of a collecting bank, Section 5–118 on the security interest of a letter-of-credit issuer or nominated person, Section 9–110 on a security interest arising under Article 2 or 2A, and Section 9–206 on security interests in investment property.

(d) A person becomes bound as debtor by a security agreement entered into by another person if, by operation of law other than this article or by contract:

(1) the security agreement becomes effective to create a security interest in the person's property; or

(2) the person becomes generally obligated for the obligations of the other person, including the obligation secured under the security agreement, and acquires or succeeds to all or substantially all of the assets of the other person.

(e) If a new debtor becomes bound as debtor by a security agreement entered into by another person:

(1) the agreement satisfies subsection (b)(3) with respect to existing or after-acquired property of the new debtor to the extent the property is described in the agreement; and

(2) another agreement is not necessary to make a security interest in the property enforceable.

(f) The attachment of a security interest in collateral gives the secured party the rights to proceeds provided by Section 9–315 and is also attachment of a security interest in a supporting obligation for the collateral.

(g) The attachment of a security interest in a right to payment or performance secured by a security interest or other lien on personal or real property is also attachment of a security interest in the security interest, mortgage, or other lien.

(h) The attachment of a security interest in a securities account is also attachment of a security interest in the security entitlements carried in the securities account.

(i) The attachment of a security interest in a commodity account is also attachment of a security interest in the commodity contracts carried in the commodity account.

§ 9–204. After-Acquired Property; Future Advances.

(a) Except as otherwise provided in subsection (b), a security agreement may create or provide for a security interest in after-acquired collateral.

(b) A security interest does not attach under a term constituting an after-acquired property clause to:

(1) consumer goods, other than an accession when given as additional security, unless the debtor acquires rights in them within 10 days after the secured party gives value; or

(2) a commercial tort claim.

(c) A security agreement may provide that collateral secures, or that accounts, chattel paper, payment intangibles, or promissory notes are sold in connection with, future advances or other value, whether or not the advances or value are given pursuant to commitment.

§ 9–205. Use or Disposition of Collateral Permissible.

(a) A security interest is not invalid or fraudulent against creditors solely because:

(1) the debtor has the right or ability to:

(A) use, commingle, or dispose of all or part of the collateral, including returned or repossessed goods;

(B) collect, compromise, enforce, or otherwise deal with collateral;

(C) accept the return of collateral or make repossessions; or

(D) use, commingle, or dispose of proceeds; or

(2) the secured party fails to require the debtor to account for proceeds or replace collateral.

(b) This section does not relax the requirements of possession if attachment, perfection, or enforcement of a security interest depends upon possession of the collateral by the secured party.

§ 9–206. Security Interest Arising in Purchase or Delivery of Financial Asset.

(a) A security interest in favor of a securities intermediary attaches to a person's security entitlement if:

(1) the person buys a financial asset through the securities intermediary in a transaction in which the person is obligated to pay the purchase price to the securities intermediary at the time of the purchase; and

(2) the securities intermediary credits the financial asset to the buyer's securities account before the buyer pays the securities intermediary.

(b) The security interest described in subsection (a) secures the person's obligation to pay for the financial asset.

(c) A security interest in favor of a person that delivers a certificated security or other financial asset represented by a writing attaches to the security or other financial asset if:

(1) the security or other financial asset:

(A) in the ordinary course of business is transferred by delivery with any necessary indorsement or assignment; and

(B) is delivered under an agreement between persons in the business of dealing with such securities or financial assets; and

(2) the agreement calls for delivery against payment.

(d) The security interest described in subsection (c) secures the obligation to make payment for the delivery.

[Subpart 2. Rights and Duties]

§ 9–207. Rights and Duties of Secured Party Having Possession or Control of Collateral.

(a) Except as otherwise provided in subsection (d), a secured party shall use reasonable care in the custody and preservation of collateral in the secured party's possession. In the case of chattel paper or an instrument, reasonable care includes taking necessary steps to preserve rights against prior parties unless otherwise agreed.

(b) Except as otherwise provided in subsection (d), if a secured party has possession of collateral:

(1) reasonable expenses, including the cost of insurance and payment of taxes or other charges, incurred in the custody, preservation, use, or operation of the collateral are chargeable to the debtor and are secured by the collateral;

(2) the risk of accidental loss or damage is on the debtor to the extent of a deficiency in any effective insurance coverage;

(3) the secured party shall keep the collateral identifiable, but fungible collateral may be commingled; and

(4) the secured party may use or operate the collateral:

(A) for the purpose of preserving the collateral or its value;

(B) as permitted by an order of a court having competent jurisdiction; or

(C) except in the case of consumer goods, in the manner and to the extent agreed by the debtor.

(c) Except as otherwise provided in subsection (d), a secured party having possession of collateral or control of collateral under Section 9–104, 9–105, 9–106, or 9–107:

(1) may hold as additional security any proceeds, except money or funds, received from the collateral;

(2) shall apply money or funds received from the collateral to reduce the secured obligation, unless remitted to the debtor; and

(3) may create a security interest in the collateral.

(d) If the secured party is a buyer of accounts, chattel paper, payment intangibles, or promissory notes or a consignor:

(1) subsection (a) does not apply unless the secured party is entitled under an agreement:

(A) to charge back uncollected collateral; or

(B) otherwise to full or limited recourse against the debtor or a secondary obligor based on the nonpayment or other default of an account debtor or other obligor on the collateral; and

(2) subsections (b) and (c) do not apply.

§ 9–208. Additional Duties of Secured Party Having Control of Collateral.

(a) This section applies to cases in which there is no outstanding secured obligation and the secured party is not committed to make advances, incur obligations, or otherwise give value.

(b) Within 10 days after receiving an authenticated demand by the debtor:

(1) a secured party having control of a deposit account under Section 9–104(a)(2) shall send to the bank with which the deposit account is maintained an authenticated statement that releases the bank from any further obligation to comply with instructions originated by the secured party;

(2) a secured party having control of a deposit account under Section 9–104(a)(3) shall:

(A) pay the debtor the balance on deposit in the deposit account; or

(B) transfer the balance on deposit into a deposit account in the debtor's name;

(3) a secured party, other than a buyer, having control of electronic chattel paper under Section 9–105 shall:

(A) communicate the authoritative copy of the electronic chattel paper to the debtor or its designated custodian;

(B) if the debtor designates a custodian that is the designated custodian with which the authoritative copy of the electronic chattel paper is maintained for the secured party, communicate to the custodian an authenticated record releasing the designated custodian from any further obligation to comply with instructions originated by the secured party and instructing the custodian to comply with instructions originated by the debtor; and

(C) take appropriate action to enable the debtor or its designated custodian to make copies of or revisions to the authoritative copy which add or change an identified assignee of the authoritative copy without the consent of the secured party;

(4) a secured party having control of investment property under Section 8–106(d)(2) or 9–106(b) shall send to the securities intermediary or commodity intermediary with which the security entitlement or commodity contract is maintained an authenticated record that releases the securities intermediary or commodity intermediary from any further obligation to comply with entitlement orders or directions originated by the secured party; and

(5) a secured party having control of a letter-of-credit right under Section 9–107 shall send to each person having an unfulfilled obligation to pay or deliver proceeds of the letter of credit to the secured party an authenticated release from any further obligation to pay or deliver proceeds of the letter of credit to the secured party.

§ 9–209. Duties of Secured Party If Account Debtor Has Been Notified of Assignment.

(a) Except as otherwise provided in subsection (c), this section applies if:

(1) there is no outstanding secured obligation; and

(2) the secured party is not committed to make advances, incur obligations, or otherwise give value.

(b) Within 10 days after receiving an authenticated demand by the debtor, a secured party shall send to an account debtor that has received notification of an assignment to the secured party as assignee under Section 9–406(a) an authenticated record that releases the account debtor from any further obligation to the secured party.

(c) This section does not apply to an assignment constituting the sale of an account, chattel paper, or payment intangible.

§ 9–210. Request for Accounting; Request Regarding List of Collateral or Statement of Account.

(a) In this section:

(1) "Request" means a record of a type described in paragraph (2), (3), or (4).

(2) "Request for an accounting" means a record authenticated by a debtor requesting that the recipient provide an accounting of the unpaid obligations secured by collateral and reasonably identifying the transaction or relationship that is the subject of the request.

(3) "Request regarding a list of collateral" means a record authenticated by a debtor requesting that the recipient approve or correct a list of what the debtor believes to be the collateral securing an obligation and reasonably identifying the transaction or relationship that is the subject of the request.

(4) "Request regarding a statement of account" means a record authenticated by a debtor requesting that the recipient approve or correct a statement indicating what the debtor believes to be the aggregate amount of unpaid obligations secured by collateral as of a specified date and reasonably identifying the transaction or relationship that is the subject of the request.

(b) Subject to subsections (c), (d), (e), and (f), a secured party, other than a buyer of accounts, chattel paper, payment intangibles, or promissory notes or a consignor, shall comply with a request within 14 days after receipt:

(1) in the case of a request for an accounting, by authenticating and sending to the debtor an accounting; and

(2) in the case of a request regarding a list of collateral or a request regarding a statement of account, by authenticating and sending to the debtor an approval or correction.

(c) A secured party that claims a security interest in all of a particular type of collateral owned by the debtor may comply with a request regarding a list of collateral by sending to the debtor an authenticated record including a statement to that effect within 14 days after receipt.

(d) A person that receives a request regarding a list of collateral, claims no interest in the collateral when it receives the request, and claimed an interest in the collateral at an earlier time shall comply with the request within 14 days after receipt by sending to the debtor an authenticated record:

(1) disclaiming any interest in the collateral; and

(2) if known to the recipient, providing the name and mailing address of any assignee of or successor to the recipient's interest in the collateral.

(e) A person that receives a request for an accounting or a request regarding a statement of account, claims no interest in the obligations when it receives the request, and claimed an interest in the obligations at an earlier time shall comply with the request within 14 days after receipt by sending to the debtor an authenticated record:

(1) disclaiming any interest in the obligations; and

(2) if known to the recipient, providing the name and mailing address of any assignee of or successor to the recipient's interest in the obligations.

(f) A debtor is entitled without charge to one response to a request under this section during any six-month period. The secured party may require payment of a charge not exceeding $25 for each additional response.

As amended in 1999.

Part 3 Perfection and Priority

[Subpart 1. Law Governing Perfection and Priority]

§ 9–301. Law Governing Perfection and Priority of Security Interests.

Except as otherwise provided in Sections 9–303 through 9–306, the following rules determine the law governing perfection, the effect of perfection or nonperfection, and the priority of a security interest in collateral:

(1) Except as otherwise provided in this section, while a debtor is located in a jurisdiction, the local law of that jurisdiction governs perfection, the effect of perfection or nonperfection, and the priority of a security interest in collateral.

(2) While collateral is located in a jurisdiction, the local law of that jurisdiction governs perfection, the effect of perfection or nonperfection, and the priority of a possessory security interest in that collateral.

(3) Except as otherwise provided in paragraph (4), while negotiable documents, goods, instruments, money, or tangible chattel paper is located in a jurisdiction, the local law of that jurisdiction governs:

(A) perfection of a security interest in the goods by filing a fixture filing;

(B) perfection of a security interest in timber to be cut; and

(C) the effect of perfection or nonperfection and the priority of a nonpossessory security interest in the collateral.

(4) The local law of the jurisdiction in which the wellhead or minehead is located governs perfection, the effect of perfection or nonperfection, and the priority of a security interest in as-extracted collateral.

§ 9–302. Law Governing Perfection and Priority of Agricultural Liens.

While farm products are located in a jurisdiction, the local law of that jurisdiction governs perfection, the effect of perfection or nonperfection, and the priority of an agricultural lien on the farm products.

§ 9–303. Law Governing Perfection and Priority of Security Interests in Goods Covered by a Certificate of Title.

(a) This section applies to goods covered by a certificate of title, even if there is no other relationship between the jurisdiction under whose certificate of title the goods are covered and the goods or the debtor.

(b) Goods become covered by a certificate of title when a valid application for the certificate of title and the applicable fee are delivered to the appropriate authority. Goods cease to be covered by a certificate of title at the earlier of the time the certificate of title ceases to be effective under the law of the issuing jurisdiction or the time the goods become covered subsequently by a certificate of title issued by another jurisdiction.

(c) The local law of the jurisdiction under whose certificate of title the goods are covered governs perfection, the effect of perfection or nonperfection, and the priority of a security interest in goods covered by a certificate of title from the time the goods become covered by the certificate of title until the goods cease to be covered by the certificate of title.

§ 9–304. Law Governing Perfection and Priority of Security Interests in Deposit Accounts.

(a) The local law of a bank's jurisdiction governs perfection, the effect of perfection or nonperfection, and the priority of a security interest in a deposit account maintained with that bank.

(b) The following rules determine a bank's jurisdiction for purposes of this part:

(1) If an agreement between the bank and the debtor governing the deposit account expressly provides that a particular jurisdiction is the bank's jurisdiction for purposes of this part, this article, or [the Uniform Commercial Code], that jurisdiction is the bank's jurisdiction.

(2) If paragraph (1) does not apply and an agreement between the bank and its customer governing the deposit account expressly provides that the agreement is governed by the law of a particular jurisdiction, that jurisdiction is the bank's jurisdiction.

(3) If neither paragraph (1) nor paragraph (2) applies and an agreement between the bank and its customer governing the deposit account expressly provides that the deposit account is maintained at an office in a particular jurisdiction, that jurisdiction is the bank's jurisdiction.

(4) If none of the preceding paragraphs applies, the bank's jurisdiction is the jurisdiction in which the office identified in an account statement as the office serving the customer's account is located.

(5) If none of the preceding paragraphs applies, the bank's jurisdiction is the jurisdiction in which the chief executive office of the bank is located.

§ 9–305. Law Governing Perfection and Priority of Security Interests in Investment Property.

(a) Except as otherwise provided in subsection (c), the following rules apply:

(1) While a security certificate is located in a jurisdiction, the local law of that jurisdiction governs perfection, the effect of perfection or nonperfection, and the priority of a security interest in the certificated security represented thereby.

(2) The local law of the issuer's jurisdiction as specified in Section 8–110(d) governs perfection, the effect of perfection or nonperfection, and the priority of a security interest in an uncertificated security.

(3) The local law of the securities intermediary's jurisdiction as specified in Section 8–110(e) governs perfection, the effect of perfection or nonperfection, and the priority of a security interest in a security entitlement or securities account.

(4) The local law of the commodity intermediary's jurisdiction governs perfection, the effect of perfection or nonperfection, and the priority of a security interest in a commodity contract or commodity account.

(b) The following rules determine a commodity intermediary's jurisdiction for purposes of this part:

(1) If an agreement between the commodity intermediary and commodity customer governing the commodity account expressly provides that a particular jurisdiction is the commodity intermediary's jurisdiction for purposes of this part, this article, or [the Uniform Commercial Code], that jurisdiction is the commodity intermediary's jurisdiction.

(2) If paragraph (1) does not apply and an agreement between the commodity intermediary and commodity customer governing the commodity account expressly provides that the agreement is governed by the law of a particular jurisdiction, that jurisdiction is the commodity intermediary's jurisdiction.

(3) If neither paragraph (1) nor paragraph (2) applies and an agreement between the commodity intermediary and commodity customer governing the commodity account expressly provides that the commodity account is maintained at an office in a particular jurisdiction, that jurisdiction is the commodity intermediary's jurisdiction.

(4) If none of the preceding paragraphs applies, the commodity intermediary's jurisdiction is the jurisdiction in which the office identified in an account statement as the office serving the commodity customer's account is located.

(5) If none of the preceding paragraphs applies, the commodity intermediary's jurisdiction is the jurisdiction in which the chief executive office of the commodity intermediary is located.

(c) The local law of the jurisdiction in which the debtor is located governs:

(1) perfection of a security interest in investment property by filing;

(2) automatic perfection of a security interest in investment property created by a broker or securities intermediary; and

(3) automatic perfection of a security interest in a commodity contract or commodity account created by a commodity intermediary.

§ 9–306. Law Governing Perfection and Priority of Security Interests in Letter-of-Credit Rights.

(a) Subject to subsection (c), the local law of the issuer's jurisdiction or a nominated person's jurisdiction governs perfection, the effect of perfection or nonperfection, and the priority of a security interest in a letter-of-credit right if the issuer's jurisdiction or nominated person's jurisdiction is a State.

(b) For purposes of this part, an issuer's jurisdiction or nominated person's jurisdiction is the jurisdiction whose law governs the liability of the issuer or nominated person with respect to the letter-of-credit right as provided in Section 5–116.

(c) This section does not apply to a security interest that is perfected only under Section 9–308(d).

§ 9–307. Location of Debtor.

(a) In this section, "place of business" means a place where a debtor conducts its affairs.

(b) Except as otherwise provided in this section, the following rules determine a debtor's location:

(1) A debtor who is an individual is located at the individual's principal residence.

(2) A debtor that is an organization and has only one place of business is located at its place of business.

(3) A debtor that is an organization and has more than one place of business is located at its chief executive office.

(c) Subsection (b) applies only if a debtor's residence, place of business, or chief executive office, as applicable, is located in a jurisdiction whose law generally requires information concerning the existence of a nonpossessory security interest to be made generally available in a filing, recording, or registration system as a condition or result of the security interest's obtaining priority over the rights of a lien creditor with respect to the collateral. If subsection (b) does not apply, the debtor is located in the District of Columbia.

(d) A person that ceases to exist, have a residence, or have a place of business continues to be located in the jurisdiction specified by subsections (b) and (c).

(e) A registered organization that is organized under the law of a State is located in that State.

(f) Except as otherwise provided in subsection (i), a registered organization that is organized under the law of the United States and a branch or agency of a bank that is not organized under the law of the United States or a State are located:

(1) in the State that the law of the United States designates, if the law designates a State of location;

(2) in the State that the registered organization, branch, or agency designates, if the law of the United States authorizes the registered organization, branch, or agency to designate its State of location; or

(3) in the District of Columbia, if neither paragraph (1) nor paragraph (2) applies.

(g) A registered organization continues to be located in the jurisdiction specified by subsection (e) or (f) notwithstanding:

(1) the suspension, revocation, forfeiture, or lapse of the registered organization's status as such in its jurisdiction of organization; or

(2) the dissolution, winding up, or cancellation of the existence of the registered organization.

(h) The United States is located in the District of Columbia.

(i) A branch or agency of a bank that is not organized under the law of the United States or a State is located in the State in which the branch or agency is licensed, if all branches and agencies of the bank are licensed in only one State.

(j) A foreign air carrier under the Federal Aviation Act of 1958, as amended, is located at the designated office of the agent upon which service of process may be made on behalf of the carrier.

(k) This section applies only for purposes of this part.

[Subpart 2. Perfection]

§ 9–308. When Security Interest or Agricultural Lien Is Perfected; Continuity of Perfection.

(a) Except as otherwise provided in this section and Section 9–309, a security interest is perfected if it has attached and all of the applicable requirements for perfection in Sections 9–310 through 9–316 have been satisfied. A security interest is perfected when it attaches if the applicable requirements are satisfied before the security interest attaches.

(b) An agricultural lien is perfected if it has become effective and all of the applicable requirements for perfection in Section 9–310 have been satisfied. An agricultural lien is perfected when it becomes effective if the applicable requirements are satisfied before the agricultural lien becomes effective.

(c) A security interest or agricultural lien is perfected continuously if it is originally perfected by one method under this article and is later perfected by another method under this article, without an intermediate period when it was unperfected.

(d) Perfection of a security interest in collateral also perfects a security interest in a supporting obligation for the collateral.

(e) Perfection of a security interest in a right to payment or performance also perfects a security interest in a security interest, mortgage, or other lien on personal or real property securing the right.

(f) Perfection of a security interest in a securities account also perfects a security interest in the security entitlements carried in the securities account.

(g) Perfection of a security interest in a commodity account also perfects a security interest in the commodity contracts carried in the commodity account.

Legislative Note: Any statute conflicting with subsection (e) must be made expressly subject to that subsection.

§ 9–309. Security Interest Perfected upon Attachment.

The following security interests are perfected when they attach:

(1) a purchase-money security interest in consumer goods, except as otherwise provided in Section 9–311(b) with respect to consumer goods that are subject to a statute or treaty described in Section 9–311(a);

(2) an assignment of accounts or payment intangibles which does not by itself or in conjunction with other assignments to the same assignee transfer a significant part of the assignor's outstanding accounts or payment intangibles;

(3) a sale of a payment intangible;

(4) a sale of a promissory note;

(5) a security interest created by the assignment of a health-care-insurance receivable to the provider of the health-care goods or services;

(6) a security interest arising under Section 2–401, 2–505, 2–711(3), or 2A–508(5), until the debtor obtains possession of the collateral;

(7) a security interest of a collecting bank arising under Section 4–210;

(8) a security interest of an issuer or nominated person arising under Section 5–118;

(9) a security interest arising in the delivery of a financial asset under Section 9–206(c);

(10) a security interest in investment property created by a broker or securities intermediary;

(11) a security interest in a commodity contract or a commodity account created by a commodity intermediary;

(12) an assignment for the benefit of all creditors of the transferor and subsequent transfers by the assignee thereunder; and

(13) a security interest created by an assignment of a beneficial interest in a decedent's estate; and

(14) a sale by an individual of an account that is a right to payment of winnings in a lottery or other game of chance.

§ 9–310. When Filing Required to Perfect Security Interest or Agricultural Lien; Security Interests and Agricultural Liens to Which Filing Provisions Do Not Apply.

(a) Except as otherwise provided in subsection (b) and Section 9–312(b), a financing statement must be filed to perfect all security interests and agricultural liens.

(b) The filing of a financing statement is not necessary to perfect a security interest:

(1) that is perfected under Section 9–308(d), (e), (f), or (g);

(2) that is perfected under Section 9–309 when it attaches;

(3) in property subject to a statute, regulation, or treaty described in Section 9–311(a);

(4) in goods in possession of a bailee which is perfected under Section 9–312(d)(1) or (2);

(5) in certificated securities, documents, goods, or instruments which is perfected without filing or possession under Section 9–312(e), (f), or (g);

(6) in collateral in the secured party's possession under Section 9–313;

(7) in a certificated security which is perfected by delivery of the security certificate to the secured party under Section 9–313;

(8) in deposit accounts, electronic chattel paper, investment property, or letter-of-credit rights which is perfected by control under Section 9–314;

(9) in proceeds which is perfected under Section 9–315; or

(10) that is perfected under Section 9–316.

(c) If a secured party assigns a perfected security interest or agricultural lien, a filing under this article is not required to continue the perfected status of the security interest against creditors of and transferees from the original debtor.

§ 9–311. Perfection of Security Interests in Property Subject to Certain Statutes, Regulations, and Treaties.

(a) Except as otherwise provided in subsection (d), the filing of a financing statement is not necessary or effective to perfect a security interest in property subject to:

(1) a statute, regulation, or treaty of the United States whose requirements for a security interest's obtaining priority over the rights of a lien creditor with respect to the property preempt Section 9–310(a);

(2) [list any certificate-of-title statute covering automobiles, trailers, mobile homes, boats, farm tractors, or the like, which provides for a security interest to be indicated on the certificate as a condition or result of perfection, and any non-Uniform Commercial Code central filing statute]; or

(3) a certificate-of-title statute of another jurisdiction which provides for a security interest to be indicated on the certificate as a condition or result of the security interest's obtaining priority over the rights of a lien creditor with respect to the property.

(b) Compliance with the requirements of a statute, regulation, or treaty described in subsection (a) for obtaining priority over the rights of a lien creditor is equivalent to the filing of a financing statement under this article. Except as otherwise provided in subsection (d) and Sections 9–313 and 9–316(d) and (e) for goods covered by a certificate of title, a security interest in property subject to a statute, regulation, or treaty described in subsection (a) may be perfected only by compliance with those requirements, and a security interest so perfected remains perfected notwithstanding a change in the use or transfer of possession of the collateral.

(c) Except as otherwise provided in subsection (d) and Section 9–316(d) and (e), duration and renewal of perfection of a security interest perfected by compliance with the requirements prescribed by a statute, regulation, or treaty described in subsection (a) are governed by the statute, regulation, or treaty. In other respects, the security interest is subject to this article.

(d) During any period in which collateral subject to a statute specified in subsection (a)(2) is inventory held for sale or lease by a person or leased by that person as lessor and that person is in the business of selling goods of that kind, this section does not apply to a security interest in that collateral created by that person.

Legislative Note: This Article contemplates that perfection of a security interest in goods covered by a certificate of title occurs upon receipt by appropriate State officials of a properly tendered application for a certificate of title on which the security interest is to be indicated, without a relation back to an earlier time. States whose certificate-of-title statutes provide for perfection at a different time or contain a relation-back provision should amend the statutes accordingly.

§ 9–312. Perfection of Security Interests in Chattel Paper, Deposit Accounts, Documents, Goods Covered by Documents, Instruments, Investment Property, Letter-of-Credit Rights, and Money; Perfection by Permissive Filing; Temporary Perfection without Filing or Transfer of Possession.

(a) A security interest in chattel paper, negotiable documents, instruments, or investment property may be perfected by filing.

(b) Except as otherwise provided in Section 9–315(c) and (d) for proceeds:

(1) a security interest in a deposit account may be perfected only by control under Section 9–314;

(2) and except as otherwise provided in Section 9–308(d), a security interest in a letter-of-credit right may be perfected only by control under Section 9–314; and

(3) a security interest in money may be perfected only by the secured party's taking possession under Section 9–313.

(c) While goods are in the possession of a bailee that has issued a negotiable document covering the goods:

(1) a security interest in the goods may be perfected by perfecting a security interest in the document; and

(2) a security interest perfected in the document has priority over any security interest that becomes perfected in the goods by another method during that time.

(d) While goods are in the possession of a bailee that has issued a nonnegotiable document covering the goods, a security interest in the goods may be perfected by:

(1) issuance of a document in the name of the secured party;

(2) the bailee's receipt of notification of the secured party's interest; or

(3) filing as to the goods.

(e) A security interest in certificated securities, negotiable documents, or instruments is perfected without filing or the taking of possession for a period of 20 days from the time it attaches to the extent that it arises for new value given under an authenticated security agreement.

(f) A perfected security interest in a negotiable document or goods in possession of a bailee, other than one that has issued a negotiable document for the goods, remains perfected for 20 days without filing if the secured party makes available to the debtor the goods or documents representing the goods for the purpose of:

(1) ultimate sale or exchange; or

(2) loading, unloading, storing, shipping, transshipping, manufacturing, processing, or otherwise dealing with them in a manner preliminary to their sale or exchange.

(g) A perfected security interest in a certificated security or instrument remains perfected for 20 days without filing if the secured party delivers the security certificate or instrument to the debtor for the purpose of:

(1) ultimate sale or exchange; or

(2) presentation, collection, enforcement, renewal, or registration of transfer.

(h) After the 20-day period specified in subsection (e), (f), or (g) expires, perfection depends upon compliance with this article.

§ 9–313. When Possession by or Delivery to Secured Party Perfects Security Interest without Filing.

(a) Except as otherwise provided in subsection (b), a secured party may perfect a security interest in negotiable documents, goods, instruments, money, or tangible chattel paper by taking possession of the collateral. A secured party may perfect a security interest in certificated securities by taking delivery of the certificated securities under Section 8–301.

(b) With respect to goods covered by a certificate of title issued by this State, a secured party may perfect a security interest in the goods by taking possession of the goods only in the circumstances described in Section 9–316(d).

(c) With respect to collateral other than certificated securities and goods covered by a document, a secured party takes possession of collateral in the possession of a person other than the debtor, the secured party, or a lessee of the collateral from the debtor in the ordinary course of the debtor's business, when:

(1) the person in possession authenticates a record acknowledging that it holds possession of the collateral for the secured party's benefit; or

(2) the person takes possession of the collateral after having authenticated a record acknowledging that it will hold possession of collateral for the secured party's benefit.

(d) If perfection of a security interest depends upon possession of the collateral by a secured party, perfection occurs no earlier than the time the secured party takes possession and continues only while the secured party retains possession.

(e) A security interest in a certificated security in registered form is perfected by delivery when delivery of the certificated security occurs under Section 8–301 and remains perfected by delivery until the debtor obtains possession of the security certificate.

(f) A person in possession of collateral is not required to acknowledge that it holds possession for a secured party's benefit.

(g) If a person acknowledges that it holds possession for the secured party's benefit:

(1) the acknowledgment is effective under subsection (c) or Section 8–301(a), even if the acknowledgment violates the rights of a debtor; and

(2) unless the person otherwise agrees or law other than this article otherwise provides, the person does not owe any duty to the secured party and is not required to confirm the acknowledgment to another person.

(h) A secured party having possession of collateral does not relinquish possession by delivering the collateral to a person other than the debtor or a lessee of the collateral from the debtor in the ordinary course of the debtor's business if the person was instructed before the delivery or is instructed contemporaneously with the delivery:

(1) to hold possession of the collateral for the secured party's benefit; or

(2) to redeliver the collateral to the secured party.

(i) A secured party does not relinquish possession, even if a delivery under subsection (h) violates the rights of a debtor. A person to which collateral is delivered under subsection (h) does not owe any duty to the secured party and is not required to confirm the delivery to another person unless the person otherwise agrees or law other than this article otherwise provides.

§ 9–314. Perfection by Control.

(a) A security interest in investment property, deposit accounts, letter-of-credit rights, or electronic chattel paper may be perfected by control of the collateral under Section 9–104, 9–105, 9–106, or 9–107.

(b) A security interest in deposit accounts, electronic chattel paper, or letter-of-credit rights is perfected by control under Section 9–104, 9–105, or 9–107 when the secured party obtains control and remains perfected by control only while the secured party retains control.

(c) A security interest in investment property is perfected by control under Section 9–106 from the time the secured party obtains control and remains perfected by control until:

(1) the secured party does not have control; and

(2) one of the following occurs:

(A) if the collateral is a certificated security, the debtor has or acquires possession of the security certificate;

(B) if the collateral is an uncertificated security, the issuer has registered or registers the debtor as the registered owner; or

(C) if the collateral is a security entitlement, the debtor is or becomes the entitlement holder.

§ 9–315. Secured Party's Rights on Disposition of Collateral and in Proceeds.

(a) Except as otherwise provided in this article and in Section 2–403(2):

(1) a security interest or agricultural lien continues in collateral notwithstanding sale, lease, license, exchange, or other disposition thereof unless the secured party authorized the disposition free of the security interest or agricultural lien; and

(2) a security interest attaches to any identifiable proceeds of collateral.

(b) Proceeds that are commingled with other property are identifiable proceeds:

(1) if the proceeds are goods, to the extent provided by Section 9–336; and

(2) if the proceeds are not goods, to the extent that the secured party identifies the proceeds by a method of tracing, including application of equitable principles, that is permitted under law other than this article with respect to commingled property of the type involved.

(c) A security interest in proceeds is a perfected security interest if the security interest in the original collateral was perfected.

(d) A perfected security interest in proceeds becomes unperfected on the 21st day after the security interest attaches to the proceeds unless:

(1) the following conditions are satisfied:

(A) a filed financing statement covers the original collateral;

(B) the proceeds are collateral in which a security interest may be perfected by filing in the office in which the financing statement has been filed; and

(C) the proceeds are not acquired with cash proceeds;

(2) the proceeds are identifiable cash proceeds; or

(3) the security interest in the proceeds is perfected other than under subsection (c) when the security interest attaches to the proceeds or within 20 days thereafter.

(e) If a filed financing statement covers the original collateral, a security interest in proceeds which remains perfected under subsection (d)(1) becomes unperfected at the later of:

(1) when the effectiveness of the filed financing statement lapses under Section 9–515 or is terminated under Section 9–513; or

(2) the 21st day after the security interest attaches to the proceeds.

§ 9–316. Continued Perfection of Security Interest Following Change in Governing Law.

(a) A security interest perfected pursuant to the law of the jurisdiction designated in Section 9–301(1) or 9–305(c) remains perfected until the earliest of:

(1) the time perfection would have ceased under the law of that jurisdiction;

(2) the expiration of four months after a change of the debtor's location to another jurisdiction; or

(3) the expiration of one year after a transfer of collateral to a person that thereby becomes a debtor and is located in another jurisdiction.

(b) If a security interest described in subsection (a) becomes perfected under the law of the other jurisdiction before the earliest time or event described in that subsection, it remains perfected thereafter. If the security interest does not become perfected under the law of the other jurisdiction before the earliest time or event, it becomes unperfected and is deemed never to have been perfected as against a purchaser of the collateral for value.

(c) A possessory security interest in collateral, other than goods covered by a certificate of title and as-extracted collateral consisting of goods, remains continuously perfected if:

(1) the collateral is located in one jurisdiction and subject to a security interest perfected under the law of that jurisdiction;

(2) thereafter the collateral is brought into another jurisdiction; and

(3) upon entry into the other jurisdiction, the security interest is perfected under the law of the other jurisdiction.

(d) Except as otherwise provided in subsection (e), a security interest in goods covered by a certificate of title which is perfected by any method under the law of another jurisdiction when the goods become covered by a certificate of title from this State remains perfected until the security interest would have become unperfected under the law of the other jurisdiction had the goods not become so covered.

(e) A security interest described in subsection (d) becomes unperfected as against a purchaser of the goods for value and is deemed never to have been perfected as against a purchaser of the goods for value if the applicable requirements for perfection under Section 9–311(b) or 9–313 are not satisfied before the earlier of:

(1) the time the security interest would have become unperfected under the law of the other jurisdiction had the goods not become covered by a certificate of title from this State; or

(2) the expiration of four months after the goods had become so covered.

(f) A security interest in deposit accounts, letter-of-credit rights, or investment property which is perfected under the law of the bank's jurisdiction, the issuer's jurisdiction, a nominated person's jurisdiction, the securities intermediary's jurisdiction, or the commodity intermediary's jurisdiction, as applicable, remains perfected until the earlier of:

(1) the time the security interest would have become unperfected under the law of that jurisdiction; or

(2) the expiration of four months after a change of the applicable jurisdiction to another jurisdiction.

(g) If a security interest described in subsection (f) becomes perfected under the law of the other jurisdiction before the earlier of the time or the end of the period described in that subsection, it remains perfected thereafter. If the security interest does not become perfected under the law of the other jurisdiction before the earlier of that time or the end of that period, it becomes unperfected and is deemed never to have been perfected as against a purchaser of the collateral for value.

[Subpart 3. Priority]

§ 9–317. Interests That Take Priority over or Take Free of Security Interest or Agricultural Lien.

(a) A security interest or agricultural lien is subordinate to the rights of:

(1) a person entitled to priority under Section 9–322; and

(2) except as otherwise provided in subsection (e), a person that becomes a lien creditor before the earlier of the time:

(A) the security interest or agricultural lien is perfected; or

(B) one of the conditions specified in Section 9–203(b)(3) is met and a financing statement covering the collateral is filed.

(b) Except as otherwise provided in subsection (e), a buyer, other than a secured party, of tangible chattel paper, documents, goods, instruments, or a security certificate takes free of a security interest or agricultural lien if the buyer gives value and receives delivery of the collateral without knowledge of the security interest or agricultural lien and before it is perfected.

(c) Except as otherwise provided in subsection (e), a lessee of goods takes free of a security interest or agricultural lien if the lessee gives value and receives delivery of the collateral without knowledge of the security interest or agricultural lien and before it is perfected.

(d) A licensee of a general intangible or a buyer, other than a secured party, of accounts, electronic chattel paper, general intangibles, or investment property other than a certificated security takes free of a security interest if the licensee or buyer gives value without knowledge of the security interest and before it is perfected.

(e) Except as otherwise provided in Sections 9–320 and 9–321, if a person files a financing statement with respect to a purchase-money security interest before or within 20 days after the debtor receives delivery of the collateral, the security interest takes priority over the rights of a buyer, lessee, or lien creditor which arise between the time the security interest attaches and the time of filing.

As amended in 2000.

§ 9–318. No Interest Retained in Right to Payment That Is Sold; Rights and Title of Seller of Account or Chattel Paper with Respect to Creditors and Purchasers.

(a) A debtor that has sold an account, chattel paper, payment intangible, or promissory note does not retain a legal or equitable interest in the collateral sold.

(b) For purposes of determining the rights of creditors of, and purchasers for value of an account or chattel paper from, a debtor that has sold an account or chattel paper, while the buyer's security interest is unperfected, the debtor is deemed to have rights and title to the account or chattel paper identical to those the debtor sold.

§ 9–319. Rights and Title of Consignee with Respect to Creditors and Purchasers.

(a) Except as otherwise provided in subsection (b), for purposes of determining the rights of creditors of, and purchasers for value of goods from, a consignee, while the goods are in the possession of the consignee, the consignee is deemed to have rights and title to the goods identical to those the consignor had or had power to transfer.

(b) For purposes of determining the rights of a creditor of a consignee, law other than this article determines the rights and title of a consignee while goods are in the consignee's possession if, under this part, a perfected security interest held by the consignor would have priority over the rights of the creditor.

§ 9–320. Buyer of Goods.

(a) Except as otherwise provided in subsection (e), a buyer in ordinary course of business, other than a person buying farm products from a person engaged in farming operations, takes free of a security interest created by the buyer's seller, even if the security interest is perfected and the buyer knows of its existence.

(b) Except as otherwise provided in subsection (e), a buyer of goods from a person who used or bought the goods for use primarily for personal, family, or household purposes takes free of a security interest, even if perfected, if the buyer buys:

(1) without knowledge of the security interest;

(2) for value;

(3) primarily for the buyer's personal, family, or household purposes; and

(4) before the filing of a financing statement covering the goods.

(c) To the extent that it affects the priority of a security interest over a buyer of goods under subsection (b), the period of effectiveness of a filing made in the jurisdiction in which the seller is located is governed by Section 9–316(a) and (b).

(d) A buyer in ordinary course of business buying oil, gas, or other minerals at the wellhead or minehead or after extraction takes free of an interest arising out of an encumbrance.

(e) Subsections (a) and (b) do not affect a security interest in goods in the possession of the secured party under Section 9–313.

§ 9–321. Licensee of General Intangible and Lessee of Goods in Ordinary Course of Business.

(a) In this section, "licensee in ordinary course of business" means a person that becomes a licensee of a general intangible in good faith, without knowledge that the license violates the rights of another person in the general intangible, and in the ordinary course from a person in the business of licensing general intangibles of that kind. A person becomes a licensee in the ordinary course if the license to the person comports with the usual or customary practices in the kind of business in which the licensor is engaged or with the licensor's own usual or customary practices.

(b) A licensee in ordinary course of business takes its rights under a nonexclusive license free of a security interest in the general intangible created by the licensor, even if the security interest is perfected and the licensee knows of its existence.

(c) A lessee in ordinary course of business takes its leasehold interest free of a security interest in the goods created by the lessor, even if the security interest is perfected and the lessee knows of its existence.

§ 9–322. Priorities among Conflicting Security Interests in and Agricultural Liens on Same Collateral.

(a) Except as otherwise provided in this section, priority among conflicting security interests and agricultural liens in the same collateral is determined according to the following rules:

(1) Conflicting perfected security interests and agricultural liens rank according to priority in time of filing or perfection. Priority dates from the earlier of the time a filing covering the collateral is first made or the security interest or agricultural lien is first perfected, if there is no period thereafter when there is neither filing nor perfection.

(2) A perfected security interest or agricultural lien has priority over a conflicting unperfected security interest or agricultural lien.

(3) The first security interest or agricultural lien to attach or become effective has priority if conflicting security interests and agricultural liens are unperfected.

(b) For the purposes of subsection (a)(1):

(1) the time of filing or perfection as to a security interest in collateral is also the time of filing or perfection as to a security interest in proceeds; and

(2) the time of filing or perfection as to a security interest in collateral supported by a supporting obligation is also the time

of filing or perfection as to a security interest in the supporting obligation.

(c) Except as otherwise provided in subsection (f), a security interest in collateral which qualifies for priority over a conflicting security interest under Section 9–327, 9–328, 9–329, 9–330, or 9–331 also has priority over a conflicting security interest in:

(1) any supporting obligation for the collateral; and

(2) proceeds of the collateral if:

(A) the security interest in proceeds is perfected;

(B) the proceeds are cash proceeds or of the same type as the collateral; and

(C) in the case of proceeds that are proceeds of proceeds, all intervening proceeds are cash proceeds, proceeds of the same type as the collateral, or an account relating to the collateral.

(d) Subject to subsection (e) and except as otherwise provided in subsection (f), if a security interest in chattel paper, deposit accounts, negotiable documents, instruments, investment property, or letter-of-credit rights is perfected by a method other than filing, conflicting perfected security interests in proceeds of the collateral rank according to priority in time of filing.

(e) Subsection (d) applies only if the proceeds of the collateral are not cash proceeds, chattel paper, negotiable documents, instruments, investment property, or letter-of-credit rights.

(f) Subsections (a) through (e) are subject to:

(1) subsection (g) and the other provisions of this part;

(2) Section 4–210 with respect to a security interest of a collecting bank;

(3) Section 5–118 with respect to a security interest of an issuer or nominated person; and

(4) Section 9–110 with respect to a security interest arising under Article 2 or 2A.

(g) A perfected agricultural lien on collateral has priority over a conflicting security interest in or agricultural lien on the same collateral if the statute creating the agricultural lien so provides.

§ 9–323. Future Advances.

(a) Except as otherwise provided in subsection (c), for purposes of determining the priority of a perfected security interest under Section 9–322(a)(1), perfection of the security interest dates from the time an advance is made to the extent that the security interest secures an advance that:

(1) is made while the security interest is perfected only:

(A) under Section 9–309 when it attaches; or

(B) temporarily under Section 9–312(e), (f), or (g); and

(2) is not made pursuant to a commitment entered into before or while the security interest is perfected by a method other than under Section 9–309 or 9–312(e), (f), or (g).

(b) Except as otherwise provided in subsection (c), a security interest is subordinate to the rights of a person that becomes a lien creditor to the extent that the security interest secures an advance made more than 45 days after the person becomes a lien creditor unless the advance is made:

(1) without knowledge of the lien; or

(2) pursuant to a commitment entered into without knowledge of the lien.

(c) Subsections (a) and (b) do not apply to a security interest held by a secured party that is a buyer of accounts, chattel paper, payment intangibles, or promissory notes or a consignor.

(d) Except as otherwise provided in subsection (e), a buyer of goods other than a buyer in ordinary course of business takes free of a security interest to the extent that it secures advances made after the earlier of:

(1) the time the secured party acquires knowledge of the buyer's purchase; or

(2) 45 days after the purchase.

(e) Subsection (d) does not apply if the advance is made pursuant to a commitment entered into without knowledge of the buyer's purchase and before the expiration of the 45-day period.

(f) Except as otherwise provided in subsection (g), a lessee of goods, other than a lessee in ordinary course of business, takes the leasehold interest free of a security interest to the extent that it secures advances made after the earlier of:

(1) the time the secured party acquires knowledge of the lease; or

(2) 45 days after the lease contract becomes enforceable.

(g) Subsection (f) does not apply if the advance is made pursuant to a commitment entered into without knowledge of the lease and before the expiration of the 45-day period.

As amended in 1999.

§ 9–324. Priority of Purchase-Money Security Interests.

(a) Except as otherwise provided in subsection (g), a perfected purchase-money security interest in goods other than inventory or livestock has priority over a conflicting security interest in the same goods, and, except as otherwise provided in Section 9–327, a perfected security interest in its identifiable proceeds also has priority, if the purchase-money security interest is perfected when the debtor receives possession of the collateral or within 20 days thereafter.

(b) Subject to subsection (c) and except as otherwise provided in subsection (g), a perfected purchase-money security interest in inventory has priority over a conflicting security interest in the same inventory, has priority over a conflicting security interest in chattel paper or an instrument constituting proceeds of the inventory and in proceeds of the chattel paper, if so provided in Section 9–330, and, except as otherwise provided in Section 9–327, also has priority in identifiable cash proceeds of the inventory to the extent the identifiable cash proceeds are received on or before the delivery of the inventory to a buyer, if:

(1) the purchase-money security interest is perfected when the debtor receives possession of the inventory;

(2) the purchase-money secured party sends an authenticated notification to the holder of the conflicting security interest;

(3) the holder of the conflicting security interest receives the notification within five years before the debtor receives possession of the inventory; and

(4) the notification states that the person sending the notification has or expects to acquire a purchase-money security interest in inventory of the debtor and describes the inventory.

(c) Subsections (b)(2) through (4) apply only if the holder of the conflicting security interest had filed a financing statement covering the same types of inventory:

(1) if the purchase-money security interest is perfected by filing, before the date of the filing; or

(2) if the purchase-money security interest is temporarily perfected without filing or possession under Section 9–312(f), before the beginning of the 20-day period thereunder.

(d) Subject to subsection (e) and except as otherwise provided in subsection (g), a perfected purchase-money security interest in livestock that are farm products has priority over a conflicting security interest in the same livestock, and, except as otherwise provided in Section 9–327, a perfected security interest in their identifiable proceeds and identifiable products in their unmanufactured states also has priority, if:

(1) the purchase-money security interest is perfected when the debtor receives possession of the livestock;

(2) the purchase-money secured party sends an authenticated notification to the holder of the conflicting security interest;

(3) the holder of the conflicting security interest receives the notification within six months before the debtor receives possession of the livestock; and

(4) the notification states that the person sending the notification has or expects to acquire a purchase-money security interest in livestock of the debtor and describes the livestock.

(e) Subsections (d)(2) through (4) apply only if the holder of the conflicting security interest had filed a financing statement covering the same types of livestock:

(1) if the purchase-money security interest is perfected by filing, before the date of the filing; or

(2) if the purchase-money security interest is temporarily perfected without filing or possession under Section 9–312(f), before the beginning of the 20-day period thereunder.

(f) Except as otherwise provided in subsection (g), a perfected purchase-money security interest in software has priority over a conflicting security interest in the same collateral, and, except as otherwise provided in Section 9–327, a perfected security interest in its identifiable proceeds also has priority, to the extent that the purchase-money security interest in the goods in which the software was acquired for use has priority in the goods and proceeds of the goods under this section.

(g) If more than one security interest qualifies for priority in the same collateral under subsection (a), (b), (d), or (f):

(1) a security interest securing an obligation incurred as all or part of the price of the collateral has priority over a security interest securing an obligation incurred for value given to enable the debtor to acquire rights in or the use of collateral; and

(2) in all other cases, Section 9–322(a) applies to the qualifying security interests.

§ 9–325. Priority of Security Interests in Transferred Collateral.

(a) Except as otherwise provided in subsection (b), a security interest created by a debtor is subordinate to a security interest in the same collateral created by another person if:

(1) the debtor acquired the collateral subject to the security interest created by the other person;

(2) the security interest created by the other person was perfected when the debtor acquired the collateral; and

(3) there is no period thereafter when the security interest is unperfected.

(b) Subsection (a) subordinates a security interest only if the security interest:

(1) otherwise would have priority solely under Section 9–322(a) or 9–324; or

(2) arose solely under Section 2–711(3) or 2A–508(5).

§ 9–326. Priority of Security Interests Created by New Debtor.

(a) Subject to subsection (b), a security interest created by a new debtor which is perfected by a filed financing statement that is effective solely under Section 9–508 in collateral in which a new debtor has or acquires rights is subordinate to a security interest in the same collateral which is perfected other than by a filed financing statement that is effective solely under Section 9–508.

(b) The other provisions of this part determine the priority among conflicting security interests in the same collateral perfected by filed financing statements that are effective solely under Section 9–508. However, if the security agreements to which a new debtor became bound as debtor were not entered into by the same original debtor, the conflicting security interests rank according to priority in time of the new debtor's having become bound.

§ 9–327. Priority of Security Interests in Deposit Account.

The following rules govern priority among conflicting security interests in the same deposit account:

(1) A security interest held by a secured party having control of the deposit account under Section 9–104 has priority over a conflicting security interest held by a secured party that does not have control.

(2) Except as otherwise provided in paragraphs (3) and (4), security interests perfected by control under Section 9–314 rank according to priority in time of obtaining control.

(3) Except as otherwise provided in paragraph (4), a security interest held by the bank with which the deposit account is maintained has priority over a conflicting security interest held by another secured party.

(4) A security interest perfected by control under Section 9–104(a)(3) has priority over a security interest held by the bank with which the deposit account is maintained.

§ 9–328. Priority of Security Interests in Investment Property.

The following rules govern priority among conflicting security interests in the same investment property:

(1) A security interest held by a secured party having control of investment property under Section 9–106 has priority over a security interest held by a secured party that does not have control of the investment property.

(2) Except as otherwise provided in paragraphs (3) and (4), conflicting security interests held by secured parties each of which has control under Section 9–106 rank according to priority in time of:

(A) if the collateral is a security, obtaining control;

(B) if the collateral is a security entitlement carried in a securities account and:

(i) if the secured party obtained control under Section 8–106(d)(1), the secured party's becoming the person for which the securities account is maintained;

(ii) if the secured party obtained control under Section 8–106(d)(2), the securities intermediary's agreement to comply with the secured party's entitlement orders with respect to security entitlements carried or to be carried in the securities account; or

(iii) if the secured party obtained control through another person under Section 8–106(d)(3), the time on which priority would be based under this paragraph if the other person were the secured party; or

(C) if the collateral is a commodity contract carried with a commodity intermediary, the satisfaction of the requirement for control specified in Section 9–106(b)(2) with respect to commodity contracts carried or to be carried with the commodity intermediary.

(3) A security interest held by a securities intermediary in a security entitlement or a securities account maintained with the securities intermediary has priority over a conflicting security interest held by another secured party.

(4) A security interest held by a commodity intermediary in a commodity contract or a commodity account maintained with the commodity intermediary has priority over a conflicting security interest held by another secured party.

(5) A security interest in a certificated security in registered form which is perfected by taking delivery under Section 9–313(a) and not by control under Section 9–314 has priority over a conflicting security interest perfected by a method other than control.

(6) Conflicting security interests created by a broker, securities intermediary, or commodity intermediary which are perfected without control under Section 9–106 rank equally.

(7) In all other cases, priority among conflicting security interests in investment property is governed by Sections 9–322 and 9–323.

§ 9–329. Priority of Security Interests in Letter-of-Credit Right.

The following rules govern priority among conflicting security interests in the same letter-of-credit right:

(1) A security interest held by a secured party having control of the letter-of-credit right under Section 9–107 has priority to the extent of its control over a conflicting security interest held by a secured party that does not have control.

(2) Security interests perfected by control under Section 9–314 rank according to priority in time of obtaining control.

§ 9–330. Priority of Purchaser of Chattel Paper or Instrument.

(a) A purchaser of chattel paper has priority over a security interest in the chattel paper which is claimed merely as proceeds of inventory subject to a security interest if:

(1) in good faith and in the ordinary course of the purchaser's business, the purchaser gives new value and takes possession of the chattel paper or obtains control of the chattel paper under Section 9–105; and

(2) the chattel paper does not indicate that it has been assigned to an identified assignee other than the purchaser.

(b) A purchaser of chattel paper has priority over a security interest in the chattel paper which is claimed other than merely as proceeds of inventory subject to a security interest if the purchaser gives new value and takes possession of the chattel paper or obtains control of the chattel paper under Section 9–105 in good faith, in the ordinary course of the purchaser's business, and without knowledge that the purchase violates the rights of the secured party.

(c) Except as otherwise provided in Section 9–327, a purchaser having priority in chattel paper under subsection (a) or (b) also has priority in proceeds of the chattel paper to the extent that:

(1) Section 9–322 provides for priority in the proceeds; or

(2) the proceeds consist of the specific goods covered by the chattel paper or cash proceeds of the specific goods, even if the purchaser's security interest in the proceeds is unperfected.

(d) Except as otherwise provided in Section 9–331(a), a purchaser of an instrument has priority over a security interest in the instrument perfected by a method other than possession if the purchaser gives value and takes possession of the instrument in good faith and without knowledge that the purchase violates the rights of the secured party.

(e) For purposes of subsections (a) and (b), the holder of a purchase-money security interest in inventory gives new value for chattel paper constituting proceeds of the inventory.

(f) For purposes of subsections (b) and (d), if chattel paper or an instrument indicates that it has been assigned to an identified secured party other than the purchaser, a purchaser of the chattel paper or instrument has knowledge that the purchase violates the rights of the secured party.

§ 9–331. Priority of Rights of Purchasers of Instruments, Documents, and Securities under Other Articles; Priority of Interests in Financial Assets and Security Entitlements under Article 8.

(a) This article does not limit the rights of a holder in due course of a negotiable instrument, a holder to which a negotiable document of title has been duly negotiated, or a protected purchaser of a security. These holders or purchasers take priority over an earlier security interest, even if perfected, to the extent provided in Articles 3, 7, and 8.

(b) This article does not limit the rights of or impose liability on a person to the extent that the person is protected against the assertion of a claim under Article 8.

(c) Filing under this article does not constitute notice of a claim or defense to the holders, or purchasers, or persons described in subsections (a) and (b).

§ 9–332. Transfer of Money; Transfer of Funds from Deposit Account.

(a) A transferee of money takes the money free of a security interest unless the transferee acts in collusion with the debtor in violating the rights of the secured party.

(b) A transferee of funds from a deposit account takes the funds free of a security interest in the deposit account unless the transferee acts in collusion with the debtor in violating the rights of the secured party.

§ 9–333. Priority of Certain Liens Arising by Operation of Law.

(a) In this section, "possessory lien" means an interest, other than a security interest or an agricultural lien:

(1) which secures payment or performance of an obligation for services or materials furnished with respect to goods by a person in the ordinary course of the person's business;

(2) which is created by statute or rule of law in favor of the person; and

(3) whose effectiveness depends on the person's possession of the goods.

(b) A possessory lien on goods has priority over a security interest in the goods unless the lien is created by a statute that expressly provides otherwise.

§ 9–334. Priority of Security Interests in Fixtures and Crops.

(a) A security interest under this article may be created in goods that are fixtures or may continue in goods that become fixtures. A security interest does not exist under this article in ordinary building materials incorporated into an improvement on land.

(b) This article does not prevent creation of an encumbrance upon fixtures under real property law.

(c) In cases not governed by subsections (d) through (h), a security interest in fixtures is subordinate to a conflicting interest of an encumbrancer or owner of the related real property other than the debtor.

(d) Except as otherwise provided in subsection (h), a perfected security interest in fixtures has priority over a conflicting interest of an encumbrancer or owner of the real property if the debtor has an interest of record in or is in possession of the real property and:

(1) the security interest is a purchase-money security interest;

(2) the interest of the encumbrancer or owner arises before the goods become fixtures; and

(3) the security interest is perfected by a fixture filing before the goods become fixtures or within 20 days thereafter.

(e) A perfected security interest in fixtures has priority over a conflicting interest of an encumbrancer or owner of the real property if:

(1) the debtor has an interest of record in the real property or is in possession of the real property and the security interest:

(A) is perfected by a fixture filing before the interest of the encumbrancer or owner is of record; and

(B) has priority over any conflicting interest of a predecessor in title of the encumbrancer or owner;

(2) before the goods become fixtures, the security interest is perfected by any method permitted by this article and the fixtures are readily removable:

(A) factory or office machines;

(B) equipment that is not primarily used or leased for use in the operation of the real property; or

(C) replacements of domestic appliances that are consumer goods;

(3) the conflicting interest is a lien on the real property obtained by legal or equitable proceedings after the security interest was perfected by any method permitted by this article; or

(4) the security interest is:

(A) created in a manufactured home in a manufactured-home transaction; and

(B) perfected pursuant to a statute described in Section 9–311(a)(2).

(f) A security interest in fixtures, whether or not perfected, has priority over a conflicting interest of an encumbrancer or owner of the real property if:

(1) the encumbrancer or owner has, in an authenticated record, consented to the security interest or disclaimed an interest in the goods as fixtures; or

(2) the debtor has a right to remove the goods as against the encumbrancer or owner.

(g) The priority of the security interest under paragraph (f)(2) continues for a reasonable time if the debtor's right to remove the goods as against the encumbrancer or owner terminates.

(h) A mortgage is a construction mortgage to the extent that it secures an obligation incurred for the construction of an improvement on land, including the acquisition cost of the land, if a recorded record of the mortgage so indicates. Except as otherwise provided in subsections (e) and (f), a security interest in fixtures is subordinate to a construction mortgage if a record of the mortgage is recorded before the goods become fixtures and the goods become fixtures before the completion of the construction. A mortgage has this priority to the same extent as a construction mortgage to the extent that it is given to refinance a construction mortgage.

(i) A perfected security interest in crops growing on real property has priority over a conflicting interest of an encumbrancer or owner of the real property if the debtor has an interest of record in or is in possession of the real property.

(j) Subsection (i) prevails over any inconsistent provisions of the following statutes:

[List here any statutes containing provisions inconsistent with subsection (i).]

Legislative Note: States that amend statutes to remove provisions inconsistent with subsection (i) need not enact subsection (j).

§ 9–335. Accessions.

(a) A security interest may be created in an accession and continues in collateral that becomes an accession.

(b) If a security interest is perfected when the collateral becomes an accession, the security interest remains perfected in the collateral.

(c) Except as otherwise provided in subsection (d), the other provisions of this part determine the priority of a security interest in an accession.

(d) A security interest in an accession is subordinate to a security interest in the whole which is perfected by compliance with the requirements of a certificate-of-title statute under Section 9–311(b).

(e) After default, subject to Part 6, a secured party may remove an accession from other goods if the security interest in the accession has priority over the claims of every person having an interest in the whole.

(f) A secured party that removes an accession from other goods under subsection (e) shall promptly reimburse any holder of a security interest or other lien on, or owner of, the whole or of the other goods, other than the debtor, for the cost of repair of any physical injury to the whole or the other goods. The secured party need not reimburse the holder or owner for any diminution in value of the whole or the other goods caused by the absence of the accession removed or by any necessity for replacing it. A person entitled to reimbursement may refuse permission to remove until the secured party gives adequate assurance for the performance of the obligation to reimburse.

§ 9–336. Commingled Goods.

(a) In this section, "commingled goods" means goods that are physically united with other goods in such a manner that their identity is lost in a product or mass.

(b) A security interest does not exist in commingled goods as such. However, a security interest may attach to a product or mass that results when goods become commingled goods.

(c) If collateral becomes commingled goods, a security interest attaches to the product or mass.

(d) If a security interest in collateral is perfected before the collateral becomes commingled goods, the security interest that attaches to the product or mass under subsection (c) is perfected.

(e) Except as otherwise provided in subsection (f), the other provisions of this part determine the priority of a security interest that attaches to the product or mass under subsection (c).

(f) If more than one security interest attaches to the product or mass under subsection (c), the following rules determine priority:

(1) A security interest that is perfected under subsection (d) has priority over a security interest that is unperfected at the time the collateral becomes commingled goods.

(2) If more than one security interest is perfected under subsection (d), the security interests rank equally in proportion to the value of the collateral at the time it became commingled goods.

§ 9–337. Priority of Security Interests in Goods Covered by Certificate of Title.

If, while a security interest in goods is perfected by any method under the law of another jurisdiction, this State issues a certificate of title that does not show that the goods are subject to the security interest or contain a statement that they may be subject to security interests not shown on the certificate:

(1) a buyer of the goods, other than a person in the business of selling goods of that kind, takes free of the security interest if the buyer gives value and receives delivery of the goods after issuance of the certificate and without knowledge of the security interest; and

(2) the security interest is subordinate to a conflicting security interest in the goods that attaches, and is perfected under Section 9–311(b), after issuance of the certificate and without the conflicting secured party's knowledge of the security interest.

§ 9–338. Priority of Security Interest or Agricultural Lien Perfected by Filed Financing Statement Providing Certain Incorrect Information.

If a security interest or agricultural lien is perfected by a filed financing statement providing information described in Section 9–516(b)(5) which is incorrect at the time the financing statement is filed:

(1) the security interest or agricultural lien is subordinate to a conflicting perfected security interest in the collateral to the extent that the holder of the conflicting security interest gives value in reasonable reliance upon the incorrect information; and

(2) a purchaser, other than a secured party, of the collateral takes free of the security interest or agricultural lien to the extent that, in reasonable reliance upon the incorrect information, the purchaser gives value and, in the case of chattel paper, documents, goods, instruments, or a security certificate, receives delivery of the collateral.

§ 9–339. Priority Subject to Subordination.

This article does not preclude subordination by agreement by a person entitled to priority.

[Subpart 4. Rights of Bank]

§ 9–340. Effectiveness of Right of Recoupment or Set-Off against Deposit Account.

(a) Except as otherwise provided in subsection (c), a bank with which a deposit account is maintained may exercise any right of recoupment or set-off against a secured party that holds a security interest in the deposit account.

(b) Except as otherwise provided in subsection (c), the application of this article to a security interest in a deposit account does not affect a right of recoupment or set-off of the secured party as to a deposit account maintained with the secured party.

(c) The exercise by a bank of a set-off against a deposit account is ineffective against a secured party that holds a security interest in the deposit account which is perfected by control under Section 9–104(a)(3), if the set-off is based on a claim against the debtor.

§ 9–341. Bank's Rights and Duties with Respect to Deposit Account.

Except as otherwise provided in Section 9–340(c), and unless the bank otherwise agrees in an authenticated record, a bank's rights and duties with respect to a deposit account maintained with the bank are not terminated, suspended, or modified by:

(1) the creation, attachment, or perfection of a security interest in the deposit account;

(2) the bank's knowledge of the security interest; or

(3) the bank's receipt of instructions from the secured party.

§ 9–342. Bank's Right to Refuse to Enter into or Disclose Existence of Control Agreement.

This article does not require a bank to enter into an agreement of the kind described in Section 9–104(a)(2), even if its customer so requests or directs. A bank that has entered into such an agreement is not required to confirm the existence of the agreement to another person unless requested to do so by its customer.

Part 4 Rights of Third Parties

§ 9–401. Alienability of Debtor's Rights.

(a) Except as otherwise provided in subsection (b) and Sections 9–406, 9–407, 9–408, and 9–409, whether a debtor's rights in collateral may be voluntarily or involuntarily transferred is governed by law other than this article.

(b) An agreement between the debtor and secured party which prohibits a transfer of the debtor's rights in collateral or makes the transfer a default does not prevent the transfer from taking effect.

§ 9–402. Secured Party Not Obligated on Contract of Debtor or in Tort.

The existence of a security interest, agricultural lien, or authority given to a debtor to dispose of or use collateral, without more, does not subject a secured party to liability in contract or tort for the debtor's acts or omissions.

§ 9–403. Agreement Not to Assert Defenses against Assignee.

(a) In this section, "value" has the meaning provided in Section 3–303(a).

(b) Except as otherwise provided in this section, an agreement between an account debtor and an assignor not to assert against an assignee any claim or defense that the account debtor may have against the assignor is enforceable by an assignee that takes an assignment:

(1) for value;

(2) in good faith;

(3) without notice of a claim of a property or possessory right to the property assigned; and

(4) without notice of a defense or claim in recoupment of the type that may be asserted against a person entitled to enforce a negotiable instrument under Section 3–305(a).

(c) Subsection (b) does not apply to defenses of a type that may be asserted against a holder in due course of a negotiable instrument under Section 3–305(b).

(d) In a consumer transaction, if a record evidences the account debtor's obligation, law other than this article requires that the record include a statement to the effect that the rights of an assignee are subject to claims or defenses that the account debtor could assert against the original obligee, and the record does not include such a statement:

(1) the record has the same effect as if the record included such a statement; and

(2) the account debtor may assert against an assignee those claims and defenses that would have been available if the record included such a statement.

(e) This section is subject to law other than this article which establishes a different rule for an account debtor who is an individual and who incurred the obligation primarily for personal, family, or household purposes.

(f) Except as otherwise provided in subsection (d), this section does not displace law other than this article which gives effect to an agreement by an account debtor not to assert a claim or defense against an assignee.

§ 9–404. Rights Acquired by Assignee; Claims and Defenses against Assignee.

(a) Unless an account debtor has made an enforceable agreement not to assert defenses or claims, and subject to subsections (b) through (e), the rights of an assignee are subject to:

(1) all terms of the agreement between the account debtor and assignor and any defense or claim in recoupment arising from the transaction that gave rise to the contract; and

(2) any other defense or claim of the account debtor against the assignor which accrues before the account debtor receives a notification of the assignment authenticated by the assignor or the assignee.

(b) Subject to subsection (c) and except as otherwise provided in subsection (d), the claim of an account debtor against an assignor may be asserted against an assignee under subsection (a) only to reduce the amount the account debtor owes.

(c) This section is subject to law other than this article which establishes a different rule for an account debtor who is an individual and who incurred the obligation primarily for personal, family, or household purposes.

(d) In a consumer transaction, if a record evidences the account debtor's obligation, law other than this article requires that the record include a statement to the effect that the account debtor's recovery against an assignee with respect to claims and defenses against the assignor may not exceed amounts paid by the account debtor under the record, and the record does not include such a statement, the extent to which a claim of an account debtor against the assignor may be asserted against an assignee is determined as if the record included such a statement.

(e) This section does not apply to an assignment of a health-care-insurance receivable.

§ 9–405. Modification of Assigned Contract.

(a) A modification of or substitution for an assigned contract is effective against an assignee if made in good faith. The assignee acquires corresponding rights under the modified or substituted contract. The assignment may provide that the modification or substitution is a breach of contract by the assignor. This subsection is subject to subsections (b) through (d).

(b) Subsection (a) applies to the extent that:

(1) the right to payment or a part thereof under an assigned contract has not been fully earned by performance; or

(2) the right to payment or a part thereof has been fully earned by performance and the account debtor has not received notification of the assignment under Section 9–406(a).

(c) This section is subject to law other than this article which establishes a different rule for an account debtor who is an individual and who incurred the obligation primarily for personal, family, or household purposes.

(d) This section does not apply to an assignment of a health-care-insurance receivable.

§ 9–406. Discharge of Account Debtor; Notification of Assignment; Identification and Proof of Assignment; Restrictions on Assignment of Accounts, Chattel Paper, Payment Intangibles, and Promissory Notes Ineffective.

(a) Subject to subsections (b) through (i), an account debtor on an account, chattel paper, or a payment intangible may discharge its obligation by paying the assignor until, but not after, the account debtor receives a notification, authenticated by the assignor or the assignee, that the amount due or to become due has been assigned and that payment is to be made to the assignee. After receipt of the notification, the account debtor may discharge its obligation by paying the assignee and may not discharge the obligation by paying the assignor.

(b) Subject to subsection (h), notification is ineffective under subsection (a):

(1) if it does not reasonably identify the rights assigned;

(2) to the extent that an agreement between an account debtor and a seller of a payment intangible limits the account debtor's duty to pay a person other than the seller and the limitation is effective under law other than this article; or

(3) at the option of an account debtor, if the notification notifies the account debtor to make less than the full amount of any installment or other periodic payment to the assignee, even if:

(A) only a portion of the account, chattel paper, or payment intangible has been assigned to that assignee;

(B) a portion has been assigned to another assignee; or

(C) the account debtor knows that the assignment to that assignee is limited.

(c) Subject to subsection (h), if requested by the account debtor, an assignee shall seasonably furnish reasonable proof that the assignment has been made. Unless the assignee complies, the account debtor may discharge its obligation by paying the assignor, even if the account debtor has received a notification under subsection (a).

(d) Except as otherwise provided in subsection (e) and Sections 2A–303 and 9–407, and subject to subsection (h), a term in an agreement between an account debtor and an assignor or in a promissory note is ineffective to the extent that it:

(1) prohibits, restricts, or requires the consent of the account debtor or person obligated on the promissory note to the assignment or transfer of, or the creation, attachment, perfection, or enforcement of a security interest in, the account, chattel paper, payment intangible, or promissory note; or

(2) provides that the assignment or transfer or the creation, attachment, perfection, or enforcement of the security interest may give rise to a default, breach, right of recoupment, claim, defense, termination, right of termination, or remedy under the account, chattel paper, payment intangible, or promissory note.

(e) Subsection (d) does not apply to the sale of a payment intangible or promissory note.

(f) Except as otherwise provided in Sections 2A–303 and 9–407 and subject to subsections (h) and (i), a rule of law, statute, or regulation that prohibits, restricts, or requires the consent of a government, governmental body or official, or account debtor to the assignment or transfer of, or creation of a security interest in, an account or chattel paper is ineffective to the extent that the rule of law, statute, or regulation:

(1) prohibits, restricts, or requires the consent of the government, governmental body or official, or account debtor to the assignment or transfer of, or the creation, attachment, perfection, or enforcement of a security interest in the account or chattel paper; or

(2) provides that the assignment or transfer or the creation, attachment, perfection, or enforcement of the security interest may give rise to a default, breach, right of recoupment, claim, defense, termination, right of termination, or remedy under the account or chattel paper.

(g) Subject to subsection (h), an account debtor may not waive or vary its option under subsection (b)(3).

(h) This section is subject to law other than this article which establishes a different rule for an account debtor who is an individual and who incurred the obligation primarily for personal, family, or household purposes.

(i) This section does not apply to an assignment of a health-care-insurance receivable.

(j) This section prevails over any inconsistent provisions of the following statutes, rules, and regulations:

[List here any statutes, rules, and regulations containing provisions inconsistent with this section.]

Legislative Note: States that amend statutes, rules, and regulations to remove provisions inconsistent with this section need not enact subsection (j).

As amended in 1999 and 2000.

§ 9–407. Restrictions on Creation or Enforcement of Security Interest in Leasehold Interest or in Lessor's Residual Interest.

(a) Except as otherwise provided in subsection (b), a term in a lease agreement is ineffective to the extent that it:

(1) prohibits, restricts, or requires the consent of a party to the lease to the assignment or transfer of, or the creation, attachment, perfection, or enforcement of a security interest in an interest of a party under the lease contract or in the lessor's residual interest in the goods; or

(2) provides that the assignment or transfer or the creation, attachment, perfection, or enforcement of the security interest may give rise to a default, breach, right of recoupment, claim, defense, termination, right of termination, or remedy under the lease.

(b) Except as otherwise provided in Section 2A–303(7), a term described in subsection (a)(2) is effective to the extent that there is:

(1) a transfer by the lessee of the lessee's right of possession or use of the goods in violation of the term; or

(2) a delegation of a material performance of either party to the lease contract in violation of the term.

(c) The creation, attachment, perfection, or enforcement of a security interest in the lessor's interest under the lease contract or the lessor's residual interest in the goods is not a transfer that materially impairs the lessee's prospect of obtaining return performance or materially changes the duty of or materially increases the burden or risk imposed on the lessee within the purview of Section 2A–303(4) unless, and then only to the extent that, enforcement actually results in a delegation of material performance of the lessor.

As amended in 1999.

§ 9–408. Restrictions on Assignment of Promissory Notes, Health-Care-Insurance Receivables, and Certain General Intangibles Ineffective.

(a) Except as otherwise provided in subsection (b), a term in a promissory note or in an agreement between an account debtor and a debtor which relates to a health-care-insurance receivable or a general intangible, including a contract, permit, license, or franchise, and which term prohibits, restricts, or requires the consent of the person obligated on the promissory note or the account debtor to, the assignment or transfer of, or creation, attachment, or perfection of a security interest in, the promissory note, health-care-insurance receivable, or general intangible, is ineffective to the extent that the term:

(1) would impair the creation, attachment, or perfection of a security interest; or

(2) provides that the assignment or transfer or the creation, attachment, or perfection of the security interest may give rise to a default, breach, right of recoupment, claim, defense, termination, right of termination, or remedy under the promissory note, health-care-insurance receivable, or general intangible.

(b) Subsection (a) applies to a security interest in a payment intangible or promissory note only if the security interest arises out of a sale of the payment intangible or promissory note.

(c) A rule of law, statute, or regulation that prohibits, restricts, or requires the consent of a government, governmental body or official, person obligated on a promissory note, or account debtor to the assignment or transfer of, or creation of a security interest in, a promissory note, health-care-insurance receivable, or general intangible, including a contract, permit, license, or franchise between an account debtor and a debtor, is ineffective to the extent that the rule of law, statute, or regulation:

(1) would impair the creation, attachment, or perfection of a security interest; or

(2) provides that the assignment or transfer or the creation, attachment, or perfection of the security interest may give rise to a default, breach, right of recoupment, claim, defense, termination, right of termination, or remedy under the promissory note, health-care-insurance receivable, or general intangible.

(d) To the extent that a term in a promissory note or in an agreement between an account debtor and a debtor which relates to a health-care-insurance receivable or general intangible or a rule of law, statute, or regulation described in subsection (c) would be effective under law other than this article but is ineffective under subsection (a) or (c), the creation, attachment, or perfection of a security interest in the promissory note, health-care-insurance receivable, or general intangible:

(1) is not enforceable against the person obligated on the promissory note or the account debtor;

(2) does not impose a duty or obligation on the person obligated on the promissory note or the account debtor;

(3) does not require the person obligated on the promissory note or the account debtor to recognize the security interest, pay or render performance to the secured party, or accept payment or performance from the secured party;

(4) does not entitle the secured party to use or assign the debtor's rights under the promissory note, health-care-insurance receivable, or general intangible, including any related information or materials furnished to the debtor in the transaction giving rise to the promissory note, health-care-insurance receivable, or general intangible;

(5) does not entitle the secured party to use, assign, possess, or have access to any trade secrets or confidential information of the person obligated on the promissory note or the account debtor; and

(6) does not entitle the secured party to enforce the security interest in the promissory note, health-care-insurance receivable, or general intangible.

(e) This section prevails over any inconsistent provisions of the following statutes, rules, and regulations:

[List here any statutes, rules, and regulations containing provisions inconsistent with this section.]

Legislative Note: States that amend statutes, rules, and regulations to remove provisions inconsistent with this section need not enact subsection (e).

As amended in 1999.

§ 9–409. Restrictions on Assignment of Letter-of-Credit Rights Ineffective.

(a) A term in a letter of credit or a rule of law, statute, regulation, custom, or practice applicable to the letter of credit which prohibits, restricts, or requires the consent of an applicant, issuer, or nominated person to a beneficiary's assignment of or creation of a security interest in a letter-of-credit right is ineffective to the extent that the term or rule of law, statute, regulation, custom, or practice:

(1) would impair the creation, attachment, or perfection of a security interest in the letter-of-credit right; or

(2) provides that the assignment or the creation, attachment, or perfection of the security interest may give rise to a default, breach, right of recoupment, claim, defense, termination, right of termination, or remedy under the letter-of-credit right.

(b) To the extent that a term in a letter of credit is ineffective under subsection (a) but would be effective under law other than this article or a custom or practice applicable to the letter of credit, to the transfer of a right to draw or otherwise demand performance under the letter of credit, or to the assignment of a right to proceeds of the letter of credit, the creation, attachment, or perfection of a security interest in the letter-of-credit right:

(1) is not enforceable against the applicant, issuer, nominated person, or transferee beneficiary;

(2) imposes no duties or obligations on the applicant, issuer, nominated person, or transferee beneficiary; and

(3) does not require the applicant, issuer, nominated person, or transferee beneficiary to recognize the security interest, pay or render performance to the secured party, or accept payment or other performance from the secured party.

As amended in 1999.

Part 5 Filing

[Subpart 1. Filing Office; Contents and Effectiveness of Financing Statement]

§ 9–501. Filing Office.

(a) Except as otherwise provided in subsection (b), if the local law of this State governs perfection of a security interest or agricultural lien, the office in which to file a financing statement to perfect the security interest or agricultural lien is:

(1) the office designated for the filing or recording of a record of a mortgage on the related real property, if:

(A) the collateral is as-extracted collateral or timber to be cut; or

(B) the financing statement is filed as a fixture filing and the collateral is goods that are or are to become fixtures; or

(2) the office of [ ] [or any office duly authorized by [ ]], in all other cases, including a case in which the collateral is goods that are or are to become fixtures and the financing statement is not filed as a fixture filing.

(b) The office in which to file a financing statement to perfect a security interest in collateral, including fixtures, of a transmitting utility is the office of [ ]. The financing statement also constitutes a fixture filing as to the collateral indicated in the financing statement which is or is to become fixtures.

Legislative Note: The State should designate the filing office where the brackets appear. The filing office may be that of a governmental official (e.g., the Secretary of State) or a private party that maintains the State's filing system.

§ 9–502. Contents of Financing Statement; Record of Mortgage as Financing Statement; Time of Filing Financing Statement.

(a) Subject to subsection (b), a financing statement is sufficient only if it:

(1) provides the name of the debtor;

(2) provides the name of the secured party or a representative of the secured party; and

(3) indicates the collateral covered by the financing statement.

(b) Except as otherwise provided in Section 9–501(b), to be sufficient, a financing statement that covers as-extracted collateral or timber to be cut, or which is filed as a fixture filing and covers goods that are or are to become fixtures, must satisfy subsection (a) and also:

(1) indicate that it covers this type of collateral;

(2) indicate that it is to be filed [for record] in the real property records;

(3) provide a description of the real property to which the collateral is related [sufficient to give constructive notice of a mortgage under the law of this State if the description were contained in a record of the mortgage of the real property]; and

(4) if the debtor does not have an interest of record in the real property, provide the name of a record owner.

(c) A record of a mortgage is effective, from the date of recording, as a financing statement filed as a fixture filing or as a financing statement covering as-extracted collateral or timber to be cut only if:

(1) the record indicates the goods or accounts that it covers;

(2) the goods are or are to become fixtures related to the real property described in the record or the collateral is related to the real property described in the record and is as-extracted collateral or timber to be cut;

(3) the record satisfies the requirements for a financing statement in this section other than an indication that it is to be filed in the real property records; and

(4) the record is [duly] recorded.

(d) A financing statement may be filed before a security agreement is made or a security interest otherwise attaches.

Legislative Note: Language in brackets is optional. Where the State has any special recording system for real property other than the usual grantor-grantee index (as, for instance, a tract system or a title registration or Torrens system) local adaptations of subsection (b) and Section 9–519(d) and (e) may be necessary. See, e.g., Mass. Gen. Laws Chapter 106, Section 9–410.

§ 9–503. Name of Debtor and Secured Party.

(a) A financing statement sufficiently provides the name of the debtor:

(1) if the debtor is a registered organization, only if the financing statement provides the name of the debtor indicated on the public record of the debtor's jurisdiction of organization which shows the debtor to have been organized;

(2) if the debtor is a decedent's estate, only if the financing statement provides the name of the decedent and indicates that the debtor is an estate;

(3) if the debtor is a trust or a trustee acting with respect to property held in trust, only if the financing statement:

(A) provides the name specified for the trust in its organic documents or, if no name is specified, provides the name of the settlor and additional information sufficient to distinguish the debtor from other trusts having one or more of the same settlors; and

(B) indicates, in the debtor's name or otherwise, that the debtor is a trust or is a trustee acting with respect to property held in trust; and

(4) in other cases:

(A) if the debtor has a name, only if it provides the individual or organizational name of the debtor; and

(B) if the debtor does not have a name, only if it provides the names of the partners, members, associates, or other persons comprising the debtor.

(b) A financing statement that provides the name of the debtor in accordance with subsection (a) is not rendered ineffective by the absence of:

(1) a trade name or other name of the debtor; or

(2) unless required under subsection (a)(4)(B), names of partners, members, associates, or other persons comprising the debtor.

(c) A financing statement that provides only the debtor's trade name does not sufficiently provide the name of the debtor.

(d) Failure to indicate the representative capacity of a secured party or representative of a secured party does not affect the sufficiency of a financing statement.

(e) A financing statement may provide the name of more than one debtor and the name of more than one secured party.

§ 9–504. Indication of Collateral.

A financing statement sufficiently indicates the collateral that it covers if the financing statement provides:

(1) a description of the collateral pursuant to Section 9–108; or

(2) an indication that the financing statement covers all assets or all personal property.

As amended in 1999.

§ 9–505. Filing and Compliance with Other Statutes and Treaties for Consignments, Leases, Other Bailments, and Other Transactions.

(a) A consignor, lessor, or other bailor of goods, a licensor, or a buyer of a payment intangible or promissory note may file a financing statement, or may comply with a statute or treaty described in Section 9–311(a), using the terms "consignor", "consignee", "lessor", "lessee", "bailor", "bailee", "licensor", "licensee", "owner", "registered owner", "buyer", "seller", or words of similar import, instead of the terms "secured party" and "debtor".

(b) This part applies to the filing of a financing statement under subsection (a) and, as appropriate, to compliance that is equivalent to filing a financing statement under Section 9–311(b), but the filing or compliance is not of itself a factor in determining whether the collateral secures an obligation. If it is determined for another reason that the collateral secures an obligation, a security interest held by the consignor, lessor, bailor, licensor, owner, or buyer which attaches to the collateral is perfected by the filing or compliance.

§ 9–506. Effect of Errors or Omissions.

(a) A financing statement substantially satisfying the requirements of this part is effective, even if it has minor errors or omissions, unless the errors or omissions make the financing statement seriously misleading.

(b) Except as otherwise provided in subsection (c), a financing statement that fails sufficiently to provide the name of the debtor in accordance with Section 9–503(a) is seriously misleading.

(c) If a search of the records of the filing office under the debtor's correct name, using the filing office's standard search logic, if any, would disclose a financing statement that fails sufficiently to provide the name of the debtor in accordance with Section 9–503(a), the name provided does not make the financing statement seriously misleading.

(d) For purposes of Section 9–508(b), the "debtor's correct name" in subsection (c) means the correct name of the new debtor.

§ 9–507. Effect of Certain Events on Effectiveness of Financing Statement.

(a) A filed financing statement remains effective with respect to collateral that is sold, exchanged, leased, licensed, or otherwise disposed of and in which a security interest or agricultural lien continues, even if the secured party knows of or consents to the disposition.

(b) Except as otherwise provided in subsection (c) and Section 9–508, a financing statement is not rendered ineffective if, after the financing statement is filed, the information provided in the financing statement becomes seriously misleading under Section 9–506.

(c) If a debtor so changes its name that a filed financing statement becomes seriously misleading under Section 9–506:

(1) the financing statement is effective to perfect a security interest in collateral acquired by the debtor before, or within four months after, the change; and

(2) the financing statement is not effective to perfect a security interest in collateral acquired by the debtor more than four months after the change, unless an amendment to the financing statement which renders the financing statement not seriously misleading is filed within four months after the change.

§ 9–508. Effectiveness of Financing Statement If New Debtor Becomes Bound by Security Agreement.

(a) Except as otherwise provided in this section, a filed financing statement naming an original debtor is effective to perfect a security interest in collateral in which a new debtor has or acquires rights to the extent that the financing statement would have been effective had the original debtor acquired rights in the collateral.

(b) If the difference between the name of the original debtor and that of the new debtor causes a filed financing statement that is effective under subsection (a) to be seriously misleading under Section 9–506:

(1) the financing statement is effective to perfect a security interest in collateral acquired by the new debtor before, and within four months after, the new debtor becomes bound under Section 9B–203(d); and

(2) the financing statement is not effective to perfect a security interest in collateral acquired by the new debtor more than four months after the new debtor becomes bound under Section 9–203(d) unless an initial financing statement providing the name of the new debtor is filed before the expiration of that time.

(c) This section does not apply to collateral as to which a filed financing statement remains effective against the new debtor under Section 9–507(a).

§ 9–509. Persons Entitled to File a Record.

(a) A person may file an initial financing statement, amendment that adds collateral covered by a financing statement, or amendment that adds a debtor to a financing statement only if:

(1) the debtor authorizes the filing in an authenticated record or pursuant to subsection (b) or (c); or

(2) the person holds an agricultural lien that has become effective at the time of filing and the financing statement covers only collateral in which the person holds an agricultural lien.

(b) By authenticating or becoming bound as debtor by a security agreement, a debtor or new debtor authorizes the filing of an initial financing statement, and an amendment, covering:

(1) the collateral described in the security agreement; and

(2) property that becomes collateral under Section 9–315(a)(2), whether or not the security agreement expressly covers proceeds.

(c) By acquiring collateral in which a security interest or agricultural lien continues under Section 9–315(a)(1), a debtor authorizes the filing of an initial financing statement, and an amendment, covering the collateral and property that becomes collateral under Section 9–315(a)(2).

(d) A person may file an amendment other than an amendment that adds collateral covered by a financing statement or an amendment that adds a debtor to a financing statement only if:

(1) the secured party of record authorizes the filing; or

(2) the amendment is a termination statement for a financing statement as to which the secured party of record has failed to file or send a termination statement as required by Section 9–513(a) or (c), the debtor authorizes the filing, and the termination statement indicates that the debtor authorized it to be filed.

(e) If there is more than one secured party of record for a financing statement, each secured party of record may authorize the filing of an amendment under subsection (d).

As amended in 2000.

§ 9–510. Effectiveness of Filed Record.

(a) A filed record is effective only to the extent that it was filed by a person that may file it under Section 9–509.

(b) A record authorized by one secured party of record does not affect the financing statement with respect to another secured party of record.

(c) A continuation statement that is not filed within the six-month period prescribed by Section 9–515(d) is ineffective.

§ 9–511. Secured Party of Record.

(a) A secured party of record with respect to a financing statement is a person whose name is provided as the name of the secured party or a representative of the secured party in an initial financing statement that has been filed. If an initial financing statement is filed under Section 9–514(a), the assignee named in the initial financing statement is the secured party of record with respect to the financing statement.

(b) If an amendment of a financing statement which provides the name of a person as a secured party or a representative of a secured party is filed, the person named in the amendment is a secured party of record. If an amendment is filed under Section 9–514(b), the assignee named in the amendment is a secured party of record.

(c) A person remains a secured party of record until the filing of an amendment of the financing statement which deletes the person.

§ 9–512. Amendment of Financing Statement.

[Alternative A]

(a) Subject to Section 9–509, a person may add or delete collateral covered by, continue or terminate the effectiveness of, or, subject to subsection (e), otherwise amend the information provided in, a financing statement by filing an amendment that:

(1) identifies, by its file number, the initial financing statement to which the amendment relates; and

(2) if the amendment relates to an initial financing statement filed [or recorded] in a filing office described in Section 9–501(a)(1), provides the information specified in Section 9–502(b).

[Alternative B]

(a) Subject to Section 9–509, a person may add or delete collateral covered by, continue or terminate the effectiveness of, or, subject to subsection (e), otherwise amend the information provided in, a financing statement by filing an amendment that:

(1) identifies, by its file number, the initial financing statement to which the amendment relates; and

(2) if the amendment relates to an initial financing statement filed [or recorded] in a filing office described in Section 9–501(a)(1), provides the date [and time] that the initial financing statement was filed [or recorded] and the information specified in Section 9–502(b).

[End of Alternatives]

(b) Except as otherwise provided in Section 9–515, the filing of an amendment does not extend the period of effectiveness of the financing statement.

(c) A financing statement that is amended by an amendment that adds collateral is effective as to the added collateral only from the date of the filing of the amendment.

(d) A financing statement that is amended by an amendment that adds a debtor is effective as to the added debtor only from the date of the filing of the amendment.

(e) An amendment is ineffective to the extent it:

(1) purports to delete all debtors and fails to provide the name of a debtor to be covered by the financing statement; or

(2) purports to delete all secured parties of record and fails to provide the name of a new secured party of record.

Legislative Note: States whose real-estate filing offices require additional information in amendments and cannot search their records by both the name of the debtor and the file number should enact Alternative B to Sections 9–512(a), 9–518(b), 9–519(f), and 9–522(a).

§ 9–513. Termination Statement.

(a) A secured party shall cause the secured party of record for a financing statement to file a termination statement for the financing statement if the financing statement covers consumer goods and:

(1) there is no obligation secured by the collateral covered by the financing statement and no commitment to make an advance, incur an obligation, or otherwise give value; or

(2) the debtor did not authorize the filing of the initial financing statement.

(b) To comply with subsection (a), a secured party shall cause the secured party of record to file the termination statement:

(1) within one month after there is no obligation secured by the collateral covered by the financing statement and no commitment to make an advance, incur an obligation, or otherwise give value; or

(2) if earlier, within 20 days after the secured party receives an authenticated demand from a debtor.

(c) In cases not governed by subsection (a), within 20 days after a secured party receives an authenticated demand from a debtor, the secured party shall cause the secured party of record for a financing statement to send to the debtor a termination statement for the financing statement or file the termination statement in the filing office if:

(1) except in the case of a financing statement covering accounts or chattel paper that has been sold or goods that are the subject of a consignment, there is no obligation secured by the collateral covered by the financing statement and no commitment to make an advance, incur an obligation, or otherwise give value;

(2) the financing statement covers accounts or chattel paper that has been sold but as to which the account debtor or other person obligated has discharged its obligation;

(3) the financing statement covers goods that were the subject of a consignment to the debtor but are not in the debtor's possession; or

(4) the debtor did not authorize the filing of the initial financing statement.

(d) Except as otherwise provided in Section 9–510, upon the filing of a termination statement with the filing office, the financing statement to which the termination statement relates ceases to be effective. Except as otherwise provided in Section 9–510, for purposes of Sections 9–519(g), 9–522(a), and 9–523(c), the filing with the filing office of a termination statement relating to a financing statement that indicates that the debtor is a transmitting utility also causes the effectiveness of the financing statement to lapse.

As amended in 2000.

§ 9–514. Assignment of Powers of Secured Party of Record.

(a) Except as otherwise provided in subsection (c), an initial financing statement may reflect an assignment of all of the secured party's power to authorize an amendment to the financing statement by providing the name and mailing address of the assignee as the name and address of the secured party.

(b) Except as otherwise provided in subsection (c), a secured party of record may assign of record all or part of its power to authorize an amendment to a financing statement by filing in the filing office an amendment of the financing statement which:

(1) identifies, by its file number, the initial financing statement to which it relates;

(2) provides the name of the assignor; and

(3) provides the name and mailing address of the assignee.

(c) An assignment of record of a security interest in a fixture covered by a record of a mortgage which is effective as a financing statement filed as a fixture filing under Section 9–502(c) may be made only by an assignment of record of the mortgage in the manner provided by law of this State other than [the Uniform Commercial Code].

§ 9–515. Duration and Effectiveness of Financing Statement; Effect of Lapsed Financing Statement.

(a) Except as otherwise provided in subsections (b), (e), (f), and (g), a filed financing statement is effective for a period of five years after the date of filing.

(b) Except as otherwise provided in subsections (e), (f), and (g), an initial financing statement filed in connection with a public-finance transaction or manufactured-home transaction is effective for a period of 30 years after the date of filing if it indicates that it is filed in connection with a public-finance transaction or manufactured-home transaction.

(c) The effectiveness of a filed financing statement lapses on the expiration of the period of its effectiveness unless before the lapse a continuation statement is filed pursuant to subsection (d). Upon lapse, a financing statement ceases to be effective and any security interest or agricultural lien that was perfected by the financing statement becomes unperfected, unless the security interest is perfected otherwise. If the security interest or agricultural lien becomes unperfected upon lapse, it is deemed never to have been perfected as against a purchaser of the collateral for value.

(d) A continuation statement may be filed only within six months before the expiration of the five-year period specified in subsection (a) or the 30-year period specified in subsection (b), whichever is applicable.

(e) Except as otherwise provided in Section 9–510, upon timely filing of a continuation statement, the effectiveness of the initial financing statement continues for a period of five years commencing on the day on which the financing statement would have become ineffective in the absence of the filing. Upon the expiration of the five-year period, the financing statement lapses in the same manner as provided in subsection (c), unless, before the lapse, another continuation statement is filed pursuant to subsection (d). Succeeding continuation statements may be filed in the same manner to continue the effectiveness of the initial financing statement.

(f) If a debtor is a transmitting utility and a filed financing statement so indicates, the financing statement is effective until a termination statement is filed.

(g) A record of a mortgage that is effective as a financing statement filed as a fixture filing under Section 9–502(c) remains effective as a financing statement filed as a fixture filing until the mortgage is released or satisfied of record or its effectiveness otherwise terminates as to the real property.

§ 9–516. What Constitutes Filing; Effectiveness of Filing.

(a) Except as otherwise provided in subsection (b), communication of a record to a filing office and tender of the filing fee or acceptance of the record by the filing office constitutes filing.

(b) Filing does not occur with respect to a record that a filing office refuses to accept because:

(1) the record is not communicated by a method or medium of communication authorized by the filing office;

(2) an amount equal to or greater than the applicable filing fee is not tendered;

(3) the filing office is unable to index the record because:

(A) in the case of an initial financing statement, the record does not provide a name for the debtor;

(B) in the case of an amendment or correction statement, the record:

(i) does not identify the initial financing statement as required by Section 9–512 or 9–518, as applicable; or

(ii) identifies an initial financing statement whose effectiveness has lapsed under Section 9–515;

(C) in the case of an initial financing statement that provides the name of a debtor identified as an individual or an amendment that provides a name of a debtor identified as an individual which was not previously provided in the financing statement to which the record relates, the record does not identify the debtor's last name; or

(D) in the case of a record filed [or recorded] in the filing office described in Section 9–501(a)(1), the record does not provide a sufficient description of the real property to which it relates;

(4) in the case of an initial financing statement or an amendment that adds a secured party of record, the record does not provide a name and mailing address for the secured party of record;

(5) in the case of an initial financing statement or an amendment that provides a name of a debtor which was not previously provided in the financing statement to which the amendment relates, the record does not:

(A) provide a mailing address for the debtor;

(B) indicate whether the debtor is an individual or an organization; or

(C) if the financing statement indicates that the debtor is an organization, provide:

(i) a type of organization for the debtor;

(ii) a jurisdiction of organization for the debtor; or

(iii) an organizational identification number for the debtor or indicate that the debtor has none;

(6) in the case of an assignment reflected in an initial financing statement under Section 9–514(a) or an amendment filed under Section 9–514(b), the record does not provide a name and mailing address for the assignee; or

(7) in the case of a continuation statement, the record is not filed within the six-month period prescribed by Section 9–515(d).

(c) For purposes of subsection (b):

(1) a record does not provide information if the filing office is unable to read or decipher the information; and

(2) a record that does not indicate that it is an amendment or identify an initial financing statement to which it relates, as required by Section 9–512, 9–514, or 9–518, is an initial financing statement.

(d) A record that is communicated to the filing office with tender of the filing fee, but which the filing office refuses to accept for a reason other than one set forth in subsection (b), is effective as a filed record except as against a purchaser of the collateral which gives value in reasonable reliance upon the absence of the record from the files.

§ 9–517. Effect of Indexing Errors.

The failure of the filing office to index a record correctly does not affect the effectiveness of the filed record.

§ 9–518. Claim Concerning Inaccurate or Wrongfully Filed Record.

(a) A person may file in the filing office a correction statement with respect to a record indexed there under the person's name if the person believes that the record is inaccurate or was wrongfully filed.

[Alternative A]

(b) A correction statement must:

(1) identify the record to which it relates by the file number assigned to the initial financing statement to which the record relates;

(2) indicate that it is a correction statement; and

(3) provide the basis for the person's belief that the record is inaccurate and indicate the manner in which the person believes the

record should be amended to cure any inaccuracy or provide the basis for the person's belief that the record was wrongfully filed.

[Alternative B]

(b) A correction statement must:

(1) identify the record to which it relates by:

(A) the file number assigned to the initial financing statement to which the record relates; and

(B) if the correction statement relates to a record filed [or recorded] in a filing office described in Section 9–501(a)(1), the date [and time] that the initial financing statement was filed [or recorded] and the information specified in Section 9–502(b);

(2) indicate that it is a correction statement; and

(3) provide the basis for the person's belief that the record is inaccurate and indicate the manner in which the person believes the record should be amended to cure any inaccuracy or provide the basis for the person's belief that the record was wrongfully filed.

[End of Alternatives]

(c) The filing of a correction statement does not affect the effectiveness of an initial financing statement or other filed record.

Legislative Note: States whose real-estate filing offices require additional information in amendments and cannot search their records by both the name of the debtor and the file number should enact Alternative B to Sections 9–512(a), 9–518(b), 9–519(f), and 9–522(a).

[Subpart 2. Duties and Operation of Filing Office]

§ 9–519. Numbering, Maintaining, and Indexing Records; Communicating Information Provided in Records.

(a) For each record filed in a filing office, the filing office shall:

(1) assign a unique number to the filed record;

(2) create a record that bears the number assigned to the filed record and the date and time of filing;

(3) maintain the filed record for public inspection; and

(4) index the filed record in accordance with subsections (c), (d), and (e).

(b) A file number [assigned after January 1, 2002,] must include a digit that:

(1) is mathematically derived from or related to the other digits of the file number; and

(2) aids the filing office in determining whether a number communicated as the file number includes a single-digit or transpositional error.

(c) Except as otherwise provided in subsections (d) and (e), the filing office shall:

(1) index an initial financing statement according to the name of the debtor and index all filed records relating to the initial financing statement in a manner that associates with one another an initial financing statement and all filed records relating to the initial financing statement; and

(2) index a record that provides a name of a debtor which was not previously provided in the financing statement to which the record relates also according to the name that was not previously provided.

(d) If a financing statement is filed as a fixture filing or covers as-extracted collateral or timber to be cut, [it must be filed for record and] the filing office shall index it:

(1) under the names of the debtor and of each owner of record shown on the financing statement as if they were the mortgagors under a mortgage of the real property described; and

(2) to the extent that the law of this State provides for indexing of records of mortgages under the name of the mortgagee, under the name of the secured party as if the secured party were the mortgagee thereunder, or, if indexing is by description, as if the financing statement were a record of a mortgage of the real property described.

(e) If a financing statement is filed as a fixture filing or covers as-extracted collateral or timber to be cut, the filing office shall index an assignment filed under Section 9–514(a) or an amendment filed under Section 9–514(b):

(1) under the name of the assignor as grantor; and

(2) to the extent that the law of this State provides for indexing a record of the assignment of a mortgage under the name of the assignee, under the name of the assignee.

[Alternative A]

(f) The filing office shall maintain a capability:

(1) to retrieve a record by the name of the debtor and by the file number assigned to the initial financing statement to which the record relates; and

(2) to associate and retrieve with one another an initial financing statement and each filed record relating to the initial financing statement.

[Alternative B]

(f) The filing office shall maintain a capability:

(1) to retrieve a record by the name of the debtor and:

(A) if the filing office is described in Section 9–501(a)(1), by the file number assigned to the initial financing statement to which the record relates and the date [and time] that the record was filed [or recorded]; or

(B) if the filing office is described in Section 9–501(a)(2), by the file number assigned to the initial financing statement to which the record relates; and

(2) to associate and retrieve with one another an initial financing statement and each filed record relating to the initial financing statement.

[End of Alternatives]

(g) The filing office may not remove a debtor's name from the index until one year after the effectiveness of a financing statement naming the debtor lapses under Section 9–515 with respect to all secured parties of record.

(h) The filing office shall perform the acts required by subsections (a) through (e) at the time and in the manner prescribed by filing-office rule, but not later than two business days after the filing office receives the record in question.

[(i) Subsection[s] [(b)] [and] [(h)] do[es] not apply to a filing office described in Section 9–501(a)(1).]

Legislative Notes:

1. States whose filing offices currently assign file numbers that include a verification number, commonly known as a "check digit," or can implement this requirement before the effective date of this Article should omit the bracketed language in subsection (b).

2. In States in which writings will not appear in the real property records and indices unless actually recorded the bracketed language in subsection (d) should be used.

3. States whose real-estate filing offices require additional information in amendments and cannot search their records by both the name of the debtor and the file number should enact Alternative B to Sections 9–512(a), 9–518(b), 9–519(f), and 9–522(a).

4. A State that elects not to require real-estate filing offices to comply with either or both of subsections (b) and (h) may adopt an applicable variation of subsection (i) and add "Except as otherwise provided in subsection (i)," to the appropriate subsection or subsections.

§ 9–520. Acceptance and Refusal to Accept Record.

(a) A filing office shall refuse to accept a record for filing for a reason set forth in Section 9–516(b) and may refuse to accept a record for filing only for a reason set forth in Section 9–516(b).

(b) If a filing office refuses to accept a record for filing, it shall communicate to the person that presented the record the fact of and reason for the refusal and the date and time the record would have been filed had the filing office accepted it. The communication must be made at the time and in the manner prescribed by filing-office rule but [, in the case of a filing office described in Section 9–501(a)(2),] in no event more than two business days after the filing office receives the record.

(c) A filed financing statement satisfying Section 9–502(a) and (b) is effective, even if the filing office is required to refuse to accept it for filing under subsection (a). However, Section 9–338 applies to a filed financing statement providing information described in Section 9–516(b)(5) which is incorrect at the time the financing statement is filed.

(d) If a record communicated to a filing office provides information that relates to more than one debtor, this part applies as to each debtor separately.

Legislative Note: A State that elects not to require real-property filing offices to comply with subsection (b) should include the bracketed language.

§ 9–521. Uniform Form of Written Financing Statement and Amendment.

(a) A filing office that accepts written records may not refuse to accept a written initial financing statement in the following form and format except for a reason set forth in Section 9–516(b):

[NATIONAL UCC FINANCING STATEMENT (FORM UCC1)(REV. 7/29/98)]

[NATIONAL UCC FINANCING STATEMENT ADDENDUM (FORM UCC1Ad)(REV. 07/29/98)]

(b) A filing office that accepts written records may not refuse to accept a written record in the following form and format except for a reason set forth in Section 9–516(b):

[NATIONAL UCC FINANCING STATEMENT AMENDMENT (FORM UCC3)(REV. 07/29/98)]

[NATIONAL UCC FINANCING STATEMENT AMENDMENT ADDENDUM (FORM UCC3Ad)(REV. 07/29/98)]

§ 9–522. Maintenance and Destruction of Records.

[Alternative A]

(a) The filing office shall maintain a record of the information provided in a filed financing statement for at least one year after the effectiveness of the financing statement has lapsed under Section 9–515 with respect to all secured parties of record. The record must be retrievable by using the name of the debtor and by using the file number assigned to the initial financing statement to which the record relates.

[Alternative B]

(a) The filing office shall maintain a record of the information provided in a filed financing statement for at least one year after the effectiveness of the financing statement has lapsed under Section 9–515 with respect to all secured parties of record. The record must be retrievable by using the name of the debtor and:

(1) if the record was filed [or recorded] in the filing office described in Section 9–501(a)(1), by using the file number assigned to the initial financing statement to which the record relates and the date [and time] that the record was filed [or recorded]; or

(2) if the record was filed in the filing office described in Section 9–501(a)(2), by using the file number assigned to the initial financing statement to which the record relates.

[End of Alternatives]

(b) Except to the extent that a statute governing disposition of public records provides otherwise, the filing office immediately may destroy any written record evidencing a financing statement. However, if the filing office destroys a written record, it shall maintain another record of the financing statement which complies with subsection (a).

Legislative Note: States whose real-estate filing offices require additional information in amendments and cannot search their records by both the name of the debtor and the file number should enact Alternative B to Sections 9–512(a), 9–518(b), 9–519(f), and 9–522(a).

§ 9–523. Information from Filing Office; Sale or License of Records.

(a) If a person that files a written record requests an acknowledgment of the filing, the filing office shall send to the person an image of the record showing the number assigned to the record pursuant to Section 9–519(a)(1) and the date and time of the filing of the record. However, if the person furnishes a copy of the record to the filing office, the filing office may instead:

(1) note upon the copy the number assigned to the record pursuant to Section 9–519(a)(1) and the date and time of the filing of the record; and

(2) send the copy to the person.

(b) If a person files a record other than a written record, the filing office shall communicate to the person an acknowledgment that provides:

(1) the information in the record;

(2) the number assigned to the record pursuant to Section 9–519(a)(1); and

(3) the date and time of the filing of the record.

(c) The filing office shall communicate or otherwise make available in a record the following information to any person that requests it:

(1) whether there is on file on a date and time specified by the filing office, but not a date earlier than three business days before the filing office receives the request, any financing statement that:

(A) designates a particular debtor [or, if the request so states, designates a particular debtor at the address specified in the request];

(B) has not lapsed under Section 9–515 with respect to all secured parties of record; and

(C) if the request so states, has lapsed under Section 9–515 and a record of which is maintained by the filing office under Section 9–522(a);

(2) the date and time of filing of each financing statement; and

(3) the information provided in each financing statement.

(d) In complying with its duty under subsection (c), the filing office may communicate information in any medium. However, if requested, the filing office shall communicate information by issuing [its written certificate] [a record that can be admitted into evidence in the courts of this State without extrinsic evidence of its authenticity].

(e) The filing office shall perform the acts required by subsections (a) through (d) at the time and in the manner prescribed by filing-office rule, but not later than two business days after the filing office receives the request.

(f) At least weekly, the [insert appropriate official or governmental agency] [filing office] shall offer to sell or license to the public on a nonexclusive basis, in bulk, copies of all records filed in it under this part, in every medium from time to time available to the filing office.

Legislative Notes:

1. States whose filing office does not offer the additional service of responding to search requests limited to a particular address should omit the bracketed language in subsection (c)(1)(A).

2. A State that elects not to require real-estate filing offices to comply with either or both of subsections (e) and (f) should specify in the appropriate subsection(s) only the filing office described in Section 9–501(a)(2).

§ 9–524. Delay by Filing Office.

Delay by the filing office beyond a time limit prescribed by this part is excused if:

(1) the delay is caused by interruption of communication or computer facilities, war, emergency conditions, failure of equipment, or other circumstances beyond control of the filing office; and

(2) the filing office exercises reasonable diligence under the circumstances.

§ 9–525. Fees.

(a) Except as otherwise provided in subsection (e), the fee for filing and indexing a record under this part, other than an initial financing statement of the kind described in subsection (b), is [the amount specified in subsection (c), if applicable, plus]:

(1) $[X] if the record is communicated in writing and consists of one or two pages;

(2) $[2X] if the record is communicated in writing and consists of more than two pages; and

(3) $[½X] if the record is communicated by another medium authorized by filing-office rule.

(b) Except as otherwise provided in subsection (e), the fee for filing and indexing an initial financing statement of the following kind is [the amount specified in subsection (c), if applicable, plus]:

(1) $_______ if the financing statement indicates that it is filed in connection with a public-finance transaction;

(2) $_______ if the financing statement indicates that it is filed in connection with a manufactured-home transaction.

[Alternative A]

(c) The number of names required to be indexed does not affect the amount of the fee in subsections (a) and (b).

[Alternative B]

(c) Except as otherwise provided in subsection (e), if a record is communicated in writing, the fee for each name more than two required to be indexed is $_______.

[End of Alternatives]

(d) The fee for responding to a request for information from the filing office, including for [issuing a certificate showing] [communicating] whether there is on file any financing statement naming a particular debtor, is:

(1) $_______ if the request is communicated in writing; and

(2) $_______ if the request is communicated by another medium authorized by filing-office rule.

(e) This section does not require a fee with respect to a record of a mortgage which is effective as a financing statement filed as a fixture filing or as a financing statement covering as-extracted collateral or timber to be cut under Section 9–502(c). However, the recording and satisfaction fees that otherwise would be applicable to the record of the mortgage apply.

Legislative Notes:

1. To preserve uniformity, a State that places the provisions of this section together with statutes setting fees for other services should do so without modification.

2. A State should enact subsection (c), Alternative A, and omit the bracketed language in subsections (a) and (b) unless its indexing system entails a substantial additional cost when indexing additional names.

As amended in 2000.

§ 9–526. Filing-Office Rules.

(a) The [insert appropriate governmental official or agency] shall adopt and publish rules to implement this article. The filing-office rules must be[:

(1)] consistent with this article[; and

(2) adopted and published in accordance with the [insert any applicable state administrative procedure act]].

(b) To keep the filing-office rules and practices of the filing office in harmony with the rules and practices of filing offices in other jurisdictions that enact substantially this part, and to keep the technology used by the filing office compatible with the technology used by filing offices in other jurisdictions that enact substantially this part, the [insert appropriate governmental official or agency], so far as is consistent with the purposes, policies, and provisions of this article, in adopting, amending, and repealing filing-office rules, shall:

(1) consult with filing offices in other jurisdictions that enact substantially this part; and

(2) consult the most recent version of the Model Rules promulgated by the International Association of Corporate Administrators or any successor organization; and

(3) take into consideration the rules and practices of, and the technology used by, filing offices in other jurisdictions that enact substantially this part.

§ 9–527. Duty to Report.

The [insert appropriate governmental official or agency] shall report [annually on or before _______] to the [Governor and Legislature] on the operation of the filing office. The report must contain a statement of the extent to which:

(1) the filing-office rules are not in harmony with the rules of filing offices in other jurisdictions that enact substantially this part and the reasons for these variations; and

(2) the filing-office rules are not in harmony with the most recent version of the Model Rules promulgated by the International Association of Corporate Administrators, or any successor organization, and the reasons for these variations.

Part 6 Default

[Subpart 1. Default and Enforcement of Security Interest]

§ 9–601. Rights after Default; Judicial Enforcement; Consignor or Buyer of Accounts, Chattel Paper, Payment Intangibles, or Promissory Notes.

(a) After default, a secured party has the rights provided in this part and, except as otherwise provided in Section 9–602, those provided by agreement of the parties. A secured party:

(1) may reduce a claim to judgment, foreclose, or otherwise enforce the claim, security interest, or agricultural lien by any available judicial procedure; and

(2) if the collateral is documents, may proceed either as to the documents or as to the goods they cover.

(b) A secured party in possession of collateral or control of collateral under Section 9–104, 9–105, 9–106, or 9–107 has the rights and duties provided in Section 9–207.

(c) The rights under subsections (a) and (b) are cumulative and may be exercised simultaneously.

(d) Except as otherwise provided in subsection (g) and Section 9–605, after default, a debtor and an obligor have the rights provided in this part and by agreement of the parties.

(e) If a secured party has reduced its claim to judgment, the lien of any levy that may be made upon the collateral by virtue of an execution based upon the judgment relates back to the earliest of:

(1) the date of perfection of the security interest or agricultural lien in the collateral;

(2) the date of filing a financing statement covering the collateral; or

(3) any date specified in a statute under which the agricultural lien was created.

(f) A sale pursuant to an execution is a foreclosure of the security interest or agricultural lien by judicial procedure within the meaning of this section. A secured party may purchase at the sale and thereafter hold the collateral free of any other requirements of this article.

(g) Except as otherwise provided in Section 9–607(c), this part imposes no duties upon a secured party that is a consignor or is a buyer of accounts, chattel paper, payment intangibles, or promissory notes.

§ 9–602. Waiver and Variance of Rights and Duties.

Except as otherwise provided in Section 9–624, to the extent that they give rights to a debtor or obligor and impose duties on a secured party, the debtor or obligor may not waive or vary the rules stated in the following listed sections:

(1) Section 9–207(b)(4)(C), which deals with use and operation of the collateral by the secured party;

(2) Section 9–210, which deals with requests for an accounting and requests concerning a list of collateral and statement of account;

(3) Section 9–607(c), which deals with collection and enforcement of collateral;

(4) Sections 9–608(a) and 9–615(c) to the extent that they deal with application or payment of noncash proceeds of collection, enforcement, or disposition;

(5) Sections 9–608(a) and 9–615(d) to the extent that they require accounting for or payment of surplus proceeds of collateral;

(6) Section 9–609 to the extent that it imposes upon a secured party that takes possession of collateral without judicial process the duty to do so without breach of the peace;

(7) Sections 9–610(b), 9–611, 9–613, and 9–614, which deal with disposition of collateral;

(8) Section 9–615(f), which deals with calculation of a deficiency or surplus when a disposition is made to the secured party, a person related to the secured party, or a secondary obligor;

(9) Section 9–616, which deals with explanation of the calculation of a surplus or deficiency;

(10) Sections 9–620, 9–621, and 9–622, which deal with acceptance of collateral in satisfaction of obligation;

(11) Section 9–623, which deals with redemption of collateral;

(12) Section 9–624, which deals with permissible waivers; and

(13) Sections 9–625 and 9–626, which deal with the secured party's liability for failure to comply with this article.

§ 9–603. Agreement on Standards Concerning Rights and Duties.

(a) The parties may determine by agreement the standards measuring the fulfillment of the rights of a debtor or obligor and the duties of a secured party under a rule stated in Section 9–602 if the standards are not manifestly unreasonable.

(b) Subsection (a) does not apply to the duty under Section 9–609 to refrain from breaching the peace.

§ 9–604. Procedure If Security Agreement Covers Real Property or Fixtures.

(a) If a security agreement covers both personal and real property, a secured party may proceed:

(1) under this part as to the personal property without prejudicing any rights with respect to the real property; or

(2) as to both the personal property and the real property in accordance with the rights with respect to the real property, in which case the other provisions of this part do not apply.

(b) Subject to subsection (c), if a security agreement covers goods that are or become fixtures, a secured party may proceed:

(1) under this part; or

(2) in accordance with the rights with respect to real property, in which case the other provisions of this part do not apply.

(c) Subject to the other provisions of this part, if a secured party holding a security interest in fixtures has priority over all owners and encumbrancers of the real property, the secured party, after default, may remove the collateral from the real property.

(d) A secured party that removes collateral shall promptly reimburse any encumbrancer or owner of the real property, other than the debtor, for the cost of repair of any physical injury caused by the removal. The secured party need not reimburse the encumbrancer or owner for any diminution in value of the real property caused by the absence of the goods removed or by any necessity of replacing them. A person entitled to reimbursement may refuse permission to remove until the secured party gives adequate assurance for the performance of the obligation to reimburse.

§ 9–605. Unknown Debtor or Secondary Obligor.

A secured party does not owe a duty based on its status as secured party:

(1) to a person that is a debtor or obligor, unless the secured party knows:

(A) that the person is a debtor or obligor;

(B) the identity of the person; and

(C) how to communicate with the person; or

(2) to a secured party or lienholder that has filed a financing statement against a person, unless the secured party knows:

(A) that the person is a debtor; and

(B) the identity of the person.

§ 9–606. Time of Default for Agricultural Lien.

For purposes of this part, a default occurs in connection with an agricultural lien at the time the secured party becomes entitled to enforce the lien in accordance with the statute under which it was created.

§ 9–607. Collection and Enforcement by Secured Party.

(a) If so agreed, and in any event after default, a secured party:

(1) may notify an account debtor or other person obligated on collateral to make payment or otherwise render performance to or for the benefit of the secured party;

(2) may take any proceeds to which the secured party is entitled under Section 9–315;

(3) may enforce the obligations of an account debtor or other person obligated on collateral and exercise the rights of the debtor with respect to the obligation of the account debtor or other person obligated on collateral to make payment or otherwise render performance to the debtor, and with respect to any property that secures the obligations of the account debtor or other person obligated on the collateral;

(4) if it holds a security interest in a deposit account perfected by control under Section 9–104(a)(1), may apply the balance of the deposit account to the obligation secured by the deposit account; and

(5) if it holds a security interest in a deposit account perfected by control under Section 9–104(a)(2) or (3), may instruct the bank to pay the balance of the deposit account to or for the benefit of the secured party.

(b) If necessary to enable a secured party to exercise under subsection (a)(3) the right of a debtor to enforce a mortgage nonjudicially, the secured party may record in the office in which a record of the mortgage is recorded:

(1) a copy of the security agreement that creates or provides for a security interest in the obligation secured by the mortgage; and

(2) the secured party's sworn affidavit in recordable form stating that:

(A) a default has occurred; and

(B) the secured party is entitled to enforce the mortgage nonjudicially.

(c) A secured party shall proceed in a commercially reasonable manner if the secured party:

(1) undertakes to collect from or enforce an obligation of an account debtor or other person obligated on collateral; and

(2) is entitled to charge back uncollected collateral or otherwise to full or limited recourse against the debtor or a secondary obligor.

(d) A secured party may deduct from the collections made pursuant to subsection (c) reasonable expenses of collection and enforcement, including reasonable attorney's fees and legal expenses incurred by the secured party.

(e) This section does not determine whether an account debtor, bank, or other person obligated on collateral owes a duty to a secured party.

As amended in 2000.

§ 9–608. Application of Proceeds of Collection or Enforcement; Liability for Deficiency and Right to Surplus.

(a) If a security interest or agricultural lien secures payment or performance of an obligation, the following rules apply:

(1) A secured party shall apply or pay over for application the cash proceeds of collection or enforcement under Section 9–607 in the following order to:

(A) the reasonable expenses of collection and enforcement and, to the extent provided for by agreement and not prohibited by law, reasonable attorney's fees and legal expenses incurred by the secured party;

(B) the satisfaction of obligations secured by the security interest or agricultural lien under which the collection or enforcement is made; and

(C) the satisfaction of obligations secured by any subordinate security interest in or other lien on the collateral subject to the security interest or agricultural lien under which the collection or enforcement is made if the secured party receives an authenticated demand for proceeds before distribution of the proceeds is completed.

(2) If requested by a secured party, a holder of a subordinate security interest or other lien shall furnish reasonable proof of the interest or lien within a reasonable time. Unless the holder complies, the secured party need not comply with the holder's demand under paragraph (1)(C).

(3) A secured party need not apply or pay over for application noncash proceeds of collection and enforcement under Section 9–607 unless the failure to do so would be commercially unreasonable. A secured party that applies or pays over for application noncash proceeds shall do so in a commercially reasonable manner.

(4) A secured party shall account to and pay a debtor for any surplus, and the obligor is liable for any deficiency.

(b) If the underlying transaction is a sale of accounts, chattel paper, payment intangibles, or promissory notes, the debtor is not entitled to any surplus, and the obligor is not liable for any deficiency.

As amended in 2000.

§ 9–609. Secured Party's Right to Take Possession after Default.

(a) After default, a secured party:

(1) may take possession of the collateral; and

(2) without removal, may render equipment unusable and dispose of collateral on a debtor's premises under Section 9–610.

(b) A secured party may proceed under subsection (a):

(1) pursuant to judicial process; or

(2) without judicial process, if it proceeds without breach of the peace.

(c) If so agreed, and in any event after default, a secured party may require the debtor to assemble the collateral and make it available to the secured party at a place to be designated by the secured party which is reasonably convenient to both parties.

§ 9–610. Disposition of Collateral after Default.

(a) After default, a secured party may sell, lease, license, or otherwise dispose of any or all of the collateral in its present condition or following any commercially reasonable preparation or processing.

(b) Every aspect of a disposition of collateral, including the method, manner, time, place, and other terms, must be commercially reasonable. If commercially reasonable, a secured party may dispose of collateral by public or private proceedings, by one or more contracts, as a unit or in parcels, and at any time and place and on any terms.

(c) A secured party may purchase collateral:

(1) at a public disposition; or

(2) at a private disposition only if the collateral is of a kind that is customarily sold on a recognized market or the subject of widely distributed standard price quotations.

(d) A contract for sale, lease, license, or other disposition includes the warranties relating to title, possession, quiet enjoyment, and the like which by operation of law accompany a voluntary disposition of property of the kind subject to the contract.

(e) A secured party may disclaim or modify warranties under subsection (d):

(1) in a manner that would be effective to disclaim or modify the warranties in a voluntary disposition of property of the kind subject to the contract of disposition; or

(2) by communicating to the purchaser a record evidencing the contract for disposition and including an express disclaimer or modification of the warranties.

(f) A record is sufficient to disclaim warranties under subsection (e) if it indicates "There is no warranty relating to title, possession, quiet enjoyment, or the like in this disposition" or uses words of similar import.

§ 9–611. Notification before Disposition of Collateral.

(a) In this section, "notification date" means the earlier of the date on which:

(1) a secured party sends to the debtor and any secondary obligor an authenticated notification of disposition; or

(2) the debtor and any secondary obligor waive the right to notification.

(b) Except as otherwise provided in subsection (d), a secured party that disposes of collateral under Section 9–610 shall send to the persons specified in subsection (c) a reasonable authenticated notification of disposition.

(c) To comply with subsection (b), the secured party shall send an authenticated notification of disposition to:

(1) the debtor;

(2) any secondary obligor; and

(3) if the collateral is other than consumer goods:

(A) any other person from which the secured party has received, before the notification date, an authenticated notification of a claim of an interest in the collateral;

(B) any other secured party or lienholder that, 10 days before the notification date, held a security interest in or other lien on the collateral perfected by the filing of a financing statement that:

(i) identified the collateral;

(ii) was indexed under the debtor's name as of that date; and

(iii) was filed in the office in which to file a financing statement against the debtor covering the collateral as of that date; and

(C) any other secured party that, 10 days before the notification date, held a security interest in the collateral perfected by compliance with a statute, regulation, or treaty described in Section 9–311(a).

(d) Subsection (b) does not apply if the collateral is perishable or threatens to decline speedily in value or is of a type customarily sold on a recognized market.

(e) A secured party complies with the requirement for notification prescribed by subsection (c)(3)(B) if:

(1) not later than 20 days or earlier than 30 days before the notification date, the secured party requests, in a commercially reasonable manner, information concerning financing statements indexed under the debtor's name in the office indicated in subsection (c)(3)(B); and

(2) before the notification date, the secured party:

(A) did not receive a response to the request for information; or

(B) received a response to the request for information and sent an authenticated notification of disposition to each secured party or other lienholder named in that response whose financing statement covered the collateral.

§ 9–612. Timeliness of Notification before Disposition of Collateral.

(a) Except as otherwise provided in subsection (b), whether a notification is sent within a reasonable time is a question of fact.

(b) In a transaction other than a consumer transaction, a notification of disposition sent after default and 10 days or more before the earliest time of disposition set forth in the notification is sent within a reasonable time before the disposition.

§ 9–613. Contents and Form of Notification before Disposition of Collateral: General.

Except in a consumer-goods transaction, the following rules apply:

(1) The contents of a notification of disposition are sufficient if the notification:

(A) describes the debtor and the secured party;

(B) describes the collateral that is the subject of the intended disposition;

(C) states the method of intended disposition;

(D) states that the debtor is entitled to an accounting of the unpaid indebtedness and states the charge, if any, for an accounting; and

(E) states the time and place of a public disposition or the time after which any other disposition is to be made.

(2) Whether the contents of a notification that lacks any of the information specified in paragraph (1) are nevertheless sufficient is a question of fact.

(3) The contents of a notification providing substantially the information specified in paragraph (1) are sufficient, even if the notification includes:

(A) information not specified by that paragraph; or

(B) minor errors that are not seriously misleading.

(4) A particular phrasing of the notification is not required.

(5) The following form of notification and the form appearing in Section 9–614(3), when completed, each provides sufficient information:

NOTIFICATION OF DISPOSITION OF COLLATERAL

To: *[Name of debtor, obligor, or other person to which the notification is sent]*

From: *[Name, address, and telephone number of secured party]*

Name of Debtor(s): *[Include only if debtor(s) are not an addressee]*

[For a public disposition:]

We will sell [or lease or license, *as applicable*] the [*describe collateral*] [to the highest qualified bidder] in public as follows:

Day and Date: ________

Time: ________

Place: ________

[For a private disposition:]

We will sell [or lease or license, *as applicable*] the [*describe collateral*] privately sometime after [*day and date*].

You are entitled to an accounting of the unpaid indebtedness secured by the property that we intend to sell [or lease or license, *as applicable*] [for a charge of $________]. You may request an accounting by calling us at [*telephone number*].

[End of Form]

As amended in 2000.

§ 9–614. Contents and Form of Notification before Disposition of Collateral: Consumer-Goods Transaction.

In a consumer-goods transaction, the following rules apply:

(1) A notification of disposition must provide the following information:

(A) the information specified in Section 9–613(1);

(B) a description of any liability for a deficiency of the person to which the notification is sent;

(C) a telephone number from which the amount that must be paid to the secured party to redeem the collateral under Section 9–623 is available; and

(D) a telephone number or mailing address from which additional information concerning the disposition and the obligation secured is available.

(2) A particular phrasing of the notification is not required.

(3) The following form of notification, when completed, provides sufficient information:

[*Name and address of secured party*]

[*Date*]

NOTICE OF OUR PLAN TO SELL PROPERTY

[*Name and address of any obligor who is also a debtor*]

Subject: [*Identification of Transaction*]

We have your [*describe collateral*], because you broke promises in our agreement.

[*For a public disposition:*]

We will sell [*describe collateral*] at public sale. A sale could include a lease or license. The sale will be held as follows:

Date: ________

Time: ________

Place: ________

You may attend the sale and bring bidders if you want.

[*For a private disposition:*]

We will sell [*describe collateral*] at private sale sometime after [*date*]. A sale could include a lease or license.

The money that we get from the sale (after paying our costs) will reduce the amount you owe. If we get less money than you owe, you [*will or will not, as applicable*] still owe us the difference. If we get more money than you owe, you will get the extra money, unless we must pay it to someone else.

You can get the property back at any time before we sell it by paying us the full amount you owe (not just the past due payments), including our expenses. To learn the exact amount you must pay, call us at [*telephone number*].

If you want us to explain to you in writing how we have figured the amount that you owe us, you may call us at [telephone number] [or write us at [*secured party's address*]] and request a written explanation. [We will charge you $________ for the explanation if we sent you another written explanation of the amount you owe us within the last six months.]

If you need more information about the sale call us at [*telephone number*] [or write us at [secured party's address]].

We are sending this notice to the following other people who have an interest in [*describe collateral*] or who owe money under your agreement:

[*Names of all other debtors and obligors, if any*]

[End of Form]

(4) A notification in the form of paragraph (3) is sufficient, even if additional information appears at the end of the form.

(5) A notification in the form of paragraph (3) is sufficient, even if it includes errors in information not required by paragraph (1), unless the error is misleading with respect to rights arising under this article.

(6) If a notification under this section is not in the form of paragraph (3), law other than this article determines the effect of including information not required by paragraph (1).

§ 9–615. Application of Proceeds of Disposition; Liability for Deficiency and Right to Surplus.

(a) A secured party shall apply or pay over for application the cash proceeds of disposition under Section 9–610 in the following order to:

(1) the reasonable expenses of retaking, holding, preparing for disposition, processing, and disposing, and, to the extent provided for by agreement and not prohibited by law, reasonable attorney's fees and legal expenses incurred by the secured party;

(2) the satisfaction of obligations secured by the security interest or agricultural lien under which the disposition is made;

(3) the satisfaction of obligations secured by any subordinate security interest in or other subordinate lien on the collateral if:

(A) the secured party receives from the holder of the subordinate security interest or other lien an authenticated demand for proceeds before distribution of the proceeds is completed; and

(B) in a case in which a consignor has an interest in the collateral, the subordinate security interest or other lien is senior to the interest of the consignor; and

(4) a secured party that is a consignor of the collateral if the secured party receives from the consignor an authenticated demand for proceeds before distribution of the proceeds is completed.

(b) If requested by a secured party, a holder of a subordinate security interest or other lien shall furnish reasonable proof of the interest or lien within a reasonable time. Unless the holder does so, the secured party need not comply with the holder's demand under subsection (a)(3).

(c) A secured party need not apply or pay over for application noncash proceeds of disposition under Section 9–610 unless the failure to do so would be commercially unreasonable. A secured party that applies or pays over for application noncash proceeds shall do so in a commercially reasonable manner.

(d) If the security interest under which a disposition is made secures payment or performance of an obligation, after making the payments and applications required by subsection (a) and permitted by subsection (c):

(1) unless subsection (a)(4) requires the secured party to apply or pay over cash proceeds to a consignor, the secured party shall account to and pay a debtor for any surplus; and

(2) the obligor is liable for any deficiency.

(e) If the underlying transaction is a sale of accounts, chattel paper, payment intangibles, or promissory notes:

(1) the debtor is not entitled to any surplus; and

(2) the obligor is not liable for any deficiency.

(f) The surplus or deficiency following a disposition is calculated based on the amount of proceeds that would have been realized in a disposition complying with this part to a transferee other than the secured party, a person related to the secured party, or a secondary obligor if:

(1) the transferee in the disposition is the secured party, a person related to the secured party, or a secondary obligor; and

(2) the amount of proceeds of the disposition is significantly below the range of proceeds that a complying disposition to a person other than the secured party, a person related to the secured party, or a secondary obligor would have brought.

(g) A secured party that receives cash proceeds of a disposition in good faith and without knowledge that the receipt violates the rights of the holder of a security interest or other lien that is not subordinate to the security interest or agricultural lien under which the disposition is made:

(1) takes the cash proceeds free of the security interest or other lien;

(2) is not obligated to apply the proceeds of the disposition to the satisfaction of obligations secured by the security interest or other lien; and

(3) is not obligated to account to or pay the holder of the security interest or other lien for any surplus.

As amended in 2000.

§ 9–616. Explanation of Calculation of Surplus or Deficiency.

(a) In this section:

(1) "Explanation" means a writing that:

(A) states the amount of the surplus or deficiency;

(B) provides an explanation in accordance with subsection (c) of how the secured party calculated the surplus or deficiency;

(C) states, if applicable, that future debits, credits, charges, including additional credit service charges or interest, rebates, and expenses may affect the amount of the surplus or deficiency; and

(D) provides a telephone number or mailing address from which additional information concerning the transaction is available.

(2) "Request" means a record:

(A) authenticated by a debtor or consumer obligor;

(B) requesting that the recipient provide an explanation; and

(C) sent after disposition of the collateral under Section 9–610.

(b) In a consumer-goods transaction in which the debtor is entitled to a surplus or a consumer obligor is liable for a deficiency under Section 9–615, the secured party shall:

(1) send an explanation to the debtor or consumer obligor, as applicable, after the disposition and:

(A) before or when the secured party accounts to the debtor and pays any surplus or first makes written demand on the consumer obligor after the disposition for payment of the deficiency; and

(B) within 14 days after receipt of a request; or

(2) in the case of a consumer obligor who is liable for a deficiency, within 14 days after receipt of a request, send to the consumer obligor a record waiving the secured party's right to a deficiency.

(c) To comply with subsection (a)(1)(B), a writing must provide the following information in the following order:

(1) the aggregate amount of obligations secured by the security interest under which the disposition was made, and, if the amount reflects a rebate of unearned interest or credit service charge, an indication of that fact, calculated as of a specified date:

(A) if the secured party takes or receives possession of the collateral after default, not more than 35 days before the secured party takes or receives possession; or

(B) if the secured party takes or receives possession of the collateral before default or does not take possession of the collateral, not more than 35 days before the disposition;

(2) the amount of proceeds of the disposition;

(3) the aggregate amount of the obligations after deducting the amount of proceeds;

(4) the amount, in the aggregate or by type, and types of expenses, including expenses of retaking, holding, preparing for disposition, processing, and disposing of the collateral, and attorney's fees secured by the collateral which are known to the secured party and relate to the current disposition;

(5) the amount, in the aggregate or by type, and types of credits, including rebates of interest or credit service charges, to which the obligor is known to be entitled and which are not reflected in the amount in paragraph (1); and

(6) the amount of the surplus or deficiency.

(d) A particular phrasing of the explanation is not required. An explanation complying substantially with the requirements of subsection (a) is sufficient, even if it includes minor errors that are not seriously misleading.

(e) A debtor or consumer obligor is entitled without charge to one response to a request under this section during any six-month period in which the secured party did not send to the debtor or consumer obligor an explanation pursuant to subsection (b)(1). The secured party may require payment of a charge not exceeding $25 for each additional response.

§ 9–617. Rights of Transferee of Collateral.

(a) A secured party's disposition of collateral after default:

(1) transfers to a transferee for value all of the debtor's rights in the collateral;

(2) discharges the security interest under which the disposition is made; and

(3) discharges any subordinate security interest or other subordinate lien [other than liens created under [cite acts or statutes providing for liens, if any, that are not to be discharged]].

(b) A transferee that acts in good faith takes free of the rights and interests described in subsection (a), even if the secured party fails to comply with this article or the requirements of any judicial proceeding.

(c) If a transferee does not take free of the rights and interests described in subsection (a), the transferee takes the collateral subject to:

(1) the debtor's rights in the collateral;

(2) the security interest or agricultural lien under which the disposition is made; and

(3) any other security interest or other lien.

§ 9–618. Rights and Duties of Certain Secondary Obligors.

(a) A secondary obligor acquires the rights and becomes obligated to perform the duties of the secured party after the secondary obligor:

(1) receives an assignment of a secured obligation from the secured party;

(2) receives a transfer of collateral from the secured party and agrees to accept the rights and assume the duties of the secured party; or

(3) is subrogated to the rights of a secured party with respect to collateral.

(b) An assignment, transfer, or subrogation described in subsection (a):

(1) is not a disposition of collateral under Section 9–610; and

(2) relieves the secured party of further duties under this article.

§ 9–619. Transfer of Record or Legal Title.

(a) In this section, "transfer statement" means a record authenticated by a secured party stating:

(1) that the debtor has defaulted in connection with an obligation secured by specified collateral;

(2) that the secured party has exercised its post-default remedies with respect to the collateral;

(3) that, by reason of the exercise, a transferee has acquired the rights of the debtor in the collateral; and

(4) the name and mailing address of the secured party, debtor, and transferee.

(b) A transfer statement entitles the transferee to the transfer of record of all rights of the debtor in the collateral specified in the statement in any official filing, recording, registration, or certificate-of-title system covering the collateral. If a transfer statement is presented with the applicable fee and request form to the official or office responsible for maintaining the system, the official or office shall:

(1) accept the transfer statement;

(2) promptly amend its records to reflect the transfer; and

(3) if applicable, issue a new appropriate certificate of title in the name of the transferee.

(c) A transfer of the record or legal title to collateral to a secured party under subsection (b) or otherwise is not of itself a disposition of collateral under this article and does not of itself relieve the secured party of its duties under this article.

§ 9–620. Acceptance of Collateral in Full or Partial Satisfaction of Obligation; Compulsory Disposition of Collateral.

(a) Except as otherwise provided in subsection (g), a secured party may accept collateral in full or partial satisfaction of the obligation it secures only if:

(1) the debtor consents to the acceptance under subsection (c);

(2) the secured party does not receive, within the time set forth in subsection (d), a notification of objection to the proposal authenticated by:

(A) a person to which the secured party was required to send a proposal under Section 9–621; or

(B) any other person, other than the debtor, holding an interest in the collateral subordinate to the security interest that is the subject of the proposal;

(3) if the collateral is consumer goods, the collateral is not in the possession of the debtor when the debtor consents to the acceptance; and

(4) subsection (e) does not require the secured party to dispose of the collateral or the debtor waives the requirement pursuant to Section 9–624.

(b) A purported or apparent acceptance of collateral under this section is ineffective unless:

(1) the secured party consents to the acceptance in an authenticated record or sends a proposal to the debtor; and

(2) the conditions of subsection (a) are met.

(c) For purposes of this section:

(1) a debtor consents to an acceptance of collateral in partial satisfaction of the obligation it secures only if the debtor agrees to the terms of the acceptance in a record authenticated after default; and

(2) a debtor consents to an acceptance of collateral in full satisfaction of the obligation it secures only if the debtor agrees to the terms of the acceptance in a record authenticated after default or the secured party:

(A) sends to the debtor after default a proposal that is unconditional or subject only to a condition that collateral not in the possession of the secured party be preserved or maintained;

(B) in the proposal, proposes to accept collateral in full satisfaction of the obligation it secures; and

(C) does not receive a notification of objection authenticated by the debtor within 20 days after the proposal is sent.

(d) To be effective under subsection (a)(2), a notification of objection must be received by the secured party:

(1) in the case of a person to which the proposal was sent pursuant to Section 9–621, within 20 days after notification was sent to that person; and

(2) in other cases:

(A) within 20 days after the last notification was sent pursuant to Section 9–621; or

(B) if a notification was not sent, before the debtor consents to the acceptance under subsection (c).

(e) A secured party that has taken possession of collateral shall dispose of the collateral pursuant to Section 9–610 within the time specified in subsection (f) if:

(1) 60 percent of the cash price has been paid in the case of a purchase-money security interest in consumer goods; or

(2) 60 percent of the principal amount of the obligation secured has been paid in the case of a non-purchase-money security interest in consumer goods.

(f) To comply with subsection (e), the secured party shall dispose of the collateral:

(1) within 90 days after taking possession; or

(2) within any longer period to which the debtor and all secondary obligors have agreed in an agreement to that effect entered into and authenticated after default.

(g) In a consumer transaction, a secured party may not accept collateral in partial satisfaction of the obligation it secures.

§ 9–621. Notification of Proposal to Accept Collateral.

(a) A secured party that desires to accept collateral in full or partial satisfaction of the obligation it secures shall send its proposal to:

(1) any person from which the secured party has received, before the debtor consented to the acceptance, an authenticated notification of a claim of an interest in the collateral;

(2) any other secured party or lienholder that, 10 days before the debtor consented to the acceptance, held a security interest in or other lien on the collateral perfected by the filing of a financing statement that:

(A) identified the collateral;

(B) was indexed under the debtor's name as of that date; and

(C) was filed in the office or offices in which to file a financing statement against the debtor covering the collateral as of that date; and

(3) any other secured party that, 10 days before the debtor consented to the acceptance, held a security interest in the collateral perfected by compliance with a statute, regulation, or treaty described in Section 9–311(a).

(b) A secured party that desires to accept collateral in partial satisfaction of the obligation it secures shall send its proposal to any secondary obligor in addition to the persons described in subsection (a).

§ 9–622. Effect of Acceptance of Collateral.

(a) A secured party's acceptance of collateral in full or partial satisfaction of the obligation it secures:

(1) discharges the obligation to the extent consented to by the debtor;

(2) transfers to the secured party all of a debtor's rights in the collateral;

(3) discharges the security interest or agricultural lien that is the subject of the debtor's consent and any subordinate security interest or other subordinate lien; and

(4) terminates any other subordinate interest.

(b) A subordinate interest is discharged or terminated under subsection (a), even if the secured party fails to comply with this article.

§ 9–623. Right to Redeem Collateral.

(a) A debtor, any secondary obligor, or any other secured party or lienholder may redeem collateral.

(b) To redeem collateral, a person shall tender:

(1) fulfillment of all obligations secured by the collateral; and

(2) the reasonable expenses and attorney's fees described in Section 9–615(a)(1).

(c) A redemption may occur at any time before a secured party:

(1) has collected collateral under Section 9–607;

(2) has disposed of collateral or entered into a contract for its disposition under Section 9–610; or

(3) has accepted collateral in full or partial satisfaction of the obligation it secures under Section 9–622.

§ 9–624. Waiver.

(a) A debtor or secondary obligor may waive the right to notification of disposition of collateral under Section 9–611 only by an agreement to that effect entered into and authenticated after default.

(b) A debtor may waive the right to require disposition of collateral under Section 9–620(e) only by an agreement to that effect entered into and authenticated after default.

(c) Except in a consumer-goods transaction, a debtor or secondary obligor may waive the right to redeem collateral under Section 9–623 only by an agreement to that effect entered into and authenticated after default.

[Subpart 2. Noncompliance with Article]

§ 9–625. Remedies for Secured Party's Failure to Comply with Article.

(a) If it is established that a secured party is not proceeding in accordance with this article, a court may order or restrain collection, enforcement, or disposition of collateral on appropriate terms and conditions.

(b) Subject to subsections (c), (d), and (f), a person is liable for damages in the amount of any loss caused by a failure to comply with this article. Loss caused by a failure to comply may include loss resulting from the debtor's inability to obtain, or increased costs of, alternative financing.

(c) Except as otherwise provided in Section 9–628:

(1) a person that, at the time of the failure, was a debtor, was an obligor, or held a security interest in or other lien on the collateral may recover damages under subsection (b) for its loss; and

(2) if the collateral is consumer goods, a person that was a debtor or a secondary obligor at the time a secured party failed to comply with this part may recover for that failure in any event an amount not less than the credit service charge plus 10 percent of the principal amount of the obligation or the time-price differential plus 10 percent of the cash price.

(d) A debtor whose deficiency is eliminated under Section 9–626 may recover damages for the loss of any surplus. However, a debtor or secondary obligor whose deficiency is eliminated or reduced under Section 9–626 may not otherwise recover under subsection

(b) for noncompliance with the provisions of this part relating to collection, enforcement, disposition, or acceptance.

(e) In addition to any damages recoverable under subsection (b), the debtor, consumer obligor, or person named as a debtor in a filed record, as applicable, may recover $500 in each case from a person that:

(1) fails to comply with Section 9–208;

(2) fails to comply with Section 9–209;

(3) files a record that the person is not entitled to file under Section 9–509(a);

(4) fails to cause the secured party of record to file or send a termination statement as required by Section 9–513(a) or (c);

(5) fails to comply with Section 9–616(b)(1) and whose failure is part of a pattern, or consistent with a practice, of noncompliance; or

(6) fails to comply with Section 9–616(b)(2).

(f) A debtor or consumer obligor may recover damages under subsection (b) and, in addition, $500 in each case from a person that, without reasonable cause, fails to comply with a request under Section 9–210. A recipient of a request under Section 9–210 which never claimed an interest in the collateral or obligations that are the subject of a request under that section has a reasonable excuse for failure to comply with the request within the meaning of this subsection.

(g) If a secured party fails to comply with a request regarding a list of collateral or a statement of account under Section 9–210, the secured party may claim a security interest only as shown in the list or statement included in the request as against a person that is reasonably misled by the failure.

As amended in 2000.

§ 9–626. Action in Which Deficiency or Surplus Is in Issue.

(a) In an action arising from a transaction, other than a consumer transaction, in which the amount of a deficiency or surplus is in issue, the following rules apply:

(1) A secured party need not prove compliance with the provisions of this part relating to collection, enforcement, disposition, or acceptance unless the debtor or a secondary obligor places the secured party's compliance in issue.

(2) If the secured party's compliance is placed in issue, the secured party has the burden of establishing that the collection, enforcement, disposition, or acceptance was conducted in accordance with this part.

(3) Except as otherwise provided in Section 9–628, if a secured party fails to prove that the collection, enforcement, disposition, or acceptance was conducted in accordance with the provisions of this part relating to collection, enforcement, disposition, or acceptance, the liability of a debtor or a secondary obligor for a deficiency is limited to an amount by which the sum of the secured obligation, expenses, and attorney's fees exceeds the greater of:

(A) the proceeds of the collection, enforcement, disposition, or acceptance; or

(B) the amount of proceeds that would have been realized had the noncomplying secured party proceeded in accordance with the provisions of this part relating to collection, enforcement, disposition, or acceptance.

(4) For purposes of paragraph (3)(B), the amount of proceeds that would have been realized is equal to the sum of the secured obligation, expenses, and attorney's fees unless the secured party proves that the amount is less than that sum.

(5) If a deficiency or surplus is calculated under Section 9–615(f), the debtor or obligor has the burden of establishing that the amount of proceeds of the disposition is significantly below the range of prices that a complying disposition to a person other than the secured party, a person related to the secured party, or a secondary obligor would have brought.

(b) The limitation of the rules in subsection (a) to transactions other than consumer transactions is intended to leave to the court the determination of the proper rules in consumer transactions. The court may not infer from that limitation the nature of the proper rule in consumer transactions and may continue to apply established approaches.

§ 9–627. Determination of Whether Conduct Was Commercially Reasonable.

(a) The fact that a greater amount could have been obtained by a collection, enforcement, disposition, or acceptance at a different time or in a different method from that selected by the secured party is not of itself sufficient to preclude the secured party from establishing that the collection, enforcement, disposition, or acceptance was made in a commercially reasonable manner.

(b) A disposition of collateral is made in a commercially reasonable manner if the disposition is made:

(1) in the usual manner on any recognized market;

(2) at the price current in any recognized market at the time of the disposition; or

(3) otherwise in conformity with reasonable commercial practices among dealers in the type of property that was the subject of the disposition.

(c) A collection, enforcement, disposition, or acceptance is commercially reasonable if it has been approved:

(1) in a judicial proceeding;

(2) by a bona fide creditors' committee;

(3) by a representative of creditors; or

(4) by an assignee for the benefit of creditors.

(d) Approval under subsection (c) need not be obtained, and lack of approval does not mean that the collection, enforcement, disposition, or acceptance is not commercially reasonable.

§ 9–628. Nonliability and Limitation on Liability of Secured Party; Liability of Secondary Obligor.

(a) Unless a secured party knows that a person is a debtor or obligor, knows the identity of the person, and knows how to communicate with the person:

(1) the secured party is not liable to the person, or to a secured party or lienholder that has filed a financing statement against the person, for failure to comply with this article; and

(2) the secured party's failure to comply with this article does not affect the liability of the person for a deficiency.

(b) A secured party is not liable because of its status as secured party:

(1) to a person that is a debtor or obligor, unless the secured party knows:

(A) that the person is a debtor or obligor;

(B) the identity of the person; and

(C) how to communicate with the person; or

(2) to a secured party or lienholder that has filed a financing statement against a person, unless the secured party knows:

(A) that the person is a debtor; and

(B) the identity of the person.

(c) A secured party is not liable to any person, and a person's liability for a deficiency is not affected, because of any act or omission arising out of the secured party's reasonable belief that a transaction is not a consumer-goods transaction or a consumer transaction or that goods are not consumer goods, if the secured party's belief is based on its reasonable reliance on:

(1) a debtor's representation concerning the purpose for which collateral was to be used, acquired, or held; or

(2) an obligor's representation concerning the purpose for which a secured obligation was incurred.

(d) A secured party is not liable to any person under Section 9–625(c)(2) for its failure to comply with Section 9–616.

(e) A secured party is not liable under Section 9–625(c)(2) more than once with respect to any one secured obligation.

Part 7 Transition

§ 9–701. Effective Date.

This [Act] takes effect on July 1, 2001.

§ 9–702. Savings Clause.

(a) Except as otherwise provided in this part, this [Act] applies to a transaction or lien within its scope, even if the transaction or lien was entered into or created before this [Act] takes effect.

(b) Except as otherwise provided in subsection (c) and Sections 9–703 through 9–709:

(1) transactions and liens that were not governed by [former Article 9], were validly entered into or created before this [Act] takes effect, and would be subject to this [Act] if they had been entered into or created after this [Act] takes effect, and the rights, duties, and interests flowing from those transactions and liens remain valid after this [Act] takes effect; and

(2) the transactions and liens may be terminated, completed, consummated, and enforced as required or permitted by this [Act] or by the law that otherwise would apply if this [Act] had not taken effect.

(c) This [Act] does not affect an action, case, or proceeding commenced before this [Act] takes effect.

As amended in 2000.

§ 9–703. Security Interest Perfected before Effective Date.

(a) A security interest that is enforceable immediately before this [Act] takes effect and would have priority over the rights of a person that becomes a lien creditor at that time is a perfected security interest under this [Act] if, when this [Act] takes effect, the applicable requirements for enforceability and perfection under this [Act] are satisfied without further action.

(b) Except as otherwise provided in Section 9–705, if, immediately before this [Act] takes effect, a security interest is enforceable and would have priority over the rights of a person that becomes a lien creditor at that time, but the applicable requirements for enforceability or perfection under this [Act] are not satisfied when this [Act] takes effect, the security interest:

(1) is a perfected security interest for one year after this [Act] takes effect;

(2) remains enforceable thereafter only if the security interest becomes enforceable under Section 9–203 before the year expires; and

(3) remains perfected thereafter only if the applicable requirements for perfection under this [Act] are satisfied before the year expires.

§ 9–704. Security Interest Unperfected before Effective Date.

A security interest that is enforceable immediately before this [Act] takes effect but which would be subordinate to the rights of a person that becomes a lien creditor at that time:

(1) remains an enforceable security interest for one year after this [Act] takes effect;

(2) remains enforceable thereafter if the security interest becomes enforceable under Section 9–203 when this [Act] takes effect or within one year thereafter; and

(3) becomes perfected:

(A) without further action, when this [Act] takes effect if the applicable requirements for perfection under this [Act] are satisfied before or at that time; or

(B) when the applicable requirements for perfection are satisfied if the requirements are satisfied after that time.

§ 9–705. Effectiveness of Action Taken before Effective Date.

(a) If action, other than the filing of a financing statement, is taken before this [Act] takes effect and the action would have resulted in priority of a security interest over the rights of a person that becomes a lien creditor had the security interest become enforceable before this [Act] takes effect, the action is effective to perfect a security interest that attaches under this [Act] within one year after this [Act] takes effect. An attached security interest becomes unperfected one year after this [Act] takes effect unless the security interest becomes a perfected security interest under this [Act] before the expiration of that period.

(b) The filing of a financing statement before this [Act] takes effect is effective to perfect a security interest to the extent the filing would satisfy the applicable requirements for perfection under this [Act].

(c) This [Act] does not render ineffective an effective financing statement that, before this [Act] takes effect, is filed and satisfies the applicable requirements for perfection under the law of the jurisdiction governing perfection as provided in [former Section 9–103]. However, except as otherwise provided in subsections (d) and (e) and Section 9–706, the financing statement ceases to be effective at the earlier of:

(1) the time the financing statement would have ceased to be effective under the law of the jurisdiction in which it is filed; or

(2) June 30, 2006.

(d) The filing of a continuation statement after this [Act] takes effect does not continue the effectiveness of the financing statement filed before this [Act] takes effect. However, upon the timely filing of a continuation statement after this [Act] takes effect and in accordance with the law of the jurisdiction governing perfection as provided in Part 3, the effectiveness of a financing statement filed in the same office in that jurisdiction before this [Act] takes effect continues for the period provided by the law of that jurisdiction.

(e) Subsection (c)(2) applies to a financing statement that, before this [Act] takes effect, is filed against a transmitting utility and satisfies the applicable requirements for perfection under the law of the jurisdiction governing perfection as provided in [former Section 9–103] only to the extent that Part 3 provides that the law of a jurisdiction other than the jurisdiction in which the financing statement is filed governs perfection of a security interest in collateral covered by the financing statement.

(f) A financing statement that includes a financing statement filed before this [Act] takes effect and a continuation statement filed after this [Act] takes effect is effective only to the extent that it satisfies the requirements of Part 5 for an initial financing statement.

§ 9–706. When Initial Financing Statement Suffices to Continue Effectiveness of Financing Statement.

(a) The filing of an initial financing statement in the office specified in Section 9–501 continues the effectiveness of a financing statement filed before this [Act] takes effect if:

(1) the filing of an initial financing statement in that office would be effective to perfect a security interest under this [Act];

(2) the pre-effective-date financing statement was filed in an office in another State or another office in this State; and

(3) the initial financing statement satisfies subsection (c).

(b) The filing of an initial financing statement under subsection (a) continues the effectiveness of the pre-effective-date financing statement:

(1) if the initial financing statement is filed before this [Act] takes effect, for the period provided in [former Section 9–403] with respect to a financing statement; and

(2) if the initial financing statement is filed after this [Act] takes effect, for the period provided in Section 9–515 with respect to an initial financing statement.

(c) To be effective for purposes of subsection (a), an initial financing statement must:

(1) satisfy the requirements of Part 5 for an initial financing statement;

(2) identify the pre-effective-date financing statement by indicating the office in which the financing statement was filed and providing the dates of filing and file numbers, if any, of the financing statement and of the most recent continuation statement filed with respect to the financing statement; and

(3) indicate that the pre-effective-date financing statement remains effective.

§ 9–707. Amendment of Pre-Effective-Date Financing Statement.

(a) In this section, "Pre-effective-date financing statement" means a financing statement filed before this [Act] takes effect.

(b) After this [Act] takes effect, a person may add or delete collateral covered by, continue or terminate the effectiveness of, or otherwise amend the information provided in, a pre-effective-date financing statement only in accordance with the law of the jurisdiction governing perfection as provided in Part 3. However, the effectiveness of a pre-effective-date financing statement also may be terminated in accordance with the law of the jurisdiction in which the financing statement is filed.

(c) Except as otherwise provided in subsection (d), if the law of this State governs perfection of a security interest, the information in a pre-effective-date financing statement may be amended after this [Act] takes effect only if:

(1) the pre-effective-date financing statement and an amendment are filed in the office specified in Section 9–501;

(2) an amendment is filed in the office specified in Section 9–501 concurrently with, or after the filing in that office of, an initial financing statement that satisfies Section 9–706(c); or

(3) an initial financing statement that provides the information as amended and satisfies Section 9–706(c) is filed in the office specified in Section 9–501.

(d) If the law of this State governs perfection of a security interest, the effectiveness of a pre-effective-date financing statement may be continued only under Section 9–705(d) and (f) or 9–706.

(e) Whether or not the law of this State governs perfection of a security interest, the effectiveness of a pre-effective-date financing statement filed in this State may be terminated after this [Act] takes effect by filing a termination statement in the office in which the pre-effective-date financing statement is filed, unless an initial financing statement that satisfies Section 9–706(c) has been filed in the office specified by the law of the jurisdiction governing perfection as provided in Part 3 as the office in which to file a financing statement.

As amended in 2000.

§ 9–708. Persons Entitled to File Initial Financing Statement or Continuation Statement.

A person may file an initial financing statement or a continuation statement under this part if:

(1) the secured party of record authorizes the filing; and

(2) the filing is necessary under this part:

(A) to continue the effectiveness of a financing statement filed before this [Act] takes effect; or

(B) to perfect or continue the perfection of a security interest.

As amended in 2000.

§ 9–709. Priority.

(a) This [Act] determines the priority of conflicting claims to collateral. However, if the relative priorities of the claims were established before this [Act] takes effect, [former Article 9] determines priority.

(b) For purposes of Section 9–322(a), the priority of a security interest that becomes enforceable under Section 9–203 of this [Act] dates from the time this [Act] takes effect if the security interest is perfected under this [Act] by the filing of a financing statement before this [Act] takes effect which would not have been effective to perfect the security interest under [former Article 9]. This subsection does not apply to conflicting security interests each of which is perfected by the filing of such a financing statement.

As amended in 2000.

Appendix D

The Sarbanes-Oxley Act of 2002 (Excerpts and Explanatory Comments)

Note: The author's explanatory comments appear in italics following the excerpt from each section.

Section 302
Corporate responsibility for financial reports[1]

(a) Regulations required

The Commission shall, by rule, require, for each company filing periodic reports under section 13(a) or 15(d) of the Securities Exchange Act of 1934 (15 U.S.C. 78m, 78o(d)), that the principal executive officer or officers and the principal financial officer or officers, or persons performing similar functions, certify in each annual or quarterly report filed or submitted under either such section of such Act that—

(1) the signing officer has reviewed the report;

(2) based on the officer's knowledge, the report does not contain any untrue statement of a material fact or omit to state a material fact necessary in order to make the statements made, in light of the circumstances under which such statements were made, not misleading;

(3) based on such officer's knowledge, the financial statements, and other financial information included in the report, fairly present in all material respects the financial condition and results of operations of the issuer as of, and for, the periods presented in the report;

(4) the signing officers—

(A) are responsible for establishing and maintaining internal controls;

(B) have designed such internal controls to ensure that material information relating to the issuer and its consolidated subsidiaries is made known to such officers by others within those entities, particularly during the period in which the periodic reports are being prepared;

(C) have evaluated the effectiveness of the issuer's internal controls as of a date within 90 days prior to the report; and

(D) have presented in the report their conclusions about the effectiveness of their internal controls based on their evaluation as of that date;

(5) the signing officers have disclosed to the issuer's auditors and the audit committee of the board of directors (or persons fulfilling the equivalent function)—

(A) all significant deficiencies in the design or operation of internal controls which could adversely affect the issuer's ability to record, process, summarize, and report financial data and have identified for the issuer's auditors any material weaknesses in internal controls; and

(B) any fraud, whether or not material, that involves management or other employees who have a significant role in the issuer's internal controls; and

(6) the signing officers have indicated in the report whether or not there were significant changes in internal controls or in other factors that could significantly affect internal controls subsequent to the date of their evaluation, including any corrective actions with regard to significant deficiencies and material weaknesses.

(b) Foreign reincorporations have no effect

Nothing in this section shall be interpreted or applied in any way to allow any issuer to lessen the legal force of the statement required under this section, by an issuer having reincorporated or having engaged in any other transaction that resulted in the transfer of the corporate domicile or offices of the issuer from inside the United States to outside of the United States.

(c) Deadline

The rules required by subsection (a) of this section shall be effective not later than 30 days after July 30, 2002.

* * * *

Explanatory Comments:

Section 302 requires the chief executive officer (CEO) and chief financial officer (CFO) of each public company to certify that they have reviewed the company's quarterly and annual reports to be filed with the Securities and Exchange Commission (SEC). The CEO and CFO must certify that, based on their knowledge, the reports do not contain any untrue statement of a material fact or any half-truth that would make the report misleading, and that the information contained in the reports fairly presents the company's financial condition.

In addition, this section also requires the CEO and CFO to certify that they have created and designed an internal control system for their company and have recently evaluated that system to ensure that it is effectively providing them with relevant and accurate financial information. If the signing officers have found any significant deficiencies or weaknesses in the company's system or have discovered any evidence of fraud, they must have reported the situation, and any corrective actions they have taken, to the auditors and the audit committee.

1. This section of the Sarbanes-Oxley Act is codified at 15 U.S.C. Section 7241.

Section 306
Insider trades during pension fund blackout periods[2]

(a) Prohibition of insider trading during pension fund blackout periods

(1) In general

Except to the extent otherwise provided by rule of the Commission pursuant to paragraph (3), it shall be unlawful for any director or executive officer of an issuer of any equity security (other than an exempted security), directly or indirectly, to purchase, sell, or otherwise acquire or transfer any equity security of the issuer (other than an exempted security) during any blackout period with respect to such equity security if such director or officer acquires such equity security in connection with his or her service or employment as a director or executive officer.

(2) Remedy

(A) In general

Any profit realized by a director or executive officer referred to in paragraph (1) from any purchase, sale, or other acquisition or transfer in violation of this subsection shall inure to and be recoverable by the issuer, irrespective of any intention on the part of such director or executive officer in entering into the transaction.

(B) Actions to recover profits

An action to recover profits in accordance with this subsection may be instituted at law or in equity in any court of competent jurisdiction by the issuer, or by the owner of any security of the issuer in the name and in behalf of the issuer if the issuer fails or refuses to bring such action within 60 days after the date of request, or fails diligently to prosecute the action thereafter, except that no such suit shall be brought more than 2 years after the date on which such profit was realized.

(3) Rulemaking authorized

The Commission shall, in consultation with the Secretary of Labor, issue rules to clarify the application of this subsection and to prevent evasion thereof. Such rules shall provide for the application of the requirements of paragraph (1) with respect to entities treated as a single employer with respect to an issuer under section 414(b), (c), (m), or (o) of Title 26 to the extent necessary to clarify the application of such requirements and to prevent evasion thereof. Such rules may also provide for appropriate exceptions from the requirements of this subsection, including exceptions for purchases pursuant to an automatic dividend reinvestment program or purchases or sales made pursuant to an advance election.

(4) Blackout period

For purposes of this subsection, the term "blackout period", with respect to the equity securities of any issuer—

(A) means any period of more than 3 consecutive business days during which the ability of not fewer than 50 percent of the participants or beneficiaries under all individual account plans maintained by the issuer to purchase, sell, or otherwise acquire or transfer an interest in any equity of such issuer held in such an individual account plan is temporarily suspended by the issuer or by a fiduciary of the plan; and

2. Codified at 15 U.S.C. Section 7244.

(B) does not include, under regulations which shall be prescribed by the Commission—

(i) a regularly scheduled period in which the participants and beneficiaries may not purchase, sell, or otherwise acquire or transfer an interest in any equity of such issuer, if such period is—

(I) incorporated into the individual account plan; and

(II) timely disclosed to employees before becoming participants under the individual account plan or as a subsequent amendment to the plan; or

(ii) any suspension described in subparagraph (A) that is imposed solely in connection with persons becoming participants or beneficiaries, or ceasing to be participants or beneficiaries, in an individual account plan by reason of a corporate merger, acquisition, divestiture, or similar transaction involving the plan or plan sponsor.

(5) Individual account plan

For purposes of this subsection, the term "individual account plan" has the meaning provided in section 1002(34) of Title 29, except that such term shall not include a one-participant retirement plan (within the meaning of section 1021(i)(8)(B) of Title 29).

(6) Notice to directors, executive officers, and the Commission

In any case in which a director or executive officer is subject to the requirements of this subsection in connection with a blackout period (as defined in paragraph (4)) with respect to any equity securities, the issuer of such equity securities shall timely notify such director or officer and the Securities and Exchange Commission of such blackout period.

* * * *

Explanatory Comments:

Corporate pension funds typically prohibit employees from trading shares of the corporation during periods when the pension fund is undergoing significant change. Prior to 2002, however, these blackout periods did not affect the corporation's executives, who frequently received shares of the corporate stock as part of their compensation. Section 306 was Congress's solution to the basic unfairness of this situatiion. This section of the act required the SEC to issue rules that prohibit any director or executive officer from trading during pension fund blackout periods. (The SEC later issued these rules, entitled Regulation Blackout Trading Restriction, or Reg BTR.) Section 306 also provided shareholders with a right to file a shareholder's derivative suit against officers and directors who have profited from trading during these blackout periods (provided that the corporation has failed to bring a suit). The officer or director can be forced to return to the corporation any profits received, regardless of whether the director or officer acted with bad intent.

Section 402
Periodical and other reports[3]

* * * *

(i) Accuracy of financial reports

Each financial report that contains financial statements, and that is required to be prepared in accordance with (or reconciled to) generally accepted accounting principles under this chapter and filed

3. This section of the Sarbanes-Oxley Act amended some of the provisions of the 1934 Securities Exchange Act and added the paragraphs reproduced here at 15 U.S.C. Section 78m.

with the Commission shall reflect all material correcting adjustments that have been identified by a registered public accounting firm in accordance with generally accepted accounting principles and the rules and regulations of the Commission.

(j) Off-balance sheet transactions

Not later than 180 days after July 30, 2002, the Commission shall issue final rules providing that each annual and quarterly financial report required to be filed with the Commission shall disclose all material off-balance sheet transactions, arrangements, obligations (including contingent obligations), and other relationships of the issuer with unconsolidated entities or other persons, that may have a material current or future effect on financial condition, changes in financial condition, results of operations, liquidity, capital expenditures, capital resources, or significant components of revenues or expenses.

(k) Prohibition on personal loans to executives

(1) In general

It shall be unlawful for any issuer (as defined in section 7201 of this title), directly or indirectly, including through any subsidiary, to extend or maintain credit, to arrange for the extension of credit, or to renew an extension of credit, in the form of a personal loan to or for any director or executive officer (or equivalent thereof) of that issuer. An extension of credit maintained by the issuer on July 30, 2002, shall not be subject to the provisions of this subsection, provided that there is no material modification to any term of any such extension of credit or any renewal of any such extension of credit on or after July 30, 2002.

(2) Limitation

Paragraph (1) does not preclude any home improvement and manufactured home loans (as that term is defined in section 1464 of Title 12), consumer credit (as defined in section 1602 of this title), or any extension of credit under an open end credit plan (as defined in section 1602 of this title), or a charge card (as defined in section 1637(c)(4)(e) of this title), or any extension of credit by a broker or dealer registered under section 78o of this title to an employee of that broker or dealer to buy, trade, or carry securities, that is permitted under rules or regulations of the Board of Governors of the Federal Reserve System pursuant to section 78g of this title (other than an extension of credit that would be used to purchase the stock of that issuer), that is—

(A) made or provided in the ordinary course of the consumer credit business of such issuer;

(B) of a type that is generally made available by such issuer to the public; and

(C) made by such issuer on market terms, or terms that are no more favorable than those offered by the issuer to the general public for such extensions of credit.

(3) Rule of construction for certain loans

Paragraph (1) does not apply to any loan made or maintained by an insured depository institution (as defined in section 1813 of Title 12), if the loan is subject to the insider lending restrictions of section 375b of Title 12.

(l) Real time issuer disclosures

Each issuer reporting under subsection (a) of this section or section 78o(d) of this title shall disclose to the public on a rapid and current basis such additional information concerning material changes in the financial condition or operations of the issuer, in plain English, which may include trend and qualitative information and graphic presentations, as the Commission determines, by rule, is necessary or useful for the protection of investors and in the public interest.

Explanatory Comments:

Before this act, many corporate executives typically received extremely large salaries, significant bonuses, and abundant stock options, even when the companies for which they worked were suffering. Executives were also routinely given personal loans from corporate funds, many of which were never paid back. The average large company during that period loaned almost $1 million a year to top executives, and some companies loaned hundreds of millions of dollars to their executives every year. Section 402 amended the 1934 Securities Exchange Act to prohibit public companies from making personal loans to executive officers and directors. There are a few exceptions to this prohibition, such as home-improvement loans made in the ordinary course of business. Note also that while loans are forbidden, outright gifts are not. A corporation is free to give gifts to its executives, including cash, provided that these gifts are disclosed on its financial reports. The idea is that corporate directors will be deterred from making substantial gifts to their executives by the disclosure requirement—particularly if the corporation's financial condition is questionable—because making such gifts could be perceived as abusing their authority.

Section 403

Directors, officers, and principal stockholders[4]

(a) Disclosures required

(1) Directors, officers, and principal stockholders required to file

Every person who is directly or indirectly the beneficial owner of more than 10 percent of any class of any equity security (other than an exempted security) which is registered pursuant to section 78l of this title, or who is a director or an officer of the issuer of such security, shall file the statements required by this subsection with the Commission (and, if such security is registered on a national securities exchange, also with the exchange).

(2) Time of filing

The statements required by this subsection shall be filed—

(A) at the time of the registration of such security on a national securities exchange or by the effective date of a registration statement filed pursuant to section 78l(g) of this title;

(B) within 10 days after he or she becomes such beneficial owner, director, or officer;

(C) if there has been a change in such ownership, or if such person shall have purchased or sold a security-based swap agreement (as defined in section 206(b) of the Gramm-Leach-Bliley Act (15 U.S.C. 78c note)) involving such equity security, before the end of the second business day following the day on which the subject transaction has been executed, or at such other time as the Commission shall establish, by rule, in any case in which the Commission determines that such 2-day period is not feasible.

(3) Contents of statements

A statement filed—

(A) under subparagraph (A) or (B) of paragraph (2) shall contain a statement of the amount of all equity securities of such issuer of which the filing person is the beneficial owner; and

---

4. This section of the Sarbanes-Oxley Act amended the disclosure provisions of the 1934 Securities Exchange Act, at 15 U.S.C. Section 78p.

(B) under subparagraph (C) of such paragraph shall indicate ownership by the filing person at the date of filing, any such changes in such ownership, and such purchases and sales of the security-based swap agreements as have occurred since the most recent such filing under such subparagraph.

(4) Electronic filing and availability

Beginning not later than 1 year after July 30, 2002—

(A) a statement filed under subparagraph (C) of paragraph (2) shall be filed electronically;

(B) the Commission shall provide each such statement on a publicly accessible Internet site not later than the end of the business day following that filing; and

(C) the issuer (if the issuer maintains a corporate website) shall provide that statement on that corporate website, not later than the end of the business day following that filing.

* * * *

Explanatory Comments:

This section dramatically shortens the time period provided in the Securities Exchange Act of 1934 for disclosing transactions by insiders. The prior law stated that most transactions had to be reported within ten days of the beginning of the following month, although certain transactions did not have to be reported until the following fiscal year (within the first forty-five days). In several instances, some insider trading was not disclosed (and was therefore not discovered) until long after the transactions. So Congress added this section to reduce the time period for making disclosures. Under Section 403, most transactions by insiders must be electronically filed with the SEC within two business days. Also, any company that maintains a Web site must post these SEC filings on its site by the end of the next business day. Congress enacted this section in the belief that if insiders are required to file reports of their transactions promptly with the SEC, companies will do more to police themselves and prevent insider trading.

Section 404
Management assessment of internal controls[5]

(a) Rules required

The Commission shall prescribe rules requiring each annual report required by section 78m(a) or 78o(d) of this title to contain an internal control report, which shall—

(1) state the responsibility of management for establishing and maintaining an adequate internal control structure and procedures for financial reporting; and

(2) contain an assessment, as of the end of the most recent fiscal year of the issuer, of the effectiveness of the internal control structure and procedures of the issuer for financial reporting.

(b) Internal control evaluation and reporting

With respect to the internal control assessment required by subsection (a) of this section, each registered public accounting firm that prepares or issues the audit report for the issuer shall attest to, and report on, the assessment made by the management of the issuer. An attestation made under this subsection shall be made in accordance with standards for attestation engagements issued or adopted by the Board. Any such attestation shall not be the subject of a separate engagement.

* * * *

Explanatory Comments:

This section was enacted to prevent corporate executives from claiming they were ignorant of significant errors in their companies' financial reports. For instance, several CEOs testified before Congress that they simply had no idea that the corporations' financial statements were off by billions of dollars. Congress therefore passed Section 404, which requires each annual report to contain a description and assessment of the company's internal control structure and financial reporting procedures. The section also requires that an audit be conducted of the internal control assessment, as well as the financial statements contained in the report. This section goes hand in hand with Section 302 (which, as discussed previously, requires various certifications attesting to the accuracy of the information in financial reports).

Section 404 has been one of the more controversial and expensive provisions in the Sarbanes-Oxley Act because it requires companies to assess their own internal financial controls to make sure that their financial statements are reliable and accurate. A corporation might need to set up a disclosure committee and a coordinator, establish codes of conduct for accounting and financial personnel, create documentation procedures, provide training, and outline the individuals who are responsible for performing each of the procedures. Companies that were already well managed have not experienced substantial difficulty complying with this section. Other companies, however, have spent millions of dollars setting up, documenting, and evaluating their internal financial control systems. Although initially creating the internal financial control system is a one-time-only expense, the costs of maintaining and evaluating it are ongoing. Some corporations that spent considerable sums complying with Section 404 have been able to offset these costs by discovering and correcting inefficiencies or frauds within their systems. Nevertheless, it is unlikely that any corporation will find compliance with this section to be inexpensive.

Section 802(a)
Destruction, alteration, or falsification of records in Federal investigations and bankruptcy[6]

Whoever knowingly alters, destroys, mutilates, conceals, covers up, falsifies, or makes a false entry in any record, document, or tangible object with the intent to impede, obstruct, or influence the investigation or proper administration of any matter within the jurisdiction of any department or agency of the United States or any case filed under title 11, or in relation to or contemplation of any such matter or case, shall be fined under this title, imprisoned not more than 20 years, or both.

Destruction of corporate audit records[7]

(a) (1) Any accountant who conducts an audit of an issuer of securities to which section 10A(a) of the Securities Exchange Act of 1934 (15 U.S.C. 78j-1(a)) applies, shall maintain all audit or review workpapers for a period of 5 years from the end of the fiscal period in which the audit or review was concluded.

(2) The Securities and Exchange Commission shall promulgate, within 180 days, after adequate notice and an opportunity for comment, such rules and regulations, as are reasonably necessary, relating to the retention of relevant records such as workpapers, documents that form the basis of an audit or review, memoranda, correspondence, communications, other documents, and records (including electronic records) which are created, sent, or received in connection with an audit or review and contain conclusions, opinions, analyses, or financial data relating to such an audit or

5. Codified at 15 U.S.C. Section 7262.

6. Codified at 15 U.S.C. Section 1519.

7. Codified at 15 U.S.C. Section 1520.

review, which is conducted by any accountant who conducts an audit of an issuer of securities to which section 10A(a) of the Securities Exchange Act of 1934 (15 U.S.C. 78j-1(a)) applies. The Commission may, from time to time, amend or supplement the rules and regulations that it is required to promulgate under this section, after adequate notice and an opportunity for comment, in order to ensure that such rules and regulations adequately comport with the purposes of this section.

(b) Whoever knowingly and willfully violates subsection (a)(1), or any rule or regulation promulgated by the Securities and Exchange Commission under subsection (a)(2), shall be fined under this title, imprisoned not more than 10 years, or both.

(c) Nothing in this section shall be deemed to diminish or relieve any person of any other duty or obligation imposed by Federal or State law or regulation to maintain, or refrain from destroying, any document.

* * * *

Explanatory Comments:

Section 802(a) enacted two new statutes that punish those who alter or destroy documents. The first statute is not specifically limited to securities fraud cases. It provides that anyone who alters, destroys, or falsifies records in federal investigations or bankruptcy may be criminally prosecuted and sentenced to a fine or to up to twenty years in prison, or both. The second statute requires auditors of public companies to keep all audit or review working papers for five years but expressly allows the SEC to amend or supplement these requirements as it sees fit. The SEC has, in fact, amended this section by issuing a rule that requires auditors who audit reporting companies to retain working papers for seven years from the conclusion of the review. Section 802(a) further provides that anyone who knowingly and willfully violates this statute is subject to criminal prosecution and can be sentenced to a fine, imprisoned for up to ten years, or both if convicted.

This portion of the Sarbanes-Oxley Act implicitly recognizes that persons who are under investigation often are tempted to respond by destroying or falsifying documents that might prove their complicity in wrongdoing. The severity of the punishment should provide a strong incentive for these individuals to resist the temptation.

Section 804

Time limitations on the commencement of civil actions arising under Acts of Congress[8]

(a) Except as otherwise provided by law, a civil action arising under an Act of Congress enacted after the date of the enactment of this section may not be commenced later than 4 years after the cause of action accrues.

(b) Notwithstanding subsection (a), a private right of action that involves a claim of fraud, deceit, manipulation, or contrivance in contravention of a regulatory requirement concerning the securities laws, as defined in section 3(a)(47) of the Securities Exchange Act of 1934 (15 U.S.C. 78c(a)(47)), may be brought not later than the earlier of—

(1) 2 years after the discovery of the facts constituting the violation; or

(2) 5 years after such violation.

* * * *

8. Codified at 28 U.S.C. Section 1658.

Explanatory Comments:

Prior to the enactment of this section, Section 10(b) of the Securities Exchange Act of 1934 had no express statute of limitations. The courts generally required plaintiffs to have filed suit within one year from the date that they should (using due diligence) have discovered that a fraud had been committed but no later than three years after the fraud occurred. Section 804 extends this period by specifying that plaintiffs must file a lawsuit within two years after they discover (or should have discovered) a fraud but no later than five years after the fraud's occurrence. This provision has prevented the courts from dismissing numerous securities fraud lawsuits.

Section 806

Civil action to protect against retaliation in fraud cases[9]

(a) Whistleblower protection for employees of publicly traded companies.—

No company with a class of securities registered under section 12 of the Securities Exchange Act of 1934 (15 U.S.C. 78l), or that is required to file reports under section 15(d) of the Securities Exchange Act of 1934 (15 U.S.C. 78o(d)), or any officer, employee, contractor, subcontractor, or agent of such company, may discharge, demote, suspend, threaten, harass, or in any other manner discriminate against an employee in the terms and conditions of employment because of any lawful act done by the employee—

(1) to provide information, cause information to be provided, or otherwise assist in an investigation regarding any conduct which the employee reasonably believes constitutes a violation of section 1341, 1343, 1344, or 1348, any rule or regulation of the Securities and Exchange Commission, or any provision of Federal law relating to fraud against shareholders, when the information or assistance is provided to or the investigation is conducted by—

(A) a Federal regulatory or law enforcement agency;

(B) any Member of Congress or any committee of Congress; or

(C) a person with supervisory authority over the employee (or such other person working for the employer who has the authority to investigate, discover, or terminate misconduct); or

(2) to file, cause to be filed, testify, participate in, or otherwise assist in a proceeding filed or about to be filed (with any knowledge of the employer) relating to an alleged violation of section 1341, 1343, 1344, or 1348, any rule or regulation of the Securities and Exchange Commission, or any provision of Federal law relating to fraud against shareholders.

(b) Enforcement action.—

(1) In general.—A person who alleges discharge or other discrimination by any person in violation of subsection (a) may seek relief under subsection (c), by—

(A) filing a complaint with the Secretary of Labor; or

(B) if the Secretary has not issued a final decision within 180 days of the filing of the complaint and there is no showing that such delay is due to the bad faith of the claimant, bringing an action at law or equity for de novo review in the appropriate district court of the United States, which shall have jurisdiction over such an action without regard to the amount in controversy.

(2) Procedure.—

9. Codified at 18 U.S.C. Section 1514A.

(A) In general.—An action under paragraph (1)(A) shall be governed under the rules and procedures set forth in section 42121(b) of title 49, United States Code.

(B) Exception.—Notification made under section 42121(b)(1) of title 49, United States Code, shall be made to the person named in the complaint and to the employer.

(C) Burdens of proof.—An action brought under paragraph (1)(B) shall be governed by the legal burdens of proof set forth in section 42121(b) of title 49, United States Code.

(D) Statute of limitations.—An action under paragraph (1) shall be commenced not later than 90 days after the date on which the violation occurs.

(c) Remedies.—

(1) In general.—An employee prevailing in any action under subsection (b)(1) shall be entitled to all relief necessary to make the employee whole.

(2) Compensatory damages.—Relief for any action under paragraph (1) shall include—

(A) reinstatement with the same seniority status that the employee would have had, but for the discrimination;

(B) the amount of back pay, with interest; and

(C) compensation for any special damages sustained as a result of the discrimination, including litigation costs, expert witness fees, and reasonable attorney fees.

(d) Rights retained by employee.—Nothing in this section shall be deemed to diminish the rights, privileges, or remedies of any employee under any Federal or State law, or under any collective bargaining agreement.

Explanatory Comments:

Section 806 is one of several provisions that were included in the Sarbanes-Oxley Act to encourage and protect whistleblowers—that is, employees who report their employer's alleged violations of securities law to the authorities. This section applies to employees, agents, and independent contractors who work for publicly traded companies or testify about such a company during an investigation. It sets up an administrative procedure at the U.S. Department of Labor for individuals who claim that their employer retaliated against them (fired or demoted them, for example) for blowing the whistle on the employer's wrongful conduct. It also allows the award of civil damages—including back pay, reinstatement, special damages, attorneys' fees, and court costs—to employees who prove that they suffered retaliation. Since this provision was enacted, whistleblowers have filed numerous complaints with the U.S. Department of Labor under this section.

Section 807
Securities fraud[10]

Whoever knowingly executes, or attempts to execute, a scheme or artifice—

(1) to defraud any person in connection with any security of an issuer with a class of securities registered under section 12 of the Securities Exchange Act of 1934 (15 U.S.C. 78l) or that is required to file reports under section 15(d) of the Securities Exchange Act of 1934 (15 U.S.C. 78o(d)); or

(2) to obtain, by means of false or fraudulent pretenses, representations, or promises, any money or property in connection with the purchase or sale of any security of an issuer with a class of securities registered under section 12 of the Securities Exchange Act of 1934 (15 U.S.C. 78l) or that is required to file reports under section 15(d) of the Securities Exchange Act of 1934 (15 U.S.C. 78o(d)); shall be fined under this title, or imprisoned not more than 25 years, or both.

* * * *

Explanatory Comments:

Section 807 adds a new provision to the federal criminal code that addresses securities fraud. Prior to 2002, federal securities law had already made it a crime—under Section 10(b) of the Securities Exchange Act of 1934 and SEC Rule 10b-5, both of which are discussed in Chapter 26—to intentionally defraud someone in connection with a purchase or sale of securities, but the offense was not listed in the federal criminal code. Also, paragraph 2 of Section 807 goes beyond what is prohibited under securities law by making it a crime to obtain by means of false or fraudulent pretenses any funds or property from the purchase or sale of securities. This new provision allows violators to be punished by up to twenty-five years in prison, a fine, or both.

Section 906
Failure of corporate officers to certify financial reports[11]

(a) Certification of periodic financial reports.—Each periodic report containing financial statements filed by an issuer with the Securities Exchange Commission pursuant to section 13(a) or 15(d) of the Securities Exchange Act of 1934 (15 U.S.C. 78m(a) or 78o(d)) shall be accompanied by a written statement by the chief executive officer and chief financial officer (or equivalent thereof) of the issuer.

(b) Content.—The statement required under subsection (a) shall certify that the periodic report containing the financial statements fully complies with the requirements of section 13(a) or 15(d) of the Securities Exchange Act of 1934 (15 U.S.C. 78m or 78o(d)) and that information contained in the periodic report fairly presents, in all material respects, the financial condition and results of operations of the issuer.

(c) Criminal penalties.—Whoever—

(1) certifies any statement as set forth in subsections (a) and (b) of this section knowing that the periodic report accompanying the statement does not comport with all the requirements set forth in this section shall be fined not more than $1,000,000 or imprisoned not more than 10 years, or both; or

(2) willfully certifies any statement as set forth in subsections (a) and (b) of this section knowing that the periodic report accompanying the statement does not comport with all the requirements set forth in this section shall be fined not more than $5,000,000, or imprisoned not more than 20 years, or both.

Explanatory Comments:

As previously discussed, under Section 302 a corporation's CEO and CFO are required to certify that they believe the quarterly and annual reports their company files with the SEC are accurate and fairly present the company's financial condition. Section 906 adds "teeth" to these requirements by authorizing criminal penalties for those officers who intentionally certify inaccurate SEC filings. Knowing violations of the requirements are punishable by a fine of up to $1 million, ten years' imprisonment, or both. Willful violators may be fined up to $5 million, sentenced to up to twenty years' imprisonment, or both. Although the difference between a knowing and a willful violation is not entirely clear, the section is obviously intended to remind corporate officers of the serious consequences of certifying inaccurate reports to the SEC.

10. Codified at 18 U.S.C. Section 1348.

11. Codified at 18 U.S.C. Section 1350.

Appendix E

Sample Answers for Select *Questions with Sample Answer*

1–2A QUESTION WITH SAMPLE ANSWER.

1. The U.S. Constitution—The U.S. Constitution is the supreme law of the land. A law in violation of the Constitution, no matter what its source, will be declared unconstitutional and will not be enforced.
2. The federal statute—Under the U.S. Constitution, when there is a conflict between federal law and state law, federal law prevails.
3. The state statute—State statutes are enacted by state legislatures. Areas not covered by state statutory law are governed by state case law.
4. The U.S. Constitution—State constitutions are supreme within their respective borders unless they conflict with the U.S. Constitution, which is the supreme law of the land.
5. The federal administrative regulation—Under the U.S. Constitution, when there is a conflict between federal law and state law, federal law prevails.

2–2A QUESTION WITH SAMPLE ANSWER.

Marya can bring suit in all three courts. The trucking firm did business in Florida, and the accident occurred there. Thus, the state of Florida would have jurisdiction over the defendant. Because the firm was headquartered in Georgia and had its principal place of business in that state, Marya could also sue in a Georgia court. Finally, because the amount in controversy exceeds $75,000, the suit could be brought in federal court on the basis of diversity of citizenship. In deciding whether to file her case in a federal court or in a Georgia state court, Marya may be influenced by several factors including the distance to the respective courthouses, the reputation of the particular judges, and availability of different remedies in state versus federal court.

3–2A QUESTION WITH SAMPLE ANSWER.

Factors for the firm to consider in making its decision include the appropriate ethical standard. Under the utilitarian standard, an action is correct, or "right," when, among the people it affects, it produces the greatest amount of good for the greatest number. When an action affects the majority adversely, it is morally wrong. Applying the utilitarian standard requires the following:

(a) A determination of which individuals will be affected by the action in question;
(b) An assessment, or cost-benefit analysis, of the negative and positive effects of alternative actions on these individuals; and
(c) The choice of the alternative that will produce maximum societal utility.

Ethical standards may also be based on a concept of duty, which postulates that the end can never justify the means and that human beings should not be treated as mere means to an end. But ethical decision making in a business context is not always simple, particularly when an action will have different effects on different groups of people: shareholders, employees, society, and other stakeholders, such as the local community. Thus, another factor to consider is to whom the firm believes it owes a duty.

4–2A QUESTION WITH SAMPLE ANSWER.

To answer this question, you must first decide if there is a legal theory under which Harley may be able to recover. A possibility is the intentional tort of wrongful interference with a contractual relationship. To recover damages under this theory, Harley would need to show that:

(a) He and Martha had a valid contract,
(b) Lothar knew of this contractual relationship, and
(c) Lothar intentionally convinced Martha to break her contract with Harley.

Even though Lothar hoped that his advertisements would persuade Martha to break her contract with Harley, the question states that Martha's decision to change bakers was based solely on the advertising and not on anything else that Lothar did. Lothar's advertisements did not constitute a tort. Note, though, that although Harley cannot collect from Lothar for Martha's actions, he does have a cause of action against Martha for her breach of their contract.

7–2A QUESTION WITH SAMPLE ANSWER.

According to the question, Janine was apparently unconscious or otherwise unable to agree to a contract for the nursing services she received while she was in the hospital. As you read in the chapter, however, sometimes the law will create a fictional contract in order to prevent one party from unjustly receiving a benefit at the expense of another. This is known as a quasi contract and provides a basis for Nursing Services to recover the value of the services it provided while Janine was in the hospital. As for the at-home services that were provided to Janine, because Janine was aware that those services were being provided for her, Nursing Services can recover for those services under an implied contract. Under this type of contract, the conduct of the parties creates and defines the terms. Janine's acceptance of the services constitutes her agreement to form a contract, and she will probably be required to pay Nursing Services in full.

13–2A QUESTION WITH SAMPLE ANSWER.

The entire answer falls under UCC 2–206(1)(b) because the situation deals with a buyer's order to buy goods for prompt shipment. The law is that such an order or offer invites acceptance by a prompt promise to ship conforming goods. If the promise (acceptance) is sent by a medium reasonable under the circumstances, the acceptance is effective when sent. Therefore, a contract was formed on October 8, and it required

Fulsom to ship one hundred model HD-X television sets. Fulsom's shipment is nonconforming, and Salinger is correct in claiming that Fulsom is in breach. Fulsom's claim would be valid if Fulsom had not sent its promise of shipment. The UCC provides that shipment of nonconforming goods constitutes an acceptance unless the seller seasonably notifies the buyer that such shipment is sent only as an accommodation. Thus, had a contract not been formed on October 8, the nonconforming shipment on October 28 would not be treated as an acceptance, and no contract would be in existence to breach.

16–2A QUESTION WITH SAMPLE ANSWER.

For an instrument to be negotiable, it must meet the following requirements:

1. Be in writing.
2. Be signed by the maker or the drawer.
3. Be an unconditional promise or order to pay.
4. State a fixed amount of money.
5. Be payable on demand or at a definite time.
6. Be payable to order or to bearer, unless it is a check.

The instrument in this case meets the writing requirement in that it is handwritten and on something with a degree of permanence that is transferable. The instrument meets the requirement of being signed by the maker, as Muriel Evans's signature (her name in her handwriting) appears in the body of the instrument. The instrument's payment is not conditional and contains Muriel Evans's definite promise to pay. In addition, the sum of $100 is both a fixed amount and payable in money (U.S. currency). Because the instrument is payable on demand and to bearer (Karen Marvin or any holder), the instrument is negotiable.

18–2A QUESTION WITH SAMPLE ANSWER.

Mendez has a security interest in Arabian Knight and is a perfected secured party. He has met all the necessary criteria listed under UCC 9–203 to be a secured creditor. Mendez has given value of $5,000 and has taken possession of the collateral, Arabian Knight, owned by Marsh (who has rights in the collateral). Thus, Mendez has a security interest even though Marsh did not sign a security agreement. Once a security interest attaches, a transfer of possession of the collateral to the secured party can perfect the party's security interest without a filing [UCC 9–310(b)(6); 9–313]. Thus, a security interest was created and perfected at the time Marsh transferred Arabian Knight to Mendez as security for the loan.

23–2A QUESTION WITH SAMPLE ANSWER.

1. A limited partner's interest is assignable. In fact, assignment allows the assignee to become a substituted limited partner with the consent of the remaining partners. The assignment does not dissolve the limited partnership.
2. Bankruptcy of the limited partnership itself causes dissolution, but bankruptcy of one of the limited partners does not dissolve the partnership unless it causes the bankruptcy of the firm.
3. The retirement, death, or insanity of a general partner dissolves the partnership unless the business can be continued by the remaining general partners. Because Dorinda was the only general partner, her death dissolves the limited partnership.

27–3A QUESTION WITH SAMPLE ANSWER.

For Curtis to recover against the hotel, he must first prove that a bailment relationship was created between himself and the hotel as to the car or the fur coat, or both. For a bailment to exist, there must be a delivery of the personal property that gives the bailee exclusive possession of the property, and the bailee must knowingly accept the bailed property. If either element is lacking, there is no bailment relationship and no liability on the part of the bailee hotel. The facts clearly indicate that the bailee hotel took exclusive possession and control of Curtis's car, and it knowingly accepted the car when the attendant took the car from Curtis and parked it in the underground guarded garage, retaining the keys. Thus, a bailment was created as to the car, and, because a mutual benefit bailment was created, the hotel owes Curtis the duty to exercise reasonable care over the property and to return the bailed car at the end of the bailment. Failure to return the car creates a presumption of negligence (lack of reasonable care), and unless the hotel can rebut this presumption, the hotel is liable to Curtis for the loss of the car. As to the fur coat, the hotel neither knew nor expected that the trunk contained an expensive fur coat. Thus, although the hotel knowingly took exclusive possession of the car, the hotel did not do so with the fur coat. (But the hotel would be liable for a regular coat and other items likely to be in the car.) Because no bailment of the expensive fur coat was created, the hotel has no liability for its loss.

30–2A QUESTION WITH SAMPLE ANSWER.

Assuming that the circuit court has abandoned the *Ultramares* rule, it is likely that the accounting firm of Goldman, Walters, Johnson & Co. will be held liable to Happydays State Bank for negligent preparation of financial statements. This hypothetical scenario is partially derived from *Citizens State Bank v. Timm, Schmidt & Co.* In *Citizens State Bank,* the Supreme Court of Wisconsin enunciated various policy reasons for holding accountants liable to third parties even in the absence of privity. The court suggested that this potential liability would make accountants more careful in the preparation of financial statements. Moreover, in some situations the accountants may be the only solvent defendants, and hence, unless liability is imposed on accountants, third parties who reasonably rely on financial statements may go unprotected. The court further asserted that accountants, rather than third parties, are in a better position to spread the risks. If third parties such as banks have to absorb the costs of bad loans made as a result of negligently prepared financial statements, then the cost of credit to the public in general will increase. In contrast, the court suggests that accountants are in a better position to spread the risk by purchasing liability insurance.

Appendix F

Sample Answers for *Case Problems with Sample Answer*

1–4A CASE PROBLEM WITH SAMPLE ANSWER.

Yes, the court should issue an injunction to prevent the enforcement of the rules because they suppress free speech and are not reasonable restrictions. To be reasonable, the rules must further "an important or substantial governmental interest," be content neutral, and be unrelated to the suppression of free expression. In addition, as the court hearing the case pointed out, any "incidental restriction on alleged First Amendment freedoms [must be] no greater than is essential to the furtherance of that interest." The means chosen must not "burden substantially more speech than is necessary to further the government's legitimate interests. . . . For example, a city has a legitimate aesthetic interest in forbidding the littering of its public areas with paper, but that could not justify a prohibition against the public distribution of handbills, even though the recipients might well toss them on the street." Such a ban would not be upheld because "a free society prefers to punish the few who abuse rights of speech after they break the law than to throttle them and all others beforehand."

Here, the rules hindered young adults' access to the materials they need for lawful artistic expression. The "prohibition against young adults' possession of spray paint and markers in public places—because it applies even where the individuals have a legitimate purpose for their use—imposes a substantial burden on innocent expression." Because the regulations "burdened substantially more speech than is necessary to achieve the City's legitimate interest in preventing illegal graffiti," they were unenforceable.

2–4A CASE PROBLEM WITH SAMPLE ANSWER.

T-Mobile was not correct that Lowden had to arbitrate her dispute. Based on a recent holding by the Washington State supreme court, the federal appellate court held that the arbitration provision was unconscionable and thus invalid. Because it was invalid, the restriction on class-action lawsuits was also invalid. The state court held that for consumers to be offered a contract that restricted class actions and required individual arbitration improperly stripped consumers of rights they would normally have to attack certain industry practices. Class-action suits are often brought when the losses suffered by an individual consumer as a result of deceptive or unfair industry practices are too small to warrant the consumer bringing suit. In other words, the alleged added cell phone fees are so small that no one consumer would be likely to litigate or arbitrate the matter due to the expenses involved. Eliminating that cause of action by the arbitration clause violates public policy, so that provision is void and unenforceable.

3–5A CASE PROBLEM WITH SAMPLE ANSWER.

A firm may have acted unethically but still not be held legally accountable unless the party that was wronged can establish some basis of liability. This makes sense because rules of law are designed to require plaintiffs to prove certain elements that establish a defendant's liability in order to recover for injuries or loss. Internal ethical codes are a firm's policy statements rather than rules of law, and the violation of internal codes is not a basis for liability. In this case, even though Prudential's conduct was clearly wrongful—and may even have been illegal because of the hidden broker fee—Havensure had the burden of proving liability. Havensure did not establish that it has a valid cause of action against Prudential for violating its ethical code. The appellate court stated, "Although violations of 'recognized ethical codes' or 'established customs or practices' may be significant in evaluating the nature of an actor's conduct, Havensure has identified no authority suggesting that a violation of internal policies has . . . significance." Furthermore, even if Prudential had violated state law by including hidden broker fees, such a violation would be a matter of concern for insurance regulators, but does not, in itself, create an obligation to Havensure, according to the court.

4–5A CASE PROBLEM WITH SAMPLE ANSWER.

Eubanks could not make a case for either libel or invasion of privacy. The paper had a privilege to publish the information in a public record, and it acted in good faith (the mistake was inadvertent). The trial court awarded the newspaper summary judgment, and the appellate court affirmed. On appeal, the plaintiff claimed that the trial court erred in applying the fair-report privilege, which Section 611 of the *Restatement (Second) of Torts* defines as follows: "The publication of defamatory matter concerning another in a report of an official action or proceeding . . . is privileged if the report is accurate and complete or a fair abridgement [shortening] of the occurrence reported."

Eubanks argued that the publication was not an accurate and complete report because the second e-mail made clear that the first was not correct. Nevertheless, the court found that the original newspaper article "was a complete and accurate summary of an official report from the Lake in the Hills police department . . . that stated the plaintiff was charged with the crimes of theft and attempted obstruction of justice. The fair-report privilege applied to the publication of this information because it was an official report from a police department."

The paper had a privilege to print the information. That privilege was not abused. No information was changed, and there was no "actual malice" in the publication. There was no evidence that the later e-mail had been seen before the paper went to publication. Hence, there was no basis for a suit for libel or invasion of privacy.

5–5A CASE PROBLEM WITH SAMPLE ANSWER.

No, Hamilton's actions could not be the basis for a trade secret claim, according to the appellate court. Under Alabama law, a trade secret is information that: "a. Is used or intended for use in a trade or business;

b. Is included or embodied in a formula, pattern, compilation, computer software, drawing, device, method, technique, or process; c. Is not publicly known and is not generally known in the trade or business of the person asserting that it is a trade secret; d. Cannot be readily ascertained or derived from publicly available information; e. Is the subject of efforts that are reasonable under the circumstances to maintain its secrecy; and f. Has significant economic value."

Jones contended that information in the file boxes met this definition. Hamilton answered that the documents were not marked confidential and were in unmarked cartons left in a vehicle to which various employees had access. She had no idea what was in the boxes that Edwards' wife wanted to see. Leaving trade secrets about in such a manner is not evidence of good faith effort to protect such information. The Alabama Court of Civil Appeals agreed that the claim should be dismissed. Jones did not take adequate steps to protect the information that may, in fact, be trade secrets.

6–5A CASE PROBLEM WITH SAMPLE ANSWER.

Under the Fourth Amendment, a police officer must obtain a search warrant to search private property. In a traffic stop, however, it seems unreasonable to require an officer to obtain a warrant to search one of the vehicle's occupants. Yet it also seems reasonable to apply some standard to prevent police misconduct. An officer might be held to a standard of probable cause, which consists of reasonable grounds to believe that a person should be searched. In some situations, however, an officer may have a reasonable suspicion short of probable cause to believe that a person poses a risk of violence. In a traffic stop, the normal reaction of a person stopped for a driving infraction would not present such a risk, but it might arise from the possibility that evidence of a more serious crime might be discovered. A criminal's motivation to use violence to prevent such a discovery could be great. And because the vehicle would already be stopped, the additional intrusion would be minimal. Under these circumstances, a limited search of the person for weapons would protect the officer, the individual, and the public. Thus, an officer who conducts a routine traffic stop can perform a patdown search of a passenger on a reasonable suspicion that the person may be armed and dangerous. In this case, a jury convicted Johnson of the charge, but a state appellate court reversed the conviction. The United States Supreme Court reversed the appellate court's judgment and remanded the case.

7–4A CASE PROBLEM WITH SAMPLE ANSWER.

No, the federal district court in New York held that Gutkowski did not have a claim for *quantum meruit.* "In New York, a contract must be sufficiently "definite" to be enforceable. 'The doctrine of definiteness or certainty is well established in contract law. In short, it means that a court cannot enforce a contract unless it is able to determine what in fact the parties have agreed to . . . . [I]f an agreement is not reasonably certain in its material terms, there can be no legally enforceable contract.'"

"In this case, Plaintiff alleges that Defendant 'told Plaintiff that he would be compensated fairly for his efforts,' and, similarly, that Plaintiff would 'be fairly compensated for his idea and efforts.' It is therefore undisputed that the purported oral agreement lacks a specifically alleged price or compensation term. 'The failure to fix a sum certain, however, is not necessarily fatal to a contract.' " Gutkowski failed to explain the compensation term, however, so the purported oral agreement is indefinite. He claims he should get 2 to 3 percent of the value of YES, but no such figure was discussed, so there is no enforceable oral contract.

Gutkowski was compensated as a consultant for his expertise. For him to claim that he is due more compensation based on unjust enrichment or *quantum meruit,* he must have proof. As it is, he has only a claim that there were discussions about him being an executive or part owner of YES. Such negotiations are not the basis for a monetary claim. The claims were dismissed.

8–6A CASE PROBLEM WITH SAMPLE ANSWER.

Yes, the parties had a contract. The elements of an enforceable agreement include an offer and its acceptance. The moment of acceptance is the moment that the contract is created. For an acceptance to be effective, it must comply with the terms of the offer and be clear, unambiguous, and unequivocal. In this case, the parties' conduct established that they understood their dispute and that they intended its settlement through their agreement. The Kowalchuks' e-mail shows that Stroup made an offer. The same e-mail shows that the Kowalchuks accepted it. Because there appears to be nothing unclear, ambiguous, or equivocal about the e-mail, it constituted an effective acceptance. Stroup contended that his offer was revoked before it was accepted, because the Kowalchuks had not yet added their signatures to his signed, faxed copy of the settlement when he communicated the revocation. But the document signed by Stroup established the existence of the parties' agreement, including its offer and acceptance, and was enforceable against him. The court issued a judgment in the Kowlachuks' favor, and the state intermediate appellate court affirmed the judgment.

9–5A CASE PROBLEM WITH SAMPLE ANSWER.

Yes, the Sharabianlous have a good argument for rescission. The reviewing court concluded that "Rescission is intended to restore the parties as nearly as possible to their former positions and 'to bring about substantial justice by adjusting the equities between the parties.'" Rescission does not occur if a contract is affirmed; it means the contract is repudiated. Here, rescission is appropriate because the contracting parties were mutually mistaken as to the condition of the property. The environmental contamination substantially reduced its value. When an agreement to purchase property is subject to rescission, "the seller must refund all payments received in connection with the sale." Hence, the award of damages to the Berensteins was reversed and the Sharabianlous' deposit was refunded.

10–5A CASE PROBLEM WITH SAMPLE ANSWER.

No, the trial court should not have admitted parol evidence because the contract was clear on its face. The trial court accepted parol evidence because it believed that there was a conflict between the 10 percent termination clause and the tax-exemption termination clause. But the appellate court did not believe that the trial court had to accept parol evidence because the contract in fact could have been interpreted on its face. Under the contract, if the property was not tax-exempt, the tax-exemption termination clause took effect. That was the situation, so Evangel had the right to terminate without payment. The court should not have accepted the parol evidence because it was not needed. In any event, the parol evidence did not change the outcome of the case because the contract could be resolved without it.

11–5A CASE PROBLEM WITH SAMPLE ANSWER.

JH breached the contract because it failed to fulfill the condition precedent requiring it to obtain certification from the architect that sufficient cause existed to justify Mike's termination. Hence, JH is liable to Mike for losses it can demonstrate. The reviewing court ruled in favor of Mike. "Where a contract provides that a party must fulfill specific conditions precedent before it can terminate the agreement, those conditions are enforced as written and the party must comply with them." The clause in the construction contract is a standard clause and should have been followed. Of course, if JH can show that Mike acted improperly, then no damages may be owed to Mike, but JH failed to follow the procedure provided in the contract, which called for JH to bring the architect into the situation to decide if termination was in order for failure to perform properly.

12–5A CASE PROBLEM WITH SAMPLE ANSWER.

The requirements for recovery on a quasi-contract theory are:

(a) One party must confer a benefit on another party,

(b) The party must confer the benefit with the reasonable expectation of being paid,

(c) The party must not act as a volunteer in conferring the benefit, and

(d) The party who received the benefit would be unjustly enriched if it were retained without being paid for.

In this case, most of these requirements are apparent—Lindquist lent its manager Miller to Middleton. Lindquist did not do this as a volunteer but at Middleton's request, and Middleton would be unjustly enriched if Miller's services accrued to its ultimate benefit without being paid for. The requirement most likely to be disputed is whether Lindquist reasonably expected to be paid if Miller did not make Middleton profitable. If Lindquist did not expect to be paid unless its manager made the Wisconsin dealership profitable, the Iowa dealership could not recover on a quasi-contract basis, because Miller did not make a profit for Middleton. The court awarded damages on a quasi-contract basis, but the U.S. Court of Appeals for the Seventh Circuit reversed and remanded the case to determine what Lindquist's reasonable expectations were.

13–5A CASE PROBLEM WITH SAMPLE ANSWER.

Normally, the terms of a written contract that the parties intend to be the final expression of their agreement cannot be contradicted by evidence of prior agreements or contemporaneous oral agreements. Under the UCC, in interpreting a commercial agreement, a court will assume that the usage of trade and the course of prior dealing between the parties were considered when the contract was formed. Also, the conduct that occurs under an agreement—the course of performance—is the best indication of what the parties meant.

In this case, the court found that the parties intended "market size" to refer to fish approximating one-pound live weight and awarded the Griffiths damages. On Clear Lakes's appeal, the Idaho Supreme Court affirmed the lower court's decision. The state supreme court noted that the Griffiths "presented evidence of . . . trade usage predating the contract" that indicated "market size" refers to fish approximating one-pound live weight. The court also cited the parties' prior course of dealing. At the time of their contract "Clear Lakes and Griffith had an understanding about what fish were market size. Specifically, . . . the term is suggestive of a trout approximating one pound as the parties had considered it over the years." The court pointed out that "the course of performance between the parties over the first three years of the contract . . . confirmed that the parties intended market size to indicate trout approximating one pound live weight."

14–5A CASE PROBLEM WITH SAMPLE ANSWER.

Under UCC 2–609 (and 2A–401), if a contracting party has "reasonable grounds" to believe that the other party will not perform, he or she may "demand adequate assurance" of that performance. Until the assurance is received, the demanding party may suspend its own performance. If assurance is not provided within less than thirty days, this may be considered a repudiation of the contract, and the contract may be canceled. What constitutes "reasonable grounds" is determined by commercial standards. Concerned about the source of JAG's product, Flint Hills asked for evidence of title and suspended payment until this "lack of information" was resolved. From one perspective, this demand for proof of title could be seen as an overreaction to a rumor without substantial evidence of bad title or a conflicting claim of ownership. But under the UCC, the right to seek assurances and suspend payment can be based on a lack of information and does not require an adverse claim, proof of theft, or objective evidence of wrongdoing. Thus, in this case, Flint Hills had the right to seek assurances from JAG, and JAG was then obligated to provide "satisfactory" evidence of title. JAG's failure to provide the documents that it promised to forward—or any other substantiating proof of the chain of title to its product—was sufficient to support Flint Hills' suspension of payments and, after several weeks, its cancellation of the deal.

15–5A CASE PROBLEM WITH SAMPLE ANSWER.

No, the court should not have granted Kallestad's request to dismiss the case. On the Rothings' appeal, the Montana Supreme Court reversed the lower court's judgment on this issue and remanded the case for trial. The state supreme court found no requirement of foreseeability to determine liability for a breach of the UCC's implied warranty of merchantability. The court explained that "the Rothings' purchase of hay from Kallestad was a transaction in goods" and if Kallestad was, on remand, held to be "a merchant for purposes of the sale of his hay to the Rothings, then the provisions of the UCC, and more specifically, the Implied Warranty of Merchantability [in UCC 2–314], would apply to this transaction."

To be merchantable, goods must be, among other things, "fit for the ordinary purposes for which such goods are used." Goods "are not merchantable, if in their ordinary use, the goods cause damage to the property to which they are applied or harm to the person using them." Under these principles, livestock feed must be not only of the kind and quality ordered by its buyers, but also "free from deleterious substances, poisonous to stock." If Kallestad's hay could not meet this test, as the facts as stated in the problem seem to indicate, then he would have breached the implied warranty of merchantability. Therefore, the Rothings would likely be entitled to damages for the deaths of their horses and related losses.

16–6A CASE PROBLEM WITH SAMPLE ANSWER.

Yes, the instrument is negotiable. For an instrument to be negotiable under UCC 3–104, it must meet the following requirements:

(a) Be in writing,

(b) Be signed by the maker or the drawer,

(c) Be an unconditional promise or order to pay,

(d) State a fixed amount of money,

(e) Be payable on demand or at a definite time, and

(f) Be payable to order or to bearer unless it is a check.

Applying these principles to the facts in this problem, all of the requirements to establish the instrument as negotiable are met:

(a) The instrument is in writing.

(b) It is signed by Scotto.

(c) There are no conditions or promises other than the unconditional promise to pay.

(d) The instrument states a fixed amount—$2,970.

(e) The instrument does not include a definite repayment date, which means that it is payable on demand.

(f) The instrument is payable to Vinueza.

A writing that complies with the requirements of negotiability is a promissory note if it is a promise by one person (the maker) to pay another (usually a payee) a specified sum.

In the facts set out in this problem, Vinueza—the payee on the note and the plaintiff in the suit—is most likely to prevail. The reason is that she has the note as evidence of the promise to pay, and Scotto, the maker of the note and the defendant in the suit, admitted that he borrowed the money. His contention that he paid the note is not supported by any proof. In the actual case on which this problem is based, the court concluded that the plaintiff proved she was owed $2,970 from the defendant. The court also found that she did not prove she was owed an additional $630, as she claimed. The defendant, who failed to show that he paid the loan, was ordered to pay $2,970 to the plaintiff.

17–8A CASE PROBLEM WITH SAMPLE ANSWER.

In this situation, Brooks is likely to suffer the loss for the forged checks. When a bank pays a check on which the drawer's signature is forged, generally the bank suffers the loss. A bank may be able to recover some or all of the loss from the customer if the customer's negligence substantially contributed to the forgery. A bank—or the customer—may also obtain partial recovery from the forger of the check (if he or she can be found and there are assets against which a recovery can be enforced).

A bank typically makes available to a customer a monthly statement detailing the activity in the customer's checking account. The customer has a duty to examine promptly the statement with reasonable care on receipt and to report any forged signatures. When the same wrongdoer forges the customer's signature on a series of checks, the customer must discover and report the first forged check to the bank within thirty calendar days of the availability of the bank statement. Failure to notify the bank within this time period discharges the bank's liability for all forged checks that it pays before notification. The UCC places an absolute time limit on the liability of a bank for paying a check with a customer's forged signature. A customer who fails to report his or her forged signature within one year from the date that the statement was made available for inspection loses the right to have the bank recredit his or her account.

Here, Brooks did not exercise reasonable care in handling her accounts. She did not look at any statements for five years. When she finally examined the statements and realized that Tingstrom had taken money from her account by forging Brooks's name on checks drawn on the account, at least two years had passed since the first forged signature. Brooks's claim against Transamerica is thus precluded. Unless Brooks can find Tingstrom and the latter has assets against which a judgment could be enforced, it is most likely that Brooks alone will suffer the loss.

In the actual case on which this problem is based, the court denied a defense motion for summary judgment. On appeal, a state intermediate appellate court reversed this decision and issued a summary judgment dismissing Brooks's claim.

18–5A CASE PROBLEM WITH SAMPLE ANSWER.

A secured creditor has a variety of steps that it can take to satisfy a debt. Under the UCC, these remedies are cumulative and can be exercised simultaneously. A secured creditor can repossess and retain a debtor's collateral in full or partial satisfaction of the debt. The collateral does not have to be disposed of first unless the parties have agreed otherwise. If the collateral satisfies the debt only partially, the creditor can seek a judgment for the balance due. Of course, it would not be fair for a creditor to deprive a debtor of the possession of the collateral for an unreasonable length of time and not apply the property, or the proceeds from its sale, against the debt. The creditor must act in a commercially reasonable manner and take steps to sell, lease, retain, or otherwise dispose of the collateral.

In this problem, it does not appear that the bank failed to proceed in a commercially reasonable manner. The bank chose to retain the collateral and seek a judgment on the debt. The amount that OAI owes the bank might be at issue—how does the value of the collateral apply against the amount due on the note?—but the facts state that the debtor did not dispute the amount due. In the case on which this problem is based, the court issued a judgment in the bank's favor, and a state intermediate appellate court affirmed, on the principles stated here.

19–7A CASE PROBLEM WITH SAMPLE ANSWER.

As in this problem, certain property of a debtor is exempt under state law from creditors' actions. In most states, certain types of real and personal property are exempt from execution. Each state permits a debtor to retain the family home, either in its entirety or up to a specified dollar amount, free from the claims of unsecured creditors. In a few states, statutes allow the homestead exemption only if the judgment debtor has a family. In this problem, state law allows a $100,000 homestead exemption if the debtor or spouse lives in the home. A greater exemption of $175,000 is allowed if either the debtor or the spouse who lives in the home is disabled and "unable to engage in gainful employment."

Here, the Mas own half of a two-unit residential building. Betty and her mother live in one of the units. Her husband Bill lives in China. The Mas assert that they are entitled to the greater exemption of $175,000 because Bill cannot work as a waiter or a driver due to "gout and dizziness." But state law requires that to obtain the greater exemption, the disabled spouse must live in the home. Bill does not live on the property—he lives in China. Thus, the Mas are entitled only to an exemption of $100,000, not to the $175,000 exemption.

On the sale of the residence, most likely by public auction, the amount of the proceeds that represents the Mas' interest in the property would be distributed as follows:

(a) The Mas would be given $100,000 as Bill's homestead exemption.

(b) Zhang and the other plaintiffs would be paid the remainder toward the judgment debt, presumably leaving a deficiency, which would be subject to a deficiency judgment ("leftover debt") that could be satisfied from any other nonexempt property (personal or real) that Bill or the other defendants may own, as permitted by state law.

In the actual case on which this problem is based, on the reasoning set out above, the court issued a judgment in the plaintiffs' favor.

20–7A CASE PROBLEM WITH SAMPLE ANSWER.

The plaintiffs argued that the foreclosure was void and that they were entitled to damages because the $33,500 amount paid by the defendant-mortgagee for the property so shocked the conscience that it could be considered a wrongful foreclosure or a breach of fiduciary duty. The fair market value of the property at the time of the foreclosure was the key fact in deciding this issue. The defendant contended that the fair market value of the property at the time of the foreclosure was the price bid at the foreclosure sale—that is, $33,500. The plaintiffs contended that the fair market value of the property was $65,000.

The evidence is overwhelming that the value of the property at the time of the foreclosure was the same as the price paid at the foreclosure sale—that is, $33,500. The only direct evidence that did not agree that the fair market value of the property was $33,500 was Mr. Sharpe's testimony. Mr. Sharpe testified that the fair market value was $65,000. Although a property owner may give an opinion about the value of his or her property, the owner must be able to support that opinion with fact. As the U.S. Court of Appeals for the Eleventh Circuit recognized, any testimony by an owner may be "self-serving and unsupported by other evidence." Mr. Sharpe based his opinion on an appraisal and the local tax assessor's yearly valuation of the property. On cross-examination, he could not support his testimony. He did not produce the appraisal he mentioned, and he did not produce the appraiser, the only one who could have testified about the appraisal. Therefore, based on the legal standard applicable under Alabama law, the court held, as a conclusion of law, that the price the defendant bid at the foreclosure sale was not inadequate. The defendant bid the value of the property. Consequently, the defendant does not have any liability under wrongful foreclosure.

21–4A CASE PROBLEM WITH SAMPLE ANSWER.

The disclosure of a principal by an agent who is acting within the scope of his or her authority when entering into a contract with a third party absolves the agent of liability for the nonperformance of the contract. This is the principle that the Pappases cited in their defense to the Crisses' suit. If a principal is partially disclosed or undisclosed, the principal and the agent may both be liable for nonperformance. These are the principles that the Crisses might cite to make their case. Even if Kevin Pappas might arguably have disclosed that he was acting on behalf of a principal named Outside Creations, there is no indication that he was acting on behalf of an entity named Forever Green. He signed the contract as Outside Creations' "rep," but the payments on the contract were by checks payable to him personally, which he deposited in his personal account. There was no Outside Creations account. The contract did not mention Forever Green, the Pappases did not mention Forever Green, the Crisses knew nothing about Forever Green, and there was no Forever Green account.

In the actual case on which this problem is based, the court issued a summary judgment in the homeowners' favor, finding that the contract was between the homeowners and the Pappases personally, not Kevin Pappas as the agent of Forever Green. A state intermediate appellate court affirmed.

22–7A CASE PROBLEM WITH SAMPLE ANSWER.

Yes, Dawson has established a claim for retaliatory discharge, according to the U.S. Court of Appeals for the Ninth Circuit. Under Oregon law, it is an unlawful employment practice for an employer to discriminate against an individual based on sexual orientation. It is also unlawful for an employer to discharge an individual because that person has filed a complaint. To establish a *prima facie* case of retaliatory discharge, a plaintiff must prove that (1) the defendant intentionally retaliated against the employee because he or she filed a discrimination complaint, (2) the defendant did so with the intent of forcing the employee to leave the employment, and (3) the employee left the employment as a result of the retaliation. Dawson engaged in a protected activity when he went to the human resources department and filed a complaint. "The protected activity occurred at most two days before the discharge and the treatment of Dawson was a topic during both the protected activity and the discharge." Therefore, Dawson has offered enough evidence that "a reasonable trier of fact could find in favor of Dawson on his retaliation claim." The federal appellate court held that the district court had erred in granting a summary judgment for the employer. The court reversed the decision and remanded the case for trial.

23–7A CASE PROBLEM WITH SAMPLE ANSWER.

In a member-managed limited liability company (LLC), all of the members participate in management, and decisions are made by majority vote. The managers of an LLC—whether member or manager managed—owe fiduciary duties to the company and its members. These duties include the duty of loyalty and the duty of care. An LLC's operating agreement can include provisions governing decision-making procedures. For example, the agreement can set forth procedures for choosing or removing members or managers.

Here, Bluewater is a member-managed LLC. Under the applicable state law, every member of a member-managed LLC is entitled to participate in managing the business. The Bluewater operating agreements provide for a "super-majority" vote to remove and buy out a member—if the "member has either committed a felony or under any other circumstances that would jeopardize the company status" as a contractor. Without giving a reason, however, three of the four members of Bluewater "fired" the fourth member.

Under these facts and principles, Smith, Mosser, and Floyd breached their fiduciary duties, the Bluewater operating agreements, and the state LLC statute. The Bluewater members breached their fiduciary duties by their treatment of Williford. The defendants also breached the Bluewater operating agreements. A super-majority ouster was allowed only when the member to be ousted had committed a felony or had jeopardized the company's status as an approved contractor—the defendants' ouster notice alleged neither. And by attempting to oust Williford, the defendants violated Mississippi's LLC statute, which provides that every member of a member-managed LLC is entitled to participate in managing the business. As a member of both Bluewater LLCs, Williford was entitled to participate in the management of both, and he could not be "fired."

In the actual case on which this problem is based, the court issued a judgment in Williford's favor with a damages award of nearly $350,000. A state intermediate appellate court reversed the judgment, but the Mississippi Supreme Court reversed the appellate court's ruling and affirmed the trial court's judgment, based, in part, on the reasoning stated above.

24–5A CASE PROBLEM WITH SAMPLE ANSWER.

Yes, the court should consider piercing the corporate veil and holding Smith personally liable because he treated the corporate business carelessly and was using it to circumvent a legal debt. The appellate court reversed the trial court's dismissal. The appellate court found that genuine issues of material fact existed as to whether Smith's corporation abused the corporate form by disregarding it and using it to undermine Laker's ability to seek legal recourse on the unpaid account. The case was remanded for further proceedings consistent with the appellate court's opinion. No single factor indicating abuse of corporate form for purposes of piercing corporate veil controls. Factors bearing on abuse of corporate form for purposes of piercing corporate veil include:

(a) Whether the corporation is inadequately capitalized;

(b) Whether the owners observe corporate formalities;

(c) Whether the corporation issues stock or pays dividends;

(d) Whether it operates without a profit;

(e) Whether there is a commingling of corporate and personal assets;

(f) Whether the owners use corporate assets as their own, or in general deal with the corporation at arm's length;

(g) Whether there are nonfunctioning officers or directors;

(h) Whether the corporation is insolvent at the time of the transaction;

(i) Whether corporate records have been maintained; and

(j) Whether others pay or guarantee debts of the corporation.

These issues will be considered at trial.

25–5A CASE PROBLEM WITH SAMPLE ANSWER.

Directors and officers are fiduciaries of their corporations and owe legal and ethical duties to their firms and the shareholders, including the duty of care and the duty of loyalty. Among other things, these duties require directors and officers to act in good faith, to exercise the care that a reasonably prudent person would in like circumstances, and to act in what they believe is the best interest of their corporation. Directors and officers must not use confidential corporate information to their personal advantage. They must refrain from self-dealing. They should not oppose a tender offer in the firm's best interest simply because it may cost them their positions. With respect to other conflicts of interest, they should fully disclose any potential problem that arises in a corporate transaction.

In this problem, the bank's directors included some of its officers, as well as directors whose outside companies worked with the bank. Under the terms of the various offers to buy the bank, all of the directors might have lost their directorships, their jobs with the bank, and their firms' employment by the bank to perform services. The directors' negative responses to these offers might well have breached the fiduciary duties owed to their corporation and its shareholders. The directors' apparent failure to act in the best interest of their firm and its owners, while protecting their own personal interests, would be a breach of good faith and a use of confidential corporate information to their advantage. There could also be undisclosed conflicts of interest.

26–5A CASE PROBLEM WITH SAMPLE ANSWER.

No. The federal appellate court affirmed that there was no negligence by the officers of Orphan. There was no duty to disclose early drug trial data, nor was there a duty to give shareholders access to such data. There was no evidence of an intent to mislead investors in Orphan. Federal drug procedure is technical and lengthy. The fact that one stage of testing was successful was no guarantee that further testing would be successful or that the U.S. Food and Drug Administration would allow the drug to be widely marketed. Hence, officers had good reason to be careful not to set off speculation by releasing good news that might, in the long run, turn out not to be favorable.

27–5A CASE PROBLEM WITH SAMPLE ANSWER.

Michael and his father jointly owned the bank account while Chester was alive. Michael owned it after Chester's death. The court granted Michael's motion for summary judgment. On Joseph's appeal, a state intermediate appellate court affirmed the lower court's judgment. The appellate court concluded that the Advancial account was a joint account between Chester and Michael, and that Michael had a right of survivorship. Generally, in a joint tenancy, each of two or more persons owns an undivided share in the property, and a deceased joint tenant's interest passes to the surviving joint tenant, not to any of the decedent's other heirs through his or her estate. There must be a clear intent to establish a joint tenancy, however, or a tenancy in common, which does not feature a right of survivorship, will be presumed.

Under Texas state law, "on the death of one party to a joint account, all sums in the account . . . vest in and belong to the surviving party as his or her separate property." But the terms of the account must expressly designate the right of survivorship: "A survivorship agreement will not be inferred from the mere fact that the account is a joint account." Thus, for an account to include a right of survivorship, "there must be (1) a written agreement, (2) signed by the decedent, (3) which makes his interest 'survive' to the other party." Both Chester and Michael signed the "Account Application" and were given a copy of the "Account Agreement, Disclosures and Privacy Policy," which provided that "a multiple party account includes rights of survivorship." The court stated, "This language is sufficient to confer a right of survivorship."

28–6A CASE PROBLEM WITH SAMPLE ANSWER.

No. The appeals court affirmed that the property belonged to Hunter and ordered the encroaching structure removed because it was a continuing trespass. Since Mansell initially occupied the property under an informal agreement with the original owner of the property, adverse possession never started. Mansell was a lessee. When Hunter bought the property, the free lease of the property under the garage ended. Mansell never notified the previous owner or Hunter that she was claiming adverse possession so that the hostile possession time would begin. Hunter had objected to the possession in 2003. So Mansell's garage was trespassing on Hunter's property. Hunter may agree to sell Mansell the property, but she need not do so. In that event, the garage must be removed to end the continuing trespass.

29–7A CASE PROBLEM WITH SAMPLE ANSWER.

Once an insurer has accepted a risk and issued a policy, and an event occurs that gives rise to a claim, the insurer has a duty to investigate to determine the facts. When a policy provides insurance against a third party claim, the insurer is obligated to make a reasonable effort to settle the claim. If a settlement is not reached, the insurer has a duty to defend any consequent suit against the insured. This encompasses the duty to provide or pay an attorney to defend the insured when a complaint alleges facts that could, if proved, impose liability on the insured within the policy's coverage. The insurer also has a duty to pay any claims up to the face amount of the policy. If an insurer denies coverage in bad faith, the insured can recover in tort an amount exceeding the policy's coverage limits and may also recover punitive damages.

Here, the families of two employees of Deters Tower filed a negligence suit against Leo, one of the firm's officers. Leo's insurer USF investigated when Mary, on behalf Leo's estate, filed a claim for a defense against the suit. USF denied coverage, however, and refused to defend its insured. Because the insurer denied coverage without a reasonable basis, on behalf of Leo's estate, Mary filed a bad faith tort action to recover. Most likely, she will succeed. USF may have met its duty to investigate, but it did not make any effort to settle the third party claim or to defend its insured in the ensuing litigation. If Mary does succeed, she may recover the amount of any judgment paid or settlement entered into with the employees' families, even if the payment exceeds the policy's coverage limits. Mary may also recover punitive damages.

In the actual case on which this problem is based, the court ruled that the insurer had a duty to defend and indemnify its insured against the employees' claims. The court held that the insurer had no reasonable basis for denying benefits and awarded the amount of those benefits, plus punitive damages. A state intermediate appellate court affirmed the award.

30–5A CASE PROBLEM WITH SAMPLE ANSWER.

The key to determining liability in this case is whether the accounting firm (Grant Thornton) negligently failed to detect fraud or other misconduct during its audits of the bank's books. The appellate court vacated the order of the Comptroller. The court noted that external auditing of the books only verifies the accuracy of the books. Thornton did not participate or engage in an unsafe or unsound banking practice in violation of federal law. The accountants played no role in directing the bank's affairs. There was no showing that the audit was improper given the information the bank officers provided. Thornton had no way of knowing that the records it was provided had been falsified. The liability rests with the bank officers and managers who participated in the scheme, not Thornton.

31–5A CASE PROBLEM WITH SAMPLE ANSWER.

The key international legal principles at play here are comity and sovereign immunity. Comity requires one nation to give effect to the laws and judicial decrees of another. Sovereign immunity prevents the U.S. courts from exercising jurisdiction over foreign nations unless certain conditions are met. In this case, the United States Supreme Court reversed the decision of the U.S. Court of Appeals for the Ninth Circuit and remanded the case. The Court found that lower courts gave insufficient weight to the sovereign status of the Republic of the Philippines and its Commission in considering whether the interests of those parties would be prejudiced if the case proceeded. Giving full effect to sovereign immunity promotes the comity and dignity interest that contributed to the development of the immunity doctrine. The claims here arise from historically and politically significant events for the Republic and its people. They have a unique interest in resolving matters related to Arelma's assets. A foreign state has a comity interest in using its courts for a dispute if it has a right to do so. Other nations should not bypass the courts of the Philippines without good cause. To seize assets of the Philippines would be a specific affront. The lower courts erred in ruling on the merits of the case. The Pimentel class has interests, but the courts did not accord proper weight to the compelling sovereign immunity claim.

Appendix G

Answers to *Issue Spotters*

Chapter 1:

1A No. The U.S. Constitution is the supreme law of the land and applies to all jurisdictions. A law in violation of the Constitution (in this question, the First Amendment to the Constitution) will be declared unconstitutional.

2A Case law includes courts' interpretations of statutes, as well as constitutional provisions and administrative rules. Statutes often codify common law rules. For these reasons, a judge might rely on the common law as a guide to the intent and purpose of a statute.

Chapter 2:

1A Yes. Submission of the dispute to mediation or nonbinding arbitration is mandatory, but compliance with a decision of the mediator or arbitrator is voluntary.

2A Tom could file a motion for a directed verdict. This motion asks the judge to direct a verdict for Tom on the ground that Sue presented no evidence that would justify granting her relief. The judge grants the motion if there is insufficient evidence to raise an issue of fact.

Chapter 3:

1A Maybe. On the one hand, it is not the company's "fault" when a product is misused. Also, keeping the product on the market is not a violation of the law, and stopping sales would hurt profits. On the other hand, suspending sales could reduce suffering and could prevent negative publicity that might result if sales continued.

2A When a corporation decides to respond to what it sees as a moral obligation to correct for past discrimination by adjusting pay differences among its employees, an ethical conflict is raised between the firm and its employees and between the firm and its shareholders (not between the employees). This dilemma arises directly out of the effect of such a decision on the firm's profits. With respect to the employees and the shareholders, the firm arguably has an obligation to stay in business. If adjusting pay differences among employees increases profitability, then staying in business is not an issue, and the dilemma is easily resolved in favor of "doing the right thing."

Chapter 4:

1A Probably. To recover on the basis of negligence, the injured party as a plaintiff must show that the truck's owner owed the plaintiff a duty of care, that the owner breached that duty, that the plaintiff was injured, and that the breach caused the injury. In this problem, the owner's actions breached the duty of reasonable care. The direct cause of the injury was the billboard falling on the plaintiff, not the plaintiff's own negligence. Thus, liability turns on whether the plaintiff can connect the breach of duty to the injury. This involves the test of proximate cause—the question of foreseeability. The consequences to the injured party must have been a foreseeable result of the owner's carelessness.

2A The company might defend against the electrician's claim by asserting that it had no duty to warn of a dangerous risk that the electrician should have recognized. According to the problem, the danger is common knowledge in the electrician's field and should have been clear to this electrician, given his years of training and experience. The firm could also raise the defense of comparative negligence. Both parties' negligence, if any, could be weighed and the liability distributed proportionately. The defendant could also assert assumption of risk, claiming that the electrician voluntarily entered into a dangerous situation knowing the risk involved.

Chapter 5:

1A This is patent infringement. A software maker in this situation might best protect its product, save litigation costs, and profit from its patent by the use of a license. In the context of this problem, a license would grant permission to sell a patented item. (A license can be limited to certain purposes and to the licensee only.)

2A Yes. This may be an instance of trademark dilution. Dilution occurs when a trademark is used, without permission, in a way that diminishes the distinctive quality of the mark. Dilution does not require proof that consumers are likely to be confused by a connection between the unauthorized use and the mark. The products involved do not have to be similar. Dilution does require, however, that a mark be famous when the dilution occurs.

Chapter 6:

1A No. A mistake of fact, as opposed to a mistake of law, will constitute a defense if it negates the mental state required for the crime. The mental state required for theft involves the knowledge that the property is another's and the intent to deprive the owner of it.

2A Yes. With respect to the gas station, Daisy has obtained goods by false pretenses. She might also be charged with larceny and forgery, and most states have special statutes covering illegal use of credit cards.

Chapter 7:

1A The objective theory of contracts is the determining factor. If a reasonable person would have thought that the offeree accepted the offeror's offer when the offeree signed and returned the letter, a contract was made, and the offeree is bound. This depends in part on what was said in the letter (was it a valid offer?) and what was said in response (was it a valid acceptance?). Under any circumstances, the issue is not whether either party subjectively believed that they did, or did not, have a contract.

2A No. This "contract," although not fully executed, is for an illegal purpose and therefore void. A void contract gives rise to no legal obligation on the part of any party. A contract that is void is no contract. There is nothing to enforce.

Chapter 8:

1A Yes. An offer must be communicated to the offeree so that the offeree knows about it. For example, the offer of a reward must be communicated to offerees. An offeree who knows of the offer and performs the required act can then claim the reward.

2A First, it might be noted that the Uniform Electronic Transactions Act (UETA) does not apply unless the parties to a contract agree to use e-commerce in their transaction. In this deal, of course, the parties used e-commerce. The UETA removes barriers to e-commerce by giving the same legal effect to e-records and e-signatures as to paper documents and signatures. The UETA does not include rules for those transactions, however.

Chapter 9:

1A Yes. The original contract was executory. The parties rescinded it and agreed to a new contract. If Sharyn had broken the contract to accept a contract with another employer, she might have been held liable for damages for the breach.

2A No. Generally, an exculpatory clause (a clause attempting to absolve parties of negligence or other wrongs) is not enforced if the party seeking its enforcement is involved in a business that is important to the public as a matter of practical necessity, such as an airline. Because of the essential nature of these services, airlines have an advantage in bargaining strength and could insist that anyone contracting for their services agree not to hold them liable.

Chapter 10:

1A Yes. The accountant may be liable on the ground of negligent misrepresentation. A misrepresentation is negligent if a person fails to exercise reasonable care in disclosing material facts or does not use the skill and competence required by his or her business or profession.

2A No, although the memo would be a sufficient writing to enforce the contract against My-T if that party chose not to complete the deal. Letterhead stationery can constitute a signature. If the memo names the parties, the subject matter, the consideration, and the quantity involved in the transaction, it may be sufficient to be enforced against the party whose letterhead appears on it.

Chapter 11:

1A Yes. Generally, if a contract clearly states that a right is not assignable, no assignment will be effective, but there are exceptions, and assignment of the right to receive money cannot be prohibited.

2A Contracts that are executory on both sides—contracts on which neither party has performed—can be rescinded solely by agreement. Contracts that are executed on one side—contracts on which one party has performed—can be rescinded only if the party who has performed receives consideration for the promise to call off the deal.

Chapter 12:

1A A nonbreaching party is entitled to his or her benefit of the bargain under the contract. Here, the innocent party is entitled to be put in the position she would have been in if the contract had been fully performed. The measure of the benefit is the cost to complete the work ($500). These are compensatory damages.

2A To recover damages that flow from the consequences of a breach but that are caused by circumstances beyond the contract (consequential damages), the breaching party must know, or have reason to know, that special circumstances will cause the nonbreaching party to suffer the additional loss. That was not the circumstance in this problem.

Chapter 13:

1A A shipment of nonconforming goods constitutes an acceptance and a breach, unless the seller seasonably notifies the buyer that the nonconforming shipment does not constitute an acceptance and is offered only as an accommodation. Without the notification, the shipment is an acceptance and a breach. Thus, here, the shipment was both an acceptance and a breach.

2A Yes. In a transaction between merchants, the requirement of a writing is satisfied if one of them sends to the other a signed written confirmation that indicates the terms of the agreement, and the merchant receiving it has reason to know of its contents. If the merchant who receives it does not object in writing within ten days after receipt, the writing will be enforceable against him or her even though he or she has not signed anything.

Chapter 14:

1A Yes. A seller is obligated to deliver goods in conformity with a contract in every detail. This is the perfect tender rule. The exception of the seller's right to cure does not apply here, because the seller delivered too little too late to take advantage of this exception.

2A Yes. In a case of anticipatory repudiation, a buyer (or lessee) can resort to any remedy for breach even if the buyer tells the seller (the repudiating party in this problem) that the buyer will wait for the seller's performance.

Chapter 15:

1A Yes. The manufacturer is liable for the injuries to the user of the product. A manufacturer is liable for its failure to exercise due care to any person who sustains an injury proximately caused by a negligently made (defective) product. In this problem, the failure to inspect is a failure to use due care. Of course, the maker of the component part may also be liable.

2A Yes. Under the doctrine of strict liability, persons may be liable for the results of their acts regardless of their intentions or their exercise of reasonable care (that is, regardless of fault).

Chapter 16:

1A A statement that "I.O.U." money (or anything else) or an instruction to a bank stating, "I wish you would pay," would render any instrument nonnegotiable. To be negotiable, an instrument must contain an express promise to pay. An I.O.U. is only an acknowledgment of indebtedness. An order stating, "I wish you would pay," is not sufficiently precise.

2A No. When a drawer's employee provides the drawer with the name of a fictitious payee (a payee whom the drawer does not actually intend to have any interest in an instrument), a forgery of the payee's name is effective to pass good title to subsequent transferees.

Chapter 17:

1A Yes, to both questions. In a civil suit, a drawer (Lyn) is liable to a payee (Nan) or to a holder of a check that is not honored. If intent to defraud can be proved, the drawer (Lyn) can also be subject to criminal prosecution for writing a bad check.

2A The drawer is entitled to $6,300—the amount to which the check was altered ($7,000) less the amount that the drawer ordered the bank to pay ($700). The bank may recover this amount from the party who presented the altered check for payment.

Chapter 18:

1A A creditor can put other creditors on notice by perfecting its interest by filing a financing statement in the appropriate public office, or by taking possession of the collateral until the debtor repays the loan.

2A When collateral is consumer goods with a PMSI, and the debtor has paid less than 60 percent of the debt or the purchase price, the creditor can dispose of the collateral in a commercially reasonable manner, which generally requires notice of the place, time, and manner of sale. A debtor can waive the right to notice, but only after default. Before the disposal, a debtor can redeem the collateral by tendering performance of all of the obligations secured by it and by paying the creditor's reasonable expenses in retaking and maintaining it.

Chapter 19:

1A Each of the parties can place a mechanic's lien on the debtor's property. If the debtor does not pay what is owed, the property can be sold to satisfy the debt. The only requirements are that the lien be filed within a specific time from the time of the work, depending on the state statute, and that notice of the foreclosure and sale be given to the debtor in advance.

2A Yes. A debtor's payment to a creditor for a preexisting debt, made within ninety days of a bankruptcy filing (one year in the case of an insider or fraud), can be recovered if the payment gives the creditor more than he or she would have received in the bankruptcy proceedings. A trustee can recover this preference using his or her specific avoidance powers.

Chapter 20:

1A The major terms that must be disclosed under the Truth-in-Lending Act include the loan principal, the interest rate at which the loan is made, the annual percentage rate (APR) (the actual cost of the loan on a yearly basis), and all fees and costs associated with the loan. These disclosures must be made on standardized forms and based on uniform formulas of calculation. Certain types of loans have special disclosure requirements.

2A Foreclosure is the process that allows a lender to repossess and auction off property that is securing a loan. The two most common types of foreclosure are judicial foreclosure and power of sale foreclosure. In the former—available in all states—a court supervises the process. This is the more common method of foreclosure. In the latter—available in only a few states—a lender forecloses on and sells the property without court supervision.

If the sale proceeds cover the mortgage debt and foreclosure costs, the debtor receives any surplus. If the proceeds do not cover the debt and costs, the mortgagee can seek to recover the difference through a deficiency judgment, which is obtained in a separate action. A deficiency judgment entitles the creditor to recover this difference from a sale of the debtor's other nonexempt property. Before a foreclosure sale, a mortgagor can redeem the property by paying the debt, plus any interest and costs. This right is known as the *equity of redemption*. In some states, a mortgagor may redeem property within a certain time—called a statutory period of redemption—after the sale.

Chapter 21:

1A When a person enters into a contract on another's behalf without the authority to do so, the other may be liable on the contract if he or she approves or affirms that contract. In other words, the employer-principal would be liable on the note in this problem on ratifying it. Whether the employer-principal ratifies the note or not, the unauthorized agent is most likely also liable on it.

2A Yes. A principal has a duty to indemnify an agent for liabilities incurred because of authorized and lawful acts and transactions and for losses suffered because of the principal's failure to perform his or her duties.

Chapter 22:

1A No. A closed shop (a company that requires union membership as a condition of employment) is illegal. A union shop (a company that does not require union membership as a condition of employment but requires workers to join the union after a certain amount of time on the job) is illegal in a state with a right-to-work law, which makes it illegal to require union membership for continued employment.

2A Yes, if she can show that she was not hired solely because of her disability. The other elements for a discrimination suit based on a disability are that the plaintiff (1) has a disability and (2) is otherwise qualified for the job. Both of these elements appear to be satisfied in this problem.

Chapter 23:

1A No. A widow (or widower) has no right to take a dead partner's place. No one can become a partner without the unanimous consent of the partners. Also, if a partner dies, the surviving partners, not the heirs of the deceased partner, have the right of survivorship to the specific partnership property. Surviving partners must account to the decedent's estate for the value of the deceased partner's interest in the property, however.

2A The members of a limited liability company (LLC) may designate a group to run their firm, in which situation the firm would be considered a manager-managed LLC. The group may include only members, only nonmembers, or members and nonmembers. If instead, all members participate in management, the firm would be a member-managed LLC. In fact, unless the members agree otherwise, all members are considered to participate in the management of the firm.

Chapter 24:

1A Yes. Small businesses that meet certain requirements can qualify as S corporations, created specifically to permit small businesses to avoid double taxation. The six requirements of an S corporation are (1) the firm must be a domestic corporation, (2) the firm must not be a member of an affiliated group of corporations, (3) the firm must have less than a certain number of shareholders, (4) the shareholders must be individuals, estates, or qualified trusts (or corporations in some cases), (5) there can be only one class of stock, and (6) no shareholder can be a nonresident alien.

2A Yes. Broad authority to conduct business can be granted in a corporation's articles of incorporation. For example, the term "any lawful purpose" is often used. This can be important because acts of a corporation that are beyond the authority given to it in its articles or charter (or state statutes) are considered illegal, *ultra vires* acts.

Chapter 25:

1A Yes. A shareholder can bring a derivative suit on behalf of a corporation, if some wrong is done to the corporation. Normally, any damages recovered go into the corporate treasury.

2A Yes. A single shareholder—or a few shareholders acting together—who owns enough stock to exercise *de facto* control over a corporation owes the corporation and minority shareholders a fiduciary duty when transferring those shares.

Chapter 26:

1A The average investor is not concerned with minor inaccuracies but with facts that, if disclosed, would tend to deter him or her from buying the securities. These would include facts that have an important bearing on the condition of the issuer and its business—liabilities, loans to officers and directors, customer delinquencies, and pending lawsuits.

2A No. The Securities Exchange Act of 1934 extends liability to officers and directors in their personal transactions for taking advantage of inside information when they know it is unavailable to the persons with whom they are dealing.

Chapter 27:

1A Yes. A bailee's right of possession, even though temporary, permits the bailee to recover damages from any third persons for damage or loss to the property.

2A The shipper suffers the loss. A common carrier is liable for damage caused by the willful acts of third persons or by an accident. Other losses must be borne by the shipper (or the recipient, depending on the terms of their contract). This shipment was lost due to an act of God.

Chapter 28:

1A This is a breach of the warranty deed's covenant of quiet enjoyment. The buyer can sue the seller and recover the purchase price of the house, plus any damages.

2A Yes. An owner of a fee simple has the most rights possible—he or she can give the property away, sell it, transfer it by will, use it for almost any purpose, possess it to the exclusion of all the world, or (as in this case) transfer possession for any period of time. The party to whom possession is transferred can also transfer her or his interest (usually only with the owner's permission) for any lesser period of time.

Chapter 29:

1A No. The general test for testamentary capacity is that the testator must comprehend and remember the "natural objects of his or her bounty" (usually family members and others), that the testator comprehend the kind and character of the property being distributed, and that the testator understand and formulate a plan for disposing of the property. In this problem, the testator passes the test.

2A The estate will pass according to the state's intestacy laws. Intestacy laws set out how property is distributed when a person dies without a will. Their purpose is to carry out the likely intent of the decedent. The laws determine which of the deceased's natural heirs (including first the surviving spouse, second lineal descendants, third parents, and finally collateral heirs) inherit his or her property.

Chapter 30:

1A Yes. In these circumstances, when the accountant knows that the bank will use the statement, the bank is a foreseeable user. A foreseeable user is a third party within the class of parties to whom an accountant may be liable for negligence.

2A No. In the circumstances described in the problem, the accountant will not be held liable to a purchaser of the securities. To avoid liability, however, the accountant must prove that he or she is free of fraud and negligence.

Chapter 31:

1A Under the principle of comity, a U.S. court would defer to and give effect to foreign laws and judicial decrees that are consistent with U.S. law and public policy.

2A The practice described is known as dumping. Dumping is the sale of imported goods at "less than fair value" and is regarded as an unfair international trade practice. Based on the price of those goods in the exporting country, an extra tariff, known as an antidumping duty, can be imposed on the imports.

Glossary

A

abandoned property • Property that has been discarded by the owner, who has no intention of reclaiming it.

acceleration clause • A clause that allows a payee or other holder of a time instrument to demand payment of the entire amount due, with interest, if a certain event occurs, such as a default in the payment of an installment when due.

acceptance • A voluntary act by the offeree that shows assent, or agreement, to the terms of an offer; may consist of words or conduct. In negotiable instruments law, the drawee's signed agreement to pay a draft when it is presented.

acceptor • A drawee that is legally obligated to pay an instrument when it is presented later for payment.

accession • Occurs when an individual adds value to personal property by the use of either labor or materials. In some situations, a person may acquire ownership rights in another's property through accession.

accord and satisfaction • A common means of settling a disputed claim, whereby a debtor offers to pay a lesser amount than the creditor purports to be owed. The creditor's acceptance of the offer creates an accord (agreement), and when the accord is executed, satisfaction occurs.

accredited investors • In the context of securities offerings, "sophisticated" investors, such as banks, insurance companies, investment companies, the issuer's executive officers and directors, and persons whose income or net worth exceeds certain limits.

actionable • Capable of serving as the basis of a lawsuit. An actionable claim can be pursued in a lawsuit or other court action.

act of state doctrine • A doctrine providing that the judicial branch of one country will not examine the validity of public acts committed by a recognized foreign government within its own territory.

actual malice • The deliberate intent to cause harm, which exists when a person makes a statement either knowing that it is false or showing a reckless disregard for whether it is true. In a defamation suit, a statement made about a public figure normally must be made with actual malice for the plaintiff to recover damages.

actus reus • A guilty (prohibited) act. The commission of a prohibited act is one of the two essential elements required for criminal liability, the other element being the intent to commit a crime.

adjustable-rate mortgage (ARM) • A mortgage in which the rate of interest paid by the borrower changes periodically, often with reference to a predetermined government interest rate (the index). Usually, the interest rate for ARMs is initially low and increases over time, but there is a cap on the amount that the rate can increase during any adjustment period.

administrative law judge (ALJ) • One who presides over an administrative agency hearing and has the power to administer oaths, take testimony, rule on questions of evidence, and make determinations of fact.

adverse possession • The acquisition of title to real property by occupying it openly, without the consent of the owner, for a period of time specified by a state statute. The occupation must be actual, open, notorious, exclusive, and in opposition to all others, including the owner.

after-acquired property • Property that is acquired by the debtor after the execution of a security agreement.

agency • A relationship between two parties in which one party (the agent) agrees to represent or act for the other (the principal).

agreement • A meeting of two or more minds in regard to the terms of a contract; usually broken down into two events—an offer by one party to form a contract and an acceptance of the offer by the person to whom the offer is made.

alien corporation • A designation in the United States for a corporation formed in another country but doing business in the United States.

alienation • The process of transferring land out of one's possession (thus "alienating" the land from oneself).

alternative dispute resolution (ADR) • The resolution of disputes in ways other than those involved in the traditional judicial process. Negotiation, mediation, and arbitration are forms of ADR.

annual percentage rate (APR) • The cost of credit on a yearly basis, typically expressed as an annual percentage.

answer • Procedurally, a defendant's response to the plaintiff's complaint.

anticipatory repudiation • An assertion or action by a party indicating that he or she will not perform an obligation that the party is contractually obligated to perform at a future time.

apparent authority • Authority that is only apparent, not real. In agency law, a person may be deemed to have had the power to act as an agent for another party if the other party's manifestations to a third party led the third party to believe that an agency existed when, in fact, it did not.

appraisal right • The right of a dissenting shareholder, who objects to an extraordinary transaction of the corporation (such as a merger or a consolidation), to have his or her shares appraised and to be paid the fair value of those shares by the corporation.

appraiser • An individual who specializes in determining the value of certain real or personal property.

appropriation • In tort law, the use by one person of another person's name, likeness, or other identifying characteristic without permission and for the benefit of the user.

arbitration • The settling of a dispute by submitting it to a disinterested third party (other than a court), who renders a decision that is (most often) legally binding.

arbitration clause • A clause in a contract that provides that, in the event of a dispute, the parties will submit the dispute to arbitration rather than litigate the dispute in court.

arson • The intentional burning of another's building. Some statutes have expanded this to include any real property regardless of ownership and the destruction of property by other means—for example, by explosion.

articles of incorporation • The document filed with the appropriate governmental agency, usually the secretary of state, when a business is incorporated. State statutes usually prescribe what kind of information must be contained in the articles of incorporation.

articles of organization • The document filed with a designated state official by which a limited liability company is formed.

articles of partnership • A written agreement that sets forth each partner's rights and obligations with respect to the partnership.

artisan's lien • A possessory lien given to a person who has made improvements and added value to another person's personal property as security for payment for services performed.

assault • Any word or action intended to make another person fearful of immediate physical harm; a reasonably believable threat.

assignee • A party to whom the rights under a contract are transferred, or assigned.

assignment • The act of transferring to another all or part of one's rights arising under a contract.

assignor • A party who transfers (assigns) his or her rights under a contract to another party (called the assignee).
assumption of risk • A doctrine under which a plaintiff may not recover for injuries or damage suffered from risks he or she knows of and has voluntarily assumed.
attachment • In a secured transaction, the process by which a secured creditor's interest "attaches" to the property of another (collateral) and the creditor's security interest becomes enforceable. In the context of judicial liens, a court-ordered seizure and taking into custody of property prior to the securing of a judgment for a past-due debt.
authorization card • A card signed by an employee that gives a union permission to act on his or her behalf in negotiations with management.
automatic stay • In bankruptcy proceedings, the suspension of almost all litigation and other action by creditors against the debtor or the debtor's property. The stay is effective the moment the debtor files a petition in bankruptcy.
average prime offer rate • The mortgage rate offered to the best-qualified borrowers as established by a survey of lenders.
award • In litigation, the amount of monetary compensation awarded to a plaintiff in a civil lawsuit as damages. In the context of alternative dispute resolution, the decision rendered by an arbitrator.

B

bailee • One to whom goods are entrusted by a bailor. Under the Uniform Commercial Code (UCC), a party who, by a bill of lading, warehouse receipt, or other document of title, acknowledges possession of goods and/or contracts to deliver them.
bailee's lien • A possessory lien, or claim, that a bailee entitled to compensation can place on the bailed property to ensure that he or she will be paid for the services provided. The lien is effective as long as the bailee retains possession of the bailed goods and has not agreed to extend credit to the bailor. Sometimes referred to as an *artisan's lien*.
bailment • A situation in which the personal property of one person (a bailor) is entrusted to another (a bailee), who is obligated to return the bailed property to the bailor or dispose of it as directed.
bailor • One who entrusts goods to a bailee.
balloon mortgage • A loan that allows the debtor to make small monthly payments for an initial period, such as eight years, but then requires a large balloon payment for the entire remaining balance of the mortgage loan at the end of that period.
bankruptcy court • A federal court of limited jurisdiction that handles only bankruptcy proceedings, which are governed by federal bankruptcy law.
battery • The unexcused, harmful or offensive, intentional touching of another.
bearer • A person in possession of an instrument payable to bearer or indorsed in blank.
bearer instrument • Any instrument that is not payable to a specific person, including instruments payable to the bearer or to "cash."
bequest • A gift of personal property by will (from the verb to bequeath).
beyond a reasonable doubt • The standard of proof used in criminal cases. If there is any reasonable doubt that a criminal defendant committed the crime with which she or he has been charged, then the verdict must be "not guilty."
bilateral contract • A type of contract that arises when a promise is given in exchange for a return promise.
bilateral (mutual) mistake • A mistake that occurs when both parties to a contract are mistaken about the same material fact and the mistake is one that a reasonable person would make; either party can rescind the contract.
Bill of Rights • The first ten amendments to the U.S. Constitution.
binder • A written, temporary insurance policy.
binding authority • Any source of law that a court must follow when deciding a case. Binding authorities include constitutions, statutes, and regulations that govern the issue being decided, as well as court decisions that are controlling precedents within the jurisdiction.
blank indorsement • An indorsement that specifies no particular indorsee and can consist of a mere signature. An order instrument that is indorsed in blank becomes a bearer instrument.
blue sky laws • State laws that regulate the offering and sale of securities for the protection of the public.
bona fide occupational qualification (BFOQ) • Identifiable characteristics reasonably necessary to the normal operation of a particular business. These characteristics can include gender, national origin, and religion, but not race.
bond • A security that evidences a corporate (or government) debt. It does not represent an ownership interest in the issuing entity.
bond indenture • A contract between the issuer of a bond and the bondholder.
botnet • A network of computers that have been appropriated without the knowledge of their owners and used to spread harmful programs via the Internet; short for robot network.
breach • The failure to perform a legal obligation.
breach of contract • The failure, without legal excuse, of a promisor to perform the obligations of a contract.
bridge loan • A short-term loan that allows a buyer to make a down payment on a new home before selling her or his current home (the current home is used as collateral).
brief • A formal legal document prepared by a party's attorney for the appellant or the appellee (in answer to the appellant's brief) and submitted to an appellate court when a case is appealed. The appellant's brief outlines the facts and issues of the case, the judge's rulings or jury's findings that should be reversed or modified, the applicable law, and the arguments on the client's behalf.
browse-wrap term • A term or condition of use that is presented to an Internet user at the time certain products, such as software, are being downloaded but that need not be agreed to (by clicking "I agree," for example) before the user is able to install or use the product.
burglary • The unlawful entry or breaking into a building with the intent to commit a felony. (Some state statutes expand this to include the intent to commit any crime.)
business ethics • Ethics in a business context; a consensus as to what constitutes right or wrong behavior in the world of business and the application of moral principles to situations that arise in a business setting.
business invitee • A person, such as a customer or a client, who is invited onto business premises by the owner of those premises for business purposes.
business judgment rule • A rule that immunizes corporate management from liability for actions that result in corporate losses or damages if the actions are undertaken in good faith and are within both the power of the corporation and the authority of management to make.
business necessity • A defense to allegations of employment discrimination in which the employer demonstrates that an employment practice that discriminates against members of a protected class is related to job performance.
business tort • Wrongful interference with another's business rights.
buyout price • The amount payable to a partner on his or her dissociation from a partnership, based on the amount distributable to that partner if the firm were wound up on that date, and offset by any damages for wrongful dissociation.
bylaws • A set of governing rules adopted by a corporation or other association.

C

case law • The rules of law announced in court decisions. Case law includes the aggregate of reported cases that interpret judicial precedents, statutes, regulations, and constitutional provisions.

cashier's check • A check drawn by a bank on itself.

categorical imperative • A concept developed by the philosopher Immanuel Kant as an ethical guideline for behavior. In deciding whether an action is right or wrong, or desirable or undesirable, a person should evaluate the action in terms of what would happen if everybody else in the same situation, or category, acted the same way.

causation in fact • An act or omission without which an event would not have occurred.

certificate of deposit (CD) • A note issued by a bank in which the bank acknowledges the receipt of funds from a party and promises to repay that amount, with interest, to the party on a certain date.

certificate of limited partnership • The basic document filed with a designated state official by which a limited partnership is formed.

certification mark • A mark used by one or more persons, other than the owner, to certify the region, materials, mode of manufacture, quality, or other characteristic of specific goods or services.

certified check • A check that has been accepted in writing by the bank on which it is drawn. Essentially, the bank, by certifying (accepting) the check, promises to pay the check at the time the check is presented.

charging order • In partnership law, an order granted by a court to a judgment creditor that entitles the creditor to attach profits or assets of a partner on the dissolution of the partnership.

charitable trust • A trust in which the property held by the trustee must be used for a charitable purpose, such as the advancement of health, education, or religion.

chattel • All forms of personal property.

check • A draft drawn by a drawer ordering the drawee bank or financial institution to pay a certain amount of funds to the holder on demand.

checks and balances • The principle under which the powers of the national government are divided among three separate branches—the executive, legislative, and judicial branches—each of which exercises a check on the actions of the others.

choice-of-language clause • A clause in a contract designating the official language by which the contract will be interpreted in the event of a future disagreement over the contract's terms.

choice-of-law clause • A clause in a contract designating the law (such as the law of a particular state or nation) that will govern the contract.

citation • A reference to a publication in which a legal authority—such as a statute or a court decision—or other source can be found.

civil law • The branch of law dealing with the definition and enforcement of all private or public rights, as opposed to criminal matters.

civil law system • A system of law derived from that of the Roman Empire and based on a code rather than case law; the predominant system of law in the nations of continental Europe and the nations that were once their colonies. In the United States, Louisiana, because of its historical ties to France, has, in part, a civil law system.

clearinghouse • A system or place where banks exchange checks and drafts drawn on each other and settle daily balances.

click-on agreement • An agreement that arises when a buyer, engaging in a transaction on a computer, indicates assent to be bound by the terms of an offer by clicking on a button that says, for example, "I agree"; sometimes referred to as a *click-on license* or a *click-wrap agreement.*

close corporation • A corporation whose shareholders are limited to a small group of persons, often only family members. In a close corporation, the shareholders' rights to transfer shares to others are usually restricted.

closed shop • A firm that requires union membership by its workers as a condition of employment. The closed shop was made illegal by the Labor-Management Relations Act of 1947.

closing • The final step in the sale of real estate—also called settlement or closing escrow. The escrow agent coordinates the closing with the recording of deeds, the obtaining of title insurance, and other concurrent closing activities. A number of costs must be paid, in cash, at the time of closing, and they can range from several hundred to several thousand dollars, depending on the amount of the mortgage loan and other conditions of the sale.

cloud computing • A subscription-based or pay-per-use service that, in real time over the Internet, extends a computer's software or storage capabilities. By using the services of large companies with excess storage and computing capacity, a company can increase its information technology capabilities without investing in new infrastructure, training new personnel, or licensing new software.

codicil • A written supplement or modification to a will. A codicil must be executed with the same formalities as a will.

collateral • Under Article 9 of the UCC, the property subject to a security interest, including accounts and chattel paper that have been sold.

collateral promise • A secondary promise that is ancillary (subsidiary) to a principal transaction or primary contractual relationship, such as a promise made by one person to pay the debts of another if the latter fails to perform. A collateral promise normally must be in writing to be enforceable.

collecting bank • Any bank handling an item for collection, except the payor bank.

collective bargaining • The process by which labor and management negotiate the terms and conditions of employment, including working hours and workplace conditions.

collective mark • A mark used by members of a cooperative, association, union, or other organization to certify the region, materials, mode of manufacture, quality, or other characteristic of specific goods or services.

comity • The principle by which one nation defers to and gives effect to the laws and judicial decrees of another nation. This recognition is based primarily on respect.

commerce clause • The provision in Article I, Section 8, of the U.S. Constitution that gives Congress the power to regulate interstate commerce.

commercial impracticability • A doctrine under which a seller may be excused from performing a contract when (1) a contingency occurs, (2) the contingency's occurrence makes performance impracticable, and (3) the nonoccurrence of the contingency was a basic assumption on which the contract was made. Although UCC Section 2–615 expressly frees only sellers under this doctrine, courts have not distinguished between buyers and sellers in applying it.

commingle • To put funds or goods together into one mass so that they are mixed to such a degree that they no longer have separate identities. In corporate law, if personal and corporate interests are commingled to the extent that the corporation has no separate identity, a court may "pierce the corporate veil" and expose the shareholders to personal liability.

common law • The body of law developed from custom or judicial decisions in English and U.S. courts, not attributable to a legislature.

common stock • Shares of ownership in a corporation that give the owner of the stock a proportionate interest in the corporation with regard to control, earnings, and net assets. Shares of common stock are lowest in priority with respect to payment of dividends and distribution of the corporation's assets on dissolution.

community property • A form of concurrent ownership of property in which each spouse technically owns an undivided one-half interest in property acquired during the marriage. This form of joint ownership occurs in only ten states and Puerto Rico.

comparative negligence • A rule in tort law that reduces the plaintiff's recovery in proportion to the plaintiff's degree of fault, rather than barring recovery completely; used in the majority of states.

compensatory damages • A monetary award equivalent to the actual value of injuries or damage sustained by the aggrieved party.

complaint • The pleading made by a plaintiff alleging wrongdoing on the part of the defendant; the document that, when filed with a court, initiates a lawsuit.

computer crime • Any wrongful act that is directed against computers and computer parts or that involves the wrongful use or abuse of computers or software.

concurrent conditions • Conditions that must occur or be performed at the same time; they are mutually dependent. No obligations arise until these conditions are simultaneously performed.
concurrent jurisdiction • Jurisdiction that exists when two different courts have the power to hear a case. For example, some cases can be heard in a federal or a state court.
concurrent ownership • Joint ownership.
condemnation • The process of taking private property for public use through the government's power of eminent domain.
condition • A qualification, provision, or clause in a contractual agreement, the occurrence or nonoccurrence of which creates, suspends, or terminates the obligations of the contracting parties.
condition precedent • In a contractual agreement, a condition that must be met before a party's promise becomes absolute.
condition subsequent • A condition in a contract that, if it occurs, operates to terminate a party's absolute promise to perform.
confession of judgment • The act or agreement of a debtor permitting a judgment to be entered against him or her by a creditor, for an agreed sum, without the institution of legal proceedings.
confiscation • A government's taking of a privately owned business or personal property without a proper public purpose or an award of just compensation.
conforming goods • Goods that conform to contract specifications.
confusion • The mixing together of goods belonging to two or more owners to such an extent that the separately owned goods cannot be identified.
consequential damages • Special damages that compensate for a loss that does not directly or immediately result from the breach (for example, lost profits). For the plaintiff to collect consequential damages, they must have been reasonably foreseeable at the time the breach or injury occurred.
consideration • Generally, the value given in return for a promise; involves two elements—the giving of something of legally sufficient value and a bargained-for exchange. The consideration must result in a detriment to the promisee or a benefit to the promisor.
consignment • A transaction in which an owner of goods (the consignor) delivers the goods to another (the consignee) for the consignee to sell. The consignee pays the consignor only for the goods that are sold by the consignee.
consolidation • A contractual and statutory process in which two or more corporations join to become a completely new corporation. The original corporations cease to exist, and the new corporation acquires all their assets and liabilities.
constitutional law • The body of law derived from the U.S. Constitution and the constitutions of the various states.
construction loan • A loan that the borrower takes out to finance the building of a new home. Construction loans are often set up to release funds at particular stages of the project.
constructive delivery • An act equivalent to the actual, physical delivery of property that cannot be physically delivered because of difficulty or impossibility. For example, the transfer of a key to a safe constructively delivers the contents of the safe.
constructive discharge • A termination of employment brought about by making the employee's working conditions so intolerable that the employee reasonably feels compelled to leave.
constructive eviction • A form of eviction that occurs when a landlord fails to perform adequately any of the duties (such as providing heat in the winter) required by the lease, thereby making the tenant's further use and enjoyment of the property exceedingly difficult or impossible.
constructive trust • An equitable trust that is imposed in the interests of fairness and justice when someone wrongfully holds legal title to property. A court may require the owner to hold the property in trust for the person or persons who should rightfully own the property.
consumer-debtor • An individual whose debts are primarily consumer debts (debts for purchases made primarily for personal, family, or household use).
continuation statement • A statement that, if filed within six months prior to the expiration date of the original financing statement, continues the perfection of the original security interest for another five years. The perfection of a security interest can be continued in the same manner indefinitely.
contract • An agreement that can be enforced in court; formed by two or more competent parties who agree, for consideration, to perform or to refrain from performing some legal act now or in the future.
contractual capacity • The threshold mental capacity required by law for a party who enters into a contract to be bound by that contract.
contributory negligence • A rule in tort law that completely bars the plaintiff from recovering any damages if the damage suffered is partly the plaintiff's own fault; used in a minority of states.
conversion • Wrongfully taking or retaining possession of an individual's personal property and placing it in the service of another.
conveyance • The transfer of title to land from one person to another by deed; a document (such as a deed) by which an interest in land is transferred from one person to another.
copyright • The exclusive right of an author or originator of a literary or artistic production to publish, print, or sell that production for a statutory period of time. A copyright has the same monopolistic nature as a patent or trademark, but it differs in that it applies exclusively to works of art, literature, and other works of authorship (including computer programs).
corporate governance • A set of policies or procedures affecting the way a corporation is directed or controlled.
corporate social responsibility • The idea that corporations can and should act ethically and be accountable to society for their actions.
corporation • A legal entity formed in compliance with statutory requirements that is distinct from its shareholder-owners.
correspondent bank • A bank in which another bank has an account (and vice versa) for the purpose of facilitating fund transfers.
cost-benefit analysis • A decision-making technique that involves weighing the costs of a given action against the benefits of that action.
co-surety • A joint surety; a person who assumes liability jointly with another surety for the payment of an obligation.
counterclaim • A claim made by a defendant in a civil lawsuit against the plaintiff. In effect, the defendant is suing the plaintiff.
counteroffer • An offeree's response to an offer in which the offeree rejects the original offer and at the same time makes a new offer.
course of dealing • Prior conduct between the parties to a contract that establishes a common basis for their understanding.
course of performance • The conduct that occurs under the terms of a particular agreement. Such conduct indicates what the parties to an agreement intended it to mean.
covenant not to compete • A contractual promise of one party to refrain from conducting business similar to that of another party for a certain period of time and within a specified geographic area.
covenant not to sue • An agreement to substitute a contractual obligation for some other type of legal action based on a valid claim.
cover • Under the UCC, a remedy that allows the buyer or lessee, on the seller's or lessor's breach, to purchase the goods, in good faith and within a reasonable time, from another seller or lessor and substitute them for the goods due under the contract. If the cost of cover exceeds the cost of the contract goods, the breaching seller or lessor will be liable to the buyer or lessee for the difference, plus incidental and consequential damages.
cram-down provision • A provision of the Bankruptcy Code that allows a court to confirm a debtor's Chapter 11 reorganization plan even though only one class of creditors has accepted it.

creditors' composition agreement • An agreement formed between a debtor and his or her creditors in which the creditors agree to accept a lesser sum than that owed by the debtor in full satisfaction of the debt.

crime • A wrong against society proclaimed in a statute and, if committed, punishable by society through fines and/or imprisonment—and, in some cases, death.

criminal law • Law that defines and governs actions that constitute crimes. Generally, criminal law has to do with wrongful actions committed against society for which society demands redress.

cross-collateralization • The use of an asset that is not the subject of a loan to collateralize that loan.

cure • The right of a party who tenders nonconforming performance to correct that performance within the contract period [UCC 2–508(1)].

cyber crime • A crime that occurs online, in the virtual community of the Internet, as opposed to in the physical world.

cyber fraud • Any misrepresentation knowingly made over the Internet with the intention of deceiving another and on which a reasonable person would and does rely to his or her detriment.

cyberlaw • An informal term used to refer to all laws governing electronic communications and transactions, particularly those conducted via the Internet.

cyber mark • A trademark in cyberspace.

cybernotary • A legally recognized authority that can certify the validity of digital signatures.

cybersquatting • The act of registering a domain name that is the same as, or confusingly similar to, the trademark of another and then offering to sell that domain name back to the trademark owner.

cyberstalking • The crime of stalking committed in cyberspace though the use of the Internet, e-mail, or another form of electronic communication. Generally, stalking involves harassing a person and putting that person in reasonable fear for his or her safety or the safety of the person's immediate family.

cyberterrorist • A person who uses the Internet to attack or sabotage businesses and government agencies with the purpose of disrupting infrastructure systems.

cyber tort • A tort committed in cyberspace.

D

damages • Money sought as a remedy for a breach of contract or a tortious action.

debtor • Under Article 9 of the Uniform Commercial Code, any party who owes payment or performance of a secured obligation.

debtor in possession (DIP) • In Chapter 11 bankruptcy proceedings, a debtor who is allowed to continue in possession of the estate in property (the business) and to continue business operations.

deed • A document by which title to property (usually real property) is passed.

deed in lieu of foreclosure • An alternative to foreclosure in which the mortgagor, rather than fighting to retain possession, voluntarily conveys the property to the lender in satisfaction of the mortgage.

defalcation • Embezzlement; the misappropriation of funds by a party, such as a corporate officer or public official, in a fiduciary relationship with another.

defamation • Anything published or publicly spoken that causes injury to another's good name, reputation, or character.

default • Failure to observe a promise or discharge an obligation; commonly used to refer to failure to pay a debt when it is due.

default judgment • A judgment entered by a court against a defendant who has failed to appear in court to answer or defend against the plaintiff's claim.

defendant • One against whom a lawsuit is brought; the accused person in a criminal proceeding.

defense • A reason offered and alleged by a defendant in an action or lawsuit as to why the plaintiff should not recover or establish what she or he seeks.

deficiency judgment • A judgment against a debtor for the amount of a debt remaining unpaid after the collateral has been repossessed and sold.

delegatee • A party to whom contractual obligations are transferred, or delegated.

delegation of duties • The act of transferring to another all or part of one's duties arising under a contract.

delegator • A party who transfers (delegates) her or his obligations under a contract to another party (called the delegatee).

depositary bank • The first bank to receive a check for payment.

deposition • The testimony of a party to a lawsuit or a witness taken under oath before a trial.

destination contract • A contract for the sale of goods in which the seller is required or authorized to ship the goods by carrier and tender delivery of the goods at a particular destination. The seller assumes liability for any losses or damage to the goods until they are tendered at the destination specified in the contract.

devise • As a noun, a gift of real property by will; as a verb, to make a gift of real property by will.

devisee • One designated in a will to receive a gift of real property.

digital cash • Funds contained on computer software, in the form of secure programs stored on microchips and on other computer devices.

disaffirmance • The legal avoidance, or setting aside, of a contractual obligation.

discharge • The termination of an obligation. In contract law, discharge occurs when the parties have fully performed their contractual obligations or when events, conduct of the parties, or operation of law releases the parties from performance. In bankruptcy proceedings, the extinction of the debtor's dischargeable debts, thereby relieving the debtor of the obligation to pay the debts.

disclosed principal • A principal whose identity is known to a third party at the time the agent makes a contract with the third party.

discovery • A phase in the litigation process during which the opposing parties may obtain information from each other and from third parties prior to trial.

dishonor • To refuse to pay or accept a negotiable instrument, whichever is required, even though the instrument is presented in a timely and proper manner.

disparagement of property • An economically injurious falsehood made about another's product or property; a general term for torts that are more specifically referred to as *slander of quality* or *slander of title*.

disparate-impact discrimination • A form of employment discrimination resulting from certain employer practices or procedures that, although not discriminatory on their face, have a discriminatory effect.

disparate-treatment discrimination • A form of employment discrimination resulting when an employer intentionally discriminates against employees who are members of protected classes.

dissociation • The severance of the relationship between a partner and a partnership when the partner ceases to be associated with the carrying on of the partnership business.

dissolution • The formal disbanding of a partnership or a corporation. It can take place by (1) an act of the state; (2) acts of the partners or, in a corporation, acts of the shareholders and board of directors; (3) the subsequent illegality of the firm's business; (4) the expiration of a time period stated in a partnership agreement or a certificate of incorporation; or (5) judicial decree.

distributed network • A network that can be used by persons located (distributed) around the country or the globe to share computer files.

distribution agreement • A contract between a seller and a distributor of the seller's products setting out the terms and conditions of the distributorship.

diversity of citizenship • Under Article III, Section 2, of the U.S. Constitution, a basis for federal district court jurisdiction over a lawsuit between (1) citizens of different states, (2) a foreign country and citizens of a state or of different states, or (3) citizens of a state and citizens or subjects of a foreign country. The amount in controversy must be more than $75,000 before a federal district court can take jurisdiction in such cases.
dividend • A distribution to corporate shareholders of corporate profits or income, disbursed in proportion to the number of shares held.
docket • The list of cases entered on a court's calendar and thus scheduled to be heard by the court.
document of title • A paper exchanged in the regular course of business that evidences the right to possession of goods (for example, a bill of lading or a warehouse receipt).
domain name • The last part of an Internet address, such as "westlaw.com." The top level (the part of the name to the right of the period) indicates the type of entity that operates the site (com is an abbreviation for "commercial"). The second level (the part of the name to the left of the period) is chosen by the entity.
domestic corporation • In a given state, a corporation that does business in, and is organized under the law of, that state.
dominion • Ownership rights in property, including the right to possess and control the property.
double jeopardy • A situation occurring when a person is tried twice for the same criminal offense; prohibited by the Fifth Amendment to the U.S. Constitution.
down payment • The part of the purchase price of real property that is paid in cash up front, reducing the amount of the loan or mortgage.
draft • Any instrument drawn on a drawee that orders the drawee to pay a certain sum of money, usually to a third party (the payee), on demand or at a definite future time.
dram shop act • A state statute that imposes liability on the owners of bars and taverns, as well as those who serve alcoholic drinks to the public, for injuries resulting from accidents caused by intoxicated persons when the sellers or servers of alcoholic drinks contributed to the intoxication.
drawee • The party that is ordered to pay a draft or check. With a check, a bank or a financial institution is always the drawee.
drawer • The party that initiates a draft (such as a check), thereby ordering the drawee to pay.
due diligence • A required standard of care that certain professionals, such as accountants, must meet to avoid liability for securities violations.
due process clause • The provisions in the Fifth and Fourteenth Amendments to the U.S. Constitution that guarantee that no person shall be deprived of life, liberty, or property without due process of law. Similar clauses are found in most state constitutions.
dumping • The selling of goods in a foreign country at a price below the price charged for the same goods in the domestic market.
duress • Unlawful pressure brought to bear on a person, causing the person to perform an act that she or he would not otherwise perform.
duty of care • The duty of all persons, as established by tort law, to exercise a reasonable amount of care in their dealings with others. Failure to exercise due care, which is normally determined by the reasonable person standard, constitutes the tort of negligence.

E

e-agent • A computer program that by electronic or other automated means can independently initiate an action or respond to electronic messages or data without review by an individual.
easement • A nonpossessory right to use another's property in a manner established by either express or implied agreement.
e-contract • A contract that is formed electronically.
e-evidence • Evidence that consists of computer-generated or electronically recorded information, including e-mail, voice mail, spreadsheets, document preparation systems, and other data.
electronic fund transfer (EFT) • A transfer of funds through the use of an electronic terminal, a telephone, a computer, or magnetic tape.
emancipation • In regard to minors, the act of being freed from parental control; occurs when a child's parent or legal guardian relinquishes the legal right to exercise control over the child. Normally, a minor who leaves home to support himself or herself is considered emancipated.
embezzlement • The fraudulent appropriation of funds or other property by a person to whom the funds or property has been entrusted.
eminent domain • The power of a government to take land from private citizens for public use on the payment of just compensation.
e-money • Prepaid funds recorded on a computer or a card (such as a smart card or a stored-value card).
employment at will • A common law doctrine under which either party may terminate an employment relationship at any time for any reason, unless a contract specifies otherwise.
employment contract • A contract between an employer and an employee in which the terms and conditions of employment are stated.
employment discrimination • Treating employees or job applicants unequally on the basis of race, color, national origin, religion, gender, age, or disability; prohibited by federal statutes.
encryption • The process by which a message is transmitted into a form or code that the sender and receiver intend not to be understandable by third parties.
entrapment • In criminal law, a defense in which the defendant claims that he or she was induced by a public official—usually an undercover agent or police officer—to commit a crime that he or she would otherwise not have committed.
entrepreneur • One who initiates and assumes the financial risk of a new business enterprise and undertakes to provide or control its management.
entrustment rule • The transfer of goods to a merchant who deals in goods of that kind and who may transfer those goods and all rights to them to a buyer in the ordinary course of business.
equal dignity rule • In most states, a rule stating that express authority given to an agent must be in writing if the contract to be made on behalf of the principal is required to be in writing.
equal protection clause • The provision in the Fourteenth Amendment to the U.S. Constitution that guarantees that no state will "deny to any person within its jurisdiction the equal protection of the laws." This clause mandates that the state governments must treat similarly situated individuals in a similar manner.
equitable principles and maxims • General propositions or principles of law that have to do with fairness (equity).
equitable right of redemption • The right of the mortgagor who has breached (defaulted on) the mortgage agreement to redeem or purchase the property prior to foreclosure proceedings.
escrow account • An account that is generally held in the name of the depositor and escrow agent; the funds in the account are paid to a third person only on fulfillment of the escrow condition.
e-signature • As defined by the Uniform Electronic Transactions Act, "an electronic sound, symbol, or process attached to or logically associated with a record and executed or adopted by a person with the intent to sign the record."
establishment clause • The provision in the First Amendment to the U.S. Constitution that prohibits the government from establishing any state-sponsored religion or enacting any law that promotes religion or favors one religion over another.
estate in property • In bankruptcy proceedings, all of the debtor's interests in property currently held, wherever located, together with certain jointly owned property, property transferred in transactions voidable by the trustee, proceeds and profits from the property of the estate, and certain property interests to which the debtor becomes entitled within 180 days after filing for bankruptcy.
estopped • Barred, impeded, or precluded.
estray statute • A statute defining finders' rights in property when the true owners are unknown.
ethical reasoning • A reasoning process in which an individual links his or her moral convictions or ethical standards to the particular situation at hand.

ethics • Moral principles and values applied to social behavior.
eviction • A landlord's act of depriving a tenant of possession of the leased premises.
exclusionary rule • In criminal procedure, a rule under which any evidence that is obtained in violation of the accused's constitutional rights guaranteed by the Fourth, Fifth, and Sixth Amendments to the U.S. Constitution, as well as any evidence derived from illegally obtained evidence, will not be admissible in court.
exclusive jurisdiction • Jurisdiction that exists when a case can be heard only in a particular court or type of court.
exculpatory clause • A clause that releases a contractual party from liability in the event of monetary or physical injury, no matter who is at fault.
executed contract • A contract that has been completely performed by both parties.
execution • An action to carry into effect the directions in a court decree or judgment.
executor • A person appointed by a testator in a will to see that her or his will is administered appropriately.
executory contract • A contract that has not as yet been fully performed.
export • The sale of goods and services by domestic firms to buyers located in other countries.
express contract • A contract in which the terms of the agreement are stated in words, oral or written.
express warranty • A seller's or lessor's oral or written promise or affirmation of fact ancillary (secondary) to an underlying sales or lease agreement, as to the quality, condition, description, or performance of the goods being sold or leased.
expropriation • The seizure by a government of a privately owned business or personal property for a proper public purpose and with just compensation.
extension clause • A clause in a time instrument that allows the instrument's date of maturity to be extended into the future.

F

family limited liability partnership (FLLP) • A type of limited liability partnership owned by family members or fiduciaries of family members.
federal form of government • A system of government in which the states form a union and the sovereign power is divided between the central government and the member states.
federal question • A question that pertains to the U.S. Constitution, acts of Congress, or treaties. A federal question provides a basis for federal jurisdiction.
Federal Reserve System • A network of twelve district banks and related branches located around the country and headed by the Federal Reserve Board of Governors. Most banks in the United States have Federal Reserve accounts.
fee simple • An absolute form of property ownership entitling the property owner to use, possess, or dispose of the property as he or she chooses during his or her lifetime. On death, the interest in the property descends to the owner's heirs.
fee simple absolute • An ownership interest in land in which the owner has the greatest possible aggregation of rights, privileges, and power. Ownership in fee simple absolute is limited absolutely to a person and her or his heirs.
felony • A crime—such as arson, murder, rape, or robbery—that carries the most severe sanctions, ranging from one year in a state or federal prison to the death penalty.
fictitious payee • A payee on a negotiable instrument whom the maker or drawer does not intend to have an interest in the instrument. Indorsements by fictitious payees are treated as authorized indorsements under Article 3 of the UCC.
fiduciary • As a noun, a person having a duty created by his or her undertaking to act primarily for another's benefit in matters connected with the undertaking. As an adjective, a relationship founded on trust and confidence.
filtering software • A computer program that is designed to block access to certain Web sites, based on their content. The software blocks the retrieval of a site whose URL or key words are on a list within the program.
financing statement • A document prepared by a secured creditor, and filed with the appropriate state or local official, to give notice to the public that the creditor has a security interest in collateral belonging to the debtor named in the statement. The financing statement must contain the names and addresses of both the debtor and the secured party and must describe the collateral by type or item.
firm offer • An offer (by a merchant) that is irrevocable without the necessity of consideration for a stated period of time or, if no definite period is stated, for a reasonable time (neither period to exceed three months). A firm offer by a merchant must be in writing and must be signed by the offeror.
fixed-rate mortgage • A standard mortgage with a fixed, or unchanging, rate of interest. The loan payments on these mortgages remain the same for the duration of the loan, which ranges between fifteen and forty years.
fixed-term tenancy • A type of tenancy under which property is leased for a specified period of time, such as a month, a year, or a period of years; also called a tenancy for years.
fixture • An item that was once personal property but has become attached to real property in such a way that it takes on the characteristics of real property and becomes part of that real property.
floating lien • A security interest in proceeds, after-acquired property, or collateral subject to future advances by the secured party (or all three); a security interest in collateral that is retained even when the collateral changes in character, classification, or location.
forbearance • The act of refraining from an action that one has a legal right to undertake.
***force majeure* clause** • A provision in a contract stipulating that certain unforeseen events—such as war, political upheavals, or acts of God—will excuse a party from liability for nonperformance of contractual obligations.
foreclosure • A proceeding in which a mortgagee either takes title to or forces the sale of the mortgagor's property in satisfaction of the debt.
foreign corporation • In a given state, a corporation that does business in the state without being incorporated therein.
foreign exchange market • A worldwide system in which foreign currencies are bought and sold.
forgery • The fraudulent making or altering of any writing in a way that changes the legal rights and liabilities of another.
formal contract • A contract that by law requires a specific form, such as being executed under seal, for its validity.
forum-selection clause • A provision in a contract designating the court, jurisdiction, or tribunal that will decide any disputes arising under the contract.
fraudulent misrepresentation • Any misrepresentation, either by misstatement or by omission of a material fact, knowingly made with the intention of deceiving another and on which a reasonable person would and does rely to his or her detriment.
free exercise clause • The provision in the First Amendment to the U.S. Constitution that prohibits the government from interfering with people's religious practices or forms of worship.
free-writing prospectus • Any type of written, electronic, or graphic offer that describes the issuing corporation or its securities and includes a legend indicating that the investor may obtain the prospectus at the Securities and Exchange Commission's Web site.
frustration of purpose • A court-created doctrine under which a party to a contract will be relieved of her or his duty to perform when the objective purpose for performance no longer exists (due to reasons beyond that party's control).
fungible goods • Goods that are alike by physical nature, by agreement, or by trade usage (for example, wheat, oil, and wine that are identical in type and quality). When owners hold fungible goods as tenants in common, title and risk can pass without actually separating the goods being sold from the larger mass.

G

garnishment • A legal process used by a creditor to collect a debt by seizing property of the debtor (such as wages) that is being held by a third party (such as the debtor's employer).

general partner • In a limited partnership, a partner who assumes responsibility for the management of the partnership and liability for all partnership debts.

generally accepted accounting principles (GAAP) • The conventions, rules, and procedures that define accepted accounting practices at a particular time. The source of the principles is the Financial Accounting Standards Board.

generally accepted auditing standards (GAAS) • Standards concerning an auditor's professional qualities and the judgment exercised by him or her in the performance of an examination and report. The source of the standards is the American Institute of Certified Public Accountants.

gift • Any voluntary transfer of property made without consideration, past or present.

gift *causa mortis* • A gift made in contemplation of death. If the donor does not die of that ailment, the gift is revoked.

gift *inter vivos* • A gift made during one's lifetime and not in contemplation of imminent death, in contrast to a gift *causa mortis*.

good faith purchaser • A purchaser who buys without notice of any circumstance that would cause a person of ordinary prudence to inquire as to whether the seller has valid title to the goods being sold.

Good Samaritan statute • A state statute stipulating that persons who provide emergency services to, or rescue, someone in peril cannot be sued for negligence, unless they act recklessly, thereby causing further harm.

grand jury • A group of citizens called to decide, after hearing the state's evidence, whether a reasonable basis (probable cause) exists for believing that a crime has been committed and that a trial ought to be held.

guarantor • A person who agrees to satisfy the debt of another (the debtor) only after the principal debtor defaults.

H

hacker • A person who uses one computer to break into another.

holder • Any person in possession of an instrument drawn, issued, or indorsed to him or her, to his or her order, to bearer, or in blank.

holder in due course (HDC) • A holder who acquires a negotiable instrument for value; in good faith; and without notice that the instrument is overdue, that it has been dishonored, that any person has a defense against it or a claim to it, or that the instrument contains unauthorized signatures, has been altered, or is so irregular or incomplete as to call into question its authenticity.

holding company • A company whose business activity is holding shares in another company.

holographic will • A will written entirely in the signer's handwriting and usually not witnessed.

home equity loan • A loan in which the lender accepts a person's home equity (the portion of the home's value that is paid off) as collateral, which can be seized if the loan is not repaid on time. Borrowers often take out home equity loans to finance the renovation of the property or to pay off debt that carries a higher interest rate, such as credit-card debt.

homeowners' insurance • Insurance that protects a homeowner's property against damage from storms, fire, and other hazards. Lenders may require that a borrower carry homeowners' insurance on mortgaged property.

homestead exemption • A law permitting a debtor to retain the family home, either in its entirety or up to a specified dollar amount, free from the claims of unsecured creditors or trustees in bankruptcy.

hybrid mortgage • A mortgage that starts as a fixed-rate mortgage and then converts to an adjustable-rate mortgage.

I

I-9 verification • A process that all U.S. employers must perform within three business days of hiring a new worker to verify the employment eligibility and identity of the worker by completing an I-9 form.

I-551 Alien Registration Receipt • A document, commonly known as a green card, that shows that a foreign-born individual has been lawfully admitted for permanent residency in the United States. Persons seeking employment can prove to prospective employers that they are legally in the United States by showing this receipt.

identification • In a sale of goods, the express designation of the goods provided for in the contract.

identity theft • The theft of identity information, such as a person's name, driver's license number, or Social Security number. The information is then usually used to access the victim's financial resources.

implied contract • A contract formed in whole or in part from the conduct of the parties (as opposed to an express contract). Also known as an *implied-in-fact contract*.

implied warranty • A warranty that arises by law because of the circumstances of a sale rather than by the seller's express promise.

implied warranty of fitness for a particular purpose • A warranty that goods sold or leased are fit for a particular purpose. The warranty arises when any seller or lessor knows the particular purpose for which a buyer or lessee will use the goods and knows that the buyer or lessee is relying on the skill and judgment of the seller or lessor to select suitable goods.

implied warranty of habitability • An implied promise by a seller of a new house that the house is fit for human habitation—that is, in a condition that is safe and suitable for people to live there. Also, the implied promise by a landlord that rented residential premises are habitable.

implied warranty of merchantability • A warranty that goods being sold or leased are reasonably fit for the general purpose for which they are sold or leased, are properly packaged and labeled, and are of proper quality. The warranty automatically arises in every sale or lease of goods made by a merchant who deals in goods of the kind sold or leased.

impossibility of performance • A doctrine under which a party to a contract is relieved of his or her duty to perform when performance becomes objectively impossible or totally impracticable (through no fault of either party).

imposter • One who, by use of the mails, Internet, telephone, or personal appearance, induces a maker or drawer to issue an instrument in the name of an impersonated payee. Indorsements by imposters are treated as authorized indorsements under Article 3 of the UCC.

incidental beneficiary • A third party who incidentally benefits from a contract but whose benefit was not the reason the contract was formed. An incidental beneficiary has no rights in a contract and cannot sue to have the contract enforced.

incidental damages • Damages awarded to compensate for expenses that are directly incurred because of a breach of contract—such as those incurred to obtain performance from another source.

incontestability clause • A clause within a life or health insurance policy that states that after the policy has been in force for a specified length of time—most often two or three years—the insurer cannot contest statements made in the policyholder's application.

independent contractor • One who works for, and receives payment from, an employer but whose working conditions and methods are not controlled by the employer. An independent contractor is not an employee but may be an agent.

indictment • A charge by a grand jury that a named person has committed a crime.

indorsement • A signature placed on an instrument for the purpose of transferring one's ownership rights in the instrument.

informal contract • A contract that does not require a specified form or formality to be valid.

information • A formal accusation or complaint (without an indictment) issued in certain types of actions (usually criminal actions involving lesser crimes) by a government prosecutor.

information return • A tax return submitted by a partnership that only reports the income and losses earned by the business. The partnership as an entity does not pay taxes on the income received by the partnership.

inside director • A person on the board of directors who is also an officer of the corporation.
insider trading • The purchase or sale of securities on the basis of *inside information*—that is, information that has not been made available to the public.
insolvent • Under the UCC, a term describing a person who ceases to pay his or her debts in the ordinary course of business or cannot pay his or her debts as they become due or is insolvent within the meaning of federal bankruptcy law.
installment contract • Under the UCC, a contract that requires or authorizes delivery in two or more separate lots to be accepted and paid for separately.
insurable interest • An interest either in a person's life or well-being or in property that is sufficiently substantial that insuring against injury to (or the death of) the person or against damage to the property does not amount to a mere wagering (betting) contract. In regard to the sale or lease of goods, a property interest in the goods that is sufficiently substantial to permit a party to insure against damage to the goods.
insurance • A contract in which, for a stipulated consideration, one party agrees to compensate the other for loss on a specific subject by a specified peril.
intangible property • Property that cannot be seen or touched but exists only conceptually, such as corporate stocks and bonds, patents and copyrights, and ordinary contract rights. Article 2 of the UCC does not govern intangible property.
integrated contract • A written contract that constitutes the final expression of the parties' agreement. If a contract is integrated, evidence extraneous to the contract that contradicts or alters the meaning of the contract in any way is inadmissible.
intellectual property • Property resulting from intellectual, creative processes.
intended beneficiary • A third party for whose benefit a contract is formed. An intended beneficiary can sue the promisor if such a contract is breached.
intentional tort • A wrongful act knowingly committed.
interest-only (IO) mortgage • A mortgage that gives the borrower the option of paying only the interest portion of the monthly payment and forgoing the payment of any of the principal for a specified period of time, such as five years. After the interest-only payment option is exhausted, the borrower's payment will increase to include payments on the principal.
intermediary bank • Any bank to which an item is transferred in the course of collection, except the depositary or payor bank.
international law • The law that governs relations among nations. International customs, treaties, and organizations are important sources of international law.
international organization • Any membership group that operates across national borders. These organizations can be governmental organizations, such as the United Nations, or nongovernmental organizations, such as the Red Cross.
interrogatories • A series of written questions for which written answers are prepared by a party to a lawsuit, usually with the assistance of the party's attorney, and then signed under oath.
***inter vivos* trust** • A trust created by the grantor (settlor) and effective during the grantor's lifetime; a trust not established by a will.
intestacy laws • State statutes that specify how property will be distributed when a person dies intestate (without a valid will); also called *statutes of descent and distribution.*
intestate • As a noun, one who has died without having created a valid will; as an adjective, the state of having died without a will.
investment company • A company that acts on the behalf of many smaller shareholders/owners by buying a large portfolio of securities and professionally managing that portfolio.
investment contract • In securities law, a transaction in which a person invests in a common enterprise reasonably expecting profits that are derived primarily from the efforts of others.

J

joint and several liability • In partnership law, a doctrine under which a plaintiff may sue, and collect a judgment from, all of the partners together (jointly) or one or more of the partners separately (severally, or individually). This is true even if one of the partners sued did not participate in, ratify, or know about whatever it was that gave rise to the cause of action.
joint liability • Shared liability. In partnership law, partners incur joint liability for partnership obligations and debts. For example, if a third party sues a partner on a partnership debt, the partner has the right to insist that the other partners be sued with him or her.
joint tenancy • The joint ownership of property by two or more co-owners in which each co-owner owns an undivided portion of the property. On the death of one of the joint tenants, his or her interest automatically passes to the surviving joint tenant(s).
joint venture • A joint undertaking of a specific commercial enterprise by an association of persons. A joint venture normally is not a legal entity and is treated like a partnership for federal income tax purposes.
judicial foreclosure • A court-supervised foreclosure proceeding in which the court determines the validity of the debt and, if the borrower is in default, issues a judgment for the lender.
judicial review • The process by which a court decides on the constitutionality of legislative enactments and actions of the executive branch.
junior lienholder • A party that holds a lien that is subordinate to one or more other liens on the same property.
jurisdiction • The authority of a court to hear and decide a specific case.
jurisprudence • The science or philosophy of law.
justiciable controversy • A controversy that is not hypothetical or academic but real and substantial; a requirement that must be satisfied before a court will hear a case.

L

larceny • The wrongful taking and carrying away of another person's personal property with the intent to permanently deprive the owner of the property. Some states classify larceny as either grand or petit, depending on the property's value.
law • A body of enforceable rules governing relationships among individuals and between individuals and their society.
lease • Under Article 2A of the UCC, a transfer of the right to possess and use goods for a period of time in exchange for payment.
lease agreement • In regard to the lease of goods, an agreement in which one person (the lessor) agrees to transfer the right to the possession and use of property to another person (the lessee) in exchange for rental payments.
leasehold estate • An estate in realty held by a tenant under a lease. In every leasehold estate, the tenant has a qualified right to possess and/or use the land.
legacy • A gift of personal property under a will.
legatee • One designated in a will to receive a gift of personal property.
lessee • A person who acquires the right to the possession and use of another's goods in exchange for rental payments.
lessor • A person who transfers the right to the possession and use of goods to another in exchange for rental payments.
letter of credit • A written instrument, usually issued by a bank on behalf of a customer or other person, in which the issuer promises to honor drafts or other demands for payment by third parties in accordance with the terms of the instrument.
levy • The obtaining of funds by legal process through the seizure and sale of nonexempt property, usually done after a writ of execution has been issued.
libel • Defamation in writing or other form having the quality of permanence (such as a digital recording).
license • A revocable right or privilege of a person to come onto another person's land. In the context of intellectual property law, an agreement permitting the use of a trademark, copyright, patent, or trade secret for certain limited purposes.

lien • An encumbrance on a property to satisfy a debt or protect a claim for payment of a debt.
life estate • An interest in land that exists only for the duration of the life of some person, usually the holder of the estate.
limited liability company (LLC) • A hybrid form of business enterprise that offers the limited liability of a corporation and the tax advantages of a partnership.
limited liability limited partnership (LLLP) • A type of limited partnership in which the liability of all of the partners, including general partners, is limited to the amount of their investments.
limited liability partnership (LLP) • A hybrid form of business organization that is used mainly by professionals who normally do business in a partnership. An LLP is a pass-through entity for tax purposes, but the personal liability of the partners is limited.
limited partner • In a limited partnership, a partner who contributes capital to the partnership but has no right to participate in the management and operation of the business. The limited partner assumes no liability for partnership debts beyond the capital contributed.
limited partnership (LP) • A partnership consisting of one or more general partners (who manage the business and are liable to the full extent of their personal assets for debts of the partnership) and one or more limited partners (who contribute only assets and are liable only up to the extent of their contributions).
liquidated damages • An amount, stipulated in a contract, that the parties to the contract believe to be a reasonable estimation of the damages that will occur in the event of a breach.
liquidated debt • A debt for which the amount has been ascertained, fixed, agreed on, settled, or exactly determined. If the amount of the debt is in dispute, the debt is considered unliquidated.
liquidation • The sale of all of the nonexempt assets of a debtor and the distribution of the proceeds to the debtor's creditors. Chapter 7 of the Bankruptcy Code provides for liquidation bankruptcy proceedings.
litigation • The process of resolving a dispute through the court system.
lockout • An employer's act of shutting down the business to prevent employees from working. A lockout is the employer's counterpart to the workers' right to strike and normally is used when a strike is imminent.
long arm statute • A state statute that permits a state to obtain personal jurisdiction over nonresident defendants. A defendant must have certain "minimum contacts" with that state for the statute to apply.
lost property • Property with which the owner has involuntarily parted and then cannot find or recover.

M

mailbox rule • A rule providing that an acceptance of an offer becomes effective on dispatch (on being placed in an official mailbox), if mail is, expressly or impliedly, an authorized means of communication of acceptance to the offeror.
maker • One who promises to pay a fixed amount of money to the holder of a promissory note or a certificate of deposit (CD).
malpractice • Professional misconduct or unreasonable lack of skill; the failure of a professional to use the skills and learning common to the average reputable members of the profession or the skills and learning the professional claims to possess, resulting in injury, loss, or damage to those relying on the professional. Negligence—the failure to exercise due care—on the part of a professional, such as a physician, is commonly referred to as malpractice.
malware • Any program that is harmful to a computer or a computer user; for example, worms and viruses.
market-share liability • A theory under which liability is shared among all firms that manufactured and distributed a particular product during a certain period of time. This form of liability sharing is used only when the true source of the harmful product is unidentifiable; it is not recognized in many jurisdictions.
material fact • A fact to which a reasonable person would attach importance in determining his or her course of action.
mechanic's lien • A statutory lien on the real property of another to ensure payment for work performed and materials furnished in the repair or improvement of real property, such as a building.
mediation • A method of settling disputes outside the courts by using the services of a neutral third party, who acts as a communicating agent between the parties and assists them in negotiating a settlement.
member • A person who has an ownership interest in a limited liability company.
mens rea • Mental state, or intent. Normally, a wrongful mental state is as necessary as a wrongful act to establish criminal liability. What constitutes such a mental state varies according to the wrongful action. Thus, for murder, the *mens rea* is the intent to take a life.
merchant • A person who is engaged in the purchase and sale of goods. Under the UCC, a person who deals in goods of the kind involved in the sales contract or who holds herself or himself out as having skill or knowledge peculiar to the practices or goods being purchased or sold [UCC 2–104].
merger • A contractual and statutory process in which one corporation (the surviving corporation) acquires all of the assets and liabilities of another corporation (the merged corporation).
meta tag • A key word in a document that can serve as an index reference to the document. On the Web, search engines return results based, in part, on these tags in Web documents.
minimum wage • The lowest wage, either by government regulation or union contract, that an employer may pay an hourly worker.
mirror image rule • A common law rule that requires that the terms of the offeree's acceptance adhere exactly to the terms of the offeror's offer for a valid contract to be formed.
misdemeanor • A lesser crime than a felony, punishable by a fine or incarceration in jail for up to one year.
mislaid property • Property with which the owner has voluntarily parted and then cannot find or recover.
mitigation of damages • A rule requiring a plaintiff to do whatever is reasonable to minimize the damages caused by the defendant.
money laundering • Engaging in financial transactions to conceal the identity, source, or destination of illegally gained funds.
moral minimum • The minimum degree of ethical behavior expected of a business firm, which is usually defined as compliance with the law.
mortgage • A written instrument giving a creditor an interest in (lien on) the debtor's real property as security for payment of a debt.
mortgage assignee • An entity that purchases a mortgage from the current mortgage holder and assumes all rights and liabilities of that mortgage, including the right to collect and foreclose.
mortgagee • Under a mortgage agreement, the creditor who takes a security interest in the debtor's property.
mortgagor • Under a mortgage agreement, the debtor who gives the creditor a security interest in the debtor's property in return for a mortgage loan.
motion for a directed verdict • In a jury trial, a motion for the judge to take the decision out of the hands of the jury and to direct a verdict for the party who filed the motion on the ground that the other party has not produced sufficient evidence to support her or his claim.
motion for a new trial • A motion asserting that the trial was so fundamentally flawed (because of error, newly discovered evidence, prejudice, or another reason) that a new trial is necessary to prevent a miscarriage of justice.
motion for judgment *n.o.v.* • A motion requesting the court to grant judgment in favor of the party making the motion on the ground that the jury's verdict against him or her was unreasonable and erroneous.
motion for judgment on the pleadings • A motion by either party to a lawsuit at the close of the pleadings requesting the court to decide the issue

solely on the pleadings without proceeding to trial. The motion will be granted only if no facts are in dispute.

motion for summary judgment • A motion requesting the court to enter a judgment without proceeding to trial. The motion can be based on evidence outside the pleadings and will be granted only if no facts are in dispute.

motion to dismiss • A pleading in which a defendant asserts that the plaintiff's claim fails to state a cause of action (that is, has no basis in law) or that there are other grounds on which the suit should be dismissed. Although the defendant normally is the party requesting a dismissal, either the plaintiff or the court can also make a motion to dismiss the case.

mutual fund • A specific type of investment company that continually buys or sells to investors shares of ownership in a portfolio.

mutual rescission • An agreement between the parties to cancel their contract, releasing the parties from further obligations under the contract. The object of the agreement is to restore the parties to the positions they would have occupied had no contract ever been formed.

N

national law • Law that pertains to a particular nation (as opposed to international law).

necessaries • Necessities required for life, such as food, shelter, clothing, and medical attention; may include whatever is believed to be necessary to maintain a person's standard of living or financial and social status.

negative amortization • Occurs when the payment made by the borrower is less than the interest due on the loan and the difference is added to the principal. The result of negative amortization is that the balance owed on the loan increases rather than decreases over time.

negligence • The failure to exercise the standard of care that a reasonable person would exercise in similar circumstances.

negligence *per se* • An action or failure to act in violation of a statutory requirement.

negotiable instrument • A signed writing (record) that contains an unconditional promise or order to pay an exact sum on demand or at an exact future time to a specific person or order, or to bearer.

negotiation • A process in which parties attempt to settle their dispute informally, with or without attorneys to represent them. In the context of negotiable instruments, the transfer of an instrument in such form that the transferee (the person to whom the instrument is transferred) becomes a holder.

nominal damages • A small monetary award (often one dollar) granted to a plaintiff when no actual damage was suffered.

nonpossessory interest • In the context of real property, an interest in land that does not include any right to possess the property.

normal trade relations (NTR) status • A status granted by each member country of the World Trade Organization to other member countries. Each member is required to treat other members at least as well as it treats the country that receives its most favorable treatment with respect to trade.

notary public • A public official authorized to attest to the authenticity of signatures.

notice of default • A notification that the lender records in the county where the property is located that informs a borrower, who is behind on mortgage payments, of a possible foreclosure if the payments are not brought current.

notice of sale • A notice that the lender sends to a borrower who is in default on a mortgage that informs the borrower that the property will be sold in a foreclosure proceeding. The notice of sale is also typically recorded with the county, posted on the property, and published in the local newspaper.

novation • The substitution, by agreement, of a new contract for an old one, with the rights under the old one being terminated. Typically, novation involves the substitution of a new person who is responsible for the contract and the removal of the original party's rights and duties under the contract.

nuncupative will • An oral will (often called a *deathbed will*) made before witnesses; usually limited to transfers of personal property.

O

objective theory of contracts • A theory under which the intent to form a contract will be judged by outward, objective facts (what the party said when entering into the contract, how the party acted or appeared, and the circumstances surrounding the transaction) as interpreted by a reasonable person, rather than by the party's own secret, subjective intentions.

obligee • One to whom an obligation is owed.

obligor • One who owes an obligation to another.

offer • A promise or commitment to perform or refrain from performing some specified act in the future.

offeree • A person to whom an offer is made.

offeror • A person who makes an offer.

online dispute resolution (ODR) • The resolution of disputes with the assistance of organizations that offer dispute-resolution services via the Internet.

operating agreement • In a limited liability company, an agreement in which the members set forth the details of how the business will be managed and operated. State statutes typically give the members wide latitude in deciding for themselves the rules that will govern their organization.

option contract • A contract under which the offeror cannot revoke the offer for a stipulated time period. During this period, the offeree can accept or reject the offer without fear that the offer will be made to another person. The offeree must give consideration for the option (the irrevocable offer) to be enforceable.

order for relief • A court's grant of assistance to a complainant. In bankruptcy proceedings, the order relieves the debtor of the immediate obligation to pay the debts listed in the bankruptcy petition.

order instrument • A negotiable instrument that is payable "to the order of an identified person" or "to an identified person or order."

ordinance • A regulation enacted by a city or county legislative body that becomes part of that state's statutory law.

output contract • An agreement in which a seller agrees to sell and a buyer agrees to buy all or up to a stated amount of what the seller produces.

outside director • A person on the board of directors who does not hold a management position at the corporation.

overdraft • A check that is paid by the bank when the checking account on which the check is written contains insufficient funds to cover the check.

P

parol evidence rule • A substantive rule of contracts, as well as a procedural rule of evidence, under which a court will not receive into evidence the parties' prior negotiations, prior agreements, or contemporaneous oral agreements if that evidence contradicts or varies the terms of the parties' written contract.

partially disclosed principal • A principal whose identity is unknown by a third party, but the third party knows that the agent is or may be acting for a principal at the time the agent and the third party form a contract.

participation loan • A loan that gives the lender some equity rights in the property, such as the right to receive a percentage of revenue, rental income, or resale income. Also known as an *equity participation loan.*

partnering agreement • An agreement between a seller and a buyer who frequently do business with each other concerning the terms and conditions that will apply to all subsequently formed electronic contracts.

partnership • An agreement by two or more persons to carry on, as co-owners, a business for profit.

pass-through entity • A business entity that has no tax liability. The entity's income is passed through to the owners, and the owners pay taxes on the income.
past consideration • An act that takes place before the contract is made and that ordinarily, by itself, cannot be consideration for a later promise to pay for the act.
patent • A government grant that gives an inventor the exclusive right or privilege to make, use, or sell his or her invention for a limited time period.
payee • A person to whom an instrument is made payable.
payor bank • The bank on which a check is drawn (the drawee bank).
peer-to-peer (P2P) networking • The sharing of resources (such as files, hard drives, and processing styles) among multiple computers without the need for a central network server.
penalty • A contractual clause that states that a certain amount of monetary damages will be paid in the event of a future default or breach of contract. The damages are a punishment for a default and not an accurate measure of compensation for the contract's breach. The agreement as to the penalty amount will not be enforced, and recovery will be limited to actual damages.
per capita • A Latin term meaning "per person." In the law governing estate distribution, a method of distributing the property of an intestate's estate so that each heir in a certain class (such as grandchildren) receives an equal share.
perfection • The legal process by which secured parties protect themselves against the claims of third parties who may wish to have their debts satisfied out of the same collateral; usually accomplished by filing a financing statement with the appropriate government official.
performance • In contract law, the fulfillment of one's duties arising under a contract with another; the normal way of discharging one's contractual obligations.
periodic tenancy • A lease interest in land for an indefinite period involving payment of rent at fixed intervals, such as week to week, month to month, or year to year.
personal defense • A defense that can be used to avoid payment to an ordinary holder of a negotiable instrument but not a holder in due course (HDC) or a holder with the rights of an HDC.
personal property • Property that is movable; any property that is not real property.
per stirpes • A Latin term meaning "by the roots." In the law governing estate distribution, a method of distributing an intestate's estate so that each heir in a certain class (such as grandchildren) takes the share to which her or his deceased ancestor (such as a mother or father) would have been entitled.
persuasive authority • Any legal authority or source of law that a court may look to for guidance but on which it need not rely in making its decision. Persuasive authorities include cases from other jurisdictions and secondary sources of law.
petition in bankruptcy • The document that is filed with a bankruptcy court to initiate bankruptcy proceedings. The official forms required for a petition in bankruptcy must be completed accurately, sworn to under oath, and signed by the debtor.
petty offense • In criminal law, the least serious kind of criminal offense, such as a traffic or building-code violation.
phishing • The attempt to acquire financial data, passwords, or other personal information from consumers by sending e-mail messages that purport to be from a legitimate business, such as a bank or a credit-card company.
piercing the corporate veil • An action in which a court disregards the corporate entity and holds the shareholders personally liable for corporate debts and obligations.
plaintiff • One who initiates a lawsuit.
plea bargaining • The process by which a criminal defendant and the prosecutor in a criminal case work out a mutually satisfactory disposition of the case, subject to court approval; usually involves the defendant's pleading guilty to a lesser offense in return for a lighter sentence.
pleadings • Statements made by the plaintiff and the defendant in a lawsuit that detail the facts, charges, and defenses involved in the litigation. The complaint and answer are part of the pleadings.
pledge • A common law security device (retained in Article 9 of the UCC) in which personal property is transferred into the possession of the creditor as security for the payment of a debt and retained by the creditor until the debt is paid.
police powers • Powers possessed by the states as part of their inherent sovereignty. These powers may be exercised to protect or promote the public order, health, safety, morals, and general welfare.
policy • In insurance law, a contract between the insurer and the insured in which, for a stipulated consideration, the insurer agrees to compensate the insured for loss on a specific subject by a specified peril.
power of attorney • A written document, which is usually notarized, authorizing another to act as one's agent; can be special (permitting the agent to do specified acts only) or general (permitting the agent to transact all business for the principal).
power of sale foreclosure • A foreclosure procedure that is not court supervised and is available only in some states.
precedent • A court decision that furnishes an example or authority for deciding subsequent cases involving identical or similar facts.
predominant-factor test • A test courts use to determine whether a contract is primarily for the sale of goods or for the sale of services.
preemption • A doctrine under which certain federal laws preempt, or take precedence over, conflicting state or local laws.
preemptive rights • Rights held by shareholders that entitle them to purchase newly issued shares of a corporation's stock, equal in percentage to shares already held, before the stock is offered to any outside buyers. Preemptive rights enable shareholders to maintain their proportionate ownership and voice in the corporation.
preference • In bankruptcy proceedings, property transfers or payments made by the debtor that favor (give preference to) one creditor over others. The bankruptcy trustee is allowed to recover payments made both voluntarily and involuntarily to one creditor in preference over another.
preferred creditor • In the context of bankruptcy, a creditor who has received a preferential transfer from a debtor.
preferred stock • Classes of stock that have priority over common stock as to both payment of dividends and distribution of assets on the corporation's dissolution.
premium • In insurance law, the price paid by the insured for insurance protection for a specified period of time.
prenuptial agreement • An agreement made before marriage that defines each partner's ownership rights in the other partner's property. Prenuptial agreements must be in writing to be enforceable.
prepayment penalty clause • A clause in a mortgage loan contract that requires the borrower to pay a penalty if the mortgage is repaid in full within a certain period. A prepayment penalty helps to protect the lender should the borrower refinance within a short time after obtaining a mortgage.
presentment • The act of presenting an instrument to the party liable on the instrument in order to collect payment. Presentment also occurs when a person presents an instrument to a drawee for a required acceptance.
presentment warranties • Implied warranties, made by any person who presents an instrument for payment or acceptance, that (1) the person obtaining payment or acceptance is entitled to enforce the instrument or is authorized to obtain payment or acceptance on behalf of a person who is entitled to enforce the instrument, (2) the instrument has not been altered, and (3) the person obtaining payment or acceptance has no knowledge that the signature of the drawer of the instrument is unauthorized.
***prima facie* case** • A case in which the plaintiff has produced sufficient evidence of his or her claim that the case can go to a jury; a case in

which the evidence compels a decision for the plaintiff if the defendant produces no affirmative defense or evidence to disprove the plaintiff's assertion.

primary source of law • A document that establishes the law on a particular issue, such as a constitution, a statute, an administrative rule, or a court decision.

principle of rights • The principle that human beings have certain fundamental rights (to life, liberty, and the pursuit of happiness, for example). Those who adhere to this "rights theory" believe that a key factor in determining whether a business decision is ethical is how that decision affects the rights of various groups. These groups include the firm's owners, its employees, the consumers of its products or services, its suppliers, the community in which it does business, and society as a whole.

private equity capital • A financing method by which a company sells equity in an existing business to a private or institutional investor.

privilege • A legal right, exemption, or immunity granted to a person or a class of persons. In the context of defamation, an absolute privilege immunizes the person making the statements from a lawsuit, regardless of whether the statements were malicious.

privity of contract • The relationship that exists between the promisor and the promisee of a contract.

probable cause • Reasonable grounds for believing that a person should be arrested or searched.

probate • The process of proving and validating a will and settling all matters pertaining to an estate.

probate court • A state court of limited jurisdiction that conducts proceedings relating to the settlement of a deceased person's estate.

procedural law • Law that establishes the methods of enforcing the rights established by substantive law.

proceeds • Under Article 9 of the UCC, whatever is received when collateral is sold or otherwise disposed of, such as by exchange.

product liability • The legal liability of manufacturers, sellers, and lessors of goods to consumers, users, and bystanders for injuries or damage that are caused by the goods.

profit • In real property law, the right to enter onto and remove something of value from the property of another (for example, the right to enter onto another's land and remove sand and gravel).

promise • An assertion that something either will or will not happen in the future.

promisee • A person to whom a promise is made.

promisor • A person who makes a promise.

promissory estoppel • A doctrine that applies when a promisor makes a clear and definite promise on which the promisee justifiably relies. Such a promise is binding if justice will be better served by the enforcement of the promise.

promissory note • A written promise made by one person (the maker) to pay a fixed amount of money to another person (the payee or a subsequent holder) on demand or on a specified date.

property • Legally protected rights and interests in anything with an ascertainable value that is subject to ownership.

prospectus • A written document, required by securities laws, that describes the security being sold, the financial operations of the issuing corporation, and the investment or risk attaching to the security. It is designed to provide sufficient information to enable investors to evaluate the risk involved in purchasing the security.

protected class • A group of persons protected by specific laws because of the group's defining characteristics. Under laws prohibiting employment discrimination, these characteristics include race, color, religion, national origin, gender, age, and disability.

proximate cause • Legal cause; exists when the connection between an act and an injury is strong enough to justify imposing liability.

proxy • In corporate law, a written agreement between a stockholder and another party in which the stockholder authorizes the other party to vote the stockholder's shares in a certain manner.

puffery • A salesperson's often exaggerated claims concerning the quality of property offered for sale. Such claims involve opinions rather than facts and are not considered to be legally binding promises or warranties.

punitive damages • Monetary damages that may be awarded to a plaintiff to punish the defendant and deter similar conduct in the future.

purchase-money security interest (PMSI) • A security interest that arises when a seller or lender extends credit for part or all of the purchase price of goods purchased by a buyer.

Q

qualified indorsement • An indorsement on a negotiable instrument in which the indorser disclaims any contract liability on the instrument. The notation "without recourse" is commonly used to create a qualified indorsement.

quantum meruit • An expression (meaning "as much as he deserves") that describes the extent of liability on a quasi contract. An equitable doctrine based on the concept that one who benefits from another's labor and materials should not be unjustly enriched by them but should be required to pay a reasonable amount for the benefits received, even if there is no contract.

quasi contract • A fictional contract imposed on the parties by a court in the interests of fairness and justice; usually imposed to avoid the unjust enrichment of one party at the expense of another.

question of fact • In a lawsuit, an issue that involves only disputed facts, and not what the law is on a given point. Questions of fact are decided by the jury in a jury trial (by the judge if there is no jury).

question of law • In a lawsuit, an issue involving the application or interpretation of a law. Only a judge, not a jury, can rule on questions of law.

quitclaim deed • A deed intended to pass any title, interest, or claim that the grantor may have in the property without warranting that such title is valid. A quitclaim deed offers the least amount of protection against defects in the title.

quorum • The number of members of a decision-making body that must be present before business may be transacted.

quota • A set limit on the amount of goods that can be imported.

R

ratification • The act of accepting and giving legal force to an obligation that previously was not enforceable.

reaffirmation agreement • An agreement between a debtor and a creditor in which the debtor voluntarily agrees to pay, or reaffirm, a debt dischargeable in bankruptcy. To be enforceable, the agreement must be made before the debtor is granted a discharge.

real property • Land and everything attached to it, such as trees and buildings.

reamortize • A restart of the amortization schedule—a table of the periodic payments the borrower makes to pay off a debt—changing the way a loan's payments are configured.

reasonable person standard • The standard of behavior expected of a hypothetical "reasonable person"; the standard against which negligence is measured and that must be observed to avoid liability for negligence.

receiver • In a corporate dissolution, a court-appointed person who winds up corporate affairs and liquidates corporate assets.

record • According to the Uniform Electronic Transactions Act, information that is either inscribed on a tangible medium or stored in an electronic or other medium and is retrievable.

recording statutes • Statutes that allow deeds, mortgages, and other real property transactions to be recorded so as to provide notice to future purchasers or creditors of an existing claim on the property.

reformation • A court-ordered correction of a written contract so that it reflects the true intentions of the parties.

Regulation E • A set of rules issued by the Federal Reserve System's Board of Governors to protect users of electronic fund transfer systems.

release • A contract in which one party forfeits the right to pursue a legal claim against the other party.
remedy • The relief given to an innocent party to enforce a right or compensate for the violation of a right.
replevin • An action to recover identified goods in the hands of a party who is wrongfully withholding them from the other party. Under the UCC, this remedy is usually available only if the buyer or lessee is unable to cover.
reply • Procedurally, a plaintiff's response to a defendant's answer.
requirements contract • An agreement in which a buyer agrees to purchase and the seller agrees to sell all or up to a stated amount of what the buyer needs or requires.
rescission • A remedy whereby a contract is canceled and the parties are returned to the positions they occupied before the contract was made; may be effected through the mutual consent of the parties, by the parties' conduct, or by court decree.
res ipsa loquitur • A doctrine under which negligence may be inferred simply because an event occurred, if it is the type of event that would not occur in the absence of negligence. Literally, the term means "the facts speak for themselves."
respondeat superior • Latin for "let the master respond." A doctrine under which a principal or an employer is held liable for the wrongful acts committed by agents or employees while acting within the course and scope of their agency or employment.
restitution • An equitable remedy under which a person is restored to his or her original position prior to loss or injury, or placed in the position he or she would have been in had the breach not occurred.
restrictive indorsement • Any indorsement on a negotiable instrument that requires the indorsee to comply with certain instructions regarding the funds involved. A restrictive indorsement does not prohibit the further negotiation of the instrument.
resulting trust • An implied trust arising from the conduct of the parties. A trust in which a party holds the actual legal title to another's property but only for that person's benefit.
retained earnings • The portion of a corporation's profits that has not been paid out as dividends to shareholders.
reverse mortgage • A loan product typically provided to older homeowners that allows them to extract cash (either in a lump sum or in multiple payments) for the equity in their home. The mortgage does not need to be repaid until the home is sold or the owner leaves or dies.
revocation • In contract law, the withdrawal of an offer by an offeror. Unless the offer is irrevocable, it can be revoked at any time prior to acceptance without liability.
right of contribution • The right of a co-surety who pays more than her or his proportionate share on a debtor's default to recover the excess paid from other co-sureties.
right of reimbursement • The legal right of a person to be restored, repaid, or indemnified for costs, expenses, or losses incurred or expended on behalf of another.
right of subrogation • The right of a person to stand in the place of (be substituted for) another, giving the substituted party the same legal rights that the original party had.
right-to-work law • A state law providing that employees may not be required to join a union as a condition of retaining employment.
risk • A prediction concerning potential loss based on known and unknown factors.
risk management • Planning that is undertaken to protect one's interest should some event threaten to undermine its security. In the context of insurance, risk management involves transferring certain risks from the insured to the insurance company.
robbery • The act of forcefully and unlawfully taking personal property of any value from another. Force or intimidation is usually necessary for an act of theft to be considered a robbery.
rule of four • A rule of the United States Supreme Court under which the Court will not issue a writ of *certiorari* unless at least four justices approve of the decision to issue the writ.

S

sale • The passing of title to property from the seller to the buyer for a price.
sales contract • A contract for the sale of goods under which the ownership of goods is transferred from a seller to a buyer for a price.
sale on approval • A type of conditional sale in which the buyer may take the goods on a trial basis. The sale becomes absolute only when the buyer approves of (or is satisfied with) the goods being sold.
sale or return • A type of conditional sale in which title and possession pass from the seller to the buyer, but the buyer retains the option to return the goods during a specified period even though the goods conform to the contract.
scienter • Knowledge by the misrepresenting party that material facts have been falsely represented or omitted with an intent to deceive.
S corporation • A close business corporation that has met certain requirements set out in the Internal Revenue Code and thus qualifies for special income tax treatment. Essentially, an S corporation is taxed the same as a partnership, but its owners enjoy the privilege of limited liability.
search warrant • An order granted by a public authority, such as a judge, that authorizes law enforcement personnel to search particular premises or property.
seasonably • Within a specified time period or, if no period is specified, within a reasonable time.
secondary source of law • A publication that summarizes or interprets the law, such as a legal encyclopedia, a legal treatise, or an article in a law review.
SEC Rule 10b-5 • A rule of the Securities and Exchange Commission that makes it unlawful, in connection with the purchase or sale of any security, to make any untrue statement of a material fact or to omit a material fact if such omission causes the statement to be misleading.
secured party • A lender, seller, or any other person in whose favor there is a security interest, including a person to whom accounts or chattel paper have been sold.
secured transaction • Any transaction in which the payment of a debt is guaranteed, or secured, by personal property owned by the debtor or in which the debtor has a legal interest.
securities • Generally, stocks, bonds, notes, debentures, warrants, or other items that evidence an ownership interest in a corporation or a promise of repayment by a corporation.
security agreement • An agreement that creates or provides for a security interest between the debtor and a secured party.
security interest • Any interest in personal property or fixtures that secures payment or performance of an obligation.
self-defense • The legally recognized privilege to protect oneself or one's property against injury by another. The privilege of self-defense usually applies only to acts that are reasonably necessary to protect oneself, one's property, or another person.
self-incrimination • The giving of testimony that may subject the testifier to criminal prosecution. The Fifth Amendment to the U.S. Constitution protects against self-incrimination by providing that no person "shall be compelled in any criminal case to be a witness against himself."
seniority system • In regard to employment relationships, a system in which those who have worked longest for the employer are first in line for promotions, salary increases, and other benefits. They are also the last to be laid off if the workforce must be reduced.
service mark • A mark used in the sale or advertising of services to distinguish the services of one person from those of others. Titles, character names, and other distinctive features of radio and television programs may be registered as service marks.

sexual harassment • In the employment context, the demanding of sexual favors in return for job promotions or other benefits, or language or conduct that is so sexually offensive that it creates a hostile working environment.

share exchange • In a share exchange, some or all of the shares of one corporation are exchanged for some or all of the shares of another corporation, but both corporations continue to exist.

shareholder's derivative suit • A suit brought by a shareholder to enforce a corporate cause of action against a third person.

shelter principle • The principle that the holder of a negotiable instrument who cannot qualify as a holder in due course (HDC), but who derives his or her title through an HDC, acquires the rights of an HDC.

shipment contract • A contract for the sale of goods in which the seller is required or authorized to ship the goods by carrier. The seller assumes liability for any losses or damage to the goods until they are delivered to the carrier.

short-form (parent-subsidiary) merger • A merger of companies in which one company (the parent corporation) owns at least 90 percent of the outstanding shares of each class of stock of the other corporation (the subsidiary corporation). The merger can be accomplished without the approval of the shareholders of either corporation.

short sale • A sale of real property for an amount that is less than the balance owed on the mortgage loan, usually due to financial hardship. Both the lender and the borrower must consent to a short sale. Following a short sale, the borrower still owes the balance of the mortgage debt (after the sale proceeds are applied) to the lender—unless the lender agrees to forgive the remaining debt.

short-swing profits • Profits earned by a purchase and sale, or sale and purchase, of the same security within a six-month period; under Section 16(b) of the 1934 Securities Exchange Act, must be returned to the corporation if earned by company insiders from transactions in the company's stock.

shrink-wrap agreement • An agreement whose terms are expressed in a document located inside a box in which goods (usually software) are packaged; sometimes called a *shrink-wrap license*.

slander • Defamation in oral form.

slander of quality (trade libel) • The publication of false information about another's product, alleging that it is not what its seller claims.

slander of title • The publication of a statement that denies or casts doubt on another's legal ownership of any property, causing financial loss to that property's owner.

small claims court • A special court in which parties may litigate small claims (such as $5,000 or less). Attorneys are not required in small claims courts and, in some states, are not allowed to represent the parties.

smart card • A card containing a microprocessor that permits storage of funds via security programming, can communicate with other computers, and does not require online authorization for fund transfers.

sole proprietorship • The simplest form of business organization, in which the owner is the business. The owner reports business income on his or her personal income tax return and is legally responsible for all debts and obligations incurred by the business.

sovereign immunity • A doctrine that immunizes foreign nations from the jurisdiction of U.S. courts when certain conditions are satisfied.

spam • Bulk e-mails, particularly of commercial advertising, sent in large quantities without the consent of the recipient.

special indorsement • An indorsement on an instrument that indicates the specific person to whom the indorser intends to make the instrument payable; that is, it names the indorsee.

special warranty deed • A deed in which the grantor warrants only that the grantor or seller held good title during his or her ownership of the property and does not warrant that there were no defects of title when the property was held by previous owners.

specific performance • An equitable remedy requiring exactly the performance that was specified in a contract; usually granted only when monetary damages would be an inadequate remedy and the subject matter of the contract is unique (for example, real property).

spendthrift trust • A trust created to protect the beneficiary from spending all the funds to which she or he is entitled. Only a certain portion of the total amount is given to the beneficiary at any one time, and most states prohibit creditors from attaching assets of the trust.

stale check • A check, other than a certified check, that is presented for payment more than six months after its date.

standing to sue • The requirement that an individual must have a sufficient stake in a controversy before he or she can bring a lawsuit. The plaintiff must demonstrate that he or she has been either injured or threatened with injury.

stare decisis • A common law doctrine under which judges are obligated to follow the precedents established in prior decisions.

Statute of Frauds • A state statute under which certain types of contracts must be in writing to be enforceable.

statute of limitations • A federal or state statute setting the maximum time period during which a certain action can be brought or certain rights enforced.

statutory law • The body of law enacted by legislative bodies (as opposed to constitutional law, administrative law, or case law).

statutory right of redemption • A right provided by statute in some states under which mortgagors can redeem or purchase their property back after a judicial foreclosure for a limited period of time, such as one year.

stock • An equity (ownership) interest in a corporation, measured in units of shares.

stock buyback • The purchase of shares of a company's own stock by that company on the open market.

stock certificate • A certificate issued by a corporation evidencing the ownership of a specified number of shares in the corporation.

stock option • An agreement that grants the owner the option to buy a given number of shares of stock, usually within a set time period.

stock warrant • A certificate that grants the owner the option to buy a given number of shares of stock, usually within a set time period.

stop-payment order • An order by a bank customer to his or her bank not to pay or certify a certain check.

stored-value card • A card bearing a magnetic strip that holds magnetically encoded data, providing access to stored funds.

strict liability • Liability regardless of fault. In tort law, strict liability is imposed on those engaged in abnormally dangerous activities, on persons who keep dangerous animals, and on manufacturers or sellers that introduce into commerce goods that are unreasonably dangerous when in a defective condition.

strike • An action undertaken by unionized workers when collective bargaining fails; the workers leave their jobs, refuse to work, and (typically) picket the employer's workplace.

sublease • A lease executed by the lessee of real estate to a third person, conveying the same interest that the lessee enjoys but for a shorter term than that held by the lessee.

subprime mortgage • A high-risk loan made to a borrower who does not qualify for a standard mortgage because of his or her poor credit rating or high debt-to-income ratio. Lenders typically charge a higher interest rate on subprime mortgages.

substantive law • Law that defines, describes, regulates, and creates legal rights and obligations.

substitute check • A paper reproduction of the front and back of an original check that contains all of the same information required on checks for automated processing.

summary jury trial • A method of settling disputes, used in many federal courts, in which a trial is held, but the jury's verdict is not binding. The verdict acts only as a guide to both sides in reaching an agreement during the mandatory negotiations that immediately follow the summary jury trial.

summons • A document informing a defendant that a legal action has been commenced against her or him and that the defendant must appear in court on a certain date to answer the plaintiff's complaint.

supremacy clause • The requirement in Article VI of the U.S. Constitution that provides that the Constitution, laws, and treaties of the United States are "the supreme Law of the Land." Under this clause, state and local laws that directly conflict with federal law will be rendered invalid.

surety • A person, such as a cosigner on a note, who agrees to be primarily responsible for the debt of another.

suretyship • An express contract in which a third party to a debtor-creditor relationship (the surety) promises to be primarily responsible for the debtor's obligation.

symbolic speech • Nonverbal expressions of beliefs. Symbolic speech, which includes gestures, movements, and articles of clothing, is given substantial protection by the courts.

T

takeover • The acquisition of control over a corporation through the purchase of a substantial number of the voting shares of the corporation.

taking • The taking of private property by the government for public use. The government may not take private property for public use without "just compensation."

tangible employment action • A significant change in employment status, such as a change brought about by firing or failing to promote an employee; reassigning the employee to a position with significantly different responsibilities; or effecting a significant change in employment benefits.

tangible property • Property that has physical existence and can be distinguished by the senses of touch and sight. A car is tangible property; a patent right is intangible property.

target corporation • The corporation to be acquired in a corporate takeover; a corporation whose shareholders receive a tender offer.

tariff • A tax on imported goods.

tenancy at sufferance • A type of tenancy under which a tenant who, after rightfully being in possession of leased premises, continues (wrongfully) to occupy the property after the lease has terminated. The tenant has no rights to possess the property and occupies it only because the person entitled to evict the tenant has not done so.

tenancy at will • A type of tenancy that either party can terminate without notice; usually arises when a tenant who has been under a tenancy for years retains possession, with the landlord's consent, after the tenancy for years has terminated.

tenancy in common • Co-ownership of property in which each party owns an undivided interest that passes to her or his heirs at death.

tender • An unconditional offer to perform an obligation by a person who is ready, willing, and able to do so.

tender of delivery • Under the Uniform Commercial Code, a seller's or lessor's act of placing conforming goods at the disposal of the buyer or lessee and giving the buyer or lessee whatever notification is reasonably necessary to enable the buyer or lessee to take delivery.

tender offer • An offer made by one company directly to the shareholders of another (target) company to purchase their shares of stock; sometimes referred to as a *takeover bid.*

testamentary trust • A trust that is created by will and therefore does not take effect until the death of the testator.

testate • Having left a will at death.

testator • One who makes and executes a will.

third party beneficiary • One for whose benefit a promise is made in a contract but who is not a party to the contract.

tippee • A person who receives inside information.

tort • A civil wrong not arising from a breach of contract; a breach of a legal duty that proximately causes harm or injury to another.

tortfeasor • One who commits a tort.

Totten trust • A trust created when a person deposits funds in his or her own name as a trustee for another. It is a tentative trust, revocable at will until the depositor dies or completes the gift in his or her lifetime by some unequivocal act or declaration.

trade dress • The image and overall appearance of a product—for example, the distinctive decor, menu, layout, and style of service of a particular restaurant. Basically, trade dress is subject to the same protection as trademarks.

trademark • A distinctive mark, motto, device, or emblem that a manufacturer stamps, prints, or otherwise affixes to the goods it produces so that they may be identified on the market and their origins made known. Once a trademark is established (under the common law or through registration), the owner is entitled to its exclusive use.

trade name • A term that is used to indicate part or all of a business's name and that is directly related to the business's reputation and goodwill. Trade names are protected under the common law (and under trademark law, if the name is the same as the firm's trademarked product).

trade secret • Information or process that gives a business an advantage over competitors that do not know the information or process.

transfer warranties • Implied warranties, made by any person who transfers an instrument for consideration to subsequent transferees and holders who take the instrument in good faith.

traveler's check • A check that is payable on demand, drawn on or payable through a financial institution (bank), and designated as a traveler's check.

Treasury securities • Government debt issued by the U.S. Department of the Treasury. The interest rate on Treasury securities is often used as a baseline for measuring the rate on loan products with higher interest rates.

treaty • In international law, a formal written agreement negotiated between two nations or among several nations. In the United States, all treaties must be approved by the Senate.

treble damages • Damages that, by statute, are three times the amount that the fact finder determines is owed.

trespass to land • The entry onto, above, or below the surface of land owned by another without the owner's permission or legal authorization.

trespass to personal property • The unlawful taking or harming of another's personal property; interference with another's right to the exclusive possession of his or her personal property.

trust • An arrangement in which title to property is held by one person (a trustee) for the benefit of another (a beneficiary).

trust indorsement • An indorsement for the benefit of the indorser or a third person; also known as an *agency indorsement.* The indorsement results in legal title vesting in the original indorsee.

U

ultra vires • A Latin term meaning "beyond the powers"; in corporate law, acts of a corporation that are beyond its express and implied powers to undertake.

unconscionable (contract or clause) • A contract or clause that is void on the basis of public policy because one party, as a result of disproportionate bargaining power, is forced to accept terms that are unfairly burdensome and that unfairly benefit the dominating party.

underwriter • In insurance law, the insurer, or the one assuming a risk in return for the payment of a premium.

undisclosed principal • A principal whose identity is unknown by a third person, and the third person has no knowledge that the agent is acting for a principal at the time the agent and the third person form a contract.

unenforceable contract • A valid contract rendered unenforceable by some statute or law.

uniform law • A model law created by the National Conference of Commissioners on Uniform State Laws and/or the American Law Institute for the states to consider adopting. Each state has the option of adopting or rejecting all or part of a uniform law. If a state adopts the law, it becomes statutory law in that state.

unilateral contract • A contract that results when an offer can be accepted only by the offeree's performance.

unilateral mistake • A mistake that occurs when one party to a contract is mistaken as to a material fact; the contract normally is enforceable.

union shop • A firm that requires all workers, once employed, to become union members within a specified period of time as a condition of their continued employment.

universal defense • A defense that is valid against all holders of a negotiable instrument, including holders in due course (HDCs) and holders with the rights of HDCs.

unreasonably dangerous product • In product liability law, a product that is defective to the point of threatening a consumer's health and safety. A product will be considered unreasonably dangerous if it is dangerous beyond the expectation of the ordinary consumer or if a less dangerous alternative was economically feasible for the manufacturer, but the manufacturer failed to produce it.

usage of trade • Any practice or method of dealing having such regularity of observance in a place, vocation, or trade as to justify an expectation that it will be observed with respect to the transaction in question.

U.S. trustee • A government official who performs certain administrative tasks that a bankruptcy judge would otherwise have to perform.

usury • Charging an illegal rate of interest.

utilitarianism • An approach to ethical reasoning that evaluates behavior in light of the consequences of that behavior for those who will be affected by it, rather than on the basis of any absolute ethical or moral values. In utilitarian reasoning, a "good" decision is one that results in the greatest good for the greatest number of people affected by the decision.

V

valid contract • A contract that results when the elements necessary for contract formation (agreement, consideration, legal purpose, and contractual capacity) are present.

venture capital • Capital (funds and other assets) provided by professional, outside investors (venture capitalists, usually groups of wealthy investors and securities firms) to start new business ventures.

venue • The geographic district in which a legal action is tried and from which the jury is selected.

vesting • The creation of an absolute or unconditional right or power.

vicarious liability • Legal responsibility placed on one person for the acts of another; indirect liability imposed on a supervisory party (such as an employer) for the actions of a subordinate (such as an employee) because of the relationship between the two parties.

virus • A computer program that can replicate itself over a network, such as the Internet, and interfere with the normal use of a computer. A virus cannot exist as a separate entity and must attach itself to another program to move through a network.

vishing • A variation of phishing that involves some form of voice communication. The consumer receives either an e-mail or a phone call from someone claiming to be from a legitimate business and asking for personal information; instead of being asked to respond by e-mail as in phishing, the consumer is asked to call a phone number.

void contract • A contract having no legal force or binding effect.

voidable contract • A contract that may be legally avoided (canceled, or annulled) at the option of one or both of the parties.

voir dire • An Old French phrase meaning "to speak the truth." In legal language, the process in which the attorneys question prospective jurors to learn about their backgrounds, attitudes, biases, and other characteristics that may affect their ability to serve as impartial jurors.

voluntary consent • The knowing and voluntary agreement to the terms of a contract; sometimes called *mutual assent*. If a contract is formed as a result of a mistake, misrepresentation, undue influence, or duress, voluntary consent is lacking, and the contract will be voidable.

W

warranty deed • A deed in which the grantor assures (warrants to) the grantee that the grantor has title to the property conveyed in the deed, that there are no encumbrances on the property other than what the grantor has represented, and that the grantee will enjoy quiet possession of the property; a deed that provides the greatest amount of protection for the grantee.

watered stock • Shares of stock issued by a corporation for which the corporation receives, as payment, less than the stated value of the shares.

whistleblowing • An employee's disclosure to government authorities, upper-level managers, or the media that the employer is engaged in unsafe or illegal activities.

white-collar crime • Nonviolent crime committed by individuals or corporations to obtain a personal or business advantage.

will • An instrument directing what is to be done with the testator's property on his or her death, made by the testator and revocable during his or her lifetime. No interests in the testator's property pass until the testator dies.

will substitutes • Various documents that attempt to dispose of an estate in the same or similar manner as a will, such as trusts or life insurance plans.

winding up • The second of two stages in the termination of a partnership or corporation. Once the firm is dissolved, it continues to exist legally until the process of winding up all business affairs (collecting and distributing the firm's assets) is complete.

workers' compensation laws • State statutes establishing an administrative procedure for compensating workers for injuries that arise out of—or in the course of—their employment, regardless of fault.

working papers • The various documents used and developed by an accountant during an audit. Working papers include notes, computations, memoranda, copies, and other papers that make up the work product of an accountant's services to a client.

workout • In bankruptcy proceedings, an out-of-court agreement between a debtor and creditors in which the parties work out a payment plan or schedule under which the debtor's debts can be discharged.

workout agreement • In the mortgage-lending business, a formal contract between a debtor and his or her creditors in which the parties agree to negotiate a payment plan for the amount due on the loan instead of proceeding to foreclosure.

worm • A computer program that can automatically replicate itself over a network such as the Internet and interfere with the normal use of a computer. A worm does not need to be attached to an existing file to move from one network to another.

writ of attachment • A court's order, issued prior to a trial to collect a debt, directing the sheriff or other public officer to seize nonexempt property of the debtor. If the creditor prevails at trial, the seized property can be sold to satisfy the judgment.

writ of *certiorari* • A writ from a higher court asking a lower court for the record of a case.

writ of execution • A court's order, issued after a judgment has been entered against a debtor, directing the sheriff to seize and sell any of the debtor's nonexempt real or personal property.

wrongful discharge • An employer's termination of an employee's employment in violation of the law.

Table of Cases

A

A&M Records, Inc. v. Napster, Inc., 99, 100
Adams v. Gateway, Inc., 39
Alberty-Vélez v. Corporación de Puerto Rico para la Difusión Publica, 398Alden v. Maine, 429
Alexander v. Lafayette Crime Stoppers, Inc., 147–148
Alexander, State v., 231
Allan v. Nersesova, 199
Amazon.com, LLC v. New York State Department of Taxation and Finance, 463
American Civil Liberties Union v. Ashcroft, 12
American Library Association, United States v., 12
American Standard, Inc. v. OakFabco, Inc., 476
Angelo Todesca Corp., Commonwealth v., 464
Angelos, United States v., 118
APL Limited v. State of Washington Department of Revenue, 542–543
Apple, Inc. v. Samsung Electronics Co., 94–95
Arizona, United States v., 433
Armenian Assembly of America v. Cafesjian, 470
Armory v. Delamirie, 530
Ashcroft v. American Civil Liberties Union, 12
Ashcroft v. Free Speech Coalition, 14
AT&T Mobility, LLC v. Concepcion, 44
Atlanta, City of, v. Hotels.com, 228
Auto-Owners Insurance Co. v. Bank One, 320
Autry v. Republic Productions, 205
A.V. ex rel Vanderhye v. iParadigms, LLC, 124
Azur v. Chase Bank USA, 404

B

B-Sharp Musical Productions, Inc. v. Haber, 215
Bad Frog Brewery, Inc. v. New York State Liquor Authority, 11–12
Bates v. United Parcel Service, Inc., 431
Baze v. Rees, 117
Beneficial Homeowner Service Corp. v. Steele, 186–187
Bernhard-Thomas Building Systems, LLC v. Dunican, 75
Bessemer & Lake Eric Railroad Co. v. Seaway Marine Transport, 69
Beydoun, United States v., 92
Bezirdjian v. O'Reilly, 494–495
BHP Land Services, Inc. v. Seymour, 355
Biglane v. Under the Hill Corp., 543
Billings v. Town of Grafton, 427
Bilski, *In re,* 95
Blackman v. Iverson, 164
Board of Trustees of the University of Alabama v. Garrett, 429
Boles v. Sun Ergoline, Inc., 279
Booker, United States v., 118
Bortell v. Eli Lilly & Co. 270
Boschetto v. Hansing, 32
Braddock v. Braddock, 223–224
Bridgeport Music, Inc. v. Dimension Films, 98
Brodie v. Jordan, 496
Brown v. Board of Education of Topeka, 6
Brown v. Entertainment Merchants Association, 290
Brown v. Plata, 106
Brown v. W. P. Media, Inc., 469
Bruesewitz v. Wyeth, LLC, 275
BUC International Corp. v. International Yacht Council, Ltd., 96
Buis, *In re,* 370
Bullock v. Philip Morris USA, Inc., 277
Burlington Industries, Inc. v. Ellerth, 427
Bush v. Department of Justice, 33

C

Camtech Precision Manufacturing, *In re,* 340–341
Cape-France Enterprises v. Estate of Peed, 206
Cardinal Health, Inc. Securities Litigation, *In re,* 586
Casserlie v. Shell Oil Co., 286–287
Central Virginia Community College v. Katz, 393–394
Chavers v. Epsco, Inc., 447
CITGO Asphalt Refining Co. v. Paper, Allied-Industrial, Chemical, and Energy Workers International Union Local No. 2-991, 423
Citizens National Bank of Jessamine County v. Washington Mutual Bank, 344
Citizens United v. Federal Election Commission, 11
City of ______________. *See* name of city
Coca-Cola Co. v. Babyback's International, Inc., 186
Coca-Cola Co. v. Koke Co. of America, 89
Collier v. Turner Industries Group, LLC, 426
Colt v. Mt. Princeton Trout Club, Inc., 477
Columbia Pictures v. Brunnell, 39

Commonwealth v. ________________. *See* name of opposing party
Consolidated Edison Co. v. Public Service Commission, 11
Corona Fruits and Veggies, Inc. v. Frozsun Foods, Inc., 340
Cotton v. U.S. Department of Education, 292
Cousins v. Realty Ventures, Inc., 402
Craton Capital, LP v. Natural Pork Production II, LLP, 452–453
Crawford v. Metropolitan Government of Nashville and Davidson County, Tennessee, 427
Credit Alliance Corp. v. Arthur Andersen & Co., 583
Crespo, Commonwealth v., 92
Crummey v. Morgan, 32
Cumis Mutual Insurance Society, Inc. v. Rosol, 325

D

Dalton v. 933 Peachtree, LP, 398
De La Concha v. Fordham University, 215
Diamond v. Diehr, 95
Dodson v. Shrader, 167
Dole Food Co. v. Patrickson, 608–609
Downey v. Bob's Discount Furniture Holdings, Inc., 40

E

eBay, Inc. v. MercExchange, LLC, 96
Edmondson v. Macclesfield L-P Gas Co., 279
Equal Employment Opportunity Commission v. Cheesecake Factory, Inc., 427
EPCO Carbondioxide Products, Inc. v. St. Paul Travelers Insurance Co., 156
ESPN, Inc. v. Quiksilver, Inc., 91
Espresso Roma Corp. v. Bank of America, N.A., 321
Estate of ________________. See name of party

F

Family Winemakers of California v. Jenkins, 9–10
Faragher v. City of Boca Raton, 427
Fehr v. Algard, 26–27
Findlay, City of v. Hotels.com, 228
First National Bank of Boston v. Bellotti, 11
Fitl v. Strek, 263
Freeman v. Brown Hiller, Inc., 170
Frosty Treats, Inc. v. Sony Computer Entertainment America, Inc., 91

G

Gaming Venture, Inc. v. Tastee Restaurant Corp., 177
Garrigus v. Viarengo, 568–569
Garware Polyester, Ltd. v. Intermax Trading Corp., 600
Gavengno v. TLT Construction Corp., 183
Gebhart v. Securities and Exchange Commission, 512–513
Gibbons v. Ogden, 8
Gillespie v. Sears, Roebuck & Co., 277
Gilmer v. Interstate/Johnson Lane Corp., 44
Glacial Plains Cooperative v. Lindgren, 234
Gleeson v. Preferred Sourcing, LLC, 106100
Goldberg v. UBS AG, 594
Gomez-Perez v. Potter, 429
Gonzales v. Raich, 9
Goodlettsville, City of v. Priceline.com, Inc., 228
Goodman v. Atwood, 528
Gould & Lamb, LLC v. D'Alusio, 170
Greenman v. Yuba Power Products, Inc., 275
Gross v. FBL Financial Services, 429
Grote, *In re* Estate of, 527
Gubbons v. Herson, 82
Gucci America, Inc. v. Wang Huoqing, 32
Guth v. Loft, Inc., 488

H

Hadley v. Baxendale, 213–214
Hall v. Geiger-Jones Co., 513
Hamlin v. Hampton Lumber Mills, Inc., 69–70
Hammett v. Deutsche Bank National Co., 299–300
Harris v. Forklift Systems, 427
Harvey v. Dow, 165–166
Hasbro, Inc. v. Internet Entertainment Group, Ltd., 93
Hausman, *In re,* 469
Hawkins v. McGee, 146
Henrichs v. Chugach Alaska Corp., 487
Herring v. United States, 117
Hicklin v. Onyx Acceptance Corp., 348
Hochster v. De La Tour, 203
Houseman v. Dare, 260
Hustler Magazine, Inc. v. Falwell, 72
Hyatt Corp. v. Palm Beach National Bank, 301

I

In re, ________________. *See* name of party
Indiana Surgical Specialists v. Griffin, 357
Industrial Risk Insurers v. American Engineering Testing, Inc., 280
Inglimo, 581
Inn Foods, Inc., United States v., 598–599
Intel Corp. Microprocessor Antitrust Litigation, *In re,* 39

International Shoe Co. v. Washington, 29
Izquierdo v. Gyroscope, Inc., 79

J

Jamieson v. Woodward & Lothrop, 280
Jamison Well Drilling, Inc. v. Pfeifer, 212–213
Jannusch v. Naffziger, 229
Jaynes v. Commonwealth of Virginia, 120
Jesmer v. Retail Magic, Inc., 153
Ji-Haw Industrial Co. v. Broquet, 29
Jiann Min Chang v. Alabama Agricultural and Mechanical University, 425
Joel v. Morison, 407
John B. v. Goetz, 39
Johnson, *In re* Estate of, 562–563
Johnson, State v., 115
Jones v. Star Credit Corp., 236
Juaregui v. Bobb's Piano Sales & Service, Inc., 262

K

Kelleher v. Eaglerider, Inc., 155
Kelley v. Buckley, 581–582
Kelo v. City of New London, Connecticut, 548
Khulumani v. Barclay National Bank, Ltd., 603–604
Kim v. Park, 203
Kitts, *In re,* 383
Koch Materials Co. v. Shore Slurry Seal, Inc., 256
Kovarik v. Kovarik, 575–576
Krasner v. HSH Nordbank AG, 53–54
Kuhn v. Tumminelli, 455

L

Laasko v. Xerox Corp., 600
L&H Construction Co. v. Circle Redmont, Inc., 180
LaPlace v. Briere, 534
Laurel Creek Health Care Center v. Bishop, 400–401
Las Vegas Sands, LLC v. Nehme, 296–297
Leadsinger, Inc. v. BMG Music Publishing, 97
Ledbetter v. Goodyear Tire Co., 426
Les Enterprises Jacques Defour & Fils, Inc. v. Dinsick Equipment Corp., 261–262
Lhotka v. Geographic Expeditions, Inc., 172
Litwin v. Blackstone Group, LP, 507
Lopez, United States v., 8
Lopez v. El Palmar Taxi, Inc., 399
Lucy v. Zehmer, 145
Lumley v. Gye, 76
Lutfi v. Spears, 74
Lyons, United States v., 112

M

Malone v. Flattery, 195
Maple Farms, Inc. v. City School District of Elmira, 255
Mathews v. B and K Foods, Inc.,52–53
Maverick Recording Co. v. Harper, 89–90
McBride v. Taxman Corp., 405
Media General Operations, Inc. v. National Labor Relations Board, 441–442
Medimmune, Inc. v. Genentech, Inc., 129–130
Meinhard v. Salmon, 448–449
Merrill Lynch, Pierce, Fenner & Smith, Inc. v. Dabit, 510
Methyl Tertiary Butyl Ether (MTBE) Products Liability Litigation, *In re,* 277
Metro-Goldwyn-Mayer Studios, Inc. v. Grokster, Ltd., 100
Microsoft Corp. v. AT&T Corp., 94
MidAmerica Bank, FSB v. Charter One Bank, 316–317
Midland, Town of v. Morris, 548–549
Miller v. California, 12
Mims v. Starbucks Corp., 417
Mineral Park Land Co. v. Howard, 205
Miranda v. Arizona, 118
Mitchell v. Valteau, 387
MM Companies v. Liquid Audio, Inc., 484
M'Naghten's Case, 114
Moren v. Jax Restaurant, 449
Morningstar v. Hallett, 272
Moroni v. Medco Health Solutions, Inc., 416
Morrison, United States v., 8
Moseley v. V. Secret Catalogue, Inc., 90
Motorsport Marketing, Inc. v. Wiedmaier, Inc., 401

N

Naldi v. Grunberg, 416
National Aeronautics and Space Administration v. Nelson, 423
Nelson v. United States, 120
Nevada Department of Human Resources v. Hibbs, 430
Nomo Agroindustrial Sa De CV v. Enza Zaden North America, Inc., 270
Notz v. Everett Smith Group, Ltd., 523–524

O

O'Bryan v. Holy See, 596
Office Supply Store.com v. Kansas City School Board, 233
Oliver, United States v., 121

Oncale v. Sundowner Offshore Services, Inc., 428
One Hundred Sixty-Five Thousand Five Hundred Eighty Dollars, United States v., 531
Ontario, California, City of v. Quon, 422
Ora, Commonwealth v., 11
Oregon Steel Mills, Inc. v. Coopers & Lybrand, LLP, 580
Orlando v. Cole, 20, **72–73**
ORX Resources, Inc. v. MBW Exploration, LLC, 453
Ostolaza-Diaz v. Countrywide Bank, N.A., 382
Overseas Private Investment Corp. v. Kim, 358

P

Pack 2000, Inc. v. Cushman, 201
Paduano v. American Honda Motor Co., 64–65
Payne v. Hurwitz, 205
Pelman v. McDonald's Corp., 280
Pennsylvania State Police v. Suders, 427
People v. ______________. *See* name of opposing party
Perez v. Stern, 584
Pichardo v. C. S. Brown Co., 279
Piper, *In re* Estate of, 529
Plessy v. Ferguson, 6
Polk v. Polk, 455
Portnoy v. Cryo-Cell International, Inc., 492
Powerhouse Custom Homes, Inc. v. 84 Lumber Co., 151
Prestridge v. Bank of Jena, 333–334
Printz v. United States, 8
Purdue Frederick Co., United States v., 51

Q

Qualcomm, Inc. v. Broadcom Corp., 39
Quill Corp. v. North Dakota, 463

R

Raffles v. Wichelhaus, 180
Ransom v. FIA Card Services, N.A., 371
Rebel Rents, Inc., *In re,* 345
Reger Development, LLC v. National City Bank, 295
Reno v. American Civil Liberties Union, 12
Roman Catholic Church of Our Lady of Sorrows v. Prince Realty Management, 545
Romero v. Scoggin-Dickey Chevrolet-Buick, Inc., 257
Roscoe, People v., 109
RSN Properties, Inc. v. Engineering Consulting Services, Ltd., 218
Rubin v. Murray, 465–466

S

Sandoval, State v., 115
Scarborough v. Rollins, 547–548
Scheerer v. Fisher, 137–138
Schmude v. Tricam Industries, Inc., 276
Schultz v. General Electric Healthcare Financial Services, 471
Schwarzrock v. Remote Technologies, 135
SEC v. Alpha Telcom, Inc., 503
SEC v. Rocklage, 511
SEC v. Texas Gulf Sulphur Co., 509–510
SEC v. W. J. Howey Co., 503
Securities and Exchange Commission. *See* SEC
Security State Bank v. Visiting Nurses Association of Telfair County, Inc., 321
Selleck v. Cuenca, 181
Shar's Cars, LLC v. Elder, 449
Shaw Family Archives, Ltd. v. CMG Worldwide, Inc., 75
SHI Imaging v. Artisan House, Inc., 399
Shlahtichman v. 1-800 Contacts, Inc., 155
Shoop v. Daimler-Chrysler Corp., 271
Simkin v. Blank, 180
Singh, United States v., 109
Sisuphan, People v., 111
Six Flags, Inc. v. Steadfast Insurance Co., 147
Skilling v. United States, 51–52
Slack v. Truitt, 563
Smith v. Cutter Biological, Inc., 277
Smith v. Eli Lilly & Co., 278
Smith v. Ingersoll-Rand Co., 280
Smith v. Johnson and Johnson, 417–418
Southern Prestige Industries, Inc. v. Independence Plating Corp., 30
Spectrum Stores, Inc. v. Citgo Petroleum Corp., 595
Sprint Communications Co. v. APCC Services, Inc., 33
Stagno v. Hoover Owners Corp., 398
Stainbrook v. Low, 217
Stander v. Dispoz-O-Products, Inc., 398
Stanley, *In re,* 359
Starbucks Corp. v. Lundberg, 90
State Farm Mutual Automobile Insurance Co. v. Campbell, 69
State Street Bank & Trust Co. v. Signature Financial Group, Inc., 95
State v. ______________. *See* name of opposing party
Stevens v. Publicis, 416
Stewart, United States v., 513
Stone v. Jetmar Properties, LLC, 469

Stultz v. Safety and Compliance Management, Inc., 170
Sturdza v. United Arab Emirates, 169
Sutowski v. Eli Lilly & Co., 277

T

Tennessee v. Lane, 429
Tepperwien v. Energy Nuclear Operations, Inc., 429
Terwilliger, State v., 115
Thompson v. North American Stainless, LP, 428
Thyroff v. Nationwide Mutual Insurance Co., 77
Toro Co. v. Krouse, Kern & Co., 583
Totten, *In re,* 568
Town of ________________. *See* name of town
Toyota Motor Manufacturing, Kentucky, Inc. v. Williams, 430
TransTexas Gas Corp., In the Matter of, 364
Treiber & Straub, Inc. v. United Parcel Service, Inc., 535
Trell for American Association for the Advancement of Science, 146
Triffin v. Liccardi Ford, Inc., 303
Triple E, Inc. v. Hendrix & Dail, Inc., 270
Trunk v. City of San Diego, 14
Trustees of Dartmouth College v. Woodward, 464
02 Development, LLC v. 607 South Park, LLC, 453
2007 Custom Motorcycle, United States v., 237–238

U

Ultramares Corp. v. Touche, 583
UMG Recordings, Inc. v. Augusto, 97–98
United States v. ________________. *See* name of opposing party
United Student Aid Funds, Inc. v. Espinosa, 372
U.S. Bank, N.A. v. Tennessee Farmers Mutual Insurance Co., 139–140
U.S. Bank National Association v. Ibanez, 386

V

Valero v. Florida Insurance Guaranty Association, Inc., 559
Van Horn v. Watson, 82
Van Orden v. Perry, 14
Van Zanen v. Qwest Wireless, LLC, 138
Vanegas v. American Energy Services, 164
Verigy US, Inc. v. Mayder, 100
Video Software Dealers Association v. Schwarzenegger, 278

W

Wal-Mart Stores, Inc. v. Dukes, 424
Walsh v. State, 582
Watkins v. Schexnider, 188
Webster v. Blue Ship Tea Room, Inc., 271
Weidner v. Carroll, 97
Wendeln v. The Beatrice Manor, Inc., 415
White v. Experian Information Solutions, Inc., 368
White v. Samsung Electronics America, Inc., 75
Whitehead v. Humphrey, 546
Wickard v. Filburn, 8
Williams, United States v., 13
Williams v. Pike, 420
Wingnut Films v. Katjia Motion Pictures, 41
Winschel v. Brown, 280
Wisconsin Electric Power Co. v. Union Pacific Railroad Co., 202
Wolf v. Don Dingmann Construction, Inc., 81
WorldCom, Inc. Securities Litigation, *In re,* 586
Wright v. Moore, 82

Z

Z4 Technologies, Inc. v. Microsoft Corp., 96
Zurich American Insurance Co. v. ABM Industries, Inc, 557

Index

A

Abatement, 561
Abuse of process, 75–76
Acceptance,
  of bribe, 112
  contractual, 150–154, 232–234, 242, 257–258, 262
  of gift, 529
  of negotiable instrument, 291, 317
  trade, 291, 304
Acceptor, 295, 304
Accession, 530
Accommodation shipment, 232
Accord and satisfaction, 164, 204
Account party, 601
Accountant(s). *See also* Professional(s)
  duties of, 60, 579–580
  liability of, 578–589
    common law, to client, 578–583
    criminal, 568
    statutory, 586–588
    to third parties, 583–585
  public accounting firms and, 578, 585–586
  relationship of, with clients, 509
Accounting
  agent's duty of, 402
  debtor's request for, 345–346
  global rules for, 579–580
  partner's right to, 447–448
Act
  of commission, 108
  of God (*force majeure*), 535, 600
  guilty (*actus reus*), 108
  of maker, will revocation by, 564
  of omission, 108
Act of state doctrine, 595–596
Actual malice, 74
Actus reus (guilty act), 108
Adjustable-rate mortgage (ARM), 379
Administrative agencies, 4–5, 140
Administrative law, 4–5, 19, 23
Administrator, 560
Admissions, 37–38, 183n, 185, 234
ADR. *See* Alternative dispute resolution
Advertisements, 11, 76, 146
Affidavit, 37, 356, 564
Age
  discrimination based on, 423, 424, 429–430, 603
  legal, for executing a will, 562
  of majority, 166
  misrepresentation of, 167
Age Discrimination in Employment Act (ADEA)(1967), 424, 429–430, 603
Agency relationships, 396–413
  bank-customer relationships and, 318
  defined, 396
  duties in, 401–403
  employment status and, 397–399
  exclusive, 403
  with foreign firm, 596
  formation of, 400–401, 404
  liability in, 405–408, 462
  termination of, 408–410
Agent(s)
  agency termination by, 409
  authority of, 211, 401, 403–405
  authorized acts of, 405–406
  bankruptcy of, agency termination and, 409
  contractual capacity and, 400
  corporate officers and executives as, 462–464
  crimes of, 408
  death or insanity of, agency termination by, 409
  defined, 396
  duties of, to principal, 401–402
  e- (electronic), 406
  escrow, 545
  insurance, 397, 557
  liability of, 405–408
  principal's duties to, 401, 402–403
  real estate, 545
  registered, 467, 468
  torts of, 407–408
  unauthorized acts of, 404, 406
Agreement(s). *See also* Contract(s)
  agency formation by, 400–401
  agency termination by, 409
  to agree, 146–147
  bailment, 531–536
  bilateral, 594
  click-on (click-wrap), 153
  contract discharge by, 203
  contractual, 133, 144–154. *See* also Contract(s)
  creditors' composition, 357
  distribution, 596
  family settlement, 564–565
  illegal, withdrawal from, 181–182
  international, 594
  lease. *See* Lease contract(s)
  multilateral, 594
  operating, for LLC, 454–456
  partnering, 154
  partnership, 445
  prenuptial, 184
  reaffirmation, 363, 367
  security, 337. *See also* Secured transaction(s); Security interest(s)
  shareholder, 465, 491, 493
  shrink-wrap, 153
Alien Registration Receipt ("green card"), 432–433
Alien Tort Claims Act (ATCA), 602–603
Alienation, 195–196
Alternative dispute resolution (ADR), 42–45
America Invents Act (2011), 94
Americans with Disabilities Act (ADA)(1990), 424, 430–431, 603
Answer, 36–37
Anticybersquatting Consumer Protection Act (ACPA), 92–93
Appeals, 34, 35, 36,41
Appellant, 25
Appellate courts. *See* Federal court system, appellate courts of; State court system, appellate courts of
Appellate review, 41
Appellee, 25
Appropriation, 75
Arbitration, 43–45, 600–601
Arraignment, 119

Arrest, 118, 119
Arson, 110
Articles
of consolidation, 474
of dissolution, 475, 477
of incorporation, 467–468, 468, 469, 485, 489
of merger, 474
of organization, 453, 497
of partnership, 446–447
Assault, 71
Assignment(s), 550
of contract rights, 193–196, 198
relationships in, illustrated, 197
defined, 193
of interest in partnership, 450
negotiable instruments transferred by, 297–298
notice of, 196
of security interest, 345
Assignor, assignee, 194
Assurance, right of, 256
Attachment, 341–342, 356
Attorney(s)
accused person's right to, 10, 116
-client relationship, 588
district (D.A.), 7, 107
durable power of, 404
duties of, 83–84, 580–582
in fact, versus at law, 403
liability of, 578–589
malpractice (professional negligence) and, 79, 581–582
power of, 400n, 403–404
Attribution, 156
Auctions, 120, 146
Audits, 431, 580, 588
Auditors, 580, 583, 585, 588. *See also* Accountant(s)
Authority(ies)
of agent, 403–405
apparent, 401, 404
binding, 5
certificate of, 464
express, 403–404
implied, 404, 406
of partner, 449
persuasive, 6
Automated teller machines (ATMs), 326
Avoidance powers, 363
Award, jury, 40, 41, 43

B

Bailee
acknowledgment by, of buyers rights, 253n, 259
defined, 240, 531
duties of, 533–534
goods held by, delivery and, 240–241, 259
liability of, 533, 535, 534
lien of, 533
rights of, 533
Bailment(s), 531–536
agreement creating, 531, 532
defined, 531
elements of, 531–532
gratuitous, 533
for hire (commercial), 532–533
involuntary (constructive), 532
for mutual benefit of bailor and bailee, 532–533, 534, 535
ordinary, 532–535
for sole benefit of bailee, 532, 533, 534, 535
for sole benefit of bailor, 532, 533, 534
special (extraordinary), 532, 535–536
warranties and, 535
Bailor
defined, 531
duties of, 535
Balloon mortgage, 380
Bank(s), 315–334
advising, 601
check collection and clearing process of, 323–326
collecting, 323
correspondent, 601
-customer relationship, 318. *See also* Bank customer(s)
defined by UCC, 315
depositary, 323
depository, 323n
duty of
to accept deposits, 323–326
to honor checks, 318–323
electronic fund transfers and, 326–327, 601–603
intermediary, 323
liability of, 319, 321–323, 327
negligence of, 321
online banking and, 327
paying, 601
payor, 323
Bank customer(s)
bank's relationship with, 318
check collection and clearing process and, 323–326
death or incompetence of, 319,
liability of, 319
negligence of, 319, 320–321
Bankruptcy. *See also* Bankruptcy Code
adequate protection doctrine and, 362, 367
automatic stay in, 362–363, 367
creditors and, 355, 361, 362, 365, 367, 369
debtor in, 360. *See also* Debtor(s)
debtor's property in (bankruptcy estate) in, 360, 361, 363–367
bankruptcy trustee's right to possess, 363–364
distribution of, to creditors, 365–366
exempted, 364–365
discharge in, 204, 308, 360, 366–367, 370, 371–372
foreclosure versus, 396n
fraud and, 112, 363, 364, 366
involuntary, 362–363
means testing in, 361–362, 363
order for relief in, 362
ordinary (straight), 360–367
petition in, 360–361, 362, 363, 368n, 370
dismissal of, 362, 363
preferences in, 364
prepackaged, 385
priority of perfected secured parties and, 343
special requirements for consumer-debtors in, 360
substantial abuse and, 361–362, 363
tax returns and, 361
trustee in, 360, 361, 363–364
types of relief in, summarized, 360
voluntary, 360, 361–362
Bankruptcy Abuse Prevention and Consumer Protection Act (2005), 360n
Bankruptcy Code (Title 11 of the *United States Code*), 360. *See also* Bankruptcy
Chapter 7 of (liquidation proceedings), 360–367
Chapter 11 of (reorganization), 367–369, 370n
Chapter 12 of (adjustment of debts by family farmers and fishermen), 365n, 369–372
Chapter 13 of (adjustment of debts by individuals), 365n, 269, 370–372
dollar amounts in, adjustment of, 364n
Bankruptcy Reform Act (1978), 360
Bankruptcy Reporter (Bankr.), 20
Bargain
basis of, 163, 270
loss of, 212
Bargained-for exchange, 162, 163
Battery, 71
Bearer, 292, 296

Bearer instrument, 296–297, 298
Beneficiary(ies)
  creditor, 198
  donee, 198
  insurance and, 555
  on letter of credit, 601
  third party, 193, 198–200
  of trust, 566, 569
  trustee's duties to, 569
Bequest, 560
Berne Convention (1886), 101
Beyond a reasonable doubt, 107, 118
Bill of lading, 227, 238, 240, 601
Bill of Rights, 8, 10–15, 462
Board of directors. *See* Directors, corporate
Bond indenture, 471, 503
Bonds, 471, 502, 503
Boycotts, 8
Brady Handgun Violence Prevention Act (1993), 8n
Bribery
  commercial, 112
  of foreign officials, 59–60, 112, 599
  of public officials, 112
Broker(s)
  insurance, 397, 557
  real estate, 397, 545
Burden of proof
  in civil cases, 74, 75, 107
  in criminal cases, 107
  shifting of, under Title VII, 424, 429, 431
Burglary, 110
Business(es)
  Bill of Rights and, 8, 10–15, 462
  legal environment of, 2–15
  place of, seller's, 253
  sale of ongoing, covenant not to compete and, 170
  wrongful interference with, 76
Business ethics, 2–3, 50–54. *See also* Ethics
  defined, 51
  codes of conduct and, 54
  ethical reasoning and, 55–57
  on global level, 58–60
  "gray areas" in law and, 52–53
  importance of, 51
  management and, 53–55
  moral minimum and, 51
  transgressions of, by financial institutions, 54–55
  Web-based reporting systems and, 54
Business invitees, 79
Business judgment rule, 486–487
Business necessity, 431
Business organization(s), 444–460
  corporation as. *See* Corporation(s)
  family limited liability partnership (FLLP) as, 451
  limited liability company (LLC) as, 453–456, 497
  limited liability partnership (LLP) as, 451, 497
  limited partnership (LP) as 451–453
  major forms of, compared, 496–497
  partnership as. *See* Partnership(s)
  sole proprietorship as, 444–445, 496
Buyer(s)
  breach by, 241, 258–260
  goods in possession of, on breach, 260
  insolvency of, 258
  inspection of goods by, 257
  insurable interest of, 241
  in the ordinary course of business, 238, 344
  performance obligations of, 256–258
  rejection of goods by, 253, 262
  rights and remedies of, 253n, 259, 260–263
  risk of loss and, 239–241
Bystanders, 278

C

Cancellation. *See also* Rescission
  of contract, 6, 258, 260
  of insurance policy, 559
  of negotiable instrument, 309
CAN-SPAM (Controlling the Assault of Non-Solicited Pornography and Marketing) Act (2003), 123
Capacity
  contractual, 133, 166–168
  testamentary, 562
Care
  due, 274, 501
  duty of, 78–80
    accountant's, 579–580
    agent's, 402
    attorney's, 580–582
    bailee's, 533, 535–536
    bank's, 321
    breach of, 78, 579
    corporate directors' and officers', 486
    defined, 78
    landowner's, 77
    LLC member's, 455
    partner's, 448
  ordinary, 402
Carrier(s)
  common, 535
  delivery via, 253
  substitution of, 254
  timely notice to, 259
Case(s)
  abstract of, 41
  brief of, 41
  citations to, 20–22
  of first impression, 6
  "no-asset," 365
  prima facie, 424–425, 429
  sample, 25–27
  terminology of, 25
  titles of, 25
Case law
  common law doctrines and, 5
  defined, 5
  finding, 19–23
  old, 20
  as primary source of law, 4
  reading and understanding, 20, 25–27
Cash, digital (virtual), 327–328
Catalogues, 146
Categorical imperative, 56
Causation, 78, 79–80
Cause
  challenge of prospective juror for, 38
  probable, 116, 118
  proximate (legal), 80, 270n, 275, 579
  superseding, 80, 81
Central America–Dominican Republic–United States Fair Trade Agreement (CAFTA-DR), 599
Certificate(s)
  of authority, 464
  of credit counseling, 361
  of deposit (CD),
  of incorporation, 468
  of limited partnership, 446
  of merger or consolidation, 474
  stock, 492. *See also* Stock(s)
Certification mark, 91
Challenges, of prospective jurors, 38
Chancellor, 6
Chattel paper, 338
Chattels, 77, 526. *See also* Personal property

Check(s), 290, 291–292, 293, 315–323
    altered, 322–323
    cashier's, 316–317
    certified, 304, 317–318
    collection and clearance of, 323–325
    dating of, 297, 318
    defined, 291, 315
    dishonor of, 318
    forged indorsements on, 321–322
    forged signatures on, 319–321
    poorly filled out, 322
    postdated, 318
    stale, 319
    stop-payment orders and, 319
    substitute, 325
    teller's, 316
    traveler's, 317
Check Clearing in the 21st Century Act (Check 21)(2001), 325
Child Online Protection Act (COPA)(1998), 12
Children
    child labor and, 417
    intestacy laws and, 565
    pornography and, 12–13
Child Pornography Prevention Act (CPPA(1996), 13
Children's Internet Protection Act (CIPA)(2000), 12
Choice-of-language clause, 600
Choice-of-law clause, 600, 601
Circulars, 146
Circumstances, changed, agency termination and, 409
Citations, 4, 19–24
Civil law, 7
    criminal law versus, 7, 107–108
Civil law system, 7
Civil Rights Act (1964), Title VII of, 58, 424–429, 603
Claim(s)
    priority of, to debtor's collateral, 343–345, 347–348
    proof of, in bankruptcy, 365
    settlement of, 164–166
Class Action Fairness Act (2005), 71
Clearinghouse, 325
Client(s)
    accountant's relationship with, 589
    attorney's relationship with, 588
    professionals' common law liability to, 578–583
    defalcation (embezzlement) by, 579
    misconduct of, 588
Closed shop, 434
Closing, 545
Cloud computing, 99
COBRA (Consolidated Omnibus Budget Reconciliation Act)(1985), 421–422
Code of Federal Regulations (C.F.R.), 19
C.O.D. (collect on delivery) shipments, 257
Codicil, 564
Collateral
    after-acquired, 354–355
    buyers of, versus secured creditors, 345
    claims to, priorities and, 343–345, 346, 347–348, 354
    classifications of, 337, 338
    consumer goods as, 339, 341–342, 348, 347
    of debtor, 336
        creditors' or secured parties' rights in, 343–350, 354
        debtor's rights in, 337
    defined, 337
    description of, 329–330
    disposition of, 347–348
    intangible, 338, 339
    methods of perfecting security interest and, 358–360
    redemption of, 349
    release of, 345
    repossession of, 347
    retention of, by secured party, 347
    sale of, 342, 348–349
        proceeds from, 342, 349
    surrender or impairment of, 358
    tangible, 338, 339
Collective bargaining, 422–423, 434–435
Collective mark, 91
Color, discrimination based on, 423, 424, 425, 603
Comity, principle of, 594–595
Commerce clause, 8–10, 433
Commercial activity, 596
Commercial impracticability, 205–206, 254–256
Commercial paper, 290. *See also* Negotiable instrument(s)
Commercial reasonableness, 230, 252, 259, 302, 347, 348
Commercial unit, 257
Common law, 5–6
Common law system, 7
Communications Decency Act (CDA)(1996), 12, 83
Communication(s)
    of acceptance, 150–152, 232
    of offer, 145, 147–148
    employer's monitoring of, 422
    privileged, 73–74, 588–589
Compensation
    bailments and, 533
    acorporate directors and, 484
    foreign investments and, 597
    just, 548, 595
    partners and, 447
    principal's duty of, 403
    unemployment, 397, 421
    workers', 397, 403, 420
Compensation committee, 532
Complaint, 36
Computer Fraud and Abuse Act (Counterfeit Access Device and Computer Fraud and Abuse Act)(CFAA)(1984), 124
Computer Software Copyright Act (1980), 98
Condition(s)
    concurrent, 201–202
    defined, 200
    of performance, 200–202
    precedent, 187, 200–201
    subsequent, 201
Conduct
    ethical code of, 54
    implied contracts and, 136
    misrepresentation by, 181
    oppressive, 485–486
    pattern of, apparent authority and, 404
    rejection of offer by, 149
    sexually offensive, 442. *See also* Sexual harassment
Conference, pretrial, 38
Confirmation, debtor's request for, 345–346
Confiscation, 595, 597
Conflict of interest, 488–489
Confusion, acquisition of personal property by, 530
Consent, voluntary, 71, 134, 178–182
Consideration
    adequacy of, 163
    in contracts, 133, 147, 162–166, 231n, 233–234
    defined, 162
    gifts and, 528
    lack or failure of, 163–164, 308
    past, 164
    contract rescission and, 203–204
Consolidation, 473, 474–475, 490–491
Constitutional law, 4. *See also* United States Constitution
Consumer(s)
    as debtor. *See* Consumer-debtor(s)
    electronic fund transfers by, 326–327
    financial data of, privacy rights and, 328
    protections for, mortgages and, 382, 383
Consumer-debtor(s)
    accuracy of bankruptcy petition and, 361

bankruptcy discharge and, 366
defined, 368
special Bankruptcy Code treatment of, 360
Contract(s), 132–224. *See also* Agreement(s); E-contract(s); Lease contract(s); Sales contract(s)
acceptance in, 133, 150–152, 154, 232–234, 242, 257–258, 262
adhesion, 171
agency relationships and, 405–406, 415
agreement in, 133, 144–154
anticipatory repudiation of, 203, 258
arbitration clauses in, 43–44
assignment of rights in, 193–196, 198
bank-customer relationship and, 318
bilateral, 134–145
breach of
as defense to liability on negotiable instrument, 308
defined, 3, 203
material versus minor, 202, 203
professionals' liability and, 579
remedies for. *See* Contract(s), remedies for breach of
capacity and, 133, 166–168
collateral, 182, 184
consideration in. *See* Consideration
construction, 212–213
contrary to public policy, 170–172
contrary to statute, 168–169
covenants not to compete in, 170, 217
defined, 133
delegation of duties under, 193, 196–198
destination, 238, 240, 253
disaffirmance and, 166–167
discharge of, 200–210
by agreement, 203–204
commercial impracticability and, 205–206, 254–256
by operation of law, 204–205
by performance, 202–203
elements of, 133–134, 136
employment. *See* Employment contract(s)
enforceability of, 136, 136, 168–173, 178–192. *See also* Parol evidence rule; Statute of Frauds
exculpatory clauses in, 170, 172, 218, 280, 533
executed, 136
executory, 136
express, 135–136
form of, 135
formal, 135
formation of, 134–136
function of, 133
implied, 135–136, 415
incomplete, 187
informal (simple), 135
installment, 253
insurance. *See* Insurance, contract (policy) for
integrated, 188–189, 235
investment, 503
involving interests in land, Statute of Frauds and, 182, 183
international. *See* International contract(s)
interpretation of, 138–140, 235
lacking consideration, 163–164, 308
law governing, 327
sources of, 132–133
legality of, 133, 168–173
limitation-of-liability clauses in, 118, 228, 535
material alteration of, 204, 241
mirror image rule and, 149, 150, 232
mistakes and, 178–180
modification of, 187, 233–234
objective theory of, 133
offer in, 133, 145–150, 152–153, 230–232, 242
option, 148, 231n
oral, 182–185. *See also* Parol evidence rule; Statute of Frauds
output, 231
parol evidence rule and, 187–189, 235–236
performance of. *See* Performance
for personal services. *See* Personal-service contract(s)
preincorporation, 466–467
privity of, 193, 274, 583–584
proposed, supervening illegality of, 149, 150
quasi (implied in law), 136–138, 218
ratification of, 167, 404–405
reformation of, 170, 181, 211, 217
remedies for breach of. *See also individual remedies*
damages as, 211–216, 218. *See also* Damages
equitable, 211, 216–218
limitation of, 218
repudiation of, 203, 258
requirements, 231
rescission of. *See* Rescission
in restraint of trade, 170
severable (divisible), 173
shipment, 238, 239–240, 253
within Statute of Frauds, 182–185, 186, 358, 380. *See also* Statute of Frauds
subsequently modified, 187
terms of. *See* Term(s)
types of, 134–136
unconscionability and. *See* Unconscionability
unenforceable, 136
unilateral, 134–135
with unlicensed practitioner, 169–170
valid, 136, 168
void, 136, 168, 187
voidable, 136, 168, 187
written (confirmatory) memorandum of, 185, 186–187, 234
wrongful interference with, 76
Contribution, co-surety's right of, 359
Control(s)
de facto (actual), 595
dominion and complete, 529
export, 597–598
import, 598–599
right to
bailee's, 533
employer's, worker's status and, 397, 399
Controlled Substances Act (CSA), 9
Conversion, 77–78, 531
Conveyance, 385, 543. *See also* Real property, ownership of, transfer of
Cooperation, duty of, 256, 403
Copyright(s), 88, 96–102, 399
Copyright Act (1976), 96–97, 399
Corporate citizenship, 57
Corporate governance, 514–517
Corporate social responsibility, 56–57
Corporation(s), 461–522
acquiring, 476
alien, 464
assets of
commingling, 470–471
misapplication or wasting of, 494
purchase or sale of, 475–476, 489
bankruptcy of, 360, 367–369, 370n
bylaws of, 467, 468, 485, 489
classification of, 461, 464–466
close, 464–466, 470–471
compared with other major business forms, 496
consolidations and, 471, 474–475
constitutional rights of, 462
criminal liability and, 109, 462–464, 489
de facto, 469
de jure, 468
defined, 109, 461
directors of. *See* Directors, corporate
dissolution and winding up of, 477, 494
dividends and, 462, 493–494
domestic, 464, 466

duration of, 468, 496
by estoppel, 469
ethics and, 52–63. *See also* Business ethics; Ethics
financing of, 471–473. *See also* Bond(s); Security(ies); Stock(s)
first organizational meeting of, 468
foreign, 464
formation of, 466–469, 496. *See also* Incorporation
freedom of speech and, 11–12, 462
incorporation of. *See* Incorporation
jurisdiction and, 29–30
as legal ("artificial") person, 29–30, 109, 116, 360, 462, 483
management of, 53–55, 465, 467, 484, 487–489
mergers and, 473–475, 489
nature of, 461–464
nonprofit (not-for-profit), 464
officers of. *See* Officers, corporate
parent, 462, 474–475
piercing the corporate veil of, 453n, 462, 470–471
powers of, 469–470
private, 464
professional (P.C.), 466
profits of, 462, 493
public, 464
publicly held, 464
purpose of, 467, 468
registered office of, 467, 468,
retained earnings of, 462, 493
S, 466
service (S.C.), 466
stakeholders and, 57
surplus of, 493
surviving, 474, 475
takeovers and, 476, 490
target, 476
termination of, 477
Corporations commissioner, 514
Cost-benefit analysis, 60
Counterclaim, 36
Counterfeiting, 92–93
Counteroffer, 149
Course of (prior) dealing, 139, 187, 235, 272
Course of performance, 139, 187, 235
Courts(s)
adaptation to online world by, 41–42
of appeals, appellate. *See* Federal court system, appellate courts of; State court system, appellate courts of
bankruptcy, 30, 360
chancery, 6
cyber, 42
decisions of, 19–20
finding, 19–23
reading and understanding, 20, 25–27
docket of, 42
early English, 5, 6, 20, 23
of equity, 6
federal. *See* Federal court system
judicial review by, 28–29
jurisdiction of. *See* Jurisdiction
king's, 6
of law, 6
online, 42
opinions of, 25
probate, 30
role of, 28–29
small claims, 33–34
state. *See* State court system
trial. *See* Trial court(s)
Covenant(s)
not to compete, 170, 217
not to sue, 165
of quiet enjoyment, 546, 550
warranty deeds and, 546
Cover, 260–261
Co-workers, sexual harassment by, 428
Credit, continuing line of, 342–343
Credit cards, 122, 155, 327
Credit reporting, 367, 384n
Creditor(s)
automatic stay and, 362–363, 367
best interests of, 367–368
claims of
in bankruptcy, 361, 365
false, 112
committees of, 369
composition agreements of, 357
–debtor relationship, bank-customer relationship as, 318
distribution of bankruptcy estate to, 365–366
duties of, 345–347
involuntary bankruptcy and, 362
laws assisting, 354–359, 380–381
meetings of, 365
preferred, 363, 364
priorities among, 343–3445, 346, 354
rights of, 345–349
in collateral, 343–345
Crime(s)
civil liability for, 107–108
classification of, 113
computer, 120–124
cyber, 120–124
defined, 107
intent and, 108–109
organized, 112–113
persons accused of, rights of, 10, 115–118. *See also individual protections*
property, 110
public order, 110
prosecution for, tort lawsuit for same act versus, 407–108
types of, 109–113
violent, 109–110
white-collar, 111–113, 463
Criminal law, 7, 116–127. *See also* Crime(s)
burden of proof under, 107
civil law versus, 7, 107
Criminal liability
corporate, 109, 462–464, 489
defenses to, 113–115
professionals and, 588
requirements for, 108–109
Criminal procedures, 115–118
Criminal process, 118–120
Crops, sale of, 228, 542
Cure, 254, 262
Customs, international, 594
Cyber marks, 92–93
Cyber theft, 120–122
Cyberlaw, 7
Cybernotary, 154
Cyberspace. *See* Internet
Cybersquatting, 92–93
Cyberterrorism, 122–123

D

Damages, 6
for breach of contract, 211–215, 218, 259, 261–262
compensatory, 69 80, 211–213
consequential (special), 211, 213–214, 263
incidental, 212, 259
injury requirement and, 84
liquidated, versus penalties, 215–216
measurement of, 212–213
mitigation of, 214–215
nominal, 214
punitive, 69–70, 214

treble, 327
Danger, commonly known, 280
"Danger invites rescue" doctrine, 82
Davis-Bacon Act (1931), 416
Death
  of agent or principal, 409
  of bank customer, 319
  of LLC member, 456
  of offeror or offeree, 149–150
  of partner, 450, 451452
  of party to personal-service contract, 205
  of sole proprietor, 445
  work-related, of employee, 420
Debentures, 471, 503
Debit cards, 326
  Debt(s)
  in dispute, 164
  liquidated, 164
  preexisting, 364
  reaffirmation of, 363, 367
  unliquidated, 164
Debtor(s)
  in bankruptcy, income of, 361–362, 365, 370
  consumer as. *See* Consumer-debtor(s)
  -creditor relationship, bank-customer relationship as, 318
  default of, 337, 347–349, 358
  duties of, 345–347
  defined, 337
  laws assisting, 359–360. *See also* Bankruptcy
  name of, in financing statement, 338–339
  in possession (DIP), 368–369
  property of, 360, 363–366
    as bankruptcy estate (estate in property), 363
    bankruptcy trustee's right to possess, 363–364
    distribution of, in bankruptcy, 365–366
    exempted, 359, 364–365
    garnishment of, 356–357
    involuntary bankruptcy and, 362
  request for confirmation of debt by, 345–346
  rights of, 345–347
    in collateral, 338
Decision(s)
  court, 19–22, 25–27. *See also* Opinion(s)
  duty to make informed and reasonable, 486
Deed(s)
  defined, 546
  easement or profit created by, 544
  in lieu of foreclosure, 385
  types of, 546–547
Defamation, 72–74, 83
Default
  of debtor, 303, 386, 337, 347–349, 358, 386–387
  judgment, 36
Defendant, 6, 25, 36–37
Defense(s)
  affirmative, 37, 80, 427
  to assault and battery, 71
  bona fide occupational qualification (BFOQ), 431
  business necessity, 431
  to contract enforceability, 131–132, 178–192
  to criminal liability, 113–115
  to defamation, 73–74
  defined, 71
  to employment discrimination, 427, 431
  "ignorance," 114, 517
  knowledge of, HDC status and, 504
  knowledgeable user, 280
  to liability on negotiable instruments, 307–309
  under securities laws, 507, 586–587
  to negligence, 80–82
  notice of, HDC status and, 304
  of others, 71
  to payment
    of insurance claim, 560
    on negotiable instrument, 303, 307–309
    personal (limited), 308–309
  to product liability, 278–280
  of property, 71
  self-, 71, 113
  of surety or guarantor, 358
  to trespass, 77
  to violations of securities laws, 507, 586–587
  universal (real), 320–321
  to wrongful interference, 76
Delegatee, delegator, 196
Delegations, 193, 198–198
Delivery
  constructive, 528–529, 532
  contract term regarding, 231
  of deed, 546
  ex-ship, 240
  of gift, 528–529
  in installments, 253
  with movement of goods, 239–240
  without movement of goods, 239–240
  of nonconforming goods, by seller or lessor, 262–263
  place of, 253
  of possession, 532
  requirements for stopping, 259–260
  seller's or lessor's refusal to make, 260–262
  seller's or lessor's right to withhold, 258
  tender of, 240, 253
Demand, payment on, 292, 295–296
Demand instrument, 290–291, 303
Deposit(s)
  bank's duty to accept, 323–326
  certificate of (CD), 290, 292, 293, 294n, 503
  direct, 326
  indorsement for, 300
Deposited acceptance rule, 151
Depositions, 37
Descendants, lineal, 565
Design defects, 276–277
Devise, devisee, 561
Digital Millennium Copyright Act (1998), 98
Dilution, trademark, 89–90
Directors, corporate
  approval of mergers and other combinations by, 474
  audit committee of, 515
  conflicts of interest and,488–489
  corporate governance and, 514–517
  corporate management and, 53–55, 465, 467, 484, 487–489
  crimes of, 462–464, 489
  dissenting, 486
  duties of, 486–489
  election of, 484
  failure of, to declare dividend, 493
  initial, 467 468
  liability of, 109, 462–464, 486, 489
  meetings of, 484–485
  removal of, 484
  rights of, 485
  role of, 462, 483–486
  torts of, 462–464, 489
Disability, discrimination based on, 423, 424, 430–431, 603
Disaffirmance, 166–167
Discharge
  in bankruptcy, 204, 308, 360, 366–367, 370, 371–372
  constructive, 426–427
  contract, 200–206
  from liability on negotiable instrument, 309
  wrongful, 415–416
Disclosure
  of defects

to bailee, 535
to buyer of real property, 545–546
under EFTA, 326–327
public, of private facts, 74
under SEC Rule 10b–5, 509–510
under TILA, 381
Discovery, 37–38
Discrimination
employment. *See* Employment discrimination
jury selection and, 39
reverse, 425
Disparagement of property, 78
Distributed network, 99
Distributorship, 596
Diversity of citizenship, 30–31
Dividends, 462, 493–494
Divorce, wills and, 564
Docket, 42
Documents of title, 227, 238, 240, 253, 259, 536
Dodd-Frank Wall Street Reform and Consumer Protection Act (2010), 502
Domain names, 92–93
Donor, donee, 528
"Dormant" commerce clause, 9–10
Double jeopardy, 10, 116, 462
Drafts, 291–292, 293. *See also* Check(s)
Drawee, 291, 204–305, 315
Drawer, 291, 304–305, 315, 319–323
Due diligence, 507, 586
Due process
constitutional guarantee of, 10, 15, 69, 116, 356, 462
procedural, 15
substantive, 15
Dumping, 599
Duress, 114, 173, 308
Duty(ies)
antidumping, 599
of care. *See* Care, duty of
delegation of, 196–198
ethics and, 55–56
fiduciary. *See* Fiduciary(ies); Fiduciary relationships
of loyalty. *See* Loyalty, duty of
preexisting, 163–164

E

Early neutral case evaluation, 44
Easements, 183, 544
Economic Espionage Act (1996), 100, 112
E-contract(s)
agreement in, 152–154
defined, 152
dispute resolution and, 153
e-signatures and, 153–157
Eighth Amendment, 10, 116–117
Electronic Communications Privacy Act (ECPA)(1986), 327, 422
Electronic Fund Transfer Act (EFTA)(1978), 326–327
Electronic fund transfers (EFTs), 326–327, 601–602
Eleventh Amendment, 429, 430
E-mail
contract formation and modification by, 416
credit-card receipts sent by, 155
employers' policies and, 422
fraudulent, 517
spam and, 123
Embezzlement, 111, 479
Emergency Economic Stabilization Act (2008), 381n
Eminent domain, 545, 548–549
Employee(s)
agency law and, 397–399
drug testing of, 422–423
ethics training for, 54
family and medical leave for, 419
health and safety of, 419–420
income security for, 420–422
key, 419
layoffs of, 418–419
overtime provisions of FLSA and, 417–418
privacy rights of, 422–423
private pension plans and, 421
reasonable supervision of, 486
recruiting and retaining, 57
safety of, 403, 407, 417, 419–420
state, age discrimination and, 429–430
status of, determining, 397–399
travel by, liability and, 408
whistleblowing by, 415
work-related death of, OSHA and, 420
Employee Retirement Income Security Act (ERISA)(1974), 421
Employer(s)
liability of, 405–408
reasonable accommodation by
for employee's disability, 430–431
for employee's religious beliefs, 15, 425
undue hardship versus, 430
retaliation by, 427–428
self-insured, 420
Employment, 397, 414–440. *See also* Employee(s); Employer(s); Employment contract(s)
foreign suppliers' practices and, 58–59
fraud and, 122
immigration laws and, 431–433
labor laws and, 433–436
scope of, *respondeat superior* and, 407–408
at will, 414–416
Employment contract(s)
arbitration clauses in, 44
covenants not to compete in, 170, 217
implied, 415
modification of, by e-mail, 416
Employment discrimination, 423–431
based on
age, 423, 424, 429–430, 603
color, 423, 424, 425, 603
disability, 423, 424, 430–431, 603
gender, 58, 423, 424, 425–426, 603. *See also* Sexual harassment
national origin, 423, 424, 425, 603
pregnancy, 426
race, 423, 424, 425, 603
religion, 423, 424, 425, 603
union affiliation, 434
burden of proof and, 424, 429, 431
defenses to, 427, 431
defined, 424
disparate-impact (unintentional, 424–425
disparate-treatment (intentional), 425
foreign workers and, 58–59, 603
independent contractor status and, 398
prima facie case of, 424–425, 429
protected classes and, 423
remedies for, under Title VII, 429
reverse discrimination and, 425
tangible employment action and, 427
wages and, 426
Entrapment, 114
Entrepreneur, 444
Entrustment rule, 238–239
Equal dignity rule, 400, 403
Equal Employment Opportunity Commission (EEOC), 424, 425,429, 430
Equal Pay Act (1963), 426
Equity
courts of, 6
home, 380
merging of law and, 6
remedies in, 6, 211, 216–217
Error(s). *See also* Mistake(s)

banking, 327
clerical (typographical), 179, 188
UETA and 157
Escrow account, 545
E-SIGN (Electronic Signatures in Global and National Commerce) Act (2000), 162, 154–155
E-signatures, 153, 153–157
attribution and, 156
defined, 153, 154
errors and, 157
permissible uses of, 154
Estate(s)
leasehold, 549–550
life, 543–544, 569
in property, 360, 361, 363–364–367
Estoppel
agency formation by, 401, 404
corporation by, 469
partnership by, 447
promissory. *See* Promissory estoppel
Ethics, 50–63. *See also* Business ethics
codes of conduct and, 54
defined, 50–51
duty-based, 55–56
ethical reasoning and, 55–57
management and, 53–55
outcome-based, 56–57
Event, occurrence of
agency termination and, 409
partnership termination and, 450, 451
Eviction, 550
Evidence
after-acquired, 431
e- (electronic), 38, 39
extrinsic, 139
illegally obtained, 117
parol, 187–189, 235–236
preponderance of, 107
prima facie, 579
Exclusionary rule, 117
Execution
fraud in the, 308
and levy, as judicial remedy, 347, 356
writ of, 356
Exemption(s)
in bankruptcy, 364–365
homestead, 359, 365
Expedited Funds Availability Act (1987), 323
Export Administration Act (1979), 598
Export-Import Bank of the United States, 597, 598
Export Trading Company Act (1982), 598
Exporting, 596–598
Expression. *See also* Speech, freedom of
of opinion, offer and, 145–146
protected, 96. *See also* Copyright(s)
Expropriation, 595, 597

F

Fact(s)
affirmation of, 270
compilations of, 96
justifiable of, 172–173
material, 179, 180, 582, 586–587
misrepresentation of, 75, 180–181, 582, 586–587
mistake of, 114, 178–179
promise of, 270
question of, 34
statement of, 72–73, 75
Fair and Accurate Credit Transactions (FACT) Act (2003), 154
Fair Credit Reporting Act (FCRA), 368
Fair Labor Standards Act (FLSA)(1938), 416–418, 426, 429–430
False imprisonment, 71
Family and Medical Leave Act (FMLA)(1993), 419
Family limited liability partnership (FLLP), 451
Farmer(s)
defined, 369n
family, 369–370
involuntary bankruptcy and, 362n
Federal Bureau of Investigation, 12
Federal Communications Commission, 12
Federal court system
appellate courts of, 19, 34, 35. *See also* United States Supreme Court
citations to, 20–23
decisions of, 19, 20
illustrated, 34
jurisdiction of, 30–31
trial (district) courts of, 19, 20, 23, 30, 34, 35
Federal Insurance Contributions Act, 420
Federal Reporter (F., F2d, or F.3d), 20, 23
Federal Reserve System
Board of Governors of, 323
Regulation CC of, 323
Regulation E of, 326, 327
Regulation Z of, 382
check clearance by, 325
Federal Supplement (F.Supp. or F.Supp.2d), 20, 23
Federal Trade Commission (FTC)
HDC doctrine and, 309
merger guidelines of, 475
regulation of spam by, 123
Federal Trademark Dilution Act (1995), 89
Federal Unemployment Tax Act (FUTA)(1935), 421
Fee simple, 526–527, 561
Felonies, 113
Fiduciary(ies), 410–411
agent as, 401, 445
corporate directors and officers as, 486–489
defined, 396–397, 401
at heart of agency law, 396–397
inside information and, 510–511
majority shareholder as, 489, 495–496
manager in member-managed LLC as, 455–456
partner as, 445, 448–449
principal as, 401
Fiduciary relationship(s)
agency relationship as, 396–397, 401
of corporate directors and officers
with corporation, 486–489
with shareholders, 486
defined, 181
loyalty and, 402
misrepresentation and, 181
undue influence and, 182
Fifth Amendment, 10, 15, 116, 117, 462, 548
Filing
of appeal, 41
electronic, 42
perfection of security interest by, 338–341
perfection of security interest without, 341–342
Financial institutions, ethical transgressions by, 54–55
Financial Privacy Act (1978), 328
Financial Services Modernization Act (Gramm-Leach-Bliley Act)(1999), 328
First Amendment, 10, 11–15, 72, 422, 462
Fishermen, family, 370–371
Fixed-rate mortgage, 379
Fixtures, 183, 336, 542–543
Food, merchantable, 271
Forbearance, 162, 384
Force
deadly versus nondeadly, 113–114, 115
justifiable use of, 113–114, 115
reasonable, 71
Force majeure clause, 600

Foreclosure, 384–388
deed in lieu of, 385
defined, 384
friendly, 385
Home Affordable Modification Program (HAMP) and, 384–385
how to avoid, 384–385
judicial, 385
on liens, 355, 356, 384n
power of sale, 384–385
procedures for, 385–388
redemption rights and, 387–388
Foreign Corrupt Practices Act (FCPA)(1977), 59–60, 112, 599
Foreign exchange market, 601
Foreign investors, in LLC, 454
Foreign Sovereign Immunities Act (FSIA)(1976), 596
Foreseeability
of contingencies, 254–255
of product misuse, 277, 277, 280
of risk, 277, 278, 279
unforeseen difficulties and, 163
of users of accountants' statements or reports, 584
Forfeiture, 112
Forgery(ies), 116
as defense to liability on negotiable instrument, 306, 307–308
failure to detect, 321
as form of property crime, 110
on negotiable instrument, 319–322
Forum-selection clauses, 153, 600, 601
Forum shopping, in class-action lawsuits, 70
Fourteenth Amendment, 1, 15, 122, 356
Fourth Amendment, 10, 116, 117, 118, 422–423
Fraud. *See also* Misrepresentation
actual, 582
bankruptcy, 112, 364, 368
constructive, 582
contract illegal through, 173
in the execution, 308
in the inducement, 309
mail, 111–112
online, 120, 517–518
professional's liability and, 582
securities, 506–514, 517–518
wire, 111–112
Fraudulent misrepresentation. *See* Fraud; Misrepresentation
Freedom
of religion, 10, 11, 13–15
of speech, 10, 11–13, 72, 422, 462
"Fruit of the poisonous tree," 117
Fund(s)
assignment of right to receive, 195
commingling of personal and corporate, 470–471
electronic transfers of, 326–327, 601–602
misappropriation of, 465–466
mutual, 505
trust, 566, 569

G

GAAP (generally accepted accounting principles), 579–580, 586
GAAS (generally accepted auditing standards), 579, 586
Gambling, 168–169, 296–27
Garnishee, 356
Garnishment, 356–357
Gender
discrimination based on, 38, 58, 423, 424, 425–426, 603
same-, harassment and, 428–429
sexual harassment and, 58, 427–429
Genuineness of assent. *See* Consent, voluntary
Gift(s)
acquisition of personal property by, 527–530
causa mortis, 529–530
deathbed, 529–530
defined, 520
inter vivos, 529–530
by will, 561–562
Good faith
defined, 302
insurance contracts and, 559–560
performance of contract and, 133
taking in, HDC status and, 301–302
UCC and, 230, 231, 233, 252, 261, 301–302, 363, 370
Good faith purchaser, 238, 261
Goods. *See also* Product(s)
acceptance of, 257–258
revocation of, 262–263
associated with real estate, 228–229
commingling of, 530
conforming, 232, 252–253, 270
conforming/nonconforming, remedies of parties and, 258–263
consumer, as collateral, 339, 341–342, 348
counterfeit, 91–92
defective, 275, 535. *See also* Product(s), defective
defined, 227–228
description of, warranties and, 270
destruction of, 256
dumping of, 599
existing, 236–237
fungible, 237, 530
future, 237
identification of, 236–237
inspection of, 257, 273
location of, 253
merchantable, 271
nonconforming, 232, 254, 254, 258, 262–263
obtaining, by false pretenses, 110
in possession
of bailee, 240
of buyer or lessee, 260
of seller or lessor, 240, 258–259
reclamation of, 260
rejection of, 253, 257, 262
replevy of, 261
resale or disposal of, 258–259, 262
sale of. *See* Sales contract(s)
seller's or lessor's refusal to deliver, 260
services combined with, 229
specially manufactured, 234
stolen, receiving, 111
title to, 236–239
in transit, 259–260
Government
judiciary's role in, 28–29
local, 4, 9
regulation by. *See* Government regulation
substantial interest of, 11
Government regulation(s)
by administrative agencies, 4–5
commerce clause and, 8–10
of common carriers, 535
concurrent, 515
finding, 19, 23
garnishment proceedings and, 357
of insurance industry, 557
international business transactions and, 597–599
online banking and, 327
plain language laws and, 138
as primary source of law, 4–5
of real estate financing, 381–383
of securities, 502–514, 517–518
of spam, 123
of warehousing, 535–536
Gramm-Leach-Bliley Act (Financial Services Modernization Act)(1999), 328
Grandchildren, intestacy laws and, 565–566
Grantor, grantee, 546, 566
Guarantor, 357–359

Guaranty, 357–359
Gun-Free School Zones Act (1990), 8n

H

Hackers, hacking, 122–123, 517
Hague Convention on the Law Applicable to Contracts for the International Sale of Goods (Choice-of-Law Convention)(1986), 600
Health Care and Education Reconciliation Act (2010), 421n
Health insurance, 430–432
Hearing, preliminary, 119
Heirs, collateral, 565
Higher-Priced Mortgage Loans (HPML), 383
Holder, 296, 302, 304, 309
Holder in due course (HDC), 298, 301–304, 308, 309, 317n
Holding company, 462, 474
Home Ownership and Equity Protection Act (HOEPA)(1994), 382–383
Hostile-environment harassment, 427
Hotel operators, 535, 536
Housing and Economic Recovery Act (2008), 381n

I

ICANN (Internet Corporation for Assigned Names and Numbers), 92, 93,
Identification
- of author of online defamation, 83
- of goods, 236
- of parties to contract, offer and, 147
- prosecuting cyber crime and, 123–124

Illegality
- of contract, effect of, 172
- as defense to liability on negotiable instrument, 308, 309
- of performance, change in law and, 206
- supervening, of proposed contract, 149, 150

Immigration, 431–433
Immigration Act (1990), 432–433
Immigration and Nationality Act (1952), 431n, 433
Immigration Reform and Control Act (IRCA)(1986), 431–432
Immunity
- from prosecution, 115
- sovereign, doctrine of, 596
- of states, from lawsuits, 429

Implied warranties, 270–273
- arising from course of dealing or usage of trade, 272
- of authority, 406
- defined, 270
- of fitness
  - for the intended purpose of the bailment, 535
  - for a particular purpose, 272, 273, 535
- of habitability, 545, 550
- of merchantability, 229n, 270–271, 273, 535

Importing, 598–599
Impossibility of performance, 204–205, 404
Imposter rule, 306
Incapacity, mental. *See* Mental incompetence
Income
- of debtor in bankruptcy, 361–362, 365, 370
- security, employment and, 420–422

Incompetence. *See* Mental incompetence
Incorporation
- articles of, 467–468, 469, 489, 490
- certificate of, 468
- improper, 468–469
- procedures for, 467–468

Incorporators, 467, 468
Indemnification
- corporate director's right to, 485
- principal's duty of, 403

Independent contractor(s)
- agency relationships and, 397–399, 415. *See also* Agency relationship(s)
- defined, 397
- insurance broker as, 397
- torts of, 398, 407, 408
- "works for hire" and, 399

Indictment, 10, 118, 119
Individual retirement account (IRA), as will substitute, 565
Indorsee, 298
Indorsement(s), 294, 298–301. *See also* Signature(s)
- alternative or joint payees and, 301
- blank, 298, 299
- defined, 298
- forged, 321–322
- misspelled names and, 301
- qualified, 299–300
- restricted, 300
- special, 298–299
- unauthorized, 306

Indorser, 298, 304–305
Information
- in criminal process, 118, 119
- digital, copyrights in, 98
- inside, 112, 509
- requests for, 37–38, 345
- untruthful denial of, misrepresentation and, 181

Information return, 446
Infringement
- copyright, 96–98
- patent, 94–96
- trademark, 90
- warranty of title and, 269, 270

Initial public offering (IPO), 475, 504
Injunction, 6
Injury(ies)
- to bystanders, 278
- causation and, 79–80
- to employee, 420
- to innocent party, 182, 278, 579
- legally recognizable, 80
- as requirement for damages, 80, 582
- strict liability and, 276

Innkeepers. *See* Hotel operators
Insanity, 114. *See also* Mental incompetence
Inside information, 112, 509
Insider trading, 112, 488, 509–511
Insider Trading and Securities Fraud Enforcement Act (1988), 530
Insider Trading Sanctions Act (1984), 530n
Insiders, preferences to, 364
Insolvency
- balance-sheet, 360n
- bankruptcy relief and, 360
- of buyer or lessee, 259
- defined, 238
- equitable, 360n
- of seller or lessor, 238, 260

Inspection(s)
- of business records, right of
  - corporate director's, 485
  - partner's, 447
  - shareholder's, 464n, 493
- of goods, 257, 273
- by ICE officers, 447

Instrument. *See* Negotiable instrument(s)
Insurance, 555–560
- agent v. insurance broker, 397
- binder and, 558
- classifications of, 556
- contract (policy) for, 557–560
  - cancellation of, 559
  - clauses in, 558
- defined, 555
- homeowners', 381
- insurable interest and, 241, 557
- interpreting, 558–559
- key-person, 557
- life, 363, 365, 557,
- premium (payment) for, 422, 557

property, 557
terminology of, 557
title, 545
unemployment, 397, 421
Insurer, insured, 557
Intellectual property, 88–105
copyrights as. *See* Copyright(s)
defined, 88
forms of, summarized, 101
international protection for, 101–102
licensing of, 93, 618
patents as, 93–96, 101
trade secrets as, 100–101, 112
trademarks as. *See* Trademark(s)
Intent, intention
bailments and, 532
contracts and, 138–139, 145–147
contractual offer and, 144–147
in criminal law, 108–109, 111
to deceive, 180–181
deeds and, 546
donative, 528
employment discrimination and, 425
fixtures and, 542–543
forged indorsements and, 306
future, statement of, 146
third party beneficiaries and, 198
torts and, 70–78. *See also* Tort(s), intentional
wills and, 562–563, 564
Intentional infliction of emotional distress, 771–72
Interest(s)
commingling of personal and corporate, 470
conflict of, 488–489
insurable, 241, 557
leasehold, 550–551. *See also* Lease(s); Lease contract(s)
nonpossessory, 544–545
partner's, in partnership, 447
protected, 68–69
rate of, 294, 297, 379–381, 383
annual percentage (APR), 381
average prime offer, 383
usury and, 56
remainder, 569
security. *See* Security interest(s)
Interest-only (IO) mortgage, 379
Internal Revenue Code, 589, 588
Internal Revenue Service (IRS), 361, 399
International business transactions, 238, 593, 596–603
business ethics and, 58–60
government regulation and, 597–599
extraterritoriality of U.S. laws and, 58–59, 602–603
jurisdictional issues and, 32
making payment on, 601–602
International contract(s), 241–242, 600–601. *See also* International business transactions; International law(s)
acceptance in, 242
CISG and, 241–242
clauses in, 600
dispute resolution and, 601
offer in, 242
sample (Starbucks Coffee Company), 248–241, 600
International law(s), 593–609
defined, 7–8, 593
international principles and doctrines and, 593, 594–596
national law compared with, 7–8, 593–594
sources of, 593–594
International organizations, 8, 594
Internet
banking services via, 327
company financial information on, 491, 508
"corporate watch" groups on, 58, 59
courts adapting to, 41–42
crimes committed via, 120–124
defamation and, 83
e-contracts and, 152–157
e-prospectus delivery via, 503
fraud on, 120, 519–520
hacking and, 122–123, 517
investment newsletters and forums and, 517
investment scams and, 517
jurisdictional issues and, 31–33
obscenity and, 12, 13
online dispute resolution (ODR) via, 45
payment systems and, 326
proxy materials on, 491
retail fraud and, 120
sales via, taxation of, 227, 228, 463
securities fraud and, 517–518
spam and, 123
terrorism and, 122–123
theft via, 120–122
torts and, 83
trade secrets and, 100
trademark dilution and, 93
Internet service providers (ISPs), 83
Internet Tax Freedom Act (1998), 463n
Interrogatories, 37
Intestacy laws, 560, 565–566
Intestate, 560
Intoxication, contractual capacity and, 167–168
Intrusion into individual's affairs, 74
Inventory, 338, 339, 343, 345
Investing, international business transactions and, 597
Investment company, 505, 522
Involuntary servitude, 217

J

Joint venture, 597
Judge, justice versus, 25
Judgment(s)
default, 36
deficiency, 349, 387
enforcement of, 41, 601
as a matter of law, 39, 40–41
n.o.v. (notwithstanding the verdict), 40
on the pleadings, 37
summary, 37
Judiciary, role of, 28–29. *See also* Court(s)
Jurisdiction, 5, 29–32
appellate, 30
concurrent, 31
over corporations, 29–30
defined, 5, 29
e-contracts and, 153
exclusive, 31
of federal courts, 30–31, 453–454
general, 33
international issues and, 32, 594, 596
Internet and, 31–32, 45, 123
limited, 33–34
LLCs and, 453–454
minimum contacts and, 29
over nonresident defendants, 29
original, 30
over persons (*in personam*), 29–30
over property (*in rem*), 29–30
prosecution of cyber crime and, 123
"sliding-scale" standard and, 31–32
over subject matter, 30
of United States Supreme Court, 36
Jury
award of, 40, 41, 43
challenges to prospective members of, 38
charges (instructions) to, 40

grand, 10, 118
right to trial by, 10, 38–39, 116
selection of, 38
verdict of, 40, 41, 43
Justice, judge versus, 25
Justiciable controversy, 33

L

Labor-Management Relations Act (LMRA)(Taft-Hartley Act)(1947), 424
Labor unions, 414, 433–435
Land. *See also* Real property
contracts involving interests in
breach of 211, 216–217
Statute of Frauds and, 183
defined, 183, 541
fixtures and, 183, 542–543
legally sufficient description of, 546
trespass to, 77
Landlord (lessor), 550–551
Landlord-tenant relationships, 550–551
Landowners, duty of, 77
Language
choice of, in international contracts, 600
plain, 138
Lanham Act (1946), 89–90, 92
Larceny, 110
Law(s)
areas of, affecting business, illustrated, 3
administrative, 4–5
assisting creditors, 354–359, 380–381
bankruptcy, 360–372. *See also* Bankruptcy
blue sky, 173
case. *See* Case(s); Case law
change in
agency termination and, 409
rendering performance impossible, 206
choice of, 600, 601
civil, 7
classifications of, 6–8
code, 7
constitutional, 4. *See also* United States Constitution
courts of, 6
criminal. *See* Criminal law
cyber-, 7
defined, 2
due process of. *See* Due process
"duty to retreat," 115
employment, 414–440
equity and, merging of, 6
"gray areas" in, 52–53
immigration, 431–433
international. *See* International law(s)
intestacy, 560, 565–566
Islamic, 8
labor, 433–436
lemon, 273–274
misrepresentation of, 181
mistake of, 114
national, 7–8, 593
operation of. *See* Operation of law
plain language, 138
procedural, 6
protecting debtors, 359. *See also* Bankruptcy
question of, 34
regulating business. *See* Government regulation(s)
remedies at, 6, 211. *See also* Damages
right-to-work, 434
sources of, 3–5
"stand-your-ground," 114
statutory, 4
substantive, 6
tort. *See* Tort(s)
U.S., extraterritorial application of, 58–59, 602–603
uniform, 4
wage and hour, 416–418
workers' compensation, 397, 403, 420
Lawsuit(s). *See also* Litigation
basic judicial requirements for, 29–33
class-action, 70
covenant not to bring, 165
parties to, 25, 36–37
procedures in, 36–41
shareholder's derivative, 464n, 489, 494–495
standing to bring, 33
terminology of, 25
tort, criminal prosecution versus, for same act, 107–108
Lawyers' Edition of the Supreme Court Reports (L.Ed. or L.Ed.2d), 20
Lease(s). *See also* Lease contract(s)
anticipatory repudiation of, 258
assignment of, 551
consumer, 230
defined, 229
by nonowners, 238–239
of real property, 183, 550–551
Lease contract(s), 238–280. *See also* Contract(s), Lease(s); Uniform Commercial Code (UCC)
acceptance in, 232–233
breach of, 258–263
consideration in, 233–234
defined, 230
formation of, 230–236
landlord-tenant relationship and, 550–551
law governing, 133, 226, 229–230
offer in, 230–232
parol evidence and, 235–236
payment under, 256–257, 260
performance of, 252–258
remedies for breach of, 258–263
limitation of, 18, 263–264
risk of loss and, 239–241
Statute of Frauds and, 183, 234–235
Leaseback, sale and, 384
Legacy, 561
Legatee, 561
Lessee
breach by, 241, 258–260
defined, 230
goods in possession of, on breach, 260
inspection of goods by, 273
performance obligations of, 256–258
remedies of, 260–263
Lessor
breach by, 241, 260–263
defined, 230
goods held by, 258–259
performance obligations of, 252–256
remedies of, 258–260
Letter of credit, 135, 601–602
Levy, 347, 356
Liability(ies)
civil and criminal, for same act, 107–108
criminal. *See* Criminal liability
joint, 449
joint and several, 449
limitation or disclaimer of, 118, 152, 533. *See also* Contract(s), exculpatory clauses in
market-share, 277–278
primary, 184, 304, 358
product. *See* Product liability
secondary (contingent), 184, 304–305, 358
signature, 304–306
strict. *See* Strict liability
successor, 479–480
vicarious (indirect), 99n, 407

warranty, 306–307, 535
without fault, 87. *See also* Strict liability
Libel, 72, 73–74, 78
License, licensing
click-on (click-wrap agreement), 153
to come onto land, 544–545
common carriers and, 535
defined, 93
of intellectual property, 93
manufacturing abroad and, 597
of professionals, NAFTA and, 599
shrink-wrap (shrink-wrap agreement), 153
software, 151
state regulation of, 169
Lien(s), 354–356
artisan's, 77, 356
bailee's, 533
bankruptcy trustee's avoidance of, 363
defined, 269–270, 354
floating, 343
judicial, 302, 337n, 356, 356
mechanic's, 347, 354–355
possessory, 356, 533
statutory, 354
title warranties and, 269–270
Lily Ledbetter Fair Pay Act (2009), 426
Limited liability company (LLC), 453–456, 497
Limited liability partnership (LLP), 451, 497
Limited partnership (LP), 451–453, 497
Lineal descendants, 565
Liquidation, under Chapter 7, 360–367
Litigation. *See also* Case(s); Lawsuit(s)
abusive or frivolous, 75–76
defined, 36
international contracts and, 601
workers' compensation versus, 420
Loan(s). *See also* Mortgage(s)
acceleration clauses and, 386
assignment of, 204
bridge, 383
construction, 380
high-cost mortgage, 382–383
higher-priced mortgage (HPML), 383
home equity, 380
negative amortization of, 382
predatory lending and, 381
reamortization of, 385
student, bankruptcy and, 372
Lockouts, 414, 435
Loss(es)
of the bargain, 212
of goods, 253
profits and, in partnership, 446, 447, 451
risk of, 239–241
Loyalty, duty of, 487
agent's, 402
breach of, 402, 448–449
corporate director's and officer's, 487–489
LLC member's, 455
partner's, 448–449

M

Madrid Protocol (2003), 102
Magnuson-Moss Warranty Act (1975), 273
Mail Fraud Act (1990), 111
Mailbox rule, 151
Main purpose rule, 184, 358
Maker
act of, will revocation by, 564
of promissory note, 292, 304
Malpractice, 80, 581–582
Malware, 122
Manufacturing, manufacturers
abroad, 597
defective products and, 276–278
duty to warn and, 277, 288
Marriage, promises made in consideration of, 182, 184
Mediation, 43, 45–46
Medicare, 420–421, 445
Member (of LLC), 455
Mens rea (wrongful state of mind), 108–109
Mental incapacity. *See* Mental incompetence
Mental incompetence
of agent or principal, agency termination and, 409
of bank customer, 319
contractual capacity and, 168
as defense
to criminal liability, 114
to payment on negotiable instrument, 308, 309
of LLC member, dissociation and, 456
of offeror or offeree, offer termination and, 149–150
of partner, dissociation or dissolution and, 450, 451, 452
of party to personal-service contract, 205
Merchant(s)
both parties as, 233
defined, 229
duties of, when goods are rejected, 262
firm offer of, 148, 231–232
one or both parties as, 232–233
"privilege to detain" granted to, 71
special rules for, under UCC, 185, 229, 231–234, 262
written confirmation between 185, 234
Merger, 473–475, 505
Meta tags, 93
Minor(s). *See also* Children
age of majority and, 166
contractual capacity of, 166–167
disaffirmance by, 166–167
emancipation of, 166
legal, for executing a will, 562
negotiable instruments and, 308
parents' liability and, 167
Miranda rule, 117, 118
Mirror image rule, 149, 150, 232
Misappropriation theory, 510, 511
Misconduct
after-acquired evidence of, 431
professional, 581. *See also* Malpractice
Misdemeanors, 113
Misrepresentation. *See also* Fraud
by agent, 407
by conduct, 181
of fact, 75, 180–181, 602, 586–587
fraudulent, 75, 180–182
injury caused by, 75
insurance procured by, 557
of law, 181
product liability based on, 274
reliance on, 75, 148, 180, 181, 582, 584
by silence, 181
voluntary consent and, 180–182
Mistake(s), 187–189. *See also* Error(s)
bilateral (mutual), 178–180
as defense to criminal liability, 114
of fact, 114, 178, 179
of law, 114
of quality, 178
unilateral, 179
of value, 178, 179
voluntary consent and, 178–180
M'Naghten test, 114
Model Business Corporation Act (MBCA), 461
Model Penal Code, 109, 114
Monetary systems, 601

Money
e- (electronic), 327
fixed amount of, 292, 294–295
laundering of, 112–113
Moral minimum, 51
Mortgage Disclosure Improvement Act (2008), 381
Mortgage(s). *See also* Loan(s)
defined, 378, 379
foreclosures on, 384–388
important provisions in, 380–381
laws governing, 381–384
reverse, 380
Statute of Frauds and, 183, 380
subprime, 55, 379
types of, 379–381
Mortgagor, mortgagee, 379
Motion(s)
for directed verdict, 39
to dismiss, 37
for judgment as a matter of law, 39, 40–41
for judgment *n.o.v.* (notwithstanding the verdict), 40–41
for judgment on the pleadings, 37
for new trial, 41
posttrial, 40–41
pretrial, 37
for summary judgment, 37
MP3, 98–100
Mutual fund, 505

N

National Labor Relations Act (NLRA)(1935), 434, 435
National Labor Relations Board (NLRB), 434
National origin, discrimination based on, 423, 424, 425, 603
National Reporter System (West), 20, 21
National Securities Markets Improvement Act (1996), 514
Necessaries, 167
Necessity
business, 431
as defense to criminal liability, 114
easement created by, 544
Negligence, 70, 78–83
of agent, 407–408
of bailee or bailor, 533, 534, 535, 536
of bank, 319, 321
of bank customer, 320–321, 322
comparative, 80, 81–82, 280
contributory, 80, 81
criminal, 109
defenses to, 80–83
defined, 78
elements of, 78–83, 579
gross, 69, 179
per se, 82
product liability based on, 274
professional's liability and, 579
reasonable person standard and, 71, 78–79, 120, 222, 402, 416
special doctrines and statutes relating to, 82–83
Negotiable instrument(s), 290–314
acceleration clauses and, 296, 386
defined, 290
dishonor of, 303, 304, 305–306
extension clauses and, 296
forgery on, 319–322
as formal contract, 135
indorsements on, 298–301, 321–322
irregular or incomplete, 303
liability on, 304–307
defenses to, 307–309
discharge from, 309
signature, 304–306. *See also* Signature(s)
warranty, 304, 306–307
material alteration of, 303, 308
negotiability of, 292–297
overdue, 303–304
presentment of, 295, 305, 307, 325
signatures on, 292, 293, 304–306. *See also* Signature(s)
transfer of, 296, 290, 297–298
types of, 290–292, 293
Negotiation(s)
as ADR option, 42–43
preliminary, 146
transfer of negotiable instruments by, 298
Ninth Amendment, 10
Nonemployees, sexual harassment by, 428
Nonmerchant, one or both parties as, 232–233
Normal trade relations (NTR) status, 599
Norris-LaGuardia Act (1932), 434
North American Free Trade Agreement (NAFTA), 598, 590
Notary public, 404, 563n
Note, promissory, 292, 293
Notice
of agency termination, 409
agent's duty to give, 402
constructive, 409n
proper, of dishonor, 306
of sale, 348, 386–387
seasonable, 232
taking without, HDC status and, 303
Novation, 204, 470, 483
Nuisance, 77, 550, 561

O

Obedience, agent's duty of, 402
Obligor, obligee, 194
Obscenity, 12–13
Occupational Safety and Health Act (1970), 419–420
Occupational Health and Safety Administration (OSHA), 419–420
Offer(s)
of bribe, 112
contractual, 133, 145–150, 152–153, 230–232
irrevocable, 148, 231–232, 242
tender, 476
termination of, 148–150
Offeree
counteroffer by, 149
death of, offer termination and, 149–150
defined, 134, 144
incompetence of, offer termination and, 149–150
rejection of offer by, 148–149
Offeror
death of, offer termination and, 149–150
defined, 134, 144
incompetence of, offer termination and, 149–150
intent of, 145–147
Officers, corporate,
corporate governance and, 514–517
crimes of, 462–464, 489
duties of, 486–489
implied powers of, 486
insider trading and, 526
interests of, shareholders' interests and, 514
liability of, 109, 486, 489
reasonable supervision of, 486, 515, 517
role of, 462, 485–486
torts of, 462–464, 489
One-year rule, 183, 218n
Online dispute resolution (ODR), 45
Operation of law
agency formation by, 401
agency termination by, 409–410
contract discharge by, 204–205
offer termination by, 149–150
partnership termination by, 451
will revocation by, 564

Opinion(s)
auditor's, 580
court, 20
expressions of, 145–146
statements of, 72–73, 75, 282
unpublished, 20
Order(s)
cease-and-desist, 434
to pay, 290, 292, 294–297
for relief, 362
stop-payment, 319
Order instrument, 296, 297
Ordinance, 4
Organized Crime Control Act (1970), 113
Outsiders, 510–511
Overtime, 417–418
Ownership
concurrent, 527
in fee simple, 526–527, 543
of property. *See* Personal property, ownership of; Property, ownership of; Real property, ownership of

P

Paris Convention (1883), 101
Parol evidence rule, 187–189, 235–236
Partial performance, 185, 235, 255–256
Participation, corporate director's right of, 485
Partner(s). *See also* Partnership(s)
as agent, 445, 449
bankruptcy or mental incompetence of, 450, 451, 452
death of, 450, 451, 452
dissociation of, 450, 451, 452–453
duties of, 448–449
general, 451, 452
interest of, in partnership, 447
liability of, 448–449, 451–452, 496
limited, 451, 452
rights of, 447–448
withdrawal of, 450, 452
Partnerships(s), 461–467. *See also* Partner(s)
agency concepts and, 445, 448–449
as aggregate versus entity, 446
articles of, 446
compared with other major business forms, 496
defined, 445, 446
determining existence of, 446
dissolution of, 450–451
duration of, 446–447, 496
formation of, 446–447, 496
liability and, 448–449, 451–452, 496
limited (special) (LP), 451–453, 497
limited liability (LLP), 451, 497
management of, 446, 447, 451, 452, 496
partner's interest in, 447, 451
profits and losses of, 446, 447, 451
property of, 448
termination of, 450–451, 496
winding up of, 451
Patents, 93–96, 101, 597
Paycheck Fairness Act (2009), 426
Payee(s)
alternative, 301
defined, 291
fictitious, 306
joint, 301
Payment(s)
to bearer, 292, 296–297
at definite time, 295, 296,
on demand, 295–296
down, 380
e-contracts and, 152
in e-money, 327–328
"grease," to government officials, 59–60
international transactions and, 601–602
Internet systems for, 326
lease, 259
on negotiable instrument. *See* Negotiable instrument(s)
to order, 292, 296–297
prepayment penalties and, 380
promise to make, 292, 294
wrongful, bank's liability for, 319
Peer-to-peer (P2P) networking, 98
Penalties, liquidated damages versus, 213–214
Pension plans, 421
Pension Protection Act (2006), 421
Per capita distribution, 566
Per curiam opinion, 25
Per stirpes distribution, 565–566
Perfect tender rule, 253–256
Perfection, of security interest, 338–342, 354
Performance
agent's duty of, 402
complete, 202
conditions of, 200–202
of contract, 136, 184, 196–197, 202–203, 212, 252–258
course of, 139, 187, 235
defined, 200
impossibility of, 204–205, 409
partial, 185, 235, 255–256
to the satisfaction of another, 202
specific. *See* Specific performance
substantial, 202
tender of, 202
Person(s),
accused, rights of, 10, 115–118
intentional torts against, 70–76
jurisdiction over, 29–30
legal, 29–30, 109, 116, 360, 462
Personal (limited) defenses, 208–309
Personal identification number (PIN), 326
Personal property, 526–531. *See also* Property
bailment of, 532. *See also* Bailment(s)
conversion and, 77–78, 531
defined, 76, 544
exempted, 359, 376–377
fixtures and, 183, 336, 542–543
gift of, 528–530, 581
liens on, 77, 356
ownership of, 526–531
trespass to 77
Personal representative, 560
Personal-service contracts
assignments and, 194–195
death or incapacity of party to, 206
delegations and, 196
impossibility of performance and, 206
specific performance and, 217
Personalty, 77. *See also* Personal property
Petition
to appellate court, 36, 41
in bankruptcy, 360–361, 362, 363, 368n, 370
Petty offenses, 113
Phishing, 121
Piercing the corporate veil, 453n, 462, 470–471
Plagiarism, 124
Plain meaning rule, 138
Plaintiff, 6, 25, 36
Plant life, as real property, 542
Plea bargaining, 115, 119
Pleadings, 36
Pledge, 341
Point-of-sale systems, 326
Ponzi scheme, 50n, 518
Pornography, 12–13

Possession
acquisition of personal property by, 527
actual versus constructive, 528–529, 363n, 532
adverse, 547–548
artisan's lien and, 356
bailee's right of, 532, 533
debtor in, 368–369
of leased property, 550
perfection of security interest by, 341
Precedent, 5–6
Predominant-factor test, 229
Preemption, 433
Pregnancy Discrimination Act (1978), 426
Presentment
defined, 295
electronic, 325
payment on, 305
proper and timely, 305, 307
warranties regarding, 307
Pretext, for discrimination, 429
Price(s)
buyout, 450
purchase, seller's right to recover, 259, 260
Price lists, 146
Price term, 230
Primary liability, 184, 304, 358
Principal(s)
agency termination by, 409
agent's duties to, 401–402
bankruptcy of, agency termination and, 409
death or insanity of, agency termination and, 409
defined, 396
disclosed, 405
duties of, to agent, 401, 402–403
liability of, 405–408
partially disclosed, 405
torts of, 407
undisclosed, 405–406
Prior dealing, course of, 147–148, 197
Privacy right(s)
consumer data and, 328
e-contracts and, 152
e-money records and, 328
of employees, 422–423
invasion of, as tort, 74
online banking and, 328
Private equity capital, 472, 472
Private Securities Litigation Reform Act (1995), 510, 586, 588
Privilege, 73–74, 609
Privity of contract, 193, 274, 583–584, 607
Probate, 543n, 564–565
Proceeds, 349, 342
Product(s). *See also* Goods
defective, product liability and, 274–278
misuse of, 277, 280
trademarks and, 92
unreasonably dangerous, 275, 276
Product liability, 83, 274–278
defenses to, 278–280
defined, 274
privity of contract and, 274
strict, 83, 274–278
Production, acquisition of personal property by, 527
Professional(s)
duty of, 79, 579–582
liability of, 578–501
common law, to clients, 578–583
criminal, 588
statutory, 586–588
to third parties, 583-585
Profit(s)
corporate, 462, 493
and losses, shared by partners, 446, 447, 451
maximizing, business ethics and, 51–52
in real property law, 544
short-swing, 511
Promise(s)
collateral (secondary), 182, 184
defined, 132
of fact, 270
illusory, 164
made in consideration of marriage, 182, 184
to pay, 290, 292, 294–297
Promisor, promisee, 133
Promissory estoppel. *See also* Reliance, detrimental
defined, 165
as exception to Statute of Frauds, 185
irrevocable offers and, 148
requirements for, 165
Promissory notes, 292, 293
Proof
burden of. *See* Burden of proof
of claim, creditor's, 377
Property. *See also* Personal property; Real property
abandoned, 531, 549
after-acquired, 341
appraisers of, 381–382
bailed. *See* Bailment(s)
community, 363, 527
conveyance of. See Real property, ownership of, transfer of
crimes involving, 110
defined, 526
disparagement of, 78
dominion and control over, 529
estate in (bankruptcy estate), 361–362, 365, 370
intangible, 228, 529
intellectual. *See* Intellectual property
intentional torts against, 76–78
jurisdiction over, 29–30
liens on, 354–356
lost, 530–531
mislaid, 530
ownership of, 526–531, 543–545
concurrent, 517
in fee simple, 517–518, 543
transfer of, 206, 537–531, 543n, 545–549, 565
partnership, 448
personal. *See* Personal property
private, taken for public use, 10, 548–549, 595–597
real. *See* Real property
tangible, 227–228
testamentary disposition of, 561. *See also* Will(s)
Prosecution
criminal, and tort lawsuit for same act, 107–108
of cyber crime, 123–124
malicious, 75
Prospectus, 503, 503, 504, 506
Protect (Prosecutorial Remedies and Other Tools to End the Exploitation of Children Today) Act (2003), 15
Protected classes, 173, 423
Proximate cause, 80, 270n, 579
Proxy, 489–490, 491
Proxy materials, 490, 511
Public accounting firms, 578, 585–586
Public Company Accounting Oversight Board, 515, 585
Public figures, 74
Public policy
contracts contrary to, 168–172
exception to at-will employment based on, 415
strict product liability and, 83, 274–275
Publication
of defamatory statement, 73
of information placing person in false light, 74
of will, 563

Puffery (seller's talk), 75, 181, 270
Purpose
  achievement of, agency termination and, 409
  frustration of, 206
  proper, 510

Q

Quality
  mistake of, 178
  slander of, 78
Quantity term, 231
Quantum meruit, 137–138, 218
Quasi contract, 136–138, 218
Question
  of fact, 34
  federal, 30
  of law, 34
Quid pro quo harassment, 427
Quorum, 485, 490
Quotas, import, 598

R

Race, discrimination based on, 38, 423, 424, 425, 603
Racketeer Influenced and Corrupt Organizations Act (RICO)(1970), 113
Railway Labor Act, 434
Ratification
  agency formation by, 401, 404–405
  defined, 167
  by minor, of contract, 167
  by principal, of agent's unauthorized act, 401, 404–405
  of signature, 306
  of voidable contract, 136
Real estate. *See* Land; Real property
Real property. *See also* Land; Property
  contract for sale of, 545–547. *See also* Contract(s)
    breach of, 212, 216
    financing for. *See* Loan(s); Mortgage(s)
    fixtures and, 183, 542–543
    plant life and vegetation and, 542
    specific performance and, 216–217
    Statute of Frauds and, 183
  defined, 76, 526
  goods associated with, 228–229
  nature of, 541–543
  ownership interests in, 543–545
    nonpossessory, 544–545
    transfer of, 543–544, 560–569
  private, taking of, for public use, 10, 548–549, 595, 597
Realty. *See* Land; Real property
Reasonable manner, 71, 253
Reasonable person standard, 71, 78–79, 120, 222, 402, 416
Receiver, 477
Record(s)
  on appeal, 41
  attribution and, 156
  corporate, shareholder's right to inspect, 464n, 493
  defined, under UETA, 154
  electronic, 154–157
  financial, privacy and, 328
  security agreement and, 337
Redemption, right of, 349, 385, 387–388
Reformation, 170, 181, 211, 217
Registration
  of domain names, 92–93
  of securities. *See* Security(ies), registration of
  of trademark, 90
Reimbursement
  principal's duty of, 403
  surety's right of, 359
Rejection
  of goods, buyer's or lessee's right of, 253, 257, 262
  of offer, 157
Release, 165, 345, 358
Reliance
  detrimental, 148, 165–166, 185. *See also* Promissory estoppel
  justifiable, 75, 148, 180, 181, 185, 582, 584
Religion
  accommodation of, 13, 15, 440
  discrimination based on, 423, 424, 425, 603
  ethical standards and, 56
  freedom of, 10, 11, 13–15
Remedy(ies). *See also individual remedies*
  for breach of contract. *See* Contract(s), remedies for breach of; Lease contract(s), remedies for breach of; Sales contract(s), remedies for breach of
  defined, 6, 211
  in equity (equitable), 6, 211, 216–217
  exclusive, 263
  judicial, 356–357
  at law, 6, 211. *See also* Damages
  prejudgment, 356
  "self-help," 347
Rent, 550–551
Renunciation, of agency relationship, 409
Reorganization, under Chapter 11, 360, 367–369, 370n
Replevin, 261
Reply, 36
Reports (reporters), 20
Repossession of collateral, 347
Repudiation
  of agency relationship, 409
  of contract, 203, 256
Res ipsa loquitur, 82
Rescission. *See also* Cancellation
  of affirmation agreement, 367
  of contract, 6, 203–204, 211, 258, 260
  defined, 163
  misrepresentation and, 181
  mutual, 203–204
  new contract and, 163–164
  and restitution, 211, 216
  right to, under TILA, 382
Residuary (residuum) of estate, 562
Respondeat superior, 407–408
Responsible corporate officer doctrine, 109
Restatement (Second) of Agency, 407
Restatement (Third) of Agency, 396, 397
Restatement (Second) of Contracts, 153, 199
Restatement of Torts, 100
Restatement (Second) of Torts, 275
Restatement (Third) of Torts: Products Liability, 276, 277, 583–584
Restatement (Second) of Trusts, 569n
Restatement (Third) of Trusts, 569n
Restatements of the Law, 4 *See also individual restatements*
Restitution, 211, 216
Restraint(s)
  against alienation, 196
  of trade, contracts in, 170
Revised Model Business Corporation Act (RMBCA), 461, 474, 484
Revised Uniform Limited Partnership Act (RULPA), 451–452
Revised Uniform Principal and Income Act, 569n
Revocation
  of agent's authority, 409
  of acceptance of goods, 262–263
  declaration of, 564
  of offer, 135, 143, 148
  of trust, 566–567
  of will, 563–564
RICO (Racketeer Influenced and Corrupt Organizations Act)(1970), 113
Right(s)
  airspace, 541, 542
  appraisal, 475
  constitutional. *See* Bill of Rights; United States Constitution
  of inspection. *See* Inspection, right of

preemptive, 491–492
principle of, 59–60
privacy. *See* Privacy rights
subsurface, 541. 542
survivorship, 527
voidable, 363
Right to Financial Privacy Act (1978), 328
Risk
assumption of, 80–81, 279
defined, 555
duty to warn of, 79, 277
foreseeability of, 277, 279
of loss, 239–241
management of, 555
negligence and, 78–79
Robbery, 109
Rules of construction, 235

S

Sale(s)
of collateral, 342, 348–349
of corporate assets, 475–476
defined, 227
and leaseback, 384
by nonowners, 238–239
notice of, 386–387
of ongoing business, covenant not to compete and, 170
power of, 387n, 385–386
sheriff's, 546
short, 384, 511n
Sales contract(s), 226–268. *See also* Contract(s); Uniform Commercial Code (UCC)
acceptance in, 232–233, 258–258
anticipatory repudiation of, 258
breach of, 258–263
assignment of right to receive damages on, 196
measurement of damages and, 212
risk of loss and, 239–241
cancellation of, as remedy, 258, 260
consideration in, 234–235
defined, 241
definiteness of terms and, 185, 230–231
formation of, 230–236
interpretation of, 245–246
law governing, 133, 226–229
between merchants, special rules for 185, 229, 231–234, 262
mirror image rule and, 149–150, 232
modification of, 246
offer in, 230–232. *See also* Term(s)
merchant's firm offer and, 231–232
open terms and, 230–231
ongoing, 231
output, 231
parol evidence and, 235–236
payment under, 256–257
performance of, 252–258
remedies for breach of, 258–263. *See also individual remedies*
buyer's, 260–263
damages as, 212, 259, 263
limitation of, 152, 118, 263–264
seller's, 258–260
requirements, 231
rescission of, 260
risk of loss and, 239–241
sample, 248–251
Statute of Frauds and, 184–185, 234–235
statute of limitations and, 264
unconscionability and, 273
Sarbanes-Oxley Act (2002), 54, 168, 463n, 515–517, 578, 585–586, 588
key provisions of, 516, 586
Satisfaction, accord and, 164, 204
Scienter, 181, 511–513, 587
Searches and seizures, unreasonable, 10, 116, 422–423, 462
Second Amendment, 10
Secondary (collateral) promises, 182, 184
Secondary (contingent) liability, 184, 304–305, 358
Secondary sources of law, 4
Secured party(ies)
defined, 336
priorities among, 343–345, 346, 347–348, 354
remedies of, 347–349
retention of collateral by, 347–348
rights and duties of, 343–350
value given by, 337
Secured transactions, 227, 336–353. *See also* Security interest(s)
defined, 336
rights and duties of parties to, 345–347
terminology of, 336–337
Securities Act (1933), 582–507, 509, 517, 585, 586–587
potential liability of accountants under, 586–587
violations of, 506–507, 586–587, 588
Securities and Exchange Commission (SEC), 490, 491, 502, 503, 508–513, 516, 517–518, 586, 587, 588
EDGAR (Electronic Data Gathering, Analysis and Retrieval) database of, 503
International Financial Reporting Standards (IFRS) adopted by, 579
online securities fraud and, 517–518
proxies and, 490
Public Company Accounting Oversight Board and, 515, 585
Regulation A of, 504
Regulation D of, 504–506
resales of securities regulated by, 506
Rule 10b-5 of, 508–511, 512, 513, 587
Web site of, 503, 504
Securities Exchange Act (1934), 507–513
potential liability of accountants under, 585, 587, 588
Section 10(b) of, 508–511, 513, 608
Section 16(b) of, 511, 512
violations of, 511–513, 587, 588
Securities Litigation Uniform Standards Act (SLUSA)(1998), 527
Security(ies)
debt, 471
defined, 471, 502, 503
equity, 471
fixed-income, 471
registration of, 503–504, 513–514, 585, 586–587
electronic prospectus and, 503
exemptions from, 504–506, 514
restricted, 505
state laws governing, 513–514
Treasury, 382
unrestricted, 505
well-known seasoned issuers (WKSI) of, 504
Security interest(s)
in accounts, 339
in after-acquired property, 342
assignment of, 345
in consumer goods, 339, 341–342, 348
creating, 337–338
defined, 337, 354
in equipment, 339
in future advances, 342
in inventory, 339, 343, 345
in negotiable instrument, 302, 336, 339
perfection of, 338–342, 354
in personal property, 336. *See also* Mortgage(s)
priority of claims to debtor's collateral and, 343–345, 346, 347–348, 354
in proceeds, 342
purchase-money (PMSI), 341–342, 344–345, 347
scope of, 342–343
termination of, 346
warranty of title and, 270
Self-defense, 71, 113
Self-incrimination, 10, 116, 462
Self-tender, 476

Seller(s)
as beneficiary of letter of credit, 601
breach by, 241, 260–263
goods held by, 240, 258–259
insurable interest of, 241
performance obligations of, 252–256
place of business of, 253, 600
remedies of, 258–260
residence of, 253
risk of loss and, 239–241
Seniority systems, 431
Sentencing guidelines, 118, 463
Sentencing Reform Act (1984), 118
Service mark, 91, 101
Services
goods combined with, 229
personal, contracts for. *See* Personal-service contract(s)
Settlement of claims, 164–166
Settlor, 566
Seventh Amendment, 10, 38
Sexual harassment, 58, 427–429
Share(s)
number of authorized, 467–468
par value of, 468, 495
transfer of, 465, 474, 493
Shareholder(s)
appraisal rights of, 475
approval of merger and other combinations by, 474, 475m, 489
derivative action by, 464n, 489, 494–495
duties of, 495–496
liability of, 462, 495–496
majority, 489, 495–496
meetings of, 489–490
minority, 495–496
powers of, 489
proposals by, 490
rights of, 472, 474, 492–495
role of, 462, 489–492
voting by, 489–492
Sharia, 8
Shelter principle, 304
Short-form merger, 474–475
Sight draft, 291
Signature(s)
on deed, 546
e- (electronic), 154–157
forged, 319–321
on merchant's firm offer, 231–232
on negotiable instruments, 291, 294, 307, 319–321
ratification of, 306
UCC's requirements for, 232n, 294
unauthorized, 303, 306, 321
on will, 563
on written(confirmatory) memorandum, 185, 186–187
Signature liability, 304–306
Sixth Amendment, 10, 116, 117
Slander, 72, 73, 78
Small Business Administration, 360
Smart cards, 327
Social hosts, 83
Social Security, 397, 420, 445
Social Security Act (1935), 420
Social Security Administration, 420–421
Société Anonyme (S.A.), 416n
Software
copyright protection for, 98
e-agents and, 406
file-sharing, 98–100
filtering, 12
licensing and, 151
shrink-wrap agreements and, 153
warning labels for, 278
Sole proprietorships, 444–445, 496
Spam, 123
Specific performance
buyer's or lessee's right to obtain, 260
construction contracts and, 217n
contract for sale of land and, 212, 216–217
defined, 5, 216
personal-service contracts and, 217
as remedy for breach of contract, 6, 211, 216–217
Speech
commercial, 11–12, 462
freedom of, 10, 11, 72, 422, 462
political, corporate, 11, 462
symbolic, 11
unprotected, 12, 72
Spouse, surviving, intestacy laws and, 565
Standing to sue, 33
Starbucks Coffee Company, international sales contract of, 248–251, 600
Stare decisis, 5
State(s)
administrative agencies of, 5
constitutions of, 4
courts of. *See* State court system
immunity of, from lawsuits, 429
law codes of, 4, 19
powers of, 8
police, 9
regulatory, 9
Tenth Amendment and, 4, 9, 10
uniform laws and, 4
State court system, 33–34
appellate courts of, 20, 33, 34, 41
citations to, 19–20
decisions of, 19–20, 25–27
electronic filing and, 42
following a case through, 36–41
jurisdiction of. *See* Jurisdiction
supreme (highest) courts of, 22, 29n, 33, 34
trial courts of, 19–20, 29, 33–34
Statement(s)
bank, examination of, 320, 326
continuation, 342
of fact, 72–73, 75, 181
false
constituting slander *per se*, 73
defamation and, 72–73
fraudulent misrepresentation and, 75
on insurance application, 557
liability of professionals and, 586–588
financial, 580, 583, 586–588, 589, 590
financing, 337–341, 342, 345, 354
of future intention, 146
misleading, 586–588
of opinion, 72–73, 74, 181, 270
about public figures, 74
registration, 503–504, 507, 585, 586–587
termination, 346–347
of value, 270
Statute(s)
arbitration required by, 43–44
assignments prohibited by, 194
certificate-of-title, 342
citations to, 19–20–23
contracts contrary to, 168–169
dram shop, 83
estray, 531
federal, 4
of Frauds. *See* Statute of Frauds.
Good Samaritan, 82
licensing, 169
of limitations. *See* Statute of limitations
long arm, 29

as primary source of law, 4
recording, 547
state and local, 4
Statute of Frauds
contracts within, 182–185, 186, 380
defined, 182
exceptions to, 184–185, 234–235
one-year rule under, 183, 218n, 416
UCC and, 184–185, 234–235
Statute of limitations
contract discharge and, 204
as defense
to criminal liability, 114–115
to product liability, 279
under UCC, 264
Statutory law, 4, 19, 23
Stock(s), 466, 471–473, 502, 503 *See also* Share(s)
bonds versus, 472
common, 472, 473
defined, 471, 502
preemptive rights and, 491–492
preferred, 472, 473
purchase of, gaining control of corporation by, 476
S corporations and, 466
types of, listed, 473
watered, 405
Stock buybacks, 54–55
Stock certificate(s)
restrictions on transfer and, 493
shareholder's right to, 492
Stock options, 55, 503, 514
Stock warrants, 493, 503
Stop Counterfeiting in Manufactured Goods Act (SCMGA), 91–92
Stored-value cards, 327
Strict liability
of common carriers, 535
defined, 83
hotel operators and, 536
market-share liability and, 277–278
product liability and, 83, 274–278
requirements for, 275–276
Strikes, 414, 434, 435
Strong-arm power, 363
Subject matter
of contract, identification of, 147
destruction of
agency termination and, 409
impossibility of performance and, 205
offer termination and, 149
jurisdiction over, 29
Sublease, 551
Subrogation, right of, 359
Summons, 36
Supervisors, sexual harassment by, 427
Suppliers
foreign, employment practices of, 58–59
of component parts, product liability and, 279
Supreme Court Reporter (S.Ct.), 20
Surety, 357–359
Suretyship, 357–359

T

Taking
of negotiable instrument, HDC status and, 314–316
of private property, for public use, 10, 548–549, 595–597
Tariffs, 598–599
Tax, taxation
"Amazon," 463
bankruptcy and, 361, 366n, 370
corporations and, 462
double, 462, 496
estate, 569
exports and, 597–598
holding (parent) companies and, 462
on imports, 598–599
independent contractors and, 398
on Internet sales, 227, 228, 463
limited liability companies and, 453, 454, 497
limited liability partnerships and, 451, 497
Medicare, 420–421
partnerships and, 445, 446, 451, 496
pass-through entities and, 446, 451, 454
S corporations and, 466
Social Security, 420, 445
sole proprietorships and, 445, 496
"tort," 70
trusts and, 566
unemployment, 397
use, 228
withholding, 397
Tax preparers, 588
Tax Relief, Unemployment Insurance Reauthorization, and Job Creation Act (2010), 420
Tax returns
accountant's duties and, 588
bankruptcy and, 361
Technology
e-signature, 153–154
file-sharing, 98–100
Tenancy
in common, 527
fixed-term, 548
joint, 527, 565
periodic, 549
at sufferance, 549–550
at will, 549
Tenant(s)
in common, 237
duties of, 550
life, 543–544
rights of
assignment of, 551
subleases and, 551
Tender
of delivery, 238, 240
of documents, to buyer, 253
perfect, 253–258
of performance, 202
Tender offer, 476, 504
Tenth Amendment, 4, 9, 10
Term(s)
additional, 230–231, 233, 235
ambiguous, 187
browse-wrap, 153
C.I.F (or C&F)(cost, insurance, and freight), 240
conditioned on offeror's assent, 233
definiteness of, 145, 147, 185, 230–231
e-contracts and, 152–153
F.A.S. (free alongside ship), 240, 253
F.O.B. (free on board), 240, 253
generic, 91
handwritten versus printed/typewritten, 297
interpretation of contracts and, 139
of loan, 380–381. *See also* Mortgage(s)
open, 185, 230–231, 242
partnership for a, 446–447
shrink-wrap, 153
Testamentary disposition, 560
Testate, 560
Testator, 560
Theft
credit-card, 122
cyber, 120–122

identity, 120–121
of trade secrets, 112
Third Amendment, 10
Third party(ies)
collateral promises by, 184
as contract beneficiaries, 193, 198–200, 584
incidental, 199–200
intended, 199–210
professional's liability to, 583–584
promise benefiting, 208
Thirteenth Amendment, 217
Time
for acceptance of offer, 151–152, 151
definite, payment due at, 292, 295–296
for examination of bank statements, 320–321, 326
financing statement's duration and, 342
lapse of
agency termination and, 408
offer termination and, 149
for proper presentment, 305
reasonable, 71, 147, 166, 240, 253, 256, 262
for rejection of goods, 254, 262
of shipment, 253
UETA and, 157
Time draft, 291
Time instrument, 291, 303–304
Tipper/tippee theory, 510–511
Title(s)
case, 25
documents of, 227, 238, 240, 253, 536
good, 269
passage of, 236–239
slander of, 78
void, 238
voidable, 238
warranty of, 269–270
Tort(s), 68–87
actionable, 72
agency relationships and, 407–408
business, 68, 76
classification of, 70
corporate, 462–464, 489
cyber, 68, 83
defined, 68
intentional, 70–78
law governing
basis of, 68–70
exception to at-will employment based on, 415
extraterritorial application of, 602–603
lawsuit for, criminal prosecution versus, for same act, 107–108
strict liability for, 83. *See also* Strict liability
unintentional. *See* Negligence
Tort reform, 71
Tortfeasor, 70, 407
Trade
barriers to, minimizing, 599
restraint of, 170
usage of, 139, 187, 235, 272
Trade dress, 91
Trade libel, 78
Trade names, 92, 338–339
Trade secrets, 100–101, 100, 112, 448
Trademarks, 89–92, 101, 597
Transactions, under UETA, 154–157
Transfer(s)
fraudulent, 364
of funds, 326–327, 601–602
of property, 206, 527–531, 545–549
ourside the probate process, 543n, 565
of shares, 465, 474, 493
Treaties, 594
Trespass, 77
Trial(s)
civil, 39–40, 107
criminal, 107, 118, 119
by jury, right to, 10, 38, 116
mini-, 44
new, motion for, 41
speedy and public, right to, 10, 116
summary jury, 45
Trial court(s)
federal (district), 19–20, 30,
state, 19–20, 29, 33–34
TRIPS (Agreement on Trade-Related Aspects of Intellectual Property Rights) (1994), 101, 102
Trust(s), 566–569
charitable, 567
constructive, 568–569
defined, 566
express, 566–568
funds of, 566
implied, 568–569
living (*inter vivos*), 566–567
resulting, 568
spendthrift, 567–568
testamentary, 567
Totten, 568
Trustee(s)
bankruptcy, 360, 361, 363–364
of trust, 566, 569
United States, 361, 362
Truth-in-Lending Act (TILA), 381–382
Twenty-seventh Amendment, 10n

U

Ultra vires doctrine, 470
Ultramares rule, 583
Unconscionability
of contracts or clauses, 170–172, 264
defined, 170–171
procedural, 171
substantive, 171–172
under UCC, 171, 235, 263
warranty disclaimers and, 273
Underwriter, 557
Undue hardship, 366, 367, 425, 430
Undue influence
contract illegal through, 173
on testator, 562
voluntary consent and, 182
Unemployment compensation, 397, 421
Unfair labor practices, 434
Uniform Commercial Code (UCC), 132
adoption of, 4, 227
Article 2 of (Sales Contracts)
scope of, 226–229
Article 2A of (Leases)
scope of, 226, 229–230
Article 3 of (Negotiable Instruments), 226–227, 290, 307, 315
Article 4 of (Bank Deposits and Collection), 227, 290, 315, 323
Article 4A of (Funds Transfers), 227, 326, 327
Article 5 of (Letters of Credit), 227
Article 7 of (Documents of Title), 227, 535
Article 9 of (Secured Transactions), 227, 339, 336
auctions and, 146n
choice of law and, 600
CISG compared with, 242, 594
citations to, 23
commercial reasonableness under, 230, 252, 259, 302, 347, 348
consideration under, 231n, 233–234
creation of, 4
definiteness of terms and, 185, 232–233

entrustment rule under, 238–239
E-SIGN Act and, 154, 155
fictitious payee rule of, 306
form of contracts and, 135
good faith and, 230, 231, 233, 252, 261, 301–302, 363, 370
imposter rule of, 306
insurable interest and, 241
liquidated damages under, 215n
limitation of remedies under, 263–264
merchant's firm offer under, 231–232
mirror image rule under, 232
modification of contract and, 246–247
online acceptance and, 153
open terms and, 185, 230–231, 242
parol evidence rule and, 235–236
partial performance under, 185
passage of title under, 237–239
perfect tender rule under, 253–258
rescission of contract under, 203
risk of loss under, 236, 239–241
rules of construction under, 235
sale of growing crops and, 544
signature requirements of, 294
special rules for merchants under, 185, 229, 231–234, 262
Statute of Frauds under, 194–195, 234–235
statute of limitations under, 264
UETA and, 155, 262
unconscionability under, 171, 237, 263
warranties under, 229n, 269–273
Uniform Electronic Transactions Act (UETA), 151, 154–157, 406
Uniform laws, 4
Uniform Limited Liability Company Act (ULLCA), 454
Uniform Limited Partnership Act (ULPA), 451
Uniform Partnership Act (UPA), 445, 496
Uniform Probate Code (UPC), 562, 563, 564
Uniform Residential Landlord and Tenant Act (URLTA), 550
Uniform Securities Act, 514
Uniform Trade Secrets Act, 100
Union shop, 434
Unions, 414, 433–435
United Nations
Commission on International Trade Law, 594
Convention
on Contracts for the International Sale of Goods (CISG), 226, 241–242, 594, 600
UCC compared with, 242, 594
on the Recognition and Enforcement of Foreign Arbitral Awards (New York Convention), 600–601
United States Citizenship and Immigration Services, 432
United States Code (U.S.C.), 2, 19, 23, 360
United States Code Annotated (U.S.C.A.), 19
United States Commerce Department, 597
United States Constitution
Bill of Rights of, 88, 10–15, 462
business and, 9–15
checks and balances established by, 29
commerce clause of, 8–10, 433
due process clause of. *See* Due process
eminent domain and, 549–550
establishment clause of, 13–14
excessive bail and fines prohibited by, 10, 116
export taxes prohibited by, 597–598
free exercise clause of, 13, 14–15
intellectual property protected by, 88
president's treaty making power under, 594
as primary source of law, 3
privileges and immunities clause of, 462
protections guaranteed by, 10, 115–118. *See also individual protections*
supremacy clause of, 433
Supreme Court established by, 36
as supreme law of land, 4
takings clause of, 10, 547–548
unreasonable searches and seizures prohibited by, 10, 116, 422–423, 462
United States Copyright Office, 96
United States Department of Homeland Security, 432
United States Department of Housing and Urban Development (HUD), 384
United States Department of Justice, 475, 507, 587
United States Department of Labor, 416, 432, 433
United States Department of Transportation, 431
United States Department of the Treasury, 378n, 384–385
United States Food and Drug Administration, 4
United States Immigration and Customs Enforcement (ICE), 432
United States Patent and Trademark Office, 90, 94
United States Reports (U.S.), 20, 22
United States Safe Web Act (2006), 123
United States Sentencing Commission, 118
United States Statutes at Large, 19
United States Supreme Court, as nation's highest court, 34, 35–36
appeals to, 36, 41
decisions of
as binding authorities, 5
online availability of, 42
petitions granted by, 36
"rule of four" of, 36
United States Trustee, 361–362
Universal defenses, 307–308
Usage of trade, 139, 187, 235, 272
Usury, 168
Utilitarianism, 56

V

Value
fair, for land, 548, 595
given by secured party, 338–339
good faith purchaser for, 238, 261
legally sufficient, 162–163
mistake of, 178–179
statement of, 270
taking for, HDC status and, 302, 314, 315
Vegetation, as real property, 542
Venture capital, 472–473
Venue, 33
Verdict, 39, 40, 118
Vesting, 199, 421
Vicarious (indirect) liability, 99n, 407
Violence against Women Act (1994), 8n
Virus, 122
Visas, 433
Vishing, 121–122
Voir dire, 38
Voting, by shareholders, 489–493
Voting lists, 490

W

Wage(s)
discrimination based on, 426
foreign workers and, 58
and hour laws, 416–418
minimum, 417
overtime, 417–418
Social Security tax based on, 420
subject to garnishment, 357
Walsh-Healey Act (1936), 416
War, 8, 410
Warehouse companies, 535–536
Warehouse receipts, 227, 238, 240, 536
Warehouseman, 535n
Warnings
by landowner, 79
product liability and, 277, 278
Warrant
search, 113, 116, 117

stock, 509, 520, 528
Warranty(ies), 269–73
breach of, as defense to liability on negotiable instrument, 308
disclaimers of, 272–273
in deeds, 546
express, 270, 272
full, 273
implied. *See* Implied warranty(ies)
limited, 273
overlapping, 272
presentment, 307
of title, 269–270
transfer, 307
under UCC, 229n, 269–273
Warranty liability, 306–307, 535
Watered stock, 405
Westlaw®, 20, 24
Whistleblowing, 415
Will(s), 560–566
amendment to (codicil), 564
deathbed, 563
defined, 560
easement or profit created by, 544
employment at, 414–416
holographic, 563
nuncupative, 563
oral, 563
partnership at, 447
probate of, 543n, 564–565
publication of, 563
real property transferred by, 545, 547
requirements for valid, 562–563
residuary clause in, 562
revocation of, 563–564
tenancy at, 549
terminology of, 560–561
trusts created by, 567
UETA and, 155
valid, requirements for, 562–563
Will substitutes, 565
Wire fraud, 111–112
Withdrawal
direct, 326
from illegal agreement, 173
from partnership, 450, 452
Witnesses, 38, 39–40, 563
Worker. *See* Employee(s)
Worker Adjustment and Retraining Notification (WARN) Act, 418
Workers' compensation, 397, 403, 420
Working papers, 585, 586
Workouts, 367, 384 Workplace safety, 403, 407, 417, 419–420
"Works for hire," 399
World Intellectual Property Organization (WIPO), 98
World Trade Organization (WTO), 620
Worm, 122
Writ
of attachment, 356
of *certiorari,* 36
of execution, 356
Writing
defined, 185
equal dignity rule and, 400n, 403
material alteration of, 241, 303, 308, 334–335
requirements for, relating to
agency agreements, 400, 403–404
bailments, 532
collateral promises, 184
deeds, 546
easements and profits, 544
guaranty contracts, 358
leases of real property, 550
LLC operating agreements, 454
merchant's firm offer, 231–232
mortgages, 183, 380
negotiable instruments, 292, 292–294
partnership agreements, 446
power of attorney, 400n, 403–404
rescission, 203
security agreements, 337
TILA transactions, 382
wills, 563, 564
signed, defined, by UCC, 232n, 294
Statute of Frauds and. *See* Statute of Frauds
sufficiency of, 185–187, 234
Written memorandum, 185, 234, 234
Wrongful interference, 76
Wrongul mental state (*mens rea*), 108–109

Y

Year Books, 5

Z

"Zero-tolerance" policies, 423